PRENTICE HALL

UNITED STATES HISTORY

PART 1

Emma J. Lapsansky-Werner
Peter B. Levy
Randy Roberts
Alan Taylor

PEARSON

Taken from:

Prentice Hall: United States History

Published by Prentice Hall
Upper Saddle River, New Jersey 07458

This special edition published in cooperation with Pearson Learning Solutions.

Pearson Learning Solutions, 501 Boylston Street, Suite 900
Boston, MA 02116
A Pearson Education Company
www.pearsoned.com

Printed in the United States of America

9 10 0BRV 16 15 14

000200010271276223

EG

Cover Images: Bkgd, Corbis Royalty-Free; BM, NASA/Johnson Space Center; M, Getty Images; BL, Barry Rosenthal/Getty Images; BFL, Bettmann/CORBIS; TR, Bettmann/CORBIS; BR, George K.Warren/Corbis; TL, Illustration by Michael J. Deas; B, Getty Images; **Title page** Corbis Royalty-Free; **Spine**: Corbis Royalty-Free; **Back cover**: Corbis Royalty-Free

Acknowledgments appear on page 1258, which constitutes an extension of this copyright page.

PEARSON

ISBN-10: 1-256-33196-1
ISBN-13: 978-1-256-33196-4

AUTHORS

Emma J. Lapsansky-Werner

Emma J. Lapsansky-Werner is Professor of History and Curator of the Quaker Collection at Haverford College. After receiving her doctorate from the University of Pennsylvania, she taught at Temple University for almost two decades. Dr. Lapsansky-Werner's recent publications include *Quaker Aesthetics,* coauthored with Ann Verplanck, and *Back to Africa: Benjamin Coates and the Colonization Movement in America, 1848–1880,* coedited with Margaret Hope Bacon.

Peter B. Levy

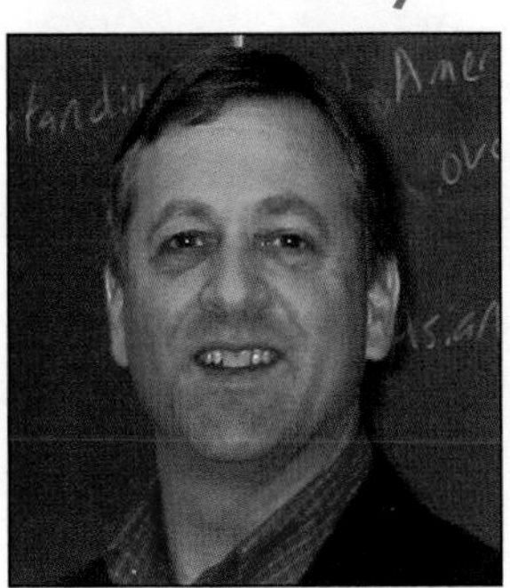

Peter B. Levy is a Full Professor in the Department of History at York College of Pennsylvania, where he teaches a wide variety of courses in American history. He received his B.A. from the University of California, Berkeley, and his Ph.D. from Columbia University. Dr. Levy is the author of eight books and many articles, including: *The New Left and Labor in the 1960s; Civil War on Race Street: The Civil Rights Movement in Cambridge, Maryland;* and *100 Key Documents in American Democracy.* He lives in Towson, Maryland, with his wife, two children, and a yellow Labrador.

Randy Roberts

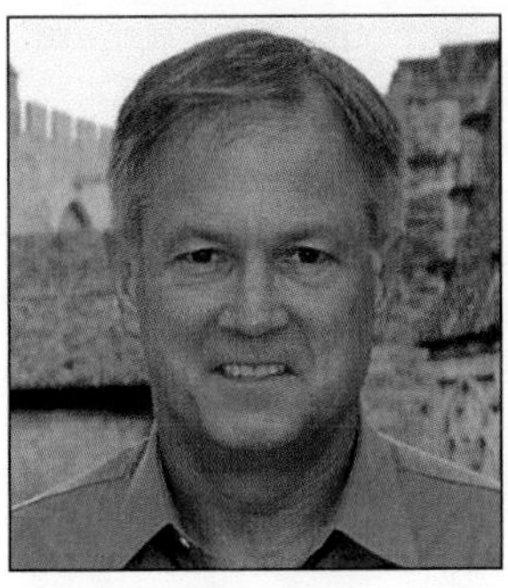

Randy Roberts, Professor of History at Purdue University, specializes in twentieth-century American history and the history of popular culture. He has written, cowritten, or edited more than 20 books, including biographies of John Wayne, Jack Johnson, and Oscar Robertson. Dr. Roberts has also written histories of American sports and of the Vietnam War. His books have been nominated for and won a number of national prizes. At Purdue University, he has won the University Teacher of the Year award. Dr. Roberts has also appeared frequently on the History Channel and in documentaries for HBO, NBC, ESPN, and PBS.

Alan Taylor

Alan Taylor, Professor of History at the University of California, Davis, earned his Ph.D. in history from Brandeis University and did a postdoctoral fellowship at the Institute of Early American History and Culture in Williamsburg, Virginia. He teaches courses in early American history and the history of the American West. Dr. Taylor is the author of five books, including *American Colonies* and *William Cooper's Town,* which won the Bancroft and Beveridge prizes, as well as the 1996 Pulitzer Prize for American history. He is a contributing editor for *The New Republic.*

Program Consultant

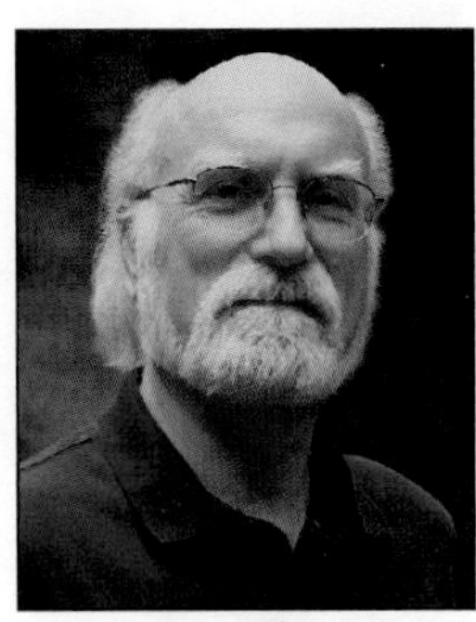

Grant Wiggins, Ed.D., is the President of Authentic Education in Hopewell, New Jersey. He earned his Ed.D from Harvard University and his B.A. from St. John's College in Annapolis. Dr. Wiggins consults with schools, districts, and state education departments on a variety of reform matters. He organizes conferences, workshops, and develops print materials and Web resources on curricular change. He is the co-author, with Jay McTighe, of *Understanding by Design* and *The Understanding by Design Handbook,* the award-winning and highly successful materials on curriculum.

Senior Consultants

John R. Chávez is Professor of History at Southern Methodist University, Clements Department of History. He earned his Ph.D. from the University of Michigan, with a specialty in Mexican American history. Dr. Chávez's publications include *Eastside Landmark: A History of the East Los Angeles Community Union, The Lost Land: The Chicano Image of the Southwest,* and *Teaching Mexican American History,* co-authored with Neil Foley.

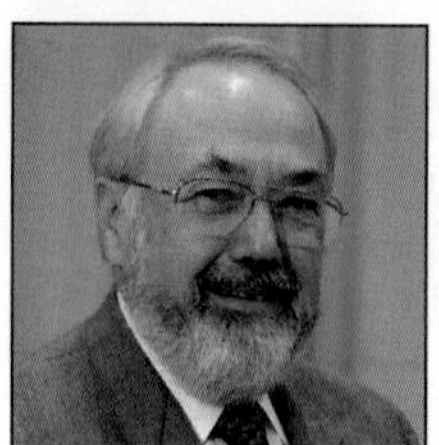

Herman J. Viola specializes in the history of the American West, the American Indian, and the Civil War. He has published books on historic subjects, including *After Columbus* and *Little Bighorn Remembered: The Untold Indian Story of Custer's Last Stand.* Dr. Viola earned his Ph.D. from Indiana University and currently serves as curator emeritus at the Smithsonian's National Museum of Natural History.

Senior Reading Consultants

Kate Kinsella, Ed.D., Adjunct faculty member, Department of Secondary Education at San Francisco State University. A specialist in second-language and adolescent literacy, she teaches coursework addressing language and literacy development across the secondary curricula. Dr. Kinsella earned her M.A. in TESOL from San Francisco State University and her Ed.D. in Second Language Acquisition from the University of San Francisco.

Kevin Feldman, Ed.D., is the Director of Reading and Early Intervention with the Sonoma County Office of Education (SCOE) and an independent educational consultant. At the SCOE, he develops, organizes, and monitors programs related to K–12 literacy. Dr. Feldman has an M.A. from the University of California, Riverside, in Special Education, Learning Disabilities, and Instructional Design. He earned his Ed.D. in Curriculum and Instruction from the University of San Francisco.

Differentiated Instruction Consultants

Don Deshler

Don Deshler, Ph.D., is the director of the Center for Research on Learning (CRL) at the University of Kansas. Dr. Deshler's expertise centers on adolescent literacy, learning strategic instruction, and instructional strategies for teaching content areas to academically diverse classes. He is the author of *Teaching Content to All: Evidence-Based Inclusive Practices in Middle and Secondary Schools,* a text which presents the instructional practices that have been tested and validated through his research at CRL.

Anthony S. Bashir
Director, Academic and Disability Services
Emerson College
Boston, Massachusetts

Cathy Collins Block, Ph.D.
Professor of Curriculum and Instruction
Texas Christian University
Fort Worth, Texas

Anna Uhl Chamot
Professor of Secondary Education (ESL)
The George Washington University
Washington, D.C.

John Guthrie
Professor of Human Development
University of Maryland
College Park, Maryland

Susan P. Miller
Professor of Special Education
University of Nevada, Las Vegas
Las Vegas, Nevada

Jennifer Platt
Executive Associate Dean for Academic Affairs
College of Education
University of Central Florida
Orlando, Florida

Reviewers

Academic Reviewers

William R. Childs
Professor of History
The Ohio State University
Columbus, Ohio

Dr. Huping Ling
Professor of History
Department of History
Editor, *Journal of Asian American Studies*
Truman State University
Kirksville, Missouri

Judith Ridner
Department of History
Muhlenberg College
Allentown, Pennsylvania

Carol Schneider
Rock Point Community School
Rock Point, Arizona

Contributing Editor

Richard Snow
former Editor in Chief
American Heritage Magazine
New York, New York

Accuracy Panel

Barbara Whitney Petruzzelli, M.L.S.

Amy Raff, M.L.S.

Bernard Rosen, Ph.D.

Wilma Schmidt, M.L.S.

Teacher Reviewers

Tom Berve
Papillion–LaVista High School
Papillion, Nebraska

Janet K. Chandler
Social Studies Department Chair
Hamilton Southeastern High School
Fishers, Indiana

Joyce Cooper
Dallas Independent School District
Dallas, Texas

Scott Crump
Bingham High School
South Jordan, Utah

Peter DiNardo
Mt. Lebanon High School
Pittsburgh, Pennsylvania

Robert Hasty
Lawrence Central High School
Indianapolis, Indiana

Dee Ann Holt
Mann Magnet School
Little Rock, Arkansas

Bruce A. Lesh
Franklin High School
Reisterstown, Maryland

Seth Massey
Station Camp High School
Gallatin, Tennessee

Dr. Robert McAdams
East Burke High School, retired
Connelly Springs, North Carolina

Roxanna Mechem
Curriculum Director, Social Studies, Education, and Assessment
Rockwood School District
Eureka, Missouri

Cynthia Mostoller
Alice Deal Middle School
Washington, D.C.

Brent Muirhead, Ph. D
University of Phoenix
Atlanta, Georgia

Deborah W. Powers
Westlake High School
Atlanta, Georgia

Jeanne T. Salvado
Montgomery County Public Schools
Rockville, Maryland

Dr. Francis N. Sheboy
Principal
Cornwall Central High School
New Windsor, New York

Jim Thovson
Rapid City Central High School
Rapid City, South Dakota

Social Studies Master Teacher Board

Peggy Altoff
K-12 Social Studies Facilitator
District 11 Colorado Springs
Colorado Springs, Colorado

David Burns
Foothill High School
Sacramento, California

Katherine A. Deforge
Chair, Social Studies Dept.
Marcellus Central School
Marcellus, New York

Roceal N. Duke
District of Columbia Public Schools
Content Specialist, retired
Washington, D.C.

Thomas E. Gray
De Ruyter Central School, retired
De Ruyter, New York

Sandra Person
Sunnyside High School
Fresno, California

Teacher's Edition Consultants

Diane Hart
Social Studies Author and Assessment Consultant
Menlo Park, California

Sam M. Intrator
Professor of Education and Child Studies
Smith College
Northampton, Massachusetts

John Poggio
Professor, Department of Educational Psychology and Research
University of Kansas
Lawrence, Kansas

Program Advisers

Michal Howden
Social Studies Consultant
Zionsville, Indiana

TABLE OF CONTENTS

ORIGINS OF A NEW NATION Prehistory–1765

We the People
Article. I.

CHANGING AND ENDURING ISSUES 1980–Today

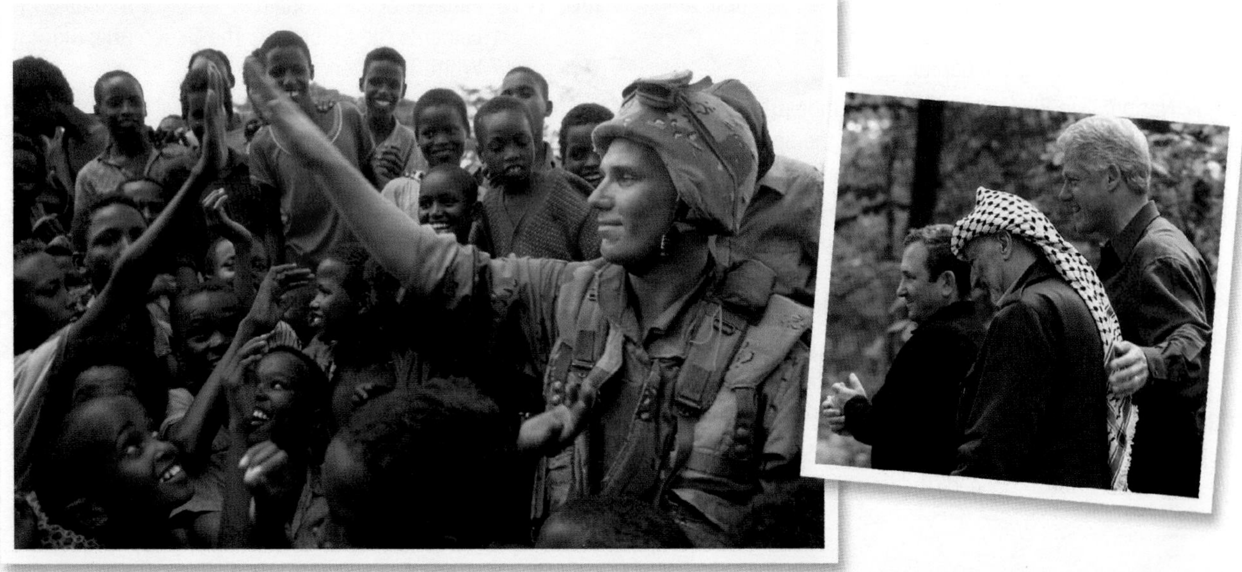

SPECIAL FEATURES AND MULTIMEDIA

Witness History: The Latest Fad

As baby boomers went to school, new fads came and went with amazing speed. One such fad revolved around a popular television show about the American folk hero Davy Crockett. Steven Spielberg, who later would become one of Hollywood's most successful movie directors, recalled the craze.

> "I was in third grade at the time. Suddenly, the next day, everybody in my class but me was Davy Crockett. And because I didn't have my coonskin cap and my powder horn, or Old Betsy, my rifle, and my chaps, I was deemed the Mexican leader, Santa Anna. And they chased me home from school until I got my parents to buy me a coonskin cap."

—Steven Spielberg, recalling the Davy Crockett craze of 1955

WITNESS HISTORY

Primary source accounts throughout the text bring the voices of history to life.

Chapter 1 The Discovery; The First People; Prince Henry the Navigator; Timbuktu; The First Meeting

Chapter 2 The Mayflower Compact; Cities of Gold; A Profitable Fur Trade; Pocahontas; The Pilgrims Leave for America; The Dutch in New Amsterdam

Chapter 3 The Colonies Prosper; New Arrivals; An Illegal Trade; Paul Revere: A Silversmith; Rogers Rangers

Chapter 4 A Revolution of Ideas; Rights of the Colonists; The Spirit of Independence; Could England Win the War?; Cornwallis Surrenders

Chapter 5 Creating a Government for the New Nation; Creating a Republic; The Father of the Constitution; A Hopeful Future

Chapter 6 The First American President; The First Inaugural; A Great Orator Speaks; Jefferson Calls for Free Speech; Burning the Capital

Chapter 7 Nationalism Revived; Dawn of the Industrial Age; A Nation of Farming and Industry; In the Spirit of Nationalism; The "People's President"; Debate Over States' Rights

Chapter 8 Another Great Awakening; Religious Revival; Improving Society; The Evils of Slavery; Equality for Women

Chapter 9 Westward Ho!; A Pioneer Woman Heads West; A Child at the Alamo; Seeking a Mountain of Gold

Chapter 10 Can Slavery Be Regulated in the Territories?; Why Limit Slavery Only in the Territories?; Slavery and Union; A House Divided; The President Falters

Chapter 11 War Between the States; Marching Off to War; A Memorable Day; The Hardships of War; Gettysburg: A Soldier's Story; The South Surrenders

Chapter 12 All Is Now Lost; Nothing Left but the Bare Land; An African American in the Senate; A Stormy Election

Chapter 13 "The March of American Progress"; Celebrating the Nation's Centennial; From Rags to Riches; The Right to Strike

Chapter 14 The New American City; Looking Forward and Back; A Fiery Tide; America Takes to Wheels

Chapter 15 Businesses Running Full Blast; Creating a "New South"; My Heart Feels Like Bursting; A Test of Courage

Chapter 16 Paupers and Millionaires; Frederick Douglass Laments the Color Line; The Gilded Age; Black and White Together

Chapter 17 Slum Sisters; Children in the Coal Mines; Women at Work; Voices of Protest; A Bold Leader Takes Control; A History of Reform

Chapter 18 Americans Charge to Victory; America Eyes Hawaii; Remember the *Maine*!; A Plea for Peace; Dollars for Bullets

Chapter 19 American Soldiers Arrive "Over There"; To Fight or Not to Fight?; Supporting the War; War Enthusiasm; A Difficult Transition

Events That Changed America

See how certain events changed the course of our nation's history.

History *Interactive*

Audio, video, and animation-filled features help you explore major turning points in history.

Primary Source

Full-page excerpts allow you to relive history through eyewitness accounts and documents.

American Humanities

Experience great American literature and art.

In-Text Primary Source

Gain insights as you read by reading the words of people who were there.

Comparing Viewpoints

Explore issues by analyzing two opposing viewpoints.

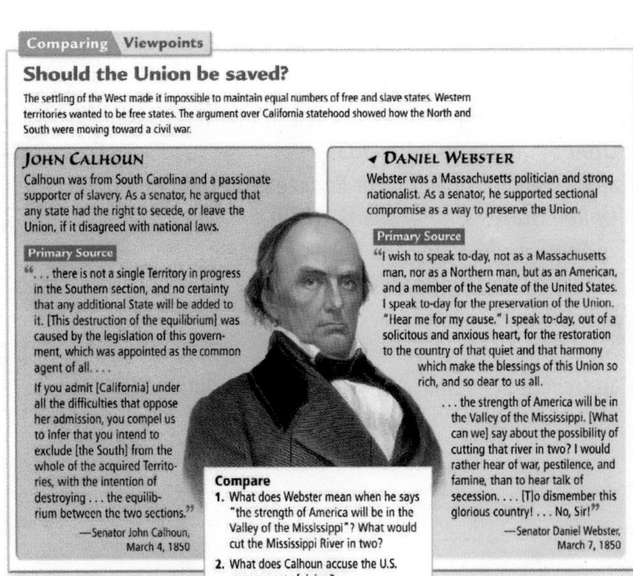

Comparing Viewpoints

Should the Union be saved?

The settling of the West made it impossible to maintain equal numbers of free and slave states. Western territories wanted to be free states. The argument over California statehood showed how the North and South were moving toward a civil war.

JOHN CALHOUN

Calhoun was from South Carolina and a passionate supporter of slavery. As a senator, he argued that any state had the right to secede, or leave the Union, if it disagreed with national laws.

Primary Source

"... there is not a single Territory in progress in the Southern section, and no certainty that any additional State will be added to it. [This destruction of the equilibrium] was caused by the legislation of this government, which was appointed as the common agent of all. . . .

If you admit [California] under all the difficulties that oppose her admission, you compel us to infer that you intend to exclude [the South] from the whole of the acquired Territories, with the intention of destroying . . . the equilibrium between the two sections."

—Senator John Calhoun, March 4, 1850

DANIEL WEBSTER

Webster was a Massachusetts politician and strong nationalist. As a senator, he supported sectional compromise as a way to preserve the Union.

Primary Source

"I wish to speak to-day, not as a Massachusetts man, nor as a Northern man, but as an American, and a member of the Senate of the United States. I speak to-day for the preservation of the Union. "Hear me for my cause." I speak to-day, out of a solicitous and anxious heart, for the restoration to the country of that quiet and that harmony which make the blessings of this Union so rich, and so dear to us all.

. . . the strength of America will be in the Valley of the Mississippi. [What can we] say about the possibility of cutting that river in two? I would rather hear of war, pestilence, and famine, than to hear talk of secession. . . . [T]o dismember this glorious country! . . . No, Sir!"

—Senator Daniel Webster, March 7, 1850

Compare

1. What does Webster mean when he says "the strength of America will be in the Valley of the Mississippi"? What would cut the Mississippi River in two?
2. What does Calhoun accuse the U.S. government of doing?

Decision Point

Consider how you would have decided key questions in American history.

Cause and Effect

Diagrams help you see the short- and long-term causes and effects of history's most important events.

Landmark Decisions of the Supreme Court

Explore key Supreme Court cases and link the decisions to today.

History Makers

Meet many fascinating people.

History Makers

Helen Hunt Jackson
(1830–1885)
Helen Hunt Jackson grew up in Massachusetts. In the late 1870s, she heard some Native Americans speak about their peoples' plight. Deeply moved, she was determined to publicize their cause. In *A Century of Dishonor,* she sharply criticized the U.S. government's history of shattered treaties. She elaborated on the situation in a report on Indian policy written for the government and in the highly popular novel *Ramona.* Jackson's work helped build sympathy for the plight of Native Americans.

American Issues Connector

Examine key issues that have endured throughout American history.

☑ Quick Study Timeline

Illustrated timelines help you review and explore key events.

INFOGRAPHIC

Photographs, maps, charts, illustrations, and text help you understand the significance of important historical events and developments.

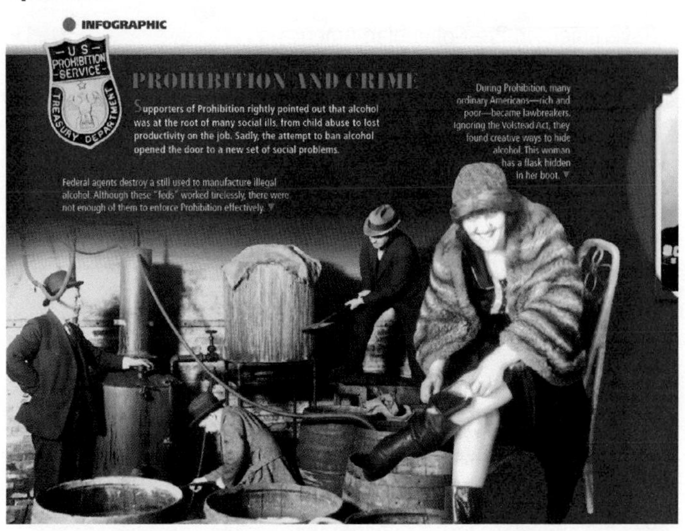

Document-Based Assessment

Practice the art and science of a historian by analyzing an event through multiple historical documents, data, and images.

Focus On Geography

See how geography has affected events in American history.

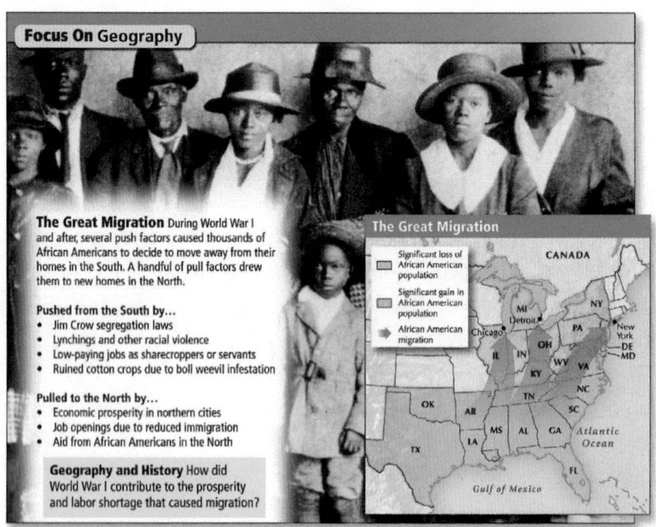

Charts and Graphs

Diagrams and data help you understand history through visuals.

Maps Geography *Interactive*

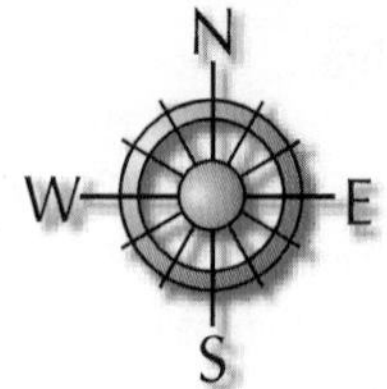

Interactive maps help you understand where history happened.

Political Cartoons

Examine how artists have expressed their points of view about events of their day.

Discover

the enduring issues of our nation's history

The **American Issues Connector** explores the enduring questions that frame our American past, present, and future.

Here's how it works:

1. **Highlight issues as you learn**
   Review issues in every chapter using the American Issues Connector Cumulative Review.

2. **Study Issues in depth**
   The American Issues Connector feature focuses on a modern debate about an enduring issue.

3. **Track Issues over time**
   Take notes in the Study Guide to prepare for thematic essays on enduring issues.

Here's an example:

What is the proper balance between national security and civil liberties?

Patrick Henry addressing Congress

1

American Issues Connector

By connecting prior knowledge with what you have learned in this chapter, you can gradually build your understanding of enduring questions that still affect America today. Answer the questions below. Then, use your American Issues Connector study guide (or go online: www.PHSchool.com **Web Code:** neh-1211).

Issues You Learned About

• **Civil Liberties and National Security** From the beginning of the American republic, Americans have debated to what extent individual freedom should be limited when the safety of the nation is at stake.

1. How does the Bill of Rights guarantee the rights of people accused of crimes?
2. During the Civil War, what action did President Lincoln take that limited these guaranteed rights? Why?
3. During the Cold War, what effect did the actions of HUAC and McCarthy have on individual rights?

• **America Goes to** ... debate whether U.S. en...

7. What were argumen... against North Korea
8. What were argumen...

Connect to You...

America and the W... when dealing with thre...

2

American Issues Connector **Civil Liberties and National Security**

TRACK THE ISSUE

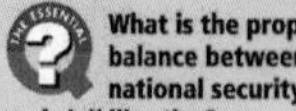

What is the proper balance between national security and civil liberties?

The Constitution guarantees rights and freedoms to all American citizens. But during war and other crises, government leaders have limited such civil liberties in order to protect citizens' lives. Should they? Use the timeline below to explore this enduring issue.

1790s Undeclared War With France
Alien Act allows President to imprison or deport resident aliens. Sedition Act limits freedoms of speech and press.

1860s Civil War
Lincoln suspends the right of habeas corpus.

1940s World War II
Government sends more than 100,000 Japanese Americans into internment camps.

A traveler has his baggage searched at an airport security checkpoint.

DEBATE THE ISSUE

Terrorism and the Patriot Act After the devastating terrorist attacks of September 11, 2001, the United States declared a "War on Terrorism." Congress passed the Patriot Act to help law enforcement agencies prevent future terrorist attacks. The Act was to expire in 2005. In spite of controversy regarding it, Congress voted to extend the provisions of the Patriot Act to 2009.

"I have a lot of problems with the ... "Right after 9-11, the President ...

3

Name ___ Class ___ Date ___

American Issues Journal

Civil Liberties and National Security

Essential Question: What is the proper balance between national security and civil liberties?

1780 — 1790s Undeclared War with France, Alien and Sedition Acts — 1820 — 1860s Civil War, Habeas Corpus suspended — 1860 — 1900 — 1940s World War II, Internment of Japanese Americans — 1950s Cold War, Red Scare — 1940 — 1980 — 200... War... Terr... Patri... Act

...ts history, the U.S. government has faced moments when the safety of the ... more important than preserving all the rights and liberties of its citizens. ...n this page shows when this issue surfaced in U.S. history. ...tween national security and civil liberties affects all Americans. But how ...ce between safety and liberty surface in your life?

...ou define the term "safe?" 1. (b) How do you define the term "freedom?"

...where students assemble to learn, discuss ideas, and acquire essential ...ve citizens. Schools are also organizations with rules and regulations ...fety.

...things that you think 2. (b) What three freedoms do you think ...

Contents

A series of handbooks provides skills instruction to help you read, learn, and demonstrate your knowledge of American history.

Reading Informational Texts

Writing Handbook

Critical Thinking About Visuals and Text Sources

Speaking and Listening

Reading Informational Texts

Reading a newspaper, a magazine, an Internet page, or a textbook differs from reading a novel. You read nonfiction texts to acquire new information. Researchers have shown that the reading strategies presented below will help you maximize your understanding of such informational texts.

Strategies to Use Before You Read

Before you read informational text, it's important to take the time to do some prereading. These strategies will help.

Set a Purpose for Reading

Try to focus on a goal when you're reading the text. Preview a section by reading the objectives and looking at the illustrations. Then, write a purpose for your reading, such as:

- "I'll learn about the development of the North and South and find ways to compare these regions."
- "I'll find out about the growth of railroads."

Ask Questions

Before you read a section, consider what you'd like to know about a topic. Then, ask questions that will yield relevant information. Scan the section headings and illustrations and write a few questions in a chart like the one below. As you read, try to answer each of your questions. Use phrases and words to fill in the chart.

Question	Answer
Why did immigrants come to the United States in the late 1800s?	To find religious freedom, to escape poverty, to flee persecution
What was life like for immigrants when they arrived?	It was hard at first, but opportunities opened up; sometimes they faced hostility and prejudice.

Predict

Engage in the reading process by making predictions about what you are preparing to learn. Scan the section headings and the visuals. Then, write a prediction, such as:

- "I will find out what caused the United States to fight Spain in 1898."

Keep your predictions in mind as you read—do they turn out to be accurate or do you need to revise them?

Use Prior Knowledge

Research shows that if you connect the new information in your reading to your prior knowledge, you'll be more likely to remember the new information. You'll also see the value of studying history if you see how it connects to the present. After previewing a section, create a chart like this one. Complete the chart as you read the section.

What I Know	What I Want to Know	What I Learned
Older Americans are worried about Social Security and whether it will provide for them when they retire.	When did Social Security start?	Social Security was a program that started during the Great Depression of the 1930s to help provide for older Americans when they retire.

Strategies to Use As You Read

It's important to be an active reader. Use these strategies as you read informational text.

Reread or Read Ahead

If you do not understand a certain passage, reread it to look for connections among the words and sentences. For example, look for cause-and-effect words that link ideas or sequence words that show when events took place. Or, try reading ahead to see if the ideas are clarified later on. Once you find new clarifying information, return to the confusing text and read it again with the new information in mind.

Paraphrase/Summarize

To paraphrase is to restate information in your own words. Summarizing—a version of paraphrasing—can also help you confirm your understanding of the text. Summarizing focuses on restating the main ideas of a passage, as you can see in the example below. Include a few important details, such as the time period, to orient yourself or other readers to the text.

Original Paragraph	Summary
During the 1920s, the National Women's Party took a more militant position, demanding complete economic, social, and political equality with men. Its primary goal was the passage of the Equal Rights Amendment. Most women, however, believed that a new constitutional amendment was premature.	In the 1920s, the National Women's Party demanded complete equality with men, working for passage of the Equal Rights Amendment. Most women thought it was too soon for such an amendment.

Reading Informational Texts

Identify Main Ideas and Details

A main idea is the most important point in a paragraph or section of text. Some main ideas are stated directly, but others are implied. You must determine these yourself by reading carefully. Pause occasionally to make sure you can identify the main idea.

Main ideas are supported by details. Record main ideas and details in an outline format like the one shown here.

Changes in the South and West, 1880–1900

Main Idea → I. The South changed economically

Details → A. Industry developed

B. Train and road transportation grew

C. Cities attracted workers

Analyze the Text's Structure

Just as you might organize a story about your weekend to highlight the most important parts, authors will organize their writing to stress their key ideas. Analyzing text structure can help you tap into this organization. In a social studies textbook, the author frequently uses one of the structures listed in the chart at right to organize information. Learn to identify structures in texts and you'll remember text information more effectively.

Structures for Organizing Information

Compare and Contrast Here, an author highlights similarities and differences between two or more ideas, cultures, processes, people, etc. Look for clue words such as *on the other hand* or *similarly*.

Sequence Here, an author recounts the order in which events occurred or steps were taken. History is often told in chronological sequence but can also involve flashbacks from later times to earlier times. Look for sequence words such as *initially*, *later*, and *ultimately*.

Cause and Effect Here, an author highlights the impact of one event on another or the effects of key events. Cause and effect is critical to understanding history because events in one time often strongly influence those in later times. Look for clue words such as *because*, *so*, or *as a result*.

Analyze the Author's Purpose

Different reading materials are written with different goals, or purposes. For example, this textbook is written to teach you about American history. The technical manual that accompanies a cell phone is written to explain how to use the product.

An author's purpose influences not only how the material is presented but also how you read it. Thus you must identify the purpose, whether it is stated directly or merely suggested. If it is not directly stated, use clues in the text—such as opinion words in an editorial—to identify the author's purpose.

Vocabulary

Here are several strategies to help you understand the meaning of a word you do not recognize.

Use Context Clues You can often define an unfamiliar word with clues from the surrounding text. For example, in the sentence "One campaign of the Progressives had the goal of improving sanitation in cities," the words *campaign* and *improve* are clues that Progressives were reformers. Context clues can be in the same sentence as the unfamiliar word or in nearby sentences or paragraphs.

Analyze Word Parts Use your knowledge of word parts to help you define unfamiliar words. Break the word into its parts—root, prefix, suffix. What do you know about these parts? For example, the prefix *inter* means "between" and the suffix *ism* means "belief in." The word *international* means "between nations" and *internationalism* means "belief in relations between nations."

Recognize Word Origins Another way to figure out the meaning of an unfamiliar word is to understand the word's origins. Use your experience with Greek or Latin roots, for example, to build meaning. The word *bilingual* contains the Latin root *lingua,* which means "tongue." *Bilingual* means "two tongues" or "two languages."

Distinguish Between Facts and Opinions/Recognize Bias

It's important to read actively, especially when reading informational texts. Decide whether information is factual—which means it can be proven—or if it includes opinions or bias—that is, people's views or evaluations.

Anytime you read material that conveys opinions, such as an editorial, keep an eye out for author bias. This bias might be revealed in the use of emotionally charged words or faulty logic. For example, the newspaper editorial below includes factual statements (in blue) and opinion statements (in red). The emotionally charged words (underlined) will get a rise out of people. Faulty logic may include circular reasoning that returns to its beginning and either/or arguments that ignore other possibilities.

Editorial

Some day, Dwight Eisenhower will be remembered as the best President of the 20th century. He kept government small; he left the states alone to tend to their affairs; and the economy hummed. Any American with any sense will agree that these things contributed to the overall well-being of the nation.

Identify Evidence

Read critically. Do not accept an author's conclusion automatically. Identify and evaluate the author's evidence. Does it justify the conclusion in quantity and content? An author may present facts to support a claim, but there may be more to the story than facts. For example, what evidence does the writer of the editorial above present to support the claim that Eisenhower was a great President? Perhaps Americans who didn't prosper in the 1950s would disagree with the assertion.

Evaluate Credibility

After you evaluate evidence, check an author's credentials. Consider his or her level of experience and expertise about the topic. Is he or she likely to be knowledgeable *and* objective about the topic? Evaluating credibility is especially important with Web sites you may visit on the Internet. Ask the following questions to determine if a Web site and its author are reliable.

- Who sponsors the Web site? Is it a respected organization, a discussion group of individuals, or a single person?
- What is the source of the Web site's information? Does the site list sources for facts and statements?
- Does the Web site creator include his or her name and credentials?
- Is the information on the Web site balanced and objective or biased to reflect only one point of view?
- Can you verify the Web site's information using two other sources, such as an encyclopedia or news agency?
- Is the information current? Is there a date on the Web site to show when it was created or last updated?

Strategies to Use After You Read

Evaluate Understanding

Evaluate how well you understand what you've read.

- Go back to the questions you asked yourself before reading. Try to answer each of them.
- Check the predictions you made and revise them if appropriate.
- Draw a conclusion about the author's evidence and credibility.
- Check meanings of unfamiliar words in the dictionary to confirm your definitions.

Recall Information

Before moving on to new material, you should be able to answer the following questions fully:

- What was the text about?
- What was the purpose of the text?
- How was the text structured?

You should also be able to place the information you have just read in the context of your prior knowledge of the topic.

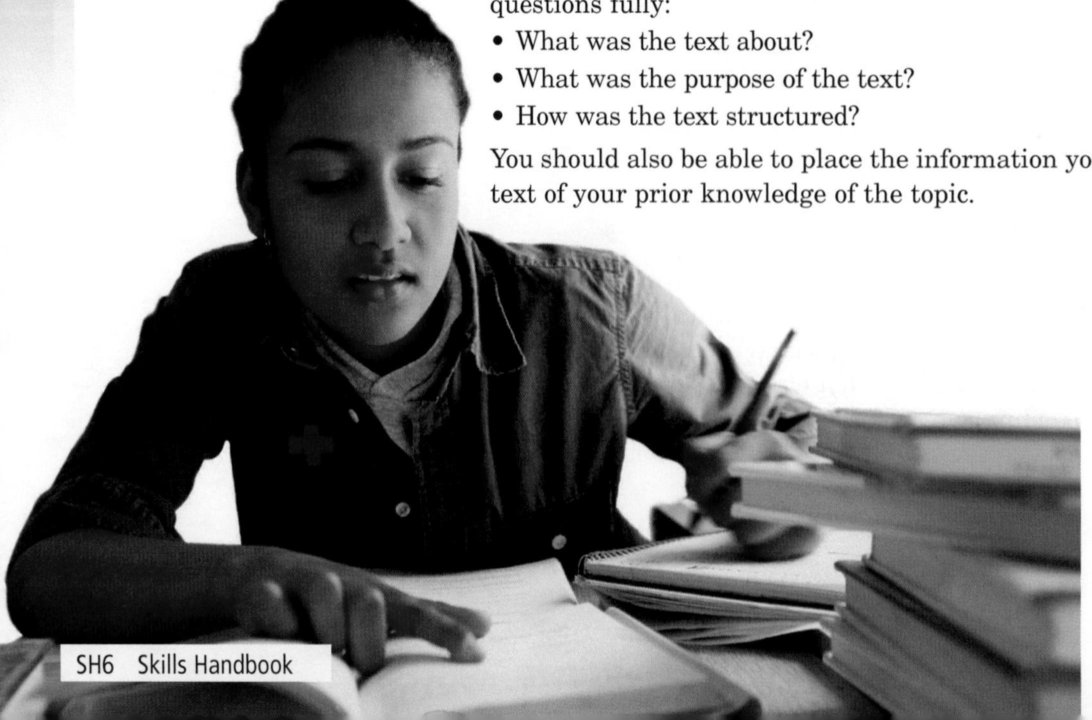

Writing Handbook

Writing is one of the most powerful communication tools you will use for the rest of your life. Research shows that writing about what you read actually helps you learn new information and ideas. A systematic approach to writing—including prewriting, drafting, revising, and proofreading—can always help you write better.

Narrative Essay

Narrative writing tells a story about a personal experience or a historical event. This story might also recount a person's life or tell about an important accomplishment.

1 Prewriting

Choose a topic. The focus of your essay will often be about a historical event from a particular point of view. Use these ideas as a guide.

- **Review the details of the event** you will be writing about.
- **Choose a person,** actual or fictional, who would have experienced the event.
- **List words** describing why the person caused the event or how he or she might have reacted to it.
- **Brainstorm** about the story you will write. Jot down ideas like the ones below.

Teenager in the 1920s responds to hearing jazz music for the first time.
• Circumstances: standing in the street outside an apartment building, overhearing a musician practicing
• Reactions: startled at first because the music is different; intrigued; spellbound; wants to dance to the music; goes home and tries to play jazz

Consider audience and purpose.

- Keep your **audience's** knowledge and experience level in mind. Make sure you provide any necessary background information.
- Choose a **purpose** as well. If you want to entertain, include humorous details. You might also include more serious insights.

Gather details.

- Collect the facts and details you need to tell your story.
- Research any background about the historical event that readers might need to know about.

2 Drafting

Identify the climax, or most interesting part of your story. Then, logically organize your story into a beginning, middle, and end. Narratives are often told in chronological order.

Open strongly with an engaging sentence, such as the one below, that will catch your reader's attention.

Use sensory details, such as sights, sounds, or smells, to make the story vivid for readers. Describe people's actions and gestures. Pinpoint and use detail to describe locations.

Write a conclusion that sums up the significance of the event or situation you are writing about.

Strong opening engages the reader.

Sensory details help the reader envision the experience.

Insight or significance tells the reader what this event means to the person in the narrative or to history.

I never could have imagined how a simple stroll down the street would change my life. I was walking down the street yesterday, whistling to myself, when the most strange and enticing harmonies drifted toward me from an open third-floor window. Now, I'm pretty cool, but I've never heard such music before. It set me tingling; it set me to swaying. It made me want to dance right there on the spot. I emerged from the trance as the saxophonist let the last full note drift into the air. Then, I rushed home to see if I could replicate the smooth new sound on my clarinet. I know this chance encounter has changed my life forever.

3 Revising

Add dialogue or description. Dialogue, or conveying a person's thoughts or feelings in his or her own words, can make a narrative more effective. Look for places where the emotions are especially intense. In the model, this might be when the writer began to "feel" the music.

First Draft	Revised Original
The music made me feel very involved. It made me want to dance.	It set me tingling; it set me to swaying. It made me want to dance right there on the spot.

Revise word choice. Replace general words with more specific, colorful ones. Choose vivid action verbs, precise adjectives, and specific nouns to convey your meaning. Look at the example above. Notice how much more effective the revised version is at conveying the experience.

Read your draft aloud. Listen for grammatical errors and statements that are unclear. Revise your sentences as necessary.

4 Publishing and Presenting

Share by reading aloud. Highlight text you want to emphasize and then read your essay aloud to the class. Invite and respond to questions.

Expository Writing

Expository writing explains ideas or information in detail. The strategies on these pages examine each of several types of expository writing.

1 Prewriting

Choose a topic. In social studies, the focus of your writing might be comparing and contrasting economic trends, explaining causes and effects of current events, or exploring problems the nation has faced and the solutions it has sought. These ideas are a guide.

- **Create a compare/contrast grab bag.** With a small group, write on separate slips of paper examples from each category: ideas, events, or time periods. Mix the slips in a bag and choose two. Compare and contrast the two ideas, events, or time periods.
- **Interview** someone who made a major change in lifestyle, such as moving from one part of the country to another. Find out how and why the person did this. Understanding why is the basis of any cause-and-effect essay.
- **Take a mental walk.** Study a map and envision taking a tour of the region. Think about problems each area you visit might face, such as economic challenges or natural disasters. Choose a problem and suggest solutions for it.

Consider audience and purpose. Consider how much your readers know about the problem, comparison, or event you will address. Suit your writing to your audience's knowledge or plan to give explanations of unfamiliar terms and concepts.

Gather details. Collect the facts and details you need to write your essay.

Research the topic. Use books, the Internet, or interviews of local experts. List facts, details, and other evidence related to your topic. Also consider your personal experience. For example, you might know about a problem from your own experience or have witnessed the effects of a historic legal decision.

Create a graphic organizer. For cause-and-effect or problem-solution essays, use a two-column chart. Process writing can be listed as a bulleted list of steps. A Venn diagram can help you compare and contrast.

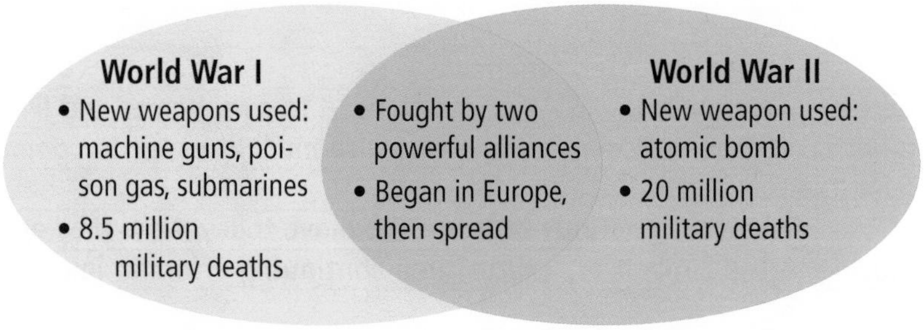

World War I
- New weapons used: machine guns, poison gas, submarines
- 8.5 million military deaths

Both
- Fought by two powerful alliances
- Began in Europe, then spread

World War II
- New weapon used: atomic bomb
- 20 million military deaths

Identify causes and effects. List possible explanations for events. Remember that many events result from multiple causes. Identify effects both large and small. Note that some events may have effects that in turn cause other events. Look for causes and effects in all your expository essays. But be aware that sometimes there are limitations on determining cause and effect.

2 Drafting

Match structure to purpose. Typically, cause-and-effect essays are written in sequence order. Problem-solution essays benefit from block organization, which presents the entire problem and proposes a solution. For compare/contrast essays, you can organize by subject or by point.

By subject: Discuss the events and outcomes of World War I, and then compare and contrast these with those of World War II.
By point: Introduce a category, such as use of new weapons. Relate both wars to this category, comparing or contrasting them along the way.

Give background. To discuss events from history, first orient the reader to time and place. Choose the important facts but don't overwhelm the reader with detail. If you need to, return to prewriting to narrow your topic further.

Elaborate for interest and emphasis. Give details about each point in your essay. For example, add facts that make the link between events so that a cause-and-effect relationship is clear. Also, readers will support proposed solutions more if your details clearly show how these solutions will solve the stated problem. Use facts and human experiences to make your essay vivid.

Connect to today. Even when you write about historical events, you may find links to today. Explore these links in your essay.

Identify the topic to orient readers.

The United States population underwent tremendous change in the first half of the twentieth century. In the early part of the century, Americans moved from rural to urban areas. Later, people moved out of cities into suburbs in increasing numbers. These changes resulted from many causes.

Chronological order walks readers through the cause-and-effect sequence.

Lured by jobs in the cities' factories, rural Americans and growing numbers of immigrants settled in cities during the late nineteenth and early twentieth centuries. By 1920, urban population had surpassed rural population.

Elaboration supports the relationship you are highlighting.

Thirty years later, Americans were again on the move. Cities had become overcrowded, and Americans longed to own homes and live in more space. The explosion of highways also made it easier to commute from the suburbs to the cities for work.

Connection to today tells readers why this matters to them.

Americans continue to be on the move today. Now they are moving to the Sunbelt or "exurbs" in a continuing effort to improve their lives.

 Revising

Add transition words. Make cause-and-effect relationships clear with words such as *because, as a result,* and so on. To compare or contrast ideas, use linking words, such as *similarly, both,* and *equally* or *in contrast, instead,* and *yet.* Use words such as *first, second, next,* and *finally* to help readers follow steps in a sequence or chain of causes. Look at the following examples. In the revised version, a reader knows the correct order in which to perform the steps.

First Draft	Revised
Historians form an educated guess called a hypothesis. They test that hypothesis with further research.	Next, historians form an educated guess called a hypothesis. Then, they test that hypothesis with further research.

Remember purpose. Shape your draft so that it answers the question or thesis you began with. For a problem-solution essay—in which your purpose is to sell your solution—that means anticipating opposing arguments and responding to them. For a cause-and-effect essay, you want to stress the way one event leads to the next. Always tell readers why they should care about your topic.

Review organization. Confirm that your ideas flow in a logical order. Write main points on index cards. Reorganize these until you are satisfied that the order best strengthens your essay.

Add details. Make sure you have not left out any steps in your essay, and do not assume readers will make the connections. For example, you might forget to state explicitly that your narrative represents a particular point of view. Add more background if necessary for clarity.

Revise sentences and words. Look at your sentence length. Vary it to include both short and long sentences. Then scan for vague words, such as *good.* Replace them with specific and vibrant words, such as *effective.* Use technical terms only when necessary, and then define them.

Peer review. Ask a peer to read your draft. Is it clear? Can he or she follow your ideas? Revise areas of confusion.

4 Publishing and Presenting

Contribute to a class manual. Include your comparison essay in a class History Journal.

Submit to a library. Find a specialized library, such as a presidential library. Mail your essay to the library's publications or public relations department.

Seek publication. If your historical events or issues are local, seek publication in a local historical magazine or contact a historical society. You might speak to its members.

Mail to an advocacy group. Find a local, national, or international organization that is concerned with your topic. Send it your essay and ask for comments on its ideas. Make sure to include a self-addressed stamped envelope and a note explaining your essay and offering thanks for its review.

Research Writing

1 Prewriting

Choose a topic. Often, a teacher will assign your research topic. You may have flexibility in choosing your focus or you may have the opportunity to completely define your topic. These ideas are a guide.

- **Catalog scan.** Using a card or electronic catalog in a library, or Internet search engine, search for topics that interest you. When a title looks promising, find the book on the shelves. Or follow up on your Internet search results by reviewing the linked Web sites. You can use what you find to decide on your final topic.
- **Notes review.** Review your social studies notes from the last month or so. Jot down topics that you found interesting. Then repeat the process with your other classes. For example, you might find a starting point for research into an environmental issue from a biology experiment.
- **Social studies categories game.** With a group, brainstorm categories in social studies. For example, you might list key American leaders or important wars. Within each category, take turns adding subtopics. The chart below shows different topics related to agriculture.

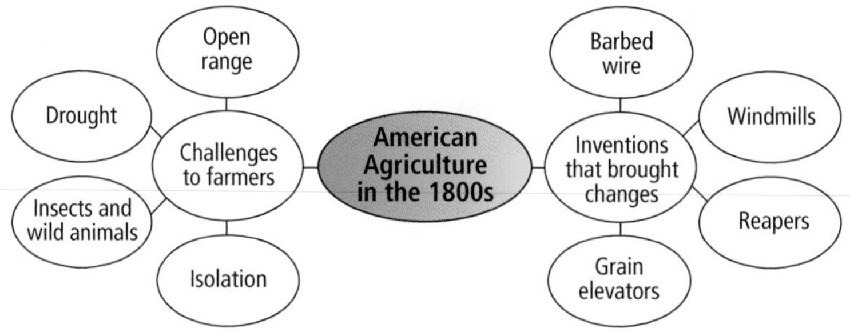

You can use sources such as newspapers to get ideas.

Daily News

December 17, 1903

Volume 1

Men Prove They Can Fly!

Analyze the audience. Your research and your paper should be strongly influenced by the audience. How much will readers know about this topic and how much will you have to teach them?

Gather details. Collect the facts and details you need to write your paper. Use resources beyond the typical history books. Look at nonfiction books such as memoirs or collections of letters. Also look at magazine and newspaper articles. Consider news magazines, as well as those focused on topics such as history or travel. Search the Internet, starting with online encyclopedias, news organizations, and history Web sites. Remember to check Web sites for reliability.

Organize evidence and ideas. Use note cards to record information and to help you organize your thoughts. Start with a general thesis statement in mind. Then begin reading and taking notes. Write a heading at the top of each note card to group it under a subtopic. Note a number or title to identify the information source. In the examples below, the number 3 is used. Use the same number for an additional source card containing the bibliographic information you will need.

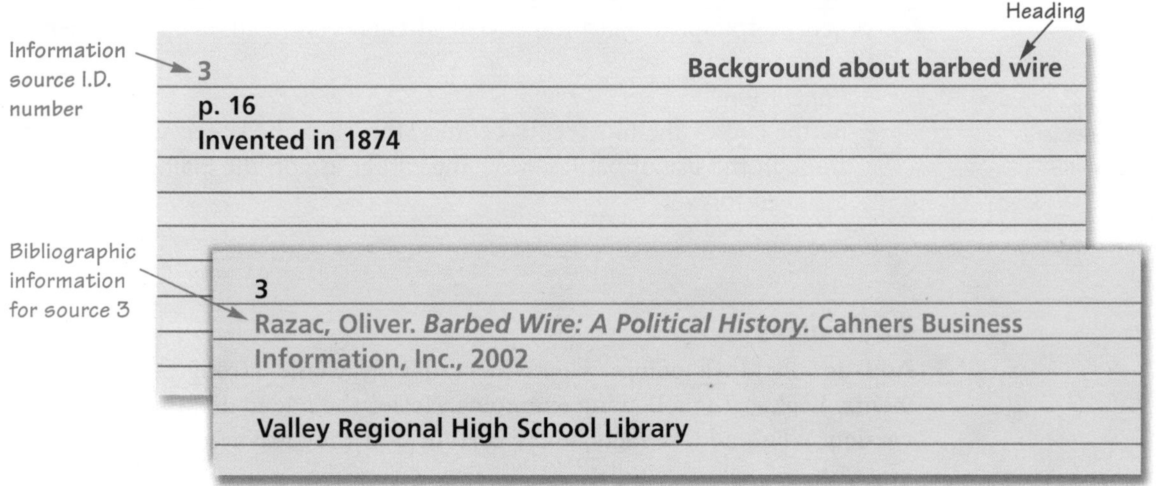

2 Drafting

Fine-tune your thesis. Review your notes to find relationships between ideas. Shape a thesis that is supported by the majority of your information, then check that it is narrow enough to address thoroughly in the allotted time and space. Remember, you can fine-tune your thesis further as you draft or even when you revise.

Organize to fit your purpose. Do you want to persuade readers of a particular position about your topic, compare and contrast aspects of the topic, or show a cause-and-effect relationship? Organize appropriately.

Make an outline. Create an outline in which you identify each topic and subtopic in a single phrase. You can then turn these phrases into sentences and later into the topic sentences of your draft paragraphs. Study the example at the top of the next page to see how to do this well.

Write by paragraph. Write an introduction, at least three body paragraphs, and a conclusion. Address a subtopic of your main topic in each body paragraph. Support all your statements with the facts and details you gathered.

An outline helps you structure your information.

Each body paragraph looks at a part of the whole topic.

The introduction puts the topic in a context of time and place. The entire paragraph conveys the thesis: dividing up the Plains with barbed wire had lasting effects for the region.

The conclusion recaps key points and leaves readers with a final statement to remember.

The Importance of Barbed Wire
Outline

I. Introduction
II. Why barbed wire was invented
III. How barbed wire was used
IV. Effects of the use of barbed wire
  A. End of open grazing lands for cattle
  B. End of cowboys' way of life
  C. Increased importance of farming on the Plains
V. Conclusion

Introduction
No invention was more important to the development of the American Plains than barbed wire. Until its widespread use in the late 1800s, cattle herds roamed the Plains region and farmers worried about their crops getting trampled. With the advent of barbed wire, all of this changed.

Conclusion
By the end of the nineteenth century, the Plains had been sectioned off through the use of barbed wire. The earlier life on the Plains had been changed forever.

3 Revising

Add detail. Mark points where more details would strengthen your statements. Look at the following examples. Notice the added details in the revised version. When adding facts, make certain that they are accurate.

Make the connection for readers. Help readers find their way through your ideas. First, check that your body paragraphs and the information within them flow in a logical sequence. If they do not, revise to correct this. Then, add transition words to link ideas and paragraphs.

Give credit. Check that you have used your own words or given proper credit for borrowed words. You can give credit easily with parenthetical notes. These include the author's last name and the relevant page number from the source. For example, you could cite the note card on the previous page as "(Razac, 16)."

First Draft	Revised
Cowboys would ride the range with huge herds of cattle. Their goal was to bring the herd to Kansas for shipping to markets in Chicago and the East.	Cowboys worked long hours on the dusty Plains, keeping constant vigilance on their herd of hundreds of cattle. They always kept the goal in sight: reaching Kansas, a key shipping center, then taking a well-deserved rest.

4 Publishing and Presenting

Plan a conference. Gather a group of classmates and present your research projects. You may each wish to create visual materials to accompany your presentations. After you share your papers, hold a question-and-answer session.

Persuasive Essay

Persuasive writing supports an opinion or position. In social studies, persuasive essays often argue for or against positions on historical or current issues.

1 Prewriting

Choose a topic. Choose a topic that provokes an argument and has at least two sides. Use these ideas as a guide.

- **Round-table discussion.** Talk with classmates about issues you have studied recently. Outline pro-and-con positions about these issues.
- **Textbook flip.** Scan the table of contents or flip through the pages of your textbook. Focus on historical issues that engage your feelings.
- **Make connections.** Relate current events to history. Develop a position for or against a situation of importance today using historical evidence.

Narrow your topic.

- **Cover part of the topic** if you find too many pros and cons for a clear argument of the whole topic.
- **Use looping.** Write for five minutes on the general topic. Circle the most important idea. Then write for five minutes on that idea. Continue looping until the topic is manageable.

Consider your audience. Choose arguments that will appeal to the audience for your writing and that are likely to persuade them to agree with your views.

Gather evidence. Collect the evidence to support your position convincingly.

- **Identify pros and cons.** Use a graphic organizer like the one below to list points on both sides of the issue.

The United States should increase its efforts to send astronauts to Mars.	
Pro	**Con**
• Space travel increases human knowledge about Earth and inspires young people to learn about science. • Space travel leads to technologies that can be used to improve life on Earth. • The United States has a history of exploration beyond its borders; this would be just one more step.	• Space travel is too expensive. • Space travel is a luxury; the nation should concentrate on needs at home. • There is no need to send humans to Mars when we can learn as much from robots traveling there.

- **Interview** adults who remember the first moon landing. What do they think about sending astronauts to Mars? Ask them for reasons to support their views.
- **Research** to get your facts straight. Read articles or books about the space program.

2 Drafting

State your thesis. Clearly state your position, as in this example:

> The United States should strongly promote the space program by sending people to Mars. We have so much to learn from the challenge of space travel that can help us at home.

Use your introduction to provide a context for the issue. Tell your readers when and why the issue arose, and identify the important people involved.

Sequence your arguments. Open or close with your strongest argument. If you close with the strongest argument, open with the second-best argument.

Acknowledge opposition. State, and then refute, opposing arguments.

Use facts and details. Include quotations, statistics, or comparisons to build your case. Include personal experiences or reactions to the topic, such as those a family member might have shared when interviewed.

Write a conclusion that restates your thesis and closes with a strong, compelling argument.

Background orients readers.

Thesis identifies your main argument.

Supporting argument clarifies your thesis.

Opposing argument, noted and refuted, adds to your position.

For a long time, the United States led the world in space exploration. But recently, the space program has become more limited. This situation should change. The United States should strongly promote the space program by sending people to Mars. We have so much to learn from meeting the challenge of space travel that can help us here at home.

Sending people into space has already yielded great rewards in the development of technology and other advances. Improved computers, medicines, and GPS systems are all positive by-products of space exploration. Some people might argue that space exploration is too expensive and that we have problems to tackle right here at home. However, the benefits of space exploration will help us at home today and in the future. The benefits outweigh the costs....

3 Revising

Add information. Extra details can generate interest in your topic. For example, in the essay on space travel, add a quotation from a news article that assesses the importance of space exploration to solving problems on Earth.

Review arguments. Make sure your arguments are logically sound and clearly developed. Avoid faulty logic such as circular reasoning (arguing a point by merely restating it differently). Evidence is the best way to support your points. Look at the following examples. Notice how much more effectively the revised version supports the argument.

First Draft	Revised
Space exploration will help our nation in many ways.	Space exploration will provide jobs, new technologies, and inspiration to young scientists.

Use transition words to guide readers through your ideas.

- **To show contrast:** *however, although, despite*
- **To point out a reason:** *since, because, if*
- **To signal conclusion:** *therefore, consequently, so, then*

4 Publishing and Presenting

Persuasive Speech. Many persuasive essays are delivered orally. Prepare your essay as a speech, highlighting words for emphasis and adding changes in tone, volume, or speed.

Writing for Assessment

Assessment writing differs from all other writing that you do. You have many fewer choices as a writer, and you almost always face a time limit. In social studies, you'll need to write both short answers and extended responses for tests. While these contrast in some ways, they share many requirements.

1 Prewriting

Choose a topic. Short-answer questions seldom offer a topic choice. For extended-response questions, however, you may have a choice of more than one question. Use the following strategies to help you navigate that choice.

- **Examine the question.** To choose a question you can answer effectively, analyze what each question is asking. Use key words such as those listed below to help you choose topics and respond to short-answer questions in which the topic is given.

Key Words	What You Need in an Answer
Explain	Give a clear, complete account of how something works or why something happened.
Compare/Contrast	Show how two or more things are alike and different.
Define	Give examples to explain meaning.
Argue, Convince, Support, Persuade	Take a position on an issue and present strong reasons to support your side of the issue.
Summarize	Provide the most important elements of a subject.
Evaluate/Judge	Assign a value or explain an opinion.
Interpret	Support a thesis with examples from the text.

Notice in the examples below that the key words are underlined:

Short answer: <u>Describe</u> one way that Chief Joseph showed his <u>military expertise</u>.
Extended response: According to the author of this article, Chief Joseph was both a <u>peace chief</u> and a <u>military genius</u>. Use information from the article to <u>support this conclusion</u>.

- **Plot your answer.** After choosing a question, quickly plot the answer in your mind. Do you have the information to answer this question? If the answer is no, try another question.

Measure your time. Your goal is to show the instructor that you've mastered the material. To stay focused on this goal, divide your time: one-quarter on prewriting; half on drafting; one-quarter on revising. For short-answer questions, determine how much of the overall test time you can spend on each question. Don't spend more than that.

Gather details. Organize the facts and details you need to write your answer. For short-answer questions, this usually involves identifying exactly what information is required.

Use a graphic organizer. For extended-response questions, divide your topic into subtopics that fit the type of question. Jot down facts and details for each. For the question on Chief Joseph, the following organizer would be effective:

Chief Joseph of the Nez Percés
Peace Chief
- traded peacefully with white settlers (1)
- reluctantly went to war (2)
- famous speech, "I will fight no more forever." (3)

Military Genius
- won battles with fewer warriors than opposing troops had (a)
- avoided capture for many months (b)
- led his people more than 1,000 miles (c)
- knew when to surrender for the good of his people (d)

2 Drafting

Choose an organization that fits the question. With a short-answer question, write one to three complete sentences. With extended responses, you'll need more elaborate organization. For the question on Chief Joseph, organize your points by importance within each subtopic. For a summary or explanation, use chronological order. For compare/contrast, present similarities first, then differences.

Open and close strongly. Start your answer by restating the question or using its language to state your position. This helps you focus and shows the instructor that you understand the question. Finish with a strong conclusion that restates your position. For short answers, include some language from the question in your response.

One way that Chief Joseph showed his military expertise was by defeating U.S. Army troops despite having fewer warriors than they had.

Support your ideas. Each paragraph should directly or indirectly support your main idea. Choose facts that build a cohesive argument. The numbered sentences in the draft below show how this writer organized support.

The opening restates the question and presents the writer's main idea.

The writer uses information from the graphic organizer, in order of importance.

The writer supports the second subtopic in a separate paragraph.

The conclusion recaps the main idea and again references the question's language.

Chief Joseph was both a peace chief and a military genius. He was a peace chief because he traded peacefully with white settlers for many years. (1) He went to war reluctantly after the government ordered his people to move to a reservation. (2) When he finally surrendered, he said in a famous speech, "I will fight no more forever." (3)

Chief Joseph was also a military genius. He fought off U.S. Army forces with fewer warriors than they had, (a) and he avoided capture for many months. (b) He led his people more than 1,000 miles (c) before he made the decision to surrender. (d) Chief Joseph will long be remembered for his dual roles as peace chief and military genius.

3 Revising

Examine word choice. Replace general words with specific words. Add transitions where these improve clarity. Read the following examples. The revised version shows the relative importance of the writer's supporting evidence.

First Draft	Revised
Chief Joseph was both a peace chief and a military genius. He was a peace chief because he traded peacefully with whites for many years. He went to war reluctantly....	Chief Joseph was both a peace chief and a military genius. He was a peace chief for several reasons. First, he traded peacefully with whites for many years. Second, he went to war reluctantly....

Check organization. Make sure your introduction includes a main idea and defines subtopics. Review each paragraph for a single main idea. Check that your conclusion summarizes the information you've presented.

4 Publishing and Presenting

Edit and proof. Check spelling, grammar, and mechanics. Make sure that tenses match, that subjects agree with verbs, and that sentences are not too long. Finally, confirm that you have responded to all the questions you were asked to answer.

Writing Rubrics

Use these charts, or rubrics, to evaluate your writing.

SAT	
SCORE OF 6 An essay in this category is **outstanding**, demonstrating **clear and consistent mastery**, although it may have a few minor errors. A typical essay • effectively and insightfully develops a point of view on the issue and demonstrates outstanding critical thinking, using clearly appropriate examples, reasons, and other evidence to support its position • is well organized and clearly focused, demonstrating clear coherence and smooth progression of ideas • exhibits skillful use of language, using a varied, accurate, and apt vocabulary • demonstrates meaningful variety in sentence structure • is free of most errors in grammar, usage, and mechanics	**SCORE OF 3** An essay in this category is **inadequate**, but demonstrates **developing mastery**, and is marked by **one or more** of the following weaknesses: • develops a point of view on the issue, demonstrating some critical thinking, but may do so inconsistently or use inadequate examples, reasons, or other evidence to support its position • is limited in its organization or focus, and may demonstrate some lapses in coherence or progression of ideas • displays developing facility in the use of language, but sometimes uses weak vocabulary or inappropriate word choice • lacks variety or demonstrates problems in sentence structure • contains an accumulation of errors in grammar, usage, and mechanics
SCORE OF 5 An essay in this category is **effective**, demonstrating **reasonably consistent mastery**, although it will have occasional errors or lapses in quality. A typical essay • effectively develops a point of view on the issue and demonstrates strong critical thinking, generally using appropriate examples, reasons, and other evidence to support its position • is well organized and focused, demonstrating coherence and progression of ideas • exhibits facility in the use of language, using appropriate vocabulary • demonstrates variety in sentence structure • is generally free of most errors in grammar, usage, and mechanics	**SCORE OF 2** An essay in this category is **seriously limited**, demonstrating **little mastery**, and is flawed by **one or more** of the following weaknesses: • develops a point of view on the issue that is vague or seriously limited, demonstrating weak critical thinking, providing inappropriate or insufficient examples, reasons, or other evidence to support its position • is poorly organized and/or focused, or demonstrates serious problems with coherence or progression of ideas • displays very little facility in the use of language, using very limited vocabulary or incorrect word choice • demonstrates frequent problems in sentence structure • contains errors in grammar, usage, and mechanics so serious that meaning is somewhat obscured
SCORE OF 4 An essay in this category is **competent**, demonstrating **adequate mastery**, although it will have lapses in quality. A typical essay • develops a point of view on the issue and demonstrates competent critical thinking, using adequate examples, reasons, and other evidence to support its position • is generally organized and focused, demonstrating some coherence and progression of ideas • exhibits adequate but inconsistent facility in the use of language, using generally appropriate vocabulary • demonstrates some variety in sentence structure • has some errors in grammar, usage, and mechanics	**SCORE OF 1** An essay in this category is **fundamentally lacking**, demonstrating **very little** or **no mastery**, and is severely flawed by **one or more** of the following weaknesses: • develops no viable point of view on the issue, or provides little or no evidence to support its position • is disorganized or unfocused, resulting in a disjointed or incoherent essay • displays fundamental errors in vocabulary • demonstrates severe flaws in sentence structure • contains pervasive errors in grammar, usage, or mechanics that persistently interfere with meaning
	SCORE OF 0 Essays not written on the essay assignment will receive a score of zero.

ACT	Scores of 4–6	Scores of 1–3
Purpose	shows a clear understanding of the essay's purpose by articulating a perspective and developing ideas	does not clearly articulate a perspective
Support	most generalizations developed with specific examples to support the perspective	demonstrates some development of ideas but may be overly general or repetitious
Focus	clear focus maintained throughout	focus maintained on general prompt topic but is not sufficiently specific
Language	shows competent use of language	language is mostly understandable, organization is clear but simple
Mechanics	minimal errors that only occasionally distract and do not interfere with meaning	errors frequently distract and interfere with meaning

Critical Thinking About Visuals and Text Sources

Analyze Graphic Data

The study of history requires that you think critically about the text you're reading as well as any visuals or media sources. This section will allow you to practice and apply some important skills for critical thinking.

Graphs show numerical facts in picture form. Bar graphs and line graphs compare things at different times or places, such as changes in school enrollment. Circle graphs show how a whole is divided into parts. To interpret a graph, look closely at its features. Use the graphs below and the steps that follow to practice analyzing graphic data.

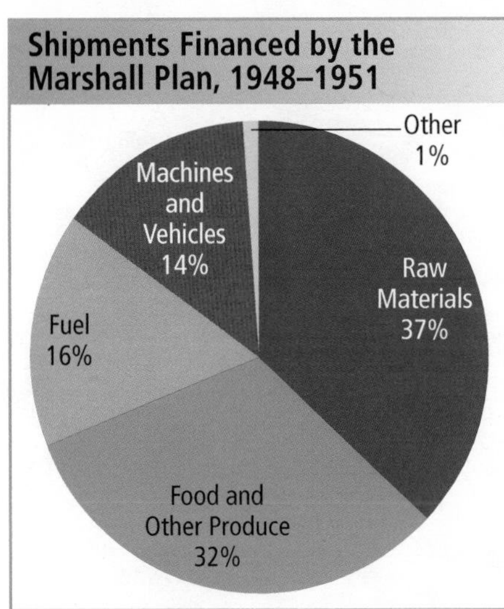

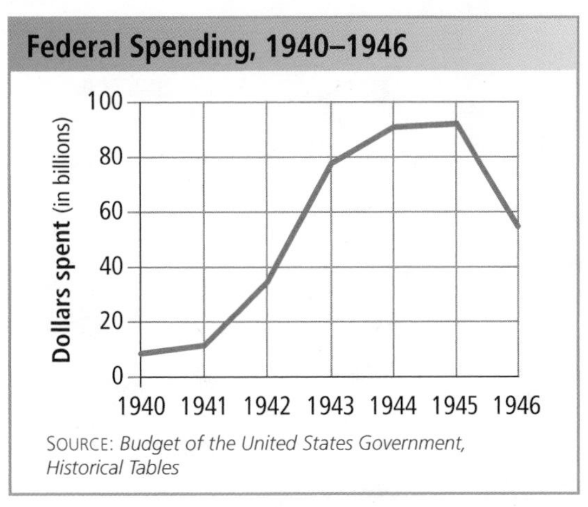

Read the title to learn the main topic of the graph.

Use labels and the key to read the data given in the graph. The line graph is labeled in years, with single-year intervals. The different colors on the circle graph represent the different shipments.

Interpret the graph. Look for interesting patterns in the data. Look at changes over time or compare information for different categories.

Practice and Apply the Skill

Use the graphs above to answer the following questions:

1. What is the title of the line graph? What is its topic?
2. In which year did federal spending increase at the fastest rate? State two generalizations that are supported by the graph.
3. The Marshall Plan was a program under which the United States helped European countries devastated by World War II. According to the circle graph, what proportion of shipments contained fuel? What proportion of shipments contained items that could help factories run?
4. Could the information in the circle graph be shown as a line graph? Explain.

Critical Thinking: Analyze Maps

Analyze Maps

Maps can show many different types of information. A physical map represents what a region looks like by showing its major physical features, such as mountains and plains. A political map focuses on elements related to government, such as nations, borders, and cities.

A special-purpose map provides information on a specific subject—for example, land use, population distribution, natural resources, or trade routes. Road maps are special-purpose maps, as are weather maps. These maps often use a variety of colors and symbols to show different pieces of information, so the key is very important. Use the map below and the steps that follow to practice analyzing a special-purpose map.

Louisiana Purchase

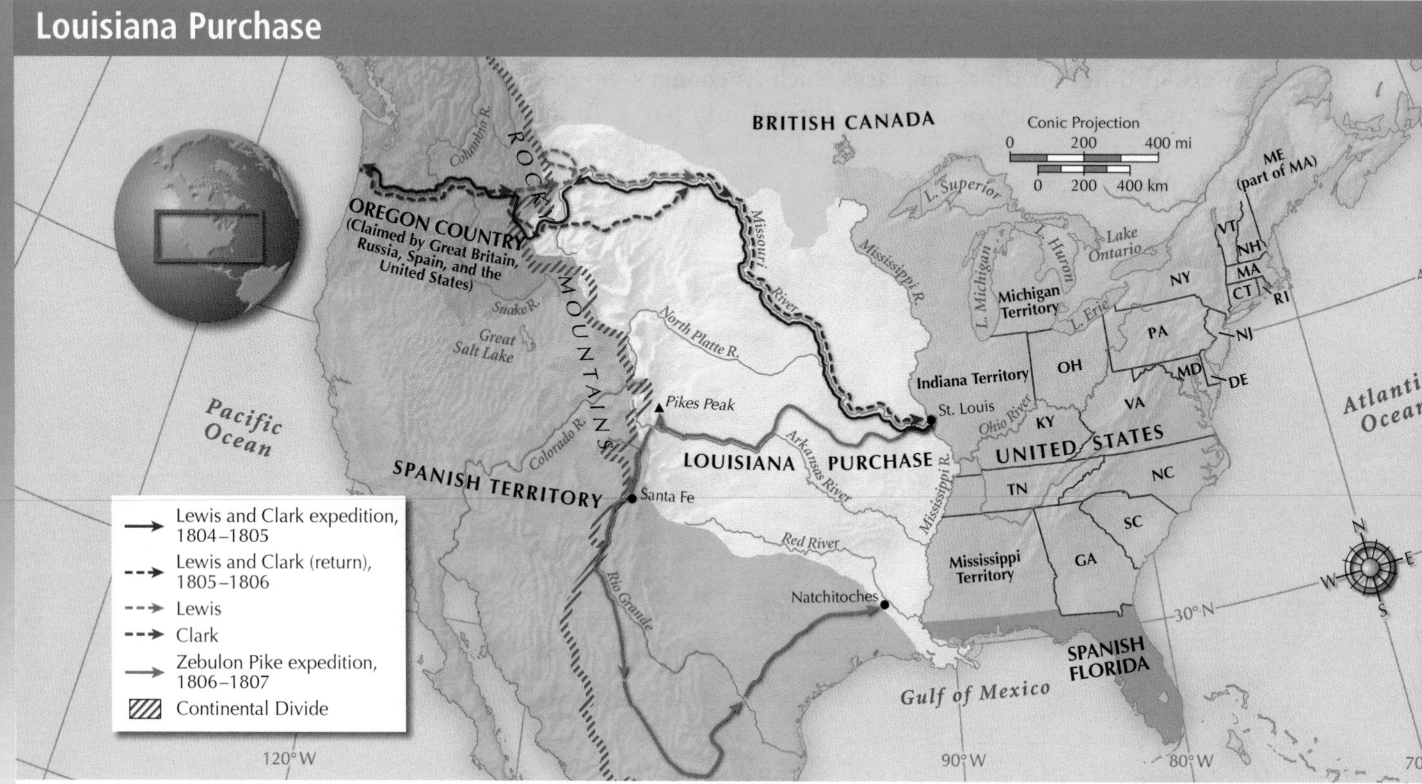

Study the title, locator globe, scale bar, and compass rose. Together, these features tell you the map's context—what part of the world it shows and why.

Read the key. Use the key to learn the specific details shown on the map.

Apply the key and labels to the map. Locate the symbols, lines, or colors from the key on the map. Also, read any labels on the map. Then, use the information given in the key and labels to understand what the map shows.

Practice and Apply the Skill

Use the map above to answer the following questions:

1. What is the purpose of this map? What part of the world does it show?
2. What does the red dotted line on the map represent?
3. Where did Zebulon Pike's expedition end?
4. Through which region did Lewis and Clark travel on their way to Oregon Country?
5. Does the map provide information about the effects of the Louisiana Purchase? Explain.

Analyze Images

Television, film, the Internet, and print media all carry images that seek to convey information or influence attitudes. To respond, you must develop the ability to understand and interpret visuals. Use the photograph below and the steps that follow to practice analyzing images.

In the 1950s, people everywhere worried about nuclear attacks. This 1952 image shows schoolchildren and their teacher ducking under desks during a nuclear air raid drill.

Identify the content. Look at all parts of the image and determine which are most important.

Note emotions. Study facial expressions and body positions. Consider the emotions they may suggest.

Read captions/credits. Gather information about the image, such as when it was produced.

Study purpose. Consider who might have created this image. Decide if the purpose was to entertain, inform, or persuade.

Consider context. Determine the context in which the image was created—in this case, the Cold War between the United States and the Soviet Union.

Respond. Decide if a visual's impact achieves its purpose—to inform, to entertain, or to persuade.

Practice and Apply the Skill

Use the photograph above to answer the following questions:

1. What is the focus of this photograph?

2. What feelings are conveyed by the children's facial expressions?

3. What do you think the photograph's purpose is?

4. When was this image produced? How did historical context influence its production?

Critical Thinking: Analyze Primary Sources

Analyze Primary Sources

Primary sources include official documents and firsthand accounts of events or visual evidence such as photographs, paintings, and political cartoons. Such sources provide valuable information about the past. Use the excerpt below and the steps that follow to learn to analyze primary sources.

In 1914, a great war broke out in Europe. Americans debated whether the United States should take sides in the war. In this excerpt, President Wilson expresses his views:

> **Primary Source** "The people of the United States are drawn from many nations, and chiefly from the nations now at war. It is natural and inevitable that there should be the utmost variety of sympathy and desire among them. . . . Some will wish one nation, others another, to succeed in the momentous struggle. . . . The people of the United States, whose love of their country and whose loyalty to its government should unite them as Americans all, . . . may be divided in camps of hostile opinion. . . .
>
> Such divisions amongst us would be fatal to our peace of mind and might seriously stand in the way of the proper performance of our duty as the one great nation at peace."
>
> —speech by Woodrow Wilson, August 19, 1914

Read the headnote, caption, or attribution line. Determine the source's historical context—who wrote it, when, and why.

Read the primary source. Identify and define unfamiliar words. Then, look for the writer's main point.

Identify facts and opinions. Facts can be proven. Opinions reflect a person's views or feelings. Use clues to help identify opinion words: exaggeration, phrases such as *I think,* or descriptive words such as *gorgeous.*

Identify bias and evaluate credibility. Consider whether the author's opinions suggest bias. Evaluate other factors that might lead to author bias, such as his or her previous experiences. Decide if the author knows enough to be credible and was objective enough to be reliable. Determine whether the source might be propaganda, that is, material published to promote a policy, an idea, or a cause.

Practice and Apply the Skill

Political cartoons reflect an artist's observations about events of the time. They often use symbols to represent things or exaggeration to make a point. Use the cartoon at left to answer the following questions.

1. What was happening in Europe when this cartoon was published?
2. What does the kneeling woman represent? the man?
3. What is exaggerated in this cartoon?
4. What opinion is the cartoonist expressing?

Compare Viewpoints

A person's viewpoint is shaped by subjective influences such as feelings, prejudices, and past experiences. For example, two politicians may recommend two different policies to address the same problem. Likewise, historians often have different interpretations of past events, based on their research and review of other historians' work. Comparing such viewpoints will help you understand issues and develop your own interpretations. The excerpts below offer two different views on why the founders wrote a new U.S. Constitution in 1787. Use the excerpts and the steps that follow to learn about comparing viewpoints.

Comparing Viewpoints

"[People who favored the Constitution] believed the slogans of 1776 were outmoded; . . . that certain political processes such as war, foreign affairs, and commerce, were national by nature; that the right to tax was essential to any government; and that powers wrested from king and parliament should not be divided among thirteen states, if the American government was to have any influence in the world."

—Samuel E. Morison and Henry S. Commager, *The Growth of the American Republic.* New York: Oxford University Press, 1962.

"The 55 delegates [to the Constitutional Convention] had much in common. All were white, male, and well educated, and many already knew one another. . . . Not surprisingly, all seemed to agree that the contagion of liberty had spread too far. . . . Most delegates hoped to replace the existing Confederation structure with a national government capable of controlling finances and creating [lender]-friendly [economic] policies. . . ."

—Jacqueline Jones, Peter W. Wood, Elaine Tyler May, Thomas Borstelmann, and Vicki L. Ruiz, *Created Equal: A Social and Political History of the United States.* Boston: Pearson Education, 2003.

Identify the authors. Determine when the historians studied or wrote.

Examine the viewpoints. Identify each author's main idea and evaluate his or her supporting arguments. Determine whether the arguments are logical and the evidence is sufficient to support the main idea. Confirm that the evidence is valid by doing research if necessary.

Determine the author's frame of reference. Consider how the author's background and historical specialty might affect his or her viewpoint.

Recognize facts and opinions. Identify which statements are opinions and which are facts. Opinions represent the author's viewpoint.

Evaluate each viewpoint's validity. Decide whether the viewpoints are based on facts and/or reasonable arguments. Consider whether or not you agree with the viewpoints.

Practice and Apply the Skill

Use the excerpts above to answer the following questions.

1. Who are the authors of these two excerpts? When was each excerpt written?
2. What is each historian's main argument about the U.S. Constitution? What evidence or supporting arguments does each provide?
3. How might each historian's frame of reference affect the viewpoint?
4. Are these two viewpoints based on reasonable arguments? Explain.

Synthesize Information

Just as you might ask several friends about a movie before deciding to see it, you can combine information from different sources to develop a fuller understanding of any topic. This process, called synthesizing, will help you become better informed. Study the documents below about developments during the Great Depression in the 1930s. Then, use the steps that follow to learn to synthesize information.

Document A

Rural poverty during the Great Depression of the 1930s.

Document B

Unemployment, 1928–1933

People (in millions)
15
12
9
6
3
0
3% of workforce
25% of workforce
1928 1929 1930 1931 1932 1933

SOURCE: *Historical Statistics of the United States*

Document C

Primary Source “This great nation will endure as it has endured, will revive and will prosper. So, first of all, let me assert my firm belief that the only thing we have to fear is fear itself—nameless, unreasoning, unjustified terror which paralyzes needed efforts to convert retreat into advance.”

—President Franklin Roosevelt, First Inaugural Address, 1933

Identify thesis statements. Before you can synthesize, you must understand the thesis, or main idea, of each source. Analyze how the information and ideas in the sources are the same or different. When several sources agree, the information is more reliable and thus more significant.

Draw conclusions and generalize. Look at all the information. Use it to draw conclusions that form a single picture of the topic. Make a generalization, or statement that applies to all the sources.

Construct and test hypotheses. As you learn new information about history, you can begin to form hypotheses, or educated guesses, about events and trends. You might form a hypothesis about why something happened or about the connection between two events. Then, as you learn more, you should test your hypothesis against new information. You should continue to refine your hypothesis based on the new information.

Practice and Apply the Skill

Use the documents above to answer the following questions.

1. What is the main idea of each source?
2. Which sources support the idea that the depression affected people throughout the United States?
3. Form a hypothesis about the Great Depression, based on the information presented.

Analyze Cause and Effect

One of a historian's main tasks is to understand the causes and effects of the event he or she is studying. Study the facts below, which are listed in random order. Then, use the steps that follow to learn how to analyze cause and effect.

The United States, with other nations, fought a war in North and South Korea in the 1950s. This list shows key trends and events related to that war.

- South Korea and its allies fight a 3-year war against North Korea and its allies.
- At the end of World War II, Korea was divided into North Korea, a communist nation, and South Korea, a noncommunist nation, divided at the 38th parallel.
- President Truman worried about the spread of communism in Europe and Asia.
- Communists gained control of mainland China.
- By the end of the Korean War, the border between North Korea and South Korea stood at about the 38th parallel, where it still is today.
- North Korea invaded South Korea.
- As a result of the north's invasion, the south and its allies pushed back.
- The United States continues to station troops along the border dividing North Korea from South Korea.
- Thousands of Americans were killed in the Korean War.
- The United States stations thousands of troops in West Germany.

Identify the central event. Determine to what event or issue all the facts listed relate.

Locate clue words. Use words such as *because, so,* and *due to* to spot causes and effects.

Identify causes and effects. Causes precede the central event and contribute to its occurrence. Effects come after the central event. They occur or emerge as a result of it.

Consider time frame. Decide if causes have existed for a long period of time or if they emerged just prior to the central event. Short-term causes are usually single or narrowly defined events. Long-term causes usually arise from conditions that are ongoing.

Notice relationships that are not causal. Sometimes events are related, but the earlier event did not cause the later event. For example, although there are parallels, the Russian Revolution was not caused by the American Revolution.

Practice and Apply the Skill

Use the list above to answer the following questions:

1. Which item on the list describes the central event whose causes and effects can be determined?
2. Name two facts that are long-term effects.
3. Name two facts that are probably causes of the central event.
4. Name one fact that is not a cause or effect of the central event, though it is related.

Critical Thinking:
Problem Solving and Decision Making

Problem Solving and Decision Making

When you have a problem to solve or decision to make, you can find solutions if you think in a logical way. Study the situation outlined below. Then use the steps that follow to learn the skills of problem solving and decision making.

Ending the Woes of the Great Depression

In 1929, the United States entered a period of extreme economic difficulties, known as the Great Depression. Thousands of businesses closed, millions of people lost their jobs, and many people had to leave their homes because they couldn't afford the rent or other costs. When the Depression began, Herbert Hoover was President. Later, Franklin Roosevelt was elected to replace Hoover. Both Presidents tried strategies to solve the problems brought on by the Depression.

Options for Presidents Hoover and Roosevelt

Option	Advantages	Disadvantages
1. Allow the economy to correct itself.	• The economy works better when left alone. • The government does not have the right to intervene in local economic affairs.	• This could take a long time, while people continue to suffer. •
2. Let the federal government do whatever is necessary to relieve the effects of the Depression.	• •	• •
3. Take certain federal actions, but rely mainly on the states and on private economic activities.	• •	• •

The Decisions

- President Hoover decided to follow Option 3.
- President Roosevelt decided to follow Option 2.

Effects of the Decisions

- Hoover's actions did not relieve the problems of the Depression quickly enough and he lost his bid for reelection in 1932.
- Roosevelt's actions put some people back to work and relieved some hunger, but did not end the Depression.

Identify the problem. You cannot solve a problem until you examine it and understand it.

Gather information and identify options. Most problems have many solutions. Identify as many solution options as possible.

Consider advantages and disadvantages. Analyze each option by predicting benefits and drawbacks.

Decide on and implement the solution. Pick the option with the most desirable benefits and least important drawbacks.

Evaluate the decision. After awhile, reexamine your solution. If necessary, make a new decision.

Practice and Apply the Skill

Use information from the box above to answer the following questions:

1. What problems did Presidents Hoover and Roosevelt face?
2. Identify at least one advantage and one disadvantage of Options 2 and 3.
3. Why do you think that neither President was able to end the Depression?

Draw Inferences and Conclusions

Text and artwork may not contain all the facts and ideas you need to understand a topic. You may need to draw inferences, that is, to add information from your own experience or knowledge, or use information that is implied but not directly stated in the text or artwork. Study the biography below. Then, use the steps that follow to learn how to draw inferences and conclusions.

HISTORY MAKERS

Ida B. Wells (1862–1931)

Wells had gained fame for her campaign against the lynching of African Americans. But she was also a tireless worker for women's suffrage and joined in the famous 1913 march for universal suffrage that took place in Washington, D.C. Not able to tolerate injustice of any kind, Ida B. Wells, along with Jane Addams, successfully blocked the establishment of segregated schools in Chicago. In 1930, she ran for the Illinois State legislature, which made her one of the first black women to run for public office in the United States.

Study the facts. Determine what facts and information the text states.

Summarize information. Confirm your understanding of the text by briefly summarizing it.

Ask questions. Use who, what, when, where, why, and how questions to analyze the text and learn more. For example, you might compare and contrast, or look for causes or effects.

Add your own knowledge. Consider what you know about the topic. Use this knowledge to evaluate the information.

Draw inferences and conclusions. Use what you learned from the text and your own knowledge to draw inferences and conclusions about the topic.

Practice and Apply the Skill

Use the biography above to answer these questions.

1. Who is discussed in the biography? When did she live?
2. Briefly summarize the text.
3. How might Wells's activities have been unusual for her time?
4. What inferences can you draw about Wells's character from the information in the biography?

Speaking and Listening

Speaking and listening are forms of communication you use every day. In certain situations, however, specific skills and strategies can increase the effectiveness of your communication. The strategies offered in this section will help you improve both your speaking and listening skills.

Participate in Group Discussions

A group discussion is an informal meeting of people that is used to openly discuss ideas and topics. You can express your views and hear those of others.

Identify Issues

Before you speak, identify the issues and main points you want to address. Incorporate what you already know about these issues into your views. Then find the best words to convey your ideas effectively.

Interact With the Group

As with persuasive writing, in a discussion it helps to accept the validity of opposing views, then argue your position. Always acknowledge the views of others respectfully, but ask questions that challenge the accuracy, logic, or relevance of those views.

Debating

A debate is a formal argument about a specific issue. Explicit rules govern the procedure of a debate, with each debater or team given an allotted time to make arguments and respond to opposing positions. You may also find yourself arguing a position you do not personally hold.

Prepare Your Arguments

If you support a position, use your existing knowledge of it to direct your research. If you personally oppose an assigned position, use that knowledge to identify likely opposing arguments. Generate an outline and then number note cards to highlight key information for each of your main points.

Avoid Common Pitfalls

Stay focused on your arguments. Be aware of words that may reveal bias, such as *unpatriotic*. Speak assertively, but avoid getting overly emotional. Vary the pitch and tone of your voice to keep listeners engaged. Try to speak actively, rather than just reading aloud, and use eye contact and gestures to emphasize your message.

Give an Oral or Multimedia Presentation

An oral or multimedia presentation provides an audience with information through a variety of media.

Choose Media

If you are limited to speaking only, focus your time on developing a presentation that engages listeners. If you can include other media, consider what kind of information each form of media conveys most effectively.

Maps	Graphs/Charts	Pictures	Diagrams	Audio/Video
Clarify historical or geographical information	Show complicated information in an accessible format	Illustrate objects, scenes, or other details	Show links between parts and a whole or a process	Bring the subject to life and engage audiences

Prepare Your Presentation

Gather information using library and online sources. Develop your most important ideas in the body of your presentation. Back up assertions with solid facts and use multimedia examples to illustrate key points.

Present With Authority

Practice your presentation to gain comfort with the ideas and the presentation sequence. Experiment with the timing of how to include multimedia elements. Make sure you have the necessary equipment and know how to use it.

Active Listening

Active listening is a key component of the communication process. Like all communication, it requires your engaged participation.

Focus Your Attention on Ideas

Look at and listen to the speaker. Think about what you hear and see. Which ideas are emphasized or repeated? What gestures or expressions suggest strong feelings? Can you connect the speaker's ideas to your own experiences?

Listen to Fit the Situation

Active listening involves matching your listening to the situation. Listen critically to a speech given by a candidate for office. Listen empathetically to the feelings of a friend. Listen appreciatively to a musical performance.

Ask Questions

Try to think of questions while you're listening. Look at these examples:

Open-ended	Closed	Fact
Why do you think it is so important for young people to vote?	Do you support the current voting age of 18?	How many people between the ages of 18 and 25 voted in the most recent election?

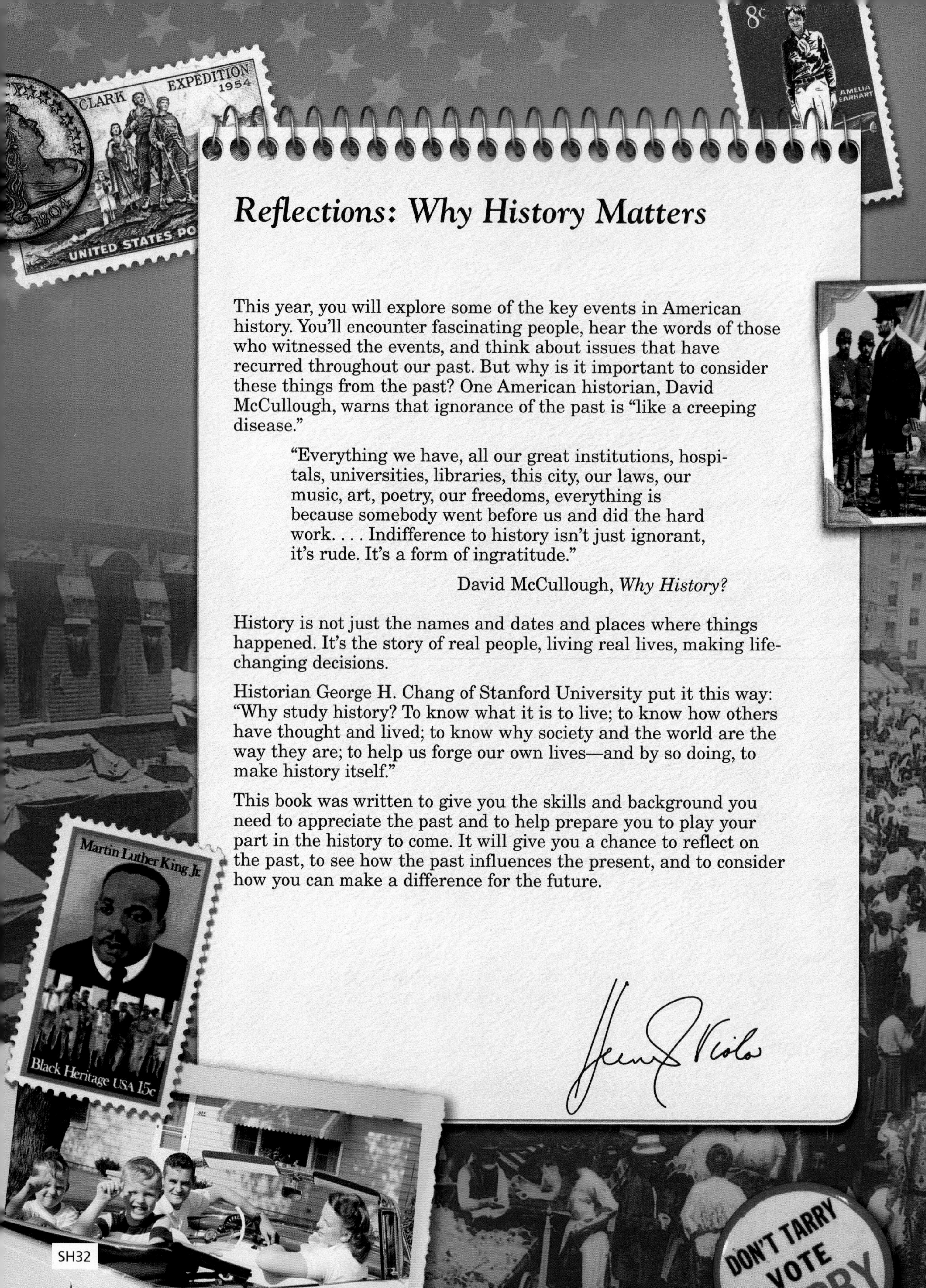

Reflections: Why History Matters

This year, you will explore some of the key events in American history. You'll encounter fascinating people, hear the words of those who witnessed the events, and think about issues that have recurred throughout our past. But why is it important to consider these things from the past? One American historian, David McCullough, warns that ignorance of the past is "like a creeping disease."

> "Everything we have, all our great institutions, hospitals, universities, libraries, this city, our laws, our music, art, poetry, our freedoms, everything is because somebody went before us and did the hard work. . . . Indifference to history isn't just ignorant, it's rude. It's a form of ingratitude."
>
> David McCullough, *Why History?*

History is not just the names and dates and places where things happened. It's the story of real people, living real lives, making life-changing decisions.

Historian George H. Chang of Stanford University put it this way: "Why study history? To know what it is to live; to know how others have thought and lived; to know why society and the world are the way they are; to help us forge our own lives—and by so doing, to make history itself."

This book was written to give you the skills and background you need to appreciate the past and to help prepare you to play your part in the history to come. It will give you a chance to reflect on the past, to see how the past influences the present, and to consider how you can make a difference for the future.

Origins of a New Nation

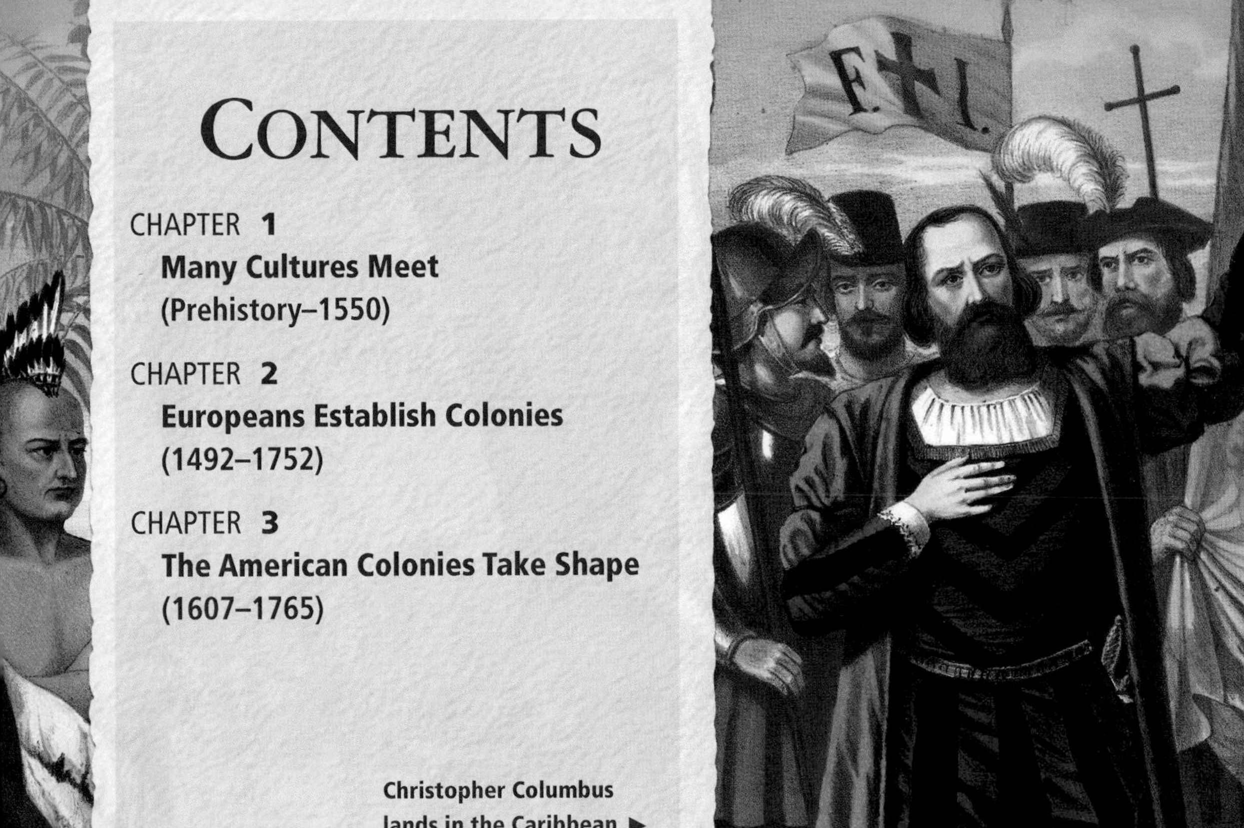

Contents

Christopher Columbus lands in the Caribbean. ▶

CHAPTER

1 Many Cultures Meet
Prehistory–1550

WITNESS HISTORY

The Discovery

Since departing from Spain, Christopher Columbus and his crew of 90 men had traveled westward across the Atlantic Ocean for more than 3,000 miles. After more than a month at sea, they finally sighted land on October 12, 1492.

The Europeans had hoped to find Asian lands. They had no idea that the islands upon which they landed were not near Asia but near two other continents about which they knew nothing. Columbus's accidental discovery began a chain of events that would bring death and devastation to some and wealth and success to others. In 1776, economist Adam Smith described the effects of European exploration:

> "The discovery of America, and . . . a passage to the East Indies by the Cape of Good Hope, are the . . . most important events recorded in the history of mankind. By uniting, in some measure, the most distant parts of the world, by enabling them to relieve one another's wants, to increase one another's enjoyments, and to encourage one another's industry, their general tendency would seem to be beneficial."
>
> —Adam Smith, *The Wealth of Nations,* 1776

◀ Columbus approaches an island near North America in 1492

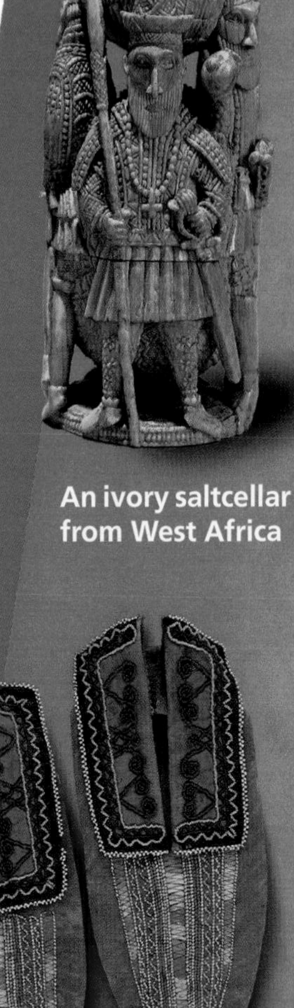

An ivory saltcellar from West Africa

Beaded leather moccasins from the Iroquois

Chapter Preview

Chapter Focus Question: How did the interaction of many cultures after 1492 affect the Americas?

Section 1
The American Indians

Section 2
The Europeans

Section 3
The West Africans

Section 4
First Encounters

Hohokam plates made from buffalo skin and decorated with red designs

Use the ☑ **Quick Study Timeline** at the end of this chapter to preview chapter events.

Note Taking Study Guide *Online*
For: Note Taking and American Issues Connector
www.pearsonschool.com/ushist

SECTION 1

▲ Portrait of a Blackfoot woman by artist George Catlin

WITNESS HISTORY

The First People

Scholars have studied where the first people of the Americas came from. Many American Indian groups have their own stories about how they came into being. This story comes from the Blackfoot people:

“One day Old Man decided that he would make a woman and a child. So he formed them both of clay. . . . After he had made the clay into human shapes, he said to it, "You must be people." And then he covered it up and went away. The next morning he went to the place and took off all the covering, but the clay had changed little. The fourth morning, he went to the place . . . and said "Get up and walk. They did so. . . . And that is how we came to be people. It was he who made us.”

—Story of the origin of the Blackfoot people

The American Indians

Objectives

- Explain how American Indians may have come to North America.
- Describe the process by which different American Indian groups and cultures developed.
- Describe the major culture areas prior to the arrival of Europeans in North America.

Terms and People

ice age	Aztecs
migrate	adobe
Mayas	Iroquois League

NoteTaking

Reading Skill: Identify Main Ideas As you read this section, complete an outline like the one below with the main ideas.

I. The First People of the Americas
  A. Paleo-Indians
    1.
    2.

Why It Matters The people who first inhabited North and South America found a land rich in resources and varied in geographic features. As they spread out across the land, they developed distinctive ways of living and surviving. Their cultures represent a central part of our heritage and history. **Section Focus Question: How did the spread of civilization begin in the Americas?**

The First People of the Americas

Scholars refer to the first humans to live in the Americas as Paleo-Indians. They think these people came from Siberia, a region in Asia that lies just across the narrow Bering Strait from Alaska. Scholars disagree, however, about when and how the Paleo-Indians arrived.

People Migrate to the Americas Until recently, most scholars insisted that the first Americans were hunters who arrived about 15,000 years ago. At that time, the world was experiencing an **ice age,** a time lasting thousands of years during which the Earth was covered by ice and glaciers. Much of the planet's seawater was frozen in polar ice caps. Therefore, the sea level fell as much as 360 feet below today's level. The lower sea levels exposed a land bridge between Siberia and Alaska. Scholars believe Paleo-Indian hunters crossed this land bridge in pursuit of their favored prey—immense mammals such as mammoths, mastodons, and giant bison.

However, some scholars today theorize that the first Americans **migrated,** or traveled, from Asia as many as 40,000 years ago. These were coastal peoples who gathered wild plants and hunted seals and small whales. According to this view, the first people to arrive in the Americas arrived in small boats, eventually working their way down the west coasts of North and South America.

Paleo-Indians Adapt to Climate Change Scholars do agree that about 12,000 to 10,000 years ago, the climate warmed. As temperatures rose, the polar ice melted and the oceans rose close to present-day levels. Together, the warming climate and the spread of skilled Paleo-Indian hunters killed off the mammoths and other large mammals. Meanwhile, the environment became more diverse. The northern grasslands shrank while forests expanded northward.

Vocabulary Builder
diverse–(duh VERS) *adj.* varied

Paleo-Indians adapted by relying less on hunting large mammals and more on fishing and on gathering nuts, berries, and roots. They also developed tracking techniques needed for hunting small, mobile animals such as deer, antelope, moose, elk, and caribou. The broader array of new food sources led to population growth. As the population grew, it expanded throughout the North and South American continents.

Diverse Cultures Emerge The Indians became culturally diverse as they adapted to their varying local climates and environments. Over time, their languages, rituals, mythic stories, and kinship systems became more complex and varied. By 1492, American Indians spoke at least 375 distinct languages, including Athapaskan, Algonquian, Caddoan, Siouan, Shoshonean, and Iroquoian. Each language group divided into many ethnic groups later called tribes or nations. In turn, these subdivided into many smaller groups that identified with a particular village or hunting territory. Each group was headed by a chief, who was usually advised by a council of elders.

The Beginnings of Agriculture Some of these peoples learned how to domesticate wild plants, so that they could be planted and grown for food. About 3,500 years ago in central Mexico, American Indians developed three important crops: maize (corn), squashes, and beans. The expanded food supply promoted population growth, which led to larger, permanent villages. In Mexico, some villages grew into great cities ruled by powerful chiefs. Residents built large pyramids topped with temples. By carefully studying the sun, moon, and stars, the Mexican peoples developed precise calendars of the seasons and the days. Along the Gulf of Mexico and the Caribbean coast, the leading peoples were the Olmecs and later the **Mayas.** In the highlands of central Mexico, the **Aztecs** became the most powerful people.

From Mexico, the methods of learning how to plant, cultivate, and harvest crops slowly spread northward. By about A.D. 1200, crop cultivation was common in the American Southwest, Midwest, Southeast, and parts of the Northeast.

In some places, people clung to a traditional mix of hunting, gathering, and fishing. Some lived in regions that were too cold or dry for farming, such as

Geography *Interactive*
For: Interactive map
www.pearsonschool.com/ushist

Migration to the Americas

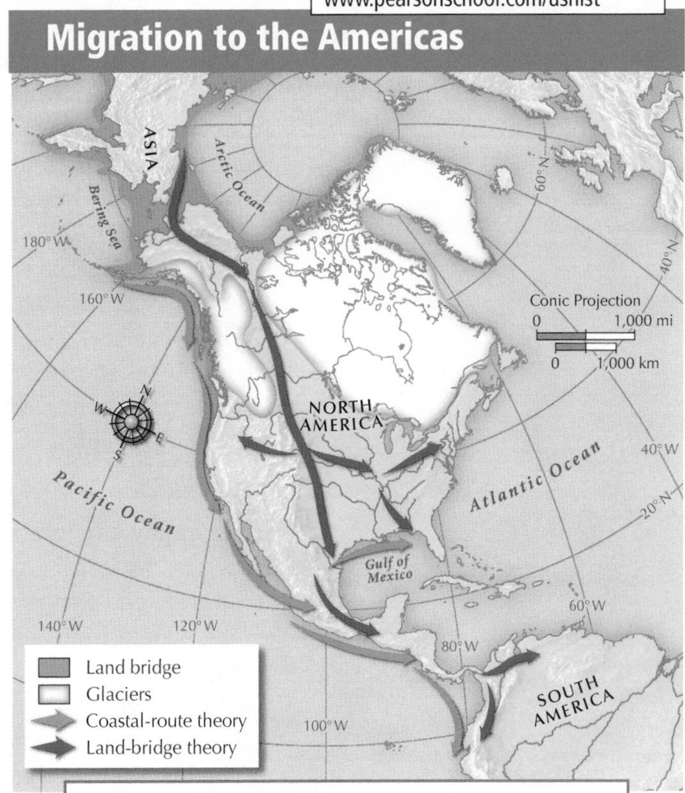

Map Skills The first people to come to the Americas spread slowly across the continents.

1. **Regions** What part of North America was filled with glaciers?
2. **Analyze Information** What geographical features may have caused people to keep moving south?

the frigid subarctic regions of Alaska, the Sierra Nevada, the Rocky Mountains, and the arid western Great Plains and Great Basin. In addition, coastal peoples in what is now California and the Pacific Northwest did not need to farm because their fishing—usually for salmon—and their gathering of nuts, seeds, and berries was so productive.

✓ **Checkpoint How did the ice age lead to the migration of people to the Americas?**

Early American Indian Cultures

As you just read, early people grew in numbers and developed permanent villages in areas where farming was practiced. A little more than 2,000 years ago, such villages began to appear in what would later become the United States.

The Southwest The first farming villages north of present-day Mexico emerged in the arid Southwest. There, the cultivation of crops required building ponds, dams, and ditches in order to irrigate, or bring water to, the fields. Building such complex systems required leadership by a group of priests and chiefs.

The Hohokams lived in the Gila and Salt river valleys of present-day southern Arizona. Over the course of their history, they built more than 500 miles of irrigation canals. The Hohokam irrigation canals were so elaborate that later peoples referred to the Hohokams as Canal Builders. In their largest village, about 1,000 people inhabited row houses built of **adobe,** a type of sun-dried brick. Some of the houses were three stories tall.

The Anasazis occupied the upland canyons in the Four Corners region at the intersection of Arizona, New Mexico, Utah, and Colorado. At Chaco Canyon, the Anasazis built an especially complex village that required 30,000 tons of sandstone blocks. This site became the center of the Anasazi world. Some of the multistory dwellings, known as pueblos, rose five stories and had about 600 rooms.

Between A.D. 1100 and 1300, both the Hohokams and the Anasazis experienced a severe crisis as a prolonged drought reduced crops. The resulting famine led to violence between rival villages that were competing for scarce resources.

The crisis broke up both the Hohokam and Anasazi villages. Most of the Anasazis moved south and east in search of water. They resettled along the Rio Grande and Pecos River, in present-day New Mexico. Today, they are known as the Pueblo peoples.

The Mississippi River Valley Unlike the arid Southwest, the Mississippi River valley enjoys a humid and temperate climate. The Mississippi River collects the waters of wide-ranging tributaries, including the Ohio, Missouri, Arkansas, and Red rivers.

The people from this area, known as the Mississippians, were influenced by the great cultures of Mexico. They built large towns around central plazas, featuring pyramids made of earth. At the top of the pyramids, they built wooden temples that also served as the residences of chiefs.

The largest and wealthiest city of the Mississippian culture was at Cahokia, in present-day southwestern Illinois. Cahokia benefited from being located near the junctures of the Missouri, Tennessee, Ohio, and Mississippi rivers. The site provided fertile soil and excellent trade connections with distant groups. At its peak in the year 1100, Cahokia had a population of at least 10,000 people and perhaps as many as 40,000.

During the twelfth century, Cahokia's residents abandoned the city. As in the Southwest, evidence suggests that an environmental crisis led to social conflict. The growing population had depleted the soil and deer. Hunger led to disease

INFOGRAPHIC

Ancient Cliff Dwellers

The word *Anasazi* has come to mean "ancient people." However, the term is not a Pueblo word but a Navajo word meaning "enemy ancestors." Today, Pueblo Indians refer to their ancestors as Ancestral Puebloans.

Before the ancient Pueblo people moved into cliff dwellings, they lived on the flat tops of mountains. As the population increased, residences built from hand-cut stone blocks rose along the sides of canyon walls. Shown here is Cliff Palace, built nearly 900 years ago. It is located in Mesa Verde National Park in Colorado. Embedded in the mountainside, the building gained heat from the sun in winter, while overhanging rock protected the structure from rain and snow.

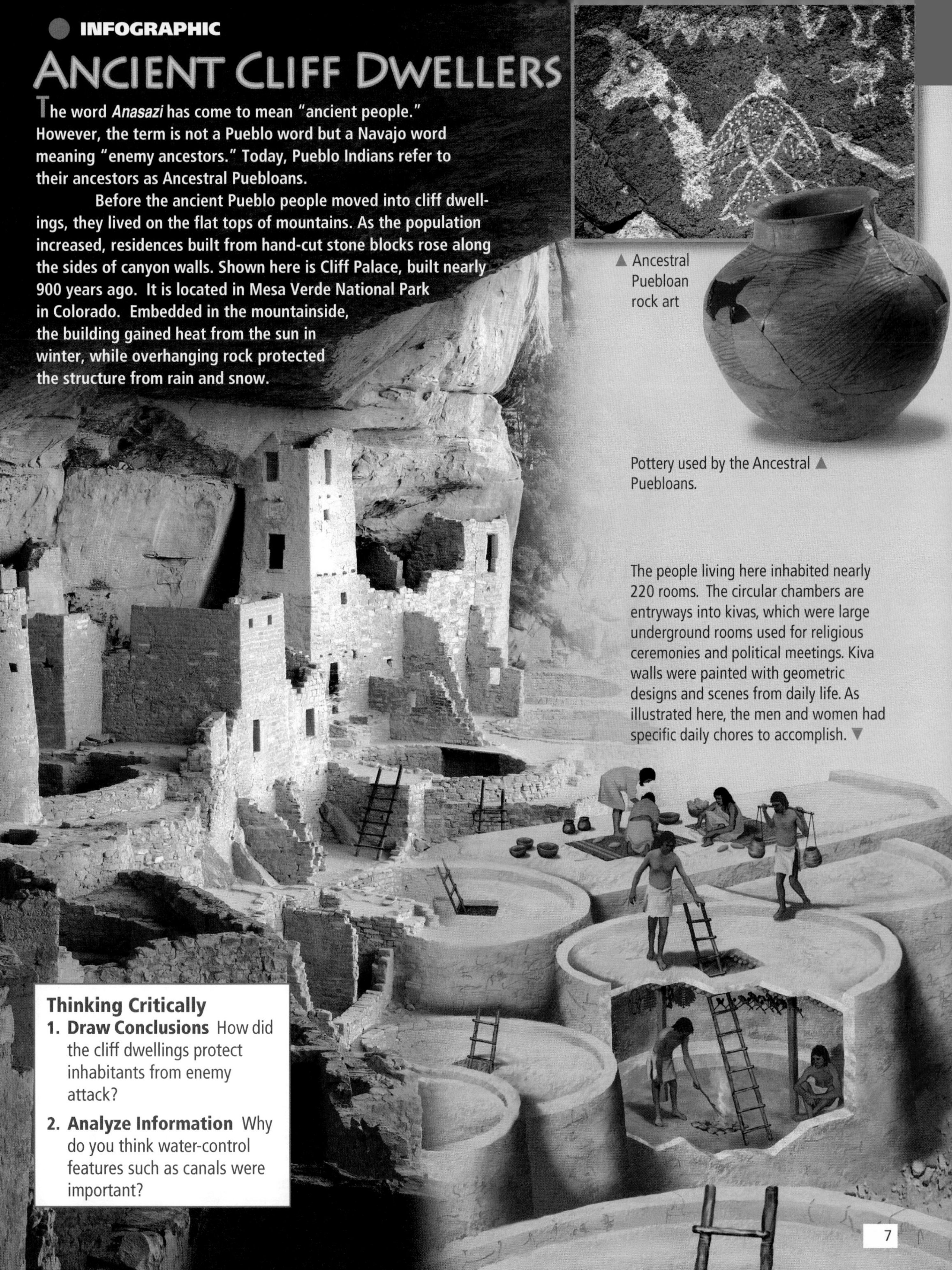

▲ Ancestral Puebloan rock art

Pottery used by the Ancestral Puebloans. ▲

The people living here inhabited nearly 220 rooms. The circular chambers are entryways into kivas, which were large underground rooms used for religious ceremonies and political meetings. Kiva walls were painted with geometric designs and scenes from daily life. As illustrated here, the men and women had specific daily chores to accomplish. ▼

Thinking Critically

1. **Draw Conclusions** How did the cliff dwellings protect inhabitants from enemy attack?
2. **Analyze Information** Why do you think water-control features such as canals were important?

Geography ***Interactive***
For: Interactive map
www.pearsonschool.com/ushist

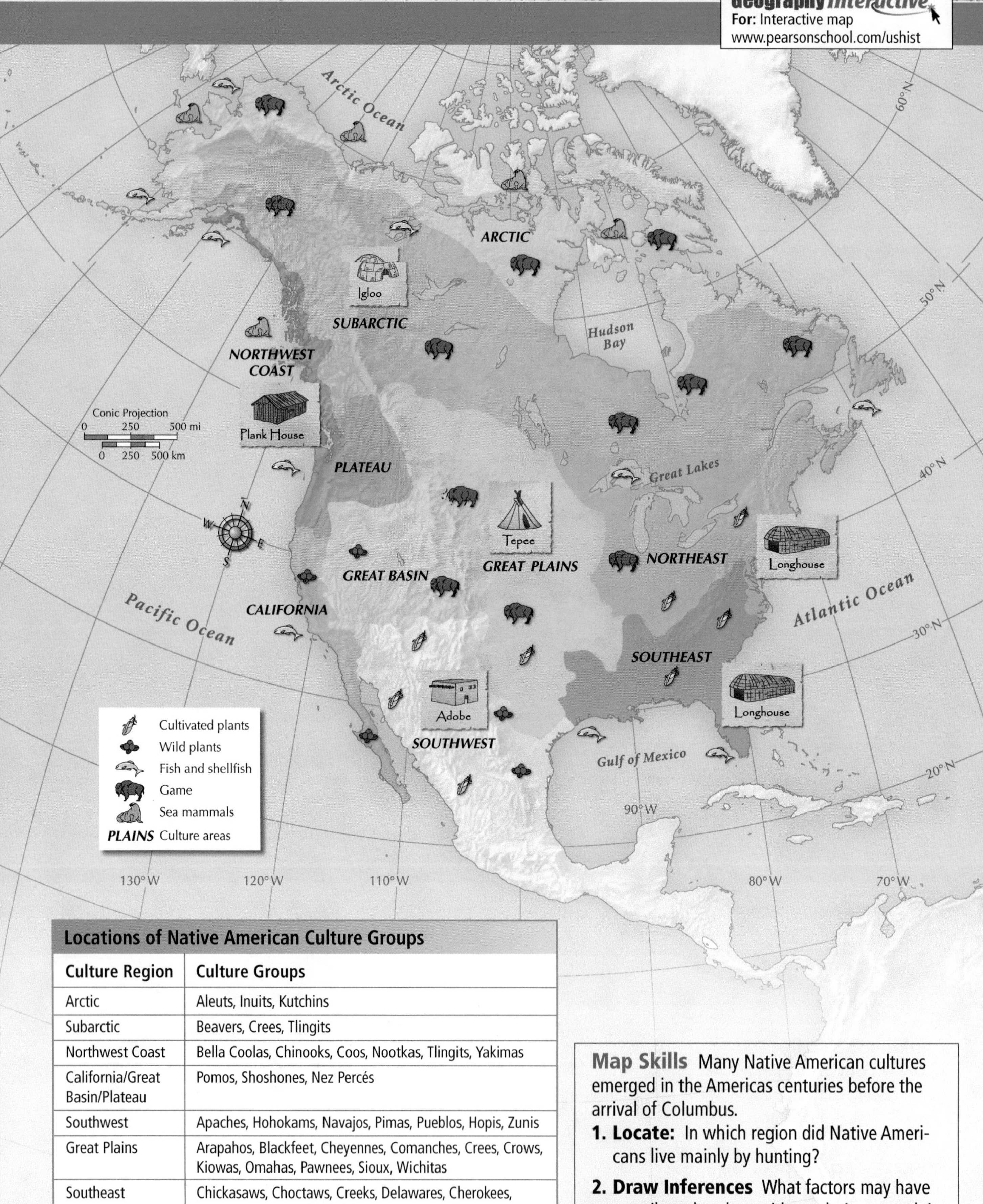

Locations of Native American Culture Groups

Culture Region	Culture Groups
Arctic	Aleuts, Inuits, Kutchins
Subarctic	Beavers, Crees, Tlingits
Northwest Coast	Bella Coolas, Chinooks, Coos, Nootkas, Tlingits, Yakimas
California/Great Basin/Plateau	Pomos, Shoshones, Nez Percés
Southwest	Apaches, Hohokams, Navajos, Pimas, Pueblos, Hopis, Zunis
Great Plains	Arapahos, Blackfeet, Cheyennes, Comanches, Crees, Crows, Kiowas, Omahas, Pawnees, Sioux, Wichitas
Southeast	Chickasaws, Choctaws, Creeks, Delawares, Cherokees, Tuscaroras, Mississippians, Natchez, Seminoles
Northeast	Algonquins, Hopewells, Iroquois, Leni-Lenapes, Winnebagos

Map Skills Many Native American cultures emerged in the Americas centuries before the arrival of Columbus.

1. **Locate:** In which region did Native Americans live mainly by hunting?
2. **Draw Inferences** What factors may have contributed to the rapid population growth in the Northeast?

and to fighting among villages. Although Cahokia disappeared, Mississippian culture still thrived to the south at Moundville in Alabama, Etowah in Georgia, and Spiro in Oklahoma.

The Great Plains Between the Rocky Mountains and the Mississippi River, the Great Plains is an immense, windy, and arid grassland in the heart of North America. The Great Plains receive only between 12 and 20 inches of rain a year. Only a few major rivers flow year-round. Instead of trees, drought-resistant grasses cover the land. Thus, the Great Plains favor grazing animals, especially the bison, or buffalo. When Europeans first arrived, the Great Plains probably supported more than 20 million bison.

During the ninth century, some Mississippians moved westward up the major river valleys onto the Great Plains. They built villages and planted crops beside the rivers. In the hotter southern valleys, people lived in well-ventilated beehive-shaped houses made from wooden frames covered with grass thatch. In colder northern valleys, villagers built log lodges well insulated with earth. In the summer, villagers ventured on foot onto the plains to hunt bison. While on the hunt, they lived in mobile camps. Their shelters were called tepees—cone-shaped tents of tanned bison hides stretched over a frame of cottonwood poles.

Great Plains villagers sometimes clashed with nomads who came from the Rocky Mountains to the west. Devoted to hunting, the nomads did not cultivate crops. By the fifteenth century, most of these nomads were Athapaskan speakers. Their enemies called them Apaches.

Some nomad bands established economic ties with the villagers of the valleys. The nomads traded buffalo meat and hides for maize, beans, squash, turquoise, pottery, and cotton blankets. The villagers would forgo this trade, however, when they lacked surplus food. Angered, the nomads raided the villages.

Vocabulary Builder
forgo–(for GOH) *v.* to decide not to do something

Eastern Woodlands The eastern region featured a vast forest atop rolling hills and a low range of mountains, the Appalachians. Many streams, rivers, and lakes drained this wooded land.

Stretching from eastern Texas to the Atlantic Ocean, the Southeast has mild winters and warm summers with plenty of rainfall. The Cherokees were the largest group in the Southeast. They lived in present-day western North Carolina and eastern Tennessee. Other people in the Southeast included Choctaws, Chickasaws, Natchez, and Creeks. Because of the long growing season, the Choctaws, the Creeks, and other southeastern groups were primarily farmers, but they also depended on hunting and fishing. They knew what plants to use to make rope, medicine, and clothing. Their main crops were corn, beans, squashes, and pumpkins.

Northeastern people developed into two major language groups: the Algonquians and the Iroquoians. The Algonquins occupied the Atlantic seaboard from present-day Virginia north to the mouth of the St. Lawrence River. The Iroquois lived around Lake Ontario and Lake Erie and along the upper St. Lawrence River.

A chief difference between the two cultures lay in their housing. Algonquins lived in wigwams: oval frames between 10 and 16 feet in diameter that are made of saplings covered with bark sheets or woven mats. Using similar materials, the Iroquois built larger multifamily longhouses, some more than 200 feet in length.

Five Iroquois peoples—the Mohawks, Oneidas, Onondagas, Cayugas, and Senecas—united to form a loose confederation, known as the **Iroquois League.** The Iroquois League was not a European-style nation. Lacking central authority, it was mainly a ritual forum for promoting peaceful cooperation among the member nations.

▼ Painting of an Algonquin village

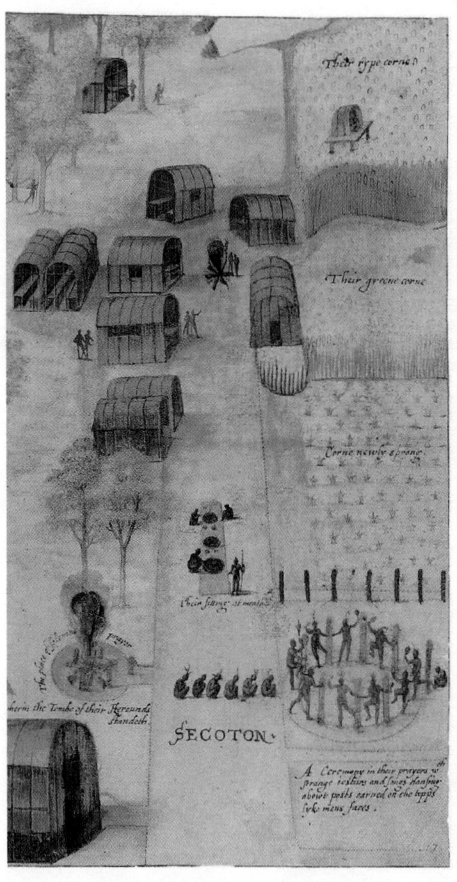

The Iroquois League's guiding law was a constitution, which was passed down by oral tradition. One version of this constitution includes the following:

> **Primary Source** "The Lords of the Confederacy of the Five nations shall be mentors of the people for all time. . . . Their hearts shall be full of peace and good will and their minds filled with a yearning for the welfare of the people of the Confederacy."
>
> —The Iroquois Constitution

✓ **Checkpoint What building style did the Mississippian culture take from Mexican culture?**

Common Cultural Features

Despite their cultural diversity, most Native American groups shared several cultural features. For example, most American Indians did not have centralized nations like those in Europe. Instead, political power was spread among many local chiefs with limited authority.

American Indians believed that spirits could be found in every plant, animal, rock, cloud, and body of water. If properly honored, the spirits could help people catch or grow what they needed. If offended, spirits might hide the animals or fish or destroy the corn crop. The spiritual leaders of a tribe, known as shamans, mediated between their people and the spirit beings. They conducted rituals to promote hunts, secure crops, and protect warriors.

American Indians owned little private property. Some families owned garden plots and hunting territories, but they could not sell them. Most local land was considered a common ground for every resident to use.

There was a respectful equality among the various groups of Indians. Usually, work was divided along gender lines. Men assumed more dangerous tasks, such as hunting and warfare. Women, meanwhile, cared for the children, wove baskets and made pottery, prepared meals, and gathered food. If their people cultivated crops, that work also usually fell to women.

Checkpoint What were three common cultural characteristics shared by most Native Americans?

SECTION 1 Assessment

Progress Monitoring *Online*
For: Self-test with vocabulary practice
www.pearsonschool.com/ushist

Comprehension

1. **Terms and People** Explain how each of the following terms is significant in understanding American Indian culture in North America.
   - ice age
   - migrate
   - Mayas
   - Aztecs
   - adobe
   - Iroquois League
2. **NoteTaking Reading Skill: Identify Main Ideas** Use your outline to answer the Section Focus Question: How did the spread of civilization begin in the Americas?

Writing About History

3. **Quick Write: Gather Details** Narrative essays tell a story and challenge you to use your imagination. List the details you will use to write a narrative essay about how life changed when your group shifted from a nomadic life to farming.

Critical Thinking

4. **Identify Points of View** What two leading theories explain how the first humans came to the Americas?
5. **Summarize** What sequence of events led to the expansion of people throughout the continents of North America and South America?
6. **Analyze Information** Why do you think more technologically advanced cultures would develop among farming societies rather than among hunting-and-gathering societies?

SECTION 2

◀ Prince Henry

▲ Portuguese sailors traveled in caravels, a new kind of sailing ship.

WITNESS HISTORY

Prince Henry the Navigator

For some time, Europeans dreamed of finding a shorter and easier route to Asia. Portugal led the way. Prince Henry the Navigator established a school where his sailors learned about navigation, mapmaking, and ship design. His sailors breached the unknown, taking voyages to islands off the coast of Africa. Duarte Pacheco Pereira, a Portuguese sea captain and explorer, explained the significance of the explorations in his navigation manual:

> "The benefits conferred on Portugal by the virtuous Prince Henry are such that its kings and people are greatly indebted to him, for a great part of the Portuguese people now earn their livelihood in the lands which he discovered, and the kings of Portugal derive great profit from this commerce."
>
> —from *Esmeraldo de situ orbis,* by Duarte Pacheco Pereira, 1505–1508

The Europeans

Objectives

- Describe the conditions in Europe in the fifteenth century.
- Analyze how the changes taking place in Europe affected its inhabitants.
- Describe the major developments on the Iberian Peninsula at the end of the Middle Ages and the start of the Renaissance.

Terms and People

Middle Ages
Renaissance
reconquista
Prince Henry the Navigator

NoteTaking

Reading Skill: Summarize As you read this section, fill in a chart like the one below to describe Europe before and after the 1400s.

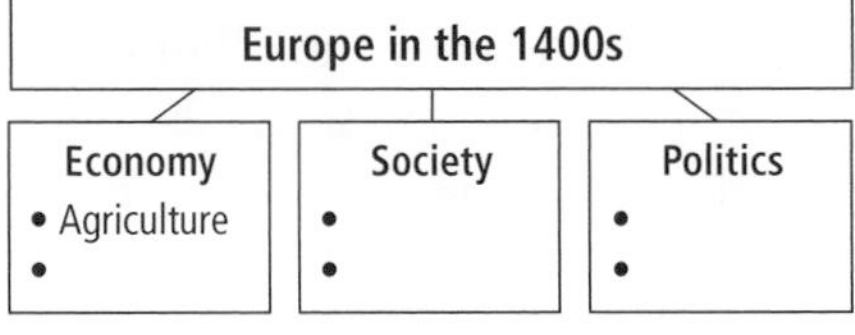

Europe in the 1400s		
Economy	Society	Politics
• Agriculture •	• •	• •

Why It Matters Europe in the 1400s experienced enormous cultural, economic, and technological changes. As new ideas swept the continent, some Europeans began to look beyond their shores to satisfy their growing ambitions. They were about to enter an age of discovery and exploration that would change not only Europe but much of the world as well. **Section Focus Question: How did Europeans begin to explore more of the world?**

Life in Europe in the 1400s

As the 1400s dawned, Europe concentrated on developing its political and cultural institutions. The earlier years of the **Middle Ages,** which began with the collapse of the Roman Empire, were marked by the absence of an effective central government and the constant threat of famine, disease, and foreign invasion. However, as new institutions and ideas slowly took hold, a new civilization emerged in Europe.

An Economy Based on Agriculture Hand tools and draft animals sustained an economy that was overwhelmingly agricultural. The population was recovering from the drastic effects of bubonic plague, known as the Black Death. During the 1340s, that epidemic had killed about a third of all Europeans. The great majority of the people lived in the countryside. Cities, however, were growing, especially in northern Italy and in the Netherlands. There, the small-scale manufacturing of cloth, tools, weapons, and ceramics came

Trade Towns
As trade increased during the Middle Ages, towns located near rivers prospered. Large trade fairs were set up in some cities, where the townspeople and merchants bought and sold goods. *How might location near a river or ocean lead to the economic growth of a town?*

from many workshops of artisans rather than from mechanized factories. The cities also served as bases for the merchants.

A Society of Unequal Classes Extremes of wealth and poverty characterized European society. A ruling elite of less than 5 percent of the population controlled almost all of the land. The most prestigious men were aristocrats—people who had inherited social rank and title and, generally, landed estates worked by peasants. Less honored, but often wealthier, were the great merchants who shipped cargoes between cities for profit. The elite also included leaders of the Roman Catholic Church. A monarch—usually a king but sometimes a queen—sat on top of the social pyramid in each kingdom.

Under the domination of this small elite class were the commoners. About three fifths of western Europeans were working poor. In good years, they subsisted by farming on land rented from an aristocrat or by selling their labor. In hard times, many fell into the ranks of the beggars. The most prosperous commoners were middle-class families. They owned enough property to employ themselves as farmers, artisans, and shopkeepers. Such people, however, accounted for only a fifth of the population.

Warring Kingdoms Western Europe was divided into a number of warring kingdoms. The most important were Castile, Portugal, France, and England. Each was ruled by a monarch who, in turn, depended on the elite class to do much of the governing. By waging war to conquer new territories, monarchs hoped to build their own power and to distract their often unruly aristocrats.

 **Checkpoint What was the structure of European society during the 1400s?**

Europe Looks Beyond Its Borders

Vocabulary Builder
adhere–(ad HEER) *v.* to stay firm in supporting or approving

During the Middle Ages, the Church strictly controlled intellectual life. Church leaders sought to ensure that all thought adhered to their understanding of the world. Church leaders felt that everything worth knowing had either been discovered by the Greeks and Romans or recorded in the Bible. Those who pursued scientific discoveries that went against Church teachings risked prosecution for heresy by Church courts.

Europe in the 1400s was in an era of rapid change. Though old ways of thinking persisted, many factors, especially rapidly widening trade, were broadening people's views of the world.

The Crusades and the Expansion of Trade In the latter half of the Middle Ages, European Christians and Southwest Asian Muslims fought one another in a series of religious wars known as the Crusades. The goal was to capture and hold Jerusalem and all of the Holy Land where Jesus had lived and died. In the end, the Muslims defeated the Christian Crusaders.

However there were other lasting effects of the Crusades that benefited the people of Europe. Europeans became aware of distant lands and different ways of life. Trade was encouraged. Crusaders returned home with goods and raw materials from the East, including silks, gems, and spices. Increasing demand for these products caused European traders to expand their businesses to Asia.

Trade Routes in Europe, 1000–1300

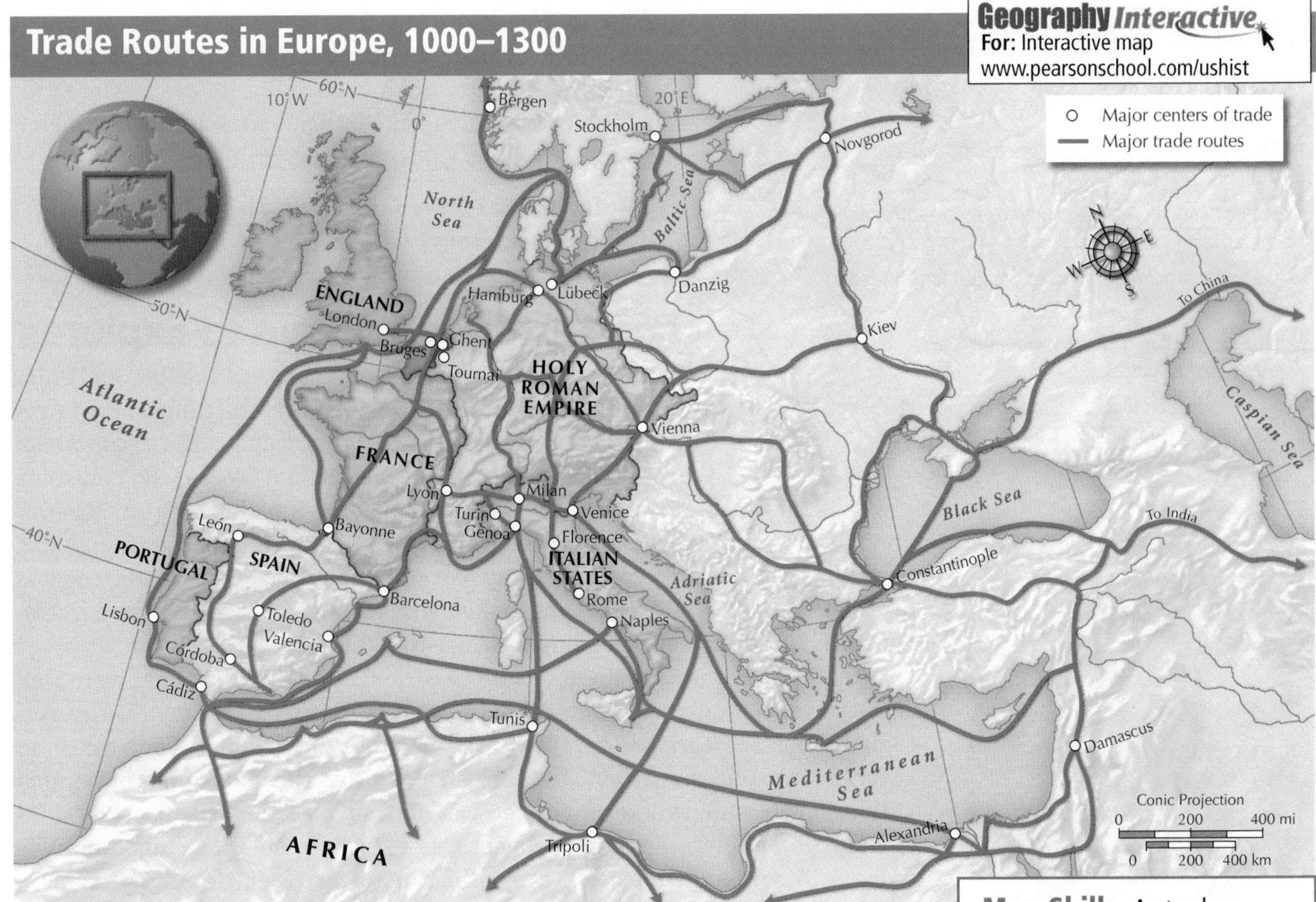

Map Skills As trade increased after the Middle Ages in Europe, major trade routes were established across the Mediterranean.

1. **Region** What major trade cities were located in Africa and Asia?
2. **Synthesize Information:** How do you think the lives of people living in the trade cities were affected?

The Renaissance and New Ideas By the mid-1400s, a new era had begun in Europe. Known as the **Renaissance,** it featured renewed interest in learning and the advancement of the arts and sciences. During the Renaissance, trade with and awareness of the world beyond Europe expanded. This, in turn, produced wealth for the increasingly powerful nations of Europe. This wealth and power would fuel more explorations. The effect for the people of Europe—and for the rest of the world—would be profound.

Popular literature reinforced the European longing for access to the fabled riches of India and China. During the fifteenth century, the development of the printing press lowered the cost and increased the volume of publishing. Books became available to more than the wealthy and leisured elite. The spread of literature helped promote the daring new Renaissance ideas of individualism and experimentation.

Readers especially delighted in vivid reports of the wealth and power of India and China. The most famous travel account came from Marco Polo, a thirteenth-century Italian merchant who had traveled across Asia to visit the emperor of China. Inspired by such accounts, Europeans longed to enlist Asian peoples and Asian wealth for a renewed crusade against Islam.

Europeans Seek New Trade Routes The Europeans, who were Christian, felt hemmed in by the superior wealth, power, and technology of their rivals and neighbors, the Muslims. Muslims followed the religion of Islam. Dominated by the Ottoman Turks, the vast Muslim realm stretched across North Africa and around the southern and eastern Mediterranean Sea to embrace parts of Eastern Europe and Southwest Asia. It also continued east through Central

Renaissance Changes Europe  Quick Study

- Increased trade and exploration bring knowledge of other lands.
- Printing press spreads literature and new ideas throughout Europe.
- Prince Henry the Navigator improves navigation and shipbuilding techniques.
- Competing monarchs sponsor voyages to gain wealth and territory.
- Portuguese shipbuilders develop the caravel, designed to travel long distances.
- New navigation tools such as the compass, the astrolabe, and more accurate maps allow longer voyages.

and Southeast Asia. The long and usually secure trade routes of the Muslim world extended from Morocco to the East Indies and from Mongolia to West Africa. The Ottoman Turks even invaded southeastern Europe, capturing the strategic city of Constantinople in 1453.

✓ **Checkpoint** **How did the Crusades help to expand Europe's horizons?**

The Portuguese Begin to Explore

European expansionists found hope on the Iberian Peninsula of southwestern Europe. There, the kingdoms of Aragon, Castile, and Portugal were waging the ***reconquista*** (reconquest) to drive out the Muslim Moors who had ruled Iberia for centuries. In 1469, the marriage of Prince Ferdinand and Queen Isabella united Aragon and Castile to create "Spain." In 1492, Ferdinand and Isabella completed the *reconquista* by seizing Granada, the last Muslim stronghold in Iberia. Long and violent, the *reconquista* promoted a zealous crusading spirit for spreading the Christian faith.

The Astrolabe
Navigators could determine a ship's latitude, as well as local time, with an astrolabe.

Facing the Atlantic Ocean and close to Africa, Spain and Portugal were well situated to seek new trade routes and to expand European influence. The Portuguese took the early lead in venturing out into the Atlantic. They relied on several new devices: the compass, the astrolabe, and the quadrant. These innovations helped sailors determine their location and direction when beyond sight of land. Shipbuilders were producing sturdier ships capable of sailing hundreds of miles. A ship known as the caravel had a stern rudder, three masts, and a combination of square and triangular *lateen* sails.

Starting in 1419, **Prince Henry the Navigator** directed Portuguese efforts to sail into the Atlantic, spread Christianity, and reduce Muslim domination of trade. Henry founded a school of navigation and sponsored several expeditions down the coast of West Africa. By sailing southward, the Portuguese hoped to reach the sources of the gold, ivory, and enslaved people that Muslim merchants transported across the great Sahara.

 **Checkpoint** **Why were the Portuguese venturing into the Atlantic Ocean?**

SECTION 2 Assessment

Progress Monitoring *Online*
For: Self-test with vocabulary practice
www.pearsonschool.com/ushist

Comprehension

1. **Terms and People** Explain how each of the following terms describes Europe in the fifteenth century.
   - Middle Ages
   - Renaissance
   - *reconquista*
2. **NoteTaking Reading Skill: Summarizing** Use your chart to answer the Section Focus Question: How did Europeans begin to explore more of the world?

Writing About History

3. **Quick Write: Use Sensory Details** You are a traveler entering a trade city. Use the image of the trade town to describe the sights and sounds that you encounter.

Critical Thinking

4. **Draw Inferences** Why do you think European technology became more advanced after the 1500s?
5. **Analyze Information** How did the Renaissance affect Europeans in the fifteenth century?
6. **Synthesize Information** Why do you think the *reconquista* sparked Spain's interest in exploration?

SECTION 3

▲ Mansa Musa, ruler of Mali

WITNESS HISTORY

Timbuktu

The city of Timbuktu first flourished as a trade center in the kingdom of Mali before becoming the intellectual center of West Africa. In the early 1500s, Leo Africanus, a Muslim of Spanish birth who had traveled widely in Africa, published his description of the great West African city of Timbuktu. It tells of the learned populace—and of a practice that would have a deep impact on West Africa's future.

"The people of Timbuktu are of a peaceful nature. They have a custom of almost continuously walking about the city in the evening (except for those that sell gold), between 10 P.M. and 1 A.M., playing musical instruments and dancing. The citizens have at their service many slaves, both men and women."

—Leo Africanus, *The Description of Africa,* 1526

The West Africans

Objectives

- Describe the development and cultural characteristics of West Africa in the fifteenth century.
- Summarize the events that led to contact between Europeans and West Africans.
- Explore the roots of the system of slavery practiced in the Americas.

Terms and People

Ghana	Mansa Musa
Mali	Songhai

NoteTaking

Reading Skill: Identify Details As you read, complete a concept web like the one below with details about major West African kingdoms.

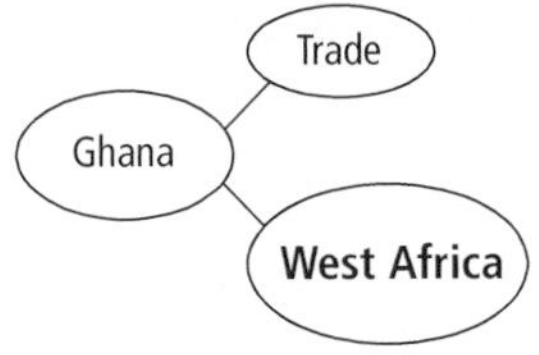

Why It Matters While American Indian cultures developed in the Americas and Europeans experienced the Renaissance, rich and varied cultures emerged in West Africa. The interaction between European and West African cultures in the 1400s helped set the stage for the transatlantic system of slavery. **Section Focus Question: What was life like in West Africa before the age of European exploration?**

West African Kingdoms

Throughout the 1400s, Portuguese sailors explored farther and farther south along the West African coast. By 1470, they had passed the equator to reach the Gulf of Guinea. Initially, the sailors acted as pirates, seizing gold, pepper, and slaves. But African resistance soon forced the Portuguese to shift to trade. The West Africans possessed civilizations that compelled grudging respect from the European explorers.

Geography Encourages Trade Western Africa is a varied land. An enormous desert—the Sahara—dominates the northern part. To the south of the Sahara lies a broad grassland, or savanna. South of this savanna is a lush region that is well watered by several major rivers, including the Niger and the Senegal. The West African landscape abounds with valuable natural resources—in particular, salt, found in the Sahara, and gold, located in the valleys along the Atlantic coast.

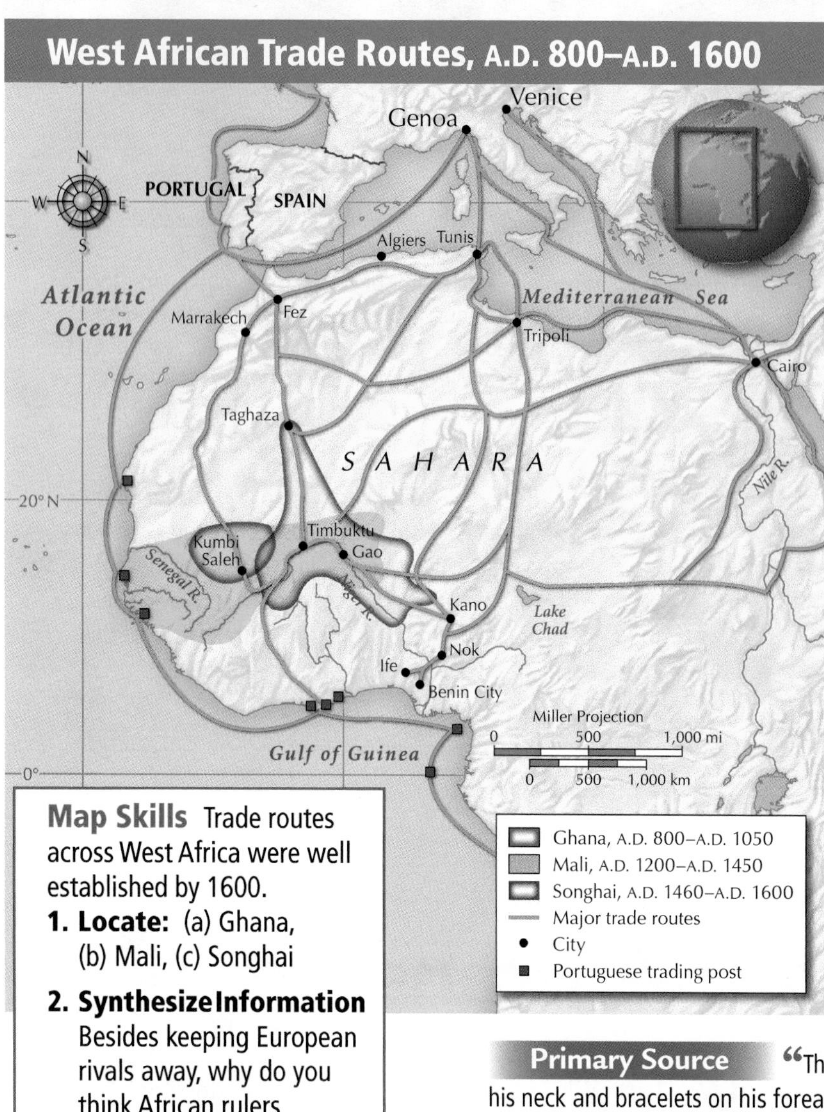

Map Skills Trade routes across West Africa were well established by 1600.

1. **Locate:** (a) Ghana, (b) Mali, (c) Songhai
2. **Synthesize Information** Besides keeping European rivals away, why do you think African rulers allowed only Portuguese trading posts along the coast?

Geography *Interactive*
For: Interactive map
www.pearsonschool.com/ushist

Hundreds of years ago, these resources provided for a thriving trade network among the people of West Africa. This trade revolved around certain trading towns, which grew into great and powerful empires. The trading empires of West Africa commanded trading routes that linked the region with North Africa, the Mediterranean, and Asia. Trade promoted rich and thriving cultures.

Ghana Between A.D. 300 and 1500, three kingdoms rose and fell in West Africa. The earliest kingdom, **Ghana,** would expand from the Sahara to the Gulf of Guinea and from the Atlantic Ocean to the Niger River. Ghana rose to prominence around A.D. 800.

A thriving caravan trade with African peoples across the Sahara to Morocco resulted in extensive Muslim influence in North Africa. By the eleventh century, Ghana supplied much of the gold for the Mediterranean region.

The ancient kingdom had large towns, beautifully designed buildings, a system of commerce, and a complex political structure. A Spanish Muslim writer from the eleventh century recorded this account of the lavish lifestyle of Ghana's king:

Primary Source "The King adorns himself . . . wearing necklaces around his neck and bracelets on his forearms, and he puts on a high cap decorated with gold and wrapped in a turban of fine cotton. He sits in audience to hear grievances against officials in a domed pavilion around which stand ten horses covered with gold-embroidered materials."

—Al-Bakri, *The Book of Routes and Realms*

Vocabulary Builder
domain–(doh MAYN) *n.* an area of land owned or controlled by one person, group, or government

Mali Attacks from outsiders eventually weakened Ghana's control of West African trade. The kingdom's power faded until, finally, Ghana was supplanted around A.D. 1200 by a new kingdom known as **Mali.** The most famous ruler of Mali was a king named **Mansa Musa.** During his reign in the early 1300s, he expanded Mali's domain westward to the Atlantic coast and increased the role of Islam, a religious faith that spread slowly through North Africa in the early 700s, when the region was under Muslim conquest. His promotion of Islamic scholarship helped lead to the founding of the famous university at Timbuktu. This great center of learning and culture was known throughout the Islamic world. The kingdom of Mali weakened after the death of Mansa Musa in 1332.

Songhai By the 1400s, another empire emerged: **Songhai.** Under the rule of Askia Muhammad, Songhai sustained an Islamic system of education based at the capital of Timbuktu. Like Ghana and Mali, Songhai grew rich from trade. In 1468, Songhai's armies conquered Mali and its capital. As a result, Songhai became the most powerful and largest kingdom in West Africa.

Other Kingdoms In addition to the great empires of Ghana, Mali, and Songhai, West Africa also hosted smaller kingdoms. For example, to the south of

INFOGRAPHIC

TRADE FLOURISHES IN ANCIENT GHANA

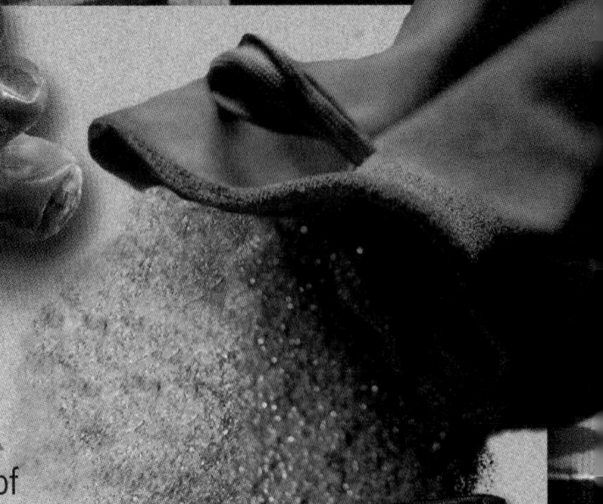

Gold and salt dominated the trans-Sahara trade in ancient Africa. Caravans carried salt from mines in the Sahara to trading areas along the Niger River in present-day Mali. Traders from these caravans hoped to exchange salt for gold that was mined in forests near the source of the Niger River. This trade established the wealth of ancient Ghana because salt traders, after crossing the Sahara, passed through the capital of Ghana, where they paid a tax on goods brought into Ghana.

Ghana markets ▲ offered a variety of food products, including dates.

Standard weights, such as the one shown, were used to weigh gold. ▶

The salt trade still exists in some parts of Africa. Here, a worker in Mali prepares slabs for market. ▼

Thinking Critically

1. **Draw Inferences** Why do you think the ruler of Ghana guarded the location of the gold mines?
2. **Analyze Information** The king of Ghana built a special city to receive Muslim merchants, traders, and foreigners. Why do you think the king felt this was needed?

History *Interactive*

For: To discover more about Ancient Ghana
www.pearsonschool.com/ushist

The route taken by most traders to Ghana would have started in North Africa and ended in Kumbi Saleh, the capital of ancient Ghana. Built on the edge of the Sahara, the city became an important trade center. After traveling many months through the desert in large camel caravans (sometimes taking as long as three months), prosperous Muslim merchants, as illustrated below, arrived to trade and sell goods.

Songhai, the kingdom of Benin occupied the tropical forest along the Gulf of Guinea. Known as "obas," the kings of Benin promoted art, especially sculptures in bronze or ivory. The Hausa people built seven cities in present-day Nigeria and Niger. Both became well known for producing beautiful cloth and for establishing extensive trade.

 **Checkpoint** **Why did West Africa become an important trade center?**

West African Life

The peoples of West Africa, like the peoples of the Americas, were a diverse group with highly developed civilizations. Religious beliefs and family bonds were among the ways of life that reinforced a sense of community.

Religious Beliefs West African spiritual beliefs varied. Caravans brought Islam across the Sahara to the people of the savanna. In many places, such as along the coast of the Gulf of Guinea, Africans held traditional beliefs. These involved a supreme creator supplemented by many spirit beings who inhabited every object and creature of the natural world. The people of West Africa believed, just as the Amerian Indians did, that spirits lived in rain, trees, rocks, and animal life. Furthermore, these spirit beings could also intervene in human affairs. Therefore, the spirits were specially honored. Ancestors, too, became spirits of enduring influence in the extended families that formed the major support system of African society.

Economy and Society Land did not belong to individuals as private property. Instead, land belonged to extended kinship networks derived from an ancient ancestor. Powerful kings could assign particular territories to favored officials to collect tribute from the peasants. But these favorites could not sell the land to others or pass it on to their heirs. Furthermore, the kings could readily replace these officials, reassigning that particular land to a new favorite. The peasants who worked the land could not be removed from it, nor could they sell it or rent it to others. Often the people of a village worked the land in common and divided the harvest according to the number of people in each household. Owning slaves (or wives), rather than property, determined one's wealth.

 **Checkpoint** **What role did landownership hold in West African culture?**

Slavery in Africa

Slavery was common in West Africa. In fact, human beings were frequently used as items of trade, along with gold, salt, ivory, and other valuable resources found in the region.

African Rulers and Arab Traders West African rulers sold about 1,000 slaves annually to Arab traders, who carried them in caravans across the Sahara to the Mediterranean. Thus, the slave trade was an important part of West Africa's economy.

Slavery was a common fate for people who were conquered or captured during warfare. People who committed crimes or were otherwise found undesirable to the community might also be enslaved.

African slavery was certainly brutal in many ways. Individual slaves were often mistreated, and some even died. In general, however, African slavery differed from the system that would eventually develop in the Americas. In Africa, slaves were usually adopted by the families into which they were sold. They could also marry and, as a rule, their children did not inherit the status of slaves. They could even become important officials and soldiers. Powerful kings relied on slave armies and slave officials to control local nobles. Although dependent upon the king, successful slave commanders and officials could become wealthy from the rewards of their positions. Most importantly, slavery was not based on the notion of racial superiority or inferiority.

The Portuguese Exploit the Slave Trade When the Portuguese first sailed along the coast of Africa, they were largely interested in gold. As they began to extend their influence, Portuguese explorers established a profitable trade with the people of West Africa. They exported a variety of goods, including peppers, ivory, copper, and African slaves. In this way, Europeans in the mid-1400s first became involved in the long-standing slave trade of Africa.

To conduct their African trade, the Portuguese mariners needed the assent of the powerful West African kings. Commercial treaties permitted the Portuguese to construct fortified trading posts at key harbors along the coast. The forts served to keep away rival European vessels. Indeed, the Portuguese treated rivals brutally, confiscating their vessels and casting their crews into the ocean to drown.

The Portuguese did not invent the slave trade, but they did greatly expand it. The first major European trading fort was established in 1482. It became a major trading center for slaves. By 1500, Europeans purchased about 1,800 African slaves a year. This nearly doubled the previous trade of some 1,000 slaves between Arab traders and the West African rulers. Some slaves were shipped to Europe. Most, however, worked on sugar plantations located on the Madeira, Canary, and Azore islands. These were islands in the East Atlantic claimed in the 1400s by Iberian explorers. Growing numbers went across the Atlantic to new plantations in the Americas. Thus began the brutal exploitation of West Africans enslaved by Europeans—a fate that would befall millions more African men and women in the centuries ahead.

✓ **Checkpoint** **How did the Portuguese come into contact with West Africans?**

Slave Trade

Local African rulers allowed Europeans to build slaveholding compounds. Captured Africans were marched to these compounds.

SECTION 3 Assessment

Progress Monitoring *Online*
For: Self-test with vocabulary practice
www.pearsonschool.com/ushist

Comprehension

1. **Terms and People** Explain how each term or person below describes West African culture between 1400 and 1600.
   - Ghana
   - Mali
   - Mansa Musa
   - Songhai
2. **NoteTaking Reading Skill: Identify Details** Use your concept web to answer the Section Focus Question: What was life like in West Africa before the age of European exploration?

Writing About History

3. **Quick Write: Research Details** Mansa Musa has invited several well-known scholars to teach at a university in Timbuktu. Research a description of the city. Then, write an account of the scholars' visit to the city.

Critical Thinking

4. **Understanding Cause and Effect** How did the presence of resources such as gold and salt help lead to the development of great kingdoms in West Africa?
5. **Compare and Contrast** How did slavery as practiced in West Africa differ from that later practiced in the Americas?
6. **Summarize** How did the Portuguese benefit from the slave trade?

SECTION 4

▲ In this painting, Native Americans and newly arriving Europeans greet one another.

WITNESS HISTORY

The First Meeting

The arrival of Europeans in the Americas dramatically affected the native peoples who had lived there for centuries. The consequences included the rapid spread of devastating diseases among the Indian population. These not only claimed lives but also demoralized the survivors. One eyewitness described an epidemic of smallpox in Mexico:

"[The victims] could no longer walk about, but lay in their dwellings and sleeping places. . . . The pustules [fluid-filled sores] that covered people cause great desolation; very many people died of them, and many just starved to death; starvation reigned, and no one took care of the others any longer."

—Bernardino de Sahagún, *General History of the Things of New Spain,* c. 1575–1580

First Encounters

Objectives

- Identify the goals of Christopher Columbus.
- Explain the consequences of his journey to the Americas.
- Analyze the effects of European contact with the people of the Americas.

Terms and People

Bartolomeu Dias
Vasco da Gama
Christopher Columbus
John Cabot
Pedro Alvarez Cabral
Amerigo Vespucci
Ferdinand Magellan
conquistador
Hernán Cortés
Moctezuma
Columbian Exchange

NoteTaking

Reading Skill: Understand Effects As you read, complete the chart below with the effects of the arrival of the Europeans in the Americas.

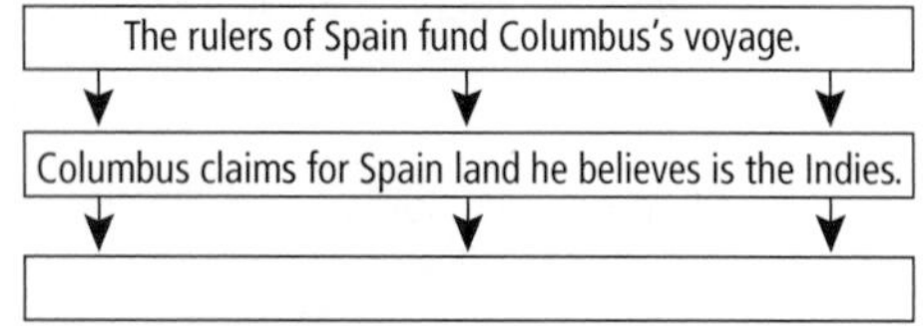

Why It Matters With financial backing from Spain's monarchs, Isabella and Ferdinand, Christopher Columbus found the Americas. He then returned to conquer the land, exploit its wealth, and convert its people to Christianity. That process changed the Americas, Europe, and Africa. **Section Focus Question: How did European exploration affect the Americas?**

Spain Looks to the West

Throughout the 1400s, the Portuguese continued to sail farther and farther from home. They sought a route around Africa's southern tip into the Indian Ocean. Then, their ships could continue east in search of India, the East Indies, and eventually China. In 1487, the Portuguese mariner **Bartolomeu Dias** learned how to use the counterclockwise winds of the South Atlantic to get around southern Africa. In 1498, **Vasco da Gama** exploited that discovery to reach India, opening an immensely profitable trade route. The Portuguese dominated the southern and eastern trade routes around Africa.

By default, in the late 1400s the Spanish looked westward into the open Atlantic. They took inspiration from the profitable discovery and exploitation earlier in the century of islands in the Atlantic—the Azores, Madeiras, and Canaries. Perhaps, they thought, similar islands could be found farther to the west. Furthermore, by leaping from one set of islands to another, perhaps mariners could one day reach the coveted coast of China.

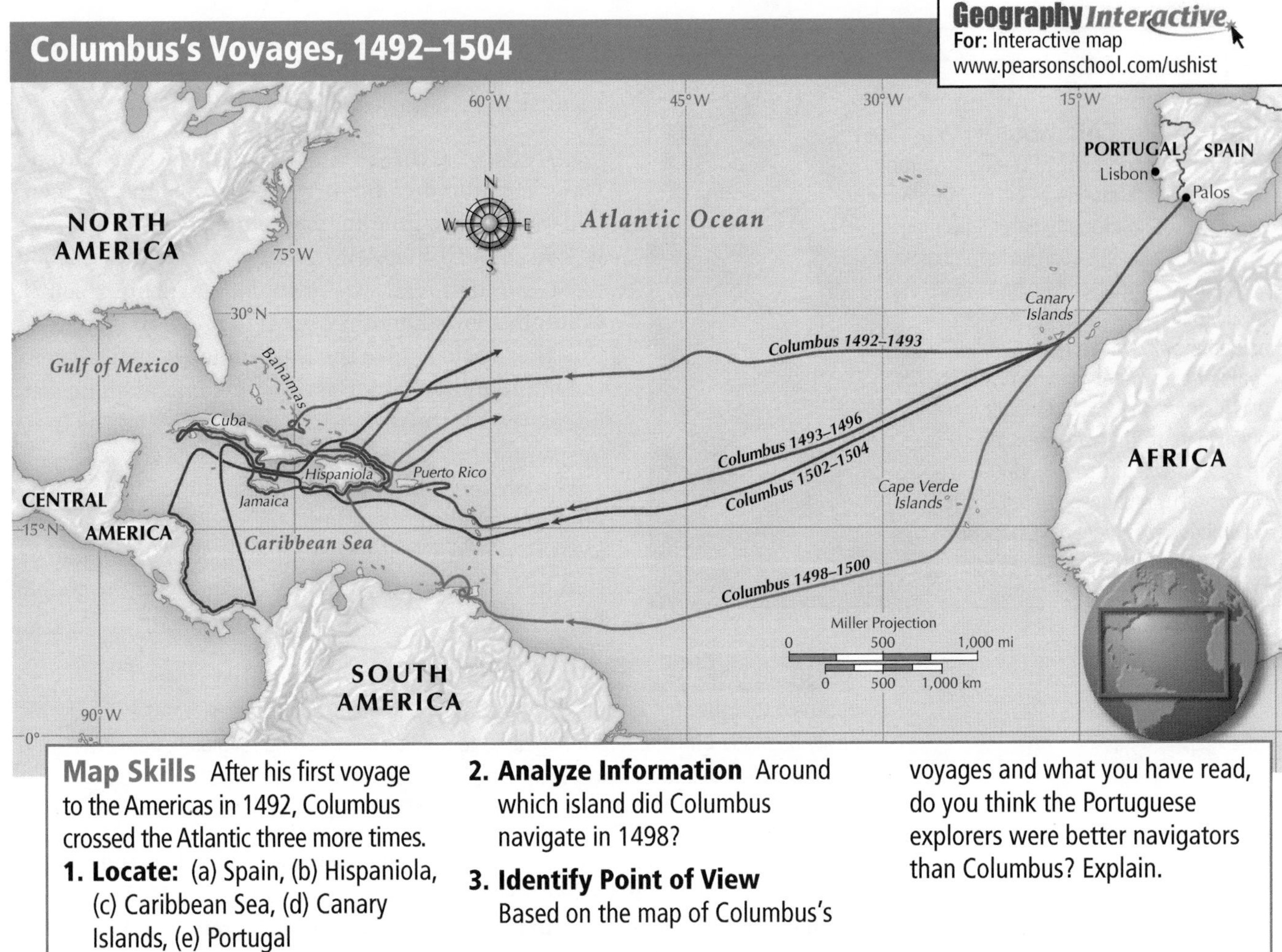

Columbus's Voyages, 1492–1504

Map Skills After his first voyage to the Americas in 1492, Columbus crossed the Atlantic three more times.

1. **Locate:** (a) Spain, (b) Hispaniola, (c) Caribbean Sea, (d) Canary Islands, (e) Portugal
2. **Analyze Information** Around which island did Columbus navigate in 1498?
3. **Identify Point of View** Based on the map of Columbus's voyages and what you have read, do you think the Portuguese explorers were better navigators than Columbus? Explain.

Contrary to popular belief, fifteenth-century Europeans did not think that the world was flat. They did, however, worry that China lay too far away and that ships could not complete a voyage west over what they believed was a vast, open ocean.

✓ **Checkpoint** **Why was Spain eager to find a new route across the Atlantic?**

The Voyages of Christopher Columbus

To pursue the western dream, Spain relied on an Italian mariner from the city of Genoa named **Christopher Columbus.** He sought a route to China as a means of reviving the Christian struggle against Islam. By converting the Chinese to Christianity, he hoped to recruit their people and use their wealth to assist Europeans in a new crusade.

Columbus dared the westward trip because he underestimated the size of Earth. He believed the planet was 18,000 miles around—almost 7,000 miles smaller than it actually is.

Columbus Investigates Viking Stories An experienced Atlantic mariner, as a young man, Columbus had investigated stories about mysterious lands to the west. He may have sailed to Iceland. If so, he probably heard about the western discoveries by the Vikings from Scandinavia. During the ninth and tenth centuries, Viking mariners had probed the North Atlantic to discover and colonize Iceland and then Greenland. From Greenland, some mariners reached the northeastern coast of North America. About the year 1000, they founded a little

History Makers

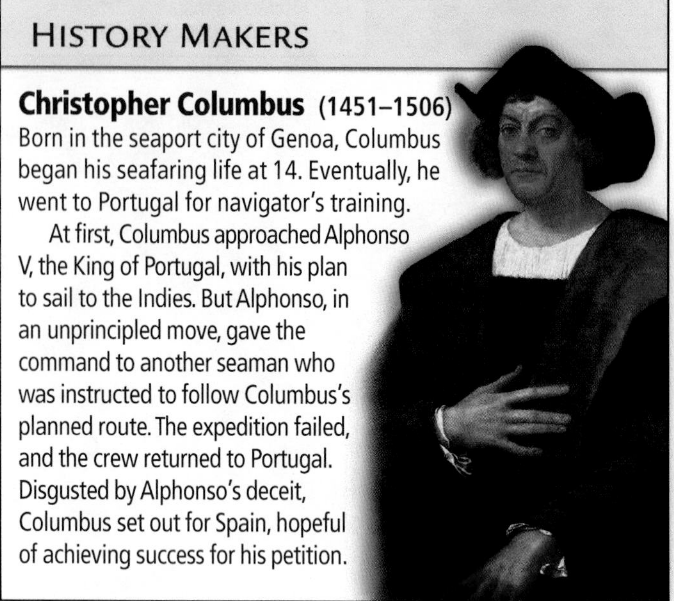

Christopher Columbus (1451–1506)
Born in the seaport city of Genoa, Columbus began his seafaring life at 14. Eventually, he went to Portugal for navigator's training.

At first, Columbus approached Alphonso V, the King of Portugal, with his plan to sail to the Indies. But Alphonso, in an unprincipled move, gave the command to another seaman who was instructed to follow Columbus's planned route. The expedition failed, and the crew returned to Portugal. Disgusted by Alphonso's deceit, Columbus set out for Spain, hopeful of achieving success for his petition.

settlement on the northern tip of Newfoundland. But they soon abandoned it because of the isolation and because of resistance by American Indians.

Columbus Sets Sail In 1492, Queen Isabella and King Ferdinand of Spain provided 3 ships, 90 men, and most of the funding for Columbus's voyage west in search of China. After 33 days at sea, he reached what we now call the Bahamas. Turning south, Columbus found another set of islands. He supposed that these belonged to the East Indies, which lay near the mainland of Asia. Based on his mistaken notion, he referred to the people living on the islands as Indians, a name that has endured to this day.

The presence of native people did not stop Columbus from claiming the land for Spain. As the representative of a Christian nation, Columbus believed that he had the right and duty to dominate the people he found. In his journal, he recorded:

Primary Source "They should be good servants and intelligent, for I observed that they quickly took in what was said to them, and I believe that they would easily be made Christians, as it appeared to me that they had no religion. I, our Lord being pleased, will take hence, at the time of my departure six natives. . . ."

—Journal of Christopher Columbus, October 1492

Reaction to Columbus's Voyage Columbus continued to explore the islands of the Caribbean. He established a settlement on the island he called Hispaniola. Then, in early 1493, leaving a number of his crew behind, he returned to Spain.

Later that year, Columbus returned to the Caribbean to colonize Hispaniola. The new colony was supposed to produce profits by shipping gold, sugar, and Indian slaves to Spain. The Spanish planned to dominate the natives and forge an empire based in Europe.

Upon his return to Hispaniola, Columbus discovered that the natives had killed the colonists he had left behind. Columbus turned to force. Employing the military advantages of horses, gunpowder, and steel, Columbus killed and captured hundreds of Indians on Hispaniola and the adjacent islands.

Vocabulary Builder
adjacent–(uh JAY suhnt) *adj.* near or close

Unfortunately for Columbus, his bullying angered the European colonists, who persuaded the king and queen to recall him in 1500. Columbus returned to Spain and died in 1506. The Spanish colonization of the Americas, however, continued.

Columbus had not reached Asia, but he had found a source of riches that enabled European Christendom to grow more powerful and wealthy than the Muslim world. During the next three centuries, the mineral and plantation wealth of the Americas—produced by the labor of African slaves—helped finance the expansion of European commerce. In turn, that commerce promoted the development of new technologies and the growth of military power.

Spain and Portugal Divide the Americas With the assistance of the pope, the Spanish and the Portuguese negotiated the 1494 Treaty of Tordesillas. They agreed to split the world of new discoveries by drawing a north-south boundary line through the mid-Atlantic west of the Azores. The Portuguese secured a monopoly to exploit the coast of Africa and the Indian Ocean. In return, the Spanish claimed Columbus's western lands. Further exploration later determined that South America bulged eastward beyond the treaty line, placing Brazil in the Portuguese sphere.

In dividing the world, no one bothered to consult the Native Americans. The Iberians and the pope considered them pagan savages without any rights. The other European kings refused to honor the treaty, for they claimed an equal right to explore and exploit the new lands. But no European leaders thought that the Native Americans could, or should, be left alone in their former isolation and native beliefs.

✓ **Checkpoint What was Columbus's purpose in sailing west across the Atlantic?**

The Spanish Expand Their American Empire

Until his last breath, Columbus insisted that his discoveries lay close to the coast of China. Other explorers, however, demonstrated that he had reached the margins of two previously unknown continents. In 1497, **John Cabot,** a Genoese mariner employed by the English, sailed to Newfoundland. In tropical waters far to the south, a Portuguese fleet commanded by **Pedro Alvarez Cabral** discovered the coast of Brazil in 1500. A year later, **Amerigo Vespucci,** another Genoese mariner, explored enough of South America's coast to deem it a new continent. European mapmakers began to call the new continents by a variant of Vespucci's first name—America. Between 1519 and 1522, a voyage begun by **Ferdinand Magellan** succeeded in encircling the entire globe, filling in even more of the increasingly detailed picture of Earth.

Cortés Conquers the Aztecs At the start of the 1500s, the Spanish learned of a spectacular Indian empire in central Mexico. Those soldiers who explored central Mexico and defeated the Indian civilizations there were called **conquistadors.** In 1519, the brilliant and ruthless **Hernán Cortés** led a group of about 600 volunteers from Cuba to the coast of Mexico. Born in 1485, Cortés had university training as a lawyer. An ambitious man, he left Spain in 1504 to try his luck in Cuba, where he became rich by acquiring plantations and gold mines. But he hungered for more.

Marching inland, Cortés reached the great central valley, home of the Aztec Empire. The approach of Cortés's army alarmed the Aztec ruler, **Moctezuma.** Hoping to intimidate them with his own power, Moctezuma invited the Spanish into his great city.

The largest and richest city in the Americas, Tenochtitlán occupied a cluster of islands in a large lake. The population of about 200,000 dwarfed Spain's largest city, Seville, which had about 70,000 inhabitants. The Aztec city's central plaza of tall stone pyramid-temples dazzled with a combination of red, blue, and ochre stucco. Bernal Diaz, a soldier, recalled, "These great towns and pyramids and buildings arising from the water, all made of stone seemed like an enchanted vision. . . . Indeed, some of our soldiers asked whether it was not all a dream."

The city's gold and silver inflamed the Spanish desire to conquer and plunder. By seizing and killing Moctezuma, the Spanish provoked violent street fighting that initially drove them from the city. Returning with reinforcements, including many revenge-seeking local Indians who had themselves been brutalized by the Aztecs, Cortés captured Tenochtitlán. The cost, however, was high. Four months of fighting had reduced the city to a bloody rubble.

The Conquistadors
Eager for wealth and fame, the men known as conquistadors established a Spanish empire in the Americas. *What factors allowed a small force of conquistadors to overwhelm larger numbers of Indians?*

The victors put thousands of captive Indians to work raising a Spanish capital, Mexico City, on the ruins of Tenochtitlán. The slaves reworked stones from the great pyramids into a Christian cathedral. They transformed the shell of Moctezuma's palace into a residence for Cortés. Grateful for the stunning conquest and a share in the immense plunder, the Spanish king appointed Cortés to govern Mexico.

The Conquistadors March On The Spanish extended their empire deep into North and South America. During the 1530s, Francisco Pizarro conquered the powerful Incas of Peru with just 180 soldiers.

Aside from wealth, conquistadors were motivated by their religious faith and by loyalty to their monarch. They reasoned that riches were wasted on the non-Christian Indians. Those riches should belong to Christians who served the Spanish Crown—and who were willing to help convert the native people. These notions had been deeply ingrained in Spanish culture as a result of the centuries-long *reconquista.*

The conquistadors benefited from their superior weapons. These included steel-edged swords, pikes, and crossbows. Such weapons were far more durable and deadly than the stone-edged swords, axes, and arrows of the Indians. Because sixteenth-century guns were so heavy, inaccurate, and slow to reload, only a few conquistadors carried them. Yet their few guns gave the Spanish a psychological advantage. Belching fire and smoke, they produced a thunderous roar that was terrifying.

Although most conquistadors fought on foot, the few with horses proved especially dreadful. The Indians had never experienced the shocking power and speed of mounted men. "The most essential thing in new lands is horses," observed a conquistador. "They instill the greatest fear in the enemy and make the Indians respect the leaders of the army." But the greatest advantage came from something the conquistadors did not even know they carried—disease.

The Devastation of Disease Brutal exploitation and disease combined to destroy the natives of Hispaniola. From about 300,000 in 1492, the island's population declined to a mere 500 by 1548. The Spanish forced the natives, known as the Tainos, to labor in mines and on ranches and plantations. Those who resisted suffered deadly raids on their villages by colonial soldiers. Overworked and underfed, the native population was especially vulnerable to disease.

The ravages of these diseases were not confined to Hispaniola. In the century after the arrival of the Europeans in the Americas, experts believe that successive epidemics reduced the native population to about one fifth of its pre-1492 numbers.

The great European killers included smallpox, typhus, diphtheria, bubonic plague, and cholera. These were diseases that had existed in Europe for centuries. As a result, the European population over the generations had developed some natural defenses against them. That is, among the population there was a percentage of people whose bodies were able to fight off the diseases before they became fatal. The native populations of the Americas had not built up such natural defenses. The European diseases hit with devastating effect. In some cases, entire villages simply disappeared.

For the Spanish, the reduction of the Indian population complicated their colonization plans. They had depended on Indians to provide the labor for their new enterprises. Left with large tracts of fertile but depopulated lands, the colonists needed a new source of workers. They turned to importing Africans as slaves to work the new sugar plantations on the tropical coasts.

 **Checkpoint What role did disease play in the defeat of the native populations of the Americas?**

● **INFOGRAPHIC**

The Columbian Exchange

In 1972, Alfred W. Crosby, a social historian, used the term Columbian Exchange to describe the exchange of plants, animals, and diseases between Europe and the Americas. The term held. The exchange also included the continents of Africa and Asia. As people, products, animals, and ideas flowed, their impact was greater than anyone could have imagined. The images below represent some results of the global exchange.

▼ Aztecs fell victim to European diseases, such as smallpox.

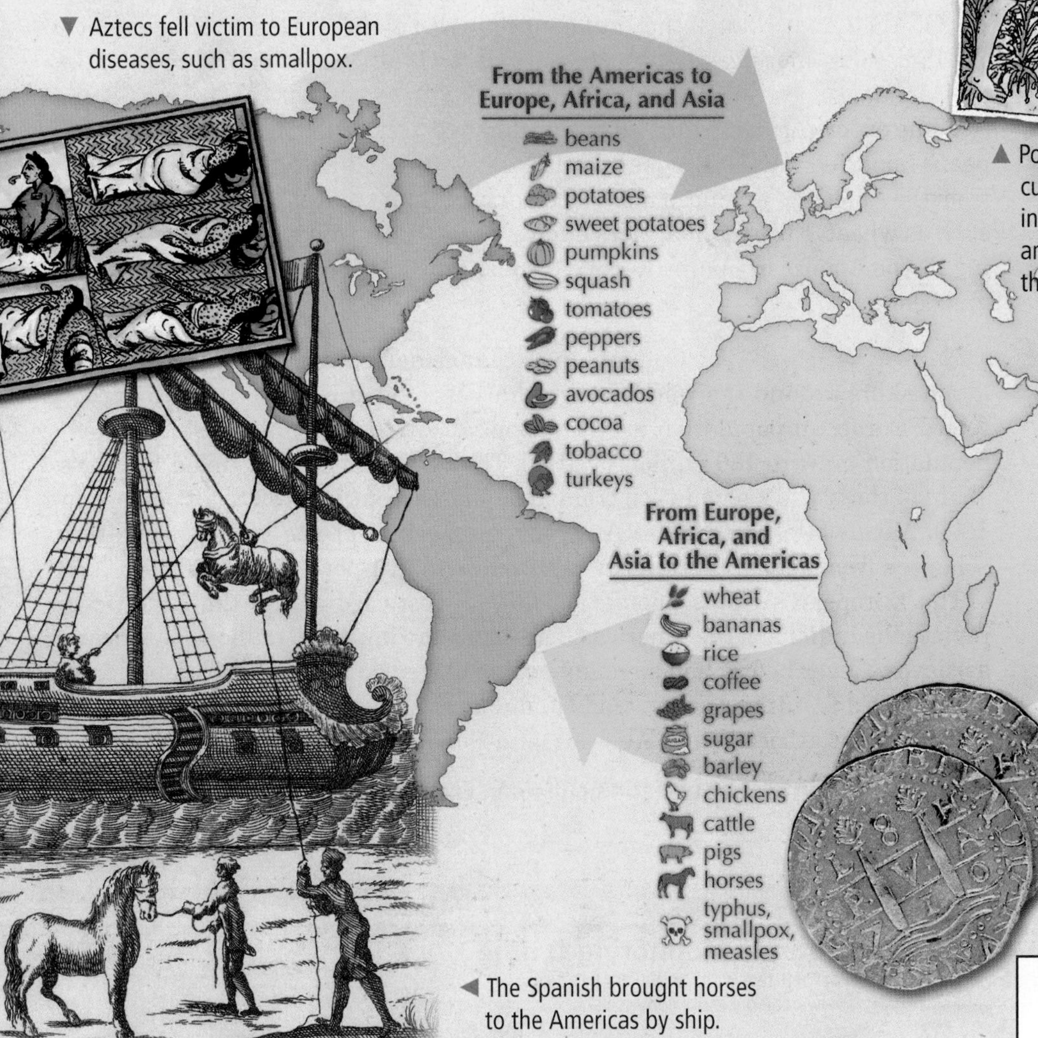

◀ The Spanish brought horses to the Americas by ship.

▲ Potatoes from Peru, cultivated by the farmers in this drawing, became an important staple of the European diet.

Quinine, native to South America, provided a cure for people in Africa suffering from malaria. ▲

◀ Silver and gold for coins like these came from the Americas.

Thinking Critically

1. **Draw Inferences** How do you think the Columbian Exchange affected the environment in the Americas?
2. **Analyze Information** Is there still a global exchange among the continents? Explain.

The Transatlantic Exchange

The Europeans who began arriving in the Americas in the late 1400s brought more than weapons, diseases, and a thirst for wealth and power. The colonizers also brought plants and animals that were new to the Americas. Indeed, the European arrival brought about an ecological revolution. Never before in human history had so many of the world's plants, animals, and microorganisms been so thoroughly and so abruptly mixed and dispersed. We call this phenomenon the **Columbian Exchange.**

Vocabulary Builder
disperse–(dih SPERS) *v.* to spread about; distribute widely

Exchange of Plants and Animals Determined to farm the American land in a European manner, the colonists introduced their domesticated livestock: pigs, horses, mules, sheep, and cattle. They also brought seeds for their domesticated plants. These included wheat, barley, rye, oats, grasses, and grapes.

In a land where large mammals such as cattle and horses did not live, the new plants and animals brought drastic changes to the environment. Ranging cattle and pigs consumed the wild plants and the shellfish that the Indians needed for their own diet. The livestock also invaded the Indians' fields to consume their maize, beans, and squashes.

The Indians proved remarkably resilient as they adapted to the new plants and animals. In time, the Indians learned to raise and consume European cattle. On the Great Plains, the Indians acquired runaway horses. This enabled the Indians to more easily hunt bison and forcefully resist efforts to colonize their land.

While exporting domesticated plants and livestock to the Americas, the Europeans imported productive plants cultivated by the Indians. Maize and potatoes from the Americas produced more food per acre than traditional European crops such as wheat. European farmers enjoyed larger harvests by adding, or switching to, the American plants. Europeans also adopted tomatoes, beans, peppers, and peanuts.

Population Shifts The Columbian Exchange helped trigger enormous population shifts around the world. Larger harvests aided by new American crops fueled European population growth. From about 80 million in 1492, Europe's population grew to 180 million by 1800. That growth nearly doubled Europe's share of the world's population from about 11 percent in 1492 to 20 percent in 1800. Meanwhile, the Native American proportion of the global population collapsed from about 7 percent in 1492 to less than 1 percent in 1800.

The European surplus population flowed westward across the Atlantic to replace the Indians in the Americas. The colonizers imported millions of Africans as slaves. Never before had so many people moved so far with such a powerful impact. As a result, maritime trade and migration integrated four great continents: Europe, Africa, South America, and North America.

 **Checkpoint** **What was the Columbian Exchange?**

SECTION 4 Assessment

Progress Monitoring *Online*
For: Self-test with vocabulary practice
www.pearsonschool.com/ushist

Comprehension

1. **Terms and People** Explain the role of the people listed below in the European exploration of the Americas.
   - Christopher Columbus
   - John Cabot
   - Pedro Alvarez Cabral
   - Amerigo Vespucci
   - Ferdinand Magellan
   - Hernán Cortés
2. **NoteTaking Reading Skill: Understand Effects** Use your chart to answer the Section Focus Question: How did European exploration affect the Americas?

Writing About History

3. **Quick Write: Write a Monologue** Stories about the Aztec ruler Moctezuma claim that he feared newcomers. Write a monologue—a long speech by one person—by Moctezuma upon his learning about the arrival of the Spaniards in his empire.

Critical Thinking

4. **Understanding Cause and Effect** How did the success of Portugal's exploration of Africa affect Spain?
5. **Analyze Information** How did the conquistadors justify their conquest of the Aztec and Inca empires?
6. **Make Generalizations** How did the Columbian Exchange affect population size and movement?

American Issues Connector

Global Interdependence

TRACK THE ISSUE

Is global interdependence good for the American economy?

Like many nations, the United States depends on trade and commerce with other countries to support its economy. Employment is a part of the global economy, as a growing number of U.S. companies outsource jobs overseas. Use the timeline below to explore this enduring issue.

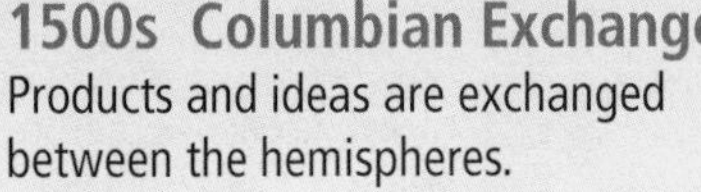

1500s Columbian Exchange Products and ideas are exchanged between the hemispheres.

1812 War of 1812 United States goes to war in part to protect its trade rights.

1944 World Bank The World Bank and International Monetary Fund are established at Bretton Woods Conference.

1990s World Trade Increases NAFTA joins the United States, Mexico, and Canada in a free-trade pact, and the World Trade Organization is founded.

2000s Globalization Debated Critics and advocates debate benefits of globalization.

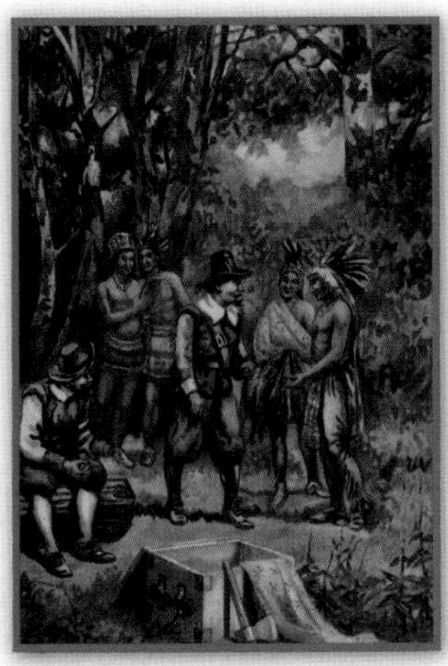

Europeans trade goods with Native Americans.

U.S. firms outsource work to such nations as India and Nigeria.

DEBATE THE ISSUE

Outsourcing Jobs Many American companies send work overseas where wages are lower. This is called outsourcing. In the past, most of the jobs lost through outsourcing were factory jobs. Now, office work and computer jobs are being sent abroad, too. How does outsourcing affect America?

"Sending jobs overseas is part of corporate America's quest for short-term profits at the expense of the well-being of our workers. In effect, forcing the middle class to compete with the cheapest foreign labor can only result in a decline in our nation's standard of living and a diminished quality of life."

—Lou Dobbs, News Anchor, CNN

"Will [the outsourcing of services] lead to jobs going overseas? You bet, but that is not a disaster. For a start, America runs a large and growing surplus in services with the rest of the world. The jobs lost will be low-paying ones. . . . By contrast, jobs will be created that demand skills to handle the deeper incorporation of information technology, and the pay for these jobs will be high."

—*The Economist* magazine

TRANSFER Activities

1. **Compare** How do these two views on outsourcing differ?
2. **Analyze** Do you think either Lou Dobbs or the writer in *The Economist* would have considered the Columbian Exchange a danger to European or Native American economies? Explain.
3. **Transfer** Use the following Web site to see a video, try a WebQuest, and write in your journal. www.pearsonschool.com/ushist

CHAPTER 1

Quick Study Guide

Progress Monitoring *Online*
For: Self-test with vocabulary practice
www.pearsonschool.com/ushist

Native American Cultures

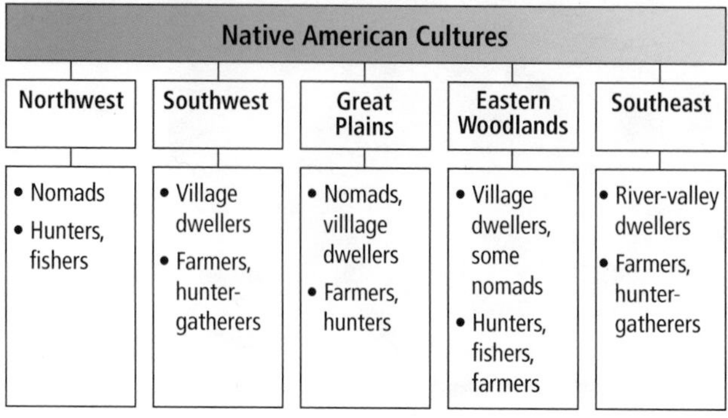

Native American Cultures				
Northwest	Southwest	Great Plains	Eastern Woodlands	Southeast
• Nomads • Hunters, fishers	• Village dwellers • Farmers, hunter-gatherers	• Nomads, villlage dwellers • Farmers, hunters	• Village dwellers, some nomads • Hunters, fishers, farmers	• River-valley dwellers • Farmers, hunter-gatherers

West African Kingdoms, A.D. 800–A.D. 1600

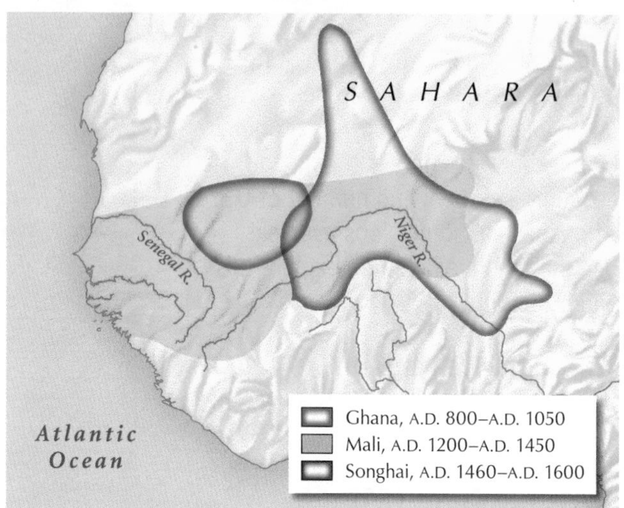

Europe, 1400s

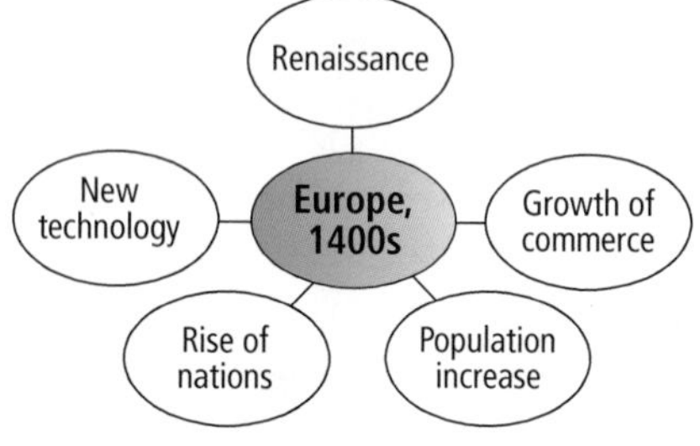

European Exploration

Causes	Events	Effects
• Europeans search for route to Asia and Africa. • Countries desire to accumulate wealth through trade. • Navigation technology is improved.	• Portuguese make voyages to Africa and India. • Columbus reaches the West Indies. • Columbus makes other voyages to the Americas. • After Columbus, other European explorers set sail for the Americas.	• Portugal establishes gold and slave trade in Africa. • Spain establishes colonies in the Americas. • Europeans enter the West African slave trade. • European diseases devastate Native Americans. • The Columbian Exchange begins.

Quick Study Timeline

1200s
Anasazi culture declines

1300s
Mansa Musa rules the kingdom of Mali

Around the World

Prehistory — **1200** — **1300**

30,000–10,000 years ago
First people arrive in the Americas

Late 1300s
Renaissance begins in Europe

American Issues Connector

By connecting prior knowledge with what you have learned in this chapter, you can gradually build your understanding of enduring questions that still affect America today. Answer the questions below. Then, use your American Issues Connector study guide (or go online: www.pearsonschool.com/ushist).

Issues You Learned About

● **Global Interdependence** As Europeans explored the Americas, these regions became linked by culture and economics.

1. Write a short essay explaining why Europeans began to set sail for new lands and what effects their journeys had on the people of the Americas and on the Europeans. Consider:
   - the religious wars in Europe
   - the importance of trade
   - settlements in the Americas
   - American Indian empires
   - the Columbian Exchange

● **Technology and Society** Throughout history, people have developed new technologies that changed culture, economics, and international relations.

2. How did technology help some Native Americans develop agricultural societies?
3. How did technology benefit the Spanish conquistadors?

● **Interaction With the Environment** American Indians adapted to their environment and modified their environment.

4. How did Paleo-Indians adapt to the changes brought by the end of the ice age?
5. In some areas of North America, people did not turn to farming. Why not?
6. Give at least one example of the way that some American Indian groups modified their environment.

Connect to Your World — Activity

America and the World Go online or to your local library to research the role that the United States currently plays in the international community. Find information such as the placement of American troops, the locations of humanitarian workers, the recipients of foreign aid, and efforts to develop other countries' economies and promote democratic governments. Use the information you learn to create your own map of the world that illustrates the important role of the United States in the international community.

History *Interactive*
For: Interactive timeline
www.pearsonschool.com/ushist

Mid–1400s Europe's first books are printed on a printing press

1492 Columbus reaches America

1591 Songhai Empire falls to invaders from Morocco

1400 — 1500 — 1600

Chapter Assessment

Terms and People

1. Define **adobe.** Which American Indian group used adobe, and what did they use it for?
2. What was the **Iroquois League**? What were its key characteristics?
3. What were the **Middle Ages** and the **Renaissance**? In what way were these two eras different?
4. Who was **Mansa Musa**? How did Mansa Musa increase the influence of Islam?
5. Who was **Hernán Cortés**? What role did he play in Spanish Mexico?

Focus Questions

The focus question for this chapter is **How did the interaction of many cultures after 1492 affect the Americas?** Build an answer to this big question by answering the focus questions for Sections 1 through 4 and the Critical Thinking questions that follow.

Section 1

6. How did the spread of civilization begin in the Americas?

Section 2

7. How did Europeans begin to explore more of the world?

Section 3

8. What was life like in West Africa before the age of European exploration?

Section 4

9. How did European exploration affect the Americas?

Critical Thinking

10. **Analyze Information** How did the environment influence the American Indian way of life?
11. **Draw Inferences** What effect do you think the printing press had on European exploration?
12. **Make Generalizations** How would you describe the social class and ruling system in western Europe in the fifteenth century?
13. **Compare Points of View** How were the views on land use similar between American Indians and West Africans? How were these views different?
14. **Synthesize Information** How did the Columbian Exchange impact the food traditions of Europe and the Americas?
15. **Analyze Visuals** The map below, drawn in the 1400s, shows only an accurate location for Europe. How and why would the rendering of this map change by the 1500s?

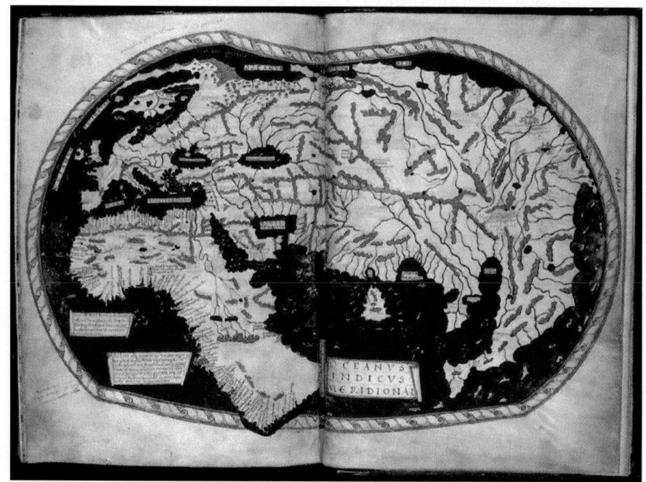

Writing About History

Write a Narrative Essay Research the life of Dekanawidah, who, according to Iroquois tradition, helped found the Iroquois League. Write an account of how he worked to persuade Native American nations to unite. Use dialogue and details to make the narrative more vivid.

Prewriting

- Research any background information you need to tell your story.
- List details.
- Consider your audience.

Drafting

- Open strongly with an engaging sentence.
- Use sensory details to make the story more interesting for the readers.
- Add dialogue or descriptions.

Revising

- Use the guidelines on page SH14 of the Writing Handbook to revise your report.

Document-Based Assessment

Government in Pre-Columbian America

By the time of European contact, the Americas were home to millions of people. Hundreds of different cultures had developed and adapted to the various environments of their particular regions. Were the governments as varied as the cultures? Use your knowledge of the history of American Indian cultures and Documents A, B, and C to answer questions 1 through 4.

Document A

"For most Native North Americans . . . there existed no institutionalized forms of social or political power—no state, no bureaucracy, and no army. Native American societies, as a rule, were egalitarian, without the kind of centralized authority and social hierarchy typical of modern societies. Custom and tradition rather than law and coercion regulated social life. While there were leaders, their influence was generally based on personal status and not any formal or permanent status. As an early French missionary, Father LeJeune, observed in 1634 of the Montagnais-Naskapis of Labrador, Indians would not "endure in the least those who seem desirous of assuming superiority over others." Authority within a group derived from the ability to make useful suggestions and knowledge of tribal tradition and lore. Among the Eskimos, for example, a person of importance was called *Isumatag*, 'he who thinks.'"

—*Carl Waldham,* Atlas of the North American Indian

Document B

"All the business of the Five Nations Confederate Council shall be conducted by the two combined bodies of Confederate Lords. First the question shall be passed upon by the Mohawk and Seneca Lords, then it shall be discussed and passed by the Oneida and Cayuga Lords. Their decisions shall then be referred to the Onondaga Lords (Fire Keepers), for final judgment. . . .

"In all cases the procedure must be as follows: when the Mohawk and Seneca Lords have unanimously agreed upon a question, they shall report their decision to the Cayuga and Oneida Lords who shall deliberate upon the question and report a unanimous decision to the Mohawk Lords. The Mohawk Lords will then report the standing of the case to the Fire Keepers, who shall render a decision as they see fit in case of a disagreement by the two bodies, or confirm the decisions of the two bodies if they are identical. The Fire keepers shall then report their decision to the Mohawk Lords who shall announce it to the open council."

—*the Iroquois Constitution*

Document C

"Inca society and government were hierarchal and pyramidal in form. The Sapa Inca, or emperor, was believed to be a descendant of the sun god and stood at the apex of the pyramid as the absolute ruler of Inca lands. His senior councilors and provincial governors, each of whom was responsible for 10,000 people, were chosen from the aristocracy which consisted principally of his relatives. Beneath them came lesser bureaucrats and military officers, some drawn from the leaders of assimilated conquered peoples, who in turn controlled smaller numbers of imperial citizens. The system continued downward to the smallest unit, the nuclear family, with each official responsible to the Sapa Inca through the administrator who was ranked directly above him."

—*Margaret Oliphant,* The Atlas of the Ancient World

---

1. Which term best describes the majority of government systems in pre-Columbian America?
A hierarchical
B bureaucratic
C constitutional
D egalitarian

2. What can you conclude from Document B?
A that the Iroquois valued consensus
B that the Iroquois created a dictatorship
C that the Iroquois rejected hierarchy
D that the Iroquois encouraged conflict

3. In comparing Document A and Document C, a reader should conclude that Inca government was
A a typical pre-Columbian American government.
B an early stage of pre-Columbian American government.
C the most advanced pre-Columbian American government.
D an unusual form of pre-Columbian American government.

4. Writing Task What categories, or types, of government existed in pre-Columbian America? What are some examples of Native American people who developed each type of government? Use your knowledge of American history and evidence from the sources above to explain your answer.

CHAPTER

2 Europeans Establish Colonies

1492–1752

WITNESS HISTORY

The Mayflower Compact

On September 16, 1620, the *Mayflower* set sail from England to North America. Some of the passengers were religious dissenters called Puritans, who hoped to establish a colony of their own.

After a journey of about two months, the colonists sighted land. Before landing, the men aboard signed an agreement establishing a government—one that derived from the consent of the governed:

> "... [we] hereof to enact, constitute, and frame, such just and equal Laws, Ordinances, Acts, Constitutions and Offices, from time to time, as shall be thought most meet and convenient for the General good of the Colony; unto which we promise all due Submission and Obedience."
>
> —The Mayflower Compact, November 11, 1620

◄ Colonists aboard the *Mayflower* sign the Mayflower Compact.

Spanish coin, called a doubloon

Beaver hat

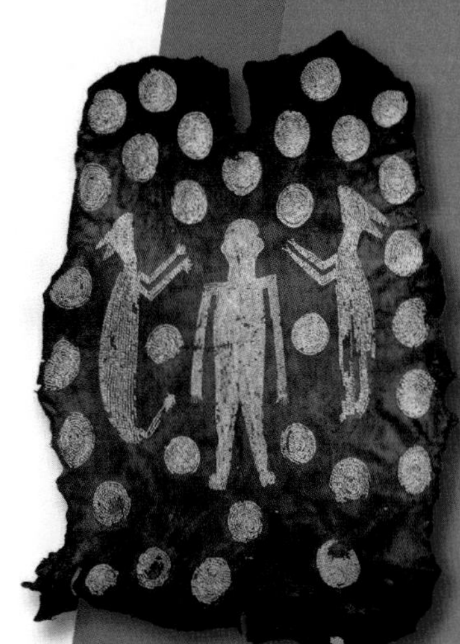

Powhatan's deerskin cloak

Chapter Preview

Chapter Focus Question: How and why did Europeans establish colonies in the Americas?

Section 1
Spain's Empire in the Americas

Section 2
The French Empire

Section 3
England's Southern Colonies

Section 4
The New England Colonies

Section 5
The Middle Colonies

Use the **Quick Study Timeline** at the end of this chapter to preview chapter events.

Note Taking Study Guide *Online*
For: Note Taking and American Issues Connector
www.pearsonschool.com/ushist

SECTION 1

◀ Francisco Vásquez de Coronado

WITNESS HISTORY

Cities of Gold

In 1540, the Spanish explorer Francisco Vásquez de Coronado, along with 300 soldiers, set out to find Cibola, one of the fabled Seven Cities of Gold. Hoping to discover riches that equaled those found in Mexico, the expedition journeyed into the lands north of Mexico (the present-day U.S. Southwest). Instead of Cibola, the group found:

"... a little, crowded village, looking as if it had been crumpled all up together. There are ranch houses in New Spain which make a better appearance at a distance. It is a village of about 200 warriors...."

—Pedro de Casteneda, *The Journey of Coronado,* 1596

Disappointment turned to rage as Coronado's men searched the village for gold. When they found none, they attacked the village, defeating it in about an hour.

Spain's Empire in the Americas

Objectives

- Explain Spanish explorers' achievements.
- Describe Spanish society in New Spain and Peru.
- Evaluate the causes and effects of Spanish imperial policies in the American Southwest.

Terms and People

missionary
presidio
viceroy
mestizo
mission

NoteTaking

Reading Skill: Summarize Complete a concept web to summarize how each item strengthened the Spanish American Empire.

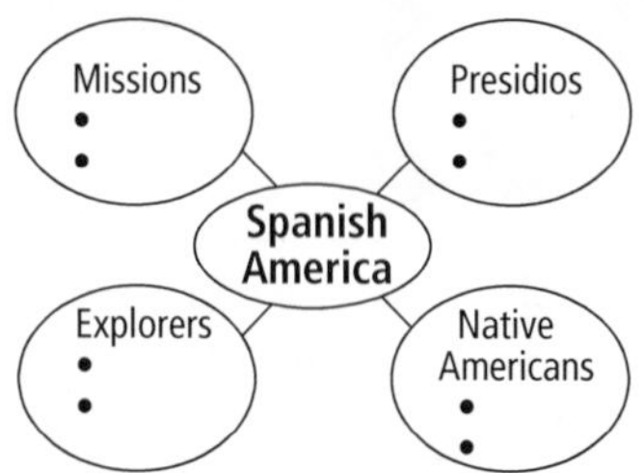

Why It Matters During the sixteenth century, the Spanish created a great empire by conquering and colonizing the lands in the Caribbean as well as large portions of North and South America. This American empire was more than ten times larger than Spain and rich in gold and silver. The potential for great wealth motivated other European nations to join the quest for colonies in the Americas. Soon rivalries emerged in the Americas as European empires vied for territory. **Section Focus Question: How did Spain strengthen its colonies in the Americas?**

Religious Divisions Cause Conflict

Enriched by conquests in the Americas, Spain financed an aggressive military policy in Europe. This aggression alarmed the Dutch, French, and English, who sought their own share of the riches in the Americas. These nations probed the coast of North America, seeking places where they might establish their own colonies. They also encouraged pirates to rob Spanish treasure ships.

Religious divisions added to the conflict among nations in Europe. In 1517, a movement called the Protestant Reformation began in Germany when a monk named Martin Luther challenged the authority of the Catholic Church. Luther and other dissenters became known as Protestants because they protested against the power of the pope and against the Church, which they viewed as corrupt and materialistic.

Protestants favored the individual's right to seek God by reading the Bible and by heeding ministers who delivered evangelical sermons. Without the unifying power of the pope, Protestants soon divided into many different denominations, including Lutherans, Calvinists, Baptists, Anglicans, and Quakers.

The Protestant movement spread throughout northern Europe, including the Netherlands and England. The French divided into hostile Protestant and Catholic camps, but the Spanish remained Catholic. Indeed, Spanish monarchs led the Catholic effort to suppress Protestantism. Rival nations carried the conflict across the Atlantic to their new colonies in the Americas.

✓ **Checkpoint** **What issues divided the nations of Europe during the 1500s?**

Spain Organizes Its American Empire

Although the conquistadors were successful at conquering territory and establishing colonies for Spain, they were not effective at running the colonies. Under Spanish rule, Indians were enslaved and forced to labor on encomiendas, large Spanish-owned plantations. They were also forced to mine for silver and gold. They suffered harsh treatment and were often beaten or worked to death.

The Spanish king worried that the conquistadors killed too many Indians, who might otherwise have become tax-paying subjects. Eager to stabilize the new conquests, the king heeded priests such as Bartolomé de Las Casas, who urged the royal government to adopt laws protecting Indians. Catholic friars served as **missionaries**—people who work to convert others to their religion. The friars aimed to convert Indians to Christianity and to persuade them to adopt Spanish culture.

Although less brutal than the conquistadors, the friars demanded that the Indians surrender their traditions in favor of Christian beliefs and Spanish ways. The friars destroyed Indian temples and sacred images. Then, missionaries ordered the Indians to build new churches and adopt the rituals of the Catholic faith. The missionaries also forced Indians to work for them. The friars relied on Spanish soldiers who set up **presidios,** or forts, near the missions.

Missionaries and Indians

Soon after the Spanish conquest of a region, missionaries arrived to convert Indians to Christianity and to persuade them to adopt Spanish culture. In this painting, friars and conquistadors watch in approval as an Indian is baptized.

New Spain and Peru Established

During the 1530s and 1540s, the Spanish Crown divided the American empire into two immense regions, known as viceroyalties, each ruled by a **viceroy** appointed by the king. The viceroyalty of New Spain consisted of Mexico, Central America, and the Caribbean islands. The viceroyalty of Peru included all of South America except Portuguese Brazil. To control the viceroys, the Spanish Crown forced them to share power with a Crown-appointed council and an archbishop. The Spanish did not permit elected assemblies in their colonies.

Society in Spain's American Colonies

During the sixteenth century, about 250,000 Spanish people, mostly men, immigrated across the Atlantic to the American empire. The male colonists generally took Indian wives. Children of mixed Spanish and Indian ancestry became known as **mestizos.** As the Native American population declined from diseases, the mestizos became the largest segment of Spain's colonial population by the eighteenth century. Next in proportion were enslaved Africans, especially in the Caribbean region.

To maintain their authority, colonial officials developed a complex system of racial hierarchy known as the *castas.* At the bottom lay the pure Africans and Indians, while

Geography Interactive
For: Interactive map
www.pearsonschool.com/ushist

Europeans Explore the Americas, 1497–1682

Map Skills After Columbus's voyages, other European explorers sailed on behalf of any power that would sponsor them. For example, Verrazano was Italian but sailed for France.

1. **Locate:** (a) Mississippi River, (b) St. Lawrence River, (c) Gulf of Mexico
2. **Movement** Describe the journey of Jolliet and Marquette.
3. **Predict Consequences** Based on this map, what regions do you think France will control in North America?

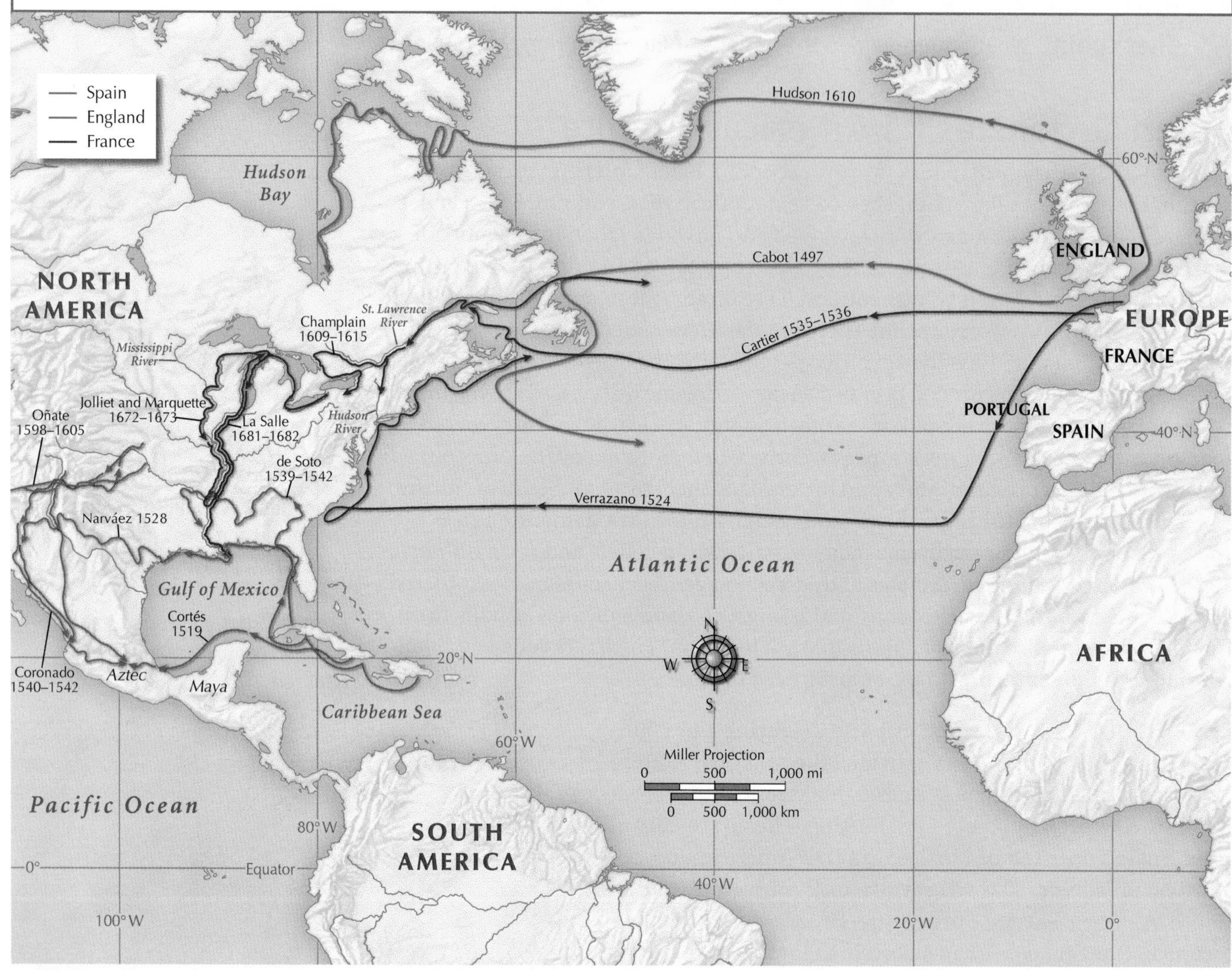

Vocabulary Builder
urban–(UHR buhn) *adj.* relating or belonging to a city

Spaniards were at the pinnacle. The higher *castas* enjoyed superior status and greater legal privileges at the expense of those of lower status.

In both New Spain and Peru, the Spanish developed an urban and cosmopolitan culture. Carefully planned towns possessed a spacious grid of streets, with the town hall and a church arranged around a central plaza. The wealthiest families dwelled near the central plaza. The common people lived in the outer districts of the towns.

✓ **Checkpoint How did Spain maintain control over its American colonies?**

Spanish Explorers Push North

Cortés's success in conquering and plundering Mexico inspired later conquistadors. Seeking their own golden empires, Hernando de Soto and Francisco Vásquez de Coronado led expeditions into the lands north of Mexico.

De Soto Explores Florida In 1539, de Soto's conquistadors crossed present-day Florida, Georgia, South Carolina, North Carolina, Tennessee, Alabama, Mississippi, and Arkansas. Frustrated in their search for riches, the conquistadors massacred Indian villages, ravaged fields, emptied storehouses, and burned towns. After de Soto died of disease in 1542, his men gave up and fled to Mexico in boats. They left behind deadly new diseases, which continued to spread among the Indians of the Southeast.

Coronado Searches for Golden Cities Coronado marched north from Mexico into the Rio Grande valley in 1540. Unable to defeat the Spanish, the Pueblo Indians in the region tried to get rid of them by appealing to their greed. The Pueblos told alluring stories of a golden kingdom named Quivira to the northeast, on the far side of a great, grassy plain. In pursuit of Quivira, Coronado and his men crossed the Great Plains to what is now Kansas. They found only villages of grass-thatched lodges inhabited by Wichita Indians, who possessed neither gold nor silver. Returning to the Rio Grande in a rage, the Spanish took a bloody revenge on the Pueblos before retreating to Mexico in 1542.

Spain Colonizes Florida After the expensive failures of de Soto and Coronado, the Spanish Crown lost interest in the northern lands. Lacking tangible wealth, the northern frontier did not seem worth the effort to conquer and colonize. But attacks by French, Dutch, and English pirates began to change Spanish minds during the 1560s. By occupying Florida and the Rio Grande valley, the Spanish hoped to create a defensive zone, to keep hostile European rivals far from the precious mines and towns of Mexico. This plan became urgent when the Spanish learned that the French had built a small base on the Atlantic coast of Florida. Worse still, these French colonists were Protestants, whom the Spanish hated as heretics.

Vocabulary Builder
tangible–(TAN juh buhl) *adj.* solid; capable of being touched or understood

In 1565, Pedro Menendez de Avilés attacked and destroyed the French base, slaughtering the captured Protestants. He then founded the fortified town of St. Augustine, which became the first enduring colonial town within what would later become the United States. However, Florida failed to attract a large number of Spanish colonists, who numbered a mere 1,000 by the end of the century. Friars tried to convert Indians to Christianity by building **missions** in the native villages. By 1675, the friars had gathered 20,000 native converts in 36 mission churches spread across northern Florida. (See the infographic on the next page.)

Pueblo Indians create *katsinas*, images that represent ancestral spirits.

Spain Colonizes New Mexico During the 1590s, a Spanish expedition led by Juan de Oñate returned to the lands explored by Coronado in the Rio Grande valley. There, Spain established the colony of New Mexico, with Santa Fe as the capital (after 1607). The colony's isolation from Mexico, however, reduced the colonists' income and drove up the cost of their imported goods. Because few Spanish settlers wished to join such an isolated and poor colony, New Mexico's colonial population stagnated. In 1638, the 2,000 colonists were greatly outnumbered by the 40,000 Pueblo Indians. A soldier described New Mexico as "at the ends of the earth . . . remote beyond compare."

As in Florida, only the friars thrived in New Mexico. By 1628, they had founded 50 missions. The progress was remarkable because the friars demanded so much from their converts. Christian churches replaced the circular *kivas,* the sacred structures for religious dances and ceremonies. The priests smashed or burned the *katsina* figures held sacred by the Indians. (*Katsinas* are wooden figures that represent ancestral spirits.) The friars also expected the Indians to dress, cook, eat, and speak like Spaniards.

For a couple of generations, the Pueblos did their best to adapt to the friars. In part, the Indians acted from fear of the Spanish soldiers, who backed up the

INFOGRAPHIC

Missions and Forts

As Spanish conquistadors explored and conquered territory in the Americas, Spanish missionaries worked to convert American Indians to Christianity. During the 1500s and 1600s, Spanish soldiers and missionaries established a number of settlements in New Mexico and Florida. Missions, or religious settlements run by friars or priests, included a church, a friary, houses, and often a fort to protect settlements from attacks by European rivals or Indian adversaries. The illustrations and pictures here depict the Spanish settlement at San Luis de Apalachee in Florida, established in 1656. San Luis was the western capital of Spanish Florida, while St. Augustine was its eastern capital. Today, archaeologists and historians are re-creating the site.

▼ Silver crucifix and rosary beads belonging to Christian Indians

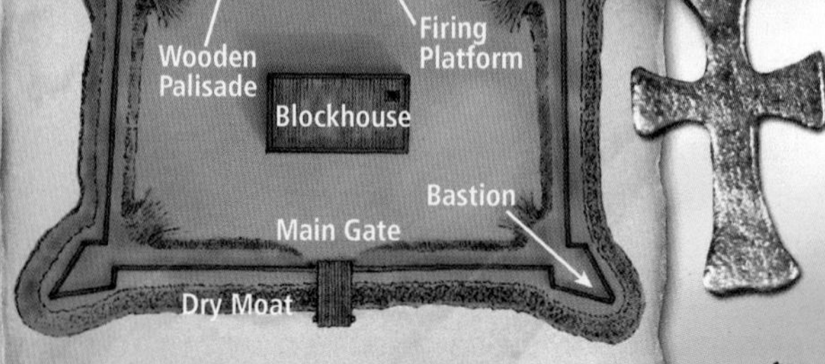

▲ A drawing shows the plan of the fort at San Luis de Apalachee.

▼ This illustration shows the construction of the fort at San Luis de Apalachee. Spaniards direct Apalachee Indians to complete the walls of the fort.

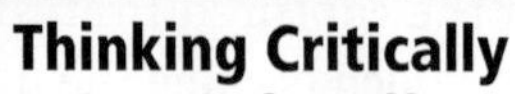

Thinking Critically

1. **Recognize Effects** How did Spanish missionaries affect Indian culture?
2. **Draw Conclusions** Why do you think the Spanish built forts as well as missions in many of the places they settled?

▲ A reconstruction of the church at San Luis

friars with firearms and horses. The Pueblos were also interested in the domesticated animals and metal tools provided by the missions.

But the Pueblos would not give up all of their traditional beliefs. Instead, they considered Christianity a supplement to their own sacred practices. To please the priests, the Indians became public Christians, but they privately mixed Christianity with traditional ways, keeping in secret their *kivas* and *katsinas*. When the missionaries discovered these secrets, they felt the fury of betrayal. The harsh punishments inflicted by the friars angered the Pueblos.

✓ **Checkpoint** **Why did the Spanish explore and colonize New Mexico and Florida in the 1600s?**

The Pueblos Revolt Against the Spanish

Conditions worsened during the 1660s and 1670s. A prolonged drought undercut the harvests, reducing many Pueblos to starvation. Disease, famine, and violence cut their population from 40,000 in 1638 to 17,000 by 1680. The losses made it harder for the Pueblos to pay tribute in labor and crops to the missionaries and colonists.

Fed up, in 1680 the Pueblos revolted under the leadership of a shaman named Popé. Encouraging resistance to Spanish ways, Popé urged a return to the traditional Pueblo culture and religion. The rebels also drew support from the Apaches, who had their own scores to settle with the Spanish slave raiders. The Indians destroyed and plundered missions, farms, and ranches. Abandoning Santa Fe, the colonial survivors and Christian Indians fled to El Paso, which at the time was on the southern margin of New Mexico. The Pueblo Revolt was the greatest setback that the Indians ever inflicted on colonial expansion.

History Makers

Popé (1630?–1690?)
In 1675, the Spanish governor of New Mexico ordered more than 40 Pueblo shamans publicly whipped for following traditional religious practices. One of those punished that day was Popé. That mistreatment spurred him to plan the Pueblo Revolt of 1680. He even convinced the Apaches, traditionally the Pueblos' enemies, to join the fight to rid the region of the Spanish. The Spanish fled and did not return for 12 years. During that time, Popé worked to restore Pueblo ways of life and religion. When and where he died is not certain, but it likely happened before the Spanish return in 1692.

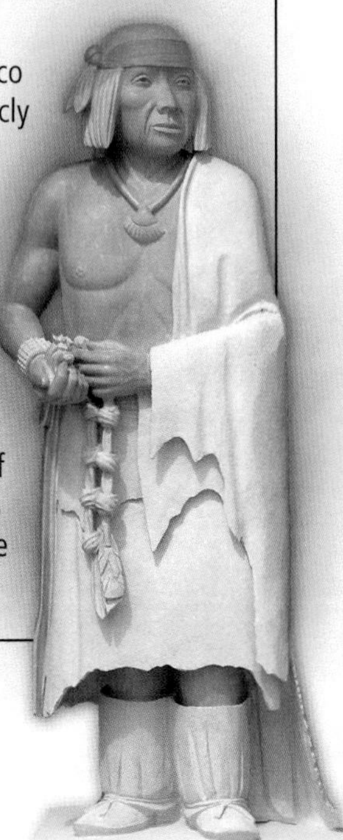

After victory deprived them of a common enemy, the Pueblos resumed feuding with one another and with the Apaches. The renewed violence discredited Popé, who had promised that the rebellion would bring peace and prosperity. Losing influence, he died sometime before 1690. During the following three years, the Spanish reclaimed New Mexico.

The bloody revolt taught the Pueblos and the Spanish to compromise. The Pueblos accepted Spanish authority, while the Spanish colonists practiced greater restraint. The Pueblos once again became public Catholics while quietly maintaining traditional ceremonies in their *kivas.* The Spanish and the Pueblos increasingly needed one another for mutual protection against the Apaches of the surrounding plains and mountains.

✓ **Checkpoint** **How did Popé manage to defeat the Spanish settlers?**

SECTION 1 Assessment

Progress Monitoring *Online*
For: Self-test with vocabulary practice
www.pearsonschool.com/shist

Comprehension

1. **Terms and People** For each term below, write a sentence explaining its relationship to Spain's American colonies.
   - missionary
   - presidio
   - viceroy
   - mestizo
   - mission
2. **NoteTaking Reading Skill: Summarize** Use your concept web to answer the Section Focus Question: How did Spain strengthen its colonies in the Americas?

Writing About History

3. **Quick Write: Identify Effects** Write a paragraph describing the effects of the Spanish in the Americas from a Native American point of view. Your paragraph should state a main idea and contain supporting details.

Critical Thinking

4. **Recognize Ideologies** How did Spanish friars view Native American religions? Explain.
5. **Analyze Information** What was the *casta* system, and why was it created?
6. **Recognize Cause and Effect** What were the causes and effects of the Pueblo Revolt?

▲ French fur trader

SECTION 2

A beaver ▶

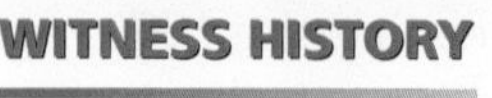

WITNESS HISTORY

A Profitable Fur Trade

While the Spanish grew rich mining silver and gold in South America, the French profited from the fur trade in Canada. But the trade relied on good relations with the Indians, who hunted and traded valuable beaver pelts with the French. At times, conflicts with the Iroquois halted the trade. As one missionary reported, New France faced ruin:

> "At no time in the past were the beavers more plentiful in our lakes and rivers and more scarce in the country's stores. . . . The war against the Iroquois has exhausted all the sources. . . . The Montréal store has not purchased a single beaver from the Natives in the past year. At Trois-Rivières, the few Natives that came were employed to defend the place where the enemy is expected. The store in Québec is the image of poverty."
>
> —François Joseph Le Mercier, *Relations des Jésuites,* 1653

The French Empire

Objectives

- Explain how the fur trade affected the French and the Indians in North America.
- Explain how and why Quebec was founded.
- Describe the French expansion into Louisiana.

Terms and People

Northwest Passage	*coureurs de bois*
Quebec	*metis*
Samuel de Champlain	

NoteTaking

Reading Skill: Compare and Contrast Fill in a Venn diagram like the one below comparing Spanish America and French America.

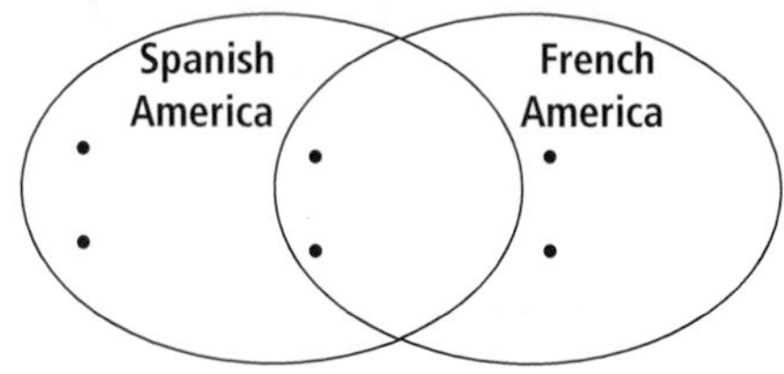

Why It Matters Spain's success with its American colonies encouraged other European nations to establish colonies. French explorers led expeditions along the North American Atlantic seaboard during the 1500s. These explorers established a number of French settlements along the St. Lawrence River and began trading fish and animal furs with Native Americans in the region. In time, these small settlements grew and became the nucleus of present-day Canada. **Section Focus Question: How did France's American colonies differ from Spain's American colonies?**

The French Establish a Fur Trade

During the early 1500s, explorers who sailed for France, including Giovanni da Verrazano and Jacques Cartier, were less interested in establishing colonies and more interested in finding a **Northwest Passage**—a water route to Asia through the cold waters of present-day Canada. They probed the eastern coastline of North America, from present-day North Carolina to Newfoundland. During the 1530s and 1540s, Cartier investigated the St. Lawrence River.

France Establishes New France The French king claimed the region that Cartier explored as New France. At the mouth of the St. Lawrence River, French mariners fished for cod and hunted for whales and seals. The mariners met Indian hunters, who offered furs in trade. Rendered scarce in Europe by excessive hunting, furs, especially beaver fur, commanded high prices.

Indians eagerly traded fur for metal arrowheads, hoes, axes, knives, and hatchets, all useful both as tools and weapons, and for iron or brass kettles, which made it easier to boil their meals. A Montagnais Indian explained, "The Beaver does everything perfectly well, it makes kettles, hatchets, swords, knives, bread; in short, it makes everything." Increasingly, the Indians hunted for a foreign market rather than just for their own subsistence.

Killing the beaver faster than the animals could reproduce, the coastal Indians sought new stocks by invading the hunting territories of their neighbors. This provoked wars between Indian groups. Those without metal weapons lost these wars, which also gave them a powerful incentive to trade with the French. Every American Indian nation tried to attract European traders and keep them away from their Indian enemies.

Quebec

Founded in 1608, Quebec was the first permanent European settlement in Canada. *How did Quebec's location contribute to its defense and economic prosperity?*

Just as the Indians fought one another over trade, the traders plundered and killed one another in their competition for furs. To repel rivals, a French company built a fortified trading post at Quebec on the St. Lawrence River in 1608. **Quebec** was the first permanent European settlement in Canada.

French–Indian Relations Unlike the Spanish in Mexico, the Canadian French could not afford to intimidate, dispossess, or enslave the Indians. The French needed them as hunters and suppliers of furs—roles that the Indians eagerly performed. Few in number, the French took little land, which lessened conflict with Canada's Native Americans.

Samuel de Champlain, Quebec's founder, traded with the Montagnais, Algonquin, and Huron Indians. In return, they expected Champlain to help them against their foes: the Iroquois, who lived to the south in what is now New York. In 1609, Champlain and nine French soldiers helped their allies attack an Iroquois camp beside the lake later named after Champlain. The Iroquois, expecting a traditional Indian battle, rich in display and light in casualties, assembled their warriors in a mass formation. They counted on their wooden shields, helmets, and body armor for protection from arrows. They were shocked when Champlain and his soldiers fired their guns, instantly killing Iroquois chiefs and warriors. Bewildered, the Iroquois warriors retreated.

Champlain won the battle at a high long-term cost. He made enemies of the powerful Iroquois, who for decades thereafter raided the French settlements. The battle also revolutionized Indian warfare. The Iroquois abandoned wooden armor, and they avoided massed formations. Instead, they relied on trees for cover and shifted their tactics to hit-and-run raids. They also demanded guns as the price of trade. Obtaining guns from Dutch traders on the Hudson River, the Iroquois became better armed than their Algonquin, Montagnais, and Huron enemies.

Exploring the Mississippi
French explorers Louis Joliet and Father Jacques Marquette traveled together from the Great Lakes to the Mississippi River in 1673.

Jesuit Missionaries Like the Spanish, the French dispatched Catholic priests as missionaries to convert the Indians. Most French Catholic missionaries belonged to the Jesuit order. They enjoyed their greatest success among the Huron Indians of the Great Lakes region. But that success attracted Iroquois warriors, who destroyed the Huron villages between 1648 and 1649. Killing hundreds, including most of the priests, the raiders carried away thousands of Huron captives. Many were adopted by the Iroquois. The Jesuit missions survived only in the St. Lawrence Valley, between the major towns of Montreal and Quebec.

✓ **Checkpoint How did the battle at Lake Champlain change the methods used by the Iroquois to fight the French?**

Life in New France

New France's government resembled that of New Spain. Both were strictly controlled by the powerful monarchs of the homeland. The French king appointed a military governor-general, a civil administrator known as the *intendant,* and a Catholic bishop. Like the Spanish, the French king did not permit an elected assembly in Canada.

New France Grows Slowly Attracting few immigrants, New France grew slowly. By 1700, the colony still had only 15,000 colonists. Potential colonists objected to the hard work of clearing dense forests to plant new farms. The long Canadian winter shocked newcomers from temperate France. Worst of all, immigrants dreaded the Iroquois raids.

Most French colonists were farmers who settled in the St. Lawrence Valley. To the west, Indians dominated the vast hinterland of forests and lakes, where the colonists were few and scattered. In the Great Lakes and Illinois countries, the French established a handful of small settlements, including Detroit. Settlers lived by a mix of farming and trade.

Vocabulary Builder
dominate–(DAHM uh nayt) *v.* to have control, power, or authority over somebody or something

Alliances With Indians Bring Benefits To survive and prosper in an Indian world, the French had to adopt some of the Indians' ways. Known as ***coureurs de bois*** (koo rer duh BWAH), many fur traders married Indian women. The children of these marriages became known as the ***metis.***

With the help of the *coureurs de bois* and the *metis,* the French allied with the Great Lakes Indians, who primarily spoke an Algonquian language. The allies defeated the Iroquois during the 1680s and 1690s, compelling them to make peace in 1701. At last, the fur traders of the Great Lakes and the grain farmers of the St. Lawrence Valley could work in safety from Iroquois raids.

Louisiana and New Orleans In 1682, the French explorer Robert de LaSalle was hoping to find a Northwest Passage. Guided by Native Americans, he made his way south on the Mississippi River toward what he hoped was an opening to the Pacific Ocean. Instead, he found the Gulf of Mexico. La Salle claimed the territory around the Mississippi River basin for France, naming it Louisiana, in honor of King Louis XIV. In 1718, near the river's mouth, the French founded New Orleans, which became the colony's largest town and leading seaport.

Like Canada, Louisiana struggled to attract colonists. The economy provided few opportunities beyond trading with the Indians for deerskins or raising tobacco of poor quality. The hot climate and swampy landscape also promoted deadly diseases, especially dysentery and malaria. By 1731, Louisiana had lost two-thirds of its settlers. The colony had just 2,000 whites and 4,000 enslaved Africans.

The French primarily valued Louisiana as a military base to keep the English from taking control of the immense Mississippi watershed. As in the Great Lakes country, the French sought Indian allies to help them confine the English colonies that were growing to the east along the Atlantic coast.

New Orleans
Despite a hot, humid climate and the danger of coastal storms, the French built a settlement at New Orleans. *Why was control of New Orleans important to the French?*

 **Checkpoint** **Why did New France attract few colonists?**

SECTION 2 Assessment

Progress Monitoring *Online*
For: Self-test with vocabulary practice
www.pearsonschool.com/ushist

Comprehension

1. **Terms and People** For each entry below, write a sentence that tells how it contributed to the development of New France.
   - Northwest Passage
   - Quebec
   - Samuel de Champlain
   - *coureurs de bois*
   - *metis*
2. **NoteTaking Reading Skill: Compare and Contrast** Use your Venn diagram to answer the Section Focus Question: How did France's American colonies differ from Spain's American colonies?

Writing About History

3. **Quick Write: Identify Effects** Make a list of one or two effects of each of the following events: the search for the Northwest Passage, the fur trade, and Champlain's attack on the Iroquois in 1609.

Critical Thinking

4. **Analyze Information** Why did the economy of the French colonies in the Americas depend on a good relationship with Native Americans?
5. **Recognize Cause and Effect** How did trade and warfare with France affect the Iroquois and other Native American nations?
6. **Support Generalizations** What evidence supports the following generalization: Conflicts among the nations of Europe emerged as they competed for territory in the Americas.

SECTION 3

▲ Pocahontas in European clothing

WITNESS HISTORY

Pocahontas

The earliest English settlers at Jamestown would have perished without assistance from Native Americans. A young Indian girl named Pocahontas was especially helpful. A daughter of Chief Powhatan, Pocahontas visited the Jamestown settlement and carried messages between the settlers and her father.

Despite Pocahontas's help, conflict arose between the Native Americans and the Jamestown colonists. During a period of warfare, Pocahontas was held captive in Jamestown. During this captivity, she and settler John Rolfe became engaged and later married. Both the Indians and the English settlers viewed the marriage between Rolfe and Pocahontas as a chance to end the war.

England's Southern Colonies

Objectives

- Describe how Jamestown was settled, why the colony struggled, and how it survived.
- Explain the relationship of Indians and settlers in the Southern Colonies.
- Discuss the settlement of Maryland, the Carolinas, and Georgia.

Terms and People

charter	royal colony
joint-stock company	proprietary colony
Powhatan	Bacon's Rebellion
John Smith	Lord Baltimore
House of Burgesses	James Oglethorpe

NoteTaking

Reading Skill: Sequence As you read this section, use a flowchart to list the important events in the founding of the Southern Colonies. Add boxes as you need them.

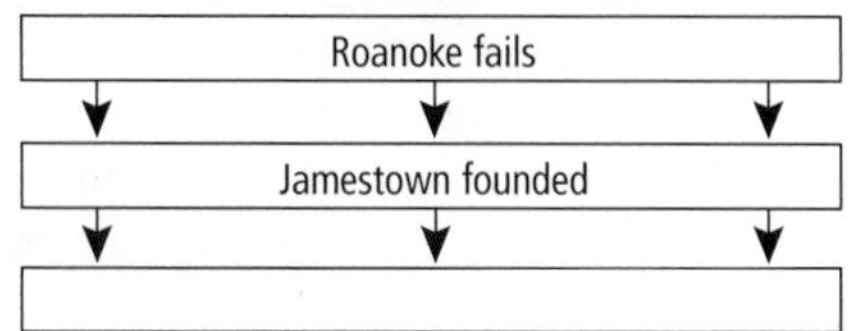

Why It Matters Neglected by the Spanish and French, the Atlantic coast remained open to English colonization during the 1580s. England's first attempts to establish a colony in North America failed, but in 1607 they succeeded in founding Jamestown, which became part of the colony of Virginia. By 1732, four more Southern Colonies had been established: Maryland, North Carolina, South Carolina, and Georgia. **Section Focus Question: What were the characteristics of the government and the economy in the Southern Colonies?**

England's First American Colonies

The first promoters of English colonies were wealthy gentlemen from southwestern England. They included Sir Walter Raleigh, a special favorite of Queen Elizabeth I. English patriots and devout Protestants, these men wanted to advance their fortunes and increase the power of England.

They promised that an American colony would solve England's problems: a growing population and increased poverty due to a stagnant economy. The promoters proposed shipping poor people across the Atlantic to work in a new colony. By mining for gold and silver and by raising plantation crops, these workers would generate new wealth for England.

Roanoke Colony Fails After obtaining a **charter,** or certificate of permission, from the king, the group formed a **joint-stock company.** This was a business venture founded and run by a group of investors who were to share in the company's profits and losses. During the 1580s, Raleigh twice tried to colonize Roanoke, a small island on the North Carolina coast (then considered part of Virginia). But English ships struggled to land supplies, and the sandy, infertile soil produced scanty crops. Raleigh's first colonists returned home in despair. The second set mysteriously vanished.

The Virginia Company Sends More Colonists The English tried again under the new leadership of the Virginia Company, a corporation of great merchants based in London. In 1607, the colonists proceeded to Chesapeake Bay, a superior location north of Roanoke. The Chesapeake offered many good harbors and navigable rivers—as well as more fertile land. But the colonists also had to deal with especially powerful Indians.

Although divided into 30 tribes, the region's 24,000 Indians shared an Algonquian language. They were also united by the rule of an unusually powerful chief named **Powhatan.** In his sixties, Powhatan impressed the English colonists with his dignity, keen mind, and powerful build.

Rather than confront the colonists at the risk of heavy casualties, Powhatan hoped to contain them and to use them against his own enemies, the Indians of the interior. He especially wanted to trade with the colonists for their metal weapons.

The colonists, however, wanted Indian lands. They refused to recognize that the Indians occupied, used, and had ancestral ties to these lands. Despite the many native villages and their large fields of maize, Captain **John Smith,** a colonist who emerged as a strong leader, described Virginia as "overgrowne with trees and weedes, being a plaine wilderness as God first made it." The English insisted on improving that "wilderness" into profitable farmland.

✓ **Checkpoint How did Powhatan deal with the English colonists?**

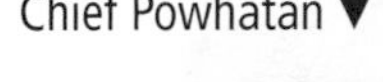
Chief Powhatan ▼

Jamestown Overcomes Hardships

The colonists founded a new settlement and named it Jamestown to honor King James I. The surrounding swamps defended the town from attack, but those swamps also bred mosquitoes that carried deadly diseases, especially malaria. The colonists also suffered from hunger, for they were often too weakened by disease to tend their crops. Between 1607 and 1622, the Virginia Company would transport some 10,000 people to the colony, but only 20 percent of them would still be alive in 1622.

Conflict With Native Americans In 1609, war broke out between the Indians and the starving colonists. In 1613, the English captured Powhatan's favorite daughter, Pocahontas. As an English captive, Pocahontas converted to Christianity and married a colonist named John Rolfe. Weary with war, Powhatan reluctantly made peace. When Powhatan died in 1618, power passed to his brother Opechancanough (oh PEHCH uhn kah noh), who hated the invaders from England.

The Tobacco Crop Saves the Colony By 1616, the Virginia Company had spent more than 50,000 English pounds—an immense sum for that time. Yet all it had to show for it was an unprofitable settlement of 350 diseased, hungry, and unhappy colonists. The company saved the colony by allowing the colonists to own and work land as their private property. As farmer-owners, rather than company employees, the colonists worked harder to grow the corn, squash, and beans that ensured their survival. But to make a profit, they still needed a commercial crop to market in England.

INFOGRAPHIC

JAMESTOWN
A COLONY SURVIVES

The first group of English settlers arrived in Jamestown on May 13, 1607. They established what would become the first permanent English settlement in America. But settling the region proved troublesome, as the colonists searched in vain for gold and refused to farm. Indians attacked the settlers for attempting to take Indian lands and food. Suffering from disease, malnutrition, and Indian attacks, two thirds of the Jamestown settlers died within the first seven months. The future looked bleak for the surviving settlers.

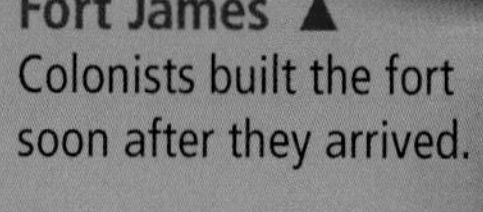

Fort James ▲ Colonists built the fort soon after they arrived.

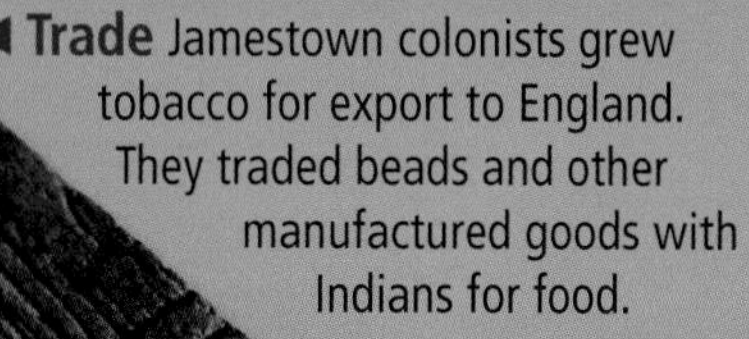

◀ Trade Jamestown colonists grew tobacco for export to England. They traded beads and other manufactured goods with Indians for food.

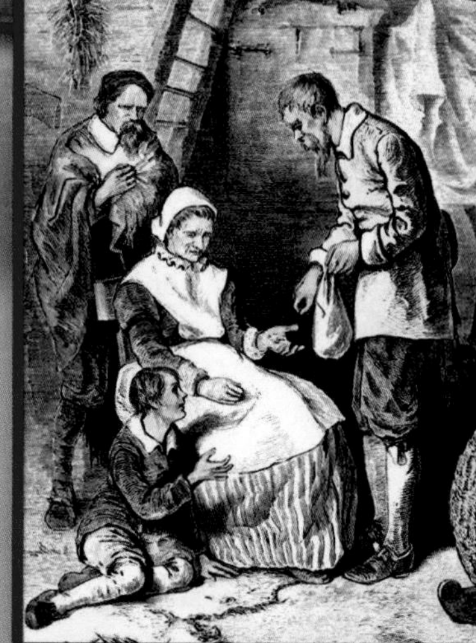

Starving Time During the ▶ winter of 1609–1610, only 60 of about 200 settlers survived. In June, as the remaining colonists prepared to leave Virginia, a supply ship arrived.

Led by John Rolfe, the colonists learned how to cultivate tobacco in 1616. West Indian tobacco had become extraordinarily popular for smoking in Europe. King James fought a losing battle when he denounced smoking as "a custom loathsome to the eye, hateful to the nose, harmful to the brain, [and] dangerous to the lungs." Eventually, though, he learned to love the revenue that the Crown reaped by taxing tobacco imports.

Because tobacco plants need a long, hot, and humid growing season, the crop thrived in Virginia but not in England. That difference gave the colonial farmers an advantage. Their tobacco production surged from 200,000 pounds in 1624 to more than 1.5 million pounds in 1640. The Chesapeake region became the principal supplier of tobacco to Europe. The profits attracted more immigrants to Virginia.

Free Land Attracts Colonists to Virginia Beginning in 1619, the Virginia Company offered free land. Under the headright system, anyone who paid for passage to Virginia or who paid for another person's passage received 50 acres of land. This enabled the wealthiest colonists to acquire large plantations. To work those plantations, landowners imported workers from England. The population of Virginia began to grow.

The House of Burgesses The Virginia Company also granted political reforms. In 1619, it allowed the planters to create the **House of Burgesses,** the first representative body in colonial America. Male landowners could elect two leaders, known as Burgesses, to represent their settlement in the colonial government. The House of Burgesses had the power to make laws and raise taxes. It began a strong tradition of representative government in the English colonies.

Success By 1615, Jamestown was growing due to the leadership of John Smith and John Rolfe. Smith forced colonists to work hard. He also established trade with the Indians. Rolfe established tobacco as a crop in Jamestown, saving the colony from financial ruin.

▲ Captain John Smith

Thinking Critically

1. **Draw Inferences** Do you think Jamestown would have survived without John Smith's leadership? Why or why not?
2. **Draw Conclusions** What evidence is there that the Jamestown colonists were prepared to trade with the Indians?

History *Interactive*
For: More about Jamestown
www.pearsonschool.com/ushist

In 1624, the Crown took over Virginia, making it the first royal colony in the English empire. During the seventeenth century, the English developed two types of colonial governments: royal and proprietary. The **royal colonies** belonged to the Crown, while the **proprietary colonies** belonged to powerful individuals or companies.

 **Checkpoint What challenges did the Jamestown settlers overcome to survive?**

The Effects of Expansion in Virginia

As the colonists expanded their tobacco plantations, they took more land from the Indians, who became enraged. In 1622, Opechancanough led a surprise attack that burned plantations and killed nearly a third of the colonists.

Wars With Algonquin Indians But counterattacks by the colonial survivors destroyed the Indian villages and their crops, reducing the natives to starvation. Defeated, Opechancanough made peace in 1632. The victors took more land and spread their settlements northward to the Potomac River.

With English settlements expanding, yet another war broke out between the colonists and Indians. In 1644, intense fighting killed hundreds of colonists and thousands of Indians, including Opechancanough. Disease and war reduced the Virginia Algonquins from 24,000 in 1607 to only 2,000 by 1670. The survivors became confined to small areas surrounded by colonial settlements. The number of settlers continued to surge, reaching 41,000 in 1670. The English had come to stay, to the alarm of Indians in the interior.

Vocabulary Builder
intense–(ihn TEHNS) *adj.* great, strong, or extreme in a way that can be felt

Bacon's Rebellion As the population of Virginia increased, settlers moved onto less fertile lands in the interior, where it cost more to transport their crops to market. They also faced greater danger from Indians angered by their intrusion.

The royal governor of Virginia, William Berkeley, worsened the growing crisis. Berkeley levied heavy taxes on the planters and used the proceeds to reward a few favorites from the wealthiest class, which dominated the House of Burgesses. He also expressed contempt for a free press and public education for common people. In 1671, he declared:

> **Primary Source** "I thank God, there are no free schools nor printing [in Virginia], and I hope we shall not have these [for a] hundred years; for learning has brought disobedience and heresy . . . into the world, and printing has divulged [spread] them, and libels [untruths] against the best government. God keep us from both!"
>
> —William Berkeley, 1671

In 1675, war erupted between the Indians and the settlers in the Potomac Valley. The settlers wanted to exterminate all of the colony's Indians. When Berkeley balked, the settlers rebelled under the leadership of the ambitious and reckless Nathaniel Bacon.

To popular acclaim, Bacon's men slaughtered Indians, peaceful as well as hostile. When Berkeley protested, Bacon marched his armed followers to Jamestown in a revolt called **Bacon's Rebellion.** In September 1676, they drove out the governor and burned the town. A month later, however, Bacon died suddenly of disease, and his rebellion collapsed. Berkeley regained power, but the rebellion had undermined his credibility. In 1677, the king appointed a new governor, and Berkeley returned to England.

Bacon's Rebellion showed that poorer farmers would not tolerate a government that catered only to the wealthiest colonists. The colony's leaders reduced the taxes paid by the farmers and improved their access to frontier land. But that frontier policy provoked further wars with the Indians of the interior.

 **Checkpoint What were the causes of Bacon's Rebellion?**

A Busy Port
Charles Town, South Carolina, was a center of trade and commerce by 1739. *How did Charles Town's location make it susceptible to attack?*

Other Southern Colonies

Virginia was the first of the Southern Colonies to be settled. During the seventeenth and eighteenth centuries, England established the Southern Colonies of Maryland, North Carolina, South Carolina, and Georgia.

Maryland In 1632, at the northern head of Chesapeake Bay, the English king established a second Southern Colony, named Maryland. The name honored Mary, the queen of the new monarch, Charles I (son of James). Charles gave Maryland to a favorite aristocrat, **Lord Baltimore,** who owned and governed it as a proprietary colony. Lord Baltimore founded Maryland as a colonial refuge for his fellow Catholics, who were discriminated against in England by the Protestant majority. Contrary to Lord Baltimore's hopes, however, more Protestants than Catholics immigrated to Maryland. Relations between the two groups deteriorated into armed conflict later in the century.

The Carolinas In 1670, the English established a new colony on the coast, north of Florida but south of Virginia. Called Carolina to honor King Charles II, the new colony included present-day North Carolina and South Carolina. The first settlement and capital was Charles Town, also named to honor the king. Carolina officially belonged to a group of English aristocrats—the Lords Proprietor—who remained in England, entrusting the colony's leadership to ambitious men from the West Indies. In 1691, the Lords Proprietor set aside the northern half of their territory as the distinct colony of North Carolina. In 1729, the North and South Carolinians rejected the control by the Lords Proprietor. The Carolinians demanded and received a Crown takeover. Thereafter, the king appointed their governors, who had to cooperate with elected assemblies in each colony.

Georgia In 1732, Georgia began as a proprietary colony intended to protect South Carolina against Spanish Florida. Led by **James Oglethorpe,** the Georgia trustees designed their colony as a haven for English debtors, who had been jailed because they could not pay their debts. Yet, most of Georgia's first colonists were poor English traders and artisans, or religious refugees from Switzerland and Germany.

Oglethorpe set strict rules for colonists. They could not drink alcohol and could not own slaves. Georgia's colonists had to work their own land and could therefore not own large plantations. These restrictions angered the colonists, who protested until the trustees surrendered to the Crown. Georgia became a royal colony in 1752.

 **Checkpoint** **Why did Lord Baltimore establish Maryland?**

Geography ***Interactive***
For: Interactive map
www.pearsonschool.com/ushist

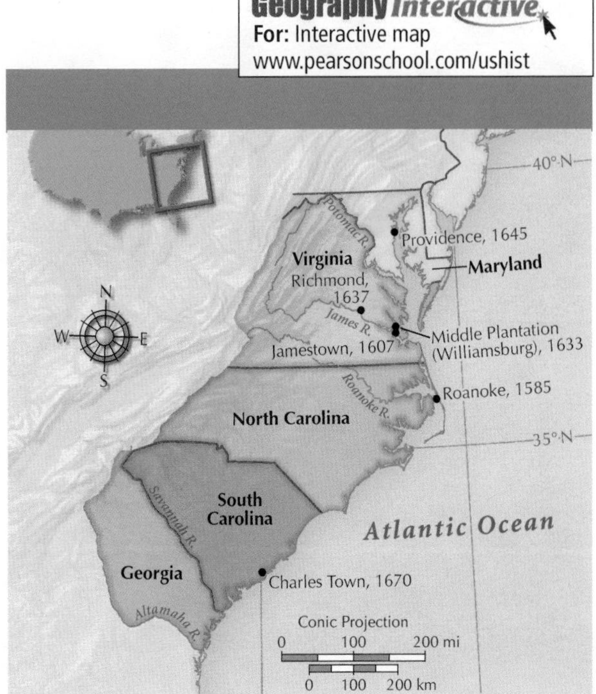

Map Skills By 1732, there were five Southern Colonies.

1. **Locate:** (a) Jamestown, (b) Charles Town, (c) Altamaha River
2. **Place** Which rivers formed Georgia's borders?
3. **Draw Conclusions** Why do you think early settlements in the Americas were founded on or near bodies of water?

SECTION 3 Assessment

Progress Monitoring *Online*
For: Self-test with vocabulary practice
www.pearsonschool.com/ushist

Comprehension

1. **Terms and People** What do the terms and people below have in common? Explain.
   - charter
   - joint-stock company
   - Powhatan
   - John Smith
   - House of Burgesses
   - royal colony
   - proprietary colony
   - Bacon's Rebellion
   - Lord Baltimore
   - James Oglethorpe
2. **NoteTaking Reading Skill: Sequence** Use your flowchart to answer the Section Focus Question: What were the characteristics of the government and the economy in the Southern Colonies?

Writing About History

3. **Quick Write: Create a Flowchart** As you prepare to write a cause-and-effect essay, you need to decide how to organize it. To do this, create a flowchart that shows the causes and effects of Bacon's Rebellion. Decide whether you want to write about the events in chronological order or in order of importance.

Critical Thinking

4. **Draw Conclusions** What combination of geographic and economic circumstances allowed Jamestown to survive?
5. **Identify Central Issues** How did the House of Burgesses distinguish the English colony of Virginia from Spanish and French colonies in the Americas?
6. **Recognize Bias** How did colonists' attitudes toward Native Americans lead to Bacon's Rebellion?

SECTION 4

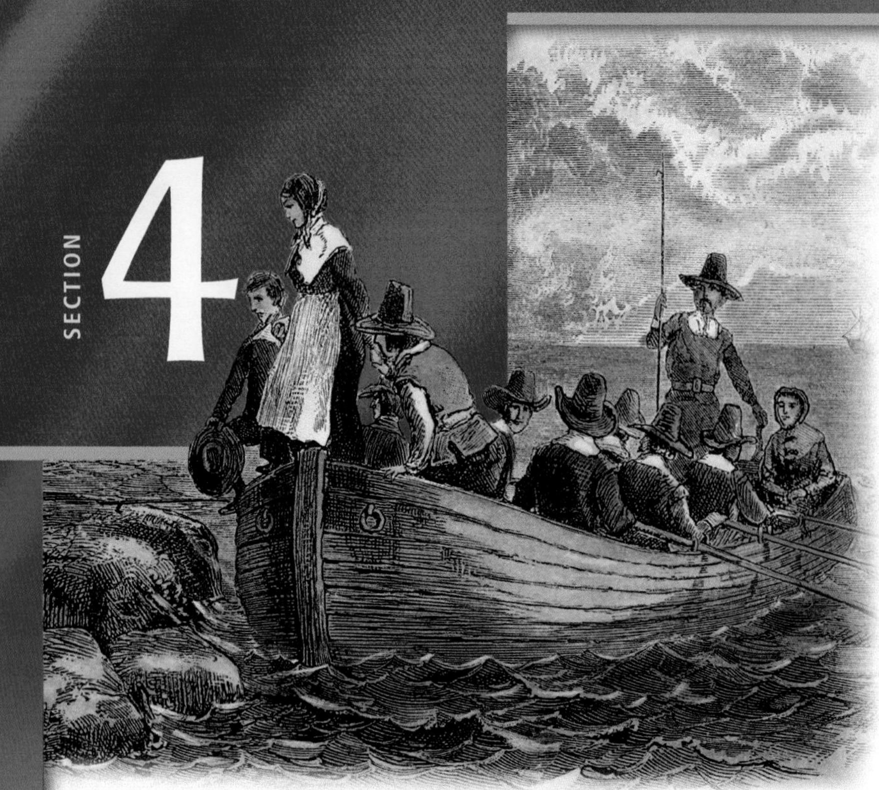

▲ Settlers land at Plymouth Rock

WITNESS HISTORY

The Pilgrims Leave for America

John Robinson, a Puritan pastor, addressed the Puritans who were about to sail to America on the *Mayflower.* Robinson spoke to them about how they should choose those who would govern them. He told the Puritans:

"... whereas you are become a body politic, using amongst yourselves civil government, and are not furnished with any persons of special eminency above the rest, to be chosen by you into office of government; let your wisdom and godliness appear, not only in choosing such persons as do entirely love and will promote the common good, but also in yielding unto them all due honor and obedience in their lawful administrations. . . ."

—John Robinson, August 5, 1620

The New England Colonies

Objectives

- Discuss why the Pilgrims left England and why they signed the Mayflower Compact.
- Summarize the government and society in the Massachusetts Bay Colony.
- Explain why Rhode Island, Connecticut, and New Hampshire were founded.
- Analyze the relationship between New Englanders and Native Americans.

Terms and People

Puritan	Roger Williams
Separatist	Anne Hutchinson
Pilgrim	Pequot War
Mayflower Compact	King Philip's War
John Winthrop	Metacom

NoteTaking

Reading Skill: Recognize Multiple Causes
Create a chart to identify the reasons the Pilgrims left Europe.

Causes for Puritans' Emigration From England		
• Disagreements with Anglican Church	•	•

Why It Matters Far to the north of the Southern Colonies, the English founded another set of colonies during the 1600s. New England was a land of dense forests, rolling hills, and a short growing season. New England demanded hard labor to farm and offered little prospect of getting rich. Before long, however, trade and commerce would bring prosperity to New England. **Section Focus Question: What were the goals of the Plymouth and Massachusetts Bay colonies?**

Puritans and the Church of England

Most of the New England colonists were religious dissidents who disagreed with the established church. Known as **Puritans,** they wanted to purify the Church of England, or Anglican Church, the only official and legal church in that kingdom. The Puritans believed that the Anglican Church, although Protestant, retained too many ceremonies from the Catholic Church. And a Catholic-style hierarchy of bishops controlled the local congregations. While some Puritans sought to reform the Anglican Church, others known as **Separatists** began their own churches.

Puritan Beliefs and Values The Puritans followed the teachings of the theologian John Calvin. They believed that they could prepare for God's saving grace by leading moral lives, praying devoutly, reading the Bible, and heeding their ministers' sermons. But not even the most devout could claim salvation as a right and a certainty, for they believed God alone determined who was saved. Salvation depended on the will of God rather than good behavior or adherence to church rules.

Puritans came from all ranks of English society, including aristocrats. Most belonged to "the middling sort"—a term used to describe small-property holders, farmers, shopkeepers, and skilled artisans. Their modest properties put them economically ahead of much of the English population.

Puritanism reinforced the values of thrift, diligence, and morality. Puritans insisted that men honored God by working hard in their occupations. One Puritan explained, "God sent you unto this world as unto a Workhouse, not a Playhouse."

Puritans Challenge the Anglican Church By challenging England's official church, the Puritans troubled the English monarchs, who led the Anglican Church. During the 1620s, King Charles I began to persecute the Puritans. His bishops dismissed Puritan ministers from their parishes and censored or destroyed Puritan books. Some Puritans sought a colonial refuge in North America, where they could escape the supervision of Anglican bishops. In their own colony, the Puritans could worship in their own churches and make their own laws, which they derived from the Bible. By living morally and prospering economically, they hoped to inspire their countrymen in England to adopt Puritan reforms.

 **Checkpoint** **Why did Puritans challenge the Anglican Church?**

Puritans Arrive in Massachusetts

In 1620, the first Puritan emigrants, who were later called **Pilgrims,** crossed the Atlantic in the ship the *Mayflower* to found the Plymouth Colony on the south shore of Massachusetts Bay. Before they disembarked, the group of about 100 made an agreement called the **Mayflower Compact.** The settlers agreed to form a government and obey its laws. This idea of self-government would later become one of the founding principles of the United States.

Massachusetts Bay Colony In 1630, **John Winthrop** led a much larger group of Puritans to America. Winthrop exhorted his fellow Puritans to make their new colony "A City upon a Hill," an inspirational example for the people of England. Winthrop explained:

> **Primary Source** "For we must consider that we shall be as a City upon a hill. The eyes of all people are upon us. [So] that if we shall deal falsely with our God in this work we have undertaken, and so cause him to withdraw his present help from us, we shall be made a story and a byword throughout the world."
>
> —John Winthrop, 1630

Beginning with the town of Boston, these Puritans established the Massachusetts Bay Colony on the north shore of that broad bay. In Massachusetts, settlers established a republic, where the Puritan men elected their governor, deputy governor, and assembly. This was the most radical government in the colonies because it was the only one that elected its governor.

From the towns of Plymouth and Boston, colonists spread rapidly along the coast and into the interior. To the northeast, New

Plymouth Colony

Puritans established Plymouth Colony in 1620. They built English-style houses and survived due to help from Native Americans. *Why did the colonists build a stockade around their settlement?*

Hampshire and Maine emerged, where Puritans settled uneasily in fishing communities that were Anglican. To the southeast, Rhode Island became a haven for especially radical Puritans. More conservative Puritans founded Connecticut along the Connecticut River and New Haven beside Long Island Sound. By the end of the seventeenth century, the Massachusetts Bay Colony included Maine and Plymouth, while Connecticut absorbed New Haven.

Vocabulary Builder
toleration–(tahl uhr AY shuhn) *n.* government acceptance of religious beliefs and ideas that are different from established ones

Religious Dissenters Form New Colonies Most of the Puritans immigrated to New England to realize their own ideal society—and certainly not to champion religious toleration. A leading New Englander denounced "the lawlessnesse of liberty of conscience" as an invitation to heresy and anarchy. No Catholics, Baptists, or Quakers need come to New England—except to Rhode Island. Dissenters were given, in the words of one Puritan, "free Liberty to keep away from us." To make that point, the Massachusetts government executed four Quakers and burned their books. The Puritans feared that God would punish any people who tolerated individual choice in religion.

The Puritans also purged their own people for expressing radical religious opinions. During the 1630s, **Roger Williams** and **Anne Hutchinson** angered the authorities by arguing that Massachusetts had not done enough to break with Anglican ways. Williams argued that settlers had no right to take land from the Indians. He said they needed to purchase the land from the Indians.

As a woman, Hutchinson seemed doubly dangerous to Puritan leaders who insisted that only men should exercise public influence. Though she ably defended herself in a trial, John Winthrop banished Hutchinson from Massachusetts.

Prosecuted by the authorities, Williams fled to Rhode Island, where he founded Providence in 1636. Rhode Island was a rare haven for religious toleration in the colonial world. Hutchinson and her family moved to the colony after she was exiled from Massachusetts. Rhode Island attracted Baptists, Quakers, and Jews. Lacking a majority for any one faith, the Rhode Islanders agreed to separate church and state. They believed that mingling church and state corrupted religion.

HISTORY MAKERS

Roger Williams
(1603–1683)
Roger Williams, a Puritan minister, came to Massachusetts in 1631. He held that the king had no right to give to English colonists land that belonged to Native Americans. After a Massachusetts court banished him and his followers, Williams founded Providence, Rhode Island—on land purchased from Native Americans. He established religious freedom and separation of church and state. Williams also allowed all males who headed families the right to vote. In Massachusetts, only church members could vote.

Anne Hutchinson
(1591–1643)
Hutchinson arrived in Massachusetts in 1634, where she held meetings in her home to boldly promote her idea that God's grace alone was the key to salvation. But the colony's leaders opposed preaching by a woman. In 1637, they declared her ideas heresy and banished her. She moved first to Rhode Island and later to New Netherland, where she was killed in a Native American attack.

Salem Witch Trials In addition to punishing religious dissenters, the New England Colonies prosecuted suspected witches. Whenever cattle and children sickened and died, the New Englanders suspected evil magic. For the safety of the community, witches had to be identified, prosecuted, and neutralized. The supposed victims of magic blamed neighbors who seemed to bear them ill will.

The most spectacular accusations occurred in and around Salem, Massachusetts, in 1692. The authorities there tried, convicted, and executed 19 suspected witches. But when the accusations reached members of prominent families, including the governor's wife, the judges dropped any further trials. Reassessed as a fiasco, the Salem mania ended the prosecution of witches in New England.

✓ **Checkpoint** **Why did Rhode Island become a haven for people of various religious faiths?**

Conflict With the Native Americans

The Puritans saw the Indians as lazy savages who accepted life in the wild, instead of laboring to conquer nature. The colonists remade the land to resemble England by clearing and fencing fields for cultivation in the English fashion. They built English-style houses, barns, mills, and churches. They introduced domesticated cattle, sheep, horses, and pigs. Colonists also killed wild animals that preyed on livestock.

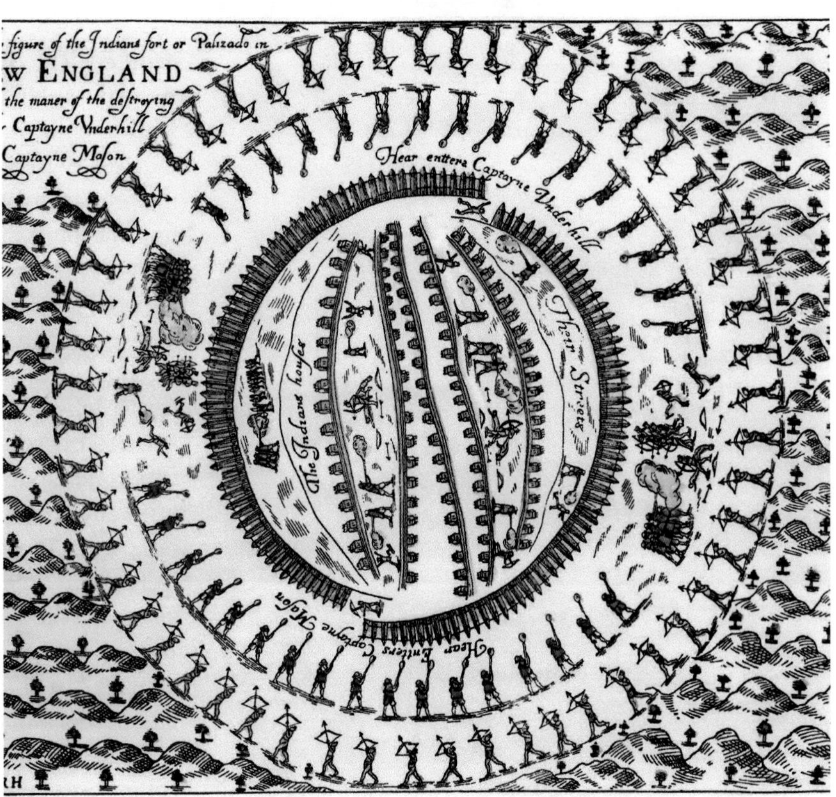

The Pequot War
In 1637, Puritans led an assault against the Pequot, destroying their villages. This woodcut shows Puritans and their Indian allies attacking a Pequot fort.

The Pequot War

By the 1630s, the Puritans of New England were engaged in a brisk fur trade with the Pequots and several other Indian nations. However, it was an uneasy relationship. Rivalry over control of the trade, coupled with Indian opposition to English territorial expansion, led to the outbreak of the **Pequot War.**

In 1636, Puritans accused the Pequots of murdering an English trader. But the Pequots denied the accusation. Allied with Narragansett and Mohegan Indians—enemies of the Pequots—the Puritans attacked several Pequot villages. In turn, the Pequots raided a Puritan village. Outraged, the Puritans burned a Pequot village filled with mostly women and children and killed most of its 600 to 700 inhabitants. The carnage was so complete that even the Puritans' Indian allies were shocked by the "manner of the Englishmen's fight . . . because it is too furious, and slays too many men." In 1638, by the Treaty of Hartford, the victorious English, Narragansetts, and Mohegans virtually eliminated the Pequot nation. The Pequots lost all their lands and surviving Pequots went to live among other Indian peoples.

Praying Towns

After the Pequot War, the Puritans worked to convert and transform the Indians into replicas of English Christians. They pressured the Indians to move into special "praying towns," where they could be closely supervised by missionaries. By 1674, Massachusetts had 14 praying towns with 1,600 Indian inhabitants. After restricting the Indians to a few special towns, the Puritans claimed most of their lands for colonial settlement. The missionaries forced the praying-town Indians to abandon their traditional ways and to don English clothing. The missionaries insisted upon the English division of gender roles. They urged the Indian men to forsake hunting and fishing in favor of farming. The Indian women were supposed to withdraw from the cornfields to tend the home and to spin and weave cloth—just as English women did.

Vocabulary Builder
gender–(JEHN duhr) *n.* condition of being male or female, especially regarding how the condition affects social status

However, only a minority agreed to enter the praying towns. As the colonists continued to expand their settlements at the Indians' expense, most Native Americans despaired of keeping their lands without a war.

Geography *Interactive*
For: Interactive map
www.pearsonschool.com/ushist

The New England Colonies

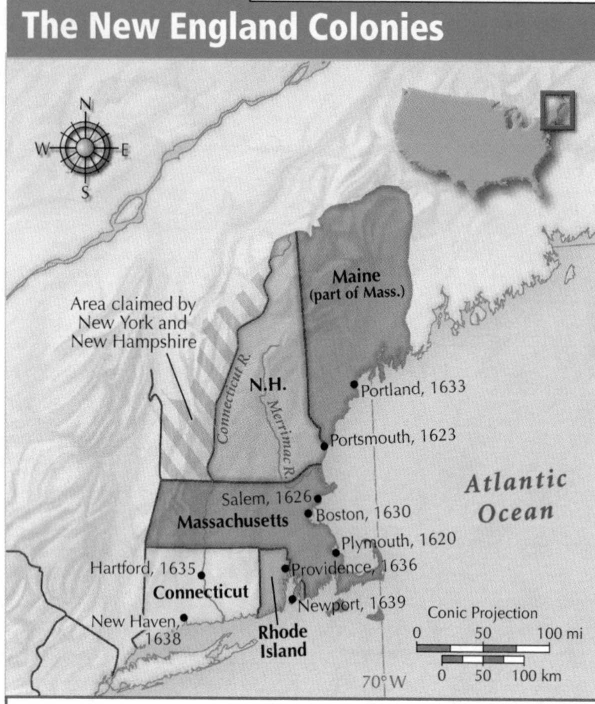

Map Skills The New England colonists found a cool climate and a rocky terrain.

1. **Place** Which settlement was established three years after Plymouth?
2. **Draw Conclusions** How did New England's geography affect its economy?

King Philip's War In 1675, a massive Indian rebellion erupted. The colonists called it **King Philip's War,** after a chief named **Metacom** who was known to the colonists as "King Philip." They imagined that he plotted and led the rebellion. In fact, every Indian village fought under its own leader. Far from any masterful plot by Metacom, the uprising consisted of many angry groups of Indians acting separately but similarly.

With guns acquired from traders, the Indians at first devastated the New England settlements, destroying 12 towns. But the tide of war turned in 1676, when the rebels began to starve because their crops were destroyed by colonial counterattacks. The Indians also ran out of ammunition after losing their access to colonial traders. In August, Metacom died in battle, shot down by a praying-town Indian who served with the colonists. The war killed at least 1,000 English colonists and about 3,000 Indians.

The defeated Indians lost most of their remaining lands in southern New England. They survived only as a small minority on limited lands within a region dominated by the newcomers. In 1700, the 92,000 colonists outnumbered New England's 9,000 Indians.

Some of the defeated Indians fled northward to the French colony of Canada, where they found refuge. Whenever the French waged war on the English, the refugee Indians sought revenge by raiding the New England frontier. Those wars became frequent and bloody after 1689, as the English and the French escalated their struggle to dominate North America.

 **Checkpoint How did Puritan praying towns compare with Spanish missions?**

SECTION 4 Assessment

Progress Monitoring *Online*
For: Self-test with vocabulary practice
www.pearsonschool.com/ushist

Comprehension

1. **Terms and People** Write a sentence for each entry below that explains how it is related to the founding of the New England Colonies.
   - Puritan
   - Separatist
   - Pilgrim
   - Mayflower Compact
   - John Winthrop
   - Roger Williams
   - Anne Hutchinson
   - Pequot War
   - King Philip's War
   - Metacom
2. **NoteTaking Reading Skill: Recognizing Multiple Causes** Use your chart to answer the Section Focus Question: What were the goals of the Plymouth and Massachusetts Bay colonies?

Writing About History

3. **Quick Write: List Effects** List the effects of one of the following events: the Mayflower Compact, the founding of Rhode Island, or the Salem witch trials. Then, rank the effects in order of importance.

Critical Thinking

4. **Identify Point of View** Read the following quotation and explain how it reflects Puritan values: "God sent you unto this world as unto a Workhouse, not a Playhouse."
5. **Make Comparisons** Compare the governments of the Virginia and Massachusetts colonies. How were the governments similar? How were they different?
6. **Recognize Bias** Consider the relationship between Indians and the following groups: Puritans, Virginians, Spanish colonists, and French colonists. How did each group's relationship with Native Americans reflect that group's bias toward Indians?

SECTION 5

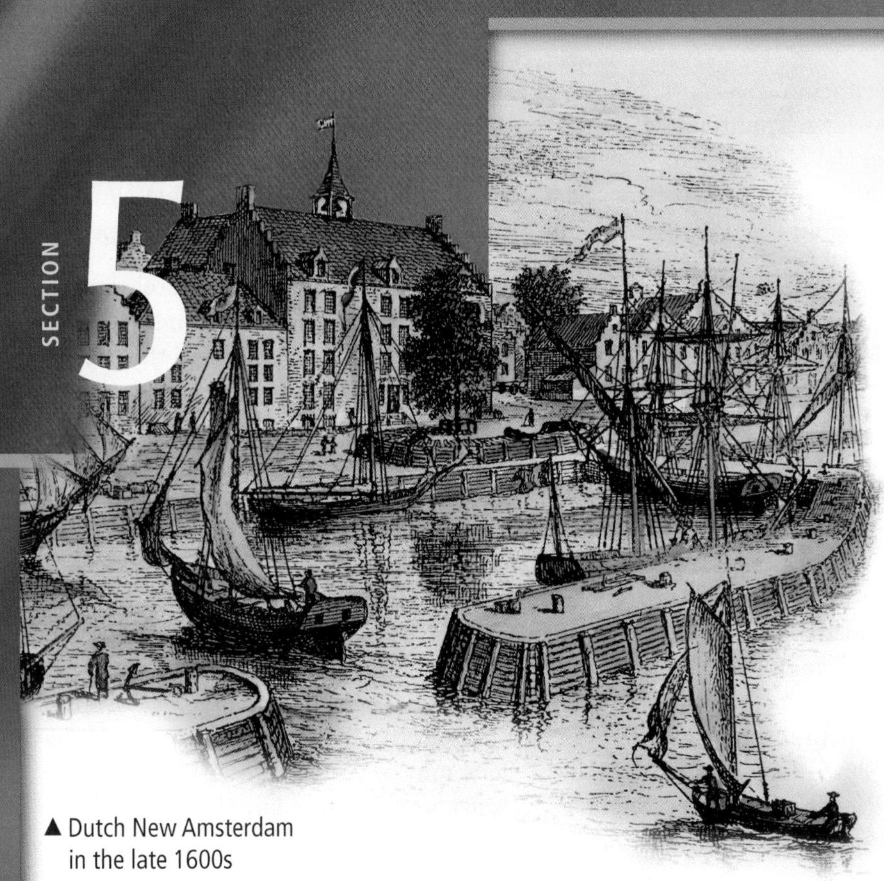

▲ Dutch New Amsterdam in the late 1600s

WITNESS HISTORY

The Dutch in New Amsterdam

At about the same time English colonists were establishing the Jamestown and Plymouth colonies, the Dutch founded New Netherland. New Amsterdam, the site of present-day Manhattan, was the Dutch capital. In the letter below, Peter Schaghen, an official of the Dutch West India Company, tells the directors of the purchase of Manhattan:

"High and Mighty Lords,
Yesterday the ship the *Arms of Amsterdam* arrived here. It sailed from New Netherland . . . on the 23d of September. They report that our people are in good spirit and live in peace. The women also have borne some children there. They have purchased the Island Manhattes [Manhattan] from the Indians for the value of 60 guilders."

—Peter Schaghen, 1626

The Middle Colonies

Objectives

- Explain how Dutch New Netherland became English New York.
- Describe William Penn's relationship with Indians in Pennsylvania.
- Compare and contrast the Pennsylvania Colony to other colonies.

Key Terms and People

push factor	William Penn
pull factor	Quaker

NoteTaking

Reading Skill: Identifying Main Ideas and Details As you read this section, prepare an outline like the one below.

I. The Dutch Establish New Netherland
  A. Government in New Netherland
    1. No elected assembly
    2. Religious tolerance
    3.
  B. Push–Pull Factors

Why It Matters During the early seventeenth century, the English developed two distinct clusters of settlements along the Atlantic coast: the Chesapeake to the south and New England to the north. Along the mid-Atlantic coast, the Dutch and Swedes established their own small colonies. Growing English power threatened the Dutch and the Swedes. Soon, England would control most of the Atlantic seaboard. **Section Focus Question: What were the characteristics of the Middle Colonies?**

The Dutch Establish New Netherland

Beginning in 1609, Dutch merchants sent ships across the Atlantic and up the Hudson River to trade for furs with the Indians. In 1614, they founded a permanent settlement at Fort Nassau (later called Fort Orange) on the upper river. To guard the mouth of the river, the Dutch built New Amsterdam at the tip of Manhattan Island in 1625. With the finest harbor on the Atlantic coast, New Amsterdam served as the colony's largest town, major seaport, and government headquarters. Coming to trade or to farm, the Dutch—in contrast to the French, Spanish, and Puritan English—made virtually no missionary effort to convert the Indians.

Government in New Netherland The Dutch West India Company appointed the governor and an advisory council of leading colonists, but they did not permit an elected assembly. Although run by authoritarian governors, New Netherland tolerated various religious groups, including Jews. That toleration drew an especially diverse group of colonists, not only from the Netherlands, but also from France, Germany, and Norway. As in New England, most of the colonists were of the middle class and poor. They came as families—unlike the unmarried, young men who prevailed in the early Chesapeake.

Push-and-Pull Factors Despite an appealing location and religious toleration, the Dutch colony attracted few immigrants. In 1660, New Netherland had only 5,000 colonists—better than the 3,000 in New France, but far behind the 25,000 in the Chesapeake and the 33,000 in New England. Why did the colonization of New Netherland falter?

In mobilizing migration to the colonies, push factors were stronger than pull factors. **Push factors** motivate people to leave their home countries. For example, religious persecution pushed the Puritans out of England. **Pull factors** attract people to a new location. For example, the promise of a better life and fertile soil may pull people to a new land. During the seventeenth century, push was stronger in England than in the Netherlands. With the Netherlands' booming economy and a high standard of living, the Dutch had less cause to leave home than did the English, who suffered from a stagnant economy. The Dutch did not have the masses of roaming poor who became servants in the Southern Colonies. And the tolerant Dutch lacked a disaffected religious minority, such as the Puritans who founded New England. The English succeeded as colonizers largely because their troubled society failed to satisfy their people at home.

 **Checkpoint Why did New Netherland have a diverse population?**

New Sweden Is Founded

In 1638, traders founded New Sweden on the lower Delaware River, within the present state of Delaware. Settlers built Fort Christina at the site of present-day Wilmington. Like the Dutch colony, New Sweden had a dual economy: the fur trade with Indians and grain farming by colonists. Some of the colonists were Swedes, but most came from Finland, then under Swedish rule. Skilled at pioneer farming in heavily forested Scandinavia, these colonists adapted quickly to America. They introduced many frontier techniques that eventually became adopted in America, including the construction of log cabins.

Eventually, New Sweden extended to both sides of the Delaware River, into present-day New Jersey, Pennsylvania, and Maryland. Although highly skilled, the approximately 500 New Sweden colonists were too few to hold the land after a violent confrontation with their Dutch neighbors. In September 1655, the Dutch governor, Peter Stuyvesant, appeared with seven warships, compelling the Swedish commander to surrender.

 **Checkpoint How did the Dutch take over New Sweden?**

The English Conquest

Thinly populated, New Netherland suffered when the Dutch and English empires came to blows. The Dutch and English became violent rivals in global commerce during the 1650s and 1660s. The English leaders resented that the more efficient Dutch shippers captured most of the trade exporting Chesapeake tobacco and West Indian sugar.

New York Becomes an English Colony In 1664, an English expedition forced Governor Stuyvesant to surrender his colony. The English renamed it New

York, after the Duke of York, who received it as a proprietary colony. New Amsterdam became the city of New York, while Fort Orange became known as Albany. Victory secured the mid-Atlantic coast for the English, closing the gap between the Chesapeake Colonies to the south and the New England Colonies to the north. Under English rule, the conquered region became known as the Middle Colonies.

The Dutch Surrender New Amsterdam

As English warships approach, Peter Stuyvesant (center) readies for surrender.

New Jersey Is Established In 1664, the Duke of York granted the lands between the Hudson and the Delaware rivers as a distinct new colony called New Jersey. Puritans and Scots settled the eastern half, while the western half attracted English Quakers. Relatively small and poor, New Jersey was dominated by its larger and wealthier neighbors: New York to the north and Pennsylvania to the west.

✓ **Checkpoint What colonies were established after the English took lands from the Dutch?**

William Penn Founds Pennsylvania

Pennsylvania began as a debt paid to **William Penn** by King Charles II of England. Although the son of an admiral, Penn had embraced the Quaker faith, a radical form of Protestantism. As a wealthy gentleman, Penn was an unusual Quaker. Most Quakers were tradespeople, shopkeepers, and small farmers who distrusted rich and powerful men. In turn, the gentry of England generally despised the Quakers.

Vocabulary Builder
radical–(RAD ih kuhl) *adj.* favoring or making extreme changes in political, social, religious, or economic thought or practice

Quaker Beliefs In contrast to the Puritan emphasis on sacred scripture and sermons by ministers, the **Quakers** sought an "Inner Light" to understand the Bible. The Quakers did not have clergy, and considering women spiritually equal to men, Quakers established both men's and women's leadership for their meetings. Pacifists, the Quakers refused to bear arms. They also tolerated other faiths. Unlike Puritan Massachusetts, Pennsylvania would have no privileged church with tax support.

Pennsylvania Prospers In 1680, the king granted to Penn the land west of the Delaware River as the colony of Pennsylvania, which means "Penn's Woods." In 1682, Penn arrived with 23 ships bearing 2,000 colonists. For his capital, Penn established a city named Philadelphia, which means "City of Brotherly Love."

Thanks to a temperate climate, fertile soil, and a navigable river, the colonists prospered and multiplied, reaching 18,000 inhabitants by 1700. As with the New England Puritans—but unlike the Chesapeake colonists—most early Pennsylvanians came in freedom as families of middle-class means. Most were Quakers, but the colony also attracted Anglicans as well as German Baptists and Lutherans.

Cultivating peace with the local Indians, the Pennsylvanians avoided the sort of native rebellions that devastated Virginia, New England, and New Mexico. Called Delawares by the English, the local Indians were Algonquian speakers.

INFOGRAPHIC

William Penn's Holy Experiment

William Penn, a member of the aristocracy, became a Quaker as a young man. Persecuted in England for their religious beliefs, many Quakers were jailed—including Penn. In 1681, Penn founded Pennsylvania as a safe haven for Quakers. He called Pennsylvania a "holy experiment" because it was a place that guaanteed religious and political freedom for its inhabitantsThis policy of toleration attracted Europeans with a variety of religious beliefs to immigrate to Pennsylvania, including Jews, Mennonites, Huguenots, and Lutheans.

Penn wrote a constitution for Pennsylvania that was unlike any other at the time. It guaranteed many fundamental liberties, limited the power of government, and contained provisions for amending the constitution. Many years later, these same ideas would appear in the U.S. Constitution.

A Planned Community ▲
Penn planned Philadelphia to include wide streets, parks, and hospitals.

Rights for Women ►
Quakers encouraged women to speak during religious services and supported education for women.

▲ **A New Kind of Colony** When he received the charter for Pennsylvania from King Charles, Penn envisioned his colony as one that would offer religious freedom. Penn also guaranteed many other freedoms.

▼ **Dealing Fairly With the Indians** Although Penn had been granted the land by the king of England, he purchased Pennsylvania from the Indians in the region and maintained good relations with them.

Thinking Critically

1. **Analyze Information** Why did King Charles II give William Penn land in North America?
2. **Draw Conclusions** Why was Penn considered an unusual Quaker?

Unlike most other colonial leaders, Penn treated Native Americans with respect and paid fair prices for their land.

✓ **Checkpoint** **How did William Penn's treatment of the Native Americans differ from the Puritans' treatment?**

Diversity in the Middle Colonies

The Middle Colonies developed an ethnic and religious diversity greater than either the Chesapeake area or New England, where almost all of the white colonists came from England. The Middle Colonies included Dutch, Swedes, Finns, French Protestants, Germans, Norwegians, and Scots—as well as English. By faith, they were Quakers, Baptists, Anglicans, Presbyterians, Lutherans, Dutch Reformed, German Reformed, and Jews. No single ethnic group or specific religious denomination possessed a majority in any Middle Colony. In 1644, a Jesuit priest described New Amsterdam:

> **Primary Source** "No religion is publicly exercised but the Calvinist, and orders are to admit none but Calvinists, but this is not observed, for there are, besides Calvinists, in the Colony Catholics, English Puritans, Lutherans, Anabaptists, [etc.]"
>
> —Reverend Isaac Jogues, 1644

The diversity of the Middle Colonies violated the traditional belief that political order depended on ethnic and religious uniformity. Thrown together in unexpected combinations, the various colonists had to learn how to tolerate their differences. In their ethnic and religious pluralism, the Middle Colonies anticipated the American future.

✓ **Checkpoint** **Why were the Middle Colonies more diverse than either the Southern or New England colonies?**

Geography ***Interactive***
For: Interactive map
www.pearsonschool.com/ushist

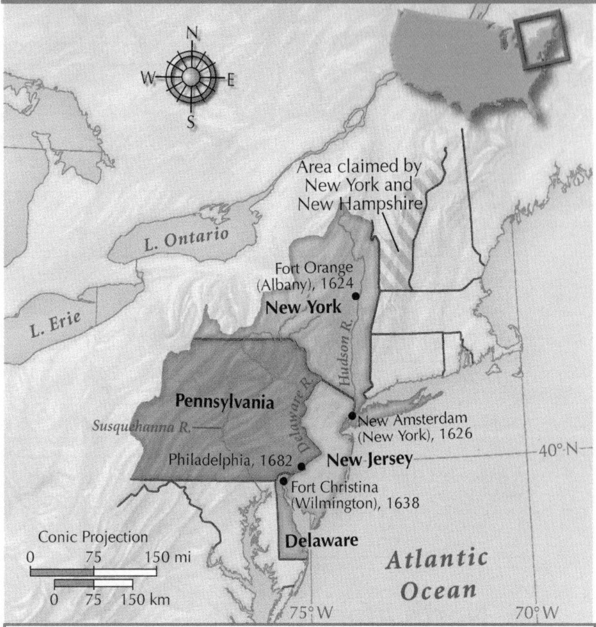

Map Skills The Middle Colonies offered settlers fertile lands and a mild climate.

1. **Locate:** (a) Fort Orange, (b) New Amsterdam, (c) Philadelphia
2. **Interaction** Which rivers were important to settlers in the Middle Colonies? Explain.
3. **Compare and Contrast** How were the Middle Colonies similar to and different from the New England and Southern colonies?

SECTION 5 Assessment

Progress Monitoring *Online*
For: Self-test with vocabulary practice
www.pearsonschool.com/ushist

Comprehension

1. **Terms and People** Write a sentence for each person or term below that tells how it contributed to the growth of the Middle Colonies.
   - push factor
   - pull factor
   - William Penn
   - Quaker
2. **NoteTaking Reading Skill: Identifying Main Ideas and Supporting Details** Use your completed outline to answer the Section Focus Question: What are the characteristics of the Middle Colonies?

Writing About History

3. **Quick Write: Provide Elaboration** Add interest to your cause-and-effect essay by finding supporting details, facts, and examples. Choose one of the events below and list as many specific details as possible. Then, write a paragraph using the details you listed to explain what caused the event.
   - The English defeat the Dutch and take over New Amsterdam.
   - William Penn gains a charter for Pennsylvania from King Charles II.

Critical Thinking

4. **Analyze Information** Why did fewer Dutch than English immigrate to the American colonies? Describe both the push factors and the pull factors that contributed to the difference.
5. **Draw Conclusions** How did geography help the colonies of New York and Pennsylvania prosper?
6. **Make Comparisons** How did religious toleration in the Middle Colonies differ from that in the New England Colonies?

CHAPTER 2

Quick Study Guide

Progress Monitoring *Online*
For: Self-test with vocabulary practice
www.pearsonschool.com/ushist

Europeans in America, 1600s–1700s

European Nation	Major Economic Activities	Government
Spain	• gold and silver mining • trading • farming	• Crown-appointed viceroys or governors • no elected officials
France	• fur trading • some farming	• Crown-appointed governors • no elected officials
England	• farming • fishing • trading	• Crown-appointed governors • elected assemblies

North America, 1753

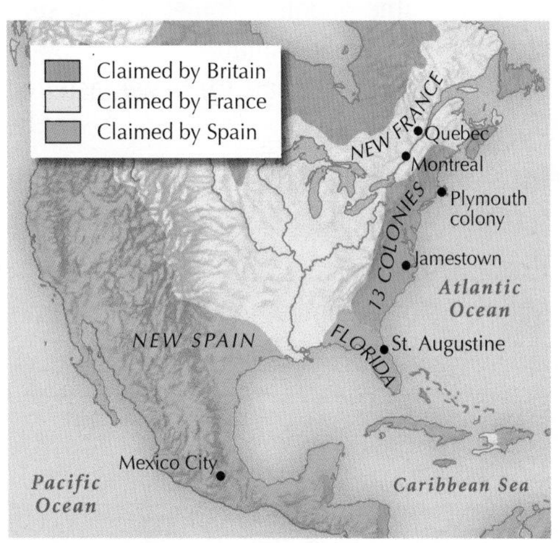

The 13 British Colonies

Colony	European Settlement
Southern Colonies	
Virginia	1607
Maryland	1632
Carolina	
North Carolina	1655
South Carolina*	1670
Georgia	1732
New England Colonies	
Massachusetts	1620
New Hampshire	1623
Connecticut	1634
Rhode Island	1636
Middle Colonies	
New York	1624
New Jersey	1630
Delaware	1638
Pennsylvania	1644

*North and South Carolina formed a single colony, Carolina, until they were separated in 1712.

Quick Study Timeline

In America

1607 English found Jamestown

1608 French found Quebec

1619 House of Burgesses established

1620 Pilgrims found Plymouth Colony

1500 | 1600 | 1620

Around the World

1517 The Protestant Reformation begins

1519–1522 Magellan circumnavigates the world

1630s Japan bars western merchants

American Issues Connector

By connecting prior knowledge with what you have learned in this chapter, you can gradually build your understanding of enduring questions that still affect America today. Answer the questions below. Then, use your American Issues Connector study guide (or go online: www.pearsonschool.com/ushist).

Issues You Learned About

● **Global Interdependence** Events, ideas, and items that come from one region often reach and influence people in other regions.

1. Explain how religious conflicts that took place in Germany in the early 1500s impacted people throughout Europe.
2. Describe the economic relationship between French settlers and the Native Americans who lived around the St. Lawrence River.
3. How did global commerce affect events in New Netherland?

● **Church and State** In colonial days, religious beliefs had a strong influence on the development of society.

4. Why did the Puritans first come to North America? What religious groups were not welcome in Massachusetts?
5. Why did leaders of Massachusetts banish Roger Williams and Anne Hutchinson?
6. What vision did Lord Baltimore have for his Maryland colony? Did he achieve this vision?
7. How did the beliefs of the Quakers lead to separation between church and state in Pennsylvania?

● **American Indian Policy** From the moment that Europeans began settling in North America, they developed policies for dealing with the Native Americans who already lived on the land.

8. How did Spanish policy toward the Pueblos change after the Pueblo revolt?
9. What benefits did the Puritans gain from pressuring Indians to move into special "praying towns"?
10. Think about the different groups of European settlers who came to North America. Which group do you think changed the lives of American Indians the least? Explain your answer.

Connect to Your World — Activity

Interaction With the Environment The early colonists in North America established thriving economies using the continent's abundant natural resources. Go online or to your local library and conduct research to learn more about the economic activities in the states that make up these regions today, especially those that relate to natural resources. Then, use your findings to write a summary of the interaction between people in these regions and their natural environment.

History *Interactive*
For: Interactive timeline
www.pearsonschool.com/ushist

1664 New York and New Jersey become English colonies

1671 Bacon's Rebellion

1680 Pueblo Revolt

1752 Georgia becomes a royal colony

1640 — 1660 — 1680 — 1750

1642 English Civil War begins

1652 Dutch build Cape Town in South Africa

1682 Peter the Great becomes czar of Russia

Chapter Assessment

Terms and People

1. Define **viceroy.** Where did the viceroys have power?
2. Who was **Samuel de Champlain**? What relationship did he have with the Native Americans?
3. How did **royal colonies** differ from **proprietary colonies**? Give an example of each type.
4. What was the **Mayflower Compact**? What was its most important principle?
5. Who were the **Quakers**? What ideas did Quakers support?

Focus Questions

The focus question for this chapter is **How and why did European nations establish colonies in the Americas?** Build an answer to this big question by answering the focus questions for Sections 1 through 5 and the Critical Thinking questions that follow.

Section 1

6. How did Spain strengthen its colonies in the Americas?

Section 2

7. How did France's American colonies differ from Spain's American colonies?

Section 3

8. What were the characteristics of the government and the economy in the Southern Colonies?

Section 4

9. What were the goals of the Plymouth and Massachusetts Bay colonies?

Section 5

10. What were the characteristics of the Middle Colonies?

Critical Thinking

11. **Make Generalizations** What was life like for Native Americans who lived on or near Spanish missions?
12. **Categorize** How did colonists in Spanish America categorize members of society? Explain your answer.
13. **Explain Effects** What effect did the fur trade with Europe have on relations between Native American groups?
14. **Analyze Information** Why did the Spanish colonists begin importing enslaved Africans?
15. **Explain Causes and Effects** What were the causes and effects of Samuel Champlain's battle with the Iroquois in 1609?
16. **Identify Assumptions** What ideas did the English in Virginia and Massachusetts hold about the way that the Native Americans interacted with the land of North America? How does their treatment of Indians reflect their attitude?
17. **Draw Inferences** How did James Oglethorpe make Georgia different from other Southern Colonies?
18. **Recognize Cause and Effect** What led to the outbreak of King Philip's War? What results did it have?
19. **Make Comparisons** Was Rhode Island more similar to other colonies in New England or to those in the Middle Colonies? Give several reasons to support your answer.
20. **Compare and Contrast** How did colonial governments in New Spain, New France, and in the 13 British colonies differ? What similarities were there?

Writing About History

Expository Essay: Cause and Effect Choose one colony in North America and write an essay that explains the causes and effects of its founding.

Prewriting

- Consider what you know about the founding of each colony, and choose one that you think best shows cause and effect.
- Take time to research facts, descriptions, and examples to clearly illustrate the causes and effects in your essay.

Drafting

- Choose one of the following to organize the causes and effects in your essay: Show the chronological order of events, or order the events from the least important to the most important.
- As you draft your essay, illustrate each cause and effect with supporting facts and details.

Revising

- Review your entire draft to ensure that you show a clear relationship between the causes and effects.
- Analyze each paragraph to check that you have provided a thorough set of facts and details.
- Use the guidelines on page SH11 of the Writing Handbook to revise your report.

Document-Based Assessment

European Motivations for Colonization

Why did European countries want colonies in North America? What motivated people to leave their homes to live on the edge of a distant continent they knew little about? Use your knowledge of colonial America and Documents A, B, and C to answer questions 1 through 4.

Document A

"It will be a service to the Church of great consequence to carry the Gospel into those parts of the world. . . . The whole earth is the Lord's garden. . . . Why . . . suffer a whole continent as fruitful and convenient for the use of man to lie waste without any improvement? . . . What can be a better work, and more honorable and worthy of a Christian than to help rise and support a particular church while it is in its infancy, and to join his forces with such a company of faithful people, as by a timely assistance may grow strong and prosper. . . ."

—*John Winthrop,* Reasons for the Plantation in New England, *c. 1628*

Document B

"Whereas . . . several lands, Islands, Places, Colonies, and Plantations have been obtained and settled in that Part of the Continent of America called New England, and thereby the Trade and Commerce there, hath been of late Years much increased: And whereas We have been informed by the hirable Petition of our Trusty and Well beloved John Winthrop [and others], being Persons principally interested in Our Colony or Plantation of Connecticut, in New England, that the same Colony . . . was Purchased and obtained for great and valuable Considerations, and some other Part thereof gained by Conquest . . . and at the only Endeavors . . . of theirs and their Associates . . . Subdued, and Improved, and thereby become a considerable Enlargement and Addition of Our Dominions and Interest there. Now Know YE, That in consideration thereof . . . We have ordained . . . the said John Winthrop [and others] . . . One Body Corporate and politique, in Fact and Name, by the Name of, Governor and Company of the English colony of Connecticut in New-England, in America. . . ."

—*from the* Charter of Connecticut, *1662*

Document C

"Carolina is a fair and spacious Province on the Continent of America. . . . This Province lying so neer Virginia, and yet more Southward, enjoys the fertility and advantages thereof; and yet is so far distant, as to be freed from the inconstancy of the Weather, which is a great cause of the unhealthfulness thereof. . . .

The Land is of divers sorts as in all Countryes of the world, that which lyes neer the Sea, is sandy and barren, but beareth many tall Trees, which make good timber for several uses; . . . up the River about 20 or 30 mile, where they have made a Town, called Charles-Town, there is plenty of as rich ground as any in the world. . . . The Woods are stored with Deer and Wild Turkeys, of a great magnitude, weighing many times above 50lbs a piece, and of a more pleasant tast than in England; . . . other sorts of Beasts in the Woods that are good for food; and also Fowls. . . . Here are as brave Rivers as any in the World, stored with great abundance of Sturgeon, Salmon, Bass, Plaice, Trout, and Spanish Mackrill, with many other most pleasant sorts of Fish, both flat and round, for which the English Tongue hath no name. . . . Last of all, the Air comes to be considered . . . and this is it which makes this Place so desireable, being seated in the most temperate Clime, where the neighbour-hood of the glorious Light of Heaven brings many advantages. . . . The Summer is not too hot, and the Winter is very short and moderate, best agreeing with English Constitutions. . . ."

—*Robert Horne,* A Brief Description of the Province of Carolina, *1666*

1. Document B suggests that England valued its New England Colonies for
   A commercial reasons.
   B religious reasons.
   C strategic reasons.
   D political reasons.

2. Which documents are most likely advertisements?
   A Document A only
   B Documents A and B
   C Documents B and C
   D Documents A and C

3. Which documents suggest a religious motive for establishing colonies?
   A Document A only
   B Document B only
   C Documents A and C
   D Documents A and B

4. **Writing Task** What role do you think economics played in the establishment of European colonies in North America? Use your knowledge of the colonial period and evidence from the sources above to explain your answer.

CHAPTER

3 The American Colonies Take Shape

1607–1765

WITNESS HISTORY

The Colonies Prosper

As the American colonies grew and prospered, England encouraged colonists to import English goods. Colonists eagerly purchased imported cloth, tea, furniture, books, and other items. And as manufacturing grew in England, colonists could buy a greater variety of goods at lower prices than ever before. One visitor to America noted:

> "... [colonists] import from London stuffs and every other article of English growth or manufacture, together with all sorts of foreign goods. England, and especially London, profits immensely by its trade with the American colonies; for not only New York but likewise all the other English towns on the continent, import so many articles from England that all their [currency] must go to Old England. . . ."
>
> —Peter Kalm, *Travels into North America,* 1748

◀ Colonial artist Charles Willson Peale painted an image of his family that shows that they valued art and culture.

An eighteenth-century colonial hornbook

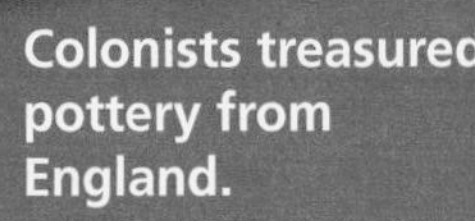

Colonists treasured pottery from England.

Chapter Preview

Chapter Focus Question: What factors shaped life in colonial America in the seventeenth and eighteenth centuries?

Section 1
Immigration and Slavery

Section 2
The American Colonies and England

Section 3
Comparing Regional Cultures

Section 4
Wars of Empire

A political cartoon urges the 13 colonies to work together.

Use the **Quick Study Timeline** at the end of this chapter to preview chapter events.

Note Taking Study Guide *Online*
For: Note Taking and American Issues Connector
www.pearsonschool.com/ushist

SECTION 1

▲ James Oglethorpe, founder of Georgia, greets Scottish immigrants.

WITNESS HISTORY

New Arrivals

In the 1700s, thousands of European immigrants crossed the Atlantic Ocean, hoping to acquire land, earn a good living, and enjoy the freedoms that existed in colonial America. In 1739, a German immigrant noted that "Liberty of conscience [thought]" was the "chief virtue of this land. . . . But for this freedom, I think this country would not improve so rapidly."

Yet, there were others who crossed the Atlantic under drastically different circumstances. These were Africans, who were forced from their homeland and crammed onto slave ships. Thrust into a hostile world, they were expected to work from sunup to sundown under terrible conditions. Their experiences in North America were different in every way from that of European immigrants.

Immigration and Slavery

Objectives

- Explain how European immigration to the colonies changed between the late 1600s and 1700s.
- Analyze the development of slavery in the colonies.
- Describe the experience of enslaved Africans in the colonies.

Terms and People

indentured servant
triangular trade
Middle Passage
Phillis Wheatley

NoteTaking

Reading Skill: Identify Main Ideas As you read the section, use a concept web to list main ideas about population in the colonies.

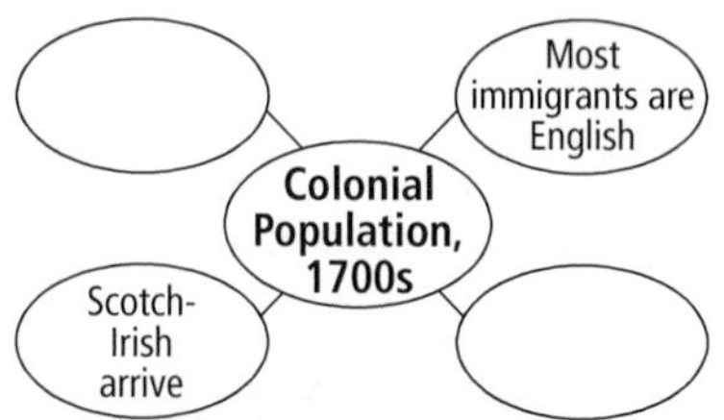

Why It Matters As the colonies developed, Europeans began to arrive in greater numbers. At first, most immigrants were English, but during the 1700s larger numbers of Germans and Scotch-Irish arrived. Enslaved Africans were taken unwillingly from their homelands and forced to work in a distant land. These newcomers would reshape American colonial society. **Section Focus Question: Which major groups of immigrants came to Britain's American colonies in the 1700s?**

Europeans Migrate to the Colonies

After a difficult start, England's American colonies grew steadily. By 1700, approximately 250,000 people of European background lived in the colonies. That number would rise tenfold during the next 75 years. Much of this growth came as a result of emigration from Europe.

Migration From England During the 1600s, about 90 percent of the migrants to the English colonies came from England. About half of these immigrants were **indentured servants**—poor immigrants who paid for passage to the colonies by agreeing to work for four to seven years. Instead of receiving a wage, indentured servants received basic food, clothing, and shelter—generally just enough to keep them alive. At the end of their term, they were supposed to receive clothes, tools, food, and sometimes land.

Developments in England caused the percentage of immigrants to drop dramatically. Prior to 1660, many English left their homeland because of religious and political turmoil. High unemployment and low wages in England added to the troubles. After 1660, however, the English economy improved and political and religious conflicts diminished. Increasingly, English people chose to stay in England.

The Scots and Scotch-Irish While English emigration shrank, Scottish emigration soared. Generally poorer than the English, the Scots had more reasons to seek their fortunes elsewhere. They also gained easier legal access to the colonies after 1707. In that year, Great Britain was formed by the union of England, Wales, and Scotland.

After the formation of Great Britain, many Scots became colonial officials. Some became royal governors. Scottish merchants also captured a growing share of the colonial commerce, especially the tobacco trade from the Chesapeake Bay.

The Scots emigrated to the 13 colonies in three waves. The first wave came from the Scottish lowlands. The second came from the Scottish highlands, and the third came from the province of Ulster in Northern Ireland. In the colonies, the Ulster Scots became known as the Scotch-Irish.

Nearly 250,000 Scotch-Irish people came to the colonies in the 1700s. They were descendants of Protestant Scots who had settled in Northern Ireland. The Scotch-Irish arrived in the American colonies in search of land. Many moved west to the mountainous "back country" that stretched from Pennsylvania to the Carolinas. There, they built farms on the frontier lands recently taken from the Indians.

The Germans Germans were second only to the Scotch-Irish as eighteenth-century emigrants from Europe to British America. Most of the 100,000 who immigrated to the colonies were Protestant. Almost all came from the Rhine Valley in southwestern Germany and northern Switzerland.

What factors explain the flood of German immigrants? They felt pushed by war, taxes, and religious persecution. During the 1700s, Germany was divided into many small principalities, frequently involved in wars. To build palaces and to wage war, German princes heavily taxed their people and forced young men to join the army. Most princes also demanded religious conformity. Germany also lacked enough farmland for its growing population.

In 1682, William Penn recruited a few Germans to settle in Pennsylvania, where they prospered. In letters to relatives and friends, immigrants reported that wages were high while land and food were cheap. In Pennsylvania, an immigrant could obtain a farm six times larger than a typical peasant holding in Germany. Pennsylvania demanded almost no taxes and did not force its young men to become soldiers.

Geography Interactive
For: Interactive map
www.pearsonschool.com/ushist

Diversity in the 13 Colonies

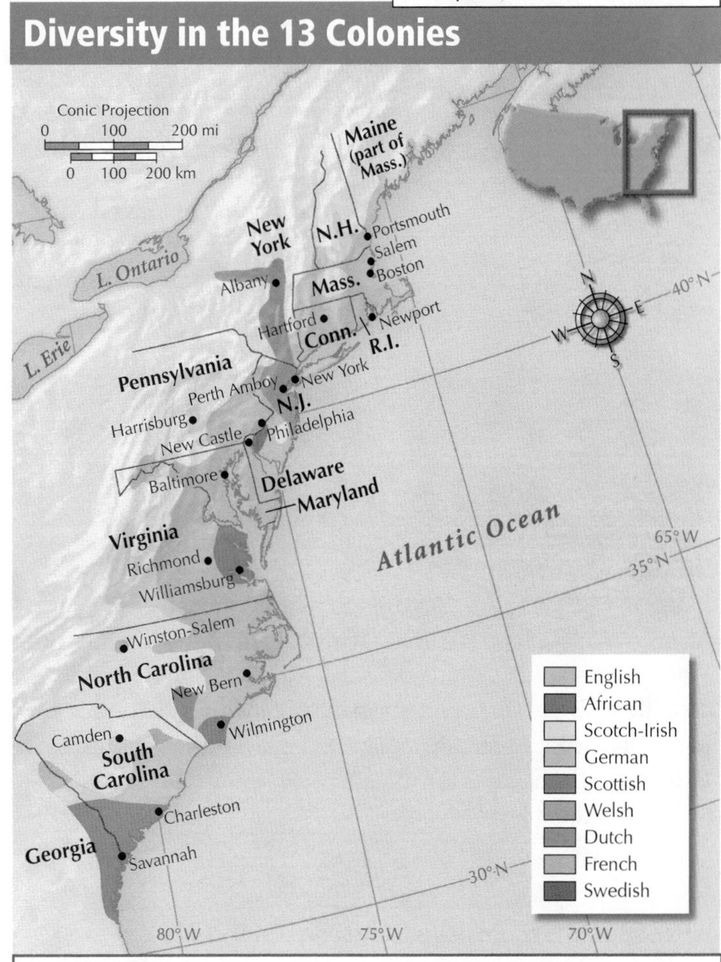

Map Skills Seeking land and liberty, Europeans from a number of nations immigrated to the 13 colonies during the 1700s. Hundreds of thousands of Africans were forced to migrate to the colonies.

1. **Locate:** (a) Pennsylvania, (b) Massachusetts, (c) South Carolina
2. **Region** Which colonies have the largest concentrations of people of African descent?
3. **Compare and Contrast** How does the diversity of the populations of New England and the Middle Colonies compare?

Immigration Brings Diversity Immigration brought changes to the colonies. In Pennsylvania, for instance, new waves of Scottish and German immigrants made the Quakers a minority in that colony. Although the different groups often distrusted one another at first, no group was large enough to impose its beliefs or to drive the others out of the colony. Instead, they all gradually accepted that a diverse society was an economic boon and the best guarantee for their own faith.

✓ **Checkpoint** **Why did Scots and Germans emigrate from their homelands?**

Africans Are Transported to America

During the 1600s, landowning colonists in the Chesapeake region needed workers to raise crops. Indentured servants filled this need, and most early indentured servants were English. Yet, as English immigration began to decline in the late 1600s, the demand for labor in the colonies grew. As a result, many colonists began to turn to another source of labor: enslaved Africans.

Slavery in the Colonies Begins Early in the 1600s, colonists often treated African workers just as they treated indentured servants, giving them their freedom after several years of service. Freed blacks could own land, vote, and even buy enslaved Africans of their own.

By the mid-1600s, however, most colonies began to pass laws that supported the permanent enslavement of Africans. In 1705, Virginia's General Assembly

INFOGRAPHIC

The Middle Passage

From the 1400s to the 1800s, more than 10 million enslaved Africans made a forced journey across the Atlantic Ocean to the Americas. Called the Middle Passage, Africans endured horrific conditions as they were crammed onto ships "like herring in a barrel" and sent to unfamiliar lands. The illustration shows enslaved Africans shackled together and jammed into spaces just 3 feet and 3 inches high.

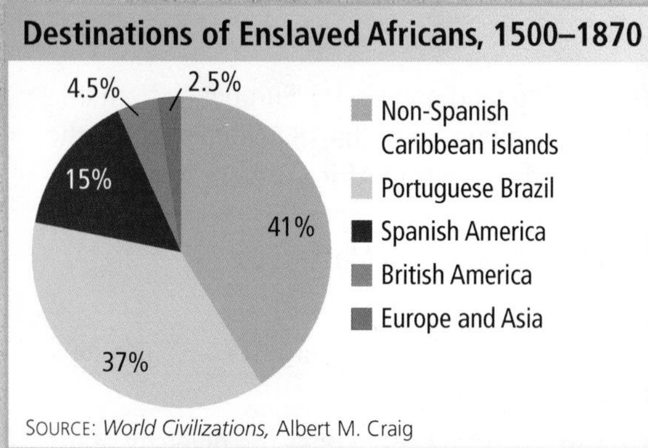

▲ The pie graph shows where slave traders sent captured Africans.

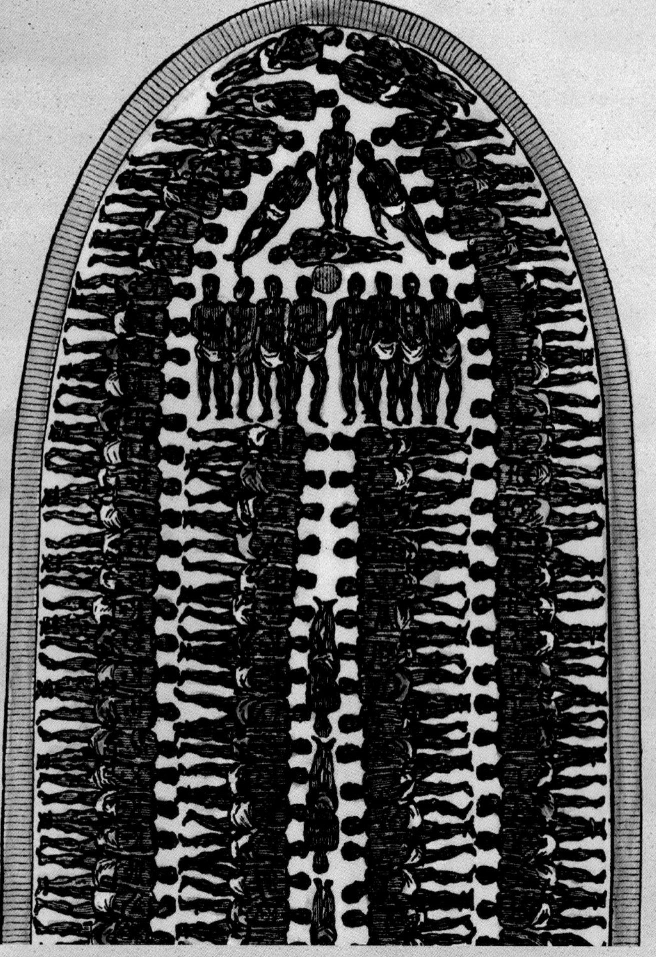

declared that "All servants imported . . . who were not Christians in their native Country . . . shall be accounted and be slaves." Other laws stated that the children of enslaved African Americans were also enslaved. This change in legal status promoted the racist idea that people of African origin were inferior to whites.

Vocabulary Builder
status–(STAT uhs) *n.* legal position or condition of a person, group, country, etc.

The Transatlantic Slave Trade Once established, slavery expanded rapidly. During the 1700s, the British colonies imported approximately 1,500,000 enslaved Africans. The great majority went to the West Indies, but at least 250,000 came to the 13 colonies to labor on plantations and in homes.

Traders purchased slaves from African merchants and chiefs in the coastal kingdoms of West Africa. Most of those enslaved were kidnapped by armed men or taken in wars between kingdoms. Although they did not directly seize slaves, Europeans promoted the trade by offering high prices for captives.

Enslaved Africans came to the Americas as part of a three-part voyage called the **triangular trade.** Slave traders sailed from Europe to Africa, where they traded manufactured goods for enslaved Africans. Then, in the **Middle Passage,** shippers carried the enslaved Africans across the Atlantic to the American colonies. After selling the slaves for colonial goods, the traders returned to the mother country.

The brutality of the Middle Passage was extreme. On a voyage that lasted two months or more, enslaved Africans suffered the psychological trauma of separation from their families and villages—as they sailed toward a strange land and an unknown future. Slave traders branded their cargo with hot irons, placed them in shackles, and jammed them into dark holds so crowded that the slaves

▼ **Crossing the Atlantic** The voyage from West Africa to the Americas could take from three weeks to three months depending on the winds and the weather. The map shows where the enslaved came from and where they were going.

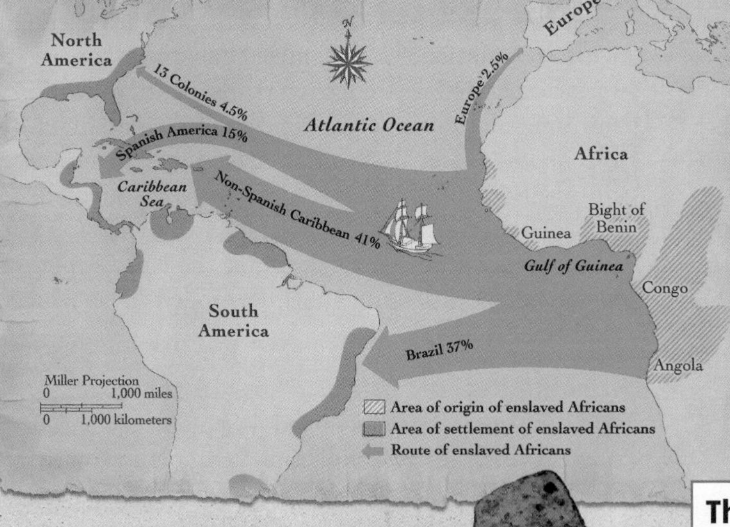

▲ Shackles

A Forced Migration

Born in West Africa, Olaudah Equiano (1745–1797) was captured when he was 11 years old. In his memoir, he vividly described the ship that would take him across the Atlantic.

"I was soon put down under the decks, and there I received such a salutation in my nostrils as I had never experienced in my life: so that, with the loathsomeness of the stench, and crying together, I became so sick and low that I was not able to eat, nor had I the least desire to taste anything. I now wished for the last friend, death, to relieve me..."

—*The Interesting Narrative of the Life of Olaudah Equiano,* by Olaudah Equiano

Thinking Critically

1. **Compare Points of View** How might Equiano's memoir compare with the journal of the captain of a slave ship?
2. **Synthesize Information** Based on the map and the pie graph, from what region of Africa did most enslaved Africans come? To what region did most go?

could hardly move. The foul air promoted disease, and the ill might be thrown overboard to prevent the spread of disease. Some Africans, hoping for death, refused to eat. One ship's surgeon witnessed the following shocking scene:

> **Primary Source** "Upon the Negroes refusing to take sustenance [food], I have seen coals of fire, glowing hot, put on a shovel and placed so near their lips as to scorch and burn them. And this has been accompanied with threats of forcing them to swallow the coals if they any longer persisted in refusing to eat."
>
> —Alexander Falconbridge, 1788

Slave traders had an interest in delivering a large and healthy cargo. However, due to the conditions, at least 10 percent of those making the Middle Passage in the 1700s did not survive.

✓ **Checkpoint How did the laws concerning enslaved Africans sent to the 13 colonies change in the 1700s?**

Africans in the Americas

Following the ordeal of the Middle Passage, enslaved Africans faced a bleak future in America. At slave auctions, colonial buyers often broke up families to make it more difficult to plot escape or rebellion. The newly enslaved were ordered about in an unfamiliar language and put to work beside strangers who shared only their skin color. Arriving with distinct languages and identities as Ashantis, Fulanis, Ibos, and many others, the enslaved forged a new culture as African Americans.

Slavery in the North and the South Slavery varied considerably by region. In 1750, enslaved African Americans were small minorities in New England and the Middle Colonies. In those two regions, most enslaved African Americans labored as farmhands, dockworkers, sailors, and house servants.

Many more enslaved African Americans lived in the Southern Colonies, where they raised labor-intensive crops of tobacco, rice, indigo, or sugar. In the Chesapeake, they comprised 40 percent of the population. In coastal South Carolina, enslaved African Americans outnumbered the white population. To maximize their profits, masters demanded as much work as possible while minimizing the cost of feeding, clothing, and housing slaves. Most of the enslaved lived in crude huts with dirt floors, no windows, and few furnishings. Their work was long and hard: at least 12 hours a day, 6 days a week under the close supervision of a white overseer, who whipped those who resisted.

This watercolor, painted on a South Carolina plantation in the late 1700s, shows a dance form and musical instruments that have their roots in Africa.

Developing a New Culture In the colonies, African Americans developed a rich culture based on African traditions and their circumstances in America. These traditions represented a blend of African cultures, as plantations, farms, and cities contained Africans from many different ethnic groups. Most African Americans adopted the Christianity of their masters, blending it with some African religious traditions. They modified African instruments, crafting banjos, rattles, and drums to create a music that emphasized rhythm and percussion.

Rebels and Runaways Slaveholders could never break enslaved African Americans' longing to be free. In the South and especially in the West Indies, some enslaved African Americans rebelled. On the mainland, the largest uprising erupted in 1739 at Stono in South Carolina, where about 100 slaves killed 20 whites before suffering defeat and execution.

Running away was more common. In the West Indies and the Carolinas, enslaved African Americans became *maroons*, a name for those who hid in forests or swamps. Other runaways fled to remote Native American villages or to Florida, where the Spanish welcomed them with food, land, and freedom. The Spanish sought to weaken the British colonies and to strengthen their own frontier militia with freed African Americans. In the Chesapeake and northern colonies, runaways tried to fit into the small free black communities.

Many more of the enslaved, however, opted for a more subtle form of rebellion. They stayed on the plantations, but they resisted by working slowly, feigning illness, pretending ignorance, or breaking tools.

HISTORY MAKERS

Phillis Wheatley
(1753?–1784)

Phillis Wheatley was the first African American to publish a book of poems. Captured at about age seven in West Africa, she was sold to John Wheatley, a Boston tailor. The Wheatleys allowed Phillis to learn to read, write, and study. She had her first poem published in 1767 in a Rhode Island newspaper. She won praise in the colonies and in Britain for her 1770 poem about the preacher George Whitefield. However, colonial publishers refused to publish a book of her poetry. Phillis and the Wheatleys found a London publisher to print her volume of poetry, *Poems on Various Subjects, Religious and Moral,* in 1773. That year the Wheatleys granted Phillis her freedom. She married in 1778 but lived in poverty until her death.

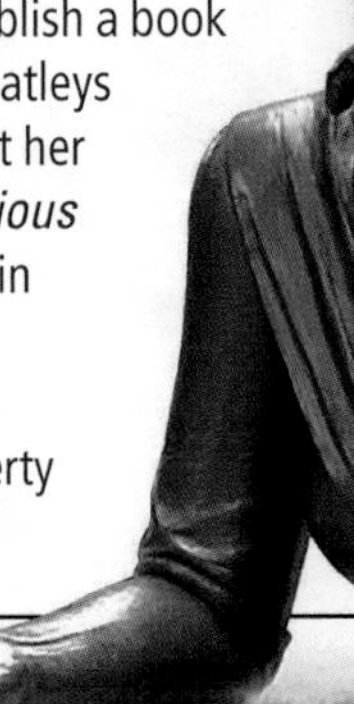

Free African Americans Although most African Americans remained slaves for life, a few did obtain their freedom. For example, an enslaved African American might manage to earn money and purchase his or her freedom or might be set free by a slave owner.

Free African Americans tended to live in cities, where they faced discrimination. A rare few managed to overcome enormous obstacles to distinguish themselves. One example was **Phillis Wheatley** of Boston (see the History Maker on this page).

✓ **Checkpoint** **How did slavery differ in the North and the South?**

SECTION 1 Assessment

Progress Monitoring *Online*
For: Self-test with vocabulary practice
www.pearsonschool.com/ushist

Comprehension

1. **Terms and People** What is the relationship between each of the following terms and people and the population of the 13 colonies?
   - indentured servant
   - triangular trade
   - Middle Passage
   - Phillis Wheatley
2. **NoteTaking Reading Skill: Main Ideas** Use your concept web to answer the Section Focus Question: Which major groups of immigrants came to Britain's American colonies in the 1700s?

Writing About History

3. **Quick Write: Define a Problem** Choose one topic from this section that you could use to write a problem-and-solution essay. For example, you could write about the experiences of European immigrants, indentured servants, or enslaved Africans. Make a list of details, facts, and examples that define the problems one of these groups faced.

Critical Thinking

4. **Understand Cause and Effect** Based on the description of European immigration to the American colonies, what were the main causes of immigration to the Americas?
5. **Analyze** Why did slavery become a permanent condition in the colonies?
6. **Draw Conclusions** Why do you think enslaved African Americans living in the South were able to preserve parts of African culture as well as build a new African American culture?

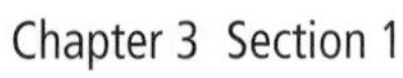

SECTION 2

▲ At busy colonial ports, merchants shipped raw materials to England and received manufactured goods from England.

American colonists imported English pottery. ▶

WITNESS HISTORY

An Illegal Trade

According to English law, the colonies could import manufactured goods only through English ports, where an additional tax was collected. Yet, the letter below holds that colonial importers evaded the law.

"... There has lately been carried on here a large illicit [illegal] trade....

A considerable number of ships have ... lately come into this country directly from Holland, laden ... with reels of yarn or spun hemp, paper, gunpowder, iron, and goods of various sorts used for men and women's clothing."

—William Bollan, advocate general of Massachusetts, 1743

The American Colonies and England

Objectives

- Explore how English traditions influenced the development of colonial governments.
- Analyze the economic relationship between England and its colonies.
- Describe the influence of the Enlightenment and the Great Awakening on the 13 colonies.

Terms and People

Magna Carta	mercantilism
Parliament	Navigation Acts
English Bill of Rights	Enlightenment
habeas corpus	Benjamin Franklin
salutary neglect	Great Awakening

NoteTaking

Reading Skill: Identify Supporting Details Use the format below to outline the section's main ideas and supporting details.

I. Government in the Colonies
  A. Traditions of English government
    1. Magna Carta
    2.
  B.
  C.
II.

Why It Matters During the eighteenth century, the colonists looked to England as their model for literature, government, and their economy. Important English documents, such as the Magna Carta and the English Bill of Rights, were the basis of colonial government and law. In addition, the colonial economy was dependent on trade with England. Although the relationship between England and the 13 colonies was a close one, during the 1700s, the distant American colonies began to form their own ideas about government and the economy. **Section Focus Question: How did English ideas about government and the economy influence life in the 13 colonies?**

Government in the Colonies

England developed an empire of many disunited colonies during the 1600s. Lacking money, the English Crown granted charters to private companies or lords proprietors, individuals who supported the monarchy. Compared to the Spanish or French, the English monarch exercised little direct control over the colonists.

Traditions of English Government Also unlike the kings of France and Spain, the English monarchs were bound to uphold the provisions of the **Magna Carta,** a document English nobles forced King John to accept in 1215. The Magna Carta protected English nobles by limiting the king's ability to tax them and by guaranteeing due process, or the right to a trial. Before levying a tax, the king needed the consent of the nobles.

After the Magna Carta, a council of nobles continued to advise English monarchs. The nobles also maintained the right to approve taxes—one of their most important powers. During the 1300s, the council of nobles gained more power and evolved into the lawmaking body known as Parliament. The English **Parliament** became a bicameral, or two-house, legislature. Members of the House of Lords were nobles, who inherited their positions, and church leaders. Commoners elected members of the House of Commons. However, only men with property could vote. Although this limited the number of eligible voters, England allowed more people to vote than any other European nation at the time.

A Measure of Self-Rule in America Although they were thousands of miles away from their homeland, most settlers in the North American English colonies asserted that they were entitled to the same rights as any other English subject. Nevertheless, the type of government in the American colonies varied from region to region.

Vocabulary Builder
assert–(uh SURT) *v.* to state positively; declare

In New England, the Puritans established republics with elected governors. Elsewhere, the distant Crown or lords proprietors appointed the governor of a colony. But that governor had to share power with the propertied colonists. Those colonists refused to pay taxes unless authorized by their own elected representatives in a colonial assembly. Colonists also claimed they were protected by English common law, which emphasized individual liberties.

King James II Asserts Royal Power In 1685, James II became king of England and tried to rule without Parliament. An open Catholic, he alarmed the Protestant majority of England. The new king also tightened control over the New England Colonies by revoking their government charters. Then, he combined them with New York and New Jersey into a larger colony known as the Dominion of New England. The Dominion replaced the colonies' elected assemblies with a Crown-appointed governor-general and council. The Dominion angered the colonists, who insisted upon their right to refuse to pay taxes unless approved by their own elected representatives.

The Glorious Revolution Results in a Bill of Rights In 1689, the colonists learned that James II had been overthrown in England in a coup called the Glorious Revolution. The plotters replaced him with two Protestant monarchs, King William and Queen Mary. The new monarchs promised to cooperate with Parliament and to support the Anglican church. William and Mary also agreed to sign an **English Bill of Rights,** a document guaranteeing a number of freedoms and restating many of the rights granted in the Magna Carta. These rights included **habeas corpus,** the idea that no one could be held in prison without being charged with a specific crime. The English Bill of Rights also stated that a monarch could not keep a standing army in times of peace without Parliament's approval. (See the primary source at right.)

The English Bill of Rights
The Glorious Revolution ousted James II. King William and Queen Mary took the throne and signed the English Bill of Rights. A few of the provisions of the Bill of Rights appear below.

Primary Source **"That levying money for or to the use of the Crown by pretence of prerogative, without grant of Parliament . . . is illegal;**
That the raising or keeping a standing army within the kingdom in time of peace, unless it be with consent of Parliament, is against law;
That excessive bail ought not to be required, nor excessive fines imposed, nor cruel and unusual punishments inflicted;"

—English Bill of Rights, 1689

INFOGRAPHIC

Roots of Democracy

Although the United States is more than 200 years old, the ideas of democracy and representative government are far older. The roots of democracy reach back to civilizations in southwest Asia and Europe.

Judeo-Christian Roots

The values found in the Bible, including the Ten Commandments and the teachings of Jesus, inspired American ideas about government and morality.

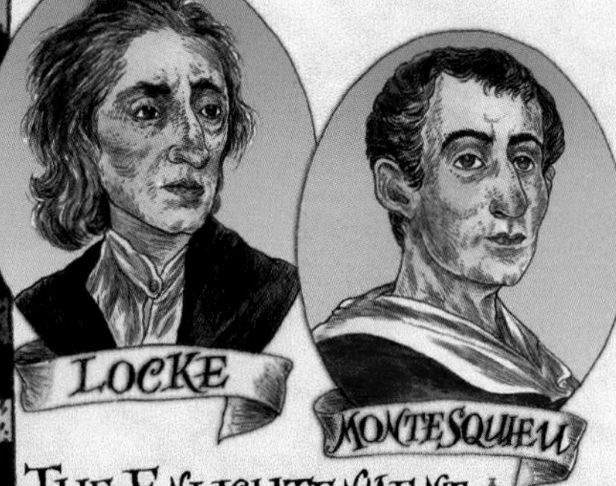

The Enlightenment

Two Enlightenment philosophers who influenced American ideas about government were John Locke and Baron de Montesquieu. Locke stated that all people have natural rights and that if a monarch violates those rights, then the people have the right to overthrow the monarch. Montesquieu declared that the powers of government should be clearly defined and limited.

DEMOCRACY

Greco-Roman Roots

Ancient Greek democracy and Roman republicanism have influenced American government.

English Parliamentary Traditions

Two key English documents inspired Americans. The Magna Carta (1215) and the English Bill of Rights (1689) guaranteed certain rights to citizens, including the right to trial by jury. The ideas of a two-house lawmaking body and voting rights also influenced Americans.

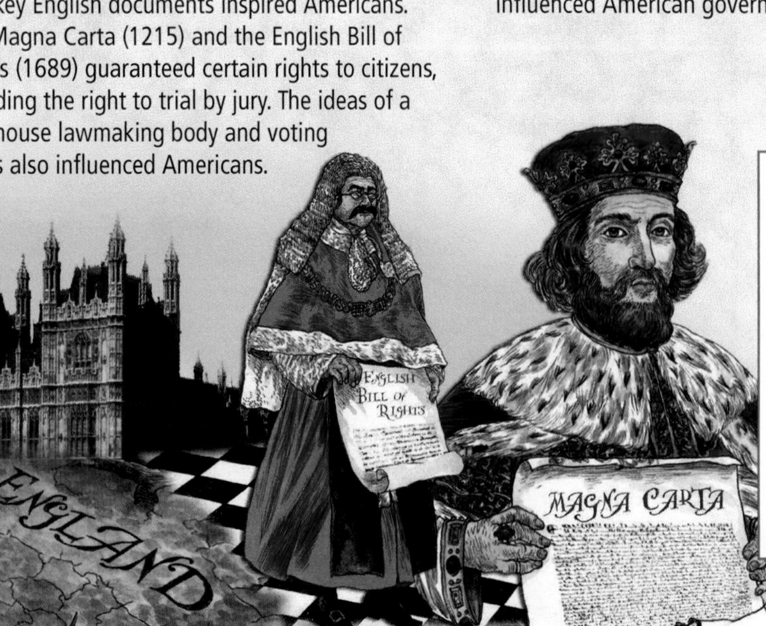

Thinking Critically

1. **Draw Conclusions** How did the Magna Carta and the English Bill of Rights limit English monarchs?
2. **Make Inferences** What Enlighten-ment values appear in the Declaration of Independence?

History *Interactive*

For: More about the roots of democracy www.pearsonschool.com/ushist

News of the English upheaval inspired rebellions among colonists in Massachusetts, New York, and Maryland. In Boston, colonial militia arrested the king's appointed governor-general, the hated Sir Edmond Andros.

All the rebels claimed loyalty to the new monarchs. And Protestant rebels in Maryland were delighted when William and Mary converted their colony into a royal colony. The new monarchs merged the Massachusetts and Plymouth colonies into a single royal colony, called Massachusetts. The new charter provided a royal governor assisted by an appointed council and an elected assembly. The assembly was permitted to choose council members, subject to the governor's approval. The king let Rhode Island and Connecticut keep their old charters, which allowed them to elect their governors as well as their assemblies.

Compromise was harder in New York. There, the leader of the rebellion, Jacob Liesler, had seized the position of governor. Liesler, however, made many political enemies. When England appointed a new governor, Liesler was made to surrender. He was quickly tried, convicted, and executed in 1691. That hasty trial and execution left a bitter legacy. For the next generation, Liesler's supporters and enemies feuded, souring politics in New York.

The Glorious Revolution encouraged England to adopt a colonial policy that historians would later call **salutary neglect.** England allowed its colonies local self-rule. In return, the Crown expected colonial cooperation with its economic policies and assistance in the empire's wars against France and Spain.

Freedom of the Press About 50 years after the Glorious Revolution, conflict broke out between the English-appointed governor and colonists in New York City. In 1734, articles criticizing the governor appeared in the *New York Weekly Journal,* a newspaper printed by John Peter Zenger. Although Zenger did not write the articles, the governor had Zenger imprisoned for libel—printing falsehoods that are intended to damage a person's reputation. He sat in jail for eight long months awaiting trial. When Zenger came to trial, his lawyer argued that the articles were not libelous but truthful. The jury agreed and found Zenger not guilty. Today, Zenger's case is considered an early victory for freedom of the press.

✓ **Checkpoint How did the Glorious Revolution affect the 13 colonies?**

England's Economic Relationship With the Colonies

England's colonization of the Americas was driven in large part by financial concerns. The purpose of the English colonies was to increase the wealth and power of England—the mother country. The economic policy of mercantilism supported those ideas.

Mercantilism Drives the British Economy The policy of **mercantilism** holds that a nation or an empire could build wealth and power by developing its industries and exporting manufactured goods in exchange for gold and silver. This policy encouraged monarchs to minimize imports from rival empires and to drive those rivals out of colonial markets. By selling more than it purchased, the empire could build wealth in the form of gold or silver.

In general, the colonies fit nicely into the mercantile system because they offered different economic strengths to the empire. In England, land was scarce whereas people

Chart Skills The Navigation Acts were a series of laws that regulated trade between Britain and the colonies. *What benefits did the act passed in 1663 provide to Britain? How did it affect the colonies?*

The Navigation Acts

1651	Goods imported to England from Asia, Africa, and the Americas could be transported only in English ships.
1660	The American colonies could export sugar, tobacco, cotton, and indigo only to England.
1663	All foreign goods shipped to the colonies had to pass through English ports where a duty was collected.
1733	Duties were increased on sugar traded between the French Indies and the American colonies.

Brown Rice

Sugar

were numerous, which meant that labor was cheap. Money for investment was abundant. This combination favored the development of industry. In the colonies, however, there was more land but fewer people and less money for investment. That combination favored agriculture. As a result, more than 90 percent of the colonists lived and worked on farms or plantations. They exported their produce in ships to buy tropical goods from Africa or the Caribbean or manufactured goods from England.

The Navigation Acts Regulate Trade The English regarded colonial commerce as the key to imperial power. By controlling colonial trade, they could collect more customs duties—taxes on imported goods. They used this money to build a stronger navy, which enabled them to defeat the Dutch and later the French. To obtain more sailors, ships, and trade, Parliament in the mid-1600s enacted a series of trade laws called the **Navigation Acts.**

The Navigation Acts stated that only English ships with English sailors could trade with English colonies. The acts also specified that especially valuable colonial goods, including tobacco and sugar, be shipped only to the mother country. Colonial ships were free to take their other products elsewhere. For example, New Englanders could export fish to Portugal and Spain.

Finally, the colonies had to import all their European goods via an English port, where they paid customs duties. For example, if a Virginian wanted a bottle of French wine, the wine had to come to America by way of an English port, rather than directly from France. Violators risked the confiscation of their ships and cargoes.

The Navigation Acts promoted the dramatic growth of English colonial commerce and the nation's prosperity. During the 1600s, English merchant shipping doubled. The value of imports and exports increased at least sixfold. In 1600, England had been a relatively poor nation, trading primarily with nearby northern Europe. By 1700, England's commerce was global, and London had become Europe's leading seaport.

At first, the Navigation Acts hurt the colonists economically because they had depended upon Dutch ships and Dutch manufactured goods. That changed by 1700. Protected by the Navigation Acts, British manufacturing and shipping improved in quality and quantity, outstripping the Dutch. The colonists could obtain better goods from British suppliers at lower costs. Thereafter, colonists often protested some particular feature of the Navigation Acts, but not the whole system.

Global Trade

This young colonial girl enjoys tea from India, sugar from the West Indies, and wears a dress of cloth made in England. *What products do people in the United States import in the twenty-first century?*

The Consumer Revolution Most colonists lived on farms or plantations. There, they produced most of their own food, fuel, and homespun cloth. But no farm or plantation could produce everything that a family needed. The colonists wanted to purchase expensive imported goods, such as sugar from the West Indies, tea from India, and manufactured goods from Britain. To obtain those goods, every colonial farm and plantation needed to produce a surplus of produce that they could export.

The expanding transatlantic commerce produced a "consumer revolution" that brought more and cheaper goods to the colonies. Between 1720 and 1770, colonial imports per person increased by 50 percent. An immigrant from Germany marveled that "it is really possible to obtain all the things one can get in Europe in Pennsylvania, since so many merchant ships arrive there every year."

British manufacturers increasingly needed the growing American market. In 1700, the American colonies consumed about 10 percent of British exports. The rate of consumption rose to 37 percent by 1772.

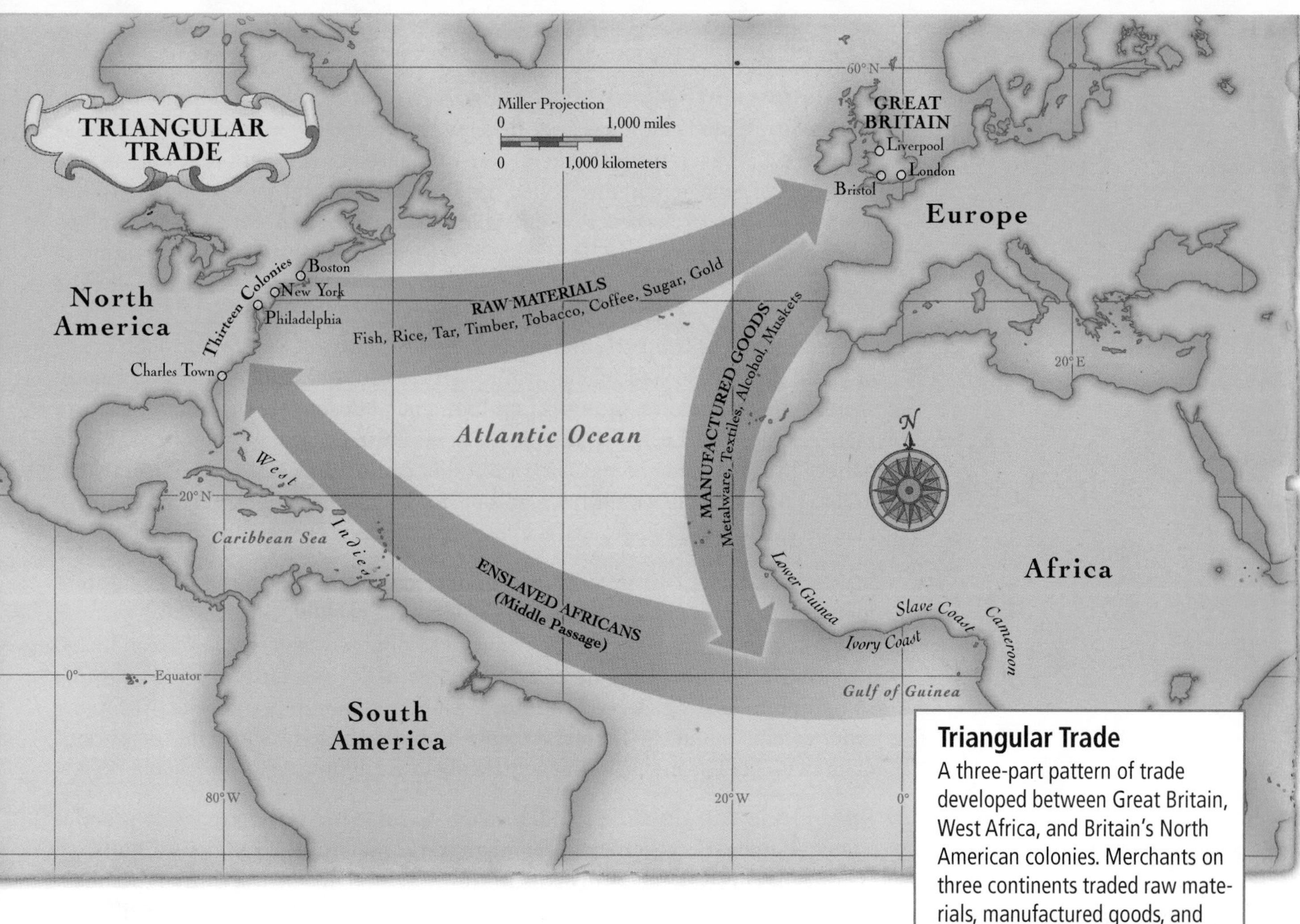

Triangular Trade
A three-part pattern of trade developed between Great Britain, West Africa, and Britain's North American colonies. Merchants on three continents traded raw materials, manufactured goods, and enslaved Africans. *What goods did England provide to West Africa? What did the colonies send to England?*

Grateful for the prosperity and consumer goods, the British as well as the colonists felt greater pride in their shared empire.

Both the middle class and the poorer class, however, bought more than they could afford. Americans suffered from a chronic trade imbalance, as they imported more than they exported. Most colonists bore mounting debts. The shortage of cash and the increasing debts fed a nagging unease at odds with the overall prosperity and general contentment with the empire.

Triangular Trade Route During the 1700s, a pattern of trade emerged that connected England, its colonies, and West Africa. Trade among the three continents had three main parts and formed a triangular shape (see the map on this page). On the first leg of the journey, British ships loaded with manufactured goods sailed to Africa's west coast. There, they swapped British manufactures—such as guns and cloth—for enslaved Africans. On the second, or middle, leg, the traders then carried the enslaved Africans to the American colonies. After selling the slaves for colonial raw material—such as sugar, timber, and tobacco—the traders returned to Europe.

✓ **Checkpoint** **What was the purpose of the Navigation Acts?**

New Ideas Affect the American Colonies

During the 1600s and 1700s, Europe experienced an intellectual movement known as the **Enlightenment**—a movement headed by thinkers who believed that all problems could be solved using human reason. The Enlightenment challenged old ways of thinking about science, religion, and government in Europe. Enlightenment thinkers changed the way many American colonists viewed the world as well.

Enlightenment Thinkers Offer New Worldviews Enlightenment philosophers formulated new ideas and suggested radically new ways of thinking about the world. However, these thinkers were influenced by the work of scientists who were part of a movement now called the Scientific Revolution. During the 1500s, scientists began to use observation and experimentation to learn about the physical world. Scientists, such as Sir Isaac Newton, used reason and observation to formulate new ideas about mathematics and physics. Those ideas challenged the traditional power of religious leaders to explain the physical world.

Enlightenment thinkers, like Rousseau and Voltaire of France and John Locke of Great Britain, looked for natural laws that could be applied to government, society, and economics. Many Enlightenment philosophers focused on government. Some, like Locke, challenged the unlimited power of monarchs. Locke believed that people had natural rights that came from God, and not from monarchs. Locke's ideas would have an enormous influence on American political leaders in the late 1700s. (See the infographic Roots of Democracy in this section.)

Impact on the Colonies A number of colonists were inspired by Enlightenment ideas. One such person was **Benjamin Franklin.** A successful printer, Franklin's hunger for knowledge embodied Enlightenment ideals. He conducted scientific experiments and invented a number of devices, including the lightning rod and bifocal eyeglasses. Franklin authored almanacs and books. Not many other colonists had the financial means to build their lives around the pursuit of knowledge. The majority knew little about Enlightenment philosophers.

A Fiery Preacher
Jonathan Edwards's sermon "Sinners in the Hands of an Angry God" was reprinted many times. It warned readers to ask God's forgiveness.

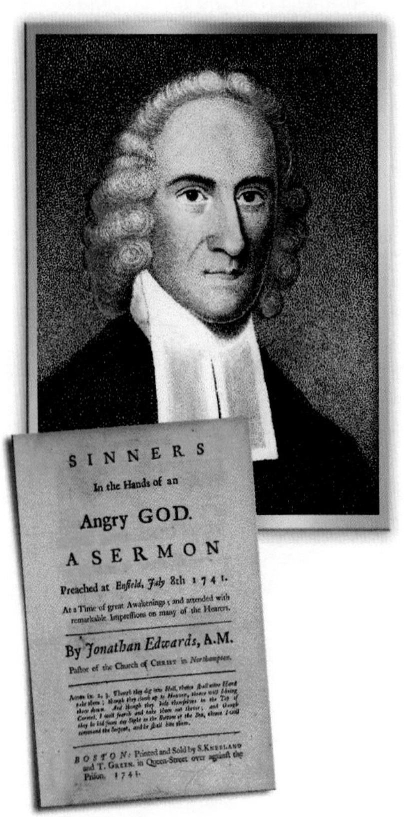

Religion in the Colonies Many colonists came to America to freely practice their religions. However, most colonists were intolerant of religions other than their own. This was especially true in New England, where the church establishment was strongest. Because of its ethnic and religious diversity, many different churches were tolerated in the Middle Colonies.

Churches filled a key role in social life, especially in rural areas. Families who lived on widespread farms and plantations looked to the church as a place to gather with members of their community. Churches also served as a public space for reading government proclamations, for posting new laws, and for holding elections.

The Great Awakening During the mid-eighteenth century, a religious movement swept through the colonies. Known as the **Great Awakening,** it was a time when powerful evangelical preachers traveled from town to town giving emotion-packed sermons that deeply touched listeners. Hundreds, sometimes thousands, of people would come from miles around to be inspired by a preacher's words.

Preachers stressed that personal religious experience was important in seeking God's salvation. They rejected the Enlightenment view that everything in the world could be explained by natural law and logic. Jonathan Edwards of Massachusetts was a leading preacher during the period of the Great Awakening. Edwards used the vivid images of an angry God dangling unbelievers like a spider over a roaring fire to inspire listeners to repent of their sins. In his well-known sermon "Sinners in the Hands of an Angry God," Edwards urged people to ask forgiveness for their sins:

> **Primary Source** "O sinner! Consider the fearful danger you are in: it is a great furnace of wrath, a wide and bottomless pit, full of the fire of wrath, that you are held over in the hands that God, whose wrath is provoked and incensed as much against you, as against many of the damned in hell. You hang by a slender thread."
>
> —Jonathan Edwards, 1741

In 1739, George Whitefield, England's most celebrated preacher, came to tour the colonies. For two years, he attracted large and enthusiastic crowds. Like Edwards, he promoted an emotional style of worship. Indeed, Whitefield urged common people to forsake ministers who favored a more subdued and rational style. Many other preachers copied Whitefield to spread the revivals. Indeed, the Great Awakening did much to inspire the American people with a sense of their own power as individuals.

> **HISTORY MAKERS**
>
> **George Whitefield** (1714–1770)
>
> A celebrated preacher, George Whitefield moved audiences with his message—and his powerful voice—in both Great Britain and the American colonies. In school, Whitefield developed skill at speaking and a passion for the Bible. In college at Oxford, he met John and Charles Wesley, who founded the Methodist Church. Whitefield had a powerful conversion experience and devoted the rest of his life to preaching. He gave more than 18,000 sermons, sometimes speaking to crowds so large that the meetings had to be held outside. Along with travels across Britain, he journeyed to the colonies to preach, where the emotional power of his words and the message of salvation help launch the Great Awakening.

Effects of the Great Awakening The Great Awakening had a profound impact on the colonies. Preaching that individuals could find their own salvation, the movement led to the formation of new churches in the colonies. Many Presbyterian, Dutch Reformed, and Congregationalist congregations were split between those who followed the preachers of the Great Awakening and those who did not. Eventually, the acceptance of the new churches contributed to an increase in tolerance. The movement also led to a rise in democratic belief in the colonies. Many preachers stressed that formal church rites were not as important as feeling God's spirit. Many colonists began to believe that if they could choose their method of worship, they could decide on their form of government.

✓ **Checkpoint** **What was the significance of the Great Awakening on the colonies?**

SECTION 2 Assessment

Progress Monitoring *Online*
For: Self-test with vocabulary practice
www.pearsonschool.com/ushist

Comprehension

1. **Terms and People** For each term or name below, write a sentence explaining its impact on the political or economic life of the English colonies in North America.
   - Magna Carta
   - Parliament
   - English Bill of Rights
   - habeas corpus
   - salutary neglect
   - mercantilism
   - Navigation Acts
   - Enlightenment
   - Benjamin Franklin
   - Great Awakening

2. **NoteTaking Reading Skill: Identify Supporting Details** Use your completed outline to answer the Focus Question: How did English ideas about government and the economy influence life in the 13 colonies?

Writing About History

3. **Quick Write: Brainstorm for Possible Solutions** Choose one topic from this section, such as the Glorious Revolution, about which you could write a problem-solution essay. Use the text and your own knowledge to create a list of possible solutions to the problem that you have chosen to write about. Next, organize your list to rank the solutions from most effective to least effective.

Critical Thinking

4. **Make Inferences** How do you think England's policy of salutary neglect toward the 13 colonies would affect the colonies' future political and economic development?

5. **Summarize** How did England's economic policies serve the interests of the British as well as the American colonists?

6. **Recognize Cause and Effect** How did the ideas of the Enlightenment lead to the Great Awakening? How did the Great Awakening lead to the growth of democratic ideas in the 13 colonies?

SECTION 3

▲ In a portrait by John Singleton Copley, Paul Revere holds a silver teapot.

WITNESS HISTORY

Paul Revere: A Silversmith

Paul Revere is best remembered as a Patriot during the American Revolution. But even before the Revolution, Revere made outstanding contributions to the growing colonial economy. Like most boys, Revere learned a trade. His father taught him to be a silversmith, and when Revere achieved master craftsman status, he produced fine works of silver. Silver working was just one of his talents. Revere also learned to engrave copper plates for printing, make surgical instruments, clean teeth and replace missing teeth, and make and sell eyeglasses. After the American Revolution, Revere opened a hardware store, foundry, and a copper-rolling mill.

Clever and ambitious business owners like Revere contributed to a growing colonial economy. His contributions were acknowledged in his obituary, which read in part, "seldom has the tomb closed upon a life so honorable and useful."

Comparing Regional Cultures

Objectives

- Explain the impact of geography on the economies of the New England, Middle, and Southern colonies.
- Compare and contrast differences in the social structure of the three major colonial regions.
- Describe the cultural life in the British colonies.

Terms and People

staple crop
cash crop
dame school

NoteTaking

Reading Skill: Compare and Contrast
Complete a chart like this one comparing the three regions of the 13 colonies.

	New England	Middle Colonies	Southern Colonies
Economy	• Fishing •	• •	• •
Society	• •	• Religious diversity •	• •

Why It Matters By the early 1700s, the economic and social foundations of Britain's 13 colonies were in place. As the colonies developed, three distinct regions emerged, each with its own economic and social structure: New England, the Middle Colonies, and the South. Despite their differences, the regions were part of Britain's North American empire. Later in the eighteenth century, events would cause the colonies to unite against a common cause: British rule. **Section Focus Question: How did life differ in each of the three main regions of the British colonies?**

Regional Economic Patterns

The vast majority of people in the 13 colonies made their living as farmers. Other than shipbuilding and some ironworks, the colonies lacked industries. The few small cities were all seaports that focused on trade with England.

In spite of these broad similarities, the colonies had by the mid-1700s developed important regional distinctions. Variations in geography and climate helped explain the differences between life in New England, the Middle Colonies, and the South.

New England New England is an area with cold winters, a short growing season, and a rugged landscape. For these reasons, New Englanders could not raise the crops most in demand by Europeans: tobacco, sugar, rice, and indigo. Instead, most New Englanders worked small farms where they raised livestock and grew wheat, rye, corn, and potatoes for their own use. None of these commodities could profitably be shipped to England, where a similar climate permitted production of the same crops.

Vocabulary Builder
commodity–(kuh MAHD uh tee) *n.* anything bought or sold; any item that is traded

New Englanders did ship some products from their shores. They exported lumber from their forests and fish—especially cod—from the sea. They salted and then shipped the fish to Europe or to the West Indies to feed enslaved Africans working on sugar plantations. New Englanders also used wood harvested from regional forests to build ships.

The principal seaport in the region was Boston, which had about 16,000 people in 1750. There, merchants did a lively business carrying out the busy trade between the colonies and Great Britain.

The Middle Colonies As in New England, family farms prevailed in the Middle Colonies. But those farms were more prosperous than those in New England. With a more temperate climate, farmers in the Middle Colonies were able to produce more and better wheat than did the New Englanders.

Thanks to a growing export trade in wheat, the Middle Colonies boomed during the eighteenth century—while New England's economy stagnated. Philadelphia and New York became the two great seaports of the prospering Middle Colonies. Still, neither of these cities was large by today's standards. In 1760, Philadelphia had a population of only 25,000.

The South Because of an even warmer climate and longer growing season, the Southern Colonies could raise the most valuable and profitable colonial crops. In the Chesapeake colonies of Virginia and Maryland, planters raised staple crops of tobacco, though some in the 1700s were switching to wheat. **Staple crops** are crops that are in steady demand. These crops were also **cash crops,** crops grown for sale. North Carolina produced cattle and lumber, while South Carolina and Georgia harvested rice and indigo. (Cotton would not become an important crop until the 1790s.) Charleston, South Carolina, was the region's largest port. Near the coast, most of the population consisted of enslaved Africans working on plantations. In the hillier areas inland from the coast, white settlers and family farms prevailed.

✓ **Checkpoint In what ways did agriculture differ in the three colonial regions?**

Regional Social Patterns

The three colonial regions also varied in the shape and form of the social life that developed there. Factors such as availability of education and patterns of settlement helped create distinct differences between the regions.

Differences in Population In New England and the Middle Colonies, there were relatively few African Americans. In parts of the South, they formed the majority of the population.

The three regions also attracted different types of free settlers. During the seventeenth century, most immigrants to the South were poor, young, single men. Seeking work for the short term and a farm for the long term, they worked as indentured servants. In contrast, most of the immigrants to seventeenth-century New England were of the middle class and could pay their own way. They immigrated to the colony

Philadelphia was a large city by colonial standards.

Geography**Interactive**
For: Interactive map
www.pearsonschool.com/ushist

Focus On Geography

Geography and Regional Economies

The geography of a region determines what type of housing people build, what type of clothing they wear, and how they make a living. Each region of the 13 colonies developed an economy based on its geography.

New England's geography lent itself to fishing, lumber, and small-scale farming. Trade and commerce took hold in the New England city of Boston and in other towns along the coast. For their thriving wheat, rye, and barley crops, the Middle Colonies became known as the "breadbasket" of colonial America. Flour and other products were shipped to England and the West Indies from busy ports in New York and Philadelphia. Large plantations in the South grew tobacco, rice, indigo, and eventually cotton. Enslaved Africans tended these labor-intensive crops. Backcountry farmers in the Middle and Southern colonies scratched out a living on small farms.

▲ **New England Colonies**
Fishing for cod off the coast of New England

Middle Colonies ▲
Family harvesting its crop

▼ **Southern Colonies**
Virginia planter watching enslaved Africans pack tobacco leaves for export

Geography and History

- How did geography affect the economy in each of the three regions?
- How do you think geography affects your town or city?

as families, which meant a better balance between males and females. For example, in 1650, New England had six males for every four females, compared with four men for every woman in the Chesapeake area.

European immigrants seemed to prefer the Middle Colonies most of all. These colonies became the most ethnically and culturally diverse region in the entire British Empire. In addition to religious tolerance, the Middle Colonies offered immigrants greater economic opportunities.

Though a less desirable destination for immigrants than the other regions, New England provided a healthier environment. A hilly land with fast-flowing rivers and streams, New England was free of the malaria and dysentery that killed so many colonists elsewhere. In New England, people who survived childhood could expect to live to about 70 years, compared to 45 years in the Chesapeake region.

With a healthier environment and better balance between men and women, New England enjoyed rapid population growth. During the seventeenth century, New England received only 21,000 immigrants—a fraction of the 120,000 transported to the Chesapeake area. Yet in 1700, New England had 91,000 colonists, more than any other region.

Graph Skills As the graph illustrates, population in the American colonies grew steadily from the mid-1600s to the mid-1700s. *What was the white population in 1720? What were some of the reasons for the increase in both the white and African American populations?*

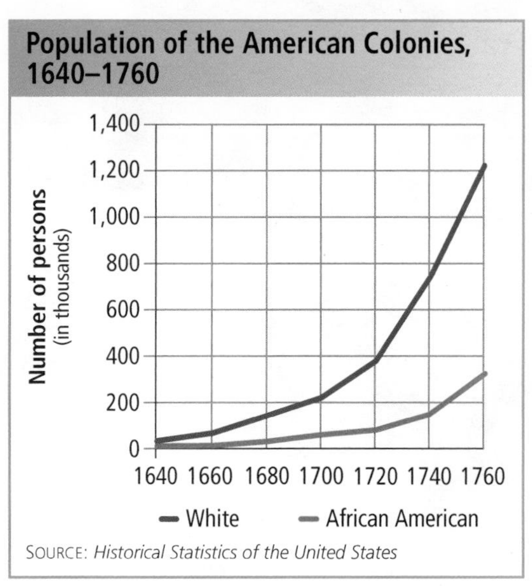

Women in the Colonies By law and custom, there were few opportunities for women outside the home. Most women were legal dependents of men, and men held all the power in colonial households. Married women could not own property, could not vote, could not hold political office, and could not serve on a jury. Although women who were widowed could inherit a portion of their husband's property, they did not have any political rights.

Both men and women depended on one another to run farms, businesses, and households. Men generally did the work of planting, raising, and harvesting crops. Women usually managed the household duties, such as cooking, gardening, sewing, and child care.

Community Life The New England Colonies granted land to men who banded together to establish a town. New England leaders favored compact settlement in towns to support public schools and to sustain a local church. As a result, more adults were literate in New England than in the other colonial regions. In addition, while New England had fewer wealthy families than in the other regions, there was a greater degree of economic equality. Most men in New England owned their own farm, shop, or fishing boat.

In the Southern Colonies, the plantation economy based on slavery produced great profits. However, each large plantation was far from the next, and backcountry farmers were excluded from plantation society. With a population that was spread far and wide, Southern colonists found it harder to sustain churches and schools. Illiteracy was more common in the South. Slavery also promoted greater economic inequality. A few white landowners became rich planters, but most remained common farmers.

Education As you have read, schooling was more available in New England than elsewhere in the colonies. By the mid-1600s, Massachusetts law required towns to provide schools where students could learn the basics of reading and writing. The goal was to enable students to read the Bible.

Larger New England towns offered a more advanced "grammar school" education—generally to boys only. Some girls did receive a grammar school education in **dame schools**—private schools operated out of a woman's home.

One-room schoolhouses were common in colonial New England. Hornbooks helped students learn to read.

Outside of New England, education was less widely available. Many colonists taught reading and mathematics to their own children. Wealthier families might hire a tutor to teach their children or send them to England to get an education.

Colleges were few, small, and very expensive. Most colonies had none, and only New Jersey had more than one—the College of New Jersey (Princeton) and Queens (Rutgers). Even the oldest and largest colleges—Harvard in Massachusetts, William and Mary in Virginia, and Yale in Connecticut—had fewer than 150 students. Only young men from prosperous families could attend. Most graduates became ministers.

During the colonial era, rules and regulations at colleges were quite strict. Students were expected to live moral and righteous lives, risking punishment or expulsion if they broke a rule. One rule stated:

Primary Source "If any scholar shall be guilty of profane swearing, cursing, vowing, any petty or implicit oath, profane . . . use of the [name of God], . . . fighting, striking, quarreling, challenging, turbulent words or behavior, . . . idleness, lying, defamation, talebearing, or any other suchlike immoralities, he shall be punished by fine, confession, . . . or expulsion, as the nature and circumstances of the case may require."

—Regulations at Yale College, 1745

The highly educated minority were expected to lead the common people. Although most colonists attended only grammar schools, most were better educated than their counterparts in Europe, many of whom were illiterate.

✓ **Checkpoint** **How did education differ from one region to the other?**

SECTION 3 Assessment

Progress Monitoring *Online*
For: Self-test with vocabulary practice
www.pearsonschool.com/ushist

Comprehension

1. **Terms and People** How does each term below relate to life in the colonies? Answer the question in one or two sentences that use each term.
   - staple crop
   - cash crop
   - dame school

2. **NoteTaking Reading Skill: Compare and Contrast** Use your completed chart to answer the Section Focus Question: How did life differ in each of the three main regions of the British colonies?

Writing About History

3. **Quick Write: Write a Thesis Statement** Immigrants to the colonies decided in which region they would live. Based on what you have read in this section, write a thesis statement for a problem-solution essay on deciding where to live from the point of view of a new immigrant.

Critical Thinking

4. **Compare and Contrast** In what ways were each of the major regions of the British colonies similar to one another, and in what ways were they different?

5. **Draw Conclusions** Why do you think more immigrants moved to the Middle Colonies and the Southern Colonies?

6. **Analyze** How do the goals and opportunities for education differ between colonial times and today?

SECTION 4

▲ Robert Rogers

▲ Rogers' Rangers

WITNESS HISTORY

Rogers' Rangers

The struggle for territory between England and France in North America broke into open conflict during the French and Indian War. From 1754 to 1763, the region between the Ohio Valley and Canada became a battlefield. To help win the war, England authorized units of Rangers—groups of colonial militiamen who served as scouts and soldiers—to aid English Crown soldiers. Rogers' Rangers, led by Robert Rogers of New Hampshire, became famous for including Indians and freed slaves in its ranks and for its unusual but highly effective tactics. As Rogers explained, his goals were:

> "... from time to time, to use my best endeavours to distress the French and their allies, by sacking, burning, and destroying their houses, barns, barracks, canoes, ... and by killing their cattle ... and at all times to endeavor to way-lay, attack and destroy their convoys of provisions by land and water, in any part of the country where I could find them."
>
> —Robert Rogers, 1756

Wars of Empire

Objectives

- Describe the causes and major events of the French and Indian War.
- Analyze the causes and effects of Pontiac's Rebellion.
- Summarize how the wars and their outcomes changed the relationship between Britain and the colonies.

Terms and People

George Washington
French and Indian War
Pontiac's Rebellion
Proclamation of 1763
Albany Plan of Union

NoteTaking

Reading Skill: Recognize Sequence As you read, keep track of the sequence of events that led to the French and Indian War.

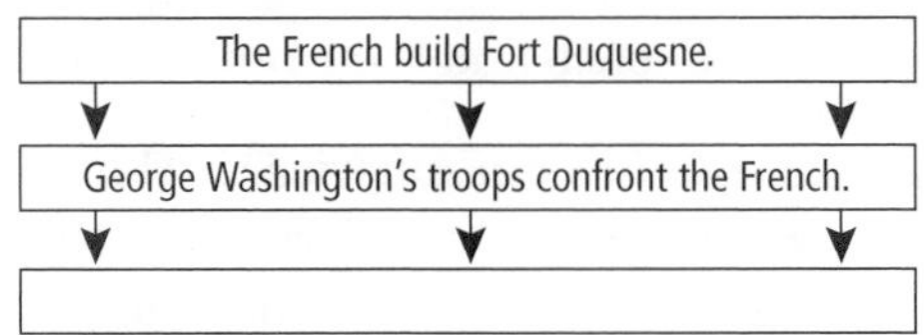

Why It Matters Conflict between the great European empires spread to the American colonies throughout the late seventeenth and early eighteenth centuries. The British and the colonists fought a series of wars against the French and their American Indian allies . In the process, however, the relationship between the British and their colonies became strained. **Section Focus Question: How did Great Britain's wars with France affect the American colonies?**

European Competition and the Colonies

By the mid-eighteenth century, England, France, Spain, and the Netherlands were locked in a worldwide struggle for empire. In North America, Britain's greatest rival was France. While Britain controlled the 13 colonies on the Atlantic seaboard, France controlled a vast territory that extended from the St. Lawrence River to the Gulf of Mexico.

Between 1689 and 1748, the British and the French fought a series of wars. Most of the fighting took place in Europe, but some spilled over into North America. Before long, British colonists were drawn into the war.

American Indians Affect the Balance of Power Each war between England and France was followed by a treaty that resolved nothing. Great Britain longed to drive the French from North America, and to accomplish this, the British needed to neutralize the great

French advantage: French support from most of the American Indians in the region. Native Americans dominated the forest passages between the frontiers of the rival empires.

The Indians benefited from their middle position between the competing empires. The British and French both gave generous gifts, especially of arms and ammunition, to woo the Indians. If one empire won a total victory, the Indians would lose their leverage and receive harsher treatment from the victors. They also were aware that the land they lived on was at stake. In the words of one Iroquois leader:

> **Primary Source** "We know our Lands are now become more valuable. The white People think we do not know their value; but we are sensible [aware] that the Land is everlasting, and the few Goods we receive for it are soon worn out that gone. . . . Besides, we are not well used [treated] with respect to the lands still unsold by us. Your people daily settle on these lands, and spoil our hunting. . . . Your horses and cows have eaten the grass our deer used to feed on."
>
> —Canasatego, Iroquois leader, July 7, 1742

Thus, the Indians recognized the importance of preserving the balance of power between the French and the British.

The Balance Shifts That balance began to tip as the British colonial population grew. In 1754, the 1,500,000 British colonists greatly outnumbered the 70,000 French. The increasingly powerful British often treated the Indians harshly and did little to stop settlers from taking Indian lands.

Vocabulary Builder
restrain–(rih STRAYN) *v.* to hold back from action

Compared to the British, the French were more restrained. Needing Indian allies, the French treated most Native Americans with respect and generosity. The outnumbered French worked with their Indian allies to resist British colonial expansion. The French built a string of small forts and trading posts along the Great Lakes and down the Ohio and Mississippi rivers. Lightly built and thinly manned, the posts depended upon the Indians for protection. Most Indians accepted these posts because, as one chief explained, "we can drive away the French when we please." That was not true of the British. Yet, while most Native Americans supported the French, some fought for the British.

✓ **Checkpoint Why did the French and British fight frequently during the 1600s and 1700s?**

A young George Washington led British troops against the French in 1754.

The French and Indian War

One point of conflict between France and Great Britain was the fertile Ohio River valley, which was claimed by both countries but was largely unsettled. To discourage British colonists from moving into this area, the French built Fort Duquesne in what is now western Pennsylvania.

The new fort angered the British governor of Virginia, Robert Dinwiddie. In 1754, he sent colonial troops to evict the French. Dinwiddie entrusted the command to a young, ambitious Virginian named **George Washington.** His troops attacked and defeated a small French force. But Washington had to surrender when the French counterattacked. His defeat touched off a world war that eventually spread from America to Europe, Asia, Africa, and the West Indies. In Europe, the war was called the Seven Years' War. The British colonists called the conflict the **French and Indian War,** after the French and their Indian allies.

Early Battles At first, the British fared poorly in North America. In 1755, a combined British and colonial force did overwhelm two French forts near Nova Scotia. Those troops evicted the French settlers, known as Acadians, and gave

British and French Wage War
This hand-colored engraving shows General Braddock's death after the battle at Fort Duquesne. The map shows the theater of war during the French and Indian War. *When did the British win Quebec and Montreal?*

their farms to New Englanders. But the British army suffered a disastrous defeat when General Edward Braddock marched into a French and Indian ambush near Fort Duquesne. Braddock died, but Washington led a skillful retreat that saved half of that army. Later, Washington recalled the battle in a letter to his mother:

> **Primary Source** "... [We] were attacked by a body of French and Indians, whose number (I am certain) did not exceed 300 men. Ours consisted of about 1,300 well-armed troops, chiefly of the English soldiers, who were struck with such a panic that they behaved with more cowardice than it is possible to conceive. The officers behaved gallantly in order to encourage their men, for which they suffered greatly, there being near 60 killed and wounded—a large proportion out of the number we had!"
>
> —George Washington, 1755

In 1756 and 1757, French General Louis-Joseph de Montcalm destroyed British forts on Lake Ontario and Lake George. Meanwhile, Indians raided British frontier settlements in Pennsylvania and Virginia.

The tide of war shifted in 1758 and 1759. The British managed to cut off French shipping to the Americas. As a result, many Indians deserted the French in favor of the better-supplied British. This allowed the British to capture Fort Duquesne. The British also seized the key French fortress of Louisbourg, which guarded the entrance to the St. Lawrence River. That victory cleared the way for General James Wolfe to attack the stronghold of Quebec in 1759. In a daring gamble, Wolfe's men used the cover of night to scale a cliff and occupy the Plains of Abraham, just outside the city walls. Marching out to attack, Montcalm suffered defeat and death.

In 1760, the British captured Montreal and forced the French governor general to surrender the rest of Canada, including the forts around the Great Lakes. The British had succeeded in their major North American goal.

Geography *Interactive*
For: Interactive map
www.pearsonschool.com/ushist

North America, 1754–1763

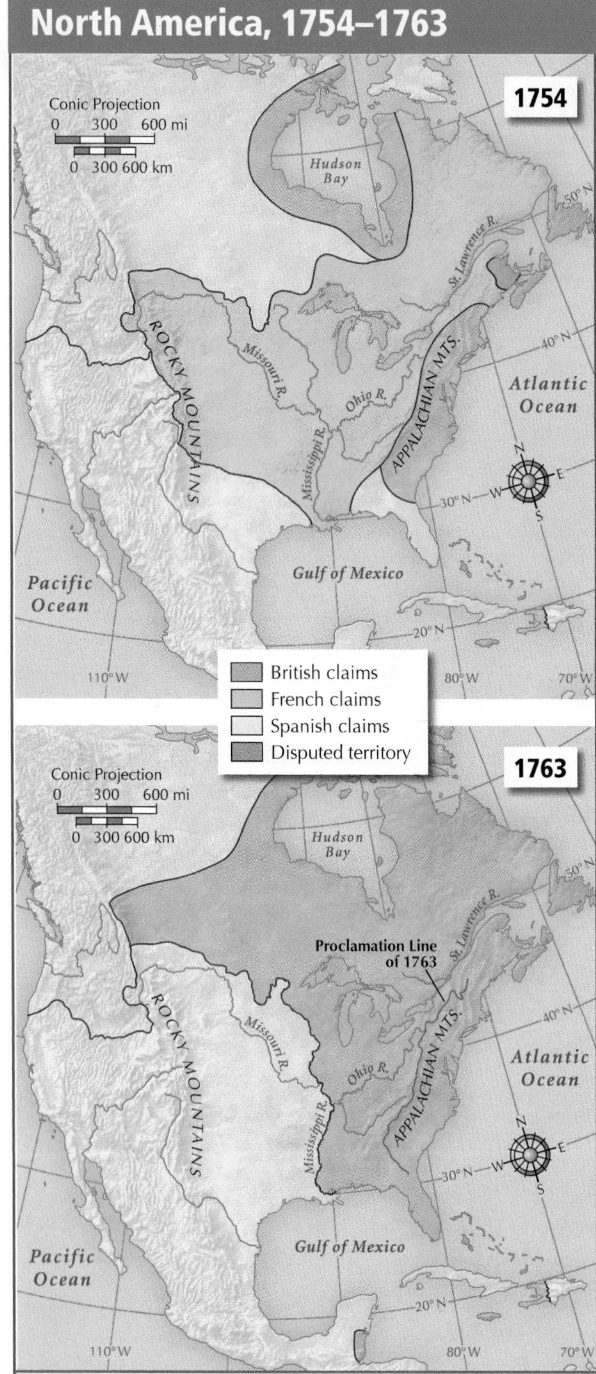

Map Skills The French and Indian War changed the colonial boundaries of North America.

1. **Locate:** (a) Mississippi River, (b) Ohio River, (c) Appalachian Mountains
2. **Regions** How did British claims in North America change from 1754 to 1763?
3. **Analyze Information** Which nation was Britain's main rival in 1754? How might this have changed in 1763?

Treaty of Paris (1763) Fighting continued in other parts of the world. The British also won major victories in India, the Philippines, West Africa, and the West Indies. In 1763, the Treaty of Paris ended the war triumphantly for the British, who kept Canada, the Great Lakes region, the Ohio River valley, and Florida. They had driven the French from North America. Thereafter, the Mississippi River became the boundary between British and Spanish claims in North America.

✓ **Checkpoint What was the outcome of the French and Indian War?**

Pontiac's Rebellion

The conquest of Canada was dreadful news to Indians of the interior. No longer could they play the French and the British off against each other. Indeed, the British military commander Lord Jeffrey Amherst quickly cut off delivery of goods to Indians. British settlers flooded onto Indian lands in western Pennsylvania and Virginia.

The Indians affected included Mississauga, Ottawa, Potawatomi, Ojibwa, Wyandot, Miami, Kickapoo, Mascouten, Delaware, Shawnee, and Seneca. During the spring of 1763, members of these groups surprised and captured most of the British forts in the Ohio River valley and along the Great Lakes. Through the summer and fall, they also raided settlements of western Pennsylvania, Maryland, and Virginia. The British called this uprising **Pontiac's Rebellion,** after an Ottawa chief who organized an attack on Detroit.

The Indians' goal was to weaken the British and lure the French back into North America. But they failed to capture the three largest and strongest British posts: Detroit, Niagara, and Fort Pitt (formerly Fort Duquesne).

During 1764, the Indian attackers ran short of gunpowder, shot, and guns. Without a European supplier, their rebellion fizzled. At the same time, the British government sought a quick end to the expensive war. The Crown blamed Amherst for the crisis, recalling him in disgrace. Thomas Gage, the new commander, recognized that respect for the Indians would cost less than military expeditions against them.

The various Indian nations made peace in return for British promises to restrain the settlers. The British rebuilt their forts, but they also tried to enforce the **Proclamation of 1763.** This document ordered colonial settlers to remain east of the Appalachian Mountains:

> **Primary Source** "And whereas it is just and reasonable, and essential to our Interest, and to the Security of our Colonies, . . . the several Nations or Tribes of Indians with whom We are connected, and who live under our Protection, should not be molested or disturbed in the Possession of such Parts of our Dominions and Territories as . . . are reserved to them, or any of them, as their Hunting Grounds."
>
> —Proclamation of 1763

The British troops, however, were too few to restrain the thousands of colonists who pushed westward. Troops burned a few log cabins, but the settlers simply rebuilt them. It was clear that the boundary set by the proclamation could not protect the Indians. At the same time, it irritated the colonists, who resented efforts to limit their expansion.

✓ **Checkpoint** **What did the Indians involved with Pontiac's Rebellion hope to accomplish?**

Aftermath of the War

The French and Indian War, as well as Pontiac's Rebellion, revealed the tensions between the British and their colonists. After investing so much blood and money to conquer North America, the British wanted greater control over their colonies. They also had a large war debt, plus the expensive job of guarding the vast territories taken from the French. The British thought that colonists should help pay these costs.

Bickering between the 13 colonies had also complicated the war effort and had angered the British. With British encouragement, colonial delegates had met in 1754 to review the **Albany Plan of Union.** Drafted by Benjamin Franklin, the plan called on the colonies to unite under British rule and to cooperate with one another in war. It created an American continental assembly that would include delegates from each colony. However, none of the colonies would accept the plan for fear of losing some of their own autonomy. The British also dropped the plan, fearing that 13 united colonies might be too difficult to manage.

During the 1760s, the British acted on their own to impose new taxes and new regulations on colonial trade. Those changes angered colonists who wanted to preserve the sort of loose empire that had, for so long, produced so many benefits at so little cost to them.

 **Checkpoint** **What was the effect of the French and Indian War and Pontiac's Rebellion on the relationship between the colonies and Great Britain?**

Benjamin Franklin supported the idea of colonial unity and created the "Join, or Die" political cartoon. *How is the idea of unity expressed in the political cartoon?*

SECTION 4 Assessment

Progress Monitoring *Online*
For: Self-test with vocabulary practice
www.pearsonschool.com/ushist

Comprehension

1. **Terms and People** How does each term below help explain how the relationship between Great Britain and its North American colonies began to change in the 1760s? For each term, write a sentence that explains your answer.
   - French and Indian War
   - Pontiac's Rebellion
   - Proclamation of 1763
   - Albany Plan of Union
2. **NoteTaking Reading Skill: Recognize Sequence** Use your completed flowchart to answer the Section Focus Question: How did Great Britain's wars with France affect the American colonies?

Writing About History

3. **Quick Write: Support a Solution** Based on what you have read, list supporting information for the following solution: What facts might Britain have used to support the decision to issue the Proclamation of 1763?

Critical Thinking

4. **Draw Conclusions** Why do you think French and British colonists in the Americas fought in the wars of their home countries?
5. **Compare and Contrast** How did the French and British differ in their efforts to gain control in North America?
6. **Make Inferences** What can you infer from the fact that the British were unable to enforce the Proclamation of 1763?

CHAPTER 3

Quick Study Guide

Progress Monitoring *Online*
For: Self-test with vocabulary practice
www.pearsonschool.com/ushist

Diversity in the Colonies

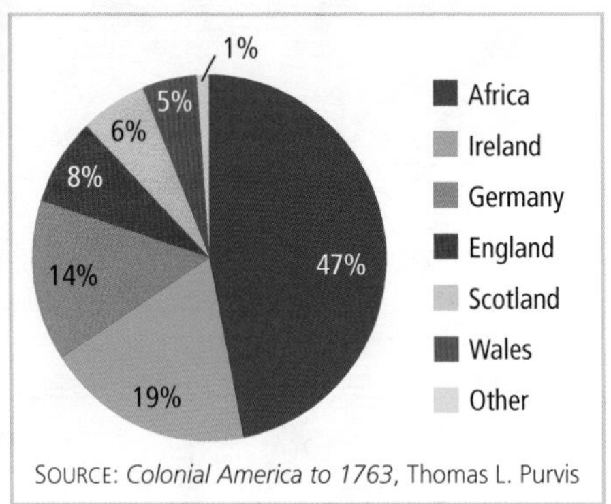

SOURCE: *Colonial America to 1763*, Thomas L. Purvis

English Ideas Influence the Colonies

English Ideas

Magna Carta	Parliament	English Bill of Rights
• Limited monarch's right to tax • Guaranteed due process	• A bicameral legislature • An elected lower house • Power to tax	• Right to habeas corpus • Bars cruel or unusual punishment

The Three Regions of the 13 Colonies

Region	Climate	Economy	Population
New England Colonies	Cold winters; short growing season	Fishing; shipbuilding; trade; lumber; small subsistence farms	Few slaves or immigrants; more families; fast-growing population
Middle Colonies	Temperate; moderate growing season	Wheat, barley, and rye crops grown on moderate-sized farms; trade	Attractive to immigrants; tolerant of religious and ethnic differences
Southern Colonies	Warm climate; long growing season	Cash crops of tobacco, rice, and indigo grown on large plantations using slave labor	More men than women; indentured servants; enslaved African Americans a majority in some areas

The French and IndianWar

Cause and Effect

Causes
- England and France vie for power in Europe
- French and English make alliances with Indians
- Conflict between French and English over territory in North America

↓

The French and Indian War

↓

Effects
- France loses colonies in North America
- England gains Canada
- Proclamation of 1763 limits colonial settlement

Quick Study Timeline

In America

1705 Virginia introduces harsher slave codes

1735 John Paul Zenger's trial becomes foundation for freedom of the press

1700 — **1720**

Around the World

1689 England's Glorious Revolution brings a bill of rights

1707 England, Scotland, and Wales join to form United Kingdom of Great Britain

1736 Qianlong becomes emperor of China

American Issues Connector

By connecting prior knowledge with what you have learned in this chapter, you can gradually build your understanding of enduring questions that still affect America today. Answer the questions below. Then, use your American Issues Connector study guide (or go online. www.pearsonschool.com/ushist).

Issues You Learned About

● **America Goes to War** Since colonial days, people in North America have taken part in local as well as global skirmishes.

1. **The French and Indian War** Colonial troops participated in the French and Indian War, which was fought in North America in the mid-1700s. Write a summary of the war, including its key events, its outcome, and its aftermath. Consider:
   - the conflict over the Ohio River valley
   - the progress of the war
   - the Treaty of Paris
   - the settlement of the western lands
   - the reaction of American Indians
   - the Native American alliances and motives

● **Interaction With the Environment** The colonists relied on farming to provide for the needs of their families as well as to raise cash crops for export.

2. Farmers in the Middle Colonies and the South sold crops to England. Why were New Englanders unsuccessful in the export of farm products?
3. Why did the Middle Colonies economically boom during the eighteenth century?
4. Is the following statement true: All farmers grew crops only for subsistence. Explain your answer.

● **Church and State** Religion played a strong role in colonial government as well as in the daily lives of the colonists.

5. In which of the three colonial regions did organized religion and religious leaders have the most influence? Why?
6. Provide at least two examples of the ties between established churches in colonial America and the colonial governments.
7. How did Rhode Island and Pennsylvania differ from the other colonies in terms of religion?

Connect to Your World — Activity

Education and American Society: Institutions of Higher Education As you have read, the colonies had no uniform school system and few institutions of higher learning. Today, the United States has more than 4,000 colleges and universities. Think of three colleges or universities that interest you, such as schools in your region or schools you might like to attend someday. Go online or to your local library and conduct research to learn more about these institutions. Find out information that could help a student make a decision about attending the school, such as enrollment, public or private status, academic strengths, cost, and historical background. Then, use your findings to create a chart.

1740 Great Awakening begins

1754 Benjamin Franklin draws up the Albany Plan of Union

1754–1763 French and Indian War

1763–1764 Pontiac's Rebellion

1740 — 1760

History *Interactive*
For: Interactive timeline
www.pearsonschool.com/ushist

1748 Montesquieu's *The Spirit of the Laws*

1760 George III becomes king of England

1763 Treaty of Paris ends war between French and British

Chapter Assessment

Terms and People

1. Define **indentured servant.** What future could an indentured servant expect?
2. What was the **Magna Carta**? What impact did it have on English political traditions?
3. What was the **Great Awakening**? What ideas did it stress?
4. What was the **French and Indian War**? How did it change North America?
5. What was **Pontiac's Rebellion**? How did this rebellion affect the colonies?

Focus Questions

The focus question for this chapter is **What factors shaped life in colonial America in the seventeenth and eighteenth centuries?** Build an answer to this big question by answering the focus questions for Sections 1 through 4 and the Critical Thinking questions that follow.

Section 1

6. Which major groups of immigrants came to Britain's American colonies in the 1700s?

Section 2

7. How did English ideas about government and the economy influence life in the 13 colonies?

Section 3

8. How did life differ in each of the three main regions of the British colonies?

Section 4

9. How did Great Britain's wars with France affect the American colonies?

Critical Thinking

10. **Draw Inferences** How did Britain's policy of mercantilism affect the colonies?
11. **Summarize** Identify the three cultural groups that dominated immigration to the colonies in the 1600s and 1700s, and briefly explain their reasons for coming to America.
12. **Evaluate Credibility of Sources** Do you think *The Interesting Narrative of Olaudah Equiano, or Gustavus Vassa the African* is a reliable source of information about the African American experience in colonial America? Why or why not?
13. **Categorize** Name the three colonial regions and their primary resources and economic activities.
14. **Make Comparisons** Compare and contrast the opportunities available to immigrants in the three colonial regions.
15. **Explain Causes** What caused the French and Indian War to erupt in 1754?
16. **Analyze Visuals** Study the political cartoon below, created by Benjamin Franklin, and then answer the questions.

What do the different parts of the snake represent? What does the cartoon's title mean? What do you think inspired Franklin to create this drawing?

17. **Synthesize Information** Do you think the Proclamation of 1763 ended the British policy of following salutary neglect when it came to governing the colonies? Explain your answer.

Writing About History

Writing a Problem-Solution Essay Immigrants in colonial America had to adapt to a diverse society, and they also had to deal with Native Americans who were defending their homelands.

Write a problem-solution essay about one of these topics, or choose your own topic relating to the content of this chapter.

Prewriting

- Choose the topic that interests you most. If you have a personal interest in a problem and its solution, your essay will be easier to develop.
- Narrow your topic.
- Make a list of details, facts, and examples that proves there is a problem. Then, identify the specific parts of your solution.

Drafting

- Develop a working thesis and choose information to support it.
- Organize the paragraphs in a logical order so that readers can understand the solution you propose.

Revising

- Use the guidelines on page SH11 of the Writing Handbook to revise your essay.

Document-Based Assessment

Colonial Labor

The English colonists in North America faced many daunting tasks. They needed to fell timber, establish farms, and build settlements. The amount of work required was overwhelming. Who did that work? Use your knowledge of colonial America and Documents A, B, and C to answer questions 1 through 4.

Document A

"This Indenture, Made the Fourth Day of August in the Twenty-ninth Year of the Reign of our Sovereign Lord George the Second King of Great Britain, &, And in the Year of our Lord, One Thousand Seven Hundred and fifty five Between William Buckland of Baford Carpenter & Joiner of the one Part, and Thomson Mason of London, Esq. of the other Part,

Witnesseth, That the said William Buckland . . . shall and will, as a faithful Covenant Servant, well and truly serve the said Thomas Mason his Executors and assigns in the Plantation of Virginia beyond the Seas, for the Space of Four Years, next ensuing his Arrival in the said Plantation in the Employment of a Carpenter and Joiner. . . .

And the said Thomas Mason . . . shall and will at his . . . proper Costs and Charges, with what convenient Speed [he] may, carry and convey, or cause to be carried and conveyed over unto the said Plantation, the said Wm Buckland and from henceforth, and during the said Voyage, and also during the said Term, shall and will at the like Costs and Charges, provide for and allow the said Wm Buckland all necessary Meat, Drink, Washing, Lodging, fit and convenient for Wm as Covenant Servants in such Cases are usually provided for and allowed and pay and allow William Buckland Wages on Salary at the Rate of Twenty Pounds Sterling per Annum Payable Quarterly."

—*Indenture Contract of William Buckland, 1755*

Document B

"Ran away from the Subscriber, living near James-Town, last Sunday was Fort-night, a Negroe Man, named Harry, who formerly belonged to Col. Grymes, of Richmond County: He is about 5 Feet 7 Inches high, thin visag'd, has small Eyes, and a very large Beard; is about 35 Years old; and plays upon the Fiddle. He had a dark-colour'd cloth Coat, double breasted, 2 cotton Jackets, dy'd of a dark Colour, a Pair of Buckskin Breeches, flourish'd at the Knees, and a blue Great Coat. It is suppos'd he is gone to Richmond County, where he has a Wife. Whoever apprehends him, so that he be brought to me near James-Town, shall have a Pistole [gold coin] Reward, besides what the Law allows. William Newgent. N.B. As he ran away without any Cause, I desire he may be punish'd by Whipping, as the Law directs."

—*advertisement in the* Virginia Gazette, *March 20 to March 27, 1746*

Document C

"And as for the general sort that shall go to be planters, be they [very] poor, so they be honest, . . . the place will make them rich: all kinds of [workers] we must first employ, are carpenters, shipwrights, masons, sawyers, brick makers, bricklayers, plowmen, sowers, planters, fishermen, coopers, smiths, . . . tailors, turners, and such like, to make and fit all necessaries, for comfort and use of the Colony, and for such as are of no trades (if they be industrious) they shall have their employment enough, for there is a world of means to set many thousands to work, partly in such things as I mentioned before, and many other profitable works, for no man must lie idle there. . . ."

—*Virginia Company pamphlet recruiting Jamestown settlers, 1609*

---

1. Where was Document A probably written?
A in England
B aboard ship
C in Virginia
D in Jamestown

2. In Document B, the advertiser states that Harry ran away "without any Cause." Yet the advertisement hints at a likely cause. What is it?
A to escape whipping
B to practice his trade
C to enjoy stolen goods
D to join his wife

3. What reasonable conclusion about Jamestown in 1611 might you draw from Document C?
A Jamestown needed new leadership.
B Jamestown had no enslaved people.
C Jamestown needed many types of workers.
D Jamestown was moving from farming to industry.

4. Writing Task Based on Documents A, B, and C, and on what you have learned in Chapter 3, write a letter from the point of view of an indentured servant in Jamestown. Use information from the documents and the chapter to give your family or friends an impression of what life as an indentured servant in Jamestown might have been like.

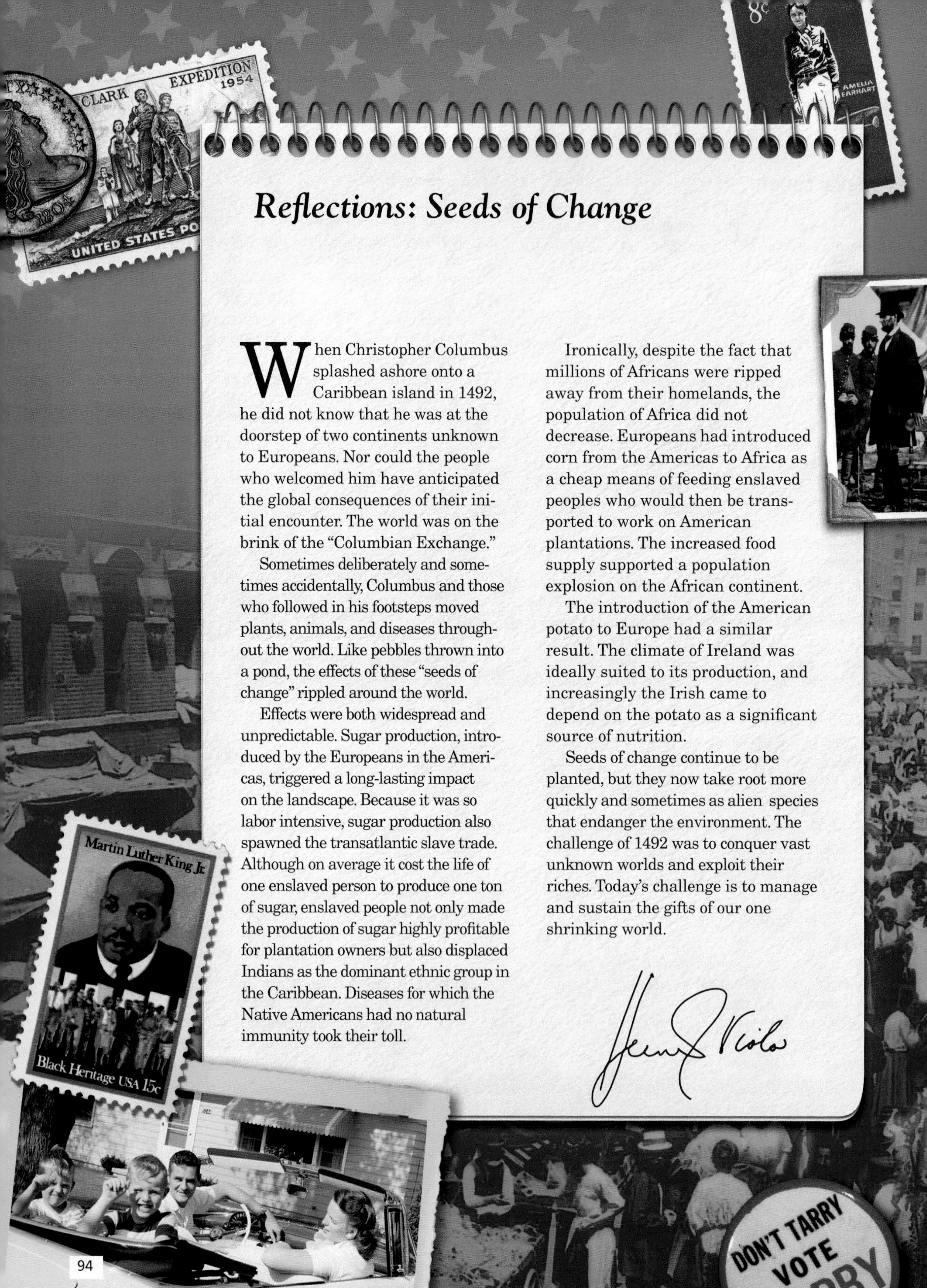

Reflections: Seeds of Change

When Christopher Columbus splashed ashore onto a Caribbean island in 1492, he did not know that he was at the doorstep of two continents unknown to Europeans. Nor could the people who welcomed him have anticipated the global consequences of their initial encounter. The world was on the brink of the "Columbian Exchange."

Sometimes deliberately and sometimes accidentally, Columbus and those who followed in his footsteps moved plants, animals, and diseases throughout the world. Like pebbles thrown into a pond, the effects of these "seeds of change" rippled around the world.

Effects were both widespread and unpredictable. Sugar production, introduced by the Europeans in the Americas, triggered a long-lasting impact on the landscape. Because it was so labor intensive, sugar production also spawned the transatlantic slave trade. Although on average it cost the life of one enslaved person to produce one ton of sugar, enslaved people not only made the production of sugar highly profitable for plantation owners but also displaced Indians as the dominant ethnic group in the Caribbean. Diseases for which the Native Americans had no natural immunity took their toll.

Ironically, despite the fact that millions of Africans were ripped away from their homelands, the population of Africa did not decrease. Europeans had introduced corn from the Americas to Africa as a cheap means of feeding enslaved peoples who would then be transported to work on American plantations. The increased food supply supported a population explosion on the African continent.

The introduction of the American potato to Europe had a similar result. The climate of Ireland was ideally suited to its production, and increasingly the Irish came to depend on the potato as a significant source of nutrition.

Seeds of change continue to be planted, but they now take root more quickly and sometimes as alien species that endanger the environment. The challenge of 1492 was to conquer vast unknown worlds and exploit their riches. Today's challenge is to manage and sustain the gifts of our one shrinking world.

Henry J. Viola

CREATING THE AMERICAN REPUBLIC

CONTENTS

The Spirit of '76 **by Archibald M. Willard, honors the heroes of the American Revolution. ▶**

CHAPTER

4 The American Revolution

1765–1783

WITNESS HISTORY

A Revolution of Ideas

Many years after the Revolutionary War ended, John Adams—a Patriot and the second President of the United States—reflected on the meaning of the Revolution. In his mind, the war itself was not the Revolution.

"What do we mean by the American Revolution? Do we mean the American war? The Revolution was effected before the war commenced. The Revolution was in the minds and hearts of the people. . . . This radical change in the principles, opinions, sentiments, and affections of the people was the real American Revolution."

—John Adams, February 13, 1818

Teapot with slogan

◀ In this nineteenth-century painting, General George Washington looks over his troops during the harsh winter at Valley Forge.

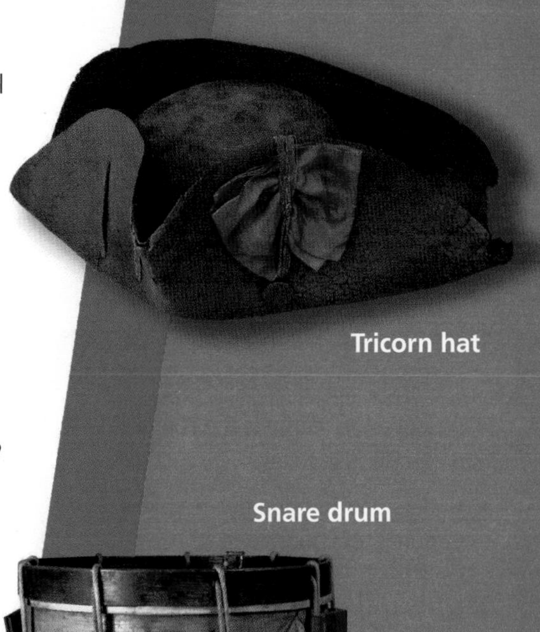

Tricorn hat

Chapter Preview

Chapter Focus Question: What aspects of the American Revolution were revolutionary?

Section 1
Causes of the Revolution

Section 2
Declaring Independence

Section 3
Turning Points of the War

Section 4
War's End and Lasting Effects

Snare drum

Use the **Quick Study Timeline** at the end of this chapter to preview chapter events.

Note Taking Study Guide *Online*
For: Note Taking and American Issues Connector
www.pearsonschool.com/ushist

SECTION 1

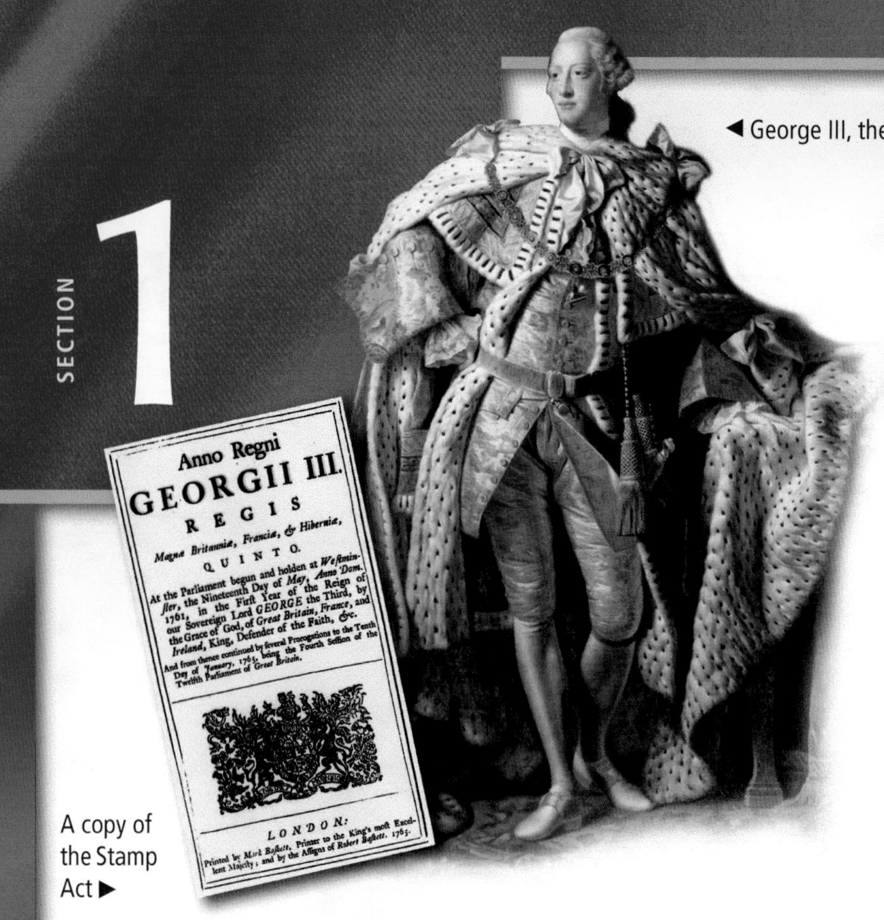
Anno Regni
GEORGII III.
REGIS
Magnæ Britanniæ, Franciæ, & Hiberniæ,
QUINTO.
At the Parliament begun and holden at Westminster, the Nineteenth Day of May, Anno Dom. 1761, in the First Year of the Reign of our Sovereign Lord GEORGE the Third, by the Grace of God, of Great Britain, France, and Ireland, King, Defender of the Faith, &c.
And from thence continued by several Prorogations to the Tenth Day of January, 1765, being the Fourth Session of the Twelfth Parliament of Great Britain.

LONDON:
Printed by Mark Baskett, Printer to the King's most Excellent Majesty; and by the Assigns of Robert Baskett. 1765.

◀ George III, the king of England

A copy of the Stamp Act ▶

WITNESS HISTORY

Rights of the Colonists

James Otis, a leading patriot, argued that British taxes threatened colonists' rights and would make them slaves to the king and Parliament.

"I can see no reason to doubt but the imposition of taxes . . . in the colonies is absolutely irreconcilable with the rights of the colonists as British subjects and as men. . . .

We all think ourselves happy under Great Britain. We love, esteem, and reverence our mother country, and adore our King. And could the choice of independency be offered the colonies or subjection to Great Britain upon any terms above absolute slavery, I am convinced they would accept the latter."

—James Otis, from *The Rights of the British Colonies Asserted and Proved*, 1763

Causes of the Revolution

Objectives

- Describe the colonists' political heritage.
- Explain the colonists' reaction to new taxes.
- Describe the methods the colonists used to protest British taxes.
- Understand the significance of the First Continental Congress in 1774.

Terms and People

Stamp Act	Boston Massacre
John Adams	committee of correspondence
Patrick Henry	Boston Tea Party
Sons of Liberty	Intolerable Acts
nonimportation agreement	First Continental Congress

NoteTaking

Reading Skill: Recognize Sequence Record the events that increased tension between Britain and its colonies.

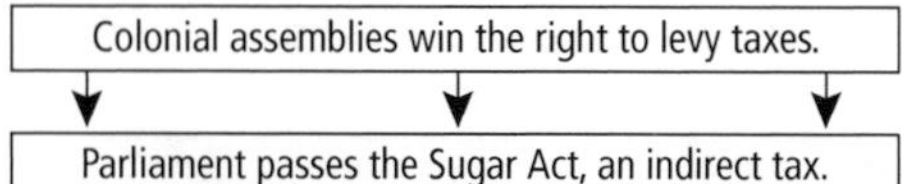

Why It Matters The American colonists enjoyed the protection of Britain during the Indian wars while paying very little of the cost. Meanwhile, they profited from trade within the British Empire. Most importantly, they cherished the political rights they enjoyed as British subjects. When Parliament began to tax the colonists to raise revenue, they protested. Eventually, the protests turned to rebellion and rebellion turned to war. **Section Focus Question: What caused the colonists to rebel against the British?**

The Colonists' Political Heritage

The colonists believed that Great Britain enjoyed the best government on Earth. British liberty included due process of common law, trial by jury, and freedom of the press from censorship. Above all, the colonists cherished the right to pay no tax unless it was levied by their representatives. Colonial governments followed the British model, but the colonists' protests of the 1760s revealed that there were some important differences.

British Government Is a Model The British government had three branches. Executive power belonged to the monarch. Legislative power was divided between two houses of Parliament: the House of Lords and the House of Commons. Aristocrats inherited seats in the House of Lords. Only the House of Commons depended on elections by a small percentage of the people.

Similarly, each colony except Pennsylvania had a two-house legislature: an elected assembly and a council of prominent colonists appointed to life terms by the governor. Colonial governors were appointed by, represented, and served the king. Only Connecticut and Rhode Island elected their own governor, while Pennsylvania's entire assembly was elected. The colonists did not elect any members of British Parliament.

By modern standards, the British system was far from democratic. To those in power, democracy seemed dangerous in a society where people inherited wildly unequal property and status. In 1770, the British prime minister, Lord North, insisted, "I can never acquiesce in the absurd opinion that all men are equal." Most Britons and colonists agreed, and wealthy men controlled government in the colonies as in Great Britain.

Differences in Colonial Governments Despite the similarities, colonial politics differed from the British model in several ways. The British constitution was not a formal document but a collection of laws and traditions accumulated over centuries. In contrast, the colonists' rights had traditionally been spelled out in formal legal documents such as the royal charters of Maryland or South Carolina, as well as informal written agreements like the Mayflower Compact.

In addition, two thirds of free colonial men owned enough property to qualify to vote, compared to less than a fourth of British men. By 1760, political upheaval in Great Britain and European wars had allowed the elected colonial assemblies to increase their powers at the expense of the royal governors. Since the colonies lacked aristocrats with inherited titles, most leaders in the assembly and council were wealthy planters and merchants related by blood or marriage. The assemblies often withheld salaries from unpopular governors.

British officials hoped to change the situation by taxing the colonists to provide salaries to royal governors and judges. Crown salaries would make them less responsive to the assemblies and councils. But that prospect alarmed the colonists, who began to cherish their deviations from Britain as important advantages. Members of Parliament believed that they "virtually represented" every British subject, including the colonists. While Parliament expected the colonists to obey, the colonists saw themselves as equal members of the British political body. These differences quickly became a problem when Parliament tried to levy taxes on the colonies. The colonists believed that only their own elected officials had that right.

Vocabulary Builder
virtual–(VER choo uhl) *adv.* being such in practice or effect, though not in actual fact; implied

✓ **Checkpoint** **How did colonial governments differ from the British government?**

Comparing British and Colonial Governments — Quick Study

Great Britain	American Colonies
King	**Governor**
• Inherited executive power	• Appointed by and served the king but paid by the colonial legislature
Parliament	**Colonial Legislatures**
House of Lords • Aristocrats with inherited titles also inherited legislative power	**Upper House or Council** • Appointed by governor • Prominent colonists but without inherited titles
House of Commons • Elected by men who held significant amounts of property • Less than 1/4 of British men qualified to vote	**Lower House or Assembly** • Elected by men who held property • About 2/3 of colonial men qualified to vote

New Taxes Upset Colonists

The Seven Years' War—called the French and Indian War in the colonies—nearly doubled Britain's national debt and greatly expanded its colonial territories. Parliament needed to raise money, both to pay the debt and to protect the colonies. People in Britain paid far more taxes than the colonists did. This imbalance seemed unfair, for the war had been fought largely to protect the colonists. Parliament decided that the colonists could and should pay more to help the Empire.

The Sugar, Quartering, and Stamp Acts Colonial merchants had grown rich from trade, often smuggling or bribing officials to avoid duties, or taxes, on imports. In 1764, the new prime minister, George Grenville, proposed raising money by collecting duties already in effect. The law, known as the Sugar Act when put into effect, actually lowered the duty on foreign molasses. However, it also assigned customs officers and created courts to collect the duties and prosecute smugglers. Grenville hoped that these measures would encourage colonists to pay the tax.

In early 1765, Parliament passed another unpopular law, the Quartering Act. This act required the colonies to provide housing and supplies for the British troops stationed there after the French and Indian War. Colonists complained but most went along with the changes because they accepted Parliament's right to regulate trade and provide for defense.

In March 1765, Parliament passed a bill intended to raise money from the colonies. The **Stamp Act** required colonists to pay a tax on almost all printed materials, including newspapers, books, court documents, contracts, and land deeds. This was the first time that Parliament had imposed a direct tax within the colonies.

Symbols of New Taxes
Printed materials were supposed to be marked with stamps like these to show that the tax had been paid. *Why do you think there were stamps of different values?*

Taxation Without Representation The colonists angrily protested the Stamp Act, which was to take effect in November. They claimed that it threatened their prosperity and liberty. Colonial leaders questioned Parliament's right to tax the colonies directly. They argued that the colonies had no representation in Parliament, so Parliament had no right to tax them. Some colonists believed that if they accepted this tax, Parliament would add ever more taxes, stripping away their property and political rights. Many colonists thought that the stamp tax revealed a conspiracy by British officials to destroy American liberties.

The colonists' arguments puzzled the members of Parliament. After all, most Britons paid taxes although they could not vote. Many large British cities did not elect representatives to Parliament, which claimed to represent everyone in the Empire. Parliament dismissed the colonial opposition as selfish and narrow-minded. The Empire needed money, and Parliament had the right to levy taxes anywhere in the Empire. Of course, Parliament's argument did not sway the colonists, who were appalled to discover that the British were denying their right to tax themselves.

Checkpoint Why did the British impose new taxes on the colonies?

Colonial Protests Intensify

Tax resistance among the colonists took three forms: intellectual protest, economic boycotts, and violent intimidation. All three forms combined to force the British to back down. Colonial leaders wrote pamphlets, drafted resolutions, gave speeches, and delivered sermons to persuade colonists to defy the new taxes. The surge in political activity astonished **John Adams,** a prominent Massachusetts lawyer who observed "our presses have groaned, our pulpits have thundered, our legislatures have resolved, our towns have voted."

Enlightenment Ideas Colonial protests drew upon the liberalism of the Enlightenment. Europe's leading liberal writers included Baron de Montesquieu of France and John Locke of England. They argued that people had divinely granted natural rights, including life, liberty, and property. A good government protected these individual rights. Locke insisted that government existed for the good of the people. Therefore, people had the right to protest any government that violated this "social contract" by failing to protect their rights.

Patrick Henry, a young Virginia representative, used these ideas to draft a radical document known as the Virginia Resolves. He argued that only the colonial assemblies had the right to tax the colonists:

> **Primary Source** "Resolved therefore, That the General Assembly of this colony, together with his majesty or his substitutes have, in their representatives capacity the only exclusive right and power to lay taxes and imposts upon the inhabitants of this colony; and that every attempt to vest such power in any other person or persons whatever than the General Assembly aforesaid is illegal, unconstitutional, and unjust, and has a manifest tendency to destroy British as well as American liberty."
>
> —Patrick Henry, May 29, 1765

On May 30, 1765, the Virginia House of Burgesses accepted most of Henry's resolves, but rejected two—including the one above—because they were deemed too radical. Colonial newspapers, however, printed all six, believing that they had been accepted. Eight other colonies then adopted resolves similar to Henry's original proposal.

Patriot Leaders Emerge Colonists violently opposed the Stamp Act, which affected every colonist. In the months following the passage of the act, colonists began to work together to fight it, which created a new, but still fragile, sense of American unity. Those who opposed the British taxes called themselves "Patriots." In the seaport streets, people showed a powerful new interest in politics. To lead the popular protests, some men formed associations known as the **Sons of Liberty.** Their most famous leader was Boston's Samuel Adams, a cousin of John Adams.

As the protests continued, angry crowds assaulted colonists who supported or helped to collect the taxes. The crowds were especially violent in Boston. In August 1765, a mob led by the Sons of Liberty tore down the office and damaged the house of the stamp tax collector. The Massachusetts lieutenant governor, Thomas Hutchinson, denounced this riot. He insisted that the colonists had a legal duty to pay Parliament's taxes. Another mob destroyed Hutchinson's house. Thereafter, no one in Boston dared to voice support for the stamp tax. By the end of the year, every stamp collector in the colonies had resigned, leaving no one to collect the taxes.

Leaders Organize a Boycott Some colonial leaders opposed the tax but feared the violence of the crowds. To control and coordinate their protest activities, nine colonies sent delegates to a Stamp Act Congress held in New York City in October 1765. Members of this congress encouraged a consumer boycott of goods imported from Britain. Local committees enforced these **nonimportation agreements,** which threatened British merchants and manufacturers with economic ruin.

Tarring and Feathering

In this painting, Bostonians pour hot tea down the throat of a tax collector who has been tarred and feathered. *How do you think this type of artwork affected colonists still loyal to the British Crown?*

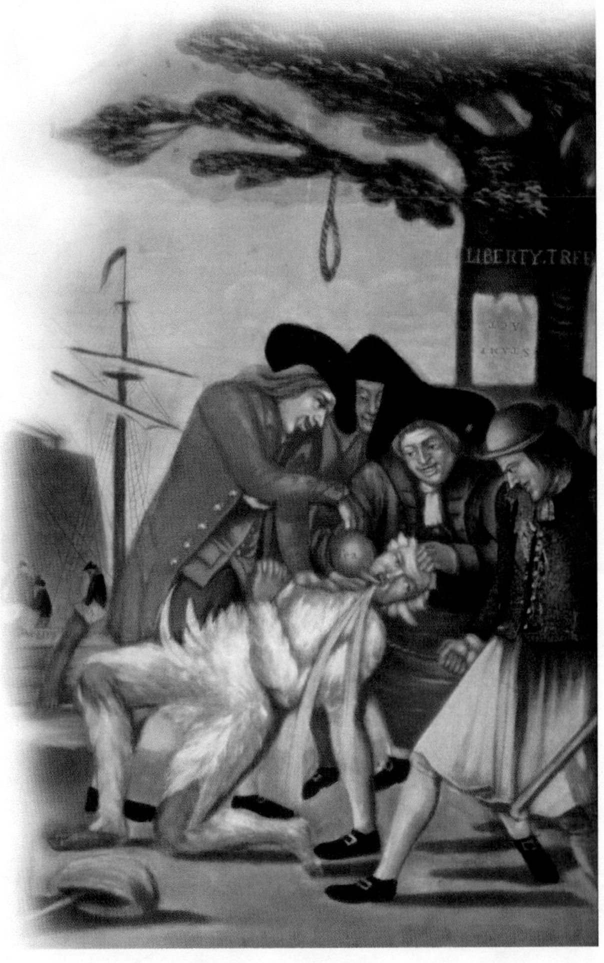

Women played an important economic role in the boycotts. When colonists stopped buying British goods, they needed "homespun" cloth to substitute for British-manufactured cloth. Colonial women organized to weave cloth. Their work was cheered by spectators and by Patriot newspapers. Women also gave up certain comforts when they pledged not to buy any manufactured British goods. Known as "Daughters of Liberty," these women won respect for their efforts in the political struggle.

The combination of tactics worked. Under pressure from British merchants and manufacturers, Parliament repealed the Stamp Act in 1766. But the struggle was not over, for Parliament also passed an act declaring its right to levy taxes on the colonists.

✓ **Checkpoint** **What three tactics did colonists use to protest British taxes?**

New Taxes Lead to New Protests

The Stamp Act crisis showed that the colonists would not accept a direct tax. But the British government still needed to raise money to pay its debt and support troops in the colonies. Charles Townshend, the Crown's chief financial officer, thought that colonists would accept indirect taxes on commerce. After all, they had long accepted customs duties in principle, though evading them in practice. In 1767, Parliament passed the Townshend Acts, which levied new import duties on everyday items such as glass, lead, paint, paper, and tea.

To Townshend's surprise, the colonists insisted that they would pay no new taxes of any sort to Parliament. They also resented Townshend's plans to use the money to pay the salaries of colonial governors and judges, making them more independent of the colonial assemblies. That prospect alarmed the colonists, who valued their financial control of the governors.

Analyzing Political Cartoons

Death of the Stamp Act This cartoon shows British government ministers mourning the end of the Stamp Act. George Grenville carries a coffin to a tomb containing the remains of other unpopular acts. In the background, warehouses are empty because the contents have quickly been shipped to America.

1. Why is Grenville portrayed as the father of a dead child?
2. What is the significance of the ships and warehouses?

Violence Erupts in Boston

In response to the Townshend Acts, the colonists revived their protests, boycotts, and street violence. Once again, the largest riots occurred in Boston, where many of the British customs officials abused their power. The Massachusetts legislature issued a circular letter denouncing the Townshend duties. Few other colonial legislatures paid attention to it until the governor dissolved the Massachusetts legislature in retaliation for their protest.

In an already tense situation, customs officers seized the merchant ship *Liberty* in June 1768 for smuggling. The ship belonged to John Hancock, a wealthy merchant and a prominent colonial politician. The seizure set off riots against the customs officers. To suppress the riots, the Crown sent 4,000 troops to occupy Boston, a city of only 16,000 people. For over a year, the presence of British troops inflamed popular anger, especially because the poorly paid soldiers competed with unskilled workers for jobs.

The Boston Massacre

Paul Revere helped demonize the British by engraving this picture of the Boston Massacre. British troops were known as Redcoats because of their red jackets. *How can you tell that Revere intended this engraving to be used as propaganda?*

One night in March 1770, a group of colonists hurled snowballs and rocks at British soldiers guarding the Customs House. The nervous soldiers fired into the crowd, killing five colonists. The dead included Crispus Attucks, a sailor who may have been an escaped slave of mixed Indian and African ancestry. Under the leadership of Samuel Adams, Patriots called the killings the **Boston Massacre.** Adams later organized a network of local **committees of correspondence** throughout Massachusetts. The committees provided leadership and promoted cooperation. By 1773, several other colonies had created committees, which helped build colonial unity.

Once again, Parliament backed down. The British withdrew troops from Boston and dropped most of the Townshend duties. But to preserve the principle of Parliamentary supremacy, Parliament kept the tax on tea. Therefore, colonists continued to boycott British tea and to drink smuggled Dutch tea.

The Boston Tea Party The tea boycott worsened financial problems for the already struggling British East India Company. To help the company and encourage the colonists to pay the tax, Parliament passed a law allowing the company to sell directly to the colonists. This made their tea cheaper than the smuggled tea, even with the tax.

Instead of buying the cheaper tea, the colonists protested that the British were trying to trick them into paying the tax. If the East India Company sold tea directly, it would also hurt the wealthy colonists who smuggled tea. On the night of December 16, 1773, Boston Patriots took matters into their own hands. Dressed as Indians, they boarded three British ships laden with tea and dumped the tea into the harbor. The event became known as the **Boston Tea Party.**

✓ **Checkpoint How did tensions between the colonists and Britain escalate after 1767?**

▼ A British soldier's cap badge

Colonists Unite Against Harsh Measures

The Bostonians' actions outraged Parliament and the Crown. To punish Boston, Parliament passed the Coercive Acts. They closed the port to trade until the inhabitants paid for the destroyed tea, including the tax. They also increased the power of the governor at the expense of the elected assembly and town meetings. To enforce these measures, the British sent warships and troops to Boston.

The Intolerable Acts

The colonists were outraged. In addition to closing the port, the acts forced colonists to house British troops and allowed British officials to be tried in Britain for crimes committed in the colonies. In addition, the Quebec Act extended Canada's southern border, cutting off lands claimed by several colonies. The horrified colonists called the new laws the **Intolerable Acts.** They rejected the idea that the British could shut down trade and change colonial governments at will.

In rural Massachusetts, people reacted to the British actions with violence. Armed with clubs and guns, they forced the courts of law to shut down. They also assaulted anyone who accepted an office under the governor or spoke in favor of obeying Parliament. They coated some victims in hot tar and feathers—a punishment both humiliating and painful.

The Colonies Take Action

Fortunately for Massachusetts, the other colonies also opposed the Coercive Acts and viewed them as a threat to their freedom.

In the fall of 1774, delegates from every colony except Georgia met in Philadelphia, Pennsylvania, for the **First Continental Congress.** Virginia's delegates included the fiery Patrick Henry, who became famous for declaring,

Soldiers Arrive in Boston
British troops row to shore from their ships in Boston Harbor (below). *How does the artist use the size and placement of ships to convey the force used by the British in Boston?*

"Give me liberty, or give me death." He delighted the New England delegates by declaring, "The distinctions between Virginians, Pennsylvanians, New Yorkers, and New Englanders are no more. I am not a Virginian, but an American."

To pressure Parliament to withdraw the Coercive Acts, the delegates announced a boycott of all British imports. Throughout the colonies, the Patriots established local committees and provincial congresses to enforce the boycotts. In effect, the Patriots established new governments that bypassed Parliament and the Crown. By including common shopkeepers, artisans, and farmers, the committees expanded the ranks of the politically active. In the spring of 1775, a newly arrived immigrant marveled, "They are all liberty mad."

By 1774, Patriot John Adams had decided that he already lived in a new country named America. He also believed that Americans could unite to defeat the British. But Adams was ahead of most colonists, who still hoped to remain within the British Empire, provided that Parliament would revoke the Coercive Acts and stop trying to tax them. Far from blaming the king, most colonists still expected that he would side with them against Parliament. Within two years, however, events would prove Adams right.

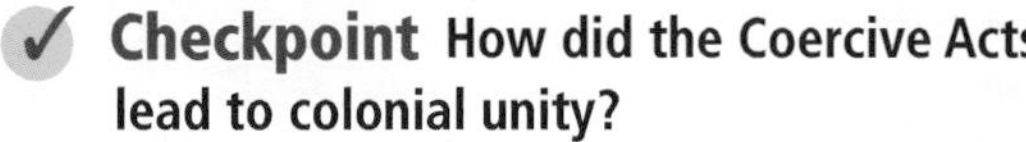

Checkpoint **How did the Coercive Acts lead to colonial unity?**

▲ Patrick Henry, a radical Patriot, encouraged the Continental Congress to embrace independence as their goal.

SECTION 1 Assessment

Progress Monitoring *Online*
For: Self-test with vocabulary practice
www.pearsonschool.com/ushist

Comprehension

1. **Terms and People** Explain how each term or person below increased tensions in the colonies or helped colonial leaders organize for action.
   - Stamp Act
   - John Adams
   - Patrick Henry
   - Sons of Liberty
   - nonimportation agreement
   - Boston Massacre
   - committee of correspondence
   - Boston Tea Party
   - Intolerable Acts
   - First Continental Congress

2. **NoteTaking Reading Skill: Recognize Sequence** Use your flowchart to answer the Section Focus Question: What caused the colonists to rebel against the British?

Writing About History

3. **Quick Write: Contrast** List each of the taxes levied by Parliament on the American colonists. Then, make a chart showing how the British justified each tax and why the colonists protested each one.

Critical Thinking

4. **Compare Points of View** Explain why Parliament did not understand the colonists' argument "no taxation without representation."

5. **Recognize Ideologies** Why did the colonists first accept and then later reject indirect taxes such as duties on trade?

6. **Determine Relevance** How did the Intolerable Acts aid Patriot leaders?

American Experience History Interactive

EXPERIENCE THE ROAD TO REVOLUTION

WILLIAM JACKSON,
an IMPORTER; at the
BRAZEN HEAD,
North Side of the TOWN-HOUSE,
and Oppoſite the Town-Pump, in
Corn-hill, BOSTON.

It is deſired that the SONS and DAUGHTERS of LIBERTY, would not buy any one thing of him, for in ſo doing they will bring Diſgrace upon themſelves, and their Poſterity, for ever and ever, AMEN.

BOSTON, September, 27, 1774.

GENTLEMEN,

THE committees of correſpondence of this and ſeveral of the neighbouring towns, having taken into conſideration the vaſt importance of withholding from the troops now here, labour, ſtraw, timber, ſlitwork, boards, and in ſhort every article excepting proviſions neceſſary for their ſubſiſtance; and being under a neceſſity from their conduct of conſidering them as real enemies, we are fully ſatisfied that it is our bounden duty to withhold from them every thing but what meer humanity requires; and therefore we muſt beg your cloſe and ſerious attention to the incloſed reſolves which were paſſed unanimouſly; and as unanimity in all our meaſures in this day of ſevere trial, is of the utmoſt conſequence, we do earneſtly recommend your co-operation in this meaſure, as conducive to the good of the whole.

We are,

Your Friends and Fellow Countrymen,

Signed by Order of the joint Committee,

William Cooper Clerk.

Fighting between Patriots and the British did not begin until 10 years after the Stamp Act caused an uproar in the colonies. In 1765, not many colonists wanted independence from Britain. Over the next decade, a few organizers rallied colonists to join the Patriots. These printers, merchants, and lawyers used the language of the Enlightenment to attract converts to the cause of independence.

In response to British taxes, early Patriots began organizing the resistance. Samuel Adams created committees of correspondence in Massachusetts to inform the colony about events in Boston. Other colonies quickly followed. Later, Sons and Daughters of Liberty employed the masses of people in their anti-British actions.

Prominent Patriots joined ▶ the Sons and Daughters of Liberty and committees of correspondence.

On August 26, 1765, Boston colonists attacked the home of the Lieutenant Governor during riots opposing the Stamp Act. ▼

▲ James Otis was a leader of the Massachusetts committee of correspondence.

▲ Joseph Reed joined the Philadelphia committee of correspondence.

April 5, 1764

The Sugar Act lowers the tax on molasses, but increases penalties for smuggling, denying a jury trial to accused smugglers.

March 22, 1765

Passage of the Stamp Act results in riots and the formation of the Sons of Liberty.

June 29, 1767

Passage of the Townshend Acts leads to colonial nonimportation agreements.

THE Massachusetts Spy

Or, Thomas's Boston Journal.

Do thou Great LIBERTY inspire our Souls—And make our Lives in thy Possession happy—Or, our Deaths glorious in thy just Defence.

Vol. IV.) THURSDAY, July 7, 1774. (Numb. 179.

JOIN OR DIE

▲ Printing presses were powerful tools for Patriots. The press for this paper had to be slipped out of Boston to prevent the British from destroying it.

▲ Pictures of these coffins, with the initials of colonists who died in the Boston Massacre, were printed in newspapers throughout the colonies.

▼ In response to the Tea Act, Boston Patriots dressed as Indians and dumped British tea into the harbor.

Thinking Critically

1. **Recognize Propaganda** How did newspapers win support for the Patriots?
2. **Identify Point of View** How would Parliament have interpreted the colonists' reactions?

Connect to Today Research a group that is working to gain support for a specific cause today. Write a report evaluating the tactics they use to spread their message.

History *Interactive*

For: Experience the Road to Revolution activities
www.pearsonschool.com/ushist

March 5, 1770

The Boston Massacre results in greater support for the Patriots, who use newspapers to advance their cause.

April 27, 1773

Parliament passes the Tea Act, leading to the Boston Tea Party in December.

April 1, 1774

Parliament closes the port of Boston; Virginia calls for every colony to create committees of correspondence.

SECTION 2

WITNESS HISTORY

The Spirit of Independence

In 1776, the Continental Congress decided to declare independence. But some colonists were hesitant.

"Some people among us seem alarmed at the *name of Independence,* while they support . . . the *spirit* of it. Have we not made laws, . . . levied war, and regulated commerce, not only without his Majesty's intervention, but absolutely against his will? Are we not as criminal in the eyes of Britain for what we have done as for what we can yet do? If we institute any government at all, for heaven's sake let it be the best government we can. We shall be as certainly hanged for a bad as a good one. . . . If, therefore, we incur the danger, let us not decline the reward. . . ."

—letter from a member of the Virginia Convention, February 10, 1776

◀ Signing the Declaration of Independence

Declaring Independence

Objectives

- Explain why fighting broke out to begin the American Revolution and the response of the Second Continental Congress.
- Describe the Loyalists' view of the Patriots.
- Analyze the impact of Thomas Paine's *Common Sense.*
- Assess why Congress declared independence and the ideas underlying the Declaration of Independence.

Terms and People

militia
Loyalist
Second Continental Congress
Continental Army
George Washington
Thomas Paine
Declaration of Independence
Thomas Jefferson
natural rights

NoteTaking

Reading Skill: Recognize Sequence Use a timeline to keep track of events in this section.

April 18, 1775 Battles of Lexington and Concord — July 4, 1776

Why It Matters In 1776, the colonists of British America made three important decisions. First, they declared independence from Britain. Second, they chose a republican model for their new government. Third, they confederated the 13 states as the United States of America. These decisions were unprecedented and risky. The colonists gambled their lives and property but found a strength that surprised and changed the world. **Section Focus Question: What events led the colonists to declare their independence from Britain?**

War Begins

In early 1775, the dispute between the British government and the colonists took a drastic turn. Following the passage of the Coercive Acts, military commander General Thomas Gage had been named governor of Massachusetts. John Hancock, Samuel Adams, and other colonial leaders then convened a Provincial Congress to govern Massachusetts without Gage. They also began to stockpile arms and ammunition.

The Battles of Lexington and Concord On April 19, 1775, war erupted at Lexington and Concord, two country towns west of Boston. Gage provoked the battles by sending troops to arrest Hancock and Adams in Lexington and to seize Patriot weapons stockpiled in Concord. Tipped off by men, including Paul Revere, who had ridden into the countryside to warn of the approaching British troops, the local Patriots rallied to drive the troops back to Boston. The Patriot fighters were **militia,** full-time farmers and part-time soldiers.

By morning, about 70 Patriots had gathered on the Lexington Green. As the British soldiers, called Redcoats, marched into town at dawn, the British commander ordered the militia to disperse. As they did, someone fired a shot. When the shooting stopped, eight Patriots were dead. The Redcoats marched on to Concord. What happened next stunned the British. The British troops began their march back to Boston following a skirmish with Patriots in Concord. However, hundreds of minutemen, Patriot militia who earned their name by their ability to respond quickly to calls for soldiers, lined the roads, firing at the British from behind trees and stone walls. The Patriots killed or wounded more than 200 British soldiers.

Stunned and exhausted, the British reached the safety of Boston in the late afternoon. From throughout New England, thousands of Patriot militiamen rushed to confine the British troops in the city. Provincial assemblies of Patriots seized control of the New England colonies. **Loyalists,** or colonists who remained loyal to Britain, fled to take refuge in Boston. But would the rest of the colonies help New England fight the British?

The Second Continental Congress The answer came in May 1775 when delegates from all the colonies assembled in Philadelphia for the **Second Continental Congress.** To the relief of New Englanders, Congress assumed responsibility for the war. Armed volunteers from the Middle and Southern colonies marched north to join the Patriot siege of Boston. Congress gave the command of the new **Continental Army** to **George Washington.** Washington had served as a colonial officer in the French and Indian War and he came from Virginia, the largest and most powerful colony. New England needed Virginia's help to win the war.

Some radical members of the Continental Congress wanted to declare American independence from Britain, but they recognized that most of their constituents were not yet ready to do so. Most colonists still hoped to remain within the British Empire but without paying taxes to Parliament. In July 1775, after three months of bloodshed, Congress sent an "Olive Branch Petition" to King George III. The petition reaffirmed the colonists' allegiance to the king but not to Parliament. The king rejected the petition and sent more troops to Boston.

✓ **Checkpoint What actions did the Second Continental Congress take in response to the outbreak of war with Britain?**

The First Battle

The engraving below shows the battle on Lexington Green. Patriots hung the lantern below from the steeple in a Boston church to signal that British troops were on the move. *Based on this picture, does it seem likely that the Patriots would defeat the British?*

Patriots Abuse Loyalists
Loyalists were subjected to harsh treatment by their Patriot neighbors. In this picture, a Loyalist is paraded through town, followed by drummers. *Why did Patriots publicly humiliate Loyalists?*

Patriots and Loyalists Disagree

Most colonists supported the Continental Congress and the boycott of British imports, but a large minority preferred British rule. These colonists were later called Loyalists. Champions of law and order, many Loyalists dreaded the Patriot crowds and committees, viewing them as illegal and brutal. One Loyalist declared, "If I must be enslaved, let it be by a King at least, and not by a parcel of upstart, lawless committeemen. If I must be devoured, let me be devoured by the jaws of a lion, and not gnawed to death by rats and vermin."

Loyalists Fear Disorder Although many Loyalists opposed Britain's taxes, they felt that Parliament and the Crown must be obeyed as the legitimate government of the Empire. The Loyalists feared that the resistance would lead to a deadly and destructive war that Britain seemed certain to win. They doubted that the colonists could defeat an empire that had recently crushed the combined powers of France and Spain.

During the summer of 1774, two old friends and lawyers walked together to discuss the crisis: John Adams, a Patriot, and Jonathan Sewell, a Loyalist. During the conversation, Sewell warned Adams, "Great Britain is determined on her system. Her power is irresistible, and it will certainly be destructive to you, and all those who . . . persevere in opposition to her designs."

Adams boldly replied, "I know that Great Britain is determined in her system, and that . . . [has] determined me on mine. . . . Swim or sink, live or die, survive or perish with my country—that is my unalterable determination."

Loyalists Oppose the Patriots' Demands About a fifth of the colonists remained loyal, and many more wished to remain neutral. According to stereotype, Loyalists were wealthy elitists who sold out their fellow colonists to reap profitable offices in the British government. A few Loyalists did fit that description, but many more were ordinary farmers and artisans. Others belonged to cultural minorities who feared oppression by the Patriot majority.

Vocabulary Builder
stereotype–(STER ee uh tīp) *n.* an oversimplified image of a group of people

Loyalists disliked the taxes, oaths of allegiance, and militia drafts demanded by the new Patriot authorities to support the Patriots' war. They also resented the Patriots for shutting down Loyalist newspapers and for punishing people who criticized the Patriots' actions. Loyalists concluded that the Patriots demanded more in taxes and allowed less free speech than did the British.

Loyalism also appealed to Native Americans and to enslaved people. The Indians wanted British help to keep out the settlers pressing westward. Because slaveholders led the revolution in the Southern Colonies, their slaves saw the British as the true champions of liberty. Thousands of enslaved people sought their freedom by running away to join the British forces.

✓ **Checkpoint** **Why did Loyalists oppose the Patriots' cause?**

Opinion Swings Toward Independence

In January 1776, a short but powerful book swung popular opinion in the colonies in favor of independence. Entitled *Common Sense,* the book was by **Thomas Paine,** a recent immigrant from England who had been both an artisan and a tax collector. In *Common Sense*, many Americans read what they longed to believe but had not known how to express. Similar ideas would soon appear in a declaration of the colonists' independence.

Thomas Paine's Radical Proposal In simple but forceful and direct language, Paine proposed a radical course of action for the colonies: independence from Britain, republican state governments, and a union of the new states.

Paine denounced the king and aristocrats of Britain as frauds and parasites. He wanted the common people to elect all of their government, not just a third

Thomas Paine's Common Sense

The printing press was vital to Patriot success before and during the American Revolution. The book *Common Sense* (below right) was the first great American bestseller. At least 150,000 copies were produced, a stunning total for a population of only 2.5 million people.

Thomas Paine (right), the author of *Common Sense,* appealed to common people by writing more clearly and directly than any previous political writer had. John Adams later noted that no man had "more influence on [the world's] inhabitants or affairs for the last thirty years than Thomas Paine."

One of Jefferson's drafts of the Declaration of Independence ▼

of it. Paine depicted the king, rather than Parliament, as the greatest enemy of American liberty. He hated the rigid class structure of Britain for smothering the hopes of common people without a noble title or money. A republic, he argued, would provide opportunities to reward merit rather than inherited privilege. Freed from the empire, Americans could trade with the entire world.

By uniting to create a republic, Americans could create a model that would inspire common people everywhere to reject kings and aristocrats. Paine concluded, "The cause of America is in a great measure the cause of all mankind." This view was new and powerful in 1776, when the revolution was a desperate gamble.

The Colonists Declare Independence By the spring of 1776, Paine's ideas had built momentum for American independence. Noting the shift in public opinion, Congress selected a committee to draft a document declaring American independence and explaining the reasons for it. On July 2, Congress voted that America was free. Two days later, they approved the **Declaration of Independence.**

Drafted by **Thomas Jefferson,** the Declaration drew upon Paine's ideas to denounce the king as a tyrant who made American independence necessary. Although primarily a long list of colonial grievances, the Declaration also advanced the bold idea that "all men are created equal." Congress embraced the Enlightenment ideas that all men are born with **natural rights** that cannot be taken away by a government. Jefferson called them "unalienable rights."

This sweeping statement was far ahead of the social and economic reality in the new United States. For example, many of the signers of the Declaration owned slaves. But the idea of equality would inspire future generations of Americans, including enslaved people, to make a better, more equal society.

Declaring independence on paper was one thing. Achieving it was another. The colonists faced many challenges before they could become an independent nation. No colony in the Americas had yet won independence from a European empire. Fighting the British for independence would pit the poorly organized colonists against the greatest military power on Earth.

Checkpoint What ideas were expressed in the Declaration of Independence?

SECTION 2 Assessment

Progress Monitoring *Online*
For: Self-test with vocabulary practice
www.pearsonschool.com/ushist

Comprehension

1. **Terms and People** For each entry below, write a sentence explaining its significance to the Revolutionary War.
   - militia
   - Loyalist
   - Second Continental Congress
   - Continental Army
   - George Washington
   - Thomas Paine
   - Declaration of Independence
   - Thomas Jefferson
   - natural rights
2. **NoteTaking Reading Skill: Recognize Sequence** Use your completed timeline to answer the Section Focus Question: What events led the colonists to declare their independence from Britain?

Writing About History

3. **Quick Write: Compare** Write a paragraph comparing the Patriot and Loyalist viewpoints. Explain their shared concerns and why they thought that the British or the Patriots were the best hope for America.

Critical Thinking

4. **Draw Inferences** Why did the Second Continental Congress send the Olive Branch Petition to the king?
5. **Recognize Ideologies** Why did Loyalists oppose independence from Britain?
6. **Recognize Bias** Why did Thomas Paine argue so forcefully for independence?
7. **Explain Effects** How did the Enlightenment affect the American Revolution?

Declaration of Independence

In Congress, July 4, 1776

THE UNANIMOUS DECLARATION OF THE THIRTEEN UNITED STATES OF AMERICA,

When in the Course of human events, it becomes necessary for one people to dissolve the political bands which have connected them with another, and to assume among the powers of the earth, the separate and equal station to which the Laws of Nature and of Nature's God entitle them, a decent respect to the opinions of mankind requires that they should declare the causes which impel them to the separation.

We hold these truths to be self-evident, that all men are created equal, that they are endowed by their Creator with certain unalienable Rights, that among these are Life, Liberty and the pursuit of Happiness.—That to secure these rights, Governments are instituted among Men, deriving their just powers from the consent of the governed,—That whenever any Form of Government becomes destructive of these ends, it is the Right of the People to alter or to abolish it, and to institute new Government, laying its foundation on such principles and organizing its powers in such form, as to them shall seem most likely to effect their Safety and Happiness. Prudence, indeed, will dictate that Governments long established should not be changed for light and transient causes; and accordingly all experience hath shewn, that mankind are more disposed to suffer, while evils are sufferable, than to right themselves by abolishing the forms to which they are accustomed. But when a long train of abuses and usurpations, pursuing invariably the same Object evinces a design to reduce them under absolute Despotism, it is their right, it is their duty, to throw off such Government, and to provide new Guards for their future security.—Such has been the patient sufferance of these Colonies; and such is now the necessity which constrains them to alter their former Systems of Government. The history of the present King of Great Britain is a history of repeated injuries and usurpations, all having in direct object the establishment of an absolute Tyranny over these States. To prove this, let Facts be submitted to a candid world.

He has refused his Assent to Laws, the most wholesome and necessary for the public good.

He has forbidden his Governors to pass Laws of immediate and pressing importance, unless suspended in their operation till his Assent should be obtained; and when so suspended, he has utterly neglected to attend to them.

He has refused to pass other Laws for the accommodation of large districts of people, unless those people would relinquish the right of Representation in the Legislature, a right inestimable to them and formidable to tyrants only.

He has called together legislative bodies at places unusual, uncomfortable, and distant from the depository of their public Records, for the sole purpose of fatiguing them into compliance with his measures.

Commentary

Preamble
The document first lists the reasons for writing the Declaration.

Protection of Natural Rights
People set up governments to protect their basic rights. These rights are unalienable; they cannot be taken away. The purpose of government is to protect these natural rights. When a government does not protect the rights of the people, the people must change the government or create a new one. The colonists feel that the king's repeated usurpations, or unjust uses of power, are a form of despotism, or tyranny, that has denied them their basic rights.

Grievances Against the King
The list of grievances details the colonists' complaints against the British government and King George III. The colonists have no say in determining the laws that govern them, and they feel King George's actions show little or no concern for the well-being of the people.

The colonists refuse to relinquish, or give up, the right to representation, which they feel is inestimable, or priceless.

Commentary

The king has refused to allow new legislators to be elected. As a result, the colonies have not been able to protect themselves against foreign enemies and convulsions, or riots, within the colonies.

The king has tried to stop foreigners from coming to the colonies by refusing to pass naturalization laws. Such laws set up the process for foreigners to become legal citizens.

The king alone has decided a judge's tenure, or term. This grievance later would result in Article 3, Section 1, of the Constitution, which states that federal judges hold office for life.

Forced by the king, the colonists have been quartering, or lodging, troops in their homes. This grievance found its way into the Constitution in the Third Amendment.

The king has taken away the rights of the people in a nearby province (Canada). The colonists feared he could do the same to the colonies if he so wished.

 **Checkpoint**

Why does the Declaration list the colonists' many grievances?

He has dissolved Representative Houses repeatedly, for opposing with manly firmness his invasions on the rights of the people.

He has refused for a long time, after such dissolutions, to cause others to be elected; whereby the Legislative powers, incapable of Annihilation, have returned to the People at large for their exercise; the State remaining in the mean time exposed to all the dangers of invasions from without, and convulsions within.

He has endeavored to prevent the population of these States; for that purpose obstructing the Laws for Naturalization of Foreigners; refusing to pass others to encourage their migration hither, and raising the conditions of new Appropriations of Lands.

He has obstructed the Administration of Justice, by refusing his Assent to Laws for establishing Judiciary powers.

He has made Judges dependent on his Will alone, for the tenure of their offices, and the amount and payment of their salaries.

He has erected a multitude of New Offices, and sent hither swarms of Officers to harass our people and eat out their substance.

He has kept among us in time of peace, Standing Armies, without the Consent of our legislatures.

He has affected to render the Military independent of and superior to the Civil power.

He has combined with others to subject us to a jurisdiction foreign to our constitutions, and unacknowledged by our laws; giving his Assent to their Acts of pretended Legislation:

For Quartering large bodies of armed troops among us:

For protecting them, by a mock Trial, from punishment for any Murders which they should commit on the Inhabitants of these States:

For cutting off our Trade with all parts of the world:

For imposing Taxes on us without our Consent:

For depriving us in many cases, of the benefits of Trial by Jury:

For transporting us beyond Seas to be tried for pretended offenses:

For abolishing the free System of English Laws in a neighbouring Province, establishing therein an Arbitrary government, and enlarging its Boundaries so as to render it at once an example and fit instrument for introducing the same absolute rule into these Colonies:

For taking away our Charters, abolishing our most valuable Laws, and altering fundamentally the Forms of our Governments:

For suspending our own Legislature, and declaring themselves invested with power to legislate for us in all cases whatsoever.

He has abdicated Government here, by declaring us out of his Protection, and waging War against us.

He has plundered our seas, ravaged our Coasts, burned our towns, and destroyed the lives of our people.

He is at this time transporting large Armies of foreign Mercenaries to compleat the works of death, desolation and tyranny, already begun with circumstances of Cruelty and perfidy scarcely paralleled in the most barbarous ages, and totally unworthy the Head of a civilized nation.

He has constrained our fellow Citizens taken Captive on the high Seas to bear Arms against their Country, to become the executioners of their friends and Brethren, or to fall themselves by their Hands.

He has excited domestic insurrections amongst us, and has endeavored to bring on the inhabitants of our frontiers the merciless Indian Savages, whose known rule of warfare, is an undistinguished destruction of all ages, sexes and conditions.

In every stage of these Oppressions We have Petitioned for Redress in the most humble terms: Our repeated Petitions have been answered only by repeated injury. A Prince, whose character is thus marked by every act which may define a Tyrant, is unfit to be the ruler of a free people.

Nor have We been wanting in attentions to our British brethren. We have warned them from time to time of attempts by their legislature to extend an unwarrantable jurisdiction over us. We have reminded them of the circumstances of our emigration and settlement here. We have appealed to their native justice and magnanimity, and we have conjured them by the ties of our common kindred to disavow these usurpations, which, would inevitably interrupt our connections and correspondence. They too have been deaf to the voice of justice and of consanguinity. We must, therefore, acquiesce in the necessity, which denounces our Separation, and hold them, as we hold the rest of mankind, Enemies in War, in Peace Friends.

We, therefore, the Representatives of the United States of America, in General Congress, Assembled, appealing to the Supreme Judge of the world for the rectitude of our intentions, do, in the Name, and by the Authority of the good People of these Colonies, solemnly publish and declare, That these United Colonies are, and of Right ought to be Free and Independent States; that they are Absolved from all Allegiance to the British Crown, and that all political connection between them and the State of Great Britain, is and ought to be totally dissolved; and that as Free and Independent States, they have full Power to levy War, conclude Peace, contract Alliances, establish Commerce, and to do all other Acts and Things which Independent States may of right do. And for the support of this Declaration, with a firm reliance on the protection of Divine Providence, we mutually pledge to each other our Lives, our Fortunes and our sacred Honor.

Commentary

The king has hired foreign mercenaries, or soldiers, to bring death and destruction to the colonists. The head of a civilized country should never act with the cruelty and perfidy, or dishonesty, that the king has.

The colonists have repeatedly asked the king to correct these wrongs. Each time, he has failed to do so. Because of the way he treats his subjects, the king is not fit to rule.

The colonists have appealed to the British people. They have asked their fellow British subjects to support them. However, like the king, the British people have ignored the colonists' requests.

◀ **Declaring Independence**
The resolution of independence boldly asserts that the colonies are now "free and independent states." The Declaration concludes by stating that these new states have the power to wage war, establish alliances, and trade with other countries.

✓ Checkpoint

What powers does the new nation have, now that it is independent?

Signatories of the Declaration of Independence

JOHN HANCOCK
PRESIDENT OF THE CONTINENTAL CONGRESS 1775–1777

NEW HAMPSHIRE
Josiah Bartlett
William Whipple
Matthew Thornton

MASSACHUSETTS BAY
Samuel Adams
John Adams
Robert Treat Paine
Elbridge Gerry

RHODE ISLAND
Stephen Hopkins
William Ellery

CONNECTICUT
Roger Sherman
Samuel Huntington
William Williams
Oliver Wolcott

NEW YORK
William Floyd
Philip Livingston
Francis Lewis
Lewis Morris

NEW JERSEY
Richard Stockton
John Witherspoon
Francis Hopkinson
John Hart
Abraham Clark

DELAWARE
Caesar Rodney
George Read
Thomas McKean

MARYLAND
Samuel Chase
William Paca
Thomas Stone
Charles Carroll of Carrollton

VIRGINIA
George Wythe
Richard Henry Lee
Thomas Jefferson
Benjamin Harrison
Thomas Nelson, Jr.
Francis Lightfoot Lee
Carter Braxton

PENNSYLVANIA
Robert Morris
Benjamin Rush
Benjamin Franklin
John Morton
George Clymer
James Smith
George Taylor
James Wilson
George Ross

NORTH CAROLINA
William Hooper
Joseph Hewes
John Penn

SOUTH CAROLINA
Edward Rutledge
Thomas Heyward, Jr.
Thomas Lynch, Jr.
Arthur Middleton

GEORGIA
Button Gwinnett
Lyman Hall
George Walton

New Yorkers tear down a statue of King George III after a reading of the Declaration of Independence on Bowling Green. The statue was later melted down to make ammunition for the Continental Army.

SECTION 3

Continental soldiers ▶

Washington's canteen ▶

WITNESS HISTORY

Could England Win the War?

During the war, Thomas Paine wrote several pamphlets supporting the Patriot cause. Paine directed this passage to Britain's commander, Lord Howe:

"By what means, may I ask, do you expect to conquer America? If you could not effect it in the summer, when our army was less than yours, nor in the winter, when we had none, how are you to do it? . . . [Y]ou have been outwitted . . . your advantages turn out to your loss and show us that it is in our power to ruin you. . . . You cannot be so insensible as not to see that we have two to one the advantage of you, because we conquer by a drawn game, and you lose by it."

—Thomas Paine, *The American Crisis II,* 1777

Turning Points of the War

Objectives

- Explain the advantages the British held at the start of the war and the mistakes they made by underestimating the Patriots.
- Describe the frontier war.
- Evaluate the major military turning points of the war.

Terms and People

William Howe
mercenary
Battle of Trenton
Charles Cornwallis
Battle of Princeton
Saratoga
Marquis de Lafayette
Benjamin Franklin
Valley Forge
Monmouth

NoteTaking

Reading Skill: Summarize Record the British and Patriot strengths and weaknesses on a chart like the one below.

British	
Strengths	Weaknesses
• •	• •

Why It Matters To make their independence a reality, the Patriots had to win a hard and bloody war against the world's most powerful empire. Britain's population was nearly four times larger than the 2.5 million people in the colonies. And at least a fifth of the colonists were Loyalists. Another fifth were slaves, who were likely to join the British to escape enslavement. Many others remained neutral for as long as possible. **Section Focus Question: What factors helped the Patriots win the war?**

The Opposing Sides

At the beginning of the war, Britain seemed to have great advantages. A leader in manufacturing, Britain produced more ships and weapons than the colonists did. The British also had an established government, while the Americans were starting from scratch. Meanwhile, the Continental Congress struggled to pay for the war. Lacking the authority to collect taxes, Congress and the states printed paper money to pay their debts, producing inflation that damaged the economy. The Continental soldiers suffered from hunger and cold, while the British troops were well trained and had plenty of supplies. The odds seemed slight that the Patriots could win.

The British Make Mistakes In 1775, the British did not take the Patriots seriously as an enemy. Two months after the defeat at Concord, they repeated their mistake at the Battle of Bunker Hill. By fortifying hills overlooking Boston, the Patriots hoped to drive the British from that seaport. To retake the hills, the new British commander, Lord **William Howe,** ordered a frontal assault by soldiers in the middle of the day. Carrying heavy packs and wearing red uniforms, his men marched uphill straight into a murderous fire from entrenched Patriots. Why did Howe put his soldiers in such a dangerous position?

Howe wanted to win the battle despite giving the Patriots every advantage. That would prove, in another general's words, "that trained troops are invincible against any numbers or any position of untrained rabble." Instead of proving Howe's point, the British suffered a bloodbath as two charges failed. A third charge captured the hills only because the Patriots ran out of ammunition. Technically, the British had won the battle, but they suffered more than twice the Patriot casualties. The Patriots had won a psychological victory.

In January 1776, six months after the Battle of Bunker Hill, Colonel Henry Knox arrived with cannons to reinforce the Patriots outside Boston. His men had hauled the cannons hundreds of miles from upstate New York, where Ethan Allen's men had captured them from Fort Ticonderoga. With Patriot cannons shelling both Boston and the British ships in the harbor, the British abandoned the city in March.

The British Misunderstand the Conflict Lord Howe continued to pursue a misguided strategy. The British thought that they were fighting a traditional European war. They believed that the Patriots would surrender if Howe could defeat the Continental Army and capture the major seaports, including Philadelphia, the Patriot capital. In fact, the British accomplished these goals but still lost the war.

The British never fully understood that they were fighting a different type of war, a revolutionary war. The Patriots understood that it was a struggle to win the hearts and minds of the civilian population. Instead of surrendering after setbacks, the Patriots kept on fighting. Thomas Paine wrote an inspiring series of essays, *The American Crisis,* which George Washington read to encourage his troops. Meanwhile, the British further angered colonists when they hired German **mercenaries,** or soldiers who fought for hire. These "Hessians," as they were called, had a particularly brutal reputation.

The Patriots' Strengths Patriot persistence owed much to Washington's leadership. He realized that to preserve his Continental Army from destruction, he could not risk all on a major battle under unfavorable conditions. Outnumbered and often outmaneuvered, Washington lost most of the battles, but his skillful retreats saved his army to fight another day. By preserving and inspiring his soldiers, Washington sustained them through incredible hardships. His small but committed army hung together despite the casualties and the soldiers' hunger and ragged clothing.

By preoccupying the British army, Washington's Continental Army freed the local militias to suppress the Loyalists in the countryside.

Colonists Endure Hard Times To succeed, the Continental Army needed aid and support from the civilian population. Throughout the war, women's work was crucial. Women freed their husbands and sons for military service by running farms and shops. They also made clothing, blankets, and shoes for the soldiers. Without these contributions, the Patriots could not have sustained their army.

History Makers

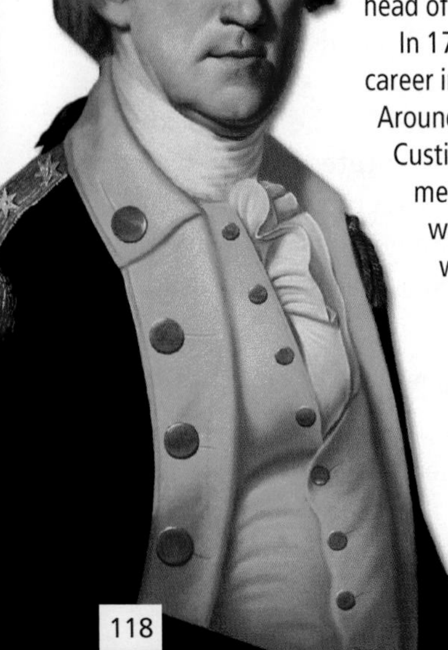

George Washington (1732–1799)
The son of a wealthy Virginia planter, George Washington became a surveyor at age 16 and inherited his brother's estate, Mount Vernon, a few years later. Washington led a militia in the French and Indian War, becoming the head of all Virginia troops in 1755.

In 1758, Washington began his political career in the Virginia House of Burgesses. Around the same time, he married Martha Custis, a wealthy widow. Between meetings of the Burgesses, Washington was a farmer, though a particularly wealthy one. When the dispute between the colonies and Great Britain began, he sided with the colonies. He would lead the Continental Army to victory before his election as the first President of the United States.

The Battle of Princeton

On January 3, 1777, Washington attacked Cornwallis in Princeton, New Jersey. *How did the Patriots' tactics in this battle differ from the way they attacked the troops retreating from Concord in 1775?*

However, the British navy also blockaded the ports, making many items scarce and expensive. A few colonists took advantage of the shortages by profiteering, or selling in demand items at a very high price. Furthermore, the Patriots caused inflation by issuing paper money. As a result, the value of money decreased. If farmers sold their crops to the Patriots, they would be paid in "Continentals," paper money issued by the Continental Congress. It would be worth nothing if the Patriots lost. The British army, however, paid for their food in gold.

During the war, some women followed their husbands into the army. They received rations for maintaining the camps and washing clothing. A few women even helped fire cannons or served as soldiers by masquerading as men. For her service, Deborah Sampson later won a military pension from Congress. Another story says that Mary Hays became known as Molly Pitcher for delivering water to troops during the battle at Monmouth. Legend says that she stepped in and took her husband's place at the cannon.

 **Checkpoint What were the Patriots' strengths?**

The War Shifts to the Middle States

After the British left Boston in early 1776, they decided to attack New York City and cut off New England from the rest of the colonies. After winning a series of battles, Howe captured the city on September 15. About 30,000 British and German troops nearly crushed the poorly trained Continentals. Forced to retreat across New Jersey, Washington saved his army and the Revolution by counterattacking on December 26. Crossing the Delaware River in the middle of Christmas night, he surprised a garrison of more than 1,000 German mercenaries at the **Battle of Trenton.** This modest victory raised the spirits of the troops and Patriot supporters at a critical moment.

NoteTaking

Reading Skill: Recognize Sequence Use a timeline to record the sequence of important events and battles during the war.

September 15, 1776
British capture
New York City

Military Turning Points Washington began 1777 with another victory. Again moving his troops in the night, Washington inflicted heavy casualties on General **Charles Cornwallis**'s troops at the **Battle of Princeton.** During the remainder of 1777, however, Washington suffered more defeats. In the fall, he lost Philadelphia to Howe's army.

Led by General John Burgoyne, another British army marched from Canada to invade New York's Hudson Valley. Falling into a Patriot trap at **Saratoga,** Burgoyne surrendered in October. The greatest Patriot victory yet, Saratoga suggested that the United States might just win the war.

European Allies Enter the War The victory at Saratoga took on greater importance because it encouraged France to recognize American independence and to enter the war. France welcomed the opportunity to weaken an old enemy, Britain. During the early years of the war, however, the French had doubted that the Patriots could win. Unwilling to risk an open alliance, they had limited their assistance to secret shipments of arms and ammunition. But that covert aid kept the Patriot army alive and fighting. Some French volunteers, including the aristocrat and Patriot general **Marquis de Lafayette,** also provided military expertise.

After Saratoga, the French risked an open alliance with the United States. Negotiated in February 1778, the alliance reflected the diplomatic genius of **Benjamin Franklin,** the leading American negotiator in Paris. A cunning gentleman, Franklin became popular in France by presenting himself in public as a simple American who loved the French. As the French army and navy began attacking the British, the war became more equal. Although the first joint operations failed miserably, the alliance would produce the biggest victory of the war in 1781.

Vocabulary Builder
ally– (AL ī) *n.* person, group, or country joined with another or with others to achieve a common purpose

The British suffered another blow in 1779 when Spain entered the war as a French ally. The Spanish also wanted to weaken the British, but they feared that American independence would inspire their own colonists to rebel against Spanish rule. Spain was not an official American ally, but the Spanish governor of Louisiana, Bernardo de Gálvez, provided money and supplies to the Patriots and prevented British ships from entering the Mississippi River at New Orleans.

The Continental Army Faces Challenges Back in Pennsylvania, Washington's army spent the harsh and hungry winter of 1777 to 1778 at **Valley Forge,** outside of Philadelphia. The soldiers suffered from a lack of supplies and food. Washington reported to Congress that nearly a third of his 10,000 soldiers had no coats or shoes.

Primary Source "Unless some great . . . change suddenly takes place . . . this Army must inevitably be reduced to one or other of these three things. Starve, dissolve, or disperse in order to obtain subsistence in the best manner they can."

—George Washington, Valley Forge, December 23, 1777

Baron Von Steuben drills soldiers at Valley Forge.

Despite their hardships, the soldiers improved from careful drilling supervised by a German volunteer, Baron Von Steuben, who had come to help the Patriots. In June 1778, the British evacuated Philadelphia, retreating across New Jersey to New York City. On the way, they fought off Washington's pursuit at **Monmouth,** New Jersey. The Continental soldiers demonstrated their improved discipline under fire.

Despite having won most of the battles, the British had little to show for it beyond their headquarters in New York City. Despairing of winning in the North, the British turned their attention to the South.

✓ **Checkpoint Describe the course of the war in 1777 and 1778.**

Geography Interactive
For: Interactive map and timeline
www.pearsonschool.com/ushist

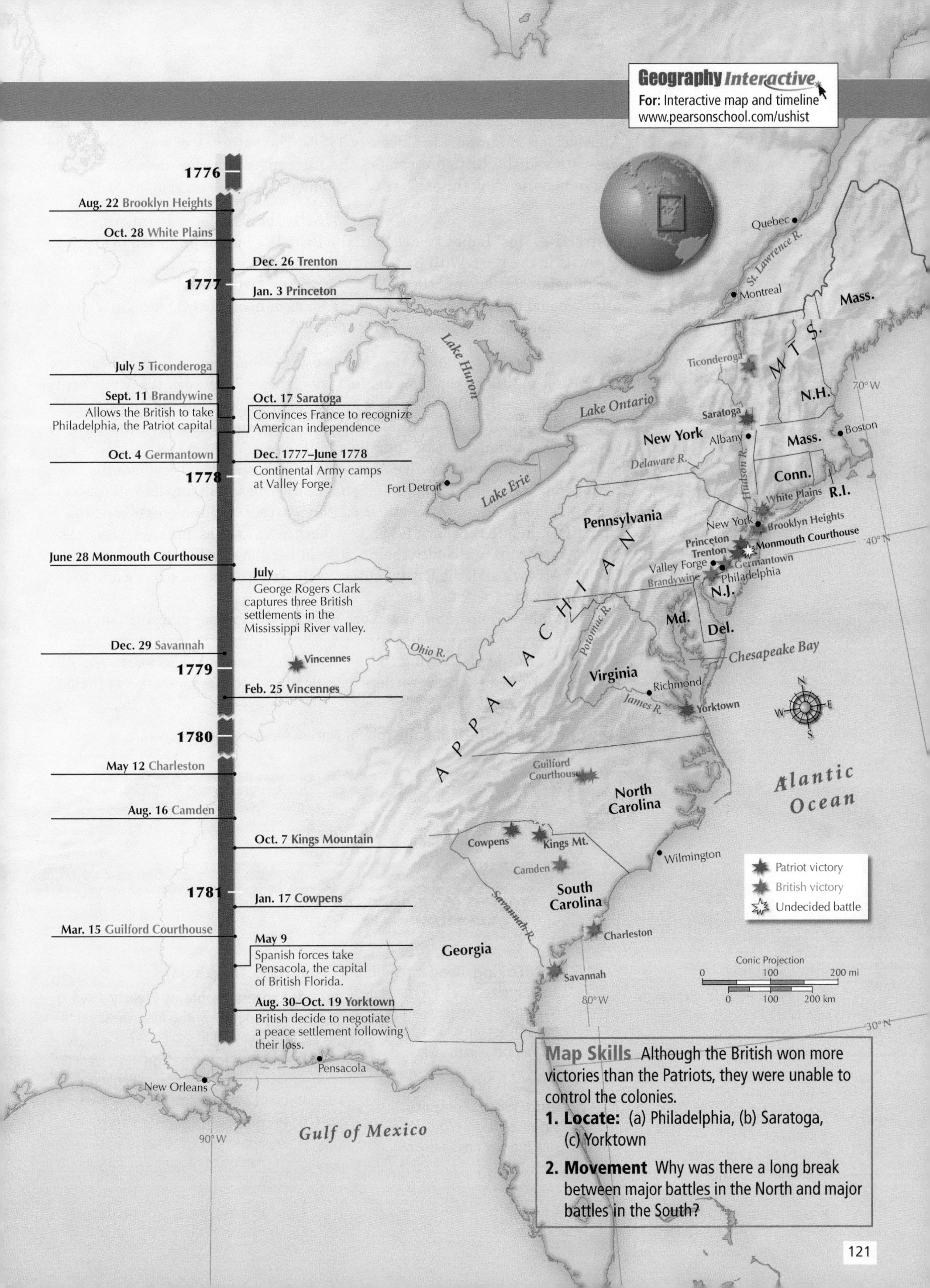
1776
Aug. 22 Brooklyn Heights
Oct. 28 White Plains
Dec. 26 Trenton
1777
Jan. 3 Princeton
July 5 Ticonderoga
Sept. 11 Brandywine
Allows the British to take Philadelphia, the Patriot capital
Oct. 17 Saratoga
Convinces France to recognize American independence
Oct. 4 Germantown
Dec. 1777–June 1778
Continental Army camps at Valley Forge.
1778
June 28 Monmouth Courthouse
July
George Rogers Clark captures three British settlements in the Mississippi River valley.
Dec. 29 Savannah
1779
Feb. 25 Vincennes
1780
May 12 Charleston
Aug. 16 Camden
Oct. 7 Kings Mountain
1781
Jan. 17 Cowpens
Mar. 15 Guilford Courthouse
May 9
Spanish forces take Pensacola, the capital of British Florida.
Aug. 30–Oct. 19 Yorktown
British decide to negotiate a peace settlement following their loss.
Quebec
St. Lawrence R.
Montreal
Mass.
Lake Huron
Ticonderoga
MTS.
N.H.
70° W
Lake Ontario
Saratoga
New York
Albany
Mass.
Boston
Delaware R.
Hudson R.
Conn.
Fort Detroit
Lake Erie
White Plains
R.I.
Pennsylvania
New York
Brooklyn Heights
Princeton
Trenton
Monmouth Courthouse
40° N
Valley Forge
Germantown
Brandywine
Philadelphia
N.J.
APPALACHIAN
Potomac R.
Md.
Del.
Ohio R.
Vincennes
Chesapeake Bay
Virginia
Richmond
James R.
Yorktown
N
W
E
S
Guilford Courthouse
Atlantic Ocean
North Carolina
Cowpens
Kings Mt.
Wilmington
Camden
South Carolina
Savannah R.
Charleston
Georgia
Savannah
80° W
Patriot victory
British victory
Undecided battle
Conic Projection
0
100
200 mi
0
100
200 km
30° N
Pensacola
New Orleans
Gulf of Mexico
90° W

Map Skills Although the British won more victories than the Patriots, they were unable to control the colonies.

1. **Locate:** (a) Philadelphia, (b) Saratoga, (c) Yorktown
2. **Movement** Why was there a long break between major battles in the North and major battles in the South?

The Frontier War

Defying the Proclamation of 1763, colonists had begun to settle west of the Appalachian Mountains in the early 1770s. The outbreak of war between the colonists and the British escalated the frequent skirmishes between settlers and Indians, leading the settlers to claim more Native American lands.

Native Americans Support the British The frontier war was especially destructive. Most Indians sided with the British, who had promised to keep the colonists in the East. With British urging, Native Americans increased attacks on colonial settlements in 1777. Meanwhile, white settlers increasingly attacked and killed neutral Native Americans or disregarded truces, beginning a cycle of revenge that continued for years.

The War Moves West In the Northwest, Colonel George Rogers Clark led the Patriot militia in the fight against the British. They took the settlements of Kaskaskia and Cahokia in the spring of 1778. By late summer, Clark's 175 soldiers and their French settler allies had captured all the British posts in the areas that would become Indiana and Illinois.

The British and their Native American allies responded a few months later, recapturing a fort at Vincennes, Indiana. Clark's men—all unpaid volunteers—quickly rallied, marching from their winter quarters on the shores of the Mississippi River. In late February 1779, they reached Vincennes and convinced many Native Americans to abandon their British allies, allowing the Patriots to recover the fort. At war's end, the Patriot outposts allowed Americans to lay claim to the Ohio River valley.

Meanwhile, in upstate New York, Native American and British forces attacked several frontier outposts in 1779. In return, Patriot troops burned 40 Iroquois towns, destroying the power of the Iroquois Federation. But the Indians continued to attack settlers with deadly effect, forcing many of them to return east.

✓ **Checkpoint** Describe the role of Native Americans in the war.

Weapons of the Revolution

Patriots used weapons like the musket below. The mold was used to make musket balls.

SECTION 3 Assessment

Progress Monitoring *Online*
For: Self-test with vocabulary practice
www.pearsonschool.com/ushist

Comprehension

1. **Terms and People** Explain the significance of each of the terms or people listed below.
   - William Howe
   - mercenary
   - Battle of Trenton
   - Battle of Princeton
   - Saratoga
   - Marquis de Lafayette
   - Benjamin Franklin
   - Valley Forge
   - Monmouth
2. **NoteTaking Reading Skill: Summarize** Use your completed chart to help you answer the Section Focus Question: What factors helped the Patriots win the war?

Writing About History

3. **Quick Write: Compare** Make an outline comparing the war in the North with the war on the frontier.

Critical Thinking

4. **Express Problems Clearly** In what ways did the British misunderstand the conflict with the colonies?
5. **Analyze Information** How were the Patriots able to continue fighting, despite losing most of the battles?
6. **Predict Consequences** How important was French assistance to the Patriots' struggle? Explain your answer.

SECTION 4

WITNESS HISTORY

Cornwallis Surrenders

More than 15 years after colonists began protesting new taxes, the Patriots defeated the British army.

"I have the Honor to inform Congress, that a Reduction of the British Army under the Command of Lord Cornwallis, is most happily effected. The unremitting Ardor which actuated every Officer and Soldier in the combined Army on this Occasion, has principally led to this Important Event, at an earlier period than my most sanguine Hopes had induced me to expect."

—George Washington, October 19, 1781

Redcoats surrender at Yorktown ▶

War's End and Lasting Effects

Objectives

- Assess why the British failed to win the war in the South.
- Describe how the British were finally defeated.
- List the terms of the peace treaty.
- Explain how the war and the peace treaty affected minority groups and women.
- Assess the impact of the American Revolution on other countries.

Terms and People

Kings Mountain	Treaty of Paris
Yorktown	manumission

NoteTaking

Reading Skill: Recognize Sequence Use a flowchart to record the events leading up to the Treaty of Paris.

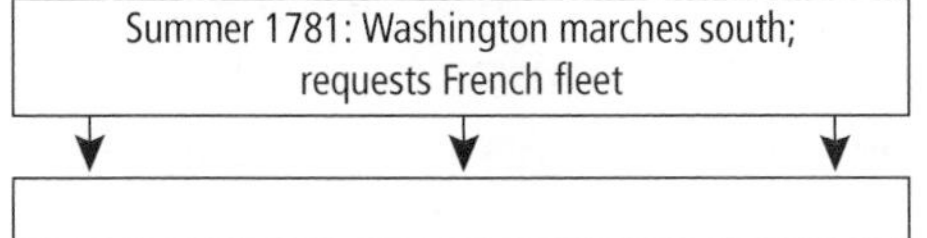

Why It Matters By eighteenth-century standards, the American Revolution was very radical. For the first time, overseas colonies rejected their empire to create a republican union—something long dismissed as a dangerous fantasy. By defying the conventional wisdom of their time, the Patriots began an enormous experiment aimed at creating a more open and equal society. **Section Focus Question: What did the Revolution accomplish, and what ideas did it set in motion?**

The British Invade the South

As the war continued, the British expected Loyalist support in the South, especially among the farmers of North Carolina, South Carolina, and Georgia. But the British wasted this support by continuing their misguided strategy. Instead of supporting Loyalist militias, the British continued to wage a conventional war.

The British Win Early Victories In the South, as in the North, the British won most of the battles and captured the leading seaports. In late 1778, they seized Savannah, Georgia. During the spring of 1780, they captured Charleston, South Carolina—along with 5,000 Patriot soldiers. That summer, the British crushed another Patriot army at Camden, South Carolina.

Just as the British began their offensive in the South, Spanish forces under Bernardo de Gálvez made key attacks on British forts in the Gulf Coast region. In 1780, they captured the British fort at Mobile, Alabama. The next year, they took Pensacola, the capital of British

History Makers

Benjamin Franklin **(1709–1795)**

A printer, author, scientist, and diplomat, Franklin was perhaps the best-known American of his time. He proposed the 1754 Albany Plan of Union and helped to draft the Declaration of Independence. He secured French assistance during the Revolutionary War and negotiated favorable terms for the United States upon war's end. In addition, he was instrumental in creating the new nation's Constitution.

As a scientist, Franklin is famous for his experiments with electricity. But he also invented bifocal glasses, a wood stove that was safer than an open fire, and other items still used today.

West Florida. These moves were intended to solidify Spanish power in North America, but they also diverted British troops from the offensive against the Patriots.

Patriots Drive the British Back Despite winning major battles, the British failed to control the southern countryside, where the Revolution became a brutal civil war between Patriot and Loyalist militias. Both sides plundered and killed civilians. A German officer in the British service observed, "This country is the scene of the most cruel events. Neighbors are on opposite sides, children are against their fathers."

In October 1780, at **Kings Mountain** in South Carolina, the Patriots crushed a Loyalist militia and executed many of the prisoners. As the Loyalists lost men and territory, neutral civilians swung over to the Patriot side. They increasingly blamed the British troops for bringing chaos into their lives. A disgusted Loyalist explained to a British officer, "The lower sort of People, who were . . . originally attached to the British Government, have suffered so severely, [and] been so frequently deceived, that Great Britain has now a hundred enemies, where it had one before." Instead of destroying the Patriots, the British army helped create more of them.

Vocabulary Builder
frustrated–(FRUHS trayt ehd) *adj.* unable to achieve an objective

As the countryside became sympathetic to the Patriots, General Cornwallis became frustrated. The Continental Army in the South was small, but it was led by two superb new commanders, Nathanael Greene and Daniel Morgan. In early 1781, the Continental Army inflicted heavy losses on the British at the battles of Cowpens in South Carolina and Guilford Courthouse in North Carolina. Despairing of winning in the Carolinas, Cornwallis marched north into Virginia. But he was leading his troops directly into a trap.

 **Checkpoint** **Describe the war in the South.**

The War Ends

Although it seemed unlikely at the start, the Patriots ultimately won the war. Four main factors contributed to their success. First, the British made tactical mistakes because they initially underestimated the Patriots. Second, the British misunderstood the political nature of the conflict. Third, the Patriots were highly motivated and benefited from Washington's shrewd leadership. Fourth, the Patriots received critical assistance from France.

Cornwallis Surrenders During the late summer of 1781, Washington boldly and rapidly marched most of his troops south. He planned to trap Cornwallis's army at **Yorktown,** Virginia. For the plan to work, however, Washington needed a French fleet to arrive at the right moment to prevent the British navy from evacuating their army by sea. Although Washington thought that a French fleet was on its way, he could not be certain when it would arrive.

The French fleet appeared at just the right moment to block the mouth of the Chesapeake Bay, trapping the British navy. Given the lack of efficient long-distance communication, this coordination was an incredible stroke of luck for the Patriots. Trapped by land and by sea, Cornwallis surrendered his army of 8,000 at Yorktown on October 19. The French had made the critical difference. At Yorktown, their soldiers and sailors outnumbered Washington's Americans.

The Treaty of Paris The loss of 8,000 soldiers was a crushing blow to the British war effort. After seven years of fighting, the British public was fed up with the casualties and with heavy taxes to pay for the war. In early 1782, a new administration came to power, determined to make peace. An American delegation, including Benjamin Franklin, negotiated a treaty with appealing terms. In 1783, the **Treaty of Paris** recognized American independence and granted generous boundaries to the United States. At the negotiating table, Franklin secured far more territory than the Patriots had won in the war. By making a

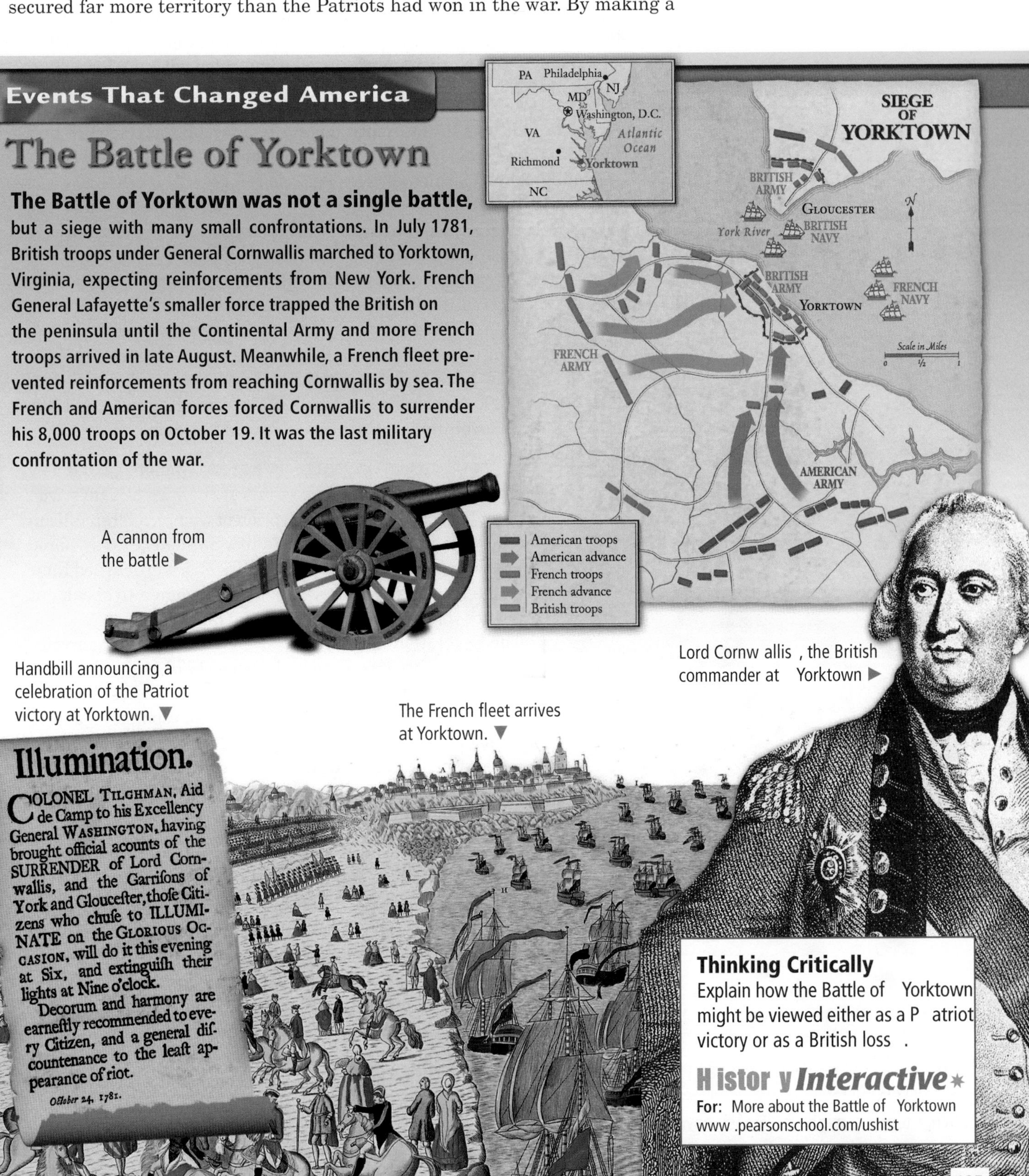

Events That Changed America

The Battle of Yorktown

The Battle of Yorktown was not a single battle, but a siege with many small confrontations. In July 1781, British troops under General Cornwallis marched to Yorktown, Virginia, expecting reinforcements from New York. French General Lafayette's smaller force trapped the British on the peninsula until the Continental Army and more French troops arrived in late August. Meanwhile, a French fleet prevented reinforcements from reaching Cornwallis by sea. The French and American forces forced Cornwallis to surrender his 8,000 troops on October 19. It was the last military confrontation of the war.

A cannon from the battle ▶

Lord Cornwallis, the British commander at Yorktown ▶

Handbill announcing a celebration of the Patriot victory at Yorktown. ▼

Illumination.

COLONEL TILGHMAN, Aid de Camp to his Excellency General WASHINGTON, having brought official acounts of the SURRENDER of Lord Cornwallis, and the Garrisons of York and Gloucester, those Citizens who chuse to ILLUMINATE on the GLORIOUS OCCASION, will do it this evening at Six, and extinguish their lights at Nine o'clock.

Decorum and harmony are earnestly recommended to every Citizen, and a general discountenance to the least appearance of riot.

October 24, 1781.

The French fleet arrives at Yorktown. ▼

Thinking Critically

Explain how the Battle of Yorktown might be viewed either as a Patriot victory or as a British loss.

History Interactive ★

For: More about the Battle of Yorktown
www.pearsonschool.com/ushist

NoteTaking

Reading Skill: Summarize Use a concept web to summarize how the Revolution affected different groups.

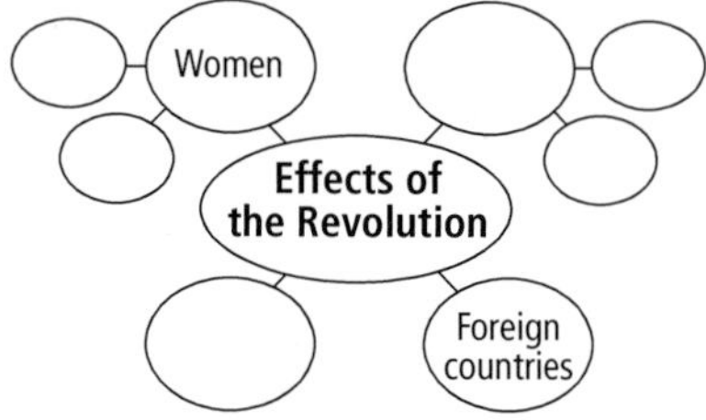

separate peace with the British, the Americans strained their alliance with the French, who had expected to control the negotiations.

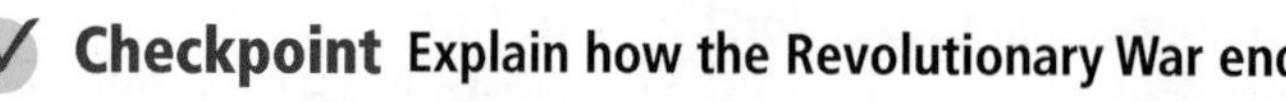

✓ Checkpoint Explain how the Revolutionary War ended.

The Revolution Impacts Society

The Patriots promised liberty and opportunity, but some Americans won more than others. The greatest winners were Patriot men of at least modest prosperity. They secured political rights and the economic benefits of western expansion. The losers were Loyalists and Native Americans who had sided with the British.

The British Abandon Their Allies The British tried to protect their Loyalist allies by setting conditions in the treaty, but state laws and mob violence prevented most Loyalists from returning to their homes after the war. About 90,000—including 20,000 former slaves—became refugees. About half of them resettled in Britain's northern colonies. Many slaves were re-enslaved in the British West Indies. In effect, the American Revolution spawned two new nations: the American Republic and the future Dominion of Canada.

Native Americans were also stunned when the British abandoned them in 1783. The Treaty of Paris ignored the Indians, leaving them vulnerable to expanding American settlements. In treaties at Fort Stanwix in 1784 and Hopewell in 1785, the Patriots forced the Indians to give up massive tracts of land as the price of peace. Settlers surged westward. More than 100,000 Americans lived in Tennessee and Kentucky by 1790. The Revolution was a disaster for the Indians.

Geography Interactive
For: Interactive map
www.pearsonschool.com/ushist

America in 1783

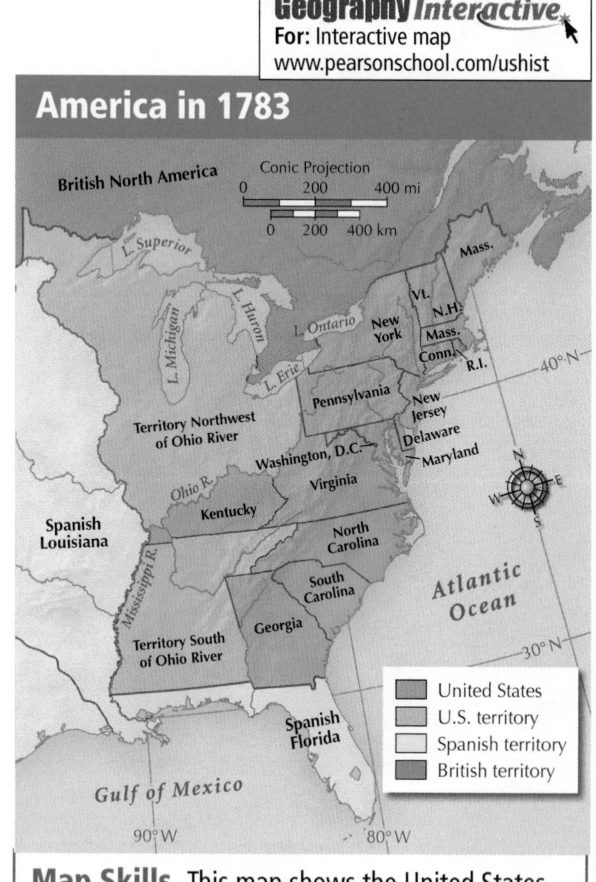

Map Skills This map shows the United States after the Treaty of Paris.

1. Why might the Spanish have been upset about the new borders?
2. What territory might the French have wanted?

The Revolution Impacts Women Women gained few political or legal rights as a result of the war, but they won respect based on the new conception of women as "republican mothers." Abigail Adams and Judith Sargent Murray noted that the Republic needed virtuous citizens, who learned their virtue from their mothers. This invited women to speak out on issues that affected their ability to raise virtuous children.

The Revolution inspired some women to seek a larger voice in public affairs. In a famous letter of 1776, Abigail Adams asked her husband, John, to "remember the Ladies" in drafting the new nation's laws. In particular, she sought legal protection for wives beaten by their husbands. Although John Adams respected his wife, he dismissed her request.

The law reserved legal and political rights to husbands. Widows could vote in New Jersey but nowhere else. As was the norm in most of Europe at the time, wives could not own property or make contracts.

Changes for African Americans Slavery seemed inconsistent with the ideals of the Revolution, but in 1776, one of every five Americans was of African ancestry, and a majority of African Americans were enslaved. Most Americans—including some Patriot leaders—accepted slavery as natural. British and Loyalist critics mocked the Patriots as hypocrites who spoke of liberty while holding slaves. In 1778, the Patriot governor of New Jersey confessed that slavery was "utterly inconsistent with the principles of Christianity and humanity; and in Americans, who have idolized liberty, peculiarly odious and disgraceful."

The Revolution inspired many slaves to demand freedom. In the northern states, some slaves petitioned legislatures for emancipation and sued their owners in the courts. About 5,000 African Americans joined Patriot militias, the Continental Army, or the small Continental Navy in return for a promise of freedom. However, the southern states feared armed blacks as a threat to the slave system, so at least 50,000 southern slaves escaped to join the British.

The Revolution led to emancipation in the North, where slavery was not critical to the economy and slaves numbered only 5 percent of the population. Although laws eventually banned slavery in the northern states, many northern masters sold their slaves to the South before they could become free.

Emancipation failed in the South, where slaves amounted to about one third of the population and were essential to the plantation economy. In Maryland and Virginia, some planters voluntarily freed their slaves, a practice known as **manumission.** After 1800, however, southern states passed laws to discourage further manumissions. Southern whites feared that freed blacks would seek revenge for past treatment as slaves. However, by 1810, about 20,000 southern slaves had been freed, including 300 liberated by George Washington.

This 1779 woodcut shows a female Continental soldier.

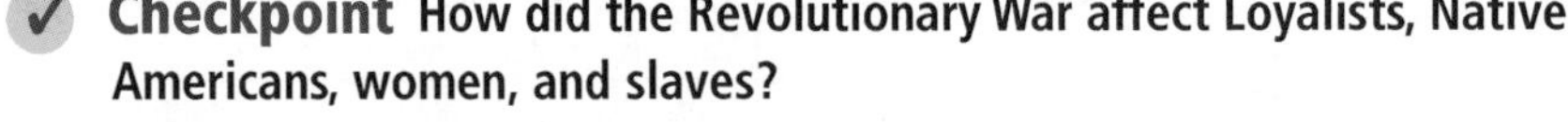
✓ **Checkpoint** **How did the Revolutionary War affect Loyalists, Native Americans, women, and slaves?**

Revolutionary Ideas Spread

Perhaps the greatest effect of the Revolution was to spread the idea of liberty, both at home and abroad. The statement that "all men are created equal" was radical when Jefferson drafted the Declaration of Independence. Although Jefferson probably intended his statement to apply to white men, African Americans and women repeated those words to claim their rights.

Over the next three centuries, the Patriots' principles inspired revolutions around the world. Beginning with the French Revolution in 1789, European republicans cited the American precedent to overthrow kings and aristocrats. In the nineteenth century, independent republics emerged throughout Latin America. During the twentieth century, Africans and Asians began national liberation movements. As Thomas Paine had predicted, the American Revolution changed the world.

✓ **Checkpoint** **How has the Revolution inspired other groups?**

SECTION 4 Assessment

Progress Monitoring *Online*
For: Self-test with vocabulary practice
www.pearsonschool.com/ushist

Comprehension

1. **Terms and People** Explain the significance of each of the terms below.
   - Kings Mountain
   - Yorktown
   - Treaty of Paris
   - manumission
2. **NoteTaking Reading Skill: Summarize** Use your completed flowchart and concept web to answer the Section Focus Question: What did the Revolution accomplish, and what ideas did it set in motion?

Writing About History

3. **Quick Write: Compare and Contrast** Write a short essay comparing and contrasting the results of the Revolution for two of these groups: white Patriot men, women, African Americans, or Loyalists.

Critical Thinking

4. **Identify Central Issues** Why did the British lose the war?
5. **Summarize** Summarize the terms of the Treaty of Paris.
6. **Draw Inferences** Explain the effects of the Revolution on minority groups and women.

CHAPTER 4

Quick Study Guide

Progress Monitoring *Online*
For: Self-test with vocabulary practice
www.pearsonschool.com/ushist

Key British Legislation, 1764–1774

Date	Act	Outcome
1764	Sugar Act	Although it reduced the tax on molasses, the Sugar Act was strictly enforced, so colonists ended up paying more taxes.
1765	Stamp Act	This tax on printed items was the first direct tax on the colonists. It added a fee to printed materials such as legal documents and newspapers.
1765	Quartering Act	Following the French and Indian War, Britain maintained a standing army in the colonies. This act required colonial assemblies to house and provision the soldiers.
1766	Declaratory Act	This act repealed the Stamp Act but asserted Parliament's right to rule the colonies as it saw fit.
1767	Townshend Acts	Import taxes on a variety of goods were collected to support royal officials in the colonies, removing the responsibility from the colonial assemblies. They were so unpopular that all the taxes were repealed, except the one on tea.
1773	Tea Act	This act was created to save the East India Tea Company. Although it lowered the price of tea, it gave the company a monopoly and threatened the business of colonial importers.
1774	Intolerable Acts	Officially called the Coercive Acts, these laws were meant to force Massachusetts to pay for the tea destroyed in the Boston Tea Party. The laws closed Boston Harbor and forced colonists to house British soldiers in their homes.

Major Events of the American Revolution

Date	Major Turning Point
1774	September 5, First Continental Congress meets
1775	April 19, Battles of Lexington and Concord May 10, Second Continental Congress meets June 17, Battle of Bunker Hill
1776	January 9, Paine publishes *Common Sense* July 4, Declaration of Independence
1777	October 17, Patriots win at Saratoga
Winter 1777–1778	Baron Von Steuben trains the Continental Army at Valley Forge, Pennsylvania
1778	February 6, France signs an alliance with the United States
1780	May, General Clinton captures 3,000 Patriot soldiers as he takes Charleston, South Carolina
1781	October 19, Cornwallis surrenders at Yorktown
1783	September 3, Treaty of Paris signed

Quick Study Timeline

In America

1763
Proclamation of 1763 prohibits white settlement west of the Appalachian Mountains

1768
British troops land in Boston

1760 — 1765

Around the World

1763
Seven Years' War ends, giving Britain control of Canada

1768
War breaks out between Russia and the Ottomans

1769
James Watt patents a steam engine

American Issues Connector

By connecting prior knowledge with what you have learned in this chapter, you can gradually build your understanding of enduring questions that still affect America today. Answer the questions below. Then, use your American Issues Connector study guide (or go online: www.pearsonschool.com/ushist).

Issues You Learned About

● **America Goes to War** The American Revolution pitted the world's most powerful empire against a small group of dedicated colonists.

1. Write one or two paragraphs explaining how the Patriots were able to defeat Britain. Consider:
   - the Patriots' strengths
   - Britain's tactical strategy
   - Britain's understanding of the conflict
   - military turning points
   - the involvement of foreign nations

● **Women in American Society** The roles and responsibilities of women in America have changed over time.

2. Why was the support of women crucial to the effort of the Patriots, both before and during the war?
3. How did the idea of "republican motherhood" enhance women's status in society?

● **Global Interdependence** Foreign nations provided valuable assistance to the Patriots fighting the American Revolution.

4. Why did France enter the American Revolution on the side of the Patriots? What aid did France provide?
5. Although Spain entered the war as a French ally, the nation remained fearful of helping the Patriots. Why?
6. What events did the American Revolution inspire in other countries?

Connect to Your World — Activity

New Tax Laws In the 1760s, the British government levied a series of new taxes on the colonists that were intended to make them pay a share of the debts incurred by the Seven Years' War. In the United States today, the federal government has the right to levy taxes on the American public. Americans hold varying ideas about what income, goods, and property should be taxed, as well as the appropriate distribution and level of taxation. Some people feel that citizens are forced to pay too many taxes. Others feel that more taxes should be collected in order to fund important services. Go online or to your local library and conduct research to learn more about recent changes in taxation, such as tax reform or new taxes that were initiated. Then, use your research to write a short report about current taxation in the United States.

1770 The Boston Massacre

1775 George Washington becomes commander in chief of the Continental Army

1776 Congress signs the Declaration of Independence

1781 Cornwallis surrenders at Yorktown

1770 — 1775 — 1780

1770 Explorer James Cook claims Australia for Britain

1776 Adam Smith publishes *The Wealth of Nations*

History Interactive
For: Interactive timeline
www.pearsonschool.com/ushist

Chapter Assessment

Terms and People

1. What were the **Intolerable Acts**? How did colonists in Massachusetts and throughout the colonies respond to them?
2. What was the **Declaration of Independence**? What basic propositions did it make?
3. Define **natural rights.** How did Jefferson use this concept to justify the Declaration of Independence?
4. Who were **William Howe** and **Charles Cornwallis**? Who were their counterparts from the Continental Army?
5. What was the **Treaty of Paris**? What effect did it have on the territory of North America?

Focus Questions

The focus question for this chapter is **What aspects of the American Revolution were revolutionary?** Build an answer to this big question by answering the focus questions for Sections 1 through 4 and the Critical Thinking questions that follow.

Section 1

6. What caused the colonists to rebel against the British?

Section 2

7. What events led the colonists to declare their independence from Britain?

Section 3

8. What factors helped the Patriots win the war?

Section 4

9. What did the Revolution accomplish, and what ideas did it set in motion?

Critical Thinking

10. **Make Comparisons** In what ways were the colonial governments different from the British government?
11. **Recognize Propaganda** Study the illustration of the Boston Massacre earlier in the chapter. Then, answer the questions that follow: Why did Paul Revere create and circulate this engraving? Is it an accurate representation of what took place? Explain.
12. **Synthesize Information** How were the goals of the First and Second Continental Congresses related?
13. **Identify Central Issues** Briefly explain the proposals Thomas Paine put forth in *Common Sense*.
14. **Analyze Information** Why was the Battle of Bunker Hill a technical victory for the British but a real victory for the Patriots?
15. **Analyze Evidence** Think about the progress of the Revolutionary War in the South. How do the events that took place there support the idea held by many colonists that the 13 colonies would fail to unite into one republic?
16. **Determine Relevance** What was the significance of the Battle of Yorktown?
17. **Draw Conclusions** Think about the ideas expressed in the Declaration of Independence. Did the American Revolution succeed at living up to the ideals expressed in this document? Support your answer with information from the text.

Writing About History

Comparing and Contrasting The American Revolution was a complicated event having many players with differing viewpoints and desired outcomes. Native Americans also became involved in the conflict. Write an essay comparing and contrasting the viewpoints of pro-British Indians (such as the Shawnee, Mohawk, Seneca, Delaware, and Ottawa) and pro-Patriot Indians (such as the Oneida and Tuscarora).

Prewriting

- Write down some questions you have about the Indian involvement in the Revolutionary War.
- Use your questions to direct your research about several different Indian nations.
- Narrow your research by choosing two Indian nations on which to focus.

Drafting

- Make an outline that shows the specific points you are going to compare and contrast.
- Develop a working thesis based on the information in your outline.
- Write an introduction that explains what the actions of these Indian nations tell historians about the Revolutionary War. Then, write a body and conclusion.

Revising

- Use the guidelines on page SH22 of the Writing Handbook to revise your essay.

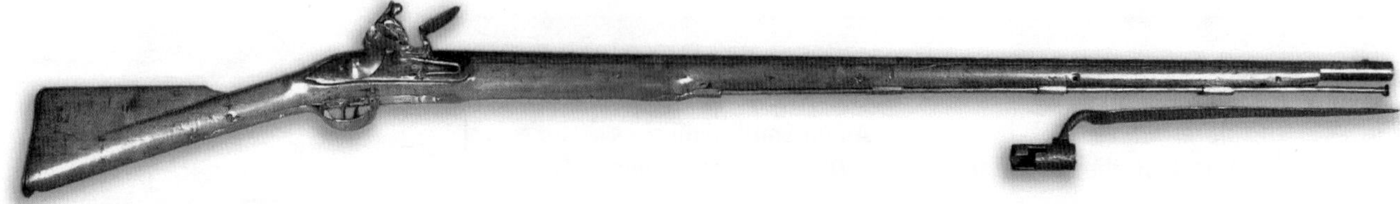

Document-Based Assessment

Slavery and the American Revolution

The American Revolution was fought for the ideals of freedom and liberty. However, thousands of African Americans were enslaved. How did the colonists and enslaved people react to this incongruity, or inconsistency? Use your knowledge of the American Revolution and Documents A, B, C, and D to answer questions 1 through 4.

Document A

I wish most sincerely there was not a slave in the province—it allways appeard a most iniquitous [vicious] scheme to me. fight ourselfs for what we are daily . . . plundering from those who have as good a right freedom as we have—you know my mind upon this subject.

—*Abigail Adams, September 22, 1774*

Document B

[I]n every human Breast, God has implanted a Principle, which we call Love of Freedom; it is impatient of Oppression. . . . I will assert, that the same Principle lives in us. God grant Deliverance [rescue] . . . and get him honour upon all those whose Avarice [greediness] impels them to countenance [allow] . . . Calamities [affliction] of their fellow Creatures. This I desire not for their Hurt, but to convince them of the strange Absurdity of their Conduct whose Words and Actions are so . . . opposite.

—*Phillis Wheatley, a black poet, March 11, 1774*

Document C

[King George] has waged cruel war on human nature itself, violating its most sacred rights of life and liberty in the persons of a distant people who never offended him, captivating and carrying them into slavery in another hemisphere, or to incur miserable death in their transportation thither.

—*from a draft of the* Declaration of Independence

Document D

The petition of A Great Number of Blackes detained in a State of slavery in the bowels of a free & Christian County Humbly sheweth that your Petitioners apprehend that they have in Common with all other men a Natural and Unalienable Right to . . . freedom . . . which they have Never forfeited by any Compact or agreement whatever. . . .

[T]hey therfor[e] humble Beseech your honours to . . . cause an act of the legislature to be pas[sed]Wherby they may be Restored to the Enjoyments of that which is the Natural right of all men—and their Children who wher Born in this Land of Liberty may not be held as Slaves after they arrive at the age of twenty one years so may the Inhabitance of this States No longer chargeable with the inconstancy of acting themselves that part which they condemn and oppose in others Be prospered in their present Glorious struggle for Liberty

—*letter to the Massachusetts House of Representatives, January 13, 1777*

---

1. Who is the writer of Document D?
   A a group of white Patriot men
   B a group of black slaves
   C a group of British soldiers
   D a group of enslaved and free women

2. What assumption is included in Document C?
   A Slavery is the colonists' fault.
   B Slavery is acceptable, but the slave trade is evil.
   C The slave trade is acceptable, but slavery is evil.
   D Slavery is fundamentally wrong.

3. The writer of Document B believes slavery is
   A natural.
   B ordained by God.
   C absurd.
   D honorable.

4. **Writing Task** In what ways do each of these writers agree? Which argument is most convincing? Consider the background of each writer and use your knowledge of the chapter content and specific evidence from the primary sources above to support your opinion.

CHAPTER

5 Creating the Constitution

1781–1789

WITNESS HISTORY

Creating a Government for the New Nation

During the Revolutionary War, the Patriots knew they needed to create a national government to coordinate the colonies' actions. The challenge after the war was to determine the kind of government the new nation needed and how to create it. After much debate, perseverance, and dedication, the United States Constitution became the blueprint for the government we know today. The following quote by statesman and constitutional lawyer Daniel Webster has been quoted by former President Ronald Reagan and other speakers at various celebrations of the Constitution.

> "We may be tossed upon an ocean where we can see no land—nor, perhaps, the sun and stars. But there is a chart and a compass for us to study, to consult, and to obey. The chart is the Constitution."
>
> —Daniel Webster, American statesman

◄ Delegates at the Constitutional Convention as visualized by artist J.H. Froelich, 1935

Ink and quill pen set used by the signers of the Constitution

Surveying compass

Benjamin Franklin ceramic figurine

Chapter Preview

Chapter Focus Question: What led to the creation of the United States Constitution, and what are its key principles?

Section 1
A Confederation of States

Section 2
Drafting the Constitution

Section 3
Ratifying the Constitution

Use the **Quick Study Timeline** at the end of this chapter to preview chapter events.

Note Taking Study Guide *Online*
For: Note Taking and American Issues Connector
www.pearsonschool.com/ushist

SECTION 1

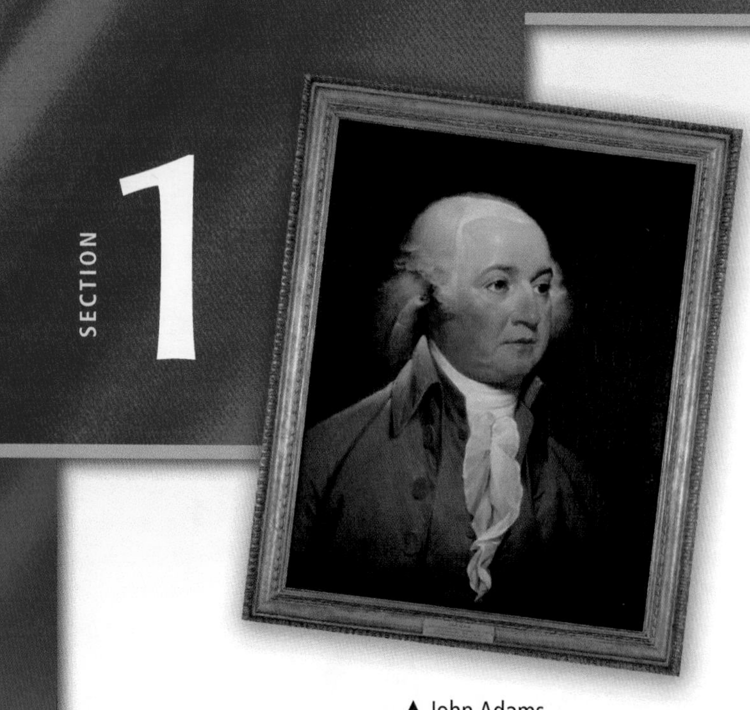
▲ John Adams

WITNESS HISTORY

Creating a Republic

During the American Revolution, each state created its own constitution, or plan of government. But the states also needed some form of government to hold them together, however loosely. In 1777, John Adams wrote to Richard Henry Lee:

> "You and I, dear friend, have been sent into life at a time when the greatest lawgivers of antiquity would have wished to live. How few of the human race have ever enjoyed an opportunity of making election of government . . . for themselves or their children."
>
> —John Adams

A Confederation of States

Objectives

- Explain how the states' new constitutions reflected republican ideals.
- Describe the structure and powers of the national government under the Articles of Confederation.
- Summarize the Congress's plan for the settlement and governance of western lands.
- List the main weaknesses of the Articles.

Terms and People

republic	Northwest Territory
unicameral legislature	Land Ordinance of 1785
bicameral legislature	Northwest Ordinance of 1787
Articles of Confederation	Shays' Rebellion
John Dickinson	
federal	

NoteTaking

Reading Skill: Identify Main Ideas Use a table to list characteristics of early state governments and characteristics of the national government under the Articles of Confederation.

Early State Governments	Early National Government
• All states established republics, in which voters chose representatives. •	• Each state had one vote, regardless of size. •

Why It Matters After the Revolutionary War, the Patriots feared the creation of another tyrannical or abusive government, so they refused to entrust the new Union with much power. As a result, most authority remained with the states. Within a short time, the powerful states and weak national government faced severe problems. **Section Focus Question: What form of national government did the Patriots create initially, and what events revealed that a new government was necessary?**

Early State Governments

Upon declaring independence in 1776, the Congress invited each new state to create a constitution to establish a government. Although these documents varied, they all called for **republics,** or governments in which the people elect their representatives. But the Patriots disagreed over the proper design for those republics. Some Patriots, such as Thomas Paine, sought changes that would promote democracy by putting more power in the hands of the people. But more conservative Patriots distrusted the ability of the common people. They hoped instead to preserve many colonial institutions.

Some States Reject Executive Power The more democratic Patriots wanted to create state governments with strong legislatures and weak governors (or with no governor at all). Seeking greater rights for the people, these leaders preferred a **unicameral legislature,** or one with a single house, whose members were elected by the people. Pennsylvania and Georgia adopted these more democratic constitutions.

Most States Preserve Colonial Traditions Most states, however, including Massachusetts and New York, chose to create more conservative state constitutions. These state governments had a bicameral legislature and a strong governor. A **bicameral legislature** is a lawmaking body with two houses—a Senate and a House of Representatives. These constitutions counterbalanced the power of the common voters in the House with the power of wealthy, well-educated gentlemen in the Senate.

Democratic Gains Even the conservative constitutions, however, dramatically expanded the power of the common people. In contrast to the colonial era, voters chose the members of both houses of the new legislatures, rather than just the members of the lower house. Almost all of the states also enlarged their legislatures. Creating smaller districts and a greater number of representatives made representatives more accountable to their constituents, or voters . In almost all of the states, the voters also elected their governor—something only two colonies had previously done.

Still, democratic and conservative Patriots disagreed about who would vote . The democratic Patriots wanted equal political rights for almost all free men, even those who had little or no property. Pennsylvania's state constitution opened voting to all men over the age of 21 who paid any taxes.

In most of the states, however, the conservatives preserved the colonial property requirements to vote. Adams warned that allowing poor men to vote would "confound and destroy all distinctions, and prostrate all ranks to the common level." Valuing distinctions, he opposed political equality as foolish and unworkable. But even in the conservative states, most free men qualified to vote because owning farms was so widespread. Both theory and practice excluded slaves and women from voting.

Over time, in most states, the most democratic institution—the House of Representatives—gained power at the expense of the Senate and the governor . By the mid-1780s, this concentration of legislative power troubled conservative Patriots who feared the "tyranny of the majority."

Freedom of Religion Because the American Revolution promoted greater religious liberty, most states also guaranteed freedom of religion in their constitutions. Before this time, states collected taxes to support religious establishments. The freedom to choose among several faiths had been controversial. After the Revolution, however, religious liberty and pluralism became the norm. This came about with the passage of the Virginia Statute for Religious Freedom in 1786, drafted by Thomas

Election Day in Philadelphia, 1764

Pennsylvania was the first state to open voting to all men over the age of 21 who paid taxes, as seen in the engraving here where men in Philadelphia are voting. *Why did most states not want to grant poor men the right to vote?*

Jefferson. Massachusetts and Connecticut were exceptions. They kept their Congregational established churches, which continued to draw fire from Baptists and Methodists.

✓ **Checkpoint** **Why did most states choose a bicameral legislature?**

Religious Freedom

The Virginia Statute for Religious Freedom, still part of Virginia's constitution today, embraced the idea of religious liberty without state interference. Children often made needlework samplers (above) that included aspects of religion such as biblical stories or verses. *What was the significance of the Virginia Statute for Religious Freedom?*

Congress Creates the Articles of Confederation

In 1777, the Continental Congress drafted the original constitution for the union of the states, known as the **Articles of Confederation.** A confederation is a league or alliance of states that agree to work together. Under the leadership of **John Dickinson** of Pennsylvania, the Congress designed a loose confederation of 13 states, rather than a strong and centralized nation. The Articles reflected the principles of the Declaration of Independence and rejected the centralized power of the British Empire as a threat to liberty. As Article II reads, "Each state retains its sovereignty, freedom, and independence, and every power, jurisdiction, and right, which is not by this Confederation expressly delegated to the United States, in Congress assembled."

The Structure of the New National Government The new **federal,** or national, government consisted of a congress of delegates, chosen by state legislatures rather than by voters. Although states could choose to send as many as seven delegates, each state—no matter how large or small—had a single vote. Enormous Virginia had no more power than tiny Rhode Island. The powers to make, implement, and enforce the laws were all placed with the Congress. The national government included no President or executive branch. Instead, executive power was spread among several committees of congressmen.

Vocabulary Builder
implement–(IHM pluh mehnt) *v.* to carry into effect

Powers of the National Congress The Articles granted certain limited powers to Congress. These powers were mostly external: to declare and conduct war and to negotiate peace, to regulate foreign affairs and to administer relations with Indian nations. The Congress had no power to raise money through taxes. Therefore, it relied on contributions from the states, which were unreliable.

On some minor issues, a majority of seven states could pass a law. But on the major issues, including declaring war and making treaties, two thirds of the states (nine) had to approve. Amending the Articles was almost impossible because all 13 states had to approve any change. In 1781, all states finally ratified the Articles.

✓ **Checkpoint** **What was the structure of the new government under the Articles of Confederation?**

Congress Creates a Plan for Western Lands

One of the most important accomplishments of the national Congress under the Articles of Confederation was the creation of plans for both settling and governing a vast territory that they had authority over. This territory, called the **Northwest Territory,** lay north of the Ohio River and west of Pennsylvania to the Mississippi River. By selling this land to speculators and farmers, the Congress hoped to raise revenue and extend America's republican society westward.

Distributing Western Lands Western settlement, however, threatened to escape the government's control. By 1784, hundreds of settlers had already crossed the Ohio River to make their own farms. This provoked war with the Native Americans, who defended their land. Already strapped for cash, the federal leaders could not afford to fight wars provoked by unregulated settlement. Congressmen also feared that the settlers would secede from the Union, form their own states, and turn to the British or the Spanish empire for protection. If deprived of thewestern lands, the federal government would be hard-pressed to pay its debts and would probably collapse. To save the Union, the federal leaders needed to regulate frontier settlement.

In ordinances, or laws, adopted in 1785 and 1787, the Congress defined a program for managing the Northwest Territory. In the **Land Ordinance of 1785,** the Congress designed a system for dispensing, or distributing, the public lands. By running a grid of lines north to south and east to west, federal surveyors divided the land into hundreds of townships, each six square miles. They then subdivided each township into 36 "sections" of one square mile (640 acres), to be sold for at least one dollar per acre.

Since ordinary farmers could not afford to pay $640, the price and size of the sections favored wealthy land speculators who had cash. To obtain land, ordinary settlers had to buy it from the speculators. The Congress sometimes broke its own rules to further benefit speculators. For example, in 1787, the Congress sold 1.5 million acres for a mere 10 cents per acre to the Ohio Company, a politically powerful group of land speculators and army officers from New England.

Governing Western Lands The **Northwest Ordinance of 1787** provided a government for the western territory based on Thomas Jefferson's ideas. At first, the Congress would appoint a territorial government led by a governor, secretary, and three judges. The citizens would enjoy freedom of religion, trial by jury, and the rights of common law, including habeas corpus. Once a territory had 5,000 men, they could establish an elected assembly—but the governor retained an absolute veto over its laws. When the population of a territory reached 60,000, the people could request admission to the Union as a state on equal terms with the original 13 states, provided the new state adopted a republican constitution. The Northwest Territory later formed the midwestern states of Ohio, Indiana, Illinois, Michigan, Wisconsin, and part of Minnesota.

The Northwest Ordinance of 1787 also barred slavery from this territory, which meant that the five new states would enter the Union as free states rather than slave states. This federal restriction set a precedent that would

Settling the Northwest Territory

This newspaper clipping spread the word to potential settlers with an early printed version of the Northwest Ordinance. Surveyors used instruments such as the compass shown here to divide land into areas of uniform size *How do you think these ordinances in 1785 and 1787 affected the settlement and development of the territory?*

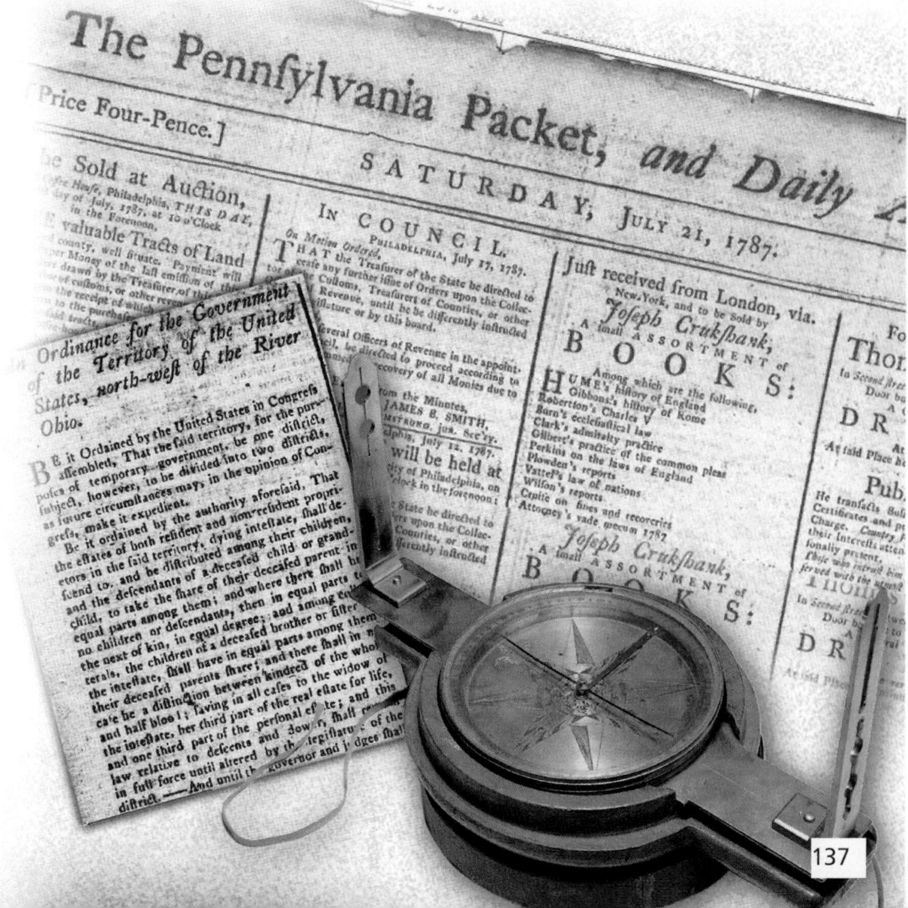

Focus On Geography

Settling the Northwest Territory

With the adoption of the Land Ordinance of 1785, Congress had an official plan for settling the Northwest Territory, a territory that belonged to the United States after the American Revolution. (Previously, individual states claimed the territory.) The plan under the ordinance was to divide public lands into uniform sizes that could be sold at standardized prices. The old system used natural features to mark off parcels of land in varying sizes and shapes.

Under the 1785 ordinance, surveyors first laid out a grid of lines spaced six miles apart, which resulted in a grid of squares. These squares represented individual townships. Then, each township was divided into 36 sections, and these 1-mile-square sections could be divided into smaller units for sale to farmers. The land and income from the sixteenth section of each township provided funding for public education.

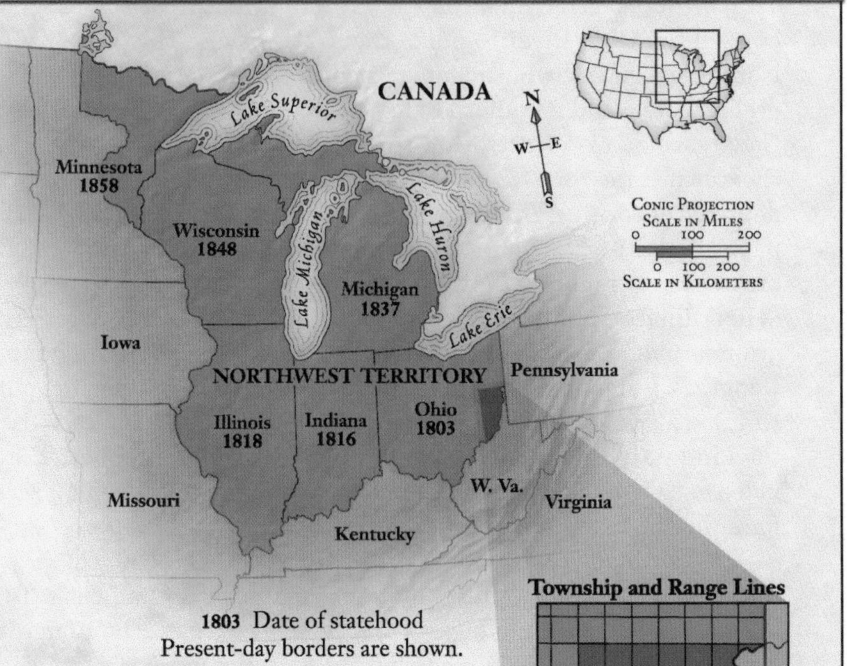

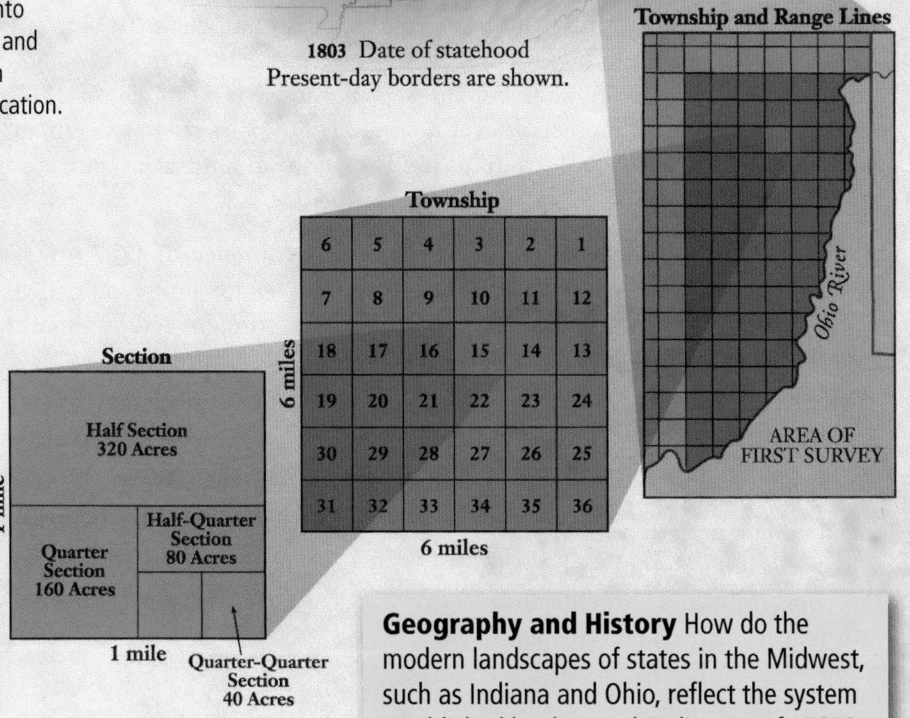

▼ The rectangular grid established in 1785 remains visible in landscapes across the Midwest today.

Geography and History How do the modern landscapes of states in the Midwest, such as Indiana and Ohio, reflect the system established by the Land Ordinance of 1785?

later alarm people in southern states who wanted to expand slavery throughout the territories.

By adopting the Northwest ordinances, the Congress discarded the British model of keeping colonies in permanent subordination. The Congress designed the territories to attract American settlers and to assure their acceptance of federal rule. In the wake of the Revolution, few Americans would settle where they could not enjoy basic freedoms, including the right to elect those who would set their taxes.

But freedom and opportunity for Americans came at the expense of the region's 100,000 Indians, who were expected to give up their lands and relocate elsewhere. During the mid-1780s, however, the Indians resisted, and the federal government lacked the means to defeat them. After the Revolution, Congress lacked money, so the national army was reduced to only 350 men, who could barely defend themselves much less conquer the territory.

✓ **Checkpoint What were the plans for settling and governing the Northwest Territory under the Articles of Confederation?**

Conflicts With Spain and Britain

During the mid-1780s, the Spanish and British did not take the new United States seriously. To them, the republican Confederation seemed weak to the point of anarchy, or lawlessness.

The Spanish Forbid American Trade The Spanish had never liked American independence, and they distrusted American expansion westward because they feared it threatened their colonies of Louisiana and Mexico. To discourage settlements west of the Appalachian Mountains, the Spanish forbade American trade with New Orleans. American settlers expected to ship their produce down the Mississippi River to market in Spanish-held New Orleans. The Congress lost support from western settlers when it almost accepted the closure of New Orleans in return for commercial agreements to benefit northeastern merchants. George Washington observed, "The Western settlers . . . stand, as it were, upon a pivot; the touch of a feather would turn them any way."

Relations With Britain Deteriorate Relations with the British Empire were also strained. In the peace treaty that ended the American Revolution in 1783, the British had tried to cultivate American goodwill. A year later, the British abandoned that policy in favor of making the Americans pay for their independence. Rejecting the new doctrine of free trade championed by Adam Smith, the British renewed their traditional mercantilism as defined by the Navigation Acts.

This meant that Americans could only trade with the British Empire under rules that favored British interests. They could certainly import all the British manufactures that they wanted, but they could no longer freely send their ships to trade with the British West Indies—the most important market for American fish, lumber, and grains. During the 1780s, the British reserved this valuable trade for their ships to benefit their merchants. They alone could carry the American produce needed by West Indian consumers.

This restriction especially hurt Massachusetts, which had more ships than any other state and a greater need for the West Indian market for its fish and lumber. In retaliation, Massachusetts prohibited British ships from transporting its exports. But this retaliation did not work because the other states did not support Massachusetts. In addition, the Congress was too weak to coordinate a common front against

Tensions With Britain

The British retained their hold on forts such as Fort Michilimackinac (the sketch shown below) even after the forts rightfully belonged to the Americans. *What did this reveal about the organization of the United States government?*

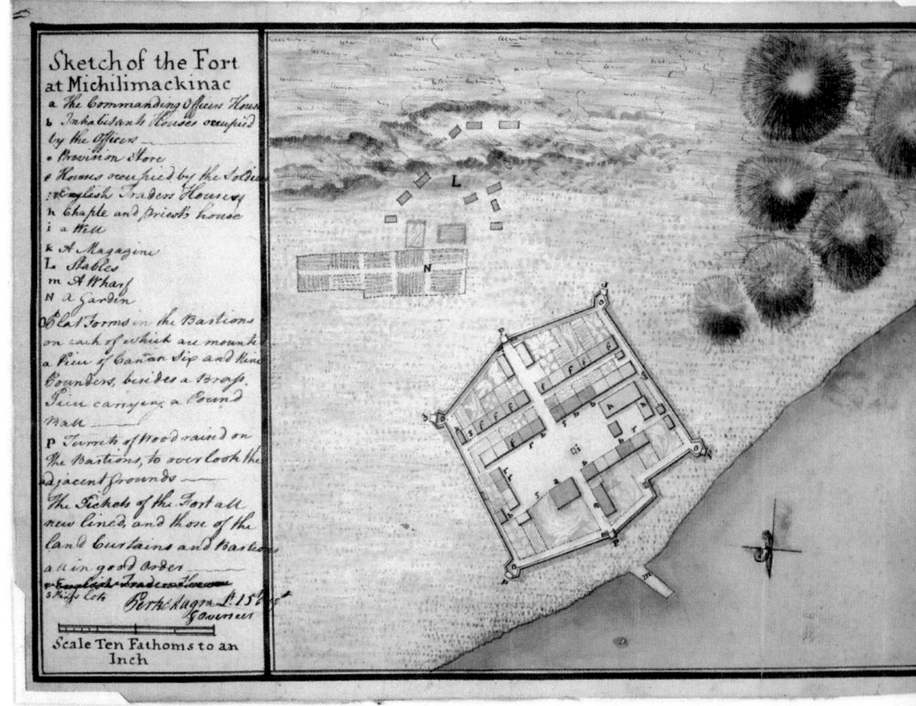

Britain's mercantile policy. American merchants began to call for a stronger national government.

The British Empire also embarrassed the Confederation by keeping frontier forts on the American side of the boundary set by the peace treaty. To please the Indians, the British kept their forts at Niagara, Detroit, and Michilimackinac. For justification, the British cited American violations of the peace treaty. Contrary to the spirit of the treaty, some states had blocked attempts by British merchants to collect debts and attempts by Loyalists to reclaim their confiscated properties. The Congress could not make the states honor the treaty.

The British hold on the forts angered Americans, but they could do nothing because they could not afford an army. Like the merchants, many settlers wanted a national government strong enough to compel British respect on the frontier.

 **Checkpoint What Spanish and British actions showed that they did not take the new American nation seriously?**

Weaknesses of the Articles of Confederation

The fledgling government under the Articles of Confederation found itself facing a host of difficulties. It soon became clear to many that the Articles themselves were part of the problem.

Economic Weaknesses Under the Articles, the federal Congress could not establish a common currency, nor could it regulate interstate commerce or levy taxes. For financial support, the Congress relied solely on contributions from the states, which were unreliable. And the Congress could do nothing to compel states to pay their share. Without money, the federal government could not fund its immense war debts. Between 1781 and 1786, the Congress received only one sixth of what it requested from the states. By 1786, it needed $2.5 million to pay the interest on its debts but had only $400,000 on hand. The states had bankrupted the nation.

To survive, the Congress sought a constitutional amendment to permit a federal 5 percent duty on imported goods. Twice, that amendment failed when a single state balked: Rhode Island in 1782 and New York in 1786. If amending the Articles was so difficult, perhaps only a new constitution could save the Union.

Farmers Revolt in Massachusetts Meanwhile, a slowdown in the trading of goods increased unemployment in the seaports and reduced the prices paid to farmers for their produce. Without the West Indian market for their shipping, Americans could not pay for their imported manufactured goods. Their debts to British suppliers mounted. In 1785, those suppliers curtailed their credit and demanded payments from the American import merchants. These demands sent a shock wave through the weak American economy as the importers sought to collect from their own debtors in the countryside. Most Americans were farmers, and most farmers were in debt. They lacked the cash to pay their debts on short notice, especially when prices fell for their crops. Losing lawsuits for debt, they faced the loss of their crops, livestock, and even their farms to foreclosure.

In western Massachusetts in 1786, farmers took up arms to shut down the courts to block any foreclosure hearings. Farmers did not want to lose their property or go to prison, but they could not pay the higher taxes imposed by the Massachusetts government. One of their leaders was Daniel Shays, a veteran of the Revolutionary War. In 1787, he led about 1,000 farmers to seize

Weaknesses of the Articles of Confederation ☑ Quick Study

- Congress could not levy or collect taxes.
- Congress was powerless to regulate interstate commerce and foreign trade.
- Each state had only one vote in Congress, regardless of its size.
- A two-thirds majority (9 out of 13 states) was required to pass laws.
- Articles could only be amended with the consent of all states.
- No separate executive branch to enforce acts of Congress
- No system of federal courts

weapons from the Springfield Armory and again attempted to shut down the courts. But the elected leaders of Massachusetts insisted that the new Republic could not survive if people violently interfered with the courts. In eastern Massachusetts, the state raised an army, which marched west to suppress what became known as **Shays' Rebellion.**

Most other states avoided rebellion by satisfying their debtors with relief measures. Some states suspended lawsuits for debt until the depression lifted. More common were state laws to flood the money supply with paper money. Paper money made it easier for debtors to pay, while reducing the value that creditors could collect. Naturally, what relieved the debtors infuriated their creditors, who felt cheated.

Creditors blamed the relief measures on excessive democracy. They saw the state governments as too responsive to the opinion of the public, which had wanted debtor relief. James Madison agreed: "Liberty may be endangered by the abuses of liberty as well as [by] the abuses of power." Some thought of abandoning republicanism in favor of an American monarchy. But most hoped to save the Republic by establishing a stronger national government. This stronger government would therefore be capable of controlling the states whenever they threatened commercial property.

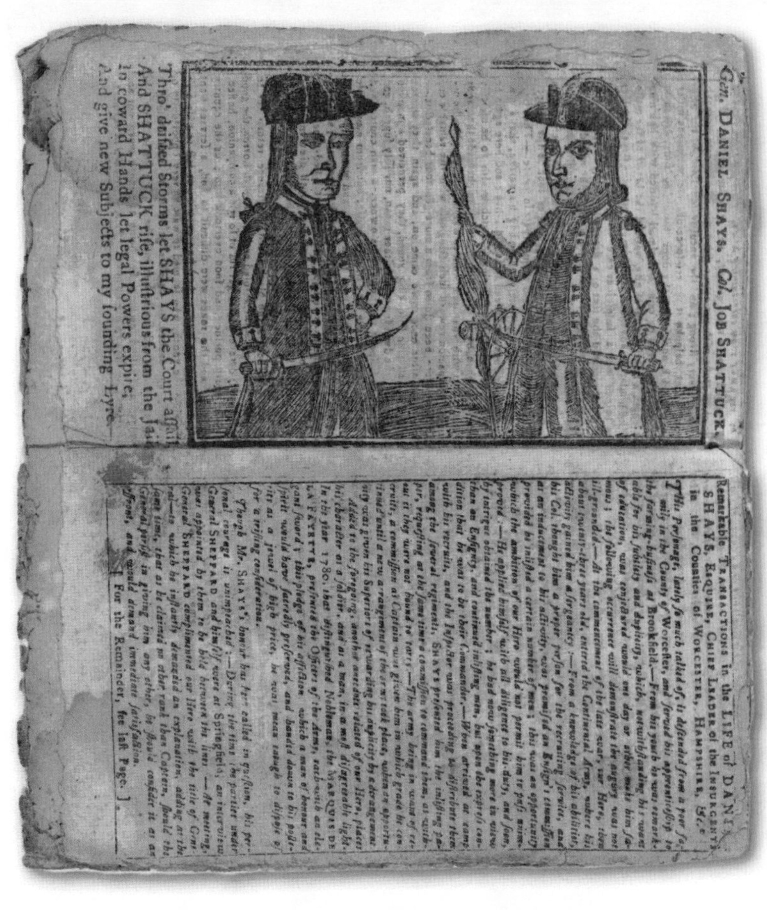

Shays' Rebellion
An engraving made during Shays' march to Springfield, Massachusetts, depicts Shays and another leader of the rebellion, Job Shattuck. *What was the significance of Shays' Rebellion?*

✓ **Checkpoint What events suggested that a stronger national government was necessary?**

SECTION 1 Assessment

Progress Monitoring *Online*
For: Self-test with vocabulary practice
www.pearsonschool.com/ushist

Comprehension

1. **Terms and People** For each entry listed below, write a sentence explaining its significance to the formation of a new national government.
   - John Dickinson
   - Northwest Territory
   - Land Ordinance of 1785
   - Northwest Ordinance of 1787
   - Shays' Rebellion
2. **NoteTaking Reading Skill: Identify Main Ideas** Use your completed table to answer the Section Focus Question: What form of national government did the Patriots create initially, and what events revealed that a new government was necessary?

Writing About History

3. **Quick Write: Combine Visuals to Synthesize** Based on the images in this section and the chart listing the weaknesses of the Articles, write a brief newspaper article summarizing the events that led many people to believe the nation needed a stronger national government.

Critical Thinking

4. **Make Comparisons** What were the similarities and differences among early state governments?
5. **Synthesize Information** In what ways was the early government under the Articles of Confederation tested?
6. **Identify Central Issues** What would you consider the greatest weakness of the Articles of Confederation? Explain.

◀ James Madison

▲ Inkstand and quill pen

WITNESS HISTORY

The Father of the Constitution

James Madison, often referred to as the Father of the Constitution, took detailed notes at the Constitutional Convention. After his death, his notes were published as *The Debates in the Federal Convention of 1787.* In the Preface, Madison describes the pressure on the delegates:

> "At the date of the Convention, the aspect & retrospect of the pol[itical] condition of the U.S. could not but fill the pub[lic] mind with a gloom which was relieved only by a hope that so select a Body would devise an adequate remedy for the existing and prospective evils so impressively demanding it."
>
> —James Madison, Preface to *The Debates in the Federal Convention of 1787*

Drafting the Constitution

Objectives

- Understand the reasons leaders called for the Constitutional Convention.
- Summarize the rival plans of government proposed at the convention.
- Describe the compromises made in order to reach agreement on the Constitution.

Terms and People

Alexander Hamilton
James Madison
Virginia Plan
New Jersey Plan
Great Compromise
federalism
Three-Fifths Compromise

NoteTaking

Reading Skill: Identify Supporting Details In a concept web like the one below, write details about each plan or compromise that led to the creation of the United States Constitution.

Why It Matters After Shays' Rebellion, many Americans agreed that they needed a stronger federal government to preserve the Union. The Congress called for a convention to meet in Philadelphia in 1787 "for the sole and express purpose of revising the Articles of Confederation." Instead of revising the Articles of Confederation, however, the delegates created an entirely new constitution that replaced the confederation of the national Union. **Section Focus Question: What new system of national government did the delegates agree upon at the Constitutional Convention of 1787?**

The Constitutional Convention

By 1787, most Americans agreed that the Articles of Confederation were flawed and needed at least two major changes. First, almost everyone wanted Congress to have the power to regulate interstate and international commerce. Second, most Americans also supported granting Congress the power to tax the people. To draft proposed amendments to the Articles, 12 of the 13 states sent delegates to a special convention in Philadelphia in May 1787. (Rhode Island declined to participate.) Once done, the delegates were supposed to submit the proposed amendments to ratification by the 13 state legislatures.

The convention, then known as the Federal Convention, was slated to begin on May 14. However, only the delegates from Pennsylvania and Virginia made it there on time. More than a week would pass before there were enough delegates to begin the convention.

The Convention Begins The Federal Convention opened in the Pennsylvania State House, now known as Independence Hall, on May 25, when 29 delegates had finally arrived. Other delegates continued to arrive during the subsequent weeks and months. The proceedings of the convention were shrouded in secrecy so the delegates could speak freely. Because of this, the windows of the hall were often closed for privacy. It was an especially hot summer in 1787 so the delegates were frequently uncomfortable in their closed-off space.

Vocabulary Builder
subsequent–(SUHB sih kwehnt) *adj.* following; coming after

Although Thomas Jefferson and John Adams were away in Europe serving as diplomats, the convention included most of the other leading statesmen of the day. Several leaders emerged, including Alexander Hamilton of New York and James Madison of Virginia. The eldest delegate was Benjamin Franklin of Pennsylvania, who added great prestige to the proceedings. Other leaders in attendance were Roger Sherman, Gouverneur Morris, James Wilson, Elbridge Gerry, William Paterson, John Dickinson, Charles Pinckney, Edmund Randolph, and George Mason. These delegates were not typical Americans. They were all white males, many were wealthy, and more than half of them were lawyers. Many of the delegates had helped to write their state constitutions, and seven had been state governors. Twenty-one had fought in the American Revolution, and eight had signed the Declaration of Independence. After reading the names of those in attendance, Jefferson remarked that it was "an assembly of demi-gods." The delegates unanimously elected George Washington as the president of the convention.

Hamilton and Madison The convention's leading thinkers were Alexander Hamilton and James Madison. Bold in action, **Alexander Hamilton** was very conservative in principles. Disliking democracy, he praised the British constitution, including its king and House of Lords, as "the best model the world has ever produced." He insisted that a balanced government should have elements of aristocracy and monarchy as well as of republicanism. Hamilton believed that such a government would have real power to command its citizens and impress foreign empires. Gouverneur Morris of Pennsylvania also advocated a strong central government at the Convention. Morris thought the President should hold office for life.

James Madison showed his eagerness to participate in the convention by arriving in Philadelphia 11 days early. He had also sent a letter to George Washington in April outlining his thoughts about what should be debated at the convention. Madison had concluded that only a strong nation could rescue the states from their own democratic excesses. Although a critic of democracy, Madison favored republicanism rather than a constitution modeled after the British system. His challenge was to design a government that was both strong and republican. Rejecting the old notion that a republic needed to be small and homogeneous, he insisted that a large republic with diverse interests would best preserve the common good. He reasoned that the numerous

The Pennsylvania State House
Today, visitors can tour Independence Hall in Philadelphia, where the delegates met in 1787.

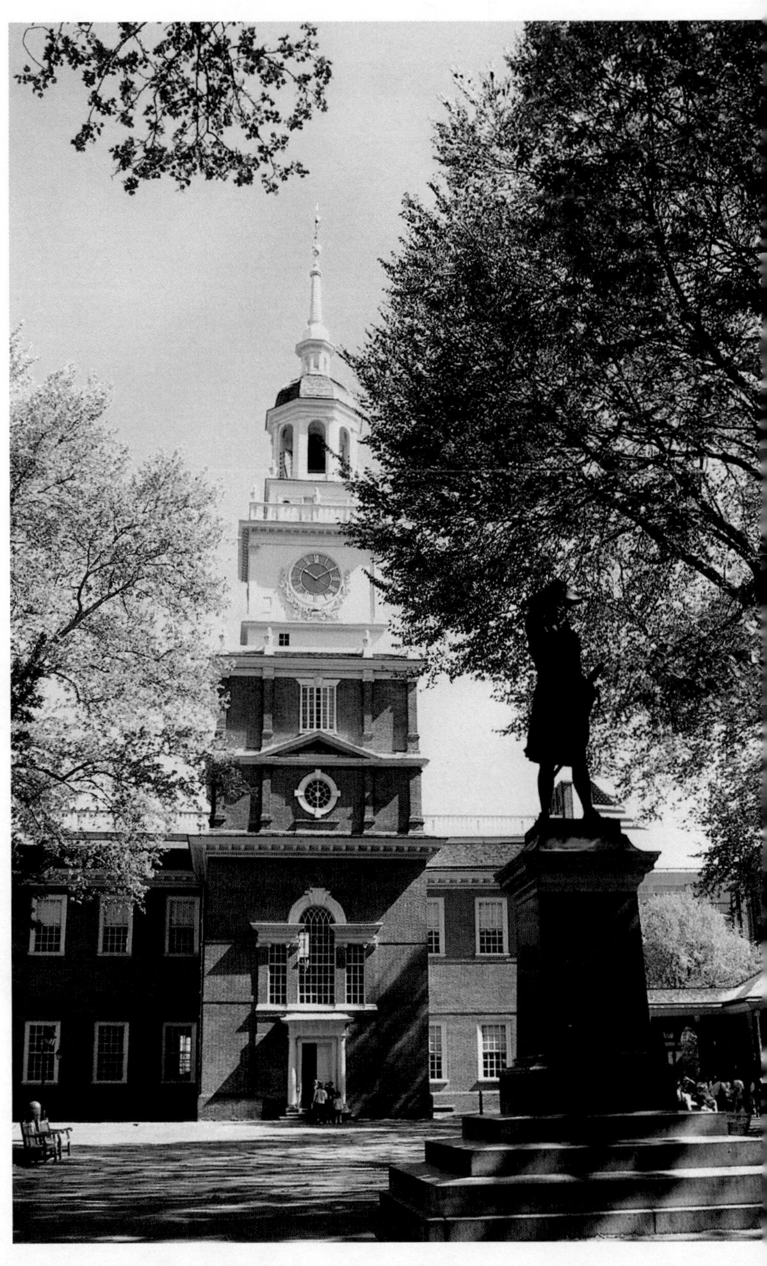

interests would "check" one another. Madison hoped that the nation's most learned men, rather than the many local political leaders he saw in the state legislatures, would govern the new national Republic. In addition to providing the basic blueprint for the Constitution, Madison kept the notes that are the best record of the convention.

✓ **Checkpoint What were some of the characteristics of the delegates to the Constitutional Convention?**

Rival Plans of Government

Before a constitution could be written and approved, the delegates needed to come to an agreement about what it should contain. To achieve this goal, they advanced and debated a number of proposals for several months.

The Virginia Plan Most of the delegates preferred an ambitious scheme proposed by Madison called the **Virginia Plan.** In addition to securing the power to

INFOGRAPHIC

Meet the Framers

Who wer e the men who attended the Constitutional Convention during the steaming summer of 1787? They were some of the most famous and important men in America. Accor ding to one historian, the delegates were the "well-bred, well-fed, well-wed, and well-read." In all, there wer e 55 who attended these secret proceedings, though they were never there all at once. The four illustrated here were among the most influential.

Alexander Hamilton
Hamilton was born on an island in the British West Indies. His thirst for education brought him to New York for schooling three years before the American Revolution. Not long after arriving in the United States, he picked up the Patriots' cause and served as a colonel during the Revolution on George Washington's staff. He and Washington developed a lifelong alliance. Hamilton was confident and was considered more ambitious than all the other delegates at the convention. He argued strongly for a powerful central government.

Benjamin Franklin
There was not much that Franklin had not crossed off his list by the time he arrived at the convention. He had started a newspaper, published a colonial bestseller, started a volunteer fire department, and was also a philosopher, scientist, inventor, and diplomat. Eighty-one years old at the time of the convention, Franklin was in poor health but nonetheless contributed his prestige, common sense, and wit to the proceedings. When the convention ended after four months of secrecy, a woman asked him what the delegates had produced. His reply? "A republic, if you can keep it."

tax and to regulate commerce, Madison proposed creating a government that divided power among three branches—the legislative, executive, and judicial branches. The plan proposed a bicameral legislature with a House of Representatives and a Senate. In both houses, the states with larger populations would have more members. Madison's plan also included a daring feature—the national Congress would have the power to veto any state law, just as Parliament had done with colonial laws.

The Virginia Plan also called for a strong President. The President would enjoy a relatively long term in office of seven years but could not be elected a second time. The President would command the armed forces and manage foreign relations. He would appoint all executive and judicial officers, subject only to approval by the Senate. A critic of the plan, Patrick Henry, worried that such a powerful President could "easily become a king."

The New Jersey Plan Some delegates advocated only modest changes to the Articles of Confederation. Favored by the small states, their proposal, introduced by William Paterson of New Jersey, became known as the **New Jersey Plan.** This

◄ *The Foundation of American Government,* by Henry Hintermeister, depicts the delegates signing the U.S. Constitution

George Washington
The leader of the Continental Army during the American Revolution, Washington was truly a national hero. When he arrived in Philadelphia May 13 for the convention, the city suddenly came to life. Although heat, humidity, black flies, and rain had kept most residents locked inside for several weeks, a crowd of people formed outside to cheer Washington's arrival. Chosen as the presiding officer at the convention, Washington never missed a session or arrived late.

James Madison
Madison was 36 years old when he arrived at the convention. Shy and scholarly, he chose a seat up front and did not miss a single day. Despite the fact that Madison stood to speak over 100 times at the convention, his voice was so feeble that oftentimes, many could not hear him. Of all the delegates, Madison was the most prepared, arriving with an idea for a plan of government that he had previously outlined in letters to Thomas Jefferson and George Washington.

Thinking Critically

Draw Conclusions How do you think the experiences and backgrounds of the Framers influenced the way the Constitution was shaped? Do you think a more diverse group would have written a different document altogether? Explain.

History *Interactive*

For: Interactive Constitutional Convention
www.pearsonschool.com/ushist

plan gave Congress the powers to regulate commerce and to tax, but it kept the three chief principles of the Articles of Confederation. First, it retained a unicameral legislature representing the states as equals, no matter how large or small. Second, it preserved an executive committee rather than adopting a singular President. Third, the states remained sovereign except for those few powers specifically granted to the national government. Under the New Jersey Plan, the United States would remain a loose confederation.

✓ **Checkpoint** **What were the differences between the Virginia and New Jersey plans?**

Settling Differences Through Compromise

Something had to be done in order to prevent the convention from ending in a stalemate. The delegates were far from a unanimous decision concerning the structure of the new government, and without the compromises laid out below, they may never have reached an agreement.

The Great Compromise Led by Roger Sherman of Connecticut, the delegates reached a compromise between the Virginia and the New Jersey plans, known as the Connecticut Compromise, or the **Great Compromise.** John Dickinson

Diagram Skill The Great Compromise, calling for representation based on a state's population in the House and equal representation in the Senate, was critical to resolving the debate between the small states and the large states. As the diagram shows, the Constitution reflects characteristics of each plan because of the Great Compromise. *What was the main concern of the small states before a compromise was reached?*

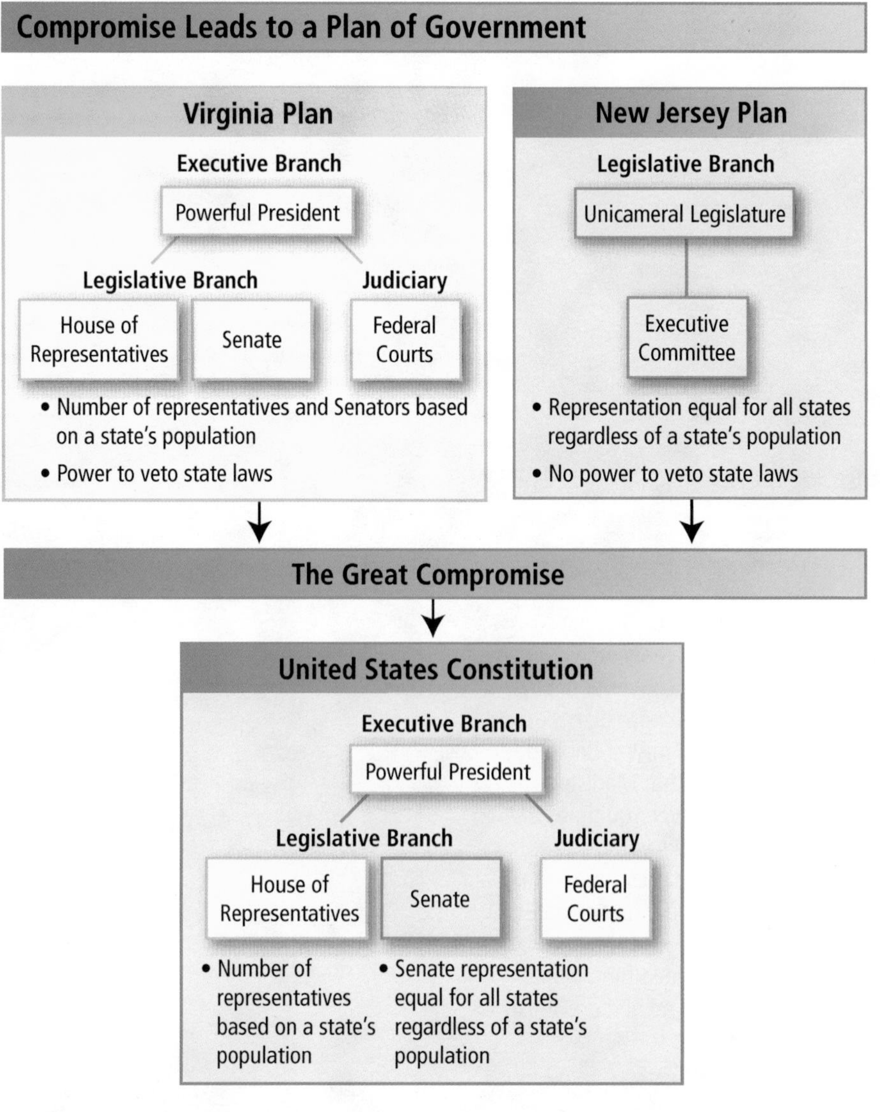

of Delaware played a key role in creating this compromise, which made a concession to the small states: The Senate would equally represent every state, regardless of size, by allowing two senators per state. In keeping with the Virginia Plan, the House of Representatives would represent population, granting more power to the larger states.

Federal Power and States' Rights In another concession, Madison abandoned his cherished national veto over state laws. Instead, the compromise simply forbade the states from enacting the sorts of laws that offended many during the 1780s. For instance, the states could no longer issue their own money or provide debtor relief at creditors' expense. By compromising between the Virginia Plan and the New Jersey Plan, the delegates supported a system known as **federalism** that divided government power between the federal government and state governments.

Slavery and the Three-Fifths Compromise During the debates over the Constitution, the delegates discovered that their greatest division pitted the southern against the northern delegates. The southerners feared future domination by the northern states, which had more free people. They worried that northern domination would threaten the slave system, which they viewed as essential to the southern economy and society. The delegates from South Carolina and Georgia threatened to walk out unless the Constitution protected the institution of slavery.

The subject tore at Madison. On the one hand, he wanted a powerful nation, and he despised slavery as "the most oppressive dominion ever exercised by man over man." On the other hand, he owned slaves, and he knew that southern

Decision Point

Should the states ratify the Constitution?

Delegates at the Constitutional Convention in 1787 debated the pros and cons of the new Constitution. In order for the Constitution to become law, at least 9 of the 13 states had to ratify the document. Read the options below. Then, you decide.

Patrick Henry Opposes Ratifying the Constitution

Primary Source

"I review . . . the subject . . . and . . . the dangers . . . in this new plan of government, and compare . . . my poor abilities to secure our rights, it will take much more time to traverse the objectionable parts of it. . . . [T]he change is dangerous . . . and the experiment ought not be made. . . ."

—Patrick Henry, June 9, 1788

Alexander Hamilton Favors Ratifying the Constitution

Primary Source

"The establishment of a Constitution, by the voluntary consent of a whole people, is a prodigy, to the completion of which I look forward. . . . I dread . . . the consequences of new attempts, because I know that powerful individuals, in this and other states, are enemies to a general national government in every possible shape."

—Alexander Hamilton, *The Federalist Papers*

You Decide

1. Why did Henry oppose ratifying the Constitution?
2. Why did Hamilton favor ratifying the Constitution?
3. What decision would you have made? Why?

voters would reject a constitution that threatened slavery. So he assured his constituents in Virginia that the Constitution offered slavery "better security than any that now exists."

That security took three forms. First, the Constitution forbade Congress from blocking the importation of slaves for twenty years. Georgia and South Carolina would import another 100,000 slaves by 1808. Second, a compromise known as the **Three-Fifths Compromise** counted each slave as three fifths of a person to be added to a state's free population in allocating representatives to the House of Representatives and electoral college votes. The three-fifths clause gave the southern states more seats in Congress and more power in presidential elections than they would have enjoyed had only free people been counted—as the northern delegates preferred. Third, the Constitution committed all states to return fugitive slaves to their owners. In other words, running away to a free state did not free a slave. Northerners were required to help enforce the slave system as the price of union.

Most state constitutions had adopted bills of rights to protect civil liberties from the power of government. But the federal delegates declined to include a bill of rights in their constitution. A South Carolina delegate, Charles C. Pinckney, explained, "such bills generally begin with declaring that all men are by nature born free." Such a declaration would come "with a very bad grace when a large part of our property consists in men who are actually born slaves." Unlike the Declaration of Independence, the Constitution did not proclaim that all men were born free and equal in their rights.

On September 17, the Constitutional Convention concluded with 42 delegates still present. Many, including Madison, disliked the compromises, but Franklin appealed to all to unite in support of the "federal experiment." Hamilton reluctantly accepted the Constitution as the only alternative to "anarchy and Convulsion." In the end, 39 delegates signed the document, while three refused to sign out of protest. George Mason and Edmund Randolph of Virginia and Elbridge Gerry of Massachusetts considered the document to be flawed. Next came the greater challenge of winning approval from the states.

Checkpoint **What was the significance of the Three-Fifths Compromise?**

SECTION 2 Assessment

Progress Monitoring *Online*
For: Self-test with vocabulary practice
www.pearsonschool.com/ushist

Comprehension

1. **Terms and People** For each entry listed below, write a sentence explaining its significance to the new Constitution.
   - Alexander Hamilton
   - James Madison
   - Virginia Plan
   - New Jersey Plan
   - Great Compromise
   - Three-Fifths Compromise

2. **NoteTaking Reading Skill: Identify Supporting Details** Use your completed concept web to answer the Section Focus Question: What new system of national government did the delegates agree upon at the Constitutional Convention of 1787?

Writing About History

3. **Quick Write: Combine Quotes and Visuals** Based on the quote by Madison and the images of the delegates in this section, what can you conclude about the characters of the delegates? Write one or two paragraphs with your conclusion.

Critical Thinking

4. **Determine Relevance** Why did leaders call for the Constitutional Convention?
5. **Identify Alternatives** In addition to the two proposed frameworks for a new constitution, what other plan might the delegates have considered?
6. **Compare Points of View** How did the Great Compromise satisfy both the small and the large states?

Primary Source

John Locke: *Two Treatises of Government*

The Framers of the Constitution relied upon the writings of Enlightenment philosophers Baron de Montesquieu, Jean Jacques Rousseau, and John Locke. English philosopher John Locke (1632–1704) published *Two Treatises of Government* in 1690. Locke believed that all people had the same natural rights of life, liberty, and property. In this essay, he states that the primary purpose of government is to protect these natural rights. He also states that governments hold their power only with the consent of the people.

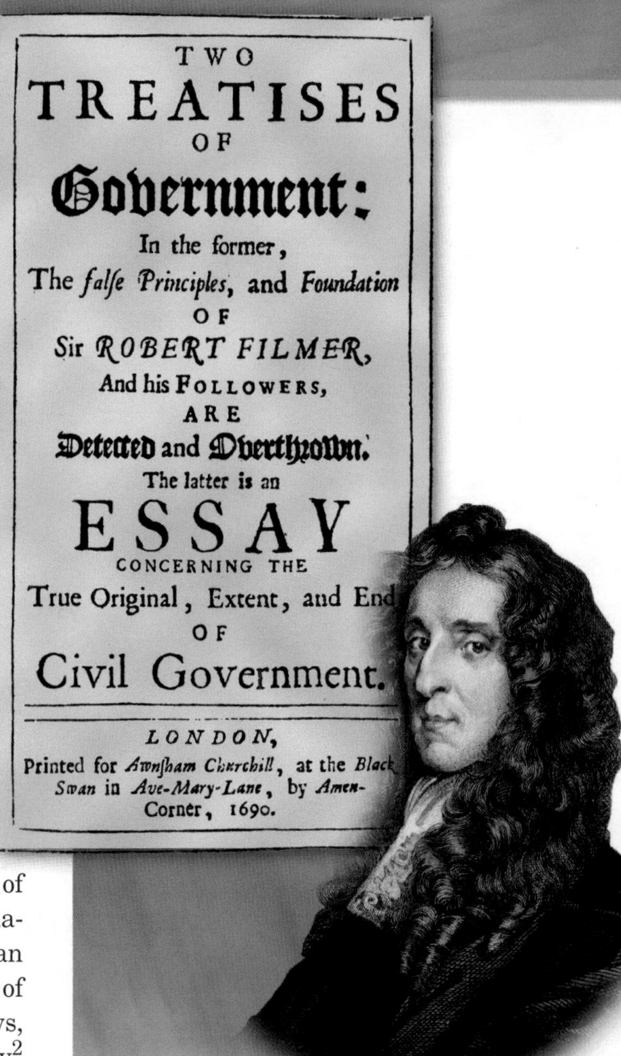
TWO TREATISES OF Government: In the former, The false Principles, and Foundation OF Sir ROBERT FILMER, And his FOLLOWERS, ARE Detected and Overthrown. The latter is an ESSAY CONCERNING THE True Original, Extent, and End OF Civil Government. LONDON, Printed for Awnsham Churchill, at the Black Swan in Ave-Mary-Lane, by Amen-Corner, 1690.

▲ John Locke and the title page of *Two Treatises of Government*

But though men, when they enter into society, give up the equality, liberty, and executive power they had in the state of nature, into the hands of society . . . the power of the society, or legislative constituted by them, can never be supposed to extend farther than the common good. . . . Whoever has the legislative or supreme power of any commonwealth, is bound to govern by established standing laws, promulgated[1] and known to the people, and not by extemporary[2] decrees, by indifferent and upright judges, who are to decide controversies by those laws; and to employ the force of the community at home only in the execution of such laws, or abroad to prevent or redress foreign injuries, and secure the community from inroads[3] and invasion. And all this to be directed to no other end but the peace, safety, and public good of the people. . . .

The reason why men enter into society, is the preservation of their property; and the end while they chuse [choose] and authorize a legislative, is, that there may be laws made, and rules set, as guards and fences to the properties of all the members of the society. . . .

Whensoever therefore the legislative [power] shall transgress[4] this fundamental rule of society; and either by ambition, fear, folly or corruption, endeavour to grasp themselves, or put into the hands of any other, an absolute power over the lives, liberties, and estates of the people; by this breach of trust they forfeit the power the people had put into their hands for quite contrary ends, and it devolves[5] to the people; who have a right to resume their original liberty, and, by the establishment of a new legislative, (such as they shall think fit) provide for their own safety and security. . . .

1. **promulgated** (PRAHM uhl gayt ihd) *v.* published or made known.
2. **extemporary** (ehk STEHM puh rer ee) *adj.* without any preparation.
3. **inroads** (IHN rohdz) *n.* advances at the expense of someone.
4. **transgress** (trans GREHS) *v.* to go beyond; break.
5. **devolves** (dih VAHLVZ) *v.* passes.

Thinking Critically

1. **Draw Inferences** According to Locke, how should a society be governed? Why do you think he felt this way?
2. **Identify Central Issues** What does Locke say can happen if a government fails to protect the rights of its people?

SECTION 3

◄ Benjamin Franklin and the U.S. Constitution

WITNESS HISTORY

A Hopeful Future

After the hard work was completed at the Constitutional Convention, the delegates set out to win the approval of the states for the document they had created. With amendments, that document—the United States Constitution—has now endured for more than 200 years. At the time, however, the system of government established by the document was in no way secure. Benjamin Franklin wryly observed:

"Our Constitution is in actual operation; everything appears to promise that it will last; but in this world nothing is certain but death and taxes."

—Benjamin Franklin, 1789

Ratifying the Constitution

Objectives

- Summarize the arguments for and against ratification of the Constitution.
- Describe how the Constitution was ratified.
- Explain the principles of the Constitution.

Terms and People

ratification
Federalist
Antifederalist
The Federalist
John Jay
Bill of Rights
popular sovereignty
limited government
separation of powers
checks and balances
electoral college

NoteTaking

Reading Skill: Identify Main Ideas Use a table to record the arguments for and against ratification of the Constitution.

Ratification of the Constitution	
Arguments For	Arguments Against
• A strong central government would be able to handle the problems that faced the nation. • •	• A strong central government would undermine basic liberties. • •

Why It Matters The delegates to the Constitutional Convention had designed a strong federal government. As you learned, all but three delegates endorsed the new Constitution, despite the fact that many felt it was imperfect. After most of the delegates signed it, the proposed Constitution was printed, circulated, and hotly debated. The question remained whether the states would accept the proposed plan. If they did not, what would become of the new nation? **Section Focus Question: How did Americans ratify the Constitution, and what are its basic principles?**

The Struggle Over Ratification

By drafting a new Constitution, the delegates had exceeded their mandate. They were only supposed to propose amendments to the Articles of Confederation. Official approval, or **ratification,** of an entirely new constitution was doomed if all 13 states had to approve it as the Articles required. To improve the odds of ratification, the delegates arbitrarily decided to change the rules. They determined that approval by nine states would suffice. They also took the ratification decision away from the state legislatures, for they would most certainly oppose a new constitution that would deprive them of some power. Instead, the delegates ruled that specially elected conventions would determine a state's choice for or against the Constitution. Two groups soon emerged in the debate: the Federalists, who favored ratification, and the Antifederalists, who opposed it.

Federalists Favor Strong Government Those who favored ratification of the Constitution were known as **Federalists.** The group included George Washington, James Madison, and Alexander Hamilton. The Federalists stressed the weaknesses of the Articles. They argued that only a new government based on the proposed Constitution could overcome the difficulties facing the new nation.

Antifederalists Fear a Strong Government Critics of the Constitution, known as **Antifederalists,** denounced it as a retreat from the liberty won by the Revolution. The Antifederalists especially disliked the lack of a bill of rights that would provide basic liberties, protecting the people from the powers of the government. They noted that the Constitution greatly increased the powers of the central government and provided a more elitist government by concentrating power in relatively few hands at a great distance from most voters. The Antifederalists believed that liberty could not survive unless the federal government remained weak, which meant that most power would belong to the democratic state governments. One Antifederalist asked:

> **Primary Source** "What have you been contending for these ten years past? Liberty! What is Liberty? The power of governing yourselves. If you adopt this Constitution, have you this power? No: you give it into the hands of a set of men who live one thousand miles distant from you."
>
> —James Lincoln, South Carolina delegate

The Antifederalists included such leading Patriots as Samuel Adams and John Hancock of Massachusetts, George Clinton of New York, and Richard Henry Lee and Patrick Henry of Virginia. Successful state politicians, they distrusted the Federalist effort to subordinate the states to a stronger national Union.

The Federalists Gain Support Most farmers recognized that the Constitution threatened the state debtor-relief laws that had rescued their farms from foreclosure. Common farmers also distrusted the lawyers, merchants, and other wealthy men who promoted the Constitution, viewing them as aristocrats hostile to the Republic. In South Carolina, farmers protested by staging a mock funeral around a coffin with the word *Liberty* painted on the side. Because most citizens were farmers, the proposed Constitution lacked majority support in 1787.

However, the Constitution had the support of two of the most popular and trusted men in America—George Washington and Benjamin Franklin. Their support allayed the fears of many rural Americans. Some frontier farmers also endorsed the Constitution because they hoped that a stronger nation would defeat the Native Americans and take control of the British forts along the Great Lakes.

The Federalists also enjoyed popular support in key places—the seaports—which hosted most of the ratifying conventions. Unlike the common farmers, most urban artisans supported the Constitution. Hurt by the depression of the 1780s, the artisans hoped that a strong national government could expand American commerce. The seaports also had most of the nation's newspapers, the printers of which strongly endorsed the Constitution.

The Federalists were also better organized than the Antifederalists. Acting quickly after the Constitutional Convention, the Federalists built a nationwide network of support. Their national experience and connections gave them a great advantage in coordinating the first national political campaign. By contrast, the Antifederalists were state politicians who struggled to build alliances across state lines.

The Federalist Papers Outline Key Ideas The Federalists' case for ratification of the Constitution appeared in ***The Federalist,*** a series of 85 essays that came to be called the Federalist Papers. Three leading Federalists—Madison, Hamilton, and **John Jay**—wrote the essays, which were published in New York newspapers in 1787 and 1788, a time of heated debate in New York's ratifying convention. The essays argued that the separation of powers in three branches of government would prevent the concentration of power dreaded by the Antifederalists.

The authors were also eager for the United States to have a strong central government, as supported by Madison in *The Federalist,* No. 10. Federalist leaders feared that the United States would dissolve without a strong government. (See Primary Source at the end of the section.) They argued in *The Federalist,* No. 51, that the checks and balances in the Constitution prevented any of the three branches from gaining too much power. The authors insisted that the real threat to liberty came from the state legislatures, which lacked sufficient checks and balances. Hamilton wrote of the importance of a judicial branch in *The Federalist,* No. 78. Today, these essays help scholars, judges, and lawyers understand the meaning of the Constitution.

 **Checkpoint Why did the Federalists have more support than the Antifederalists?**

Ratifying Conventions

Exploiting their advantages, the Federalists pushed for quick ratifying conventions in five states. By mid-January 1788, the Federalists had won ratification in Delaware, Pennsylvania, New Jersey, Georgia, and Connecticut. These early victories created momentum. To complete ratification, the Federalists needed only four of the remaining eight states. But the Antifederalists mounted a stronger fight in those states.

The Federalists Triumph In Massachusetts, the Federalists faced defeat until they made two key concessions to sway the moderate Antifederalists, led

History Makers

James Madison (1751–1836)
Madison wrote 29 of the Federalist Papers, including three he wrote with Hamilton. He wrote the essays while he was living in New York and serving as a member of the Confederation Congress. After he returned home to Virginia in the spring of 1788, he was elected to the Virginia convention to ratify the Constitution that he played a large role in creating. Madison also helped frame the Bill of Rights.

Alexander Hamilton (1755–1804)
It was Hamilton's idea to write the essays that became known as the Federalist Papers. He came up with the idea in order to help win the ratification vote in New York. Hamilton wrote 51 of the 85 essays. In Federalist Paper No. 1, Hamilton laid out the plan for all the essays. In later essays, he tackled such topics as the office of the President and the authority of the Supreme Court to rule on the constitutionality of a law.

John Jay (1745–1829)
A successful New York attorney, John Jay wrote four of the first five Federalist Papers—Nos. 2, 3, 4, and 5. In them, he argued for a strong federal government to protect the Union from foreign force and influence. His contributions to the essays were cut short when he fell ill, though he wrote No. 64 when he recovered.

by Governor John Hancock. First, the Federalists appealed to Hancock's vanity. They hinted that he could become the nation's first Vice President by switching sides. Second, to make that switch easier, they promised to support key amendments to the Constitution. They would add a bill of rights but only after ratification—not as a condition for it. In early February, following Hancock's lead, the Massachusetts convention ratified the Constitution.

The promise of a bill of rights helped the Federalists win most of the remaining states. Maryland ratified in April; South Carolina, in May; and New Hampshire, in early June. They provided the winning nine, but the new nation would not last without the support of Virginia and New York. In late June, Virginia narrowly ratified, despite the forceful opposition of Patrick Henry, the greatest political orator of his generation. In July, New York also narrowly approved after Hamilton threatened New York City's secession from the state to join the Union if the state rejected the Constitution.

A Celebration

This engraving shows the celebration of New York's ratification of the Constitution. *Who is identified with the success of ratification here?*

With the ratification of 11 states, the Congress of the Confederation made plans for the establishment of the new government and chose New York City as the temporary capital. The new Congress convened there on March 4, 1789, in Federal Hall. Plans for electing the nation's first President and Vice President were made. Within a short time, Rhode Island and North Carolina, which had previously rejected the Constitution, reconsidered and joined the Union.

Vocabulary Builder
convene–(kuhn VEEN) *v.* to meet or assemble

Adding the Bill of Rights If the Federalists deserve credit for the Constitution, the Antifederalists deserve credit for the federal **Bill of Rights,** the first ten amendments to the Constitution. Only the forceful resistance of the Antifederalists obliged the Federalists to add a bill of rights.

In the newly elected Congress, Madison drafted the Bill of Rights. Many of these amendments relied on an earlier Virginia bill of rights. Madison limited the amendments to guarantees of individual rights, leaving the federal framework the same. He also avoided any sweeping preamble that declared all men equal in their creation and rights. That omission enabled slave owners to persist in denying rights to their slaves. The protected rights included freedom of religion, speech, press, assembly, and petition; protection from unreasonable searches and seizures; and the right to a speedy and public trial.

Madison feared that any finite list of rights would later be abused to deny any left unmentioned. So the Ninth Amendment provided: "The enumeration in the Constitution, of certain rights, shall not be construed to deny or disparage others retained by the people." That left open the subsequent development of additional rights. Congress passed the Bill of Rights in 1789.

✓ **Checkpoint What was the importance of the inclusion of a bill of rights in the Constitution?**

Principles of the New Constitution

The Republic established by the Constitution of the United States became a symbol of freedom not only to Americans but to countries in Europe and republics in Latin America as well. The authors of the Constitution established a representative government based on these basic principles: popular sovereignty,

American Issues Connector

Expanding and Protecting Civil Rights

TRACK THE ISSUE

What should the federal government do to expand and protect civil rights?

The U.S. Constitution guarantees equal rights for all Americans. In 1789, though, African Americans, women, and Native Americans did not have the same rights given white males. Over the years, however, rights have been extended to these groups. A major question remains, though: How far should the government go to expand rights? Use the timeline below to explore this enduring issue.

1791 Bill of Rights
The first 10 amendments to the U.S. Constitution guarantee certain basic rights and freedoms.

1868 Fourteenth Amendment
Guarantees citizenship to everyone born or naturalized in the United States.

1920 Nineteenth Amendment
Women gain the right to vote.

1964 Civil Rights Act
Bans race or gender discrimination in public accommodations and jobs.

1990 Americans With Disabilities Act
Bans discrimination against people with disabilities.

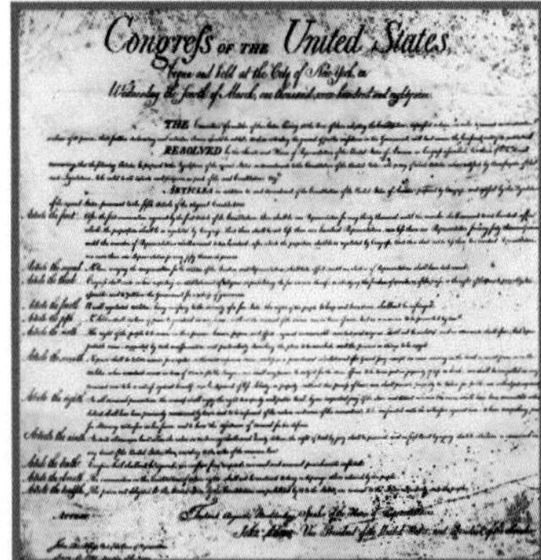

The Bill of Rights

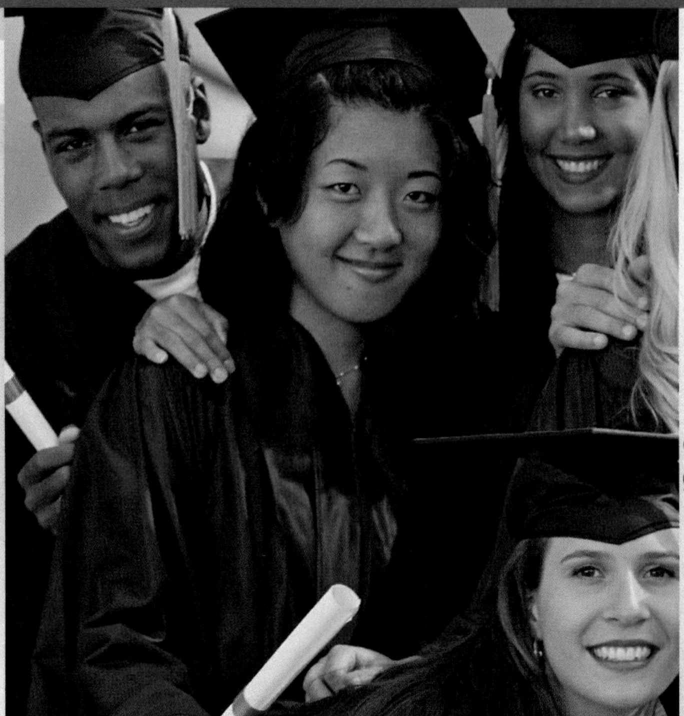

College graduates celebrate their achievements.

DEBATE THE ISSUE

Affirmative Action Some urge companies, colleges, and the government to use affirmative action programs to expand opportunities for women and minorities. Others argue that such steps are unfair.

"You do not take a man who for years has been hobbled by chains, liberate him, bring him to the starting line of a race, saying 'you are free to compete with all the others,' and still justly believe you have been completely fair. . . . We seek not just freedom but opportunity . . . not just equality as a right and a theory, but equality as a fact and as a result."

—President Lyndon Johnson, speech, June 4, 1965

"The civil rights laws themselves forbade employers to discriminate on the basis of race, sex, national origin, color, or religion. They didn't say anything about guaranteeing a certain number of slots to minorities or women. . . . The supporters of affirmative action everywhere seemed to believe that the only way to eliminate racial discrimination against blacks, Latinos, and women was to discriminate against white men."

—Linda Chavez, essay, October 2002

TRANSFER Activities

1. **Compare** Choose a statement about affirmative action you disagree with. Explain why you disagree.
2. **Analyze** Do you think either Johnson or Chavez believed that affirmative action is a basic right? Why or why not?
3. **Transfer** Use the following Web site to see a video, try a WebQuest, and write in your journal. www.pearsonschool.com/ushist

limited government, separation of powers, federalism, checks and balances, and representative government.

Popular Sovereignty The Constitution abides by the principle of **popular sovereignty,** in which all government power comes from the people. In other words, the government derives its political authority from the people.

Limited Government Popular sovereignty ensures that a government's power is restricted, or limited. In a **limited government,** the Constitution specifically states what powers the government has. The principle of limited government also refers to the rule of law. Government leaders are not supposed to be above the law.

Separation of Powers The Constitution mandated the **separation of powers** within the federal government. The Constitution, therefore, defined distinct legislative, executive, and judicial branches with different responsibilities to prevent misuse of power by any of the three branches.

The Constitution assigns certain specific powers to each of the three branches of the federal government. The legislative branch, or Congress, enacts laws. The executive branch, headed by the President, carries out the laws, negotiates treaties, and commands the armed forces. The judicial branch interprets the Constitution and applies the law. The Constitution established a Supreme Court and authorized Congress to establish other courts as needed.

Federalism Just as the Constitution divides power among the three branches of the federal government, it also divides power between the states and the nation, a division known as federalism. At the time, this meant that the states could no longer issue their own paper money or provide debtor relief at creditors' expense. These delegated powers belonged exclusively to the federal government. Federalism also reserves some powers to the state governments. For example, states regulate all elections. The federal and state governments also hold some overlapping concurrent powers, among them parallel court systems.

Principles of the Constitution	☑ Quick Study
Popular sovereignty	The people are the only source of the government's power.
Limited government	The government has only the powers that the Constitution gives it.
Separation of powers	The government's power is divided among three branches: the legislative, the executive, and the judicial branches.
Federalism	The federal government and the state governments share power.
Checks and balances	Each branch of government has the power to limit the actions of the other two.
Representative government	Citizens elect representatives to government to make laws.

Checks and Balances The Constitution also limits the power of government by creating a system of **checks and balances** designed to prevent one branch from seizing too much power. For example, while only Congress has the power to enact laws, the President may veto them. However, a two-thirds majority in both houses of Congress can override the President's veto. The President nominates judges, but the Senate must approve them.

Representative Government The writers of the new Constitution had misgivings about the democratic rule of the majority. Many saw democracy as something that would lead to mob rule. Instead of creating a direct democracy in which all citizens vote on every matter, the writers created an indirect democracy in which voters elect representatives to be their voice in government.

For example, the Constitution stipulated that the citizens would directly elect only the representatives to the House of Representatives. The state legislatures, rather than the voters, would choose the members of the Senate (who would serve for six years, rather than the two years representatives served). Similarly, an **electoral college,** or group of persons chosen from each state, would indirectly elect the President. Each state legislature would determine whether to choose those electors or let the citizens elect them.

In addition, the indirectly elected President and senators would choose the least democratic branch of all: the judiciary. By giving the federal judges (including the Supreme Court Justices) life terms, the delegates meant to insulate them from democratic politics.

✓ **Checkpoint** **What are the major principles of the Constitution?**

The Constitution Endures

The Constitution became the supreme law of the land in 1789, and with amendments, it has endured for more than 200 years. At about 7,000 words, the Constitution is relatively brief and often ambiguous. Therefore, it invites debate. Some politicians, including Thomas Jefferson, argued that the Constitution should be interpreted narrowly and literally to restrict federal power. But most Federalists, including George Washington, insisted that the Constitution be read broadly to allow for the expansion of federal power when necessary.

How is it that a Constitution written when the nation was little more than a union of 13 states continues to guide the actions of the government today? The Framers knew they could not anticipate future social, economic, or political events. They, therefore, worded parts of the Constitution to permit flexibility. The Constitution has survived and thrived in part because it provides a process for changes in its content. The Constitution makes amendment possible but difficult. Two thirds of both houses of Congress must approve an amendment, which becomes law only when ratified by three fourths of the states. Since the Bill of Rights, only 17 amendments have been added to the Constitution.

Checkpoint **What has enabled the Constitution to endure for more than 200 years?**

SECTION 3 Assessment

Progress Monitoring *Online*
For: Self-test with vocabulary practice
www.pearsonschool.com/ushist

Comprehension

1. **Terms and People** For each term listed below, write a sentence explaining why it is an important principle in the Constitution.
   - popular sovereignty
   - limited government
   - separation of powers
   - checks and balances
2. **NoteTaking Reading Skill: Identify Main Ideas** Use your completed table to answer the Section Focus Question: How did Americans ratify the Constitution, and what are its basic principles?

Writing About History

3. **Quick Write: Compare Evidence** Describe the relationship between the plans of government that were proposed at the Constitutional Convention and the plan that was chosen. Review the plan of government diagram in the previous section and the Constitution chart in this section. Write your description in one or two paragraphs.

Critical Thinking

4. **Compare Points of View** What was the main argument of the Antifederalists?
5. **Summarize** Why did Madison feel it was necessary to add the Ninth Amendment?
6. **Draw Conclusions** Why do you think the delegates made amending the Constitution difficult?

Primary Source

James Madison: *The Federalist,* No. 10

One of the most notable essays in the Federalist Papers is *The Federalist,* No. 10. In it, Madison argues that a national government on a continental scale would strengthen rather than weaken liberty. He believed that in a large and diverse republic, no single faction, or interest group, could control the government because the numerous factions would check one another.

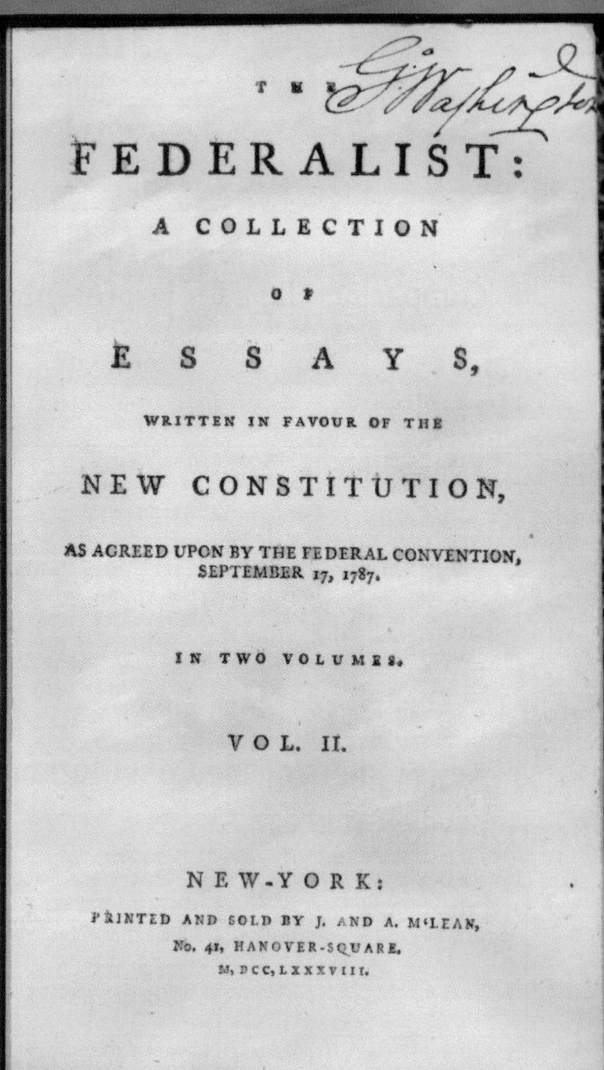
THE FEDERALIST: A COLLECTION OF ESSAYS, WRITTEN IN FAVOUR OF THE NEW CONSTITUTION, AS AGREED UPON BY THE FEDERAL CONVENTION, SEPTEMBER 17, 1787. IN TWO VOLUMES. VOL. II. NEW-YORK: PRINTED AND SOLD BY J. AND A. M'LEAN, No. 41, HANOVER-SQUARE. M,DCC,LXXXVIII.

▲ Title page from *The Federalist* signed by George Washington

The latent causes of faction are thus sown in the nature of man; and we see them everywhere brought into different degrees of activity. . . . A zeal for different opinions concerning religion, concerning government, and many other points, . . . have, in turn, divided mankind into parties, inflamed them with mutual animosity, and rendered them much more disposed to vex and oppress each other than to cooperate for their common good. . . .

From this . . . it may be concluded that a pure democracy, by which I mean a society consisting of a small number of citizens, who assemble and administer the government in person, can admit of no cure for the mischiefs of faction. . . . Hence it is that such democracies have ever been spectacles of turbulence and contention; have ever been found incompatible with personal security or the rights of property; and have in general been as short in their lives as they have been violent in their deaths. . . .

A republic, by which I mean a government in which the scheme of representation takes place, opens a different prospect, and promises the cure for which we are seeking. Let us examine the points in which it varies from pure democracy, and we shall comprehend both the nature of the cure and the efficacy which it must derive from the Union. . . .

The two great points of difference between a democracy and a republic are: first, the delegation of the government, in the latter, to a small number of citizens elected by the rest; secondly, the greater number of citizens, and greater sphere of country, over which the latter may be extended. . . .

The influence of factious leaders may kindle a flame within their particular States, but will be unable to spread a general conflagration through the other States. A religious sect may degenerate into a political faction in a part of the Confederacy; but the variety of sects dispersed over the entire face of it must secure the national councils against any danger from that source. A rage for paper money, for an abolition of debts, for an equal division of property, or for any other improper or wicked project, will be less apt to pervade the whole body of the Union than a particular member of it; in the same proportion as such a malady is more likely to taint a particular county or district, than an entire State. . . .

Thinking Critically

1. According to Madison, what are the differences between a democracy and a republic? Which does he support and why?
2. Does Madison consider factions to be good or bad for the nation? Explain.

CHAPTER 5

Quick Study Guide

Progress Monitoring *Online*
For: Self-test with vocabulary practice
www.pearsonschool.com/ushist

Comparing Plans for Representation in the New Federal Government

	Virginia Plan	New Jersey Plan	U.S. Constitution Provisions
Number of houses in legislature	2 (Bicameral)	1 (Unicameral)	2 (Bicameral)
How representation is determined	Varies based on each state's population or by the financial support each state gives to the central government	Equal representation for each state	Equal representation for each state in the Senate; representation in the House of Representatives varies based on each state's population
How representatives are chosen	Members of House of Representatives elected by popular vote; members of Senate nominated by state legislatures and then chosen by House	Elected by state legislatures	Members of House of Representatives elected by popular vote in each state; members of Senate chosen by state legislatures*

*Seventeenth Amendment later provided for popular election of senators

Key Framers of the Constitution

Name	State	Background
George Washington	Virginia	Planter; commander of the Continental Army in the American Revolution
James Madison	Virginia	Legislator; major proponent of replacing Articles
Benjamin Franklin	Pennsylvania	Writer; printer; inventor; legislator; diplomat
Gouverneur Morris	Pennsylvania	Lawyer; merchant; legislator
Alexander Hamilton	New York	Lawyer; legislator; champion of strong central government
Roger Sherman	Connecticut	Merchant; mayor of New Haven; legislator; judge
John Dickinson	Delaware	Lawyer; historian; major advocate of independence

The Bill of Rights

1st:	Guarantees freedom of religion, speech, press, assembly, and petition
2nd:	Guarantees right to bear arms
3rd:	Prohibits quartering of troops in private homes
4th:	Protects people from unreasonable searches and seizures
5th:	Guarantees due process for accused persons
6th:	Guarantees the right to a speedy and public trial in the state where the offense was committed
7th:	Guarantees the right to jury trial for civil cases tried in federal courts
8th:	Prohibits excessive bail and cruel and unusual punishments
9th:	Provides that people have rights beyond those stated in the Constitution
10th:	Provides that powers not granted to the national government belong to the states and to the people

Quick Study Timeline

In America

1777
Continental Congress adopts the Articles of Confederation, which established a limited national government in 1781

1786
Shays' Rebellion breaks out

Presidential Terms

1775 **1780** **1785**

Around the World

1782
James Watt builds first rotary steam engine

1784
Pitt's India Act establishes dual control of India

American Issues Connector

By connecting prior knowledge with what you have learned in this chapter, you can gradually build your understanding of enduring questions that still affect America today. Answer the questions below. Then, use your American Issues Connector study guide (or go online: www.pearsonschool.com/ushist).

Issues You Learned About

- **Expanding and Protecting Civil Rights** Most democracies include safeguards to protect the individual rights and freedoms of their citizens.

1. How did the Federalists' promise to support a bill of rights influence the ratification battle?
2. What are some of the rights guaranteed to American citizens by the Bill of Rights?
3. What is the significance of the Ninth Amendment?

- **Checks and Balances** The federal Constitution provided a system of checks and balances to prevent any of the three branches from dominating the others.

4. Prove or disprove this statement: The Articles of Confederation provided a strong system of checks and balances for the federal government.
5. What are the three branches of the federal government and their powers? Give an example of how one branch might check the power of another branch.
6. What prior experiences may have led the delegates at the Constitutional Convention to create a national government with a separation of powers and a system of checks and balances?

- **Federal Power and States' Rights** Questions about the power of the federal government versus the power of state governments date to the earliest days of the nation.

7. Under the Articles of Confederation, did the state governments or the federal government have more power? Explain.
8. Explain whether James Madison supported federal power or state power. Use evidence from the text to support your answer.
9. Why did the Antifederalists support a weak national government?

Connect to Your World — Activity

Voting Rights In the early years of the country, relatively few Americans enjoyed the right to vote. Several amendments eventually expanded suffrage. These changes brought voting rights to millions more Americans. In the 2008 presidential election, 63 percent of voting-age citizens actually voted. This meant that 132 million people voted, a strong turnout for a presidential election. Go online or to your local library to learn more about the trends of voter participation in the United States. Write a short report with your findings.

1787 Constitutional Convention drafts a new plan of government; Northwest Ordinance passed

1791 Bill of Rights added to the Constitution

1792 George Washington unanimously wins reelection

History Interactive
For: Interactive timeline
www.pearsonschool.com/ushist

George Washington 1789–1797

1790 — 1795 — 1800

1789 Parisians storm the Bastille, starting the French Revolution

1793 France declares war on Britain and Spain

1795 Russia, Prussia, and Austria divide Poland

1799 Napoleon seizes control of France

Chapter Assessment

Terms and People

1. Define **unicameral legislature** and **bicameral legislature.** Which type of legislature did most states have?
2. What was the **Land Ordinance of 1785**? What groups of Americans benefited from this land ordinance, and why?
3. What was the **Great Compromise**? What were its specific details?
4. Define **federalism.** How did the introduction of federalism affect the rights of the state governments?
5. What is the **Bill of Rights**? Who insisted on the creation of the Bill of Rights?

Focus Questions

The focus question for this chapter is **What led to the creation of the United States Constitution, and what are its key principles?** Build an answer to this big question by answering the focus questions for Sections 1 through 3 and the Critical Thinking questions that follow.

Section 1

6. What form of national government did the Patriots create initially, and what events revealed that a new government was necessary?

Section 2

7. What new system of national government did the delegates agree upon at the Constitutional Convention of 1787?

Section 3

8. How did Americans ratify the Constitution, and what are its basic principles?

Critical Thinking

9. **Compare Points of View** How did the views of democratic Patriots and conservative Patriots diverge regarding Americans and voting rights? How were they similar?
10. **Express Problems Clearly** Think about the challenges the United States faced with Britain in its early years of nationhood. Then, identify one challenge and explain why Congress failed to solve it.
11. **Recognize Causes** Why did the national government under the Articles of Confederation face bankruptcy?
12. **Draw Conclusions** Did the Virginia Plan or the New Jersey Plan represent a more radical departure from the Articles of Confederation? Explain.
13. **Identify Central Issues** How did the northern delegates at the Constitutional Convention convince the southern delegates to support the new Constitution?
14. **Analyze Political Cartoons** Study the political cartoon below, which shows the gradual ratification of the Constitution by the states. Then, answer the questions that follow.

To what does the cartoonist compare the ratification of the Constitution? What opinion do you think the artist had about the new Constitution?

15. **Categorize** Identify which branch of the federal government each official belongs to: the President, a senator, a Supreme Court Justice, and a member of the House of Representatives.
16. **Make Comparisons** How did the national government under the Constitution differ from the government under the Articles of Confederation?

Writing About History

Synthesis Writing Coming up with a plan for a new national government was a daunting task for the delegates at the Constitutional Convention. Consider the characters and events of the convention, and then write an essay that answers the following question: How did the Constitution reach its final form?

Prewriting

- Refresh your memory by flipping through the chapter or find other sources relating to the essay question. Compare visuals, quotes, and features.
- Using what you learn from the various sources, compile a list of significant people and events that shaped the plan that came to be the Constitution.
- Record similarities or differences among the various sources to help identify the main idea you will develop.

Drafting

- Develop a thesis statement that identifies the focus of your essay.
- Make an outline for your essay with facts and examples.
- Begin each paragraph with a clear sentence about the topic of the paragraph.
- Organize your essay so that your reader sees where information from sources overlap.

Revising

- Use the guidelines on page SH11 of the Writing Handbook to revise your essay.

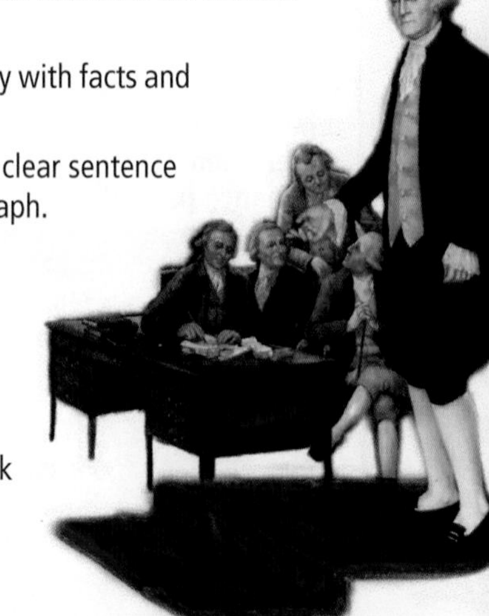

Document-Based Assessment

Religious Freedom in Early America

Many early colonists who settled in North America had faced religious discrimination in their home countries. How did the religious diversity of the nation influence the formation of state and federal governments? Use your knowledge of colonial society and Documents A, B, and C to answer questions 1 through 4.

Document A

"Whereas Almighty God has created the mind free; that all attempts to influence it by temporal punishments . . . are a departure from the plan of the Holy author of our religion, . . . that to compel a man to furnish contributions of money for the propagation of opinions which he disbelieves, is sinful and tyrannical; . . . that our civil rights have no dependence on our religious opinions, any more than our opinions in physics or geometry. . . .

Be it enacted by the General Assembly, That no man shall be compelled to frequent or support any religious worship, place, or ministry whatsoever, nor shall be enforced, restrained, molested, or burthened in his body or goods, nor shall otherwise suffer on account of his religious opinions or belief; but that all men shall be free to profess, and by argument to maintain, their opinion in matters of religion, and that the same shall in no wise diminish, enlarge, or affect their civil capacities. . . . [Y]et we are free to declare, and do declare, that the rights hereby asserted are the natural rights of mankind, and that if any act shall hereafter be passed to repeal the present, or to narrow its operation, such act will be an infringement of natural right."

—*Thomas Jefferson,* Virginia Statute for Religious Freedom, *1786*

Document B

"Congress shall make no law respecting an establishment of religion, or prohibiting the free exercise thereof; or abridging the freedom of speech, or of the press; or the right of the people peacefully to assemble, and to petition the government for a redress of grievances."

—*First Amendment to the United States Constitution, 1791*

Document C

Religion in the Colonies, 1776

Denomination	Number of Congregations
Congregational	668
Presbyterian	588
Baptist	497
Episcopal	495
Quaker	310
German Reformed	159
Lutheran	120
Methodist	65
Catholic	56
Moravian	31
Separatist and Independent	27
Dunker	24
Mennonite	16
Huguenot	7
Sandemanian	6
Jewish	5
Total	**3,074**

SOURCE: *The Churching of America, 1776–2005,* Roger Finke and Rodney Stark

1. What civil right does Document A protect?
   - A freedom of speech
   - B freedom of the press
   - C freedom of education
   - D freedom of religion

2. What can you conclude about religion in the colonies based on Document C?
   - A By 1776, there were fewer than 2,000 congregations in America.
   - B There were a variety of religious denominations in colonial America.
   - C Most colonists did not practice their religion on a regular basis.
   - D Most colonists belonged to two establishment churches.

3. How are Documents A and B related?
   - A Both established the right of assembly.
   - B Both prohibited the government from imposing religious taxes.
   - C Both guaranteed the separation of church and state.
   - D Both guaranteed freedom of the press.

4. **Writing Task** What effect did religious liberty have on the development of the new nation? Use your knowledge of the new government and specific evidence from the primary and secondary sources above to support your answer.

THE SIX BASIC PRINCIPLES

The classic textbook *Magruder's American Government* outlines the six basic principles of the Constitution. Below is a description of these principles:

1 Popular Sovereignty

The Preamble to the Constitution begins with the bold phrase, "We the people . . ." These words announce that in the United States, the people are sovereign. The government receives its power from the people and can govern only with their consent.

2 Limited Government

Because the people are the ultimate source of all government power, the government has only as much authority as the people give it. Government's power is thus limited. Much of the Constitution, in fact, consists of specific limitations on government power.

3 Separation of Powers

Government power is not only limited, but also divided. The Constitution assigns certain powers to each of the three branches: the legislative (Congress), executive (President), and judicial (federal courts). This separation of government's powers was intended to prevent the misuse of power.

4 Checks and Balances

The system of checks and balances gives each of the three branches of government the ability to restrain the other two. Such a system makes government less efficient but also less likely to trample on the rights of citizens.

5 Judicial Review

Who decides whether an act of government violates the Constitution? Federal courts have the power to review acts of the federal government and to cancel any acts that are unconstitutional, or violate a provision in the Constitution.

6 Federalism

A federal system of government is one in which power is divided between a central government and smaller governments This sharing of powers is intended to ensure that the central government is powerful enough to be effective, yet not so powerful as to threaten states or individuals.

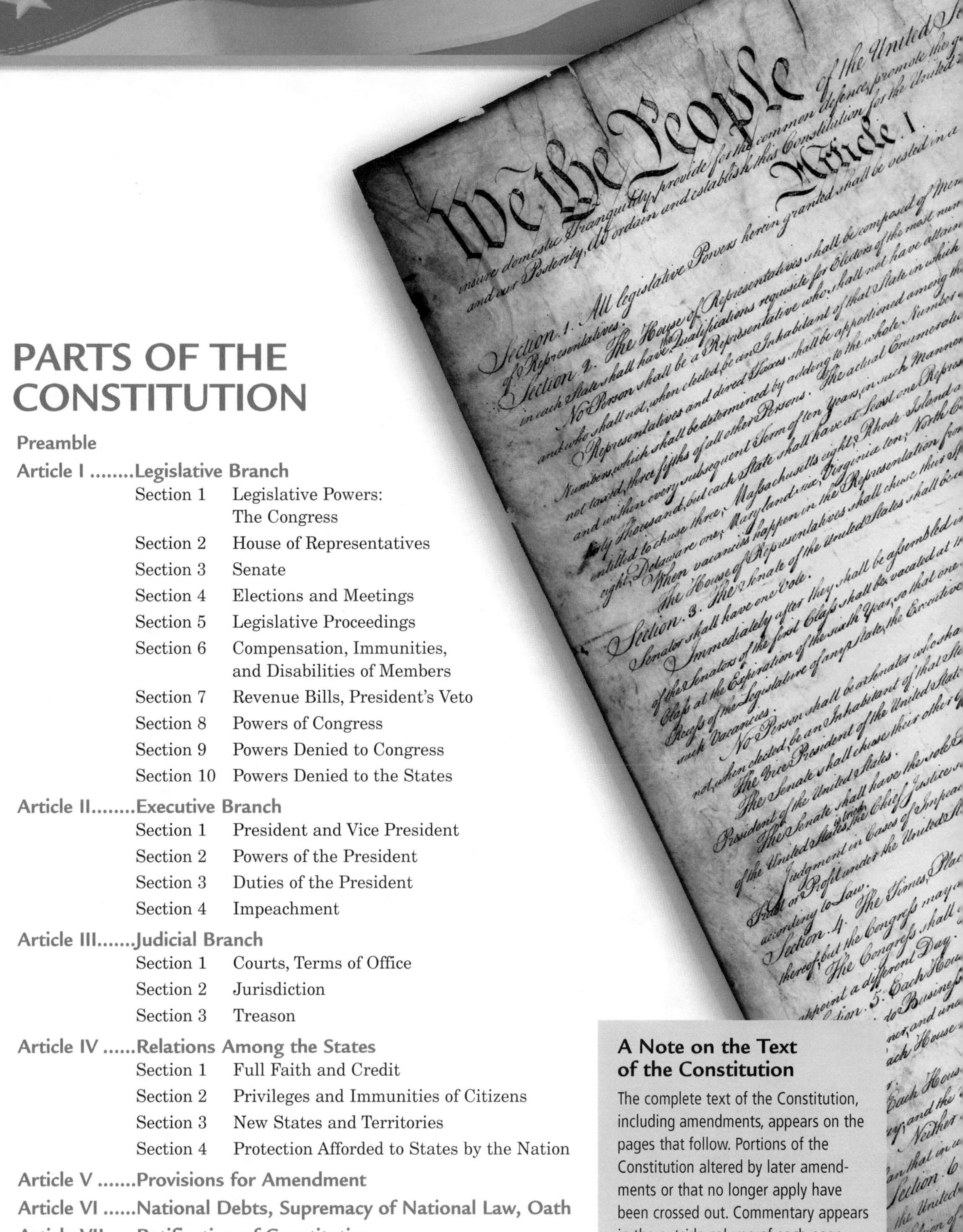

PARTS OF THE CONSTITUTION

Preamble

Article I ....Legislative Branch

Section 1	Legislative Powers: The Congress
Section 2	House of Representatives
Section 3	Senate
Section 4	Elections and Meetings
Section 5	Legislative Proceedings
Section 6	Compensation, Immunities, and Disabilities of Members
Section 7	Revenue Bills, President's Veto
Section 8	Powers of Congress
Section 9	Powers Denied to Congress
Section 10	Powers Denied to the States

Article II........Executive Branch

Section 1	President and Vice President
Section 2	Powers of the President
Section 3	Duties of the President
Section 4	Impeachment

Article III.......Judicial Branch

Section 1	Courts, Terms of Office
Section 2	Jurisdiction
Section 3	Treason

Article IV ......Relations Among the States

Section 1	Full Faith and Credit
Section 2	Privileges and Immunities of Citizens
Section 3	New States and Territories
Section 4	Protection Afforded to States by the Nation

Article V ....Provisions for Amendment

Article VI ......National Debts, Supremacy of National Law, Oath

Article VII .....Ratification of Constitution

Amendments

A Note on the Text of the Constitution

The complete text of the Constitution, including amendments, appears on the pages that follow. Portions of the Constitution altered by later amendments or that no longer apply have been crossed out. Commentary appears in the outside column of each page.

Commentary

The Preamble ▶
The Preamble describes the purpose of the government as set up by the Constitution. Americans expect their government to defend justice and liberty and provide peace and safety from foreign enemies.

Clause 4 ▶
Executive authority means the governor of a state. If a member of the House leaves office before his or her term ends, the governor must call a special election to fill the seat.

Preamble

We the People of the United States, in Order to form a more perfect Union, establish Justice, insure domestic Tranquility, provide for the common defence, promote the general Welfare, and secure the Blessings of Liberty to ourselves and our Posterity, do ordain and establish this Constitution for the United States of America.

Article I. Legislative Branch

Section 1. Legislative Powers; The Congress

All legislative Powers herein granted shall be vested in a Congress of the United States, which shall consist of a Senate and House of Representatives.

Section 2. House of Representatives

1. The House of Representatives shall be composed of Members chosen every second Year by the People of the several States, and the Electors in each State shall have the Qualifications requisite for Electors of the most numerous Branch of the State Legislature
2. No Person shall be a Representative who shall not have attained to the Age of twenty-five Years, and been seven Years a Citizen of the United States, and who shall not, when elected, be an Inhabitant of that State in which he shall be chosen.
3. Representatives ~~and direct Taxes~~* shall be apportioned among the several States which may be included within this Union, according to their respective Numbers, ~~which shall be determined by adding to the whole Number of free Persons, including those bound to Service for a Term of Years and excluding Indians not taxed, three fifths of all other Persons.~~ The actual Enumeration shall be made within three Years after the first Meeting of the Congress of the United States, and within every subsequent Term of ten Years, in such Manner as they shall by Law direct. The Number of Representatives shall not exceed one for every thirty Thousand, but each State shall have at Least one Representative; ~~and, until such enumeration shall be made, the State of New Hampshire shall be entitled to choose three, Massachusetts eight, Rhode Island and Providence Plantations one, Connecticut five, New York six, New Jersey four, Pennsylvania eight, Delaware one, Maryland six, Virginia ten, North Carolina five, South Carolina five, and Georgia three.~~
4. When vacancies happen in the Representation from any State, the Executive Authority thereof shall issue Writs of Election to fill such Vacancies.

*Portions of the Constitution altered by later amendments or that no longer apply are crossed out.

5. The House of Representatives shall choose their Speaker and other Officers; and shall have the sole Power of Impeachment.

Section 3. Senate

1. The Senate of the United States shall be composed of two Senators from each State ~~chosen by the Legislature thereof~~ for six Years; and each Senator shall have one Vote.
2. Immediately after they shall be assembled in Consequences of the first Election, they shall be divided, as equally as may be, into three Classes. The Seats of the Senators of the first Class shall be vacated at the Expiration of the second Year; of the second Class, at the Expiration of the fourth Year; and of the third Class, at the Expiration of the sixth Year; so that one-third may be chosen every second Year; ~~and if Vacancies happen by Resignation, or otherwise, during the Recess of the Legislature of any State, the Executive thereof may make temporary Appointments until the next Meeting of the Legislature, which shall then fill such Vacancies.~~
3. No Person shall be a Senator who shall not have attained to the Age of thirty Years, and been nine Years a Citizen of the United States, and who shall not, when elected, be an Inhabitant of that State for which he shall be chosen.

Commentary

◀ **Clause 5** The House elects a Speaker. Also, only the House has the power to impeach, or accuse a federal official of wrongdoing.

◀ **Clause 1** Each State has two senators.

◀ **Clause 2** Every two years, one third of the senators run for reelection. The Seventeenth Amendment changed the way of filling vacancies, or empty seats. Today, the governor of a state must choose a senator to fill a vacancy that occurs between elections.

✓ Checkpoint
What is the main job of Congress?

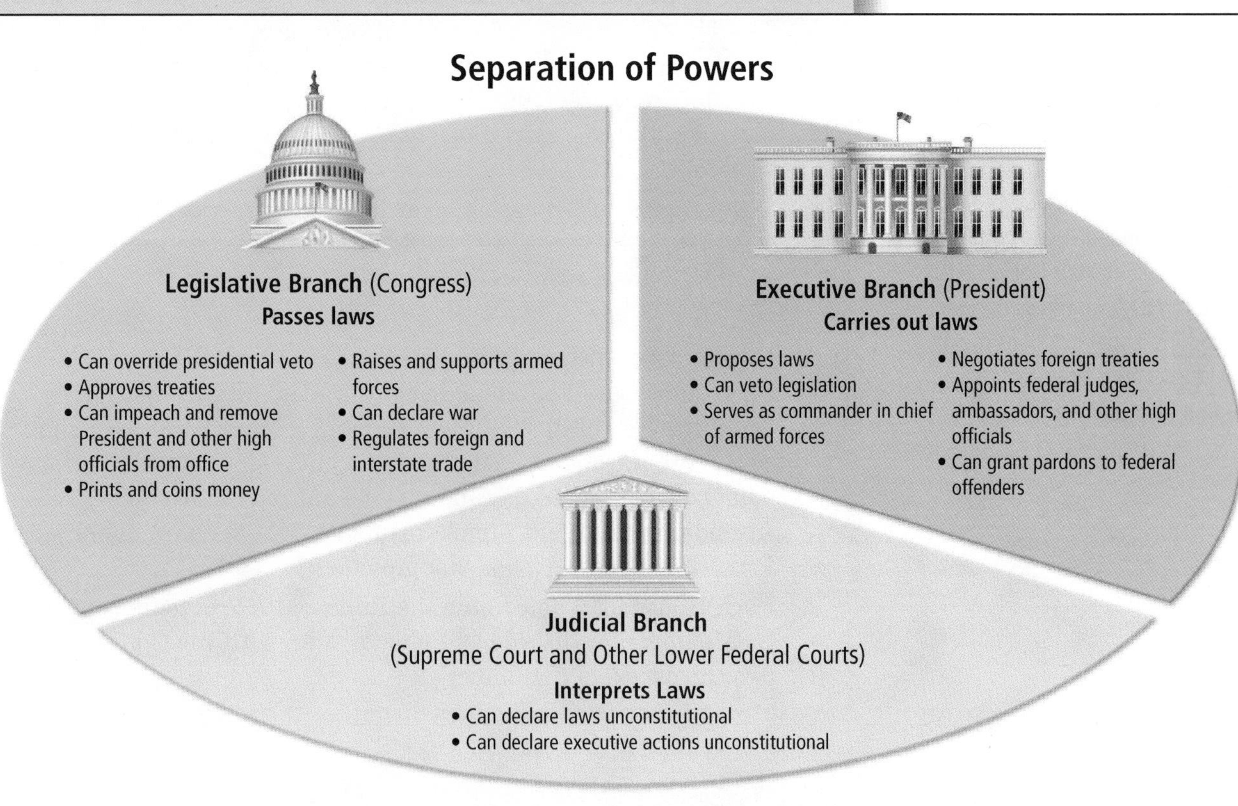

Commentary

Clause 5 ▶
The Senate chooses its own officers, including a President pro tempore when the Vice President is absent.

Clause 6 ▶
The Senate acts as a jury if the House impeaches a federal official. The Chief Justice of the Supreme Court presides if the President is on trial. Two thirds of all senators present must vote for conviction, or finding the accused guilty. No President has ever been convicted.

 **Checkpoint**

Which branches are involved in presidential impeachment?

Clause 1 ▶
Each state legislature can decide when and how congressional elections take place, but Congress can overrule these decisions. In 1842, Congress required each state to set up congressional districts with one representative elected from each district. In 1872, Congress decided that congressional elections must be held in every state on the same date in even-numbered years.

4. The Vice President of the United States shall be President of the Senate but shall have no Vote, unless they be equally divided.
5. The Senate shall choose their other Officers, and also a President pro tempore, in the Absence of the Vice President, or when he shall exercise the Office of President of the United States
6. The Senate shall have the sole Power to try all Impeachments. When sitting for that Purpose, they shall be on Oath or Affirmation. When the President of the United States is tried, the Chief Justice shall preside: And no Person shall be convicted without the Concurrence of two thirds of the Members present.
7. Judgment in Cases of Impeachment shall not extend further than to removal from Office, and disqualification to hold and enjoy any Office of honor, Trust, or Profit under the United States: but the Party convicted shall nevertheless be liable and subject to Indictment, Trial, Judgment and Punishment, according to Law.

Section 4. Elections and Meetings

1. The Times, Places and Manner of holding Elections for Senators and Representatives, shall be prescribed in each State by the Legislature thereof; but the Congress may at any time by law make or alter such Regulations, except as to the Places of choosing Senators.
2. The Congress shall assemble at least once in every Year, ~~and such Meeting shall be on the first Monday in December, unless they shall by Law appoint a different Day.~~

Section 5. Legislative Proceedings

1. Each House shall be the Judge of the Elections, Returns and Qualifications of its own Members, and a Majority of each shall constitute a Quorum to do Business; but a smaller Number may adjourn from day to day, and may be authorized to compel the Attendance of absent Members, in such Manner, and under such Penalties, as each House may provide.
2. Each House may determine the Rules of its Proceedings, punish its Members for disorderly Behavior, and, with the Concurrence of two thirds, expel a Member

3. Each House shall keep a Journal of its Proceedings, and from time to time publish the same, excepting such Parts as may in their Judgment require Secrecy; and the Yeas and Nays of the Members of either House on any question shall, at the Desire of one fifth of those Present, be entered on the Journal.
4. Neither House, during the Session of Congress, shall, without the Consent of the other, adjourn for more than three days, nor to any other Place than that in which the two Houses shall be sitting.

Section 6. Compensation, Immunities, and Disabilities of Members

1. The Senators and Representatives shall receive a Compensation for their Services, to be ascertained by Law, and paid out of the Treasury of the United States. They shall in all Cases, except Treason, Felony, and Breach of the Peace, be privileged from Arrest during their Attendance at the Session of their respective Houses, and in going to and returning from the same; and for any Speech or Debate in either House, they shall not be questioned in any other Place.
2. No Senator or Representative shall, during the Time for which he was elected, be appointed to any civil Office under the Authority of the United States, which shall have been created, or the Emoluments whereof shall have been increased during such time; and no Person holding any Office under the United States, shall be a Member of either House during his Continuance in Office.

Section 7. Revenue Bills, President's Veto

1. All Bills for raising Revenue shall originate in the House of Representatives; but the Senate may propose or concur with amendments as on other Bills.
2. Every Bill which shall have passed the House of Representatives and the Senate, shall, before it become a Law, be presented to the President of the United States: If he approve he shall sign it, but if not he shall return it, with his Objections to that House in which it shall have originated, who shall enter the Objections at large on their Journal, and proceed to reconsider it. If after such Reconsideration two thirds of the House shall agree to pass the Bill, it shall be sent, together with the Objections, to the other House, by which it shall likewise be reconsidered, and if approved by two thirds of that House, it shall become a Law. But in all such Cases the Votes of both Houses shall be determined by Yeas and Nays, and the Names of the Persons voting for and against the Bill shall be entered on the Journal of each House respectively. If any Bill shall not be returned by the President within ten Days

Commentary

◄ **Clause 4** Neither house can adjourn, or stop meeting, for more than three days unless the other house approves. Both houses must meet in the same city.

◄ **Clause 1** Tax bills must be introduced in the House, but the Senate can make changes in those bills.

◄ **Clause 2** A bill, or proposed law, that is passed by a majority of the House and Senate is sent to the President. If the President signs the bill, it becomes law. The President can veto, or reject, a bill by sending it back to the house where it was introduced. Congress can override the President's veto if each house of Congress passes the bill again by a two-thirds vote.

Commentary

Checkpoint

What is the role of Congress and the President in making laws?

(Sunday excepted) after it shall have been presented to him,the Same shall be a law, in like Manner as if he had signed it,unless the Congress by their Adjournment, prevent its Return,in which Case it shall not be a Law.

3. Every Order, Resolution, or Vote to which the Concurrence of the Senate and House of Representatives may be necessary (except on a question of adjournment) shall be presented to the President of the United States; and before the Same shall take Effect,shall be approved by him, or, being disapproved by him, shall be repassed by two thirds of the Senate and House of Representatives, according to the Rules and Limitations prescribed in the Case of a Bill.

How a Bill Becomes a Law

Start: Senate

Introduction
Bill introduced in Senate.

Committee Action
Bill referred to standing committee. Moves to subcommittee for study, hearings, revisions, approval. Moves back to full committee for more hearings and revisions.

Floor Action
Bill is debated, then passed or defeated. If passed, the bill goes to the House of Representatives. If the bill has already passed in House, the bill goes to Conference Committee.

Conference Committee
Conference Committee resolves differences between House and Senate versions of the bill.

Congressional Approval
House and Senate vote on final passage. Approved bill is sent to the President.

Presidential Action
President signs, vetoes, or allows the bill to become a law without signing. Vetoed bill returns to Congress. Veto may be overridden by two-thirds majority vote of each house.

Floor Action
Bill is debated, then passed or defeated. If passed, the bill goes to Senate If the bill has already passed through Senate, the bill goes to Conference Committee.

Committee Action
Bill referred to standingcommittee. Moves to subcommittee for study hearings, revisions, approval. Moves back to full committee for more hearings and revisions. Moves to Rules Committee to set conditions for debate and amendments.

Introduction
Bill introdued in House

Start: House

Section 8. Powers of Congress

The Congress shall have Power

1. To lay and collect Taxes, Duties, Imposts and Excises to pay the Debts and provide for the common Defence and general Welfare of the United States; but all Duties, Imposts and Excises, shall be uniform throughout the United States;
2. To borrow Money on the credit of the United States;
3. To regulate Commerce with foreign Nations, and among the several States, and with the Indian Tribes;
4. To establish an uniform Rule of Naturalization, and uniform Laws on the subject of Bankruptcies throughout the United States;
5. To coin Money, regulate the Value thereof, and of foreign Coin, and fix the Standard of Weights and Measures;
6. To provide for the Punishment of counterfeiting the Securities and current Coin of the United States;
7. To establish Post Offices and post Roads;
8. To promote the Progress of Science and useful Arts, by securing for limited Times to Authors and Inventors the exclusive Right to their respective Writings and Discoveries;
9. To constitute Tribunals inferior to the supreme Court;
10. To define and punish Piracies and Felonies committed on the high Seas, and Offences against the Law of Nations;

Commentary

◀ **Section 8** The Constitution is our social contract in which the people consent to the form and powers of government. An important part of the contract is the enumeration of legislative powers which sets the scope and limits of government authority over the people. Article I, Section 8, lists most of the expressed powers of Congress. Numbered from 1 to 18, these powers are also known as enumerated powers.

◀ **Clause 1** Duties are tariffs, or taxes on imports. Imposts are taxes in general. Excises are taxes on the production or sale of certain goods.

◀ **Clause 4** Naturalization is the process whereby a foreigner becomes a citizen. Bankruptcy is the condition in which a person or business cannot pay its debts. Congress has the power to pass laws on these two issues.

◀ **Clause 6** Counterfeiting is the making of imitation money. Securities are bonds. Congress can make laws to punish counterfeiters.

Commentary

Clause 11 ▶
Only Congress can declare war. Declarations of war are granted at the request of the President. Letters of marque and reprisal were documents issued by a government allowing merchant ships to arm themselves and attack ships of an enemy nation. They are no longer issued.

 **Checkpoint**

Which powers of Congress relate to taking in and spending money?

Clause 18 ▶
Congress has the power to make laws as needed to carry out the previous 17 clauses. It is sometimes known as the "Necessary and Proper Clause."

Clause 1 ▶
Such persons means slaves. In 1808, as soon as Congress was permitted to abolish the slave trade, it did so.

Clause 2 ▶
A writ of habeas corpus is a court order requiring government officials to bring a prisoner to court and explain why he or she is being held. A writ of habeas corpus protects people from unlawful imprisonment. The government cannot suspend this right except in times of rebellion or invasion.

11. To declare War, grant Letters of Marque and Reprisal, and make Rules concerning Captures on Land and Water;
12. To raise and support Armies, but no Appropriation of Money to that Use shall be for a longer Term than two Years;
13. To provide and maintain a Navy;
14. To make Rules for the Government and Regulation of the land and naval Forces;
15. To provide for calling forth the Militia to execute the Laws of the Union, suppress Insurrections and repel Invasions;
16. To provide for organizing, arming, and disciplining the Militia, and for governing such Part of them as may be employed in the Service of the United States, reserving to the States respectively, the Appointment of the Officers, and the Authority of training the Militia according to the discipline prescribed by Congress;
17. To exercise exclusive Legislation in all Cases whatsoever, over such District (not exceeding ten Miles square) as may, by Cession of Particular States, and the Acceptance of Congress, become the Seat of the Government of the United States, and to exercise like Authority over all Places purchased by the Consent of the Legislature of the State in which the Same shall be, for the Erection of Forts, Magazines, Arsenals, Dockyards and other needful Buildings;—And
18. To make all Laws which shall be necessary and proper for carrying into Execution the foregoing Powers and all other Powers vested by this Constitution in the Government of the United States, or in any Department or Officer thereof.

Section 9. Powers Denied to Congress

1. ~~The Migration or Importation of such Persons as any of the States now existing shall think proper to admit, shall not be prohibited by the Congress prior to the Year one thousand eight hundred and eight, but a Tax or duty may be imposed on such Importation, not exceeding ten dollars for each Person.~~
2. The Privilege of the Writ of Habeas Corpus shall not be suspended, unless when in Cases of Rebellion or Invasion the public Safety may require it.

3. No Bill of Attainder or ex post facto Law shall be passed.
4. No Capitation, ~~or other direct, Tax~~ shall be laid, unless in Proportion to the Census of Enumeration hereinbefore directed to be taken.
5. No Tax or Duty shall be laid on Articles exported from any State.
6. No Preference shall be given by any Regulation of Commerce or Revenue to the Ports of one State over those of another: nor shall Vessels bound to, or from, one State, be obliged to enter, clear or pay Duties in another.
7. No Money shall be drawn from the Treasury, but in Consequence of Appropriations made by Law; and a regular Statement and Account of the Receipts and Expenditures of all public Money shall be published from time to time.
8. No Title of Nobility shall be granted by the United States: And no Person holding any Office of Profit or Trust under them, shall, without the Consent of the Congress, accept of any present, Emolument, Office, or Title, of any kind whatever, from any King, Prince, or foreign State.

Section 10. Powers Denied to the States

1. No State shall enter into any Treaty, Alliance, or Confederation; grant Letters of Marque and Reprisal; coin Money; emit Bills of Credit; make any Thing but gold and silver Coin a Tender in Payment of Debts; pass any Bill of Attainder, ex post facto Law, or Law impairing the Obligation of Contracts, or grant any Title of Nobility.

Commentary

◀ **Clause 3** A bill of attainder is a law declaring that a person is guilty of a particular crime without a trial. An ex post facto law punishes an act which was not illegal when it was committed.

◀ **Clause 1** The writers of the Constitution did not want the states to act like separate nations, so they prohibited states from making treaties or coining money. Some powers denied to the federal government are also denied to the states.

The Federal System

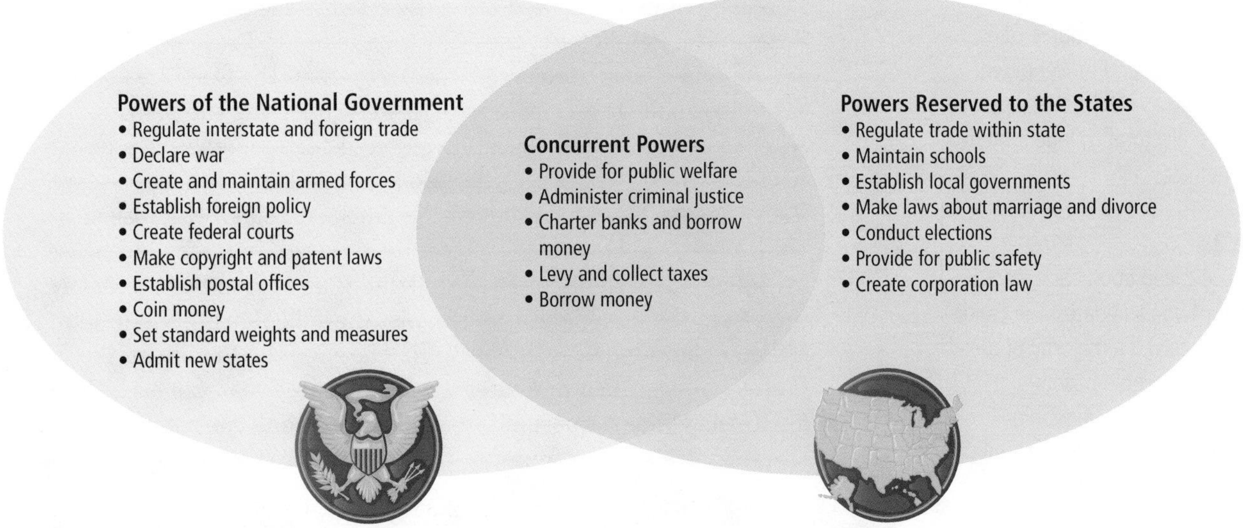

Powers of the National Government
- Regulate interstate and foreign trade
- Declare war
- Create and maintain armed forces
- Establish foreign policy
- Create federal courts
- Make copyright and patent laws
- Establish postal offices
- Coin money
- Set standard weights and measures
- Admit new states

Concurrent Powers
- Provide for public welfare
- Administer criminal justice
- Charter banks and borrow money
- Levy and collect taxes
- Borrow money

Powers Reserved to the States
- Regulate trade within state
- Maintain schools
- Establish local governments
- Make laws about marriage and divorce
- Conduct elections
- Provide for public safety
- Create corporation law

Commentary

Clauses 2, 3 ▶

Powers listed here are forbidden to the states, but Congress can pass laws that give these powers to the states. Clause 2 forbids states from taxing imports and exports without the consent of Congress.

Clause 3 ▶

This clause forbids states from keeping an army or navy without the consent of Congress. States cannot make treaties or declare war unless an enemy invades or is about to invade.

2. No State shall, without the Consent of the Congress, lay any Imposts or Duties on Imports or Exports, except what may be absolutely necessary for executing its inspection Laws; and the net Produce of all Duties and Imposts, laid by any State on Imports or Exports, shall be for the Use of the Treasury of the United States; and all such Laws shall be subject to the Revision and Control of the Congress.

3. No State shall, without the Consent of Congress, lay any Duty of Tonnage, keep Troops, or Ships of War in time of Peace, enter into any Agreement or Compact with another State, or with a foreign Power, or engage in War, unless actually invaded, or in such imminent Danger as will not admit of delay.

Article II Executive Branch

Section 1. President and Vice President

1. The executive Power shall be vested in a President of the United States of America. He shall hold his Office during the Term of four Years, and, together with the Vice President, chosen for the same Term, be elected as follows:

Clauses 2, 3 ▶

Some writers of the Constitution were afraid to allow the people to elect the President directly. Therefore, the Constitutional Convention set up the electoral college. Clause 2 directs each state to choose electors, or delegates to the electoral college, to vote for President. A state's electoral vote is equal to the combined number of senators and representatives. Each state may decide how to choose its electors. Members of Congress and federal officeholders may not serve as electors. This part of the original electoral college system is still in effect.

Clause 3 ▶

This clause called upon each elector to vote for two candidates. The candidate who received a majority of the electoral votes would become President. The runner-up would become Vice President. If no candidate won a majority, the House

2. Each State shall appoint, in such Manner as the Legislature thereof may direct, a Number of Electors, equal to the whole Number of Senators and Representatives to which the State may be entitled in the Congress: but no Senator or Representative, or Person holding an Office of Trust or Profit, under the United States, shall be appointed an Elector.

3. ~~The Electors shall meet in their respective States, and vote by Ballot for two Persons, of whom one at least shall not be an Inhabitant of the same State with themselves. And they shall make a List of all the Persons voted for, and of the Number of Votes for each; which List they shall sign and certify, and transmit sealed to the Seat of the Government of the United States, directed to the President of the Senate. The President of the Senate shall, in the Presence of the Senate and House of Representatives, open all the Certificates, and the Votes shall then be counted. The Person having the greatest Number of Votes shall be the President, if such Number be a majority of the whole Number of Electors appointed; and if there be more than one who have such Majority, and have an equal Number of Votes, then, the House of Representatives shall immediately choose by Ballot one of them for President; and if no Person have a Majority, then from the five highest on the List the said House shall in like Manner choose the President. But in choosing the President, the Votes shall be taken by States, the Representatives from each State having one Vote; a quorum for this Purpose shall consist of a Member or Members from two thirds of the States, and a Majority of~~

~~all the States shall be necessary to a Choice. In every Case, after the Choice of the President, the Person having the greatest Number of Votes of the Electors shall be the Vice President. But if there should remain two or more who have equal Votes, the Senate shall choose from them by Ballot the Vice President.~~

4. The Congress may determine the Time of choosing the Electors, and the Day on which they shall give their Votes; which Day shall be the same throughout the United States.
5. No Person except a natural born Citizen, or a Citizen of the United States, at the time of the Adoption of this Constitution, shall be eligible to the Office of President; neither shall any person be eligible to that Office who shall not have attained to the Age of thirty-five Years, and been fourteen Years a Resident within the United States.
6. ~~In Case of the Removal of the President from Office, or of his Death, Resignation, or Inability to discharge the Powers and Duties of the said Office, the Same shall devolve on the Vice President,~~ and the Congress may by Law provide for the Case of Removal, Death, Resignation or Inability, both of the President and Vice President, declaring what Officer shall then act as President, and such Officer shall act accordingly, until the Disability be removed, or a President shall be elected.
7. The President shall, at stated Times, receive for his Services, a Compensation, which shall neither be increased nor diminished during the Period for which he shall have been elected, and he shall not receive within that Period any other Emolument from the United States, or any of them.
8. Before he enter on the Execution of his Office, he shall take the following Oath or Affirmation:

"I do solemnly swear (or affirm) that I will faithfully execute the Office of President of the United States, and will to the best of my Ability, preserve, protect and defend the Constitution of the United States."

Section 2. Powers of the President

1. The President shall be Commander in Chief of the Army and Navy of the United States, and of the Militia of the several States, when called into the actual Service of the United States; he may require the Opinion, in writing, of the principal Officer in each of the executive Departments, upon any Subject relating to the Duties of their respective Offices, and he shall have Power to Grant Reprieves and Pardons for Offences against the United States, except in Cases of Impeachment.

Commentary

would choose the President. The Senate would choose the Vice President. The election of 1800, however, ended in a tie in the electoral college between Thomas Jefferson and Aaron Burr. The Twelfth Amendment changed the electoral college system so that this could not happen again.

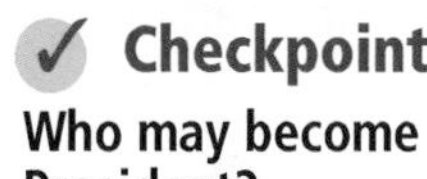

Checkpoint

Who may become President?

Clause 6 The powers of the President pass to the Vice President if the President leaves office or cannot discharge his or her duties. The Twenty-fifth Amendment clarifies this clause.

Clause 7 The President is paid a salary. It cannot be raised or lowered during his or her term in office. The President is not allowed to hold any other state or federal position while in office.

Clause 1 The President is the head of the armed forces and the state militias when they are called into national service. The military is under civilian, or nonmilitary, control. The President has the power to grant a reprieve, or pardon. A reprieve suspends punishment. A pardon prevents prosecution for a crime or overrides the judgment of a court.

Commentary

Clause 2 ▶
The President has the power to make treaties with other nations. Under the system of checks and balances, all treaties must be approved by two thirds of the Senate. The President has the power to appoint ambassadors to foreign countries and to appoint other high officials. The Senate must confirm, or approve, these appointments.

2. He shall have Power, by and with the Advice and Consent of the Senate, to make Treaties, provided two thirds of the Senators present concur; and he shall nominate, and by and with the Advice and Consent of the Senate, shall appoint Ambassadors, other public Ministers and Consuls, Judges of the supreme Court, and all other Officers of the United States, whose Appointments are not herein otherwise provided for, and which shall be established by Law: but the Congress may by Law vest the Appointment of such inferior Officers, as they think proper, in the President alone, in the Courts of Law, or in the Heads of Departments.
3. The President shall have Power to fill up all Vacancies that may happen during the Recess of the Senate, by granting Commissions which shall expire at the End of their next Session.

Section 3. Duties of the President
He shall from time to time give to the Congress Information of the State of the Union, and recommend to their Consideration such Measures as he shall judge necessary and expedient; he may, on extraordinary Occasions, convene both Houses, or either of them, and in Case of Disagreement between them, with Respect to the Time of Adjournment, he may adjourn them to such Time as he shall think proper; he shall receive Ambassadors and other public Ministers; he shall take Care that the Laws be faithfully executed, and shall Commission all the Officers of the United States.

Section 4 ▶
Civil officers include federal judges and members of the Cabinet. High crimes are major crimes. Misdemeanors are lesser crimes. The President, Vice President, and others can be forced out of office if impeached and found guilty of certain crimes.

Section 4. Impeachment
The President, Vice President and all Civil Officers of the United States, shall be removed from Office on Impeachment for and Conviction of, Treason, Bribery, or other high Crimes and Misdemeanors.

Article III Judicial Branch

Section 1. Courts, Terms of Office
The judicial Power of the United States, shall be vested in one supreme Court, and in such inferior Courts as the Congress may from time to time ordain and establish. The Judges, both of the supreme and inferior Courts, shall hold their Offices during good Behavior, and shall, at stated Times, receive for their Services, a Compensation, which shall not be diminished during their Continuance in Office.

Section 2. Jurisdiction

1. The judicial Power shall extend to all Cases, in Law and Equity, arising under this Constitution, the Laws of the United States, and Treaties made, or which shall be made, under their Authority;— to all Cases affecting Ambassadors, other public Ministers, and Consuls;— to all Cases of Admiralty and maritime Jurisdiction;— to Controversies to which the United States shall be a Party;— to Controversies between two or more States;— ~~between a State and Citizens of another State~~;— between Citizens of different States;— between Citizens of the same State claiming Lands under Grants of different States, and between a State, or the Citizens thereof, and foreign States, Citizens, or Subjects.
2. In all Cases affecting Ambassadors, other public Ministers and Consuls, and those in which a State shall be a Party, the supreme Court shall have original Jurisdiction. In all the other Cases before mentioned, the supreme Court shall have appellate Jurisdiction, both as to Law and Fact, with such Exceptions, and under such Regulations as the Congress shall make.
3. The trial of all Crimes, except in Cases of Impeachment, shall be by Jury; and such Trial shall be held in the State where the said Crimes shall have been committed; but when not committed within any State, the Trial shall be at such Place or Places as the Congress may by Law have directed.

Commentary

◀ **Clause 1** Jurisdiction refers to the right of a court to hear a case. Federal courts have jurisdiction over cases that involve the Constitution, federal laws, treaties, foreign ambassadors and diplomats, naval and maritime laws, disagreements between states or between citizens from different states, and disputes between a state or citizen and a foreign state or citizen.

◀ **Clause 2** Original jurisdiction means the power of a court to hear a case when it first arises. The Supreme Court has original jurisdiction over only a few cases, such as those involving foreign diplomats. More often, the Supreme Court acts as an appellate court. An appellate court considers whether the trial judge made errors during the trial or incorrectly interpreted or applied the law in reaching a decision.

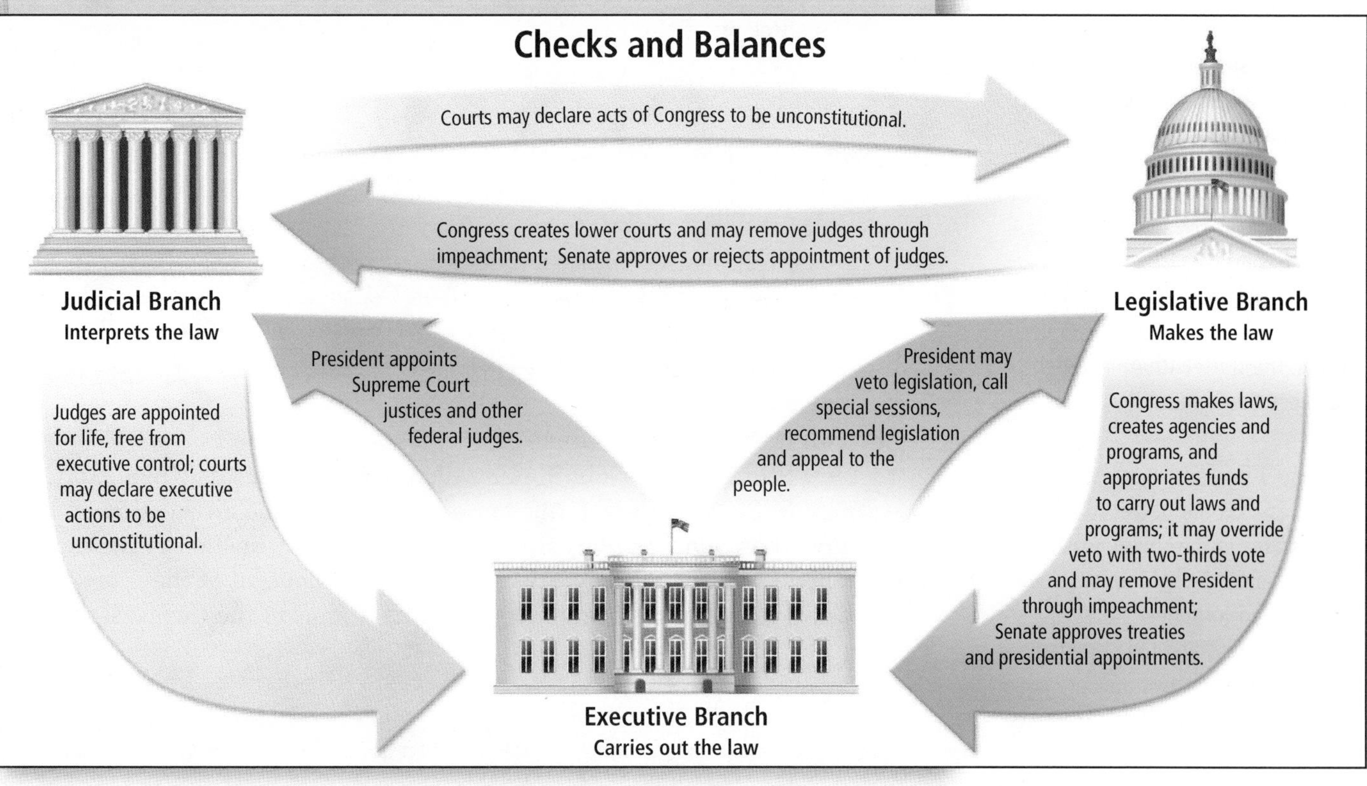

Commentary

 **Checkpoint**

How does the Constitution define treason?

Section 3. Treason

1. Treason against the United States shall consist only in levying War against them, or in adhering to their Enemies, giving them Aid and Comfort. No Person shall be convicted ofTreason unless on the Testimony of two Witnesses to the same overtAct, or on Confession in open Court.
2. The Congress shall have Power to declare the Punishment of Treason, but no Attainder of Treason shall work Corruption of Blood, or Forfeiture except during the Life of the Person attainted.

Article IV Relations Among the States

Section 1. Full Faith and Credit

Full Faith and Credit shall be given in each State to the public Acts, Records, and judicial Proceedings of every other State And the Congress may by general Laws prescribe the Manner in which such Acts, Records and Proceedings shall be proved,and the Effect thereof.

Section 2. Privileges and Immunities of Citizens

1. The Citizens of each State shall be entitled to all Privileges and Immunities of Citizens in the several States.
2. A Person charged in any State with Treason,Felony, or other Crime, who shall flee from justice, and be found in another State, shall on Demand of the executive Authority of the State from which he fled, be delivered up, to be removed to the State having Jurisdiction of the Crime.

Clause 2 ▶
The act of returning a suspected criminal or escaped prisoner to a state where he or she is wanted is called <u>extradition</u>. State governors must return a suspect to another state. However, the Supreme Court has ruled that a governor cannot be forced to do so if he or she feels that justice will not be done.

3. ~~No Person held to Service or Labor in one State, under the Laws thereof, escaping into another, shall, in Consequence of any Law or Regulation therein, be discharged from Service or Labor, but shall be delivered up on Claim of the Party to whom such Service or Labor may be due.~~

Clause 3 ▶
<u>Persons held to service or labor</u> refers to slaves or indentured servants. The Thirteenth Amendment replaces this clause.

Section 3. New States and Territories

1. New States may be admitted by the Congress into this Union;but no new State shall be formed or erected within the Jurisdiction of any other State; nor any State be formed by the Junction of two or more States, or Parts of States, without the Consent of the Legislatures of the States concerned as well as of the Congress

Clause 1 ▶
Congress has the power to admit new states to the Union. Existing states cannot be split up or joined together to form new states unless both Congress and the state legislatures approve. New states are equal to all other states.

2. The Congress shall have Power to dispose of and make all needful Rules and Regulations respecting the Territory or other Property belonging to the United States; and nothing in this Constitution shall be so construed as to Prejudice any Claims of the United States, or of any particular State.

Section 4. Protection Afforded to the States by the Nation
The United States shall guarantee to every State in this Union a Republican Form of Government, and shall protect each of them against Invasion; and on Application of the Legislature, or of the Executive (when the Legislature cannot be convened) against domestic Violence.

Article V Provision for Amendments

The Congress, whenever two thirds of both Houses shall deem it necessary, shall propose Amendments to this Constitution, or, on the Application of the Legislatures of two thirds of the several States, shall call a Convention for proposing Amendments, which, in either Case, shall be valid to all Intents and Purposes, as Part of this Constitution, when ratified by the Legislatures of three fourths of the several States, or by Conventions in three fourths thereof, as the one or the other Mode of Ratification may be proposed by the Congress; Provided ~~that no Amendment which may be made prior to the Year One thousand eight hundred and eight shall in any Manner affect the first and fourth Clauses in the Ninth section of the first Article; and~~ that no State, without its Consent, shall be deprived of its equal Suffrage in the Senate.

Article VI National Debts, Supremacy of National Law, Oath

Section 1.
All Debts contracted and Engagements entered into, before the Adoption of this Constitution, shall be as valid against the United States under this Constitution, as under the Confederation.

Section 2.
This Constitution, and the Laws of the United States which shall be made in Pursuance thereof; and all Treaties made, or which shall be made, under the Authority of the United States, shall be the supreme Law of the Land; and the Judges in every State shall be bound thereby, anything in the constitution or Laws of any State to the Contrary notwithstanding.

Commentary

◀ **Article V** The Constitution can be amended, or changed, if necessary. An amendment can be proposed by (1) a two-thirds vote of both houses of Congress or (2) a national convention called by Congress at the request of two thirds of the state legislatures. (This second method has never been used.) An amendment must be ratified, or approved, by (1) three fourths of the state legislatures or (2) special conventions in three fourths of the states. Congress decides which method will be used.

◀ **Section 2** The "supremacy clause" in this section establishes the Constitution, federal laws, and treaties that the Senate has ratified as the supreme, or highest, law of the land. Thus, they outweigh state laws. A state judge must overturn a state law that conflicts with the Constitution or with a federal law.

Commentary

Section 3.

The Senators and Representatives before mentioned, and the Members of the several State legislatures, and all executive and judicial Officers, both of the United States and of the several States, shall be bound by Oath or Affirmation, to support this Constitution; but no religious Test shall ever be required as a Qualification to any Office or public Trust under the the United States.

Article VII ▶

During 1787 and 1788, states held special conventions. By October 1788, the required nine states had ratified the United States Constitution.

Checkpoint

What had to happen before the Constitution would go into effect?

Article VII Ratification of Constitution

The ratification of the Conventions of nine States, shall be sufficient for the Establishment of this Constitution between the States so ratifying the same.

Done in Convention by the Unanimous Consent of the States present the Seventeenth Day of September in the Year of our Lord one thousand seven hundred and Eighty seven and of the Independence of the United States of America the twelfth. In witness whereof We have hereunto subscribed our Names.

Attest: William Jackson, SECRETARY
George Washington, PRESIDENT and deputy from Virginia

New Hampshire
John Langdon
Nicholas Gilman

Massachusetts
Nathaniel Gorham
Rufus King

Connecticut
William Samuel Johnson
Roger Sherman

New York
Alexander Hamilton

New Jersey
William Livingston
David Brearley
William Paterson
Jonathan Dayton

Pennsylvania
Benjamin Franklin
Thomas Mifflin
Robert Morris
George Clymer
Thomas Fitzsimons
Jared Ingersoll
James Wilson
Gouverneur Morris

Delaware
George Read
Gunning Bedford, Jr.
John Dickinson
Richard Bassett
Jacob Broom

Maryland
James McHenry
Dan of St. Thomas Jenifer
Daniel Carroll

Virginia
John Blair
James Madison, Jr.

North Carolina
William Blount
Richard Dobbs Spaight
Hugh Williamson

South Carolina
John Rutledge
Charles Cotesworth Pinckney
Charles Pinckney
Pierce Butler

Georgia
William Few
Abraham Baldwin

AMENDMENTS

First Amendment Freedom of Religion, Speech, Press, Assembly, and Petition

Congress shall make no law respecting an establishment of religion, or prohibiting the free exercise thereof, or abridging the freedom of speech, or of the press; or the right of the people peaceably to assemble, and to petition the Government for a redress of grievances.

Second Amendment Bearing Arms

A well-regulated Militia being necessary to the security of a free State, the right of the people to keep and bear Arms, shall not be infringed.

Third Amendment Quartering of Troops

No Soldier shall, in time of peace be quartered in any house, without the consent of the Owner, nor, in time of war, but in a manner to be prescribed by law.

Commentary

The Amendments The Amendments are changes made to the Constitution, which has been amended 27 times since it was originally ratified in 1788. The first 10 amendments are referred to as the Bill of Rights.

◄ **First Amendment** The First Amendment protects five basic rights: freedom of religion, speech, the press, assembly, and petition. Congress cannot set up an established, or official, church or religion for the nation, nor can it forbid the practice of religion.

Congress may not abridge, or limit, the freedom to speak or write freely. The government may not censor, or review, books and newspapers before they are printed. This amendment also protects the right to assemble, or hold public meetings. Petition means ask. Redress means to correct. Grievances are wrongs. The people have the right to ask the government for wrongs to be corrected.

◄ **Second Amendment** The Supreme Court decision in the case of *District of Columbia* v. *Heller* in 2008 ruled that a ban on handguns in the District of Columbia violated the Second Amendment. This is the first case since *U.S.* v. *Miller* in which the Court moved to interpret the Second Amendment.

◄ **Third Amendment** In colonial times, the British could quarter, or house, soldiers in private homes without permission of the owners. The Third Amendment prevents such abuses.

Commentary

Fourth Amendment ▶
This amendment protects Americans from unreasonable searches and seizures. Search and seizure are permitted only if a judge issues a warrant, or written court order. A warrant is issued only if there is probable cause. This means an officer must show that it is probable, or likely, that the search will produce evidence of a crime.

Fifth Amendment ▶
This amendment protects the rights of the accused. Capital crimes are those that can be punished with death. Infamous crimes are those that can be punished with prison or loss of rights. The federal government must obtain an indictment, or formal accusation, from a grand jury to prosecute anyone for such crimes. A grand jury is a panel of between 12 and 23 citizens who decide if the government has enough evidence to justify a trial.

Double jeopardy is forbidden by this amendment. This means that a person cannot be tried twice for the same crime. However, if a court sets aside a conviction because of a legal error, the accused can be tried again. A person on trial cannot be forced to testify, or give evidence, against himself or herself. A person accused of a crime is entitled to due process of law, or a fair hearing or trial.

The government cannot seize private property for public use without paying the owner a fair price for it.

Fourth Amendment Searches and Seizures

The right of the people to be secure in their persons, houses, papers, and effects, against unreasonable searches and seizures, shall not be violated, and no Warrants shall issue, but upon probable cause, supported by Oath or affirmation, and particularly describing the place to be searched, and the persons or things to be seized.

Fifth Amendment Criminal Proceedings; Due Process; Eminent Domain

No person shall be held to answer for a capital, or otherwise infamous crime, unless on a presentment or indictment of a Grand Jury, except in cases arising in the land or naval forces, or in the Militia, when in actual service in time of War or public danger; nor shall any person be subject for the same offence to be twice put in jeopardy of life or limb; nor shall be compelled in any criminal case to be a witness against himself, nor be deprived of life, liberty, or property, without due process of law; nor shall private property be taken for public use, without just compensation.

Sixth Amendment Criminal Proceedings

In all criminal prosecutions, the accused shall enjoy the right to a speedy and public trial, by an impartial jury of the State and district wherein the crime shall have been committed, which district shall have been previously ascertained by law, and to be informed of the nature and cause of the accusation; to be confronted with the witnesses against him; to have compulsory process for obtaining witnesses in his favor, and to have the Assistance of Counsel for his defence.

Seventh Amendment Civil Trials

In Suits at common law, where the value in controversy shall exceed twenty dollars, the right of trial by jury shall be preserved, and no fact tried by a jury, shall be otherwise re-examined in any Court of the United States, than according to the rules of the common law.

Eighth Amendment Punishment for Crimes

Excessive bail shall not be required, nor excessive fines imposed, nor cruel and unusual punishment inflicted.

Ninth Amendment Unenumerated Rights

The enumeration in the Constitution, of certain rights, shall not be construed to deny or disparage others retained by the people.

Tenth Amendment Powers Reserved to the States

The powers not delegated to the United States by the Constitution, nor prohibited by it to the States, are reserved to the States respectively, or to the people.

Commentary

◀ **Sixth Amendment** In criminal cases, the jury must be impartial, or not favor either side. The accused is guaranteed the right to a trial by jury. The trial must be speedy. The accused must be told the charges and be allowed to question all witnesses. The accused must be allowed a lawyer.

◀ **Seventh Amendment** Common law refers to rules of law established by judges in past cases. An appeals court can set aside a verdict only if legal errors make the trial unfair.

◀ **Eighth Amendment** Bail is money that the accused leaves with the court as a pledge to appear for trial. If the accused does not appear, the court keeps the money. This amendment prevents the court from imposing bail or fines that are excessive, or too high. The amendment also forbids cruel and unusual punishments, such as physical torture.

◀ **Ninth Amendment** The rights of the people are not limited to those listed in the Bill of Rights. In the Ninth Amendment, the government is prevented from claiming these are the only rights people have.

◀ **Tenth Amendment** Powers not given to the federal government belong to the states. Powers reserved to the states are not listed in the Constitution.

Commentary

Eleventh Amendment ▶
A private citizen from one state cannot sue the government of another state in federal court. However, a citizen can sue a state government in a state court.

Twelfth Amendment ▶
This amendment changed the way the electoral college voted as outlined in Article II, Section 1, Clause 3. This amendment provides that each elector choose one candidate for President and one candidate for Vice President. If no candidate for President receives a majority of electoral votes, the House of Representatives chooses the President. If no candidate for Vice President receives a majority, the Senate elects the Vice President. The Vice President must be a person who is eligible to be President.

It is possible for a candidate to win the popular vote and lose the electoral college. This happened in 1888 and 2000.

Eleventh Amendment Suits Against States

The Judicial power of the United States shall not be construed to extend to any suit in law or equity, commenced or prosecuted against one of the United States by Citizens of another State, or by Citizens or Subjects of any Foreign State.

Twelfth Amendment Election of President and Vice President

The Electors shall meet in their respective States and vote by ballot for President and Vice President, one of whom, at least, shall not be an inhabitant of the same State with themselves; they shall name in their ballots the person voted for as President, and in distinct ballots the person voted for as Vice President, and they shall make distinct lists of all persons voted for as President, and of all persons voted for as Vice President, and of the number of votes for each, which lists they shall sign and certify, and transmit sealed to the seat of the government of the United States, directed to the President of the Senate;— The President of the Senate shall, in the presence of the Senate and the House of Representatives, open all the certificates and the votes shall then be counted;— the person having the greatest Number of votes for President shall be the President, if such number be a majority of the whole number of Electors appointed; and if no person have such a majority, then, from the persons having the highest numbers not exceeding three on the list of those voted for as President, the House of Representatives shall choose immediately, by ballot, the President. But in choosing the President, the votes shall be taken by States, the representation from each State having one vote; a quorum for this purpose shall consist of a member or members from two thirds of the States, and a majority of the States shall be necessary to a choice. ~~And if the House of Representatives shall not choose a President whenever the right of choice shall devolve upon them, before the fourth day of March next following, then the Vice President shall act as President, as in case of death or other constitutional disability of the President.~~ The person having the greatest number of votes as Vice President, shall be the Vice President, if such number be a majority of the whole number of Electors appointed, and if no person have a majority, then from the two highest numbers on the list, the Senate shall choose the Vice President; a quorum for the purpose shall consist of two thirds of the whole number of Senators, a majority of the whole number shall be necessary to a choice. But no person constitutionally ineligible to the office of President shall be eligible to that of Vice President of the United States.

Thirteenth Amendment Slavery and Involuntary Servitude

Section 1. Neither slavery nor involuntary servitude, except as a punishment for crime whereof the party shall have been duly convicted, shall exist within the United States, or any place subject to their jurisdiction.

Section 2. Congress shall have power to enforce this article by appropriate legislation.

Fourteenth Amendment Rights of Citizens

Section 1. All persons born or naturalized in the United States and subject to the jurisdiction thereof, are citizens of the United States and of the State wherein they reside. No State shall make or enforce any law which shall abridge the privileges or immunities of citizens of the United States; nor shall any State deprive any person of life, liberty, or property, without due process of law; nor deny to any person within its jurisdiction the equal protection of the laws.

Section 2. Representatives shall be apportioned among the several States according to their respective numbers, counting the whole number of persons in each State, excluding Indians not taxed. But when the right to vote at any election for the choice of electors for President and Vice President of the United States, Representatives in Congress, the Executive and Judicial officers of a State, or the members of the Legislature thereof, is denied to any of the male inhabitants of such State, being twenty-one years of age, and citizens of the United States, or in any way abridged, except for participation in rebellion, or other crime, the basis of representation therein shall be reduced in the proportion which the number of such male citizens shall bear to the whole number of male citizens twenty-one years of age in such State.

Section 3. No person shall be a Senator or Representative in Congress, or elector of President and Vice President, or hold any office, civil or military, under the United States, or under any State, who, having previously taken an oath, as a member of Congress, or as an officer of the United States, or as a member of any State legislature, or as an executive or judicial officer of any State, to support the Constitution of the United States, shall have engaged in insurrection or rebellion against the same, or given aid or comfort to the enemies thereof. But Congress may, by a vote of two thirds of each House, remove such disability.

Commentary

◀ **Thirteenth Amendment** The Emancipation Proclamation (1863) freed slaves only in areas controlled by the Confederacy. This amendment freed all slaves. It also forbids involuntary servitude, or labor done against one's will. However, it does not prevent prison wardens from making prisoners work. Congress can pass laws to carry out this amendment.

◀ **Fourteenth Amendment, Section 1** This amendment defines citizenship for the first time in the Constitution. It was intended to protect the rights of the freed slaves by guaranteeing all citizens "equal protection under the law."

◀ **Fourteenth Amendment, Section 2** This section replaced the three-fifths clause. It provides that representation in the House of Representatives is decided on the basis of the number of people in the states. It also provides that states that deny the vote to male citizens aged 21 or over will be punished by losing part of their representation. This provision has never been enforced.

 **Checkpoint**

What is one key provision of the Fourteenth Amendment?

Commentary

Section 4. The validity of the public debt of the United States, authorized by law, including debts incurred for payment of pensions and bounties for services in suppressing insurrection or rebellion, shall not be questioned. But neither the United States nor any State shall assume or pay any debt or obligation incurred in aid of insurrection or rebellion against the United States, or any claim for the loss or emancipation of any slave; but all such debts, obligations and claims shall be held illegal and void.

Section 5. The Congress shall have power to enforce, by appropriate legislation, the provisions of this article.

Fifteenth Amendment, ▶ Section 1 This amendment gave African Americans the right to vote. In the late 1800s, however, southern states used grandfather clauses, literacy tests, and poll taxes to keep African Americans from voting.

Fifteenth Amendment Right to Vote—Race, Color, Servitude

Section 1. The right of citizens of the United States to vote shall not be denied or abridged by the United States or by any State on account of race, color, or previous condition of servitude.

Fifteenth Amendment, ▶ Section 2 Congress can pass laws to carry out this amendment. The Twenty-fourth Amendment barred the use of poll taxes in national elections. The Voting Rights Act of 1965 gave federal officials the power to register voters where there was voting discrimination.

Section 2. The Congress shall have power to enforce this article by appropriate legislation.

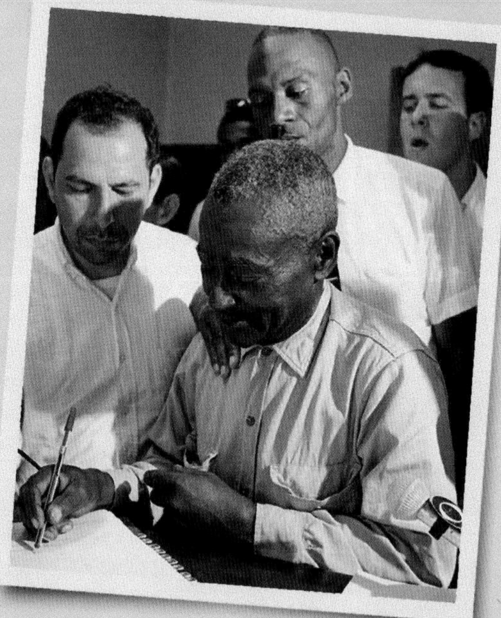

Sixteenth Amendment ▶ Congress has the power to collect taxes on people's income. An income tax can be collected without regard to a state's population. This amendment changed Article I, Section 9, Clause 4.

Sixteenth Amendment Income Tax

The Congress shall have power to lay and collect taxes on incomes, from whatever source derived, without apportionment among the several States, and without regard to any census or enumeration.

Commentary

Seventeenth Amendment Popular Election of Senators

Section 1. The Senate of the United States shall be composed of two Senators from each State, elected by the people thereof, for six years; and each Senator shall have one vote. The electors in each State shall have the qualifications requisite for electors of the most numerous branch of the State legislatures.

Section 2. When vacancies happen in the representation of any State in the Senate, the executive authority of such State shall issue writs of election to fill such vacancies: *Provided,* That the legislature of any State may empower the executive thereof to make temporary appointments until the people fill the vacancies by election as the legislature may direct.

Section 3. ~~This amendment shall not be so construed as to affect the election or term of any Senator chosen before it becomes valid as part of the Constitution.~~

◀ **Seventeenth Amendment**
This amendment replaced Article I, Section 3, Clause 2. Before it was adopted, state legislatures chose senators. This amendment provides that senators are elected directly by the people of each state.

Eighteenth Amendment Prohibition of Alcoholic Beverages

Section 1. ~~After one year from the ratification of this article the manufacture, sale, or transportation of intoxicating liquors within, the importation thereof into, or the exportation thereof from the United States and all territory subject to the jurisdiction thereof for beverage purposes is hereby prohibited.~~

Section 2. ~~The Congress and the several States shall have concurrent power to enforce this article by appropriate legislation.~~

Section 3. ~~This article shall be inoperative unless it shall have been ratified as an amendment to the Constitution by the legislatures of the several States, as provided in the Constitution, within seven years of the date of the submission hereof to the States by Congress.~~

◀ **Eighteenth Amendment**
This amendment, known as Prohibition, banned the making, selling, or transporting of alcoholic beverages in the United States. Later, the Twenty-first Amendment repealed, or canceled, this amendment.

Nineteenth Amendment Women's Suffrage

Section 1. The right of citizens of the United States to vote shall not be denied or abridged by the United States or by any State on account of sex.

Section 2. Congress shall have power to enforce this article by appropriate legislation.

◀ **Nineteenth Amendment**
Neither the federal government nor state governments can deny the right to vote on account of sex.

Commentary

Twentieth Amendment, ▶ Section 1 The date for the inauguration of the President was changed to January 20, and the date for Congress to begin its term changed to January 3. Prior to this amendment, the beginning-of-term date was set in March. The outgoing officials with little or no influence on matters were not effective in office. Being so inactive, they were called "lame ducks."

Twentieth Amendment, ▶ Section 3 If the President-elect dies before taking office, the Vice President-elect becomes President. If no President has been chosen by January 20 or if the elected candidate fails to qualify for office, the Vice President-elect acts as President, but only until a qualified President is chosen. Finally, Congress has the power to choose a person to act as President if neither the President-elect nor the Vice President-elect is qualified to take office.

Twenty-first Amendment, ▶ Section 1 The Eighteenth Amendment is repealed, making it legal to make and sell alcoholic beverages. Prohibition ended on December 5, 1933.

Twentieth Amendment Presidential Terms; Sessions of Congress

Section 1. The terms of the President and Vice President shall end at noon on the 20th day of January, and the terms of Senators and Representatives at noon on the 3d day of January, of the years in which such terms would have ended if this article had not been ratified; and the terms of their successors shall then begin.

Section 2. The Congress shall assemble at least once in every year, and such meeting shall begin at noon on the 3d day of January, unless they shall by law appoint a different day.

Section 3. If, at the time fixed for the beginning of the term of the President, the President elect shall have died, the Vice President elect shall become President. If a President shall not have been chosen before the time fixed for the beginning of his term, or if the President elect shall have failed to qualify, then the Vice President elect shall act as President until a President shall have qualified; and the Congress may by law provide for the case wherein neither a President elect nor a Vice President elect shall have qualified, declaring who shall then act as President, or the manner in which one who is to act shall be selected, and such person shall act accordingly until a President or Vice President shall have qualified.

Section 4. The Congress may by law provide for the case of the death of any of the persons from whom the House of Representatives may choose a President whenever the right of choice shall have devolved upon them, and for the case of the death of any of the persons from whom the Senate may choose a Vice President whenever the right of choice shall have devolved upon them.

Section 5. ~~Sections 1 and 2 shall take effect on the 15th day of October following the ratification of this article.~~

Section 6. This article shall be inoperative unless it shall have been ratified as an amendment to the Constitution by the legislatures of three fourths of the several States within seven years from the date of its submission.

Twenty-first Amendment Repeal of Prohibition

Section 1. The eighteenth article of amendment to the Constitution of the United States is hereby repealed.

Section 2. The transportation or importation into any State, Territory, or possession of the United States for delivery or use therein of intoxicating liquors, in violation of the laws thereof, is hereby prohibited.

Section 3. ~~This article shall be inoperative unless it shall have been ratified as an amendment to the Constitution by conventions in the several States, as provided in the Constitution, within seven years from the date of the submission hereof to the States by the Congress.~~

Twenty-second Amendment Presidential Tenure

Section 1. No person shall be elected to the office of the President more than twice, and no person who has held the office of President, or acted as President, for more than two years of a term to which some other person was elected President shall be elected to the office of the President more than once. ~~But this Article shall not apply to any person holding the office of President, when this Article was proposed by the Congress, and shall not prevent any person who may be holding the office of President, or acting as President, during the term within which this Article becomes operative from holding the office of President or acting as President during the remainder of such term.~~

Section 2. ~~This article shall be inoperative unless it shall have been ratified as an amendment to the Constitution by the legislatures of three fourths of the several states within seven years from the date of its submission to the States by the Congress.~~

Twenty-third Amendment Presidential Electors for The District of Columbia

Section 1. The District constituting the seat of Government of the United States shall appoint in such manner as the Congress may direct:

A number of electors of President and Vice President equal to the whole number of Senators and Representatives in Congress to which the District would be entitled if it were a State, but in no event more than the least populous State; they shall be in addition to those appointed by the States, they shall be considered, for the purposes of the election of President and Vice President, to be electors appointed by a State; and they shall meet in the District and perform such duties as provided by the twelfth article of amendment.

Section 2. The Congress shall have power to enforce this article by appropriate legislation.

Commentary

◄ **Twenty-second Amendment, Section 1** This amendment provides that no President may serve more than two terms. A President who has already served more than half of someone else's term can serve only one more full term. Before Franklin Roosevelt became President, no President served more than two terms in office. Roosevelt broke with this custom and was elected to four terms.

◄ **Twenty-third Amendment, Section 1** This amendment gives the residents of Washington, D.C., the right to vote in presidential elections. Until this amendment was adopted, people living in Washington, D.C., could not vote for President because the Constitution had made no provision for choosing electors from the nation's capital. Washington, D.C., has three electoral votes.

Commentary

Twenty-fourth Amendment, ▶ Section 1 A poll tax is a tax on voters. This amendment bans poll taxes in national elections. Some states used poll taxes to keep African Americans from voting. In 1966, the Supreme Court struck down poll taxes in state elections, also.

Twenty-fourth Amendment Right to Vote in Federal Elections

Section 1. The right of citizens of the United States to vote in any primary or other election for President or Vice President, for electors for President or Vice President, or for Senator or Representative in Congress, shall not be denied or abridged by the United States or any State by reason of failure to pay any poll tax or other tax.

Section 2. The Congress shall have power to enforce this article by appropriate legislation.

Twenty-fifth Amendment, ▶ Section 1 If the President dies or resigns, the Vice President becomes President. This section clarifies Article II, Section 1, Clause 6.

Twenty-fifth Amendment, ▶ Section 3 If the President declares in writing that he or she is unable to perform the duties of office, the Vice President serves as acting President until the President recovers.

Twenty-fifth Amendment, ▶ Section 4 Two Presidents, Woodrow Wilson and Dwight Eisenhower, fell gravely ill while in office. The Constitution contained no provision for this kind of emergency.

Twenty-fifth Amendment Presidential Succession; Vice Presidential Vacancy; Presidential Inability

Section 1. In case of the removal of the President from office or of his death or resignation, the Vice President shall become President.

Section 2. Whenever there is a vacancy in the office of the Vice President, the President shall nominate a Vice President who shall take office upon confirmation by a majority vote of both Houses of Congress.

Section 3. Whenever the President transmits to the President pro tempore of the Senate and the Speaker of the House of Representatives his written declaration that he is unable to discharge the powers and duties of his office, and until he transmits to them a written declaration to the contrary, such powers and duties shall be discharged by the Vice President as Acting President.

Section 4. Whenever the Vice President and a majority of either the principal officers of the executive departments or of such other body as Congress may by law provide, transmit to the President pro tempore of the Senate and the Speaker of the House of Representatives their written declaration that the President is unable to discharge the powers and duties of his office, the Vice President shall immediately assume the powers and duties of the office as Acting President.

Thereafter, when the President transmits to the President pro tempore of the Senate and the Speaker of the House of Representatives his written declaration that no inability exists, he shall resume the powers and duties of his office unless the Vice President and a majority of either the principal officers of the executive department or of such other body as Congress may by law provide, transmit within four days to the President pro tempore of the Senate and the Speaker of the House of Representatives their written declaration that the President is unable to discharge the powers and duties of his office. Thereupon Congress shall decide the issue, assembling within forty-eight hours for that purpose if not in session. If the Congress, within twenty-one days after receipt of the latter written declaration, or, if Congress is not in session, within twenty-one days after Congress is required to assemble, determines by two-thirds vote of both Houses that the President is unable to discharge the powers and duties of his office, the Vice President shall continue to discharge the same as Acting President; otherwise, the President shall resume the powers and duties of his office.

Twenty-sixth Amendment Right to Vote—Age

Section 1. The right of citizens of the United States, who are eighteen years of age or older, to vote shall not be denied or abridged by the United States or by any State on account of age.

Section 2. The Congress shall have the power to enforce this article by appropriate legislation.

Twenty-seventh Amendment Congressional Pay

No law varying the compensation for the services of the Senators and Representatives, shall take effect, until an election of Representatives shall have intervened.

Commentary

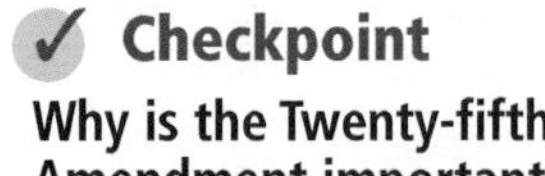

Why is the Twenty-fifth Amendment important?

◀ **Twenty-sixth Amendment, Section 1** In 1970, Congress passed a law allowing 18-year-olds to vote. However, the Supreme Court decided that Congress could not set a minimum age for state elections.

◀ **Twenty-seventh Amendment** If members of Congress vote themselves a pay increase, it cannot go into effect until after the next congressional election. This amendment was proposed in 1789. In 1992, Michigan became the thirty-eighth state to ratify it.

CHAPTER

6 The New Republic
1789–1816

WITNESS HISTORY

The First American President

On April 14, 1789, a horse and rider arrived at George Washington's home in Virginia, bearing a letter telling Washington that he had been unanimously elected President of the new United States. Washington spent eight days traveling to the capital at New York. So many people crowded the roads to see and applaud him that he said he could barely see through the dust they kicked up. Abigail Adams—the wife of John Adams, who would become Vice President—spoke for the nation when she described Washington as "polite with dignity . . . modest, wise, and good."

◀ George Washington had to leave his comfortable estate at Mount Vernon, Virginia, and move to New York to assume the presidency of the United States.

1789 button from Washington's inauguration

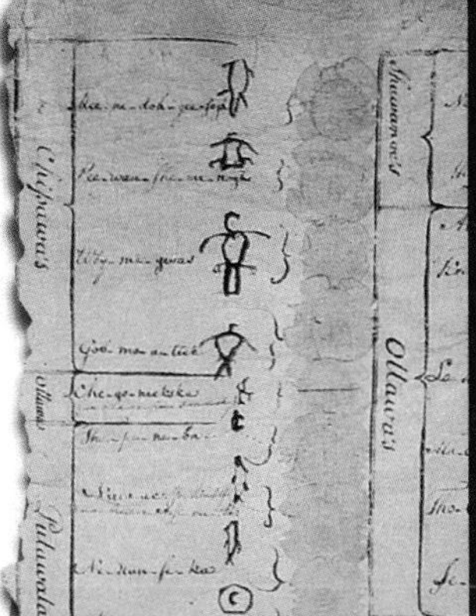

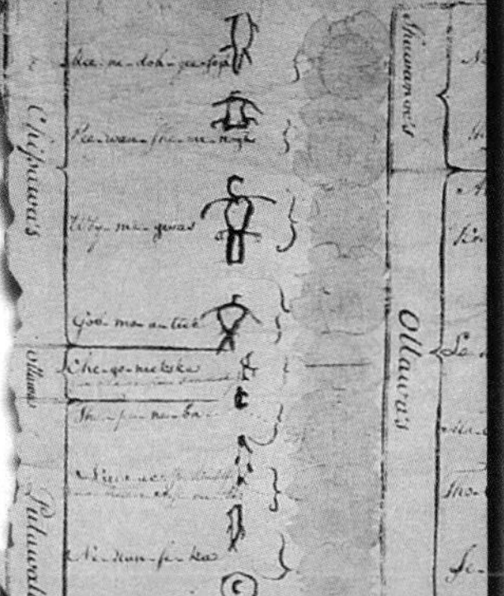

The 1795 Treaty of Greenville signed between Native Americans and the United States

Thomas Jefferson's writing desk

Chapter Preview

Chapter Focus Question: How did the United States build a government, expand its territory, and conduct foreign policy in its early years?

Section 1
Government and Party Politics

Section 2
The Struggle Over Foreign Policy

Section 3
The Age of Jefferson

Section 4
The War of 1812

Use the ☑ **Quick Study Timeline** at the end of this chapter to preview chapter events.

Note Taking Study Guide *Online*
For: Note Taking and American Issues Connector
www.pearsonschool.com/ushist

▲ Women pay respect to the new President.

A button from Washington's inauguration ▶

SECTION 1

WITNESS HISTORY

The First Inaugural

When George Washington gave his Inaugural Address in 1789, he was well aware of the extraordinary responsibility of leading "the experiment entrusted to the hands of the American people." An official at the inauguration described the ceremony in a letter to his wife:

> "It was with difficulty a passage could be made by the troops through the pressing crowds, who seemed to be incapable of being satisfied by gazing at this man of the people. . . . The streets were lined with the inhabitants as thick as the people could stand. . . . The houses were filled with gentlemen and ladies, the whole distance being half a mile, and the windows to the highest stories were illuminated by the sparkling eyes of innumberable companies of ladies, who seemed to vie with each other to show their joy on this great occasion."
>
> —Elias Boudinot, April 30, 1789

Government and Party Politics

Objectives

- Describe the steps Washington's administration took to build the federal government.
- Analyze Hamilton's plans for the economy and the opposition to them.
- Explain how a two-party system emerged in the new nation.

Terms and People

administration	strict construction
precedent	Whiskey Rebellion
Cabinet	political party
tariff	Democratic Republican
loose construction	

NoteTaking

Reading Skill: Summarize Summarize information about the early American government in an outline like the one below.

I. Building the Federal Government
  A. Electing Washington as President
  B. Forming the Cabinet
  C. Setting up the Judiciary
II.

Why It Matters In 1789, the leaders of the new federal government of the United States gathered in New York City. Besides ideals, they had very little to guide them. The newly ratified Constitution was clear on some points but vague on others. It was also entirely untested. Those who had written the Constitution, along with the new President, George Washington, knew full well that a good start would secure the daring experiment in republican union. But early mistakes could doom it. **Section Focus Question: How did debate over the role of government lead to the formation of political parties?**

Building the Federal Government

The new government started out with huge problems. It had inherited a national debt of $52 million from the Confederation—a huge burden for a nation with a farm economy and only about 3 million people. With no navy and an army of only around 400 men, the United States was not respected by other countries. At New Orleans, the Spanish closed the Mississippi River to American trade. Along the Great Lakes, the British kept forts within American territory.

Electing a President Fortunately, the new government enjoyed extraordinary leaders. In 1789, the new electoral college unanimously elected George Washington as President of the United States. As a revolutionary leader, Washington enjoyed widespread respect and popularity. Yet he took the difficult job reluctantly.

Primary Source "About ten o'clock I bade farewell to Mount Vernon, to private life, and to domestic felicity, and with a mind oppressed with more anxious and painful sensations than I have words to express, set out for New York."

—George Washington, April 16, 1789

Massachusetts patriot John Adams was elected Vice President. Washington's **administration,** or the officials in the executive branch of government, began with just himself, Adams, and about a dozen clerks. Besides the newly elected Congress, there were few other federal officers. There were also few set rules to guide the administration. Quickly after taking office, Washington began setting important **precedents,** or acts or statements that become traditions to be followed.

Setting Up the Judiciary The Constitution called for one Supreme Court and several smaller ones, but intentionally left to Congress the details of organizing a federal court system. Madison, who had been elected to the House of Representatives in the first Congress, helped to pass the Judiciary Act of 1789. This act established a judiciary, or a system of courts. The U.S. judiciary was made up of thirteen federal district courts, one for each state. Three circuit courts would hear appeals from the state courts and a six-member Supreme Court would decide contested cases. The Supreme Court also served as a trial court in certain cases involving states or foreign affairs. The act also established the office of Attorney General to prosecute and defend cases on behalf of the federal government. Washington appointed John Jay as the first Chief Justice of the Supreme Court.

Setting Up the Cabinet One of Washington's most important precedents was the formation of a **Cabinet,** or the group of federal leaders who headed the major departments of the executive branch and advised the President. The first four executive departments were the departments of State, Treasury, and War, and the Attorney General. The State Department, led by Thomas Jefferson, conducted foreign policy. The War Department supervised national defense. The Secretary of the Treasury, Alexander Hamilton, managed the nation's finances. Nominated by the President, the Cabinet members were approved by the Senate. In 1907, the Cabinet was officially recognized by law.

✓ **Checkpoint Why was setting up the Cabinet an important precedent?**

Hamilton's Plans Stir Debate

Hamilton was tasked with organizing the young nation's immense debts and setting it on a course of economic security. A true Federalist, he believed that a strong, centralized government was necessary to preserve the Union. As he developed his plans, Hamilton faced fierce and vocal opposition from Antifederalists, who feared that a strong national government would threaten states' rights and people's freedoms. Their struggles and debates made clear that two very different views of government were emerging in the new nation.

The First Cabinet

An engraving from the 1800s shows the first Cabinet. Henry Knox was the Secretary of War, and Edmund Randolph was the Attorney General.

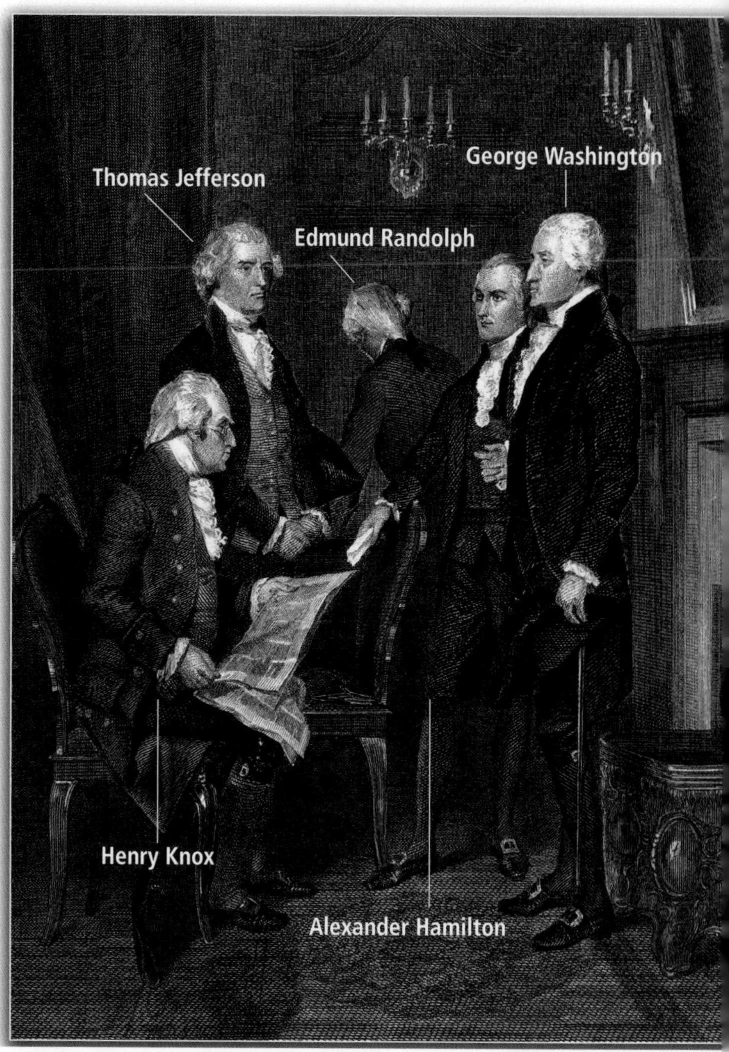

Hamilton's Plan for Restructuring Debt

Action	Result	Lasting Legacy
Pay foreign debt and interest in full	Restore national credit	Established United States as trustworthy
Federal government assumes state debts	Bring stability to country; stimulate economy	Unified country
Impose excise taxes and tariffs	Pay debts and increase manufacturing	Established precedent of nation paying its debts
Create national bank and national currency	Help government regulate economy and commerce; generate income through loans	Created model on which today's Federal Reserve System is based

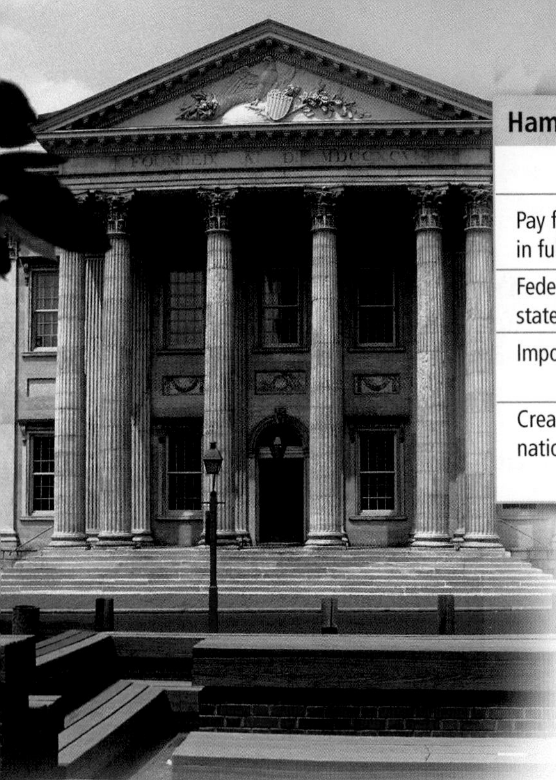

Stabilizing the Economy
Though Jefferson and Madison fiercely opposed Hamilton's plans, Congress eventually adopted them. The first bank of the United States, founded in 1791, stands in Philadelphia. *What did Hamilton plan to do about states' debts?*

Handling the National Debt Hamilton despised the nation's agricultural economy as backward. He wanted to quickly develop a commercial and industrial economy that could support a large federal government along with a strong army and navy. He saw the national debt of $52 million and the additional $25 million in debts owed by the individual states as assets. Rather than pay down those debts using cash reserves, he meant to fund them by selling government bonds, which would pay annual interest to the holders. Such bonds delighted investors, who welcomed an opportunity to reap annual profits.

To pay the annual interest on the bonds, Hamilton proposed new excise taxes and high **tariffs,** or taxes on imported goods, to raise revenue for the federal government and protect struggling American manufacturers from foreign competition. He also asked Congress to charter a Bank of the United States that could regulate state banks, strengthen the national government, and ensure that business interests were closely aligned with those of the government.

Hamilton's Strategy Hamilton saw three great benefits from his system. First, it would establish the nation's financial credibility, making it easier to borrow money in the future. Second, it would buy political support from the wealthiest Americans, which Hamilton believed was essential for the government's stability. Third, it would enrich investors, who could then build new ships, wharves, storehouses, and factories. In other words, his plan would promote the accumulation of capital needed for commercial and industrial growth.

Hamilton's program was intended to redistribute wealth in two ways: from farmers to merchants and from the South to the North. About eighty percent of the nation's debt was owed to merchants in the seaport cities of the Northeast. During the 1780s, they had bought up notes issued by the Congress or by the states. Those notes had lost most of their value but the merchants had bought them anyway as an investment. Because they paid only a fraction of the original value of the notes, and because Hamilton proposed paying them at full value, the merchants would profit under Hamilton's plan. But to pay those debts, the federal government would tax the American people, who were mainly farmers.

 **Checkpoint** **Why did Hamilton want to add to the national debt?**

Opposing Hamilton

The southern states, which were overwhelmingly agricultural, had done a better job of paying their own debts. Why, southerners wondered, should they pay federal taxes to bail out the northern states? And why should their tax dollars flow into the pockets of creditors in the Northeast? Opposition to Hamilton's plans grew steadily in the South.

Interpreting the Constitution To justify his ambitious program, Hamilton interpreted the Constitution broadly, relying on its "implied powers" and its clause empowering Congress to enact laws for the "general welfare." His broad interpretation, or **loose construction,** appalled his critics, including Jefferson and Madison. They favored a **strict construction,** or limiting the federal government to powers explicitly granted by the Constitution. They opposed Hamilton's plans for assuming state debts. Fearing that a national bank would benefit the North at the expense of the South, they also argued that the Constitution did not authorize Congress to charter one.

Compromise Over a National Capital As Americans aligned themselves either with Hamilton or with Madison and Jefferson, debate heated up. Jefferson declared that Hamilton's system "flowed from principles adverse to liberty and . . . calculated to undermine and demolish the republic." Jefferson and Madison insisted that Hamilton was betraying the American Revolution to establish a "kingly government." They pointed to Great Britain, where factories made owners wealthy but kept most of the workers in poverty. Fearing that industrial development led to greater inequality, they concluded that America needed to keep a farm economy in order to sustain the Republic.

In 1791, by a narrow vote, Congress approved full funding of the federal debt, the implementation of new excise taxes, and the creation of a national bank. But in order to get southerners to agree to the assumption of state debts, Hamilton promised that in ten years the national capital would move southward to the banks of the Potomac River, between Maryland and Virginia. To honor the first President, who was reelected in 1792, the new capital became known as Washington, District of Columbia.

The Whiskey Rebellion In western Pennsylvania, mountains made it difficult to transport bulky bushels of grain to eastern markets. So people distilled their grain into whiskey, which was more compact and of higher value. Rural farmers hated the excise tax on whiskey, which reminded them of the British taxes that had led to the Revolution. In 1794, farmers resisted the tax by intimidating and attacking tax collectors.

Hamilton welcomed the opportunity to demonstrate the new power of the nation by suppressing the **Whiskey Rebellion.** Washington agreed, observing, "We had given no testimony to the world of being able or willing to support our government and laws." Under Hamilton's command, 12,000 militiamen marched west into the troubled region. The rebellion quickly dissolved. Rather than resist such overwhelming force, most rebels stayed home or ran away. Hamilton arrested twenty suspects, but only two were convicted. Jefferson mocked that "an insurrection was announced and proclaimed and armed against, but could never be found."

✓ **Checkpoint On what grounds did some people oppose Hamilton's plans?**

Analyzing Political Cartoons

The Whiskey Rebellion A cartoon published in 1794 added to the intense debate over the Whiskey Rebellion.

1. Which figures in the cartoon are rebels? Which represent the government?
2. Does the cartoonist side with the government or the rebels? How can you tell?

A Two-Party System Emerges

The Whiskey Rebellion highlighted the growing division in American politics. The federal government, headed by Washington and Hamilton, sought to secure its power and authority. Meanwhile the opposition, led by Madison and Jefferson, grew stronger.

Debating the Whiskey Rebellion The Whiskey Rebellion, and its outcome, fueled disagreement. The Federalists blamed the rebellion in part on a set of political clubs known as the Democratic Societies. The clubs had formed to oppose the Federalists. Although these clubs were small and scattered, Washington

INFOGRAPHIC

◄ An early political cartoon honors Washington and demonizes Jefferson.

▲ A farmer plows a North Carolina field in 1787.

▼ Wealthy merchants stroll along the harbor in New York City.

Political Parties Grow

With the ink barely dry on the Constitution, distinct political parties were already forming in the United States. The intense debate over ideas that had surrounded the writing of the Constitution shaped the rise of the Federalist and Democratic Republican parties in the new nation.

Federalists

- Led by Alexander Hamilton
- Favored a strong centralized government
- Wanted to base economy on industry and trade
- Were pro-British
- Supported a loose construction of the Constitution

Democratic Republicans

- Led by Thomas Jefferson
- Thought states should have more power
- Wanted to base economy on farming
- Were pro-French
- Supported a strict construction of the Constitution

Thinking Critically

1. **Contrast** What were the major differences between the Federalists and the Democratic Republicans?
2. **Draw Inferences** Though George Washington supported most Federalist beliefs, he refused to declare himself a Federalist. Why do you think this was so?

denounced them as "the most diabolical attempt to destroy the best fabric of human government and happiness." Jefferson and Madison defended the societies, fearing that aristocracy would triumph if leaders were immune from constant public scrutiny and criticism. They were alarmed that the Federalists had sent so many troops to suppress popular dissent in western Pennsylvania. As debate over the rebellion continued, the two sides gradually emerged as distinct political groups.

Vocabulary Builder
suppress–(suh PREHS) *v.* to put an end to with force

Political Parties Compete for Power The authors of the Constitution wanted to avoid organized **political parties,** or groups of people who seek to win elections and hold public office in order to shape government policy. They deemed these groups to be "factions" that threatened the unity of a republic. Despite these intentions, politicians eventually formed two parties: the Federalists, led by Hamilton and John Adams, and the **Democratic Republicans,** led by Jefferson and Madison.

Northerners, especially merchants, tended to favor the Federalists. In contrast, southerners, especially farmers, voted mainly for the Democratic Republicans. Still, Federalists and Democratic Republicans could be found in every social class, in every type of community, in every region, and in every state. Political elections were closely contested most of the time.

The first two Presidents and most of the governors, state legislators, and congressmen were Federalists. Their early electoral success indicates that they were able to attract a majority of voters. Voters credited the Federalists with the new Constitution and with the nation's increased prosperity and stability during the 1790s.

But many common people continued to support the Democratic Republicans. They worried that the Federalists would concentrate wealth and power in the hands of the elite. Many voters also believed that the Democratic Republican Party offered more social mobility.

✓ **Checkpoint** **Who were the leaders of the two emerging political parties?**

SECTION 1 Assessment

Progress Monitoring *Online*
For: Self-test with vocabulary practice
www.pearsonschool.com/ushist

Comprehension

1. **Terms and People** For each term below, explain its impact on early American government.
   - administration
   - precedent
   - Cabinet
   - tariff
   - loose construction
   - strict construction
   - Whiskey Rebellion
   - political party
   - Democratic Republican

2. **NoteTaking Reading Skill: Summarize** Use your completed outline to answer the Section Focus Question: How did debate over the role of government lead to the formation of political parties?

Writing About History

3. **Quick Write: Frame Research Questions** Choose an event from this section. Write two or three questions to generate ideas for a research paper. For example, if you choose the Whiskey Rebellion, you could ask, "Why was it in some people's interest to call this event a rebellion?"

Critical Thinking

4. **Predict Consequences** Would the federal government have survived if the first President had not had widespread respect? Explain.
5. **Analyze Information** Why did Hamilton believe that wealthy Americans were necessary to secure the nation's economic future?
6. **Recognize Ideologies** How did Americans structure their debates about the economy in terms of interpreting the Constitution?
7. **Draw Conclusions** Is it possible to govern a democracy without political parties? Explain.

SECTION 2

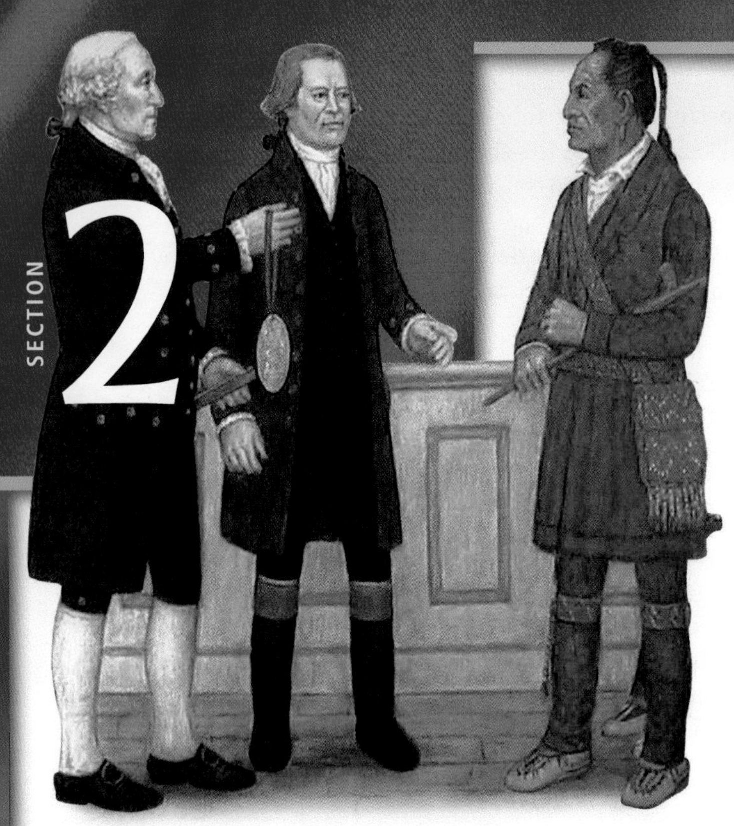

▲ Washington presents Red Jacket with a peace medal at the 1792 meeting.

WITNESS HISTORY

A Great Orator Speaks

In 1792, government officials met with Native Americans in Philadelphia to discuss treaty issues and continuing skirmishes between settlers and Indians in the Northwest. In response to a plea from President Washington for peace, a famous Seneca orator replied,

> "When you Americans and the king made peace [in 1783], he did not mention us, and showed us no compassion, notwithstanding all he said to us, and all we had suffered . . . he never asked us for a delegation to attend our interests. Had he done this, a settlement of peace among all the western nations might have been effected. . . ."
>
> —Red Jacket, 1792

The Struggle Over Foreign Policy

Objectives

- Explain how territorial expansion brought Americans into conflict with the British and with Native Americans.
- Describe American relations with Britain, France, and Spain.
- Analyze how the political parties' debates over foreign policy further divided them.

Terms and People

Little Turtle
Battle of Fallen Timbers
French Revolution
John Jay
XYZ Affair
Alien and Sedition Acts
Virginia and Kentucky resolutions
Aaron Burr

NoteTaking

Reading Skill: Identify Supporting Details Record details about early U.S. foreign policies in a chart like this one.

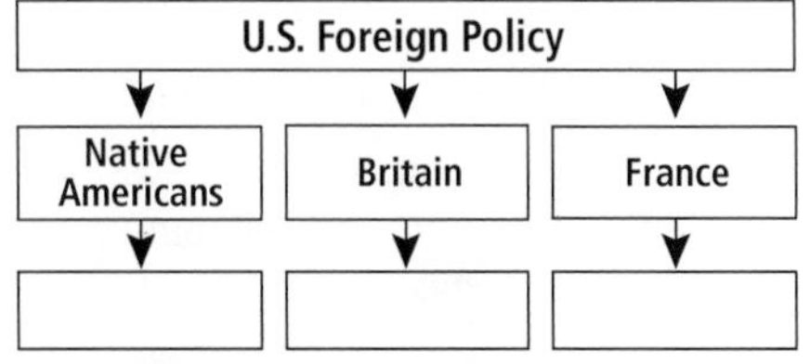

Why It Matters In addition to building a government, making peace with Native Americans, and maintaining control over expanded borders, the young United States had to establish itself in the international community during a volatile time. By 1793, Britain and France had resumed war, and it became difficult for the United States to stay neutral. Debate over America's response to a war and to a revolution in France affected the nation's foreign policy as well as its domestic structure. **Section Focus Question: How did foreign policy challenges affect political debate and shape American government?**

Conflict in the Ohio Valley

Although the United States had gained a vast new territory west of the Appalachians from the Treaty of Paris, the British kept their forts on the American side of the Great Lakes. Hoping to limit American settlement in the Northwest Territory, the British provided arms and ammunition to the Miami Indians and their allies, who were actively resisting American expansion into their lands. In 1790, Native Americans led by the war chief **Little Turtle** defeated a small force sent by President Washington to stop attacks against settlers. In 1791 in the Ohio Valley, British guns helped a confederacy of many Indian nations, again led by Little Turtle, to crush a larger American force commanded by General Arthur St. Clair.

But the tide turned in August 1794 when federal troops led by General Anthony Wayne defeated the Native American confederacy at the **Battle of Fallen Timbers,** named for the fallen trees that covered the battle site. Wayne's decisive victory forced the Native Americans to accept his peace terms. In the Treaty of Greenville, Native American leaders ceded most of the present state of Ohio to the U.S. government. This also opened the Northwest Territory to settlement.

✓ **Checkpoint** **Why was the Battle of Fallen Timbers significant?**

American Relations With Europe

While the British were helping Native Americans take a stand against the United States, the young nation struggled to chart a steady course in the area of foreign policy.

Responding to the French Revolution In 1789, Americans welcomed news of the **French Revolution,** a republican uprising in France. Grateful for French help during the American Revolution, Americans now saw the French as fellow republicans in a hostile world of aristocrats and kings. In 1793, however, leaders of the French Revolution began executing thousands of opponents, including the French king and his family. They also declared war on the monarchies of Europe, including Great Britain.

In response, Americans divided along party lines. The Democratic Republicans regretted the executions but still preferred the French Republic to its monarchical foes. Jefferson regarded the French Revolution as "the most sacred cause that ever man was engaged in." But the Federalists decided that the French revolutionaries were bloody anarchists out to destroy religion and social order. They suspected that the Democratic Republicans meant to do the same.

Proclaiming Neutrality By 1793, Britain and France were at war. Both American political parties agreed that the United States was too weak to participate in the war and too dependent on trade with Britain, which provided nearly 90 percent of American imports. That trade generated most of the federal revenue, which came primarily from tariffs and only secondarily from excise taxes.

Battle of Fallen Timbers

An engraving from the mid-1800s shows the 1794 battle that weakened Native American resistance. General Anthony Wayne, commander in chief of the United States Army, is shown below and on horseback.

If the United States entered the conflict, it could bankrupt the federal government. In 1793, President Washington, therefore, issued a proclamation of American neutrality, which became a foundation of American policy toward Europe until the twentieth century. The powerful British navy tested that neutrality by seizing American ships trading with the French colonies in the West Indies. Those seizures added to American outrage at the British policy along the new nation's western frontier.

Signing Treaties With Britain and Spain To avoid war with Britain, Washington sent Chief Justice **John Jay** to London to negotiate a compromise with the British. In the Jay Treaty of 1794, the British gave up their forts on American soil, but they kept most of their restrictions on American ships. The treaty also required Americans to repay prewar debts to the British. Washington and the Federalists favored this compromise, but the Democratic Republicans denounced the Jay Treaty as a sellout. After a heated debate, the Senate narrowly ratified the treaty, keeping the peace.

In 1795, the United States also signed a treaty with Spain. American settlers needed to move their goods down the Mississippi River to New Orleans, where they could be shipped to markets in the East. But, Spain controlled the Mississippi River and New Orleans. To ensure a free flow of trade, an American diplomat, Thomas Pinckney, negotiated a favorable treaty with the Spanish, who feared that an Anglo-American alliance might threaten their American possessions. Pinckney's Treaty guaranteed Americans free shipping rights on

INFOGRAPHIC

Americans Debate the French Revolution

As the French Revolution grew increasingly violent, American debate about it sharpened along party lines. Jefferson and his followers praised the Revolution, while Hamilton and other Federalists opposed it. Newspapers like the one on the far right (top) stoked the fires of the debate.

The Democratic Republican Response

Jefferson penned the introduction to a treatise Thomas Paine wrote defending the French Revolution, which sold a million and a half copies. Though the Democratic Republicans decried the violence, they believed it was necessary to bring about democracy. Jefferson wrote about the bloodshed in 1793: "Were there but an Adam and an Eve left in every country, and left free, it would be better than it is now."

◀ A 1789 French painting shows revolutionaries planting a "liberty tree" in France.

the Mississippi River and access to New Orleans. The treaty also established the northern boundary of Spanish Florida.

The removal of British forts, victories over Native Americans, and secure access to New Orleans encouraged thousands of Americans to move westward. By 1800, nearly 400,000 Americans lived beyond the Appalachian Mountains. By selling land to these settlers, the federal government gained revenue that helped to pay off the national debt.

Washington's Farewell In 1792, Washington had won reelection without opposition, but he declined to run again in 1796. In ailing health, he longed to escape the political turmoil by returning to his beloved plantation, Mount Vernon. He also recognized that the young nation needed him to set an example by walking away from power, proving that he was no king. His voluntary retirement after two terms set a precedent honored by all Presidents until the 1940s.

Washington retired with a record of astounding achievements. On the frontier, the Indians had been defeated, the western lands opened to settlement, and the Whiskey rebels suppressed. He had kept the nation out of the war in Europe. A booming foreign trade boosted tariffs, which funded the government and the national debt. Many historians have concluded that without Washington's skillful leadership, the nation may not have survived the harsh tests of the early 1790s. In a farewell address, Washington offered sound political advice for his successors, calling on them to temper their political strife in favor of national unity and to avoid "entangling alliances" that might lead to overseas wars.

✓ **Checkpoint** **What treaties were signed during Washington's presidency?**

—Revolution in France.—

FRANCE, June 21.

AT the moment when France thought herfelf happy in her eftablifhment of her RIGHTS and LIBERTIES, every thing is again thrown into confufion.

On Friday the National Affembly (that is t... part of the States, late called ... voted the pro-vi... of Th...

THE PROVIDENTIAL DETECTION

The Federalist Response

While the Federalists sympathized with the French drive for democracy, they distrusted the common people who were bringing it about. Adams wrote that public affairs should be left to "the rich, the well-born and the able." In cartoons like the one above on the right, Federalists attacked Jefferson for worshipping the French and destroying the American Constitution.

Thinking Critically

1. **Identify Point of View** What do each of the paintings suggest about their authors' viewpoints toward the French Revolution?
2. **Recognize Ideologies** What did the parties' response to the Revolution reveal about their basic ideas regarding political power and government?

The Parties Debate Foreign Policy

The Federalist candidate, John Adams, narrowly defeated Thomas Jefferson in the 1796 presidential election. The nation voted along regional lines, with Jefferson winning most of the southern electoral votes and Adams carrying almost all of the northern states. Due to an awkward feature of the Constitution, Jefferson, as the second place finisher, became Adams's Vice President.

Adams Confronts Crisis With France Although honest and dedicated, Adams could also be stubborn and pompous. Lacking tact, he made few friends and many enemies. Those foes included Hamilton, who had retired from public office but who tried to control the Federalist Party and the national government from behind the scenes. His meddling weakened the Adams administration.

Vocabulary Builder
unify–(YOO nuh fī) *v.* to bring together; to make into one unit

A French crisis briefly unified the nation. The Jay Treaty of 1794 had offended the French as a betrayal of their 1778 treaty of alliance with the United States. To show their irritation, in 1796 the French began seizing American merchant ships. Adams sent envoys to Paris to negotiate peace. But three French officials—known in code as X, Y, and Z—demanded humiliating terms, including $250,000 in bribes. Adams broke off negotiations. Called the **XYZ Affair,** the insult roused public sentiment against France. In 1798, the Federalist majority in Congress expanded the army and authorized a small navy, which won some surprising victories over French warships. To pay for the expanded military, Congress imposed unpopular taxes on stamps and land.

The Alien and Sedition Acts The Federalists exploited the war fever by passing the controversial **Alien and Sedition Acts** in 1798. The Alien Act authorized the President to arrest and deport immigrants who criticized the federal government. Because most immigrants supported the Democratic Republicans, the Federalists made it difficult for them to become citizens. The Sedition Act made it a crime for citizens to publicly discredit the federal government. Arguing that criticism undermined trust in the government, the Federalists used this act to silence Democratic Republican opposition.

The Sedition Act did allow juries to acquit defendants who could prove the literal truth of their statements. But that still put the burden of proof on the defendants, reversing the tradition of presuming someone innocent until proven guilty. In the end, the federal government convicted ten men of sedition, including those in Massachusetts who erected a liberty pole comparing the Federalists to the Loyalists who had supported the British king.

Analyzing Political Cartoons

Fighting Over the Sedition Act A 1798 cartoon shows a fight that broke out in Congress between Federalist Roger Griswold (with cane) and Democratic Republican Matthew Lyon (with tongs). Lyon, the first person tried and jailed under the Sedition Act, was considered a Democratic Republican hero and won reelection while in his jail cell.
What is the cartoonist's view of Congress during the Adams administration? How can you tell?

The Virginia and Kentucky Resolutions In two Democratic Republican states, the state legislatures passed controversial resolves in response to the acts. Written by Jefferson and Madison in 1798 and 1799, the **Virginia and Kentucky resolutions**

declared the Sedition Act unconstitutional. The resolves even hinted that states had the power to nullify federal laws that were unconstitutional. Though this doctrine of nullification threatened to dissolve the union, no other state legislatures adopted it. Instead, the presidential election of 1800 would decide the balance of federal power and states' rights.

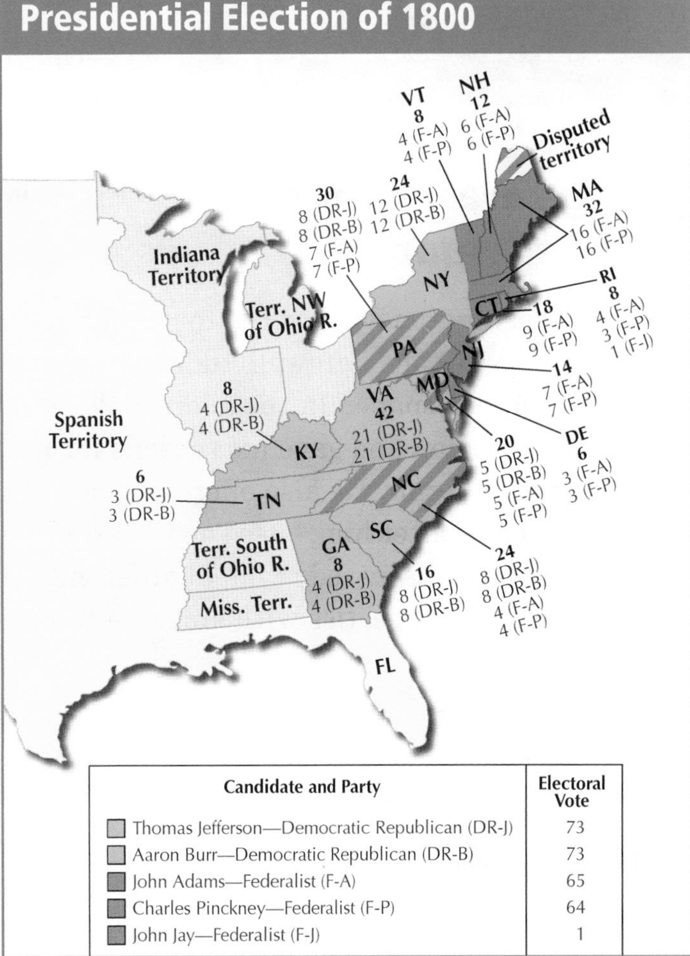

Candidate and Party	Electoral Vote
Thomas Jefferson—Democratic Republican (DR-J)	73
Aaron Burr—Democratic Republican (DR-B)	73
John Adams—Federalist (F-A)	65
Charles Pinckney—Federalist (F-P)	64
John Jay—Federalist (F-J)	1

 **Checkpoint** **What was the XYZ Affair?**

The Election of 1800

By 1800, the Sedition Act and the new federal taxes had become very unpopular. Sensing that trend, in 1799 Adams had suspended expansion of the army and sent new diplomats to France to seek peace. Those moves angered many Federalists, including Hamilton, who worked to undermine Adams's reelection. Adams lost the heated election to Jefferson.

Jefferson and his running mate, **Aaron Burr,** tied. The voters had meant for Jefferson to become President and Burr to become Vice President. But because the Constitution did not then allow a distinction between electoral votes, the House of Representatives had to decide between the two. Hamilton preferred Jefferson, so in early 1801 the Federalist congressmen allowed Jefferson to become President. This peaceful transfer of power from one party to another set a valuable precedent. To avoid another electoral crisis, in 1804 the Constitution was amended to require electors to vote separately for President and Vice President. Offended by Hamilton's criticism, Burr killed him in a duel in 1804.

 **Checkpoint** **Compare the election of 1796 to the election of 1800.**

SECTION 2 Assessment

Progress Monitoring *Online*
For: Self-test with vocabulary practice
www.pearsonschool.com/ushist

Comprehension

1. **Terms and People** What is the relationship between each of the following terms or people and American foreign policy during the 1790s?
   - Little Turtle
   - Battle of Fallen Timbers
   - French Revolution
   - John Jay
   - XYZ Affair
   - Alien and Sedition Acts

2. **NoteTaking Reading Skill: Identify Supporting Details** Use your completed chart to answer the Section Focus Question: How did foreign policy challenges affect political debate and shape American government?

Writing About History

3. **Quick Write: Narrow Your Topic** Choose a topic from this section to research. Then, narrow it down by creating a concept web. Choose one of the outer circles as a manageable topic for a research paper.

Critical Thinking

4. **Identify Central Issues** Why did the British support Native American resistance to westward expansion in the United States?
5. **Recognize Ideologies** How did American debates about foreign policy in the 1790s reflect the beliefs of the political parties?
6. **Draw Inferences** Does having a President and Vice President from different parties help or hinder government? Explain.

Primary Source

Washington asked Hamilton to revise his farewell address; Hamilton's version appears to the right. ▶

George Washington: *Farewell Address*

In 1796, Washington decided not to run for reelection. On September 19, his Farewell Address ran in a Philadelphia newspaper. In the address Washington thanked the nation and gave his reasons for leaving office after two terms. He also offered advice to those who would come after him, based on his experience and observations. He discussed regional differences, foreign policy, and political parties with amazing foresight.

Let me now take a more comprehensive view, and warn you in the most solemn manner against the baneful[1] effects of the spirit of party generally.

This spirit, unfortunately, is inseparable from our nature, having its root in the strongest passions of the human mind. It exists under different shapes in all governments, more or less stifled, controlled, or repressed; but, in those of the popular form, it is seen in its greatest rankness,[2] and is truly their worst enemy. . . .

It agitates the community with ill-founded jealousies and false alarms, kindles the animosity of one part against another, foments[3] occasionally riot and insurrection. It opens the door to foreign influence and corruption, which finds a facilitated access to the government itself through the channels of party passions. Thus the policy and the will of one country are subjected to the policy and will of another. . . .

So likewise, a passionate attachment of one nation for another produces a variety of evils. Sympathy for the favorite nation, facilitating the illusion of an imaginary common interest in cases where no real common interest exists, and infusing into one the enmities of the other, betrays the former into a participation in the quarrels and wars of the latter without adequate inducement or justification. It leads also to concessions to the favorite nation of privileges denied to others which is apt doubly to injure the nation making the concessions. . . .

The jealousy of a free people ought to be constantly awake, since history and experience prove that foreign influence is one of the most baneful foes of republican government. But that jealousy to be useful must be impartial.[4] . . .

1. **baneful** (BAYN fuhl) *adj.* harmful; destructive.
2. **rankness** (RANGK nehs) *n.* state of being excessive and unpleasant.
3. **foments** (foh MEHNTS) *v.* stirs up.
4. **impartial** (ihm PAHR shuhl) *adj.* fair; not favoring one side.

▲ George Washington, as painted by Gilbert Stuart in 1796

Thinking Critically

1. **Synthesize Information** What does Washington say are the many "baneful effects" of political parties?
2. **Draw Inferences** What event was Washington thinking of when he warned about "foreign influence"?

SECTION 3

◀ President Thomas Jefferson, and a banner (right) from his 1800 presidential campaign

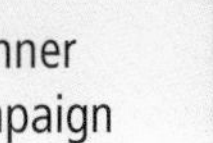

WITNESS HISTORY

Jefferson Calls for Free Speech

In 1801, Thomas Jefferson became the nation's third President. He emphasized that the federal government should respect public opinion and should allow public criticism—implying that the previous Federalist administration had fallen short in those areas. In an eloquent Inaugural Address, Jefferson insisted that the Republic needed free speech and constant debate.

> "If there be any among us who wish to dissolve the union, or to change its republican form, let them stand undisturbed as monuments of the safety with which error of opinion may be tolerated where reason is left free to combat it."
>
> —Thomas Jefferson, Inaugural Address, 1801

The Age of Jefferson

Objectives

- Understand why some saw Jefferson's election as a "republican revolution."
- Explain the impact of John Marshall's tenure as Chief Justice of the United States.
- Identify the importance of the Louisiana Purchase.
- Analyze Jefferson's foreign policies.

Terms and People

bureaucracy	Lewis and Clark Expedition
John Marshall	Barbary War
judicial review	impressment
Marbury v. *Madison*	embargo
Louisiana Purchase	

NoteTaking

Reading Skill: Identify Main Ideas Record main ideas about Jefferson's presidency in a concept web like the one below.

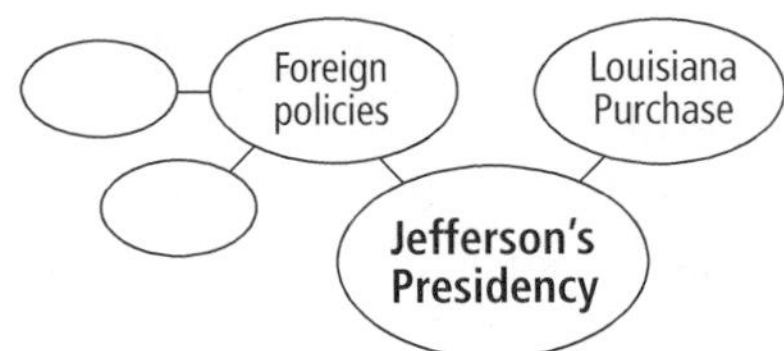

Why It Matters In addition to capturing the presidency in 1800, the Democratic Republicans won control of Congress and most of the state governments. The Federalists would never reclaim national power. Besides taking government in a new direction, the Jefferson administration left a profound legacy with its acquisition of new territory. **Section Focus Question: What were the successes and failures of the Jefferson administrations?**

Pursuing Republican Principles

When the Democratic Republicans took power, they spoke of the election as a "revolution." Jefferson insisted that "the Revolution of 1800 was as real a Revolution in the principles of our government as that of 1776 was in its form." In that view, those in the Jefferson administration set out to do things quite differently from their predecessors, who had copied the style of the British monarchy.

New Government Policies Jefferson encouraged Congress to abandon the Alien and Sedition Acts, as well as the hated taxes on stamps, land, and alcoholic spirits. Unlike Hamilton, Jefferson wanted to retire the national debt by paying it down. Despite reducing taxes, he cut the national debt from $80 million when he took office to $57 million in 1809. To do this he made major cuts to the army and navy and streamlined the government's **bureaucracy,** or the departments and workers that make up the government. He also benefited when customs revenue from imports increased with a dramatic growth in foreign trade. In addition, the westward movement of American farm families increased the sale of federal lands. These two revenues drove down the federal debt.

A Change in Style The Federalists believed that expensive displays taught the public to respect their leaders. Without that respect, they did not think that the government could survive. But, the Democratic Republicans hated the Federalist displays of wealth as an aristocratic threat to the republic. Although Jefferson was a very wealthy, refined, and educated gentleman, he recognized the popularity of a common style. A friend described Jefferson in this way:

> **Primary Source** "If his dress was plain, unstudied, and sometimes old-fashioned in its form, it was always of the finest materials . . . and if in his manners he was simple, affable, and unceremonious, it was not because he was ignorant of but because he despised the conventional and artificial usages of courts and fashionable life."
>
> —Mrs. Samuel Harrison Smith, c. 1801

Checkpoint Why was Jefferson's election considered a "republican revolution"?

John Marshall's Supreme Court

When Thomas Jefferson became President in 1801, **John Marshall** became Chief Justice of the Supreme Court. Although the two men were cousins, they were political enemies. Marshall was a Federalist, a last-minute appointee by the outgoing President, John Adams. Marshall's appointment had a major impact on the Supreme Court and on its relationship with the rest of the federal government. Over 35 years, he participated in more than 1,000 court decisions, writing over half of them—more than any other Supreme Court Justice in U.S. history.

NoteTaking

Reading Skill: Recognize Sequence As you read, trace events that led to the recognition that the Supreme Court would have the power to review federal laws.

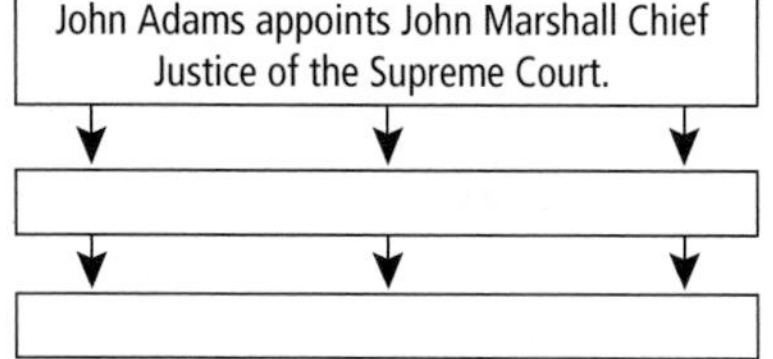

Marshall's Four-Part Legacy Marshall applied four of Hamilton's principles to interpret the Constitution. First, his Supreme Court claimed the power to review the acts of Congress and of the President to determine if they were constitutional. This power is known as **judicial review.** Second, he insisted that federal laws were superior to state laws. Third, like Hamilton, Marshall broadly interpreted the Constitution to find implied powers for the national government. Fourth, he insisted upon the "sanctity of contracts." This limited the power of state governments to interfere with business.

Marbury* v. *Madison In 1803, Marshall first asserted the power of judicial review in the case of ***Marbury* v. *Madison.*** In early 1801, outgoing President John Adams had appointed William Marbury, a Federalist, a justice for the District of Columbia. The incoming Secretary of State, James Madison, refused to deliver the official papers of appointment. When Marbury complained to the Supreme Court, Marshall ruled in favor of Madison by declaring unconstitutional part of the Judiciary Act of 1789.

This ruling was a stroke of genius. Marshall gave the Democratic Republicans what they wanted by denying Marbury his appointment. But in doing so, Marshall claimed a sweeping power for the Supreme Court that the Democratic Republicans did not want that Court to have. After all, the Constitution was silent on what institution should judge the constitutionality of congressional actions. In the Kentucky and Virginia resolutions of 1798, Jefferson and Madison had claimed that power for the state legislatures. Because of Marshall, today we accept that the Supreme Court will review the constitutionality of federal laws.

Establishing Important Precedents After establishing the precedent of judicial review, Marshall never again ruled a federal law unconstitutional. Instead, most of his decisions overruled state laws, usually to defend businesses and interstate commerce from state interference, or strengthened judicial review.

Landmark Decisions of the Supreme Court

How Can the Supreme Court Declare Laws to Be Unconstitutional?

The Constitution grants each branch of government certain powers. To prevent any one branch from becoming too powerful, a system of checks and balances is part of this framework. While the Constitution specifies balancing powers for the executive and legislative branches, it says little about the judicial branch. One challenge facing the young government was to decide how the judiciary could balance the powers of the President and the legislature.

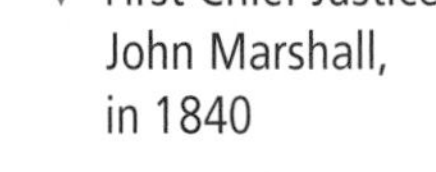

▼ First Chief Justice John Marshall, in 1840

Marbury v. *Madison* (1803)

The Facts	The Issue	The Decision
William Marbury asked the Supreme Court to grant him a job as a federal judge, which had been promised to him by the Adams administration but denied by the incoming Jefferson administration. He also sued Secretary of State James Madison.	Marbury argued that the Judiciary Act of 1789, gave the Supreme Court the power to make a government official perform a certain duty.	The Court ruled that in passing the 1789 law, Congress had exceeded the powers granted by the Constitution. Since the law was unconstitutional, the Supreme Court could not order Madison to grant Marbury his commission.

Why It Matters

Marbury v. *Madison* established the power of judicial review, ensuring that the Supreme Court had the final authority to interpret the meaning of the Constitution. In his majority opinion, Marshall wrote: "It is emphatically the province and duty of the judicial department to say what the law is. Those who apply the rule to particular cases, must of necessity expound and interpret that rule. If two laws conflict with each other, the courts must decide on the operation of each."

Marbury v. *Madison* established the judiciary branch as an equal partner in government. Since 1803, the Supreme Court and other courts have used judicial review in thousands of cases.

Connect to Your World

Supreme Court Justices serve lifetime terms and are responsible for interpreting the Constitution. When one of the nine seats of the Supreme Court must be filled, the President nominates a replacement. Then, the Senate must approve the President's nomination with a vote. In this way, both the executive and legislative branches can check and balance the power of the judiciary.

Who are the judges that can declare laws to be unconstitutional in today's Supreme Court? Research the Court's current makeup. Create a Supreme Court profile, indicating which Justices were appointed by Democratic Presidents, which by Republican Presidents, and whether they can be described as strict or loose constructionists.

For: Supreme Court cases
www.pearsonschool.com/ushist

◀ Current Chief Justice John Roberts

These decisions set precedents critical to the development of the new nation's legal and economic systems. Like Hamilton, Marshall interpreted the Constitution broadly to find the implied powers needed for a strong national government.

✓ **Checkpoint** **Why was *Marbury* v. *Madison* so important?**

The Nation Expands

Jefferson insisted that farm ownership—which freed citizens from dependence on a landlord or on an employer—was essential to the freedom of white Americans. Yet without expansion there would not be enough farms for the rapidly growing population. With the population doubling every 25 years, the nation needed twice as much land every generation to maintain farm ownership.

Eyeing the Louisiana Territory To get more land, Jefferson wanted the United States to expand to the Pacific—despite the fact that much of the continent was already inhabited by Native Americans and European colonists. At first, Jefferson believed that Spain's vast Louisiana Territory west of the Mississippi River would be easy to conquer. He noted that the Spanish colonists were few, their empire was weak, and they were distracted by the war in Europe. Jefferson's plans went awry, however, when the United States got a new and far

The United States, 1803

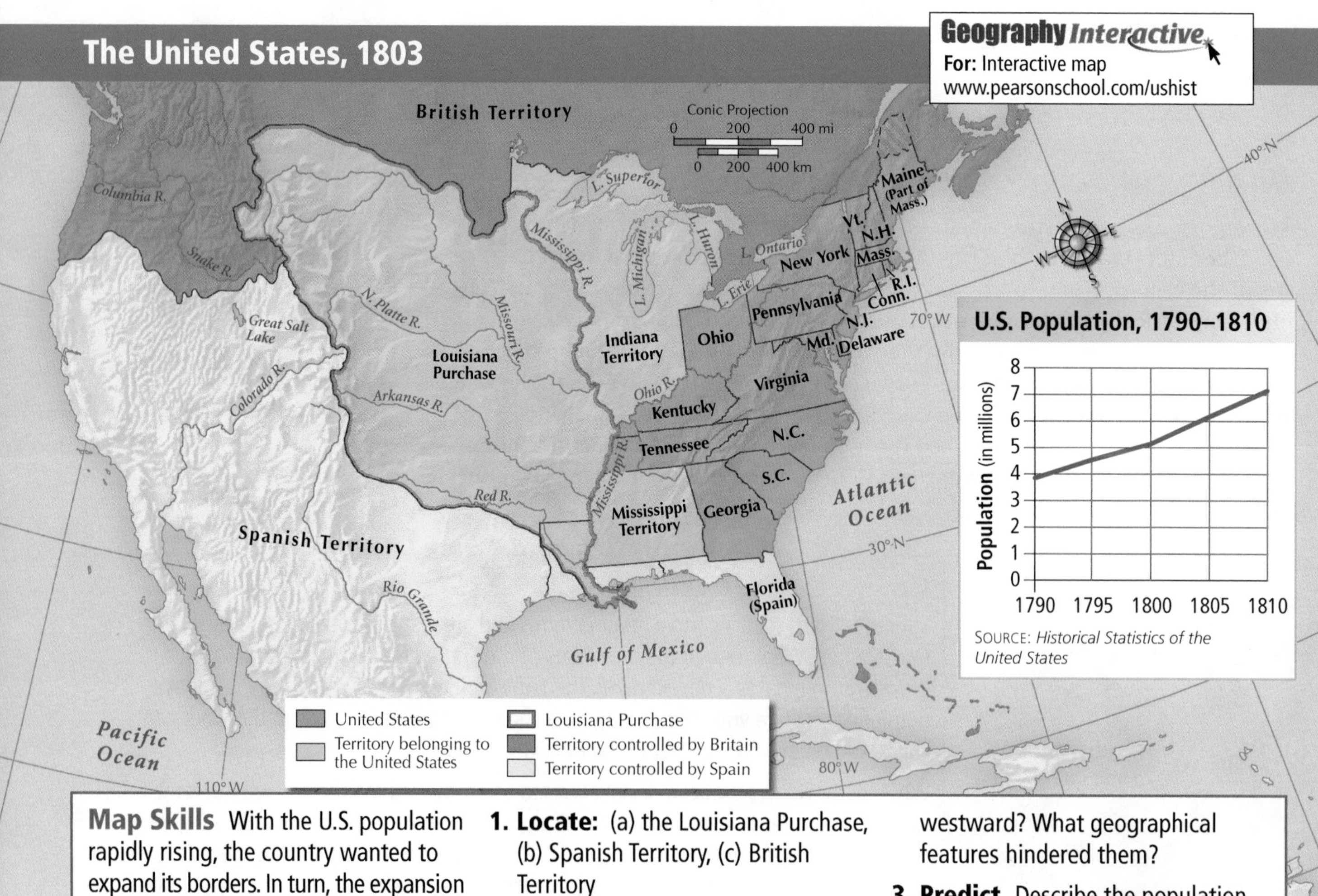

Map Skills With the U.S. population rapidly rising, the country wanted to expand its borders. In turn, the expansion of land brought about by the Louisiana Purchase encouraged population growth.

1. **Locate:** (a) the Louisiana Purchase, (b) Spanish Territory, (c) British Territory
2. **Movement** What geographical features helped settlers move westward? What geographical features hindered them?
3. **Predict** Describe the population growth in the years 1790–1810. How would this growth affect U.S. foreign relations?

more dangerous neighbor to the west. In 1801, France's military dictator, Napoleon Bonaparte, had forced Spain to give him the Louisiana Territory, including the strategic city of New Orleans. The French threatened to block American access to the market in New Orleans. An alarmed Jefferson considered joining the British in an alliance to fight France.

The Louisiana Purchase Jefferson reasoned that he could avoid war by offering to buy New Orleans from the French. When James Monroe and Robert Livingston, the American minister in France, approached Napoleon, they found him surprisingly receptive. Napoleon's imperial plans had been foiled by slave rebels in the Caribbean colony of Saint Domingue, which is now Haiti. Led by Toussaint L'Ouverture, the rebels defeated a French army sent to suppress them. Without that army to occupy Louisiana, and needing money to fight the British, Napoleon decided to sell all of the Louisiana Territory.

In the **Louisiana Purchase** of 1803, Jefferson obtained a vast territory extending from the Mississippi River to the Rocky Mountains. At about 828,000 square miles, the Louisiana Territory nearly doubled the size of the United States. For all of this, the United States paid only $15 million. Although a great bargain, the Louisiana Purchase was also something of an embarrassment, as it contradicted Jefferson's constitutional principles. He had long argued for a minimal federal government, and the Constitution did not authorize the federal government to buy territory from a foreign country. Jefferson confessed that he had "done an act beyond the Constitution."

In 1804, Jefferson sent Meriwether Lewis and William Clark to explore the new territory, in what became known as the **Lewis and Clark Expedition** (see American Experience feature in this chapter). The men were guided much of the way by a Shoshone woman, named Sacajawea, and her husband.

HISTORY MAKERS

Thomas Jefferson
(1743–1826)
Along with being a statesman, Thomas Jefferson was an amateur scientist. His deep interest in plants and animals contributed to the Lewis and Clark Expedition. His plantation, Monticello, served as a laboratory for experimenting with plants. Jefferson grew hundreds of varieties of fruits and vegetables, recording their growth in detailed journals. He imported many plants from around the world, including Italian broccoli and Mexican peppers. Some plant samples Lewis and Clark brought back from the West ended up in his garden, where they still thrive today. Jefferson was an enthusiastic experimenter, trying new varieties of those plants that did not flourish. "The greatest service which can be rendered any country," he said, "is to add an useful plant to its culture."

▲ Portable writing desk designed by Jefferson

✓ **Checkpoint How did the United States gain the Louisiana Territory?**

Jefferson's Foreign Troubles

While Jefferson succeeded in his plans to expand to the west, he faced a number of significant challenges to solidifying the stability and economy of the United States.

Fighting the Barbary War The Barbary States of North Africa—Morocco, Algiers, Tunis, and Tripoli—were profiting by seizing American ships and sailors in the Mediterranean Sea. To buy immunity from that piracy, the Washington and Adams administrations had paid protection money to the Barbary States. Jefferson was willing to do the same until the ruler of Tripoli increased his price. In 1801, Jefferson sent the small American navy to blockade the port of Tripoli, winning a favorable peace in 1805, concluding the **Barbary War.**

Entering the Reexport Trade As the population grew and spread westward, the United States needed to expand overseas markets for the surplus

Vocabulary Builder
surplus–(SUHR pluhs) *adj.* more than is needed

produce raised on its new farms. From 1793 to 1807, war in Europe aided this goal. The dominant British navy quickly captured most of France's merchant ships. To supply food to the French colonies in the West Indies, and to export their sugar, the French turned to American ships. Because the British had banned direct American voyages between the French West Indies and France, American merchants picked up cargoes in the French colonies and took them to ports in the United States, where they unloaded them. Then the merchants reshipped the cargoes to France as if they were American products.

The value of this "reexport" trade soared from about $300,000 in 1790 to nearly $59 million in 1807, creating a boom for the American economy. To meet the new demand, American shipyards produced hundreds of new ships, tripling the size of the nation's merchant marine by 1807. Prosperous American merchants built new wharves, warehouses, and mansions, boosting the construction trades in seaport cities. Farmers also benefited by selling their produce to feed French soldiers in Europe and enslaved Africans and plantation owners in the West Indies.

The British hated the reexport trade for two reasons. First, it helped the French economy, which sustained Napoleon's army. Second, the new trade helped the United States become Britain's greatest commercial competitor. In 1805, as British merchants lost markets and profits to American shippers, British warships began to stop and confiscate growing numbers of American merchant ships for trading with the French.

Facing British Impressment The British navy also angered the United States by relying on **impressment,** or taking American sailors from their ships and forcing them to serve in the British navy. Engaged in a tough war, the British desperately needed sailors for their huge fleet. Britain insisted that anyone born within its empire was a British subject for life. Yet British naval officers also took American-born sailors. By 1812, about 6,000 American citizens had been impressed for the harsh duty of serving on a British warship.

At first, Federalist merchants were willing to regard the British abuses as unfortunate costs of doing business on the high seas. They

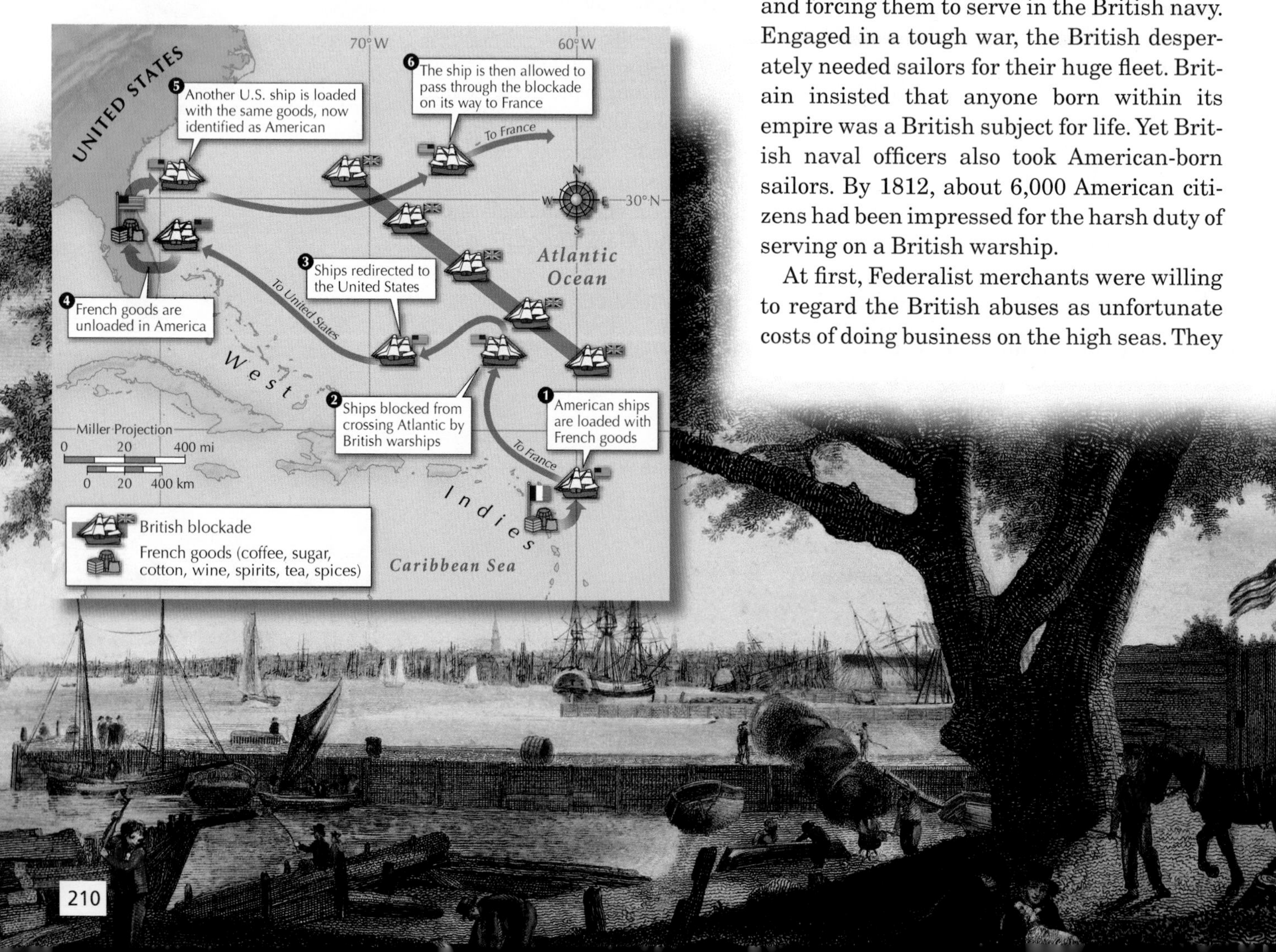

The Reexport Trade in Action
American ports like Philadelphia, shown here, thrived during the reexport trade. *Why couldn't American ships carry French goods directly to France?*

pointed out that the old trade with Great Britain remained even more valuable than the new reexport trade with France. But Democratic Republicans insisted that the British actions insulted the United States and threatened the country's economic growth. In 1807, when the British attacked an American warship, the *Chesapeake,* in order to take some of its sailors, many Americans—including many Federalists—were outraged.

Attacking the *Chesapeake*
This engraving from 1816 shows British sailors taking over the *Chesapeake* and impressing the American sailors on board.

Jefferson Asks for an Embargo The United States lacked a navy large enough to challenge the British fleet. Jefferson balked at the high cost of building a bigger navy, which would undermine his policies of reducing the national debt and keeping taxes low. He also worried that a large military would become a threat to the Republic.

As an alternative to war, in 1807 Jefferson persuaded Congress to declare an **embargo,** suspending trade by ordering American ships to stay in port. He expected the embargo to starve the British and close their factories, creating riots in the streets. Instead, the British found other markets in South America. Meanwhile, the embargo bankrupted American merchants, threw American sailors out of work, and hurt farmers, who could no longer export their crops. Exploiting voter anger, the Federalists gained support in the northern states, especially in New England.

Even Jefferson had to admit failure, lifting the embargo just before he retired from the presidency in 1809. Despite having been easily reelected in 1804, the embargo had caused his popularity to lag. Still, he was succeeded by his friend James Madison, who defeated a Federalist rival in the election of 1808.

✓ **Checkpoint** **Why did Jefferson call for an embargo?**

SECTION 3 Assessment

Progress Monitoring *Online*
For: Self-test with vocabulary practice
www.pearsonschool.com/ushist

Comprehension

1. **Terms and People** Explain the impact of the following people or terms on the development of the United States in the early 1800s.
   - bureaucracy
   - John Marshall
   - judicial review
   - *Marbury* v. *Madison*
   - Louisiana Purchase
   - Lewis and Clark Expedition
   - Barbary War
   - impressment
   - embargo
2. **NoteTaking Reading Skill: Identify Main Details** Use your completed chart to answer the Section Focus Question: What were the successes and failures of the Jefferson administrations?

Writing About History

3. **Quick Write: Develop a Thesis Statement** Introduce your topic by summarizing it in a single, clear statement. For example, if your topic for this section is John Marshall's Supreme Court, your thesis statement might be "John Marshall had a profound and lasting impact on the Supreme Court and its role in the federal government."

Critical Thinking

4. **Apply Information** How did Jefferson view the Supreme Court precedent of judicial review?
5. **Identify Central Issues** What was Jefferson's main reason for purchasing the Louisiana Territory from France?
6. **Recognize Cause and Effect** What was the impact of the embargo on the American economy?

American Experience **History Interactive**

EXPERIENCE LEWIS AND CLARK

Lewis and Clark discovered ▶ many species new to science, including 15 mammals, 16 birds, 7 fish, 7 reptiles, and dozens of plants.

In 1800, the lands west of the Appalachians were as foreign to Americans as the moon is to many people today. Therefore, when Thomas Jefferson sent Meriwether Lewis and William Clark on their expedition, he handed them a set of remarkable instructions. The President had spent years crafting them, and they reflected his own impressive range of scientific knowledge. Jefferson called for specific data such as local temperatures, when native plants flowered, and what Native Americans wore and ate. Jefferson named the group the "Corps of Discovery," and meant it literally. He saw the expedition as an unprecedented chance to combine scientific discovery with commercial knowledge that would stimulate the nation's growth. Jefferson spent two years as Lewis's mentor, hiring experts to train the expedition leader in botany, taxidermy, paleontology, and other related fields.

1 Meriwether Lewis **2** William Clark **3** The compass Clark carried on the expedition. **4** A woodpecker species observed by Lewis and named for him. **5** Clark's detailed diary of the expedition, including hundreds of sketches. **6** A sketch of a trout from Clark's diary. **7** A drawing of a prairie bird. **8** Black Moccasin, a Minitari chief who met Lewis and Clark and was painted by George Catlin three decades later. **9** A peace medal that the expedition gave to Native American chiefs; Jefferson's likeness appears on the other side.

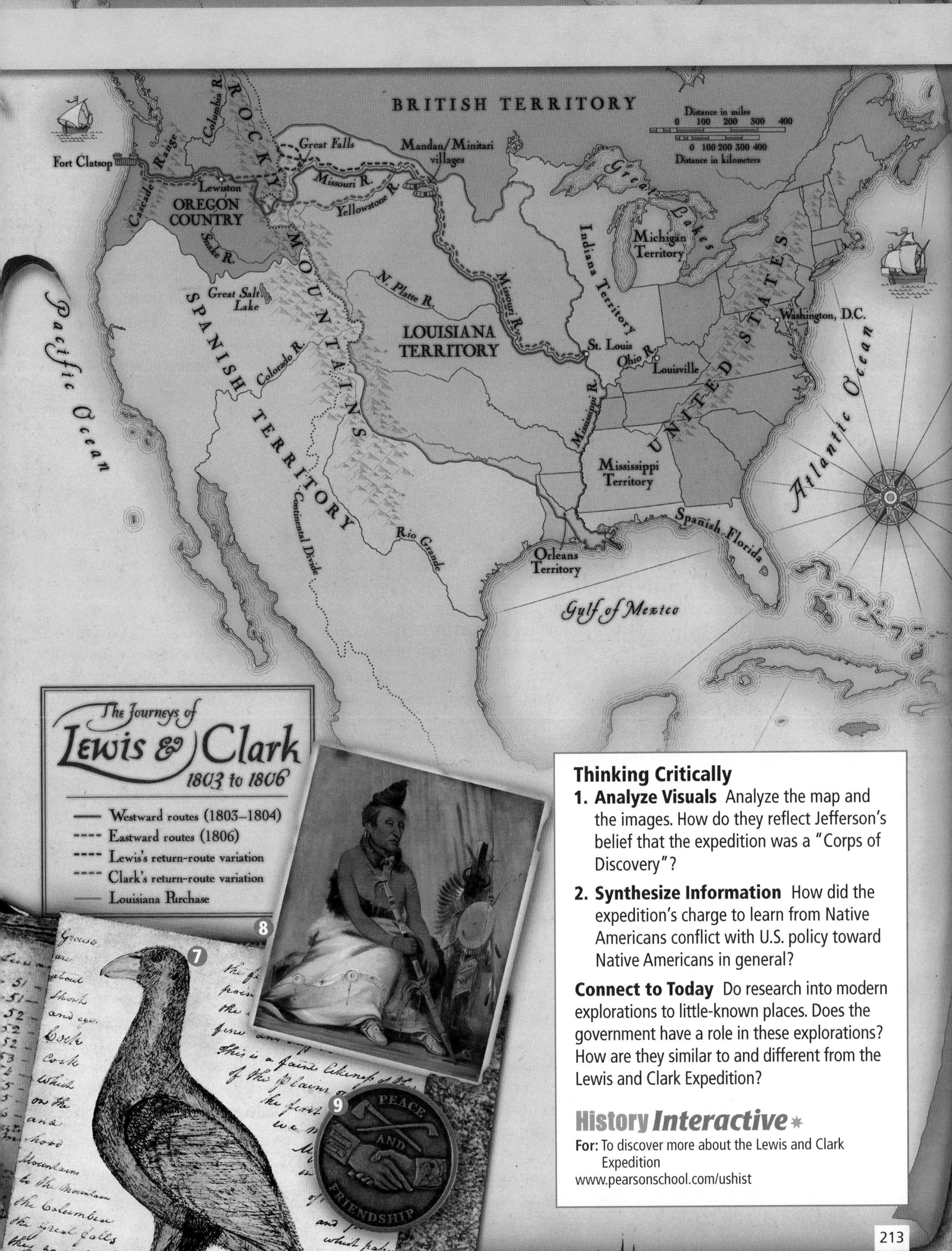

Thinking Critically

1. **Analyze Visuals** Analyze the map and the images. How do they reflect Jefferson's belief that the expedition was a "Corps of Discovery"?
2. **Synthesize Information** How did the expedition's charge to learn from Native Americans conflict with U.S. policy toward Native Americans in general?

Connect to Today Do research into modern explorations to little-known places. Does the government have a role in these explorations? How are they similar to and different from the Lewis and Clark Expedition?

History *Interactive*

For: To discover more about the Lewis and Clark Expedition
www.pearsonschool.com/ushist

▲ The burning of Washington, D.C., by British troops in 1814.

WITNESS HISTORY

Burning the Capitol

In 1814, the British entered Washington, D.C., during the War of 1812. They drove President Madison and his Cabinet into the woods before burning the city. Madison's wife, Dolley, heroically saved a painting of George Washington before joining the others. Years later, a British officer described the scene:

> "Of the Senate house, the President's palace, the barracks, the dockyard, etc., nothing could be seen except heaps of smoking ruins, and even the bridge, a noble structure upwards of a mile in length, was almost wholly demolished."
>
> —George Robert Gleig, 1826

The War of 1812

Objectives

- Identify the events that led to the War Hawks's call for war.
- Analyze the major battles and conflicts of the War of 1812.
- Explain the significance of the War of 1812.

Terms and People

Tecumseh
Battle of Tippecanoe
War Hawks
War of 1812
Andrew Jackson
Francis Scott Key
"The Star-Spangled Banner"
Battle of New Orleans
Treaty of Ghent
Hartford Convention

NoteTaking

Reading Skill: Recognize Sequence Record the causes of the War of 1812 in a chart like this one.

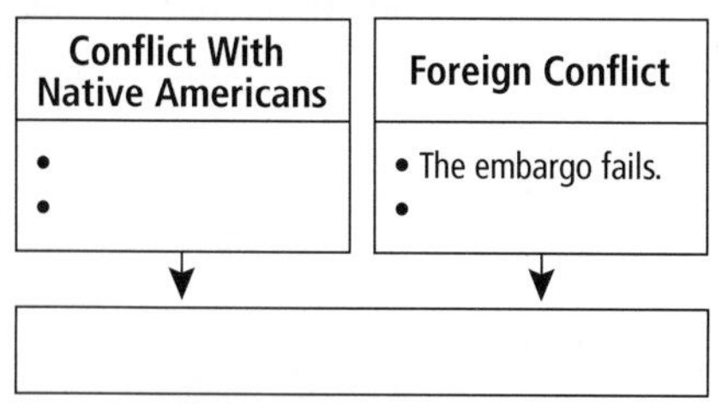

Why It Matters Just a few decades after its founding, the United States found itself involved in a major war. The war tested not only the young nation's resources and strength but the solidarity of its people as well. Despite their political divisions, Americans managed both to fight a war and to get the country back on track in the war's aftermath. **Section Focus Question: Why did the United States go to war with Britain, and what was the outcome of that war?**

Gearing Up for War

Democratic Republicans felt humiliated by the failure of the 1807 embargo against Britain. With persistent British abuses on the oceans, and Native American resistance in the West, Americans increasingly blamed the British.

Replacing the Embargo In 1809, Congress replaced the embargo with the Nonintercourse Act. Aimed at Britain and France, the act stated that the United States would resume trade with whichever of those countries lifted their restrictions on American shipping. The following year, Congress passed legislation that went a step further. Macon's Bill No. 2 restored trade with both Britain and France but also promised that if either country actively recognized American neutrality, then the United States would resume trading sanctions against the other country. When France agreed to withdraw decrees against American shipping, President Madison ordered sanctions against the British. In the meantime, however, France continued to seize American ships.

Battling Native Americans On the western frontier, two Shawnee Indian brothers, the prophet Tenskwatawa and the warrior **Tecumseh,** wanted to preserve Native American culture and unite the Indian nations in armed resistance against American expansion. They were angered by the government's repeated use of dishonest treaties to take their lands. In late 1811, while Tecumseh was seeking allies in the South, Governor William Henry Harrison of the Indiana Territory led troops into the brothers' village of Prophetstown, along the Tippecanoe River. After the **Battle of Tippecanoe,** the Americans burned Prophetstown. The Native American movement lost some momentum, though most Native Americans escaped to fight again.

Vocabulary Builder
momentum–(moh MEHN tuhm)
n. force or speed of motion

The War Hawks Demand War In 1811 some aggressive young politicians, known as the **War Hawks,** took the lead in Congress. Representing farmers and settlers from the southern and western states, the War Hawks included John C. Calhoun of South Carolina and Henry Clay of Kentucky. Strongly nationalist, they denounced the impressments of American sailors and British support for Native Americans. The War Hawks pushed for a war against Britain to restore national honor. They insisted that invading British-held Canada would deprive the Indians of their main source of arms and drive the British out of North America. The War Hawks also believed that the British would make maritime concessions to get Canada back from the Americans. They underestimated the value that the British put on their domination of world trade.

✓ **Checkpoint** **Why did many Americans blame Britain for their problems?**

Decision  **Point**

Should the United States Declare War on Britain?

No American disputed the fact that Britain was interfering with American shipping. Yet while the War Hawks called for war, some people questioned their motives. Read the opinions below, and then decide whether war against Britain was justified.

Grundy Urges War

Primary Source

"What, Mr. Speaker, are we now called on to decide? It is, whether we will resist by force the attempt, made by [Britain], to subject our maritime rights to the arbitrary and capricious rule of her will. . . . Sir, I prefer war to submission. [This] unjust and lawless invasion of personal liberty, calls loudly for the interposition of this Government. . . ."

—Senator Felix Grundy (KY)
December 9, 1811

Randolph Opposes War

Primary Source

"Sir, if you go to war it will not be for the protection of, or defense of your maritime rights. Gentlemen from the North have been taken up to some high mountain and shown all the kingdoms of the earth; and Canada seems tempting to their sight. . . . Agrarian [greed], not maritime right, urges the war. [We hear] but one word—Canada! Canada! Canada!"

—Senator John Randolph (VA)
December 16, 1811

You Decide

1. What is Grundy's reason for war?
2. Does Randolph believe Grundy? Explain.
3. What decision would you have made? Why?

History Makers

Tecumseh (1768–1813)

Tecumseh, a Shawnee warrior from the Ohio Valley, spearheaded a spiritual and military resistance movement among Native Americans. He called for them to return to traditional values as a way of preserving their culture. At the same time, he actively resisted the United States, fighting in battles, rejecting treaties, and traveling widely to convince Indian groups that they were all one people and that no one group had the right to make a treaty. He also mocked the very idea of owning land. Meeting with William Henry Harrison in 1810, he scoffed, "Sell a country! Why not sell the air, the clouds and the great sea, as well as the earth?"

War Breaks Out

Humiliated by British interference with American trade, impressments, and support for Indian attacks on settlers, President Madison urged Congress to declare war on Britain in June of 1812. Although the **War of 1812** deeply divided the nation, Madison narrowly won reelection later that year. Disunited, unprepared, and with only a small army and navy, the United States went to war once again with the world's greatest power.

The Invasion of Canada Fails Thomas Jefferson acted as adviser to Madison. He argued that with a population of 8 million, the United States could easily conquer Canada, which had only 250,000 people. Indeed, the prospects for a victory looked favorable. An overland invasion would save the cost of building a bigger navy to fight the British. In addition, Jefferson argued that the United States did not even need a professional army. The citizen militia of the states could do the job quickly and with little expense. He called the conquest of Canada "a mere matter of marching."

Jefferson's assumptions proved to be wrong. In fact, the small British and Indian forces in Canada repeatedly defeated the American invasion attempts in 1812 and 1813. Reliance on the state militias proved a disaster. Having had no professional training, many militiamen broke rank and ran when attacked. The American regular army performed almost as poorly. One blundering general, William Hull, surrendered Detroit to a much smaller British force commanded by Isaac Brock and assisted by Indians led by Tecumseh. Instead of bolstering American pride, the attempted invasion of Canada only further embarrassed the nation.

Defeating the Native Americans To the surprise of many Americans—and to the shock of the British—the small American navy performed well, capturing four British ships during 1812. On Lake Erie, American ships led by Oliver Hazard Perry defeated a British flotilla in 1813, enabling an American army, commanded by William Henry Harrison, to retake Detroit.

The Americans made little progress in conquering Canada, but they did defeat Britain's Indian allies within the United States. In October 1813, Harrison's army killed Tecumseh and scattered his supporters. In 1814, **Andrew Jackson** of Tennessee crushed the Creek Indians of Alabama, who had allied with the British. To make peace, the survivors surrendered most of their lands. Jackson then invaded the Spanish colony of Florida, defeating the Seminole Indians and seizing the Spanish fort at Pensacola.

The British Invade During 1812 and 1813, most of the British forces were in Europe fighting Napoleon. In early 1814, however, the French dictator's defeat freed thousands of British troops to fight in North America. During the summer and fall, the British took the offensive. While the British navy blockaded the coast, British forces invaded the United States. One army occupied eastern Maine, easily brushing aside the weak defense by local militia. From Montreal, a second army invaded northern New York, while a third British force landed in Maryland and marched on Washington, D.C. In late 1814, a British fleet carried a fourth army into the Gulf of Mexico to attack New Orleans.

On the defensive, the Americans fought better than they had when invading Canada. Except for the occupation of Maine, the British attacks ended in defeat. The British did capture the national capital, easily accessible by ship via the Chesapeake Bay, and burned the White House and Capitol in revenge for some American arson in Canada. But the British suffered defeat when they moved on to attack Baltimore. Lawyer **Francis Scott Key,** who observed the British attack on Fort McHenry, celebrated the American victory by writing a poem that later became the national anthem known as **"The Star-Spangled Banner."**

Primary Source

"O say, can you see, by the dawn's early light,
What so proudly we hail'd at the twilight's last gleaming,
Whose broad stripes and bright stars, thro' the perilous fight,
O'er the ramparts we watch'd, were so gallantly streaming?"

—Francis Scott Key, 1814

Meanwhile, on Lake Champlain near Plattsburgh, New York, American ships defeated a British fleet, forcing British troops to retreat to Canada.

✓ **Checkpoint What were some American successes and failures during the war?**

Geography *Interactive*
For: Interactive map
www.pearsonschool.com/ushist

Major Battles of the War of 1812

Map Skills Though Americans claimed victory, neither side actually gained or lost any territory during the War of 1812.

1. **Locate:** (a) Fort McHenry, (b) New Orleans, (c) Lake Champlain
2. **Place** In what kinds of places were most of the major battles fought?
3. **Determine Relevance** How did the British naval blockade affect the outcome of the war?

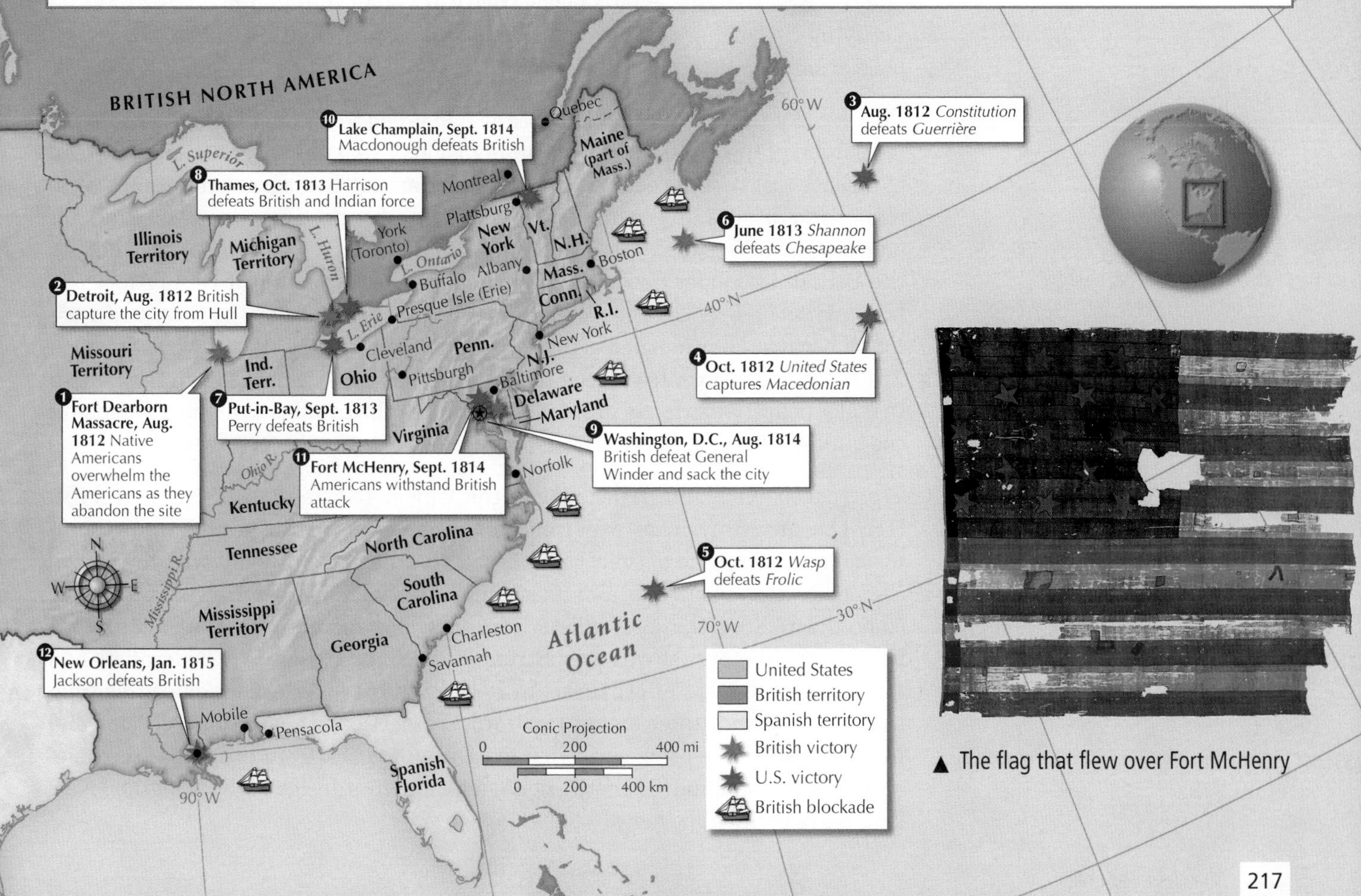

▲ The flag that flew over Fort McHenry

Battle of New Orleans
This engraving from the 1800s depicts Andrew Jackson inspiring his soldiers to fight the British. *How does the engraving show that the United States lacked a regular standing army?*

War's Aftermath and Effects

The Americans won their greatest victory at the **Battle of New Orleans** in January 1815. From a strong and entrenched position, General Andrew Jackson routed the British attack. In this lopsided battle, the Americans suffered only 71 casualties, compared to 2,036 British casualties. The bloodshed at New Orleans was especially tragic because it came two weeks after the Americans and the British had signed a peace treaty at Ghent in Belgium. Unfortunately, notifying the soldiers in North America took over a month because of the slow pace of sailing ships.

The Treaty of Ghent The Americans had failed to conquer Canada, while the British had failed in their American invasions. Weary of war, both sides agreed to a peace treaty that restored prewar boundaries. They agreed to set up a commission to discuss any boundary disputes at a future time. The treaty did not address the issues of neutrality or impressments. But after Napoleon's defeat, the British no longer needed to impress American sailors or to stop American trade with the French. The Americans interpreted the **Treaty of Ghent** as a triumph because they learned of it shortly after hearing of Jackson's great victory. That sequence of events created the illusion that Jackson had forced the British to make peace. Americans preferred to think of the conflict as a noble defense of the United States against British aggression.

The Hartford Convention After the War of 1812 and Jackson's victory in New Orleans, Americans experienced a surge of nationalism and a new confidence in the strength of their republic. By weathering a difficult war, the nation seemed certain to endure, and most Americans were giddy with relief. The outcome discredited the Federalists, who looked weak for opposing a war that became popular once it was over. Strongest in New England, the Federalists had undermined the war effort there. In December 1814, Federalist delegates from the New England states met at Hartford, Connecticut, to consider secession and making a separate peace with Britain. Drawing back from the brink, the delegates instead demanded constitutional amendments designed to strengthen New England's political power.

Unfortunately for the delegates of the **Hartford Convention,** their demands reached Washington, D.C., at the same time as news of the peace treaty and Jackson's victory. That combination embarrassed the Federalists, who were mocked as defeatists and traitors. Madison ignored their demands, and the voters punished the Federalists in the elections that followed. By 1820 the Federalist Party was dead—a sad fate for the party that had created the federal government only to lose faith in it during the War of 1812.

The Nation Continues to Grow Events during the War of 1812 ended most Indian resistance east of the Mississippi River for the time being. As a result of various defeats of Native Americans in the South, millions of acres of southern land also opened up for settlement. Settlement in the South and West led to the establishment of the new states of Indiana (1816), Mississippi (1817), Illinois (1818), and Alabama (1819). The union became bigger and stronger.

Meanwhile, American settlers had been pouring into Spanish Florida, resulting in cross-border conflict among the region's Seminole Indians, Americans, and the Spanish. Fugitive slaves from the United States, seeking sanctuary in Florida, added to the tensions. Over the next decade, the conflict would contribute to Spain's decision to cede Florida to the United States. In return the United States renounced its claims to Texas, as part of the Adams-Onís Treaty signed in 1819.

Checkpoint **What was the Hartford Convention?**

Cause and Effect

Causes

- British interfere with American shipping
- British interfere with American expansion into the western frontier
- Southerners want Florida, which is owned by Britain's ally Spain
- War Hawks want to expel Britain completely from North America

The War of 1812

Effects

- Revealed need for a strong standing army
- Encouraged American nationalism
- Brought end to the Federalist Party
- Shattered the strength of Native American resistance
- Paved the way for American acquisition of Florida

Analyze Cause and Effect Despite ending in stalemate, the War of 1812 had a major impact on the United States. *How did it affect American settlers?*

SECTION 4 Assessment

Progress Monitoring *Online*
For: Self-test with vocabulary practice
www.pearsonschool.com/ushist

Comprehension

1. **Terms and People** Write a sentence for each item below, explaining its relation to the War of 1812.
   - Tecumseh
   - Battle of Tippecanoe
   - War Hawks
   - Andrew Jackson
   - Francis Scott Key
   - "The Star-Spangled Banner"
   - Battle of New Orleans
   - Treaty of Ghent

2. **NoteTaking Reading Skill: Recognize Sequence** Use your completed chart to answer the Section Focus Question: Why did the United States go to war with Britain, and what was the outcome of that war?

Writing About History

3. **Quick Write: Give Details** Choose a topic for a research paper. Then, note the kinds of details that you should include to support a thesis. For example, if your thesis is that the American military was weaker than the British military during the War of 1812, you could include facts, statistics, quotations, and paraphrased information.

Critical Thinking

4. **Synthesize Information** Why were farmers and settlers especially likely to support the War of 1812?

5. **Make Comparisons** Compare American military strengths and weaknesses during the War of 1812 to those during the Revolutionary War.

6. **Identify Alternatives** What alternatives did Native Americans have during the war? Would the outcome have been different for them if they had chosen a different course of action?

CHAPTER 6

Quick Study Guide

Progress Monitoring *Online*
For: Self-test with vocabulary practice
www.pearsonschool.com/ushist

Establishing Important Precedents

Date	Precedent
1789	**Cabinet** Washington sets up the group of federal leaders who head major departments and advise the President.
1789	**Judiciary** Judiciary Act establishes a Supreme Court, the federal court system, and the office of Attorney General.
Around 1792	**Political parties** A two-party system, made up of Federalists and Democratic Republicans, emerges.
1797	**Two terms for Presidents** Washington retires after two terms in office.
1801	**Peaceful transfer of power** With Jefferson's election, power transfers peacefully from one party to the other.
1803	**Judicial review** The Supreme Court case *Marbury* v. *Madison* establishes judicial review.

Major U.S. Conflicts, 1794–1812

Date	Event	Cause/Significance
1794	Whiskey Rebellion	People on frontier protest whiskey taxes; First challenge facing the new government
1794	Battle of Fallen Timbers	Native Americans resist American expansion, aided by the British; American victory opened Northwest Territory
1801	Barbary War	Barbary States seize American ships and sailors; First American victory overseas
1811	Battle of Tippecanoe	Native Americans led by Tecumseh resist American expansion; American victory weakens Native American movement
1812	War of 1812	Americans blame Britain for various problems; War strengthens national unity; defeat of Native Americans opens up vast lands for settlement

U.S. Territorial Expansion

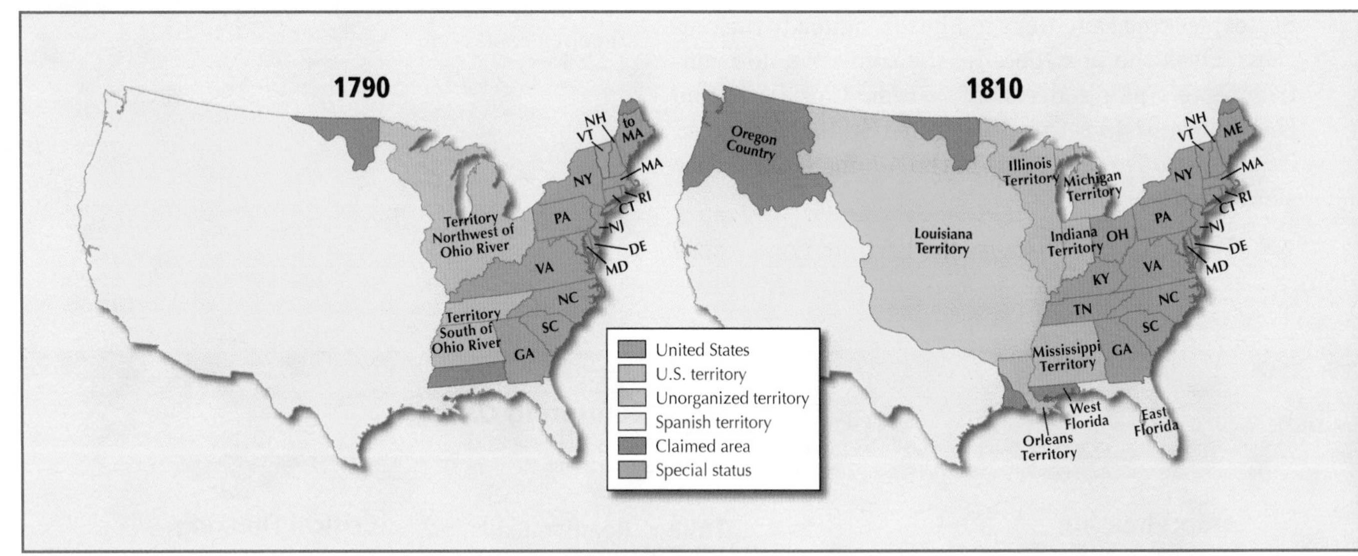

Quick Study Timeline

In America

1789
Washington elected President

1795
Treaty of Greenville signed

Presidential Terms

George Washington 1789–1797

John Adams 1797–1801

1790 | 1795 | 1800

Around the World

1789
Revolution breaks out in France

1793
China rejects British diplomatic mission

1801
United Kingdom of Great Britain and Ireland established

American Issues Connector

By connecting prior knowledge with what you have learned in this chapter, you can gradually build your understanding of enduring questions that still affect America today. Answer the questions below. Then, use your American Issues Connector study guide (or go online: www.pearsonschool.com/ushist).

Issues You Learned About

● **U.S. Foreign Policy** As a new nation, the United States had to establish a foreign policy. Deciding on foreign policies that are in the best interest of the nation has been an enduring issue.

1. In his Farewell Address, George Washington stated, "The great rule of conduct for us, in regard to foreign nations, is in extending our commercial relations to have with them as little political connection as possible." Write an evaluation of whether or not future Presidents followed Washington's advice and kept out of foreign alliances. Consider the following:
   - the funding of the military
   - laws and actions regarding trade with foreign nations
   - wars the United States has become involved in
   - international organizations the United States has become part of

● **Federal Power and States' Rights** The struggle for power between state governments and the federal government was sparked in the early years of the Republic.

2. According to Jefferson and Madison, what institution had the power to judge whether or not a federal law was constitutional?
3. Did Chief Justice John Marshall believe that federal laws were superior or inferior to state laws? Explain.
4. Would a strict constructionist be more likely to support a strong federal government or a weak federal government? Explain your answer.

● **Territorial Expansion of the United States** From its original 13 states along the eastern seaboard, the United States has expanded across the continent.

5. What were the results of the Treaty of Greenville?
6. What was the importance of the Louisiana Purchase?
7. How did the United States gain new land for settlement in Florida?

Connect to Your World | **Activity**

Sectionalism and National Politics: Political Parties
The Federalists and the Democratic Republicans were the first political parties in the United States. Today, the two main parties are the Democrats and the Republicans. Go online or to your local library and conduct research to learn more about each party. Then, use your findings to create a chart, similar to the one in the Infographic in Section 1, contrasting the two parties today. Make sure to include background information as well as details about the foreign, domestic, and economic policies each party supports.

History Interactive
For: Interactive timeline
www.pearsonschool.com/ushist

1803 Jefferson makes Louisiana Purchase

1807 Embargo Act passed

1814 Treaty of Ghent ends the War of 1812

Thomas Jefferson 1801–1809 | James Madison 1809–1817

1805 | 1810 | 1815

1804 Haiti declares independence from France

1810 Colombia gains independence from Spain

1815 French leader Napoleon is defeated at Waterloo

Chapter Assessment

Terms and People

1. Define **tariff.** Why did Hamilton favor tariffs?
2. What do **loose construction** and **strict construction** mean? Explain which view Thomas Jefferson held, and why.
3. What was the **Battle of Fallen Timbers**? What was the result of this battle?
4. Define **judicial review.** Explain how the power of judicial review developed.
5. What was the **War of 1812**? Explain its major causes.

Focus Questions

The focus question for this chapter is **How did the United States build a government, expand its territory, and conduct foreign policy in its early years?** Build an answer to this big question by answering the focus questions for Sections 1 through 4 and the Critical Thinking questions that follow.

Section 1

6. How did debate over the role of government lead to the formation of political parties?

Section 2

7. How did foreign policy challenges affect political debate and shape American government?

Section 3

8. What were the successes and failures of the Jefferson administrations?

Section 4

9. Why did the United States go to war with Britain, and what was the outcome of that war?

Critical Thinking

10. **Decision Making** What was one of Washington's most important decisions in setting up the new federal government? Explain.
11. **Draw Conclusions** Would an American who supported a strong national government be more likely to vote for a Federalist or a Democratic Republican? Who would this American have likely voted for in the presidential election of 1800? Explain your answer.
12. **Draw Inferences** Why do you think Tecumseh had difficulty uniting Native Americans to resist the expansion of American settlers onto their lands?
13. **Make Inferences** Why did the Virginia and Kentucky resolutions threaten national unity?
14. **Analyze Information** How did John Marshall help establish the authority of the Supreme Court?
15. **Analyze Graphs** Describe the graph below. What event explains the data on the graph? What would cause exports to rise again in 1809?

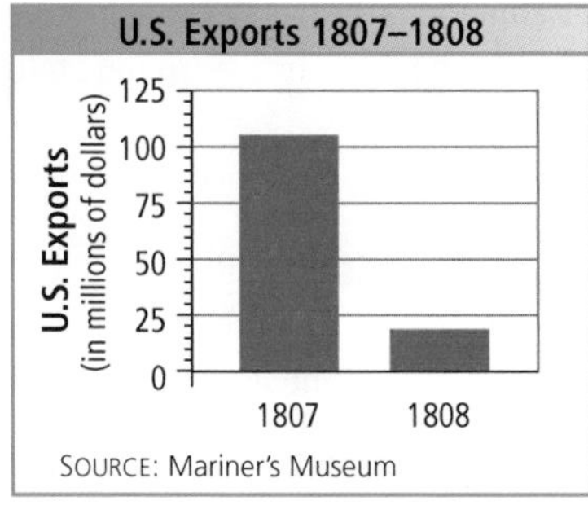

16. **Explain Effects** What effect did the War of 1812 have on political parties in the United States?

Writing About History

Writing a Research Paper The first few years of the United States were influential ones in the nation's history. Write a research paper that describes the importance of a person or an event in shaping the new republic. Choose your own topic or one of the following: George Washington, Thomas Jefferson, the Louisiana Purchase, the War of 1812.

Prewriting

- Choose the topic that most interests you, and create a set of questions about it.
- Narrow your topic to make it more manageable.
- Gather details and make a research plan.

Drafting

- Develop a thesis statement.
- Create an outline or graphic organizer to organize your information.
- Provide appropriate details from various sources.

Revising

- Use the guidelines on page SH14 of the Writing Handbook to revise your report.

Document-Based Assessment

Settling the Northwest Territory

From 1787 on, huge numbers of American settlers poured into the Northwest Territory, frequently coming into conflict with the people who already lived there. How did the newcomers and the Native Americans interact? Use your knowledge of American western expansion and Documents A, B, C, and D to answer questions 1 through 4.

Document A

"The utmost good faith shall always be observed towards the Indians; their lands and property shall never be taken from them without their consent; and, in their property, rights, and liberty, they shall never be invaded or disturbed, unless in just and lawful wars authorized by Congress; but laws founded in justice and humanity, shall from time to time be made for preventing wrongs being done to them, and for preserving peace and friendship with them."

—*Northwest Ordinance of 1787, Section 14, Article 3*

Document B

"At present, we do not think of ourselves perfectly secure from [the Indians] on account of a few lawless bandits made up of Mingos, Shawnees, and Cherokees, who reside at present on the waters of the Scioto [River]. These are a set of thievish, murdering rascals. . . . [L]et the treaty end how it may. . . . [The] little skulking parties of Indians, if they are never won over to be our friends, can never do us any considerable injury. On the other hand, should there be a general Indian war, this will be a place of general rendezvous for an army. So that, in all human probability, the settlement can never fail of the protection of government."

—*Rufus Putnam, Superintendent, Ohio Land Company, 1788*

Document C

"A white man gathers from a field, a few times bigger than his room, bread enough for a whole year. If he adds to this a small field of grass, he maintains beasts . . . while we must have a great deal of ground to live upon. A deer will serve us a couple of days, and a single deer must have a great deal of ground to put him in good condition. If we kill two or three hundred a year, 'tis the same as to eat all the wood and grass of the land they live on and that is a great deal. No wonder the whites drive us every year further before them from the sea to the Mississippi. They spread like oil on a blanket; we melt like snow before the sun."

—*Little Turtle, Miami Chief, 1792*

Document D

Movement into the Northwest Territory

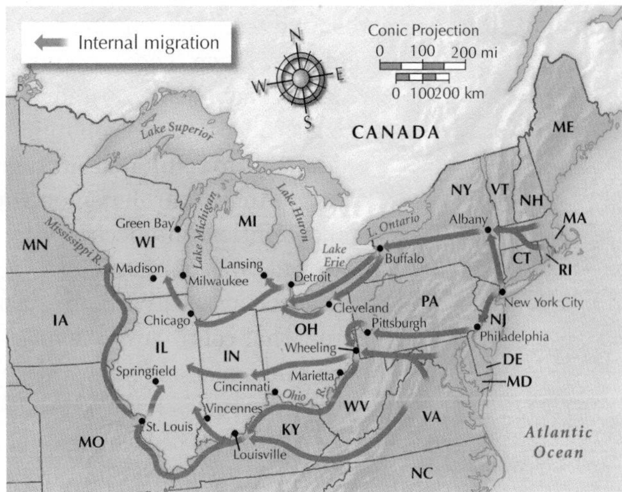

---

1. Document A could best be described as a
   - **A** treaty.
   - **B** charter.
   - **C** constitution.
   - **D** law.

2. What can you conclude from Document B?
   - **A** Native Americans were all lawless.
   - **B** Rufus Putnam opposed "a general Indian war."
   - **C** Soldiers were marching to Ohio.
   - **D** Settlers living along the Scioto River felt that Native Americans there were not a major threat.

3. According to Document C, Little Turtle thought American expansion
   - **A** was due to missionary activity.
   - **B** was fueled by racism.
   - **C** could likely be halted.
   - **D** was inevitable because of differences in land use.

4. **Writing Task** Did Americans in the Northwest Territory adhere to the provisions of the Northwest Ordinance of 1787 regarding native peoples? Use your knowledge of American history and evidence from the sources above to explain your answer.

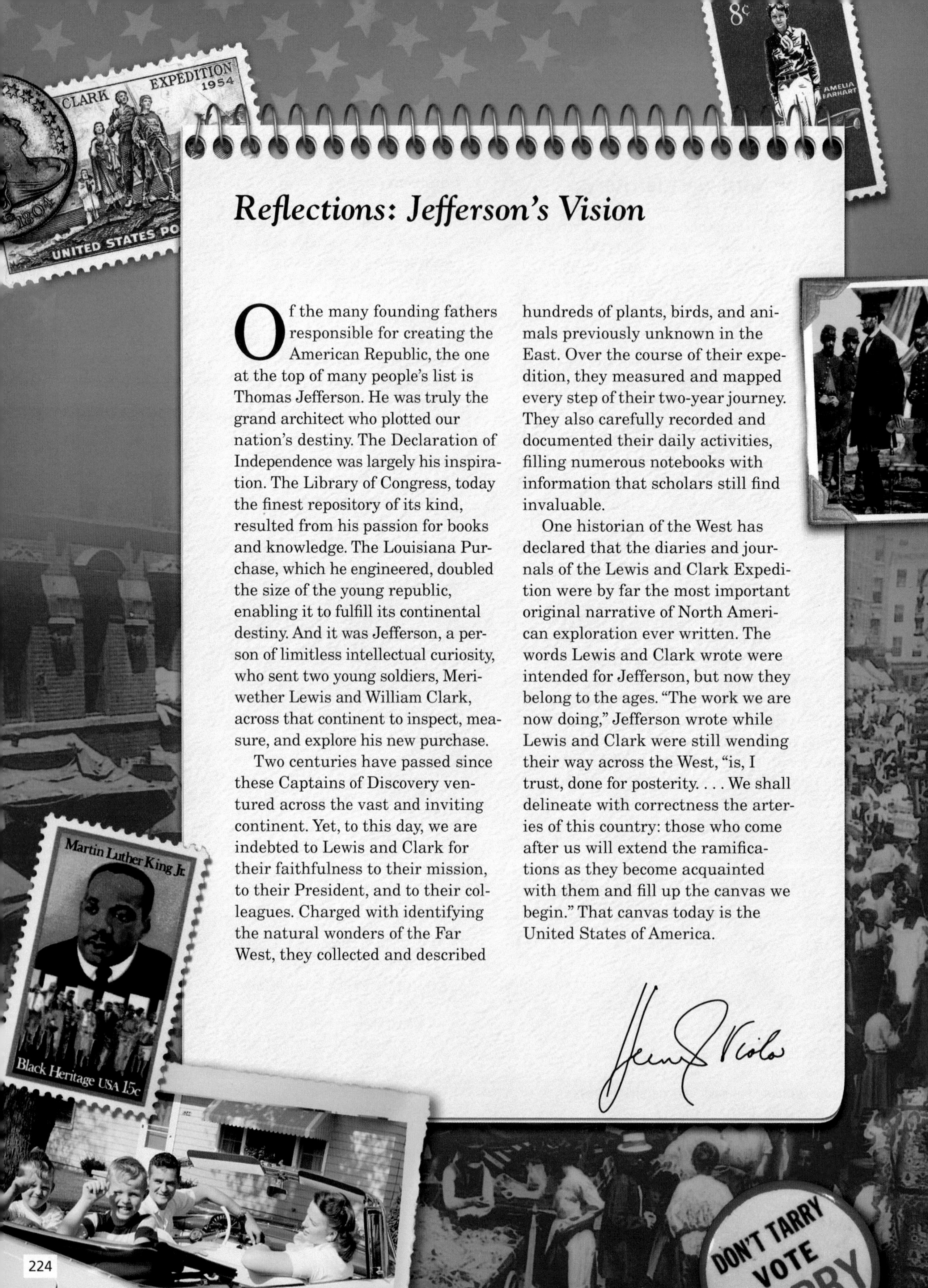

Reflections: Jefferson's Vision

Of the many founding fathers responsible for creating the American Republic, the one at the top of many people's list is Thomas Jefferson. He was truly the grand architect who plotted our nation's destiny. The Declaration of Independence was largely his inspiration. The Library of Congress, today the finest repository of its kind, resulted from his passion for books and knowledge. The Louisiana Purchase, which he engineered, doubled the size of the young republic, enabling it to fulfill its continental destiny. And it was Jefferson, a person of limitless intellectual curiosity, who sent two young soldiers, Meriwether Lewis and William Clark, across that continent to inspect, measure, and explore his new purchase.

Two centuries have passed since these Captains of Discovery ventured across the vast and inviting continent. Yet, to this day, we are indebted to Lewis and Clark for their faithfulness to their mission, to their President, and to their colleagues. Charged with identifying the natural wonders of the Far West, they collected and described hundreds of plants, birds, and animals previously unknown in the East. Over the course of their expedition, they measured and mapped every step of their two-year journey. They also carefully recorded and documented their daily activities, filling numerous notebooks with information that scholars still find invaluable.

One historian of the West has declared that the diaries and journals of the Lewis and Clark Expedition were by far the most important original narrative of North American exploration ever written. The words Lewis and Clark wrote were intended for Jefferson, but now they belong to the ages. "The work we are now doing," Jefferson wrote while Lewis and Clark were still wending their way across the West, "is, I trust, done for posterity. . . . We shall delineate with correctness the arteries of this country: those who come after us will extend the ramifications as they become acquainted with them and fill up the canvas we begin." That canvas today is the United States of America.

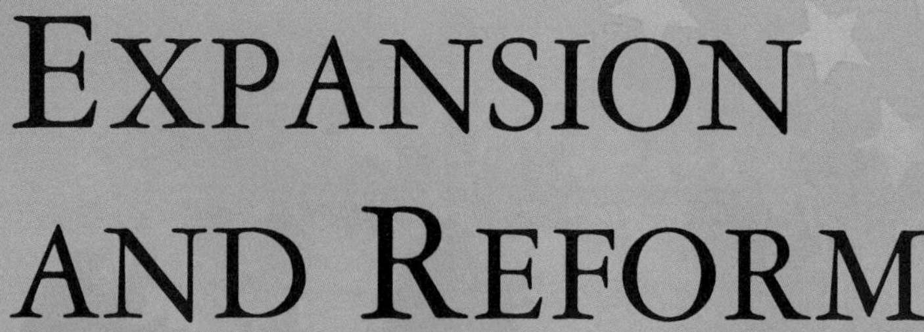

EXPANSION AND REFORM

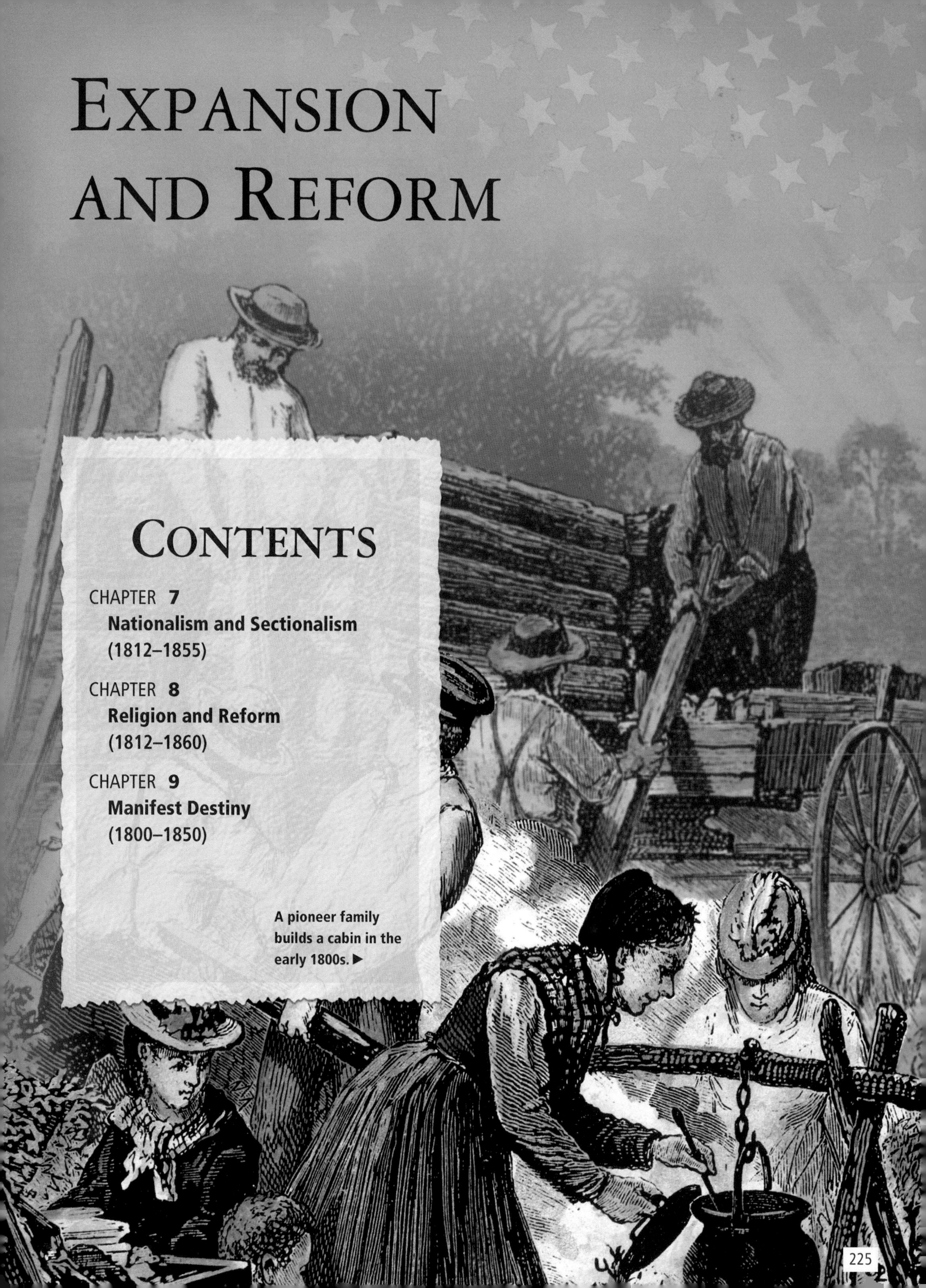

CONTENTS

A pioneer family builds a cabin in the early 1800s. ▶

CHAPTER

7 Nationalism and Sectionalism

1812–1855

WITNESS HISTORY

Nationalism Revived

After the War of 1812, the United States experienced a period of growth and renewed nationalism. Expanding markets, along with thriving industries and businesses, transformed American life. The new nationalism was reflected not only in this industrial growth, but in Supreme Court rulings and domestic and foreign policies.

> "The war [of 1812] has renewed and reinstated the national feelings and character which the Revolution had given, and which were daily lessened."
>
> —Albert Gallatin, 1816

Miniature log cabin from the Election of 1840

◄ New York Harbor, 1849

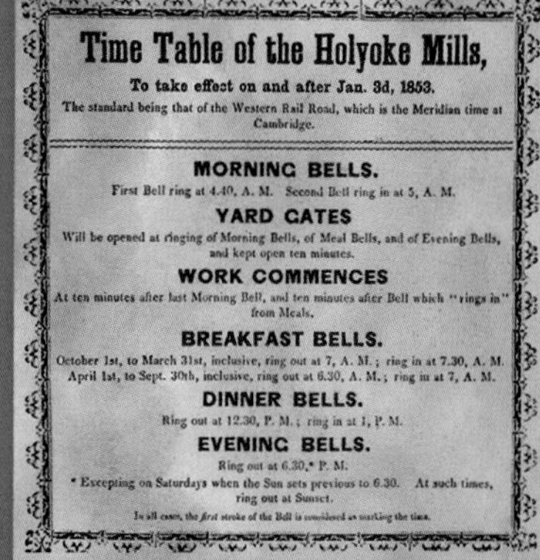

Time Table of the Holyoke Mills,

To take effect on and after Jan. 3d, 1853.

The standard being that of the Western Rail Road, which is the Meridian time at Cambridge.

MORNING BELLS.

First Bell ring at 4.40, A. M. Second Bell ring in at 5, A. M.

YARD GATES

Will be opened at ringing of Morning Bells, of Meal Bells, and of Evening Bells, and kept open ten minutes.

WORK COMMENCES

At ten minutes after last Morning Bell, and ten minutes after Bell which "rings in" from Meals.

BREAKFAST BELLS.

October 1st, to March 31st, inclusive, ring out at 7, A. M.; ring in at 7.30, A. M.
April 1st, to Sept. 30th, inclusive, ring out at 6.30, A. M.; ring in at 7, A. M.

DINNER BELLS.

Ring out at 12.30, P. M.; ring in at 1, P. M.

EVENING BELLS.

Ring out at 6.30,* P. M.

* Excepting on Saturdays when the Sun sets previous to 6.30. At such times, ring out at Sunset.

In all cases, the *first* stroke of the Bell is considered as marking the time.

Work schedule at the Holyoke Mills, 1853

Chapter Preview

Chapter Focus Question: How did nationalism and sectionalism affect the United States from the early 1800s to the mid-1800s?

Section 1
Industry and Transportation

Section 2
Sectional Differences

Section 3
An Era of Nationalism

Section 4
Democracy and the Age of Jackson

Section 5
Constitutional Disputes and Crises

Cotton gin

Use the ☑ Quick Study Timeline at the end of this chapter to preview chapter events.

Note Taking Study Guide *Online*
For: Note Taking and American Issues Connector
www.pearsonschool.com/ushist

SECTION 1

Lowell girl lunch pail ▶

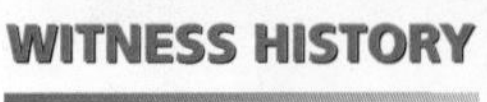

▲ Lowell girl weaving in textile mill

WITNESS HISTORY

Dawn of the Industrial Age

The United States experienced a revolution in the early 1800s—a revolution in the way many people lived and worked. This revolution introduced factory methods of production from Great Britain. Here, a Lowell mill girl writes to her father about her work schedule at the textile mill:

> "Dear Father, I am well which is one comfort. . . . At half past six [the bell] rings for the girls to get up and at seven they are called into the mill. At half past 12 we have dinner and are called back again at one and stay till half past seven. I get along very well with my work."
>
> —Mary Paul, December 21, 1845

Industry and Transportation

Objectives

- Summarize the key developments in the transportation revolution of the early 1800s.
- Analyze the rise of industry in the United States in the early 1800s.
- Describe some of the leading inventions and industrial developments in the early 1800s.

Terms and People

turnpike	Francis Cabot Lowell
National Road	Lowell girl
Erie Canal	interchangeable parts
Industrial Revolution	Eli Whitney
Samuel Slater	Samuel F.B. Morse

NoteTaking

Reading Skill: Identify Causes and Effects Fill in a table with the causes and effects of the transportation revolution and industrialization.

Transportation and Industry	
Causes	Effects
• Invention of commercial steamboat • •	• Drastically increased speed of traveling upstream • •

Why It Matters Developments in technology began to transform life in the United States in the early 1800s. New methods of transporting and manufacturing goods changed the way people lived and worked. The United States was set on a course of industrialization that would shape life in the nation for decades. **Section Focus Question: How did transportation developments and industrialization affect the nation's economy?**

The Transportation Revolution

The original 13 states hugged the Atlantic Coast, and all major settlements in the United States sprang up near a harbor or river because water provided the most efficient way to move people and goods. At the start of the nineteenth century, overland transportation consisted of carts, wagons, sleighs, and stagecoaches pulled by horses or oxen over dirt roads. Moving goods just a few dozen miles by road could cost as much as shipping the same cargo across the ocean.

Improving the Roads In an effort to improve overland transportation, some states chartered companies to operate **turnpikes**—roads for which users had to pay a toll. The term came from the turnpikes, or gates, that guarded entrances to the roads. Turnpike operators were supposed to use toll income to improve the roads and ease travel. But only a few turnpikes made a profit, and most failed to lower transportation costs or increase the speed of travel. The country's lone decent route, which was made of crushed rock, was the **National Road.** Funded by the federal government, this roadway extended west from Maryland to the Ohio River (in present-day West Virginia) in 1818.

The Steamboat Goes Commercial The first major advance in transportation was the development of the steamboat. By burning wood or coal, the engine boiled the water to create steam. The force of the steam turned a large, rotating paddle, which pushed the boat through the water. American Robert Fulton designed the first commercially successful steamboat—the *Clermont.*

The steamboat made it much easier to travel upstream against the current. For example, before the steamboat, it took about four months to travel the 1,440 miles from New Orleans to Louisville, Kentucky, along the Mississippi and Ohio rivers. In 1820, a steamboat made the same journey in just 20 days. By 1838, it took a steamboat only six days. Steamboats unlocked the great potential of the Mississippi River Basin for moving people and goods. The number of steamboats plying the rivers of that system grew from 230 in 1834 to nearly 700 in 1843.

Steam-powered ships also revolutionized transatlantic travel. By 1850, a steamship could cross the Atlantic in 10 to 14 days, compared to the 25 to 50 days for a sailing ship.

HISTORY MAKERS

Robert Fulton (1765–1815)

Although Fulton was born and raised in Pennsylvania, he spent much of his life in England and France. There, he worked first as a painter and then as an inventor and engineer, where he constructed canals and experimented with torpedoes and submarines. When he returned to the United States after 19 years, President Jefferson asked him to help build canals in the new Louisiana territory. Fulton declined, however, choosing to focus instead on the development of the steamboat. In 1807, Fulton's steamboat, the ***Clermont,*** successfully made its journey from New York to Albany, demonstrating to the world the possibilities of steam navigation. This success led Fulton and his business partner, Robert Livingston, to start the first commercial steamboat service.

Canals Boom A second transportation advance of the early 1800s was the construction of canals. The nation's canal network grew from 100 miles in 1816 to 3,300 miles in 1840. Mostly built in the Northeast, canals provided efficient water transportation that linked farms to the expanding cities.

The best-known canal of the era was the **Erie Canal.** Completed in 1825, it ran 363 miles across New York State from Lake Erie to the Hudson River. Before this canal went into service, it could cost $100 or more to ship a ton of freight overland from the city of Buffalo on the shores of Lake Erie to New York City. The canal lowered that cost to just $4.

By funneling western produce to the Hudson River, the Erie Canal helped make New York City the nation's greatest commercial center. As a result, the city grew quickly. From a population of 124,000 in 1820, its population surged to 800,000 in 1860. The canal also enhanced the value of farmland in the Great Lakes region, because farmers there now had easier access to eastern markets for their goods.

> **Primary Source** "The increase of commerce, and the growth of the country, have been very accurately measured by the growth of the business of the Canal. It has been one great bond of strength, infusing life and vigor into the whole. Commercially and politically, it has secured and maintained to the United States the characteristics of a homogeneous [sharing common features] people."
>
> —Report by the Secretary of the Treasury, 1853

Railroads Further Ease Transport The most dramatic advance in transportation in the 1800s was the arrival of a new mode of transportation—railroads. This technology, largely developed in Great Britain, began to appear in the United States in the 1820s. Horses pulled the first American trains. But clever inventors soon developed steam-powered engines, which could pull heavier loads of freight or passengers at higher speeds than horses could manage.

Focus On Geography

Geography *Interactive*
For: Interactive map
www.pearsonschool.com/ushist

A Revolution in Transportation In the early 1800s, businesses were expanding and Americans needed more efficient and reliable transportation. Roads and canals provided a good start, but they soon proved too slow and limited for a nation on the move. Beginning in the late 1820s, iron rails were laid on long tracks to connect locations such as New York City and New Haven, Connecticut. Goods could be shipped faster and more easily on trains, and cities located along railroads prospered. Via the rails, vast regions gained access to expanding markets.

Major Canals, Roads, and Railroads, 1840–1850

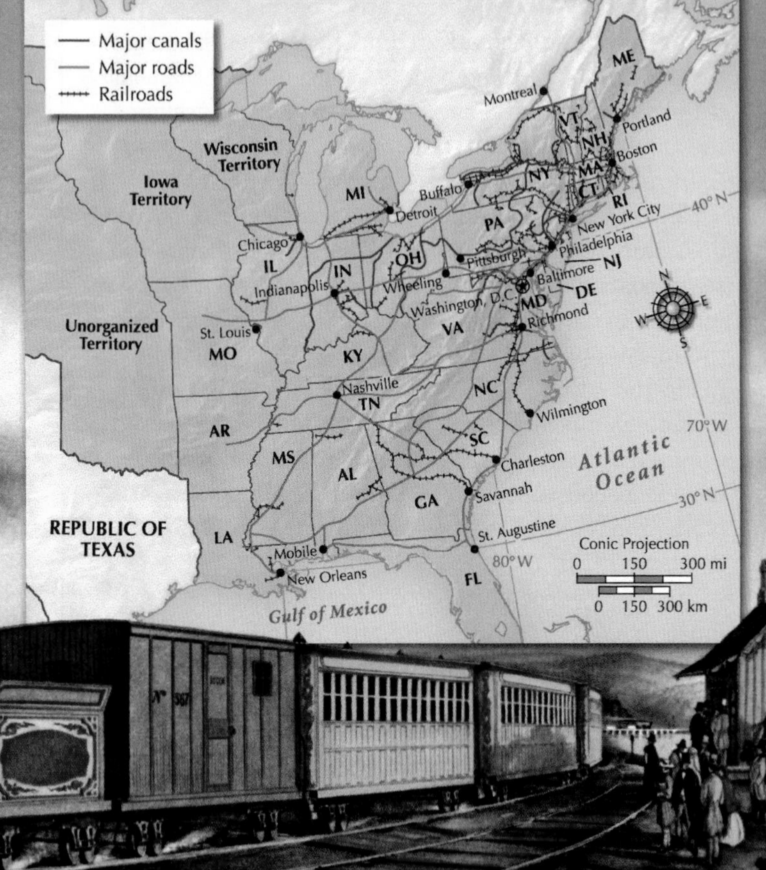

▼ Early American express train

Geography and History

- What did the transportation developments that occurred during this time period have in common?
- In what part of the country were most of the railroads located in the mid-1800s? Why do you think this was the case?

Compared to canals, railroads cost less to build and could more easily scale hills. Trains moved faster than ships and carried more weight. Their introduction put a quick end to the brief boom in canal building. Meanwhile, the American rail network expanded from 13 miles of track in 1830 to 31,000 miles by 1860. In 1800, a journey from New York City to Detroit, Michigan, took 28 days by boat. In 1857, the same trip took only two days by train.

✓ **Checkpoint What were the major developments in transportation between 1800 and 1860?**

Technology Sparks Industrial Growth

Developments in technology also transformed manufacturing. This transformation became known as the **Industrial Revolution,** which changed not only the nation's economy but also its culture, social life, and politics.

The Industrial Revolution began in Great Britain during the 1700s, with the development of machines, powered by steam or flowing rivers, to perform work that had once been done by hand. The first machines spun thread and wove cloth more quickly and cheaply.

Slater Opens First Textile Mill To protect its industrial advantage, the British banned the export of machinery, as well as the emigration of workers with knowledge of the technology. However, a skilled worker named **Samuel Slater** defied that law and moved to the United States. Slater used his detailed knowledge of the textile machinery to build the nation's first water-powered textile mill in 1793 at Pawtucket, Rhode Island. The mill used the flowing Blackstone River to power its machinery, which produced one part of the textile: cotton thread. Slater and his business partners later built more factories along New England rivers. These factories used the so-called family system, in which entire families, including parents and children, were employed in the mills. Those families settled in villages owned by factory owners and located around the mills.

Lowell Builds Fully Operational Mill Boston merchant **Francis Cabot Lowell** developed another industrial system in Massachusetts. In 1811, he toured England's factory towns to gather secret information. Returning home, Lowell organized a company called the Boston Associates. In 1813, the associates built their first mill at Waltham, Massachusetts, in which all operations in the manufacture of cloth occurred—instead of just the production of thread. During the 1820s, they built more factories on the Merrimac River and established a new town called Lowell. Their system employed young, single women recruited from area farms. The company enforced strict rules of behavior and housed the **"Lowell girls"** in closely supervised boardinghouses. After a few years of work, most of the young women married and left the factories.

Factory Work Changes Lives The growth of factories changed more than the speed and volume of production. It changed the working lives of thousands of people. Machines increased the pace of work and divided labor into many small tasks done by separate workers. This process reduced the amount of skill and training required for individual jobs. Factory owners benefited because untrained workers were more numerous and less costly to employ. In some trades, owners achieved those benefits without adopting new machines. The manufacture of clothing and shoes are two examples.

As you have read, America's first factories produced thread or cloth rather than finished clothing. During the 1820s, a garment trade developed primarily in New York City. Contractors provided cloth to poor women who made the clothes in their homes without the help of machines. They earned about $1 per week.

Shoemaking followed a similar model. Lynn, Massachusetts, led the nation in this industry. A few men performed the skilled and better-paying tasks of cutting and shaping leather for the tops of the shoes. For less pay (about 50 cents a week), women sewed the shoes together.

✓ **Checkpoint What changes occurred in the United States with the rise of industry in the early 1800s?**

Inventions Transform Industry and Agriculture

A number of key innovations paralleled the revolutions in transportation and industry in the early 1800s. These also dramatically affected the American economy and society.

New Methods of Production To improve efficiency in factories, manufacturers designed products with **interchangeable parts,** identical

▼ Samuel Slater's textile mill, Pawtucket, Rhode Island

Vocabulary Builder
component–(kuhm POH nuhnt) *n.* part; one of the parts of a whole

components that could be used in place of one another. Inventor **Eli Whitney** introduced this idea to the United States. Traditionally, items such as clocks and muskets were built one at a time by skilled artisans who made each part and assembled the device from start to finish by hand. As a result, a part that would work in one gun or clock might not work in any other. Whitney proposed making muskets in a new way—by manufacturing each part separately and precisely. Under Whitney's system, a part that would work in one musket would work in another musket. In other words, the parts would be interchangeable.

It took some years for American manufacturers to make interchangeable parts reliably. Yet the idea of interchangeable parts eventually made possible the much more efficient production of a wide range of manufactured goods. One of the products manufactured with interchangeable parts was the sewing machine. Invented by Elias Howe and improved by Isaac Singer, the sewing machine lowered the cost and increased the speed of making cloth into clothing.

Innovation Quickens Communication In 1837, American **Samuel F.B. Morse** invented the electric telegraph, which allowed electrical pulses to travel long distances along metal wires as coded signals. The code of dots and dashes is called Morse code after its inventor. Before the telegraph, a message could pass only as fast as a horse or a ship could carry a letter. By using Morse's invention, a message could be delivered almost instantly. By 1860, the nation had 50,000 miles of telegraph lines.

Agriculture Remains Strong Despite the growing size and power of the nation's factories, agriculture remained the largest industry in the United States. But change affected farming as well. American farms became more productive, raising larger crops for the market. In 1815, American farmers sold only about a third of their harvests. By 1860, that share had doubled. The gains came partly from the greater fertility of new farms in the Midwest. Farmers also adopted better methods for planting, tending, and harvesting crops and for raising livestock. After 1840, large farms also employed the steel plow invented by John Deere and the mechanical reaper developed by Cyrus McCormick.

▲ Samuel Morse's telegraph

Checkpoint What were the key inventions between 1820 and 1860?

SECTION 1 Assessment

Progress Monitoring *Online*
For: Self-test with vocabulary practice
www.pearsonschool.com/ushist

Comprehension

1. **Terms and People** For each person below, write a sentence explaining the impact of his new invention or innovation on the economy of the United States.
   - Samuel Slater
   - Francis Cabot Lowell
   - Eli Whitney
   - Samuel F.B. Morse
2. **NoteTaking Reading Skill: Identify Causes and Effects** Use your completed table to answer the Section Focus Question: How did transportation developments and industrialization affect the nation's economy?

Writing About History

3. **Quick Write: Choose a Topic** Review your notes from this section to see what topics you would like to research further. Then, write a list of questions that you will research to find the answers.

Critical Thinking

4. **Predict Consequences** How might the United States have been different if transportation had not advanced during the 1800s?
5. **Summarize** How did textile mills develop in the United States?
6. **Make Generalizations** How was the development of interchangeable parts an example of the move to make work "less skilled" in the early 1800s?

SECTION 2

◄ Northern factory

▲ Southern cotton field

WITNESS HISTORY

A Nation of Farming and Industry

Thomas Jefferson and the Democratic Republicans had once championed the idea of a nation of farmers. But Jefferson's own embargo of 1807 and the War of 1812 severely limited American access to British manufactured goods. Suddenly, Americans needed to develop factories.

> "We must now place the manufacturer by the side of the agriculturalist. . . . [S]hall we manufacture our own comforts or go without them at the will of a foreign nation? He, therefore, who is now against domestic manufactures must be for reducing us . . . to dependence on that nation. . . ."
>
> —Thomas Jefferson, in a letter to Benjamin Austin, 1816

Sectional Differences

Objectives

- Analyze why industrialization took root in the northern part of the United States.
- Describe the impact of industrialization on northern life.
- Analyze the reasons that agriculture and slavery became entrenched in the South.

Terms and People

Tariff of 1816
capital
labor union
nativist
cotton gin

NoteTaking

Reading Skill: Compare and Contrast Use a Venn diagram like the one below to compare and contrast the North and the South.

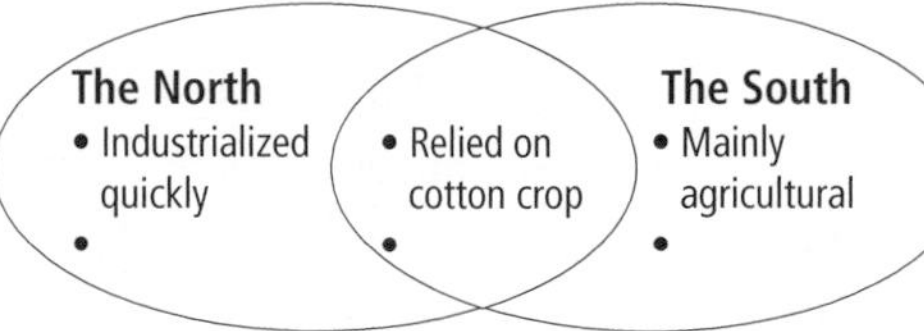

Why It Matters Industrialization occurred mainly in the Northeast, where it changed the very structure of society. In the South, a boom in cotton production helped deepen the region's commitment to slavery. The two parts of the country developed in different ways—a fact that increasingly complicated politics in the United States. **Section Focus Question: How did the North and South differ during the first half of the 1800s?**

The North Embraces Industry

Thomas Jefferson had hoped to preserve the United States as a nation of farmers. Instead, between 1815 and 1860, the United States developed an industrial sector, or a distinct part of the economy or society dedicated to industry. Without intending to do so, Democratic Republican policies contributed to that industrial development.

Why Industrialization Spread The embargo of 1807 and the War of 1812 cut off access to British manufactured goods. Eager for substitutes, Americans built their own factories in the Northeast. After the war, however, British goods once again flowed into the United States, threatening to overwhelm fledgling American manufacturers. Congress could have let those industries wither from the competition. Instead, Congress imposed the **Tariff of 1816,** a tariff on imports designed to protect American industry. This tariff increased the price of imported manufactured goods by an average of 20 to 25 percent. The inflated price for imports encouraged Americans to buy products made in the United States. The tariff helped industry, but it hurt farmers, who had to pay higher prices for consumer goods.

Vocabulary Builder
access–(AK sehs) *n.* means of getting or acquiring

Why the Northeast? Most of the new factories emerged in the Northeast. There were several reasons for this. One reason was greater access to **capital,** or the money needed to build factories or other productive assets. In the South, the land and the climate favored agriculture. Thus, people there invested capital in land and slave labor. The Northeast had more cheap labor to work in the factories. In addition, the Northeast had many swiftly flowing rivers to provide water power for the new factories.

✓ **Checkpoint** **What factors contributed to industrialization in the early 1800s?**

Social Change in the North

The arrival of industry changed the way many Americans worked by reducing the skill required for many jobs. This trend hurt highly skilled artisans, such as blacksmiths, shoemakers, and tailors, who could not compete with manufacturers working with many low-cost laborers. Most artisans suffered declining wages.

Workers Organize Troubled workers responded by seeking political change. During the 1820s, some artisans organized the Workingmen's Party to compete in local and state elections. They sought free public education and laws to limit the working day to ten hours versus the standard twelve.

The party also supported the right of workers to organize **labor unions**—groups of workers who unite to seek better pay and conditions. Most early labor unions focused on helping skilled tradesmen, such as carpenters or printers. Unions went on strike to force employers to pay higher wages, reduce hours, or improve conditions. In 1834 and 1836, for example, the Lowell mill girls held strikes when employers cut their wages and increased their charges for boarding. Singing "Oh! I cannot be a slave!" they left their jobs and temporarily shut down the factory. The Lowell strikes failed to achieve their goals, however. The women eventually returned to work and accepted the reduced pay.

Factory owners sometimes turned to the courts for protection. In 1835, a New York City court convicted 20 tailors of conspiracy for forming a union. Such convictions angered workers. But, neither the union movement nor the Workingmen's Party prospered in the early 1800s.

▲ Glass cutters' trade union ribbon

A Middle Class Emerges While hurting some working Americans, industrialization helped others. A middle class emerged, in which men helped manage businesses as bankers, lawyers, accountants, clerks, auctioneers, brokers, and retailers. The middle class stood above the working class of common laborers but below the upper class of wealthy business owners.

Most middle-class men worked in offices outside of their homes. They also began to move their homes away from the crowds, noise, and smells of the workshops and factories. Factory workers, however, could not afford that move. Neighborhoods, therefore, became segregated by class as well as by race. This contrasted with colonial cities and towns, where people of all social classes had to live close to one another.

For the middle class, work became separated from family life. These families expected wives and mothers to stay at home, tending those spaces as havens from the bustle of the working world, while the men went off to work and returned with the money to support the household. Working-class and farm families could not afford such an arrangement. In those families, women and children also had to work.

Emigration From Ireland and Germany In the 1840s, the new middle class and most of the nation's farmers had been born in the United States. Increasingly, however, the working class was comprised of immigrants. Prior to 1840, immigration consisted mainly of Protestants from England or Scotland. During the 1830s, about 600,000 immigrants arrived. That number more than doubled to 1,500,000 during the 1840s and nearly doubled again to 2,800,000 in the 1850s.

This surge primarily came from Ireland and Germany, regions suffering from political upheavals, economic depressions, and rural famines. In Ireland, mass starvation occurred in the 1840s as a result of a fungus that destroyed the potato crop. The potato had been the primary food source for the Irish poor. A few historians suggest that the famine was an act of genocide. As hundreds of thousands of Irish were starving to death, huge amounts of livestock, corn, and other foods were being exported from Ireland to England. However, most historians dismiss this idea because there was no deliberate British policy to exterminate the Irish. In fact, the British government provided some relief with soup kitchens for the starving and work projects for the jobless. Even so, it is estimated that more than a million Irish people died of starvation or famine-related diseases. Another million or more left Ireland, immigrating to Australia or North America. Those who came to America joined many other Irish and German immigrants. Germans had fled their homeland during the same period when their political revolution failed.

Irish Famine

Many Irish immigrants came to the United States in the 1840s to escape the famine. Today, there are several memorials in the United States commemorating those who suffered in Ireland. Pictured here (top) is the Irish Memorial located in Philadelphia. The etching (inset) shows a family that is homeless and starving as a result of the famine. *What drew Irish and German immigrants to the United States?*

Unlike most of their predecessors, the new immigrants tended to be Catholic or Jewish. In search of work, they arrived in the seaports of the Northeast. A small minority, mostly German, could afford to set up shops or move to the West to buy farmland. But most immigrants had to find work on the docks, in factories, at construction sites, or in middle-class homes as domestic servants.

Immigration boosted the Northeast's share of the nation's population. It also promoted urban growth. In 1860, immigrants comprised more than 40 percent of the population of New York City. Some working-class immigrants moved on to new cities in the Midwest, including Cincinnati, Chicago, Cleveland, and Detroit. Very few went to the South, which lacked factory jobs for wage workers.

The rapid influx of so many newcomers produced social and political strains. Poverty forced many immigrants to cluster in shabby neighborhoods. The newcomers competed for jobs and housing with free African Americans. Rioters attacked African Americans, killing some and burning others' homes.

Catholic immigrants also faced discrimination from American-born Protestants. Protestants distrusted the Catholic Church, thinking it to be hostile to republican government. Protestant workers also resented the competition from newcomers who were willing to work for lower wages. Riots between Protestants and Catholics occurred in Philadelphia in 1844 and in Baltimore in 1854.

Some politicians, particularly in the Whig Party, exploited ethnic tensions. Called **nativists,** they campaigned for laws to discourage immigration or to deny political rights to newcomers. To defend their interests, many immigrants became active in the Democratic Party.

✓ **Checkpoint How did industrialization change the experience of working people?**

Southern Agricultural Economy and Society

During the 1780s, Thomas Jefferson, James Madison, and George Washington hoped that slavery would gradually fade away. They thought that a shift from tobacco to wheat cultivation would slowly undermine the slave system, making it less profitable. Indeed, they saw some evidence of such a trend in Virginia and Maryland, where many slaves were freed during the 1780s.

That trend, however, did not affect the Deep South—the region to the south and southwest of Virginia. In fact, the trend did not last even in Virginia. Slavery became more profitable as cotton became the South's leading crop.

Cotton Production Surges In the Deep South, three developments worked together to boost cotton production: the cotton gin, western expansion, and industrialization.

In 1793, Eli Whitney invented the **cotton gin** while working in Georgia. This machine reduced the amount of time and the cost of separating the cotton seeds from the valuable white fiber. The cotton gin made cotton cultivation much more profitable. Previously a minor crop, cotton became the South's leading product. From 5 million pounds in 1793, cotton production surged to 170 million pounds in 1820.

In part, that surge came as planters in older states—Georgia, South Carolina, and North Carolina—switched to growing cotton. But mostly it came as planters moved west or south to make new plantations in Florida, Tennessee, Alabama, Mississippi, Arkansas, Louisiana, and east Texas. These areas offered fertile soil and a warm climate well suited for growing cotton.

The increase in the cotton supply filled a growing demand from textile factories in the Northeast and in Europe. By 1840, southern plantations produced 60 percent of the cotton used by American and European factories. Cotton and cotton textiles accounted for over half the value of all American exports. With good reason, Americans spoke of "King Cotton" as the ruler of their economy.

Cotton Boom Spreads Slavery Growing cotton required workers as well as land. Southern planters met this need with enslaved African Americans. After federal law abolished the overseas slave trade in 1808, illegal trade and interstate trade filled the gap. Many slaves came from the fading tobacco plantations of Virginia and Maryland, where planters who once grew crops now acquired their income from trading slaves.

Because cotton was so profitable, the demand for slaves soared. Slaves became more valuable to their owners. In 1802, a slave could sell for $600. By 1860, that price had tripled to $1,800. The total number of slaves increased from 1.5 million in 1820 to 4 million in 1860. Far from withering, slavery flourished and became more deeply entrenched in the southern economy.

Economic Consequences Although many plantation owners became rich, cotton production limited regional development. Most of the South became too dependent on one crop. That dependence paid off in most years, when cotton prices were high. But prices sometimes plummeted, forcing many planters into bankruptcy.

Another problem was that plantations dispersed the population. The South lost out on the urban growth needed for an industrial economy. Only one southern city, New Orleans, ranked among America's top fifteen cities in 1860. The South also lacked the commercial towns so common in the Northeast and Midwest. In 1860, a traveler in Alabama noted, "In fact the more fertile the land, the more destitute is the country of villages and towns."

The stunted commercial development in the South did not attract the immigrants who needed wage work. Consequently, the northern population grew much faster than the southern population. In 1850, the North had twice as many free people as did the South. That trend increased the political power of the North, especially in the House of Representatives. And that political trend alarmed southern whites who did not trust northerners to protect slavery.

The South also paid an economic price for keeping two fifths of its people in slavery. For lack of wages, most slaves were desperately poor and consumed very little. The South's limited consumer demand discouraged southern entrepreneurs from building factories. It was more profitable to buy a plantation.

Cultural Consequences A dispersed population and the burden of slavery affected the culture of the South. Planters opposed education for slaves and cared little about providing it to poor whites. The rate of southern white illiteracy was 15 percent—three times higher than what it was in the North and West.

Cotton Production and Slavery, 1800–1860

Slaves and bales of cotton (in millions)

4.0
3.5
3.0
2.5
2.0
1.5
1.0
0.5
0

1800 1820 1840 1860

— Cotton Production
— Number of Slaves

SOURCE: *Historical Statistics of the United States*

▲ With the invention of the cotton gin, a surge in cotton production brought about a corresponding growth in the use of slave labor.

Events That Changed America

THE COTTON GIN EXPANDS SLAVERY

Eli Whitney made cotton-growing big business with his invention of the cotton gin in 1793. Using a cotton gin, one person could clean about 50 times the amount of cotton in a day as someone working by hand. As a result, vast new areas in the South were planted with cotton, making the South the world's largest cotton supplier. But while the cotton gin decreased the amount of labor needed to remove seeds, the overall need for labor increased as cotton production went up.

◀ This ad for cotton thread illustrates the effects cotton production had on slavery and plantations in the South, as well as manufacturing towns in the North.

The cotton gin had spiked-teeth mounted on an enclosed revolving cylinder. Raw cotton was fed into the machine, and as the cylinder was turned, the seeds that were embedded in the plant were separated from the cotton fibers. Before the cotton gin, enslaved people performed this tedious task by hand. ▶

Why It Matters

Enslaved people provided cheap labor, which led to a revitalization of slavery at a time when it was on the decline. Over time, this expansion of slavery increased tensions between the North and the South, eventually resulting in the Civil War.

Thinking Critically

1. **Identify Central Issues** Why did the invention of the cotton gin eventually cause further tensions between the North and the South?
2. **Predict Consequences** What might have happened to cotton as a commodity if the cotton gin had never been invented?

Although slavery was central to life in the South, slaveholders were a minority. No more than one fourth of white men had slaves in 1860. Three fourths of these held fewer than 10 slaves, and only about 3,000 white men owned 100 or more slaves. The typical slaveholder lived in a farmhouse and owned only four or five slaves.

Why, then, did southern whites so vigorously defend the slave system? Part of the answer lies in the aspirations of common farmers. They hoped some day to acquire their own slaves and plantations. Common whites also dreaded freeing the slaves for fear they would seek bloody revenge.

All classes of whites also believed that they shared a racial bond. Even the poorest whites felt a sense of racial superiority. They also reasoned that southern whites enjoyed an equality of rights impossible in the North, where poor men depended on wage labor from rich mill owners. Southern farmers took pride in their independence. They credited that independence to a social structure that kept slaves at the bottom.

By the 1850s, proslavery forces rejected the criticism of slavery once expressed by Jefferson, Madison, and Washington. They no longer defended slavery as a necessary evil but touted the institution as a positive good. They also insisted that slavery was kinder to African Americans than industrial life was to white workers:

Primary Source "The negro slaves of the South are the happiest, and, in some sense, the freest people in the world. . . . The free laborer must work or starve. He is more of a slave than the negro, because he works longer and harder for less allowance than the slave."

—George Fitzhugh, *Cannibals All! or, Slaves Without Masters,* 1857

Despite these claims, no northern workers fled to the South to become slaves, while hundreds of slaves ran away to seek wage work in the North.

✓ **Checkpoint** **Why did slavery spread in the South, rather than fade away?**

SECTION 2 Assessment

Progress Monitoring *Online*
For: Self-test with vocabulary practice
www.pearsonschool.com/ushist

Comprehension

1. **Terms and People** What is the relationship between each of the following terms and the impact of industrialization in the northeastern United States?
   - Tariff of 1816
   - capital
   - labor union
2. **NoteTaking Reading Skill: Compare and Contrast** Use your completed Venn diagram to answer the Section Focus Question: How did the North and South differ during the first half of the 1800s?

Writing About History

3. **Quick Write: Gather Details** When writing a research report, you should include facts, examples, descriptions, and other information to help explain your findings. Make a list of details about the sectional differences between the North and the South that you read about in this section.

Critical Thinking

4. **Recognize Cause and Effect** How did the physical geography of the Northeast help influence the spread of industry there?
5. **Draw Conclusions** What can you conclude about factory workers based on the fact that there was little public support for labor unions or the policies of the Workingmen's Party in the early 1800s?
6. **Express Problems Clearly** What was the relationship between the cotton gin and the growth of slavery in the South?

American Issues Connector

Sectionalism and National Politics

TRACK THE ISSUE

How do regional differences affect national politics?

Throughout U.S. history, people in different parts of the country have had different views on important national issues. These differences have sometimes divided American politics along regional lines. Use the timeline below to explore this enduring issue.

1787 Three-fifths Compromise
North and South disagree over how to count enslaved people for congressional representation.

1812 War of 1812
Western and southern farmers favor war.

1816–1832 Tariffs
North wants protective tariffs.

1861 Civil War
Disagreements between the North and the South lead to the Civil War.

1948 Dixiecrats
Southern Democrats split from their party over civil rights.

2004 Presidential Election
Election confirms division between Democratic and Republican states.

Henry Clay, a senator from the western state of Kentucky, supported the War of 1812.

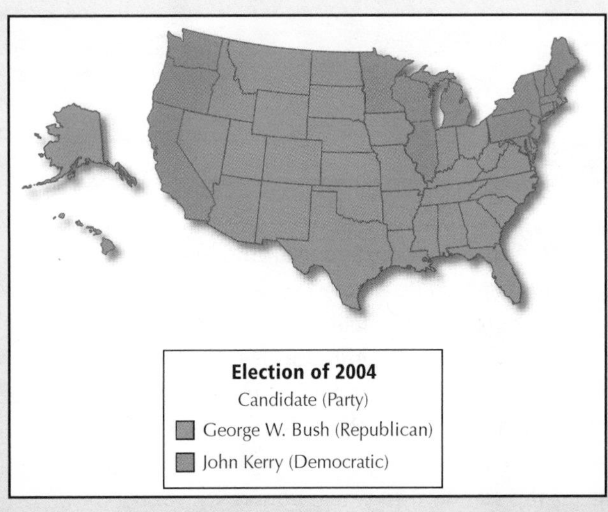

The presidential election of 2004

DEBATE THE ISSUE

Red and Blue States Recent presidential elections have revealed an alleged political divide between the states. "Red" states in the South, West, and Midwest have generally voted Republican. "Blue" states in the Northeast and Pacific West have generally voted Democratic. Are regional or sectional differences affecting voting patterns?

"Democrats and Republicans once came from the same kinds of communities. Now they don't. . . . The nation has gone through a big . . . sifting of people and politics into what is becoming two Americas. One is urban and Democratic, the other Republican, suburban and rural."

—Bill Bishop, *Austin American-Statesman*

"Very little in politics, very little in life is black and white, or in this case, red and blue. There's an awful lot of gray. . . . Truth be told, if we ask about core American values and core beliefs, about opportunity, equity and how we should go about living our lives, we see very little [if] any difference."

—Samuel Abrams, Harvard University researcher

TRANSFER Activities

1. **Compare** In what way does Bishop believe the United States is split? How does Abrams see the red-blue divide?
2. **Analyze** How do you think each of the writers quoted above would respond to the regional differences of opinion regarding the War of 1812?
3. **Transfer** Use the following Web site to see a video, try a WebQuest, and write in your journal. www.pearsonschool.com/ushist

American Experience **History Interactive**

EXPERIENCE PLANTATION LIFE

During the decades before the Civil War, and after the invention of the cotton gin, large plantations sprang up across the South as far west as Texas and Arkansas. Contrary to popular belief, very few white southerners led lives of genteel ease on plantations. Three fourths of southern whites owned no slaves at all, and of those who did, most owned fewer than 10 slaves and lived on small farms rather than plantations. Despite being few in number, white plantation owners dominated the South's economic and political life and set the standard to which poorer whites aspired.

Of the 2.5 million enslaved Africans in the United States, 1.8 million of them lived and worked on cotton plantations. Treatment of slaves was often extremely harsh and included beatings, confinement, whippings, and humiliation. The use and threat of punishment was a constant part of life as a slave. Even in cases where an owner was less harsh, slaves did not have control of their lives—they could be sold at any time and taken away from their families.

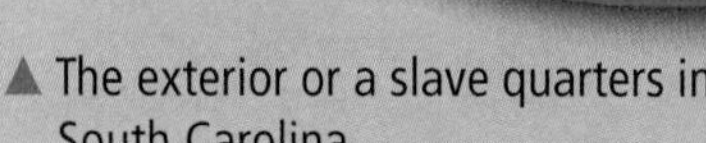

▲ The exterior or a slave quarters in South Carolina.

▼ There were many other jobs for slaves on a plantation. Some worked in the main house cooking and cleaning, and others worked as carpenters, coopers (those who make barrels), or meat curers. The vast majority of slaves, however, worked in the fields for 16 or more hours a day—planting, hoeing, weeding, and harvesting crops under backbreaking conditions. An overseer, who worked for the plantation owner, supervised them and was often demanding and brutal. Although at great human cost, plantation labor produced enormous staple crops such as cotton, sugar, and rice, which provided the backbone for the southern economy.

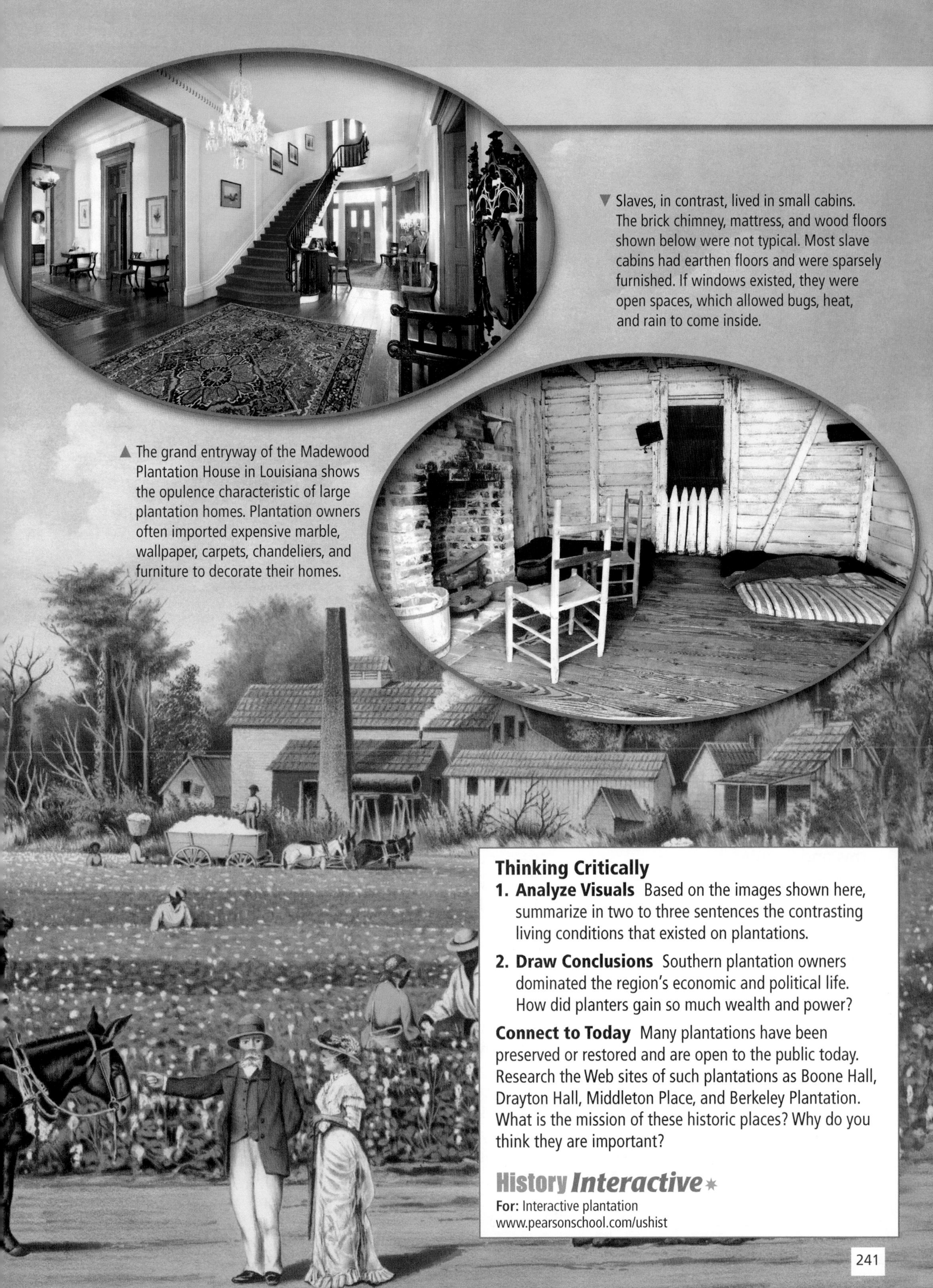

▼ Slaves, in contrast, lived in small cabins. The brick chimney, mattress, and wood floors shown below were not typical. Most slave cabins had earthen floors and were sparsely furnished. If windows existed, they were open spaces, which allowed bugs, heat, and rain to come inside.

▲ The grand entryway of the Madewood Plantation House in Louisiana shows the opulence characteristic of large plantation homes. Plantation owners often imported expensive marble, wallpaper, carpets, chandeliers, and furniture to decorate their homes.

Thinking Critically

1. **Analyze Visuals** Based on the images shown here, summarize in two to three sentences the contrasting living conditions that existed on plantations.
2. **Draw Conclusions** Southern plantation owners dominated the region's economic and political life. How did planters gain so much wealth and power?

Connect to Today Many plantations have been preserved or restored and are open to the public today. Research the Web sites of such plantations as Boone Hall, Drayton Hall, Middleton Place, and Berkeley Plantation. What is the mission of these historic places? Why do you think they are important?

History *Interactive*

For: Interactive plantation
www.pearsonschool.com/ushist

SECTION 3

◀ Henry Clay

WITNESS HISTORY

In the Spirit of Nationalism

Nationalistic feelings ran high following the War of 1812. Many Americans sought to strengthen their nation. Among them was Henry Clay, Speaker of the House, who proposed a national economic plan called the American System. He sought to protect American farmers and manufacturers from foreign competition:

> "This transformation of the condition of the country from gloom and distress to brightness and prosperity, has been mainly the work of American legislation, fostering American industry, instead of allowing it to be controlled by foreign legislation, cherishing foreign industry."
>
> —Henry Clay, "The American System," speech in the Senate, 1832

▲ Old Glory flag, 1820s

An Era of Nationalism

Objectives

- Analyze the causes and effects of nationalism on domestic policy during the years following the War of 1812.
- Describe the impact of nationalism on the nation's foreign policy.
- Summarize the struggle over the issue of slavery as the nation grew.

Terms and People

nationalism
Henry Clay
American System
John Quincy Adams
Adams-Onís Treaty
Monroe Doctrine
Missouri Compromise

NoteTaking

Reading Skill: Understand Effects Fill in a concept web to identify the effects of nationalism on the nation's domestic and foreign policies.

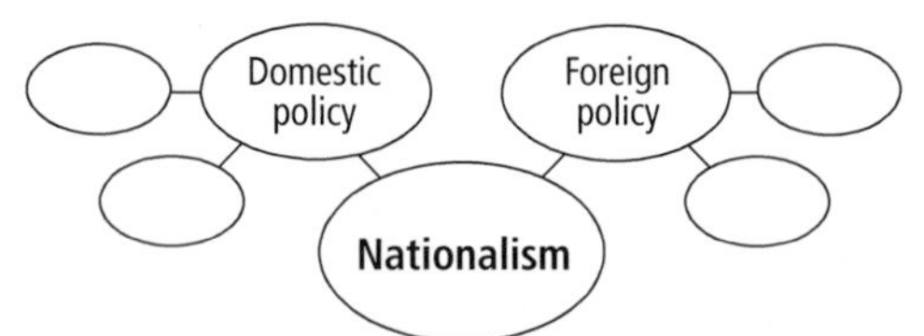

Why It Matters Nationalism was a dominant political force in the years following the War of 1812. It affected economic and foreign policy and was supported by Supreme Court rulings. The building of the nation's pride and identity was an important development that helped the country grow. **Section Focus Question: How did domestic and foreign policies reflect the nationalism of the times?**

Nationalism Shapes Domestic Policies

In 1817, a newspaper in Boston described politics as entering an "era of good feelings." The Democratic Republican Party operated almost without opposition. In the election of 1820, James Monroe won reelection as President by receiving almost all of the electoral votes cast. (John Quincy Adams received one electoral vote.) A spirit of **nationalism**—a glorification of the nation—swept the country.

Nationalist Economic Policies In the last section, you read about some of the economic policies that promoted the growth of industry. A leading example was the Tariff of 1816. By embracing a protective tariff, many Democratic Republicans betrayed their former principles. Once they had opposed federal power, supported agriculture, and favored trade unburdened by tariffs. Now they used federal power to help industrialists and their workers.

Henry Clay was one of the leading advocates of this new economic nationalism. He regarded the protective tariff as part of a larger, ambitious federal program he called the **American System.** Clay and his supporters wanted the federal government to build new roads and canals to link the Atlantic states with the Midwest. Clay insisted that the tariff and "internal improvements" would work together to tie the different regions into a harmonious and prosperous whole.

Clay also favored reestablishment of a national bank. The charter for the first Bank of the United States, created during Washington's administration, expired in 1811. That freed private and state banks to print their own money, which caused widespread uncertainty about the value of money. A national bank, Clay argued, would provide federal control over the nation's money supply and banking practices. In 1816, Congress established the second Bank of the United States. But most congressmen opposed using federal funds for internal improvements.

Vocabulary Builder
advocate–(AD vuh kiht) *n.* a person who supports or urges something

Marshall and the Supreme Court Boost Federal Power Under John Marshall, who served as Chief Justice from 1801 to 1835, the Supreme Court favored a strong federal government and a national economy. Marshall applied several Federalist principles to interpret the Constitution. For example, the Marshall Court claimed the power to review the acts of Congress and of the President for their constitutionality. This was established in the landmark decision *Marbury* v. *Madison* (1803). Marshall also insisted upon the "sanctity of contracts." In *Dartmouth College* v. *Woodward* (1819) and *Fletcher* v. *Peck* (1810), the Marshall Court limited a state government's power to interfere in business contracts.

Further, the Marshall Court insisted that federal law was superior to state law. This point was famously established in *McCulloch* v. *Maryland* (1819). The case involved the renewed Bank of the United States. When it was reestablished in 1816, branches were placed in states across the country. In effect, the bank competed with and threatened many state and local banks. In Maryland, state officials tried to defend their banks by levying a tax on the operations of the Bank of the United States.

The Marshall Court struck down this Maryland law. Embracing a broad interpretation of the Constitution, Marshall insisted that Congress had the power to charter a national bank. Further, no state could destroy such a bank with taxes.

Finally, Marshall broadly interpreted the Constitution to give greater power to the national government. In the 1824 case *Gibbons* v. *Ogden*, Marshall rejected a steamboat monopoly granted by the state of New York. The monopoly threatened the business of a steamboat operator who had run a service between New Jersey and New York. Marshall ruled that steamboat traffic was "commerce" and that the power to regulate commerce involving more than one state—interstate commerce—belonged to the federal government. As in *McCulloch* v. *Maryland,* the ruling extended federal power by creating a broad definition of commerce and by asserting the supremacy of federal over state law.

In general, Marshall's Court encouraged the development of large, far-flung business corporations by freeing them from meddling by the states. (Think, for example, how difficult it might have been to build a railroad company that covered several states if each state had the power to establish its own monopolies within its borders.) Corporations took the place of the older, smaller, and simpler forms of business—single proprietorships and limited partnerships whose reach was confined to a small area. Due in part to the Marshall Court, the United States increasingly became one large integrated market.

Primary Source "The question is, in truth, a question of supremacy. And if the right of the states to tax the means employed by the general government be conceded [accepted], the declaration that the Constitution, and the laws made in pursuance thereof, shall be the supreme law of the land, is empty and unmeaning. . . ."

—John Marshall, *McCulloch v. Maryland,* 1819

Economy Experiences Panics As the national market emerged and more enterprises became interconnected over greater distances, the economy became subject to periodic shocks, or panics. These panics were the result of "busts" in a "boom-and-bust" cycle that is common in capitalism. In capitalism, individuals own most productive property—factories

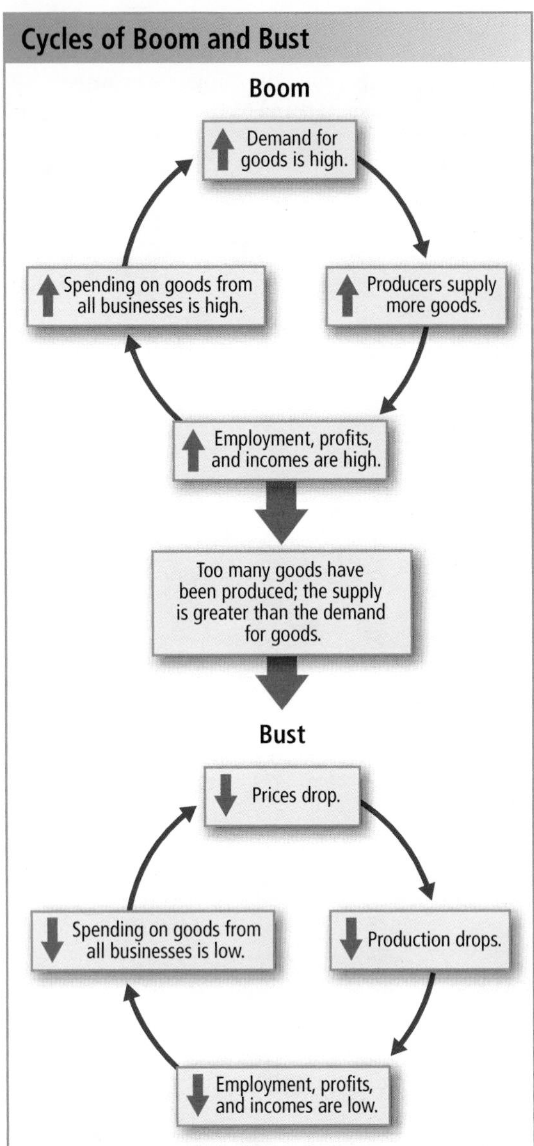

Diagram Skill Market economies experience cycles of good times, called booms, and cycles of bad times, called busts. Typically, a sharp rise or drop in an economic variable will set off a series of events that brings about the next phase of the cycle. These variables include the amount of money businesses are willing to invest, interest rates, and economic shocks, such as wars, discovery of a new oil field, or a crop failure. *What happens when producers create more goods than buyers demand?*

Vocabulary Builder
episode–(EHP uh sohd) *n.* an event or incident

and farms—and markets set prices. During the "boom" phase, high consumer demand encourages owners to expand production. But once the expanded supply of goods exceeds demand, a "bust" follows. Prices fall and producers cut back on production, closing factories and firing workers. Those jobless workers then have less to spend, hurting other businesses.

Between 1815 and 1860, there were three great panics that occurred: 1819, 1837, and 1857. Thousands of factory workers lost their jobs. The panics also hurt farmers and planters as demand declined for their grain or cotton. When farm prices fell, many farmers and planters could not pay their debts. They, therefore, lost their properties to lawsuits and foreclosures.

Panics led many workers and farmers to doubt capitalism—or at least to blame the banks, especially the Bank of the United States. The panics lifted after a year or two, however, and "boom" times returned. These economic revivals quieted the doubts.

American Art and Literature Flourish Nationalism also influenced art and literature. Artists celebrated America's beautiful landscape, while novelists expressed pride in the nation's immense potential. A period known as the American Renaissance ensued, in which literature reflected the nationalistic spirit. James Fenimore Cooper of New York became the first American to make a career as a novelist. His most celebrated novels, a series known as *The Leatherstocking Tales,* created the genre of frontier adventure tales that persists to this day. There were also several regional voices in literature. For instance, Cooper influenced William Gilmore Simms, a southern writer who gave frontier stories a more southern voice.

✓ **Checkpoint How did nationalism affect the economy starting in 1816?**

Nationalism Influences Foreign Affairs

Nationalism also influenced the nation's foreign policy. A key figure in this development was **John Quincy Adams,** James Monroe's Secretary of State and the son of former President John Adams. Monroe and Adams hoped to reduce the nation's great regional tensions by promoting national expansion.

Expanding the United States In 1819, American pressure and Adams's diplomacy persuaded Spain to sell Florida to the United States. Spain had felt pressured to give up their claims by the First Seminole War that occurred in 1818. The Seminoles were an American Indian group from southern Georgia and northern Florida, an area that was then part of Spain. Seminoles clashed often with white settlers, who were upset with the Seminoles for providing safe havens for runaway slaves. American General Andrew Jackson led a force into Florida to fight the Seminoles and seized Spanish forts. Though Jackson had not been told to act against the Spanish, the episode made it clear that Spanish control of Florida was very weak. Ratified in 1821, the **Adams-Onís Treaty** also ended Spanish claims to the vast Pacific Coast territory of Oregon. The British also claimed Oregon, but in 1818, the United States and Great Britain agreed to share the contested territory. Following the Adams-Onís Treaty, Americans began to settle in Florida and pursue the fur trade in Oregon.

The Hudson River School

American art also reflected the spirit of nationalism. The majestic scenery of the landscape inspired a group of landscape painters known as the Hudson River School. These painters used realistic detail to reflect an enormous reverence toward nature. Their dramatic depictions of towering mountains, rushing waterfalls, and plummeting gorges presented a world in which tiny, humbled humans existed in harmony with nature.

▲ **Asher B. Durand,** *Kindred Spirits* (1849)
Natural Beauty This tribute to Thomas Cole, one of the leaders of the Hudson River School, shows Cole sharing an awe-inspiring view with his friend, poet William Cullen Bryant.

◄ **Martin Johnson Heade,** *Haystacks on the Newburyport Marshes* (1862)
Light and Dark Later members of the Hudson River School were known as Luminists because of their fascination with the effects of light. Here, Martin Johnson Heade captures the glow of a late afternoon sky as the sun sets.

▲ **Jasper Cropsey,** *Autumn—on the Hudson River* (1859)
New Colors The invention of chemical pigments gave artists an exciting new palette of intense, pure colors, which were used to maximum effect by Jasper Cropsey, who became known as "the painter of autumn." His brilliant foliage created a sensation.

Thinking Critically

1. **Analyze Art** Cole and Durand often included a broken stump in their paintings. What do you think it symbolizes?
2. **Make Inferences** How might Hudson River School paintings have helped lead to the creation of national and city parks?

The Monroe Doctrine Adams also formulated the famous foreign policy doctrine named for President Monroe—the **Monroe Doctrine.** This policy responded to threats by European powers, including France, to help Spain recover Latin American colonies that had declared their independence. Monroe and Adams were eager to protect those new republics. The British shared that goal and proposed uniting with the United States to warn the other European powers to stay out of Latin America. Adams and Monroe, however, preferred to act without a British partner. In 1823, Monroe issued a written doctrine declaring that European monarchies had no business meddling with American republics. In return, the United States promised to stay out of European affairs.

Primary Source "... [T]he occasion has been judged proper for asserting, as a principle in which the rights and interests of the United States are involved, that the American continents, by the free and independent condition which they have assumed and maintain, are henceforth not to be considered as subjects for future colonization by any European powers. ..."

—James Monroe, address to Congress, December 2, 1823

The Monroe Doctrine meant little in 1823 when the Americans lacked the army and navy to enforce it. The Latin American republics kept their independence with British, rather than American, help. The doctrine did, however, reflect the nation's growing desire for power. The doctrine became much more significant in the 1890s and in the twentieth century, when the United States increasingly sent armed forces into Latin American countries.

✓ **Checkpoint What foreign policy actions did John Quincy Adams take that reflected nationalism?**

The Nation Compromises Over Slavery

The spirit of nationalism failed to suppress regional differences in the United States. Such differences made the nation more difficult to govern. In 1819, this difficulty became evident in a crisis over Missouri's admission to the Union as a new state. At that point, the Union had an equal number of slave and free states—which meant equal regional power in the United States Senate. If Missouri entered the Union as a slave state, it would tip the balance in favor of the South. This prospect alarmed northern congressmen. A New York congressman proposed banning slavery in Missouri as a price for joining the Union. The proposed ban outraged southern leaders, who claimed a right to expand slavery westward.

In 1820, after a long and bitter debate, Henry Clay crafted the **Missouri Compromise.** The northern district of Massachusetts would enter the Union as the free state of Maine to balance admission of Missouri as a slave state. To discourage future disputes over state admissions, the compromise also drew a line across the continent from the southwestern corner of Missouri to the nation's western boundary. Territories south of that line would enter as slave states. Those north of the line would become free states.

The compromise solved the short-term crisis. But that crisis had exposed the growing division between the North and the South over the expansion of slavery. Jefferson worried, "This momentous question, like a fire-bell in the night, awakened and filled me with terror. I considered it at once the [death] knell of the Union."

Southern whites felt insulted by the northern attacks on their region's reliance on slavery. They also felt threatened. In 1822, they blamed the Missouri

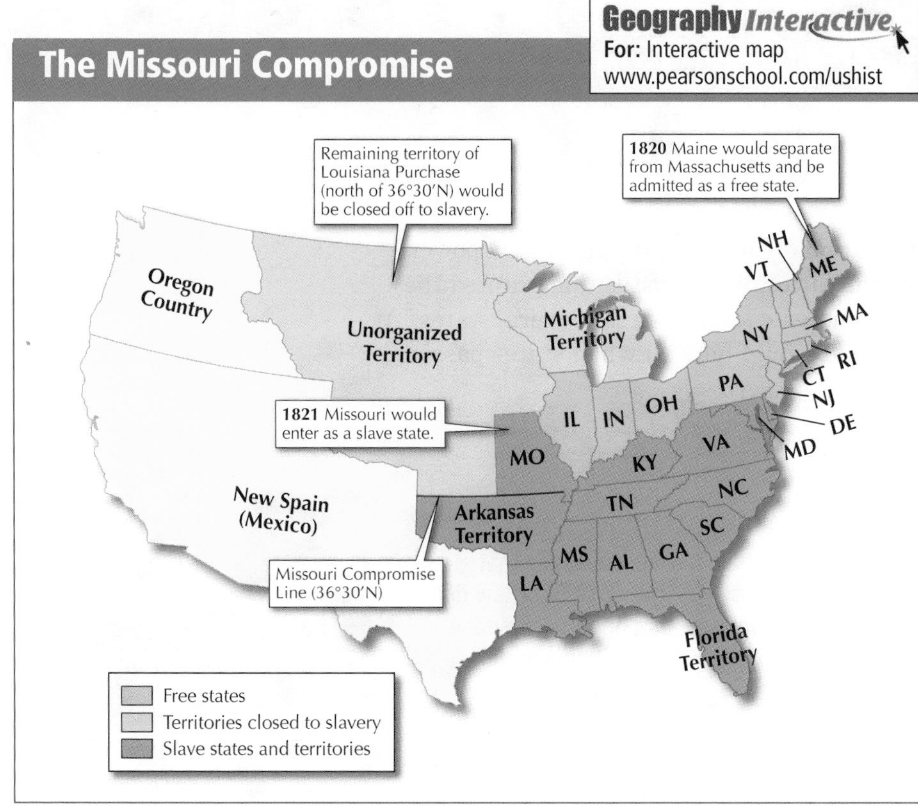

Map Skills The Missouri Compromise admitted Maine as a free state, Missouri as a slave state, and prohibited slavery north of 36°30′N latitude.

1. **Region** Which would cover more land under the compromise—new free states or new slave states?
2. **Draw Conclusions** What did the compromise reveal about the state of the Union?

debates for inspiring Denmark Vesey to plan a slave revolt. Vesey, a black freedman, prepared slaves to seize control of Charleston, South Carolina. The revolt, however, never took place because Charleston officials learned of the plot. These officials arrested, tried, convicted, and hanged Vesey and 34 others. Anxious over their close call, southern politicians insisted that their safety required northern silence on slavery.

✓ **Checkpoint How did sectionalism threaten the expansion of the Union?**

SECTION 3 Assessment

Progress Monitoring *Online*
For: Self-test with vocabulary practice
www.pearsonschool.com/ushist

Comprehension

1. **Terms and People** How does each term below demonstrate the increasing nationalism in the years following the War of 1812? Answer the question in a paragraph that uses each term.
   - American System
   - Adams-Onís Treaty
   - Monroe Doctrine
2. **NoteTaking Reading Skill: Understand Effects** Use your completed concept web to answer the Section Focus Question: How did domestic and foreign policies reflect the nationalism of the times?

Writing About History

3. **Quick Write: Write a Thesis** As in other types of essays and reports, the backbone for a research report is the thesis, or main idea. Reread the text in this section on Henry Clay's American System. Then, write a thesis statement for a research report on this topic.

Critical Thinking

4. **Recognize Sufficient Evidence** How did the fact that James Monroe won reelection in 1820 nearly unanimously reflect the nationalism of the era?
5. **Draw Conclusions** How did the spirit of nationalism contribute to the Monroe Doctrine?
6. **Analyze Information** What did the Missouri Compromise suggest about the limits of nationalism in the United States in the 1820s?

Who Has Power Over Interstate Commerce?

Under the Articles of Confederation, the national government had limited power. States controlled business within their boundaries. The Constitution granted the national Congress the power to "regulate commerce . . . among the several states." But what exactly did that power mean? What would happen when states passed laws that affected business between states?

Gibbons v. *Ogden* (1824)

The Facts	The Issue	The Decision
• Aaron Ogden had a license from the state of New York to run steamboats between New York and New Jersey. • Thomas Gibbons had a license from the federal government to run steamboats in the same area. • A New York court ruled that Gibbons had to stop running his boats but Ogden could continue to operate his. • Gibbons appealed to the Supreme Court.	Gibbons argued that the commerce clause of the Constitution gave Congress the exclusive right to regulate business between states.	• The Court said that New York State law did not apply because the Constitution was the supreme law of the land. • The Court also ruled that interstate commerce includes any business that crosses state boundaries.

New-York and Brooklyn Ferry.

SUCH persons as are inclined to compound, agreeable to law, in the Steam Ferry-Boat, Barges, or common Horse Boats, will be pleased to apply to the subscribers, who are authorized to settle the same.

GEORGE HICKS, Brooklyn,
JOHN PINTARD, 52 Wall-st.

Commutation for a single person not transferable, for 12 months, $10 00
Do. do. 8 months, 6 67

May 3, 1814 6m.

▲ Brooklyn steam ferry ad, 1814

Why It Matters

Gibbons v. *Ogden* clearly set forth the power of the national government to control commerce between states. It also did something much more far-reaching. Ogden had argued that Congress's power did not apply to the facts in this case because navigating boats on a river was not commerce. Only the buying and selling of goods, he said, should be affected by this power of Congress. John Marshall, writing the Court's decision, rejected that idea. Commerce, he said, was any kind of business interaction. It included the movement of people or goods by boat.

This decision opened broad areas of activity for the federal government. Congress has used this power to pass laws such as granting workers the right to form unions, setting limits on child labor, requiring companies to pay a minimum wage, and banning racial discrimination. Congress has also passed laws regulating radio and television, requiring that food and medicines are safe, and many others.

Connect to Your World

In recent years, the Court has moved to limit the power of Congress to use the commerce clause to pass certain laws. Research to find a case from the last 10 years involving the commerce clause. Read about the law under question and the Court's decision. Explain in one or two paragraphs whether you agree or disagree with the way the Court viewed the commerce clause.

For: Supreme Court cases
www.pearsonschool.com/ushist

◀ Today, the FCC (Federal Communications Commission) has regulations on cellphone usage.

SECTION 4

▲ A crowd gathers for Jackson's inauguration

Plate celebrating President Jackson ▶

WITNESS HISTORY

The "People's President"

After a disappointing loss in the election of 1824, Andrew Jackson rode a wave of popular support to the presidency in 1828. At his inauguration, many of those same voters caused a wild scene at the White House when they arrived in large numbers to celebrate the historic event.

> "Ladies fainted, men were seen with bloody noses and such a scene of confusion took place as is impossible to describe. . . . But it was the People's day, and the People's President, and the People would rule."
>
> —Margaret Bayard Smith in a letter to Mrs. Kirkpatrick, March 11, 1829

Democracy and the Age of Jackson

Objectives

- Analyze the movement toward greater democracy and its impact.
- Describe the personal and political qualities of Andrew Jackson.
- Summarize the causes and effects of the removal of Native Americans in the early 1800s.

Terms and People

caucus	spoils system
Andrew Jackson	Indian Removal Act
Martin Van Buren	Trail of Tears
Jacksonian Democracy	

NoteTaking

Reading Skill: Understand Effects Use a flowchart like the one below to record the effects of Jackson's presidency.

Andrew Jackson's Presidency

Why It Matters The election of 1824 signaled a shift in American political and social life. As a new political party emerged, the nation expanded its concept of democracy in some ways and narrowed it in others. The era became known for one of American history's towering and controversial figures—Andrew Jackson. **Section Focus Question: What changes did Andrew Jackson represent in American political life?**

The Election of 1824

As the presidential election of 1824 approached, two-term President James Monroe announced that he would not seek a third term. As you have read, his presidency was marked by what appeared to be general political harmony. There was only one major political party, and the nation seemed to be united in its purpose and direction. Beneath this surface, however, there were differences. These would become obvious in the election of 1824.

A Four-Way Race Four leading Democratic Republicans hoped to replace Monroe in the White House. John Quincy Adams, Monroe's Secretary of State, offered great skill and experience. A caucus of Democratic Republicans in Congress preferred William Crawford of Georgia. A **caucus** is a closed meeting of party members for the purpose of choosing a candidate. War hero **Andrew Jackson** of Tennessee and Henry Clay of Kentucky provided greater competition for Adams.

A Troubled Outcome The crowded race produced no clear winner. Jackson won more popular votes than did Adams, his next nearest competitor. Jackson did well in many southern states and in the western part of the country. Adams ran strongest in the Northeast. But neither won a majority of the electoral votes needed for election. As a result, for the second time in the nation's history (the first was in 1800), the House of Representatives had to determine the outcome of a presidential election. There, Clay threw his support to Adams, who became President. When Adams appointed Clay as Secretary of State, Jackson accused them of a "corrupt bargain," in which he thought Clay supported Adams in exchange for an appointment as Secretary of State.

Jackson's opposition weakened Adams's presidency. Taking a broad, nationalist view of the Constitution, Adams pushed for an aggressive program of federal spending for internal improvements and scientific exploration. Jackson and other critics denounced this program as "aristocratic" for allegedly favoring the wealthy over the common people. This would become a growing theme in national politics.

Jackson Begins His Next Campaign Much of the criticism of Adams's presidency came from Andrew Jackson. Indeed, Jackson and his supporters spent much of Adams's term preparing for the next election. Jackson especially relied upon New York's **Martin Van Buren,** who worked behind the scenes to build support for Jackson. Meanwhile, Jackson traveled the country drumming up support among the voters—a new practice.

Vocabulary Builder
exploit–(ehk SPLOYT) *v.* to take advantage of; utilize

Jackson hoped to exploit the increasingly democratic character of national politics. In the 1824 presidential election, a growing number of states had chosen their presidential electors based on popular vote. This was a shift from the method used in the first presidential elections, in which state legislatures chose electors. By 1836, every state but South Carolina was choosing electors based on the popular vote. Voters also had an increased role in choosing other state and local officials across the country. For example, the use of caucuses was replaced in many cases by more public conventions in which voters had a greater say in who became a candidate for office.

During the 1810s and 1820s, many states rewrote their constitutions. Those documents had originally restricted the right to vote and hold office to men who owned property. In 1776, about three fourths of all free men could meet the property-ownership requirement because they owned a farm or a shop. But that qualified proportion slipped as more men worked for wages in the expanding industries. Without their own farm or shop, they could not vote. The economic losses caused by the Panic of 1819 had also removed many voters from the rolls.

The new state constitutions expanded the electorate by abolishing the property requirement. In most states, any white man who paid a tax could vote and hold office. These changes increased participation in elections. Male voter turnout that had been less than 30 percent in the elections of the early 1800s reached almost 80 percent in 1840.

Unfortunately, the expansion of democracy did not benefit all Americans. Most of the new constitutions also took the vote away from free blacks—even those

HISTORY MAKERS

Andrew Jackson (1767–1845)

As a major general in the War of 1812, Andrew Jackson became a national hero when he defeated the British at New Orleans. Bitter over his defeat in the presidential election of 1824, Jackson came back four years later and won decisively, despite a campaign that was rife with personal attacks on his character and that of his wife. Elected by the "common man," Jackson was the first President who was not an aristocrat from Massachusetts or Virginia, but rather from the Tennessee frontier. His presidential victory was marred, however, when his wife Rachel died before he moved to Washington to assume office. Jackson believed in a strong presidency and used his power to veto 12 congressional acts—more than all the previous six Presidents combined.

with property. Nor did the new constitutions allow women to vote. (With the exception of New Jersey, in which a loophole in the state constitution allowed property-owning women to vote until 1807, no state had ever allowed women to cast a ballot.) In addition, American Indians, who were not citizens of the United States, were denied the vote. Democracy was limited to white men.

✓ **Checkpoint How did Jackson respond to his defeat in the 1824 presidential election?**

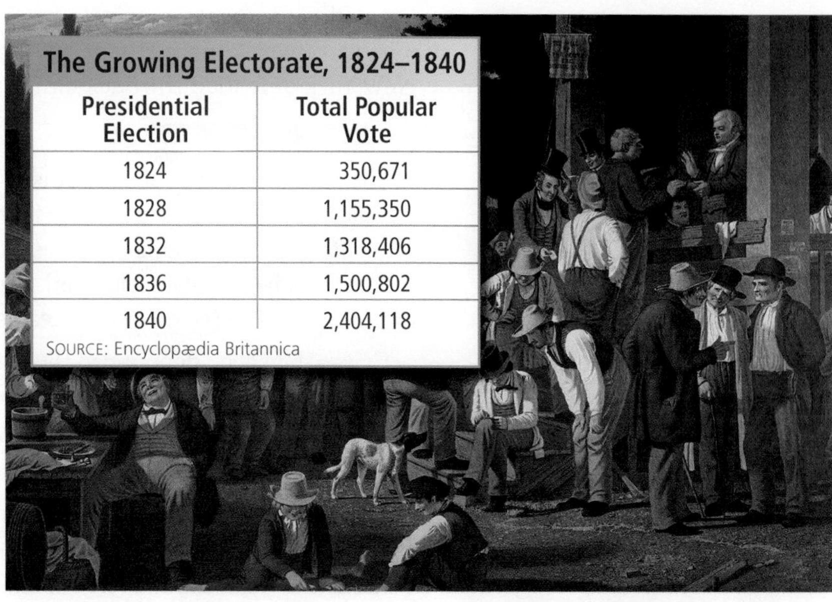

The Growing Electorate, 1824–1840

Presidential Election	Total Popular Vote
1824	350,671
1828	1,155,350
1832	1,318,406
1836	1,500,802
1840	2,404,118

SOURCE: Encyclopædia Britannica

The Growing Electorate
Before 1824, presidential election results did not include a popular vote count. By 1840, the number of voters had skyrocketed. The painting, entitled *The County Election* by George Caleb Bingham, reflects this trend. *Which Americans were not represented on the table above?*

Jackson Emerges

During the mid-1820s, Andrew Jackson became the symbol of American democracy. Historians refer to the movement as **Jacksonian Democracy.** In his speeches and writings, Jackson celebrated majority rule and the dignity of the common people. He projected himself as a down-to-earth common man with humble roots, which contrasted with the image of the aristocratic leaders of the past.

Jackson's life reflected the nation's own story of expanding opportunity. He was born in a log cabin, orphaned as a boy, and wounded during the American Revolution. Moving west to the then-frontier, he had become a wealthy lawyer and planter in Tennessee. (In fact, Jackson was wealthier than Adams.) Jackson won military fame in the War of 1812 and in the wars against the Creeks and Seminoles.

The Election of 1828 By the election of 1828, Jackson's supporters called themselves Democrats, not Democratic Republicans. Jacksonian Democracy triumphed in the presidential election of 1828. With 56 percent of the popular vote and two thirds of the electoral votes, Jackson defeated Adams. A rowdy crowd attended Jackson's inauguration in Washington, D.C. Their raucous conduct symbolized the triumph of the democratic style over the alleged aristocracy represented by John Quincy Adams.

Jackson owed his victory to his campaign manager Martin Van Buren, who revived the Jeffersonian partnership of southern planters and northern common people. The party promised a return to Jeffersonian principles: strong states and a weak federal government that would not interfere in slavery. Only those principles, Van Buren argued, could keep sectional tensions from destroying the Union.

A New Party Structure While returning to old principles, the Democrats innovated in party structure. They developed a disciplined system of local and state committees and conventions. The party cast out anyone who broke with party discipline. While becoming more democratic in style, with carefully planned appeals to voters and great public rallies, elections also became the business of professional politicians and managers.

The new party rewarded the faithful with government jobs. Where Adams had displaced only a dozen government officials when he became President, Jackson replaced hundreds. He used the government jobs to reward Democratic activists. Van Buren's "reward" was appointment as Secretary of State, the coveted steppingstone to the presidency. The Democrats defended the use of jobs as rewards for political loyalty. Here, Senator William Learned Marcy of New York defended the Jacksonians:

> **Primary Source** "They boldly preach what they practice. When they are contending for victory, they avow [state] the intention of enjoying the fruits of it. If they are defeated, they expect to retire from office. If they are successful, they claim, as a matter of right, the advantages of success. They see nothing wrong in the rule, that to the victor belongs the spoils [loot] of the enemy."
>
> —Senator William Learned Marcy, speech before Congress, January 1832

Critics, however, denounced the use of political jobs as a reward for party loyalty, a practice they called the **spoils system.**

✓ **Checkpoint** **How did Jackson's life mirror his political beliefs?**

Native American Removal

Jackson's political base lay in the South, where he captured 80 percent of the vote. Those voters expected Jackson to help them remove the 60,000 American Indians living in the region. These Indians belonged to five nations: the Cherokee, Chickasaw, Creek, Choctaw, and Seminole.

Southern voters had good reason to expect Jackson's help with Indian removal. Jackson's victory in the Creek War of 1814 had led to the acquisition of millions of

INFOGRAPHIC

THE TRAIL OF TEARS

"Perish or remove!"

In 1829, white settlers discovered gold on Cherokee lands in northwestern Georgia. It was only a matter of time before the government decided to relocate the Cherokees and other Native Americans living in the Southeast to other lands. In May 1838, soldiers forced more than 15,000 Cherokees into military stockades at bayonet point. Wahnenauhi, a Cherokee woman, wrote of the removal: "[P]erish or remove! It might be,—remove and perish! [A] long journey through the Wilderness,—could the little ones endure? [A]nd how about the sick? [T]he old people and infirm, could they possibl[y] endure the long tedious journey; Should they leave?"

But the Cherokees were not given a choice. The first leg of their journey began in October 1838. Their final destination lay 1,000 miles west in Indian Territory. The name of the route they followed is known as the "Trail of Tears," which comes from the Cherokee nunna-da-ul-tsun-yi, for the "trail where they cried."

◀ Cherokee bag, early nineteenth century

Creek acres in Georgia and Alabama. His war with the Seminoles in 1818 paved the way for the Adams-Onís Treaty and American control of Florida.

Still, many Native Americans had remained in the South. In many cases, they had even adopted white American culture. For example, many practiced Christianity, established schools, owned private property, and formed constitutional, republican governments. A Cherokee named Sequoyah invented a writing system for the Cherokee language so they could print their own newspaper and books. These Native Americans in the five southeastern tribes became known as the "five civilized tribes."

Many southern whites, however, denounced the Indian civilizations as a sham. Indians could never be civilized, southerners insisted. President Jackson agreed that the Indians should make way for white people. "What good man would prefer a country covered with forests and ranged by a few thousand savages to our extensive Republic?" he asked. Indeed, southern whites wanted the valuable lands held by the Indians. Between 1827 and 1830, the states of Georgia, Mississippi, and Alabama dissolved the Indian governments and seized these lands. In 1832, after the Indians appealed their case to the federal courts, John Marshall's Supreme Court tried to help the Indians. In *Worcester* v. *Georgia*, the Court ruled that Georgia's land seizure was unconstitutional. The federal government had treaty obligations to protect the Indians, the Court held, and federal law was superior to state law. President Jackson, however, ignored the Court's decision. "John Marshall has made his decision, now let him enforce it," Jackson boldly declared. Although often a nationalist, Jackson favored states' rights in this case.

▼ **Native American Removal, 1830–1840** The map below shows the relocation routes of Native Americans, including the Trail of Tears (in red).

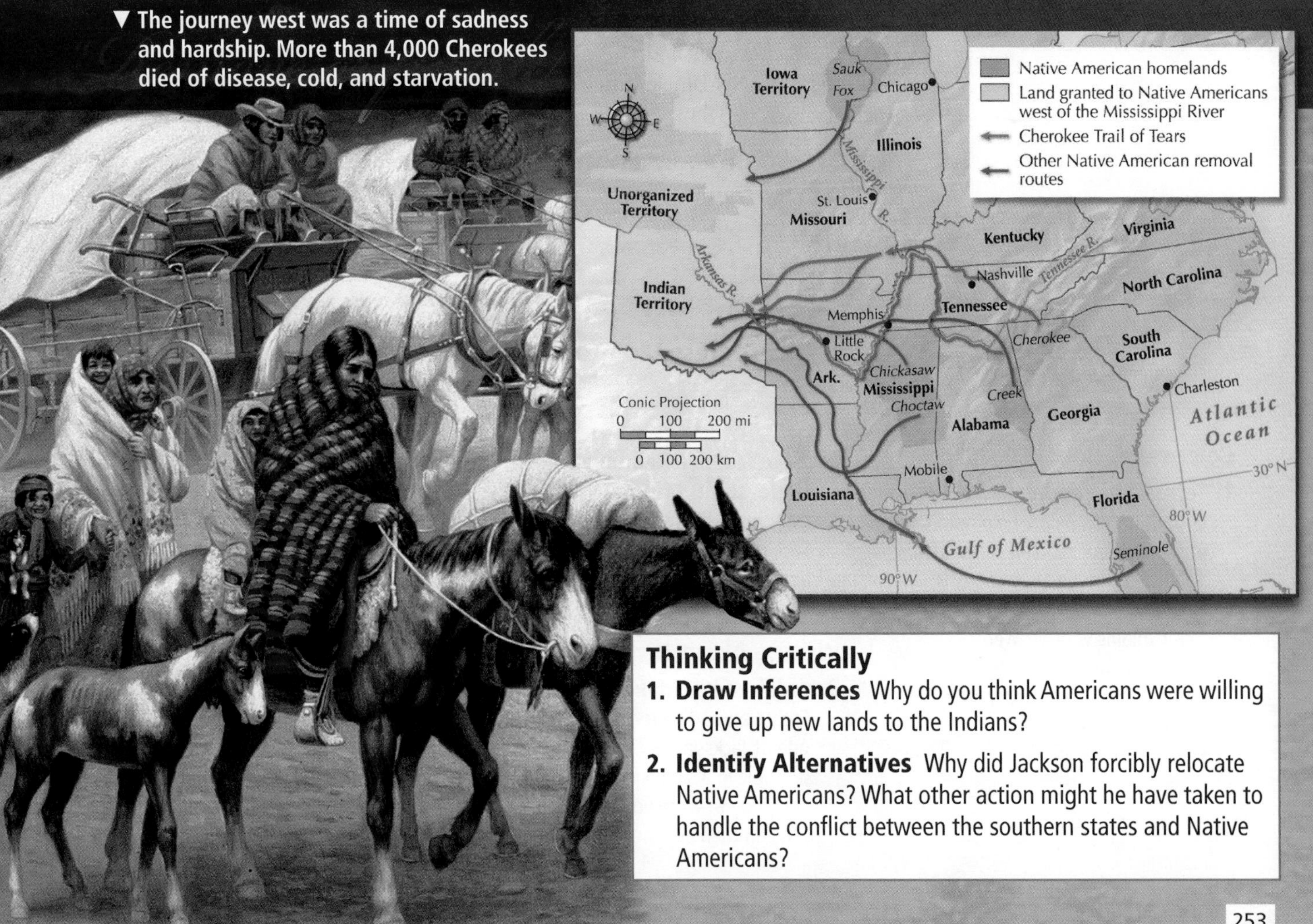

▼ **The journey west was a time of sadness and hardship. More than 4,000 Cherokees died of disease, cold, and starvation.**

Thinking Critically

1. **Draw Inferences** Why do you think Americans were willing to give up new lands to the Indians?
2. **Identify Alternatives** Why did Jackson forcibly relocate Native Americans? What other action might he have taken to handle the conflict between the southern states and Native Americans?

Even before this ruling, Jackson had urged Congress to pass the **Indian Removal Act** of 1830. This act sought to peacefully negotiate the exchange of American Indian lands in the South for new lands in the Indian Territory (modern-day Oklahoma).

Primary Source "Rightly considered, the policy of the General Government toward the red man is not only liberal, but generous. He is unwilling to submit to the laws of the States and mingle with their population. To save him from this alternative, or perhaps utter annihilation, the General Government kindly offers him a new home. . . ."

—President Andrew Jackson, message to Congress, December 8, 1830

The Choctaws and Chickasaws reluctantly agreed to leave their southeastern homelands for new lands in the West. A few stayed behind, but they suffered violent mistreatment by whites.

The Jackson administration continued pressuring remaining Indian groups to sell their lands and move west. In 1835, a small group of Cherokees who did not represent their nation made an agreement with the government under which all Cherokees would leave the South for Oklahoma. Though the rest of the Cherokees protested, the federal government sought to enforce the treaty. In 1838, U.S. soldiers forced 16,000 Cherokees to walk from their lands in the Southeast to Oklahoma along what came to be called the **Trail of Tears.** At least 4,000 Cherokees died of disease, exposure, and hunger on their long, hard journey.

Some Indians in the South resisted removal. In 1836, after a number of violent conflicts with white settlers, troops forcibly removed the Creeks from their southern lands. In Florida, the Seminoles fought the Second Seminole War between 1835 and 1842. In the end, American troops forced most Seminoles to leave Florida.

Removal also affected Native Americans in the Midwest. In Illinois, a chief named Black Hawk led the resistance by the Sauk and Fox nations. In what became known as Black Hawk's War, they fought federal troops and local militia until crushed in 1832.

Checkpoint **Why did many white people want Native Americans removed from the southeastern United States?**

SECTION 4 Assessment

Progress Monitoring *Online*
For: Self-test with vocabulary practice
www.pearsonschool.com/ushist

Comprehension

1. **Terms and People** How does each term or person below help reflect the role of Andrew Jackson in American political life in the 1820s and 1830s? For each name or term, write a sentence that explains your answer.
   - Martin Van Buren
   - Jacksonian Democracy
   - spoils system
   - Indian Removal Act
2. **NoteTaking Reading Skill: Understand Effects** Use your completed flowchart to answer the Section Focus Question: What changes did Andrew Jackson represent in American political life?

Writing About History

3. **Quick Write: Make an Outline** Create an outline for this section on the Age of Jackson. Identify each topic and subtopic in a single phrase. When you are ready to write your research report, you can then use the outline as a guide.

Critical Thinking

4. **Analyze Information** Why do you think the election of 1824 helped lead to change in national politics?
5. **Draw Conclusions** Why do you think Jackson favored and benefited from the democratic expansion that took place in the 1820s and 1830s?
6. **Summarize** What was the basic view of Jackson toward the Native Americans living in the southeastern United States in the early 1800s?

SECTION 5

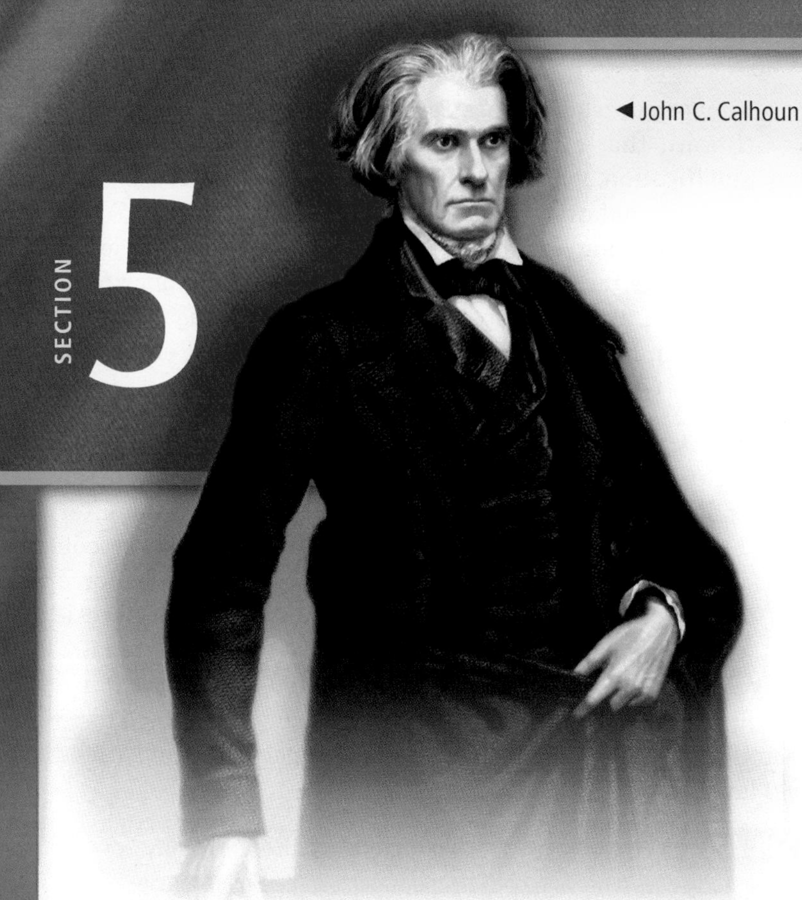

◀ John C. Calhoun

WITNESS HISTORY

Debate Over States' Rights

In 1828, John C. Calhoun wrote an anonymous document in response to the high tariff Congress adopted that year. The tariff, known as the Tariff of Abominations to people in the South who adamantly opposed it, meant high prices for goods that southern planters needed.

"So partial are the effects of the [Tariff] system that its burdens are exclusively on one side and its benefits on the other. It imposes on the agricultural interest of the South. . . . That the manufacturing States . . . bear no share of the burden of the Tariff . . ."

—John C. Calhoun, *South Carolina Exposition and Protest,* 1828

Constitutional Disputes and Crises

Objectives

- Evaluate the significance of the debate over tariffs and the idea of nullification.
- Summarize the key events of the conflict over the second Bank of the United States in the 1830s.
- Analyze the political environment in the United States after Andrew Jackson.

Terms and People

Tariff of Abominations
John C. Calhoun
nullification
Whig

NoteTaking

Reading Skill: Compare Fill in a table like the one below to compare the viewpoints of Jackson and Calhoun on the issue of nullification.

Nullification	
Andrew Jackson	John C. Calhoun
•	•
•	•
•	•

Why It Matters Jackson's presidency featured a number of conflicts and crises, and it helped bring about the formation of a rival political party. In spite of this, Jackson was able to secure the election of a handpicked successor. That administration was unable to survive its own crises and gave way to a Whig presidency. **Section Focus Question: What major political issues emerged during the 1830s?**

The Nullification Crisis

The protective tariffs had long been a topic of debate and discord in the United States. In general, the industrial North favored them, but the agricultural South disliked them.

In 1828, Congress adopted an especially high tariff. Southerners called it the **Tariff of Abominations.** This tariff had been designed by members of Congress not only to promote American industry but to embarrass President Adams and ensure a Jackson victory in that year's presidential election. In fact, Adams did sign the tariff, though reluctantly, and it did help bring about his defeat in 1828.

Calhoun Champions Nullification Jackson's Vice President, **John C. Calhoun** of South Carolina, violently opposed the tariff. During the War of 1812, he had been a strong nationalist. But his opinions changed after the the Missouri controversy of 1819 and 1820. This episode convinced him that the future of slavery, which he supported, required a stronger defense of states' rights. Toward that end, he began to champion the concept of **nullification,** which meant that states could nullify, or void, any federal law deemed unconstitutional.

Calhoun and his supporters expected Jackson to reject a protective tariff. After all, Jackson was not a supporter of the tariff, and they hoped he might take action against it on his own. He did modify the tariff rates, but not enough to satisfy Calhoun.

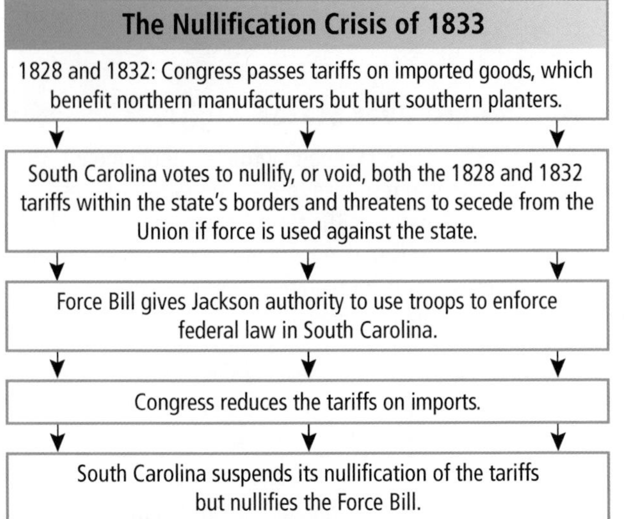

Diagram Skill The Nullification Crisis of 1833 was part of a power struggle between the states and the national government that had been present since the earliest days of the new nation. At issue was a state's power to challenge the authority of the federal government. Although the crisis was avoided, questions of nullification and secession remained. *How was the Nullification Crisis avoided?*

The Crisis Deepens In 1832, the South Carolina legislature nullified the protective tariff and prohibited the collection of federal tariff duties in South Carolina after February 1, 1833. Further, the state threatened to secede from the Union if the federal government employed force against South Carolina. Calhoun resigned the vice presidency and instead became a senator.

Jackson generally supported states' rights, and he wanted a lower tariff. He drew the line at nullification and secession, however. "Disunion by armed force is treason," Jackson thundered. He felt the Union must be perpetual and states must honor federal law.

Vocabulary Builder
perpetual–(per PECH oo ehl) *adj.* ongoing; continuous

Primary Source "I can have within the limits of South Carolina fifty thousand men, and in forty days more another fifty thousand. . . . The Union will be preserved. The safety of the republic, the supreme law, which will be promptly obeyed by me."

—President Andrew Jackson, December 9, 1832

Other state legislatures around the country supported him by passing resolutions rejecting nullification.

Webster Defends the Union In Congress, Daniel Webster of Massachusetts became the great champion of nationalism. In an 1830 debate over nullification, he had blasted the notion in a fiery speech. "Liberty *and* Union, now and forever, one and inseparable," he declared. Webster defined the Union as the creation of the American people rather than of the states. In 1833, Webster led the way in pushing for passage of a Force Bill, giving Jackson authority to use troops to enforce federal law in South Carolina.

The Crisis Avoided At the same time, with Jackson's support, Congress also reduced the tariff. This reduced South Carolina's militancy. In March, a special convention suspended that state's ordinance of nullification. Still, the convention made a political statement by nullifying the now-unnecessary Force Bill. The crisis passed. Jackson and Webster could declare victory. The difficult questions of nullification and secession, however, had been postponed rather than resolved.

 **Checkpoint How did President Jackson view nullification?**

The Bank War

Notwithstanding his fight over nullification, Jackson was a supporter of the agricultural South. Indeed, he longed to revive Jefferson's ideal of an agrarian republic, in which almost all white men owned farms and enjoyed a rough equality. But industrialization worked against that vision. Increasing numbers of Americans worked in cities for wages instead of on their own farms. In the cities, a gap widened between rich owners and poor workers. Wealth became more abstract and fluid since it was measured in bank stock versus land. The changes troubled many Americans.

Jackson Opposes the Bank Jacksonian Democrats suspected that the new economy encouraged corruption and greed. They howled when industry sought special advantages, such as protective tariffs or federal subsidies for roads and canals. Industry claimed these advantages promoted economic growth. To Jackson and his followers, they seemed mainly to enrich wealthy people at the expense of everyone else. Jacksonian Democrats promised to rescue the Republic from a new form of aristocracy they called the "Money Power."

Jacksonian Democrats especially disliked the second Bank of the United States, which had been chartered by Congress in 1816. They saw it as a dangerous, and perhaps even corrupt, special interest that favored rich investors. Many business leaders, on the other hand, valued the Bank. They believed it promoted economic growth by providing a stable currency—paper money—in which people could have confidence. They argued that a lack of confidence in the money supply could cause serious harm to the economy.

The Bank had many supporters in Congress. In 1832, they voted to renew the Bank's charter. Jackson, however, vetoed the renewal. He denounced the Bank as "unauthorized by the Constitution, subversive of the rights of the states, and dangerous to the liberties of the people." He opposed government action that led to "the advancement of the few at the expense of the many." He regretted "that the rich and powerful too often bend the acts of government to their selfish purposes." Jackson posed as the defender of "the humble members of society—the farmers, mechanics, and laborers."

Analyzing Political Cartoons

"King Andrew" Jackson exercised firm authority as President. He wielded such power that his critics sometimes referred to him as "King Andrew."

1. What details does the cartoonist use here to portray Jackson's use of power?
2. What does his trampling of the Constitution suggest?

The Whig Party Forms The Bank's supporters denounced Jackson as a power-hungry tyrant trampling on the rights of Congress. The veto shocked them because previous Presidents had so rarely used that power—only nine times in forty-two years.

Led by Henry Clay and Daniel Webster, in 1832 the Bank's friends formed a new political party known as the **Whigs.** (The name came from a British political party.) The Whigs were nationalists who wanted a strong federal government to manage the economy. Relying on a broad interpretation of the Constitution, they favored the American System of protective tariffs, internal improvements, and a national bank. Whigs also appealed to northern Protestants who wanted the government to promote moral reform.

The emergence of the Whigs renewed two-party politics in the United States. For the next twenty years, Whigs challenged Jackson's Democrats in local, state, and national elections. These close contests drew growing numbers of voters to the polls.

In the presidential election of 1832, the Whigs nominated Henry Clay. Voters, however, reelected the popular Jackson in a landslide. Longtime Jackson supporter Martin Van Buren became the new Vice President. Emboldened by the

History Makers

Henry Clay (1777–1852)
Henry Clay was born in Virginia but made his home in Kentucky—and also in the U.S. Congress. In 1811, Clay was elected to the U.S. House of Representatives and, though only 34 years old, was named Speaker of the House. Clay served most of the next 40 years in the House or the Senate. Devoted to the Union, he crafted three major compromises to settle political crises that threatened to divide the nation: the Missouri Compromise, the compromise tariff in 1833, and the Compromise of 1850. In honor of these achievements, he was called "The Great Pacificator." Clay never achieved his dearest ambition, though—he wanted to be President of the United States.

Daniel Webster (1782–1852)
Daniel Webster gained fame for his skill as an orator and lawyer when he argued and won several cases before the Supreme Court. Like Clay, Webster spent most of the four decades from 1811 to 1850 in the U.S. House and Senate representing first New Hampshire and then Massachusetts. There, he spoke forcefully in favor of preserving the Union and backed Clay's compromise to end the nullification crisis in 1833 and the Compromise of 1850. He supported the 1850 plan saying that he spoke "not as a Massachusetts man, nor as a Northern man, but as an American." Like Clay, Webster was always frustrated by his inability to win the presidency.

public support, Jackson completed his attack on the second Bank of the United States by withdrawing federal funds and placing them in state banks. Though its charter still had several years to run, Jackson's action weakened it severely. As Secretary of the Treasury, Roger B. Taney managed Jackson's plan to undermine the Bank of the United States. When John Marshall died in 1835, Jackson rewarded Taney by appointing him Chief Justice of the United States.

 **Checkpoint What did Jackson think of the second Bank of the United States?**

Politics After Jackson

Jackson reveled in his victory, but the Bank's destruction weakened the economy. Relieved from federal regulation, state banks expanded, inflating prices with a flood of paper bank notes. The face value of bank notes exploded from $10 million in 1833 to $149 million in 1837. The inflation hurt the common people that Jackson had professed to help.

Van Buren's Presidency and the Panic of 1837 Economic trouble was still in the future when Jackson retired from politics in 1836. In that year's election, voters chose Martin Van Buren, Jackson's favorite, to become President.

Soon after Van Buren took office in 1837, the economy suffered a severe panic. A key trigger was Jackson's decision, taken months earlier, to stop accepting paper money for the purchase of federal land. The effect was a sharp drop in land values and sales. As a result, hundreds of banks and businesses that had invested in land went bankrupt. Thousands of planters and farmers lost their land. One out of three urban workers lost his or her job. Those who kept their jobs saw their wages drop by 30 percent. The Panic of 1837 was the worst depression suffered by Americans to that date.

The Whigs Taste Brief Victory in the Election of 1840 The depression in 1837 revived the Whigs. In 1840, they ran William Henry Harrison for President and John Tyler for Vice President. Harrison was known as "Old Tip" for his successes at the Battle of Tippecanoe against the Indians in 1811. The Whigs ran a campaign that was light on ideas but heavy on the sort of theatrics that would become common in American politics. For example, the Whigs organized big parades and coined a catchy slogan—"Tippecanoe and Tyler too"—to garner voters' attention. With more creativity than honesty, Whig campaign managers portrayed Harrison as a simple farmer who lived in a log cabin and drank hard cider instead of the expensive champagne favored by Van Buren. Turning the political tables, the Whigs persuaded voters that Van Buren was ineffective, corrupt, and an aristocrat who threatened the Republic. This helped Harrison win the presidency, and meant that the Whigs had succeeded in capturing Congress.

The Whig victory proved brief, however. A month after assuming office, Harrison died of pneumonia. Vice President John Tyler of Virginia became the President. He surprised and horrified the Whigs by rejecting their policies. He vetoed Congress's legislation to restore the Bank of the United States and to enact Clay's American System. The Whigs would have to wait for a future election to exercise full control of the government.

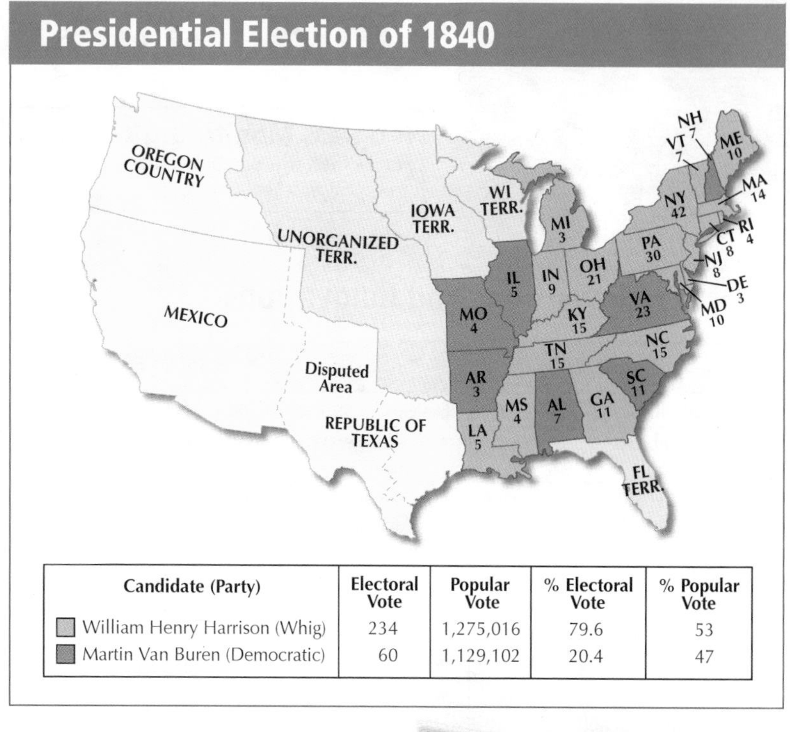

Candidate (Party)	Electoral Vote	Popular Vote	% Electoral Vote	% Popular Vote
William Henry Harrison (Whig)	234	1,275,016	79.6	53
Martin Van Buren (Democratic)	60	1,129,102	20.4	47

 **Checkpoint Who succeeded Jackson in the White House, and what happened to him?**

Presidential Election of 1840
Whig Party flag picturing William Henry Harrison's log cabin

SECTION 5 Assessment

Progress Monitoring *Online*
For: Self-test with vocabulary practice
www.pearsonschool.com/ushist

Comprehension

1. **Terms and People** For each term or person below, write a sentence explaining the significance to national politics between 1828 and 1840.
   - Tariff of Abominations
   - John C. Calhoun
   - nullification
   - Whig
2. **NoteTaking Reading Skill: Compare and Contrast** Use your completed table to answer the Section Focus Question: What major political issues emerged during the 1830s?

Writing About History

3. **Quick Write: Write an Introduction** Research more about the nullification crisis that you learned about in this section. Then, write an introductory paragraph on the topic. This paragraph should introduce the topic and map out what you will discuss within the research report.

Critical Thinking

4. **Compare Points of View** Compare the viewpoints of President Jackson and John C. Calhoun on the Tariff of Abominations.
5. **Synthesize Information** How did the attack on the second Bank of the United States lead to the formation of the Whig Party?
6. **Recognize Cause and Effect** How did Jackson's economic policies affect Van Buren?

CHAPTER 7

Quick Study Guide

Progress Monitoring *Online*
For: Self-test with vocabulary practice
www.pearsonschool.com/ushist

Key Inventions and Innovations

Invention or Innovation	Political, Economic, or Social Effect(s)
Toll roads	Expanded transportation routes
Steamboats	Allowed faster travel, shipping, and upstream movement
Canals	Expanded transportation routes; improved commerce by linking farms to cities; opened new regions to settlement
Railroads	Cost less to build than canals and could move farther and faster, and carry more weight; connected East and West
Textile mills	Provided jobs; increased the speed of producing textiles
Interchangeable parts	Made possible the efficient production of a wide range of manufactured goods

Causes and Effects of the Cotton Boom

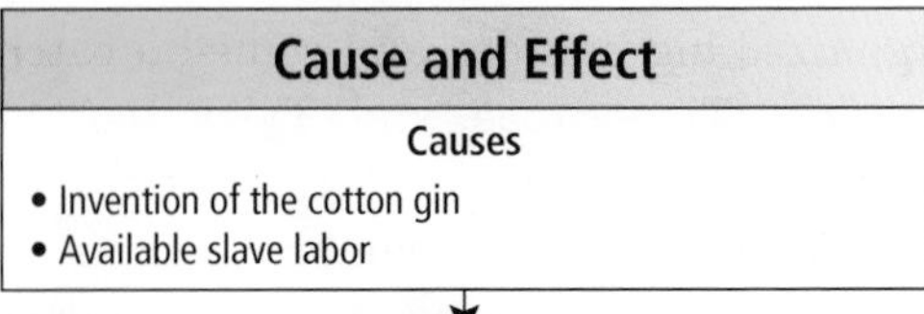

Cause and Effect

Causes
- Invention of the cotton gin
- Available slave labor

The Cotton Boom

Effects
- Creation of the Cotton Belt in the South
- Huge rise in cotton production
- Creation of state economies based on cotton production
- Westward spread of farming in the South
- Expansion of slavery system
- Slower urban growth in the South than in the North

Key Nationalist Supreme Court Cases

Case	Issues	Outcome of Decision
McCulloch v. *Maryland* (1819)	• Does the government have the power to create a national bank? • Do states have the right to tax institutions created by the federal government?	• Reinforced the principle of the power of the national government over state governments; states could not interfere with an agency of the national government and, therefore, could not tax the national bank
Gibbons v. *Ogden* (1824)	• Who has the power to regulate commerce: the states, the federal government, or both? • What if states passed laws that affected business between states?	• Established the federal government's right to regulate all aspects of interstate commerce

Quick Study Timeline

In America

1814 Francis Cabot Lowell builds first centralized textile mill

1819 Florida ceded to United States

1820 Missouri Compromise passed

1823 President Monroe issues Monroe Doctrine

New-York and Brooklyn Ferry.

SUCH persons as are inclined to compound, agreeable to law, in the Steam Ferry-Boat, Barges, or common Horse Boats, will be pleased to apply to the subscribers, who are authorized to settle the same.

GEORGE HICKS, Brooklyn,
JOHN PINTARD, 52 Wall-st.

Commutation for a single person not transferable, for 12 months, $10 00
Do. do. 6 months, 6 67
May 3, 1814 6m.

Presidential Terms James Madison 1809–1817 | James Monroe 1817–1825 | John Quincy Adams 1825–1829

1810 | 1820

Around the World

1811 Wars of independence begin in South America

1815 Napoleon defeated at Waterloo

1822 Brazil gains independence from Portugal

American Issues Connector

By connecting prior knowledge with what you have learned in this chapter, you can gradually build your understanding of enduring questions that still affect America today. Answer the questions below. Then, use your American Issues Connector study guide (or go online: www.pearsonschool.com/ushist).

Issues You Learned About

- **Sectionalism and National Politics** Because the regions of the country had different economies and cultures they developed political differences.

1. How did sectionalism affect the nation's first political parties?
2. How did the Missouri Compromise reflect the sectionalism that divided the nation in the early 1800s?
3. Why did many political leaders in the North support the so-called Tariff of Abominations while nearly all of South Carolina's leaders opposed it?

- **American Indian Policy** The U.S. government generally denied American Indians the right to hold on to their homelands.

4. How did the U.S. government acquire American Indian lands?
5. Why did many American Indians in the Southeast adopt elements of white American culture?
6. How did the Supreme Court rule in *Worcester* v. *Georgia*? What effect did this ruling have on the American Indian nations that lived in the Southeast?

- **Technology and Society** Beginning in the early 1800s, new ways of transporting and manufacturing goods transformed the United States.

7. Summarize the advances in transportation that took place in the early 1800s.
8. What invention led to the development of "King Cotton" in the South? Why?
9. How did the Industrial Revolution change the way people lived and worked in the United States?

Connect to Your World — Activity

Voting Rights: The Electoral College As you have learned, the electoral college is a group of persons chosen from each state that indirectly elect the President. Polls show that the majority of Americans today would prefer to have the President elected by a direct popular vote. They believe that this new system would allow every vote to count equally. Other Americans, however, support keeping the electoral college. Go online or to your local library to do research on the electoral college and the arguments for and against it. Use your findings to draw your own conclusion as to which method is better for electing Presidents—the electoral college or a direct popular vote. Write one or two paragraphs explaining your opinion.

1830
Indian Removal Act passed

1838
Cherokees forcibly relocated westward on the Trail of Tears

1850
U.S. slave population exceeds 3 million; cotton crop tops one billion pounds

Andrew Jackson 1829–1837 | Martin Van Buren 1837–1841 | William Henry Harrison 1841 | John Tyler 1841–1845 | James K. Polk 1845–1849

1830 — 1840 — 1850

1833
Slavery abolished in the British Empire

1839
Opium Wars between Britain and China begin

1845
Irish potato famine begins

History Interactive
For: Interactive timeline
www.pearsonschool.com/ushist

Chapter Assessment

Terms and People

1. Who was **Eli Whitney**? What were his main contributions to American society?
2. What was the **Tariff of 1816**? Why did Congress pass the tariff?
3. What was the **Monroe Doctrine**? How effective was this doctrine initially?
4. Define **caucus.** How did the use of caucuses change with the expansion of democracy?
5. Who were the **Whigs**? What policies did they support?

Focus Questions

The focus question for this chapter is **How did nationalism and sectionalism affect the United States from the early 1800s to the mid-1800s?** Build an answer to this big question by answering the focus questions for Sections 1 through 4 and the Critical Thinking questions that follow.

Section 1

6. How did transportation developments and industrialization affect the nation's economy?

Section 2

7. How did the North and South differ during the first half of the 1800s?

Section 3

8. How did domestic and foreign policies reflect the nationalism of the times?

Section 4

9. What changes did Andrew Jackson represent in American political life?

Section 5

10. What major political issues emerged during the 1830s?

Critical Thinking

11. **Explain Causes** What led to the rise of nativism in the United States in the early to mid-1800s?
12. **Categorize** Categorize and explain the factors that led to less industrial growth in the South than in the North.
13. **Make Generalizations** What domestic policies did the Marshall Court favor?
14. **Synthesize Information** How did nationalism influence domestic and foreign affairs?
15. **Draw Conclusions** Many called Andrew Jackson the "People's President." How accurate was this nickname? Explain your answer.
16. **Analyze Information** Was Jackson's refusal to uphold the Supreme Court's decision in the debate over the Cherokees a legitimate use of the system of checks and balances? Explain.
17. **Make Inferences** The Whigs supported a strong federal government to manage the economy. Could the same statement be said about the Jacksonian Democrats?

Writing About History

Writing a Research Report In this chapter, you learned about the sectionalism and nationalism that shaped the United States in the time period after the War of 1812 to the mid-1800s. Choose one of the following specific topics related to the chapter: steamboats on the Mississippi River; the Erie Canal; the Lowell mills; Irish immigration; James Fenimore Cooper; the First Seminole War; the Choctaw, Chickasaw, or Cherokee Indians. Do research at the library and online to gather additional information about the topic. Write a research report based on your findings.

Prewriting

- Review your notes and the chapter to identify links between your research topic and the contents of the chapter.
- Make a list of key ideas you want to address in your report.
- Research additional sources to gather facts. Organize your ideas and sources on note cards by topic and subtopic.

Drafting

- Write a thesis statement that reflects the main idea of your research report.
- Make an outline that breaks down the topics and subtopics.
- Write an introduction, at least three paragraphs, and a conclusion. Be sure to address all parts of your outline.

Revising

- Use the guidelines on page SH14 of the Writing Handbook to revise your report.

Document-Based Assessment

The Monroe Doctrine

The Monroe Doctrine guided American foreign policy, to greater and lesser extents, throughout the nineteenth and into the twentieth centuries. Use your knowledge of the Monroe Doctrine and Documents A, B, C, and D to answer questions 1 through 4.

Document A

In the wars of the European powers in matters relating to themselves we have never taken any part, nor does it comport with our policy so to do. . . . With the movements in this hemisphere we are of necessity more immediately connected. . . . We owe it, therefore, to candor and to the amicable relations existing between the United States and those powers to declare that we should consider any attempt on their part to extend their system to any portion of this hemisphere as dangerous to our peace and safety.

—*James Monroe, address to Congress, December 2, 1823*

Document B

The question presented by the letters you have sent me, is the most momentous which has ever been offered to my contemplation since that of Independence. . . . Our first and fundamental maxim should be, never to entangle ourselves in the broils of Europe. Our second, never to suffer Europe to intermeddle with [this side of the] Atlantic affairs. America, North and South, has a set of interests distinct from those of Europe, and peculiarly her own. She should therefore have a system of her own, separate and apart from that of Europe.

—*Thomas Jefferson, letter to James Monroe, October 24, 1823*

Document C

AND IT LOOKED EASY, TOO.

—*Political cartoon, 1850s*

Document D

Monroe essentially declared that the United States would not tolerate intervention in the Americas by European nations. Monroe also promised that the United States wouldn't interfere with already established colonies or with governments in Europe. In one sense, this declaration was an act of isolationism, with America withdrawing from the political tempests of Europe. . . . On the positive side, the Doctrine marked what might be called the last step in America's march to independence, which had begun in the Revolution and moved through post-independence foreign treaties, the Louisiana Purchase, the War of 1812, and the postwar agreements.

—*Kenneth Davis, historian*

---

1. In Document A, Monroe describes European actions in the Americas as
- **A** dangerous.
- **B** unlawful.
- **C** necessary.
- **D** amicable.

2. Which of the following statements most accurately summarizes Thomas Jefferson's ideas as expressed in Document B?
- **A** He supported the principles of the Monroe Doctrine.
- **B** He supported just one of the principles of the Monroe Doctrine.
- **C** He quietly opposed the principles of the Monroe Doctrine.
- **D** He vigorously opposed the principles of the Monroe Doctrine.

3. Which documents assert that the Monroe Doctrine had become a success?
- **A** Documents A and B
- **B** Documents B and C
- **C** Documents C and D
- **D** Documents D and A

4. **Writing Task** Did the Monroe Doctrine express a policy of isolationism? Use your knowledge of American history and specific evidence from the primary sources above to explain your answer.

CHAPTER

8 Religion and Reform 1812–1860

WITNESS HISTORY

Another Great Awakening

In the early 1800s, a wave of religious intensity once again swept the United States. Religious leaders organized meetings where people would camp out for days at a time to sing hymns and listen to ministers preaching:

> "There, on the edge of a prairie in Logan County, Kentucky, the multitudes came together and continued a number of days and nights encamped on the ground. . . . Many, very many, fell down as men slain in battle. . . . After lying there for hours, they obtained deliverance. The gloomy cloud that had covered their faces seemed gradually and visibly to disappear, and hope, in smiles, brightened into joy. They would rise, shouting deliverance . . ."
>
> —Reverend Barton W. Stone

◄ A lively camp meeting spreads the religious revival of the early 1800s

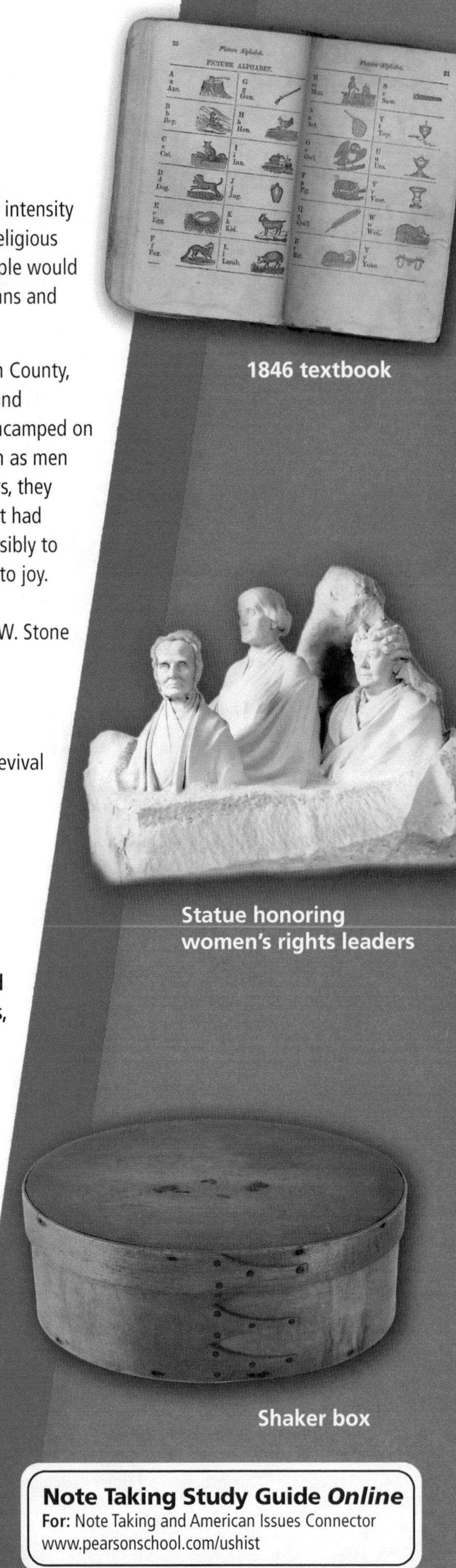

1846 textbook

Statue honoring women's rights leaders

Shaker box

Chapter Preview

Chapter Focus Question: How did the Second Great Awakening lead to several reform efforts, and what effect did those reform efforts have on American society?

Section 1
A Religious Awakening

Section 2
A Reforming Society

Section 3
The Antislavery Movement

Section 4
The Women's Movement

Use the ☑ **Quick Study Timeline** at the end of this chapter to preview chapter events.

Note Taking Study Guide *Online*
For: Note Taking and American Issues Connector
www.pearsonschool.com/ushist

SECTION 1

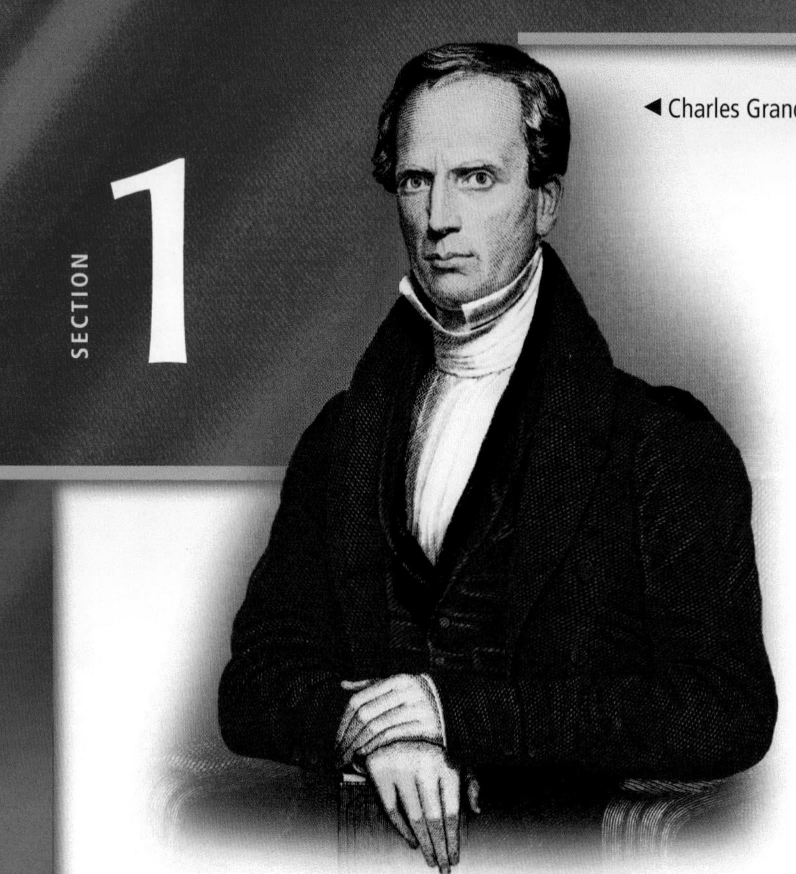

◀ Charles Grandison Finney

WITNESS HISTORY

Religious Revival

In the early 1800s, America experienced a second wave of religious enthusiasm. The famous preacher Charles Grandison Finney described the benefits of a religious revival:

"Christians will have their faith renewed. While they are in their backslidden state they are blind to the state of sinners. . . . But when they enter into a revival, . . . they see things in that strong light which will renew the love of God in their hearts. This will lead them to labor zealously to bring others to him."

—Charles Grandison Finney, *Lectures on Revivals of Religion,* 1835

A Religious Awakening

Objectives

- Describe the Second Great Awakening.
- Explain why some religious groups suffered from discrimination in the mid-1800s.
- Trace the emergence of the utopian and Transcendentalist movements.

Terms and People

Second Great Awakening
revivalist
Charles Grandison Finney
evangelical
Joseph Smith
Mormon
Unitarian
utopian community
Transcendentalist
Ralph Waldo Emerson
Henry David Thoreau

NoteTaking

Reading Skill: Identify Main Ideas Note the main ideas under each blue heading in a chart.

Religion in the Early 1800s		
Second Great Awakening	Discrimination	Other Religious Movements
• Camp meetings	•	•

Why It Matters By the early 1800s, the United States was well established as an independent, growing country. How the young country would develop was of keen interest to Americans. Many decided that the best future for the United States was one in which its citizens embraced religion. **Section Focus Question: How did the Second Great Awakening affect life in the United States?**

The Second Great Awakening Changes America

In the early 1700s, Americans had experienced a burst of religious energy known as the Great Awakening. Another revival of religious feeling called the **Second Great Awakening** swept the country beginning in the early 1800s and lasted for nearly half the century. Protestant preachers who believed that Americans had become immoral and that reviving religious participation was crucial to the country's future started and led the Second Great Awakening. These preachers were known as **revivalists,** because they wanted to revive, or reenergize, the role of religion in America.

The Second Great Awakening profoundly influenced American life. Church membership skyrocketed. Moreover, reawakened religious feeling moved Americans to work for a wide variety of social reforms.

Evangelical Revivals Fan Religious Fervor

The Second Great Awakening began on the frontier in Kentucky and then spread north and south, reaching the cities of the Northeast in the 1820s.

Its religious inspiration was spread through outdoor services known as "revivals" or "camp" meetings that lasted for as long as a week. Plentiful food and lively religious music added to the appeal of the gatherings, which were often held in isolated rural areas.

One of the most influential revivalists was former attorney **Charles Grandison Finney.** In passionate sermons, Finney dramatically proclaimed his own faith and urged his listeners to do the same. This **evangelical** style of worship, designed to elicit strong emotions and attract converts, proved highly successful: At Finney's revivals, hundreds of people at a time declared their faith.

Another leading voice was Lyman Beecher, a Yale-educated minister. Like Finney, Beecher became known for his fiery sermons. Beecher also traveled widely, urging people to read the Bible, join a church, and embrace religion. In 1832, Beecher became president of the new Lane Theological Seminary in Cincinnati, Ohio, which trained more evangelical preachers to join the revival.

Many revivalists' sermons featured the idea that the United States was leading the world into the millennium, or the thousand years of glory following the Second Coming of Jesus. Called millennialism, the belief that the millennium was at hand inspired some reformers to try to ready their society by perfecting it through reform.

Tension Between Church and State During the Second Great Awakening, some Americans wanted the government to encourage public morality by supporting religion. Others disagreed with this aim, holding that the government should protect public life from religious control. An example of the tension between the two groups is the defeat of the Sabbatarian reform movement. The Sabbatarians wanted the federal government to uphold the Christian Sabbath (a special day of each week reserved for worship) as a day of rest by not allowing any business transactions or mail delivery on that day. Congress insisted it had no authority to interfere with trade and refused to ban commerce on the Sabbath. The debate over church and state continues to this day.

African Americans Embrace the Spirit Many preachers of the Second Great Awakening welcomed African Americans at their revivals. However, some African Americans established their own, separate churches. Led by a former slave named Richard Allen, a group of Philadelphians formed their own church in 1787. African Americans in several other cities did the same. In 1816, these churches united to become the African Methodist Episcopal (AME) Church. By 1826, the AME Church had nearly 8,000 members.

For enslaved African Americans, religion had a special significance. It offered the promise of eternal freedom after a lifetime of oppression. Religious folk songs, called spirituals, gave them strength to deal with the difficulties of their lives. For some, the contradiction between religious ideals and their cruel captivity inspired them to revolt against their oppressors. Indeed, many men who led slave revolts said they were called by God to lead enslaved people out of bondage.

New Religious Groups Form Heightened religious awareness also led to the formation of two new religious groups. In New York State,

A Religious Leader

The painted serving tray below commemorates the Congregationalist minister Lemuel Haynes. In 1785, he was perhaps the first African American to be ordained by a mainstream Protestant church.

American Issues Connector

Church and State

TRACK THE ISSUE

What is the proper relationship between government and religion?

The First Amendment says that government may not establish religion or interfere with the free exercise of religion. This is often referred to as "separation of church and state." But Americans differ over how these clauses interact to prevent government from establishing religion while protecting the religious liberties of individuals. Use the timeline below to explore this enduring issue.

1791 Bill of Rights
First Amendment bars government involvement in religion.

1840s Sabbatarian Controversy
Congress debates whether to ban commerce and mail delivery on Sundays.

1947 *Everson* v. *Board of Education*
Supreme Court affirms separation of government and religion.

1984 Federal Equal Access Act
Law allows students to form religious clubs at public high schools.

2000 *Mitchell* v. *Helms*
Ruling allows private schools to receive federal funds for educational materials.

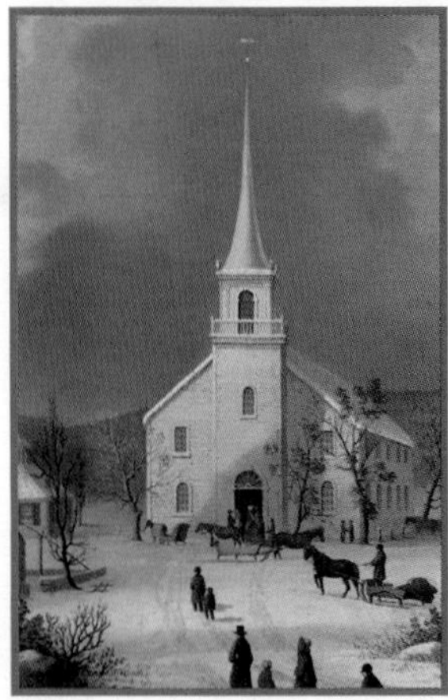

A church of the early 1800s

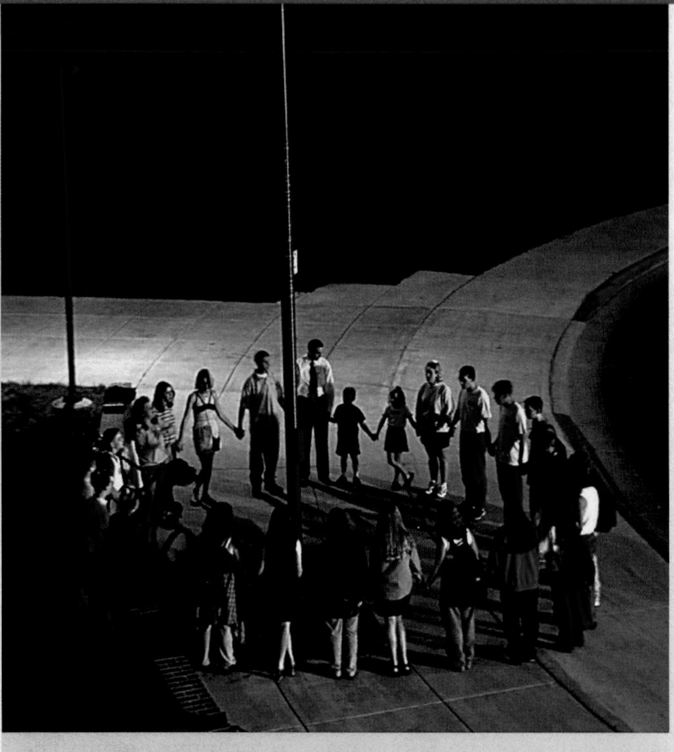

Students pray around a flagpole outside their school.

DEBATE THE ISSUE

Should prayer be allowed in public schools? One controversial topic in the church-state debate is the issue of prayer in public schools. Current law prohibits public school-sponsored prayers. Some Christians believe this ban violates their right to practice their beliefs.

"We're deeply religious. . . . And we believe that prayer in school is a necessity because, although yes, my children say blessings at home and pray at home and they learn to do that at church, most of their waking hours are spent in school. So why shouldn't they be able to pray, on the intercom, anywhere."

—Pat Mounce, high school parent, Pontotoc, Mississippi

"I'm a Catholic and I hope a devout one, but I think that the public school classroom is no place for me to try and impose my world formula for prayer on children who don't share it, and for that very reason, I don't want my children in a public school classroom to be exposed to someone else's religion or formula."

—Senator Phillip A. Hart, Michigan

TRANSFER Activities

1. **Compare** What views do Mounce and Hart share? On what point do they differ?
2. **Analyze** How do you think each of these two speakers would have reacted to the issue of outlawing commerce on Sunday?
3. **Transfer** Use the following Web site to see a video, try a WebQuest, and write in your journal. www.pearsonschool.com/ushist

Joseph Smith spoke and wrote of visions he said directed him to found a new religious group. In 1830, Smith and a few followers organized the Church of Jesus Christ of Latter-day Saints, whose members are commonly called the **Mormons.** The church grew rapidly, attracting more than 1,000 members in just a few months. It would grow to become one of the most influential religious groups in the country.

In New England, members of several Puritan or Congregational churches began to argue that, instead of seeing God as a "Trinity," people should see God as a single divine being—a unity. They organized themselves into a separate religious group called the **Unitarians,** after their belief. The Unitarians' views diverged from established religious creeds and a literal interpretation of the Bible. They reflected a growing Christian liberalism, which influenced many other religious groups in the nineteenth century.

 **Checkpoint** **What was the Second Great Awakening?**

Non-Protestants Suffer Discrimination

The preachers of the Second Great Awakening were Protestant. By the mid-1800s, well over half of all Americans were also Protestant. Non-Protestants were in the distinct minority and faced discrimination.

Mormons Are Persecuted Many Americans were wary of the new Mormon Church. Mormons isolated themselves in their own communities where they followed practices that were frowned upon by their neighbors, such as allowing men to have more than one wife. Further, the Mormons became economically powerful because they held land as a group rather than as individuals. They also voted as a group, which gave them political power.

The Mormons' power angered their neighbors. As a result, wherever they set up communities, their neighbors tried to chase them away, sometimes using violence. Mormons were chased out of Ohio, and then Missouri. They sought refuge in Illinois, founding the town of Nauvoo, which grew rapidly. In 1844, Joseph Smith declared his intention to run for President. Many non-Mormons were outraged. In the ensuing violent conflict, Smith was murdered.

The Mormons Leave Nauvoo

The Mormons were chased out of several states before finding a home in Utah. Below is a dramatic image of the Mormons being forced to leave Nauvoo, Illinois. *Looking at the map, why do you think the Mormons chose Salt Lake City as a site for resettlement?*

Mormon Migrations, 1830–1848

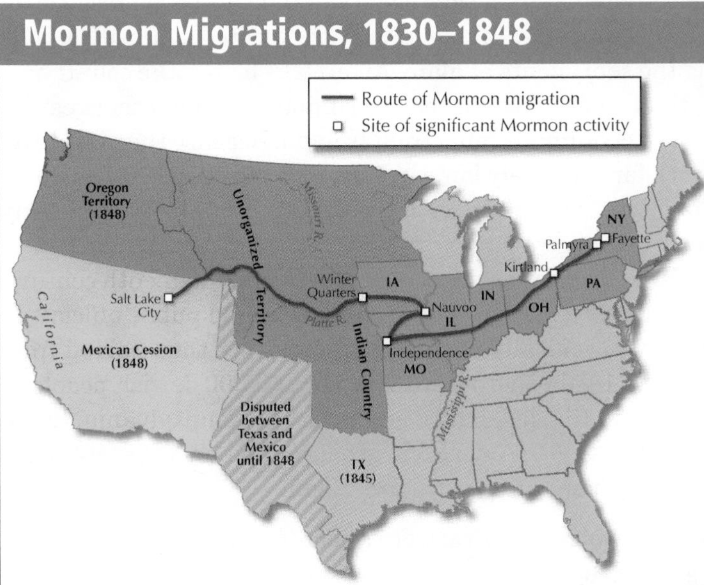

INFOGRAPHIC

Brook Farm

Living the Utopian Dream

Brook Farm was founded in 1841 by a group of Transcendentalist thinkers led by George Ripley (left). At Brook Farm, Ripley hoped to "combine the thinker and the worker, as far as possible, in the same individual." He believed that physical labor, education, and a life lived close to nature would lead to well-rounded, healthy individuals, and through them, to a more perfect society. Although considered by many to have succeeded in some of these goals, Brook Farm was troubled by financial problems from the start, causing it to fail after just six years.

George Ripley hoped that Brook Farm would "impart a greater freedom, simplicity, truthfulness, refinement and moral dignity to our mode of life."

Smith's successor, Brigham Young, led the Mormons far west, to the Great Salt Lake valley in present-day Utah, then a part of Mexico. Here, Mormon communities thrived. They recruited new members from Europe and developed irrigation systems so they could farm the dry desert land.

Vocabulary Builder
discrimination–(dih skrihm ih NAY shuhn) *n.* unfair bias in the treatment of a particular group

Catholics and Jewish People Face Discrimination Members of the Roman Catholic Church faced particularly harsh discrimination in the early 1800s. Many Protestants viewed Catholicism as incompatible with American ideals of democracy. They believed that Catholics would choose loyalty to the Pope, the leader of the Roman Catholic Church, over loyalty to the United States. "Down with Popery" yelled Protestants in Philadelphia as they rioted against Catholic worshippers, echoing the sentiments of many Americans across the country.

Moreover, most Catholics of the time faced discrimination for another reason: their poverty. Many were poor immigrants from Ireland. Because they had little money, they would work for extremely low wages, which threatened other workers. Because Irish immigrants arrived in increasingly large numbers, many feared they were growing too powerful.

Jewish people also faced discrimination. Until late in the nineteenth century, state constitutions, from New England to the South, required public officials to be Christians, sometimes specifically Protestant. Jews were then barred from holding office. In the early 1800s, there were only about 2,000 Jewish people in America, mostly clustered in Rhode Island, New York, and Pennsylvania. In the 1840s, when Jewish people came to America in greater numbers to escape political unrest in Europe, Americans often ostracized them.

✓ **Checkpoint Why did many Americans discriminate against Mormons, Catholics, and Jewish people?**

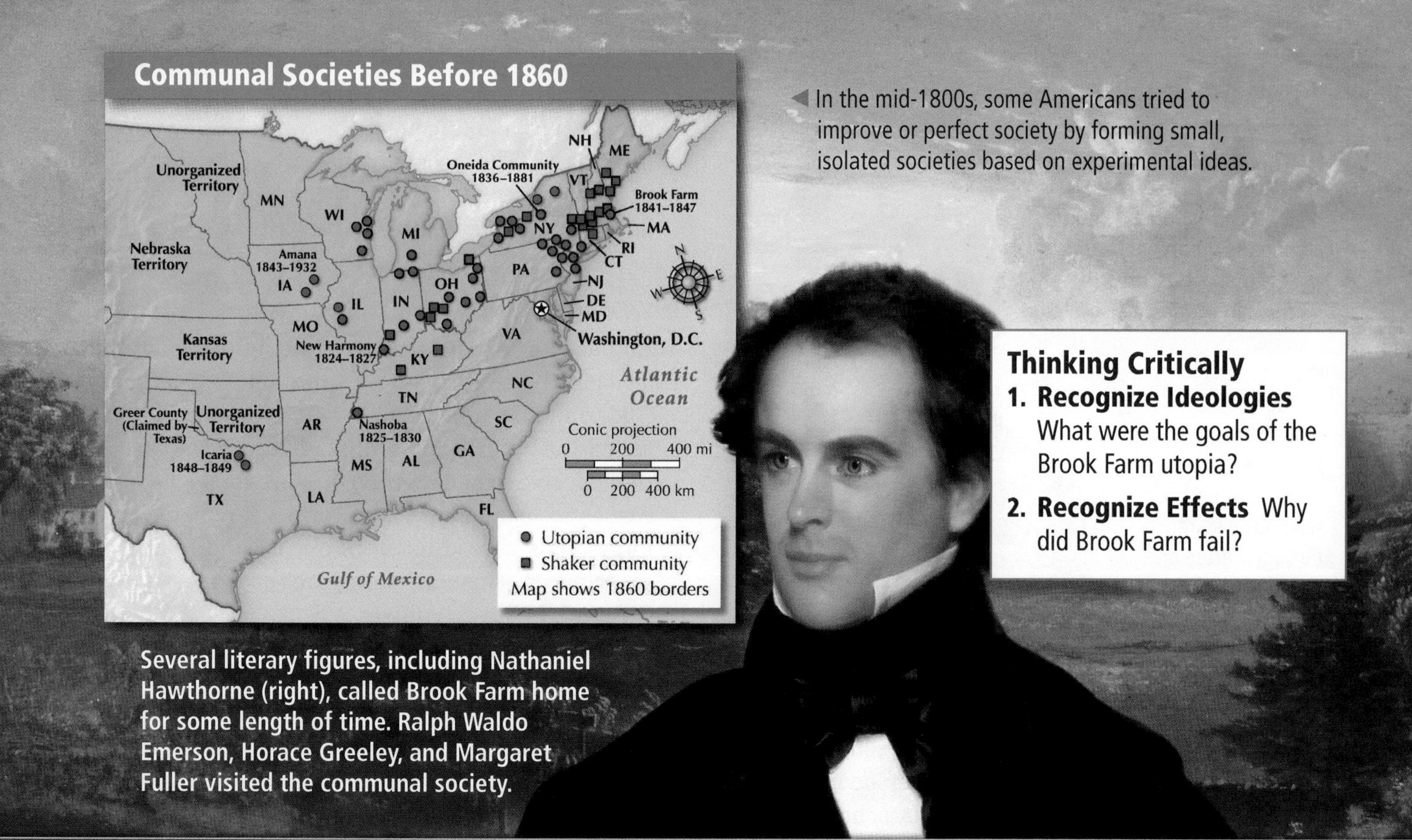

In the mid-1800s, some Americans tried to improve or perfect society by forming small, isolated societies based on experimental ideas.

Several literary figures, including Nathaniel Hawthorne (right), called Brook Farm home for some length of time. Ralph Waldo Emerson, Horace Greeley, and Margaret Fuller visited the communal society.

Thinking Critically

1. **Recognize Ideologies** What were the goals of the Brook Farm utopia?
2. **Recognize Effects** Why did Brook Farm fail?

Utopias and Transcendentalism

In the early 1800s, many Americans turned to Protestant churches, while some formed new religious groups. Still others sought different routes to try to fashion a more perfect society.

Utopian Communities Seek a Better Life During the early 1800s, dozens of groups of Americans sought to improve their lives in a unique way. They chose to distance themselves from society by setting up communities based on unusual ways of sharing property, labor, and family life. These settlements came to be called **utopian communities,** or utopias, because they aspired to be perfect communities. Organizers of utopias hoped their settlements would both engender virtue in their members and inspire those outside their communities.

Two well-known utopian communities were New Harmony, in Indiana, and Brook Farm, near Boston. In 1825, Robert Owen, a British social reformer, sought to have people from different backgrounds work together in a cooperative society at New Harmony. The society attracted some 1,000 people whom Owen described as "the industrious and well-disposed of all nations." At Brook Farm in 1841, George Ripley and 80 others sought to combine physical and intellectual labor. Brook Farm failed after only six years, while New Harmony lasted just two years. Most of the 50 or so other utopian communities were similarly short-lived.

The Shakers Succeed Another group that set up a chain of separate communal living societies was the United Society of Believers in Christ's Second Appearing, more commonly known as the Shakers. The Shakers had organized during the middle 1700s but reached their peak during the 1840s. Shakers set up independent villages in New Hampshire, New York, Ohio, and

History Makers

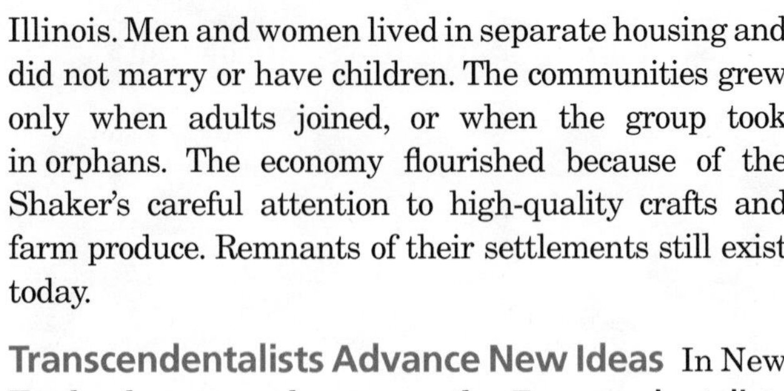

Henry David Thoreau
(1817–1862)
Henry David Thoreau is counted among the great American writers for his classic work, *Walden*. In *Walden,* he shares his experiences of subsisting alone in the woods for two years near Walden Pond in Massachusetts, living out the Transcendentalist theories of finding religious inspiration through nature and inside oneself.

Illinois. Men and women lived in separate housing and did not marry or have children. The communities grew only when adults joined, or when the group took in orphans. The economy flourished because of the Shaker's careful attention to high-quality crafts and farm produce. Remnants of their settlements still exist today.

Transcendentalists Advance New Ideas In New England, a group known as the **Transcendentalists** developed a new way to look at humanity, nature, and God, and the relationship among them. They were called the Transcendentalists because they believed that people could *transcend,* or go beyond, their senses to learn about the world. They believed that individuals should listen to nature and to their own consciences—instead of religious doctrines—to learn the truth about the universe.

Ralph Waldo Emerson, a former Unitarian minister, was the leading Transcendentalist. He celebrated the interplay between the individual and the universe in sermons, essays, and poems. "Within man," Emerson wrote, "is the soul of the whole; the wise silence; the universal beauty." Emerson gathered a group of men and women who met regularly in his Concord, Massachusetts, home to read and talk about ways to develop a rich spiritual life for individuals and for society. They published their ideas in their magazine, *The Dial*, which was edited by Margaret Fuller.

One of Emerson's most important followers was **Henry David Thoreau.** In 1846, Thoreau was jailed after refusing to pay taxes to support the Mexican-American War, which he viewed as immoral. Thoreau explained his thinking in a landmark essay, "Civil Disobedience," in which he argues that a person must be true to his or her own conscience, even if it means breaking the law. "Civil Disobedience" provided inspiration to later leaders who fought for civil rights around the world and is still widely read and admired.

Checkpoint **What did the Transcendentalists believe?**

Section 1 Assessment

Progress Monitoring *Online*
For: Self-test with vocabulary practice
www.pearsonschool.com/ushist

Comprehension

1. **Terms and People** What role did each term or person below play in the Second Great Awakening? Write your answers in complete sentences.
   - revivalist
   - Charles Grandison Finney
   - evangelical
   - Mormon
   - Unitarian
2. **NoteTaking Reading Skill: Identify Main Ideas** Use your chart to answer the Section Focus Question: How did the Second Great Awakening affect life in the United States?

Writing About History

3. **Quick Write: Identify a Viewpoint** Write a paragraph describing religion from the point of view of an evangelical preacher in the early 1800s. Include how religion would fit in with participation in the process of government.

Critical Thinking

4. **Draw Inferences** Why do you think the religious messages of the Second Great Awakening affected so many Americans?
5. **Determine Relevance** What factors led to discrimination against Irish immigrants in the early and middle 1800s?
6. **Make Comparisons** How did the methods of people who created utopian societies differ from those of other reformers?

American LITERATURE

Nature by Ralph Waldo Emerson

Ralph Waldo Emerson is considered the founder of Transcendentalism. His essay *Nature* (1836) was a statement of the movement's beliefs. Emerson came from a long line of ministers and became a Unitarian minister himself in 1829. However, he came to believe that people could get closer to God by transcending the material world and appreciating the beauties of nature rather than through following organized religion. In the excerpt below, Emerson expresses these Transcendentalist ideas.

▲ Ralph Waldo Emerson

In the woods, we return to reason and faith. There I feel that nothing can befall me in life—no disgrace, no calamity[1] (leaving me my eyes), which nature cannot repair. Standing on the bare ground—my head bathed by the blithe[2] air and uplifted into infinite space—all mean egotism[3] vanishes. I become a transparent eyeball; I am nothing; I see all; the currents of the Universal Being circulate through me; I am part or parcel of God. . . . I am the lover of uncontained and immortal beauty. In the wilderness, I find something more dear and connate[4] than in the streets or villages. In the tranquil landscape, and especially in the distant line of the horizon, man beholds somewhat as beautiful as his own nature. . . .

The waving of the boughs in the storm is new to me and old. It takes me by surprise, and yet is not unknown. Its effect is like that of a higher thought or a better emotion coming over me, when I deemed I was thinking justly or doing right.

Yet it is certain that the power to produce this delight does not reside in nature, but in man, or in a harmony of both.

The Notch of the White Mountains, Thomas Cole, 1839 ▼

Thinking Critically

1. **Draw Conclusions** What does Emerson mean by the phrase "I become a transparent eyeball"?
2. **Analyze Literature** What is the main point of this excerpt?

1. **calamity** (kuh LAM uh tee) *n.* disaster
2. **blithe** (blīth) *adj.* carefree
3. **egotism** (EE goh tihz uhm) *n.* selfishness
4. **connate** (kuh NAYT) *adj.* existing naturally

SECTION 2

▲ A print promoting the temperance cause, 1855

WITNESS HISTORY

Improving Society

In the early and middle 1800s, Americans became involved in a wide variety of reform movements, ranging from helping society's disadvantaged to trying to control alcohol abuse. Ralph Waldo Emerson eloquently expressed the feelings of many:

> "[T]he idea which now begins to agitate society has a wider scope than our daily employments, our households, and the institutions of property. We are [going] to revise the whole of our social structure, the state, the school, religion, marriage, trade, science, and explore the foundations in our own nature. . . . What is a man born for but to be a Reformer, a Remaker . . .?"
>
> —Ralph Waldo Emerson, "Man the Reformer," 1841

A Reforming Society

Objectives

- Describe the public school movement.
- Describe how reformers tried to improve the condition of prisoners and people with mental illness.
- Evaluate the effectiveness of the temperance movement.

Terms and People

public school movement
Horace Mann
Dorothea Dix
penitentiary movement
temperance movement
Neal Dow

NoteTaking

Reading Skill: Understand Effects As you read, note the different problems facing society in the early 1800s, what reformers did to address each problem, and the effects of their efforts.

Causes	Efforts to Reform	Results
Educating all Americans		

Why It Matters Many Americans embraced religion during the Second Great Awakening. Soon, many of these people began to put their religious ideals into practice by working to reshape, or reform, parts of American life. Their efforts would impact several groups of the most disadvantaged Americans. **Section Focus Question: What were the main features of the public school, penitentiary, and temperance reform movements?**

Reforming Education

The leaders of the Second Great Awakening preached that their followers had a sacred responsibility to improve life on Earth through reform, especially for the disadvantaged. Not all reformers were motivated by religion. Many were simply moved by the suffering they saw. One of most popular reform movements was in the field of education.

Reformers Value Education Since colonial times, most American children had been taught at home by their parents. Some communities established schools. *The American Spelling Book,* created by Noah Webster in the 1780s, remained the most popular schoolbook. Webster developed special spelling forms that he felt were representative of America's honesty and directness, emphasizing America's differences from England.

Still, reformers saw education in America as woefully inadequate. Because there were no public schools that children were required by law to attend, most children did not go to school. Reformers who led the **public school movement,** also called the common school movement, sought to establish such a system of tax-supported public schools. They argued that expanding education would give Americans the knowledge and <u>intellectual</u> tools they needed to make decisions as citizens of a democracy. Education would promote economic growth by supplying knowledgeable workers and help keep wealthy, educated people from oppressing the uneducated poor.

Vocabulary Builder
<u>intellectual</u>–(ihn tuh LEHK choo uhl) *adj.* related to the ability to understand difficult ideas

Horace Mann Leads the Public School Reform Movement

One of the greatest school reformers was **Horace Mann.** Mann grew up poor and had firsthand experience with inadequate schooling. He never forgot his humble beginnings. They inspired him to work to provide all children with a better education than he had received.

As a leader in the Massachusetts Senate, Mann championed the creation of a state board of education. He resigned from the Senate in 1837 to chair the first board. In this capacity, Mann advanced the idea of free public schools that all children were required by law to attend. He argued for state oversight of local schools, standardized school calendars, and adequate school funding. Mann also led the fight to abolish corporal, or physical, punishment. Further, he worked to establish training to create a body of well-educated, professional teachers.

Mann's influence was felt nationwide. Because of his work and the work of other school reformers, state legislatures across the country set aside funds to support free public schools. The reformers faced resistance from reluctant taxpayers and those who believed that education should include specific religious teaching. Despite opposition, within the next few decades, government-supported public schools became the norm across the nation. The percentage of American children attending school doubled.

Many women played key roles in the school reform movement. They petitioned their local legislatures to support public education and became teachers in the new schools. Catharine Beecher, a daughter of Lyman Beecher, and

A Place of Learning
During this period, more and more women moved into the classroom, both as students and as teachers. Students of both sexes learned from popular textbooks like the one above, which uses everyday items to illustrate the alphabet. *How does the classroom shown below differ from modern classrooms?*

Emma Willard established schools for women in Connecticut, Ohio, and New York. Elizabeth Blackwell and Ann Preston helped to establish medical training for women by the 1850s.

Checkpoint What did the public school movement accomplish?

Helping the Ill and Imprisoned

Americans who had little or no voice in how they were treated were of special concern to many reformers. That was one reason why many reformers worked tirelessly to help Americans who were imprisoned or mentally ill.

Dorothea Dix Campaigns for Change

One reformer who turned her religious ideals into action was **Dorothea Dix.** In 1841, she began teaching Sunday school in a Massachusetts prison. When she discovered that people suffering from mental illnesses were housed along with hardened criminals, she decided to act to change things.

Dix spent two years visiting every prison, almshouse (place for housing the poor), and hospital in Massachusetts. Then she wrote to the state legislature, vividly describing the horrors she had seen and demanding action:

> **Primary Source** "I tell what I have seen—painful and shocking as the details often are—that from them you may feel more deeply the imperative obligation which lies upon you to prevent the possibility of a repetition or continuance of such outrages upon humanity. . . . I come as the advocate of [the] helpless, forgotten, [and] insane. . . . Men of Massachusetts . . . raise up the fallen, succor the desolate, restore the outcast, defend the helpless."
>
> —Dorothea Dix, petition to the Massachusetts Legislature, 1843

Dix went on to campaign across the nation, encouraging other communities to build humane hospitals for people with mental illnesses. Her campaign was remarkably successful, leading directly to the creation of the first modern mental hospitals.

Reformers Target the Prison System

Dix and others also worked to reform American prisons. Until that time, most people viewed prisons as a place to punish criminals. Prison reformers, however, thought that prisons should make criminals feel penitence, or sorrow for their crimes. The prison reform movement is thus sometimes called the **penitentiary movement.**

Two types of penitentiaries were proposed by reformers. The Pennsylvania System, advocated by the Philadelphia Society for Alleviating the Miseries of Public Prisons, was embodied in the Eastern State Penitentiary. In Eastern State, prisoners were urged to repent while they lived in complete solitary confinement, working alone in their cells and exercising in individual yards. The Pennsylvania System was expensive to run, and its complete isolation of prisoners came to be viewed as cruel. The second type of penitentiary was based on a system used in Auburn Prison, in Central New York, in the 1820s. In Auburn, prisoners worked with one another during the day in strict silence but slept in individual cells at night. Many American prisons followed the Auburn model.

Checkpoint What motivated Dorothea Dix to campaign for reform?

History Makers

Dorothea Dix (1802–1887)

Dorothea Dix was an ordinary American who took extraordinary action to help other people. Despite persistent health problems, she campaigned for 40 years to win better, more humane treatment for people with mental illness—and met with amazing success. She helped to establish state mental hospitals in 15 states and Canada, and even spread her ideas in Europe. She also worked to improve prisons, favoring the Pennsylvania System of penitentiaries.

The Temperance Movement

When reformers surveyed American society, they saw a country in desperate need of reform. Ongoing industrialization caused rapid and unsettling changes. Crime, sickness, poverty, and neglected families and children seemed rampant. Many reformers attributed these problems to the widespread use of alcohol.

In response, reformers launched the **temperance movement,** an effort to end alcohol abuse and the problems created by it. Temperance means drinking alcoholic beverages in moderation. Some reformers believed in prohibition, or a complete ban, on alcohol consumption. Temperance reformers published pamphlets and posters warning that wasting money on liquor prevented people from buying food for their families. They argued that drinking alcohol led to violence and crime. The American Temperance Society, which had thousands of members in several states, held meetings where people were urged to pledge to refrain from drinking alcohol. The Washington Temperance Society sought to help drinkers through dramatic public confessions, discussion, and counseling.

However, the temperance movement had real success only when the reformers won changes in the law. **Neal Dow,** who earned a worldwide reputation for his lectures on alcohol abuse, became mayor of Portland, Maine, in 1851. He succeeded in securing the passage of the so-called "Maine Law," which restricted the sale of alcohol. Within a few years, a dozen states had passed similar temperance laws. Temperance would remain an enduring issue for the next hundred years.

Analyzing Political Cartoons

The Root of All Evil? In the illustration above, alcohol is blamed for a number of problems, including epilepsy and cholera, two medical problems unrelated to alcohol usage.

1. By what reasoning is violence related to alcohol consumption?
2. What position on the temperance debate do you think the cartoonist holds?

✓ **Checkpoint How successful was the temperance movement?**

SECTION 2 Assessment

Progress Monitoring *Online*
For: Self-test with vocabulary practice
www.pearsonschool.com/ushist

Comprehension

1. **Terms and People** Identify a leader and explain the goals of each of the following reform movements.
   - public school movement
   - penitentiary movement
   - temperance movement
2. **NoteTaking Reading Skill: Understand Effects** Use your table to answer the Section Focus Question: What were the main features of the public school, penitentiary, and temperance reform movements?

Writing About History

3. **Quick Write: State a Point of View** Write a paragraph defining the viewpoint of a mid-1800s reformer on the following issue: Should states pass laws to outlaw alcohol consumption? Give one argument someone might use to support that viewpoint.

Critical Thinking

4. **Recognize Cause and Effect** How did the Second Great Awakening lead to the launch of many reform movements?
5. **Draw Inferences** According to reformers, how would the public school movement help America's government and economy?
6. **Demonstrate Reasoned Judgment** How effective do you think the penitentiary movement was? Explain.
7. **Analyze Information** How did leaders of the temperance movement try to solve the problems of crime and poverty?

SECTION 3

▲ Slaves toil at backbreaking labor in this illustration from an 1836 geography textbook.

WITNESS HISTORY

The Evils of Slavery

In 1845, Frederick Douglass, an escaped slave, described his childhood in his autobiography. His powerful words gave many Americans their first understanding of—and compassion for—the lives of enslaved people in the South:

> "I never saw my mother . . . more than four or five times in my life; and each of these times was very short in duration, and at night. She [worked] about twelve miles from my home. She made her journeys to see me in the night, traveling the whole distance on foot, after the performance of her day's work. She was a field hand, and a whipping is the penalty of not being in the field at sunrise, unless a slave has special permission from his or her master to the contrary—a permission which they seldom get. . . . I do not recollect of ever seeing my mother by the light of day. . . . She died when I was about seven years old. . . . I was not allowed to be present during her illness, at her death, or burial."
>
> —Frederick Douglass, *Narrative of the Life of Frederick Douglass*

The Antislavery Movement

Objectives

- Describe the lives of enslaved and free African Americans in the 1800s.
- Identify the leaders and tactics of the abolition movement.
- Summarize the opposition to abolition.

Terms and People

freedman	William Lloyd Garrison
Nat Turner	Frederick Douglass
abolition movement	Gag Rule

NoteTaking

Reading Skill: Summarize Summarize what life was like for African Americans in the 1800s in a chart.

Lives of African Americans		
Daily Life	Ways of Surviving	Lives of Free Blacks
•	•	•

Why It Matters During the period of reform that swept the United States in the early and middle 1800s, reformers tried to improve life through campaigns to help children, families, and disadvantaged adults. Soon, reformers also set out to help another group of exploited people: enslaved African Americans in the South. **Section Focus Question: How did reformers try to help enslaved people?**

Life Under Slavery

Slavery, an American institution since colonial times, expanded across the South in the early 1800s with the growth of cotton farming. By 1830, from Maryland to Texas, some 2 million Africans and African Americans were held as slaves in the United States. About one third of these people were children under ten years of age. All of them struggled in their lives of captivity, knowing that they were at the mercy of slaveholders.

Suffering Cruel Treatment Most of these unfortunate men, women, and children labored from dawn to dusk at backbreaking tasks—cultivating fields of cotton, loading freight onto ships, or preparing meals in scorching hot kitchens. Their "overseers" maintained brutal work routines by punishing people physically with beatings, whipping, and maimings, and mentally, through humiliation and the threat of being separated from family members. The basics of life—food, clothing, and shelter—were barely adequate for most enslaved people.

The conditions under which enslaved people lived can be difficult to imagine. One glimpse of the heartbreak that tormented so many is provided by a letter from an enslaved woman, apparently pregnant, to her mother, who had been sold. She wrote to say that now her husband had also been sold:

> **Primary Source** "A cloud has settled upon me and produced a change in my prospect, too great for words to express. My husband is torn from me, and carried away by his master. . . . I went to see him—tried to prevail on him not to carry my husband away . . . but mother—all my entreaties and tears did not soften his hard heart. . . . A time is fast approaching when I shalt want my husband and my mother, and both are gone!"
>
> —Emily, an enslaved African American, 1836

Such anguish was commonplace. This woman was relatively lucky—she could read and write, and managed to get a letter to a distant family member. More often, enslaved people were not allowed to learn to read, and family members who were separated never heard from each other again.

Surviving Through Spirit and Strength The miserable conditions forced on enslaved people took their inevitable toll. Some, losing all hope, took their own lives. Others simply toiled through a lifetime of pain and sadness.

But, in a remarkable triumph of spirit over hardship, most enslaved people maintained their hope and their dignity. They developed many ways of coping with their inhumane conditions. They worked to maintain networks of family and friends. Parents kept family traditions alive by naming children for beloved aunts, uncles, or grandparents, and by passing on family stories that their children could cherish wherever they might find themselves. Enslaved people took comfort in their religion, a unique mix of traditional African and Christian beliefs, which shone the light of hope in the midst of their difficult lives.

Resisting Slavery Many enslaved people did whatever they could to fight back against their oppressors. Resistance took many forms including sabotage, such as breaking tools or outwitting overseers, and the more direct method of escape. Tens of thousands of enslaved people fled to the North or to Mexico, where slavery was prohibited. A loose network of ever-changing escape routes called the Underground Railroad helped many reach freedom.

Some enslaved people decided not to run but to fight. Indeed, historians estimate that nearly 200 significant slave revolts took place in the first half of the 1800s. In 1822, Denmark Vesey planned what would have been the greatest slave revolt in American history in Charleston, South Carolina. Vesey was a **freedman,** or former slave. Traveling to Haiti as a ship's carpenter, he was inspired by the successful slave rebellion that had taken place there in the 1790s. Vesey nurtured

Families Separated
This engraving shows the anguish of a mother and daughter on the auction block, while an indifferent slave-owner looks on.

his dream of a revolt after becoming frustrated with his status as a second-class citizen in Charleston. When authorities shut down Vesey's church, he was prompted into action. Vesey gathered some five-dozen conspirators and plotted a slave uprising that would involve hundreds or even thousands of people. The plan called for slaves in the city and on surrounding plantations to seize weapons from guardhouses and arsenals and use them to destroy Charleston and free all of the slaves living nearby. His plan was thwarted, however, when news of it leaked. In the end, Vesey and dozens of his accomplices were hanged.

In 1831, a slave named **Nat Turner** was more successful in carrying out his plans for revolt. Turner had taught himself to read the Bible and believed that he had received a sign from God instructing him to lead his people to freedom. In August of 1831, he led followers through the countryside near Richmond, Virginia, intending to capture a nearby armory and gain more weapons. On their journey, Turner's group killed nearly 60 people before the local militia stopped their march. In the process of the manhunt that followed, the local militia killed dozens of African Americans. Turner was captured after six weeks. He and his associates were executed.

Nat Turner's Revolt

In this dramatic image, a slave hunter apprehends Nat Turner after his failed revolt in 1831. Turner is still a controversial historical figure. Depicted in several books and films, he is sometimes shown as a visionary resisting oppression against overwhelming odds; other times he is portrayed as a delusional murderer. *How would you describe this artist's depiction of Nat Turner?*

Terrified by the idea of a successful slave revolt, southerners reacted by passing much more stringent laws and controls regarding slavery. In some places, it became illegal to teach enslaved people to read. Often, they were forbidden to gather in groups unless an overseer was present. Yet, these restrictions did nothing to dampen the spirit of the enslaved people who were determined to resist their captivity—and they inspired free people in the North to work against slavery.

Checkpoint How did enslaved people resist their captivity?

The Lives of Free African Americans

Not all people of African descent in the United States were held as slaves. Beginning with Massachusetts and Pennsylvania in the 1780s, northern states had gradually outlawed slavery by the 1840s. In Maryland and Virginia, many slaveholders were slowly manumitting, or officially freeing, their slaves. The net result was a large and growing population of free blacks. Despite their freedom, however, they suffered from persistent racial discrimination.

Moreover, the very existence of free African Americans concerned many white Americans, especially slaveholders. They felt that the large population of free African Americans made those still in bondage long all the more for freedom. In 1816, some of the South's most prominent slaveholders established the American Colonization Society (ACS). The goal of the ACS was to encourage the migration of free blacks to Africa. The ACS established Liberia, a colony on the west coast of Africa, and by 1830 some 1,100 people from the United States had been relocated there.

Most free African Americans were wary of the motives of the ACS. Most had been born in America, and they considered the United States their home. Moreover, they feared that colonization was just a plan to strengthen slavery by exiling the most able black leaders. Although several thousand free African Americans did eventually migrate to Liberia, most chose to stay in the country of their birth.

An illustration of an African American man playing the banjo

INFOGRAPHIC

African American Spirituals Give Hope

Enslaved African Americans drew strength to endure their difficult lives from community, tradition, religion, and music. Combining all of these was the African American spiritual. In these religious songs, enslaved African Americans merged African musical traditions with biblical stories and Protestant hymns to create a unique form of music. Spirituals were rarely sung the same way twice, and their original versions were never recorded. Still, many of the songs survive in some form.

Go Down, Moses

Go down, Moses,
'Way down in Egypt land,
Tell ol' Pharaoh,
Let my people go!

One of the biblical stories that slaves most identified with was the story of Moses leading the Israelites out of slavery in Egypt. Egypt stood for the American South, the Israelites for enslaved African Americans, and the Pharaoh for a particular white master or white society in general.

When Israel was in Egypt's land,
Let my people go.
Oppressed so hard they could not stand,
Let my people go.

O let us all from bondage flee,
Let my people go.
And let us all in Christ be free,
Let my people go.

In the verses, the repetition of the phrase "Let my people go!" might have been sung in the traditional African call-and-response style. In this style, a soloist or small group would have improvised while singing the first and third lines, while a larger group responded with the repeating phrase.

An African American wedding ceremony

Thinking Critically

1. **Draw Inferences** In what way did African American spirituals combine African and European influences to create something new?
2. **Recognize Causes** Why do you think few African American spirituals survive in their original forms?

Garrison Founds *The Liberator*

In 1831, Boston printer William Lloyd Garrison founded *The Liberator,* a newspaper devoted to abolishing slavery. He proclaimed his mission to speak out against slavery on the front page of the paper's first issue:

Primary Source "On this subject, I do not wish to think, or to speak, or write, with moderation. No! no! . . . I am in earnest—I will not equivocate—I will not excuse—I will not retreat a single inch—AND I WILL BE HEARD."

—*William Lloyd Garrison,* The Liberator

Considered a dangerous radical, Garrison was dragged through the streets of Boston by a mob in 1835. However, he did not let such attacks stop him from fighting against the evils of slavery. **Why do you think Garrison refused to speak or write with moderation on the subject of slavery?**

Many free African Americans worked together to establish churches and schools. Some acted to try to change and improve the lives of enslaved African Americans. In Boston, a free African American named David Walker published a pamphlet that used religion as the base for a blistering attack on slavery:

> **Primary Source** "You may do your best to keep us in wretchedness and misery, to enrich you and your children, but God will deliver us from under you. . . . Treat us then like men, and we will be your friends. And there is no doubt in my mind, but that the whole of the past will be sunk into oblivion, and we yet, under God, will become a united and happy people. The whites may say it is impossible, but remember that nothing is impossible with God."
>
> —David Walker, *Appeal to the Colored Citizens of the World,* 1829

Walker's pamphlet was outlawed in the slaveholding South. Still, it reached a wide audience in the North, where more people were beginning to view slavery as fundamentally incompatible with the religious views they embraced during the Second Great Awakening.

✓ **Checkpoint How did free blacks cope with discrimination in the mid-1800s?**

NoteTaking

Reading Skill: Contrast Use a chart like the one below to contrast the opinions held by those who supported slavery and abolitionists.

Debate Over Slavery	
Against	**For**
• Abolitionists believed that slavery was immoral. •	• Slaveholders argued that slavery was justified because it formed the basis of the South's economy. •

The Fight Against Slavery

Misgivings about slavery had been spreading across the nation since Revolutionary times. Many northerners objected to it on moral grounds. By 1804, all states north of Maryland had passed legislation to end slavery. In 1807, bringing new slaves to any part of the United States from Africa was banned. Still, slavery was an established institution in the South, where slaves played an important role in the economy.

By the early 1800s, a growing number of Americans opposed to slavery began to speak out. Because they wanted slavery abolished, or ended, they became known as abolitionists. The great reform movement they led was the **abolition movement.**

Garrison Demands Emancipation A printer named **William Lloyd Garrison,** who lived in Boston, Massachusetts, became one of the leading abolitionists. Garrison began his antislavery career by working for Benjamin Lundy, a Baltimore Quaker who published America's first antislavery newspaper. In 1831, Garrison began publishing his own antislavery newspaper, *The Liberator*. Garrison used dramatic language to attract readers and convince them that slavery was morally wrong. This technique of trying to effect change by persuading people through moral arguments is called moral suasion. It was a favorite technique of leaders of many reform movements.

Garrison was in favor of emancipation, or the freeing of enslaved people. At first he thought, like most abolitionists, that this should be accomplished gradually over time to minimize economic and social disruption. But Garrison soon took the radical step of advocating immediate emancipation and the extension of full political and social rights to African Americans.

In cities across the Northeast and the Midwest, abolitionist societies, made up of people who shared Garrison's views, sprang up. Founded by Garrison in 1833, the American Anti-Slavery Society had over 150,000 members nationally by 1840. This group implemented moral suasion by printing antislavery pamphlets and distributing them to churches and other community organizations. The American Anti-Slavery Society and similar groups also supported a team of hundreds of lecturers who spoke against slavery at camp meetings and other public gatherings. They insisted that holding slaves was counter to most Americans' religious ideals.

Many Abolitionists Spread the Word Theodore Weld, a student at the Lane Theological Seminary in Ohio, became another leading abolitionist. Weld shared Garrison's belief in the power of moral suasion. However, whereas Garrison resorted to public confrontation, Weld chose to work through the churches. Weld married Angelina Grimké, the daughter of a southern slaveholder, who was so moved by the abolition movement that she went north to join it. She and her sister Sarah Grimké spoke and wrote against slavery. Another well-known abolitionist, and arguably the most eloquent, was **Frederick Douglass,** a former slave whose booming voice filled lecture halls with touching stories about the difficulty of his life as a slave.

 **Checkpoint How did abolitionists attempt to bring about the end of slavery in the United States?**

Working Against Abolition

Despite the growing call of abolitionists, most Americans continued to support slavery. The voices against abolition came from both the slave states of the South and the free states of the North.

HISTORY MAKERS

Frederick Douglass (1818?–1895)
Frederick Douglass was born a slave in Maryland and escaped to the North in 1838. In 1841, he spontaneously shared his experiences as a slave at an antislavery convention. His remarks so stirred his audience that he soon became a valued speaker for the abolitionist cause. His autobiography, *Narrative of the Life of Frederick Douglass,* first published in 1845, reached still more people. During the Civil War, Douglass, as an adviser to President Lincoln, convinced the President to allow freedmen to fight for the North. Douglass also lent strong support to the women's movement.

Comparing Viewpoints

Should Slavery Be Abolished?

Although the answer to the question above is obvious now, debate raged on the issue in the mid-1800s. Advocates on both sides felt passionately that they were right.

Angelina Grimké

Southern-born Angelina Grimké, with her sister Sarah, was a dedicated abolitionist who worked to arouse moral outrage against slavery.

Primary Source

"Let every slaveholder apply these queries to his own heart: Am *I* willing to be a slave . . . Am *I* willing to see my mother a slave, or my father, my *white* sister, or my *white* brother? If *not,* then in holding others as slaves, I am doing what I would *not* wish to be done to me . . . and thus have broken this golden rule . . ."

—Appeal to Christian Women of the South, 1836

John C. Calhoun

One of the South's most distinguished statesman, Calhoun believed that slavery was vital to America's way of life.

Primary Source

"I hold that in the present state of civilization, where two races of different origin, and distinguished by color, and other physical differences, as well as intellectual, are brought together, the relation now existing in the slaveholding States between the two, is, instead of an evil, a good—a positive good. . . . [T]here never has yet existed a wealthy and civilized society in which one portion of the community did not . . . live on the labor of another."

—Speech to the Senate, February 6, 1837

Compare

1. What argument does Calhoun use to defend slavery?
2. Which quotation do you think is more effective? Why?

Southerners Cling to Slavery As abolitionists were developing their arguments against slavery, southern slaveholders intensified their arguments in support of it. They publicized their conviction that slavery was necessary because it formed the foundation of the South's agricultural economy. Moreover, they argued, slavery benefited the North, since the North's textile and shipping industries depended upon southern cotton.

They further maintained that a slave labor force was superior to the wage labor force of the North. They argued that northern employers and laborers would be inevitably at odds, since employers wanted workers to work more for less money while workers wanted to work less for more money. In contrast, such conflict was avoided in the South, where the well-being of slaves depended on their slaveholders' fortunes and slaveholders' fortunes depended on the well-being of their slaves.

But some southerners went even further, claiming that Christianity supported slavery, that enslaved people could not survive without slaveholders, and that the enslavement of Africans was historically inevitable. Such assertions were clearly racist, but many people of the time believed them.

Vocabulary Builder
inevitable–(ihn EHV ih tuh buhl) *adj.* impossible to prevent; unavoidable

As abolitionist rhetoric grew more strident, southern support for gradual manumission, or freeing, of slaves decreased. Southern spokespeople stepped up their arguments about the value of slavery, and southern slaveholders tried to prevent southerners from reading abolitionist publications. Post offices refused to deliver abolitionist newspapers. Southerners—even many of those who did not own slaves—embraced slavery as their preferred way of life, to be defended at all costs.

Northerners Resist Abolition Southerners were not alone in their resistance to abolition. Most northerners agreed with them. In Boston in 1835, Garrison was chased through the streets by an angry mob as a result of his antislavery views. In Philadelphia in 1838, the Grimké-Weld wedding, attended by both white and black guests, so infuriated local residents that they burned down the antislavery meeting hall. In Alton, Illinois, irate crowds destroyed abolitionist newspaper editor Elijah Lovejoy's printing press several times, killing Lovejoy himself in November 1837.

In city after city, white workers, fearing black competitors would take their jobs, launched stiff resistance to abolition. Wealthy industrialists resented the presence of black entrepreneurs in their midst. They also worried that the end of slavery would cut off the supply of southern cotton for northern textile mills.

Most white northerners disliked southerners, but they did not want to wrestle with the problems of African Americans either. They wanted to stay out of the controversy about slavery. When southern politicians pushed a **Gag Rule,** a law which prohibited debate and discussion in Congress on the subject of slavery, some northerners supported them. First passed in 1836, the Gag Rule was renewed annually for eight years.

Slavery Divides the Nation Although the abolition movement remained small and mostly confined to the North, it was vocal—and persistent. The debate over slavery divided Americans like no other issue. It widened regional cultural differences between the largely urban and industrialized North and the largely rural and agricultural South. Indeed, the divisive issue of slavery would soon prove to be a major factor in the division of the country itself.

✓ **Checkpoint Why did many Americans oppose abolishing slavery?**

SECTION 3 Assessment

Progress Monitoring *Online*
For: Self-test with vocabulary practice
www.pearsonschool.com/ushist

Comprehension

1. **Terms and People** Explain the role each of the following terms or people played in the debate over slavery.
   - freedman
   - Nat Turner
   - abolition movement
   - William Lloyd Garrison
   - Frederick Douglass
   - Gag Rule

2. NoteTaking **Reading Skill: Summarize** Use your charts to answer the Section Focus Question: How did reformers try to help enslaved people?

Writing About History

3. **Quick Write: Prioritize Arguments** List three arguments in favor of total emancipation for enslaved African Americans in 1845. Then, order the three arguments from most important to least important.

Critical Thinking

4. **Summarize** In what ways did enslaved people cope with their captivity?
5. **Identify Point of View** Why did most free African Americans not support the ACS?
6. **Draw Inferences** What role did religion play in the abolition movement?
7. **Recognize Cause and Effect** What led to the decline of manumission in the South?

SECTION 4

▲ Woman who worked in the temperance reform movement, 1851

WITNESS HISTORY

Equality for Women

The sisters Sarah Grimké and Angelina Grimké Weld were ardent abolitionists. Through their work on the behalf of slaves, they became interested in fighting for the rights of another oppressed group: women.

"I am persuaded that the rights of woman, like the rights of slaves, need only be examined to be understood and asserted, even by some of those, who are now endeavouring to smother the irrepressible desire for mental and spiritual freedom which glows in the breast of many. . . .

Men and women were CREATED EQUAL; they are both moral and accountable beings, and whatever is *right* for man to do is *right* for woman."

—Sarah Grimké, *Letters on the Equality of the Sexes and the Condition of Women,* 1838

The Women's Movement

Objectives

- Identify the limits faced by American women in the early 1800s.
- Trace the development of the women's movement.
- Describe the Seneca Falls Convention and its effects.

Terms and People

matrilineal
Sojourner Truth
women's movement
Lucretia Mott
Elizabeth Cady Stanton
Seneca Falls Convention
Amelia Bloomer
suffrage
Married Women's Property Act

NoteTaking

Reading Skill: Identify Causes and Effects Use a chart to record the causes and effects of the women's rights movement in the 1800s.

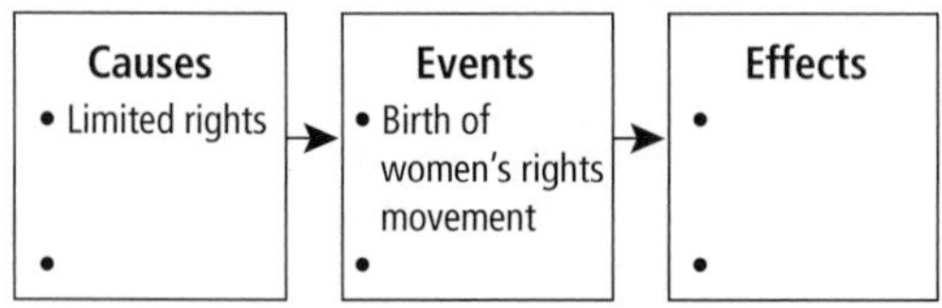

Why It Matters A spirit of reform permeated American life in the early and middle 1800s. Women took active roles in the abolition movement and other reform movements. Soon, some of these reformers began to work to gain equality for women as well. Their efforts would lay the groundwork for women's struggle for equal rights over the next hundred years. **Section Focus Question: What steps did American women take to advance their rights in the mid-1800s?**

Women Work for Change

In the 1800s, American women's freedoms and rights were sharply limited. Instead of taking a powerful role in public life, women were expected to make a difference privately, by influencing their husbands and raising their children to be good Americans. But this idealized influence was too limiting for women. Largely as a result of the Second Great Awakening, women of the early 1800s began to take on more active roles in public life.

Women Face Limits In the early 1800s, American women lacked many basic legal and economic rights. Under the British legal traditions that dominated the United States, women usually could not hold property or hold office or vote, and they usually were forbidden even to speak in public. Formal educational opportunities were virtually unheard of. In the rare instances of divorce, husbands generally gained custody of children.

Some of the groups living in America—certain Native Americans, African Americans, and Mexican Americans—had a tradition of affording women a significant amount of power. In these cultures, women controlled or influenced work patterns and family structures. Some cultures were **matrilineal,** that is, the inheritance of family names and property followed the female line in the family. Still, the legal and economic rights of the majority of American women lagged far, far behind those of American men.

Women Lead Reform Efforts The drive to reform American society created by the Second Great Awakening provided new opportunities for women. Many joined reform groups sponsored by their churches. Women played leading roles in all of the great reform movements of the day. Catharine Beecher, Emma Willard, Elizabeth Blackwell, and Ann Preston advanced education during the public school movement. Dorothea Dix almost single-handedly launched reforms in the way the country treated prisoners and people who suffered from mental illness. Most community leaders of the temperance movement were women; after all, they and their children were the primary victims of alcohol abuse among men.

The abolition movement attracted some of the most thoughtful women of the day, including Angelina and Sarah Grimké. Many abolitionist groups, like the Philadelphia Female Anti-Slavery Society, were made up entirely of women. One of the most effective abolitionist lecturers was **Sojourner Truth,** a former slave from New York who held audiences spellbound with her powerful speeches.

Women Enter the Workplace In the 1820s and 1830s, the Northeast was rapidly industrializing. This provided the first real economic opportunity in the nation's history for women outside the home. Thousands of young women, who previously would have stayed in the family home, went to work in the new mills and factories. This gave many women a small degree of economic independence (although their wages were typically sent to their husbands or fathers) and a larger degree of social independence as they developed networks of friendships with other factory workers. By 1830, a few women's labor unions had formed, and some groups had held strikes for better wages and working conditions.

✓ **Checkpoint What led to women becoming leaders of various reform movements?**

Chart Skills In the early 1800s, American women lacked many basic rights that are now taken for granted. Even the heavy and restrictive clothing women wore (below) limited what they could do. *How did the status of women in the 1800s go against the modern interpretation of the Constitution?*

Political and Economic Status of Women in the Early 1800s
Women could not vote.
Women could not hold public office.
Women could not serve on juries.
Few women received any level of higher education.
Women could not work in most trades or professions.
When they did work, women were paid less than men doing the same jobs, and their fathers or husbands often took what money they did earn.
Married women lost legal control of any money or property they owned before marriage to their husbands. Married women could not testify against their husbands in court, sue for divorce, or gain custody of their children.

Women Begin the Fight for Rights

Vocabulary Builder
virtually–(VUHR choo uh lee) *adv.* not completely, but for all practical purposes

Although many women became leading reformers, and many others entered the workforce, there had still been virtually no progress in women's rights. Real progress began only when two historical trends coincided in the 1830s. First, many urban middle-class northern women began to hire poor women to do their housework. This allowed the middle-class women more time to think about the society in which they wanted to raise their children. Second, women began to see their own social restrictions as being comparable to slavery.

The Origins of the Women's Rights Movement The parallels between the lack of power held by slaves and the lack of power held by women were hard to ignore. In fact, many women argued that their lack of rights made them almost the same as slaves. These women, along with a handful of men in the abolition movement, began to work for women's rights. They began the **women's movement,** a movement working for greater rights and opportunities for women, of the early and middle 1800s. This stage of the women's movement was active throughout the 1800s and into the early 1900s.

Women's rights reformers began to publish their ideas in pamphlets and books. One of these was the Transcendentalist Margaret Fuller, who believed that what women needed was not personal power but "as a nature to grow, as an intellect to discern, as a soul to live freely and unimpeded, to unfold such powers as were given her . . .". The Grimké sisters also published their ideas on women's rights. In *Letters on the Equality of the Sexes and the Condition of Women,* Sarah Grimké argued that God made men and women equal and that therefore men and women should be treated equally. Building on her sister's

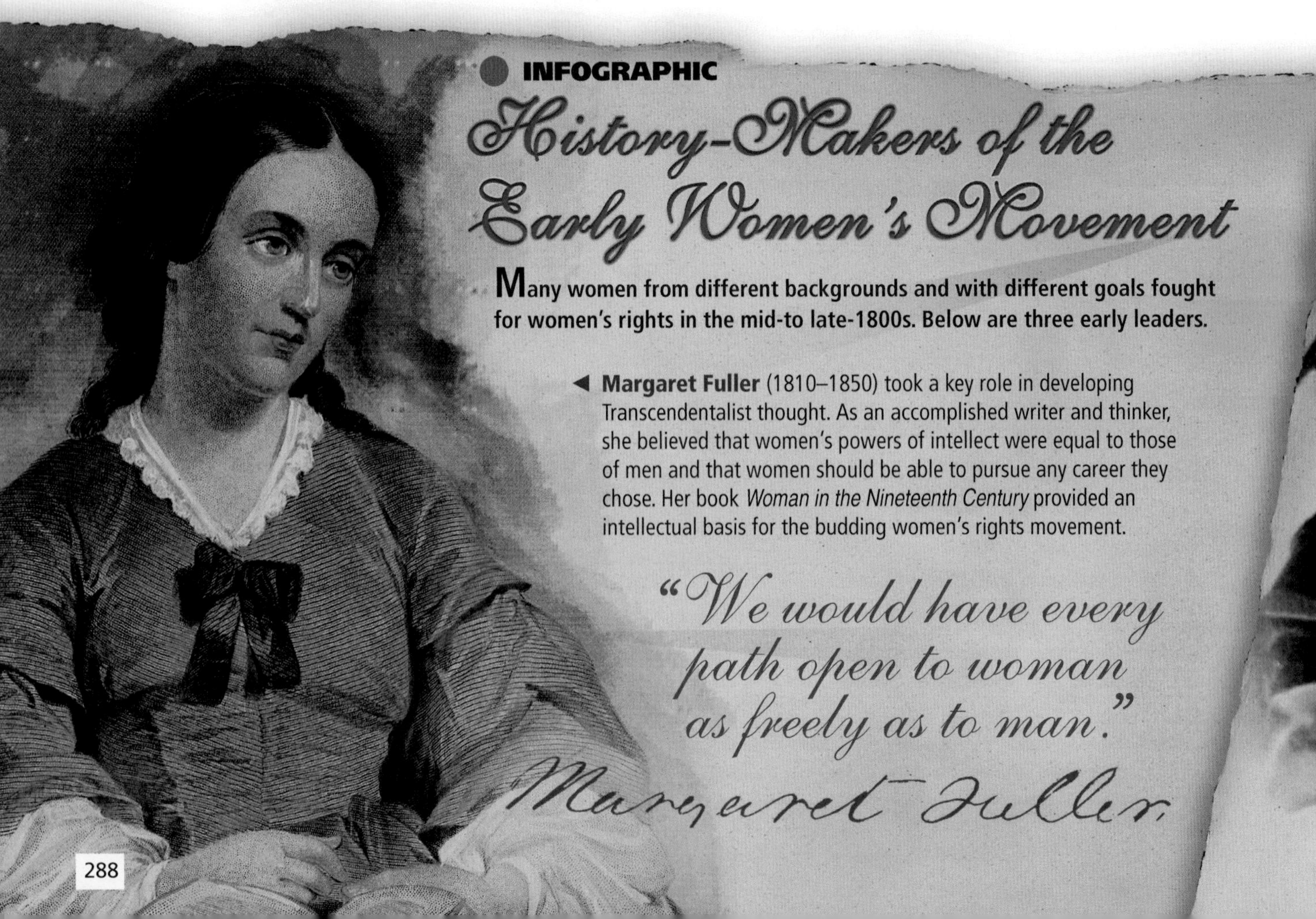

ideas, Angelina Grimké Weld defended the rights of both slaves and women on moral grounds:

> **Primary Source** "The investigation of the rights of the slave has led me to a better understanding of my own. . . . Human beings have *rights,* because they are *moral* beings. . . [I]f rights are founded on the nature of our moral being, then the *mere circumstance of sex* does not give to man higher rights and responsibilities, than to woman."
>
> —Angelina Grimké, *Letters to Catherine E. Beecher,* 1838

Women Disagree on Aims The women who spoke up for full equality were a small minority, however. Even among abolitionists there was disagreement about how much public leadership women should take. When an international abolitionist convention met in London in 1840, the group fractured over whether women should be allowed to join in the men's business meetings. Some abolitionists thought that they should not. Two who thought they should were **Lucretia Mott** and **Elizabeth Cady Stanton.**

Both Mott and Stanton were active reformers, supporting particularly the temperance and abolitionist causes. Mott had helped found the American Anti-Slavery Society and the Philadelphia Female Anti-Slavery Society. Stanton was married to a leading abolitionist, Henry Stanton. (Both Elizabeth and Henry were already keenly interested in women's rights.) These two women, outraged that women were refused full participation at a meeting to discuss the promotion of human decency and equality, were inspired to take a dramatic step to advance women's rights.

✓ **Checkpoint** **What conditions led women to start calling for equal rights?**

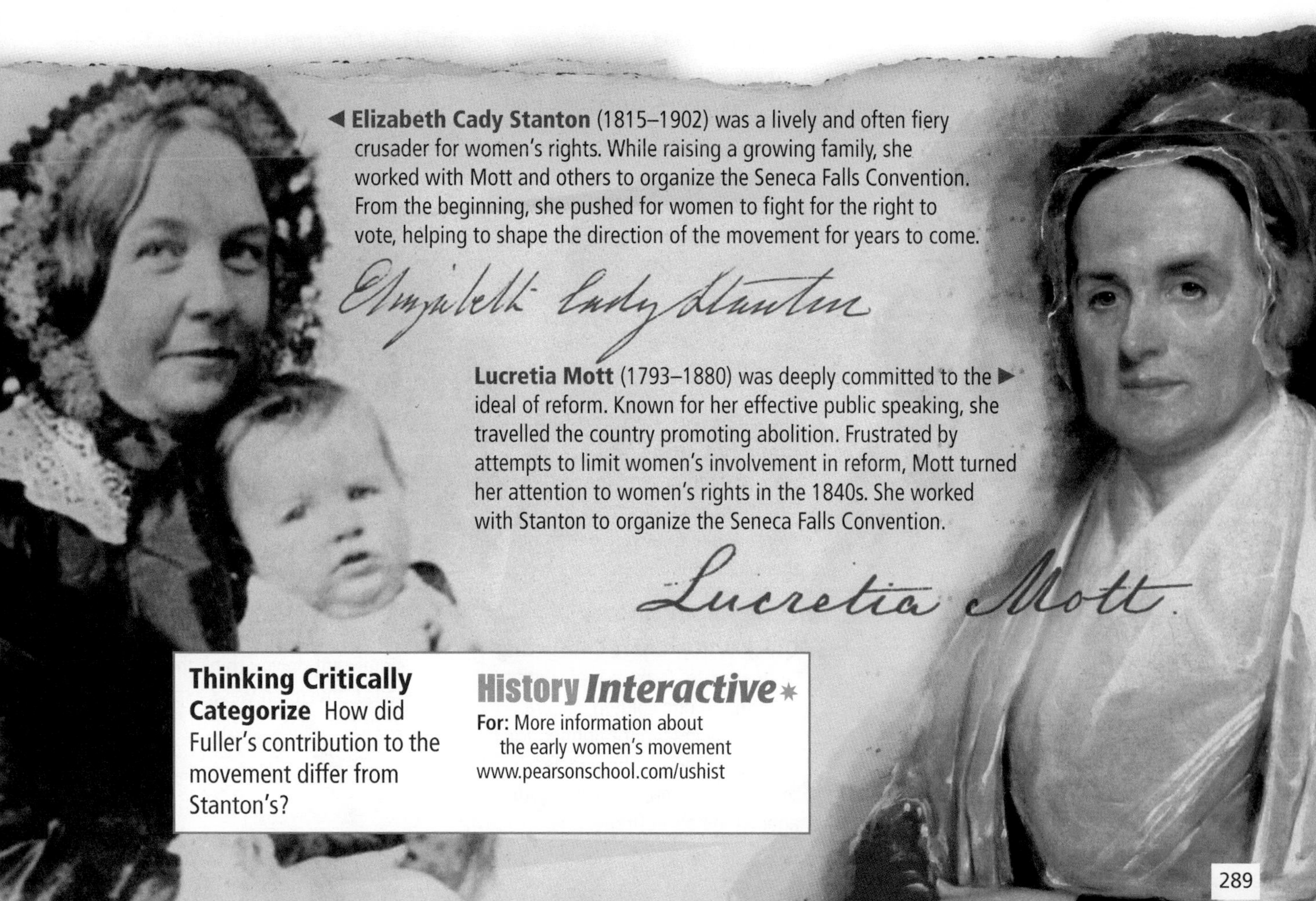

◄ **Elizabeth Cady Stanton** (1815–1902) was a lively and often fiery crusader for women's rights. While raising a growing family, she worked with Mott and others to organize the Seneca Falls Convention. From the beginning, she pushed for women to fight for the right to vote, helping to shape the direction of the movement for years to come.

Lucretia Mott (1793–1880) was deeply committed to the ideal of reform. Known for her effective public speaking, she travelled the country promoting abolition. Frustrated by attempts to limit women's involvement in reform, Mott turned her attention to women's rights in the 1840s. She worked with Stanton to organize the Seneca Falls Convention. ►

Thinking Critically

Categorize How did Fuller's contribution to the movement differ from Stanton's?

History *Interactive*

For: More information about the early women's movement
www.pearsonschool.com/ushist

A Radical Suggestion

In the mid-1800s, a number of women worked to reform the way women dressed. One of their innovations was the idea of wearing full-cut trousers under a short skirt rather than the long, heavy skirts of the day. Although she did not invent them, Amelia Bloomer wore the trousers publicly, and they were dubbed "bloomers" after her.

Women Convene in Seneca Falls

In 1848, Mott and Stanton helped organize the nation's first Women's Rights Convention in Seneca Falls, New York. Often called the **Seneca Falls Convention,** the meeting attracted hundreds of men and women. One of the most illustrious attendees was Frederick Douglass. The delegates to the convention adopted a "Declaration of Sentiments," modeled after the language of the Declaration of Independence. The Declaration of Sentiments was ridiculed, and the convention resulted in few concrete improvements in women's rights. It did, however, mark the beginning of the women's movement in the United States.

The Seneca Falls Convention Inspires Women The Seneca Falls Convention inspired generations of young women. One of these was **Amelia Bloomer,** who actually attended the convention. While she remained relatively quiet there, she would soon become a leading voice for women's rights. In the following years, Bloomer published a newspaper, *The Lily,* in which she advocated equality of women in all things—including the right to wear pants instead of dresses.

Another woman who drew inspiration from the convention was Susan B. Anthony, whose involvement in the temperance and abolition movements led her to work for greater rights for women as well. Anthony would help lead the charge to win a single, critical right for women: the right to vote. This quest for **suffrage** would prove to be a long, hard fight.

Women Make Some Gains In 1848, the same year as the Seneca Falls Convention, the state of New York passed a law, the **Married Women's Property Act,** guaranteeing many property rights for women. Elizabeth Cady Stanton had worked hard for its passage. Twelve years later, the law was amended to make it more comprehensive. New York's efforts to advance property rights for women would become a model for similar laws in other states in the years to come.

By the middle 1800s, American women had laid the foundation for a future in which equality seemed a real possibility. They had become wage earners. They had become reformers. And they had started to voice their call for justice.

 **Checkpoint What role did Lucretia Mott and Elizabeth Cady Stanton play in the women's rights movement?**

SECTION 4 Assessment

Progress Monitoring *Online*
For: Self-test with vocabulary practice
www.pearsonschool.com/ushist

Comprehension

1. **Terms and People** Explain the role each term or person listed below played in the early women's rights movement.
   - Lucretia Mott
   - Elizabeth Cady Stanton
   - Seneca Falls Convention
   - Amelia Bloomer
   - Married Women's Property Act
2. **NoteTaking Reading Skill: Identify Causes and Effects** Use your chart to answer the Section Focus Question: What steps did American women take to advance their rights in the mid-1800s?

Writing About History

3. **Quick Write: Chart Conflicting Arguments** Make a table with two columns. In one column, list two arguments in favor of fighting for female suffrage in the mid-1800s. In the other column, list two arguments against female suffrage.

Critical Thinking

4. **Draw Inferences** Why do you think women's rights were so limited in the early years of the country?
5. **Synthesize Information** Why did some abolitionists become outspoken advocates for women's rights?
6. **Determine Relevance** How significant do you think the Seneca Falls Convention was? Explain your answer.

Primary Source

The Declaration of Sentiments (1848)

Elizabeth Cady Stanton, along with four other women, created the Declaration of Sentiments to outline the aims of the Seneca Falls Convention. They purposely modeled the language of the Declaration of Sentiments on the Declaration of Independence as a potent reminder of the principles of equality upon which the United States was founded.

Notes taken at the Seneca Falls Convention (top), a statue honoring Elizabeth Cady Stanton and Lucretia Mott, as well as Susan B. Anthony

We hold these truths to be self-evident: that all men and women are created equal; that they are endowed by their Creator with certain inalienable rights; that among these are life, liberty, and the pursuit of happiness. . . .

The history of mankind is a history of repeated injuries and usurpations[1] on the part of man toward woman, having in direct object the establishment of an absolute tyranny over her. To prove this, let facts be submitted to a candid[2] world.

He has never permitted her to exercise her inalienable right to the elective franchise.

He has compelled her to submit to law in the formation of which she had no voice. . . .

He has made her, if married, in the eye of the law, civilly dead. He has taken from her all right in property, even to the wages she earns. . . .

He has denied her the facilities for obtaining a thorough education, all colleges being closed against her. . . .

He has endeavored, in every way that he could, to destroy her confidence in her own powers, to lessen her self-respect, and to make her willing to lead a dependent and abject[3] life.

Now, in view of this entire disfranchisement of one-half the people of this country, their social and religious degradation, in view of the unjust laws above mentioned, and because women do feel themselves aggrieved, oppressed, and fraudulently deprived of their most sacred rights, we insist that they have immediate admission to all the rights and privileges which belong to them as citizens of the United States.

1. **usurpations** (yoo suhr PAY shuhns) *n.* seizures
2. **candid** (KAN dihd) *adj.* fair
3. **abject** (AB jehkt) *adj.* miserable

Thinking Critically

1. **Synthesize Information** Based on the facts listed, what rights and privileges do the authors believe that women are being denied?
2. **Recognize Causes** Why do you think this declaration was modeled on the Declaration of Independence?

CHAPTER 8

Quick Study Guide

Progress Monitoring *Online*
For: Self-test with vocabulary practice
www.pearsonschool.com/ushist

Effects of the Second Great Awakening

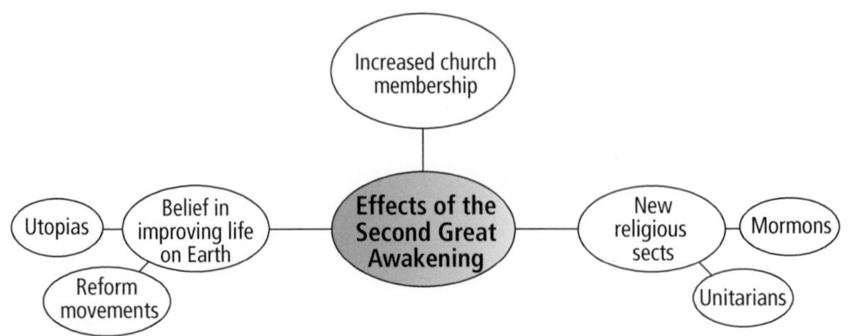

Major Reform Movements and Their Notable Leaders

Movement	Leader
School reform	Horace Mann
Prison reform	Dorothea Dix
Temperance	Neal Dow
Abolitionist	William Lloyd Garrison, Theodore Weld, Frederick Douglass, Angelina and Sarah Grimké
Women's rights	Sojourner Truth, Angelina Grimké, Margaret Fuller, Elizabeth Cady Stanton, Lucretia Mott, Susan B. Anthony

The Beginning of the Women's Rights Movement

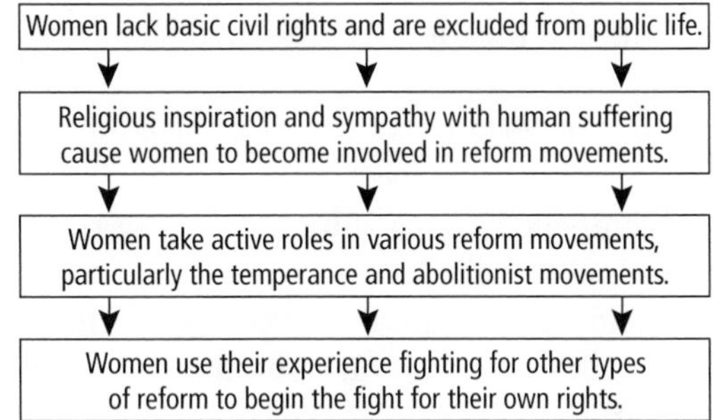

Quick Study Timeline

In America

1830
Charles Grandison Finney begins revivals in Rochester, New York

1838
Frederick Douglass escapes from slavery in Maryland

Presidential Terms — Andrew Jackson 1829–1837 — Martin Van Buren 1837–1841

1830 — 1835

Around the World

1833
Slavery abolished in British West Indies

1837
Victoria becomes queen in Great Britain

American Issues Connector

By connecting prior knowledge with what you have learned in this chapter, you can gradually build your understanding of enduring questions that still affect America today. Answer the questions below. Then, use your American Issues Connector study guide (or go online: www.pearsonschool.com/ushist).

Issues You Learned About

- **Church and State** The United States follows a policy of keeping religion separate from matters of government.

1. What guarantees the American people the right to freedom of religion?
2. As you have read, many states had laws that barred Jewish people from holding public office. Evaluate these laws with regard to the Constitution's policy on religious freedom and the prohibition of religious practices in government.
3. Some communities and states have passed "blue laws" banning the sale of certain goods on Sundays. Do you think such laws violate the separation of church and state?

- **Social Problems and Reforms** The early 1800s initiated a period of tremendous efforts to improve different aspects of American society.

4. How is the work of Dorothea Dix still felt today?
5. What methods did abolitionists use to further their cause?
6. Identify two female reformers and explain what they did.

- **Education and American Society** The United States supports a public school system that has the goal of providing a quality education for all the country's children.

7. What would be the benefit of creating tax-supported public schools?
8. Why did reformers assert that a system of public education would be an important tool of democracy?

Connect to Your World — Activity

Women in American Society: Women's Impact Today As you have read, the women's rights movement began in the early 1800s. Since that time, women have made enormous gains in economic, legal, and political rights. Conduct research to find out some key statistics about women in the United States today, such as the percentage of women in the workforce, the percentage of female voters in the most recent election, or the number of women whose level of education includes at least a bachelor's degree. Write a one-paragraph summary of how the data you found shows the impact of women on American Society today.

1843 Dorothea Dix seeks better treatment of people with mental illness

1848 Women's rights convention held in Seneca Falls, New York

William H. Harrison 1841
John Tyler 1841–1845

James K. Polk 1845–1849

Zachary Taylor 1849–1850
Millard Fillmore 1850–1853

1840 — 1845 — 1850

1839 Opium War between Great Britain and China begins

1845 Irish potato famine begins

History *Interactive*
For: Interactive Timeline
www.pearsonschool.com/ushist

Chapter Assessment

Terms and People

1. Who were **Joseph Smith** and the **Mormons**? Why did many Americans distrust them?
2. What was the **temperance movement**? What measures brought the most success to the temperance movement?
3. Who were **William Lloyd Garrison** and **Frederick Douglass**? How did they help the abolitionist cause?
4. Define **matrilineal.** Was the United States mainly a matrilineal society in the early 1800s? Explain.
5. What is **suffrage**? Why did some women consider winning suffrage a critical step?

Focus Questions

The focus question for this chapter is **How did the Second Great Awakening lead to several reform efforts, and what effect did those reform efforts have on American society?** Build an answer to this big question by answering the focus questions for Sections 1 through 4 and the Critical Thinking questions that follow.

Section 1

6. How did the Second Great Awakening affect life in the United States?

Section 2

7. What were the main features of the public school, penitentiary, and temperance reform movements?

Section 3

8. How did reformers try to help enslaved people?

Section 4

9. What steps did American women take to advance their rights in the mid-1800s?

Critical Thinking

10. **Recognize Cause and Effect** Why did the Second Great Awakening begin? What were some of the ways that it changed American society?
11. **Analyze Information** What did the Transcendentalists and people who founded utopias have in common?
12. **Draw Conclusions** How might Horace Mann's experiences as a senator have made him an ideal leader for the school reform movement?
13. **Analyze Graphs** According to the graph below, how did the amount of alcohol consumed by Americans change from 1820 to 1860?

Annual Consumption of Alcohol per Person: 1820–1860

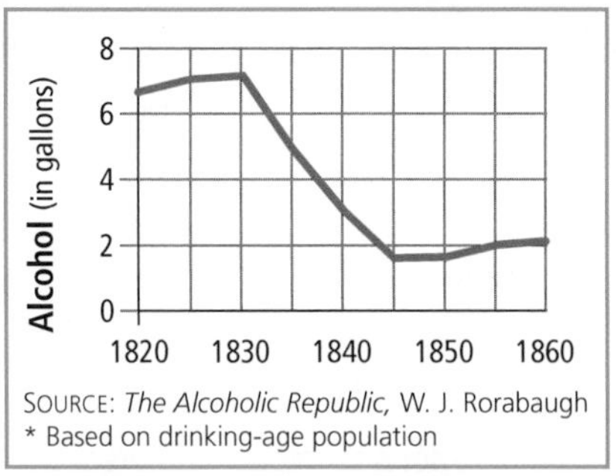

SOURCE: *The Alcoholic Republic,* W. J. Rorabaugh
* Based on drinking-age population

14. **Make Generalizations** What groups of people did reformers work hardest to help? Why?
15. **Problem Solving** How successful were slave revolts in helping enslaved African Americans resist slavery?
16. **Compare Points of View** What similar ideas did abolitionists and women's rights reformers hold?

Writing About History

Writing a Persuasive Essay In a persuasive essay, the writer identifies an issue and presents arguments that will persuade readers to support a particular viewpoint. Choose one of the reform movements described in this chapter. Write a three-paragraph essay in which you define the issue and give reasons in support of your viewpoint.

Prewriting

- Read the text in this chapter relating to the topic you have chosen.
- Use Internet or library sources to find additional descriptions and primary sources relating to your topic.
- Decide what viewpoint you wish to support.
- Make a list of arguments that might be used to support that viewpoint. Identify the two strongest arguments.

Drafting

- Make an outline identifying what aspects of your topic you want to describe.
- Write an opening paragraph in which you describe the issue and explain why it is important.
- Write two persuasive paragraphs. In each paragraph, use reasoned but forceful language that explains one of the arguments you have identified in your pre-writing. If possible, anticipate and counter possible objections to your arguments.

Revising

- Use the guidelines on page SH16 of the Writing Handbook to revise your writing.

Document-Based Assessment

Nat Turner's Revolt Shakes the South

In August 1831, Nat Turner led one of the most deadly slave revolts in American history. He and about 50 followers killed nearly 60 white people in Southampton County, Virginia, in a bloody three-day rampage. Although Turner and many of his followers were quickly caught, tried, and executed, his revolt had far-reaching repercussions. Use your knowledge of this time period and Documents A, B, C, and D to answer questions 1–4.

Document A

"A fanatic preacher by the name of Nat Turner (Gen. Nat Turner) who had been taught to read and write, and permitted to go about preaching in the country, was at the bottom of this infernal brigandage. . . . We cannot say how long they were organizing themselves—but they turned out on last Monday early (the 22d) upon their nefarious expedition. . . . They were mounted to the number of 40 or 50; and with knives and axes—knocking on the head, or cutting the throats of their victims."

—*An account of the revolt from the newspaper* The Richmond Enquirer, *August 30, 1831*

Document B

"I have received this day another number of *The Liberator,* a newspaper printed in Boston, with the express intention of inciting the slaves and free negroes in this and the other States to rebellion and to murder the men, women, and children of those states. Yet we are gravely told that there is no law to punish such an offence. . . . If this is not checked it must lead to a separation of these states."

—*Diary entry of Virginia Governor John Floyd, September 27, 1831*

Document C

"Not far from this time Nat Turner's insurrection broke out; and the news threw our town [in North Carolina] into great commotion. . . . Those who never witnessed such scenes can hardly believe what I know was inflicted at this time on innocent men, women, and children, against whom there was not the slightest ground for suspicion. Colored people and slaves who lived in remote parts of the town suffered in an especial manner. . . . Every where men, women, and children were whipped till the blood stood in puddles at their feet. Some received five hundred lashes. . . . The dwellings of the colored people, unless they happened to be protected by some influential white person, who was nigh at hand, were robbed of clothing and every thing else the marauders thought worth carrying away."

—*Harriet Jacobs, from her slave narrative* Incidents in the Life of a Slave Girl, Written by Herself

Document D

Some Measures Passed in Reaction to Nat Turner's Revolt

States	Measures
Virginia	• Passed twenty new statutes regulating the lives of free and enslaved African Americans
Alabama, Maryland, Tennessee	• Forbade free blacks from moving to the state and settling there • Further restricted the ways African Americans could meet
Mississippi	• Required all free blacks to leave the state within ninety days
Alabama, South Carolina	• Punished anyone who attempted to teach enslaved African Americans to read or write
Georgia	• Offered a reward for the arrest of the publisher or anyone caught circulating *The Liberator* or other "seditious" written material

---

1. How might Nat Turner's role as a preacher have been to his advantage in planning the revolt?
- **A** It allowed him to meet with other slaves to plan the revolt.
- **B** It allowed him to travel about the countryside freely.
- **C** It may have given him more influence over other slaves.
- **D** All of the above

2. What attitude towards William Lloyd Garrison's abolitionist newspaper *The Liberator* do both Documents B and D show?
- **A** It is a harmless scandal sheet.
- **B** It gives a good proslavery defense.
- **C** It contains dangerous, seditious propaganda.
- **D** It was of no consequence in the South.

3. How did Nat Turner's revolt affect Harriet Jacobs' town in North Carolina, according to Document C?
- **A** Laws were passed restricting the movement of African Americans.
- **B** Whites beat and stole from African Americans, regardless of their guilt or innocence.
- **C** The commotion allowed Jacobs and other slaves to escape.
- **D** It had no effect.

4. Writing Task How did Nat Turner's revolt affect the lives of slaves and the ongoing debate about slavery in the United States? Summarize the effects of the revolt. Use your knowledge of the time period and the documents above to support your main points.

CHAPTER

9 Manifest Destiny
1800–1850

WITNESS HISTORY

Westward Ho!

"Westward the course of empire takes its way," an Irish bishop wrote of North America in 1726. Little more than a century later, American empire builders fulfilled his prophecy. Thousands of pioneers moved westward along such routes as the Oregon Trail. This song of the 1850s captures their spirit:

> "The western fields give thousands wealth,
> Ho! Westward Ho!
> And yield to all a glowing health,
> Ho! Westward Ho!
> For all inclined to honest toil,
> Ho! Westward Ho!
> Secure their fortunes from the soil,
> Ho! Westward Ho!"
>
> —Ossian E. Dodge, "Ho! Westward Ho!"

◄ After traveling along the Oregon Trail in 1866, William Henry Jackson painted this view of wagon trains approaching Chimney Rock in Nebraska.

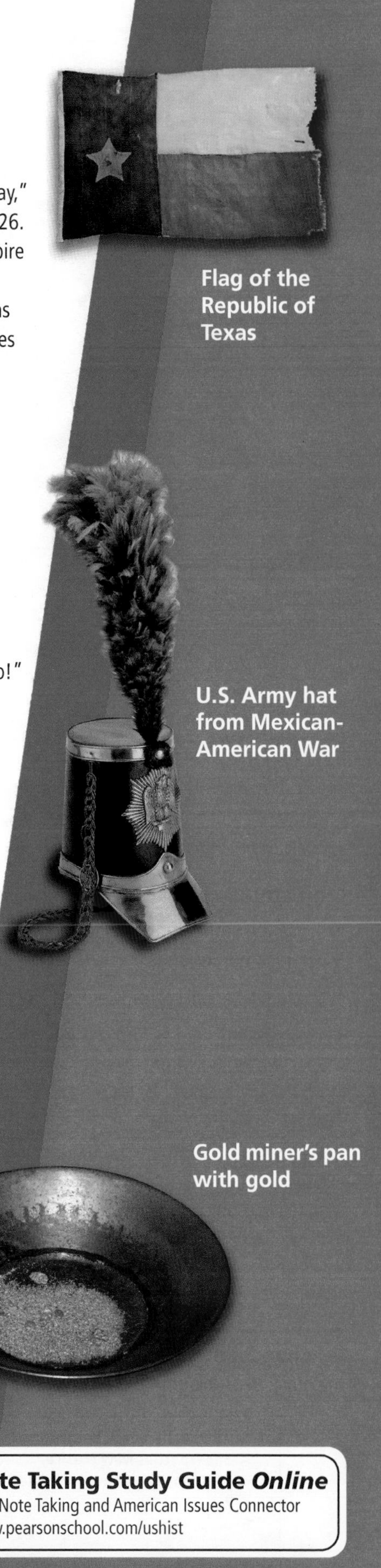

Flag of the Republic of Texas

U.S. Army hat from Mexican-American War

Gold miner's pan with gold

Chapter Preview

Chapter Focus Question: What were the causes and effects of westward expansion in the early 1800s?

Section 1
Migrating to the West

Section 2
Texas and the Mexican-American War

Section 3
Effects of Territorial Expansion

Use the ☑ **Quick Study Timeline** at the end of this chapter to preview chapter events.

Note Taking Study Guide *Online*
For: Note Taking and American Issues Connector
www.pearsonschool.com/ushist

SECTION 1

◄ Western-bound wagon train

WITNESS HISTORY

A Pioneer Woman Heads West

On April 9, 1853, Amelia Stewart Knight left Iowa with her family to join a wagon train headed for Oregon. Her diary describes many of the hazards of the five-month trek, from extreme heat or cold to poisonous water. It also reports encounters—some cordial and some tense—with Native Americans. In one entry, Knight wrote:

"After looking in vain for water, we were about to give up as it was near night, when husband came across a company of friendly Cayuse Indians about to camp, who showed him where to find water, half mile down a steep mountain, and we have all camped together, with plenty of pine timber all around us. . . . We bought a few potatoes from an Indian, which will be a treat for our supper."

—Diary of Mrs. Amelia Stewart Knight, 1853

Migrating to the West

Objectives

- Trace the settlement and development of the Spanish borderlands.
- Explain the concept of Manifest Destiny.
- Describe the causes and challenges of westward migration.

Terms and People

Junípero Serra	Mountain Men
expansionist	Oregon Trail
Manifest Destiny	Brigham Young
Santa Fe Trail	Treaty of Fort Laramie

NoteTaking

Reading Skill: Identify Main Ideas Outline the main ideas relating to westward migration.

I. Settling the Spanish Borderlands
  A. Spain Settles New Mexico
    1. Colony is sparsely populated
    2.
  B.
II.

Why It Matters Since colonial times, Americans seeking economic opportunity had looked westward. By the 1840s, migrants were crossing the Rocky Mountains to Oregon and California. In time, these and other western lands would become part of the United States, helping the nation grow in both wealth and power. **Section Focus Question: What were the causes of westward migration?**

Settling the Spanish Borderlands

In 1830, what is now the American Southwest was considered Northern Mexico. Like the former British colonies in the East, this region had a long colonial history, one that dated back to the Spanish conquest of the Americas.

Spain Settles New Mexico Founded in 1598, New Mexico was the oldest colony along New Spain's northwestern frontier. Yet, by 1765, only about 9,600 colonists lived in New Mexico, half of them in the two major towns of El Paso and Santa Fe. The rest lived on farms and ranches scattered through the long Rio Grande valley. One factor discouraging further settlement was the threat of war with nomadic Native Americans in surrounding areas. Colonists depended for protection on an alliance with local Pueblo Indians. But disease steadily reduced the Pueblo population, from about 14,000 in 1700 to about 10,000 in 1765.

At the same time, the nomads of the Great Plains, known to the Spanish as Apaches, were becoming more powerful. The Apaches lived by hunting vast herds of buffalo. These hunts became easier after 1680 when the Apaches acquired horses from the Spanish. On horseback, men could see farther, travel faster, and kill their prey more quickly and in greater safety. At the same time, the nomads began to acquire firearms from French traders. The Indians continued to hunt with bows and arrows, but they used guns to wage war.

Warfare Threatens the Colony In 1800, a trader on the Great Plains remarked, "This is a delightful country and, were it not for perpetual wars, the natives might be the happiest people on earth." The conflict stemmed largely from competition for the buffalo herds. Well-armed groups, such as the Comanches of the Rocky Mountains and the Lakotas of the Mississippi Valley, spread at the expense of Apaches and other long-time residents of the Great Plains.

The defeated Apaches fled west into New Mexico, where they raided Pueblo and Spanish settlements, taking horses, sheep, cattle, and captives. Some Apaches found a haven in the canyons of northwest New Mexico, where they became known as Navajos. The Pueblos taught their Navajo neighbors how to weave, make pottery, grow corn, and herd sheep. But most Apaches remained nomadic hunters.

Raids on Spanish settlements became more frequent and destructive, for the Apaches were now armed, mounted, and desperate. The Comanches began to attack New Mexico as well. In 1777, a governor sadly reported that Indian raids had reduced his colony "to the most deplorable state and greatest poverty."

Spanish officials rescued New Mexico by building stronger frontier defenses and using more flexible diplomacy with the nomads. By providing gifts and weapons, the new officials found it cheaper to form bonds with some nomads than to fight them all. In general, Spain paid Comanche and Navajo allies to attack the Apaches. For the most part, the strategy worked.

Although most Apache groups remained defiant, some accepted peace on Spain's terms. And the alliance program did reduce raids on New Mexico. As the colony became safer, its population grew and its economy developed. By 1821, the Hispanic population had grown to about 40,000.

Texas Attracts Few Settlers New Mexico's growth and improved security did not extend to Texas, its sister colony to the east along the Gulf of Mexico. In Texas, the nomads were more formidable and the colony remained weaker.

The Spanish had founded Texas as a buffer zone to protect the valuable towns and mines of Mexico to the south. Like New Mexico, Texas was a mixture of ranches, missions, and military *presidios.* But Texas stagnated because few settlers felt attracted to such a distant and poor region subject to nomadic raiders. In 1760, only about 1,200 colonists lived in Texas, primarily in and around San Antonio. Ranchers drove longhorn cattle southward for sale in Mexico.

Missions Thrive in California In the 1760s, the Spanish extended their northern buffer zone to the west by colonizing the California coast. They were

A Spanish Colonial Mission

Many of the oldest buildings in the Southwest are Spanish missions, like this one in Texas. Native Americans were forced to live and work on the mission grounds, where Spanish priests taught them about Christianity.

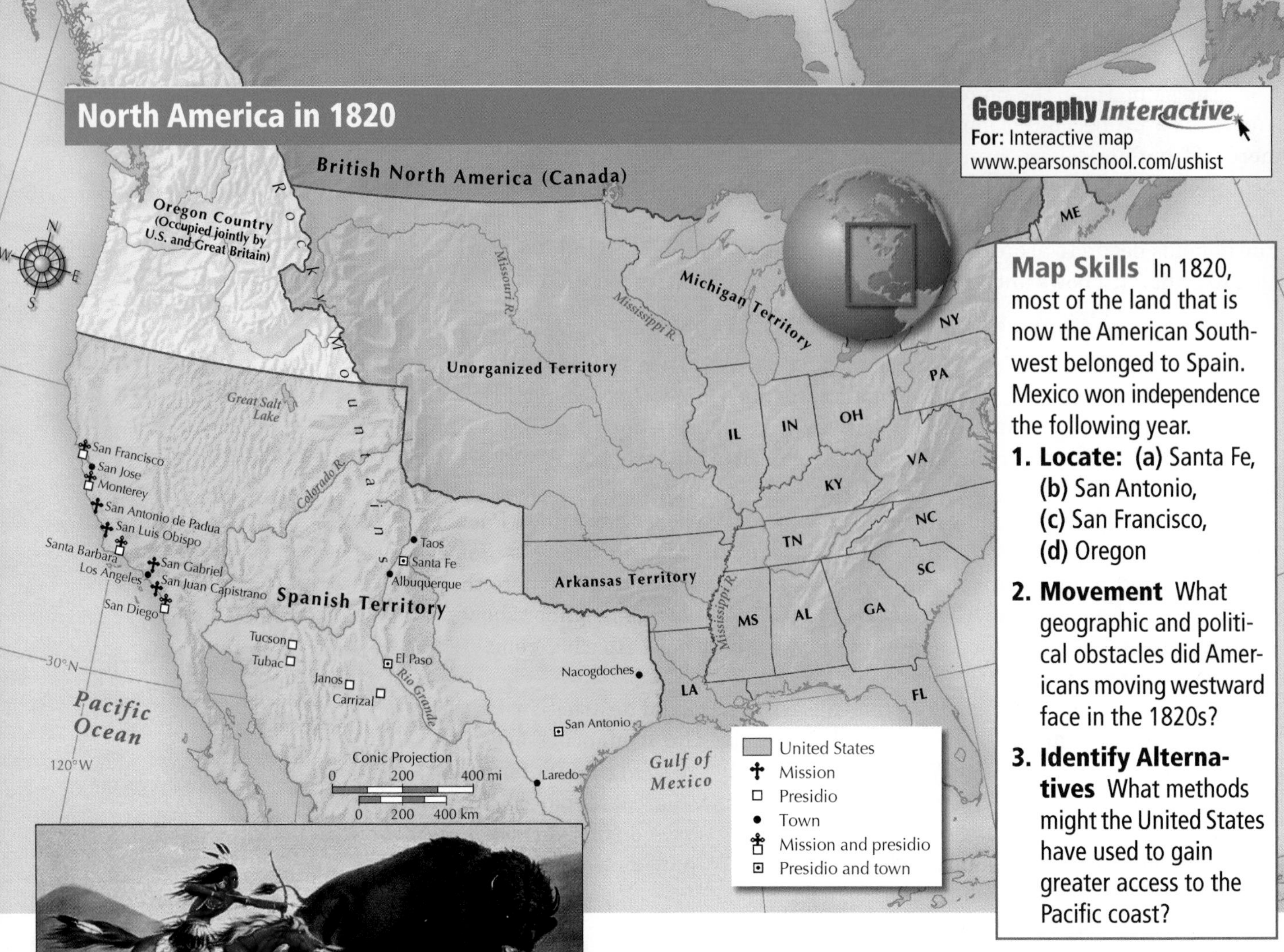

Map Skills In 1820, most of the land that is now the American Southwest belonged to Spain. Mexico won independence the following year.

1. **Locate:** (a) Santa Fe, (b) San Antonio, (c) San Francisco, (d) Oregon
2. **Movement** What geographic and political obstacles did Americans moving westward face in the 1820s?
3. **Identify Alternatives** What methods might the United States have used to gain greater access to the Pacific coast?

This 1832 painting depicts a Native American buffalo hunt on the Great Plains. Nomadic hunters depended for survival on free movement across northern Mexico and the western U.S. territories.

afraid of losing the region to Russian traders probing south from Alaska. As in Texas, Spain had trouble attracting settlers to California. Potential settlers were daunted by California's isolation from Mexico. The distance to market discouraged the export of California's livestock and grains. The limited economy depended on royal money sent to supply and pay the soldiers.

Lacking colonists, the Spanish leaders sought to convert Indians to Christianity. Led by Father **Junípero Serra,** Franciscan priests set up a string of missions. The missions were more successful in California than in Texas or New Mexico. Because the local Indians lacked guns and horses, California missions suffered few raids. By the time of Father Serra's death in 1784, California had two agricultural towns (San Jose and Los Angeles), four *presidios,* and nine missions. In 1821, when Spanish rule ended, the system had grown to 20 missions housing more than 18,000 Native American converts. The Native Americans constructed buildings, dug irrigation ditches, erected fences, herded cattle, and cultivated grain. But large numbers died of diseases, and the Spanish had to round up more Indians to replace them.

✓ **Checkpoint How did conflict develop between Spanish settlers and Native Americans in the Southwest?**

Americans Look Westward

In 1821, a revolution toppled Spanish rule and established Mexico as an independent republic. The U.S. government officially recognized its fellow republic to the south. But American **expansionists,** people who favored territorial growth, soon began to covet New Mexico, Texas, and California. Thinly settled but rich in resources, the three provinces seemed ripe for American plucking.

Expansionists Seek Manifest Destiny

Expansionists justified their views by pointing to the weakness of the Mexican government and economy. They argued that the Mexicans, whom many Americans regarded as inferior, did not deserve to keep lands so badly needed for American settlement.

In 1845, journalist John L. O'Sullivan wrote an influential editorial in favor of expansion:

Primary Source "The American claim is by the right of our manifest destiny to overspread and possess the whole of the continent which Providence has given us for the development of the great experiment of liberty and . . . self-government entrusted to us."

—John L. O'Sullivan, *New York Morning News,* December 27, 1845

Vocabulary Builder
manifest–(MAN uh fehst) *adj.* obvious; clear; plain

Expansionists were soon using the term **Manifest Destiny** to refer to the belief that God wanted the United States to own all of North America. But O'Sullivan envisioned liberty primarily for white men. Expansion would come at the expense of Indians and Mexicans. And southern expansionists hoped to add more slave states to strengthen their political position in Congress.

Americans Trade With Mexico

Mexican independence spurred American trade with northern Mexico. The Spanish had discouraged such contacts, but Mexican officials welcomed them. Indeed, trade and migration promoted economic growth in the border provinces. Still, as the Spanish had feared, American traders and settlers would come to threaten the security of Mexico's border.

Merchants from Missouri saw Mexican independence as an opportunity to open trade across the Great Plains with Santa Fe, the capital of New Mexico. Welcomed by the Mexican officials, the traders launched a growing commerce along what became known as the **Santa Fe Trail.** In exchange for American manufactured goods, the New Mexicans offered horses, mules, furs, and silver.

In the 1820s, mariners from the Northeast launched a more ambitious route. Sailing around South America to the California coast, they traded manufactured goods for tallow and hides from California ranches. Like New Mexico, California became economically dependent on commerce with the Americans.

Mountain Men Cross the Rockies

Other traders ventured up the Missouri River and into the Rockies, seeking valuable furs from the abundant beaver of the mountain streams. The daring young American trappers who hunted for beaver pelts in the Rockies were called **Mountain Men.** Most worked for two large fur companies, which provided their supplies.

Restless in pursuit of furs, the Mountain Men thoroughly probed the Rockies, making important discoveries. They blazed the best route through the mountains, via South Pass in what is now Wyoming. Some Mountain Men then pressed westward to the Great Salt Lake in the arid Great Basin of Utah. In 1826, Jedediah Smith crossed the Great Basin and the Sierra Nevada to reach California. In addition to trapping, he traded with the Mexican residents. Smith's trade and migration route became the California Trail, linking the United States with the Pacific coast.

Mountain Men
As this painting shows, Mountain Men lived a solitary, rugged existence as they hunted beaver in the Rocky Mountains. In time, they undermined their own way of life, killing beaver faster than the beaver could reproduce. *What dangers would Mountain Men face? Why do you think they were willing to face them?*

Focus On Geography

Trails to the West

During the 1840s alone, nearly 20,000 Americans migrated to California, Oregon, and Utah along the major overland trails. The trails also became trade routes, carrying merchants and goods in both directions.

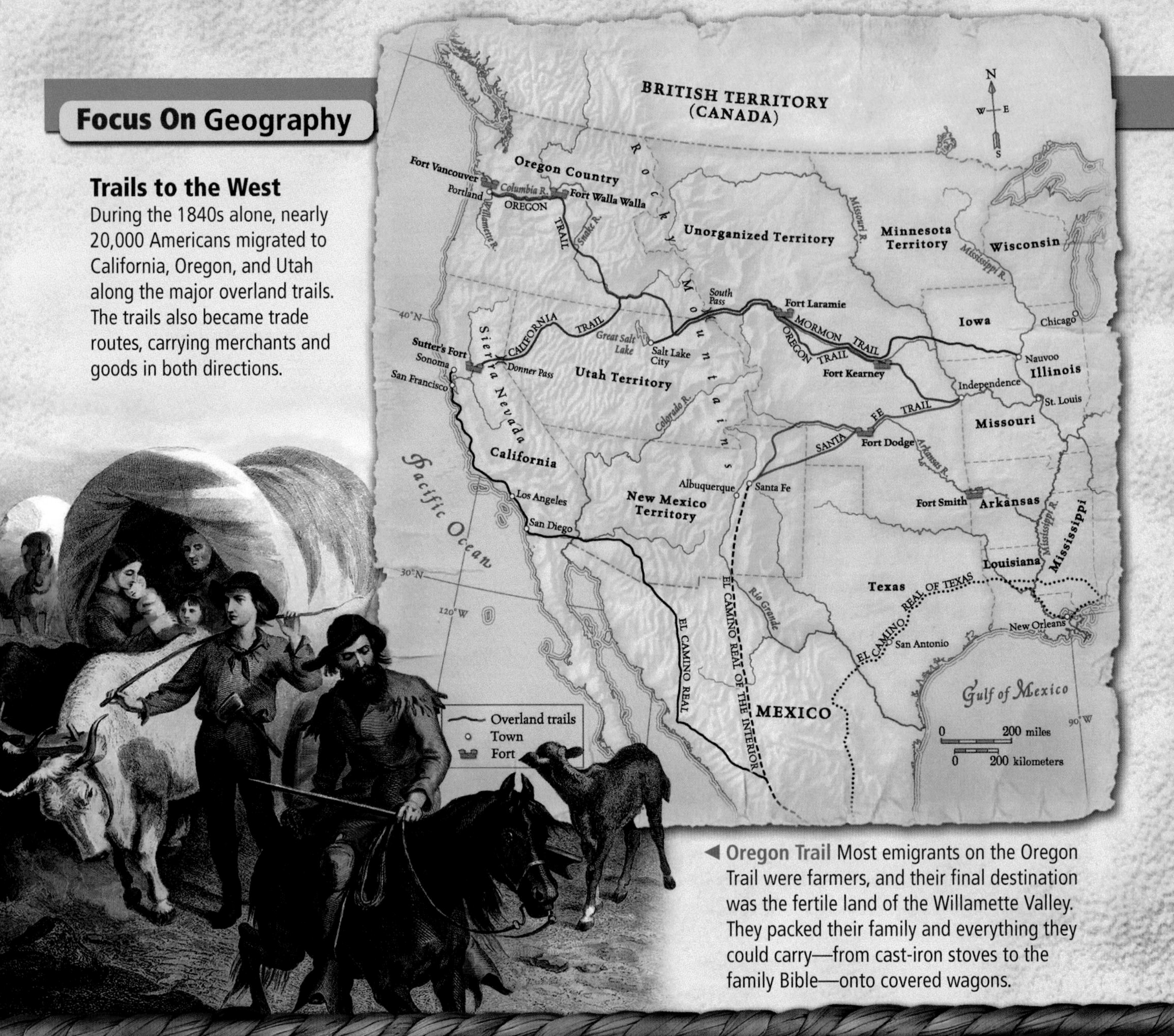

◀ **Oregon Trail** Most emigrants on the Oregon Trail were farmers, and their final destination was the fertile land of the Willamette Valley. They packed their family and everything they could carry—from cast-iron stoves to the family Bible—onto covered wagons.

Missionaries Reach Oregon A variant of this trail turned northwest at South Pass to reach Oregon Country. In 1836, Marcus and Narcissa Whitman followed this route, which became known as the **Oregon Trail,** to found an Indian mission at Walla Walla.

The Whitman compound served as a magnet and way station for farm families bound farther west to the fertile Willamette Valley. In 1847, the Whitmans were killed by Native Americans who blamed them for a deadly measles epidemic. But by then, the tide of migration to Oregon was unstoppable.

✓ **Checkpoint What role did the Mountain Men play in westward expansion?**

The Journey Westward

In 1842, an official government expedition led by John C. Frémont set off across the western country, following trails blazed by the Mountain Men and the Whitmans. Although Frémont found little that was new, his vivid and romantic reports gave wider publicity to the fertility of the Far West. In the years that followed, the overland trails drew thousands of settlers west to California and Oregon.

◀ **Mormon Trail** The final destination for Mormon emigrants was the Great Salt Lake in present-day Utah. Through extensive irrigation and farming, Mormon settlers permanently altered their desert environment.

Westward Migration, 1840s

Western Trail	Number of Settlers	Where To	When
California Trail	2,700	California	1842–1848
Mormon Trail	4,600	Utah	1847–1848
Oregon Trail	11,500	Oregon	1842–1848

SOURCE: CIA World Factbook Online

Supplies for Travelers Forts along the overland trails provided more than protection. They were also homes to trading posts, where wagon trains could replenish their supplies. ▼

◀ **Donner Pass** For emigrants, mountain passes could be a gateway to their final destination—or a snowy tomb. The Donner Pass was named for a party who got trapped in the Sierra Nevadas in the winter of 1846–1847. Nearly half died of starvation, and the survivors resorted to eating their dead.

Geography and History

- How did the goals of travelers on the Oregon and Mormon trails differ? How were they similar?
- Do deserts and mountain passes still present a hazard to travelers today? Why or why not?

Wagon Trains Journey West Commencing in springtime at the western edge of Missouri, the demanding journey covered nearly 2,000 miles and took about five months to complete. Oxen pulled the emigrants' wooden wagons covered with canvas. For security and mutual help, most emigrants traveled in trains of from 10 to 100 wagons and from 50 to 1,000 people. Eager to get to the fertile and humid Pacific, the emigrants bypassed the Great Plains, which they considered little better than a desert, and the Great Basin, which truly was a desert. They were also in a hurry to get across two cold and lofty mountain chains, the Rockies and the Sierra Nevada.

Vocabulary Builder
commence–(kuh MEHNS) *v.* to begin a project or an enterprise

Most of the emigrants were farm people from the Midwest. Men relished the journey as an adventure, while many women more keenly felt the hardships and anxieties. "What had possessed my husband, anyway, that he should have thought of bringing us away out through this God-forsaken country?" wrote one woman in her diary.

Indeed, the journey was a gamble that cost many their property and some their lives. Emigrants faced hunger, exposure, disease, poisoned streams—or worse. In 1846, the Donner Party got lost on the way to California. Trapped by snow in the Sierra Nevada, the starving survivors resorted to cannibalism.

History Makers

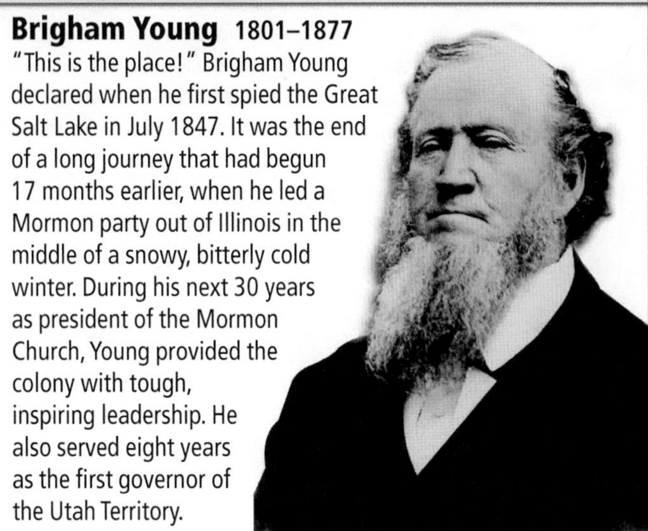

Brigham Young 1801–1877

"This is the place!" Brigham Young declared when he first spied the Great Salt Lake in July 1847. It was the end of a long journey that had begun 17 months earlier, when he led a Mormon party out of Illinois in the middle of a snowy, bitterly cold winter. During his next 30 years as president of the Mormon Church, Young provided the colony with tough, inspiring leadership. He also served eight years as the first governor of the Utah Territory.

Despite the dangers, the rewards of the journey could be great. Most of those who persevered gained bigger and better farms in Oregon or California than they had owned in the East or Midwest. Between 1840 and 1860, about 260,000 Americans crossed the continent to settle on the west coast.

Mormons Seek a Refuge One group of people preferred to settle along the way. These were the Mormons. As you read in the last chapter, Mormon founder Joseph Smith was killed in 1844 by a mob in Illinois.

Leadership passed to **Brigham Young,** a brilliant organizer with a powerful will. Convinced that the Mormons could not survive among hostile neighbors, Young organized an exodus. In 1847, he led Mormons across the Great Plains and the Rockies to establish the colony of New Zion on the eastern shore of the Great Salt Lake. Through hard work and cooperation, the Mormons made the arid land bloom by diverting water from mountain streams. By 1860, some 40,000 Mormons lived in the West.

Despite their achievements and their isolation, other Americans continued to distrust the Mormons. During the 1850s, after the territory had passed from Mexico to the United States, the government forced the Mormons to accept federal authority. New Zion became the federal territory of Utah.

Indians Face Restrictions So long as wagons kept moving west, Native Americans usually left them alone. Still, the federal government sought to protect migrants by restricting the Plains Indians. The 1851 **Treaty of Fort Laramie** bound the Indians to territories away from the major trails. But the Indians clung to their mobile way of life, pursuing buffalo across all artificial boundaries. As migration continued, the stage was set for future conflict.

✓ **Checkpoint What difficulties and opportunities awaited migrants to the West?**

SECTION 1 Assessment

Progress Monitoring *Online*
For: Self-test with vocabulary practice
www.pearsonschool.com/ushist

Comprehension

1. **Terms and People** Write a sentence explaining how each of the following was connected with westward migration.
   - Manifest Destiny
   - Santa Fe Trail
   - Mountain Men
   - Oregon Trail
   - Brigham Young
   - Treaty of Fort Laramie
2. NoteTaking **Reading Skill: Identify Main Idea** Use your outline to answer the Section Focus Question: What were the causes of westward migration?

Writing About History

3. **Quick Write: Identify an Issue** In the news media, an editorial is a statement supporting one view of a current issue. Choose a topic from this section as the subject for an editorial. Write a sentence explaining why people of the time might have held differing views on that issue.

Critical Thinking

4. **Recognize Effects** What long-term effects did the introduction of horses and firearms have on Native Americans in the West?
5. **Recognize Viewpoints** Who might have agreed with the idea of Manifest Destiny? Who might have disagreed?
6. **Make Decisions** If you were a poor farmer in 1850, would you have chosen to join a wagon train to the West? Why or why not?

Texas "Lone Star" flag ▶

SECTION 2

▲ Texans defend the Alamo

WITNESS HISTORY

A Child at the Alamo

In March 1836, Mexican troops attacked the Alamo in San Antonio, Texas. Among those inside the old mission was eight-year-old Enrique Esparza. His father, Gregorio, was one of a group of Texans engaged in a struggle to win independence from Mexico. Some 70 years later, Esparza recalled hearing sounds of shooting at two in the morning:

"I heard my mother say: 'Gregorio, the soldiers have jumped the wall. The fight's begun.' He got up and picked up his arms and went into the fight. I never saw him again. . . . It was so dark that we couldn't see anything, and the families that were in the quarters just huddled up in the corners. My mother's children were near her. Finally they began shooting through the dark into the room where we were. A boy who was wrapped in a blanket in one corner was hit and killed."

—Enrique Esparza, *San Antonio Express,* 1907

Texas and the Mexican-American War

Objectives

- Explain how Texas won independence from Mexico.
- Analyze the goals of President Polk.
- Trace the causes and outcome of the Mexican-American War.

Terms and People

Stephen F. Austin	Alamo
Antonio López de Santa Anna	Sam Houston
autonomy	James K. Polk
Lone Star Republic	Zachary Taylor
	Winfield Scott

NoteTaking

Reading Skill: Recognize Sequence Look for the steps that led to war with Mexico.

Mexico encourages Americans to settle in Texas.
↓ ↓ ↓

Why It Matters With American expansionists seeking new territory and Mexico in control of most of the land to the south and west, conflict between the two nations seemed almost inevitable. The flashpoint for conflict became Texas. In time, that conflict would lead to a war that would vastly increase the size of the United States. **Section Focus Question: How did the revolution in Texas lead to war with Mexico?**

Texas Wins Independence

Of all the Mexican provinces, Texas was most vulnerable to U.S. expansion. Offering abundant, fertile land, Texas lay closest to the United States. And it had only a small Hispanic population, known as *Tejanos* (teh HAH nohs), to defend the province. In 1821, only about 4,000 Tejanos lived in Texas.

Americans Migrate to Texas To develop and defend the province, Mexico adopted a risky strategy: It agreed to allow Americans to settle in Texas. In return for cheap land grants, Americans had to agree to become Mexican citizens, to worship as Roman Catholics, and to accept the Mexican constitution, which banned slavery. Mexico hoped this strategy would convert American settlers from a potential threat to an economic asset.

Led by **Stephen F. Austin,** American emigrants began to settle east of San Antonio, founding the town of Austin. Like settlers on other frontiers, these newcomers sought the economic opportunity of good farmland in large portions. Mostly coming from the southern United States, they raised corn, pigs, cattle, and cotton. By 1835, Texas was home to about 30,000 American settlers, known as Anglo-Texans. They outnumbered Tejanos by about six to one.

Tensions Build Relations between Anglo-Texans and the Mexican government soured by 1830. Despite their oaths of allegiance and their land grants, the settlers had not honored their part of the bargain. They remained Protestants and ignored Mexico's slavery ban by smuggling in enslaved African Americans to work their farms and plantations. In turn, the Anglo-Texans felt dismayed by the unstable Mexican government, which suffered from military coups.

In 1834, the charismatic but ruthless general **Antonio López de Santa Anna** seized power in Mexico City. Santa Anna favored a centralized, authoritarian government dominated by the military. His coup troubled those liberal Mexicans who preferred a decentralized federal system like that of the United States. Santa Anna's rule especially angered the people of Texas, both Anglo-Texans and Tejanos, who wanted greater **autonomy,** or independent control over their own affairs. One Anglo-Texan protested that Santa Anna would "give liberty to our slaves and make slaves of ourselves."

Texans Revolt In 1835, the Texans rebelled against Mexican rule. They seized the Mexican garrisons at Goliad and San Antonio. A year later, the Texans declared their independence and adopted a republican constitution. Their new nation became known as the **Lone Star Republic** because of the single star on its flag.

To crush the rebellion, Santa Anna led his army north into Texas. In March 1836, his forces attacked the small Texan garrison at the **Alamo,** a fortified former mission in San Antonio. After 12 days of cannon fire, Mexican troops overran the walls of the Alamo. Refusing to keep prisoners, Santa Anna ordered the defenders slaughtered. The victims included Anglo-Texans Jim Bowie and Davy Crockett, as well as a dozen Tejanos. A few weeks later, Santa Anna ordered a similar mass execution of Texan prisoners who had surrendered at Goliad.

Santa Anna expected the slaughter to frighten other Texans into surrendering. Instead, the fallen defenders of the Alamo became martyrs to the cause of Texan independence. The slogan "Remember the Alamo" rallied the Texans and attracted volunteers to their cause from the southern United States.

Led by **Sam Houston,** the Texans drew Santa Anna eastward into a trap. In April, they surprised and crushed the Mexican army at the Battle of San Jacinto. Houston's men killed 630 and captured 730 Mexicans, including Santa Anna himself, while suffering only 32 casualties.

Fearing execution, Santa Anna signed a treaty recognizing Texan independence. He conceded generous boundaries that stretched the new republic south and west to the Rio Grande. On paper, Texas even got half of New Mexico, including its capital of Santa Fe.

Of course, the government in Mexico City refused to honor a treaty forced on a captured and disgraced

HISTORY MAKERS

Sam Houston (1793–1863)

Sam Houston was the only American to serve as governor of two different states—first Tennessee, then Texas. In between, he was commander of the Texan army, president of the Republic of Texas, and U.S. senator from Texas.

Houston was not afraid to take unpopular stands. An adopted Cherokee, he once said that "in presenting myself as the advocate of the Indians and their rights, I shall stand very much alone." In addition, though himself a slaveholder, he angered proslavery forces by opposing the spread of slavery into the West. Finally, in 1861, when Houston spoke out against Texas seceding from the Union, he was removed from the governorship of the state he had helped create.

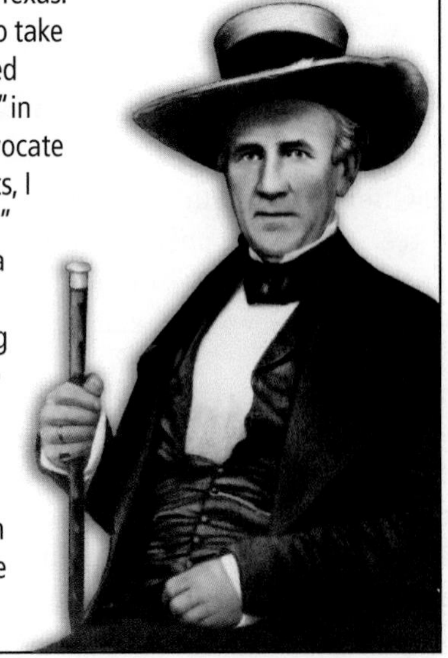

Decision Point

Should the United States Annex Texas?

From the time it achieved independence, Texas sought U.S. statehood. America's leaders had to decide whether to annex Texas. The 1844 presidential rivals James Polk and Henry Clay disagreed on the issue. Read their views below. Then, you make the call.

Polk Favors Annexation

Primary Source

"None can fail to see the danger to our safety and future peace if Texas remains an independent state or becomes an ally or dependency of some foreign nation more powerful than herself. Is there one among our citizens who would not prefer perpetual peace with Texas to occasional wars, which so often occur between bordering independent nations?"

—James K. Polk, inaugural address, 1845

Clay Opposes Annexation

Primary Source

"Annexation and war with Mexico are identical. Now, for one, I certainly am not willing to involve this country in a foreign war for the object of acquiring Texas. . . . I regard all wars as great calamities, to be avoided, if possible, and honorable peace as the wisest and truest policy of this country."

—Henry Clay, "Raleigh Letter," 1844

You Decide

1. Why did Polk think annexation would promote peace?
2. Why did Clay think annexation would lead to war?
3. What decision would you have made? Why?

dictator. The Mexicans only would accept an independent Texas that remained within its traditional boundaries, which extended no farther south than the Nueces River. For the next decade, a border war persisted between Texas and Mexico.

 **Checkpoint** **What issues led Anglo-Texans and Tejanos to seek independence from Mexico?**

Americans Debate Expansion

Texans elected Sam Houston as their first president. He quickly asked the United States to annex Texas. President Jackson privately favored the request, but he could not overcome opposition in Congress. Northern representatives balked at adding another slave state, especially one so big and potentially powerful. For nearly a decade, Texas continued to apply in vain for annexation. Houston tried to pressure Congress by pretending to consider joining the British Empire. At the time, Britain and the United States jointly occupied the Oregon Territory in the Pacific Northwest. The prospect alarmed expansionists.

An Expansionist Becomes President The annexation of Texas became a key issue in the 1844 presidential election. Southern expansionists supported **James K. Polk** of Tennessee. A Jacksonian Democrat and a slaveholder, Polk devoutly believed in Manifest Destiny. Whig candidate Henry Clay opposed annexation.

Polk reasoned that northerners would accept the annexation of Texas if they got their own prize. He promised them the Oregon Territory. Polk threatened to go to war with Britain if it did not concede all of Oregon. Polk's vow to obtain both Texas and Oregon helped him win a decisive electoral victory.

Vocabulary Builder
reluctant–(rih LUHK tuhnt) *adj.* unwilling; marked by mental hesitation or reservations

Polk Compromises on Oregon However, northern Democrats soon felt betrayed by the new President. They had reluctantly supported annexing Texas because Polk had also vowed to grab all of Oregon. Instead, in June 1846 Polk compromised with the British, agreeing to split the Oregon Territory at the 49th parallel of latitude. The United States got the future states of Washington, Oregon, and Idaho. The British kept what became the Canadian province of British Columbia. An Ohio Democrat sputtered, "Our rights to Oregon have been shamefully compromised. The administration is Southern, Southern, Southern!"

Polk compromised because the nation could not afford two wars. He wanted to fight weak Mexico rather than powerful Britain. Indeed, by the time the Oregon compromise was completed, war with Mexico had already begun.

 **Checkpoint What compromise did the United States and Britain reach regarding the Oregon Territory?**

The Mexican-American War

A month before Polk took office, Congress narrowly voted to annex Texas, which entered the Union as a slave state in December 1845. Annexation inflamed the long-standing border dispute between Texas and Mexico. Polk endorsed the Texan claim to the land south and west of the Nueces River as far as the Rio Grande. This claim tripled the traditional size of Texas. Outraged, the Mexicans refused to recognize the annexation.

Congress Declares War Polk sent American troops led by General **Zachary Taylor** to occupy the contested borderland between the two rivers. While waiting for the inevitable conflict, Polk drafted a declaration of war. He did not have to wait long. In May 1846, a Mexican patrol clashed with American soldiers, killing eleven. Polk rushed his war message to Congress:

> **Primary Source** "We have tried every effort at reconciliation. . . . But now, after reiterated menaces, Mexico has passed the boundary of the United States, has invaded our territory and shed American blood upon the American soil."
>
> —James K. Polk, war message to Congress, May 11, 1846

Of course, the Mexicans saw the clash differently: To them it was an American invasion that shed Mexican blood on Mexican soil.

Democrats, especially those from the South, were enthusiastically in favor of war with Mexico. Most Whigs, especially those from the North, opposed war. They believed that Polk had deliberately provoked the war by sending troops to Texas. Whigs also feared that Polk would not settle for even the biggest version of Texas but planned to annex the adjacent northern Mexican provinces, including New Mexico and California. The conquered territories might then become slave states, increasing southern power in Congress.

Vocabulary Builder
adjacent–(uh JAY suhnt) *adj.* neighboring; nearby

Despite their suspicions, most Whigs did not dare block the declaration of war. They knew that the war had wide popular support—and they remembered the demise of the Federalist Party after it had opposed the War of 1812. On May 13, Congress voted overwhelmingly to declare war on Mexico.

U.S. Forces Sweep to Victory In the war, the United States had great advantages. It was much larger, wealthier, and more populous than Mexico. The Mexicans lacked the industries that so quickly and abundantly supplied the Americans with arms and ammunition. The Americans also had a larger and better navy and more advanced artillery. Above all, the United States enjoyed superb officers, well trained at the military academy at West Point. Generals Zachary Taylor and

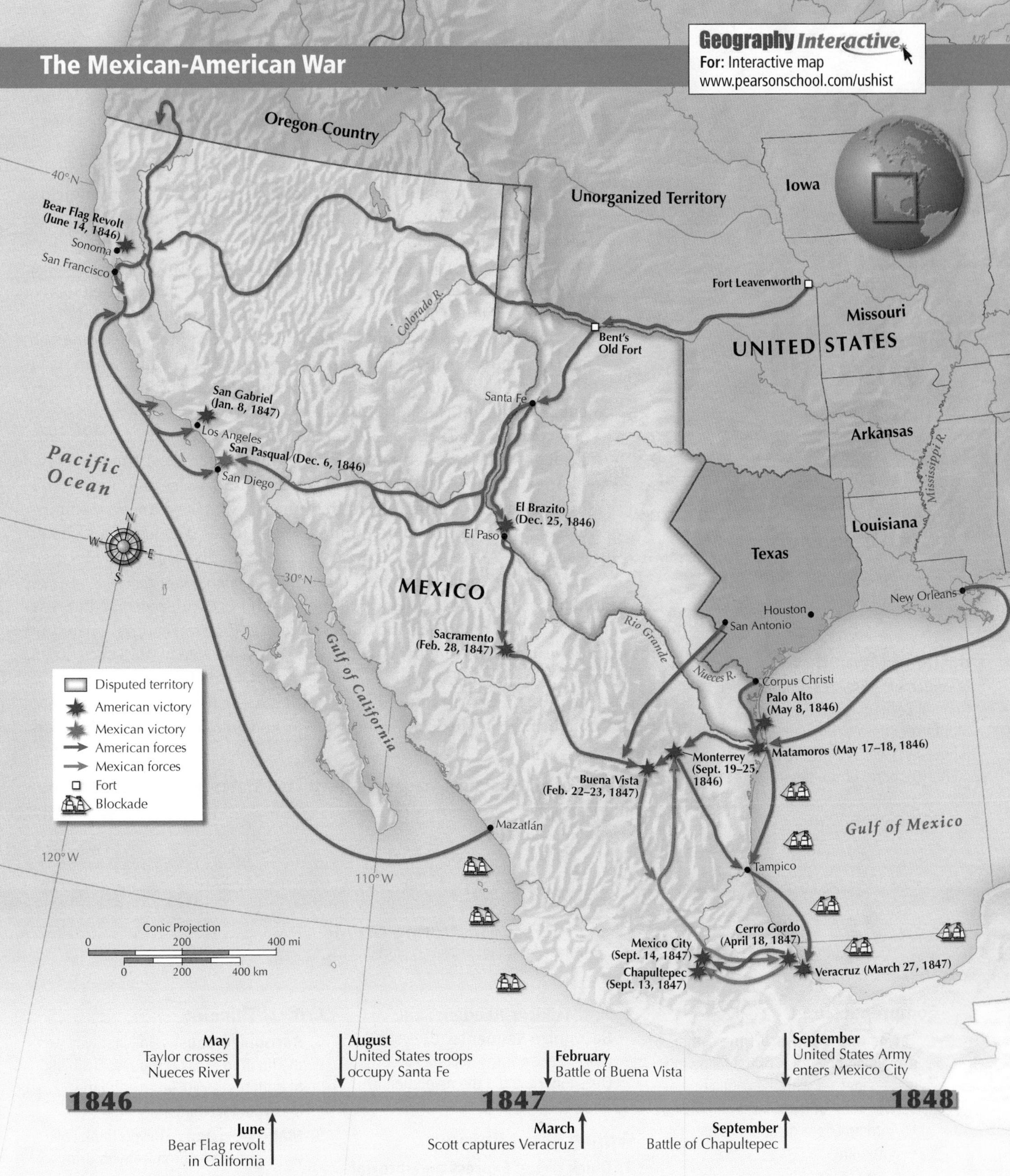

Map Skills The Mexican-American War of 1846–1847 began in Texas. During the war, the United States won every major battle.

1. **Locate:** **(a)** Nueces River, **(b)** Rio Grande, **(c)** California, **(d)** Monterrey, **(e)** Veracruz, **(f)** Mexico City
2. **Region** What region on the map was the subject of the land dispute that sparked the war?
3. **Synthesize Information** Use the map and chart to describe U.S. troop movements in the final month of the war.

Winfield Scott received exceptional support from their junior officers, including Robert E. Lee, Ulysses S. Grant, and William T. Sherman. (All these men would later play key roles in the U.S. Civil War.) Meanwhile, Mexicans were bitterly divided because Santa Anna had resumed his dictatorship.

In this one-sided war, the United States won every major battle. During the summer of 1846, General Stephen W. Kearny quickly conquered New Mexico. Meanwhile, the U.S. Navy helped American settlers, led by explorer John C. Frémont, to seize control of California. Until they could legally join the United States, these rebels organized the short-lived Bear Flag Republic. Frémont joined forces with Kearny to bring all of California under American control.

Taylor led another army deeper into northern Mexico, seizing the city of Monterrey in September. In February 1847, Santa Anna tried to retake the city. But Taylor's small army defeated the more numerous Mexicans at the bloody Battle of Buena Vista.

By early 1847, American forces had achieved all of Polk's war goals—but he wanted more. A New England critic of the war complained that with every victory, "Our Manifest Destiny higher and higher kept mounting." In March, the navy carried another American army, commanded by Winfield Scott, to the Mexican port city of Veracruz. After seizing the port, Scott boldly marched his men through 200 miles of rugged terrain to Mexico City.

Scott faced bitter resistance at Chapultepec (chah POOL tuh pehk), a fortress above Mexico City. The defenders included six young Mexican cadets—ranging in age from 13 to 19—who fought to the death. Today, Mexico honors the cadets who fell at Chapultepec as *Los Niños Héroes,* or the Child Heroes.

In September 1847, Scott captured Mexico City. After little more than a year and a half of fighting, the Mexican-American War had ended in a thorough American victory.

Battle of Monterrey
In September 1846, U.S. troops under General Zachary Taylor attacked Monterrey, Mexico. The plumed hat (above left) was part of the U.S. military uniform of the time.

Checkpoint What advantages did the United States have in the Mexican-American War?

SECTION 2 Assessment

Progress Monitoring *Online*
For: Self-test with vocabulary practice
www.pearsonschool.com/ushist

Comprehension

1. **Terms and People** Write a sentence explaining how each of the following was connected with the conflict between the United States and Mexico.
   - Antonio López de Santa Anna
   - autonomy
   - Lone Star Republic
   - Alamo
   - Sam Houston
   - James K. Polk
   - Zachary Taylor
2. **NoteTaking Reading Skill: Recognize Sequence** Use your chart to answer the Section Focus Question: How did the revolution in Texas lead to war with Mexico?

Writing About History

3. **Quick Write: Express an Editorial Position** Imagine that you are the editor of either a southern Democrat or a northern Whig newspaper in 1844. Write a topic sentence for an editorial supporting either Polk or Clay for the presidency. Make sure your sentence clearly identifies your position.

Critical Thinking

4. **Recognize Causes** In what way was the fighting in Texas the responsibility of both the Anglo-Texans and the Mexican government?
5. **Make Decisions** Do you think Polk was right to compromise with Britain over Oregon? Explain.
6. **Draw Conclusions** Do you think the U.S. declaration of war against Mexico was justified? Why or why not?

▲ Chinese miners in California

Gold mining pan with gold ▶

WITNESS HISTORY

Seeking a Mountain of Gold

By 1849, poor farmers in China had received word of a "mountain of gold" across the Pacific Ocean. Soon, thousands of Chinese men joined fortune seekers from all over the world in a rush to the gold fields of California. However, the Chinese newcomers often faced a hostile reception. In a letter home to his parents, one young American miner described the unfair treatment of Chinese miners:

> "They are coming by thousands all the time The miners in a great many plases will not let them work The miners hear drove off about 200 Chinamen about two weeks ago but they have com back about as thick as ever (I would not help drive them off as I thought they had no rite to drive them)."
>
> —Robert W. Pitkin, 1852

Effects of Territorial Expansion

Objectives

- Explain the effects of the Mexican-American War on the United States.
- Trace the causes and effects of the California Gold Rush.
- Describe the political impact of California's application for statehood.

Terms and People

Treaty of Guadalupe Hidalgo	California Gold Rush
Gadsden Purchase	forty-niners
Wilmot Proviso	placer mining
	hydraulic mining

NoteTaking

Reading Skill: Understand Effects Trace the effects of the Mexican-American War.

Why It Matters As a result of its quick victory in the Mexican-American War, the United States would finally achieve the expansionists' goal of Manifest Destiny. Yet, the long-term effects of the war served to highlight growing differences between North and South and set the stage for future conflict. **Section Focus Question: What were the effects of the Mexican-American War and the California Gold Rush?**

America Achieves Manifest Destiny

In February 1848, the defeated Mexicans made peace with the Americans. The **Treaty of Guadalupe Hidalgo** (gwah duh LOO pay ee THAHL goh) forced Mexico to give up the northern third of their country and added 1.2 million square miles of territory to the United States.

The United States Gains Territory In return for leaving Mexico City and paying $15 million, the United States kept New Mexico and California. The nation also secured the Rio Grande as the southern boundary of Texas.

The treaty angered the Mexican people who continued for decades to feel bitterness toward the United States. The treaty also dismayed Polk, but for a different reason. After Scott captured Mexico City, the President decided that he wanted to keep more of Mexico. He blamed his negotiator, Nicholas Trist, for settling for too little. But Polk had no choice but to submit the treaty to Congress because northern public opinion would not support a longer war.

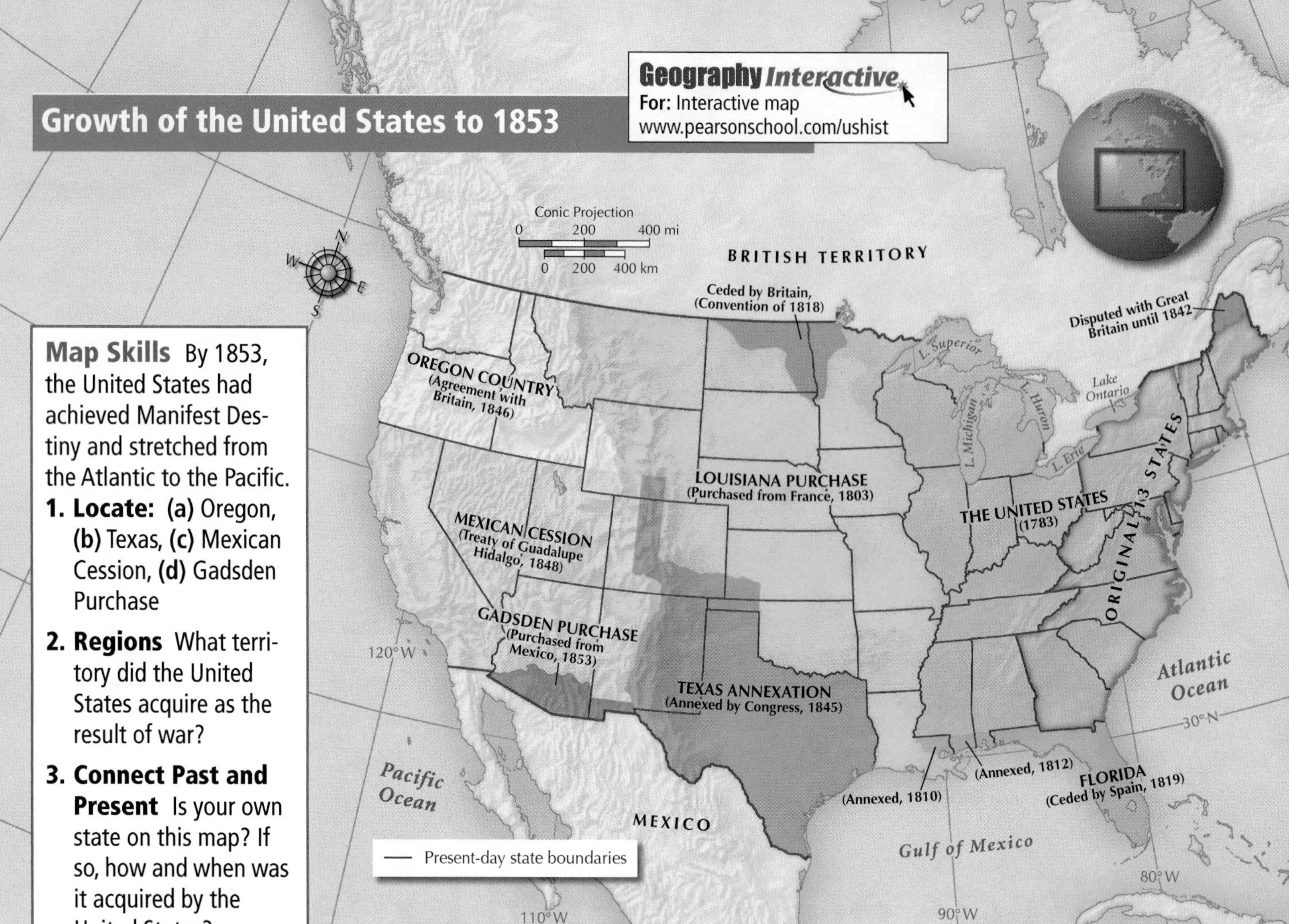

Map Skills By 1853, the United States had achieved Manifest Destiny and stretched from the Atlantic to the Pacific.

1. **Locate: (a)** Oregon, **(b)** Texas, **(c)** Mexican Cession, **(d)** Gadsden Purchase
2. **Regions** What territory did the United States acquire as the result of war?
3. **Connect Past and Present** Is your own state on this map? If so, how and when was it acquired by the United States?

In the **Gadsden Purchase** of 1853, the United States obtained from Mexico another 29,640 square miles in southern Arizona and New Mexico. The Americans bought this strip to facilitate a railroad across the continent. Along with the annexation of Texas, the Treaty of Guadalupe Hidalgo and the Gadsden Purchase increased the area of the United States by about one third. Only the Louisiana Purchase had added more territory. The new lands comprised present-day New Mexico, California, Nevada, Utah, Arizona, and half of Colorado.

Vocabulary Builder
comprise–(kuhm PRĪZ) *v.* to include; to make up

The Wilmot Proviso Divides Americans Even before the war ended, the prospect of gaining land from Mexico stirred fierce debate in the United States. In 1846, Whig congressman David Wilmot of Pennsylvania had proposed a law, known as the **Wilmot Proviso,** that would ban slavery in any lands won from Mexico. The proposal broke party unity and instead divided Congress largely along sectional lines. Most northern Democrats joined all northern Whigs to support the Wilmot Proviso. Southern Democrats joined southern Whigs in opposition. The Proviso passed in the House of Representatives, but it failed narrowly in the Senate.

The Wilmot Proviso would reappear in every session of Congress for the next 15 years. Repeatedly, it passed in the House only to fail in the Senate. The Proviso brought the slavery issue to the forefront and weakened the two major parties, which had long tried to avoid discussing the issue in Congress. Thus, the lands won from Mexico increased tensions between North and South.

✓ **Checkpoint How did the Mexican-American War serve to heighten tensions over slavery?**

The California Gold Rush

To most Americans, the new lands in the West seemed too distant for rapid settlement. But in early 1848, workers at John Sutter's sawmill found flecks of gold in the American River east of Sacramento, California.

Forty-Niners Flock to California By summer, news of the gold strike caused a sensation in the eastern United States. In a mass migration known as the **California Gold Rush,** some 80,000 fortune seekers headed for California in search of easy riches. About half of these **forty-niners** traveled by land trails. Another half went by ship around South America or via a short land passage at the Isthmus of Panama. The ships landed their human cargo in San Francisco.

The golden news also attracted miners from around the Pacific Rim. Many fortune seekers came from South America, especially Peru and Chile. Another 25,000 laborers migrated from China to California during the 1850s. From a mere 14,000 in 1847, California's population of outside settlers surged to 225,000 in just five years.

Miners Lead a Rough Life Forty-niners flocked to the gold fields with high hopes. One young man described the excitement of departing for California from Indiana:

> **Primary Source** "The diggings had been discovered but a twelve-month before, and the glowing tales of their marvelous richness were on every tongue. Our enthusiasm was wrought up to the highest pitch, while the hard-ships and perils . . . were scarcely given a passing thought."
>
> —David Rohrer Leeper, "The Argonauts of '49"

At first, the miners used cheap metal pans, picks, and shovels to harvest gold flecks from the sand along the banks and bottoms of rivers and streams. This process was known as **placer mining.** A few miners got rich, but most worked hard for little gain. Because food and clothing were so expensive, shrewd traders made more money selling goods to the miners than the miners made by panning for gold.

Conditions were hard in the crowded mining camps. Poor sanitation promoted diseases, especially cholera and dysentery, killing hundreds. In addition, life was cheap and law was scarce in the camps. Almost all of the inhabitants were men, who felt frustrated by their failure to find much gold and by their lack of family life. Competition and fights became common. One forty-niner noted, "It is surprising how indifferent people become to the sight of violence and bloodshed in this country."

In search of order, the miners carried out their own rough justice. Without official legal authority, they acted as judges, juries, and executioners.

Methods of Mining Change Placer mining soon gave way to more efficient methods that required more money and equipment. One method was to dam and divert rivers to expose their beds. Another method, **hydraulic mining,** employed jets of water to erode gravel hills into long lines of sluices to catch the gold. Hydraulic mining damaged the environment by leveling hills and clogging rivers with sediment.

The Lure of California Gold

The California gold fields attracted thousands of men and a smaller number of women (bottom). The poster (below, left) advertises ship passage to California. *What does the guidebook (below, right) suggest about the appeal of the California Gold Rush?*

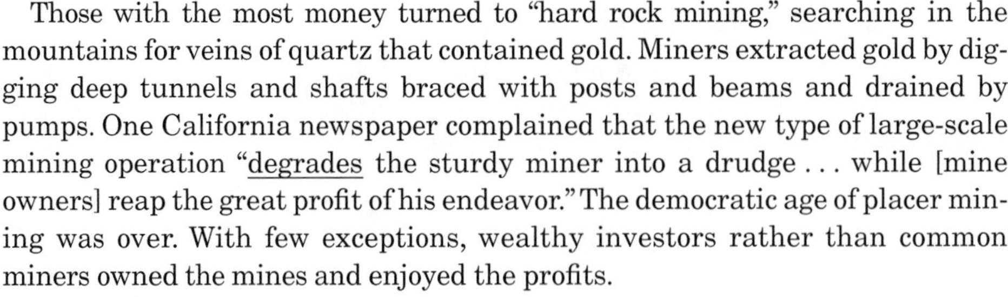

Those with the most money turned to "hard rock mining," searching in the mountains for veins of quartz that contained gold. Miners extracted gold by digging deep tunnels and shafts braced with posts and beams and drained by pumps. One California newspaper complained that the new type of large-scale mining operation "degrades the sturdy miner into a drudge . . . while [mine owners] reap the great profit of his endeavor." The democratic age of placer mining was over. With few exceptions, wealthy investors rather than common miners owned the mines and enjoyed the profits.

Vocabulary Builder
degrade–(dee GRAYD) *v.* to reduce in status or rank

Checkpoint **What problems did forty-niners face in the California gold fields?**

INFOGRAPHIC

San Francisco: GROWTH OF A CITY

For those traveling by ship, San Francisco was the gateway to the California gold fields. It was also a place where miners could come to buy supplies, exchange gold for cash, or relax. Through migration and trade, San Francisco quickly became *the* major American city on the Pacific coast in the 1800s.

A Fast Trip West
This 1851 advertisement promises a superfast trip from New York around the southern tip of South America to San Francisco—in as little as 97 days!

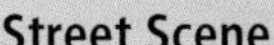

Street Scene
This painting shows a busy street market in 1850 San Francisco.

Before and After What happened to San Francisco between 1848 (above) and 1850 (below)? One word explains the rapid building boom: GOLD!

Growth of San Francisco

Year	Population
1848	800
1849	25,000
1852	36,000
1860	57,000

SOURCE: sfgenealogy.com

Thinking Critically

1. **Draw Inferences** What kind of businesses do you think sprang up in San Francisco as a result of the Gold Rush?
2. **Draw Conclusions** What other circumstances might cause rapid changes in a city's population?

History *Interactive*
For: To discover more about the growth of San Francisco
www.pearsonschool.com/ushist

Effects of the Gold Rush

Newcomers from the eastern United States quickly asserted their dominance over California. To discourage the Chinese, they levied a heavy tax on foreign miners.

Indians and Mexicans Face Discrimination White miners also terrorized and killed Native Americans by the thousands. Losing their land, many surviving Indians became workers on farms and ranches.

Mob violence drove most Mexican Americans away from the gold fields. Those who stayed had to pay the foreign miners' tax, though Mexicans had been in California long before the new American majority. *Californios*, or Mexican Californians, also lost most of their land. Contrary to the Treaty of Guadalupe Hidalgo, the courts ignored land titles created under Mexican law.

California Seeks Statehood The new Californians wanted quickly to organize a state and enter the union. In October 1849, their leaders held a convention and drew up a state constitution. The new constitution excluded African Americans, both slave and free. Most of the new Californians were northerners who did not want to compete with southern slaveholders who could use slave labor to seek gold. Nor did the miners want any free blacks to live in California.

California's application for statehood stirred discord between North and South. At the time, the Union was comprised of 15 free states and 15 slave states. Admission of a new free state would thus tip the delicate regional balance in the Senate. Over the next decade, debate over the spread of slavery into the lands won from Mexico would grow increasingly bitter. Thus, westward expansion became a major source of the division that ultimately led to the tragic Civil War.

Checkpoint **What impact did the settlement of California have on Mexicans already living there?**

HISTORY MAKERS

Mariano Vallejo
(1808–1890)

Mariano Vallejo lived under Spanish, Mexican, and U.S. rule. The son of wealthy landowners, he became a general in the Mexican army. Critical of the Mexican government, Vallejo welcomed the arrival of U.S. settlers. Though he was briefly imprisoned during the Bear Flag revolt, he continued to support the American cause, serving as a delegate to the California constitutional convention and as a state legislator. But like many Californios, he lost most of his land to white settlers when the courts refused to recognize his family land grants. Vallejo lived his final years on a small fragment of his once large ranch.

SECTION 3 Assessment

Progress Monitoring *Online*
For: Self-test with vocabulary practice
www.pearsonschool.com/ushist

Comprehension

1. **Terms and People** Write a sentence explaining how each of the following was connected with westward expansion.
   - Treaty of Guadalupe Hidalgo
   - Gadsden Purchase
   - Wilmot Proviso
   - California Gold Rush
   - forty-niners
   - placer mining
   - hydraulic mining
2. **NoteTaking Reading Skill: Recognize Effects** Use your chart to answer the Section Focus Question: What were the effects of the Mexican-American War and the California Gold Rush?

Writing About History

3. **Quick Write: Write an Editorial** Write an editorial on the Wilmot Proviso that might have appeared in an 1846 newspaper. Define the issue and give reasons to support one position.

Critical Thinking

4. **Apply Information** How did the Treaty of Guadalupe Hidalgo settle the chief issues that led to the Mexican-American War?
5. **Draw Conclusions** Who benefited most from the California Gold Rush? Who benefited least?
6. **Evaluate Information** What do you think was the most important long-term result of the Mexican-American War? Explain.

CHAPTER 9

Quick Study Guide

Progress Monitoring *Online*
For: Self-test with vocabulary practice
www.pearsonschool.com/ushist

Spain Settles the Southwest

The Spanish Borderlands

New Mexico	Texas	California
• Oldest Spanish colony in borderlands • Warfare with Apache nomads discourages settlement • Spain builds defenses; some Apaches accept life on reservations • Hispanic population grows	• Settled by Spanish as buffer zone to protect Mexico • Warfare with Native Americans discourages settlement • Cattle ranching is central to economy	• Colonized to prevent Russian settlement • Distance from Mexico discourages settlement • Strong mission system; Native Americans forced to live and work on missions

Westward Migration

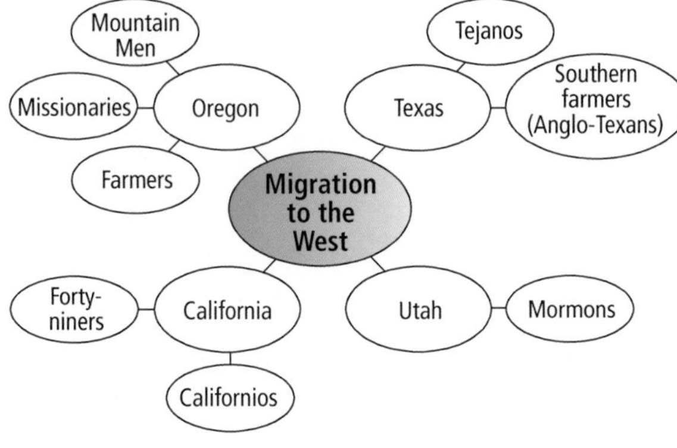

The Mexican-American War

Cause and Effect

Causes

- Expansionists pursue Manifest Destiny.
- Texas wins independence from Mexico.
- Boundary dispute arises between Mexico and Texas.
- United States annexes Texas.
- President Polk sends U.S. troops into disputed area of Texas.
- Mexican and U.S. troops clash in Texas.

↓

Mexican-American War

↓

Effects

- United States wins quick victory.
- Treaty of Guadalupe Hidalgo cedes Southwest to United States.
- Wilmot Proviso is proposed, then defeated in Congress.
- Issue of slavery in West divides nation.
- Mexican Americans in West lose many rights.
- Americans migrate to California during Gold Rush.

Quick Study Timeline

In America

1826
Jedediah Smith blazes California Trail

1836
Texas declares independence

Presidential Terms

James Monroe 1817–1825

John Quincy Adams 1825–1829

Andrew Jackson 1829–1837

Martin Van Buren 1837–1841

1820 **1830**

Around the World

1821
Mexico wins independence

1834
Santa Anna becomes dictator of Mexico

American Issues Connector

By connecting prior knowledge with what you have learned in this chapter, you can gradually build your understanding of enduring questions that still affect America today. Answer the questions below. Then, use your American Issues Connector study guide (or go online: www.pearsonschool.com/ushist).

Issues You Learned About

- **America Goes to War** Events in Texas led the United States to go to war with Mexico, its neighbor to the south.

1. Prior to the Mexican-American War, what conflicts had the United States fought?
2. What justification did the United States make for declaring war on Mexico? What do you think Mexico thought about this reasoning?
3. What advantages did the United States have over Mexico in the Mexican-American War?

- **Territorial Expansion of the United States** The United States has gradually added territory through purchase and treaties and as a result of wars.

4. What was the importance of the Louisiana Purchase?
5. Would the Mexican-American War have occurred if expansionists had not hoped to gain control of Mexico's northern territories? Explain.
6. How did the settlement of California by gold seekers impact the lives of the people already settled there?

- **Sectionalism and Nationalism** People may hold political opinions that are based on the particular needs of the region in which they live.

7. What challenge caused the greatest debate between northerners and southerners during the early to mid-1800s? Give specific examples of issues that were part of this debate.
8. Was the balance of power in the Senate tipped by the admission of California into the Union? Explain.

Connect to Your World — Activity

Migration and Urbanization The 1836 population of Los Angeles totaled 2,288 residents, including 553 Native Americans and only 29 white Americans. The vast majority were Mexican. Go online or to your local library and conduct research to learn the current population of Los Angeles. Investigate the figures, such as how many people live there, what percentage of the population is made up of immigrants, and where these immigrants came from, as well as the cultural influences that have shaped the city over the years and which are still seen in Los Angeles today. Use your findings to write a paragraph or two explaining the ethnic character of modern-day Los Angeles.

History *Interactive* For: Interactive timeline www.pearsonschool.com/ushist

1846 Mexican-American War begins

1848 Gold is discovered in California

1851 Treaty of Fort Laramie

1853 Gadsden Purchase

1861 Civil War begins

William H. Harrison 1841
John Tyler 1841–1845
James K. Polk 1845–1849
Zachary Taylor 1849–1850
Millard Fillmore 1850–1853
Franklin Pierce 1853–1857
James Buchanan 1857–1861

1840 — 1850 — 1860

1846 Britain compromises with United States on Oregon

1849 Chinese immigration to America begins

Chapter Assessment

Terms and People

1. What was the chief goal of American **expansionists**?
2. What was the **Oregon Trail**? Which settlers traveled along this trail, and why?
3. What was the goal of the **Treaty of Fort Laramie**? How did it affect Native Americans?
4. Who were **Antonio López de Santa Anna** and **Sam Houston**? How were the two men linked?
5. How did **James K. Polk** encourage territorial expansion?
6. What was the **Gadsden Purchase**? Why did the United States seek this purchase?
7. What was the **Wilmot Proviso**? Did it unite or divide Congress? Explain.
8. What was the goal of the **forty-niners**?

Focus Questions

The focus question for this chapter is **What were the causes and effects of westward expansion in the early 1800s?** Build your answer to this big question by answering the focus questions for Sections 1 through 3 and the Critical Thinking questions that follow.

Section 1

9. What were the causes of westward migration?

Section 2

10. How did the revolution in Texas lead to war with Mexico?

Section 3

11. What were the effects of the Mexican-American War and the California Gold Rush?

Critical Thinking

12. **Identify Central Issues** Why was settlement so limited in Spain's northern territories? How successful was Spain's effort to encourage settlement?
13. **Identify Point of View** Did people who believed in Manifest Destiny support the acquisition of New Mexico, Texas, and California? Explain.
14. **Predict** Why might the role of the Mormon Church in the government of the Utah Territory become a source of future conflict with the federal government?
15. **Summarize** Present a brief history of Texas that spans the period from the 1700s through the mid-1800s. What do you think were the two most important turning points in Texas history?
16. **Compare Points of View** Why did most northerners tend to oppose the Mexican-American War while most southerners tended to support it?
17. **Explain Effects** How did the Oregon settlement and the Treaty of Guadalupe Hidalgo change the map of North America?
18. **Draw Conclusions** Why do you think so few women or families made their way west to live and work in the California mining camps?
19. **Explain Effects** Identify three effects of the California Gold Rush. Which effect do you think was most important in the long term? Explain.
20. **Categorize** Throughout the 1800s, farmers traveled west in search of land. What other specific groups of Americans made their way west in the 1800s, and why?

Writing About History

Writing an Editorial The purpose of an editorial, whether in a newspaper or in the broadcast media, is to influence public opinion on a current issue. Imagine that you are a newspaper editor in the mid-1800s. Write an editorial on one of the following topics: the idea of Manifest Destiny; the Texas war for independence; the Treaty of Guadalupe Hidalgo; California's application for statehood.

Prewriting

- Identify a specific issue connected with your topic. The issue should be one on which there might have been at least two possible opposing viewpoints.
- Choose a context for your editorial. For example, are you writing for a northern or southern newspaper? An Anglo-Texan or Mexican newspaper?
- Identify your editorial viewpoint on the topic. List reasons in favor of that viewpoint.

Drafting

- Write an opening statement in which you briefly but clearly define the issue.
- State your editorial opinion.
- Clearly state the reasons why you think your readers should support your position.

Revising

- Use the guidelines for revising your writing on page SH16 of the Writing Handbook.

Document-Based Assessment

New Settlement in the Mexican Cession

After the Mexican-American War, Mexico lost about one third of its territory to the United States. This land, called the Mexican Cession, attracted American settlers. What happened to the Mexicans who now found themselves living in a different country? Use your knowledge of American history and Documents A, B, C, D, and E to answer questions 1 through 4.

Document A
The Mexican Cession

Entire State	Part of State
• Texas (Texas Annexation) • California (Mexican Cession) • Nevada (Mexican Cession) • Utah (Mexican Cession) • Arizona (Mexican Cession, Gadsden Purchase) • New Mexico (Mexican Cession, Gadsden Purchase, Texas Annexation)	• Oklahoma (Texas Annexation) • Kansas (Texas Annexation) • Colorado (Texas Annexation, Mexican Cession) • Wyoming (Texas Annexation, Mexican Cession)

Document B

"Mexicans now established in territories previously belonging to Mexico . . . shall be free to continue where they now reside. . . . In the said territories, property of every kind, now belonging to Mexicans not established there, shall be inviolably respected. . . . The Mexicans who, in the territories aforesaid, shall not preserve the character of citizens of the Mexican Republic . . . shall be incorporated into the Union of the United States and be admitted at the proper time . . . to the enjoyment of all the rights of citizens of the United States, according to the principles of the Constitution; and in the mean time, shall be maintained and protected in the free enjoyment of their liberty and property, and secured in the free exercise of their religion without restriction."

—*Treaty of Guadalupe Hidalgo, 1848*

Document C

"That ultimately the whole of Mexico will be embraced in our Union, there is very little room to doubt. That dislike to Americans of the North, which was a characteristic of the Mexicans, founded on prejudice, has to a very remarkable extent given way to admiration, and a desire for closer intimacy. . . ."

—*"Mexico and the Mexicans,"* The United States Democratic Review, *June 1850*

Document D

"What a difference between the present time and those that preceded the Americans. If the Californios could all gather together to breathe a lament, it would reach heaven as a moving sigh which would cause fear and consternation in the Universe. What misery!"

—*Mariano Vallejo, late 1800s*

Document E

"Unlike earlier [American] colonists, these new settlers came as conquerors. In most areas they were vastly outnumbered by Mexicans who had recently been given citizenship and, supposedly, equal rights. The Anglo settlers most likely felt insecure as a minority and so they, the conquerors, set out to subdue the conquered. Mexican Americans soon found that they were discriminated against and treated like aliens in lands they felt rightfully belonged to them. Their land was taken from them; their political power, or the potential for it, usurped, and their social position threatened."

—A History of the Mexican-American People, *Julian Samora, 1977*

---

1. According to Document A, which of the following states was not affected by the Treaty of Guadalupe Hidalgo?
A Oklahoma
B Nevada
C New Mexico
D Wyoming

2. According to Document B, Mexican residents in the Mexican Cession
A were required to surrender to American forces.
B were forced to sell their lands.
C would enjoy equal rights.
D would have to move to Mexico.

3. Which of the following pairs of documents express similar main ideas?
A B and D
B C and E
C C and D
D D and E

4. **Writing Task** What were the most important long-term consequences of the Mexican Cession? Use your knowledge of American history and evidence from the sources above to explain your answer.

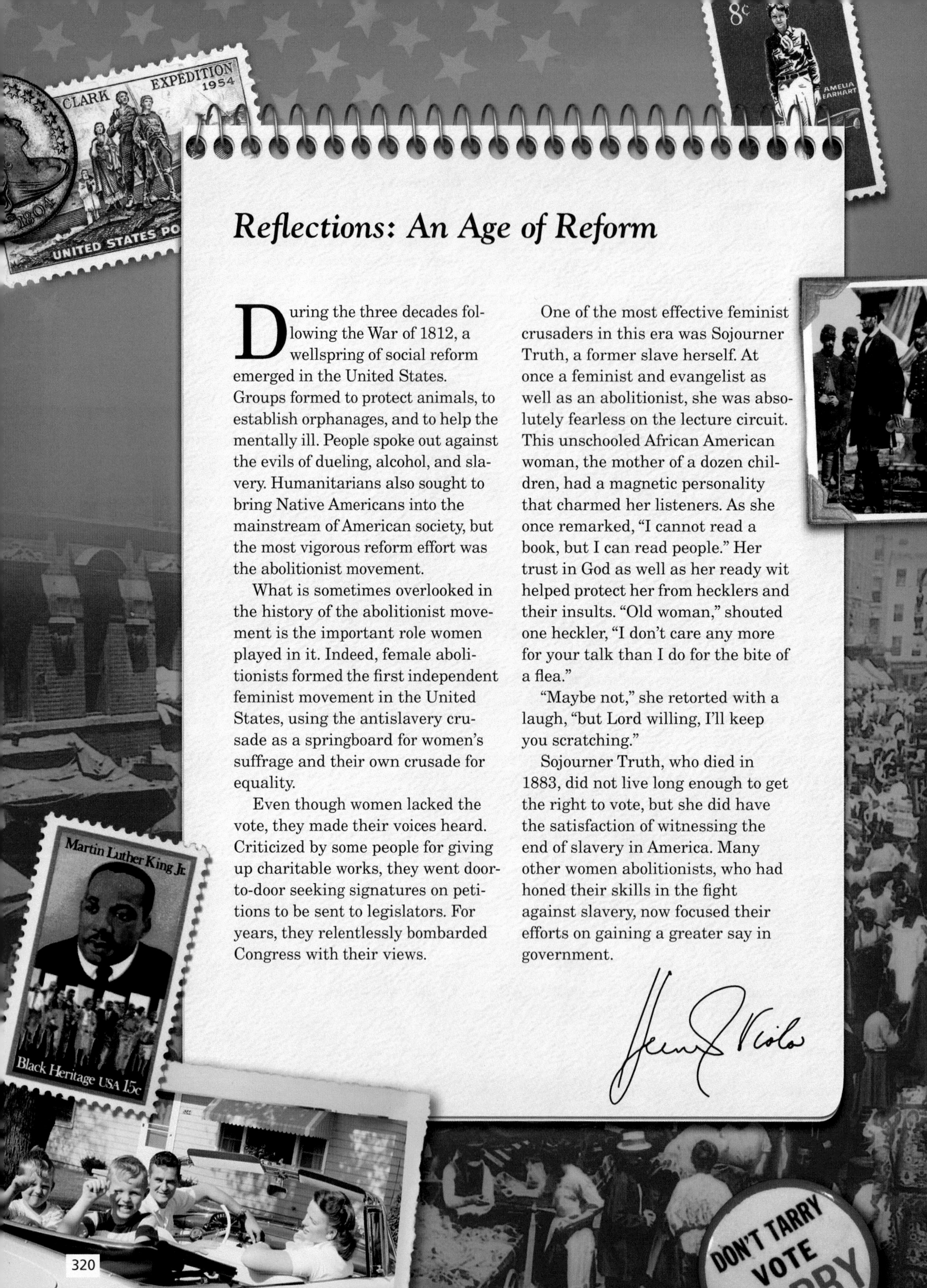

Reflections: An Age of Reform

During the three decades following the War of 1812, a wellspring of social reform emerged in the United States. Groups formed to protect animals, to establish orphanages, and to help the mentally ill. People spoke out against the evils of dueling, alcohol, and slavery. Humanitarians also sought to bring Native Americans into the mainstream of American society, but the most vigorous reform effort was the abolitionist movement.

What is sometimes overlooked in the history of the abolitionist movement is the important role women played in it. Indeed, female abolitionists formed the first independent feminist movement in the United States, using the antislavery crusade as a springboard for women's suffrage and their own crusade for equality.

Even though women lacked the vote, they made their voices heard. Criticized by some people for giving up charitable works, they went door-to-door seeking signatures on petitions to be sent to legislators. For years, they relentlessly bombarded Congress with their views.

One of the most effective feminist crusaders in this era was Sojourner Truth, a former slave herself. At once a feminist and evangelist as well as an abolitionist, she was absolutely fearless on the lecture circuit. This unschooled African American woman, the mother of a dozen children, had a magnetic personality that charmed her listeners. As she once remarked, "I cannot read a book, but I can read people." Her trust in God as well as her ready wit helped protect her from hecklers and their insults. "Old woman," shouted one heckler, "I don't care any more for your talk than I do for the bite of a flea."

"Maybe not," she retorted with a laugh, "but Lord willing, I'll keep you scratching."

Sojourner Truth, who died in 1883, did not live long enough to get the right to vote, but she did have the satisfaction of witnessing the end of slavery in America. Many other women abolitionists, who had honed their skills in the fight against slavery, now focused their efforts on gaining a greater say in government.

Herman J. Viola

CIVIL WAR AND RECONSTRUCTION

CONTENTS

An African American regiment during the Civil War ▶

CHAPTER

10 The Union in Crisis 1846–1861

WITNESS HISTORY

Can Slavery Be Regulated in the Territories?

The slavery debate dominated American politics in the 1850s. Abraham Lincoln, the Republican candidate for the Illinois Senate seat, worried that federal legislation favored slavery by allowing slavery to exist until a territory became a state. Lincoln's opponent, Senator Stephen Douglas, explained how he thought that the people of a territory could close their region to slavery:

> "[P]olice regulations can only be established by the local legislature, and if the people are opposed to slavery they will elect representatives to that body who will by unfriendly legislation effectually prevent the introduction of it into their midst. If, on the contrary, they are for it, their legislation will favor its extension. . . ."
>
> —Stephen Douglas, August 27, 1858, Freeport, Illinois

◀ Abraham Lincoln (standing) and Stephen Douglas (left) debated seven times while campaigning in 1858.

slave shackles

John Calhoun

Lincoln 1860 campaign flag

Chapter Preview

Chapter Focus Question: How did the nation's expansion lead to the Civil War?

Section 1
Slavery, States' Rights, and Western Expansion

Section 2
A Rising Tide of Protest and Violence

Section 3
Political Realignment Deepens the Crisis

Section 4
Lincoln, Secession, and War

Use the Quick Study Timeline at the end of this chapter to preview chapter events.

Note Taking Study Guide *Online*
For: Note Taking and American Issues Connector
www.pearsonschool.com/ushist

SECTION 1

◄ Jefferson Davis

WITNESS HISTORY

Why Limit Slavery Only in the Territories?

The Free-Soil Party argued that slavery should not expand into the territories. Senator Jefferson Davis questioned the new party's motives. Why would they only try to limit slavery in the territories but not in the states? Rather than true concern for the slaves, Davis believed they had another purpose.

"It is not humanity that influences you. . . . It is that you may have an opportunity of cheating [the South] that you want to limit slave territory. . . . It is that you may have a majority in the Congress of the United States and convert the Government into an engine of northern aggrandizement. It is that your section may grow in power and prosperity upon treasures unjustly taken from the South. . . . [Y]ou want . . . to promote the industry of the New England states, at the expense of the people of the South and their industry."

—Senator Jefferson Davis of Mississippi

Slavery, States' Rights, and Western Expansion

Objectives

- Contrast the economies, societies, and political views of the North and the South.
- Describe the role of the Free-Soil Party in the election of 1848.
- Analyze why slavery in the territories was a divisive issue between North and South and how Congress tried to settle the issue in 1850.

Terms and People

Wilmot Proviso	secede
Free-Soil Party	Compromise of 1850
popular sovereignty	Fugitive Slave Act

NoteTaking

Reading Skill: Categorize Organize people, groups, and ideas by their position on slavery.

Position on Slavery		
For	Against	Compromise
• •	• Wilmot Proviso •	• •

Why It Matters From the nation's earliest days, the issue of slavery divided Americans. As the nation expanded, the problem became more pressing. Should slavery be allowed in the new western territories? Southerners said yes; many northerners said no. **Section Focus Question: How did Congress try to resolve the dispute between North and South over slavery?**

Slavery Divides the Nation

After the American Revolution, the North and the South developed distinctly different ways of life. The North developed busy cities, embraced technology and industry, and built factories staffed by paid workers. As immigrants arrived in northern ports, the North became an increasingly diverse society.

The South, on the other hand, remained an agrarian, or agricultural, society. The southern economy and way of life was based largely on a single crop: cotton. To grow cotton, southern planters depended on the labor of enslaved African Americans.

By the mid-nineteenth century, cotton cultivation and slavery had spread across the Deep South—that is, through Florida and Alabama into Louisiana, Mississippi, and Texas. As the country continued to expand, Americans faced a crucial question: Should slavery be allowed to spread to new American territories west of the Mississippi River?

Wilmot Proviso Seeks to Limit Slavery Americans had long avoided the troubling issue of the expansion of slavery. But when the United States gained new territories as a result of the Mexican War in the late 1840s, the nation had to decide whether to admit these lands as slave territories or free territories. The delicate balance of power between North and South—free and slave—depended on this decision.

During the early days of the Mexican War, Pennsylvania congressman David Wilmot had predicted the dilemma. He proposed a law stating, "neither slavery nor involuntary servitude shall ever exist in any" lands won from Mexico. Southerners angrily denounced the **Wilmot Proviso.** The northern-dominated House of Representatives approved the law, but the Senate voted it down.

Northern Views of Slavery Slavery ended early in the North, but slowly. By 1800, there were about 50,000 enslaved people in the North, compared to nearly one million in the South. In 1860, there were still 18 slaves in New Jersey, but none in the other northern states. Most white northerners at the time viewed blacks as inferior. Laws in the northern states severely limited the rights of free African Americans and discouraged or prevented the migration of more. As a result, many white northerners had little personal experience with African Americans, slave or free, and only a few held strong opinions about slavery.

A vocal minority of northerners were abolitionists, or people who wanted to end slavery. They believed that slavery was morally wrong. Some abolitionists favored a gradual end, while others demanded that all slavery be outlawed at once.

Not all northerners wanted to end slavery. Some white northern bankers, mill owners, and merchants earned a lot of money on southern cotton and tobacco or by trading or transporting enslaved people. They were sympathetic to Southern plantation owners and did not want to abolish slavery. Some northern workers—especially those in unskilled, low-paying jobs—also opposed abolition, fearing that freed slaves might come north and compete with them for work.

Southern Views of Slavery Slavery was an integral part of southern life. Many southerners believed that God intended that black people should provide the labor for white "civilized" society. In a speech before Congress in 1837, planter John Calhoun of South Carolina firmly defended and even praised the virtues of slavery. "I hold it [slavery] to be a good . . . ," he said, " . . . and [it] will continue to prove so if not disturbed by the . . . spirit of abolition." Calhoun's words expressed the feelings of many white southerners.

By the 1850s, many southern politicians, journalists, and economists had begun to argue that the northern free labor system harmed society more than slavery did. Southerners claimed that enslaved people were healthier and happier than northern wage workers.

✓ **Checkpoint How did northerners and southerners view slavery?**

The Election of 1848

The Wilmot Proviso had given the nation's political parties a new focus. In the 1848 presidential campaign, both Democrats and Whigs split over the question of whether to limit the expansion of slavery. New political factions emerged, with slavery at the center of debate.

A Slave Auction

An 1861 English engraving depicts a slave auction. The horrors of slavery led to the growth of the antislavery movement.

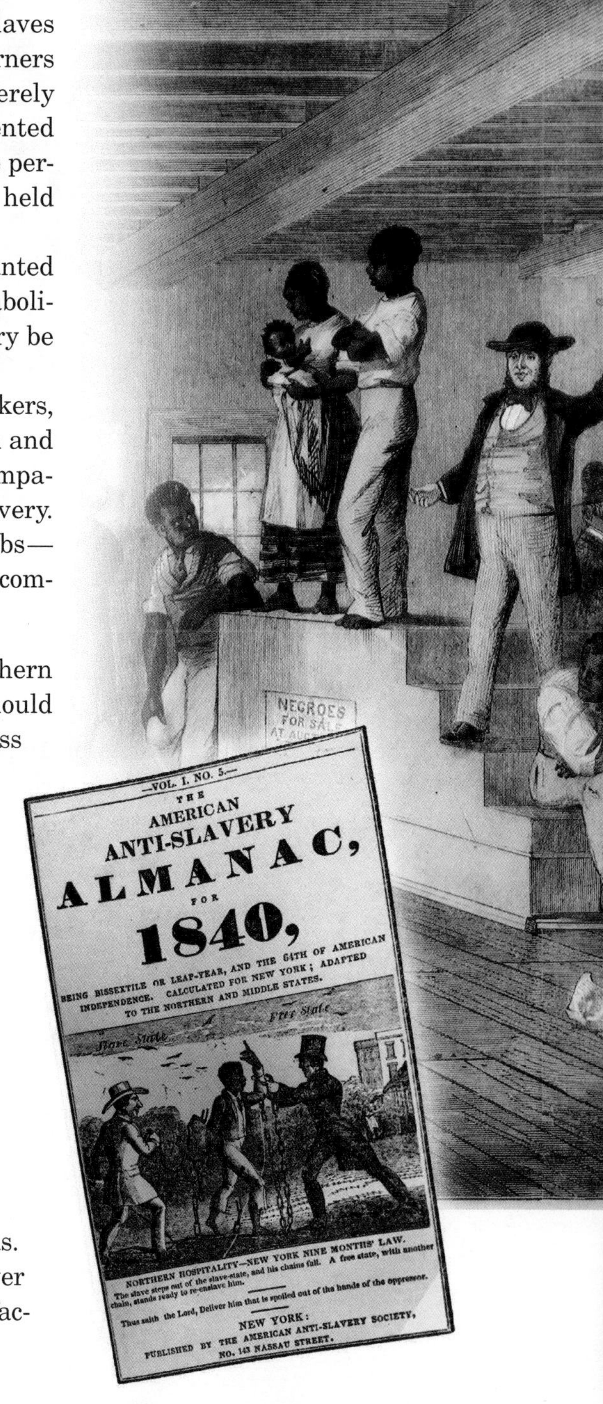

Van Buren Runs as a Free-Soil Candidate
Former President Martin van Buren was the Free-Soil candidate for the presidency in 1848. *What do the pictures on this poster tell you about the party?*

Free-Soil Party Vows to Keep Territories Free Several factions united in support of the Wilmot Proviso to form the new **Free-Soil Party.** Pledged to a "national platform of freedom" that would "resist the aggressions of the slave power," they nominated New Yorker Martin Van Buren as their candidate for President. The Free-Soil Party promised "free soil, free speech, free labor, and free men." Their main goal was to keep slavery out of the western territories.

Whigs and Democrats Dodge the Slavery Issue For decades, the major parties—the Whigs and Democrats—had avoided the slavery issue, thus managing to win support in both the North and the South. In 1848, they hoped once again to attract voters from all sides of the slavery debate. But with the Free-Soilers calling for limits to slavery in the territories, the major parties were forced to take a stand.

Both Democrats and Whigs addressed the problem by embracing the idea of **popular sovereignty,** a policy stating that voters in a territory—not Congress—should decide whether or not to allow slavery there. This idea had wide appeal, since it seemed in keeping with the traditions of American democracy. Furthermore, it allowed Whigs and Democrats once again to focus on the personal exploits and triumphs of their candidates rather than on the issues.

The Whigs nominated Zachary Taylor, a general and a hero of the Mexican War. The Democrats put forward Governor Lewis Cass of Michigan. Cass opposed the Wilmot Proviso and supported popular sovereignty. Taylor, who was primarily a military man, revealed little of his political opinions. But Taylor was a slaveholding Louisiana planter, so many southern voters automatically assumed that he supported slavery.

When the votes were counted, Taylor won the election, with slim majorities in both northern and southern states. Van Buren did not carry any states, but he did draw sufficient votes to cause Cass to lose. The Free-Soil Party, which had won 10 percent of the vote with its antislavery platform, had clearly captured Americans' attention.

 **Checkpoint What role did the Free-Soil Party play in the election of 1848?**

A Compromise Avoids a Crisis

To expand slavery or restrict it—this dilemma came to haunt the rapidly growing nation. In 1848, gold was discovered in California, and soon thousands of adventurers were headed west to seek their fortune. Before long, the burgeoning western territories would petition for entry into the Union. Should these new states allow slavery? Who would decide?

California Statehood Threatens the Balance of Power "Gold fever," as it came to be known, drew people from all over the world. They literally dug into the western foothills of California's Sierra Nevada, setting up towns with names that reflected their hopes and their origins: Gold Run, Eldorado (Spanish for "gilded one"), Dutch Flats, Chinese Camp, French Corral, Negro Bar, Iowa Hill.

Within a year, more than 80,000 people had journeyed to California. As the influx continued without a letup, California became a wild and lawless place.

Californians recognized that they needed a government to bring order to the chaos. In 1849, they drafted a constitution and asked to be admitted to the Union as a free—nonslave—state.

California's request created an uproar in the nation. For years, the North and the South had accused each other of being "aggressors" on the issue of slavery. And for years, the two sides had maintained a delicate balance of slave and free states in Congress. Now, inflamed southerners angrily noted that admission of California would tip the balance in favor of the free states.

Clay's Compromise of 1850
1. Congress would admit California as a free state.
2. The people of the territories of New Mexico and Utah would decide the slavery question by popular sovereignty.
3. The slave trade—but not slavery—would be ended in Washington, D.C.
4. Congress would pass a strict new fugitive slave law.
5. Texas would give up its claims to New Mexico in return for $10 million.

Other concerns simmered around the edges of the slavery issue, threatening to come to an explosive boil. Texas, a slave state, and the federal government were locked in a dispute over Texas's northwestern border. New Mexico and Utah were organizing to become territories but seemed likely to someday join the Union as free states. In the North, abolitionists seemed to be gaining ground in their bid to ban slavery in Washington, D.C.

In the meantime, southerners demanded that the federal government enforce the weak and often-neglected Fugitive Slave Law of 1793. The law stated that runaway slaves must be returned to their masters, but it provided no government aid to do so. The South felt that its property and its honor were at stake. Many northerners insisted that the federal government should not help to enforce slavery.

Clay Offers a Compromise Since the War of 1812, the Senate had benefited from the leadership of three extraordinary statesmen: Daniel Webster from the North, John Calhoun from the South, and Henry Clay from the West. Clay's ability to work out compromises to the thorniest problems had earned him the title the "Great Pacificator." In the crisis now brewing, Clay, although in his seventies and ailing, once again came forward.

Clay urged the North and South to reach an agreement. He advanced a series of compromise resolutions, offering concessions to both the South and the North (see chart). The most significant proposed that Congress admit California as a free state but also enact a stricter fugitive slave law. Popular sovereignty would decide the slavery issue in the Utah and New Mexico territories. Clay's attempt at sectional justice garnered wide support.

Calhoun and Webster Speak The Senate's other two giants—Calhoun and Webster—prepared long and deeply passionate responses to Clay's proposal. Calhoun was too sick and weak to deliver his own speech, but he watched defiantly from his seat as a younger colleague read it for him.

Calhoun's speech expressed his fear "that the agitation on the subject of slavery would, if not prevented by some timely and effective measure, end in disunion." But Calhoun did not believe that Clay's proposal gave the South enough protection. If the North would not submit to the South's demands, "let the states agree to separate and part in peace. If you are unwilling that we should part in peace, tell us so, and we shall know what to do." In other words, if the North did not agree, the South would **secede,** or break away, from the Union.

Daniel Webster, also ill and nearing the end of his life, tried to rally both northerners and southerners to the cause of unity. In an emotional speech, Webster urged senators to accept Clay's compromise. He suggested that the cotton and tobacco crops that flourished under slavery would not grow in California. Thus, he argued, popular sovereignty would allow the South to feel a measure of comfort but would not result in the spread of slavery to the West. (In fact, California eventually became a cotton-producing state—although a free one.)

Clay Proposes a Compromise
Henry Clay urged the Senate to adopt a compromise on the slavery issue. It was one of his last major actions in the Senate.

Comparing Viewpoints

Should the Union be saved?

The settling of the West made it impossible to maintain equal numbers of free and slave states. Western territories wanted to become free states. The argument over California statehood showed how the North and South were moving toward a civil war.

John Calhoun

Calhoun, from South Carolina, was a passionate supporter of slavery. As a senator, he argued that any state had the right to secede, or leave the Union, if it disagreed with national laws.

Primary Source

"[T]here is not a single Territory in progress in the Southern section, and no certainty that any additional State will be added to it. . . . [This destruction of the equilibrium] was caused by the legislation of this government, which was appointed as the common agent of all. . . .

If you admit [California] under all the difficulties that oppose her admission, you compel us to infer that you intend to exclude [the South] from the whole of the acquired Territories, with the intention of destroying . . . the equilibrium between the two sections."

—Senator John Calhoun, March 4, 1850

Daniel Webster

Webster [shown here], from Massachusetts, was a strong nationalist. As a senator, he supported sectional compromise as a way to preserve the Union.

Primary Source

"I wish to speak to-day, not as a Massachusetts man, nor as a Northern man, but as an American, and a member of the Senate of the United States. . . . I speak to-day for the preservation of the Union. "Hear me for my cause." I speak to-day, out of a solicitous and anxious heart, for the restoration to the country of that quiet and that harmony which make the blessings of this Union so rich, and so dear to us all.

[T]he strength of America will be in the Valley of the Mississippi. [What can we] say about the possibility of cutting that river in two? I would rather hear of war, pestilence, and famine, than to hear talk of secession. . . . [T]o dismember this glorious country! . . . No, Sir!"

—Senator Daniel Webster, March 7, 1850

Compare

1. What does Webster mean when he says "the strength of America will be in the Valley of the Mississippi"? What would cut the Mississippi River in two?
2. What does Calhoun accuse the U.S. government of doing?

Though some abolitionists felt betrayed by Webster's conciliatory three-hour speech, it persuaded many northerners to support the compromise.

✓ **Checkpoint** **How did California statehood spark a new crisis over slavery?**

Senate Adopts the Compromise of 1850

Over the years, Congress had adopted a variety of measures in order to preserve the Union. The Northwest Ordinance of 1787 had limited slavery. The Missouri Compromise of 1820 had maintained the balance between slave and free states. Now, in yet another effort to ward off division, the Senate adopted legislation based on Clay's proposals. It became known as the **Compromise of 1850.**

The debate over ratification of the compromise raged for months. Young northern radicals, such as New York's William Seward, argued that the morality of God's "higher law" against slavery was more important than popular sovereignty or national unity. Equally radical southerners organized boycotts against northern goods, and a few even promoted separation from the Union.

The proceedings erupted into violence in the Senate when Senator Thomas Hart Benton of Missouri, who supported California's admission as a free state, denounced Mississippi senator Henry Foote, who opposed it. Furious, Foote rose from his seat and aimed a loaded revolver at Benton. The alarmed senators tried to restore order. But Benton was defiant, shouting "I am not armed! I have no pistols! I disdain to carry arms! Stand out of the way, and let the assassin fire!" At last, a senator from New York seized the revolver and locked it in a desk. Order was restored.

Still, debate dragged on. With dozens of speeches—one lasting two days—an exhausted Clay struggled to gain supporters for the compromise. But in the end, the young senator Stephen A. Douglas of Illinois took charge. Working tirelessly, Douglas steered each component of Clay's plan through the Congress, persuading the Senate to adopt each measure separately.

Vocabulary Builder
component–(kuhm POH nuhnt) *n.* piece or element

By September 1850, the obstacles to agreement had melted away: Both Calhoun and the slaveholding President Taylor were dead. Unlike Taylor, the new President, Millard Fillmore, supported the compromise. At last, the Senate passed the Compromise of 1850. California was admitted as a free state, and the policy of popular sovereignty was applied to the territory acquired from Mexico. Texas relinquished its claims on New Mexico in return for $10 million from the federal government with which to settle its debts.

One by one, the other provisions passed. Slavery would remain undisturbed in Washington, D.C., but the slave trade was prohibited. And a new **Fugitive Slave Act** added stringent amendments to the earlier law, including the requirement that private citizens assist with apprehending runaway slaves. Citizens who assisted a fugitive slave could be fined or imprisoned.

Most Americans, in both the North and South, breathed a sigh of relief that the crisis had been laid to rest. Though the Compromise of 1850 restored calm for the moment, it carried the seeds of new crises to come.

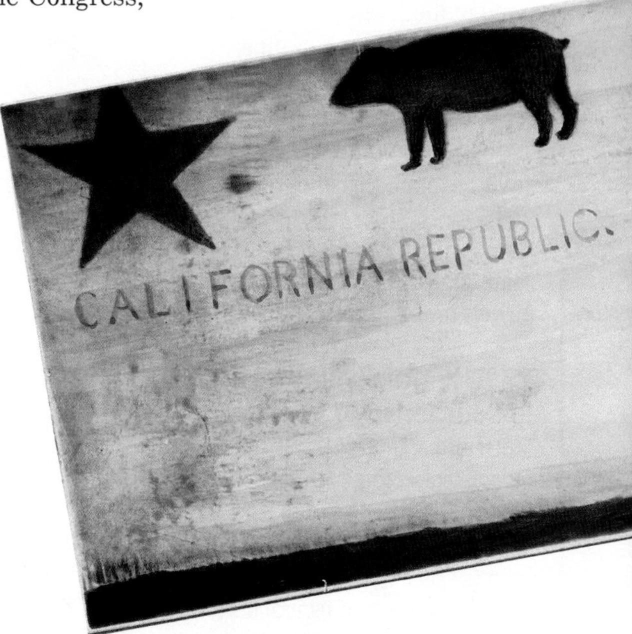

American settlers in California had declared independence from Mexico in 1846. Their symbol, the bear, later became the symbol on California's state flag.

✓ **Checkpoint What were the provisions of the Compromise of 1850?**

SECTION 1 Assessment

Progress Monitoring *Online*
For: Self-test with vocabulary practice
www.pearsonschool.com/ushist

Comprehension

1. **Terms and People** For each term below, write a sentence explaining its significance.
   - Wilmot Proviso
   - Free-Soil Party
   - popular sovereignty
   - secede
   - Compromise of 1850
   - Fugitive Slave Act

2. **NoteTaking Reading Skill: Categorize** Use your chart to answer the Section Focus Question: How did Congress try to resolve the dispute between North and South over slavery?

Writing About History

3. **Quick Write: Gather Evidence** Make a chart outlining arguments for and against adopting the Compromise of 1850. Your outline may include moral, economic, and political issues.

Critical Thinking

4. **Compare Points of View** How did the northern and southern views of slavery differ?
5. **Make Generalizations** What role did the issue of slavery play in the election of 1848?
6. **Identify Central Issues** Why did California's application for statehood cause a crisis?
7. **Draw Conclusions** How did the Compromise of 1850 appease both North and South?

American Issues Connector

Federal Power and States' Rights

TRACK THE ISSUE

How much power should the federal government have?

Under the Constitution, all powers not granted to the federal government belong to the states. Over time, however, the federal government has expanded its scope, especially in the area of social programs. Use the timeline below to explore this enduring issue.

1791 Bill of Rights
Tenth Amendment reserves most powers to the states.

1798 Kentucky and Virginia Resolutions
States argue that they can void federal legislation.

1831 Nullification Crisis
John C. Calhoun declares that states may overturn federal laws.

1857 *Dred Scott* v. *Sandford*
Supreme Court rules that federal government does not have power to outlaw slavery within territories.

1930s New Deal
Government expands power over economy and social services.

1965 Voting Rights Act
Law allows federal officers to register voters.

Dred Scott

Exhaust and waste gases from cars are just one of the many issues in the center of the continuing national debate about the environment.

DEBATE THE ISSUE

The Environment and States' Rights Since 1967, the Environmental Protection Agency (EPA) has allowed California to make its own emissions rules. California is exempt from the Clean Air Acts as long as its rules are stricter than those of the federal government and it obtains a waiver from the federal government. In November 2007, Governor Arnold Schwarzenegger sued the federal government because the EPA denied California a waiver.

"The authority of the States to address greenhouse gas emissions from motor vehicles has been supported—by the Supreme Court [and] by a federal court here in California. On this issue, the . . . EPA . . . has failed to follow the States' lead . . . we are prepared to force it out of the way . . . to protect the environment."

—Governor Arnold Schwarzenegger, April 2, 2008

"I believe that Congress by passing a . . . federal standard of 35 mpg (miles per gallon) delivers significant reductions that are more effective than a state-by-state approach. This applies to all 50 states. . . . and that's great for the economy, for national security, and for the environment."

—Stephen L. Johnson, EPA Administrator

TRANSFER Activities

1. **Compare** Why does Governor Schwarzenegger feel California should oppose the federal government? Why does Stephen Johnson disagree?
2. **Analyze** Should a state have the right to determine its own environmental standards?
3. **Transfer** Use the following Web site to see a video, try a WebQuest, and write in your journal. www.pearsonschool.com/ushist

SECTION 2

◀ This image first appeared around 1835 and became an abolitionist symbol.

WITNESS HISTORY

Slavery and Union

By the time Congress debated the Compromise of 1850, white Boston abolitionist William Lloyd Garrison had been protesting against slavery for more than two decades, and a growing number of Americans were joining his cause. He stated his resistance to compromise clearly:

"I am for union! . . . [but] I am not for SLAVERY and UNION. . . . [T]his is the issue we make before the country and the world."

—William Lloyd Garrison, 1850

A Rising Tide of Protest and Violence

Objectives

- Analyze why the Fugitive Slave Act increased tensions between the North and South.
- Assess how the Kansas-Nebraska Act was seen differently by the North and South.
- Explain why fighting broke out in Kansas and the effects of that conflict.

Terms and People

personal liberty laws
Underground Railroad
Harriet Tubman
Harriet Beecher Stowe
Kansas-Nebraska Act
John Brown
"Bleeding Kansas"

NoteTaking

Reading Skill: Understand Effects Use a concept web to record the effects of the Fugitive Slave Act on different groups of people.

Why It Matters Americans had greeted the Compromise of 1850 with relief. But the ink on the document had barely dried before the issue of slavery resurfaced, this time with violent results. **Section Focus Question: How did the Fugitive Slave Act and the Kansas-Nebraska Act increase tensions between the North and the South?**

Resistance Against the Fugitive Slave Act

The Compromise of 1850 was meant to calm the fears of Americans. But one provision, the new Fugitive Slave Act, had the opposite effect. The law, which required citizens to catch and return runaway slaves, enraged many northerners. The anger was not restricted to abolitionists; it extended to other northerners who felt forced to support the slave system.

Northerners also resented what they saw as increasing federal intervention in the affairs of the independent states. A few northern states struck back, passing **personal liberty laws.** These statutes nullified the Fugitive Slave Act and allowed the state to arrest slave catchers for kidnapping. Many northerners agreed with abolitionist William Lloyd Garrison when he demanded "nothing less than . . . a Revolution in the Government of the country."

INFOGRAPHIC

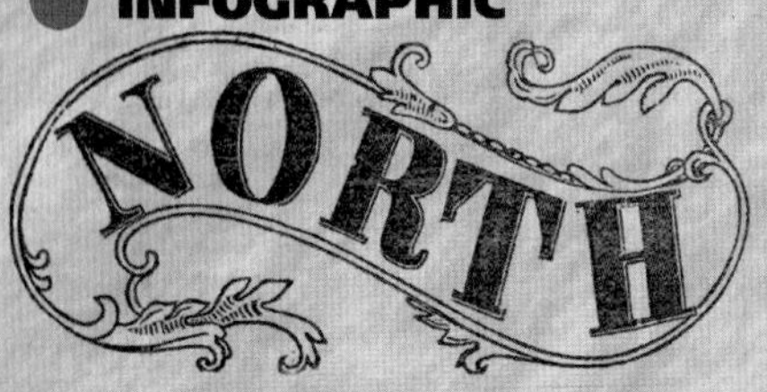

ROCHESTER NEW YORK, THURSDAY, JULY 18, 1850

THE FUGITIVE SLAVE ACT

Before 1850, many white northerners assumed that slavery was not their problem. When a new Fugitive Slave Act forced them to participate in the slave system, they resisted. In several northern cities, crowds tried to rescue fugitive slaves from their captors.

The free black community also took action. The law meant that no African American could feel safe. Through urban networks known as "Vigilance Committees," and through antislavery newspapers, African Americans remained in constant communication. The committees looked out for slave hunters and helped fugitives avoid capture.

300 DOLLARS

REWARD!

RUNAWAY from John S. Doak on the 21st inst., two NEGRO MEN; LOGAN 45 years of age, bald-headed, one or more crooked fingers; DAN 21 years old, six feet high. Both black.

Fugitive slaves were often aided by an informal network of abolitionists, known as the Underground Railroad. If fugitives were caught and returned to slavery, they could be forced to wear devices meant to prevent another escape, such as a collar with bells on it (above right).

Underground ▶ Railroad conductor Harriet Tubman

▲ The map above shows approximate routes of the Underground Railroad.

A MAN

KIDNAPPED!

A PUBLIC MEETING AT

FANEUIL HALL!

WILL BE HELD

THIS FRIDAY EVEN'G,

May 26th, at 7 o'clock,

To secure justice for A MAN CLAIMED AS A SLAVE by a

VIRGINIA

KIDNAPPER!

Soldiers sometimes escorted ▶ slave hunters and their captives because crowds often tried to free the captured men and women.

Thinking Critically

1. **Infer** Why might the Underground Railroad have been more active in free states than in slave states?
2. **Draw Conclusions** In what ways did the Fugitive Slave Act affect free African Americans?

Black Americans, of course, despised the law. Some of the captured "fugitive slaves" were really free people who had been kidnapped and sold into slavery. Although the imprisoned African Americans could appeal to a judge for their release, the law awarded $10 to judges who ruled in favor of slave owners but only $5 to those who ruled that the captive should be set free. Slaves, fugitives, and free black people plotted and carried out resistance. Through the succeeding decade, tempers flared and violence erupted as far north as Canada, as far west as Kansas, and as far south as Virginia.

Northern Blacks Mobilize In 1851, a small group of free African Americans gathered in a farmhouse in Christiana, Pennsylvania. Heavily armed, they had come to protect several fugitives from their Maryland master, who had brought a federal official to reclaim them. In the scuffle that followed, the slave owner was killed. White bystanders refused to intervene to help the slave-hunting party. Although more than 30 people were tried for conspiracy, none was found guilty. No one was tried for the murder of the slave owner.

Vocabulary Builder
intervene–(ihn tuhr VEEN) *v.* to get involved in a situation in order to prevent a certain outcome

The "Christiana Riot" was a dramatic enactment of a scene that was played out in many northern communities. In Vermont and New Hampshire, in New York City, in Oberlin, Ohio, and in Baltimore, Maryland, African Americans and white bystanders defied officials who tried to reclaim fugitives to slavery.

Underground Railroad to Freedom Northern abolitionists and free black people risked their lives and safety to help enslaved people escape to freedom through a loosely organized network known as the **Underground Railroad.** Although it was not underground and had no tracks or cars, this escape system used railroad terminology to describe its actions. A secret network of "conductors" hid runaway slaves in farm wagons and on riverboats and then moved them to destinations in the North or in Canada—sometimes even as far as England. Using complex signals and hiding places, the Underground Railroad carried its passengers over hundreds of miles of dangerous terrain.

Underground Railroad conductors had to be resourceful and daring. One of the most courageous was **Harriet Tubman,** a Maryland-born fugitive slave. She was known as "Black Moses" because, like Moses in the Bible, she led her people out of bondage. After her own escape in 1849, Tubman made almost two dozen trips into the South, guiding hundreds of slaves, including her own parents, to safety. Southern planters placed a large reward on her head, but she was never captured.

Several fugitive slaves published dramatic escape stories that inspired black Americans and struck fear in the hearts of white southerners. In one account, six-foot-tall Henry "Box" Brown described how he had himself packed into a small crate and shipped from Richmond, Virginia, to the Underground Railroad agents in Philadelphia. Light-skinned Ellen Craft and her husband, William, made their escape by posing as an invalid gentleman and his loyal servant.

Stowe and Delany Condemn Slavery In 1852, **Harriet Beecher Stowe** published *Uncle Tom's Cabin,* a powerful condemnation of slavery. Stowe's sympathetic main character, Uncle Tom, gave slavery a face for those who had never witnessed it firsthand. Set in the slave-owning South, Stowe's story features the gentle and patient Uncle Tom, a frightened slave mother, and both kind and cruel slave owners. Selling 300,000 copies in its first year, the novel spread compassion for enslaved people in the North, but it infuriated people in the South.

Black abolitionist Martin Delany also wrote an antislavery novel, called *Blake.* It is the story of an African American who chooses to rebel violently, rather than to submit like Uncle Tom. The protagonist, Blake, murders a white slave owner in order to make his escape, a scenario that terrified slave owners. In the following excerpt, Blake stands up to his master's threat to whip him:

> **Primary Source** "I won't be treated like a dog. You sold my wife away from me, after always promising that she should be free. . . . And now you talk about whipping me. Shoot me, sell me, or do anything else you please, but don't lay your hands on me, as I will not suffer you to whip me!"
>
> —Martin R. Delany, *Blake*

White southerners responded by writing their own versions of southern life. In these accounts, slaves were happy and carefree, gently cared for and taught Christianity by kind masters. They claimed that only mentally ill slaves ran away. A southern doctor even reported his discovery of a disease he called Drapetomania, which supposedly caused slaves to flee. "With the advantages of proper medical advice," he claimed "this troublesome practice" could be eliminated.

✓ **Checkpoint How did northerners respond to the Fugitive Slave Act?**

NoteTaking

Reading Skill: Understand Effects Use the chart below to trace the series of events that led up to and followed the passage of the Kansas-Nebraska Act.

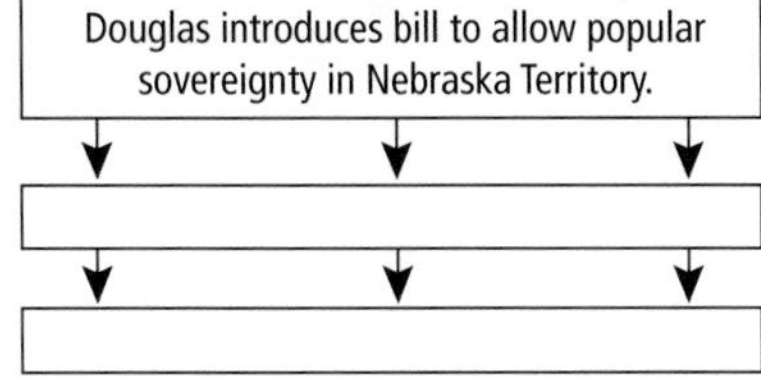

The Kansas-Nebraska Act Undoes the Missouri Compromise

Although Congress meant well, its repeated attempts to resolve the question of slavery resulted in a jumble of contradictory, and often unenforceable, policies. The Missouri Compromise, the Wilmot Proviso, the Compromise of 1850: Each seemed to offer the solution. But, in reality, the issue lay beyond the ability of patchwork legislation to resolve.

Douglas Presses for Popular Sovereignty It was Senator Douglas who forced the issue of slavery to the surface once again. In 1854, Douglas introduced a bill to set up a government in the Nebraska Territory. The area would be organized, Douglas proposed, according to the principle of popular sovereignty. That is, the people of the territory themselves would decide whether to allow slavery or outlaw it when they applied for statehood. On the surface, Douglas's plan made sense. In fact, it seemed to be a democratic solution. But would it work in practice?

Congress Debates the Kansas-Nebraska Act Once again, Congress was gripped in bitter debate. After pressure from the South, which feared Nebraska might decide to enter as a free state, Douglas amended the bill to divide the region into two distinct territories, Kansas and Nebraska. The idea was that Kansas would become a slave state and Nebraska would organize as a free state, but those assumptions were not written into the bill. In the spring of 1854, Congress accepted this proposal and passed the **Kansas-Nebraska Act.** Some northerners pointed out that, in effect, the Kansas-Nebraska Act nullified the Missouri Compromise by allowing slavery to spread to areas that had been free for more than 30 years.

✓ **Checkpoint How did the Kansas-Nebraska Act revive the issue of slavery?**

A Battle Rages in "Bleeding Kansas"

Most of the people who came to the newly opened territory of Kansas were farmers looking for land. But Kansas also attracted settlers—northern and southern—with political motives. Each group wanted to outnumber the other, so that when it came time to vote, they could control the government. Their competition to settle the territory would have deadly consequences.

Territories Open to Slavery

Geography *Interactive*
For: Interactive map skills
www.pearsonschool.com/ushist

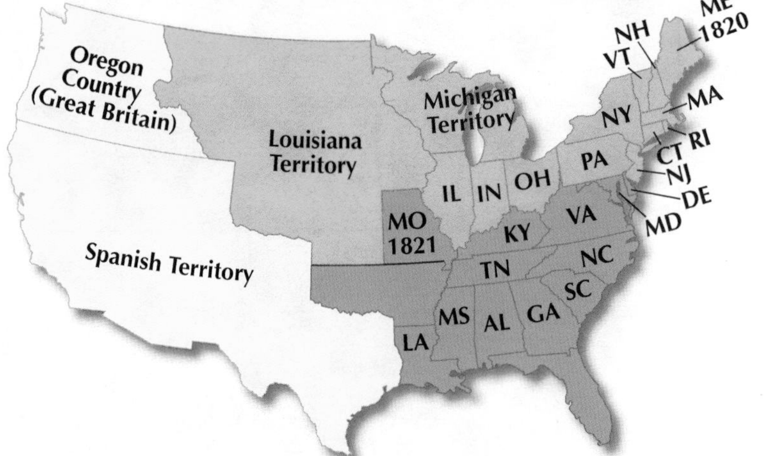

Missouri Compromise, 1820

- Slavery prohibited in the Louisiana Territory north of 36°30′, except in Missouri
- Maine entered as a free state
- Missouri entered as a slave state

Significance: Sponsored by Henry Clay, the compromise preserved the balance of free and slave states in the Senate. However, it marked the beginning of the sectional conflict that would lead to civil war.

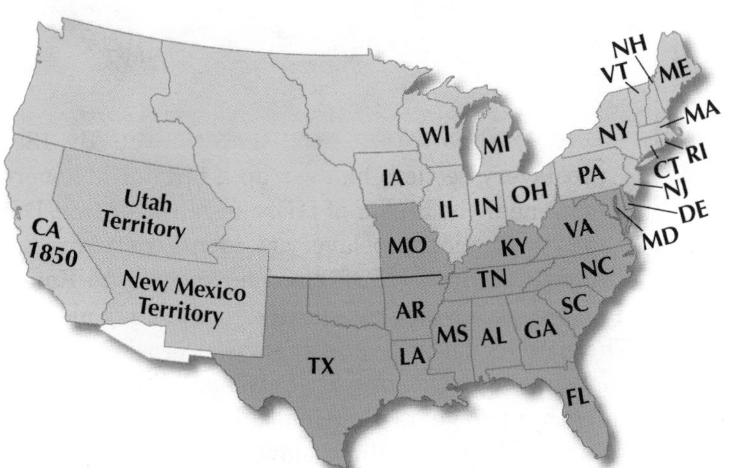

Compromise of 1850

- California entered as a free state
- Slavery issue to be decided by popular sovereignty in Utah and New Mexico territories
- New, stricter Fugitive Slave Act
- Slave trade but not slavery is ended in Washington, D.C.

Significance: Stephen Douglas steered each of the provisions though Congress as a separate bill. It showed that compromise was not a good solution to the sectional conflict, as it pushed many moderates toward more radical positions.

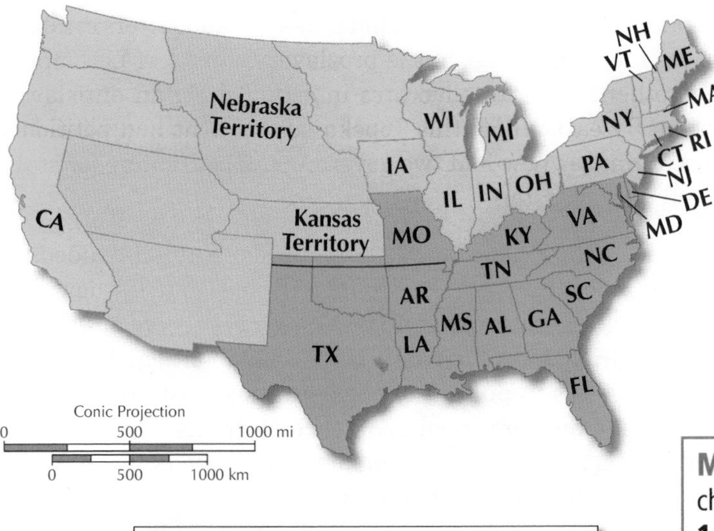

Kansas-Nebraska Act, 1854

- Created potential for slavery in Kansas and Nebraska territories by allowing for popular sovereignty

Significance: Sponsored by Stephen Douglas, this bill overturned the Missouri Compromise. Although it was meant to unite the nation, it caused further division and led to the creation of the Republican Party.

- Slave states
- Territories open to slavery by popular sovereignty
- States and territories closed to slavery
- — Missouri Compromise line (36°30′N)

Map Skills Between 1820 and 1854, three compromises changed the territories that were opened to slavery.

1. **Identify** Which territories were open to slavery after (a) the Missouri Compromise, (b) the Compromise of 1850, and (c) the Kansas-Nebraska Act?
2. **Analyze** Why were so many people upset by the Kansas-Nebraska Act?

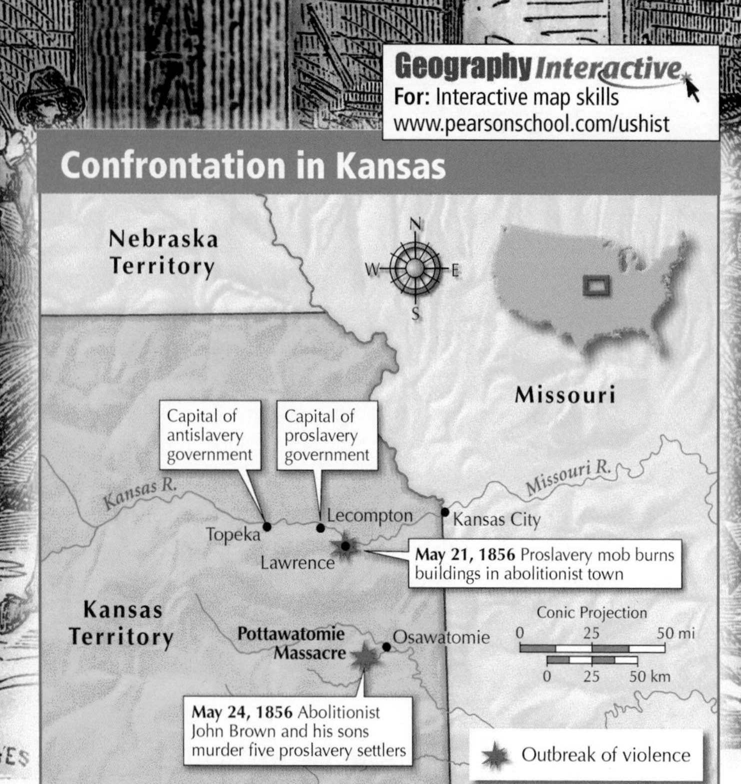

Map Skills Kansas became a battleground over slavery.

1. **Locate:** (a) Lawrence, (b) Missouri, (c) Topeka
2. **Draw Conclusions** What problems could result from having two governments in Kansas?

The Sack of Lawrence
On May 21, 1856, proslavery men attacked the Free-Soil town of Lawrence, Kansas. They burned the hotel and destroyed the newspaper. *Why did proslavery forces attack Lawrence?*

Two Governments Are Established By 1855, proslavery settlers had set up a territorial government near the border of Missouri, a slave state. During the election, proslavery residents from Missouri, known as Border Ruffians, had swept into Kansas and coerced local voters into voting for proslavery candidates. They also cast their own illegal votes. The new legislature quickly passed proslavery laws, including penalties for antislavery agitation and a requirement that officeholders take a proslavery oath. Within two years, they had called a convention and developed a constitution that would have legalized slavery and punished those who spoke or wrote against it.

Northern abolitionists also rushed into Kansas. The New England Emigrant Aid Society raised money to help several thousand free-state supporters establish the town of Lawrence, a few miles east of the proslavery capital of Lecompton. These settlers joined other free-state advocates in establishing an antislavery government in Topeka. By early 1856, this Topeka government had petitioned Congress for statehood. Kansas now had two governments petitioning for statehood. It was a sure setup for disaster.

Violence Grips the Territory On May 21, 1856, Border Ruffians raided the antislavery town of Lawrence, Kansas. They pillaged homes, burned down the Free State Hotel, and destroyed the presses of *The Kansas Free State* newspaper.

Swift retaliation came from **John Brown,** a New York abolitionist who had moved his family several times in pursuit of opportunities to confront slavery head-on and who now made his home near Lawrence. With his sons and a few friends, Brown carried out a midnight execution of five proslavery settlers near Pottawatomie Creek, about 20 miles south of Lawrence.

When stories of the incident reached the East, abolitionists were stunned. While they were outraged at the events that triggered it, they condemned Brown's massacre. In Kansas, both sides armed for battle. Throughout the fall of 1856, violent outbreaks occurred in various locales around Lawrence. Reporters characterized the territory as **"Bleeding Kansas."** By now, it was clear that popular sovereignty was not a solution to the slavery issue.

Over the next several years, the question of how to admit Kansas to the Union baffled local residents, political parties, the U.S. Congress, and the Supreme Court. Although the Border Ruffians had determined the outcome of the election, President Franklin Pierce urged Congress to admit Kansas as a slave state in 1858. However, Congress refused and Kansas submitted four constitutions before it finally entered as a free state in 1861, after the Civil War had already begun.

Violence in the Senate

Representative Brooks beat Senator Sumner with a cane meant to train dogs. *What does this depiction tell you about the event?*

Violence Spreads to the Senate The violent battles over slavery were not limited to Kansas. Tempers ran high in Congress, and some members went to work armed not only with words but with pistols and canes. In May 1856, just as fighting broke out in Kansas, Massachusetts senator Charles Sumner delivered a blistering speech on the Senate floor, which came to be known as "The Crime Against Kansas." He blasted southerners for their bullying and fraud in the Kansas elections, and he referred to the Border Ruffians from Missouri as "hirelings, picked from the drunken spew and vomit of an uneasy civilization—in the form of men."

Then, Sumner invited trouble. He insulted South Carolina senator Andrew Butler, who was absent. But a few days later, Butler's nephew, South Carolina representative Preston Brooks, attacked Sumner in the Senate, beating him unconscious with a cane.

What happened next illustrates the division of the two sides. Congress tried to punish Brooks by removing him from office. His constituency simply reelected him and sent him back. Sumner was so badly injured that he could not return to the Senate for three years. The Massachusetts voters reelected him anyway, using his empty seat as a public reminder of southern treachery. The divide between North and South grew ever wider and deeper.

✓ **Checkpoint** **Why did violence break out in Kansas?**

SECTION 2 Assessment

Progress Monitoring *Online*
For: Self-test with vocabulary practice
www.pearsonschool.com/ushist

Comprehension

1. **Terms and People** Place each of the entries below into one of these two categories: advancing slavery or working against slavery
   - personal liberty laws
   - Underground Railroad
   - Harriet Tubman
   - Harriet Beecher Stowe
   - Kansas-Nebraska Act
   - John Brown
   - "Bleeding Kansas"

2. **NoteTaking Reading Skill: Understand Effects** Use your concept web to answer the Section Focus Question: How did the Fugitive Slave Act and the Kansas-Nebraska Act increase tensions between the North and the South?

Writing About History

3. **Quick Write: Outline an Argument** List points supporting or opposing the Kansas-Nebraska Act, and then rank them in order of importance.

Critical Thinking

4. **Recognize Effects** What were the consequences of the Fugitive Slave Act for slaveholders, white northerners, free African Americans, and fugitive slaves?
5. **Summarize** How did the Kansas-Nebraska Act undo the Missouri Compromise?
6. **Synthesize** How did "Bleeding Kansas" embody the slavery controversy?

American LITERATURE

An early edition of *Uncle Tom's Cabin* ▶

UNCLE TOM'S CABIN;

OR,

LIFE AMONG THE LOWLY.

BY

HARRIET BEECHER STOWE.

▲ Harriet Beecher Stowe

Uncle Tom's Cabin by Harriet Beecher Stowe

In Harriet Beecher Stowe's controversial story, a decent Kentucky slave owner is forced to sell his slave, Tom. Tom remains kind and gentle, despite losing his family and ending up in the possession of a cruel man named Simon Legree. For the first time, readers began to think of slaves as people, rather than as possessions. In this excerpt, Tom is inspected and sold to Legree at an auction.

Various spectators, intending to purchase, or not intending, as the case might be, gathered around the group, handling, examining, and commenting on their various points and faces with the same freedom that a set of jockeys discuss the merits of a horse. . . .

Tom had been standing wistfully examining the multitude of faces thronging around him, for one whom he would wish to call master. And if you should ever be under the necessity, sir, of selecting, out of two hundred men, one who was to become your absolute owner and disposer, you would, perhaps, realize, just as Tom did, how few there were that you would feel at all comfortable in being made over to. . . .

A little before the sale commenced, a short, broad, muscular man . . . elbowed his way through the crowd, like one who is going actively into business; and, coming up to the group, began to examine them systematically. From the moment that Tom saw him approaching, he felt an immediate and revolting horror at him, that increased as he came near. He was evidently, though short, of gigantic strength. His round, bullet head . . . and stiff, wiry, sunburned hair, were rather unprepossessing items. . . . This man proceeded to a very free personal examination of the lot. He seized Tom by the jaw, and pulled open his mouth to inspect his teeth; made him strip up his sleeve, to show his muscle; turned him round, made him jump and spring to show his paces. . . .

Tom stepped upon the block, gave a few anxious looks round; all seemed mingled in a common, indistinct noise,—the clatter of the sales man crying off his qualifications in French and English, the quick fire of French and English bids; and almost in a moment came the final thump of the hammer, and the clear ring of the last syllable of the word *"dollars,"* as the auctioneer announced his price, and Tom was made over.—He had a master!

He was pushed from the block;—the short, bullet-headed man seizing him roughly by the shoulder, pushed him to one side, saying in a harsh voice, "Stand there, *you!*"

Thinking Critically

1. **Identify Point of View** Whose point of view is reflected in this selection?
2. **Demonstrate Reasoned Judgment** How accurately could a white northern woman portray the feelings of an enslaved person being auctioned? What parts of her story might have been written differently by someone who had been enslaved?

SECTION 3

WITNESS HISTORY

A House Divided

In the election of 1858, Abraham Lincoln and Stephen A. Douglas competed to represent the state of Illinois in the U.S. Senate. In a series of debates that captured the nation's attention, they argued about slavery. Douglas supported popular sovereignty as the way to resolve the slavery crisis. Lincoln, while not so certain of a solution, believed that the nation could not continue to exist half slave and half free. Lincoln kicked off his campaign with a speech summarizing his position:

> "'A house divided against itself cannot stand.' I believe this government cannot endure permanently half slave and half free. I do not expect the Union to be dissolved—I do not expect the house to fall—but I do expect it will cease to be divided. It will become all one thing, or all the other."
>
> —Abraham Lincoln, June 16, 1858

◀ Douglas and Lincoln debate

Political Realignment Deepens the Crisis

Objectives

- Analyze how deepening sectional distrust affected the nation's politics.
- Compare the positions of Abraham Lincoln and Stephen Douglas on the issue of slavery.
- Explain the effect of John Brown's raid on the slavery debate.

Terms and People

Know-Nothings
Republican Party
Dred Scott
Roger B. Taney
Abraham Lincoln
Stephen A. Douglas
Harpers Ferry

NoteTaking

Reading Skill: Sequence Use a timeline to record significant political events.

Early 1850s—Whig Party disintegrates

1850 1852 1854 1856 1858

Why It Matters Americans had always lived with sectional differences, but they temporarily resolved those differences through negotiation and compromise. By the mid-1850s, however, the battle over slavery threatened to tear the nation apart. **Section Focus Question: What developments deepened the divisions between North and South?**

The Shifting Political Scene

Traditionally, American political parties extended across sectional lines. Democrats and Whigs came from the North, South, and West. Presidents, too, had come from all areas of the country. But in the 1840s, American politics increasingly reflected regional tensions, especially over the issue of slavery.

The Whig Party Disintegrates The Compromise of 1850, as well as the policies that grew out of it, caused political upheaval. Millard Fillmore—the last Whig President—angered the South with his support for California's entry as a free state. Northerners inflamed by his support of the Fugitive Slave Act and popular sovereignty left the party in large numbers.

For the 1852 presidential election, Whigs searched unsuccessfully for a candidate and a platform to unite their members. But with their two visionary leaders—Henry Clay and Daniel Webster—dead, the party fell back on Winfield Scott, a military hero. Deeply divided over the issues, the Whigs lost to the Democrats, who solidly endorsed the 1850 Compromise that they hoped and believed would preserve the Union. The Whigs would never again achieve enough harmony to mount a presidential campaign.

Know-Nothings Attract Support By the mid-1800s, a growing immigrant population was changing the country. For example, up to that time, Protestantism—which includes Baptists, Methodists, Presbyterians, and many other groups—had been the dominant American religion. By 1850, however, Americans of Irish and German descent and Spanish-speaking natives of lands ceded by Mexico had made Catholicism the nation's largest religious group. Many native-born white Protestants were alarmed by the change. These "nativists" raised questions that reflected their prejudices. Would Catholics bring ideas that would undermine America's religious freedom? Would the newcomers take jobs away from workers who were already here? Or, alternatively, would they be lazy, not work, and become paupers, weighing down society?

These concerns fueled the growth of an anti-immigrant movement. Dubbed **"Know-Nothings"** because members responded "I know nothing" when questioned about their nativist organization, the group quickly gathered momentum. By 1855, the Know-Nothings had abandoned secrecy to form the American Party. Like the Whigs, however, the American Party soon divided over the issue of slavery in the western territories.

The Republican Party Is Born As the old parties broke up, antislavery zeal gave rise to the new **Republican Party** in 1854. Opposition to slavery was the center of the Republican philosophy. Attracting antislavery Democrats, Whigs, Free-Soilers, and Know-Nothings, the Republican Party grew rapidly in the North. It included a coalition of businessmen who believed that slavery stifled industry, as well as moral leaders who feared that slavery encouraged vice. By 1856, it was ready to challenge the older, established parties.

 **Checkpoint How did the rise and fall of political parties reflect divisions in the United States?**

American Political Parties During the 1850s	
Democratic Party (1800–present)	• Opposed strong central government • Divided over slavery issue in the 1850s
Whig Party (1834–1852)	• Favored national economic development • Opposed Andrew Jackson • Antislavery members left in the 1850s
Know-Nothings or The American Party (1843–1856)	• Opposed to immigration • Joined by antislavery Whigs • Took a proslavery platform in 1856
Free-Soil Party (1847–1854)	• Worked to prevent slavery in the western territories • Formed by antislavery Democrats and Whigs • Absorbed into the new Republican Party
Republican Party (1854–present)	• Opposed to slavery • Opposed to Kansas-Nebraska Act

Sectional Divisions Intensify

For many years, the North and South tried to ignore or patch over their differences. But by the mid-1850s, the dispute over slavery caused sectional differences to intensify.

The Election of 1856 Causes Alarm Republicans, at their first national convention, nominated for President the abolitionist John C. Frémont, a colorful Mexican War hero who had helped win California's independence. The Democrats nominated James Buchanan of Pennsylvania, while the Know-Nothings put up former President Millard Fillmore.

"Free Soil, Free Labor, Free Men, Frémont!" Under this slogan, the Republican Party tried to

THE GREAT PRESIDENTIAL SWEEPSTAKES OF 1856.

Analyzing Political Cartoons

A Race for the Presidency In this cartoon, the Know-Nothing candidate Fillmore leads the race in the "American Express" carriage, which represents his anti-immigrant platform. The outgoing Democratic president, Franklin Pierce, carries Buchanan. The Republican Frémont is last, urged on by the abolitionist Horace Greeley (wearing a top hat).

1. Explain the cartoonist's stance on abolition.
2. Did the cartoonist correctly predict the election results?

rally Americans to reject popular sovereignty and to insist that slavery be excluded from the western territories. They also campaigned to admit Kansas as a free state.

But Buchanan, who promised that as President he would stop "the agitation of the slavery issue," won the election, supported by the large majority of southerners. His running mate from the South, John C. Breckinridge, further bolstered his campaign. Still, the Republican Frémont, with his solid abolitionist platform, made a strong showing, winning one third of the popular vote and 11 northern states.

The *Dred Scott* Decision Triggers Outrage While passions still ran high from the 1856 election, another event fueled the flames of division. In 1857, the U.S. Supreme Court ruled in the case of Missouri slave **Dred Scott,** who had sued for his freedom. Scott based his case on the fact that his master had taken him to the free state of Illinois and Wisconsin Territory, where slavery was outlawed by the Missouri Compromise. In other words, between 1834 and 1838, Scott had lived mostly on free soil while remaining enslaved.

With the help of abolitionists, Scott's case reached the Supreme Court under Chief Justice **Roger B. Taney.** In its decision handed down in March 1857, the Court ruled against Scott. In a controversial decision, the Court decided that slaves and their descendants were property, not citizens, and therefore were not entitled to sue in the courts. It also said that the Missouri Compromise was unconstitutional because it was illegal for Congress to deprive an owner of property—in this case, a slave—without due process of law.

Southerners celebrated the decision, but the North viewed it with alarm. Abolitionists labeled the ruling a southern conspiracy. Some suggested that the North should secede from the Union. Others insisted that the members of the Supreme Court should be impeached. Leading black abolitionist Frederick Douglass predicted that the decision would actually hasten the end of slavery:

Does Congress Have the Power to Limit Slavery?

One of the most divisive issues facing the country in the 1850s was the question of slavery in the territories. The Missouri Compromise had banned slavery from some areas and allowed it in others. The Kansas-Nebraska Act left the question up to those people living in a territory. But if the Constitution allowed slavery to exist, did Congress have the power to take these actions?

Dred Scott v. *Sandford* (1857)

The Facts	The Issue	The Decision
• Dred Scott, an African American slave, was taken north of the Missouri Compromise line, where slavery was banned.	Scott argued that since he had lived several years in a free state and several years in a free territory, he should be free.	• The Court stated that temporary residence in a free territory did not make Scott free. • It said that Scott was property, not a citizen, and therefore had no right to sue. • It further reasoned that no African American could be a citizen. • It stated that Congress could not ban slavery from any territory because doing so would take away slave owners' property without due process of law.

Chief Justice Roger B. Taney

Why It Matters

The *Dred Scott* decision deeply split an already divided country. Southerners applauded the Court for defending their rights to hold slaves. A South Carolina newspaper victoriously declared that the decision proves that "slavery is guaranteed by the constitutional compact." Many in the North viewed the decision with dismay, however. Republicans wanted to block the spread of slavery, and the Court's decision dashed their hopes. Abraham Lincoln expressed the fears of many that the Court would act even more boldly in the future. In an 1858 speech, he warned that the Court would next force slavery onto northern soil:

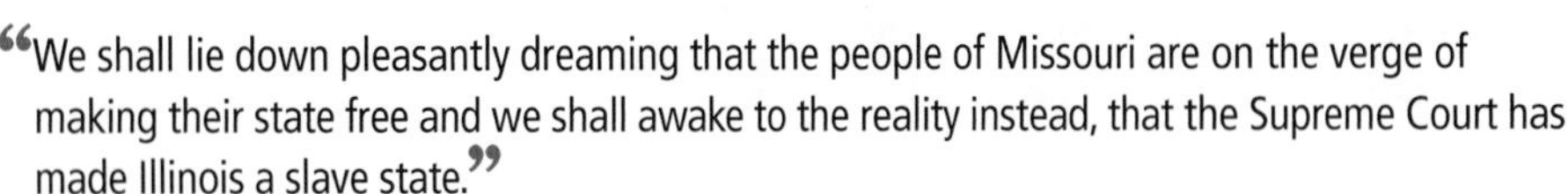

> "We shall lie down pleasantly dreaming that the people of Missouri are on the verge of making their state free and we shall awake to the reality instead, that the Supreme Court has made Illinois a slave state."

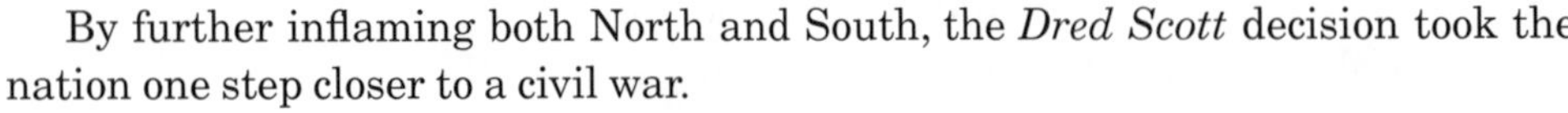

By further inflaming both North and South, the *Dred Scott* decision took the nation one step closer to a civil war.

Connect to Your World

The Court has made other controversial decisions over the years. Examples are *Engel* v. *Vitale* (1962), *Miranda* v. *Arizona* (1966), *Roe* v. *Wade* (1973), *Texas* v. *Johnson* (1989), and *Kelo* v. *New London* (2005). Read about the Court's decision in a controversial case and its aftermath. Analyze how people with different points of view have responded to the decision.

For: Supreme Court cases
www.pearsonschool.com/ushist

Primary Source "The Supreme Court . . . [is] not the only power in the world. We, the abolitionists and colored people, should meet this decision, unlooked for and monstrous as it appears, in a cheerful spirit. This very attempt to blot out forever the hopes of an enslaved people may be one necessary link in the chain of events preparatory to the complete overthrow of the whole slave system."

—Frederick Douglass, 1857

✓ **Checkpoint** **What were the reactions to the *Dred Scott* decision?**

The Lincoln-Douglas Debates

Throughout the 1850s, American attention was riveted on westward expansion. But no discussion of expansion, or any aspect of the nation's future, could get beyond the issue of slavery. In 1858, Stephen Douglas and Abraham Lincoln held a series of seven debates while competing for a seat in the U.S. Senate. Thousands of Americans attended the Lincoln-Douglas debates and listened raptly as the two candidates presented opposing views of slavery and its role in America.

Stephen A. Douglas, the "Little Giant" stood just over 5 feet tall. His opponent, Abraham Lincoln, was about 6 feet, 4 inches tall.

"Honest Abe" vs. "The Little Giant" Raised in rural poverty and largely self-taught, **Abraham Lincoln** began his political career at age 25, when he was elected to the Illinois state legislature as a Whig. By 1836, he had been admitted to the Illinois bar and was practicing law in Springfield. He soon gained a reputation for integrity and directness that earned him the title "Honest Abe." Lincoln seemed to be staunchly opposed to slavery, but his political life was marked by a desire to steer a middle course.

In the 1840s, Lincoln had served a short stint in the U.S. House of Representatives, supporting Zachary Taylor and his policy of admitting California as a free state. But Lincoln's real political career began with his opposition to the Kansas-Nebraska Act and its implicit support for the expansion of slavery promoted by rival Illinois politician **Stephen A. Douglas.**

Vocabulary Builder
implicit–(ihm PLIHS iht) *adj.* unspoken but understood

Douglas was, in many ways, the opposite of Lincoln. Lincoln was tall, lanky, and slow of speech. Douglas was short, round, and filled with energy and a commanding voice. These qualities earned him the nickname the "Little Giant." His critics, however, questioned his motives and his sincerity. Unlike Lincoln, Douglas supported the annexation of Texas, and he promoted popular sovereignty as the solution to regional tensions. But many wondered if he promoted these policies because he believed in them or because he had a financial stake in the railroads that would profit from them.

Douglas Backs Popular Sovereignty Douglas had supporters in both the North and the South. Though he was not a slaveholder, his wife had inherited slaves, and he was somewhat sympathetic to slavery. Popular sovereignty, he insisted, was the implied intent of the Constitution. He expressed this sentiment strongly in the seventh and last debate:

Primary Source "This Union was established on the right of each State to do as it pleased on the question of slavery, and every other question."

—Stephen A. Douglas, 1858

Douglas was seeking the support of both southern and northern Democrats. But while some southerners supported him, many northern Democrats distrusted what they believed were his self-serving motives.

Lincoln Wins a Reputation When Lincoln stood before these same audiences, he spoke of the "eternal struggle between right and wrong." He repeatedly

The Raid at Harpers Ferry

Marines led by Colonel Robert E. Lee smashed the armory door at Harpers Ferry and succeeded in capturing John Brown (pictured above) and his followers inside. No slaves joined Brown's rebellion. *Did John Brown's raid have a chance to succeed?*

referred to the *Dred Scott* decision as wrong. He attacked popular sovereignty as wrong. And he condemned slavery as a system whereby one person does the "work and toil to earn bread" and someone else does the eating. While Lincoln, like most white people of his day, ridiculed the idea of social and political equality with African Americans, he strongly affirmed the idea of their natural rights:

> **Primary Source** "There is no reason in the world why the negro is not entitled to all the natural rights enumerated in the Declaration of Independence—the right of life, liberty, and the pursuit of happiness. I hold that he is as much entitled to these as the white man. . . . In the right to eat the bread, without the leave of anybody else, which his own hand earns, he is my equal and the equal of Judge Douglas, and the equal of every living man."
>
> —Abraham Lincoln, 1858

The debates lasted for weeks. When they were over, Douglas won the election by a slim margin. But Lincoln had not really lost. As a result of the debates, Lincoln won a large following that would serve him well the next time he ran for national office.

 **Checkpoint How did Lincoln and Douglas differ on the issue of slavery?**

John Brown's Raid

Both Lincoln and Douglas believed the slavery crisis had to be resolved within the framework of the nation's laws. Abolitionist John Brown felt no such constraints. Brown viewed himself as an angel of God, avenging the evil of slavery. Even before one of his sons was killed in Bleeding Kansas, he had concluded that violence was the best way to reach his goal. By late 1857, Brown had begun planning his attack. For many months, he crisscrossed New England, the Midwest, and Canada, soliciting recruits and funds to mount an armed assault on slavery.

Brown Seizes the Arsenal at Harpers Ferry By the fall of 1859, Brown was ready. "Men, get your arms," he cried, "we will proceed to the ferry." Gathering his following of 21 men—including 5 free African Americans—Brown set out to seize the federal arsenal in **Harpers Ferry,** Virginia (now in West Virginia). He hoped to inspire local slaves to join a revolution that would destroy slavery in the South.

Brown had chosen Harpers Ferry because it was a hub of trains and canals, which would offer efficient escape routes. This locale was also near the borders of Pennsylvania, a free state, and Maryland, where there were many free African Americans. It seemed the ideal launching point.

But the effort failed. Few Americans—black or white—were prepared to join a rebellion organized by this intense, fanatical white man. Frederick Douglass, a close friend, refused to join, warning Brown that his mission "would array the whole country against us." A few black and white abolitionists sent money for guns, but in the end Brown's revolution came to naught. Local residents surrounded Brown's men in the arsenal, and federal troops soon arrived to arrest them. Two more of Brown's sons were killed in the fray, but a few of the rebels escaped to Canada. Brown and several others, however, went to the gallows.

Brown's Execution Deepens the Growing Divide Brown's attack increased the heat in already-boiling tempers. Similar to the *Dred Scott* decision, suspicion and rumors were widespread. Stephen Douglas accused the Republicans of instigating Brown's attack, and southern congressmen demanded an investigation. But when Abraham Lincoln and other Republicans condemned Brown, the rumors subsided. Yet, many congressmen still came armed to the Capitol. The uncertainty caused a steep drop in cotton prices, and many southerners prepared for war.

Many northerners thought abolitionist activism had gone too far. But others now saw Brown as a courageous martyr. They were moved to tears when he proclaimed his willingness to "mingle my blood . . . with the blood of my children and with the blood of millions in this slave country whose rights are disregarded by wicked, cruel, and unjust enactments."

Some admirers suggested that Brown should be buried at Boston's Bunker Hill, next to the heroes of the American Revolution. A popular song later immortalized him, celebrating the fact that "his soul goes marching on." On the morning of his execution, Brown made the prophetic prediction that "the crimes [of slavery] of this guilty land will never be purged away, . . . without very much bloodshed." Many Americans agreed with him.

Checkpoint **How did Americans respond to John Brown's raid and his execution?**

SECTION 3 Assessment

Progress Monitoring *Online*
For: Self-test with vocabulary practice
www.pearsonschool.com/ushist

Comprehension

1. **Terms and People** For each item below, write a sentence that explains its significance.
   - Know-Nothings
   - Republican Party
   - Dred Scott
   - Roger B. Taney
   - Abraham Lincoln
   - Stephen A. Douglas
   - Harpers Ferry

2. **NoteTaking Reading Skill: Sequence** Use your timeline to answer the Section Focus Question: What developments deepened the divisions between North and South?

Writing About History

3. **Quick Write: Organize Your Ideas** Write a short argument supporting a presidential candidate from the election of 1856. Explain why this candidate was the best person to lead the politically unstable nation.

Critical Thinking

4. **Recognize Ideologies** Why did the Republican Party form?
5. **Recognize Effects** How did the *Dred Scott* decision increase tensions between North and South?
6. **Determine Relevance** How successful was John Brown's raid on Harpers Ferry?

SECTION 4

◄ President Buchanan

WITNESS HISTORY

The President Falters

Outgoing President James Buchanan condemned South Carolina's secession from the Union but was unwilling to use force to stop it. Many northerners criticized his weak response to the crisis. In an address to Congress, he seemed almost baffled that the situation had deteriorated so far:

> "How easy it would be for the American people to settle the slavery question forever and to restore peace and harmony to this distracted country! . . . All that is necessary to accomplish the object, and all for which the slave States have ever contended, is to be let alone and permitted to manage their domestic institutions in their own way. As sovereign States, they, and they alone, are responsible before God and the world for the slavery existing among them."
>
> —President Buchanan, December 3, 1860

Lincoln, Secession, and War

Objectives

- Compare the candidates in the election of 1860, and analyze the results.
- Analyze why southern states seceded from the Union.
- Assess the events that led to the outbreak of war.

Terms and People

Jefferson Davis
John C. Breckinridge
Confederate States of America
Crittenden Compromise
Fort Sumter

NoteTaking

Reading Skill: Identify Causes and Effects
Use a cause-and-effect chart to show the events that led to secession.

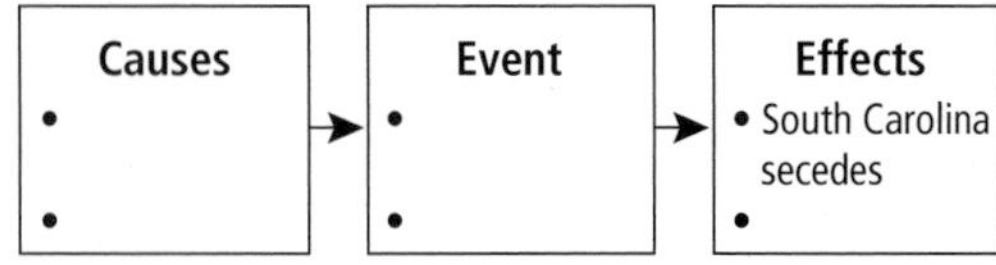

Why It Matters Despite repeated attempts at compromise, disagreement between the North and the South over the issue of slavery continued to deepen. With the election of Republican President Abraham Lincoln in 1860, the crisis came to a head. The Union of states that had been formed less than a hundred years before was about to dissolve. **Section Focus Question: How did the Union finally collapse into a civil war?**

The Election of 1860

John Brown's raid and execution were still fresh in the minds of Americans as the 1860 presidential election approached. Uncertainty about Kansas—would it be a slave state or a free state?—added to the anxiety. In the North, loss of confidence in the Supreme Court resulting from the *Dred Scott* decision and rage about the Fugitive Slave Act's intrusion into the states' independence further aggravated the situation.

The issue of states' rights was on southern minds as well. Would northern radicals conspire to eliminate slavery not only in the territories but also in the original southern states? In the spring of 1860, Mississippi senator **Jefferson Davis** convinced Congress to adopt resolutions restricting federal control over slavery in the territories. The resolutions also asserted that the Constitution prohibited Congress or any state from interfering with slavery in the states where it already existed. Even southerners who did not own slaves felt that their way of life and their honor were under attack.

With ill will running so deep, the upcoming elections posed a serious dilemma. It was hard to imagine that either northerners or southerners would accept a President from the other region. Could the Union survive?

Democrats Split Their Support The Democrats held their nominating convention in Charleston, North Carolina. For ten days, they argued about the issue that had plagued the nation for decades: slavery. The southern Democrats called for a platform supporting federal protection of slavery in the territories. The northern Democrats, who backed Stephen Douglas, supported the doctrine of popular sovereignty. When the Douglas forces prevailed, the delegates from eight southern states walked out and formed a separate convention.

The Democrats were now split into two parties. The northern Democrats nominated Stephen A. Douglas. The southern Democrats nominated the Vice President, **John C. Breckinridge** of Kentucky. Breckinridge was committed to expanding slavery into the territories.

Whigs Make a Last Effort In the meantime, the few remaining Whigs teamed up with the Know-Nothings to create the Constitutional Union Party. They hoped to heal the split between North and South. Their candidate was John Bell, a little-known moderate from Tennessee. Their platform condemned sectional parties and promised to uphold "the Constitution of the country, the Union of the States and the enforcement of the laws."

Republicans Nominate Lincoln The Republicans, who had gained great strength since their formation, held their nominating convention in Chicago. After several ballots, they nominated Abraham Lincoln as their candidate. When the party convened, seasoned politician William H. Seward of New York had been the favorite to win the nomination. But when many delegates began to worry that Seward's antislavery views were too radical, the convention went with the more moderate Lincoln.

Vocabulary Builder
stipulate–(STIHP yuh layt) *v.* to specify or indicate

The Republican platform called for the end of slavery in the territories. At the same time, the Republicans defended the right of each state to control its own institutions and stipulated that there should be no interference with slavery in the states where it already existed. Abraham Lincoln—with his great debating skills, his moderate views, and his reputation for integrity—was seen as the ideal candidate to carry the Republican platform to victory.

Lincoln Wins the Election Benefiting from the fracturing among the other political parties, Lincoln won the election handily, with 40 percent of the popular vote and almost 60 percent of the electoral vote. Still, he did not receive a single southern electoral vote. In fact, he was not even on the ballot in most southern states.

Breckinridge was the clear favorite among southern voters, carrying every cotton state, along with North Carolina, Delaware, and Maryland. The border

Events That Changed America

INTERACTIVE Whiteboard

THE ELECTION OF 1860

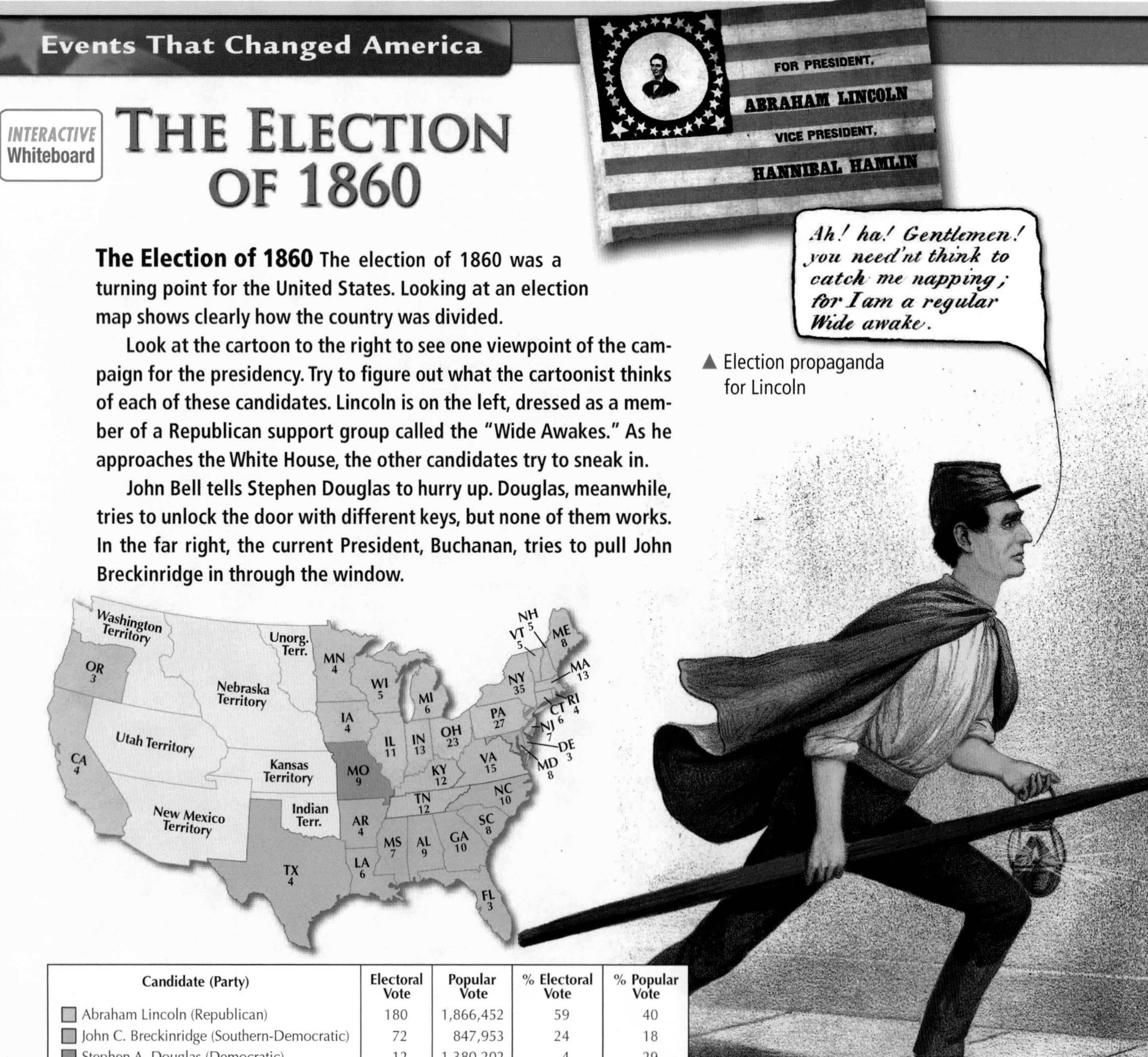

The Election of 1860 The election of 1860 was a turning point for the United States. Looking at an election map shows clearly how the country was divided.

Look at the cartoon to the right to see one viewpoint of the campaign for the presidency. Try to figure out what the cartoonist thinks of each of these candidates. Lincoln is on the left, dressed as a member of a Republican support group called the "Wide Awakes." As he approaches the White House, the other candidates try to sneak in.

John Bell tells Stephen Douglas to hurry up. Douglas, meanwhile, tries to unlock the door with different keys, but none of them works. In the far right, the current President, Buchanan, tries to pull John Breckinridge in through the window.

▲ Election propaganda for Lincoln

Candidate (Party)	Electoral Vote	Popular Vote	% Electoral Vote	% Popular Vote
Abraham Lincoln (Republican)	180	1,866,452	59	40
John C. Breckinridge (Southern-Democratic)	72	847,953	24	18
Stephen A. Douglas (Democratic)	12	1,380,202	4	29
John Bell (Constitutional Union)	39	590,901	13	13

states of Virginia, Kentucky, and Tennessee—whose economic interests were not as closely tied to slavery as the cotton states were—gave their votes to Bell. Stephen A. Douglas, although running second to Lincoln in the popular vote, won only in Missouri and New Jersey.

The election of 1860 demonstrated that Americans' worst fears had come to pass. There were no longer any national political parties. Bell and Breckinridge competed for southern votes, while Douglas and Lincoln competed in the North and West. The North and South were now effectively two political entities, and there seemed no way to bridge the gap.

Vocabulary Builder
entity–(EHN tuh tee) *n.* something that exists as a single and complete unit

✓ **Checkpoint** **How did Lincoln's election reflect the break between the North and the South?**

▲ Election propaganda for Bell

Why It Matters

The election of 1860 was the first national contest for the Republican Party, which became one of the two major political parties. More importantly, the election was the immediate cause for the secession of the southern states.

Thinking Critically

1. **Analyze** What is the meaning of the keys with which Douglas is trying to open the door?
2. **Make Comparisons** How is Lincoln portrayed in a different manner from the other candidates?

History Interactive
For: More about the election of 1860
www.pearsonschool.com/ushist

Long-term Causes of the Civil War
• Sectional economic and cultural differences • Debate over expansion of slavery into the territories • Political compromises failed to ease sectional differences and resolve question of expanding slavery —Missouri Compromise (1820) —Compromise of 1850 —Kansas-Nebraska Act (1854) • Laws and court decisions increased sectional tension —Fugitive Slave Act (1850) —Dred Scott decision —Tariff policy • Growth of the antislavery movement • *Uncle Tom's Cabin*

Short-term Causes of the Civil War
Kansas-Nebraska Act splits political parties ↓ Breakdown of the party system ↓ Lincoln elected President ↓ South Carolina secedes from the Union

The Union Collapses

Southerners were outraged that a President could be elected without a single southern vote. In the southerners' perception, the South no longer had a voice in the national government. They decided to act.

Southern States Leave the Union As soon as Lincoln's election was confirmed, the South Carolina legislature summoned a state convention. Meeting in Charleston on December 20, 1860, and without a dissenting vote, the convention declared that "the union now subsisting between South Carolina and the other States, under the name of the 'United States of America,' is hereby dissolved." They cited as their reason for seceding the election of a President "whose opinions and purposes are hostile to slavery." They further declared:

> **Primary Source** "On the 4th of March next, [a new administration] will take possession of the Government. It has announced . . . that a war must be waged against slavery until it shall cease throughout the United States. . . .
>
> The Guarantees of the Constitution will then no longer exist; the equal rights of the States will be lost. The slaveholding States will no longer have the power of self-government, or self-protection, and the Federal Government will have become their enemy."
>
> —Declaration of the Immediate Causes Which Induce and Justify the Secession of South Carolina From the Federal Union, December 20, 1860

In the next few weeks, six other states of the Deep South seceded from the Union. Sentiments favoring secession were not always unanimous, with the gravest doubts surfacing in Georgia. State senator Alexander H. Stephens, though alarmed by Lincoln's election, was devoted to the Union of states under the Constitution: "This government of our fathers, with all its defects, comes nearer the objects of all good government than any other on the face of the Earth," he said. But Georgia voted to secede anyway. Like delegates in the other slave-dependent, cotton-growing states, they believed they had to take this step to protect their property and way of life.

The Confederacy Is Formed In February 1861, the seven seceding states established the **Confederate States of America.** They then proceeded to frame a constitution for the new government. The Confederate constitution closely resembled the U.S. Constitution. However, it stressed the independence of each state and implied that states had the right to secede. It also guaranteed the protection of slavery. To win the support of Britain and France, which adamantly opposed the slave trade, it prohibited importing new slaves from other countries.

Not all southerners backed the Confederacy. Some large planters with economic ties to the North still hoped for a compromise. So, too, did many small farmers with no vested interest in slavery. To gain the loyalty of such citizens, the Confederacy chose former Mississippi senator Jefferson Davis as their president. Davis had supported the Compromise of 1850, but he had also insisted that the South should be left alone to manage its own culture and institutions—including slavery.

A Final Compromise Fails Some politicians sought a final compromise. Kentucky senator John Crittenden proposed a constitutional amendment allowing slavery in western territories south of the Missouri Compromise line. He also called for federal funds to reimburse slaveholders for unreturned fugitives.

Geography Interactive
For: Interactive map
www.pearsonschool.com/ushist

Focus On Geography

Slavery and Secession

Cotton cultivation increased substantially in the nineteenth century. Harvesting cotton (right) was a time-consuming and difficult task that required a large labor force. This led planters to buy more enslaved people. In 1861, more than 50 percent of the population was enslaved in some areas of the Deep South. Tension built over extending slavery into the territories. The states with the largest slave populations seceded. Border states, which had fewer enslaved people, stayed in the Union.

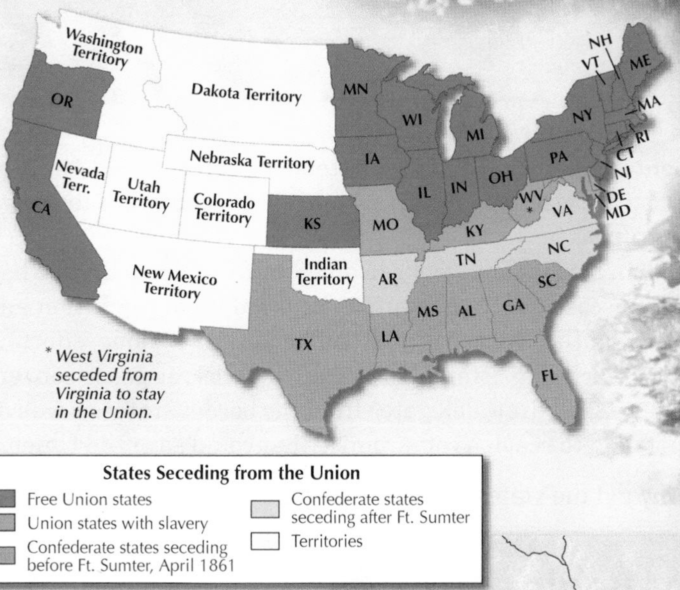

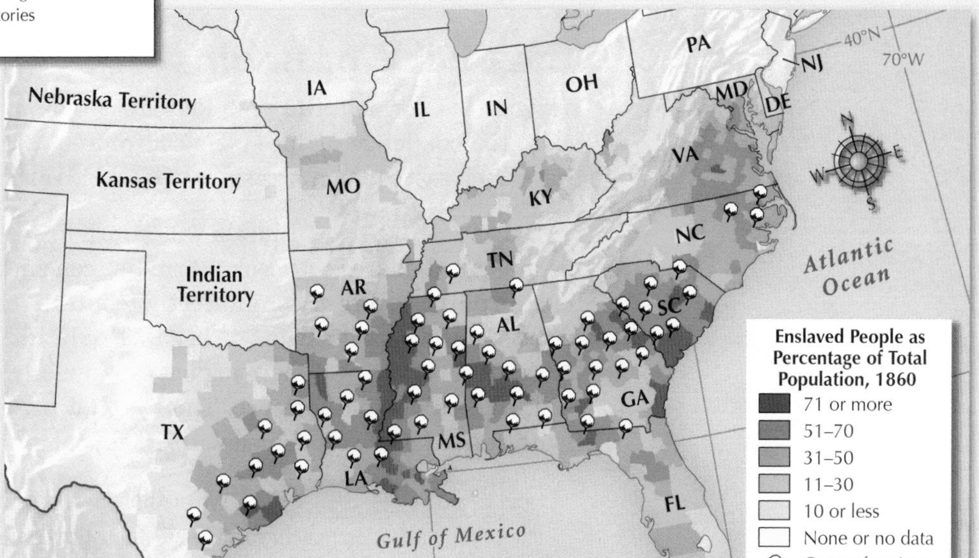

Geography and History

- Which states had the greatest concentrations of enslaved people?
- What was the relationship between the percentage of enslaved people and secession?

History Makers

Abraham Lincoln (1809–1865)
Lincoln grew up on the Kentucky frontier and moved to Illinois as a young man. Although he had little formal education, he enjoyed reading and disliked farming. In 1836, he began practicing law in Illinois.

Lincoln began his political career as a Whig in the Illinois state legislature, later serving in the U.S. Congress. Although not an abolitionist, he opposed slavery. When the Whigs fell apart, he joined the new Republican Party.

Upon assuming the presidency, Lincoln faced tough challenges. Seven states had already left the Union. Lincoln won reelection as he steered the country through the Civil War. He is best remembered for ending slavery in the United States.

Jefferson Davis (1808–1889)
Davis is best known as president of the Confederate States of America. Before the Civil War, he served in the U.S. House of Representatives. Davis left Congress in 1846 to serve in the army during the war with Mexico.

Returning to Mississippi as a hero, Davis became a U.S. Senator and the Secretary of War under Franklin Pierce. He opposed South Carolina's secession, still hoping for a compromise. But when Mississippi seceded, Davis resigned from the Senate.

Two weeks later, Davis became president of the CSA. Despite his strong leadership, the Confederacy lacked the manpower and manufacturing capability to defeat the Union. After the war, Davis was tried for treason but was pardoned by President Johnson.

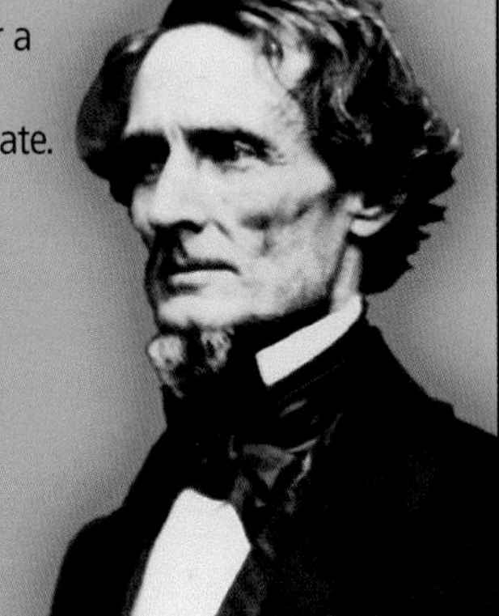

Lincoln, now President-elect, warned that Crittenden's plan would "lose us everything we gained by the election." A narrow margin of senators voted down this **Crittenden Compromise.**

President Buchanan, in his last few weeks in office, told Congress that he had no authority to prevent secession. He lamented the breakup of the Union and sympathized with the South's concerns, but he made no serious effort to resolve the crisis. Other pacifying attempts also failed. A secret peace convention held in Washington, which drew delegates from the border states as well as the North and South, failed to reach a compromise that could save the Union.

✓ **Checkpoint Why did the states of the Deep South leave the Union?**

The Civil War Begins

Amid this turmoil, the new President took office. Lincoln had no illusions about the challenge he faced. He confronted "a task," he feared, "greater than that which rested upon [President George] Washington."

Lincoln Takes Office Lincoln was sworn in as President on March 4, 1861. In his inaugural address, he took a firm but conciliatory tone toward the South. "I have no purpose, directly or indirectly, to interfere with the institution of slavery in the states where it exists," he began. But he *did* intend to preserve the Union. "No state, upon its own mere action, can lawfully get out of the Union," he said. Still, he would avoid violence. There would be no war, he pledged, unless the South started it. He concluded with an appeal to the South to live in peace:

> **Primary Source** "We are not enemies, but friends. We must not be enemies. Though passion may have strained, it must not break our bonds of affection. The mystic chords of memory, stretching from every battle-field, and patriot grave, to every living heart and hearthstone, all over this broad land, will yet swell the chorus of the Union, when again touched, as surely they will be, by the better angels of our nature."
>
> —Abraham Lincoln, March 4, 1861

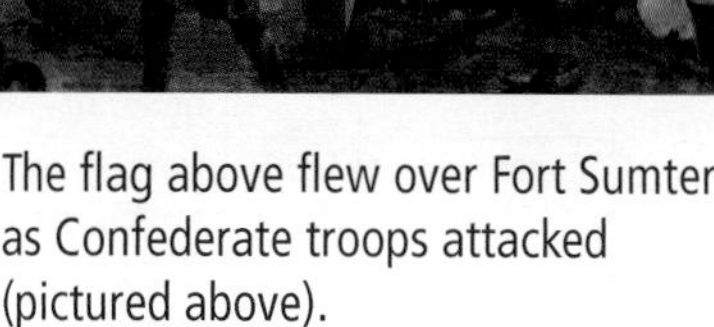

The flag above flew over Fort Sumter as Confederate troops attacked (pictured above).

Lincoln Decides to Act When the southern states seceded, they seized the federal forts and arsenals within their borders. Only four forts remained in Union hands. The most important of these was **Fort Sumter,** which guarded the harbor at Charleston, South Carolina. In January 1861, President Buchanan tried to send troops and supplies to the fort, but the unarmed supply ship sailed away when Confederate guns fired on it. Upon taking office, Lincoln had to decide whether to take the risk required to hold on to these forts or yield to Confederate demands that they be surrendered.

By April, the troops at the fort desperately needed food and supplies. Lincoln, who still hoped to bring back the South without bloodshed, faced a dilemma. Should he try to resupply the fort? Or should he let the Confederates take it? Lincoln struggled to make a decision. During his inaugural address, he had promised southerners that "the government will not assail you." But as President, he was sworn to defend the property of the United States. A wrong move could touch off a war. At last, trying to steer a middle course, Lincoln notified South Carolina that he was sending supplies—food only, no arms—to the fort.

Fort Sumter Falls South Carolinians were suspicious of Lincoln's motives and ordered the Fort Sumter garrison to surrender to the Confederacy. When the Union troops refused, the Confederates fired on the fort. The Union troops eventually ran out of ammunition, forcing the commander to surrender.

Northerners responded to the attack on Fort Sumter with shock and anger. A few days later, on April 15, President Lincoln declared that "insurrection" existed and called for 75,000 volunteers to fight against the Confederacy.

The South responded just as strongly. At the outbreak of hostilities, the states of Virginia, Arkansas, Tennessee, and North Carolina joined the Confederacy. As in the North, the South raised troops quickly and struggled to equip and train them before sending them into battle.

Both sides predicted a short skirmish, with victory only a few days or months away. These predictions were unfounded. Americans faced years of terrible suffering before the fighting that had begun at Fort Sumter finally ended.

✓ **Checkpoint** **What event led to the outbreak of war?**

SECTION 4 Assessment

Progress Monitoring *Online*
For: Self-test with vocabulary practice
www.pearsonschool.com/ushist

Comprehension

1. **Terms and People** For each item below, write a sentence explaining its significance.
   - Jefferson Davis
   - John C. Breckinridge
   - Confederate States of America
   - Crittenden Compromise
   - Fort Sumter
2. **NoteTaking Reading Skill:** Use your cause-and-effect chart to answer the Section Focus Question: How did the Union finally collapse into a civil war?

Writing About History

3. **Quick Write: Outline an Argument** Outline an answer to this question: Was secession the only option for the South?

Critical Thinking

4. **Recognize Effects** How did the election of 1860 increase sectional tensions?
5. **Recognize Causes** Why did the southern states secede?
6. **Demonstrate Reasoned Judgment** How could Buchanan have prevented war?

CHAPTER 10

Quick Study Guide

Progress Monitoring *Online*
For: Self-test with vocabulary practice
www.pearsonschool.com/ushist

Key Legislation Affecting Slavery

Legislation	Effect on Slavery
Missouri Compromise	Prohibited slavery in all federal territories north of 36° 30′, except in Missouri
Compromise of 1850	Opened New Mexico and Utah territories to slavery by applying popular sovereignty, or letting the residents decide when they applied for statehood; ended the slave trade in Washington, D.C.
Fugitive Slave Act	Part of the Compromise of 1850, this law forced all Americans to return fugitive slaves to their masters or face arrest
Personal liberty laws	State laws passed in several northern states that allowed slave catchers to be arrested for kidnapping
Kansas-Nebraska Act	Opened Kansas and Nebraska territories to slavery by applying popular sovereignty

Proslavery and Antislavery Arguments

Proslavery Arguments
• Banning slavery would deprive slave owners of their property (their slaves) • African Americans were better off enslaved than free because slave owners cared for them • Free African Americans would compete with white laborers for jobs
Antislavery Arguments
• Slavery was morally wrong • Slavery harmed society

Key People

Person	Significance
John Brown	Abolitionist who killed proslavery settlers in Kansas and tried to start a slave revolt in Virginia
James Buchanan	President from 1857–1861 who did not act to stop South Carolina's secession
Henry Clay	Kentucky senator who proposed the Compromise of 1850
John Calhoun	South Carolina senator who supported slavery and warned that the South would secede if slavery were threatened
Jefferson Davis	Mississippi senator who became president of the Confederacy
Stephen Douglas	Illinois Democrat who believed in popular sovereignty and steered the Compromise of 1850 through the Senate; he defeated Lincoln in the 1858 Senate race but lost to him in the 1860 presidential election
Frederick Douglass	Former slave and abolitionist who became the face of abolitionism
William Lloyd Garrison	White abolitionist and publisher of *The Liberator* who helped organize the American Anti-Slavery Society
Abraham Lincoln	Republican President whose election in 1860 caused South Carolina to secede
Dred Scott	The slave who sued for freedom after living in a free state and a free territory; his loss in the Supreme Court outraged many northerners and pushed the nation toward war
Daniel Webster	Massachusetts senator and nationalist who supported the Compromise of 1850 to save the Union

Quick Study Timeline

In America

1848
The Mexican War ends and northern Mexico is annexed to the United States

1850
Congress agrees to the Compromise of 1850

Presidential Terms: James K. Polk 1845–1849; Zachary Taylor 1849–1850; Millard Fillmore 1850–1853

1846 | 1849 | 1852

Around the World

1848
Revolutions take place throughout Europe

1850
Taiping Rebellion begins in China

American Issues Connector

By connecting prior knowledge with what you have learned in this chapter, you can gradually build your understanding of enduring questions that still affect America today. Answer the questions below. Then, use your American Issues Connector study guide (or go online: www.pearsonschool.com/ushist).

Issues You Learned About

- **Federal Power and States' Rights** State governments and the federal government may disagree over legislation.

1. How did the system of popular sovereignty favor state power over federal power?
2. Why and how did some northern state legislatures reject the federal government's passage of the Fugitive Slave Act?
3. How did the constitution created by the Confederacy support states' rights over federal power?

- **Sectionalism and National Politics** During the mid-1800s, the South and North were split over the issue of slavery.

4. What incidents among members of Congress emphasized the emotional nature of the debate over slavery between North and South?
5. Which groups backed each of the four candidates for the presidency in 1860, and what positions did each hold?
6. Why was the result of the presidential election of 1860 unacceptable to the South?

- **America at War** By the mid-1800s, the United States had been involved in several wars, but never one that pitted citizens against each other.

7. How did Lincoln attempt to breach the divide between North and South in his inaugural address?
8. What caused Lincoln to call for troops to fight against the Confederacy?

Connect to Your World — Activity

Social-reform literature can be described as literature that an author writes in hopes of bringing about a specific change in society. Many writers created social-reform literature as part of the debate over slavery. Think about a social problem that exists today. You may review a newspaper, newsmagazine, or online news source to help you select a social problem. Then, research the problem at the local library or online and decide what you think would be the best way to solve it. Finally, imagine that you are going to create a piece of social-reform literature to persuade people to share your side of the issue, and write an outline for your book.

History Interactive
For: Interactive timeline
www.pearsonschool.com/ushist

1854 Congress passes the Kansas-Nebraska Act

1857 The Supreme Court rules against Dred Scott

1860 Lincoln wins the presidential election, leading South Carolina to secede

1861 The Civil War begins at Fort Sumter, South Carolina

Franklin Pierce 1853–1857 | James Buchanan 1857–1861 | Abraham Lincoln 1861–1865

1855 | 1858 | 1861

1854 Britain and France join the Crimean War against Russia

1857 Hindu and Muslim soldiers in India rebel against British rule

1861 Czar Alexander II emancipates Russian serfs

Chapter Assessment

Terms and People

1. What was the **Fugitive Slave Act**? Under the Fugitive Slave Act, what would happen to people who assisted a fugitive slave?
2. What was the **Underground Railroad**? How did the Underground Railroad work?
3. Why was the territory called **"Bleeding Kansas"**? Why did Kansas become a battleground for proslavery and antislavery forces?
4. What was the strategic significance of **Harpers Ferry**? Why did abolitionists launch an attack there?
5. Who was **Jefferson Davis**? What point of view did he support on the slavery issue?

Focus Questions

The focus question for this chapter is **How did the nation's expansion lead to the Civil War?** Build an answer to this big question by answering the focus questions for Sections 1 through 4 and the Critical Thinking questions that follow.

Section 1

6. How did Congress try to resolve the dispute between North and South over slavery?

Section 2

7. How did the Fugitive Slave Act and the Kansas-Nebraska Act increase tensions between the North and the South?

Section 3

8. What developments deepened the divisions between North and South?

Section 4

9. How did the Union finally collapse into a civil war?

Critical Thinking

10. **Explain Causes** Up until the 1840s, the Whigs and the Democrats had failed to declare an opinion on the slavery issue. What caused them to change this policy?
11. **Compare Points of View** How did Calhoun and Webster respond to Clay's proposed compromise? With which side did the majority of congressmen agree?
12. **Recognize Bias** What attitudes did abolitionist writers and proslavery writers portray in their novels?
13. **Analyze Information** In what ways did the Kansas-Nebraska Act support the expansion of slavery?
14. **Draw Conclusions** How did the Republican Party grow so rapidly that within two years its candidates were challenging the established parties?
15. **Predict Consequences** What did Frederick Douglass predict might happen as a result of the *Dred Scott* decision?
16. **Analyze Charts** Study the chart below. Then, answer the question that follows. Which candidate received the fewest electoral votes in comparison with his percentage of the popular vote? Explain.

Candidate	Percentage of Popular Vote	Number of Electoral Votes
Abraham Lincoln	39.9%	180
Stephen A. Douglas	29.4%	12
John C. Breckinridge	18.1%	72
John Bell	12.6%	39

17. **Identify Point of View** Why was the Crittenden Compromise unacceptable to Lincoln?

Writing About History

Debate a Topic The decades before the Civil War were filled with political compromises, new political parties, and feuding between different sections of the country. Prepare an argument that you would use to debate the question: Was the Civil War inevitable?

Prewriting

- Make a list of the arguments for each side of the debate.
- Rank each point from most to least important.
- Decide which side you are going to argue.

Drafting

- Develop a working thesis, and choose information to support the thesis.
- Make an outline organizing your argument and addressing the points that the opposition might make.
- Write an introduction that explains your argument, provide a body of evidence, and end with a convincing conclusion.

Revising

- Use the guidelines on page SH16 of the Writing Handbook to revise your report. Review your argument and add information where it is not strong.

Document-Based Assessment

John Brown's Raid

Abolitionist John Brown dedicated his life to ending slavery in the United States. He was a deeply religious man, but he did not hesitate to use violence to achieve his goals. To what extent was John Brown's raid at Harpers Ferry successful? Use your knowledge of the raid and its consequences along with Documents A, B, C, and D to answer questions 1 through 4.

Document A

"I John Brown am now quite certain that the crimes of this guilty land: will never be purged away; but with Blood. I had as I now think: vainly flattered myself that without very much bloodshed; it might be done."

—*John Brown, December 2, 1859*

Document B

"Though it convert the whole Northern people, without an exception, into furious, armed abolition invaders, yet old Brown will be hung! That is the stern and irreversible decree, not only of the authorities of Virginia, but of the PEOPLE of Virginia, without a dissenting voice. And, therefore, Virginia, and the people of Virginia, will treat with the contempt they deserve, all the craven appeals of Northern men in behalf of old Brown's pardon. The miserable old traitor and murderer belongs to the gallows, and the gallows will have its own."

—*Richmond "Whig" newspaper editorial quoted in the* Liberator, *November 18, 1859*

Document C

"But the question is, Did John Brown fail? . . . And to this I answer ten thousand times, No! . . . When John Brown stretched forth his arm the sky was cleared. The time for compromises was gone—the harmed hosts of freedom stood face to face over the chasm of a broken Union—and the clash of arms was at hand. The South staked all upon getting possession of the Federal Government, and failing to do that, drew the sword of rebellion and thus made her own, and not Brown's, the lost cause of the century."

—*Frederick Douglass, May 30, 1881*

Document D

The Last Moments of John Brown
by Thomas Hovenden, 1884

---

1. How do Documents A, C, and D portray John Brown?
   A As a criminal who committed treason
   B As a martyr who died for a just cause
   C As an abolitionist who went too far
   D As the cause of the Civil War

2. What does Document B predict about Brown's execution?
   A It will turn southerners into abolitionists.
   B The people of Virginia will not support it.
   C People will quickly forget about Brown.
   D It may turn northerners into abolitionists.

3. According to Frederick Douglass, what did John Brown's raid achieve?
   A It pushed the nation toward the Civil War.
   B It made abolitionism a lost cause.
   C It helped the North to gain control of the government.
   D It achieved nothing of importance.

4. **Writing Task** To what extent was John Brown's raid on Harpers Ferry a success or a failure? Consider different points of view when constructing your answer. Use your knowledge of the time period and specific evidence from the primary sources above to support your answer.

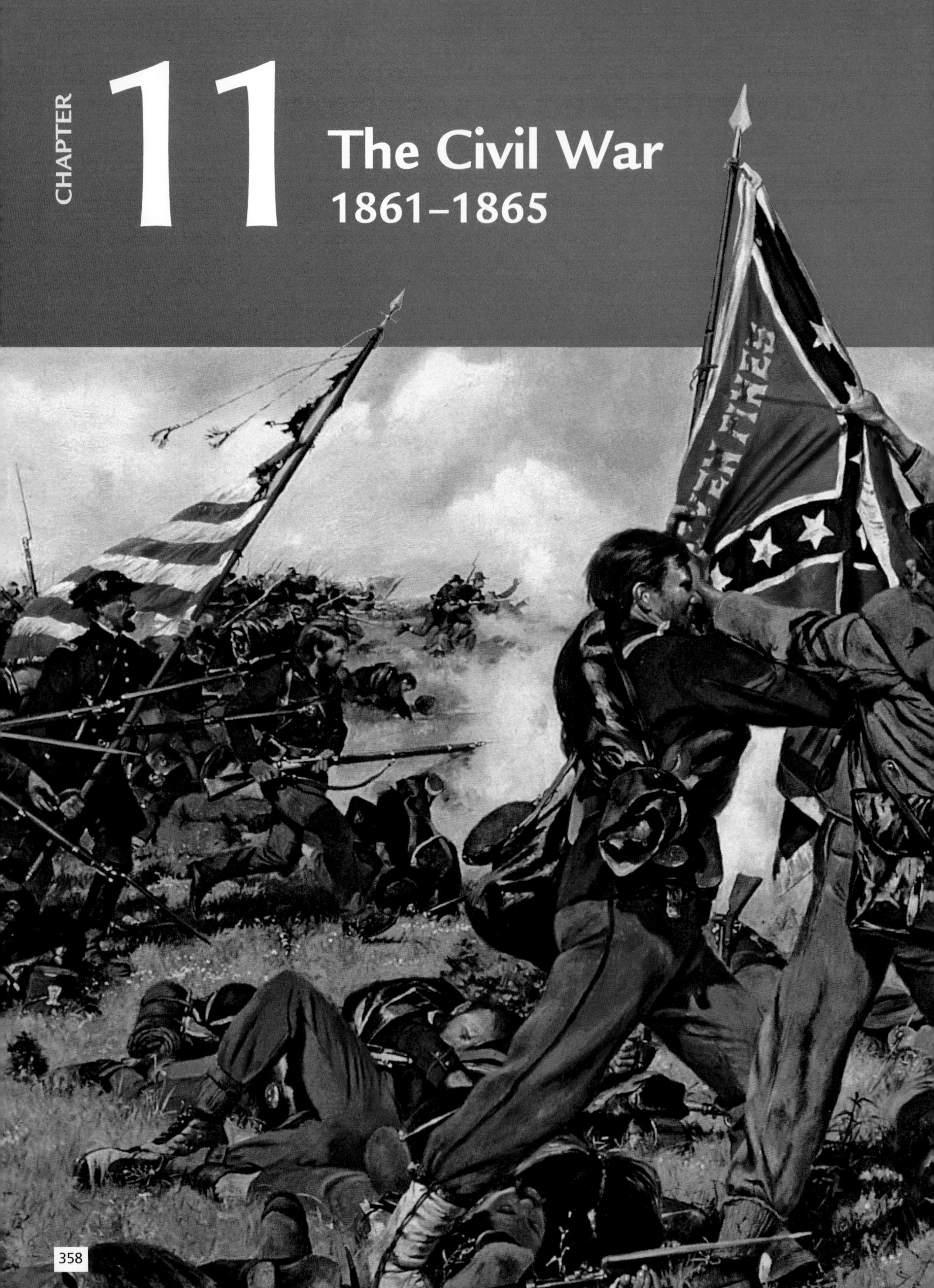

CHAPTER

11 The Civil War 1861–1865

WITNESS HISTORY

War Between the States

During the Civil War, soldiers sang marching songs to stir their spirits for battle. Union troops proclaimed:

> "The Union forever,
> Hurrah! boys, hurrah!
> Down with the traitors,
> Up with the stars!"
>
> —"The Battle Cry of Freedom"

But Confederates countered with their own battle cry:

> "But now, when Northern treachery
> Attempts our rights to mar,
> We hoist on high the Bonnie Blue Flag
> That bears a single star."
>
> —"The Bonnie Blue Flag"

◄ This painting by Don Troiani depicts the Battle of Gettysburg.

A tattered diary of a Civil War soldier

Cannonball from a battle between Union and Confederate ironclads

Chapter Preview

Chapter Focus Question: What were the causes, key events, and effects of the Civil War?

Union drummer boy

Use the ☑ **Quick Study Timeline** at the end of this chapter to preview chapter events.

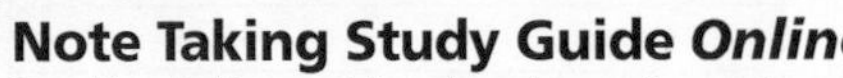

Note Taking Study Guide *Online*
For: Note Taking and American Issues Connector
www.pearsonschool.com/ushist

▲ An illustration shows Union volunteers, each dressed up like Uncle Sam, marching in a parade.

WITNESS HISTORY

Marching Off to War

When the war began, families on both sides watched as husbands and sons rushed to join the Union and Confederate armies. Often there were celebratory parades to cheer the soldiers on. As the men marched off, family members felt both sadness and pride. One Richmond resident noted these mixed emotions in her diary:

> "An old lady, the mother of several dearly loved sons, but echoed the almost universal sentiment when she said . . . 'War, I know is very dreadful, but if, by the raising of my finger, I could prevent my sons from doing their duty to their country now, though I love them as my life, I could not do it. I am no coward, nor have I brought up my boys to be cowards. They must go if their country needs them.'"
>
> —Sallie Brock Putnam, *Richmond During the War*

Resources, Strategies, and Early Battles

Objectives

- Contrast the resources and strategies of the North and South.
- Describe the outcomes and effects of the early battles of the Civil War.

Terms and People

blockade
Robert E. Lee
Anaconda Plan
border state
Stonewall Jackson
George B. McClellan
Ulysses S. Grant
Shiloh

NoteTaking

Reading Skill: Categorize As you read, use a table to note the advantages of the North and the South at the beginning of the war.

Wartime Advantages	
Union	Confederacy
• Population • •	• Strong military tradition • •

Why It Matters In 1861, the long, bitter dispute over slavery and states' rights erupted into war. The first shots at Fort Sumter set the stage for a long, costly struggle. At stake was the survival of the United States. **Section Focus Question: How did each side's resources and strategies affect the early battles of the war?**

Union and Confederate Resources

As the Civil War began, each side possessed significant strengths and notable weaknesses. At first glance, most advantages appeared to add up in favor of the Union.

Advantages of the Union The North enjoyed a tremendous advantage in population. Some 22 million people lived in the states that stayed in the Union. By contrast, the Confederacy had a population of only 9 million, of whom 3.5 million were enslaved African Americans.

The industrialized North was far better prepared to wage war than the agrarian South. Most of the nation's coal and iron came from Union mines, and the vast West was a source of gold, silver, and other resources. The densely populated urban areas of the Northeast supported a wide variety of manufacturing. With mechanized factories and a steady flow of European immigrants seeking work, the Union could produce more ammunition, arms, uniforms, medical supplies, and railroad cars than the Confederacy could. In addition, the Union had a larger railroad network for moving troops and material.

The Union had a small but well-organized navy. By late 1861, the Union had launched more than 250 warships, with dozens more under construction. The South had no navy at all, leaving it vulnerable to a naval **blockade** in which Union ships prevented merchant vessels from entering or leaving the South's few good ports, thereby crippling southern trade.

Finally, while the Confederate government was new and inexperienced, the North had an established government and an outstanding leader in Abraham Lincoln. Not everyone recognized this fact at the outset of the war, but Lincoln's leadership would prove invaluable to the Union cause.

Vocabulary Builder
thereby–(ther BĪ) *adv.* by or through that

Advantages of the Confederacy

Still, the North did have some distinct weaknesses compared to the South. One of the Confederacy's advantages was psychological. Many northerners were willing to let the slaveholding South go. To them, preserving the Union was not worth killing and dying for. But the Confederacy was fighting for survival. Although there were pockets of pro-Union feeling in places such as western Virginia, most southern whites believed passionately in the Confederate cause. Even those who were not slaveholders resented what they saw as northern efforts to dominate them.

When the war began, Union forces consisted of only 16,000 men. New recruits signed on for three months of service, hardly long enough to form an efficient fighting team. The South faced similar challenges in assembling its armies, but it had a strong military tradition and fine leaders like Virginia's **Robert E. Lee.** Lee, who had an outstanding record in the United States Army, actually opposed secession and slavery. Yet he turned down an offer to command Union forces. He wrote:

> **Primary Source** "With all my devotion to the Union, and the feeling of loyalty and duty of an American citizen, I have not been able to make up my mind to raise my hand against my relatives, my children, my home. I have therefore resigned my commission in the army, and save in defense of my native state . . . I hope I may never be called upon to draw my sword."
>
> —Robert E. Lee, letter to his sister, April 20, 1861

In fact, Lee did accept command of the Confederate army and provided the South with inspiring military leadership throughout the war. The North struggled to find a commander of such caliber.

Resources Compared

As fresh-faced soldiers marched off to war, each side's resources gave it advantages over the other. For example, in terms of population, the Union outnumbered the Confederacy by a ratio of 2.5 to 1. *Pick two pie graphs and explain what advantage those resources gave to the North or South.*

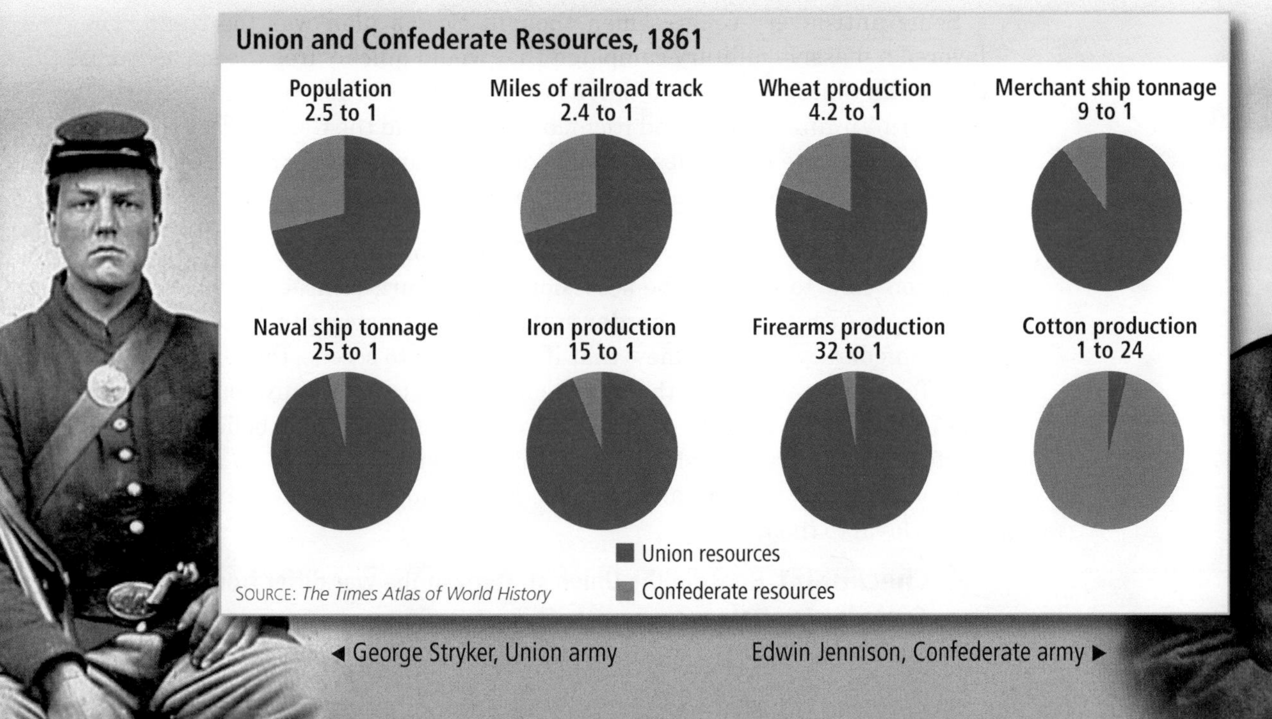

◄ George Stryker, Union army

Edwin Jennison, Confederate army ►

Finally, the Confederacy had a number of strategic advantages. It did not need to conquer the North; it simply had to avoid defeat, expecting that in time the North would give up the effort. By and large, southern forces would be fighting a defensive war on familiar, friendly ground while northern forces had to fight an offensive war in enemy territory. Union troops and supplies had to travel farther to reach the field of battle. The North also had to devote precious military resources to defending Washington, D.C. Only the Potomac River separated the Union capital from Confederate Virginia.

✓ **Checkpoint What were some of the strengths and weaknesses of the Union and the Confederacy?**

Confederate and Union Strategies

As the two sides prepared for war, Union and Confederate leaders contemplated their goals and how they might go about meeting them. While northerners hoped for a quick victory, southern strategists planned for a prolonged war.

Vocabulary Builder
erode–(ee ROHD) *v.* to eat into; wear away

The Confederacy Seeks Foreign Support

The strategy of the Confederacy had two main thrusts. Militarily, the South hoped to preserve its small armies while doing enough damage to erode the Union's will to fight. Politically, it hoped to win formal recognition from Britain and France. Trade with these nations was crucial to the South, since the supply of manufactured goods from the North was now cut off. By the same token, the European textile industry was dependent on southern cotton. Confederate leaders reasoned that if the war dragged on, French and British mills would run out of raw cotton. Therefore, these countries might be willing to provide military aid to the South.

The Union Devises the Anaconda Plan

The initial Union strategy was a two-part plan devised by General Winfield Scott, a Virginia-born hero of the Mexican-American War and the commander of all U.S. forces in 1861. First, the Union would blockade southern ports, starving the South of income and supplies. Then, Union forces would drive southward along the Mississippi River. Union control of the Mississippi would split the Confederacy in two, fatally weakening it. Scott's plan came to be known as the **Anaconda Plan,** after a type of snake that coils around its prey and squeezes it to death.

Some antislavery congressmen thought Scott's plan was too timid. They favored a massive military campaign that would quickly free the slaves across the South. Lincoln also hoped that a decisive victory over rebel forces massed in northern Virginia and around Richmond might lead the Confederacy to negotiate an end to the crisis. Despite such criticism and concentration on winning quickly, the Anaconda Plan remained central to the Union war strategy.

Lincoln Avoids the Slavery Issue

The Union also faced a tricky political question: how to prevent the secession of Missouri, Kentucky, Delaware, and Maryland. Although these **border states** allowed slavery, they had not joined the Confederacy. Lincoln knew that if they chose to secede, the Union could be lost. To reduce this threat, the President insisted that his only goal was to save the Union. In his First Inaugural Address, he announced, "I believe I have no lawful right to [free the slaves], and I have no inclination to do so." Although Lincoln's stand troubled abolitionists, he did succeed in keeping the border states loyal to the Union.

✓ **Checkpoint How did the Union strategy in the war differ from the Confederate strategy?**

INFOGRAPHIC

New Technology Changes Warfare

The Civil War revolutionized warfare. On water, new warships steamed into battle encased in thick armor plating. On land, the minié ball and the repeating rifle greatly improved soldiers' accuracy and firepower in battle. These changes resulted in staggering numbers of casualties on both sides. As the conflict dragged on, military commanders were forced to change their strategies to account for the deadly impact of new technology.

▲ Wooden ships were no match for ironclads like the Confederate *Virginia* and the Union *Monitor*.

▼ Cone-shaped minié balls were accurate at much greater ranges than round bullets.

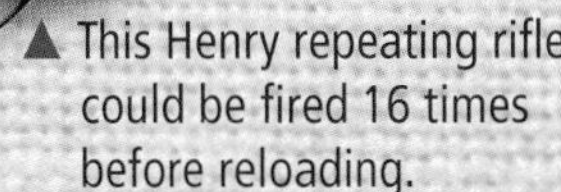

▲ This Henry repeating rifle could be fired 16 times before reloading.

▲ As casualties mounted, soldiers adapted their tactics and dug trenches for cover enemy fire.

▼ Most Civil War troops were arranged into tightly packed formations prior to marching against an enemy position. New firearms and ammunition exacted a gruesome toll on the massed attackers.

Thinking Critically

1. **Compare and Contrast** How did Civil War technology differ from earlier military technology?
2. **Draw Conclusions** How might future military tactics change because of lessons learned during the Civil War?

NoteTaking

Reading Skill: Recognize Sequence Use a timeline to note how the fighting developed during the early years of the Civil War.

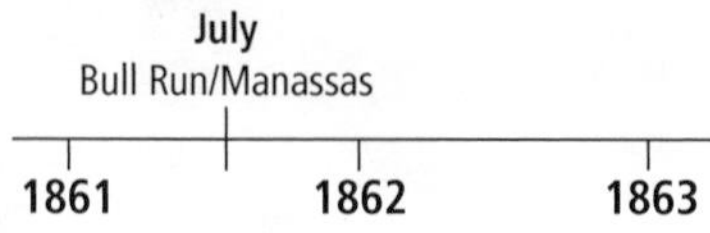

Early Battles of the Civil War

The Civil War started slowly. The first large battle did not take place until three months after the firing on Fort Sumter. Ultimately, the conflict would span nearly four years and stretch across much of the continent.

Bull Run Shakes Union Confidence In July 1861, General Scott sent General Irvin McDowell and more than 30,000 Union troops to do battle with Confederate forces waiting outside Washington. The two armies met at Bull Run, a creek near Manassas, Virginia. In the battle's first hours, Union troops gained the upper hand. But a determined stand led by Confederate General Thomas J. Jackson sent them scrambling back to Washington. Confederates nicknamed their hero **Stonewall Jackson** in honor of his refusal to yield to the Union armies.

The battle, known as the Battle of Bull Run in the North and the Battle of Manassas in the South, proved a shock to those who had hoped the war would end quickly—and who were unprepared for the carnage modern warfare could produce. Lincoln responded by calling for additional troops and by replacing McDowell with General **George B. McClellan.**

Grant Fights in Tennessee While McClellan began to organize his Army of the Potomac, General **Ulysses S. Grant** pursued the Mississippi Valley wing of the Anaconda Plan. In February 1862, he directed the attack and capture of two Confederate strongholds—Fort Henry on the Tennessee River and Fort Donelson on the Cumberland River. His bold action drove Confederate forces from western Kentucky and much of Tennessee, and boosted northern morale. However, in April, Grant's troops fought a terrible battle in southwest Tennessee. In just two days of fighting, nearly 25,000 Union and Confederate soldiers were killed or wounded. The Battle of **Shiloh** horrified both the North and South and damaged Grant's rising reputation.

Union Forces Capture New Orleans While Shiloh shocked the public, it did not slow the course of the war. Just days later, Union ships under the command of David Farragut sailed through the Gulf of Mexico and seized the vital southern port of New Orleans at the mouth of the Mississippi. Emboldened by his success, Farragut continued to sail north, hoping to capture the Confederate stronghold of Vicksburg, Mississippi. The Confederates, however, stopped Farragut's fleet more than 50 miles from his goal. Meanwhile, pushing southward from Tennessee, Grant's land forces were also checked in their advance on Vicksburg. Complete Union control of the Mississippi would have to wait.

A Fierce Fight at Shiloh

Union troops fight off a Confederate charge into the "Hornet's Nest." This sunken road saw some of the heaviest casualties at Shiloh. *Why do you think soldiers called this position the "Hornet's Nest"?*

Fighting Spreads to the Southwest The American Southwest held strategic value to both sides in the Civil War. The region held rich gold mines and offered access to California and the Pacific Ocean. Despite its importance, neither side stationed many troops in the region.

Fighting did take place as far west as Arizona. But the most significant action occurred in New Mexico in early 1862, when a Confederate force marched up the Rio Grande from Texas. The goal was to

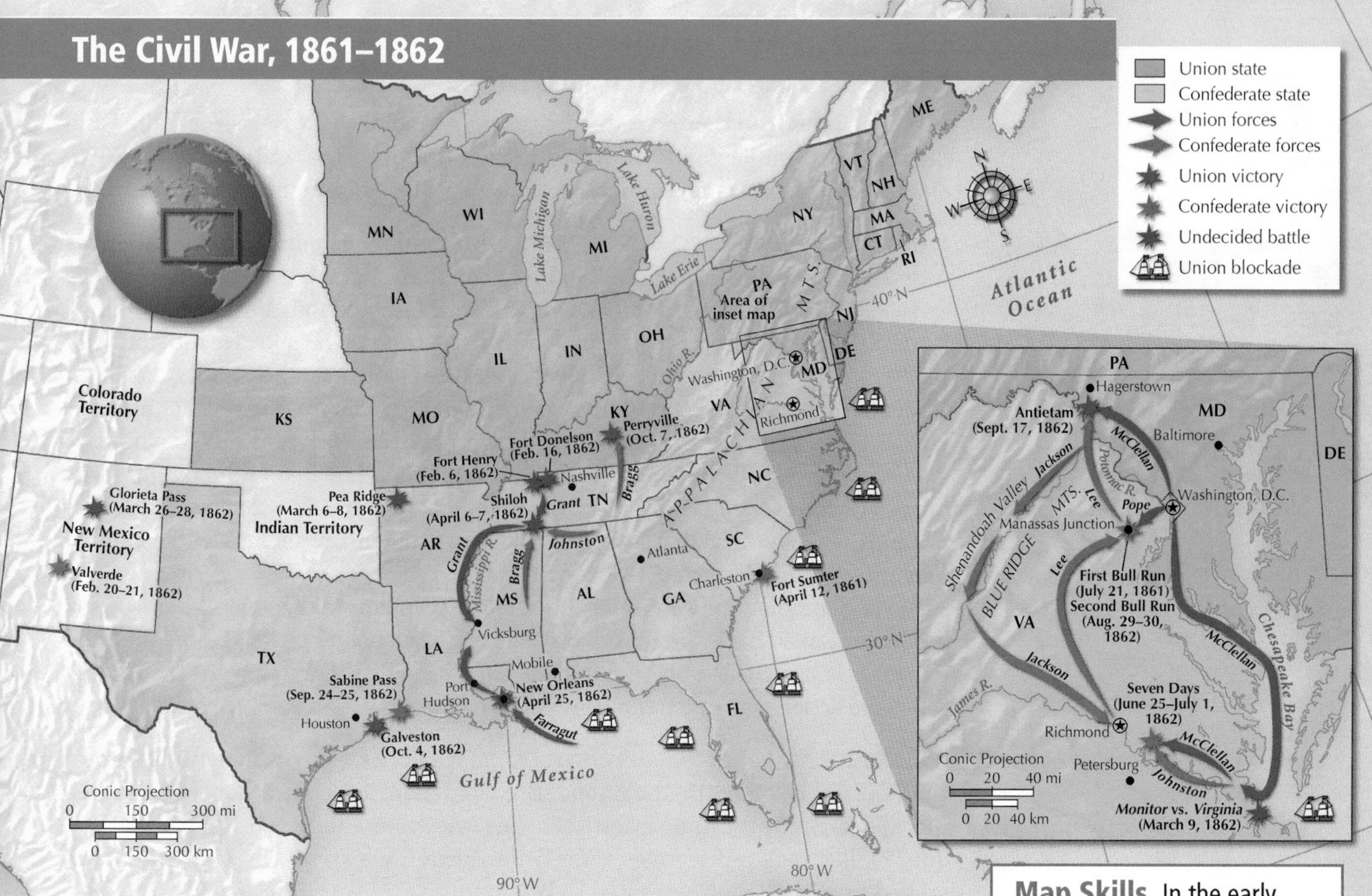

Map Skills In the early years of the war, most fighting took place in two distinct theaters of operation: one in Virginia and the other in the Mississippi River valley.

1. **Locate:** (a) Bull Run, (b) Richmond, (c) New Orleans, (d) Glorieta Pass
2. **Movement** What was McClellan's strategy for victory?
3. **Draw Inferences** How did the Union blockade affect the Confederate economy?

Geography *Interactive*
For: Interactive map
www.pearsonschool.com/ushist

drive Union troops from the Southwest and capture it for the Confederacy. The rebel troops were defeated in late March at Glorieta Pass, thanks in part to the destruction of their supply train by a Union force under Major John Chivington and Lt. Col. Manuel Chavez. The Confederates eventually retreated back into Texas, never to mount another threat to Union control of the Southwest.

The Union and Confederacy also vied for the loyalty of the Southwest's residents—many of whom in the past had been treated as outcasts. The Union got help from Mexican American militia in Texas, which worked to disrupt Confederate supply lines. Both sides also courted Native American groups throughout the entire West. The Cheyennes were able to bargain with the Union government for land in return for their aid. The Confederates persuaded the Creeks and Choctaws to support their cause. They also sought support from the Cherokee nation. The Cherokees, however, split over the question of which side to support. Such conflict within Native American groups was not uncommon as loyalties shifted during the course of the war.

The *Monitor* Battles the *Virginia* Few of the major battles of the Civil War took place at sea. However, one notable exception occurred in 1862 when the Union ship *Monitor* clashed with its Confederate opponent *Virginia* off the Virginia coast. The Union had hired a European engineer to design the *Monitor* as a model for a fleet of ships plated with iron armor. The Confederacy, meanwhile, had built the ironclad *Virginia* by refitting a Union ship previously known as the *Merrimack*. On March 9, the two ironclads met in battle. Though neither ship emerged the victor, the contest signaled the beginning of the end of wooden warships.

✓ **Checkpoint What was the outcome and impact of the first major battle of the Civil War?**

This cannonball was fired from the *Monitor* during its contest against the *Virginia. What does the photo suggest about the battle?*

Stalemate Develops in the East

While Union and Confederate forces squared off in the Mississippi Valley and farther west, major fighting in the East focused on the state of Virginia. As elsewhere, the outcomes did not prove decisive for either side.

Lincoln Urges McClellan to Attack Since taking command of Union forces after Bull Run, General McClellan had been planning what he hoped would be a decisive drive on the Confederate capital at Richmond, Virginia. A skilled leader beloved by his troops, McClellan was also very cautious. He did not want to execute his plan until he felt his troops were ready.

McClellan's caution created friction with Lincoln, who was anxious for military victories. Yet, even as he pushed McClellan to act, the President was unwilling to give the general all the forces he asked for. Lincoln insisted on holding a large force near the capital to protect it from a Confederate attack. Stonewall Jackson's brilliant campaign in the spring of 1862 in the nearby Shenandoah Valley of Virginia increased Lincoln's concerns.

By midsummer, Lincoln insisted that McClellan take action. Reluctantly, McClellan sailed his army southward across Chesapeake Bay. The force landed on a peninsula southeast of Richmond and then began its march toward the capital. Thus, the action was called the Peninsular Campaign.

McClellan Fails to Take Richmond McClellan's army was actually larger than the force defending Richmond. But Confederate General Robert E. Lee led his troops skillfully. In a series of battles known as the Seven Days (June 26–July 2), Lee took advantage of McClellan's cautious style. The Union advance stalled and McClellan retreated to Washington.

After the retreat, Lincoln replaced McClellan. The move proved to be a mistake. At the Second Battle of Bull Run in late August, Lee's Confederates handed the Union a crushing defeat. Stonewall Jackson was instrumental in outmanuevering a larger Union force and nearly destroying it before the Federals could retreat. The victory, known in the South as the Second Battle of Manassas, energized Lee and led Lincoln to return McClellan to command. Lee and McClellan would soon face off in the single bloodiest day of the Civil War.

 **Checkpoint Why did Lincoln and McClellan clash in early 1862?**

SECTION 1 Assessment

Progress Monitoring *Online*
For: Self-test with vocabulary practice
www.pearsonschool.com/ushist

Comprehension

1. **Terms and People** For each of the following items, write a sentence explaining its significance.
   - blockade
   - Robert E. Lee
   - Anaconda Plan
   - border state
   - Stonewall Jackson
   - George B. McClellan
   - Ulysses S. Grant
   - Shiloh

2. **NoteTaking Reading Skill: Categorize** Use your table to answer the Section Focus Question: How did each side's resources and strategies affect the early battles of the war?

Writing About History

3. **Quick Write: Plan a News Article** Review the information about the battle between the *Monitor* and the *Virginia*. Plan a news article you might write about the encounter by answering the questions required of every news article: *Who? What? When? Where? Why?*

Critical Thinking

4. **Predict Consequences** Which side do you think had the best long-term chances for victory at the start of the Civil War? Why?
5. **Identify Effects** Choose two battles discussed in this section and describe one effect of each.
6. **Contrast** Based on what you have read, how did Grant and McClellan differ as military leaders?

◄Frederick Douglass

▲Like the African Americans gathered in this postcard, Frederick Douglass celebrated the long-awaited Emancipation Proclamation

WITNESS HISTORY

A Memorable Day

Frederick Douglass, the foremost African American abolitionist, journalist, and orator of his time, traveled the United States and spoke out against slavery. In his autobiography, he described his reaction to the Emancipation Proclamation:

"The first of January, 1863, was a memorable day in the progress of American liberty and civilization. It was the turning-point in the conflict between freedom and slavery. A death blow was then given to the slave-holding rebellion. Until then the federal arm had been more than tolerant to that relic of barbarism. . . . We fought the rebellion, but not its cause. And now, on this day . . . the formal and solemn announcement was made that thereafter the government would be found on the side of emancipation. This proclamation changed everything."

—Frederick Douglass, *Life and Times of Frederick Douglass*

African Americans and the War

Objectives

- Analyze why Lincoln decided to issue the Emancipation Proclamation and what it achieved.
- Assess the different roles that African Americans played in the Civil War.

Terms and People

contraband
Antietam
Emancipation Proclamation
Militia Act
54th Massachusetts Regiment

NoteTaking

Reading Skill: Identify Supporting Details As you read, use an outline to record details about African Americans during the war.

I. The Push Toward Emancipation
   A. Enslaved African Americans Seek Refuge
      1. Enslaved people come under Union control
      2.
   B.
II. Emancipation at Last

Why It Matters Despite Lincoln's efforts to downplay the slavery issue, abolitionists kept up the pressure to end slavery. Soon, Lincoln himself recognized the need to include freedom for enslaved Americans among the goals of the war. His actions helped bring about the beginning of the end of slavery in the United States. At the same time, African American soldiers joined the fight for freedom. **Section Focus Question: How did the Emancipation Proclamation and the efforts of African American soldiers affect the course of the war?**

The Push Toward Emancipation

Pressures at home and abroad urged Lincoln to address the issue of slavery. Abolitionists such as Frederick Douglass and William Lloyd Garrison, as well as the thousands who supported them, were impatient with Lincoln's policies. Another reason for Lincoln to act was that slavery was unpopular in Europe. Antislavery sentiment was one of the main reasons why Great Britain was reluctant to aid the Confederacy.

Enslaved African Americans Seek Refuge On the battlefield, Union officers faced a dilemma: what to do with enslaved African Americans who came under their control. It was absurd, argued these officers, to return slaves to their owners. Early on, Union General Benjamin Butler had gathered hundreds of black refugees into his camps and set them to manual labor. He declared the fugitives under his protection to be **contraband,** or captured war supplies. General John Frémont went a step further, declaring that enslaved people who came under his command in Missouri were free. Fearing retaliation from the border states, Lincoln reversed Frémont's order.

Lincoln's Plan Needs a Victory Lincoln realized he could not avoid the slavery issue for long. He secretly began working on a plan for the emancipation of enslaved African Americans living in Confederate states. In the summer of 1862, he shared his ideas with a surprised Cabinet. The members generally supported Lincoln's plan but agreed that its announcement should wait. After the Union failure at the Second Battle of Bull Run, such a proclamation might look like an act of desperation. What was needed was a major Union victory. Several weeks later, Lincoln got his opportunity.

Victory Comes at Antietam After his army's recent victories, General Lee was brimming with confidence. In early September 1862, he led his troops into Maryland, the border state where many favored the South. Lee hoped to inspire a pro-Confederate uprising. A victory on Union soil might also spur European recognition of the Confederacy. Lee also hoped to acquire an abundance of food supplies for his hungry army in an area unmolested by war.

Vocabulary Builder
ally–(uh LĪ) *v.* to unite or associate for a specific purpose

Lee's invasion did not go according to plan. On September 8, the general issued a "Proclamation to the People of Maryland" that invited them to ally themselves with the South. But Marylanders responded to the invitation with far less enthusiasm than Lee had anticipated. A few days later, Union soldiers found a copy of Lee's battle plan wrapped around some cigars at an abandoned rebel campsite. As a result, Lee lost the crucial element of surprise. When McClellan reviewed the orders, he exclaimed, "Here is a paper with which if I cannot whip Bobbie Lee, I will be willing to go home."

The two armies converged at Sharpsburg, Maryland, and McClellan's troops fanned out near Antietam Creek. On September 17, Union troops attacked Lee's army in three phases, moving from one side of the Confederate line to the other. By the end of the day, more than 23,000 soldiers lay dead or wounded. The Battle of **Antietam** marked the bloodiest single day of the Civil War. With his army exhausted and Maryland still in the Union, Lee retreated to Virginia. Though Union losses exceeded Confederate losses, Lincoln had the victory he needed to move forward with emancipation.

✓ **Checkpoint Why did Lincoln decide to change his official stand on slavery?**

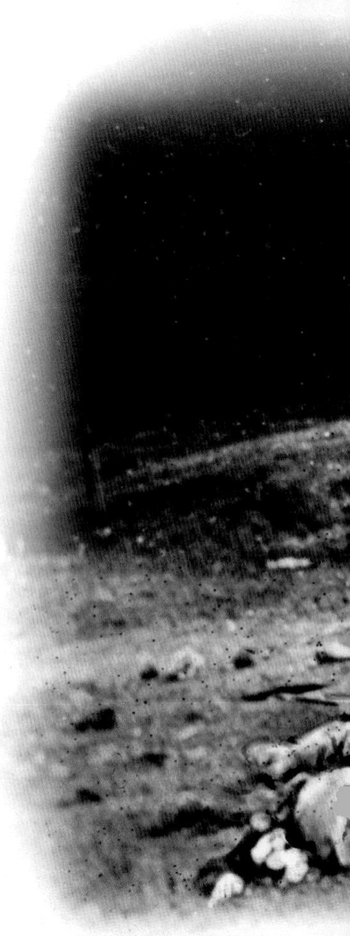

Emancipation at Last

On September 22, 1862, Lincoln formally announced the **Emancipation Proclamation.** Issued as a military decree, it freed all enslaved people in states still in rebellion after January 1, 1863. It did not, however, apply to loyal border states or to places that were already under Union military control. Lincoln hoped the proclamation might convince some southern states to surrender before the January 1 deadline.

Many northerners responded to the Emancipation Proclamation with great excitement. "We shout for joy that we live to record this righteous decree," rejoiced Frederick Douglass. Some who had once criticized Lincoln for inaction now praised his name and held rallies in honor of the proclamation. An African American minister in Philadelphia said:

> **Primary Source** "The morning dawns! The long night of sorrow and gloom is past. . . . The Proclamation has gone forth, and God is saying . . . to this nation Man must be free. . . . Your destiny as white men and ours as black men are one and the same."
>
> —Jonathan C. Gibbs, January 1, 1863

Others were less enthusiastic. William Lloyd Garrison grumbled that "what is still needed is a proclamation distinctly announcing the total abolition of slavery." British abolitionists applauded the President's move—but also wondered about Lincoln's conviction, since he attacked slavery only in areas over which he had no control. Lincoln also received criticism in Congress. Many Republicans felt the proclamation had not gone far enough, while many Democrats felt it was too drastic a step. The Proclamation may have been one factor leading to Democratic gains in the fall congressional elections.

Although the Emancipation Proclamation did not actually free a single slave, it was an important turning point in the war. For northerners, it redefined the war as being "about slavery." For white southerners, the call to free the slaves ended any desire for a negotiated end to the war. Confederate leaders now felt they must fight to the end.

For African Americans in the North, the proclamation made them eager to join the Union army and fight against slavery. Even before Lincoln's decree, growing demands by African Americans—and a growing need for soldiers on

Antietam: The Bloodiest Day of the War

The gruesome clash at Antietam claimed thousands of lives. Below, Confederate dead lie near the Dunker Church. Though the Union lost more men during the battle, Confederate losses amounted to a higher percentage of troop strength. *Why was Lincoln eager to claim victory in spite of Union losses?*

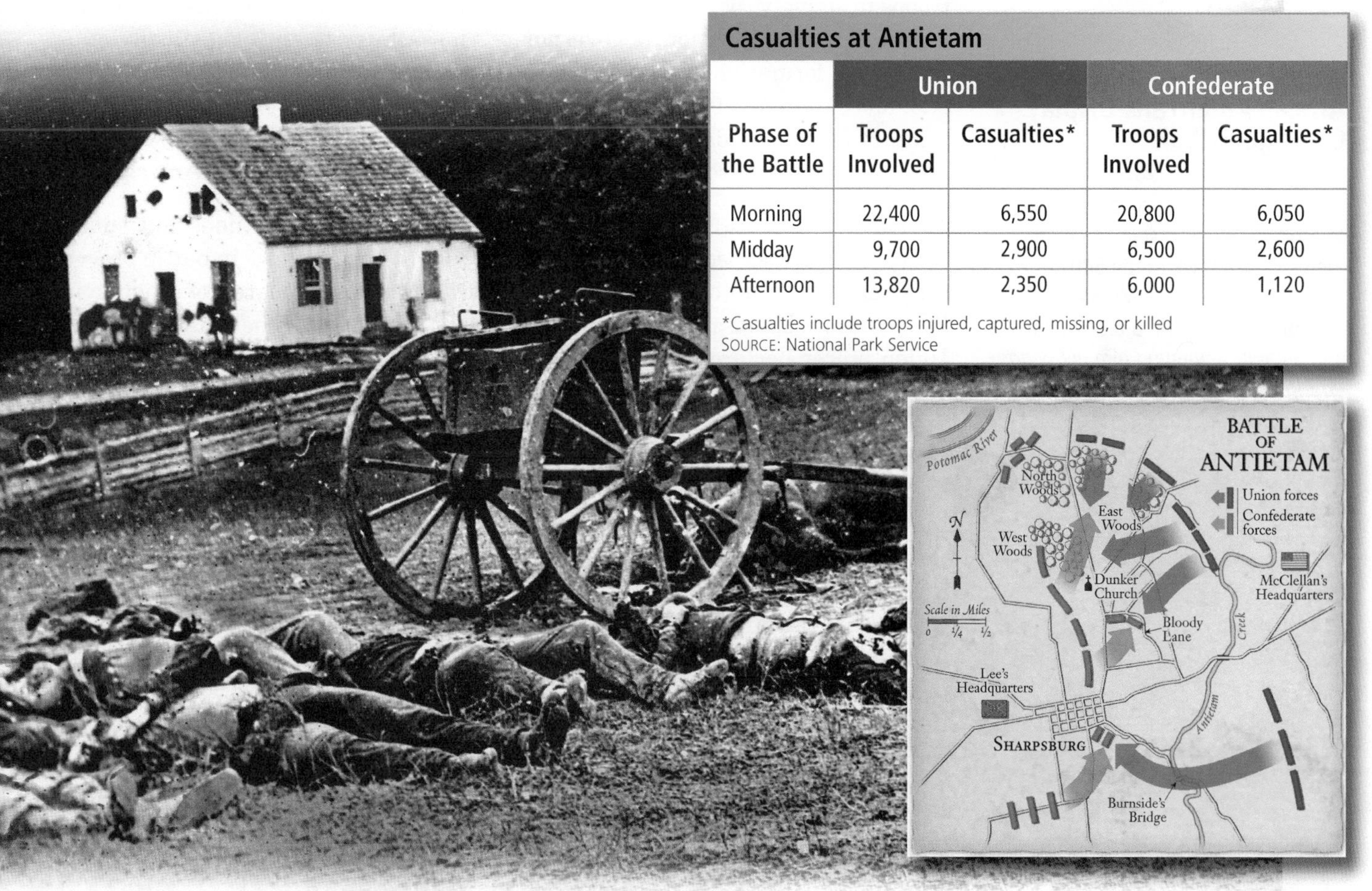

Casualties at Antietam

Phase of the Battle	Union: Troops Involved	Union: Casualties*	Confederate: Troops Involved	Confederate: Casualties*
Morning	22,400	6,550	20,800	6,050
Midday	9,700	2,900	6,500	2,600
Afternoon	13,820	2,350	6,000	1,120

*Casualties include troops injured, captured, missing, or killed
SOURCE: National Park Service

This drummer had been enslaved prior to his service in the 79th U.S. Colored Infantry. ▼

▲ Poster used to recruit African American regiments

The 54th Massachusetts Regiment storms Fort Wagner.

the frontlines—had led the Union to reconsider its ban on African American soldiers. Just two months before the proclamation, Congress had passed the **Militia Act,** mandating that black soldiers be accepted into the military.

✓ **Checkpoint What were the effects of the Emancipation Proclamation?**

African Americans Join the Fight

With the Emancipation Proclamation, the Union moved from allowing black troops to actively recruiting them. African American leaders were asked to seek volunteers. The abolitionist governor of Massachusetts enthusiastically supported the formation of the all-black **54th Massachusetts Regiment.** By war's end, more than 180,000 African American volunteers had served in the Union military. The Confederacy considered drafting slaves and free blacks in 1863 and 1864, but most southerners opposed the enlistment of African Americans.

African American Soldiers Fight Bravely Racist attitudes left many whites with low expectations for black troops. But performance in battle proved these expectations to be false. In June 1863, accounts appeared of a battle in Port Hudson, Mississippi—the first major test for African American soldiers. A Union officer declared that "my prejudices with regard to negro troops have been dispelled by the battle. . . . The brigade of negroes behaved magnificently."

A few weeks later, the 54th Massachusetts followed Robert Gould Shaw, their respected white officer, into battle at Fort Wagner in Charleston harbor. During the unsuccessful assault, Shaw and many of his men were killed. Nevertheless, the 54th had earned respect for its discipline and courage. One soldier received the Congressional Medal of Honor—the first of almost two dozen African American soldiers to be decorated for bravery.

Still, African American troops faced prejudice. They were usually assigned menial tasks, such as cooking, cleaning, or digging latrines. They often served the longest guard duty and were placed in exposed battle positions. It took a three-year effort to win equal pay. Black soldiers also knew that if captured, they would be killed. In one bloody incident, Confederates massacred more than 100 African American soldiers who were trying to surrender at Fort Pillow, Tennessee. Nevertheless, African Americans supported the Union in hundreds of battles, and some 70,000 lost their lives.

African Americans Display Courage in War

The photos and illustrations above testify to the dedication and bravery of African American soldiers during the war. The attack of the 54th Massachusetts on Fort Wagner was memorialized in both a monument and an award-winning film. *Why do you think these soldiers were so honored by succeeding generations of Americans?*

▲ Monument to the 54th Massachusetts Regiment in Boston

▲ Actor Denzel Washington in the 1989 movie *Glory*

Enslaved People Help the Union Cause Enslaved African Americans in the South also played an important role in the war, finding a variety of ways to passively or actively help the Union forces. White owners often abandoned plantations for the safety of southern cities, leaving trusted slaves to manage the farm. Advancing Union forces often enlisted these African Americans to produce food for the northern troops. Other African Americans used their familiarity with the terrain to serve as spies or scouts for Union armies. Sometimes, emancipated slaves organized their own military units. Regiments of former slaves appeared in such places as South Carolina, Kansas, and Missouri. Across the South, ambitious slaves seized the opportunity to begin to shape their own civilian lives. Some demanded, and got, wages for their work. Others simply abandoned their masters, fleeing to Union camps or to the North or West. They turned Lincoln's promise of freedom into a reality.

✓ **Checkpoint How did African Americans respond to Union recruitment efforts after the Emancipation Proclamation?**

SECTION 2 Assessment

Progress Monitoring *Online*
For: Self-test with vocabulary practice
www.pearsonschool.com/ushist

Comprehension

1. **Terms and People** For each of the following terms, write a sentence explaining its significance.
   - Antietam
   - Emancipation Proclamation
   - 54th Massachusetts Regiment
2. **NoteTaking Reading Skill: Identify Supporting Details** Use your outline to answer the Section Focus Question: How did the Emancipation Proclamation and the efforts of African American soldiers affect the course of the war?

Writing About History

3. **Quick Write: Write Headlines** Choose three events described in this section. Imagine you are writing a news article about each one. Write a headline for each article that will capture its main idea and attract the attention of readers.

Critical Thinking

4. **Make Decisions** Do you think Lincoln was right to wait so long before declaring emancipation? Why or why not?
5. **Identify Effects** What do you think was the most important effect of the Emancipation Proclamation?
6. **Draw Inferences** A corporal in the 54th Massachusetts wrote to President Lincoln: "Your Excellency, we have done a Soldier's Duty. Why can't we have a Soldier's pay?" What does this letter suggest about conditions for black soldiers in the Civil War?

Primary Source

Abraham Lincoln: *The Emancipation Proclamation*

Five days after the Union victory at Antietam, Abraham Lincoln issued the Emancipation Proclamation. The presidential decree freed all enslaved persons in states under Confederate control as of January 1, 1863. One of the most important documents in American history, it changed the nature of the Union cause and paved the way for the eventual abolition of slavery by the Thirteenth Amendment in 1865.

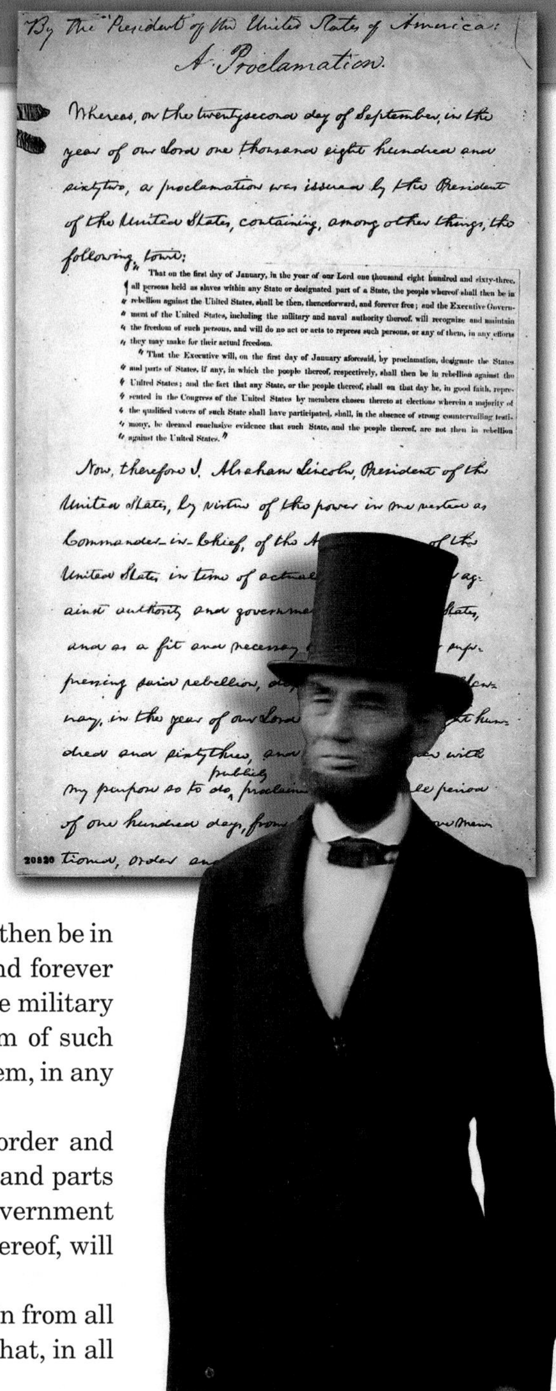

Whereas, on the twenty-second day of September, in the year of our Lord one thousand eight hundred and sixty-two, a proclamation was issued by the President of the United States, containing, among other things, the following, to wit:

That on the first day of January, in the year of our Lord one thousand eight hundred and sixty-three, all persons held as slaves within any State or designated part of a State, the people whereof shall then be in rebellion against the United States, shall be then, thenceforward,[1] and forever free; and the Executive Government of the United States, including the military and naval authority thereof, will recognize and maintain the freedom of such persons, and will do no act or acts to repress such persons, or any of them, in any efforts they may make for their actual freedom. . . .

And by virtue of the power, and for the purpose aforesaid, I do order and declare that all persons held as slaves within said designated States, and parts of States, are, and henceforward shall be free; and that the Executive government of the United States, including the military and naval authorities thereof, will recognize and maintain the freedom of said persons.

And I hereby enjoin upon the people so declared to be free to abstain from all violence, unless in necessary self-defence; and I recommend to them that, in all cases when allowed, they labor faithfully for reasonable wages.

And I further declare and make known, that such persons of suitable condition, will be received into the armed services of the United States to garrison[2] forts, positions, stations, and other places, and to man vessels of all sorts in said service.

And upon this act, sincerely believed to be an act of justice, warranted by the Constitution, upon military necessity, I invoke the considerate judgment of mankind, and the gracious favor of Almighty God. . . .

Thinking Critically

1. **Draw Conclusions** How did the emotional effects of the proclamation differ from its actual effects?
2. **Explain Effects** How did the Emancipation Proclamation benefit the Union war effort?

President Lincoln and the first page of his final draft of the proclamation ▶

1. **thenceforward** (thehns FOR werd) *adv.* from that time onward.
2. **garrison** (GAR uh suhn) *v.* to occupy and control by sending troops into.

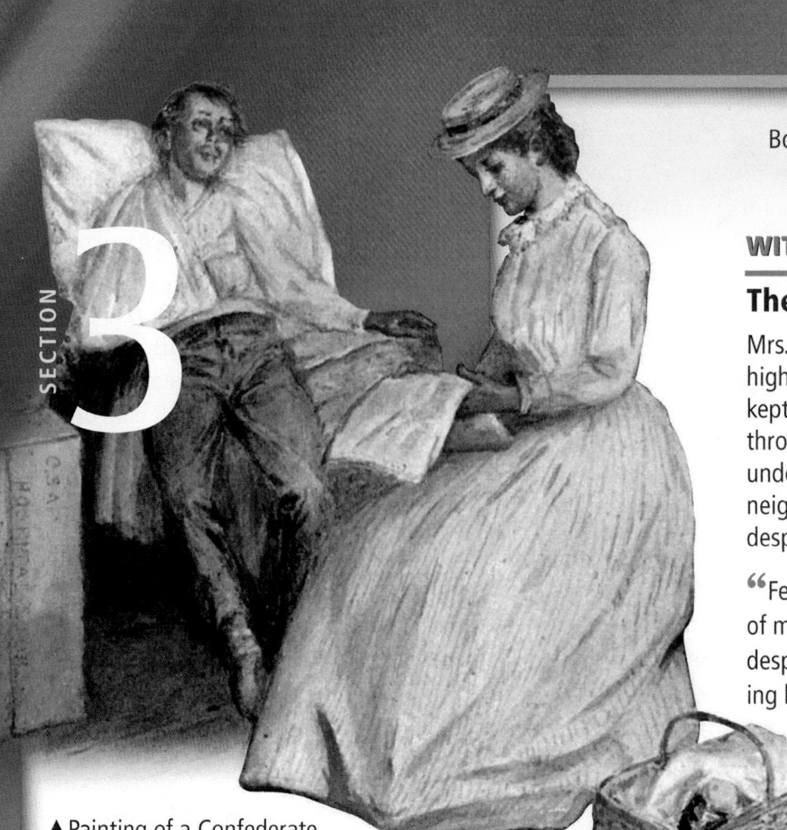

SECTION 3

▲Painting of a Confederate hospital scene

Bottle of medicine used during the Civil War▶

WITNESS HISTORY

The Hardships of War

Mrs. Judith Brockenbrough McGuire, the wife of a high school principal from Alexandria, Virginia, kept a diary that describes daily life in the South throughout the Civil War. Her record of a people under siege highlights the hardships endured by her friends and neighbors as Union soldiers confiscated the supplies they so desperately needed:

> "February 11, 1863. For ten days past I have been at the bedside of my patient in Richmond. The physicians for the third time despaired of his life; by the goodness of God he is again [recovering his health]. Our wounded are suffering excessively for tonics, and I believe that many valuable lives are lost for the want of a few bottles of [medicine]. . . . Oh, how cruel it is that the Northern Government should have made medicines and the necessaries of life to the sick and wounded, contraband articles!"
>
> —Judith Brockenbrough McGuire, Civil War diary

Life During the War

Objectives

- Analyze how the war changed the economy and society in the North and South.
- Discuss how northern and southern soldiers experienced the war.
- Explain the impact of the war on women.

Terms and People

income tax	Copperhead
bond	habeas corpus
Homestead Act	inflation
conscription	Clara Barton

NoteTaking

Reading Skill: Compare and Contrast Note the similarities and differences between the northern and southern home fronts during the war.

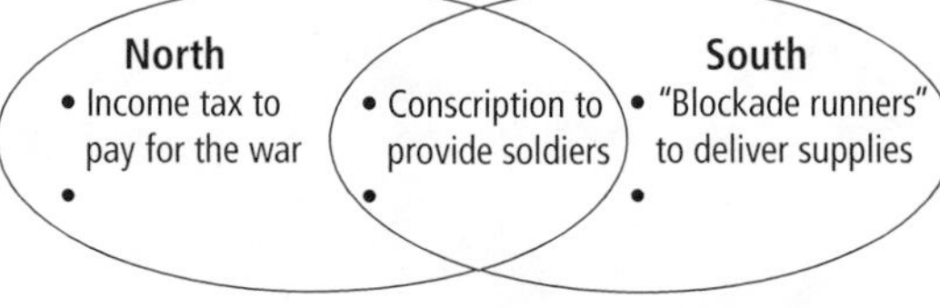

Why It Matters As African Americans rushed to join the Union ranks, the war dragged on. The fighting brought hard times to the home fronts of both North and South and helped transform many aspects of American life. Between 1861 and 1865, the economy and society of both regions underwent deep and lasting changes. These changes would help launch the North into the modern world, while the South suffered physical and social damage that persisted for decades. **Section Focus Question: How did the Civil War bring temporary and lasting changes to American society?**

The Home Front in the North

The war had a huge impact on northern industry. For example, the drop in southern cotton production severely damaged the large cotton textiles industry. At the same time, other industries boomed as demand for clothing, arms, and other supplies spiked. To meet the demand, industry became more mechanized.

War Transforms the Northern Economy Paying to supply the military was a major economic challenge. To help meet the cost, the Union government introduced a tax based on an individual's earnings. At first, the **income tax** was 3 percent on all income over $800 a year. As the war continued, the tax was increased. The Union also raised tariffs, which brought in revenue and helped northern industry by raising the cost of imported goods.

The biggest source of wartime funds came from the sale of government **bonds.** In return for the purchase price, the buyer received a certificate promising to pay the holder a larger amount of money at a future date. The Union sold billions of dollars worth of bonds to banks and individuals. Citizens were encouraged to buy bonds as an act of patriotism.

To increase the amount of cash in circulation and to help people buy war bonds, Congress passed the Legal Tender Act in 1862. This law allowed the Treasury to issue paper money, called "greenbacks" because of the color of the paper used. For the first time, the United States had a single, common currency that its citizens could use to purchase goods.

The Civil War also helped bring about far-reaching changes in the use of public land in the West. For years, the question of how to use this land had been dominated by the slavery issue. In addition, northern and southern companies squabbled over the route for a proposed rail line linking California to the East. With secession, however, these issues disappeared. In 1862, Congress passed the **Homestead Act,** making western land available at very low cost to those who would farm it. The war also resolved the argument over the route of the intercontinental railroad. The Pacific Railroad Act granted land to companies to build rail lines through Union territory.

The Draft Triggers Rioting In 1863, the Union instituted **conscription,** also called the draft, to meet the unending demand for fresh troops. Under this system, any white man between the ages of 20 and 45 might be called for required military service. However, a man could pay $300 to hire a replacement. Thus, at a time when laborers earned less than $2 per day, the burden of conscription fell mostly on recent immigrants and others who held low-paying jobs.

▼ Both the Union and the Confederacy initiated drafts to replenish the ranks of their depleted armies.

THE DRAFT.

The draft will commence in the 14th Congressional District, on

Thursday, Sept. 17th, 1863,

At 10 o'clock A. M., at the Court House in Wooster, Ohio.

The whole number required from this district is SIX HUNDRED AND NINETEEN, to which fifty per cent. will be added to cover exemptions. The following table exhibits the number to be drafted from each sub-district:

HOLMES COUNTY—To the first sub-district, 21; Second, 21; Third, 18; Fourth, 27; Fifth, 12; Sixth, 18; Seventh, 19.

ASHLAND COUNTY—Eighth sub-dist., 24; Ninth, 20; Tenth, ... Thirteenth, 18;

INFOGRAPHIC

Troubles on the Home Fronts

The Civil War introduced civilians on both sides to the hardships of life during wartime. The effects were economic, political, and social. Across the divided nation, economic troubles, political turmoil, draft riots, and attacks on civil liberties disrupted life on the home fronts.

▼ Northern anger over conscription led to violence. The worst incident was the New York Draft Riot of 1863, shown below.

Some northern Democrats called for an immediate end to the fighting. Likening these politicians to poisonous snakes, their enemies called them "Copperheads." This cartoon shows Copperheads threatening the Union. ▼

Many working men resented the fact that the rich could pay to avoid the draft. They also worried about losing their jobs to African Americans, who were not subject to conscription. Anger over the draft led to violence. In the New York Draft Riot of July 1863, a mob of poor white working men went on a four-day rampage, damaging factories that made war supplies and attacking African Americans. Blacks were also targeted in similar race riots in other northern cities.

War Threatens Civil Liberties Draft rioters were not the only northerners angered by the war effort. A faction calling themselves "Peace Democrats" opposed Lincoln's conduct of the war and demanded an end to the fighting. Their opponents dubbed them **Copperheads,** after a type of poisonous snake found in the South. While some Copperheads promoted violence against the Union, most remained loyal to it and wanted only to end the war.

Vocabulary Builder
faction–(FAK shuhn) *n.* a group of people inside a political party or government, working in a common cause against other such groups or against the main body

The President, however, viewed any effort to undermine the war effort as a grave threat to the nation. To deal with this crisis, he suspended the constitutional right of **habeas corpus,** which protects a person from being held in jail without being charged with a specific crime. Lincoln empowered the military to arrest people suspected of disloyalty to the Union, including some who had criticized the President and others who had participated in draft riots.

✓ **Checkpoint** **What was the response in the North to conscription?**

The Home Front in the South

The Civil War made great economic demands on the South as well. But, unlike the North, the Confederacy lacked the resources to meet these demands. As the war dragged on, the South seemed in danger of collapse.

▼ Confederate $500 bill

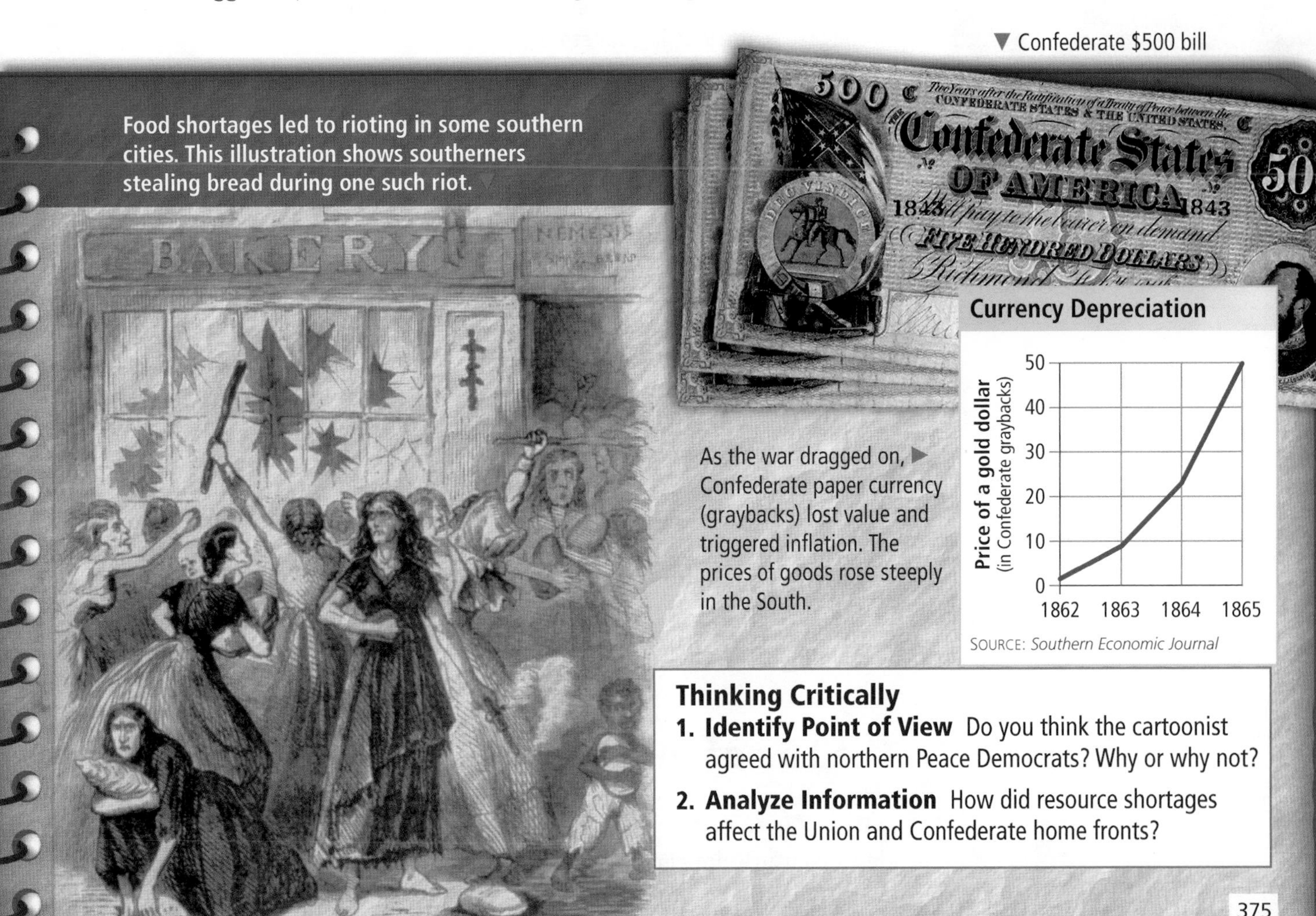

Food shortages led to rioting in some southern cities. This illustration shows southerners stealing bread during one such riot.

As the war dragged on, Confederate paper currency (graybacks) lost value and triggered inflation. The prices of goods rose steeply in the South.

Thinking Critically

1. **Identify Point of View** Do you think the cartoonist agreed with northern Peace Democrats? Why or why not?
2. **Analyze Information** How did resource shortages affect the Union and Confederate home fronts?

Blockade Brings Hardships The most pressing threat was the Union blockade of southern ports. Small, swift ships known as "blockade runners" were initially effective at avoiding capture and delivering needed supplies to the South. However, by 1863, the Union blockade was about 80 percent effective. As a result, southerners were forced to depend almost entirely on their own farms and factories. This production was often complicated by nearby military operations. Even when farmers were able to harvest crops, they had difficulty getting the food to market or to the troops because rivers and rail lines were often blocked by Union forces.

The South in Distress
Although he criticized Lincoln for suspending habeas corpus in the North, President Jefferson Davis eventually did the same to keep order in the Confederacy.

Davis Struggles to Pay for War Much of the South's wealth was invested in land and in more than 3 million slaves. Most of that slave labor was devoted to producing market crops, such as cotton, tobacco, and sugar. The war drastically reduced the value of these assets, leaving President Jefferson Davis with few sources of money with which to finance the Confederate military effort.

The South used every opportunity to ease its economic squeeze. When possible, Confederate soldiers seized Union weapons, food, and supplies—often from bodies on the battlefields. Union shoes and boots were especially prized. Although Britain remained officially neutral, British shipyards helped the Confederacy build blockade runners. Entrepreneurs built ironworks in several southern cities. Still, the costs of the war quickly outran the South's resources. Duties on the South's few imports were hard to collect, and many southerners resisted the 10 percent tax on farm produce.

Like the Union, the Confederacy issued paper money, backed only by the government's promise to pay. Many doubted the value of Confederate money. Prices soared as those with items to sell demanded more and more Confederate cash. This **inflation,** combined with the shortage of food, led to riots in some parts of the South. In a note to North Carolina Governor Zebulon Vance, one woman reported on the dire conditions in that state:

> **Primary Source** "I have threatened for some time to write you a letter—a crowd of we poor women went to Greensborough yesterday for something to eat as we had not a mouthful [of] meat nor bread—what did they do but put us in jail—we women will write for our husbands to come home and help us."
>
> —Nancy Mangum, 1863

Southern Leaders Argue Hardships quickly began to weaken southern unity. As early as August 1861, Mary Boykin Chesnut of South Carolina wrote in her diary of "the rapid growth of the party forming against Mr. Davis." Indeed, Jefferson Davis found that his attempts to build unity were often hampered by his stubborn personality and by the fierce spirit of independence that had led to secession in the first place. Some states resisted sending troops outside their own borders or having their militia serve under commanders from other states.

As in the North, the Confederate government enacted conscription laws, seized private property in support of the war effort, and suspended habeas corpus. In response, some southerners called for Davis's impeachment. In Georgia, there was even talk of seceding from the Confederacy!

 **Checkpoint** **Why did the Confederacy face severe economic problems during the Civil War?**

The Life of the Soldier

Just under half the eligible men in the Union and four out of five eligible men in the South served in the military during the Civil War. Their experiences mingled adventure, danger, comradeship, pride, and terrible hardship.

Camp Life Offers New Experiences The Civil War gave many young men their first taste of travel. A typical regiment was comprised of recruits from the same town who had all joined up together. Still, soldiers were often homesick and bored. When not preparing for battle, they passed the time writing letters home, playing games, or attending religious revivals. One Confederate chaplain noted that many southern men "have come out of this war Christian soldiers."

In the border states especially, many families suffered divided loyalties, with brothers or sons fighting on different sides. Soldiers might find themselves far from home but camped across the battlefield from family. It was not uncommon for soldiers to exchange greetings with the "enemy" between engagements.

Soldiers Face Death in Many Forms As you have read, new technology used in the Civil War resulted in killing on a scale never before seen in America. Tens of thousands of soldiers died on the battlefields and many more were injured. Powerful new weapons caused gaping wounds, and the most frequent treatment was the amputation of limbs—sometimes without anesthesia. Doctors lacked modern knowledge about infection, so even minor wounds could prove deadly.

For those who survived the fighting, life in camp had its own dangers. Poor drinking water and lack of sanitation led to a rapid spread of illness in the ranks. For every soldier killed in battle, two died of disease.

Worse yet were the prison camps. On both sides, prisoners of war faced overcrowding and filth while in captivity. African American prisoners in Confederate camps were usually killed outright. The most notorious camp was the open-pen prison at Andersonville, Georgia. By the summer of 1864, some 33,000 Union prisoners had been crowded into its confines. With their own troops starving, Confederates had little incentive to find food for Union prisoners. During the 15 months that Andersonville remained in operation, more than 12,000 Union prisoners died of disease and malnutrition.

✓ **Checkpoint What were the greatest dangers faced by wounded and captured soldiers during the Civil War?**

A soldier's tin cup

Camp Life During the Civil War

Union troops share a meal in 1863.

◀ A Union surgeon's deck of cards

For most soldiers, army life was months of tedious marching and drilling punctuated by brief periods of fierce and deadly combat. To fight boredom in camp, troops engaged in many activities to entertain themselves and one another. One Confederate marveled at a "fellow by the name of Vaughn... [who] could sing funny Songs, dance clog, make funny speeches, play tricks, turn somer saults, and [do] other things [too] numerous to mention." *What does the quotation suggest about the soldiers' mood in camp?*

A bullet ripped through this war diary. ▶

HISTORY MAKERS

Clara Barton (1821–1912)

Alarmed by the casualties at the First Battle of Bull Run in July 1861, Clara Barton—then a clerk at the U.S. Patent Office in Washington, D.C.—quickly began collecting medical supplies. She carried them to the battlefield and began nursing the wounded soldiers. Barton continued this work for the rest of the war. In 1870, while in Europe on vacation, Barton nursed soldiers wounded in a war between France and Germany. She went on to found the American branch of the International Red Cross and served as its president for more than 20 years. During this time, Barton added disaster relief to the agency's mission.

Women and the War

Many women had long sought an active role in public life. The Civil War offered them new opportunities. Even women who did not choose new roles often were forced to assume unfamiliar responsibilities.

Women Do New Work The vast majority of women did not get close to military action, but many took over family businesses, farms, or plantations. With so many men away at the front, women made inroads into professions that had previously been dominated by men. By war's end, for example, most teaching jobs had been taken over by women.

A few white women from the North and the South masqueraded as men and marched into battle. More commonly, wives joined husbands in camps, cooking and doing laundry. Like their husbands and brothers, some African American women in the South served as spies and guides.

Nurses Care for the Sick and Wounded In both the North and South, the most notable military role for women was nursing. The development of nursing as a profession began slowly, as small groups of women formed organizations to assist returning soldiers and their families. Beginning in 1861, **Clara Barton** took the effort one step further. After collecting medical supplies in her Massachusetts community, she secured permission to travel with Union army ambulances and assist in "distributing comforts for the sick and wounded of both sides."

President Lincoln approved the formation of the United States Sanitary Commission, which authorized women to oversee hospitals and sanitation in military installations. This systematic program of federal responsibility for public health would be yet another lasting effect of the Civil War.

✓ **Checkpoint** **How did women contribute to the war effort?**

SECTION 3 Assessment

Progress Monitoring *Online*
For: Self-test with vocabulary practice
www.pearsonschool.com/ushist

Comprehension

1. **Terms and People** For each of the following items, write a sentence explaining its significance.
   - income tax
   - Homestead Act
   - conscription
   - Copperhead
   - habeas corpus
   - Clara Barton
2. **NoteTaking Reading Skill: Compare and Contrast** Use your Venn diagram to answer the Section Focus Question: How did the Civil War bring temporary and lasting changes to American society?

Writing About History

3. **Quick Write: Gather Information for a News Article** Gather information for a news article about the daily life of soldiers during the Civil War. List the relevant information, using phrases and sentences.

Critical Thinking

4. **Identify Central Issues** How did wartime needs lead to limitations on individual freedom in the North? Do you think such actions were justified?
5. **Compare and Contrast** How were the wartime economic problems of the North and South similar? How were they different?
6. **Analyze Information** Why do you think nursing came to be a profession dominated by women? Is this still true today?

Songs of the Civil War

Julia Ward Howe ▶

Soldiers on both sides loved music, from the rousing marching tunes they sang to summon courage in battle to the sentimental campfire songs that longed for the day "When This Cruel War Is Over." However, North and South each embraced its own anthem that lifted the spirits of soldiers fighting in the field.

The Battle Hymn of the Republic When abolitionist and poet Julia Ward Howe visited Washington, D.C., in 1861, she heard Union troops sing a marching song called "John Brown's Body." Later that night, the stirring tune still ringing in her ears, Howe composed lyrics she believed were better suited to the noble cause of ending slavery. The first time Abraham Lincoln heard "The Battle Hymn of the Republic," he stood up, tears running down his face, and called out over the cheering crowd: "Sing it again! Sing it again!"

Dixie The song that came to represent the South was actually written by a northern musician named Daniel Decatur Emmett in 1859. The origin of the song's title is uncertain—possibly it came from the Mason-Dixon line that separated North and South—but homesick Confederate soldiers took the tune as their own. When the war ended in 1865, Lincoln ended a celebratory address to a crowd outside the White House by asking a nearby band to play "Dixie."

◀ Civil War era homemade banjo

*Mine eyes have seen the
glory of the coming of
the Lord;*

*He is trampling out the
vintage where the
grapes of wrath are
stored;*

*He hath loosed the fateful
lightning of His terrible
swift sword;*

His truth is marching on.

Glory, glory, hallelujah!

Glory, glory, hallelujah!

Glory, glory, hallelujah!

His truth is marching on.

I WISH I WAS IN DIXIE'S LAND

DAN. D. EMMETT.

W. L. HOBBS.

*Oh, I wish I was in the
land of cotton,
Cinnamon seed and
sandy bottom,
Look away, look away,
look away Dixie Land.
In Dixie Land, where
I was born in,
Early on one frosty mornin',
Look away, look away, look away Dixie
Land.
I wish I was in Dixie, Hooray! Hooray!
In Dixie Land I'll take my stand
To live and die in Dixie.
Away, away, away down south in Dixie.
Away, away, away down south in Dixie.*

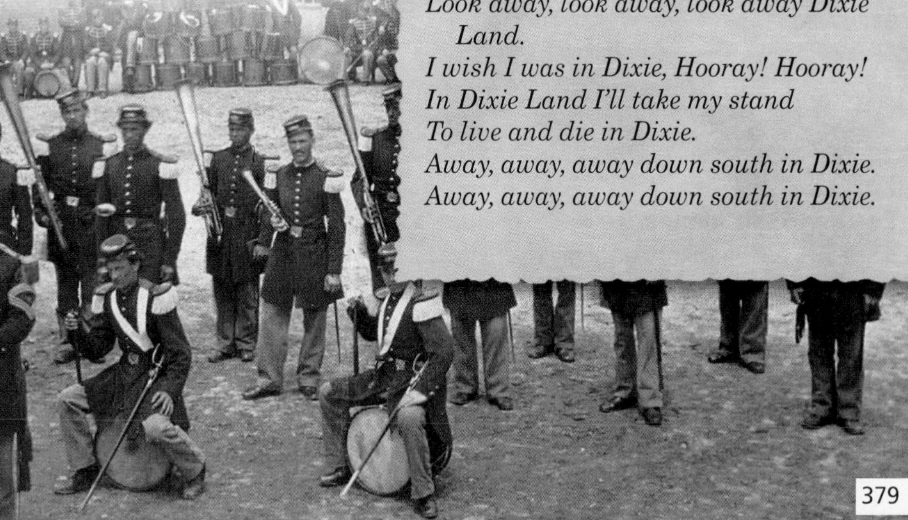

▼ A Union regimental band poses for a photograph in 1863.

Thinking Critically

1. **Analyze Lyrics** Why do you think Union soldiers found "The Battle Hymn of the Republic" so inspiring?
2. **Draw Inferences** Why might Lincoln have asked for "Dixie" to be played when the war ended?

▲ Dead soldiers at Little Round Top

Drum from a Union regiment that fought at Gettysburg ▶

WITNESS HISTORY

Gettysburg: A Soldier's Story

In early July 1863, North and South clashed near Gettysburg, Pennsylvania. A young Union officer described the fighting on a hill called Little Round Top:

"As we reached the crest a never to be forgotten scene burst upon us. A great basin lay before us full of smoke and fire, and literally swarming with riderless horses and fighting, fleeing and pursuing men. The air was saturated with the sulphurous fumes of battle and was ringing with the shouts and groans of the combatants. The wild cries of charging lines, the rattle of musketry, the booming of artillery and the shrieks of the wounded were the orchestral accompaniments of a scene like very hell itself. . . ."

—Lt. Porter Farley, 140th New York Infantry Regiment

Turning Points of the War

Objectives

- Explain what the Union gained by capturing Vicksburg.
- Describe the importance of the Battle of Gettysburg.
- Analyze how the Union pressed its military advantage after 1863.

Terms and People

siege
Vicksburg
Gettysburg
George Pickett
Gettysburg Address
total war
William Tecumseh Sherman

NoteTaking

Reading Skill: Summarize As you read, use a timeline to trace how the tide of the war turned toward Union victory.

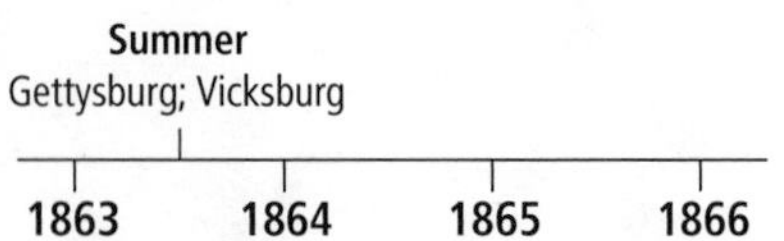

Why It Matters In the early stages of the war, the North had only limited success in achieving its military goals. But after months of difficult fighting and military setbacks, the Union enjoyed some stunning military successes in 1863. Though there was much bloodshed to come, that year marked the beginning of the end for the Confederacy. **Section Focus Question: How did the Battles of Vicksburg and Gettysburg change the course of the Civil War?**

Union Victory at Vicksburg

Although Union General U. S. Grant's troops battled the Confederates in Kentucky and central Tennessee in late 1862, the major focus of the Union's western campaign remained the Mississippi River. The Anaconda Plan depended on gaining control of the river and cutting the South in half. Yet after two years of war, the Confederacy still had strongholds at Port Hudson, Louisiana, and Vicksburg, Mississippi. "Vicksburg is the key!" Lincoln proclaimed. "The war can never be brought to a close until that key is in our pocket."

Grant Faces a Formidable Challenge Grant made several attempts to fulfill Lincoln's goal, but it was a daunting task. The mighty Vicksburg fortress towered high above the waters of the Mississippi. Along the city's western edge, Confederate gunners could rain deadly fire on any gunboats that might approach. In May 1862, they thwarted one such assault under Union Admiral David

Farragut. Grant even tried digging a canal so that Union ships could bypass the stretch of the river dominated by the Vicksburg batteries, but the attempt failed. Vicksburg's location also protected it from attack by land. A Union assault in late 1862 stalled out in the labyrinth of swamps, creeks, and woods guarding the northern approaches to the city.

Grant Initiates a Brilliant Plan In the spring of 1863, Grant devised a new plan to take the Confederate stronghold. First, he marched his troops southward through Louisiana to a point south of Vicksburg. At the same time, he ordered a cavalry attack on rail lines in central Mississippi to draw Confederate attention away from the city. On April 30, some 20,000 of Grant's men crossed the river and headed northeast to capture the Mississippi state capital at Jackson. After sacking that city, the Federals turned west toward Vicksburg, gaining control of the main rail line leading into the city and fortress. Vicksburg was completely cut off.

Grant launched two frontal assaults against the Confederates but failed to break their defenses. So, on May 22, he placed Vicksburg under **siege.** A siege is a military tactic in which an army surrounds, bombards, and cuts off all supplies to an enemy position in order to force its surrender. For over a month, Union guns kept up a steady fire from land and river. One astonished resident noted "ladies walk[ing] quietly along the streets while the shells burst above them, their heads meanwhile protected by parasol." The constant fire and lack of supplies gradually weakened Vicksburg's defenders. (See the American Experience feature at the end of this section.) Finally, on July 4, 1863, the Confederate commander concluded that his position was hopeless and ordered his forces to surrender. The siege of **Vicksburg** was over. Days later, after it learned of the Vicksburg surrender, the Confederate garrison at Port Hudson, Louisiana, also surrendered to the Union. With its last strongholds on the Mississippi in Union hands, the Confederacy was split in two.

✓ **Checkpoint** **What was the outcome of the siege of Vicksburg?**

Campaign for Vicksburg, March–July 1863

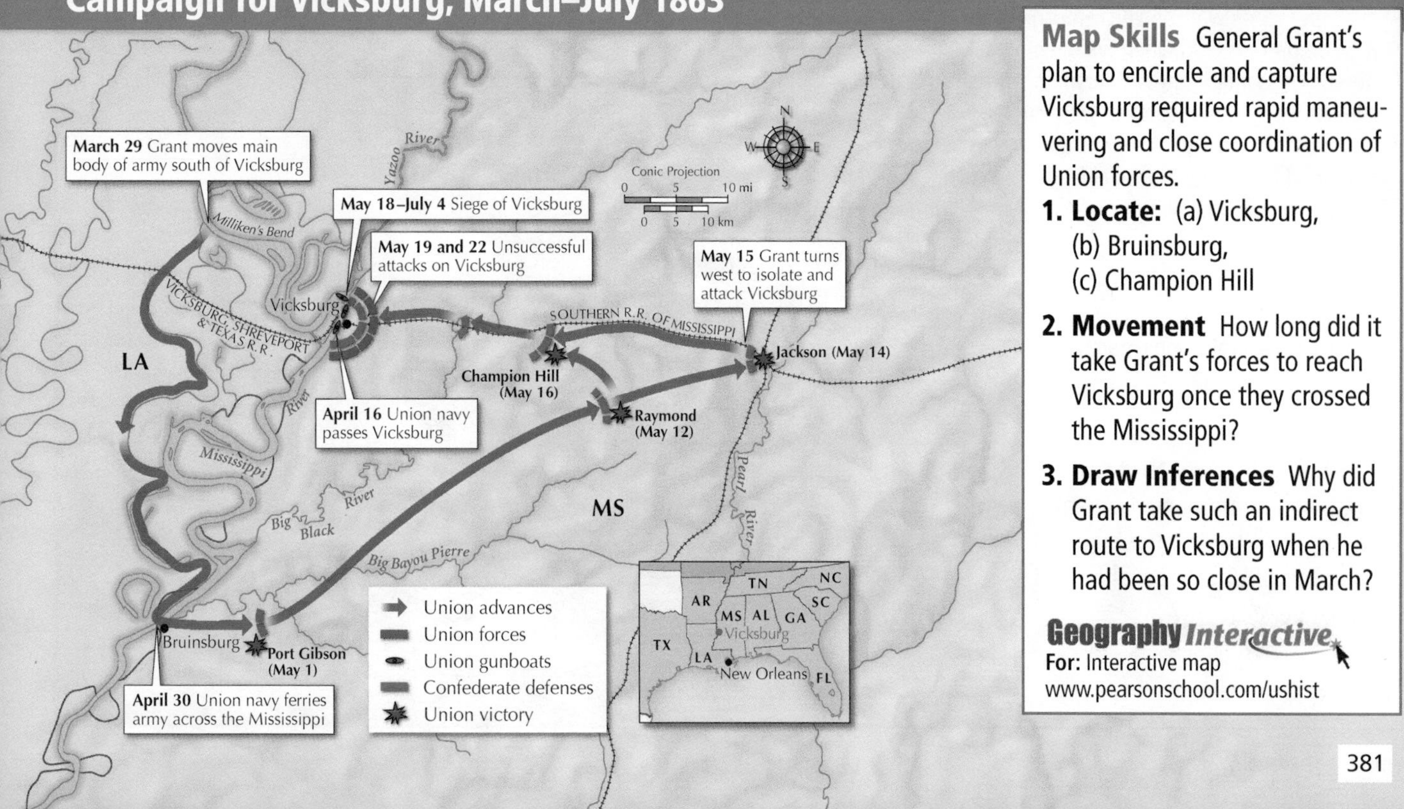

Map Skills General Grant's plan to encircle and capture Vicksburg required rapid maneuvering and close coordination of Union forces.

1. **Locate:** (a) Vicksburg, (b) Bruinsburg, (c) Champion Hill
2. **Movement** How long did it take Grant's forces to reach Vicksburg once they crossed the Mississippi?
3. **Draw Inferences** Why did Grant take such an indirect route to Vicksburg when he had been so close in March?

Geography Interactive
For: Interactive map
www.pearsonschool.com/ushist

A Turning Point in the East

Vocabulary Builder
successor–(suhk SEHS uhr) *n.* person or thing that succeeds, or follows, another

While Union troops advanced in the West, the situation was different in the East. Despite claiming victory at Antietam, Lincoln soon replaced General McClellan for failing to pursue the retreating Confederates. McClellan's successor, General Ambrose Burnside, headed south, hoping to win a decisive victory.

Lee Wins Two Victories and Pushes North The Army of the Potomac met General Lee's Army of Northern Virginia at Fredericksburg, Virginia, in December 1862. Burnside had 120,000 troops, while Lee had fewer than 80,000. But Lee, aided by generals Stonewall Jackson and James Longstreet, soundly defeated the new Union commander. Union casualties were more than double those of the Confederacy.

Lincoln replaced Burnside with General Joseph Hooker, who launched his own offensive against Lee in the spring. The two armies clashed at Chancellorsville, just west of Fredericksburg. Once again, the Confederates overwhelmed the Federals. The loss at the Battle of Chancellorsville was devastating to the Union. Upon hearing the news, President Lincoln paced the room, muttering "What will the country say? What will the country say?" Nevertheless, Lee paid dearly for his

Focus On Geography

Battle of Fredericksburg
On December 13, 1862, Union forces attempting to smash Lee's army at Fredericksburg had to cross a canal ditch and 400 yards of open ground. The Confederates commanded Marye's Heights, a low hill that gave a clear view of the attackers. The rebels were further aided by the excellent cover offered by a sunken road and stone wall. "A chicken could not live on that field when we open on it," noted one Confederate artilleryman. Almost 9,000 Union soldiers were cut down before the wall. Many of the wounded lay on the battlefield through a cold snowy night.

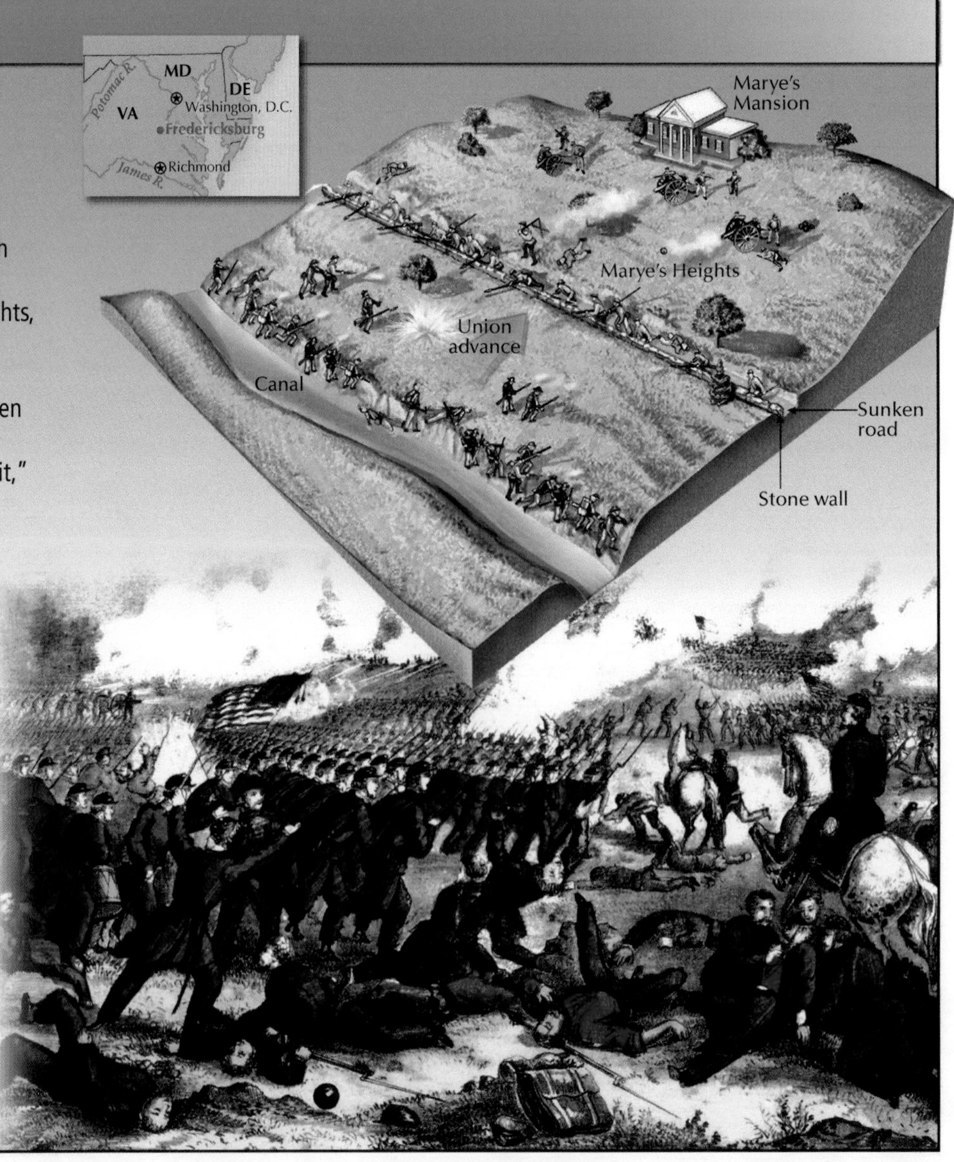

Waves of Federal troops march ▶ against Marye's Heights.

Geography and History
How did human-environment interaction lead to the high number of Union casualties at Fredericksburg?

victory, losing the incomparable Stonewall Jackson during the fighting. After being accidentally shot by his own men, Jackson died a few days after the battle.

Though he was upset by the loss of Jackson, Lee sensed an opportunity to win international support for the Confederacy, demoralize the Union, and perhaps even force an end to the war. Once again, he decided to invade the North. In June 1863, Lee's army set off through Virginia's Shenandoah Valley and crossed into Union territory, eventually reaching Pennsylvania.

Lee Loses His "Right Arm"
After Stonewall Jackson was mistakenly shot by his own troops at Chancellorsville (above), doctors had to amputate his arm. Upon hearing the news, Lee lamented, "He has lost his left arm, but I have lost my right arm." *What do you think Lee meant?*

Union Troops Engage Lee at Gettysburg Lee's invasion caused great concern throughout the Union. The Army of the Potomac, now under the leadership of General George Meade, set out to engage the Confederates. Meanwhile, a Confederate unit headed for the town of Gettysburg, hoping to seize footwear from the shoe factory there. On the morning of July 1, Lee's men ran into several brigades of Union cavalry commanded by General John Buford. Buford's men spread out northwest of town and called for reinforcements. This was the start of the decisive Battle of **Gettysburg,** which would last for the next three days. (See the Events That Changed America feature on the following page.)

As the main bodies of both armies converged on Gettysburg, the first day of the fighting went to the Confederates. They pushed the smaller Union force back through the town and onto higher ground to the south. But nightfall halted the Confederate advance. This allowed General Meade to bring up the rest of his army and strengthen the Union position. Union troops dug in along a two-and-a-half mile defense line stretching from Culp's Hill and Cemetery Hill southward along Cemetery Ridge. The Federal line ended at two more rocky hills, Little Round Top and Big Round Top. Troubled that the Union now held the high ground, Confederate General James Longstreet regretted, "It would have been better had we not fought at all than to have left undone what we did."

Lee Is Defeated and Forced to Retreat As July 2 dawned, Lee's men prepared to assault both ends of the Union line. Lee ordered one force to move against the northern part of Meade's defenses while General Longstreet attacked the southern end of Cemetery Ridge. Late in the afternoon, Longstreet's troops charged against a large body of Union soldiers that had mistakenly abandoned Little Round Top and moved westward off Cemetery Ridge. The two sides hammered at each other for several hours in some of the fiercest fighting of the war. The rebels, however, failed to breach the Union line.

Meanwhile, Union troops had noticed the undefended position on Little Round Top. They hurried forward just in time to meet the gray tide of Confederates rushing uphill. Anchoring the Union defense of the hilltop was a Maine unit under Colonel Joshua L. Chamberlain. Chamberlain's men stood firm against numerous Confederate attacks, but their numbers and ammunition eventually dwindled. Chamberlain responded by ordering a bayonet charge that shocked and scattered his exhausted enemy. Hundreds of Confederates surrendered and the fighting drew to a close. Night fell and the Union still held the high ground.

Lee was not discouraged. Despite opposition from Longstreet—and believing that victory was still within reach—the Confederate commander attacked one more time. The result was disastrous. In the early afternoon of July 3, Lee commenced an artillery barrage aimed at the center of the Union line. He had hoped his cannon would break up the Union defenses in advance of an infantry attack on Cemetery Ridge. When Lee's men, including a division under General **George Pickett,** marched toward the ridge, thousands of Confederates were mowed down by Union rifle and cannon fire. After the failure of Pickett's Charge, Lee ordered the general to reposition his division. "General Lee," replied Pickett, "I have no division now." The Battle of Gettysburg was over. On the battlefield lay over 50,000 dead and wounded. About half of these were Confederates—nearly a third of Lee's fighting force. Lee abandoned his invasion of the North and led his limping army back into Virginia. The South had suffered a crushing defeat. It would never again attempt to fight on Union soil.

Lincoln Honors the Dead In November 1863, Lincoln came to the Gettysburg battlefield to dedicate a cemetery for the fallen soldiers. There, he delivered his

INTERACTIVE Whiteboard

Events That Changed America

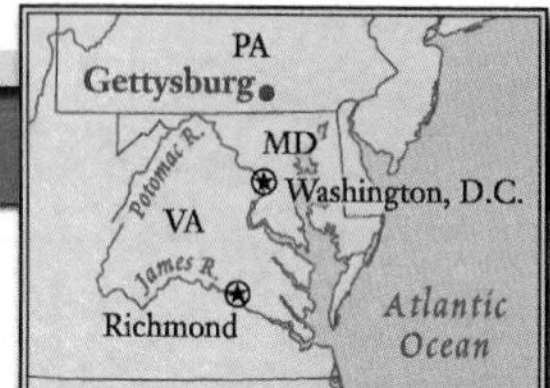

BATTLE OF GETTYSBURG

As the bloodiest battle ever fought on American soil, the Battle of Gettysburg marked a turning point in the Civil War. To halt a second Confederate invasion of the North, more than 90,000 Union soldiers faced off against General Robert E. Lee and 77,500 soldiers of the Army of Northern Virginia in early July 1863.

On July 1, Confederate troops collided with Union cavalry just outside the small Pennsylvania crossroads of Gettysburg. By the end of the day, the Confederates had routed the gathering force of Union troops and forced them onto higher ground south of town. For the next two days, Lee's army hammered at the Union lines as each side struggled to win the battle. Despite Confederate General George Pickett's heroic charge against Union positions on July 3, Lee's battered men ultimately lost the battle. They avoided destruction at the hands of the victorious Union army by retreating back to Virginia.

July 1 Late on the first day, Lee ordered General Richard Ewell to push onto Cemetery Hill "if practicable." Ewell famously decided not to press his attack, leaving the Union defenders to dig in.

The battle had begun when the Confederates attempted to raid a shoe factory in Gettysburg.

July 2 Union Colonel Joshua L. Chamberlain (right) commanded his regiment's desperate, bloody defense of Little Round Top.

Gettysburg Address. He described the Civil War as a struggle to fulfill the Declaration of Independence and to preserve a nation "dedicated to the proposition that all men are created equal." Today, the speech is recognized as an enduring statement of American values and goals. (See the Documents of Our Nation section at the back of this textbook.) The President concluded his speech by urging:

> **Primary Source** "[W]e here highly resolve that these dead shall not have died in vain—that this nation under God, shall have a new birth of freedom—and that government of the people, by the people, for the people, shall not perish from the earth."
>
> —Abraham Lincoln, November 19, 1863

✓ **Checkpoint** **What was the outcome of the Battle of Gettysburg?**

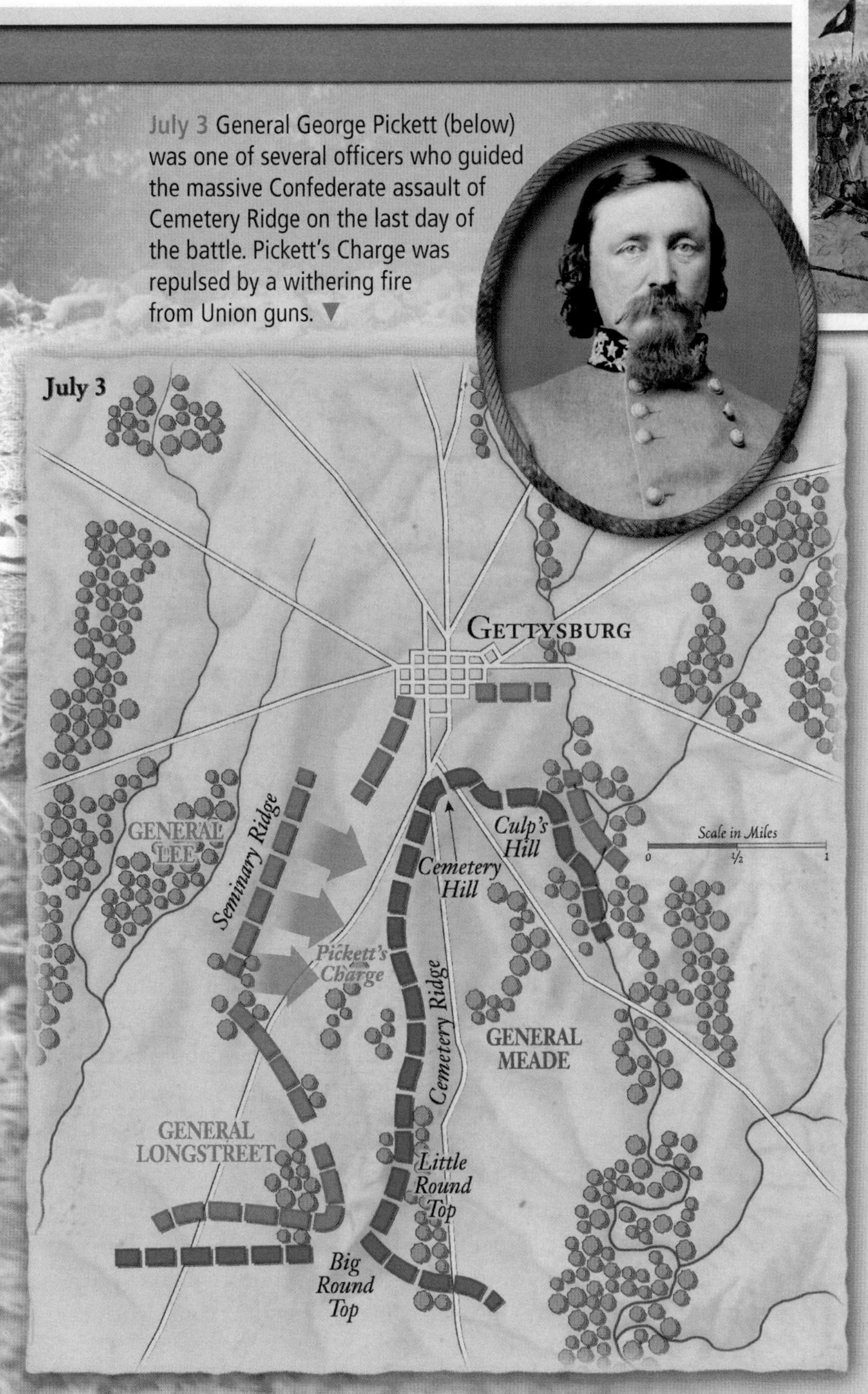

July 3 General George Pickett (below) was one of several officers who guided the massive Confederate assault of Cemetery Ridge on the last day of the battle. Pickett's Charge was repulsed by a withering fire from Union guns. ▼

▲ July 3 The peak moment of the Confederate charge came when General Lewis Armistead (above, with hat on sword) led his troops through a breach in the Union line. Armistead and many of his men were soon killed in the Union counterattack.

Why It Matters

Along with Vicksburg, Gettysburg turned the tide of the Civil War in favor of the Union. After its second invasion of the North was defeated, the Confederacy would fight the rest of the war on its own soil. Lincoln's immortal Gettysburg Address, delivered four months after the battle, motivated the Union to connect the massive human sacrifice to "a new birth of freedom" for the United States.

Thinking Critically

What might have happened if the South had won at Gettysburg? Describe a new course of events.

History *Interactive*

For: To discover more about the Battle of Gettysburg
www.pearsonschool.com/ushist

Goals of Total War ☑ Quick Study

- Strike military <u>and</u> civilian targets.
- Destroy materials and crops that enemy forces might be able to use.
- Destroy railroads and factories to damage the local economy.
- Break the people's will to continue fighting.

Sherman Unleashes Total War
Soon after occupying Atlanta, William Tecumseh Sherman (see photo) abandoned his supply lines and set off to "make Georgia howl." Above, his troops ravage the Confederate countryside. *How do you think southerners felt about Sherman?*

The Union Presses the Advantage

Coming within a day of each other, the Union victories at Gettysburg and Vicksburg dealt a severe blow to the Confederacy. Lee's troops were in retreat and the Mississippi was in Union hands. Gone, too, was any hope for the Confederacy to win recognition from Britain or France. The war was not over—indeed, the Confederacy would still win some victories, such as that at Chickamauga, Georgia, in the fall of 1863. In general, however, the situation of the South was dire.

Grant Marches Toward Richmond Lincoln recalled General Grant from the Mississippi Valley in early 1864 to take charge of the entire Union military effort. The President knew that Grant would accept nothing less than victory. He was correct. Grant set his sites on the Confederate capital of Richmond. "I propose to fight it out," he declared, "if it takes all summer." Grant's campaign did last all summer and for months beyond. He engaged Lee's army in a series of ferocious battles: the Wilderness, Spotsylvania Court House, and Cold Harbor. Grant's strategy was to inflict more losses on the Confederates than their limited resources could withstand. The cost of Grant's relentless advance was horrifying. Tens of thousands of Union and Confederate soldiers fell on the battlefields of Virginia. In the North, public outrage began to grow.

Grant's attack did not target the South's military forces alone. He was following a strategy of **total war,** which involves striking civilian as well as military targets. The purpose of total war is to weaken not just an enemy's armies but also the economy that supports them and the overall will of the people to fight. The South was suffering serious losses that it could not hope to replace.

Sherman Drives to the Sea The Union's total-war strategy was also implemented by General **William Tecumseh Sherman.** In May 1864, he set out from the Tennessee-Georgia border with 60,000 troops on a 250-mile march to capture the port of Savannah, Georgia. During his "March to the Sea," Sherman ordered his men to get supplies by looting along the way, then to destroy anything of potential value left behind. Cutting a 60-mile-wide swath through

Georgia, Sherman's army tore up railroad tracks, destroyed buildings, and vandalized hundreds of private homes. With Union forces closing in on Atlanta, Confederate troops abandoned the city. Sherman's men occupied it on September 2 and forced the residents to leave. When the mayor asked Sherman to reconsider his order, the general responded:

> **Primary Source** "You might as well appeal against the thunder-storm as against these terrible hardships of war. They are inevitable, and the only way the people of Atlanta can hope once more to live in peace and quiet at home is to stop the war. . . . We don't want your negroes or your horses or your houses or your lands . . . but we do want, and will have, a just obedience to the laws of the United States. That we will have, and if it involves the destruction of your improvements, we cannot help it."
>
> —William T. Sherman, letter to James Calhoun, September 12, 1864

Once Atlanta was emptied, Union troops burned it to the ground. "Sherman the Brute," as southerners called him, continued eastward and captured Savannah in late December.

The Election of 1864 As 1864 drew to a close, Lincoln had much to celebrate. While his military commanders were winning victories on the battlefield, he had won reelection in November.

The campaign had been difficult. Lincoln had lost some support even in his own party. Some Republicans criticized the President for grasping too much authority; others charged that he was not fully committed to ending slavery. Democrats, fractured into several factions, finally nominated George McClellan, the popular former Union commander.

Lincoln's presidency had seemed in jeopardy. However, Union victories boosted his popularity. Many Union soldiers, loyal to Lincoln, were allowed to go home to vote. When the ballots were in, McClellan won 45 percent of the popular vote, but Lincoln received 212 of the 233 electoral votes. The reelection of Abraham Lincoln destroyed any last Confederate hopes that the North would cave in and negotiate a peace.

✓ **Checkpoint What strategy did Grant follow as commander of Union forces?**

SECTION 4 Assessment

Progress Monitoring *Online*
For: Self-test with vocabulary practice
www.pearsonschool.com/ushist

Comprehension

1. **Terms and People** For each of the following items, write a sentence explaining its significance.
   - siege
   - Vicksburg
   - Gettysburg
   - George Pickett
   - Gettysburg Address
   - total war
   - William Tecumseh Sherman
2. **NoteTaking Reading Skill: Summarize** Use your timeline to answer the Section Focus Question: How did the Battles of Vicksburg and Gettysburg change the course of the Civil War?

Writing About History

3. **Quick Write: Begin to Write a News Article** Choose a battle discussed in this section. Outline the article you would write about the battle, including how you would answer the five *W* questions. Write the headline for the article.

Critical Thinking

4. **Apply Information** Using examples from this section, write a general definition of the term *turning point.*
5. **Draw Inferences** In the Gettysburg Address, Lincoln stated that the purpose of the war was to ensure "that this nation . . . shall have a new birth of freedom—and that government of the people, by the people, for the people, shall not perish from the earth." What do you think he meant?
6. **Analyze Information** Why do you think General Sherman felt justified in destroying civilian property during his march through Georgia?

EXPERIENCE
THE SIEGE OF VICKSBURG

Shots rang out over the trenches. Artillery shells slammed into houses. Frightened civilians abandoned their homes. Burrowing into hillsides overlooking the Mississippi River, the citizens of Vicksburg built bomb shelters out of earth and wood. There, they waited as the Union encircled and bombarded one of the Confederacy's last remaining strong points in the West.

If the Union army could not capture this strategic outpost on the Mississippi, the Union would be hard-pressed to fulfill the Anaconda Plan and split the Confederacy in two. Facing many obstacles, General Ulysses S. Grant decided against a final frontal assault to take Vicksburg. Instead, beginning in May 1863, Grant surrounded the city, hoping to bomb and starve it into submission. On July 4, after a six-week siege, Vicksburg surrendered. For Vicksburg's brave and battered citizens, their terrible ordeal was over. For the rest of the Confederacy, the fall of Vicksburg was a devastating loss.

Not Safe at Home In her diary, Vicksburg resident Emma Balfour described a rain of death: "We have spent the last two nights in a cave, but tonight I think we will stay at home. It is not safe I know, for the shells are falling all around us. . . ." ▼

A page from Emma Balfour's diary ▼

Life During the Siege Shell-shocked civilians seek refuge in one of Vicksburg's underground shelters as the bombs fall. ▼

Blasted to Freedom Escaping to freedom at Vicksburg, this enslaved man was blasted 300 yards across the lines when Union miners blew up a Confederate fortification. ▶

Trophy of Victory
Union soldiers captured this Confederate flag at Vicksburg. ▼

Thinking Critically

1. **Analyze Visuals** How did the civilians of Vicksburg respond to the Union attack on their city?
2. **Draw Conclusions** Do you think Grant's tactics at Vicksburg were warranted? Why or why not?

Connect to Today Do research to learn about recent natural disasters in the United States. How did those events impact Americans living in the areas where they occurred?

History *Interactive* ✶
For: To learn more about the siege of Vicksburg
www.pearsonschool.com/ushist

Battle for the River
Confederate artillery in Vicksburg fire upon passing Union ships. The Confederates desperately hoped to maintain control of the Mississippi River. ▶

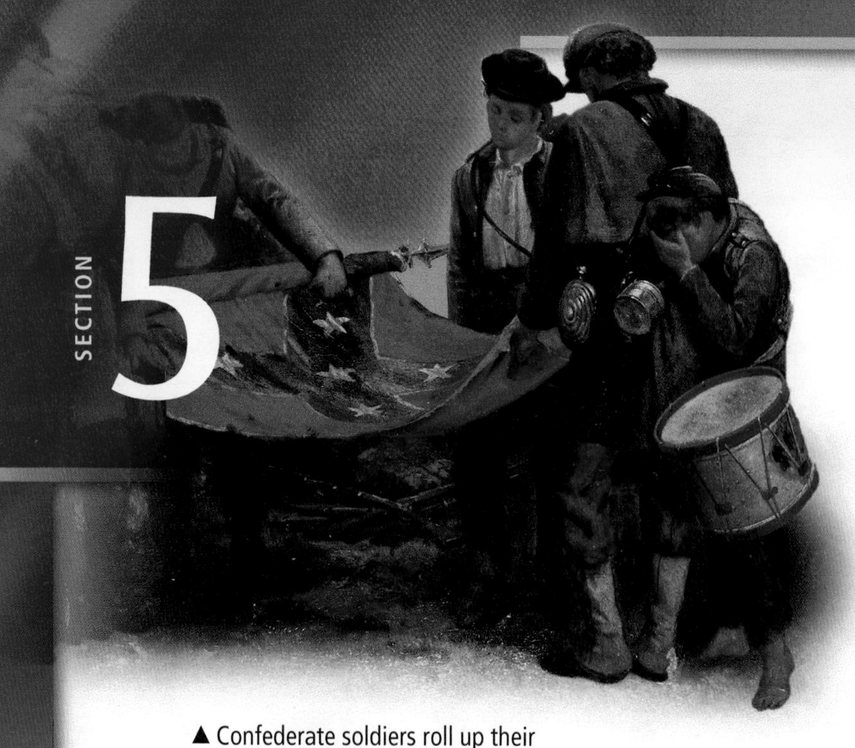

▲ Confederate soldiers roll up their flag after Lee's surrender

WITNESS HISTORY

The South Surrenders

Confederate General John B. Gordon was with General Lee at Appomattox Court House when the Army of Northern Virginia surrendered to Union troops. Gordon later described the despair of his soldiers:

> "During these last scenes at Appomattox some of the Confederates were so depressed in spirit . . . that the future seemed to them shrouded in gloom. They knew that burnt homes and fenceless farms, poverty and ashes, would greet them on their return from the war. Even if the administration at Washington should be friendly, they did not believe that the Southern States could recover in half a century from the chaotic condition in which the war had left them."
>
> —General John B. Gordon, *Reminiscences of the Civil War*

The War's End and Impact

Objectives

- Analyze the final events of the Civil War.
- Explain why the North won the war.
- Assess the impact of the Civil War on North and South.

Terms and People

Thirteenth Amendment
John Wilkes Booth
Mathew Brady
Land Grant College Act

NoteTaking

Reading Skill: Recognize Sequence As you read, use a flowchart to note what happened during the final days of the Civil War.

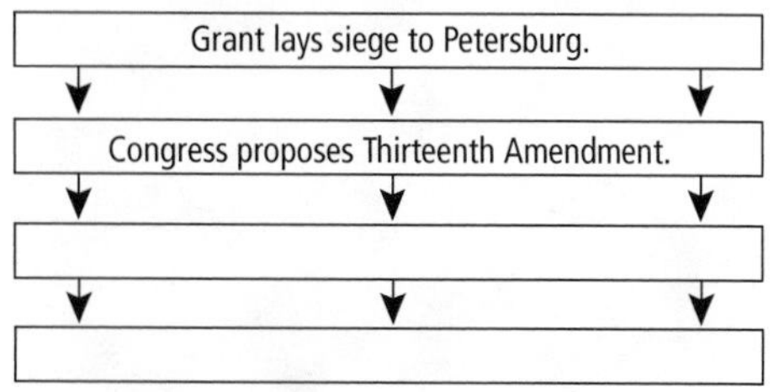

Why It Matters After four years of bitter struggle and sacrifice, the Confederacy stood on the brink of defeat. As Lee prepared to surrender to Grant, Lincoln began to plan for the future. The Civil War had lasting effects on both the North and the South. With the fighting over, Americans faced the difficult challenge of rebuilding their nation. **Section Focus Question: What was the final outcome and impact of the Civil War?**

The War's Final Days

In the summer of 1864, Grant continued his bloody drive toward Richmond. But at Petersburg, about 20 miles south of Richmond, the Confederates made a desperate stand. (See the map at the end of the section.) Petersburg was a vital railroad center. If Grant captured it, he could cut all supply lines to Richmond.

Grant Places Petersburg Under Siege As he had at Vicksburg, Grant turned to siege tactics. Throughout the summer and fall and into the winter, his forces tightened their grip around Petersburg. Both sides dug trenches and threw up fortifications to guard against attack. By March 1865, the two opposing lines of defense stretched for more than 30 miles around Petersburg.

Fighting was fierce. Union troops suffered more than 40,000 casualties. The Confederates lost 28,000 men. However, unlike Grant, Lee had no replacement troops in reserve. As the siege of Petersburg wore on, Union strength grew in comparison to the Confederate defenders.

Lincoln Looks to the Future With the Confederate position truly desperate, southerners began to talk of peace. In February 1865, a party led by Confederate Vice President Alexander Stephens met with Lincoln to discuss a feasible end to the war. However, these discussions produced no results. One reason for the failure was that the U.S. Congress, with Lincoln's support, had recently proposed the **Thirteenth Amendment** to the Constitution. If ratified, the amendment would outlaw slavery in the United States. The Confederate peace delegation was unwilling to accept a future without slavery. (The Thirteenth Amendment was ratified in December 1865.)

Vocabulary Builder
feasible–(FEE zuh buhl) *adj.* possible; practical

Despite the failure of the February meeting, Lincoln was confident of an eventual victory. He now began to turn his attention to the process of bringing the Confederate states back into the Union. This would be no easy task. Many northerners had a strong desire to punish the South harshly.

Lincoln had a different goal. While committed to the defeat of the Confederacy and an end to slavery, he believed that the Union should strike a more generous stance with the rebellious states. At the beginning of March, in his Second Inaugural Address, Lincoln declared his vision of a united and peaceful nation. "With malice toward none," Lincoln said, Americans should "do all which may achieve and cherish a just and lasting peace."

Lee Surrenders to Grant Several weeks later, the Confederates made a desperate attempt to break the siege of Petersburg. They failed. Recognizing that the situation was hopeless, Lee ordered a retreat from Petersburg on the night of April 2. Richmond, now defenseless, was evacuated and set aflame.

Lee's one hope was to join with Confederate forces in North Carolina. Setting out on the march, the men suffered from a lack of food and constant harassment by Union forces. Finally, Lee and his starving, exhausted soldiers were trapped at the town of Appomattox Court House, Virginia. On April 9, Lee formally surrendered to Grant. The Union general refused to allow his troops to gloat. "The war is over," he said, "the rebels are our countrymen again."

▼ Lee surrenders to Grant at Appomattox Court House

Lee's surrender did not officially end the war. The South still had some 170,000 soldiers under arms, and it took until June for other Confederate generals scattered around the South to complete similar surrenders. In Texas, African Americans celebrated June 19, 1865, as "Juneteenth," the day the news of surrender reached the Southwest.

Lincoln Is Assassinated On April 14, just days after Lee's surrender, Lincoln decided to relax by attending a new comedy, *Our American Cousin,* at nearby Ford's Theatre. During the performance, actor and Confederate supporter **John Wilkes Booth** approached the President's private box. Booth fired a single shot into the back of Lincoln's head. Leaping to the stage, he was heard to call out *"Sic semper tyrannis!"* ("Thus ever to tyrants," the motto of Virginia) and "the South is avenged." Mortally wounded, Lincoln died the next morning.

Booth became the target of a massive manhunt. After several days, he was shot and killed while hiding in a barn in Virginia. Soon, it was discovered that Booth had been part of a plot to kill not only Lincoln, but also the Vice President and the Secretary of State.

HISTORY MAKERS

In May and June 1864, Robert E. Lee's Army of Northern Virginia beat back Ulysses S. Grant's Army of the Potomac in several fierce battles between Washington and Richmond. After each fight, Grant sidestepped Lee to march closer to the southern capital. However, as the Union army moved, Lee followed and set up strong defensive positions, which forced Grant to attack. Neither general could maneuver to win a decisive victory. In a month's time, the two armies suffered nearly 70,000 combined casualties. By late summer, the bloody contest had settled into a siege at Petersburg, south of Richmond. In early April 1865, Lee abandoned the city and eventually surrendered to Grant.

Ulysses S. Grant (1822–1885)

Robert E. Lee (1807–1870)

A "wanted" poster showing Booth at the top (center photo)

The assassin John Wilkes Booth levels a pistol at his unsuspecting victim.

The plotters hoped to cause chaos and panic in the North, thereby giving the South time to regroup and continue the war. Although Secretary of State William Seward was attacked and seriously injured by one of Booth's accomplices, Booth was the only man to carry out his part of the plot. Four of his accomplices were later hanged as coconspirators.

Lincoln's tragic death had a deep political impact. His murder united his northern supporters and critics, who now saw him as both a hero and a symbol of freedom. Gone was the strong, skilled leader who had guided the nation through its greatest crisis. As you will read in the next chapter, his presence would be greatly missed in the difficult days ahead.

 **Checkpoint** **What event marked the end of the Confederacy's hopes in the Civil War?**

The Death of a President

After Booth shot him, Lincoln was carried to a boardinghouse across the street from Ford's Theatre. There, doctors struggled to save his life but ultimately failed. When President Lincoln died, his Secretary of War, Edwin Stanton, plainly stated, "Now he belongs to the ages." *How do you think northerners reacted to Lincoln's assassination? How do you think southerners reacted?*

Why the North Won

With hindsight, it is tempting to claim that the Union victory had been certain from the outset, but that is not the case. When the war began, the South had confidence, outstanding military leadership, and a strong determination to defend its land. By contrast, many northerners were far less committed to the fight.

But as northerners warmed to the conflict, they were able to marshal their greater technological prowess, larger population, and more abundant resources. Moreover, the Union was able to develop new advantages, particularly brilliant and fearless military leaders, such as Grant and Sherman, who were willing to do everything it took to win the war. Meanwhile, the South used up its resources, unable to call upon fresh troops and supplies. According to historian Richard Current, the Confederacy's inability to gain a European ally and northern military superiority sealed the South's fate:

Primary Source

> "[I]t seems to have become inevitable once two dangers for the Union had been passed. One of these was the threat of interference from abroad. The other was the possibility of military disaster resulting from the enemy's superior skill or luck on the battlefield. . . . Both dangers appear to have been over by midsummer, 1863. . . . Thereafter, month by month, the resources of the North began increasingly to tell, in what became more and more a war of attrition."
>
> —Richard N. Current, in *Why the North Won the Civil War*

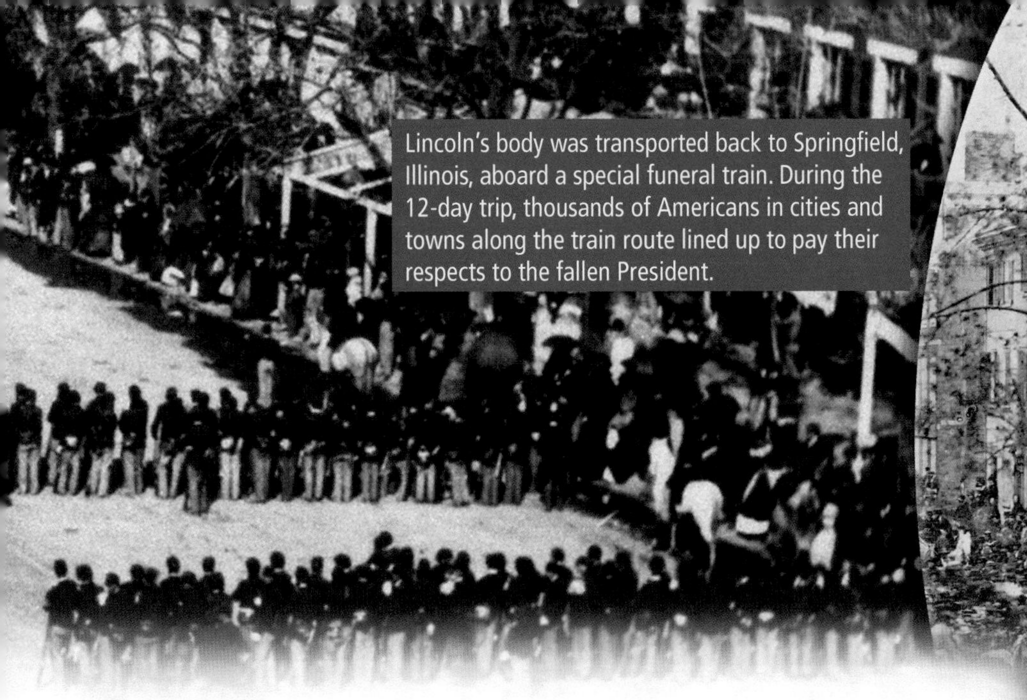

Lincoln's body was transported back to Springfield, Illinois, aboard a special funeral train. During the 12-day trip, thousands of Americans in cities and towns along the train route lined up to pay their respects to the fallen President.

The North also enjoyed the steady leadership of President Lincoln. At a time when opinion in the North was bitterly divided, he applied uncommon skill to the difficult task of keeping the nation together.

Finally, Lincoln's decision to proclaim emancipation was a fateful step that changed the nature of the war. Lincoln's determination—and the determination of thousands of African Americans in the North and South—sustained northern spirits, even as the war sapped southern resolve.

✓ **Checkpoint What were some of the reasons the North prevailed in the Civil War?**

Lincoln's funeral casket is displayed to mourners in Philadelphia, Pennsylvania.

The War's Lasting Impact

The United States had never experienced a war like the Civil War. Some individual battles produced casualties greater than the United States had previously sustained in entire wars. When the war was over, more than 600,000 Americans were dead. Hundreds of thousands more were maimed.

The Civil War ushered in the harsh reality of modern warfare. For the first time, ordinary citizens could see the carnage of the battlefield through the photographs of journalists such as **Mathew Brady.** His exhibition "The Dead at Antietam" provided graphic evidence of the terrible realities of war.

Effects on the Economy After the fighting ended, social and political disillusionment on both sides fed economic greed. The era following the war came to be labeled the Gilded Age—a term that suggested a superficial glitter and beauty covering up an underlying decay. Nevertheless, in the North, the industrial boom that was fueled by the war continued. In 1862, Congress passed both the **Land Grant College Act** and legislation authorizing a protective tariff. The Land Grant College Act gave money from the sale of public lands to states for the establishment of universities that taught "agriculture and mechanical arts." The tariff protected northern industry from foreign competition and raised much-needed revenue for the Union war effort. It also led to a surge in manufacturing that lasted far beyond the end of the war. After 1865, northern factories, banks, and cities underwent sweeping industrialization, helping the United States emerge as a global economic power.

In contrast, rebuilding the South was slow and tortured. Southern cities, such as Richmond and Atlanta, lay in ruins, as did many of the region's factories and railroads. The South struggled to regain its economic footing after the war, often

NoteTaking

Reading Skill: Understand Effects Use a concept web to identify the effects of the Civil War.

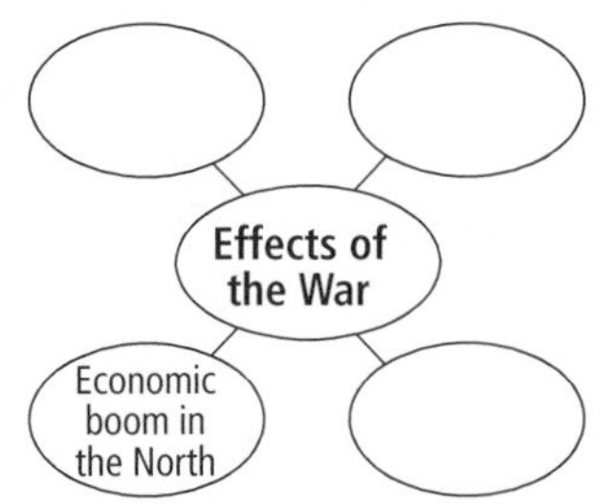

The Civil War, 1863–1865

Geography*Interactive*
For: Interactive map
www.pearsonschool.com/ushist

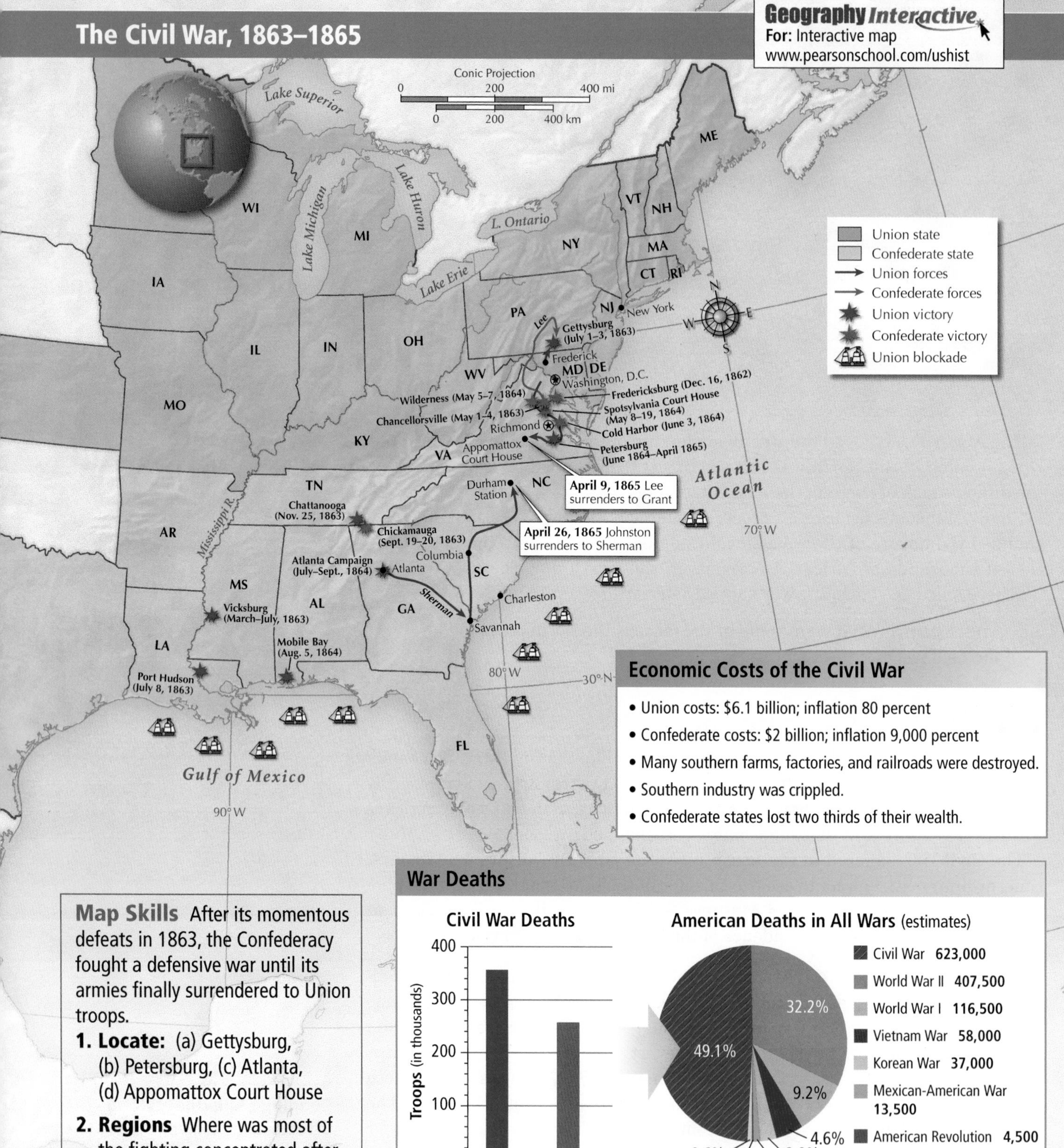

Economic Costs of the Civil War

- Union costs: $6.1 billion; inflation 80 percent
- Confederate costs: $2 billion; inflation 9,000 percent
- Many southern farms, factories, and railroads were destroyed.
- Southern industry was crippled.
- Confederate states lost two thirds of their wealth.

War Deaths

Map Skills After its momentous defeats in 1863, the Confederacy fought a defensive war until its armies finally surrendered to Union troops.

1. **Locate:** (a) Gettysburg, (b) Petersburg, (c) Atlanta, (d) Appomattox Court House
2. **Regions** Where was most of the fighting concentrated after 1863? Why?
3. **Draw Conclusions** Which side do you think suffered the most as a result of the Civil War? Why?

▲ The Costs of War

The death toll from the Civil War was staggering. More than half a million soldiers died—nearly as many were killed as in all other American wars combined. Additionally, more than 500,000 soldiers were wounded in the fighting. The material devastation of the war would plague the South for decades after its defeat.

relying on northern investment and seeking ways to enter the modern cash economy. For many decades, agriculture would remain at the center of southern economy. Northerners, forgetting Sherman's destruction of southern assets, would often blame the slow recovery on southerners' own shortcomings.

Effects on Society As a result of the war, the southern landscape was in shambles. Many Confederate soldiers returned to find their homes and farms destroyed. Millions of dislocated white southerners drifted aimlessly about the South in late 1865. Defeat had shaken them to the very core of their beliefs. Some felt that they were suffering a divine punishment, with one southerner mourning, "Oh, our God! What sins we must have been guilty of that we should be so humiliated by Thee now!" Others, however, came to view the Civil War as a lost, but noble, cause. These white southerners kept the memory of the struggle alive and believed that, eventually, the South would be redeemed.

African Americans of the South were equally disoriented. But they also had a new sense of hope. Freedom promised them a new life with new opportunities, including a chance to own land and to control their own lives. Some headed west to take advantage of the Homestead Act. Black southerners eagerly joined the migration that would mark American society for many years. However, as Reconstruction began, most African Americans in the South found that freedom was a promise not fully delivered.

Monument at Antietam National Battlefield

Effects on Government and Politics In many ways, the Civil War eased the history of disunity in American political life. While sectional differences remained strong, never again would such differences trigger threats of secession. Instead, over time, the economic, political, and social life of the nation's disparate regions would increasingly intertwine.

Debates over states' rights did not end with the Civil War. Still, the war helped cement federal authority. The government had fought a war to assert that individual states did not have the power to break the national bond forged by the Constitution. Increasingly, the federal government would come to play a larger role in Americans' lives. And more Americans would see themselves as citizens not just of a state but of a united nation.

✓ **Checkpoint** **What were some of the lasting effects of the Civil War?**

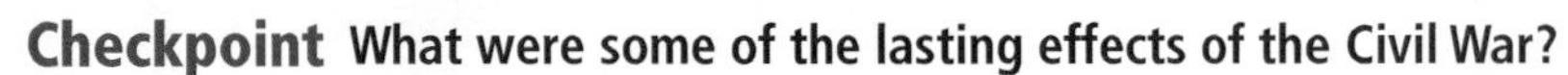

SECTION 5 Assessment

Progress Monitoring *Online*
For: Self-test with vocabulary practice
www.pearsonschool.com/ushist

Comprehension

1. **Terms and People** For each of the following items, write a sentence explaining its significance.
   - Thirteenth Amendment
   - John Wilkes Booth
   - Mathew Brady
   - Land Grant College Act
2. **NoteTaking Reading Skill: Recognize Sequence** Use your flowchart to answer the Section Focus Question: What was the final outcome and impact of the Civil War?

Writing About History

3. **Quick Write: Draft a News Article** Outline the news article you would write about the surrender at Appomattox or the assassination of President Lincoln. Then, write the headline and the first two paragraphs.

Critical Thinking

4. **Identify Alternatives** What alternatives did the South face in February 1865? Do you think they made the right choice?
5. **Predict Consequences** What was Lincoln's attitude toward the defeated South? How do you think his death might have affected plans for reuniting the country?
6. **Draw Conclusions** Why do you think a larger percentage of American troops died in the Civil War than in any other American war?

CHAPTER 11

Quick Study Guide

Progress Monitoring *Online*
For: Self-test with vocabulary practice
www.pearsonschool.com/ushist

Comparing North and South

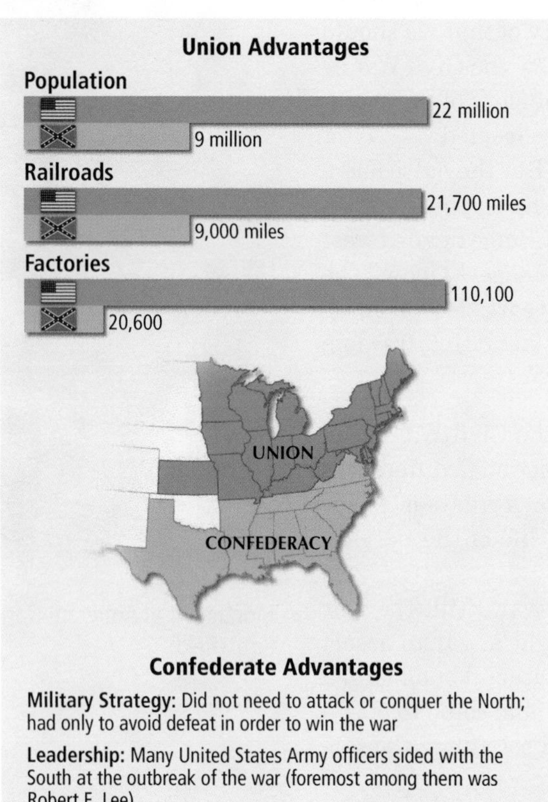

Confederate Advantages

Military Strategy: Did not need to attack or conquer the North; had only to avoid defeat in order to win the war

Leadership: Many United States Army officers sided with the South at the outbreak of the war (foremost among them was Robert E. Lee).

Morale: Most white southerners were willing to fight to protect their way of life.

Key Battles of the Civil War

Union Victories	Confederate Victories
• Glorieta Pass	• Fort Sumter
• Shiloh	• First Bull Run (First Manassas)
• New Orleans	• Seven Days
• Antietam	• Second Bull Run (Second Manassas)
• Perryville	• Sabine Pass
• Gettysburg	• Fredericksburg
• Vicksburg	• Chancellorsville
• Port Hudson	• Chickamauga
• Chattanooga	• Wilderness
• Atlanta	• Spotsylvania Court House
• Petersburg	• Cold Harbor

Extent of the Emancipation Proclamation, 1863

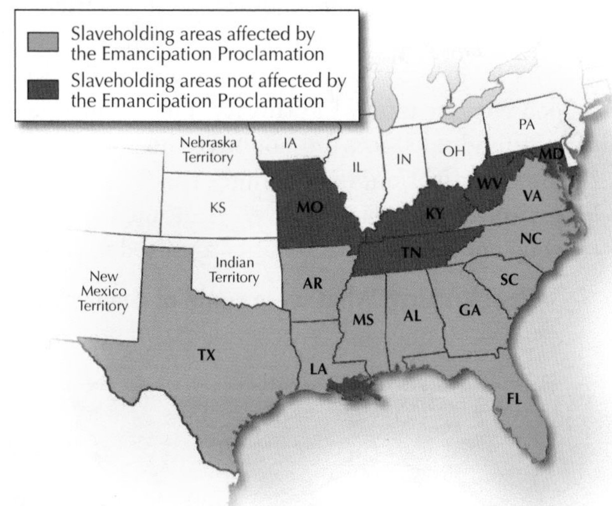

Quick Study Timeline

In America

1861 North and South clash at Bull Run

1862 Thousands die at Shiloh

January 1863 Emancipation Proclamation takes effect

Presidential Terms: Abraham Lincoln 1861–1865

1861 | 1862 | 1863

Around the World

1861 Alexander II emancipates Russian serfs

1862 Victor Hugo publishes *Les Misérables*

1863 Ismail Pasha comes to power in Ottoman Egypt

American Issues Connector

By connecting prior knowledge with what you have learned in this chapter, you can gradually build your understanding of enduring questions that still affect America today. Answer the questions below. Then, use your American Issues Connector study guide (or go online: www.pearsonschool.com/ushist).

Issues You Learned About

● **Social Problems and Reforms** Initially, the North engaged in the Civil War to prevent the breakup of the United States. Over time, however, the nature of the northern war effort changed to focus more on abolishing slavery.

1. What was the practical effect of the Emancipation Proclamation? What was the emotional effect?
2. What new right was extended to African Americans in the North around the time of the Emancipation Proclamation?
3. Is it likely that the Thirteenth Amendment, ending slavery in the United States, would have passed in 1865 if the Civil War had not been taking place? Explain.

● **Women in American Society** As with previous conflicts and movements in American history, the Civil War encouraged women to assume new responsibilities.

4. What new roles did women take on during the American Revolution?
5. How did women contribute to the antislavery movement in the early nineteenth century?
6. How did the Civil War create new opportunities for women on both sides?

● **Government's Role in the Economy** The federal government may pass new laws in response to the economic impact of a war.

7. What measures did the federal government pass to increase war funds during the Civil War?
8. What was the Homestead Act? How did the Civil War contribute to its passage?

Connect to Your World — Activity

Civil Liberties and National Security During the Civil War, Abraham Lincoln suspended the right of habeas corpus. In the aftermath of the terror attacks of September 11, 2001, the U.S. government passed several new national security laws collectively known as the Patriot Act. Some Americans feel that the Patriot Act violates civil liberties. Go online to learn more about civil liberties issues raised since 9/11. Write a summary of your findings.

Selected Provisions of the Patriot Act

Provision	Effect
Sec. 213. Authority for delaying notice of the execution of a warrant	Allows agents to search a property for which they have a warrant without notifying the subject at the time of the search.
Sec. 215. Access to records under the Foreign Intelligence Surveillance Act	Allows the government to obtain an individual's financial, medical, and other records without his or her knowledge in a terrorist investigation.

July 1863 Union victories at Gettysburg and Vicksburg

1864 Sherman's March to the Sea; Lincoln reelected

1865 Lee surrenders to Grant; Lincoln assassinated

Andrew Johnson 1865–1869

1864 — 1865 — 1866

1864 Chinese government crushes Taiping Rebellion

1865 Joseph Lister founds modern antiseptic surgery

History Interactive For: Interactive timeline www.pearsonschool.com/ushist

Chapter Assessment

Terms and People

1. Who was **Ulysses S. Grant**? Why was he important to the Union war effort?
2. What was the Battle of **Antietam**? What effect did it have on the North?
3. Define **conscription.** Which members of society did conscription fall most heavily on? Why?
4. Who were the **Copperheads**? Which people were most likely to be Copperheads, and why?
5. What were the siege of **Vicksburg** and the Battle of **Gettysburg**? What effects did they have on the progress of the war?

Focus Questions

The focus question for this chapter is **What were the causes, key events, and effects of the Civil War?** Build an answer to this big question by answering the focus questions for Sections 1 through 5 and the Critical Thinking questions that follow.

Section 1

6. How did each side's resources and strategies affect the early battles of the war?

Section 2

7. How did the Emancipation Proclamation and the efforts of African American soldiers affect the course of the war?

Section 3

8. How did the Civil War bring temporary and lasting changes to American society?

Section 4

9. How did the Battles of Vicksburg and Gettysburg change the course of the Civil War?

Section 5

10. What was the final outcome and impact of the Civil War?

Critical Thinking

11. **Analyze Evidence** Think about Robert E. Lee's reasons for turning down leadership of the Union forces and serving the South instead. What does this tell you about some of the difficulties the Civil War posed for all Americans?
12. **Analyze Information** How did African American soldiers surpass the initial expectations the Union had about them?
13. **Draw Conclusions** What is a possible explanation for Lincoln's refusal to obey the Supreme Court's ruling that only Congress had the right to suspend habeas corpus?
14. **Analyze Photographs** Study the image below of Richmond, Virginia, in 1865. What does the photograph suggest about the needs of the postwar period?

15. **Compare Points of View** How did Lincoln's ideas about the course the nation should take after the Civil War differ from those held by many northerners?
16. **Make Comparisons** Which side experienced more losses in the Civil War, the North or the South? Explain why this was the case.

Writing About History

Write a News Article People on both sides during the Civil War followed the war's events through news reports printed in local newspapers. Imagine that you are a reporter during the Civil War. Decide whether you are reporting from one of the national capitals or are traveling with one of the armies. Choose an event and write an article for your newspaper.

Prewriting

- Gather information about an event that interests you. Make sure you will be able to answer the five *W* questions: *Who? What? Where? When? Why?*
- Consider your audience and remember that a news article is an objective account of events.
- Gather additional information about the event from other sources.

Drafting

- Sort your information and write an outline of the article.
- Write the first paragraph, which should tell the most basic information about what happened.
- Write at least two more paragraphs, filling in further information. Newspaper articles include the least important information last.
- Write a headline that will help readers know what the article will be about.

Revising

- Use the guidelines on page SH11 of the Writing Handbook to revise your essay.

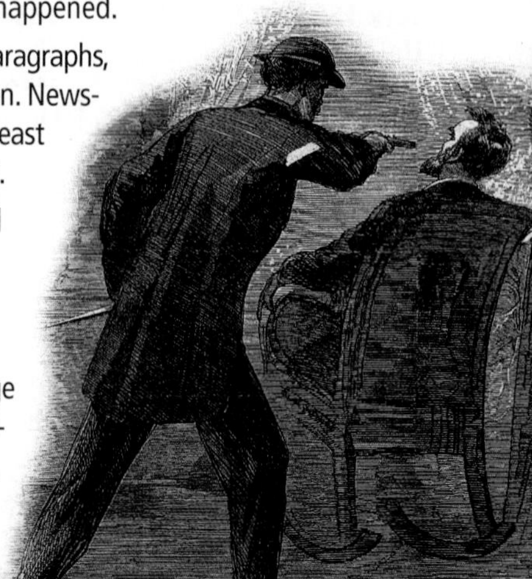

Document-Based Assessment

Total War

Union General William Tecumseh Sherman implemented a strategy of total war during his "march to the sea" in 1864. The concept of total war called for expanding military targets to include civilian economic resources. Use your knowledge of the Civil War and Documents A, B, C, and D to answer questions 1 through 4.

Document A

"Sherman's Atlanta campaign in May to September 1864 won the Confederate prize that ensured Lincoln's reelection that year. Sherman ordered a civilian evacuation of Atlanta, burned everything of any military value, and in November headed out of the city on his famous 'march to the sea.' More than any other Civil War commander, Sherman grasped the brutal logic of total war. In such a war, civilian morale and economic resources are as much military targets as the enemy's armies. For Sherman, war unleashed the fury of hell, and he refused to sentimentalize the killing and pillaging required for victory."

—*William L. Barney,* The Reader's Companion to American History

Document B

CITIZENS OF ATLANTA LEAVING THE CITY IN COMPLIANCE WITH GENERAL SHERMAN'S ORDERS.

"Citizens of Atlanta leaving the City in Compliance With General Sherman's Orders."

Document C

"Many people on both sides believed that the war would be short—one or two battles and the cowardly Yankees or slovenly rebels would give up. . . . Responsible leaders on both sides did not share the popular faith in a short war. Yet even they could not foresee the kind of conflict this war would become—a total war, requiring total mobilization of men and resources, destroying these men and resources on a massive scale, and ending only with unconditional surrender. In the spring of 1861 most northern leaders thought in terms of a limited war. Their purpose was not to conquer the South but to suppress insurrection and win back the latent loyalty of the southern people. The faith in southern unionism lingered long."

—*James M. McPherson,* Battle Cry of Freedom

Document D

"William Tecumseh Sherman was considered one of the ablest generals in the Federal army, but he was a cruel one. . . . His celebrated march through Georgia put a stain upon his name that will cling to it as it is found upon the pages of history. . . . With his grand army of veterans, almost unopposed, he had overrun and desolated the fairest sections of the South, burning cities, towns, and country dwellings; had wantonly destroyed many millions of dollars worth of property, both public and private; had made thousands of women and children and aged men homeless and destitute by burning their homes and destroying their means of subsistence. And it was to glorify him for these deeds of barbarism that 'Marching through Georgia' was written, and it is for this that it is sung."

—*Milford Overley,* "What 'Marching Through Georgia' Means"

---

1. The authors of Documents A and C define total war as
- **A** total mobilization of men and resources against both military and civilian targets.
- **B** a diplomatic effort aimed at avoiding the outbreak of hostilities.
- **C** a military effort concentrated almost entirely on civilian targets.
- **D** a policy for controlling the civilian populations of cities.

2. Which of the documents focuses on southerners reacting to total war?
- **A** Documents A and B
- **B** Documents B and C
- **C** Documents B and D
- **D** Documents A and D

3. According to Document A, why might Sherman have refused to "sentimentalize" total war?
- **A** He wanted to protect Confederate government property.
- **B** He wanted captured Confederate soldiers to help rebuild war-torn areas.
- **C** He wanted more troops and supplies from Washington.
- **D** He wanted civilian suffering to speed the collapse of the Confederate war effort.

4. **Writing Task** What impact did the military strategy of total war have on the people of the South during the Civil War? Use your knowledge of the war and specific evidence from the primary sources above to support your opinion.

CHAPTER

12 The Reconstruction Era 1865–1877

WITNESS HISTORY

All Is Now Lost

At the end of the Civil War, much of the South was in ruins. As described below by a member of a southern plantation family, all southerners faced not only the reconstruction of their cities and homes, but the reconstruction of the South as a whole.

"Our losses have been frightful, and we have, now, scarcely a support. My Father had five plantations on the coast, and all the buildings were burnt, and the negroes . . . are roaming in a starving condition. Our farm near Charleston was abandoned. . . . All is now lost, and the negroes, left to themselves . . . seek a little food, about the city. Our Residence in the city, was sacked . . . and the house well riddled by shell & shot. Our handsome Residence in the country was burnt. The Enemy passed over all our property on the coast in their march from Savannah to Charleston, the whole country, down there, is now a howling wilderness. . . . [I]t will be many years, before this once productive country will be able to support itself."

—Edward Barnwell Heyward

◀ Young African Americans sitting amid the rubble and ruins of Charleston, South Carolina

Ticket to President Johnson's impeachment trial

A carpetbag suitcase

Chapter Preview

Chapter Focus Question: What lasting consequences arose from the struggles over Reconstruction?

Section 1
Rival Plans for Reconstruction

Section 2
Reconstruction in the South

Section 3
The End of Reconstruction

Lithograph with portraits of African American politicians

Use the ☑ Quick Study Timeline at the end of this chapter to preview chapter events.

Note Taking Study Guide *Online*
For: Note Taking and American Issues Connector
www.pearsonschool.com/ushist

SECTION 1

Mary Chesnut and her husband, James ▶

WITNESS HISTORY

Nothing Left But the Bare Land

Mary Chesnut was the wife of a wealthy and respected South Carolina planter and politician. During the Civil War, her husband resigned from the United States Senate to fight for the Confederacy. Now, at war's end, the family was penniless. The world they had known was gone. Mary Chesnut described the devastation.

> "Mrs. Bartow drove me to our house at Mulberry. On one side of the house, every window was broken, every bell torn down, every piece of furniture destroyed, every door smashed in. . . . [The Yankee soldiers] carried off sacks of our books and our papers, our letters were strewed along the Charleston road. Potter's raid ruined us. He burned our mills and gins, and a hundred bales of cotton. Indeed nothing is left now but the bare land."
>
> —Mary Boykin Chesnut, May 1865

Rival Plans for Reconstruction

Objectives

- Explain why a plan was needed for Reconstruction of the South.
- Compare the Reconstruction plans of Lincoln, Johnson, and Congress.
- Discuss Johnson's political difficulties and impeachment.

Terms and People

Reconstruction	black code
Radical Republican	Civil Rights Act of 1866
Wade-Davis Bill	Fourteenth Amendment
Freedmen's Bureau	impeach
Andrew Johnson	Fifteenth Amendment

NoteTaking

Reading Skill: Identify Main Ideas Use a chart to record main ideas about Reconstruction.

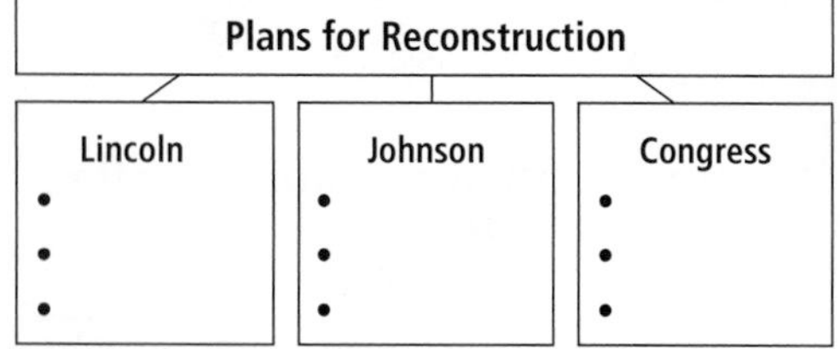

Why It Matters Even before the end of the Civil War, Congress and the President disagreed over how the seceded states would rejoin the Union. When the war ended, bitterness between the North and South was compounded by a power struggle between the executive and legislative branches of government. The issues that arose and how they were dealt with would have consequences for generations to come. **Section Focus Question: How did the Radical Republicans' plans for Reconstruction differ from Lincoln's and Johnson's?**

The Issues of Reconstruction

When the Civil War ended, parts of the South lay in ruins—homes burned, businesses closed, many properties abandoned. African Americans, though emancipated, lacked full citizenship and the means to make a living. During the era of **Reconstruction** (1865–1877), the federal government struggled with how to return the eleven southern states to the Union, rebuild the South's ruined economy, and promote the rights of former slaves.

How Will Southern States Rejoin the Union? To many Americans, the most important issue was deciding the political fate of Confederate states. Should Confederate leaders be tried for treason, or should they be pardoned so that national healing could proceed as quickly as possible? And what should be the process by which southern representatives could reclaim their seats in Congress?

The Constitution provided no guidance on secession or readmission of states. It was not clear whether Congress or the President should take the lead in forming Reconstruction policy. Some argued that states should be allowed to rejoin the Union quickly with few conditions. But many claimed that the defeated states should first satisfy certain stipulations, such as swearing loyalty to the federal government and adopting state constitutions that guaranteed freedmen's rights.

Vocabulary Builder
stipulation–(stihp yuh LAY shuhn) *n.* act of specifying a condition in an agreement

How Will the Southern Economy Be Rebuilt? The Civil War devastated the South's economy. Between 1860 and 1870, the South's share of the nation's total wealth declined from more than 30 percent to 12 percent. The Union army had destroyed factories, plantations, and railroads. Nearly half of the region's livestock and farm machinery were gone. About one fourth of southern white men between the ages of 20 and 40 had died in the war. In addition, more than 3 million newly freed African Americans were now without homes or jobs. After the war, the land was the South's most valuable asset, and arguments raged over who should control it.

During Reconstruction, some people proposed using the land to benefit former slaves. General William Tecumseh Sherman proposed that millions of acres abandoned by planters, or confiscated by the federal government, should be given to former slaves. "Forty acres and a mule," he suggested, would be sufficient to support a family. Many northerners thought this might also be a way to restore the South's productivity, reconstruct its economy, and provide employment as well as income for many African Americans.

Not everyone agreed. Southern landowners rejected the idea that the government could simply give away their land. Many white northerners worried that confiscating property violated the Constitution. Even some southern African Americans felt that the government should pay white southerners for farmland, and then sell it to former slaves on easy terms.

What Rights Will African Americans Have? The Thirteenth Amendment freed African Americans from slavery, but it did not grant them the privileges of full citizenship. The former slaves hoped that they would gain voting rights and access to education, benefits that most northern black people also did not have. Most leaders of the Republican Party, which at the time dominated the federal government, supported programs to extend full citizenship to African Americans. However, most white southerners opposed the idea. They feared it would undermine their own power and status in society.

✓ **Checkpoint** **What were three major issues of Reconstruction?**

Lincoln Sets a Moderate Course

Even while the war was in progress, Union politicians had debated programs for repairing the nation's political structure and economy. For President Lincoln, one of the first major goals was to reunify the nation.

Ten Percent Plan Offers Leniency Throughout the war, Lincoln had felt some sympathy for the South and hoped that southern states might easily rejoin the Union after the war. To this end, in 1863 he issued a Proclamation of Amnesty and Reconstruction, known as the "Ten Percent Plan." According to its terms, as soon as ten percent of a state's voters took a loyalty oath to the Union, the state could set up a new government. If the state's constitution abolished slavery and provided education for African Americans, the state would regain representation in Congress.

Destruction and Devastation
The destruction of the Richmond, Virginia, rail depot (below) and the many other stations and railroads during the Civil War contributed to the South's devastated economy during Reconstruction. *Why would destroying a region's rail system affect the local economy?*

Freedmen's Bureau
Freedmen's Bureau schools like this one brought new educational opportunities for African Americans. *How old do the students at this school appear to be?*

Vocabulary Builder
compensate–(KAHM puhn sayt) *v.* to make up for

Lincoln was generous in other ways to white southerners. He was willing to grant pardons to former Confederates, and he considered compensating them for lost property. In addition, Lincoln did not require a guarantee of social or political equality for African Americans. He recognized pro-Union governments in Arkansas, Louisiana, and Tennessee even though they denied African Americans the right to vote.

Lincoln took the position that the Union was unbreakable and therefore the southern states had never really left the Union. In his Second Inaugural Address, delivered a month before the war ended, Lincoln promised forgiveness:

> **Primary Source** "With malice toward none, and charity for all, with firmness in the right as God gives us to see the right, let us strive on to finish the work we are in, to bind up the nation's wounds . . . to do all which may achieve and cherish a just and a lasting peace among ourselves and with all nations."
>
> —Lincoln's Second Inaugural Address, March 1865

Radicals Oppose the Ten Percent Plan Members of Lincoln's own party opposed his plan. Led by Representative Thaddeus Stevens and Senator Charles Sumner, these "**Radical Republicans**" in Congress insisted that the Confederates had committed crimes—by enslaving African Americans and by entangling the nation in war.

The Radical Republicans advocated full citizenship, including the right to vote, for African Americans. They favored punishment and harsh terms for the South, and they supported Sherman's plan to confiscate Confederates' land and give farms to freedmen.

Rejecting Lincoln's Ten Percent Plan, Congress passed the **Wade-Davis Bill** in 1864. It required that a majority of a state's prewar voters swear loyalty to the Union before the process of restoration could begin. The bill also demanded guarantees of African American equality. President Lincoln killed this plan with a "pocket veto" by withholding his signature beyond the 10-day deadline at the end of the congressional session.

Government Aids Freedmen One Radical Republican plan did receive the President's support. This was the Bureau of Refugees, Freedmen, and Abandoned Lands, known as the **Freedmen's Bureau.** Created a few weeks before Lincoln's death, its goal was to provide food, clothing, health care, and education for both black and white refugees in the South.

The Freedmen's Bureau helped reunite families that had been separated by slavery and war. It negotiated fair labor contracts between former slaves and white landowners. By representing African Americans in the courts, the Bureau also established a precedent that black citizens had legal rights. The Freedmen's Bureau continued its efforts until 1872.

✓ **Checkpoint How did Lincoln's goals differ from those of the Radical Republicans?**

HISTORY MAKERS

Andrew Johnson (1808–1875)
Despite a lack of formal schooling, Andrew Johnson became a skilled public speaker and entered Tennessee politics as a Democrat. When Tennessee seceded in 1861, Johnson was the only southern senator who refused to join the Confederacy. When the Union occupied Tennessee in 1862, Lincoln appointed him military governor. Hoping to attract Democratic voters, the Republican Party chose Johnson as Lincoln's Vice President in 1864.

Johnson's Reconstruction Plan

Lincoln was assassinated in April 1865, just weeks after his second inaugural. Lincoln's death thrust his Vice President, **Andrew Johnson,** into the presidency.

Johnson Seeks to Restore the Union Like Lincoln, Johnson wanted to restore the political status of the southern states as quickly as possible. He offered pardons and the restoration of land to almost any Confederate who swore allegiance to the Union and the Constitution. His main requirement was that each state ratify the Thirteenth Amendment and draft a constitution that abolished slavery. However, Johnson resented wealthy planters and required that they and other Confederate leaders write to him personally to apply for a pardon.

Johnson's dislike of the planter class did not translate into a desire to elevate African Americans. Like many southerners, Johnson expected the United States to have a "government for white men." He did not want African Americans to have the vote. In fact, he had little sympathy for their plight. Johnson supported states' rights, which would allow the laws and customs of the state to outweigh federal regulations. States would, therefore, be able to limit the freedoms of former slaves.

By the time Congress reconvened in December 1865, most Confederate states had met Johnson's requirements for readmission. Radical and moderate Republicans were concerned about the lack of African American suffrage, but they remained hopeful that black political rights would soon follow.

Southerners Aim to Restore Old Ways That hope was soon dashed. Beginning with the state conventions required by Johnson, southern leaders proceeded to rebuild their prewar world. Many states specifically limited the vote to white men. Some states sent their Confederate officials to the United States Congress. All of the states instituted **black codes**—laws that sought to limit the rights of African Americans and keep them as landless workers.

The codes required African Americans to work in only a limited number of occupations, most often as servants or farm laborers. Some states prohibited African Americans from owning land, and all set up vagrancy laws. These laws stipulated that any black person who did not have a job could be arrested and sent to work as prison labor. Even though the South remained under Union military occupation, white southerners openly used violence and intimidation to enforce the black codes.

Congress Fights Back Both Radical and moderate Republicans were infuriated by the South's disregard of the spirit of Reconstruction. When the southern representatives arrived in Washington, D.C., Congress refused them their seats. Congress also created a committee to investigate the treatment of former slaves.

Through the spring of 1866, the political situation grew worse. While the Radicals claimed that federal intervention was needed to advance African American political and civil rights, President Johnson accused them of trying "to Africanize the southern half of our country." When Congress passed a bill to allow the Freedmen's Bureau to continue its work and provide it with authority to punish state officials who failed to extend civil rights to African Americans, Johnson vetoed it. Undaunted, Congress sought to overturn the black codes by passing the **Civil Rights Act of 1866.** This measure created federal guarantees of civil rights and superseded any state laws that limited them. But once again, Johnson used his veto power to block the law. Johnson was now openly defying Congress.

 **Checkpoint How did the southern states try to reestablish conditions before the war?**

Congressional Reconstruction

As violence against African Americans in the South increased, moderate and Radical Republicans blamed the rising tide of lawlessness on Johnson's lenient policies. Congress then did something unprecedented. With the required two-thirds majority, for the first time ever, it passed major legislation over a President's veto. The Civil Rights Act of 1866 became law.

Decision Point

Who Controls the Readmission of States?

Although their main purpose was to reunite the nation, Reconstruction policies actually created new divisions between the President and Congress. A critically divisive issue was how the southern states should be readmitted into the Union.

Johnson Opposes Tight Restrictions

Primary Source

"As eleven States are not at this time represented in either branch of Congress, it would seem to be [the President's] duty on all proper occasions to present their just claims to Congress. . . . [I]f they are all excluded from Congress, if in a permanent statute they are declared not to be in full constitutional relations to the country, they may think they have cause to become a unit in feeling and sentiment against the Government."

—President Andrew Johnson, 1866

Stevens Favors Tight Restrictions

Primary Source

"The late war between two acknowledged belligerents . . . broke all the ties that bound them together. The future condition of the conquered power depends on the will of the conqueror. . . . Hence a law of Congress must be passed before any new State can be admitted. . . . Until then no member can be lawfully admitted into either House. . . . Then each House must judge whether the members . . . possess the requisite qualifications."

—Thaddeus Stevens, 1865

You Decide

1. Why did Johnson favor immediate readmission?
2. Why did Stevens want tight restrictions?
3. What decision would you have made? Why?

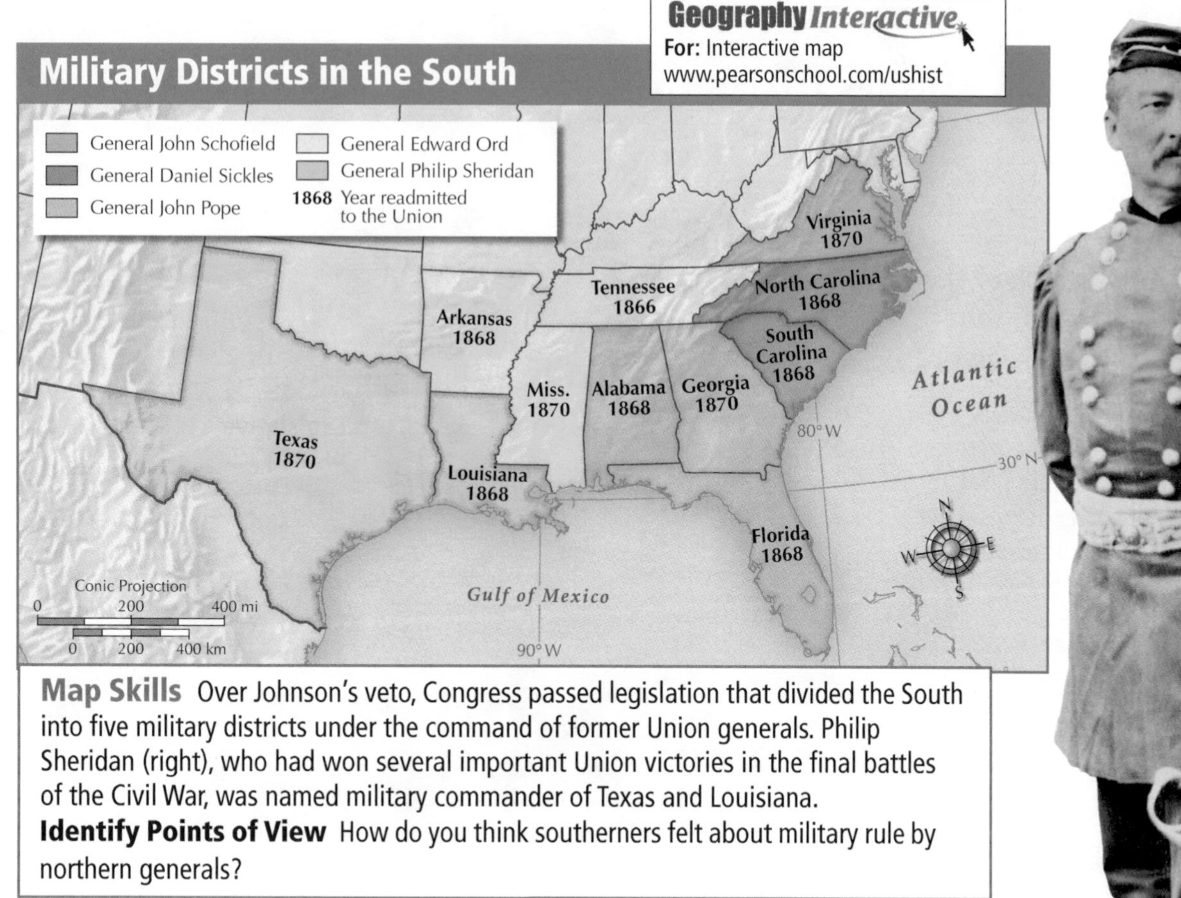

Map Skills Over Johnson's veto, Congress passed legislation that divided the South into five military districts under the command of former Union generals. Philip Sheridan (right), who had won several important Union victories in the final battles of the Civil War, was named military commander of Texas and Louisiana.
Identify Points of View How do you think southerners felt about military rule by northern generals?

Radical Reconstruction Begins Feeling their strength in Congress, a coalition of Radical and moderate Republicans spent nearly a year designing a sweeping Reconstruction program. To protect freedmen's rights from presidential vetoes, southern state legislatures, and federal court decisions, Congress passed the **Fourteenth Amendment** to the Constitution. It guaranteed equality under the law for all citizens. Under the amendment, any state that refused to allow black people to vote would risk losing the number of seats in the House of Representatives that were represented by its black population. The measure also counteracted the President's pardons by barring leading Confederate officials from holding federal or state offices.

Congress again passed legislation over Johnson's veto with the ratification of the Military Reconstruction Act of 1867. The act divided the 10 southern states that had yet to be readmitted into the Union into five military districts governed by former Union generals (see map above). The act also delineated how each state could create their new state government and receive congressional recognition. In each state, voters were to elect delegates to write a new constitution that guaranteed suffrage for African American men. Then, once the state ratified the Fourteenth Amendment, it could reenter the Union.

Congress Impeaches the President The power struggle between Congress and the President reached a crisis in 1867. To limit the President's power, Congress passed the Tenure of Office Act. Under its terms, the President needed Senate approval to remove certain officials from office. When Johnson tried to fire Secretary of War Edwin Stanton, the last Radical Republican in his Cabinet, Stanton barricaded himself in his office for about two months.

Angrily, the House of Representatives voted to **impeach** Johnson, that is, to charge him with wrongdoing in office, for trying to fire Stanton. The trial in the

American Issues Connector

Checks and Balances

TRACK THE ISSUE

Does any branch of the federal government have too much power?

Our system of checks and balances is meant to prevent any branch of government from becoming too powerful. Yet at times the balance of power between the executive, legislative, and judicial branches has shifted. Use the timeline below to explore this enduring issue.

1803 *Marbury* v. *Madison*
John Marshall affirms Supreme Court's right of judicial review.

1830s Jackson Presidency
Andrew Jackson increases executive power.

1868 Johnson Impeachment
Congress tries to remove President Andrew Johnson from office.

1930s New Deal
Franklin D. Roosevelt boosts presidential power to fight the depression.

1960s Warren Court
Supreme Court under Earl Warren becomes a force for social reform.

1973 War Powers Act
Congress limits the President's power to wage war.

2000s War on Terrorism
Congress increases executive branch powers to combat terrorism.

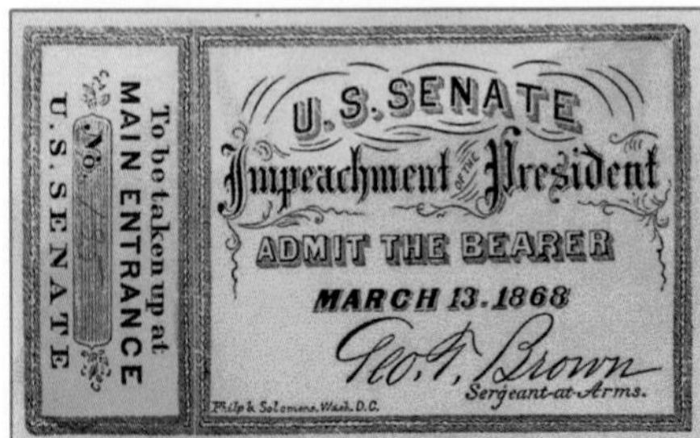

Ticket to Andrew Johnson's trial

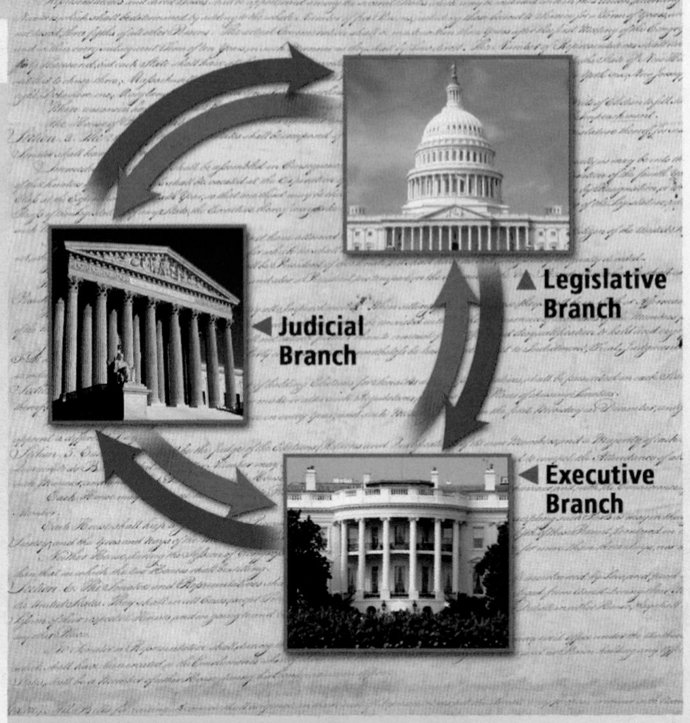

DEBATE THE ISSUE

Imbalance of Power? During the administration of President George W. Bush, much debate focused on the relative powers of the President and Congress.

"I do have the view that over the years there had been an erosion of presidential power. . . . I served in the Congress for 10 years. I've got enormous regard for the other body . . . but . . . the President of the United States needs to have his constitutional powers unimpaired, if you will, in terms of the conduct of national security policy."

—Vice President Richard Cheney, December 20, 2005

"During the early years of the post–World War II era, power was relatively well-balanced . . . but major shifts . . . have made Congress much weaker and the President dangerously stronger. . . . The Bush presidency has attained a level of power over Congress that undermines sound democratic governance."

—Walter Williams, *Seattle Times,* May 2004

TRANSFER Activities

1. **Compare** When does Vice President Cheney feel the President should have more power? Why would Walter Williams disagree?
2. **Analyze** How did the administration of President Andrew Johnson reflect a similar power struggle?
3. **Transfer** Use the following Web site to see a video, try a WebQuest, and write in your journal. www.pearsonschool.com/ushist

Senate lasted through the spring of 1868. In the end, the Radicals failed—by only one vote—to win the two-thirds majority necessary in the Senate to remove Johnson from office. Several moderate Republicans backed away from conviction. They felt that using impeachment to get rid of a President who disagreed with Congress would upset the balance of power in the government. During his impeachment trial, Johnson had promised to enforce the Reconstruction Acts. In his remaining time in office, he kept that promise.

Major Reconstruction Legislation, 1865–1870 Quick Study

Legislation	Provisions
Freedmen's Bureau Acts (1865–1866)	Create a government agency to provide services to freed slaves and war victims
Civil Rights Act of 1866	Grants citizenship to African Americans and outlaws black codes
Reconstruction Act of 1867	Divides former Confederacy into military districts
Fourteenth Amendment (1868)	Guarantees citizenship to African Americans and prohibits states from passing laws to take away a citizen's rights
Fifteenth Amendment (1870)	States that no citizen can be denied the right to vote because of "race, color, or previous condition of servitude"
Enforcement Act of 1870	Protects voting rights by making intimidation of voters a federal crime

The Fifteenth Amendment Extends Suffrage In 1868, the Republican candidate, former Union general Ulysses S. Grant was elected President. Although he won the electoral vote by a huge margin and had a significant lead in the popular vote, his opponent, Horatio Seymour, a Democrat from New York, received a majority of the white vote. Republican leaders now had another reason for securing a constitutional amendment that would guarantee black suffrage throughout the nation.

In 1869, Congress passed the **Fifteenth Amendment** forbidding any state from denying suffrage on the grounds of race, color, or previous condition of servitude. Unlike previous measures, this guarantee applied to northern states as well as southern states. Both the Fourteenth and Fifteenth amendments were ratified by 1870, but both contained loopholes that left room for evasion. States could still impose voting restrictions based on literacy or property qualifications, which in effect would exclude most African Americans. Soon the southern states would do just that.

Checkpoint How did the Fourteenth and Fifteenth amendments extend the rights of African Americans?

SECTION 1 Assessment

Progress Monitoring *Online*
For: Self-test with vocabulary practice
www.pearsonschool.com/ushist

Comprehension

1. **Terms and People** For each item below, write a sentence explaining its significance:
   - Reconstruction
   - Radical Republican
   - Wade-Davis Bill
   - Freedmen's Bureau
   - Andrew Johnson
   - black code
   - Civil Rights Act of 1866
   - Fourteenth Amendment
   - impeach
   - Fifteenth Amendment

2. **NoteTaking Reading Skill: Identify Main Ideas** Use your chart to answer the Section Focus Question: How did the Radical Republicans' plans for Reconstruction differ from Lincoln's and Johnson's?

Writing About History

3. **Quick Write: Identify Audience and Purpose** Write a letter to your constituents about the passage of the Civil Rights Acts as if you were Thaddeus Stevens. Before you begin, consider your audience and the purpose of your letter—information, persuasion, or explanation.

Critical Thinking

4. **Predict Consequences** Why was Reconstruction of the South likely to be a difficult process?

5. **Draw Conclusions** Why do you think President Lincoln proposed generous terms for Reconstruction in 1863?

6. **Analyze Information** How did the Radical Republicans try to protect the rights of African Americans?

SECTION 2

▲ Freedmen line up to vote.

◀ Portrait of Senator Hiram Revels

WITNESS HISTORY

An African American in the Senate

In 1861, Jefferson Davis left his seat in the U.S. Senate and became President of the Confederacy. In 1870, his unfinished term was resumed by Hiram Revels—an African American. A few months later, Senator Revels stood up to make his first speech. He answered those who charged that African Americans in the South were using their new political power to seek revenge on white southerners:

> "As the recognized representative of my downtrodden people, I deny the charge. . . . They bear toward their former masters no revengeful thoughts, no hatreds, no animosities. They aim not to elevate themselves by sacrificing one single interest of their white fellow-citizens. They ask but the rights which are theirs by God's universal law. . . . [to] enjoy the liberties of citizenship on the same footing with their white neighbors and friends."
>
> —Hiram Revels, speech in the U.S. Senate, March 16, 1870

Reconstruction in the South

Objectives

- Explain how Republicans gained control of southern state governments.
- Discuss how freedmen adjusted to freedom and the South's new economic system.
- Summarize efforts to limit African Americans' rights and the federal government's response.

Terms and People

scalawag
carpetbagger
segregation
integration
sharecropping
share-tenancy
tenant farming
Ku Klux Klan
Enforcement Acts

NoteTaking

Reading Skill: Identify Main Ideas Use a chart like the one below to record details about changes in the South during Reconstruction.

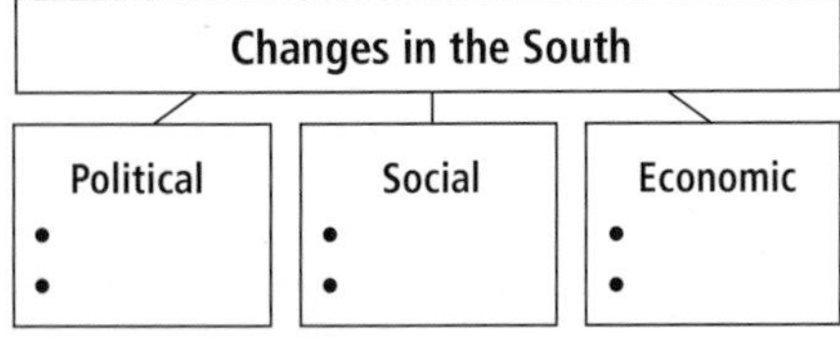

Why It Matters Before the Civil War, a limited number of powerful men had controlled the South. In the wake of the war, a very basic question needed to be resolved. Who would gain power and how would they use it? How this question was answered at the time would have both immediate and lasting consequences. **Section Focus Question: What were the immediate effects of Reconstruction?**

Republican Governments Bring Change

By 1870, all of the former Confederate states had met the requirements under Radical Reconstruction and rejoined the Union. Republicans dominated their newly established state governments.

African Americans Use Political Power Almost 1,500 black men—some born free, some recently released from slavery—helped usher the Republican Party into the South. These new black citizens served the South as school superintendents, sheriffs, mayors, coroners, police chiefs, and representatives in state legislatures. Six served as lieutenant governors. Two state legislatures—in Mississippi and South Carolina—had black Speakers of the House. Between 1870 and 1877, two African American senators and fourteen African American congressmen served in the United States Congress.

Most importantly, millions of southern African American men were now voters. Since the Radical Republicans required a loyalty oath, many white southerners were not eligible to vote, or chose to stay away from the constitutional conventions and from the elections that followed. Black men, however, quickly signed up to use their new right of suffrage. Thus, by 1868, many southern states had both African American elected officials and a strong Republican Party. Ironically, South Carolina—the state that had ignited the Civil War—became the one state where a black majority ruled the legislature, although only for a short time.

Scalawags and Carpetbaggers Take Part in Southern Politics The Republican Party attracted not only black southerners but also others who sought change and challenge. **Scalawags,** as southern white critics called them, were white men who had been locked out of pre–Civil War politics by their wealthier neighbors. The new Republican Party invited them in.

Scalawags found allies in northern white or black men who relocated to the South. These northerners came seeking to improve their economic or political situations, or to help make a better life for freedmen. Many southern white people resented what they felt was the invasion of opportunists, come to make their fortunes from the South's misfortune. Southerners labeled the newcomers **"carpetbaggers,"** after the inexpensive carpet-cloth suitcases often carried by northerners.

For carpetbaggers, the opportunities in the new South were as abundant as those in the western frontier: new land to be bought, new careers to be shaped. The progress of Blanche K. Bruce presents an example. Born a slave in Virginia, Bruce learned to read from his owner's son. When the war began, Bruce left the plantation and moved to Missouri, where he ran a school for black children for a short time before moving on to Oberlin College in Ohio. In 1866, Bruce—now 25 years old—went south to Mississippi, where he became a prosperous landowner and was elected to several local political positions. In 1874, in his mid-thirties, Bruce was elected to the United States Senate.

Bruce's story highlights several characteristics of the carpetbaggers. First, they were often young. Second, since only the wealthy minority of white southerners were literate, a northerner with even a basic education had a real advantage. Finally, for African Americans, the South was the only place to pursue a political career. Even though the Fifteenth Amendment established suffrage nationally, no black congressman was elected from the North until the twentieth century.

Analyzing Political Cartoons

The Burden of Reconstruction This cartoon appeared in a northern newspaper in the 1870s.

- **A** President Grant
- **B** Union soldiers
- **C** the South

1. What do the weapons and soldiers in the cartoon represent?
2. What is the woman doing? Is her task easy or difficult?
3. What is this cartoonist's view of Reconstruction?

Successes and Failures Result On the other hand, the Republican Party did not support women's suffrage, arguing that they could not rally national support behind the essential goal of black suffrage if they tried to include women too. Even so, the Reconstruction South offered northern women—white and black—opportunities that they could not pursue at home. In medical facilities, orphanages, and other relief agencies, single women carved out new roles and envisioned new horizons. They also participated in what was the most enduring development of the new South—the shaping of a public school system.

Mandated by Reconstruction state constitutions, public schools grew slowly, drawing in only about half of southern children by the end of the 1870s. Establishing a new school system was expensive. This was especially so since southerners opted for **segregation,** or separation of the races. Operating two school systems—one white, one black—severely strained the southern economy. A few of the most radical white Republicans suggested **integration**—combining the schools—but the idea was unpopular with most Republicans. Nevertheless, the beginning of a tax-supported public school system was a major Reconstruction success.

Vocabulary Builder
nevertheless–(nehv uhr thuh LEHS) *adv.* in spite of

Despite these successes, the South still faced many challenges. Many southerners remained illiterate. The quality of medical care, housing, and economic production lagged far behind the North and, in some cases, behind the newly settled West. Legal protection for African Americans was limited, and racial violence remained a problem until well into the twentieth century.

A new reality was sweeping the country. Political offices, which were once an honor bestowed upon a community's successful business people, were becoming a route to wealth and power rather than a result of these attributes. However, conditions in the South were not unlike the rest of the country in that respect. Ambitious people everywhere were willing to bribe politicians in order to gain access to attractive loans or contracts.

Some of the most attractive arenas for corruption involved the developing railroads. Republicans were the party of African American freedom, but they were also the party of aggressive economic development. Building railroads had two big advantages. First, the construction of tracks and rail cars created jobs. Second, the rail lines would provide the means to carry produce and industrial goods to expanded markets. Hence, in many states across the nation, legislatures gave public land or lent taxpayers' money to railroad speculators.

In some cases, the speculators delivered on their promises and repaid the loans. But southern leaders, who had fewer resources and less financial expertise than their northern peers, found that a good number of their loans were stolen or mismanaged. Though northern white speculators defaulted, too, many Americans used these examples to argue that southern black politicians were dishonest or incompetent.

✓ **Checkpoint What new groups were active in politics under Republican governments?**

Rebuilding the South

After the Civil War, the South faced the challenge of rebuilding. Some of its most important cities lay in ruins. *What evidence of rebuilding can you see in this photograph?*

African American Farmers
Although some African Americans moved to southern cities after the Civil War, many remained in rural areas. *How do you think the lives of freed African Americans compared to their lives during slavery?*

Freed People Build New Communities

For newly freed African Americans, the importance of such issues as public corruption was matched by the importance of trying to work out new social institutions and economic relationships. Some freedmen deliberately moved away from the plantation, even if the owner had been a generous person. As one minister put it, "As long as the shadow of the great house falls across you, you ain't going to feel like no free man and no free woman."

Work and Family For the first time, many African American men and women could legalize and celebrate their marriages, create homes for their families, and make choices about where they would reside (though these choices were restricted by black codes limiting what work they might do). Life presented new problems and opportunities.

> **Primary Source** "I stayed on [the plantation] 'cause I didn't have no place to go. . . . Den I starts to feeling like I ain't treated right. So one night I just put that new dress in a bundle and set foot right down the big road, a-walking west!"
>
> —Mary Lindsey, age 19

Many African Americans headed for southern cities, where they could develop churches, schools, and other social institutions. They also hoped to find work. Skilled men might find work as carpenters, blacksmiths, cooks, or house servants; women took in laundry, or did child care or domestic work. However, most often, black workers had to settle for what they had had under slavery: substandard housing and poor food, in return for hard labor.

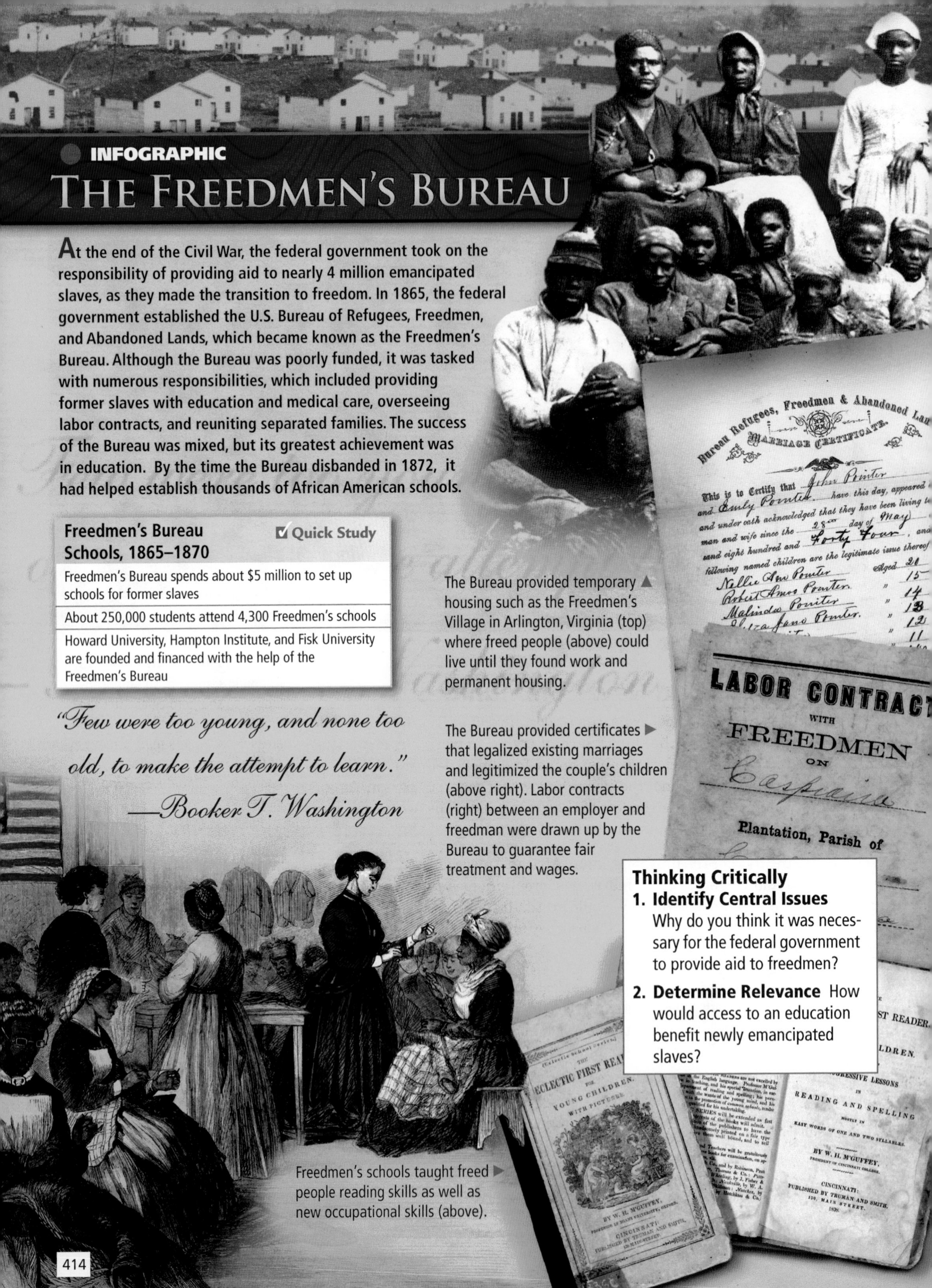

INFOGRAPHIC

THE FREEDMEN'S BUREAU

At the end of the Civil War, the federal government took on the responsibility of providing aid to nearly 4 million emancipated slaves, as they made the transition to freedom. In 1865, the federal government established the U.S. Bureau of Refugees, Freedmen, and Abandoned Lands, which became known as the Freedmen's Bureau. Although the Bureau was poorly funded, it was tasked with numerous responsibilities, which included providing former slaves with education and medical care, overseeing labor contracts, and reuniting separated families. The success of the Bureau was mixed, but its greatest achievement was in education. By the time the Bureau disbanded in 1872, it had helped establish thousands of African American schools.

Freedmen's Bureau Schools, 1865–1870 (Quick Study)
Freedmen's Bureau spends about $5 million to set up schools for former slaves
About 250,000 students attend 4,300 Freedmen's schools
Howard University, Hampton Institute, and Fisk University are founded and financed with the help of the Freedmen's Bureau

"Few were too young, and none too old, to make the attempt to learn."
—Booker T. Washington

The Bureau provided temporary housing such as the Freedmen's Village in Arlington, Virginia (top) where freed people (above) could live until they found work and permanent housing.

Bureau Refugees, Freedmen & Abandoned Lands
Marriage Certificate.
This is to Certify that John Pointer and Emily Pointer have this day, appeared and under oath acknowledged that they have been living as man and wife since the 28th day of May ... thousand eight hundred and Forty Four, and following named children are the legitimate issue thereof
Nellie Ann Pointer Aged 21
Robert Amos Pointer 15
Malinda Pointer 14
Eliza Jane Pointer 13
12
11

LABOR CONTRACT
WITH
FREEDMEN
ON
Caspiana
Plantation, Parish of

The Bureau provided certificates that legalized existing marriages and legitimized the couple's children (above right). Labor contracts (right) between an employer and freedman were drawn up by the Bureau to guarantee fair treatment and wages.

Thinking Critically

1. **Identify Central Issues** Why do you think it was necessary for the federal government to provide aid to freedmen?
2. **Determine Relevance** How would access to an education benefit newly emancipated slaves?

Freedmen's schools taught freed people reading skills as well as new occupational skills (above).

The majority of African American families remained in rural areas. There, they labored in such occupations as lumbering, railroad building, or farming land for landowners—white or black—who themselves were often poor.

Vocabulary Builder
intrinsic–(ihn TRIHN sihk) *adj.* basic; essential

Schools and Churches

Freed people immediately realized the intrinsic value of learning to read and perform basic arithmetic. Only in this way could they vote wisely and protect themselves from being cheated. So the Freedmen's Bureau schools filled quickly. By 1866, there were as many as 150,000 African American students—adults and children—acquiring basic literacy. Three years later, that number had doubled. Tuition amounted to 10 percent of a laborer's wage, but attendance at Freedmen's schools represented a firm commitment to education.

In addition to establishing its own schools, the Freedmen's Bureau aided black colleges. It also encouraged the many northern churches and charitable organizations that sent teachers, books, and supplies to support independent schools. Mostly these schools taught the basics of reading, writing, and math, but they also taught life skills such as health and nutrition, or how to look for a job.

The black church was an important component of Reconstruction education. Under slavery, slave owners sometimes allowed their slaves to hold their own religious services. Now, with freedom, black churches were established throughout the South and often served as school sites, community centers, employment agencies, and political rallying points. By providing an arena for organizing, public speaking, and group planning, churches helped develop African American leaders. A considerable number of African American politicians began their careers as ministers.

✓ **Checkpoint** **Why were schools and churches important to freed people?**

Remaking the Southern Economy

Many of the South's problems resulted from the uneven distribution of land. As an agricultural region, the South's wealth was defined by landownership. Yet, in 1860, the wealthiest 5 percent of white southerners owned almost half the region's land. Relatively few people held the rest of the land. In fact, more than 90 percent of southern land was owned by only 50 percent of the people. This meant that even before the war, the South had a large number of white citizens with little or no land. After the war, the millions of landless southern white people were competing with millions of landless black people for work as farm laborers on the land of others.

The plan developed by General Sherman and the Radical Republicans to give or sell land to freed people did not provide a solution. Congress had no interest in Thaddeus Stevens's radical suggestion that large plantations be confiscated from once-wealthy planters and redistributed to freedmen. A few African American men, however, were able to gather together the means to buy land. By 1880, about 7 percent of the South's land was owned by African Americans.

Systems For Sharing the Land

Even large land owners had no money to purchase supplies or pay workers. As a result, many southerners adopted one of three arrangements: sharecropping, share-tenancy, or tenant-farming.

The first two of these systems could be carried out without cash. Under the **sharecropping** system, which embraced most of the South's black and white poor, a landowner dictated the crop and provided the sharecropper with a place to live, as well as seeds and tools, in return for a "share" of the harvested crop. The landowner often bought these supplies on credit, at very high interest, from a supplier. The landlord passed on these costs to the sharecropper. Hence, sharecroppers were perpetually in debt to the landowner, and the landowner was always in debt to the supplier.

One problem with this system was that most landlords, remembering the huge profits from prewar cotton, chose to invest in this crop again. Dishonest landowners could lie about the cost of supplies, devaluing the sharecropper's harvest that now amounted to less than the season's expenses. Thus the sharecropper could never move, because he always owed the owner the labor for next year's crop.

Share-tenancy was much like sharecropping, except that the farmworker chose what crop he would plant and bought his own supplies. Then, he gave a share of the crop to the landowner. In this system, the farmworker had a bit more control over the cost of supplies. Therefore, he might be able to grow a variety of crops or use some of the land to grow food for his family. With these choices, it became more possible to save money.

Tenant Farmers The most independent arrangement for both farmer and landowner was a system known as **tenant farming.** In this case, the tenant paid cash rent to a landowner and then was free to choose and manage his own crop—and free to choose where he would live. This system was only viable for a farmer who had good money-management skills—and some good luck.

✓ **Checkpoint What arrangements allowed landless people to farm?**

Violence Undermines Reform Efforts

The struggle to make a living in a region devastated by war led to fierce economic competition. Economic uncertainty in turn fueled the fire of white southerners' outrage. Already resentful of the Republican takeover of local politics and of occupation by federal troops, white southerners from all economic classes were united in their insistence that African Americans not have full citizenship.

The Sharecropping System

In theory, sharecropping provided an opportunity for poor, landless freedmen and white southerners to save money to purchase their own land. However, as the chart at right illustrates, sharecropping proved to be an endless cycle of debt and poverty that southern farmers could rarely escape. As agriculture was key to the southern economy, the sharecropping system remained a major source of labor until the 1940s when mechanized farming reduced the need for human laborers.

Why was the sharecropping system considered an endless cycle for southern farmers?

◀ Cotton was the primary crop of sharecroppers.

Sharecropping Cycle of Poverty

1. Landowner provides land, seed, and tools to sharecropper in exchange for a large share of the harvested crop.
2. Sharecropper purchases supplies from landowner's store on credit, often at high interest rates.
3. Sharecropper plants and harvests the crop.
4. Landowner sells the crop and takes the predetermined share. The sharecropper's portion of the crop is worth less than the amount owed to the landowner.
5. Sharecropper must promise the landowner a larger share of the next year's crop and becomes trapped in a cycle of debt.

The Ku Klux Klan Strikes Back The more progress African Americans made, the more hostile white southerners became as they tried to keep freedmen in a subservient role. During Reconstruction, dozens of loosely organized groups of white southerners emerged to terrorize African Americans. The best known of these was the **Ku Klux Klan,** formed in Tennessee in 1866. Klan members roamed the countryside, especially at night, burning homes, schools, and churches, and beating, maiming, or killing African Americans and their white allies. Dressed in white robes and hoods, mounted on horses with hooves thundering through the woods, these gangs aimed to scare freed people away from voting.

The Klan took special aim at the symbols of black freedom: African American teachers and schools, churches and ministers, politicians, and anyone—white or black—who encouraged black people to vote. Unfortunately, often their tactics succeeded. In many rural counties, African American voters were too intimidated to go out to the polls.

The Federal Government Responds Racial violence grew even more widespread, in the North as well as in the South, after the Fifteenth Amendment guaranteed all American men the right to vote. In Arkansas, Republican legislators were murdered. In New Orleans, riots broke out. One freed woman from South Carolina reported that the Klan killed her husband, a sharecropper on the land of one Mr. Jones. The widow explained that Klan members were incensed because Mr. Jones had had "poor white folks on the land, and he [evicted them], and put all these blacks on the premises."

The United States Congress took action, passing **Enforcement Acts** (also known as Ku Klux Klan Acts) in 1870 and 1871. The acts made it a federal offense to interfere with a citizen's right to vote. Congress also held hearings inviting black politicians and other observers to describe the situation in the South. George Ruby of Texas told how he had been dragged into the woods and beaten

NoteTaking

Reading Skill: Identify Cause and Effect Use a chart like the one below to summarize the causes and effects of the Enforcement Acts.

Cause		Event		Effect
•	→	• Congress passes Enforcement Acts	→	•

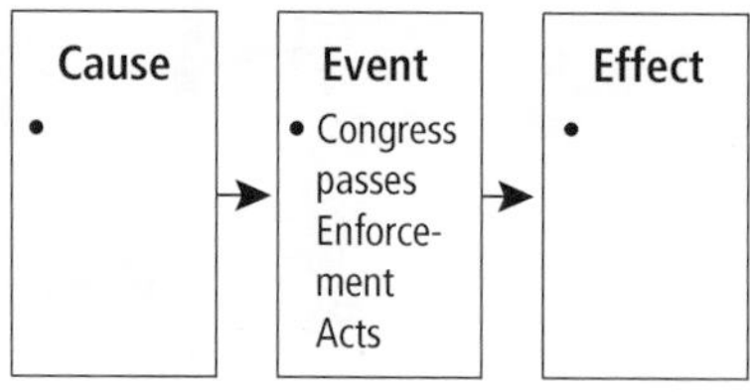

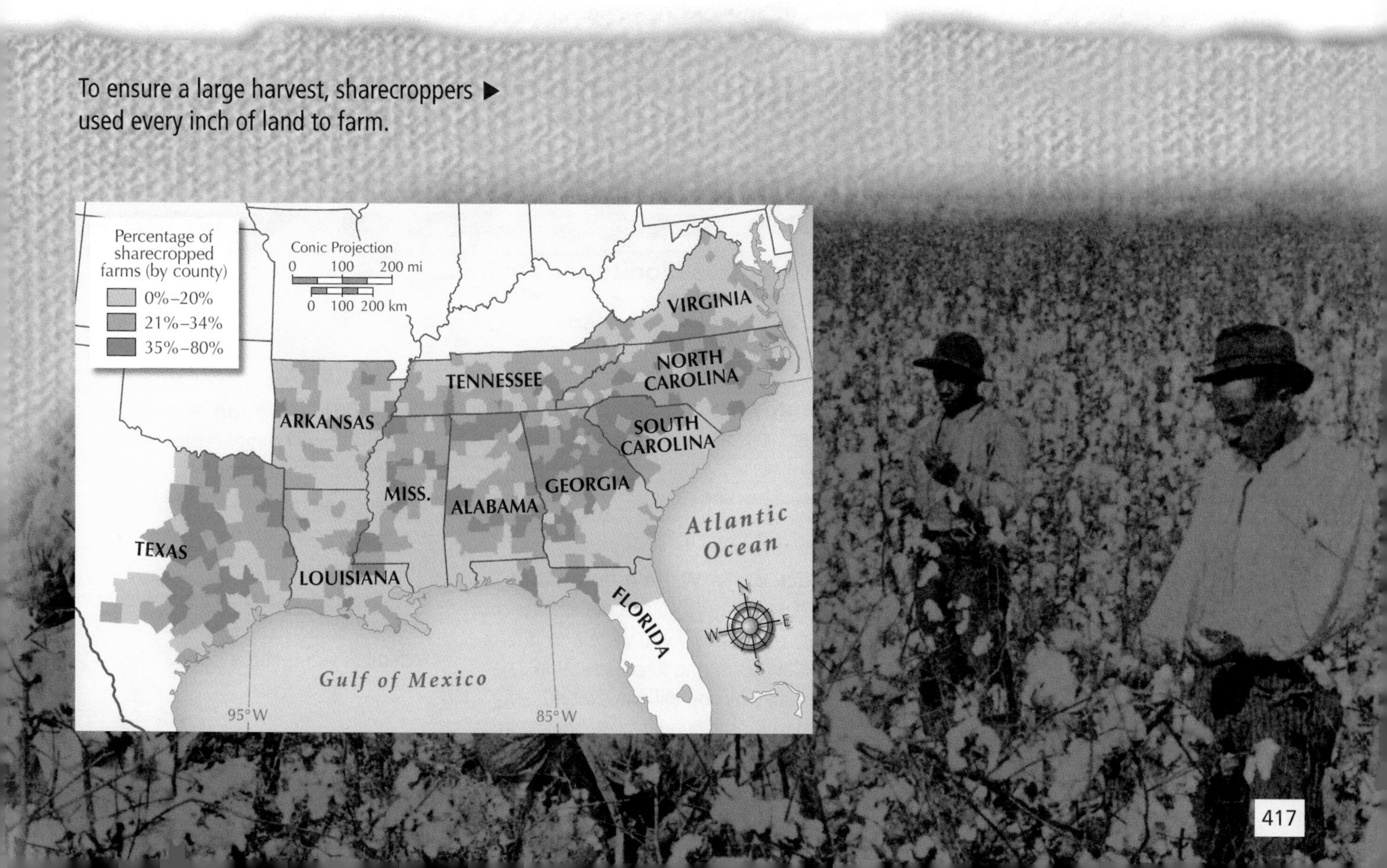

To ensure a large harvest, sharecroppers ▶ used every inch of land to farm.

because he had opened a school in Louisiana. Emanuel Fortune, one of Florida's political organizers, reported that his "life was in danger at all times" because he was "a leading man in politics."

Racial violence at the polls was not limited to the South. In the 1870 election in Philadelphia, a company of marines was sent in to protect African American voters. When no such protection was supplied for the 1871 elections, an African American teacher, Octavius Catto, was killed in antiblack political riots. At a protest meeting that followed, one African American Philadelphian spoke out:

Klan Spreads Terror

Ku Klux Klan members dressed in costumes to hide their identities. They used terror tactics to intimidate African Americans and their supporters, such as leaving miniature coffins as warnings.

Primary Source "The Ku Klux of the South are not by any means the lower classes of society. The same may be said of the Ku Klux of the North. . . . Let no man think that we ask for people's pity or commiseration. What we do ask is fairness and equal opportunities in the battle of life."

—Isaiah Wears, 1871

Congress used the Ku Klux Klan Acts to indict hundreds of Klansmen throughout the South. After 1872, on account of the federal government's readiness to use legal action, there was a decline in violence against Republicans and African Americans. The hatred may have been contained, but it was far from extinguished. Smoldering beneath the surface, it would flare up in the coming decades.

 **Checkpoint** **How did the federal government react to racial violence?**

SECTION 2 Assessment

Progress Monitoring *Online*
For: Self-test with vocabulary practice
www.pearsonschool.com/ushist

Comprehension

1. **Terms and People** For each of the following terms, write a sentence explaining its significance.
   - scalawag
   - carpetbagger
   - segregation
   - integration
   - sharecropping
   - share-tenancy
   - tenant farming
   - Ku Klux Klan
   - Enforcement Acts
2. **NoteTaking Reading Skill: Identify Main Ideas** Use your chart to answer the Section Focus Question: What were the immediate effects of Reconstruction?

Writing About History

3. **Quick Write: Write a Complaint Letter** Write to your supplier after a poor harvest as if you were a southern landowner during Reconstruction. Explain why you will have a problem paying for the supplies you bought at the beginning of the season.

Critical Thinking

4. **Analyze Information** How did Republican governments provide new opportunities in the South?
5. **Make Generalizations** How did social and economic life change for freed people?
6. **Summarize** Why did racial violence increase after 1870? How did the federal government respond?

SECTION 3

▲ Wade Hampton

WITNESS HISTORY

A Stormy Election

Wade Hampton was an old southern aristocrat from a long line of cotton planters and had been a Confederate general during the Civil War. In short, he was exactly the sort of man that Radical Republicans did not want to see in power.

In 1876, Hampton ran for governor of South Carolina. Across the state, huge crowds cheered his fiery speeches denouncing the carpetbaggers and scalawags who controlled the state government. Hampton won the election by a wide margin. But Radical Republicans charged fraud and refused to leave office. For four months, while federal troops barred Hampton from the statehouse, South Carolina had two separate governments. Not until the troops were withdrawn did Hampton take full possession of his office. The stormy election proved to be one of the last stands for Radical Republicans in the South.

The End of Reconstruction

Objectives

- Explain why Reconstruction ended.
- Evaluate the successes and failures of Reconstruction.

Terms and People

Redeemer
Rutherford B. Hayes
Compromise of 1877

NoteTaking

Reading Skill: Identify Main Ideas Use a chart like the one below to record main ideas about the factors that led to the end of Reconstruction.

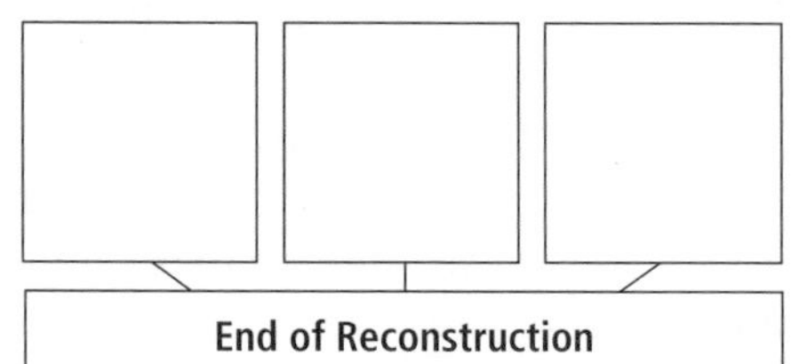

Why It Matters In the end, most northerners came to realize what southerners already knew. The rebuilding of the politics, economy, and society of the South would not be easy, nor would it happen quickly. As reformers lost their resolve, old prejudices took new shapes. It would take generations of striving before some issues were resolved. **Section Focus Question: How and why did Reconstruction end?**

The Nation Considers Other Matters

By 1872, the nation had been focusing its energies on regional strife for almost two decades. Meanwhile, other social, political, and economic issues cried out for attention. European immigration had swelled the population in the North and West. Corruption and intrigue had become part of city politics. As new technologies spurred the growth of industry and provided new opportunities for huge profits, they also provided opportunities for major corruption.

Corruption Plagues Grant's Administration Ulysses S. Grant was a popular war hero but a disappointing President. Allied with the Radical Republicans, he promised to take a strong stand against southern resistance to Reconstruction. But Grant's ability to lead was marred by scandal. He gave high-level advisory posts to untrustworthy friends and acquaintances who used their positions

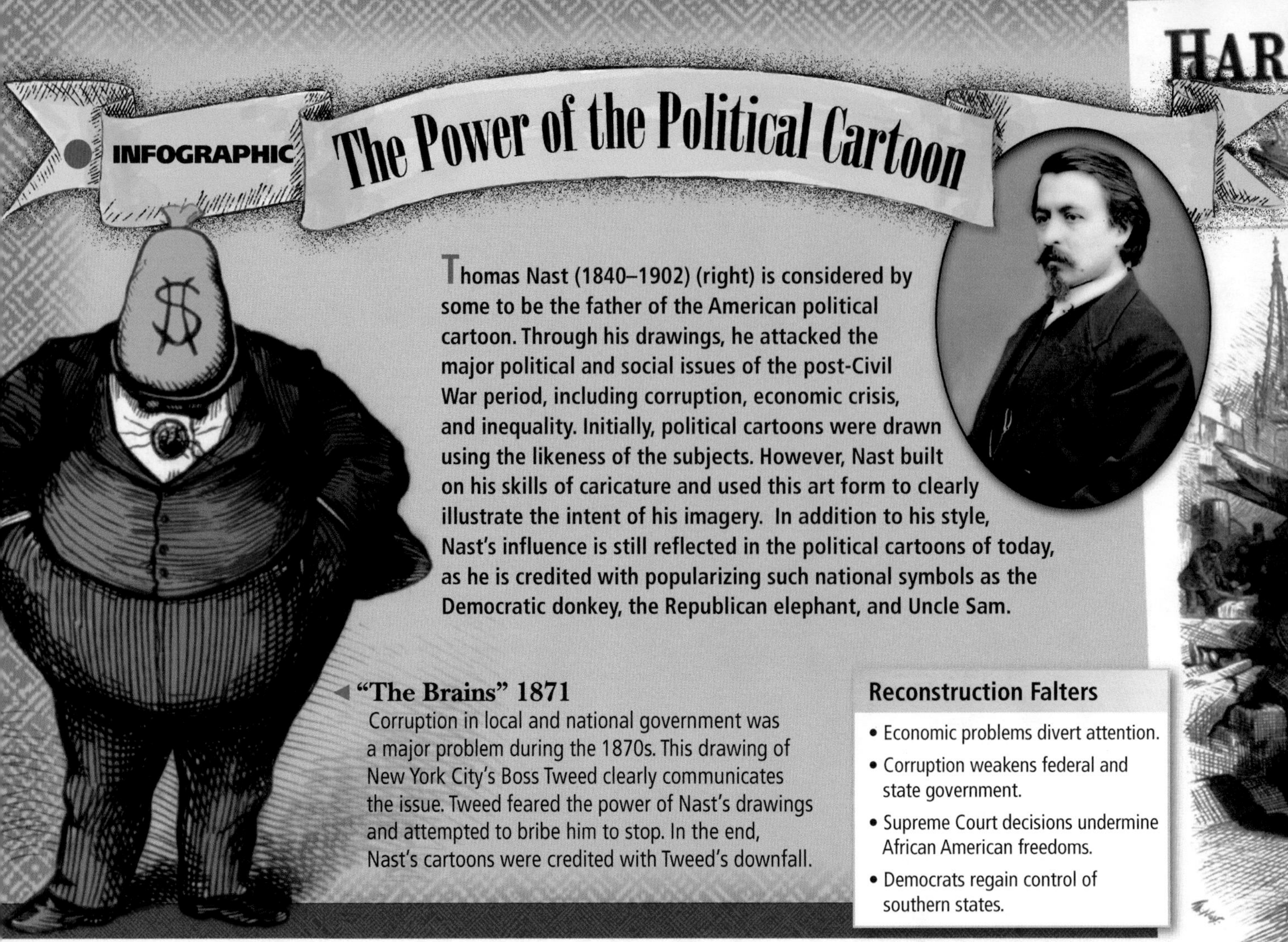

◄ **"The Brains" 1871**
Corruption in local and national government was a major problem during the 1870s. This drawing of New York City's Boss Tweed clearly communicates the issue. Tweed feared the power of Nast's drawings and attempted to bribe him to stop. In the end, Nast's cartoons were credited with Tweed's downfall.

to line their own pockets. His own Vice President, Schuyler Colfax, was investigated and implicated in a scheme to steal profits from the Union Pacific Railroad. A plan by railroad developer and financier Jay Gould to corner the gold market actually included President Grant's brother-in-law.

When Grant ran for reelection in 1872, some reform-minded Republicans withdrew their support and teamed up with some Democrats to create the Liberal Republican Party. The Liberal Republicans advocated civil service reform, removal of the army from the South, and an end to corruption in southern and national governments. Grant easily defeated their presidential candidate, the *New York Tribune* editor Horace Greeley.

Not long after the election, however, Americans sensed the aura of greed surrounding American politics. When scandal swirled around the members of his administration including his private secretary, the Secretary of War, and members of Congress, Grant seemed to look the other way. Even though he had stated, "Let no guilty man escape," he seemed to lack the will to root out this corruption. Confidence in public officials plummeted.

Across the nation, local scandals came to light. Many city officials sold lucrative public construction contracts to their friends or diverted money from city accounts. The most notorious of these scandals involved a band of New York City Democratic politicians led by state senator William "Boss" Tweed. The "Tweed Ring," as it came to be known, plundered millions of dollars from the city's treasury. By 1873, when Tweed was convicted and sentenced to prison, the public's confidence in its leaders was at a low ebb.

"Worse Than Slavery" 1874 ▶
Nast was an advocate of black civil rights and drew many cartoons addressing the issue. Here he attacks the intolerable treatment of African Americans by southern white supremacist groups.

◀ **"Out of the Ruins" 1873**
At the end of Reconstruction, the nation's economy was very unstable. Eventually, the many financial and industrial bankruptcies led to the Panic of 1873. In this cartoon, Nast illustrates the nation's financial crisis while alluding to a hopeful future.

Thinking Critically

1. **Draw Conclusions** Why do you think a cartoon such as "The Brains" would inspire fear in a political figure?
2. **Make Comparisons** How are the Nast cartoons similar to the political cartoons of today? How are they different?

History *Interactive*
For: To learn more about political cartoons
www.pearsonschool.com/ushist

Economic Panic Leads to Depression The public's discontent was worsened by economic turmoil and uncertainty. In the fall of 1873, one of the nation's most influential banks failed, apparently as a result of overextended loans to the expanding railroad industry. Suddenly, the southern economy was not the only one in trouble.

Across the nation, bank failures, job losses, and the uncertain economy added to the array of concerns that preoccupied northerners. The stamina necessary to keep pressure on the South waned.

✓ **Checkpoint** **Why did the public lose confidence in government?**

Why Did Reconstruction End?

The end of Reconstruction did not come suddenly. However, ever since the Radical Republicans failed to convict President Johnson, their power and crusading zeal had faded.

Northern Support Evaporates As the 1860s ended, voters and politicians outside the South increasingly turned their attention to other pressing issues—reforming politics and the economy, among other things. Also, the continued cost of military operations in the South worried many. Gradually and quietly, beginning in 1871, troops were withdrawn from the South. In 1872, the Freedmen's Bureau was dissolved.

Vocabulary Builder
transition–(tran ZIHSH uhn) *n.* process of moving from one stage to another

The death of Radical Republican leader Charles Sumner in 1874 also symbolized an important transition. A generation of white reformers, forged by abolitionist fervor and anxious to carry that passion into the national politics of Reconstruction, had passed away. Without such leaders to temper it, northern racial prejudice reemerged.

Supreme Court Decisions Impede Equality The Thirteenth, Fourteenth, and Fifteenth amendments guaranteed African Americans' rights. Yet it was left to the courts to interpret how these new amendments would be applied.

Vocabulary Builder
scope–(skohp) *n.* range covered by a subject

In a series of landmark cases, the Supreme Court chipped away at African American freedoms in the 1870s. In what became known as the *Slaughterhouse Cases* (1873), the Court restricted the scope of the Fourteenth Amendment. It concluded that though a citizen had certain national rights, the federal government would have no control over how a state chose to define rights for the citizens who resided there. Two years later, the Supreme Court heard the case of *United States* v. *Cruikshank*. This case involved a white mob in Louisiana who had killed a large group of African Americans at a political rally. The Court ruled that the due process and equal protection clauses of the Fourteenth Amendment protected citizens only from the action of the state and not from the action of other citizens.

Southern Whites Gain Power While the Klan intimidated with violence and the courts with legal interpretation, some southern Democrats devised a more subtle strategy for suppressing black rights. They put together a coalition to return the South to the rule of white men. To appeal to small farmers, they emphasized how Republican programs like schools and road-building resulted in higher taxes. They compromised with local Republicans by agreeing to African American suffrage. In return, southern Republicans joined their Democratic neighbors in ostracizing white southerners who supported the Radical Republicans. Playing on the national sensitivity to corruption, the new coalition seized every opportunity to discredit black politicians as being both self-serving and incompetent. These Democrats and Republicans agreed that racial segregation should be the rule of the new South.

The main focus of their strategy was compromise: finding common issues that would unite white southerners around the goal of regaining power in Congress. These compromisers have become known as **Redeemers,** politicians who aimed to repair or "redeem" the South in the eyes of Congress. Sometimes their strategy is described as being designed to "redeem" or reclaim the South from northern domination. In either case, their plan brought some success. By 1870, Virginia, North Carolina, and Tennessee had reinstated wealthy white southern men as governors and had sent Confederate leaders back to the United States Congress. Other Confederate states soon followed their lead. In the congressional elections of 1874, the Republicans lost their control over the House of Representatives.

African Americans in Congress

The montage below shows the Mississippi delegates to the 44th U.S. Congress. Blanche K. Bruce (second row, right) was the first African American to serve a full term as a U.S. senator. After Bruce, no African American was elected to the U.S. Senate until the 90th Congress almost 100 years later.

Can the Federal Government Enforce Protection of Rights?

After the Civil War, the Fourteenth Amendment declared that African Americans were citizens of the United States. Both the Fourteenth and Fifteenth amendments protected them from discrimination. But how were those rights to be enforced? Did they apply only to the federal government or also to the states?

United States v. *Cruikshank* (1876)

The Facts	The Issue	The Decision
• William J. Cruikshank belonged to a group that wanted to reestablish white government in Louisiana. • In Colfax, Louisiana, a clash between this group and some African Americans resulted in the deaths of 100 blacks. • Cruikshank was convicted of trying to take away the civil rights of African Americans.	Cruikshank claimed that his conviction was unconstitutional because his actions did not come under the authority of federal law.	The Court overturned Cruikshank's conviction saying that the Fourteenth Amendment did not apply to individuals but only to the actions of states, and that the charges did not specify that he intended to deprive African Americans of their rights.

Why It Matters

Cruikshank, along with several other Supreme Court rulings in the 1870s, severely limited the impact of the Fourteenth and Fifteenth amendments. Although Congress passed several civil rights laws giving the federal government the power to enforce the protections of these amendments, the Court stripped away the authority of those laws.

Not long after *Cruikshank,* army troops were withdrawn from the South, and the federal government abandoned its efforts to protect African Americans. In the aftermath, white southerners used unfair laws and violence to limit African Americans' right to vote and to take away other rights as well. Not until the middle of the twentieth century did federal courts begin to strike down these laws as unconstitutional.

▼ Gathering the wounded following the Colfax massacre.

Connect to Your World

Later Court decisions upheld the federal government's authority on the civil rights protections provided by the Fourteenth and Fifteenth amendments. For that reason, employers cannot turn down job seekers, schools cannot deny admissions, and restaurants cannot refuse to serve people because of their race or religion. Write an essay explaining how significant the Fourteenth Amendment is to American society today.

For: Supreme Court cases
www.pearsonschool.com/ushist

◄ **Protection of Rights**
Today, through the Fourteenth Amendment, the federal government ensures equal protection of all citizens, which includes equal access to education.

Presidential Election of 1876

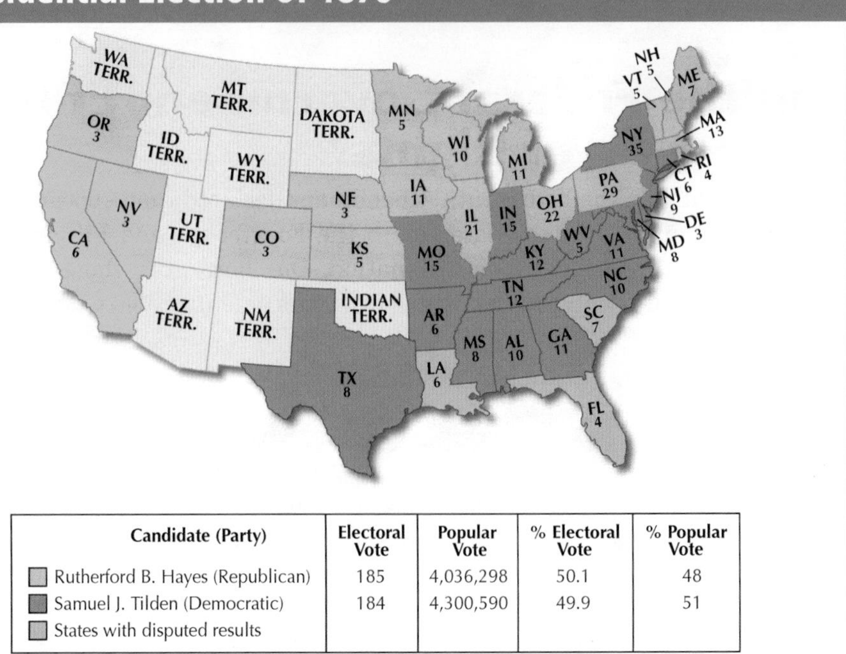

Candidate (Party)	Electoral Vote	Popular Vote	% Electoral Vote	% Popular Vote
Rutherford B. Hayes (Republican)	185	4,036,298	50.1	48
Samuel J. Tilden (Democratic)	184	4,300,590	49.9	51
States with disputed results				

Map Skills Samuel Tilden won the popular vote in the 1876 election, but there were disputes about the electoral votes.

1. **Location:** In which southern states were election results disputed?
2. **Draw Inferences** Based on the map, do you think the Civil War brought an end to sectionalism?

Geography *Interactive*
For: Interactive map
www.pearsonschool.com/ushist

Reconstruction Officially Ends With the Radical Republicans' loss of power, the stage was set to end northern domination of the South. The 1876 election pitted Ohio Republican **Rutherford B. Hayes** against New York Democrat Samuel Tilden. Hayes, a respected Union general, had served in the House of Representatives in 1866. He had resigned to become governor of Ohio, where he developed a reputation for honesty and reform-mindedness. Tilden had been active in fighting corruption in New York City. Both candidates, then, held appeal for voters who were tired of corrupt leadership.

Tilden received 51 percent of the popular vote and carried all of the southern states. However, Republicans claimed that the votes had been miscounted in three southern states, which happened to be states where Republicans controlled the reporting of ballots. Not surprisingly, in the recount, the Republicans found enough mistakes to swing the election to Hayes by one electoral vote.

When southern Democrats protested the results of this vote, Congress was charged with mediating the crisis. It created a commission of five senators (chosen by the Republican-dominated Senate), five representatives (chosen by the Democratic House of Representatives), and five Supreme Court Justices.

In what became known as the **Compromise of 1877,** Hayes was elected President. In return, the remaining federal troops were withdrawn from the South, a southerner was appointed to a powerful cabinet position, and southern states were guaranteed federal subsidies to build railroads and improve their ports.

Federal Reconstruction was over. The South and the millions of recently freed African Americans were left to negotiate their own fate.

✓ Checkpoint How did southern Redeemers gain power?

NoteTaking

Reading Skill: Identify Main Ideas Create a chart with information about the effects of Reconstruction.

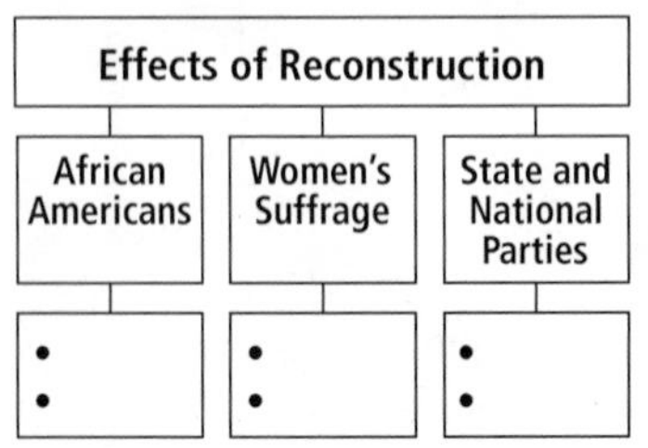

Evaluating Reconstruction's Effects

Was Reconstruction a "success" or a "failure"? There have been many different answers from southerners and northerners, black and white, then and now. All agree, however, that some things were forever changed when the victorious North tried to remake the vanquished South.

Among the enduring changes to the South were the introduction of a tax-supported school system and an infusion of federal money to modernize railroads and ports. In addition, the economy expanded from one crop—cotton—to a range of agricultural and industrial products. There was a gradual transition to a wage economy from a barter-and-credit system. But some historians say that these changes might have happened anyway, since southern planters were concerned about their debt-ridden society even before the war.

Reconstruction failed to heal the bitterness between North and South or to provide lasting protection for freed people. However, it did raise African Americans' expectations of their right to citizenship, and it placed before Americans the meaning and value of the right to vote.

Effects on African Americans Before the Civil War, no African American in the South, and only a small number in the North, had the right to vote. Few black southerners owned land. Most worked others' land, without pay, and without hope of improving their lot.

Reconstruction changed these things. By 1877, a few southern black Americans owned their own farms. That number would grow slowly through the next decades. Before the Civil War, most southern African Americans worked—involuntarily—in agriculture. Reconstruction began to give them choices. Perhaps most importantly, the Freedmen's Bureau helped reunite freed slaves with their families and promoted literacy within African American communities.

Though it fell short of its ambitious goals, Reconstruction opened new vistas for black Americans, North and South. The Thirteenth, Fourteenth, and Fifteenth amendments provided hope for full inclusion in American society, though it would take later generations to use them to gain racial equality.

Effects on Women's Suffrage Movement One of the ironies of Reconstruction is that it gave the vote to black American men, while fragmenting the women's movement that had often been supportive of black freedom. In the debate over the Fifteenth Amendment, there was disagreement about whether it should also include a clause giving women the right to vote. Some felt the Fifteenth Amendment could not get ratified if it included women's suffrage. Those who agreed with this position formed the American Woman Suffrage Association (AWSA) in 1869.

HISTORY MAKERS

Robert Smalls (1839–1915)

Born into slavery, Robert Smalls lived in Charleston, South Carolina, before the Civil War. During the war, he stole a Confederate boat full of military supplies and steamed it to a Union ship anchored in the harbor. The navy hired him as a pilot. After distinguished service in a battle, he became the first African American to command a navy ship. After the war, Smalls entered South Carolina's new state government and then was elected five times to the U.S. House of Representatives, a major post-Reconstruction achievement (see graph below). In the 1890s, he fought, unsuccessfully, against the movement in South Carolina to take away African Americans' civil rights.

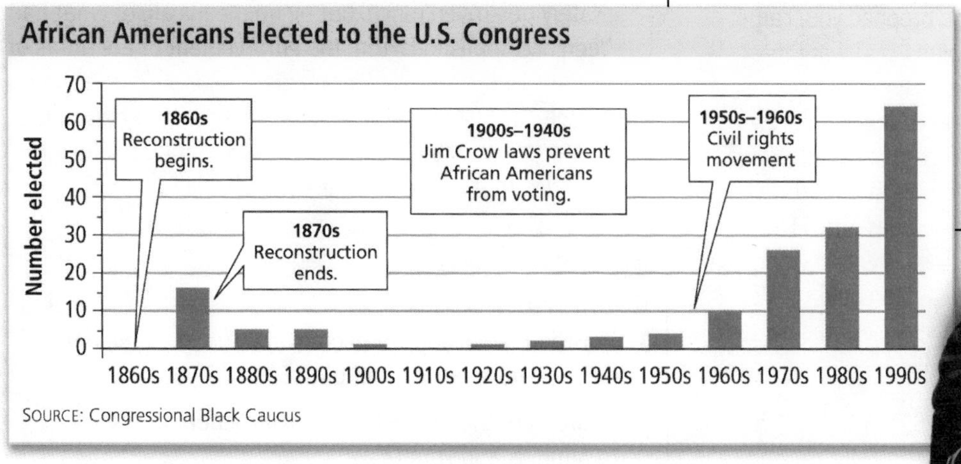

SOURCE: Congressional Black Caucus

Comparing Viewpoints

Was Reconstruction "Radical"?

After the Civil War, Congress passed a series of increasingly radical measures designed to rebuild the South. The effectiveness of these measures was hotly debated at the time, and the debate has continued into the present day. How radical was Reconstruction?

Northern Newspaper, 1865

Radical Republicans advocated harsh treatment for the South.

Primary Source

"There is one, and only one, sure and safe policy for the immediate future: namely: the North must remain the absolute Dictator of the Republic until the spirit of the North shall become the spirit of the whole country. . . . The South is still unpurged of her treason. Prostrate in the dust she is no less a traitor at this hour than when her head was erect. . . . They cannot be trusted with authority over their former slaves. . . . The only hope for the South is to give the ballot to the Negro and in denying it to the rebels."

—*The Independent,* May 5, 1865

Historian Francis Simkins

Reconstruction neglected the economic needs of the former slaves.

Secondary Source

"A truly radical program would have called for the confiscation of land for the freedmen. Land was the principal form of Southern wealth, the only effective weapon with which the ex-slaves could have battled for economic competence and social equality. . . . The dominant Radicalism of the day naively assumed that a people's salvation could be obtained through the ballot and the spelling book. . . ."

—Francis Simkins, 1939

THE "WEAK" GOVERNMENT 1877–1881.

Historian Eric Foner

Reconstruction set into motion the ongoing effort to address inequality.

Secondary Source

"Over a century ago . . . Americans made their first attempt to live up to the noble professions of their political creed. . . . The effort produced a sweeping redefinition of the nation's public life and a violent reaction that ultimately destroyed much, but by no means all, of what had been accomplished. From the enforcement of the rights of citizens to the stubborn problem of economic and racial justice, the issues central to Reconstruction are as old as the American republic, and as contemporary as the inequalities that still afflict our society today."

—Eric Foner, 2002

South Carolina Senator Benjamin Tillman

White southerners opposed northern domination and their ideas of equality.

Primary Source

"You had set us an impossible task. You had handcuffed us and thrown away the key, and you propped your carpetbag negro government with bayonets. . . . I want the country to get the full view of the Southern side of this question and the justification for anything we did. We were sorry we had the necessity forced upon us, but we could not help it, and as white men we are not sorry for it. . . . We did not disfranchise the negroes until 1895. . . . [W]e had a constitutional convention . . . with the purpose of disfranchising as many of them as we could. . . . We of the South have never recognized the right of the negro to govern white men, and we never will."

—Senator Benjamin Tillman, 1900

Compare

1. How do the opinions of Tillman and *The Independent* differ on northern control of the South?
2. What were the failures of Reconstruction according to Simkins and Foner?

Others, like Elizabeth Cady Stanton, believed that women and African Americans should get the vote immediately. They formed the National Woman Suffrage Association (NWSA). This group scored its first victory in 1869, when the Wyoming Territory became the first political unit to extend the vote to women. Both the NWSA and the AWSA included some black women. However, a further division occurred when a group of black women split off to form the Colored Women's Progressive Franchise association in 1880.

Effects of Reconstruction — Quick Study

- Union is restored.
- African Americans gain citizenship and voting rights.
- South's economy and infrastructure are improved.
- Southern states establish public school system.
- Ku Klux Klan and other groups terrorize African Americans.
- Sharecropping system takes hold in the South.

The Effects on State and National Politics American politics were irrevocably shaped by the Civil War and Reconstruction. The Republican Party, born out of the controversy over slavery, continued to be seen by many as "the party of Lincoln, that freed the slaves." White southerners therefore shunned it, while African Americans—in both the North and South—embraced it. Consequently, the Democratic Party came to dominate the white South.

Following Reconstruction, the national Republicans became the party of big business—a reputation that continues to the present. The national Democratic Party, which identified with industrial laborers, differed from the southern Democrats and had to maintain a delicate balance with the southern faction on this issue as well as on the question of race.

The Effects on State and Federal Power What political unit has more power—the federal government or the individual states? In cases of disputes of public policy, which branch of the federal government has the last word? These questions have perplexed American lawmakers since the Constitution's creation. During Reconstruction, they acquired deeper meaning as the federal government asserted its authority not only over southern states but over state laws in other regions as well.

In the end, American voters and their representatives in government opted for a balance of power, at the expense of protecting freed people in the South. With the demise of the Radical Republicans, most congressmen concluded that it was better to let the South attend to its own affairs than to leave a whole region under the control of federal military power and federal political control. That choice would have far-reaching social, political, and economic implications.

✓ **Checkpoint** **What were the positive effects of Reconstruction?**

SECTION 3 Assessment

Progress Monitoring *Online*
For: Self-test with vocabulary practice
www.pearsonschool.com/ushist

Comprehension

1. **Terms and People** For each item below, write a sentence explaining its role in bringing Reconstruction to an end.
   - Redeemer
   - Rutherford B. Hayes
   - Compromise of 1877
2. **NoteTaking Reading Skill: Identify Main Ideas** Use your chart to answer the Section Focus Question: How and why did Reconstruction end?

Writing About History

3. **Quick Write: Write an E-mail** Historians who specialize in Reconstruction disagree about the main reason that Reconstruction ended. Write an e-mail as if you were a historian expressing your point of view to a colleague. Identify the subject line you would use, and summarize the main point you would make. Use complete sentences and remember to follow proper e-mail etiquette.

Critical Thinking

4. **Identify Central Issues** What factors contributed to the refocusing of the nation away from the problems of the South?
5. **Recognize Cause and Effect** Why did the goals of the Republican Party change during the 1870s?
6. **Identify Point of View** From the perspective of an African American in the South, how was Reconstruction a success and how was it a failure?

CHAPTER 12

Quick Study Guide

Progress Monitoring *Online*
For: Self-test with vocabulary practice
www.pearsonschool.com/ushist

Congressional Reconstruction

Cause and Effect

Causes
- Southern governments pass black codes.
- Violence against African Americans in the South increases.
- Southerners disregard spirit of Reconstruction.
- Johnson defies Congress and vetoes key bills.

↓

Congressional Reconstruction

↓

Effects
- Congress overrides president's veto.
- South is put under military rule.
- Congress passes 15th Amendment.
- House impeaches Johnson.
- Republicans control southern state governments.

Democrats Regain Control

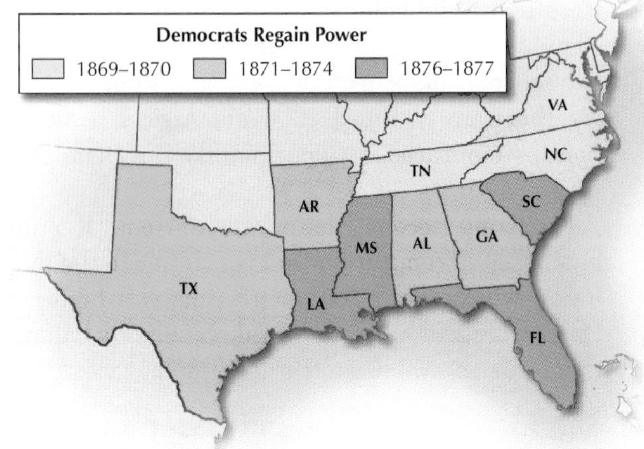

Successes and Failures of Reconstruction

Successes	Failures
• The Union is restored. • Southern economic rebuilding begins. • African Americans are granted citizenship and voting rights. • Freedmen's Bureau helps African Americans get education, housing, and jobs. • Public school system develops in the South.	• Distribution of wealth and power in the South remains unchanged. • Many southerners are caught in a cycle of poverty. • Southern governments limit African American voting. • Racism continues in the North and South. • Many southerners remain bitter toward the federal government and Republican Party.

Quick Study Timeline

In America

1863 Lincoln issues Proclamation of Amnesty and Reconstruction

1865 Freedmen's Bureau created

1866 Ku Klux Klan forms in Tennessee

1867 South placed under military rule

Presidential Terms: Abraham Lincoln 1861–1865 | Andrew Johnson 1865–1869

1862 — 1865 — 1868

Around the World

1864 Taiping Rebellion ends

1867 Russia sells Alaska to the United States

1868 Japan's Meiji Restoration

American Issues Connector

By connecting prior knowledge with what you have learned in this chapter, you can gradually build your understanding of enduring questions that still affect America today. Answer the questions below. Then, use your American Issues Connector study guide (or go online: www.pearsonschool.com/ushist).

Issues You Learned About

● **Checks and Balances** The Constitution gives each of the three branches of government the ability to check the powers of the other branches.

1. Think about the political clashes and events that surrounded Congressional Reconstruction. Then, write a paragraph that describes how the system of checks and balances worked to shape the Reconstruction era. Consider:
   - the Fourteenth Amendment
   - presidential vetoes
   - the Tenure of Office Act
   - President Johnson's impeachment trial

● **Expanding and Protecting Civil Rights** During Reconstruction, new legislation guaranteed African American civil rights.

2. Prior to the Civil War, how were the rights of free African Americans in the South restricted?
3. After the Thirteenth Amendment abolished slavery, southern states responded by passing "black codes." How did these codes affect African Americans' experience of freedom?
4. Why did Republicans in Congress believe that the Civil Rights Act of 1866 was an insufficient response to the "black codes" and work for passage of the Fourteenth Amendment?

● **Federal Power and States' Rights** In some cases, the federal government passes laws that are contrary to the laws a state would make.

5. What is the meaning of the term ***states' rights***? Why was this an important issue prior to the Civil War? How was this an important issue during Reconstruction?
6. In the 1870s, the Supreme Court issued several rulings that allowed states the opportunity to undermine federal laws. What were these cases, and how did they limit federal power?

Connect to Your World | **Activity**

Voting Rights African Americans today enjoy equal voting rights, but do they have equal political representation? What proportion of elected federal, state, and local officials are African American today? Conduct research online or go to the local library to investigate this question. Consider the percentage of African Americans in the population as it compares to the percentage of African American elected officials. Also consider the types of elected roles that African Americans hold. To conclude, write a paragraph analyzing the political power of African Americans and include your thoughts on what the future may hold.

History *Interactive*
For: Interactive timeline
www.pearsonschool.com/ushist

1870 Fifteenth Amendment gives African Americans the right to vote

1876 Supreme Court rules in *Cruikshank* case

1877 Reconstruction ends

Ulysses S. Grant 1869–1877

Rutherford B. Hayes 1877–1881

1871 | 1874 | 1877

1869 Suez Canal opens

1871 Germany is unified

1873 Slave markets abolished in Zanzibar

1876 Diaz gains power in Mexico

Chapter Assessment

Terms and People

1. Who were the **Radical Republicans**? Identify two specific policies that they supported.
2. What was the **Wade-Davis Bill**? How did it differ from Lincoln's plan for Reconstruction?
3. Define **scalawag.** Which groups of people in the South welcomed scalawags, and which groups disliked them?
4. Define **segregation** and **integration.** Which policy was generally supported in the post–Civil War South?
5. Who were the **Redeemers**? What strategy did they follow, and how successful were they?

Focus Questions

The focus question for this chapter is **What lasting consequences arose from the struggles over Reconstruction?** Build an answer to this big question by answering the focus questions for Sections 1 through 3 and the Critical Thinking questions that follow.

Section 1

6. How did the Radical Republicans' plans for Reconstruction differ from Lincoln's and Johnson's?

Section 2

7. What were the immediate effects of Reconstruction?

Section 3

8. How and why did Reconstruction end?

Critical Thinking

9. **Recognize Bias** Think about the different policies that Johnson supported for Reconstruction. Which of his policies represent the beliefs of a typical white southerner? How did these beliefs shape his policies?
10. **Draw Conclusions** Why did most African American voters support the Republican Party? What is a likely explanation for the fact that southern African Americans were elected to Congress during Reconstruction but no northern African Americans were elected to Congress until 1928?
11. **Distinguish False From Accurate Images** Study the drawing of a carpetbagger at right. Does this drawing present a faithful representation? Which elements seem accurate and which seem biased?

12. **Determine Relevance** Analyze the role that the Freedmen's Bureau played in the lives of newly freed African Americans.
13. **Make Comparisons** Explain the differences between the three farming arrangements in the South after the Civil War. Which system was best for the farmer?
14. **Make Generalizations** How did many white southerners react to the new status of African Americans in society?
15. **Predict Consequences** How do you think passage of the Fifteenth Amendment would affect the future women's suffrage movement?
16. **Analyze Information** Historians disagree about whether Reconstruction was a success or a failure. Explain what you think were Reconstruction's greatest success and greatest failure using examples and details from the text.

Writing About History

Writing a Letter Reconstruction was a period of enormous change in the South. It was an era of physical rebuilding, of great economic changes, and of adjusting social relationships. Choose one aspect of Reconstruction in the South, and, as if you have been commissioned by Congress to visit the region and investigate, write a letter reporting your observations.

Prewriting

- Choose an aspect of Reconstruction that interests you, and gather information from the text and other sources about it.
- Consider your audience and what they will be interested in reading.
- Gather additional information that you might have observed had you actually traveled to the South during Reconstruction.

Drafting

- Members of Congress are very busy, so plan to include a summary of your observations in the first paragraph or two of your letter.
- Make an outline to organize your ideas.
- Write the introductory summary and then write the rest of the letter including more details.
- Use the structure of a formal letter.

Revising

- Use the guidelines on page SH11 of the Writing Handbook to revise your letter.

Document-Based Assessment

The Freedmen's Bureau

Congress created the Freedmen's Bureau to help freed slaves in the South. What impact did the Bureau have on education? How did white southerners react to the work of the Freedmen's Bureau? Use your knowledge of the Freedmen's Bureau and Documents A, B, C, and D to answer questions 1 through 4.

Document A

"I am just returned from a tour through my district, and in reply to your note . . . have to say that at this place there are 366 colored children under 14 of which perhaps 200 might be gathered into a school. . . . The colored people here are anxious that a school may be established, and I heartily second their desire. Winchester also presents a favorable field for efforts in their behalf. There are 372 under 14, and a colored church that will accommodate about half of the pupils. . . . At Harpers Ferry I found a school of 40 pupils established by Miss Mann . . . and taught by her for four months under every discouragement illustrating heroic charity. She is about to accept a situation elsewhere, and was exceedingly anxious that the school should be continued. . . . I promised that the school should continue."

—*W. Storer How, August 31, 1865*

Document B

Freedmen's Bureau school of Edisto Island, South Carolina

Document C

Cartoon depicting President Johnson's veto of the Freedmen's Bureau bill.

Document D

"We have pronounced ourselves distinctly in favor of the education of the Freedmen. . . . It is the interest of the whites and blacks alike that education should be generally diffused, and it will prepare both classes for the better performance of their duties. Therefore, let the people of the South, even the true, and, in fact, we think, only real friends of the negro move in the matter wisely and upon system. If the negro is to possess civil rights, and those are already accorded him, a certain amount of education will be indispensable. . . . The following . . . remarks show very clearly what difficulties are in the way of the system which has been established by those who are ignorant of the nature and character of the blacks. The Southern people must take the matter in their own hands."

—*J.D.B. DeBrow, Debow's Review, July 1866*

---

1. Which documents present a constructive view of the Freedmen's Bureau's efforts?
A Documents B and C
B Documents A and D
C Documents A and B
D Documents C and D

2. In Document D, what is the author's view of educating freed slaves?
A The job should be given to the Freedmen's Bureau.
B Northern teachers should be trained for the job.
C The job should be given to educated blacks.
D Southerners who understand freed slaves should educate them.

3. Which document presents the conflict between President Johnson and Congress over the Freedmen's Bureau?
A Document A
B Document B
C Document C
D Document D

4. **Writing Task** How did the Freedmen's Bureau provide education for African Americans after the Civil War? Did everyone support its efforts to help freed slaves? Use your knowledge of the chapter content and specific evidence from the primary sources above to support your opinion.

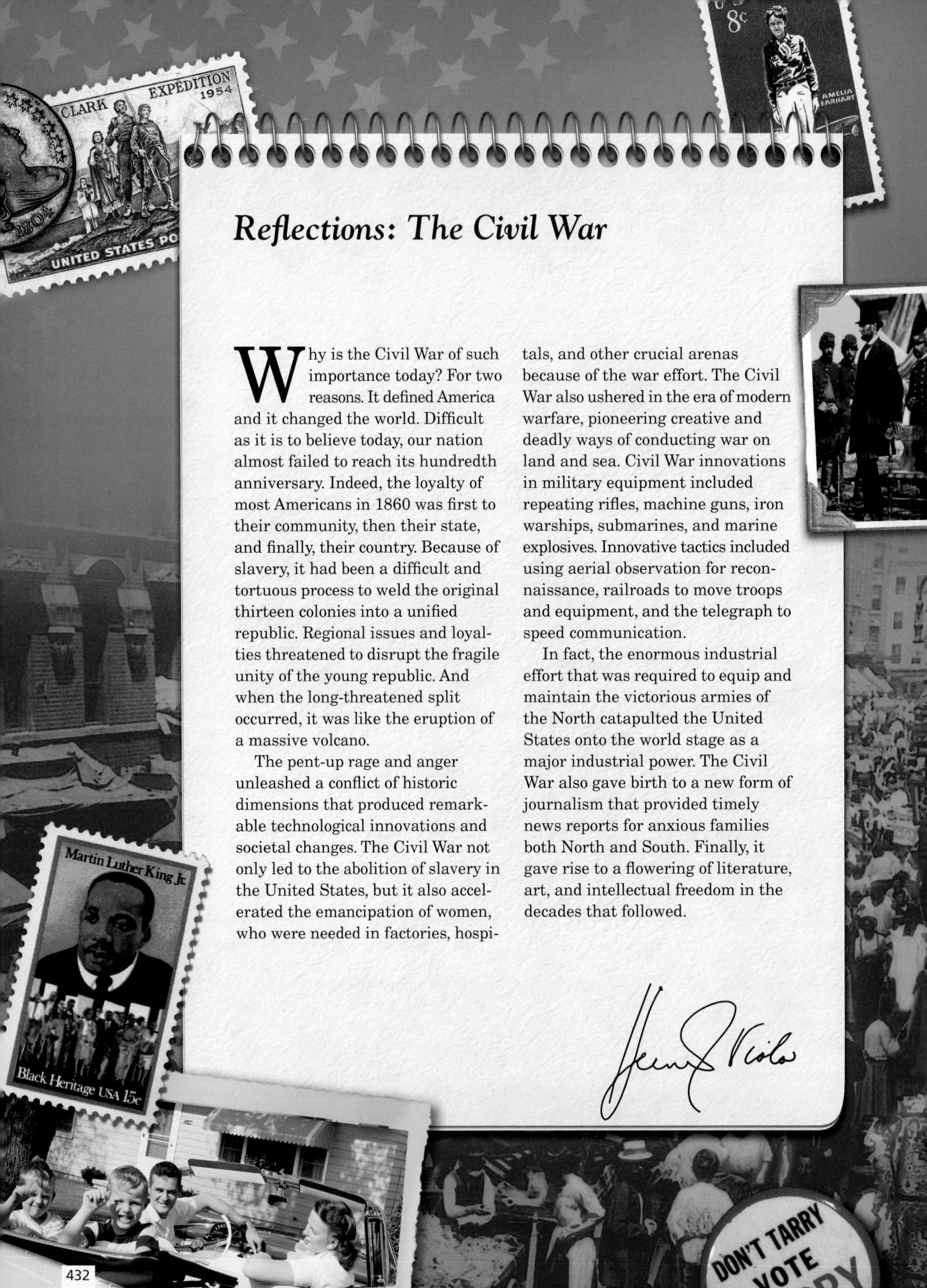

Reflections: The Civil War

Why is the Civil War of such importance today? For two reasons. It defined America and it changed the world. Difficult as it is to believe today, our nation almost failed to reach its hundredth anniversary. Indeed, the loyalty of most Americans in 1860 was first to their community, then their state, and finally, their country. Because of slavery, it had been a difficult and tortuous process to weld the original thirteen colonies into a unified republic. Regional issues and loyalties threatened to disrupt the fragile unity of the young republic. And when the long-threatened split occurred, it was like the eruption of a massive volcano.

The pent-up rage and anger unleashed a conflict of historic dimensions that produced remarkable technological innovations and societal changes. The Civil War not only led to the abolition of slavery in the United States, but it also accelerated the emancipation of women, who were needed in factories, hospitals, and other crucial arenas because of the war effort. The Civil War also ushered in the era of modern warfare, pioneering creative and deadly ways of conducting war on land and sea. Civil War innovations in military equipment included repeating rifles, machine guns, iron warships, submarines, and marine explosives. Innovative tactics included using aerial observation for reconnaissance, railroads to move troops and equipment, and the telegraph to speed communication.

In fact, the enormous industrial effort that was required to equip and maintain the victorious armies of the North catapulted the United States onto the world stage as a major industrial power. The Civil War also gave birth to a new form of journalism that provided timely news reports for anxious families both North and South. Finally, it gave rise to a flowering of literature, art, and intellectual freedom in the decades that followed.

INDUSTRIALIZATION OF THE UNITED STATES

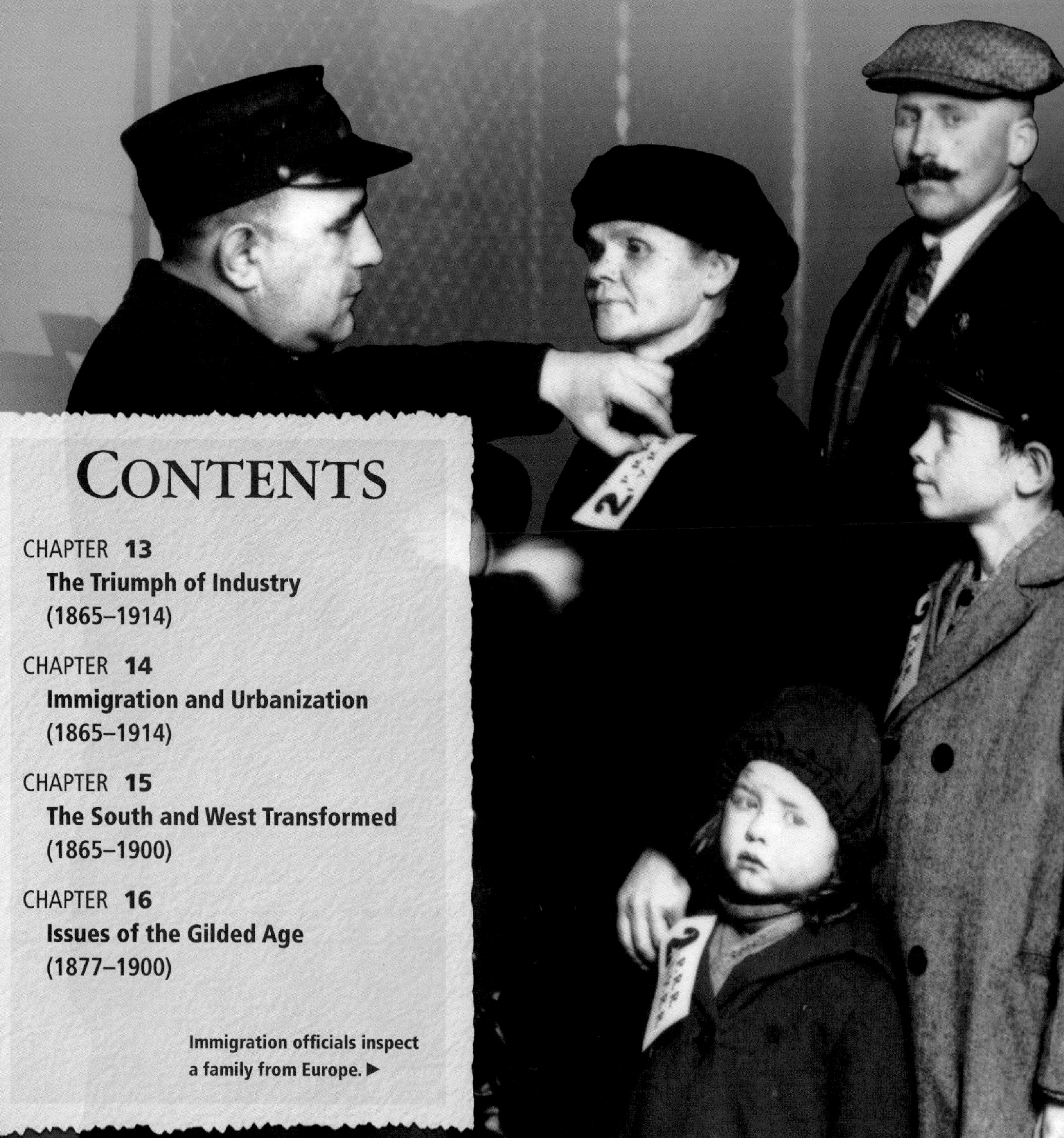

CONTENTS

Immigration officials inspect a family from Europe. ▶

CHAPTER

13 The Triumph of Industry

1865–1914

WITNESS HISTORY

The March of American Progress

On May 24, 1883, the front page of the *Brooklyn Eagle* heralded the opening of the Brooklyn Bridge:

> “Proudly uprearing its mighty towers, secure in the integrity of its massive cables, spanning the graceful arch of its splendid superstructure the perilous rush of the swiftly flowing river, the great bridge . . . stands today a completed monument to human ingenuity, mechanical genius and engineering skill. . . . With its completing are realized the hopes of millions of people, the fruition of fourteen years of faithful and persistent toil. . . . Its opening to public use marks an enormous stride in the march of American progress . . .”

◄ People take a tour on a high catwalk while work on the Brooklyn Bridge is in progress.

Early labor union ribbon

Thomas Edison's light bulb

Chapter Preview

Chapter Focus Question: How did the industrial growth of the late 1800s shape American society and the economy?

Section 1
Technology and Industrial Growth

Section 2
The Rise of Big Business

Section 3
The Organized Labor Movement

Fireworks over the new Brooklyn Bridge

Use the ☑ Quick Study Timeline at the end of this chapter to preview chapter events.

Note Taking Study Guide *Online*
For: Note Taking and American Issues Connector
www.pearsonschool.com/ushist

Section 1

Alexander Graham Bell's telephone ►

◄ President Grant and foreign visitors look in amazement at the Corliss steam engine, shown for the first time at the Centennial.

WITNESS HISTORY

Celebrating the Nation's Centennial

On May 10, 1876, the United States celebrated its 100th anniversary by opening the Centennial Exhibition in Philadelphia. At a time when the total population of the country was only 46 million people, the exhibition drew nearly 9 million visitors. The event stunned Americans and foreign visitors alike with its demonstration of new technology, including an icemaker and a telephone. It also introduced the United States to the world as a new industrial and innovative powerhouse.

Technology and Industrial Growth

Objectives

- Analyze the factors that led to the industrialization of the United States in the late 1800s.
- Explain how new inventions and innovations changed Americans' lives.
- Describe the impact of industrialization in the late 1800s.

Terms and People

entrepreneur
protective tariff
laissez faire
patent
Thomas Edison
Bessemer process
suspension bridge
time zone
mass production

NoteTaking

Reading Skill: Identify Causes and Effects
As you read, record the causes and effects of industrialization in a chart like the one below.

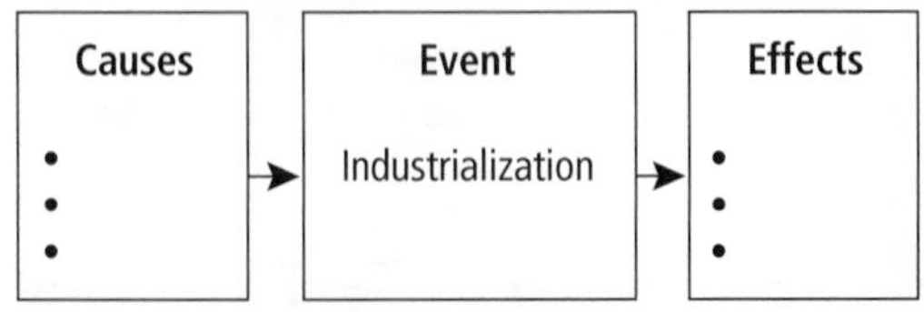

Why It Matters The Industrial Revolution began in the British textile industry in the 1700s. It soon spread to America. The first Industrial Revolution was marked by the introduction of steam power and the factory system. Coal and iron became key resources. Around the 1850s, the Industrial Revolution entered a new phase, dominated by steel, oil, and a major new power source—electricity. This second Industrial Revolution had a distinctly American character. American inventors and business leaders helped turn the United States into an industrial powerhouse. **Section Focus Question: How did industrialization and new technology affect the economy and society?**

Encouraging Industrial Growth

The Civil War challenged industries to make goods more quickly and efficiently. Using new tools and methods, factories stepped up production of guns, ammunition, medical supplies, and uniforms. The food industry developed ways to process foods so they could be shipped long distances. Railroads expanded and more efficient methods of creating power were developed. Meanwhile, the government encouraged immigration to meet the increasing demand for labor in the nation's factories.

Natural Resources Fuel Growth The country's growth was fueled, in part, by its vast supply of natural resources. Numerous coal mines along the eastern seaboard provided fuel to power steam locomotives and factories. Thick forests across the country were cut into lumber for construction. The nation's many navigable riverways transported these and other resources to cities and factories. Then, in 1859, Edwin Drake drilled what became the world's first oil well in Titusville, Pennsylvania. Before Drake's invention, oil, which was used for light and fuel, was mainly obtained from boiling down whale blubber. But whale hunting was time-consuming, and whales were becoming scarce. Drilled oil was relatively cheap to produce and easy to transport. The oil industry grew quickly after 1859 and encouraged the growth of related industries such as kerosene and gasoline.

The Workforce Grows After the Civil War, large numbers of Europeans, and some Asians, immigrated to the United States. They were pushed from their homelands by factors such as political upheaval, religious discrimination, and crop failures. In 1881 alone, nearly three quarters of a million immigrants arrived in America. That number climbed steadily, reaching almost one million per year by 1905. Immigrants were willing to work for low wages because competition for jobs was fierce. And they were prepared to move frequently in pursuit of economic opportunity. All of these factors meant that industries had a huge, and willing, workforce to fuel growth. The potential workforce grew even larger in the 1890s, when droughts and competition from foreign farmers drove American farmers in large numbers to seek jobs in the cities.

Capitalism Encourages Entrepreneurs In 1868, Horatio Alger published his first novel, *Ragged Dick, or Street Life in New York.* This wildly successful novel told the story of a poor boy who rose to wealth and fame by working hard. Alger's novels stressed the possibility that anyone could vault from poverty and obscurity to wealth and fame. In this excerpt, he describes how Ragged Dick starts his climb to success.

Primary Source

"Ten dollars a week was to him a fortune. . . . Indeed, he would have been glad, only the day before, to get a place at three dollars a week. . . . Then he was to be advanced if he deserved it. It was indeed a bright prospect for a boy who, only a year before, could neither read nor write. . . . Dick's great ambition to "grow up 'spectable" seemed likely to be accomplished after all."

—Horatio Alger, 1868

The "rags to riches" idea depended on the system of capitalism, or free enterprise, in which individuals own most businesses. The heroes of this system were **entrepreneurs,** or people who invest money in a product or enterprise in order to make a profit. Entrepreneurs fueled industrialization. The factories, railroads, and mines they established created jobs and also attracted foreign investment.

Doing Business

By 1900, large stores attracted customers with impressive displays of merchandise.

Government Policies Encourage Free Enterprise Government policies encouraged the success of businesses in the late 1800s. For example, the government gave railroad builders millions of acres of land in return for their promise to quickly link the East and West coasts. To encourage the buying of American goods, Congress enacted **protective tariffs,** or taxes that would make imported goods cost more than those made locally. The government also encouraged **laissez-faire** policies, which allowed businesses to operate under minimal government regulation. Such policies, along with a strong legal system that enforced private property rights, provided the predictability and security that businesses and industries needed to encourage investment and growth.

✓ **Checkpoint** **What factors spurred industrial growth in the late 1800s?**

Innovation Drives the Nation

By the late 1800s, the drive for innovation and efficiency seemed to touch every sphere of life in the United States. The number of patents increased rapidly during this time. A **patent** is a grant by the federal government giving an inventor the exclusive right to develop, use, and sell an invention for a set period of time. Businessmen invested heavily in these new innovations, hoping to create new industries and expand old ones.

Electricity Transforms Life In 1876, inventor **Thomas Edison,** supported by wealthy industrialists like J. P. Morgan, established a research laboratory at Menlo Park, New Jersey. Edison, a creative genius who had had only a few months of formal education, would receive more than 1,000 patents for new inventions. In 1880, for example, with the goal of developing affordable lighting for homes, Edison and his team invented the light bulb. Within a few years, they had also developed plans for central power plants to light entire sections of cities. Other inventors later improved upon Edison's work. George Westinghouse, for example, developed

Major Inventions of the 1800s

▲ **Telegraph** Samuel Morse's telegraph sends the first message from Washington, D.C., to Baltimore, Maryland, on May 24, 1844. Before the telegraph, messages were sent by horse and rider. In the early 1860s, the telegraph replaced the Pony Express—the long-distance mail service in the West.

▼ **Sewing Machine** Elias Howe's sewing machine revolutionizes the way clothes are made in homes and factories. In his original design, a hand-turned wheel moved the needle up and down.

technology to send electricity over long distances. Electricity lit city streets and powered homes and factories, extending the number of hours in the day when Americans could work and play.

Revolutionizing Communications In 1844, inventor Samuel Morse perfected telegraph technology, or the process of sending messages over wire. In 1876, Alexander Graham Bell patented the telephone. Within a few years, 148 telephone companies had strung more than 34,000 miles of wire, and long-distance lines linked several cities in the Northeast and Midwest. By 1900, there were more than one million telephones in the United States, and more than 100,000 miles of telegraph wire linked users across the land. In 1896, Guglielmo Marconi invented the wireless telegraph. Future inventors would build on this innovation in developing the radio.

Steel: A Practical Wonder In the 1850s in England, a man named Henry Bessemer developed a process for purifying iron, resulting in strong, but lightweight, steel. American industries quickly adopted the **Bessemer process,** and by 1890 the United States was outproducing British steel manufacturers. Strong steel made possible a host of innovations, including skyscrapers and the elevators to service them. However, one of its most dramatic uses was in the construction of **suspension bridges,** bridges in which the roadway is suspended by steel cables. The first suspension bridge was the Brooklyn Bridge, spanning the East River in New York City. Completed in 1883, it was at the time of its construction the longest bridge in the world.

History Makers

Thomas Edison (1847–1931)

One of history's most prolific inventors, Thomas Edison lost much of his hearing as a child, which led to poor performance in school. He began working at an early age and by 16 was a telegraph operator. His hearing problems—and an interest in machines—led him to try to invent new equipment that relied on sight rather than sound. Edison produced his first major invention, a machine to report stock prices, at the age of 22. He used the money earned from selling this and other machines to build the Menlo Park complex, where he and his team of workers developed hundreds of new devices or improved old ones.

1852

◀ **Safety Elevator** Elisha Otis develops a safety mechanism to prevent elevator cars from suddenly falling. He demonstrates his invention at an exposition in New York.

1880

◀ **Light Bulb** Thomas Edison patents the electric light bulb. Within two years, he installs a street-lighting system in New York City.

1884

▼ **Steam Boiler Furnace** African American inventor Granville Woods invents an improved steam-powered furnace for running trains.

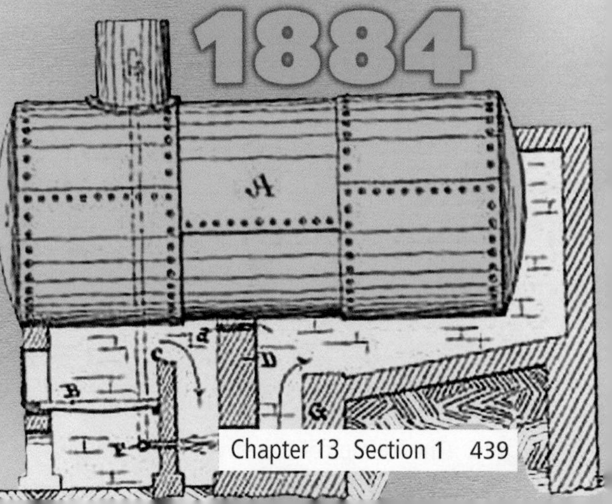

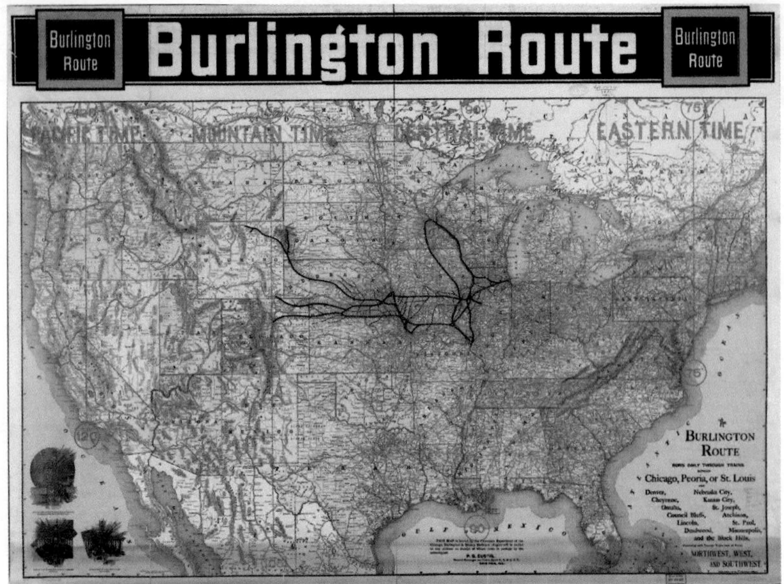

Establishing Time Zones

A map shows an early railroad route covering three time zones. *Why would making railroad schedules be difficult without time zones?*

Technology and Transportation As railroads expanded, they made use of new technologies and also encouraged innovation. George Westinghouse patented air brakes for trains in 1869, while Granville Woods patented a telegraph system for trains in 1887. Meatpacker Gustavus Swift developed refrigerated cars for transporting food. By 1883, there were three transcontinental railroad lines in the United States. The expanding transportation network caused some problems. Throughout most of the 1800s, most towns set their clocks independently. When trains started regular passenger service between towns, time differences made it hard to set schedules. In 1884, delegates from 27 countries divided the globe into 24 **time zones,** one for each hour of the day. The railroads adopted this system, which is still used today.

Technology affected how Americans traveled and where they lived. Electric streetcars, commuter trains, and subways appeared in major cities. As a result, Americans living in neighborhoods outside the city could commute to work. Factory production of automobiles with gas-powered engines began in 1902. The first successful airplane flight in 1903 by brothers Orville and Wilbur Wright, two bicycle manufacturers, marked the birth of a new industry.

A Spiral of Growth Railroads played a key role in transforming American industries and businesses. They could transport large amounts of goods quickly, cheaply, and efficiently. Because they linked the nation, they allowed businesses to obtain raw materials easily and to sell finished goods to larger numbers of people. They encouraged new methods for management and administration, which were soon adopted by the business community. In addition, the expanding railroad network stimulated innovation in many other industries.

Vocabulary Builder
stimulate–(STIHM yoo layt) *v.* to excite to action

An abundance of natural resources and an efficient transportation system to carry raw materials and finished goods set up a spiral of related growth. For example, factories turned out plate glass for windows of passenger rail cars. The factories needed freight cars to carry the windows to their destinations. Those freight cars were created in factories that used railroads to transport fuel to supply the furnaces that turned out more railroad cars. In this way, factory production generated more factory production. To meet the growing demand, factory owners developed systems for turning out large numbers of products quickly and inexpensively. Known as **mass production,** these systems depended upon machinery to carry out tasks that were once done with hand tools.

✓ **Checkpoint How did new technologies shape industrialization?**

The Impact of Industrialization

Industrialization touched every aspect of American life, from the way businesses and farms operated to the kinds of products Americans used. It also affected the country's relationship with the world and with its own environment.

Linking World Markets By the 1880s, American exports of grain, steel, and textiles dominated international markets. With almost as many miles of railroad track as the rest of the world combined, the United States could easily

Focus On Geography

The Railroads: Shaping American Cities More than any other factor, the growth of the United States in the mid-to late-1800s can be linked directly to the railroads. As the railroads expanded, they created some cities or greatly influenced the physical and economic growth of others.

Chicago, Illinois Within twenty years after the arrival of the railroads, Chicago had become the nation's main railroad hub. Livestock and grain came to Chicago from the West, while manufactured goods came from the East. Industries such as meatpacking flourished, in turn influencing the railroads. The need to keep meat fresh, for example, resulted in the development of the refrigerated train car. ▶

Pittsburgh, Pennsylvania ▶ With its extensive natural resources, Pittsburgh grew into an industrial powerhouse in the 1800s. Railroads shipped steel and other products to the rest of the country and brought immigrants into the city to begin new lives. With its strong steel-based economy, Pittsburgh became known as "The Steel City."

Geography and History

- Why is it accurate to refer to Chicago as a railroad "hub"?
- How did the railroads contribute to the growth of American cities?

Las Vegas, Nevada Once an army fort, new railroad track laid in the late 1800s turned Las Vegas into a bustling railroad town. The city's water resources allowed trains to refuel and served as a rest stop for passengers. In 1905, Las Vegas became a city. ▼

◀ **Atlanta, Georgia** Atlanta literally got its name from the railroads. It was founded in 1837 as a transportation hub where the Georgia and Atlantic rail lines began. Burned by Union forces during the Civil War, within thirty years Atlanta was once again the proud "railroad center of the southeast."

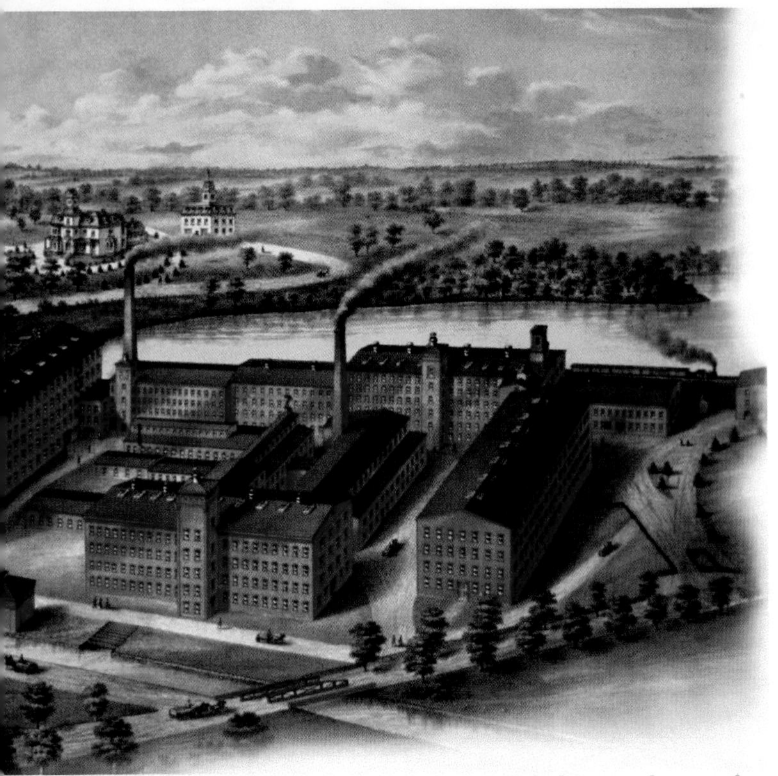

A Pleasant Scene
An attractive 1879 print of a Massachusetts factory gives no hint of the pollution the factory regularly produced.

transport goods from where they were made or grown to ports where they could be shipped around the world. Exports of food and goods greatly expanded the American economy. As the United States grew as a world economic power, it often clashed with the economic views and political policies of other countries.

Changing American Society Massive changes in industry altered how Americans lived and worked. Even farms became mechanized, meaning that fewer farm laborers were needed to feed the nation. Out-of-work farmers and their families moved to urban areas to find work, especially in the increasingly industrial North. Many moved to manufacturing centers that had sprung up around growing factories or industries. The mass production of goods meant that these new urban dwellers had easy access to clothing and supplies that they would have had to make by hand in the past. Yet they faced higher costs of living, were dependent upon cash wages to buy food, and performed repetitive work in factories.

Thinking About the Environment In the early 1800s, few worried about how industry might affect the environment. However, by the late 1800s, industrial waste had risen dramatically and mining had begun to destroy the land. In the Midwest, increasing agricultural production had led to soil erosion and dust storms. People began to raise concerns about protecting natural resources. Congress responded by setting aside protected lands that would eventually become part of the National Park Service. Its creation of Yellowstone Park in 1872 was one of the first federal responses to concerns about the environment.

 **Checkpoint** What impact did industrialization have on Americans?

SECTION 1 Assessment

Progress Monitoring *Online*
For: Self-test with vocabulary practice
www.pearsonschool.com/ushist

Comprehension

1. **Terms and People** For each item below, write a sentence explaining how it relates to industrialization.
   - entrepreneur
   - protective tariff
   - laissez faire
   - patent
   - Thomas Edison
   - Bessemer process
   - suspension bridge
   - time zone
   - mass production

2. **NoteTaking Reading Skill: Identify Causes and Effects** Use your completed chart to answer the Section Focus Question: How did industrialization and new technology affect the economy and society?

Writing About History

3. **Quick Write: Define Your Audience** Suppose that you are Thomas Edison writing a memo to J. P. Morgan requesting more financial support for work being done in your lab. Think about how much information Morgan needs to know, and summarize it in bullets.

Critical Thinking

4. **Recognize Ideologies** Would you characterize all of the government's policies in the late 1800s toward business as laissez faire? Explain your answer.

5. **Determine Relevance** How did the system of patents encourage innovation and investment?

6. **Distinguish Fact From Opinion** Explain why you agree or disagree with this statement: "The late 1800s was a time of great progress for all Americans."

SECTION 2

WITNESS HISTORY

From Rags to Riches

In 1848, 12-year-old Andrew Carnegie and his poverty-stricken family immigrated to the United States. He immediately began work in a Pennsylvania textile factory. Two years later, he got a job in a railroad office. By the time he was 40, he was a wealthy investor and the nation's most successful steelmaker, famous for his commitment to innovation. Carnegie's "rags to riches" story did not end with wealth. Believing that "the man who dies rich thus dies disgraced," he established a number of charitable organizations in the United States and around the world.

◀ Young Andrew Carnegie worked as a "bobbin boy," winding cotton thread onto a bobbin like the one at left.

The Rise of Big Business

Objectives

- Analyze different methods that businesses used to increase their profits.
- Describe the public debate over the impact of big business.
- Explain how the government took steps to block abuses of corporate power.

Terms and People

corporation	Andrew Carnegie
monopoly	vertical integration
cartel	Social Darwinism
John D. Rockefeller	ICC
horizontal integration	Sherman Antitrust Act
trust	

NoteTaking

Reading Skill: Identify Supporting Details Record supporting details about the rise of American big business in a chart like this one.

Rise of Big Business	
Corporations	Debates

Why It Matters The rapid industrial growth that occurred after the Civil War transformed American business and society. Yet it was only the beginning. The rise of big business, characterized by the investment of huge amounts of resources, turned the United States into one of the most economically powerful countries in the modern world. **Section Focus Question: How did big business shape the American economy in the late 1800s and early 1900s?**

Fighting for Profits

Until the mid-nineteenth century, most businesses were run by one person or family. This meant that no business could grow bigger than one family's ability to invest in it or run it. Businesses were also local, buying and selling to customers who lived nearby. Industrialization changed all this. Railroads provided businesses with access to raw materials and customers from farther and farther away. Business leaders, lured by the profits offered by these larger markets, responded by combining funds and resources.

The Corporation Develops To take advantage of expanding markets, investors developed a form of group ownership known as a **corporation.** In a corporation, a number of people share the ownership of a business. If a corporation experiences economic problems, the investors lose no more than they had originally invested in the business. The corporation was the perfect solution to the challenge of expanding business, especially for risky industries such as railroads

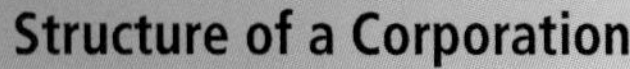

Structure of a Corporation

Public Shareholders
Give money to a company in exchange for share ownership

Board of Directors
Elected by shareholders to set business direction and to protect company

Managers
Hired by the board of directors. Run the company and hire workers

Employees
Carry out the company's jobs

Running a Corporation
Companies issue shares like those above to their investors. In every corporation, shareholders have the final say on how their money should be invested. *How does the role of director differ from that of manager?*

or mining. A corporation had the same rights as an individual: it could buy and sell property, and it could sue in the courts. If one person chose to leave the group, the others could buy out his interests.

Corporations were perfectly suited to expanding markets. They had access to huge amounts of capital, or invested money, allowing them to fund new technology, enter new industries, or run large plants across the country. Aided by railroads and the telegraph, corporations had the ability to operate in several different regions. After 1870, the number of corporations in America increased dramatically. They were an important part of industrial capitalism, or the economic free-market system centered around industries.

Gaining a Competitive Edge Corporations worked to maximize profits in several ways. They decreased the cost of producing goods or services by paying workers the lowest possible wages or paying as little as they could for raw materials. They tried to increase profits by advertising their products widely, thus increasing their potential customer base. Like J. P. Morgan, the heads of some corporations supported research laboratories where inventors could experiment with products and methods that might bring the corporations future profits. Others thought up new ways to make money. Cornelius Vanderbilt, a self-made businessman in the railroad industry, got his start in the steamboat business. He cleverly succeeded in getting his competitors to pay him to relocate because his low fares were driving them out of business.

Some corporations tried to gain a **monopoly,** or complete control of a product or service. To do this, a corporation either bought out its competitors or drove them out of business. Once consumers had no other choices for a given product or service, the sole remaining company was free to set its own prices. Other corporations worked to eliminate competition with other businesses by forming a **cartel.** In this arrangement, businesses making the same product agree to limit their production and thus keep prices high. Still other corporations came up with new methods. **John D. Rockefeller,** an oil tycoon, made deals with railroads to increase his profits:

Primary Source "[Rockefeller's company] killed its rivals, in brief, by getting the great trunk lines to refuse to give them transportation. Vanderbilt is reported to have said that there was but one man—Rockefeller—who could dictate to him."

—H. D. Lloyd, *The Atlantic,* 1881

Horizontal and Vertical Integration Businessmen continued to develop ever more effective ways to increase profits and decrease costs. One way was to create a giant company with lower production costs. This system of consolidating many firms in the same business is called **horizontal integration.** Rockefeller was one of the first businessmen to use this method. However, Ohio state law prevented one company from owning the stock of another, meaning that Rockefeller could not buy out his competitors. His lawyer had an idea to get around this law, called a **trust.** In a trust, companies assign their stock to a board of trustees, who combine them into a new organization. The trustees run the organization, paying themselves dividends on profits.

Rockefeller, steel tycoon **Andrew Carnegie,** and other businessmen also increased their power by gaining control of the many different businesses that make up all phases of a product's development. This process, called **vertical integration,** allowed companies to reduce costs and charge higher prices to competitors.

 **Checkpoint** **What strategies did corporations use to decrease costs and increase profits?**

Debating the Role of Big Business

Throughout the 1880s, business mergers created powerful empires for those who invested in steel, railroads, meat, farm equipment, sugar, lumber, and a number of other enterprises. However, while business leaders grew wealthy, many smaller companies and consumers began to question their goals and tactics.

Comparing Viewpoints

What is the Legacy of the Business Tycoons?

Business tycoons like Carnegie, Rockefeller, and Vanderbilt had a huge role in spurring America's industrial growth. Yet even today, historians debate the real legacy of those men.

Matthew Josephson

Josephson (1899–1978) was the political and economic historian who coined the phrase "robber barons."

Primary Source

"To organize and exploit the resources of a nation upon a gigantic scale . . . and to do this only in the name of an uncontrolled appetite for private profit—here surely is the great inherent contradiction whence so much disaster, outrage and misery has flowed."

Burton W. Folsom, Jr.

Folsom (born 1948) is a historian who has described the great businessmen of the time as entrepreneurs.

Primary Source

"In 1870, when Rockefeller founded Standard Oil, kerosene was 30 cents a gallon. Twenty years later, Rockefeller had almost a 90 percent market share and kerosene was only eight cents a gallon. Customers were the real winners here, because Rockefeller's size allowed him to cut costs. . . ."

Compare

1. What is the basic difference between Folsom's and Josephson's views of these businessmen?
2. What is Folsom's main defense of Rockefeller's tactics?

"Robber Barons" or "Captains of Industry"? Gradually, consumers, workers, and the federal government came to feel that systems like trusts, cartels, and monopolies gave powerful businessmen an unfair advantage. Most small businesses were bought up or squeezed out of competition. Small businesses that joined trusts found that they received few profits. Consumers were harmed by the unfairly high prices that monopolies and cartels set on their products. Because of their capacity to swindle the poor, shrewd capitalists became known as "robber barons."

At the same time, many people believed that business leaders served the nation positively, thus earning the nickname "captains of industry." Factories, steel mills, and railroads provided jobs for an ever-growing labor force. The development of efficient business practices and industrialists' support for developing technology benefited the nation's economy, stimulating innovation and shaping

INTERACTIVE Whiteboard

Events That Changed America

NEW WAYS OF DOING BUSINESS

The rise of the Standard Oil Company marked the beginning of a brand new way of building and conducting business in America. Many, though not all, of John D. Rockefeller's business practices at Standard Oil are part of mainstream corporate culture in the U.S. today. In 1904, journalist Ida Tarbell wrote, "It was the first in the field, and it has furnished the methods, the charter, and the traditions of its followers." Believing that a mix of small and large companies produced chaos and instability in prices and supplies, Rockefeller pioneered new techniques for organizing the oil industry to create a more stable and seamless business environment.

Through creativity and hard work, Rockefeller rose from a ▶ modest background to become the world's first billionaire. From his first paycheck he gave 10 percent of his earnings to his church. By the time he died, he had given away hundreds of millions of dollars.

▲ Standard Oil became a dominant symbol of the bustling American economy. At its height, the company controlled 90 percent of the nation's oil industry.

HORIZONTAL INTEGRATION

Rockefeller bought up rival businesses in Ohio, Pennsylvania, and New York to gain more control of the oil-refining industry. One of Rockefeller's harshest critics led protests against the growing power of Standard Oil—only to take a job there years later.

Clark, Payne & Company, OH

Hanna, Baslington & Company, OH

Atlantic Refining Company, OH

Charles Pratt & Company, NY

Imperial Refining Company, PA

Chess, Carley & Company, KY

Purchased by Rockefeller

Standard Oil Company

the United States into a strong international leader. Furthermore, many business leaders, like Carnegie, Rockefeller, and Vanderbilt, were important philanthropists. They established universities, museums, and libraries, believing that such institutions made it possible for the disadvantaged to rise to wealth.

Social Darwinism Catches On In 1859, biologist Charles Darwin published *On the Origin of Species,* arguing that animals evolved by a process of "natural selection" and that only the fittest survived to reproduce. Yale professor William Graham Sumner soon applied this theory to the rough-and-tumble world of American capitalism, calling it **Social Darwinism.** He declared that wealth was a measure of one's inherent value and those who had it were the most "fit."

People used Social Darwinism to justify all sorts of beliefs and conditions. Supporters of the laissez-faire economic system argued that the government

Vertical Integration

Rockefeller next sought to turn Standard Oil into a kind of empire. He invested in industries related to oil production, including pipelines, tank cars, oil barrels, railroads, and marketing companies. By taking control of the entire supply chain, Rockefeller was able to exert almost complete control over competitors.

Oil wells/ Pipelines

Tank Cars/ Railroads

Retail outlets

Purchased by Rockefeller

Standard Oil Company

Why It Matters

Rockefeller's methods—from advertising (below) to buying out competitors—changed the American business climate. In turn, big business transformed American society itself in the twentieth century, becoming the accepted means for the nation to conduct its business and produce and sell its goods. It also ushered in the globalization that would become the striking characteristic of twenty-first century life.

Following in Rockefeller's ▶ footsteps, Microsoft's Bill Gates carried the torch of modern business leadership. While praised for his philanthropy, he has also been criticized for monopolistic techniques— just as Rockefeller was.

Thinking Critically

In the late 1800s, people debated the impact of corporations, calling their leaders either "robber barons" or "captains of industry." Are such debates still relevant today?

History Interactive

For: More about big business
www.pearsonschool.com/ushist

should stay out of private business, because interference would disrupt natural selection. Many Social Darwinists believed that the nation would grow strong by allowing its most vigorous members to rise to the top. Therefore, they felt that it was wrong to use public funds to assist the poor. Social Darwinism was often used to fuel discrimination. Social Darwinists pointed to the poverty-stricken condition of many minorities as evidence of their unfitness.

 **Checkpoint** **What arguments did people use to support or oppose big business?**

NoteTaking

Reading Skill: Recognize Sequence As you read, record details about how the government gradually became involved in regulating industry.

The Government Imposes Regulations

The great industrialists' methods and their stranglehold on the nation's economy worried some Americans. The railroad industry was renowned for practices such as fixing unfair rates. Competing railroads also entered secret agreements to divide up the nation's freight, a practice called pooling.

Finally, in 1887, the United States Senate created the **Interstate Commerce Commission (ICC)** to oversee railroad operations. This was the first federal body ever set up to monitor American business operations. The ICC could only monitor railroads that crossed state lines, and it could not make laws or control the railroads' transactions. Still, the ICC could require the railroads to send their records to Congress, so that Congress could initiate investigations of unfairness. Over the next several decades, the government would set up many other federal bodies to regulate American businesses.

Vocabulary Builder
restraint–(rih STRAYNT) *n.* holding back or checking of action

Similarly, the federal government slowly became involved in regulating trusts. In 1890, the Senate passed the **Sherman Antitrust Act,** which outlawed any trust that operated "in restraint of trade or commerce among the several states." For more than a decade, the provision was seldom enforced. In fact, the law was often used in the corporations' favor, as they argued that labor unions restrained trade. However, the ICC and the Sherman Antitrust Act began a trend toward federal limitations on corporations' power.

 **Checkpoint** **How did the federal government regulate business?**

SECTION 2 Assessment

Progress Monitoring *Online*
For: Self-test with vocabulary practice
www.pearsonschool.com/ushist

Comprehension

1. **Terms and People** For each item below, write a sentence explaining how it relates to the rise of big business in the late 1800s.
   - corporation
   - monopoly
   - cartel
   - John D. Rockefeller
   - horizontal integration
   - trust
   - Andrew Carnegie
   - vertical integration
   - Social Darwinism
   - ICC
   - Sherman Antitrust Act

2. **NoteTaking Reading Skill: Identify Supporting Details** Use your completed charts to answer the Section Focus Question: How did big business shape the American economy in the late 1800s and early 1900s?

Writing About History

3. **Quick Write: Narrow Down the Topic** You are the head of a corporation and need to write a memo to your shareholders about the company's financial situation. You want to make a positive impression. What kind of information should you include? What should be the subject line of the memo?

Critical Thinking

4. **Identify Central Issues** Why did business leaders create new forms of ownership like monopolies, cartels, and trusts?
5. **Determine Relevance** How accurate is it to describe business leaders like Rockefeller and Carnegie as both "robber barons" and "captains of industry"?
6. **Draw Inferences** What does the fact that government regulation of business was not very successful at first tell you about the relationship between government and big business?

Primary Source

Andrew Carnegie: *Wealth* (1889)

One of America's wealthiest tycoons, Andrew Carnegie was also a dedicated philanthropist. By the time he died, he had given away more than 80 percent—over $350 million—of his own fortune. Carnegie wrote frequently about the role of wealthy businessmen in the American economy. In *Wealth*, Carnegie said that people had the right to accumulate as much wealth as they could, but they also had the responsibility to give it away. His ideas became popularly known as the "gospel of wealth."

ANDREW CARNEGIE

New York: 12th March 1901.

Dr J.S.Billings,
Director New York Public Library.

Dear Mr Billings,

Our conferences upon the needs of Greater New York for Branch Libraries to reach the masses of the people in every district have convinced me of the wisdom of your plans.

Sixty-five branches strike one at first as a large order, but as other cities have found one necessary for every sixty or seventy thousand of population the number is not excessive.

You estimate the average cost of these libraries at, say, $80,000 each, being $5,200,000 for all. If New York will furnish sites for these Branches for the special benefit of the masses of the people, as it has done for the Central Library, and also agree in satisfactory form to provide for their maintenance as built, I should esteem it a rare privilege to be permitted to furnish the money as needed for the buildings, say $5,200,000. Sixty-five libraries at one stroke probably breaks the record, but this is the day of big operations. and New York is soon to be the biggest of Cities,

Very truly yours,

Andrew Carnegie

Carnegie (above) built more than 2,000 public libraries around the country. A letter he wrote to the director of the New York Public Library expresses his enthusiasm for the project.

It is well, nay, essential for the progress of the race, that the houses of some should be homes for all that is highest and best in literature and the arts, and the refinements of civilization, rather than none should be so. Much better this great irregularity than universal squalor. . . .[1]

The price which society pays for the law of competition, like the price it pays for cheap comforts and luxuries, is also great; but the advantages of this law are also greater still, for it is to this law that we owe our wonderful material development, which brings improved conditions in its train. But, whether the law be benign[2] or not, we must say of it, as we say of the change in the conditions of men to which we have referred: It is here; we cannot evade[3] it; no substitutes for it have been found; and while the law may be sometimes hard for the individual, it is best for the race, because it insures the survival of the fittest in every department. . . .

What is the proper mode of administering wealth after the laws upon which civilization is founded have thrown it into the hands of the few? . . .

Individualism[4] will continue, but the millionaire will be but a trustee for the poor; intrusted for a season with a great part of the increased wealth of the community, but administering it for the community far better than it could or would have done for itself. . . . The man who dies leaving behind him millions of available wealth, which was his to administer during life, will pass away "unwept, unhonored, and unsung," no matter to what uses he leaves the dross[5] which he cannot take with him. Of such as these the public verdict will then be: The man who dies rich thus dies disgraced.

1. **squalor** (SKWAHL uhr) *n.* state of filth or of being miserable
2. **benign** (bih NĪN) *adj.* favorable; doing no harm
3. **evade** (ee VAYD) *v.* to escape or avoid
4. **individualism** (ihn duh VIHJ oo uhl ihz uhm) *n.* self-interest
5. **dross** (drahs) *n.* waste or useless substances

Thinking Critically

1. **Analyze Information** Does Carnegie believe that there is anything wrong with amassing wealth? Why or why not?
2. **Synthesize Information** How does Carnegie use the doctrine of Social Darwinism to support his argument?

SECTION 3

WITNESS HISTORY

The Right to Strike

In 1890, labor leader Samuel Gompers testified before a government labor commission. Describing the condition of workers, he argued that unions and strikes were the only way workers' rights could be expanded.

"We recognize that peaceful industry is necessary to successful civilized life, but the right to strike and the preparation to strike is the greatest preventive to strikes. If the workmen were to make up their minds to-morrow that they would under no circumstances strike, the employers would do all the striking for them in the way of lesser wages and longer hours of labor."

—Report on the (U.S.) Industrial Commission on Capital and Labor, 1890

◀ Immigrants paint machinery in a Cleveland, Ohio, factory.

The Organized Labor Movement

Objectives

- Assess the problems that workers faced in the late 1880s.
- Compare the goals and strategies of different labor organizations.
- Analyze the causes and effects of strikes.

Terms and People

sweatshop	Samuel Gompers
company town	AFL
collective bargaining	Haymarket Riot
socialism	Homestead Strike
Knights of Labor	Eugene V. Debs
Terence V. Powderly	Pullman Strike

NoteTaking

Reading Skill: Identify Main Ideas Record the main ideas about the rise of organized labor.

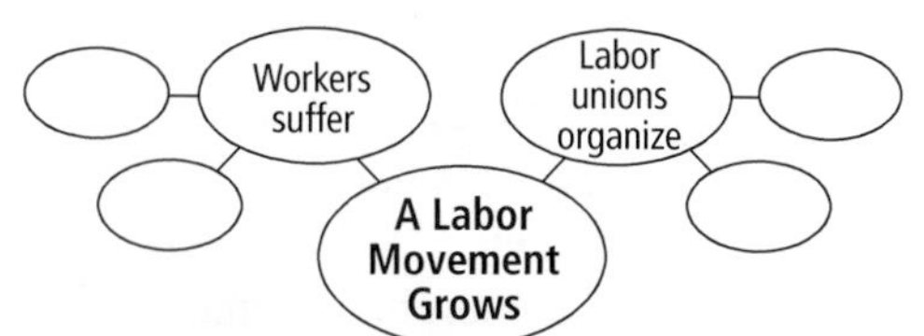

Why It Matters As industrialization intensified, the booming American economy relied heavily on workers to fuel its success. But struggles between business owners and workers also intensified, as workers rebelled against low pay and unsafe working conditions. To keep the economy thriving, Americans had to find ways to ease the tensions between business owners and workers. **Section Focus Question: How did the rise of labor unions shape relations among workers, big business, and government?**

Workers Endure Hardships

The industrial expansion in the United States made the American economy grow by leaps and bounds. Industrial growth produced great wealth for the owners of factories, mines, railroads, and large farms. It also brought general improvements to American society in the form of higher standards of living, wider availability of cheap goods, and access to public institutions like museums and schools. However, the people who actually performed the work in factories and industries struggled to survive. In addition, workers—especially immigrants, women, and minorities—often faced ridicule and discrimination.

Factory Work In the 1880s and 1890s, factory owners, seeking to maximize profits, employed people who would work for low wages. Immigrants made up a large percentage of the workforce. Far from home, lacking good English-speaking skills, and often very poor, immigrants would generally take almost any job. Factory workers toiled long hours—12 hours a day, 6 days a week—in small, hot, dark, and dirty workhouses known as **sweatshops.** These sweatshops employed thousands of people, mainly women, who worked for long hours on machines making mass-produced items. Owners ensured productivity by strictly regulating workers' days. Owners clocked work and break hours, and they fined workers for breaking rules or working slowly.

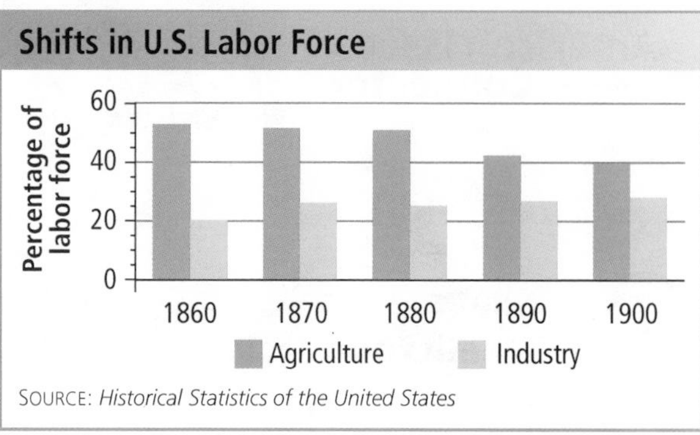

A Changing Workforce
In the late 1800s, the number of Americans working in agriculture steadily declined. *Describe the growth in the industrial workforce between 1860 and 1900.*

Factory work was often dangerous. Workspaces were poorly lit, often overheated, and badly ventilated. Some workers lost their hearing from the noisy machines. Accidents were common, both from faulty equipment and lack of proper training. Despite the harsh conditions, employers suffered no shortage of labor. There were always more people than jobs.

Families in the Workforce As industrialization advanced, more jobs opened up for women. They worked as laundresses, telegraph operators, and typists. But most women—and their families—worked in the factories. Since low wages meant that both parents needed jobs, bringing children to work kept them off the streets and close to their parents. It also meant that the children could earn a wage, which helped the family to survive. By the end of the 1800s, nearly one in five children between the ages of 10 and 16 worked rather than attending school. Conditions were especially harsh for these children. Many suffered stunted physical and mental growth. By the 1890s, social workers began to lobby to get children out of factories and into child care or schools. Eventually, their efforts prompted states to pass legislation to stop child labor.

Living in Company Towns Many laborers, especially those who worked in mines, were forced to live in isolated communities near their workplaces. The housing in these communities, known as **company towns,** was owned by the business and rented out to employees. The employer also controlled the "company store," where workers were forced to buy goods. The company store sold goods on credit but charged high interest. As a result, by the time the worker received wages, most of the income was owed back to the employer. Since workers could be arrested if they left their jobs before they repaid these loans, employers could hold workers to their jobs through a system that workers' advocates called "wage slavery." Through its management of the company town, employers could also reinforce ethnic competition and distrust. For example, Mexican, African American, or Chinese workers could be segregated in separate towns.

✓ **Checkpoint How did working conditions affect families?**

Child Laborers
Adults supervise child workers in a textile factory circa 1890. A Pennsylvania job advertisement from the late 1800s called for workers "with large families."

American Issues Connector

Technology and Society

TRACK THE ISSUE

What are the benefits and costs of technology?

Technology has had a great impact on American life. It has brought economic and social benefits for the nation, yet it has also had some negative effects. What are the benefits and costs of technological change? Use the timeline below to explore this enduring issue.

Late 1700s Factory System
Water-powered mills boost production but worsen conditions for workers.

1859 Oil Refining
Oil fuels industrial growth and raises standard of living but encourages American dependence on a single resource and worsens pollution.

1930s Polymers
Manufactured materials like plastics have many uses but also increase pollution.

1940s Nuclear Reactor
Nuclear energy holds promise but carries the threat of radioactive meltdown and nuclear waste.

2000s Genetic Engineering
Biotechnology offers benefits but may also have harmful effects.

Factory workers circa 1900

Nuclear power plant, Illinois

DEBATE THE ISSUE

Nuclear Energy Building more nuclear plants would help meet our energy needs and limit fossil-fuel emissions that contribute to global warming. But the radioactive material they produce may pose grave risks to human health and safety.

"Nuclear energy supplies clean, reliable, affordable and safe electricity and is the only emission-free source that can be readily expanded to meet our nation's growing energy needs. . . . Nuclear power plants produce electricity that otherwise would be supplied by oil-, gas-, or coal-fired generating capacity, and thus *prevent* the emissions associated with that fossil-fueled capacity."

—John E. Kane, Senior Vice President, Nuclear Energy Institute

"There is strong skepticism . . . [about] the promises of the nuclear industry. . . . This is an industry that on a daily basis, as a direct result of its work, generates the most toxic and long-lived substances known to humans. It is an industry that poses a grievous threat to the health of humans and to the wider biosphere."

—Dave Sweeney, nuclear campaigner, Australian Conservation Foundation

TRANSFER Activities

1. **Compare** Why does Mr. Kane support nuclear energy? Why does Mr. Sweeney oppose it?
2. **Analyze** Which of the authors cited here would be more likely to question the factory system's impact on workers?
3. **Transfer** Use the following Web site to see a video, try a WebQuest, and write in your journal. www.pearsonschool.com/ushist

Labor Unions Form

Industrialization lowered the prices of consumer goods, but in the late 1800s most factory workers still did not earn enough to buy them. Increasingly, working men and women took their complaints directly and forcefully to their employers. Employers usually opposed the growing labor movement, which they saw as a threat to their businesses and profits.

Early Labor Protests As early as the 1820s, factory workers tried to gain more power against employers by using the technique of **collective bargaining,** or negotiating as a group for higher wages or better working conditions. One form of collective bargaining was the strike, in which workers agreed to cease work until certain demands were met. Some strikes were local, but often they involved workers in a whole industry across a state, a region, or the country.

The first national labor union was founded in 1834 as the National Trades Union, open to workers from all trades. It lasted only a few years, and no new unions formed in the wake of the depressions of the late 1830s. However, local strikes succeeded in reducing the factory workday in some regions. The 10-hour workday became the standard in most New England factories. Gradually, national unions began to reappear.

Socialism Spreads In the 1830s, a movement called **socialism** spread throughout Europe. Socialism is an economic and political philosophy that favors public, instead of private, control of property and income. Socialists believe that society at large, not just private individuals, should take charge of a nation's wealth. That wealth, they argue, should be distributed equally to everyone.

In 1848, the German philosophers Karl Marx and Friedrich Engels expanded on the ideas of socialism in a treatise titled *Communist Manifesto.* This pamphlet denounced capitalism and predicted that workers would overturn it. Most Americans rejected these ideas, believing that they threatened the American ideals of free enterprise, private property, and individual liberty. The wealthy in particular opposed socialism because it threatened their fortunes. But many labor activists borrowed ideas from socialism to support their goals for social reform.

Founding the Knights of Labor In 1869, Uriah Smith Stephens founded a labor union called the **Knights of Labor.** Stephens, a tailor who had lived and worked around the country, included all workers of any trade, skilled or unskilled, in his union. The Knights also actively recruited African Americans. Under Stephens, the union functioned largely as a secret society, devoted to broad social reform such as replacing capitalism with workers' cooperatives. The Preamble to the Knights' Constitution, written in 1878, read:

> **Primary Source** "The recent alarming development and aggression of aggregated wealth, which, unless checked, will inevitably lead to the pauperization and hopeless degradation of the toiling masses, render it imperative, if we desire to enjoy the blessings of life, that a check should be placed upon its power . . . and a system adopted which will secure to the laborer the fruits of his toil. . . ."

In 1881, **Terence V. Powderly** took on the leadership of the Knights. The son of Irish immigrants, Powderly had worked in a menial job on the railroad before rising to become mayor of Scranton, Pennsylvania, in the 1870s. He continued to pursue ideological reforms meant to lead workers out of the bondage of wage labor. He encouraged boycotts and negotiation with employers, but he abandoned the secretive nature of the union. By 1885, the Knights had grown to include some 700,000 men and women nationwide, of every race and ethnicity. By the 1890s, however, after a series of failed strikes, the Knights had largely disappeared.

Showing Loyalty

Early unions promoted loyalty—and spread recognition—by printing their names and locations on ribbons, buttons, and posters. *Do you think employers allowed workers to display such items at work? Explain.*

Forming the AFL In 1886, **Samuel Gompers** formed the **American Federation of Labor (AFL).** Gompers was a poor English immigrant who had worked his way up to head the local cigarmakers' union in New York. While the Knights of Labor were made up of all workers, the AFL was a craft union, a loose organization of skilled workers from some 100 local unions devoted to specific crafts or trades. These local unions retained their individuality but gained strength in bargaining through their affiliation with the AFL.

Gompers set high dues for membership in the AFL, pooling the money to create a strike and pension fund to assist workers in need. Unlike the Knights of Labor, the AFL did not aim for larger social gains for workers. Instead, it focused on very specific workers' issues such as wages, working hours, and working conditions. The AFL also pressed for workplaces in which only union members could be hired. Because of its narrow focus on workers' issues, the AFL was often called a "bread and butter" union.

The AFL was not as successful as the Knights in gaining membership, partly because of its own policies. It opposed women members, because Gompers believed their presence in the workplace would drive wages down. While it was theoretically open to African Americans, local branches usually found ways to exclude them.

Checkpoint How did various labor unions differ in their goals?

Strikes Rock the Nation

As membership in labor unions rose and labor activists became more skilled in organizing large-scale protests, a wave of bitter confrontations between labor and management hit the nation. The first major strike occurred in the railroad industry in 1877. Striking workers, responding to wage cuts, caused massive property destruction in several cities. State militias were called in to protect strikebreakers, or temporary workers hired to perform the jobs of striking workers. Finally, the federal government sent in troops to restore order. In the decades to follow, similar labor disputes would affect businesses, the government, and the organization of labor unions themselves.

Violence Erupts in Haymarket Square On May 1, 1886, thousands of workers mounted a national demonstration for an eight-hour workday. Strikes erupted in several cities, and fights broke out between strikers and strikebreakers. Conflict then escalated between strikers and police who were brought in to halt the violence. On May 4, protesters gathered at Haymarket Square in Chicago. The diverse crowd included anarchists, or radicals opposed to all government. A frenzy broke out when a protester threw a bomb, killing a policemen. Dozens of people, both protesters and policemen, were killed. Eight anarchists were tried

Major Strikes of the Late 1800s — Quick Study

Strike	Cause	Effect
Railroad strikes, 1877	Response to cuts in workers' wages	Set the scene for violent strikes to come
Haymarket Square, 1886	Part of a campaign to achieve an eight-hour workday	Americans became wary of labor unions; the Knights of Labor were blamed for the riot and membership declined.
Homestead Strike, 1892	Economic depression led to cuts in steelworkers' wages	After losing the standoff, steelworker unions lost power throughout the country.
Pullman Strike, 1893	Wages cut without a decrease in the cost of living in the company town	Employers used the courts to limit the influence of unions.

Analyzing Political Cartoons

A Different Kind of Knight This cartoon appeared around 1886, at a time when people were vigorously debating the role of labor unions.

- **A** The cartoon appeared in *Puck,* a magazine that used humor and satire to explore social and political issues.
- **B** The banner is the title of the cartoon, "Knights of the Nineteenth Century."
- **C** The cooper (barrel maker) wears a huge, bloated barrel.
- **D** The plumber carries his bank book filled with profits made from the heavy bills he charges for his services.

1. What two meanings does the title of the cartoon convey?
2. How does the cartoonist's treatment of the cooper and the plumber suggest that their actions are not "knightly"?

for murder, and four were executed. The governor of Illinois, deciding that evidence for the convictions had been scanty, pardoned three of the others. The fourth had already committed suicide in jail.

The **Haymarket Riot** left an unfortunate legacy. The Knights of Labor fizzled out as people shied away from radicalism. Employers became even more suspicious of union activities, associating them with violence. In general, much of the American public at that time came to share that view.

Steelworkers Strike at Homestead In the summer of 1892, a Carnegie Steel plant in Homestead, Pennsylvania, cut workers' wages. The union immediately called a strike. Andrew Carnegie's partner, Henry Frick, responded by bringing in the Pinkertons, a private police force known for their ability to break up strikes. The Pinkertons killed several strikers and wounded many others in a standoff that lasted some two weeks. Then, on July 23, an anarchist who had joined the protesters tried to assassinate Frick. The union had not backed his plan, but the public associated the two. Recognizing that public opinion was turning against unions, the union called off the strike in November. The **Homestead Strike** was part of an epidemic of steelworkers' and miners' strikes that took place as economic depression spread across America. In each case, troops and local militia were called in to suppress the unrest.

Workers Strike Against Pullman In 1893, the Pullman Palace Car Company, which produced luxury railroad cars, laid off workers and reduced wages by 25 percent. Inventor George Pullman, who owned the company, required workers to live in the company town near Chicago and controlled their rents and the prices of goods. In May of 1894, workers sent a delegation to negotiate with Pullman. He responded by firing three workers and shutting down the plant.

Desperate, the workers turned to the American Railway Union (A.R.U.), led by **Eugene V. Debs.** Debs had begun work in a low-level railroad job while still a teenager, working his way up. He had condemned the railroad strike of 1877, which he said was a result of disorganization and corruption within the unions.

INFOGRAPHIC

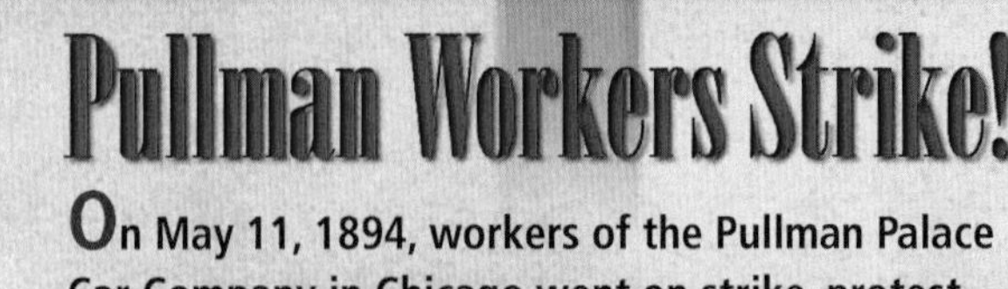

On May 11, 1894, workers of the Pullman Palace Car Company in Chicago went on strike, protesting wage cuts and worker layoffs. When the workers allied with the American Railway Union, the strike quickly spread. Railroad workers refused to service trains with Pullman cars, disrupting rail and mail service in several states. The strike grew increasingly violent, with workers destroying railroad equipment. When 12,000 federal troops were called in to end the strike, clashes between workers and troops broke out and led to riots, looting, and the deaths of over 30 people. The strike finally ended on August 3, with the arrest of Eugene Debs.

The Company Town

Pullman intended his clean, neat company town to protect workers from immoral influences—and to make a favorable impression on visitors. Life inside the town presented a different picture. Pullman owned the housing, stores, and churches, and charged steep rents for them all. Despite cutting wages several times, he never reduced rents or prices of goods. As a result, Pullman workers went further and further into debt.

After a deduction for rent, a worker's paycheck in the late 1800s totaled two cents (about forty cents in today's dollars). After the strike a worker testified that "I have seen men with families of eight or nine children crying because they got only three or four cents after paying their rent."

The Main Players

◀ **George Pullman** amassed a fortune in the railroad car business. A government investigation of the strike blamed Pullman and ruined his reputation.

Experienced labor leader and ARU head ◀ **Eugene Debs** spent six months in jail, where he read about European labor unions and became a Socialist.

Thinking Critically

1. **Distinguishing Fact From Opinion** A Pullman worker described life in the company town as "slavery worse than that of Negroes of the South." Is this factually accurate?
2. **Predict Consequences** How might the Pullman Strike have been avoided?

Debs organized the A.R.U. as an industrial union, grouping all railroad workers together rather than separating them by the job they held. He believed that industrial unions allowed groups to exert united pressure on employers.

The A.R.U. called for a nationwide strike. By June of 1894, nearly 300,000 railworkers had walked off their jobs. The **Pullman Strike** escalated, halting both railroad traffic and mail delivery. Railroad owners cited the Sherman Antitrust Act to argue that the union was illegally disrupting free trade. On July 4, President Grover Cleveland sent in federal troops, ending the strike. When he refused the government's order to end the strike, Debs was imprisoned for conspiring against interstate commerce. Though Debs appealed the conviction, claiming that the government had no authority to halt the strike, the Supreme Court upheld it in the case *In re Debs* in 1895.

Effects on the Labor Movement

The outcome of the Pullman Strike set an important trend. Employers appealed frequently for court orders against unions, citing legislation like the Sherman Antitrust Act. The federal government regularly approved these appeals, denying unions recognition as legally protected organizations and limiting union gains for more than 30 years. As the twentieth century opened, industrialists, workers, and government agencies lashed out at one another over numerous labor issues. Contract negotiations, strikes, and legislation would become the way of life for American industry.

Vocabulary Builder
trend–(trehnd) *n.* general course of events

In the decades after Pullman, the labor movement split into different factions, some increasingly influenced by socialism. By the end of the 1800s, Debs had become a Socialist. He helped organize the American Socialist Party in 1897, running for President in 1900. In 1905, he helped found the Industrial Workers of the World (IWW), or Wobblies. The IWW was a radical union of unskilled workers with many Socialists among its leaders. In the first few decades of the 1900s, the IWW led a number of strikes, many of them violent.

✓ **Checkpoint** **Why did workers increasingly turn to the strike as a tactic to win labor gains?**

SECTION 3 Assessment

Progress Monitoring *Online*
For: Self-test with vocabulary practice
www.pearsonschool.com/ushist

Comprehension

1. **Terms and People** For each item below, write a sentence explaining how it relates to the growing labor movement in the late 1800s.
   - sweatshop
   - company town
   - collective bargaining
   - socialism
   - Knights of Labor
   - Terence V. Powderly
   - Samuel Gompers
   - AFL
   - Haymarket Riot
   - Homestead Strike
   - Eugene V. Debs
   - Pullman Strike
2. **NoteTaking Reading Skill: Identify Main Ideas** Use your completed concept web to answer the Section Focus Question: How did the rise of labor unions shape relations among workers, big business, and government?

Writing About History

3. **Quick Write: Organize Information** Suppose you are a labor organizer writing a memo to union members proposing a strike. Decide on the kind of information you want to present in the main body of your memo. List the information you will cover and note what format it will be in, for example, bulleted lists, charts, and so on.

Critical Thinking

4. **Recognize Ideologies** What does the prevalence of child labor in the 1800s tell you about how society viewed children at the time?
5. **Identify Central Issues** Why were employers generally opposed to labor unions?
6. **Recognize Cause and Effect** Why did the major strikes of the late 1800s lead to a backlash against labor unions?

CHAPTER 13

Quick Study Guide

Progress Monitoring *Online*
For: Self-test with vocabulary practice
www.pearsonschool.com/ushist

Causes of Industrialization

Civil War	Natural Resources	Growing Workforce	Technology/ Innovation	Government Policies
The war encouraged production, innovation, and expansion of railroads.	Ample natural resources, including oil, fueled growth.	Immigrants willing to work for low wages flowed into the country.	New technology and innovative business practices spurred growth.	Government policies encouraged investment in businesses and new technology.

↓ Industrialization

Important People of the Late 1800s

Thomas Edison	Invented new technology, such as electric lighting, that stimulated business
Henry Bessemer	Developed process for creating strong, lightweight steel for use in construction and railroads
Andrew Carnegie	Use of vertical consolidation influenced the rise of big business; urged businessmen to also be philanthropists
John D. Rockefeller	Use of new business strategies, such as horizontal consolidation, influenced the rise of big business
Samuel Gompers	Formed the AFL, influencing the rise of labor unions
Eugene V. Debs	Challenged big business by orchestrating the Pullman Strike and helping to found the IWW

Influential Labor Unions

Name	Date Founded	Significance
National Trades Union	1834	First national union; open to workers from all trades
Knights of Labor	1869	Sought general ideological reform; open to workers from all trades
American Federation of Labor	1886	Focused on specific workers' issues; organization of skilled workers from local craft unions
American Railway Union	1893	First industrial union; open to all railway workers

Important Government Policies of the Late 1800s

- **Protective tariffs** Congress enacted tariffs on imported goods to make them cost more than locally produced goods.
- **Laissez-faire policies** The government allowed businesses to operate under minimal government regulation.
- **Subsidizing railroads** The government gave railroad builders millions of acres of land.
- **Strike breaking** Government troops routinely helped break up strikes.
- **Antiunion actions** Courts used legislation like the Sherman Antitrust Act to order unions to stop disrupting free trade.

Quick Study Timeline

In America

- **1856** Bessemer steel process ushers in new industrial age
- **1859** Drake strikes oil in Pennsylvania
- **1868** Horatio Alger publishes first book

Presidential Terms

F. Pierce 1853–1857 | J. Buchanan 1857–1861 | A. Lincoln 1861–1865 | A. Johnson 1865–1869 | U. Grant 1869–1877

1855 | 1865

Around the World

- **1850** Taiping Rebellion breaks out in China
- **1859** Darwin publishes *On the Origin of Species*
- **1869** Suez Canal is completed

American Issues Connector

By connecting prior knowledge with what you have learned in this chapter, you can gradually build your understanding of enduring questions that still affect America today. Answer the questions below. Then, use your American Issues Connector study guide (or go online: www.pearsonschool.com/ushist).

Issues You Learned About

● **Technology and Society** New technology brings both positive and negative changes to a society.

1. The industrialization of the United States changed the way Americans worked and lived. Write a paragraph or two evaluating the benefits and drawbacks of technology on American society. Consider the following:
   - new inventions and innovations
   - the growth of railroads
   - the loss of traditional jobs and the development of new ones
   - the environment
   - the rise of big business and business tycoons

● **Government's Role in the Economy** The government may pass new laws regulating business in response to changes in the economy.

2. Identify and describe one way that the federal government contributed to the success of businesses in the late 1800s.
3. What problems caused the government to create the Interstate Commerce Commission and the Sherman Antitrust Act? What were the long-term effects of these laws?
4. How did corporations and businesses transform the Sherman Antitrust Act into a tool for their own benefit?

● **Social Problems and Reform** Labor unions first formed in the early 1800s to protect workers' rights, and by the late 1800s, several national organizations had developed.

5. According to Uriah Smith Stephens, what was the best solution for leading workers out of the bondage of labor?
6. What working conditions did labor unions seek to improve? What methods did they use to achieve their aims?
7. Overall, did the efforts of the labor unions have a positive impact on workers' lives and jobs? Explain.

Connect to Your World — Activity

Poverty and Prosperity: Wealthy Companies and Individuals In this chapter, you have learned about the leading companies and entrepreneurs from the age of big business. Choose a present-day company and a present-day entrepreneur. Then, go online or to your local library to learn more about your choices. Find out the company's main business, revenue, size, area of operation, and its contributions to society, including charitable work. For the individual, research how he or she acquired wealth and what, if any, philanthropic activities he or she supports. Then, write a brief profile on the company and the individual.

1877 Great Railroad Strike

1882 Standard Oil Trust is formed

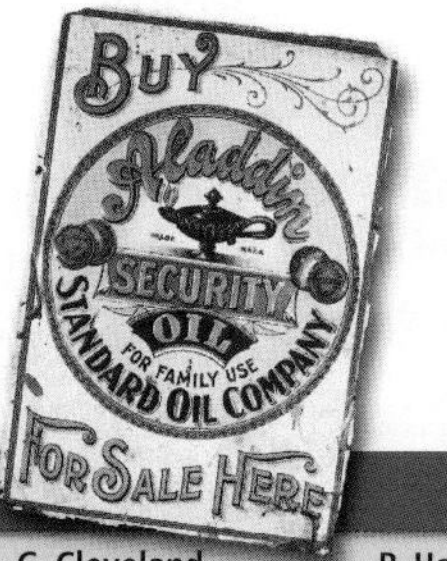

1890 Congress passes Sherman Antitrust Act

1894 Pullman Strike

History Interactive
For: Interactive timeline
www.pearsonschool.com/ushist

R. Hayes 1877–1881 | J. Garfield 1881, C. Arthur 1881–1885 | G. Cleveland 1885–1889 | B. Harrison 1889–1893 | G. Cleveland 1893–1897 | W. McKinley 1897–1901

1875 — 1885 — 1895

1876 Korea becomes an independent nation

1885 Congress Party is established in India

1899 Boer War breaks out in southern Africa

Chapter Assessment

Terms and People

1. What was the **Bessemer process**? What effect did it have on American industry?
2. Define **corporation.** List two methods that corporations used to maximize their profits.
3. Define **horizontal integration** and **vertical integration.** Identify a company or an entrepreneur that practiced each.
4. What was the **Haymarket Riot**? What impact did it have on the labor movement?
5. Who was **Eugene V. Debs**? How did the government respond to his actions in the Pullman Strike?

Focus Questions

The focus question for this chapter is **How did the industrial growth of the late 1800s shape American society and the economy?** Build an answer to this big question by answering the focus questions for Sections 1 through 3 and the Critical Thinking questions that follow.

Section 1

6. How did industrialization and new technology affect the economy and society?

Section 2

7. How did big business shape the American economy in the late 1800s and early 1900s?

Section 3

8. How did the rise of labor unions shape relations among workers, big business, and government?

Critical Thinking

9. **Analyze Causes and Effects** Was the idea of "rags to riches" a cause or a result of industrialization? Explain.
10. **Draw Inferences** Why did industrialists like J. P. Morgan support the work of inventors?
11. **Explain Effects** How did the growth of railroad technology change American society? How did it change businesses?
12. **Recognize Bias** What does the theory of Social Darwinism demonstrate about the way some Americans felt about wealth and poverty?
13. **Predict Consequences** What would a modern-day entrepreneur who believed in Carnegie's "gospel of wealth" do with his or her fortune?
14. **Analyze Information** Describe the system that critics of mining towns referred to as "wage slavery." Why did critics adopt this name?
15. **Recognize Ideologies** Would Marx and Engels have become entrepreneurs if they had lived in the United States? Explain.
16. **Analyze Charts** Mary Harris Jones played a prominent role in one of the labor unions below, traveling around the country and demanding rights for coal miners and other workers. Which union was it? Explain your answer using details from the chart.

Knights of Labor	American Federation of Labor
• Founded in 1869 by Uriah Smith Stephens • Included skilled and unskilled workers • Included women and members of all races and ethnicities • Originally operated as a secret society • Focused on achieving social reform	• Founded in 1886 by Samuel Gompers • Included skilled workers who practiced specific crafts and trades • Excluded women and African Americans as members • Set high dues for membership • Focused on addressing specific workers' issues

Writing About History

Writing a Memo In the age of industrialization and big business, long before there were cellphones and e-mail, people conveyed their ideas to one another by writing. Memos were one way to briefly convey information, such as company policy, legal matters, financial matters, and so on. Write a memo that one of the following people may have written in the late 1800s: John D. Rockefeller, Thomas Edison, Andrew Carnegie, Eugene V. Debs, Samuel Gompers, George Pullman.

Prewriting

- Use library or online resources to read about each of the people listed above.
- Choose the person who most interests you and note the kinds of information he or she would have wanted to convey.
- Choose a title line for your memo. If your topic cannot fit onto one line, it may be too broad for the purposes of a memo.

Drafting

- Present your main point as clearly and concisely as possible.
- Decide whether any of your information can be better conveyed as a chart, bulleted list, or other graphic organizer.

Revising

- Use the guidelines on page SH16 of the Writing Handbook to revise your memo.

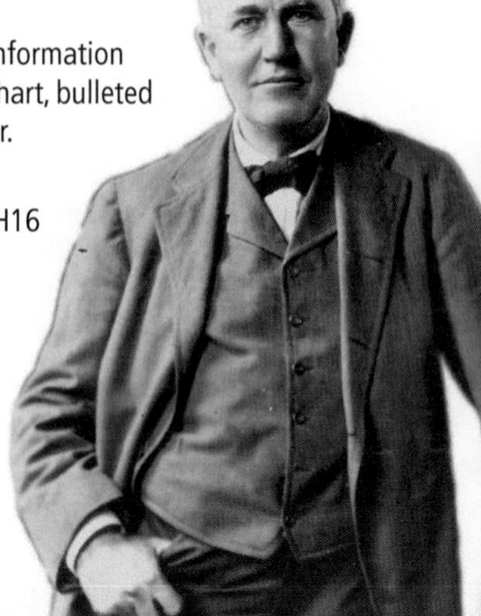

Document-Based Assessment

Attitudes Toward Organized Labor

Were labor unions successful in working out their disputes with big-business owners? Or did the federal government and the courts need to play a role in settling these disputes? Use your knowledge of the organized labor movement and Documents A, B, C, and D to answer questions 1 through 4.

Document A

"The workers at the blast furnaces in our steel-rail works once sent in a 'round-robin' stating that unless the firm gave them an advance of wages by Monday afternoon at four o'clock they would leave the furnaces. . . . Gentlemen of the Blast Furnace Committee, you have threatened our firm that you will break your agreement and that you will leave these blast furnaces . . . unless you get a favorable answer to your threat by four o'clock today. It is not three but your answer is ready. You may leave the blast furnaces. . . . The worst day that labor has ever seen in this world is that day in which it dishonors itself by breaking its agreement. You have your answer."

—The Autobiography of Andrew Carnegie, *August 1920*

Document B

"In the winter of 1893–1894 the employees of the Pullman Palace Car Company . . . joined the new American Railway Union . . . attempting to organize all workers connected with the railways. . . . The [Pullman] company refused to consider arbitration and the boycott went into effect. . . . Indictments charging Debs [president of the American Railway Union] and others of violations of the Sherman Act were secured. . . . As a result of the various injunctions, indictments, and the activities of federal troops which reached Chicago, following directions from President Cleveland, the strike and the consequent violence were practically at an end by the middle of July."

—Labor and the Sherman Act *by Edward Berman, 1930*

Document C

"There was a time when workmen were denied the right of leaving their employers, when they were part of the soil, owned by their employers. . . . Not many years ago, when workmen counseled with each other for the purpose of resisting a reduction in their wages or making an effort to secure an increase, it was held to be a conspiracy punishable by imprisonment. Through the effort of organized labor, an enlightened public sentiment changed all this until to-day the right to unite for material, moral, and social improvement on the part of workers is accepted by all."

—*Samuel Gompers to Editor,* Washington Evening Star, *May 15, 1900*

Document D

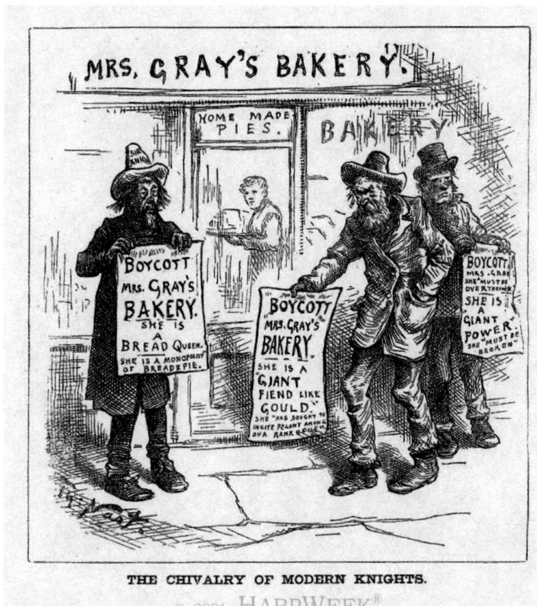

THE CHIVALRY OF MODERN KNIGHTS.

1. In Document A, what view does Andrew Carnegie take toward organized labor?
   A Businesses should bargain with employees.
   B Workers should be paid fair wages.
   C Employees should honor their original work agreement.
   D Business owners should take workers' threats seriously.

2. Which document is a secondary source that describes how the Sherman Act was used as a legal tool to end a strike?
   A Document D
   B Document A
   C Document B
   D Document C

3. Who does the cartoonist ridicule in Document D?
   A The government
   B The Knights of Labor
   C The Sherman Antitrust Act
   D George Pullman

4. **Writing Task** Who do you think was correct about the way to settle disputes between organized labor and big business: business owners, organized labor, or the government? Use your knowledge of the chapter content and specific evidence from the primary and secondary sources above to support your opinion.

CHAPTER

14 Immigration and Urbanization

1865–1914

WITNESS HISTORY

The New American City

Midwestern clergyman Josiah Strong was both fascinated and distressed by rapid urban growth. Americans bought more than 130,000 copies of his 1885 book *Our Country: Its Possible Future and Its Present Crisis.* In it, Strong explains:

> "The city is the nerve center of our civilization. It is also the storm center. . . . During the half century preceding 1880, population in the city increased more than four times as rapidly as that of the village and country. In 1800 there were only six cities . . . which had a population of 8,000 or more. In 1880 there were 286. . . . The city has become a serious menace to our civilization, because . . . it has a peculiar attraction for the immigrant. . . . Our ten larger cities contain only nine per cent of the entire population, but 23 per cent of the foreign. . . . The rich are richer, and the poor are poorer, in the city than elsewhere; and, as a rule, the greater the city, the greater are the riches of the rich and the poverty of the poor."
>
> —Josiah Strong, *Our Country: Its Possible Future and Its Present Crisis,* 1885

◀ This colorized photograph shows Mulberry Street in New York City's "Little Italy" around 1900.

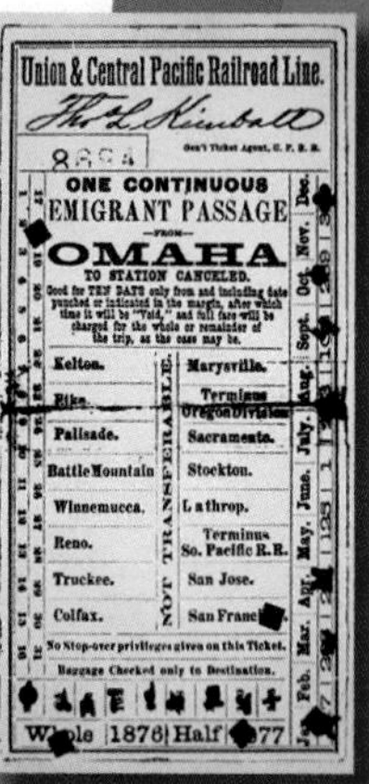

Immigrant train ticket to San Francisco

Early skyscraper

Early bicycle

Chapter Preview

Chapter Focus Question: How did American urban life change between 1875 and 1914?

Section 1
The New Immigrants

Section 2
Cities Expand and Change

Section 3
Social and Cultural Trends

Use the ☑ **Quick Study Timeline** at the end of this chapter to preview chapter events.

Note Taking Study Guide *Online*
For: Note Taking and American Issues Connector
www.pearsonschool.com/ushist

SECTION 1

◀ Two young Polish women at Ellis Island around 1910

WITNESS HISTORY

Looking Forward and Back

Life was difficult for many immigrants in the United States during the late 1800s, but it also offered freedoms they had never known in their homelands.

"Not the looking forward made me go, but the looking backward made me search a new life and struggle a hard battle. . . . [I]t is hard still now to bear the homesickness, loneliness, among strange people not knowing the language doing hard [work] without a minute of joy. But when I look back into my childhood . . . , always under a terrible fear . . . I think that there is not anything harder. . . . America means for an Immigrant a fairy promised land that came out true, a land that gives all they need for their work, a land which gives them human rights, a land that gives morality through her churches and education through her free schools and libraries."

—young Russian Jewish woman

The New Immigrants

Objectives

- Compare the "new immigration" of the late 1800s to earlier immigration.
- Explain the push and pull factors leading immigrants to America.
- Describe the challenges that immigrants faced in traveling to America.
- Analyze how immigrants adapted to American life while trying to maintain familiar cultural practices.

Terms and People

"new" immigrant	Americanization
steerage	"melting pot"
Ellis Island	nativism
Angel Island	Chinese Exclusion Act

NoteTaking

Reading Skill: Identify Main Ideas Record the main ideas of each section in an outline.

I. New Immigrants Come to America
  A.
  B.
II. Immigrants Decide to Leave Home

Why It Matters Immigration has been a central theme in American history. However, when the foreign-born population of the United States nearly doubled between 1870 and 1900, some Americans feared that the newcomers would destroy American culture. Instead, Americans adopted parts of immigrant cultures, while immigrants adopted parts of American culture. **Section Focus Question: Why did immigrants come to the United States, and what impact did they have upon society?**

New Immigrants Come to America

Immigrants had always come to America for economic opportunity and religious freedom. Until the 1870s, the majority had been Protestants from northern and western Europe. They came as families to settle in the United States, often on farms with family or friends who had come before. Many had saved some money for the journey, had a skill or trade, or were educated.

Many German and Irish Catholics had immigrated in the 1840s and 1850s, and more arrived after the Civil War. Some Americans had prejudices against Catholics, but the Irish spoke English and the German Catholics benefited from the good reputation of their Protestant countrymen. Although they lacked skills and money, the children of these immigrants were often able to blend into American society. Beginning in the 1870s, Irish and Germans were joined by **"new" immigrants** from southern and eastern Europe. They arrived in increasing numbers until the outbreak of World War I.

In contrast to "old" immigrants who had come before the Irish and Germans, "new" immigrants were often unskilled, poor, Catholic or Jewish, and likely to settle in cities rather than on farms. Many came alone, planning to save some money in the United States and return home to live. They came from Italy, Greece, Poland, Hungary, and Russia. After 1900, immigrants from Southern and Eastern Europe made up more than 70 percent of all immigrants, up from about 1 percent at midcentury. Many native-born Americans felt threatened by these newcomers with different cultures and languages.

✓ Checkpoint **Describe the "new" immigrants.**

Immigrants Decide to Leave Home

Two types of factors lead to immigration. Push factors are those that compel people to leave their homes, such as famine, war, or persecution. Pull factors are those that draw people *to* a new place, such as economic opportunity or religious freedom. Many immigrants in the late nineteenth century had both push and pull factors that helped them decide to leave the familiar for the unknown.

Reminders of Home
Immigrants often brought items of special significance, such as this Jewish prayer shawl from Russia. ▼

Push Factors In the 1880s, farmers had a difficult time. In Mexico, Poland, and China, land reform and low prices forced many farmers off their land. Some chose to come to America to get a new start. Beginning in the 1840s, China and eastern Europe experienced repeated wars and political revolutions. These events disrupted economies and left political refugees. One of the largest groups to settle in America were Russian and eastern European Jews. Beginning in the 1880s, they fled religious persecution and came to the United States to achieve a better life.

Pull Factors In addition to a vague hope for opportunity, the United States offered special attractions, including plentiful land and employment. The 1862 Homestead Act and aid from railroad companies made western farmland inexpensive. The railroads even offered reduced fares to get there because they needed customers in the West for their own business to succeed. Until 1885, immigrants were recruited from their homelands to build railroads, dig in mines, work in oil fields, harvest produce, or toil in factories. Others hoped to strike it rich by finding gold.

Many others were "chain immigrants," joining family or friends who had already settled in America. The earlier arriving immigrants promised to help the newcomers find work and housing, and sometimes they even sent them tickets for the journey. Immigrants may have lured their families and friends with the promise of religious and political freedom. In America, one could worship and vote as one chose without fear of persecution by the government.

✓ Checkpoint **List the push and pull factors for immigrants.**

Immigration, 1870–1910

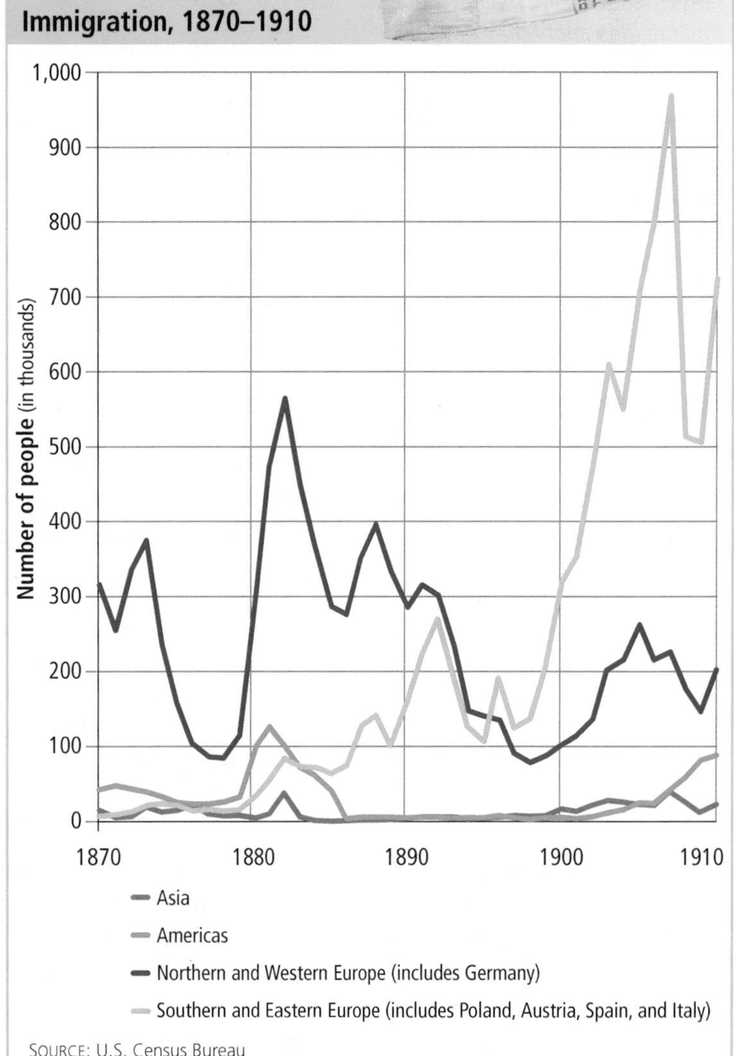

SOURCE: U.S. Census Bureau

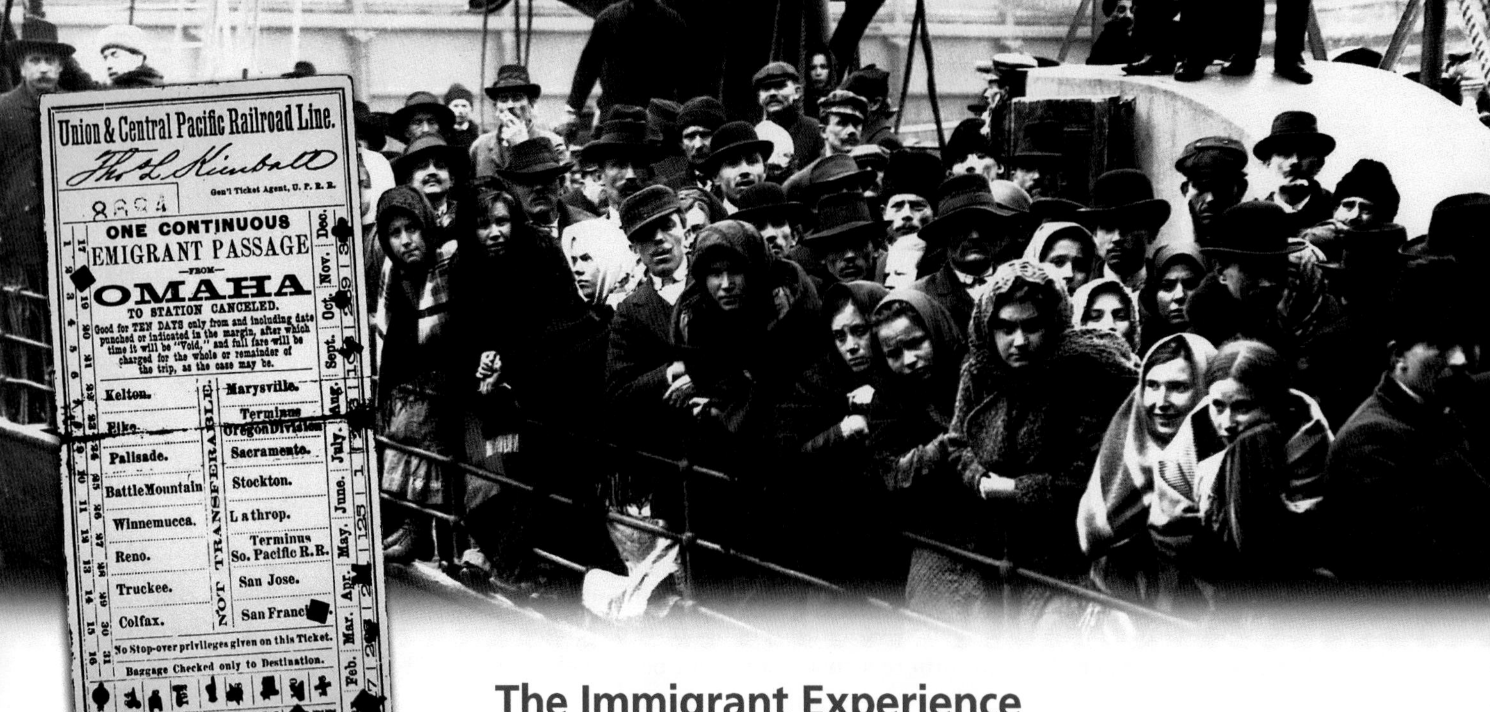

Arriving in America

Immigrants wait on the deck of the S.S. *Prince Frederick Wilhelm.* Look at the passengers' faces. *What thoughts and feelings might they have been experiencing? Why?*

The Immigrant Experience

Immigrant experiences varied greatly. However, there were common themes: a tough decision to leave home and family, a hard and costly journey with an uncertain end, and the difficulties of learning a new language and adjusting to a foreign culture. Millions of people decided that the possibilities outweighed the risks and set out for the United States.

The Long Journey Coming to America was a big task. Travelers needed money for passage and to make a new start, although some had only enough for a ticket. The immigrants' first task was to pack the items that would help them start a new life. Usually, they brought only what they could carry: clothes, maybe a photograph of loved ones, a cherished musical instrument, or the tools of their trade. Next, they made their way to a port of departure, hoping that a ship would be leaving soon. In war-torn areas, just getting to the ship could be dangerous.

By the 1870s, steamships made the trip across the Atlantic safer and faster than ever before. However, it could be an awful voyage. Most immigrants traveled in **steerage,** the worst accommodations on the ship. Located on the lower decks with no private cabins, steerage was crowded and dirty. Illness spread quickly, while rough weather could force seasick passengers to stay in cramped quarters for days at a time. Under these conditions, even healthy immigrants fell ill, while frail passengers sometimes died. Passengers on other voyages were fortunate to have beautiful weather and no illness onboard.

Immigrants Arrive at American Ports The first stop for ships at American ports was a processing station where immigration officials decided who could stay in the United States. To enter, immigrants had to be healthy and show that they had money, a skill, or a sponsor to provide for them. Most European immigrants arrived in New York Harbor. Beginning in 1892, they were processed at **Ellis Island.**

First- and second-class passengers were inspected on the ship and released, unless they had obvious medical problems. All third-class, or steerage, passengers were sent to Ellis Island. There, immigration officers conducted legal and medical inspections. Since the shipowners did a preliminary screening before passengers boarded, only about 2 percent of immigrants were denied entry; the rest took a ferry to New York City. In 1907, 10-year-old Edward Corsi arrived with his family from Italy. Years later, when he had become an immigration official, he remembered his first impressions:

Vocabulary Builder
preliminary–(pree LIHM uh ner ee) *adj.* happening before and leading up to something; initial

Primary Source "I realized that Ellis Island could inspire both hope and fear. Some of the passengers were afraid . . . ; others were impatient, anxious to get through the inspection and be off to their destinations."

—Edward Corsi, *In the Shadow of Liberty,* 1935

Chinese and other Asian immigrants crossed the Pacific Ocean, arriving in San Francisco Bay. They were processed at **Angel Island,** which opened in 1910. If Ellis Island was welcoming to some, Angel Island was always formidable and seemingly designed to filter out Chinese immigrants. After 1882, Chinese travelers were turned away unless they could prove that they were American citizens or had relatives living in America. Officials often assumed that Chinese newcomers would misrepresent themselves in order to gain entry. While most immigrants left Ellis Island within hours, Chinese immigrants at Angel Island were often held for weeks or even months in poor conditions.

 **Checkpoint** **Describe what happened to immigrants when they arrived.**

Opportunities and Challenges in America

Passing immigration inspections was just the first step. Once in America, immigrants immediately faced tough decisions such as where to settle and how to find work. On top of that, most had to learn a new language and new customs. Sometimes, immigrants worked with an agent who spoke their language for help finding work and housing, but many agents took advantage of the newcomers to make money. Lucky immigrants had contacts through family and friends who could help them navigate a new and strange world.

Immigrants Assimilate Into Society

Most new immigrants stayed in cities, close to industrial jobs in factories. There, they often lived in ethnic neighborhoods, called ghettoes, with people who shared their native language, religion, and culture. Neighbors might have come from the same country, region, or even village.

Angel Island Poetry

Detained Chinese immigrants might have spent weeks or months waiting to find out if they would be allowed to stay in the United States. To pass the time and express their frustrations, many carved poems into the walls at Angel Island. What does the poem below tell you about the author?

Primary Source

"Lin, upon arriving in America,
Was arrested, put in a wooden building,
And made a prisoner.
I was here for one autumn.
The Americans did not allow me to land.
I was ordered to be deported."

—Taoist From the Town of Iron

Analyzing Political Cartoons

Keeping Foreigners Out The caption for this cartoon entitled "Looking Backward" says, "They would close to the newcomer the bridge that carried them and their fathers over."

1. What groups of people are represented in this picture?
2. What point was the artist trying to make?

By 1890, many cities had huge immigrant populations. In San Francisco and Chicago, they made up more than 40 percent of the population. Four out of five inhabitants of New York City were foreign born or had foreign-born parents. While exclusionist policies forced some people to live in ghettoes, these neighborhoods also provided familiarity. Specialty shops, grocers, and clothing stores provided a taste of the food and culture that immigrants had left behind.

In many cities, volunteer institutions known as settlement houses ran **Americanization** programs, helping newcomers learn English and adopt American dress and diet. At the same time, immigrants helped one another through fraternal associations, such as the Polish National Alliance and the Ancient Order of Hibernians. These organizations, based on ethnic or religious identity, provided social services and financial assistance. Settlement workers and immigrants alike believed that American society was a **"melting pot"** in which white people of all different nationalities blended to create a single culture. The term came from the name of a play that opened in 1908. This model excluded Asian immigrants, who became targets of social and legal discrimination.

Despite the hopes of settlement workers, immigrants often held on to their traditions. Their children, however, became more Americanized, without memories of homes and families left behind. Some adults dreamed of returning to their homelands, but few did. Instead, they established fraternal lodges and religious institutions that made them feel more comfortable in their new surroundings. Catholics, in particular, established churches and parochial schools. In many cities, Irish Catholic churches stood side by side with Italian Catholic churches—each built to serve the needs of its own community. The immigrants' churches, schools, and institutions reminded native-born Americans that new cultures were changing American society.

New Immigrants Face Hostility Accepting immigrants into American society was not always easy. Newcomers often faced **nativism,** which was a belief that native-born white Americans were superior to newcomers. During the economic recessions of the late nineteenth century, competition for jobs and housing fueled resentment, while religious and cultural differences sparked suspicion between native-born workers and immigrants, as well as between ethnic groups. Many workers worried that immigrants would work for lower pay.

Religion was also a big problem. Protestants were suspicious of Catholicism, the religion of many Irish, German, Italian, and Polish people. Some native-born white Protestants would not hire, vote for, or work with Catholics or Jews. Some Americans even signed restrictive contracts agreeing not to rent or sell property to Catholics, Jews, African Americans, or other groups they considered "non-native."

Nativist intellectuals backed up their prejudices with dubious scientific rhetoric that linked immigrants' physical characteristics to criminal tendencies or lower intellectual abilities. Extreme hostility toward Chinese laborers led Congress to pass the **Chinese Exclusion Act** in 1882. The act prohibited immigration by Chinese laborers, limited the civil rights of Chinese immigrants already in the United States, and forbade the naturalization of Chinese residents. Many Chinese dared not visit their families in China, fearing they would not be permitted to return. In 1898, a court case established that Chinese people born in America were United States citizens and could, therefore, come and go freely. However, many immigration officials ignored this ruling.

In the same year, Congress passed another act that prohibited the entry of anyone who was a criminal, immoral, a pauper, or likely to need public assistance. In practice, the law was used to bar many poor or handicapped immigrants. These acts marked the beginning of immigration restriction into the United States. Until then, everyone had been welcomed. Immigration became a constant topic of conversation throughout America.

✓ **Checkpoint** **Why did some Americans want to restrict immigration?**

Immigrants Change America

Despite opposition, immigrants transformed American society. They fueled industrial growth, acquired citizenship, elected politicians, and made their traditions part of American culture. Mexican Americans in the Southwest developed effective ranching techniques, while Chinese, Irish, and Mexican laborers built the railroads. Equally as important, immigrants labored in coal mines, steel mills, textile mills, and factories. Immigrant women worked in factories, as seamstresses, as laundresses, and doing piecework. Others became domestic servants. Though the conditions were harsh and they received few benefits, immigrants' labor helped the United States become a world power.

Increasingly, immigrants demanded a voice, becoming active in labor unions and politics. They lobbied for policies to protect the poor and powerless and used their votes to elect favorable governments. The political leaders they supported became powerful. Union leaders demanded reforms that helped immigrants as well as all laborers. Immigrants expanded the definition of *American*.

✓ **Checkpoint** **How did immigrants assimilate to and change American culture?**

Immigrant Contributions
Immigrants made many contributions to American culture. Composer Irving Berlin immigrated in 1893 and later wrote "God Bless America" and many other well-known songs. *Can you name any other famous immigrants?*

SECTION 1 Assessment

Progress Monitoring *Online*
For: Self-test with vocabulary practice
www.pearsonschool.com/ushist

Comprehension

1. **Terms and People** What do the terms below have in common?
   - "new" immigrant
   - steerage
   - Ellis Island
   - Angel Island
   - Americanization
   - "melting pot"
   - nativism
   - Chinese Exclusion Act
2. **NoteTaking Reading Skill: Main Ideas** Use your outline to answer the Section Focus Question: Why did immigrants come to the United States, and what impact did they have upon society?

Writing About History

3. **Quick Write: Outline a Proposal** Outline a plan for helping immigrants adjust to life in America. Consider cultural and language differences.

Critical Thinking

4. **Make Comparisons** How did new immigrants differ from old immigrants?
5. **Express Problems Clearly** What problems did immigrants face in coming to America?
6. **Draw Conclusions** In what ways did immigrants affect the American economy and culture?

American Experience History Interactive

EXPERIENCE ELLIS ISLAND

▲ Ellis Island in 1926

By 1900, thousands of immigrants steamed past the Statue of Liberty and landed at Ellis Island each day. After checking their baggage, immigrants walked up a staircase toward the Great Hall on the second floor. Doctors watched closely, looking for signs of illness. At the top of the stairs, about one tenth of the immigrants were marked with chalk and sent for a closer examination. Some were quarantined on the island until they recovered their health. Others were sent home, their dreams crushed.

At the Great Hall, immigrants waited for an interview with a customs officer who checked paperwork and determined if immigrants would be able to support themselves. If they passed inspection, they could buy a train ticket before boarding a ferry for the mainland. Those with no money might stay in the dormitories until a sponsor arrived to vouch for them. Single women were detained until a relative collected them, or they could marry on the island. By 1954, more than 12 million immigrants had passed through Ellis Island on their way to a new life.

Causes of Immigration

Push Factors	Pull Factors
• Persecution • Economic hardship • Lack of jobs • War	• Religious and political freedom • Cheap land • Factory jobs • Family in the United States

▼ Immigrants arrive at Ellis Island carrying their belongings and a paper with their entry number.

THE DINING ROOM

The passenger list (below right) included each passenger's name, gender, previous address, who paid for the tickets, and other information. Immigrants often brought keepsakes like this locket and sent postcards to announce their safe arrival.

Thinking Critically

1. **Analyze Visuals** Look at the photos on this page. In what ways might Ellis Island have been an intimidating place?
2. **Make Inferences** Why were single women not allowed to leave Ellis Island on their own?

Connect to Today Do research to learn about how immigrants legally enter the United States today. How are the experiences of today's immigrants similar to and different from those of the immigrants who arrived at Ellis Island?

History *Interactive*

For: Experience Ellis Island video, audio, and analysis
www.pearsonschool.com/ushist

SECTION 2

▲ Firetruck around 1900

WITNESS HISTORY

A Fiery Tide

As cities expanded, city services, such as fire departments, became more common. But that was not enough to save Chicago from a fire that left hundreds of thousands homeless.

> "The firemen were working with extraordinary perseverance. When it seemed impossible for a man to stand without suffocation they carried their hose, sprinkling the houses opposite and endeavoring to stop its spread in a westerly direction. But it was evident by midnight that human ingenuity could not stem that fiery tide."
>
> —*Chicago Tribune,* October 11, 1869

Cities Expand and Change

Objectives

- Analyze the causes of urban growth in the late 1800s.
- Explain how technology improved city life.
- Evaluate how city dwellers solved the problems caused by rapid urban growth.

Terms and People

urbanization
rural-to-urban migrant
skyscraper
Elisha Otis
mass transit
suburb
Frederick Law Olmsted
tenement

NoteTaking

Reading Skill: Identify Main Ideas Record the main ideas of this section in a flowchart.

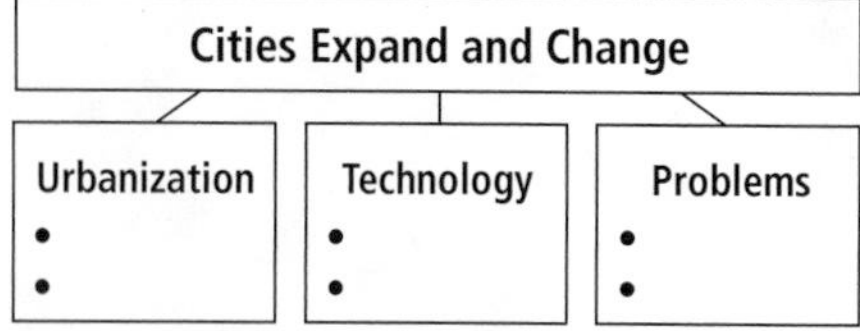

Why It Matters As one historian has noted, America was born on the farm and moved to the city. In 1860, most Americans lived in rural areas, with only 16 percent living in towns or cities with a population of 8,000 or more. By 1900, that percentage had doubled, and nearly 15 million Americans lived in cities with populations of more than 50,000. This period was the beginning of an upsurge in urbanization that both reflected and fueled massive changes in the way Americans lived. **Section Focus Question: What challenges did city dwellers face, and how did they meet them?**

America Becomes a Nation of Cities

In the late nineteenth century, America experienced a period of **urbanization** in which the number of cities and people living in them increased dramatically. Still, numbers and statistics do not tell the whole story of how Americans became city folk. Urban people lived differently from rural people. They worked on schedules, rode trolley cars, paid rents to live in apartment buildings, and interacted with many strangers. Over time, their urban values became part of American culture.

Cities Offer Advantages America's major cities were manufacturing and transportation centers clustered in the Northeast, on the Pacific Coast, and along the waterways of the Midwest. Connected

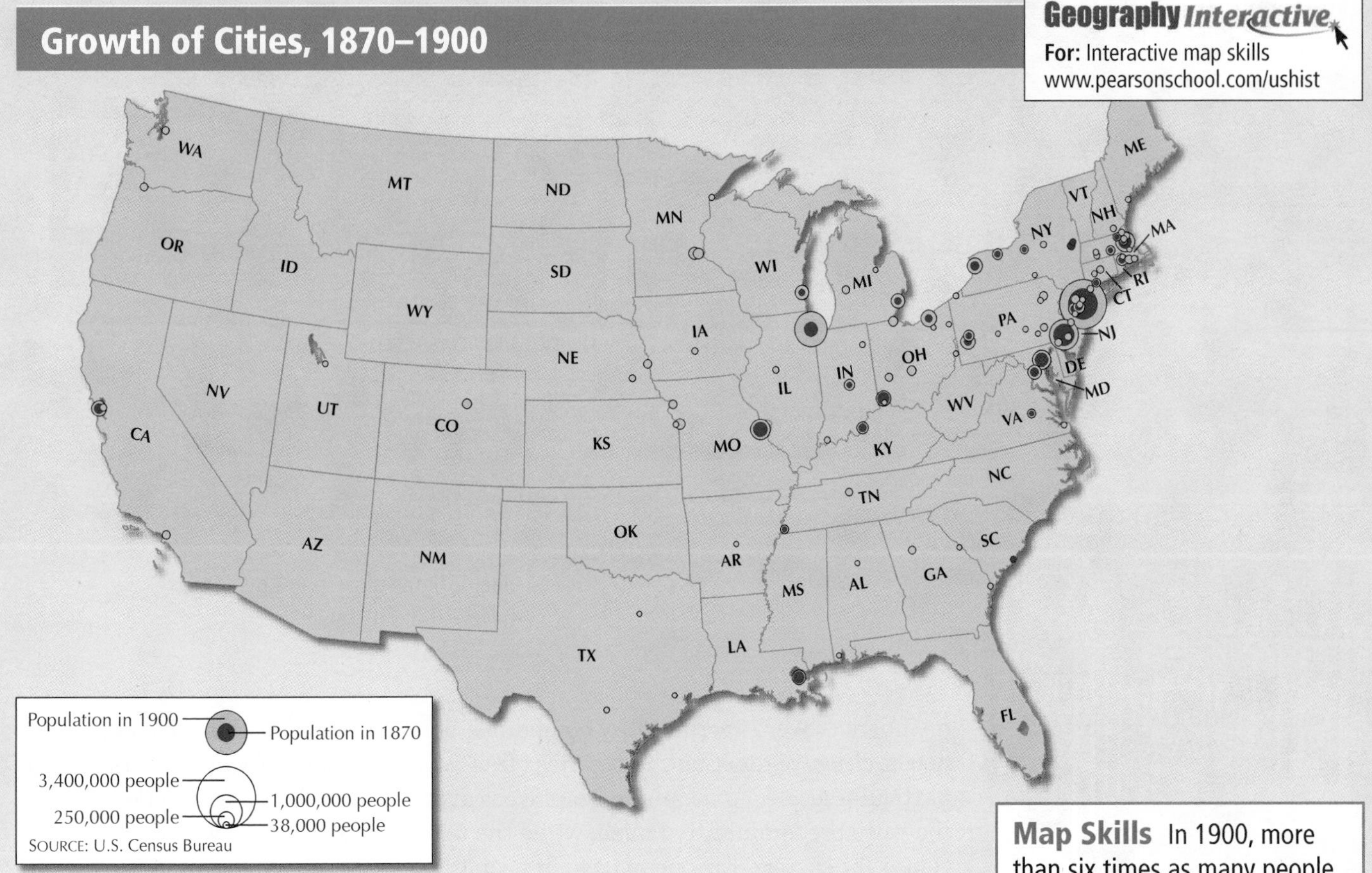

Map Skills In 1900, more than six times as many people lived in cities of 25,000 or more than in 1870.

1. **Locate:** **(a)** New York, **(b)** Chicago, **(c)** San Francisco, **(d)** Minneapolis
2. **Describe** Which areas of the country were the most urbanized?
3. **Draw Conclusions** Who settled in cities?

by the new railroad lines, cities became magnets for immigrants and rural Americans. They were attracted by jobs in factories or the service industries. Those with a little money opened shops. The educated increasingly joined the new middle-class professions, working in downtown offices.

Women's opportunities, in particular, were dramatically expanded in urban areas. In addition to factory work, they could take in boarders, do piecework, or become domestic servants. Educated women found work as teachers or in offices as secretaries and typists.

While many city jobs offered only hard work for little reward, they were an improvement over the alternatives for many. Cities offered variety, promise, and even a bit of glamour. By saving part of their wages, city workers might attain some comforts or perhaps even move into the growing middle class. At the least, they could increase their children's opportunities by sending them to school. While some laborers were trapped in an endless cycle of poverty, only the very poorest were unable to enjoy a higher standard of living in the late nineteenth century.

Life was hard in the city, but most preferred it to the country. Horace Greeley, a politician and New York City newspaper editor, wrote in the 1860s, "We cannot all live in cities, yet nearly all seem determined to do so." City churches, theaters, social clubs, and museums offered companionship and entertainment. Transportation out of the city and to other cities was easily accessible. In this period of growth and expansion, some migrants moved from city to city, trying to improve their fortunes.

Immigrants Move In to Seize Opportunities By 1900, some urban areas had a population that was more than 40 percent foreign born. Some immigrants found their way to a city through happenstance, while others joined family

Trolleys helped people travel easily around cities.

▲ Electric lights glowed in Times Square in New York City by 1910.

▲ Beginning in 1903, women in New York City could ride in female-only subway cars like this one.

members or were recruited by companies needing labor. In this way, neighborhoods, cities, regions, and industries often acquired a majority of workers from a particular locale. For example, employees at the steel mills of western Pennsylvania were predominantly Polish, while the textile factories of New York became a center for eastern European Jewish people. Domestic servants in the Northeast were primarily Irish women, while Scandinavians worked in the fish-packing industry of the Pacific Northwest.

Farmers Migrate From Country to City Many **rural-to-urban migrants** moved to cities in the 1890s. The move from farm to factory was wrenching. Former agricultural workers often found themselves working in dim light and narrow confines. The pace of work was controlled by rigid schedules, with no slow seasons. However, factory work paid wages in cash, which was sometimes scarce on family farms. The increasing difficulty of making a living on a farm, combined with the excitement and variety of city life, sparked a vigorous rural-to-urban migration.

Midwestern cities such as Minneapolis–St. Paul and Chicago exploded in the decade between 1880 and 1890. Many of the newcomers were immigrants or migrants from the rural West. They were attracted by land but also by economic opportunities. African Americans moving out of the South were also part of the migration, although on a smaller scale. The majority of these African Americans stayed in southern cities, but migrants to northern and western cities paved the way for a much larger migration after World War I.

Checkpoint What were the advantages of city life?

Technology Improves City Life

As cities swelled in size, politicians and workers struggled to keep up with the demands of growth to provide water, sewers, schools, and safety. American innovators stepped up to the task by developing new technologies to improve living conditions. The middle and upper classes benefited most from the innovations, but every city dweller was affected. Electric trolleys and subways, building codes, and other innovations kept crowded cities from slipping into pollution and chaos.

Vocabulary Builder
innovation–(ihn uh VAY shuhn) *n.* new invention or way of doing things

▲ Trolley cars, trucks, and wagons pulled by horses create a traffic jam in Chicago in 1905.

Engineers Build Skyward The cities of the late nineteenth century began to take their modern form. For the first time, skylines became recognizable by their **skyscrapers.** These ten-story and taller buildings had steel frames and used artistic designs to magnify their imposing height. Inside, they provided office space in cities that had no room left on the ground. But tall buildings were only realistic because of other new technology. In the 1850s, **Elisha Otis** developed a safety elevator that would not fall if the lifting rope broke. Central heating systems were also improved in the 1870s.

In these years, architecture emerged as a specialized career. The American Institute of Architecture was established in 1857 to professionalize the practice. Its members encouraged specific education and official licensing in order to become an architect. These professionals designed the buildings that were quickly becoming hallmarks of urban life: public schools, libraries, train stations, financial institutions, office buildings, and residences.

Electricity Powers Urban Transit In 1888, Richmond, Virginia, introduced a revolutionary invention: streetcars powered by overhead electric cables. Within a decade, every major city followed. It was the beginning of a transportation revolution. **Mass transit**—public systems that could carry large numbers of people fairly inexpensively—reshaped the nation's cities. Commuter rail lines had carried people to areas in and around cities since the 1870s. However, they were powered by coal-driven steam engines, making them slow, unreliable, and dirty. Some cities used trolleys pulled by horses, which were slower and left horse waste all over the streets. Electricity, on the other hand, was quiet, clean, and efficient. Electric cars also ran on a reliable schedule and could carry many more people than horse-drawn carts.

Electric cable cars were not practical in every city, however. Cables strung in narrow streets could block fire trucks, and traffic congestion often prevented streetcars from running on schedule. In 1897, Boston solved this problem by running the cars underground in the nation's first subway system. New York City followed in 1904.

Technology Advances

- **1868** New York City installs elevated transit with steam-driven engines
- **1873** San Francisco installs steam-driven cable cars
- **1880** First practical light bulb
- **1882** New York City installs first permanent commercial central power system
- **1888** Richmond, Virginia, introduces streetcars powered by overhead electric cables
- **1897** Boston opens public underground subway

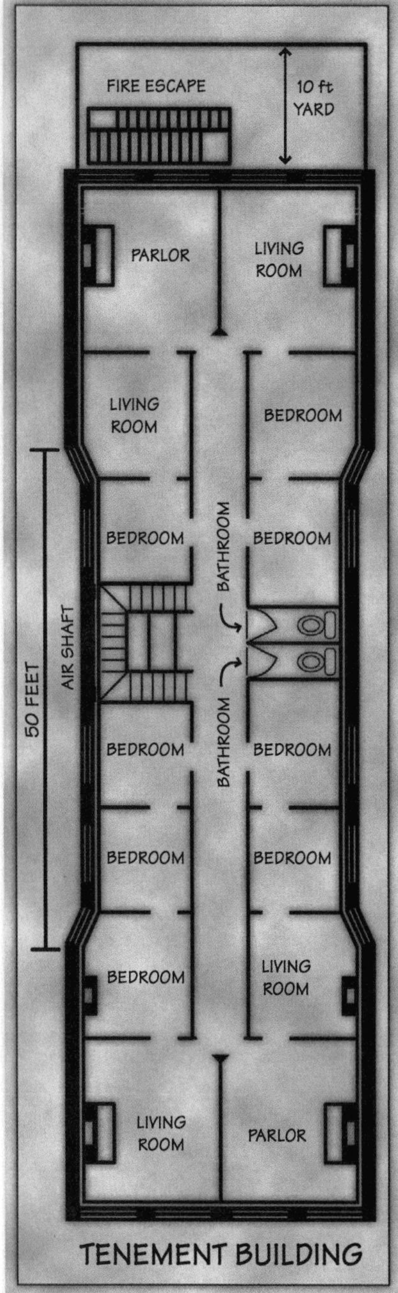

Dumbbell Tenement

Many urban workers, especially immigrants, lived in tenements with a design like the one above. The air shafts between buildings were too narrow to let in air or light. Several families often shared the same apartment, while the whole floor shared toilets located in dark, airless hallways. *What problems might tenement living cause?*

Middle and upper class people who could afford transit fares moved away from the noise and dirt of the industrial city. They built housing in the cleaner, quieter perimeter, known as streetcar **suburbs.** From there, they rode mass transit into the center of the city to work, shop, or be entertained, returning to their homes in the evening. Poorer people remained in city centers so that they could walk to work.

City Planners Control Growth As cities grew larger and more complex, architectural firms expanded to offer city-planning services designed to make cities more functional and beautiful, even as their populations skyrocketed. Architect Daniel Burnham designed his version of the ideal city for Chicago's 1893 World's Columbian Exhibition, a fair held to commemorate Columbus's arrival in the Americas. Called the White City, the integrated design included boulevards, parks, buildings, and even electric streetlights.

Mass transit allowed city planners to segregate parts of the city by zoning, or designating certain areas for particular functions. Through the 1890s, cities embraced designs that had separate zones for heavy industry, financial institutions, and residences. They also built public spaces, such as public libraries, government buildings, and universities.

Parks and recreational spaces were one of the most important aspects of city planning. Since the 1850s, cities had built parks as a solution to some of the problems of urban growth. Philadelphia purchased areas along the Schuylkill River to protect the city's water supply from industrial pollution. They hired landscape engineer **Frederick Law Olmsted** to design Fairmount Park. Olmsted had also designed New York City's Central Park and similar parks in Detroit, Michigan; Washington, D.C.; and Palo Alto, California.

✓ **Checkpoint** **How did public transportation change urban areas?**

Urban Living Creates Problems

Growing cities faced many problems caused by overcrowding and poverty. In 1890, New York's Lower East Side had a population of more than 700 people per acre. As immigrants and rural migrants arrived, they crowded into neighborhoods that already seemed to be overflowing.

Housing Conditions Deteriorate As newcomers moved into urban areas, those who could not afford to ride mass transit had to live within walking distance of the industrial plants and factories where they worked. Housing in densely populated neighborhoods was often aging and usually overcrowded. Most urban workers lived in **tenements:** low-cost multifamily housing designed to squeeze in as many families as possible. Sometimes, several families lived in one apartment or even one room. They used the space for sewing clothes or doing other piecework to earn money.

Tenement owners usually lived in the suburbs or in fashionable downtown areas, away from the industrial grime. However, they built apartments for desperate people who had little choice about where they lived. With few windows and little sanitation, tenements were unhealthy and dangerous. In 1890, journalist Jacob Riis drew attention to the plight of New York tenement dwellers:

> **Primary Source** "Go into any of the 'respectable' tenement neighborhoods . . . you shall come away agreeing [that] . . . life there does not seem worth living. . . . [T]he airshaft. . . . seems always so busy letting out foul stenches . . . that it has no time to earn its name by bringing down fresh air. . . ."
>
> —Jacob Riis, *How the Other Half Lives*

American Issues Connector

Migration and Urbanization

TRACK THE ISSUE

How does migration affect patterns of settlement in America?

Several migration trends have shaped settlement patterns in the United States. One is the movement of people to the West and to the southern "Sunbelt." Another is the movement from rural to urban areas, which then developed suburbs. These migrations have had a great influence on American life. Use the timeline below to explore this enduring issue.

1862 Homestead Act
Offer of free land brings settlers to the Great Plains.

1880–1920 Urban Migration
Millions of Americans leave farms for the city. By 1920, urban population exceeds rural population.

1910–1930 Great Migration
Southern blacks move north, giving rise to African American neighborhoods.

1950s Suburban Flight
Mass movement from central cities to suburbs begins.

1970s–Present Sunbelt Growth
Sunbelt states grow rapidly as Americans move to the warmer, southern half of the country.

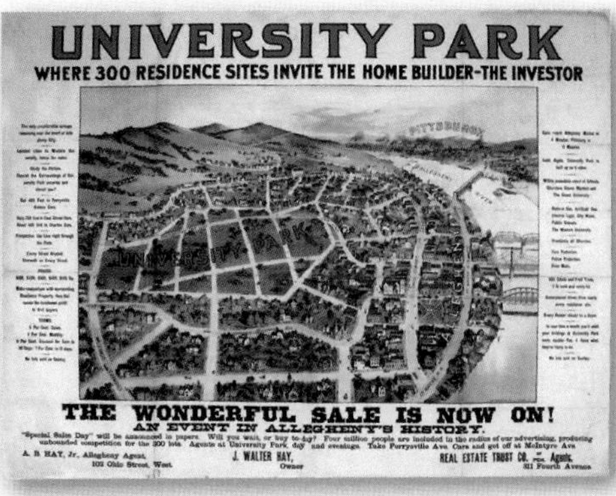

A poster advertising a "streetcar suburb" of the late nineteenth century

A modern suburb of Las Vegas, Nevada

DEBATE THE ISSUE

Expanding Suburbs American suburbs began in the 1800s but mushroomed after World War II. By 1990, nearly half of all Americans lived in suburbs. These communities offered many benefits. But critics say they have contributed to urban sprawl, traffic congestion, and other problems.

"Suburbanization represents a significant improvement in the quality of life for people who settle there. Most people who move out of their older homes do so because their needs have changed. Suburban and rural areas often meet these new needs better than older, more densely populated central cities."

—Samuel Staley, Reason Public Policy Institute

"Sprawling patterns of growth are an inefficient use of land that scatters jobs, houses, schools and shopping across the landscape. . . . It leaves people little choice but to use their auto for any trip. . . . It fragments the ecosystems that protect our drinking water and wildlife habitat and that provide recreational opportunities that we all enjoy."

—Robert J. Pirani, Regional Plan Association, New York

TRANSFER Activities

1. **Compare** How do the two quotations differ in their perspective on suburbs?
2. **Analyze** How did the growth of the suburbs affect urban life and growth?
3. **Transfer** Use the following Web site to see a video, try a WebQuest, and write in your journal. www.pearsonschool.com/ushist

City Workers
The street cleaner and police officer above worked for New York City around 1900. *Why were these city workers needed?*

Water and Sanitation Pose Risks Late nineteenth-century cities were filthy. Unpaved streets were snarled with ruts and littered with trash and even dead horses that were left to rot. Alleys between tenements were clogged with food waste and trash. Only the newest urban dwellings had indoor toilets, and the shared toilets in tenements often overflowed. These conditions were perfect for breeding epidemics, posing danger to everyone. Governments and city planners began to take steps to improve living conditions.

During the 1880s, planners attempted to regulate housing, sanitation, sewers, and public health. They began to take water from reservoirs that were separate from the polluted rivers and lakes. In the next decade, a new filtration system improved water quality even more. Private companies competed for lucrative contracts to manage water distribution. Especially in the Southwest, where water was in short supply, questions of who should profit from water delivery sent city planners into a frenzy.

Fire, Crime, and Conflict Even one careless act could have devastating consequences in crowded housing. Open fireplaces and gas lighting started fires that quickly swept through a city. A fire destroyed Chicago in 1871, killing between 200 to 300 people. It also left more than 100,000 people homeless. As the nineteenth century drew to a close, many cities developed professional firefighting teams.

At night, the streets were dangerous, yet many factory workers had to travel to and from work in the dark. In response to this challenge, professional, uniformed city police forces replaced the lone constable and the decentralized neighborhood watch. The new officers were civil servants who took exams and regularly patrolled city neighborhoods. They were aided in their task of ensuring safety by new electric streetlights.

However, the police were unable to overcome the challenge of tension between urban groups. In every big city, communities clashed along ethnic and racial fault lines. Police allowed immigrants to sleep in the station houses to avoid the violence in the streets. Even very young boys joined neighborhood gangs for safety. Race, class, and neighborhood loyalties and conflicts continued to define neighborhood life for many generations.

Checkpoint **Describe the problems created by urban living.**

SECTION 2 Assessment

Progress Monitoring *Online*
For: Self-test with vocabulary practice
www.pearsonschool.com/ushist

Comprehension

1. **Terms and People** For each item below, write a sentence explaining its significance.
   - urbanization
   - rural-to-urban migrant
   - skyscraper
   - Elisha Otis
   - mass transit
   - suburb
   - Frederick Law Olmsted
   - tenement
2. **NoteTaking Reading Skill: Identify Main Ideas** Use your flowchart to answer the Section Focus Question: What challenges did city dwellers face, and how did they meet them?

Writing About History

3. **Quick Write: Write a Proposal** Write a proposal explaining how you would fix one urban problem of the late 1800s.

Critical Thinking

4. **Draw Inferences** Why did immigrants and rural migrants move to cities?
5. **Summarize** How did city planners try to improve city life?
6. **Analyze** Why did the cities of the late nineteenth century have many problems?

American ARCHITECTURE

Skyscrapers

By the 1870s and 1880s, cities had begun to expand upward. Architects experimented with designs for taller, stronger buildings. Finally, in 1885, William LeBaron Jenney designed the Home Insurance Company building in Chicago (right). It was the first building in which a steel frame supported the outside walls, allowing more space and windows on lower floors.

▲ The Home Insurance Building in Chicago

Other projects quickly followed as engineers perfected strong but lightweight Bessemer steel supports. Louis Sullivan, Jenney's student, designed and built St. Louis's Wainwright Building in 1890. Leading architects, including Sullivan, believed that buildings must be functional first, but also artistic. This group, known as the Chicago School, designed many of the nation's early skyscrapers.

Over time the look of skyscrapers changed as architects began to experiment with materials other than stone for outer walls. Some people thought that skyscrapers were ugly and would change cities for the worse. Some cities passed laws that limited the height of buildings, allowing light to reach the streets.

▲ Cartoon showing Manhattan sinking under the weight of its skyscrapers

▶ Construction workers high above New York City

Thinking Critically

1. **Analyze Visuals** How did tall buildings change the physical landscape of urban areas?
2. **Infer** What does the cartoon tell you about the perception of skyscrapers?

SECTION 3

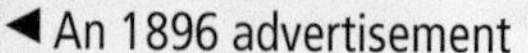

◀ An 1896 advertisement

▲ A family on a bicycle outing

WITNESS HISTORY

America Takes to Wheels

In the 1880s, the "safety bicycle" gained popularity in the United States. Cheaper than a horse, it offered an easy mode of transportation in the period before automobiles and mass transit became widespread.

"By 1893 a million bicycles were in use. It seemed as though all America had taken to wheels. . . . By physicians the therapeutic benefits were declared to be beyond compare, while dress reformers welcomed cycling as an aid to more rational fashions. . . . 'It is safe to say,' declared an expert of the census bureau in 1900, 'that few articles ever used by man have created so great a revolution in social conditions as the bicycle.'"

—Arthur M. Schlesinger, Sr., *The Rise of the City, 1878–1898*

Social and Cultural Trends

Objectives

- Explain how new types of stores and marketing changed American life.
- Analyze the ways in which Americans developed a mass culture.
- Describe the new forms of popular entertainment in the late 1800s.

Terms and People

Mark Twain
Gilded Age
conspicuous consumerism
mass culture
Joseph Pulitzer
William Randolph Hearst
Horatio Alger
vaudeville

NoteTaking

Identify Main Ideas Record the main ideas of this section in a table.

Consumerism	Mass Culture	Entertainment
• •	• •	• •

Why It Matters Novelist **Mark Twain** satirized American life in his 1873 novel, *The Gilded Age.* He depicted American society as gilded, or having a rotten core covered with gold paint. Most Americans were not as cynical. The dizzying array of things to do and buy convinced the growing middle class that modern America was in a true golden age. Still, Twain's label stuck, and historians refer to the last decades of the nineteenth century as "the **Gilded Age.**" The new lifestyle that middle-class Americans adopted during this period—shopping, sports, and reading popular magazines and newspapers—contributed to the development of a more commonly shared American culture that would persist for the next century. **Section Focus Question: What luxuries did cities offer to the middle class?**

Americans Become Consumers

Industrialization and urbanization changed the lives of American workers. More people began to work for wages rather than for themselves on farms. Some people worked in offices, drove trolleys, or became factory foremen. Even farmers made more cash as machinery improved and they sold more crops. At the same time, more products were available than ever before and at lower prices. This led to a culture of **conspicuous consumerism,** in which people wanted and bought the many new products on the market. All but the very poorest working-class laborers were able to do and buy more than they would have in the past.

Advertising Attracts Customers Rowland H. Macy opened what he called a department store in New York in 1858. It became the largest single store in America. Its sales methods—widespread advertising, a variety of goods organized into "departments," and high-quality items at fair prices—became the standard in large urban stores. By the 1870s, many big cities had department stores: Jordan Marsh in Boston, Marshall Field in Chicago, and Wanamaker's in Philadelphia.

John Wanamaker developed innovative ways to keep customers satisfied. He was the first to offer a money back guarantee. In addition, he placed large newspaper advertisements to attract customers. Later, Wanamaker became Postmaster General. In that position, he lowered the bulk shipping rates and began free delivery to rural areas, which led to a boom in the mail-order catalog business.

While department stores pioneered new marketing and sales techniques, companies began to create trademarks with distinctive logos that consumers would recognize. For the first time, consumers began to notice and buy brand-name goods. Long-distance shipping allowed consumers in Atlanta, Cincinnati, and San Francisco to purchase the same products.

Some Achieve Higher Standards of Living After the Civil War, Americans began to measure success by what they could buy. Equating purchasing power with a higher standard of living, middle-class and some working-class consumers rushed to modernize their homes and clothing styles. In this period, the cost of living decreased because manufactured products and new technology cost less. Better sanitation and medical care contributed to better health, causing life expectancy to climb. That was good news for most people.

The end of the nineteenth century is sometimes called the Victorian Era, after the queen of England. The rich were richer than ever before, and the middle class tried to imitate their lifestyle. Factory-produced clothing and prepackaged food gave homemakers a break from some activities, but rising expectations of cleanliness and more complicated meals meant that they spent more time on those tasks. Other luxuries, like indoor plumbing, also became common. On the other hand, many women had to work outside their homes to achieve a middle-class lifestyle.

Life changed for men, as well. Public transportation allowed families to live at a distance from the dirt, noise, and bustle of industry. However, it often meant that men became commuters, leaving home early in the morning and returning late in the evening. Still, their culture taught them that hard work would pay off.

✓ **Checkpoint How did consumption patterns change in the late nineteenth century?**

Mass Culture

One of the effects of the spread of transportation, communication, and advertising was that Americans all across the country became more and more alike in their consumption patterns. Rich and poor could wear the same clothing styles, although the quality of that

Changing Roles for Women
Women in the late 1800s were primarily responsible for housekeeping, though a growing number worked outside the home. *How might new appliances like these have changed women's work and expectations?*

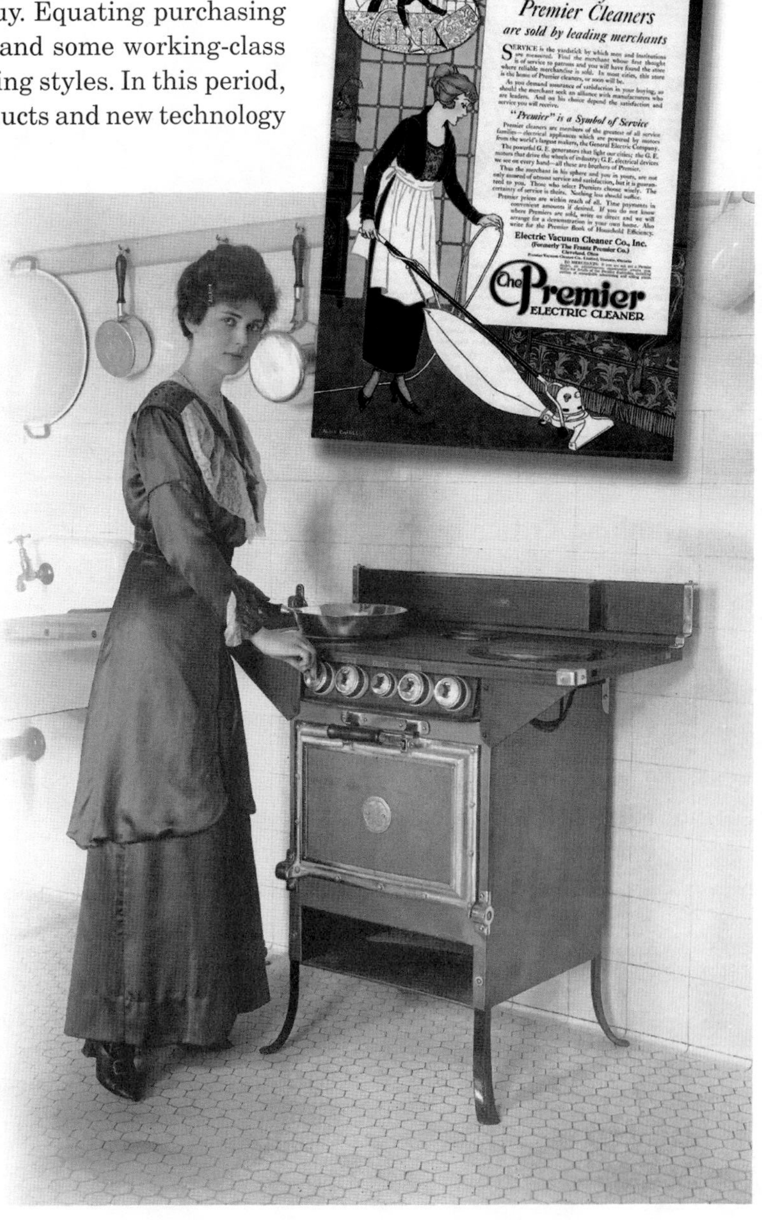

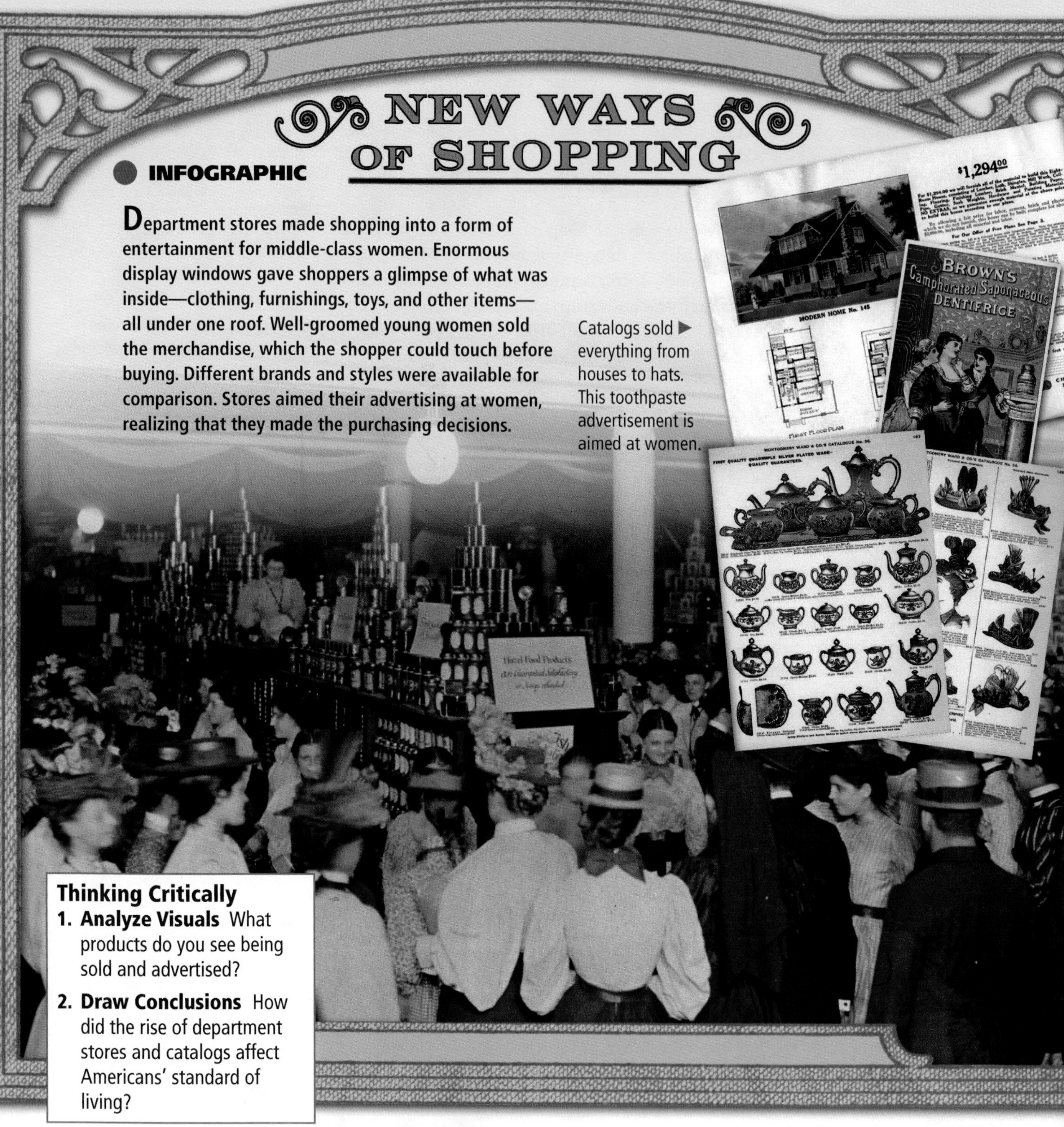

NEW WAYS OF SHOPPING

INFOGRAPHIC

Department stores made shopping into a form of entertainment for middle-class women. Enormous display windows gave shoppers a glimpse of what was inside—clothing, furnishings, toys, and other items—all under one roof. Well-groomed young women sold the merchandise, which the shopper could touch before buying. Different brands and styles were available for comparison. Stores aimed their advertising at women, realizing that they made the purchasing decisions.

Catalogs sold ► everything from houses to hats. This toothpaste advertisement is aimed at women.

Thinking Critically

1. **Analyze Visuals** What products do you see being sold and advertised?
2. **Draw Conclusions** How did the rise of department stores and catalogs affect Americans' standard of living?

clothing varied. Household gadgets, toys, and food preferences were often the same from house to house. This phenomenon is known as **mass culture.**

Newspapers Circulate Far and Wide The newspapers of the Gilded Age both reflected and helped create mass culture. Between 1870 and 1900, the number of newspapers increased from about 600 to more than 1,600. No one knew more about newspapers than **Joseph Pulitzer,** a Hungarian immigrant who had fought in the Civil War. Active in Missouri politics in the 1870s, Pulitzer moved to New York in the 1880s, where he started a morning paper, the *World*. It was so successful that Pulitzer soon started publishing the *Evening*

World. The papers were inexpensive because they were supported in part by businesses that placed advertisements in their pages.

The job of a newspaper, Pulitzer believed, was to inform people and to stir up controversy. His newspapers were sensationalistic, filled with exposés of political corruption, comics, sports, and illustrations. They were designed to get the widest possible readership, rather than simply to report the news. Pulitzer soon found a competitor in **William Randolph Hearst,** whose *Morning Journal* employed the same tactics. Their sensational styles sold many papers.

At the same time, ethnic and special-interest publishers catered to the array of urban dwellers, especially immigrants. The Philadelphia *Tribune*, begun in the 1880s, targeted the African American market. In New York, there were six Italian-language papers by 1910. Each sold more than 10,000 copies daily.

Vocabulary Builder
cater–(KAYT uhr) *v.* to supply something that is wanted or needed by a particular group

Literature and the Arts Flourish Mark Twain was not the only author to take a critical look at society during the Gilded Age. Novels that explored harsh realities were popular. Stephen Crane exposed the slums of New York in his *Maggie: A Girl of the Streets* (1893). He later wrote *The Red Badge of Courage,* which explored the psychological aspects of war. Other novelists focused on moral issues. **Horatio Alger** wrote about characters who succeeded by hard work, while Henry James and Edith Wharton questioned a society based upon rigid rules of conduct. Playwrights such as John Augustin Daly mirrored Twain's disapproval of the Gilded Age.

The vitality of city life also inspired graphic artists. Philadelphia's Thomas Eakins painted a larger-than-life illustration of a medical operation, complete with exposed flesh. Painter Robert Henri and his associates developed a style of painting known as the Ashcan School which dramatized the starkness and squalor of New York City slums and street life.

Education Newspapers and literature flourished, in part, because more Americans could read. Public education expanded rapidly. Slowly in the South and rapidly in the North, grade-school education became compulsory. Many locales provided public high schools, although only a small percentage of young people attended. In 1870, the nation had only a few hundred high schools; in 1910, there were more than 5,000. Kindergartens also appeared as a way to help working-class mothers. As a result, the literacy rate climbed to nearly 90 percent by 1900.

Schools taught courses in science, woodworking, and drafting, providing skills that workers needed in budding industries. The curriculum also included civics and business training. Urban leaders counted on schools to help Americanize immigrants, teaching them English and shaping them into good citizens. Teacher-training schools responded to the call. Not only did they grow in number, but they also developed more sophisticated ideas about teaching and learning. Reformer John Dewey sought to enhance student learning by introducing new teaching methods.

Institutions of higher education also began to provide specialized training for urban careers. Today's liberal arts curriculum was largely designed during this era. A few of

HISTORY MAKERS

John Dewey (1859–1952)
Dewey was an influential philosopher, reformer, and professor. His child-centered philosophy shaped progressive education reform. He argued that students learn by doing activities that teach them to answer their own questions, rather than by memorizing from books and lectures. His opponents argued that orderly classrooms were better for learning. Dewey's ideas declined in popularity by the 1950s, but they remain influential today.

U.S. Literacy Rates, 1870–1920

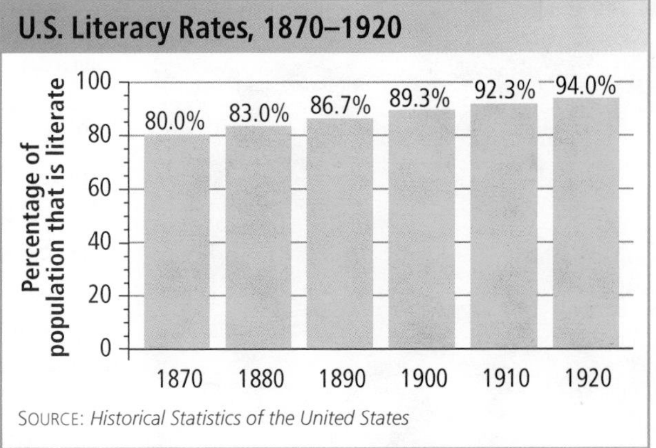

SOURCE: *Historical Statistics of the United States*

the new careers—teaching, social work, and nursing—were open to middle-class women. This led to an upsurge in women's colleges, since women were barred from many men's colleges. However, many state universities began to accept women into their classes.

Limited access to white institutions led to a growth in schools and colleges for African Americans. Across the South, the number of normal schools, agricultural colleges, and industrial-training schools mushroomed as the children of newly freed slaves set out to prepare to compete as free people.

✓ **Checkpoint** **What factors contributed to mass culture?**

New Forms of Popular Entertainment

Urban areas with thousands of people became centers for new types of entertainment in the Gilded Age. Clubs, music halls, and sports venues attracted large crowds with time and money to spend. The middle class began to take vacations at this time, while the working classes looked for opportunities to escape from the busy city, even if just for a day.

City Dwellers Escape to Amusement Parks In 1884, Lamarcus Thompson opened the world's first roller coaster. At ten cents a ride, Thompson averaged more than $600 per day in income. The roller coaster was the first ride to open at Coney Island—the nation's best-known amusement park—at the edge of the Atlantic Ocean in New York City. Soon, Coney Island added a hotel and a horse-racing track. Similar amusement parks, located within easy reach of a city, were built around the country.

Going to the Circus
Circuses such as the Ringling Brothers and the Barnum & Bailey began in the late nineteenth century, traveling around the country to perform before large audiences.

While earlier generations had enjoyed a picnic in the park, the new urbanite—even those with limited means—willingly paid the entry fees for these new, more thrilling, entertainments. Urban residents of all ethnicities and races could be found at these amusement spots, though each group was usually relegated to a particular area of the parks. The parks represented a day-long vacation for city laborers who could not afford to take the long seaside vacations enjoyed by the wealthy.

Outdoor Events Draw Audiences In 1883, "Buffalo Bill" Cody threw a Fourth of July celebration near his ranch in Nebraska. He offered prizes for competitions in riding, roping, and shooting. So many people attended that Cody took his show on the road, booking performances at points along railroad lines. Buffalo Bill's Wild West Show toured America and Europe, shaping the world's romantic notion of the American West. The show included markswoman Annie Oakley and the Sioux leader Sitting Bull, as well as displays of riding, roping, and horse-and-rider stunts.

Religious-inspired entertainment also grew in popularity. The Chautauqua Circuit, a kind of summer camp that opened in 1874, sponsored lectures and entertainment along New York's Chautauqua Lake. It began as a summer school for Methodist Sunday school teachers. Soon, Chautauqua leaders were transporting their tents to small towns all across America to deliver comic storytelling, bands and singers, and lectures on politics or morals. A family might stay at a camp for as long as two weeks. Many people saw their first "moving pictures," or movies, in a Chautauqua tent. Theodore Roosevelt called Chautauqua "the most American thing in America."

New Entertainment in the Cities Cities, with their dense populations, offered many glitzy shows and various types of entertainment. At first, **vaudeville** shows were a medley of musical drama, songs, and off-color comedy. In 1881, an entrepreneur named Tony Pastor opened a theater in New York, aiming to provide families with a "straight, clean variety show." By 1900, a few companies owned chains of vaudeville theaters, stretching all across the country.

Performance theater was not the only option. Movie theaters, called nickelodeons, soon introduced motion pictures, charging a nickel for admission. Films such as *The Great Train Robbery* became wildly popular. In music halls, ragtime bands created a style of music that would later evolve into jazz.

Some cities—including Philadelphia, Chicago, Atlanta, Buffalo, and Omaha—hosted exhibitions of new technology and entertainment. These extravaganzas stretched Americans' imaginations to see a future filled with machines and gadgets. Millions of visitors saw everything from steam engines to typewriters and telephones. In many ways, the new amusements mirrored urban life, filled with variety, drama, bright colors, and a very fast pace.

A Special Honor

This 1911 baseball card shows the pitcher Cy Young. He had the most wins of any pitcher in Major League history.

Spectator Sports Attract Fans Baseball—America's national sport—had been around for a number of years before the National League organized it into a business in 1876. Baseball soon became a public show. Major cities built stadiums that seated thousands, like Boston's Fenway Park. Billboards advertised everything from other sports to toothpaste and patent medicines. There were even baseball songs. The most famous—"Take Me Out to the Ball Game"—was written in 1908. Until 1887, teams sometimes included African American players. After the Chicago White Stockings refused to play against a team that had a black player, separate African American teams emerged by 1900.

Like baseball, horse racing, bicycle racing, boxing, and football became popular spectator sports. University football clubs formed on campuses around the country, but they faced a public outcry at the violence of the game. Rule changes made it into the sport we know today. Meanwhile, James Naismith invented basketball at the Springfield, Massachusetts, YMCA in 1891. Heroes emerged in major sports, particularly in boxing, as immigrants and ethnic Americans rooted for the boxers who shared their background.

Checkpoint **What new forms of entertainment began in the late nineteenth century?**

SECTION 3 Assessment

Progress Monitoring *Online*
For: Self-test with vocabulary practice
www.pearsonschool.com/ushist

Comprehension

1. **Terms and People** What do the following terms and people have in common?
   - Mark Twain
   - Gilded Age
   - conspicuous consumerism
   - mass culture
   - Joseph Pulitzer
   - William Randolph Hearst
   - Horatio Alger
   - vaudeville

2. **NoteTaking Reading Skill: Identify Main Ideas** Use your completed table to answer the Section Focus Question: What luxuries did cities offer to the middle class?

Writing About History

3. **Quick Write: Make a Plan** Write an itinerary for a weekend trip to a city in 1900. Consider what kinds of activities a first-time visitor from the country might like to experience.

Critical Thinking

4. **Analyze** What factors contributed to consumerism?
5. **Summarize** Describe middle-class entertainment.
6. **Make Comparisons** How did middle-class urban life differ from life for the urban poor?

CHAPTER 14

Quick Study Guide

Progress Monitoring *Online*
For: Self-test with vocabulary practice
www.pearsonschool.com/ushist

Foreign-Born Population

City	1870	1890	1910
New York, NY	44.5%	42.2%	40.8%
Chicago, IL	48.4%	41.0%	35.9%
San Francisco, CA	49.3%	42.4%	34.1%
Boston, MA	35.1%	35.3%	36.3%
Cleveland, OH	41.8%	37.2%	35.0%
Philadelphia, PA	27.2%	25.7%	24.8%
St. Louis, MO	36.1%	25.4%	18.4%
Detroit, MI	44.5%	39.7%	33.8%
Milwaukee, WI	47.3%	38.9%	29.8%
Scranton, PA	45.3%	34.0%	27.0%

SOURCE: U.S. Census Bureau

Rural and Urban Population

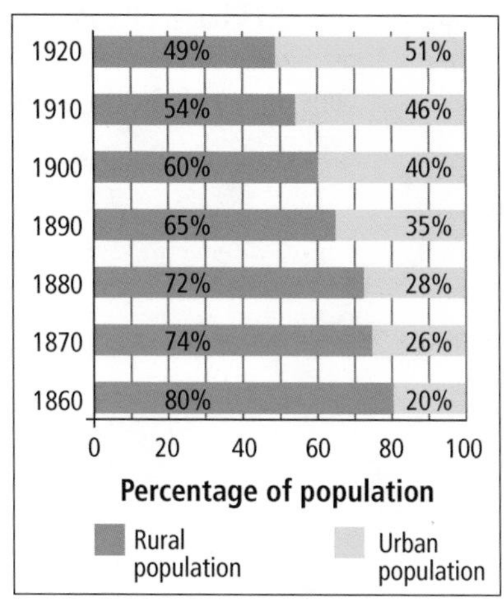

SOURCE: U.S. Census Bureau

Urban Problems

Problem →	Solution
Crowding →	Skyscrapers, city planning, parks
Poor housing →	Building codes
Danger →	Streetlights and police forces
Potential for fire →	Electric lights and fire departments
Poor sanitation →	Public-health departments

Aspects of Mass Culture

Mass Culture

- Advertising
- Department stores and mail-order catalogs
- Factory-produced clothing
- Prepackaged food
- Newspapers
- Public education
- Entertainment

Entertainment

- Amusement parks
- Outdoor shows
- The Chautauqua Circuit
- Vaudeville shows
- Movie theaters
- Exhibitions and fairs
- Spectator sports

Quick Study Timeline

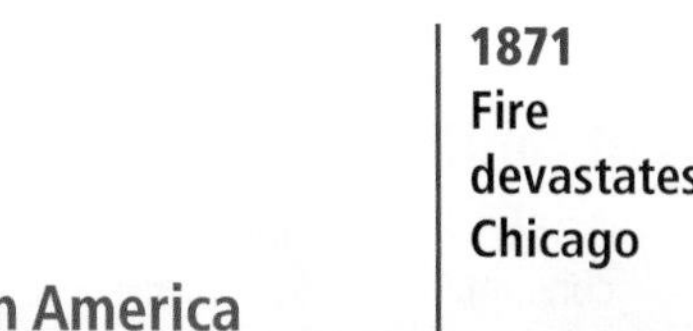

In America

1871 Fire devastates Chicago

1882 Chinese Exclusion Act closes the door to new immigration from China

1892 A processing center for immigrants opens at Ellis Island

Presidential Terms U. S. Grant 1869–1877; R. Hayes 1877–1881; J. Garfield 1881; C. Arthur 1881–1885; G. Cleveland 1885–1889; B. Harrison 1889–1893

1870 — 1880 — 1890

Around the World

1871 Britain legalizes labor unions

1881 The czar persecutes Jews in Russia

1894 Russia's last czar, Nicholas II, begins his reign

American Issues Connector

By connecting prior knowledge with what you have learned in this chapter, you can gradually build your understanding of enduring questions that still affect America today. Answer the questions below. Then, use your American Issues Connector study guide (or go online: www.pearsonschool.com/ushist).

Issues You Learned About

● **Migration and Urbanization** Immigrants have overcome many obstacles in their quest to make better lives for themselves in the United States.

1. Millions of immigrants moved to American cities in the late 1800s and early 1900s. Write a short narrative describing the life of one of these immigrants. Consider the following:
   - reasons for immigration
   - the journey to America
   - arrival at processing stations
   - life in the United States
   - the process of adopting American culture

● **Technology and Society** New technology that developed in the 1880s changed the landscape of cities.

2. How did skyscrapers reflect technology merged with art?
3. Explain the inventions that made skyscrapers a more practical form of construction.
4. Why were commuter rail lines that were powered by electricity an improvement over earlier forms of commuter rail lines?

● **Education and American Society** During the Gilded Age, education became available to more Americans.

5. What is a likely reason that the government decided to use tax dollars to support schools for all American children?
6. How might John Dewey have recommended that students at teacher-training schools study for their future careers?
7. Why was there a growth in women's colleges and African American colleges during this period?

Connect to Your World — Activity

U.S. Immigration Policy: Current Immigration Laws
Should the United States follow a policy of allowing free and open immigration? Should the United States pass new laws limiting the number of immigrants allowed into the country? These questions, and others concerning immigration, continue to trouble Americans from all backgrounds, socioeconomic classes, and professions. Decide your own answers to these questions by going online or to your local library to learn more about the current debate over immigration. Learn more about how Americans feel about immigration and why. Then, choose one side of the issue, and write an opening statement that you could present in a class or school debate.

1897 Boston opens America's first subway system

1907 Immigration to the United States reaches an all-time high

1910 A processing center for immigrants opens at Angel Island in San Francisco Bay

G. Cleveland 1893–1897 | W. McKinley 1897–1901 | T. Roosevelt 1901–1909 | W. Taft 1909–1913 | W. Wilson 1913–1921

1900 | 1910 | 1920

1901 The first "foolproof" vacuum cleaner is invented in England

1910 The Mexican Revolution begins

1914 World War I begins in Europe

History Interactive
For: Interactive timeline
www.pearsonschool.com/ushist

Chapter Assessment

Terms and People

1. Who were the **"new" immigrants**? What characteristics did they share?
2. What were **Ellis Island** and **Angel Island**? What happened at these locations?
3. Define **mass transit.** How did mass transit impact urban populations?
4. What was the **Gilded Age**? What ideas about American society did it express?
5. Who were **Joseph Pulitzer** and **William Randolph Hearst**? How did people respond to their work?

Focus Questions

The focus question for this chapter is **How did American urban life change between 1875 and 1914?** Build an answer to this big question by answering the focus questions for Sections 1 through 3 and the Critical Thinking questions that follow.

Section 1

6. Why did immigrants come to the United States, and what impact did they have upon society?

Section 2

7. What challenges did city dwellers face, and how did they meet them?

Section 3

8. What luxuries did cities offer to the middle class?

Critical Thinking

9. **Analyze Visuals** Study the photograph at right. Then, answer the question that follows: How do the activities of these immigrant children support the argument that newcomers were taught to feel patriotism toward their adopted country?
10. **Draw Conclusions** Do you think that immigrants who lived in urban ghettoes had a harder or an easier time adapting to American culture than immigrants in other locations?
11. **Compare Points of View** How did the views of settlement house workers differ from nativists over immigration?
12. **Explain Causes** What led many rural Americans to migrate to the cities in the 1890s?
13. **Problem Solving** What do you think was the most important step taken by city planners and government officials to improve city life? Explain your answer.
14. **Analyze Information** Could the United States between 1870 and 1914 be considered a "land of opportunity"? Explain your answer.
15. **Make Generalizations** What types of subjects did public high schools in the 1900s emphasize and why?
16. **Synthesize Information** Explain the relationship between the growth of the middle class, changes in the economy, and new forms of mass entertainment.

Writing About History

Writing a Proposal In the late nineteenth and early twentieth centuries, more immigrants than ever before arrived in America. Most of them settled in cities, although they usually came from rural areas. Write a proposal for a program that would help immigrants adjust to life in an American city in 1900. Focus on the most challenging aspect of an immigrant's life in an American city.

Prewriting

- Decide what type of organization will run your program. Will it be a local government, state government, federal government, or another organization?
- Decide what challenge(s) your program would address and which immigrants it would serve.
- Take notes about these topics.
- Gather additional resources.

Drafting

- Make an outline that includes the steps in your plan and explains why each step is necessary.
- Write an introduction that explains why the proposal is important, and then write a body and a conclusion.

Revising

- Use the guidelines on page SH16 of the Writing Handbook to revise your draft.

Document-Based Assessment

The Impact of Immigration, 1870 to 1910

From 1870 to 1910, more than 20 million immigrants entered the United States from Europe. How did immigrants change American society? What impact did immigrants have on the United States economy? Use your knowledge of immigration and Documents A, B, C, and D to answer questions 1 through 4.

Document A
Occupations of Immigrants, 1901

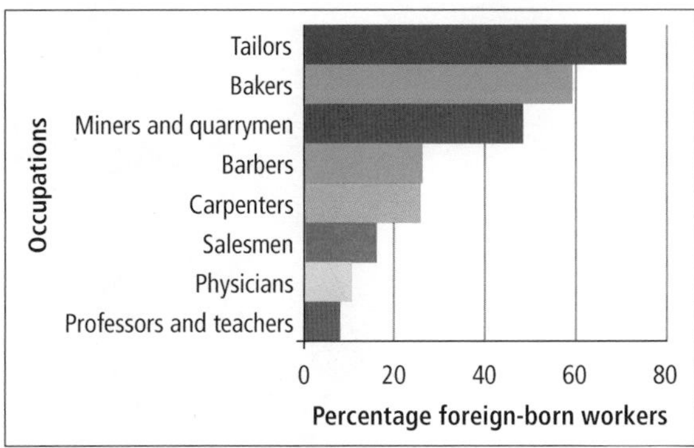

SOURCE: *Reports of the Industrial Commission on Immigration, 1901*

Document B
Uncle Sam is a man of strong features.

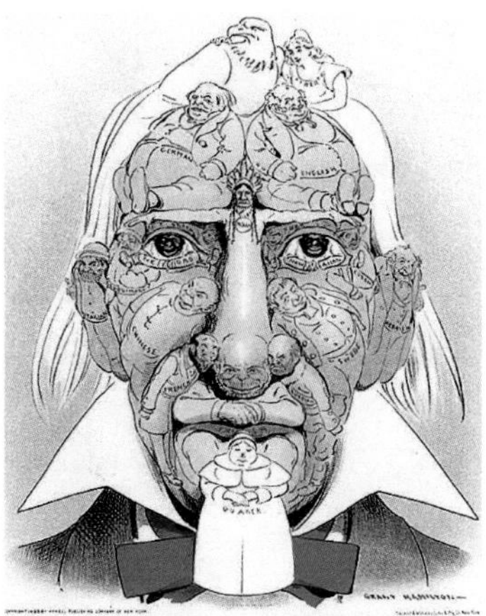

Document C

"At night we got homesick for our fine green mountains. We read all the news about home in our Lithuanian Chicago newspaper, *The Katalikas*. It is a good paper and gives all the news. . . . I joined the Cattle Butcher's Union. This union is honest and has done me a great deal of good. It has raised my wages. I am getting $11 [a week]. . . . It has given me more time to read and speak and enjoy life like an American. . . . With more time and more money I live much better and I am very happy. So is Alexandria. She came a year ago and has learned to speak English already. . . . [W]e belong to a Lithuanian society that gives two picnics in summer and two balls in winter. . . . I go one night a week to the Lithuanian Concertina Club. . . . The union is doing another good thing. . . . I help the movement by being an interpreter for the other Lithuanians who come in. . . ."

—*Antanas Kaztauskis, "From Lithuania to the Chicago Stockyards,"* Independent, *Aug. 4, 1904*

Document D

"Upon taking control of the Commonwealth of Massachusetts, the American Party proposed and passed legislation aimed at restricting the strength of the growing Irish community in Boston. The most drastic measure proposed was a constitutional amendment requiring that immigrants wait 21 years after naturalization before they could become voting citizens of the Commonwealth. . . . The Know-Nothing General Court also proposed a legislative redistricting that would reduce the number of seats in predominantly immigrant Boston. This benefited the rural areas, which were predominantly populated by 'Yankee' descendents of English settlers."

—*Steven Taylor, "Progressive Nativism: The Know-Nothing Party in Massachusetts,"* Historical Journal of Massachusetts, *2000*

---

1. According to Document A, which occupation employed the highest percentage of immigrants?
   A Teaching
   B Retail
   C Mining
   D Medicine

2. The illustrator of Document B would probably agree that
   A Only native-born white Protestants are really Americans.
   B People of many nationalities make America strong.
   C The government should restrict immigration.
   D Immigrants quickly adapt American ways of life.

3. What can you conclude about the goal of the American Party in Massachusetts?
   A It passed laws to encourage Irish immigration.
   B It wanted immigrants to move from rural areas into cities.
   C It attempted to limit the political participation of Irish immigrants.
   D It proposed legislation to increase the number of legislative seats in Boston.

4. **Writing Task** How did immigrants change American society? What impact did immigrants have on the United States economy? Use your knowledge of the chapter content and specific evidence from the primary sources above to support your opinion.

CHAPTER

15 The South and West Transformed

1865–1900

WITNESS HISTORY

Businesses Running Full Blast

The lure of gold and silver in the American West attracted prospectors from all over the country and the world. As mining camps developed, the need for merchants, innkeepers, lawyers, and others arose. Tradesmen came to alleviate this need and to enjoy the benefits of the new frontier. The western boom was so great that towns grew up in the blink of an eye, as discovered by this late 1800s miner.

"I know you won't believe it but it is true. I went out of town for five days and where the timber stood thick as I went out, when I came back it was all built up solid. On both sides of a street . . . there were stores selling goods, restaurants, boarding house, offices and all kinds of businesses running full blast, and not in tents, but in houses."

◄ Main Street of Lower Creede, Colorado, *c.* 1880s

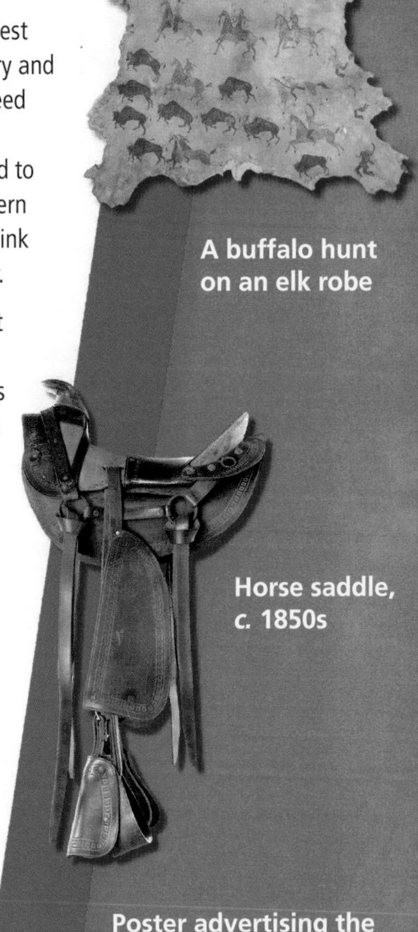

A buffalo hunt on an elk robe

Horse saddle, *c.* 1850s

Chapter Preview

Chapter Focus Question: How did the economy, society, and culture of the South and West change after the Civil War?

Section 1
The New South

Section 2
Westward Expansion and the American Indians

Section 3
Transforming the West

Poster advertising the Grand Opening of the Union Pacific Railroad

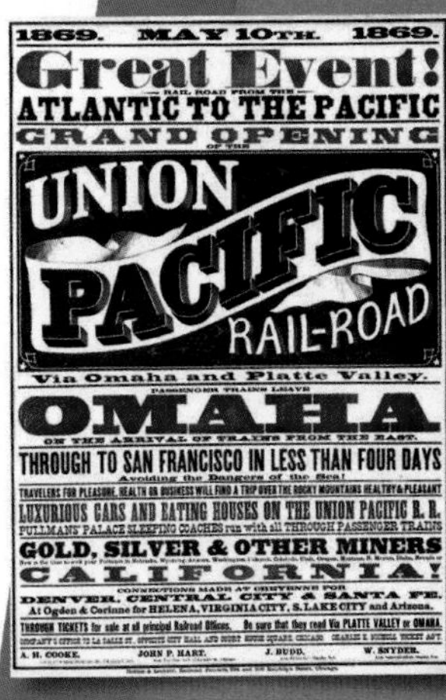

Use the **Quick Study Timeline** at the end of this chapter to preview chapter events.

Note Taking Study Guide *Online*
For: Note Taking and American Issues Connector
www.pearsonschool.com/ushist

SECTION 1

▲ A worker in an Alabama textile mill

WITNESS HISTORY

Creating a "New South"

After the Civil War, forward-looking southern businessmen sought ways to diversify the southern economy and develop more industry. Henry Grady, editor of an Atlanta newspaper, described his vision of a "New South":

> "There was a South of slavery and secession—that South is dead. There is a South of union and freedom—that South, thank God, is living, breathing, growing every hour. . . . The old South rested everything on slavery and agriculture, unconscious that these could neither give nor maintain healthy growth. The new South presents a perfect democracy, . . . a social system compact and closely knitted, less splendid on the surface, but stronger at the core . . . and a diversified industry that meets the complex needs of this complex age."
>
> —Henry Grady, 1886

The New South

Objectives

- Explain how the southern economy changed in the late 1800s.
- Analyze how southern farmers consolidated their political power.
- Describe the experience of African Americans in the changing South.

Terms and People

cash crop
Farmers' Alliance
Civil Rights Act of 1875

NoteTaking

Reading Skill: Identify Supporting Details As you read, fill in a concept web like the one below with details about how the South changed after the Civil War. Add additional circles as needed.

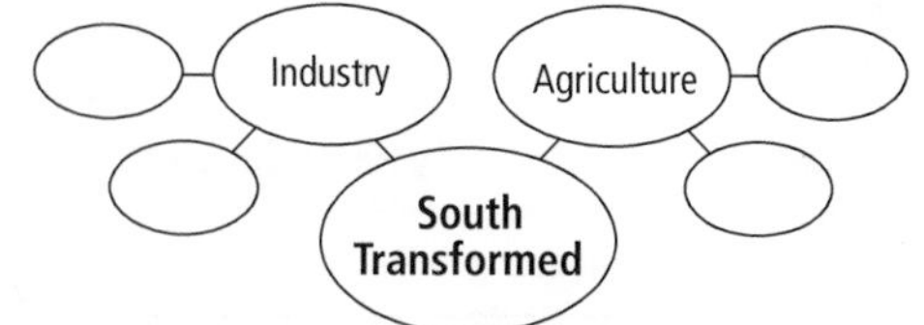

Why It Matters After Reconstruction ended, the South struggled to develop its industry. Although there were pockets of success, the South was not able to overcome its economic and social obstacles to industrial development overall. As a result, the South remained largely agricultural and poor. **Section Focus Question: How did the southern economy and society change after the Civil War?**

Industries and Cities Grow

During the Gilded Age, many southern white leaders envisioned a modernized economy that included not only agriculture but also mills and factories. Henry Grady was among those who called for a "New South" that would use its resources to develop industry.

New Industries Spread Through the South Before the Civil War, the South had shipped its raw materials—including cotton, wood, and iron ore—abroad or to the North for processing into finished goods. In the 1880s, northern money backed textile factories in western North Carolina, South Carolina, and Georgia, as well as cigar and lumber production, especially in North Carolina and Virginia. Investment in coal-, iron-, and steel-processing created urban centers in Nashville, Tennessee, and Birmingham, Alabama.

During this time, farming also became somewhat more diversified, with an increase in grain, tobacco, and fruit crops. Even the landscape of farming changed as smaller farms replaced large plantations.

Railroads Link Cities and Towns A key component of industrialization is transportation. To meet this need, southern rail lines expanded, joining rural areas with urban hubs such as Mobile and Montgomery in Alabama and the bustling ports of New Orleans, Louisiana, and Charleston, South Carolina. Yet, by the 1880s, only two rail lines—from Texas to Chicago and from Tennessee to Washington, D.C.—linked southern freight to northern markets.

To combat economic isolation, southerners lobbied the federal government for economic help and used prison labor to keep railroad construction costs down. Gradually, rail connections supported the expansion of small hubs such as Meridian, Mississippi, and Americus, Georgia. The new cities of Atlanta, Dallas, and Nashville developed and began rivaling the old.

Vocabulary Builder
component–(kuhm POH nuhnt) *n.* any of the main parts of a whole

Southern Economic Recovery Is Limited Despite these changes, the southern economy continued to lag behind the rest of the country. While the North was able to build on its strong industrial base, the South first had to repair the damages of war. Moreover, industry rests on a three-legged stool: natural resources, labor, and capital investment. The South had plenty of the first but not enough of the second and third.

Sustained economic development requires workers who are well trained and productive as well as consumers who can spend. Public education in the South was limited. In fact, the South spent less than any other part of the country on education, and it lacked the technical and engineering schools that could have trained the people needed by industry. At the same time, low wages discouraged skilled workers from coming to the South, and the lure of higher wages or better conditions elsewhere siphoned off southern workers.

Additionally, very few southern banks had survived the war, and those that were functioning had fewer assets than their northern competitors. Most of the South's wealth was concentrated in the hands of a few people. Poor tenant farmers and low-paid factory workers did not have cash to deposit. With few strong banks, southern financiers were often dependent on northern banks to start or expand businesses or farms. The southern economy suffered from this lack of labor and capital.

✓ **Checkpoint** **What factors limited southern economic recovery?**

Industry Develops in the South
With large deposits of iron ore and coal, Alabama became a center of the steel industry in the late 1800s. This photograph shows workers outside the ironworks at Ensley, Alabama. *What evidence of a "New South" can you see in this photograph?*

Wholesale Price of Cotton, 1865–1890

Cents per pound

SOURCE: *Historical Statistics of the United States*

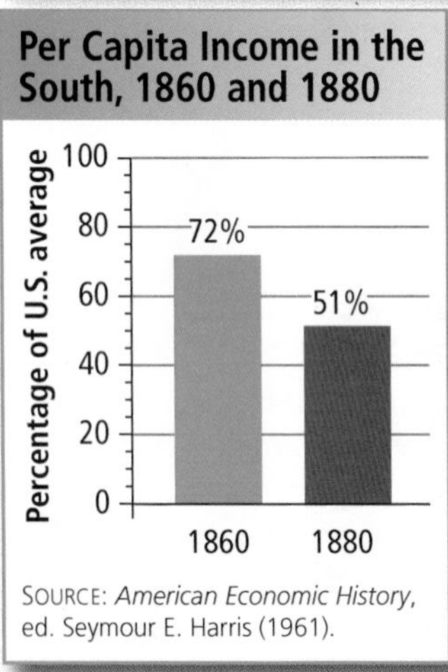

Farming in the New South
After the Civil War, farmers in the South continued to rely heavily on cotton. This made them particularly vulnerable when pests such as the boll weevil threatened their crops. *What do the graphs indicate about the economic situation in the South after the Civil War?*

Southern Farmers Face Hard Times

Before the Civil War, most southern planters had concentrated on such crops as cotton and tobacco, which were grown not for their own use but to be sold for cash. The lure of the **cash crop** continued after the war, despite efforts to diversify. One farm magazine recommended that "instead of cotton fields, and patches of grain, let us have fields of grain, and patches of cotton."

Cotton Dominates Agriculture Cotton remained the centerpiece of the southern agricultural economy. Although at the end of the Civil War cotton production had dropped to about one third of its prewar levels, by the late 1880s, it had rebounded. However, during the war, many European textile factories had found suppliers outside the South, and the price of cotton had fallen. Now, the South's abundance of cotton simply depressed the price further.

Dependence on one major crop was extremely risky. In the case of southern cotton, it was the boll weevil that heralded disaster. The boll weevil, a beetle which could destroy an entire crop of cotton, appeared in Texas in the early 1890s. Over the next decade, the yield from cotton cultivation in some states dropped by more than 50 percent. By 1900, cotton's appeal and its problems dominated the southern economy, much as they had before the Civil War.

Farmers Band Together Faced with serious difficulties, Texas farmers in the 1870s began to organize and to negotiate as a group for lower prices for supplies. The idea spread. Local organizations linked together in what became known as the **Farmers' Alliance.** These organizations soon connected farmers not only in the South but also in the West. Farmers' Alliance members tried to convince the government to force railroads to lower freight prices so members could get their crops to markets outside the South at reduced rates. Because of regularly rising rates, the Alliances also wanted the government to regulate the interest that banks could charge for loans.

✓ **Checkpoint** **Why did southern farmers face hard times?**

Black Southerners Gain and Lose

The Thirteenth, Fourteenth, and Fifteenth amendments had changed African Americans' legal status. Over time, however, these legal gains were pushed back by a series of Supreme Court decisions.

Going to School
After the Civil War, African Americans for the first time had an opportunity to get an education, although usually in segregated classrooms like this one.

Political and Economic Gains Citizenship afforded black southerners the right to vote in local and federal elections, and for a few black people it provided the means to serve their country in government or in the military. Some African Americans opened urban businesses or bought farmland. In developing the Farmers' Alliances, white leaders in some places invited black farmers to join, reasoning that the alliance would be stronger if all farmers took part. In this way, the Farmers' Alliances offered a glimpse of the political possibilities of interracial cooperation.

Perhaps the most important gain for southern African Americans, however, was access to education. Hundreds of basic-literacy schools and dozens of teachers' colleges, supported by the federal government or by northern philanthropists, enabled African Americans to learn to read and write.

White Backlash Begins Many realities of southern black lives did not change much, however. Some white southerners focused their own frustrations on trying to reverse the gains African Americans had achieved during Reconstruction.

Groups such as the Ku Klux Klan used terror and violence to intimidate African Americans. Meanwhile, many African American freedoms were whittled away. Churches that were once integrated became segregated. New laws supported the elimination of black government officials.

Congress's enactment of the **Civil Rights Act of 1875** guaranteed black patrons the right to ride trains and use public facilities such as hotels. However, in a series of civil rights' cases decided in 1883, the Supreme Court ruled that decisions about who could use public accommodations was a local issue, to be governed by state or local laws. Southern municipalities took advantage of this ruling to further limit the rights of African Americans.

✓ **Checkpoint** **How did southern blacks lose their rights?**

SECTION 1 Assessment

Progress Monitoring *Online*
For: Self-test with vocabulary practice
www.pearsonschool.com/ushist

Comprehension

1. **Terms and People** For each term below, write a sentence explaining its role in southern life.
   - cash crop
   - Farmers' Alliance
   - Civil Rights Act of 1875
2. **NoteTaking Reading Skill: Identify Supporting Details** Use your concept web to answer the Section Focus Question: How did the southern economy and society change after the Civil War?

Writing About History

3. **Quick Write: Define a Topic for an Oral Presentation** Begin planning an oral presentation on the economic recovery of the South after the Civil War. First, make a list of what you already know about that topic. Then, narrow down the list to focus on a specific topic. Describe this topic in one sentence.

Critical Thinking

4. **Categorize** What positive steps did the South take to industrialize after the Civil War?
5. **Recognize Cause and Effect** How did southern agriculture suffer from the domination of cotton?
6. **Make Comparisons** How did southern African Americans both gain and lose civil rights after the Civil War?

SECTION 2

◄ Sioux chief in the early 1900s

Painted buffalo hide ►

WITNESS HISTORY

My Heart Feels Like Bursting

Conflict between Native Americans and white settlers began almost from the moment the first Europeans arrived. The clash came to a head with the Indian Wars in the late 1800s. Satanta, a Kiowa chief, clearly expressed the Indian sentiment:

> "I don't want to settle. I love to roam over the prairies. There I feel free and happy, but when we settle down we grow pale and die. . . . A long time ago this land belonged to our fathers; but when I go up to the river I see camps of soldiers on its banks. These soldiers cut down my timber; they kill my buffalo; and when I see that my heart feels like bursting. . . . This is our country. . . . We have to protect ourselves. We have to save our country. We have to fight for what is ours."
>
> —Chief Satanta, 1867

Westward Expansion and the American Indians

Objectives

- Compare the ways Native Americans and white settlers viewed and used the land.
- Describe the conflicts between white settlers and Indians.
- Evaluate the impact of the Indian Wars.

Terms and People

reservation	Chief Joseph
Sand Creek Massacre	Wounded Knee
Sitting Bull	assimilate
Battle of the Little Big Horn	Dawes General Allotment Act

NoteTaking

Reading Skill: Identify Supporting Details As you read, fill in a concept web with details about Native Americans west of the Mississippi.

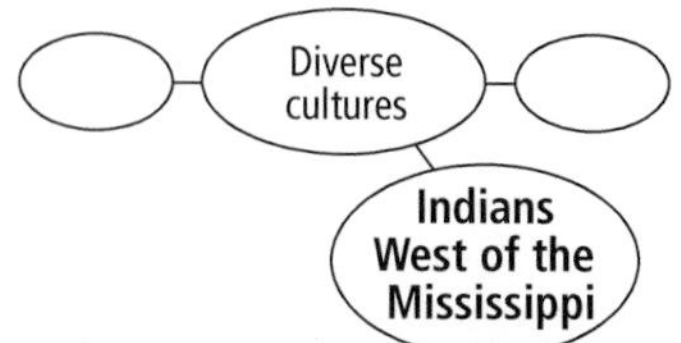

Why It Matters In 1787, the Constitution granted sole power for regulating trade with the Native Americans to the federal government. This is just one of many decrees that would establish the long, strained relationship between the federal government and Native Americans. During the 1830s, the federal government forced Native Americans from the East to resettle west of the Mississippi River and promised them the land there forever. In the 1840s through the 1860s, pressure from white settlers weakened this promise. In the ensuing contest, Native American cultures were irrevocably changed. **Section Focus Question: How did the pressures of westward expansion impact Native Americans?**

Cultures Under Pressure

By the end of the Civil War, about 250,000 Indians lived in the region west of the Mississippi River referred to as "The Great American Desert." While lumped together in the minds of most Americans as "Indians," Native Americans embraced many different belief systems, languages, and ways of life.

Diverse Cultures Geography influenced the cultural diversity of Native Americans. In the Pacific Northwest, the Klamaths, Chinooks, and Shastas benefited from abundant supplies of fish and forest animals. Farther south, smaller bands of hunter-gatherers struggled to exist on diets of small game, insects, berries, acorns, and roots. In the arid lands of New Mexico and Arizona, the Pueblos irrigated the land to grow corn, beans, and squash. They built adobe homes high in the cliffs to protect themselves from aggressive neighbors. The more mobile Navajos lived in homes made of mud or in hogans that could be moved easily. The most numerous and nomadic Native Americans were the Plains Indians, including the Sioux, Blackfeet, Crows, Cheyenne, and Comanches. The Plains Indians were expert horsemen and hunters. The millions of buffalo that roamed the Plains provided a rich source for lodging, clothing, food, and tools.

Indian cultures, however, shared a common thread—they saw themselves as part of nature and viewed nature as sacred. By contrast, many white people viewed the land as a resource to produce wealth. These differing views sowed the seeds of conflict.

Threatened by Advancing Settlers In the early 1800s, the government carried out a policy of moving Native Americans out of the way of white settlers. President Jackson moved the Cherokees off their land in Georgia and onto the Great Plains. To white settlers, Native Americans were welcome to this so-called Great American Desert as it was thought to be uninhabitable. To limit conflict, an 1834 law regulated trade relations with Indians and strictly limited the access of white people to this Indian Territory. White settlement generally paused at the eastern rim of the territory and resumed in the Far West.

By the 1850s, however, federal policy toward Native Americans was again challenged: Gold and silver had been discovered in Indian Territory as well as settled regions farther west. Americans wanted a railroad that crossed the continent. In 1851, therefore, the federal government began to restrict Indians to smaller areas. By the late 1860s, Indians were forced onto separate **reservations,** specific areas set aside by the government for the Indians' use. No longer free to roam the Plains, Indians faced suppression and poverty.

A Meeting of Cultures
Treaty signings such as this one between the Peace Commission and the Cheyenne and Arapaho Indians were a common occurrence during the late 1800s. *How does this photograph illustrate the cultural differences between the groups?*

Two more staggering blows threatened Native American civilizations: White settlers introduced diseases to which Indians had no immunity, and the vitally important buffalo herds were destroyed. In the 1870s, hunters slaughtered hundreds of buffaloes in a single day. They skinned the animals for their hides and left the meat to rot. Trainloads of tourists came to kill buffaloes purely for sport, leaving behind both the valuable meat and hides.

✓ **Checkpoint** **What three circumstances hurt Native Americans?**

New Settlers and Native Americans Clash

The rapid industrial development and expansion following the Civil War set Native Americans and white settlers on a collision course. Advances in communication and transportation that supported industrial growth also reinforced faith in manifest destiny. Horace Greeley, editor of the *New York Tribune*, encouraged the poor to move West:

> **Primary Source** "If you strike off into the broad, free West, and make yourself a farm from Uncle Sam's generous domain, you will crowd nobody, starve nobody, and neither you nor your children need evermore beg. . . ."
>
> —*New York Tribune,* February 5, 1867

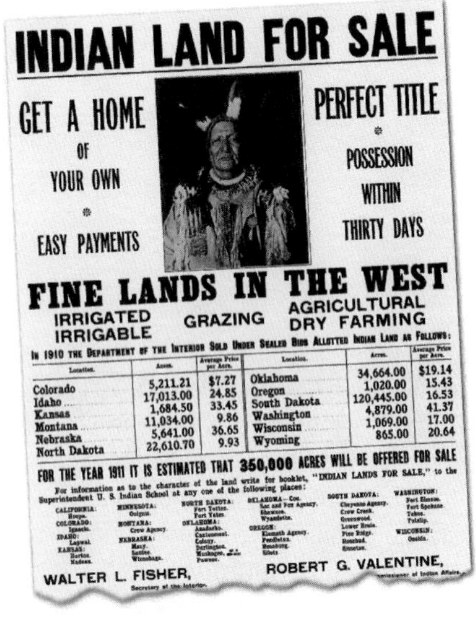

Land Rush

Posters like the one above advertised land to white settlers in areas previously promised to Native Americans.

Generally ignored was the fact that Native Americans inhabited half of the area of the United States. Indians fought to retain or regain whatever they could.

Rebellion and Tragedy on the Plains

In 1862, while the Civil War raged in the East, a group of Sioux Indians had resisted threats to their land rights by attacking settlements in eastern Minnesota. In response, the government waged a full-scale war against the Sioux, who then were pushed west into the Dakotas.

The Sioux rebellion sparked a series of attacks on settlements and stagecoach lines as other Plains Indians also saw their way of life slipping away. Each battle took its toll, raising the level of distrust on all sides. In the fall of 1864, a band of Colorado militia came upon an unarmed camp of Cheyenne and Arapaho Indians, who were under U.S. Army protection, gathered at Sand Creek. The troops opened fire, killing many men, women, and children despite the Indians' efforts to signal their friendship by raising the American flag.

Praise turned to scorn for the commanding officer, John Chivington, when the facts of the encounter became known. The **Sand Creek Massacre** spawned another round of warfare as Plains Indians joined forces to repel white settlement.

Once the Civil War ended, regiments of Union troops—both white and African American—were sent to the West to subdue the Indians. Recruitment posters for volunteer cavalry promised that soldiers could claim any "horses or other plunder" taken from the Indians. The federal government defended its decision to send troops as necessary to maintain order.

Peace Plans Fail

As the Plains Indians renewed their efforts to hold onto what they had, the federal government announced plans to build a road through Sioux hunting grounds to connect gold-mining towns in Montana. Hostilities intensified. In 1866, the legendary warrior Red Cloud and his followers lured Captain William Fetterman and his troops into an ambush, killing them all.

The human costs of the struggle drew a public outcry and called the government's Indian policy into question. As reformers and humanitarians promoted education for Indians, westerners sought strict controls over them. The government-appointed United States Indian Peace Commission concluded that lasting peace would come only if Native Americans settled on farms and adapted to the civilization of the whites.

NoteTaking

Reading Skill: Recognize Sequence Copy the timeline below, and use it to record important dates and events in the Indian Wars.

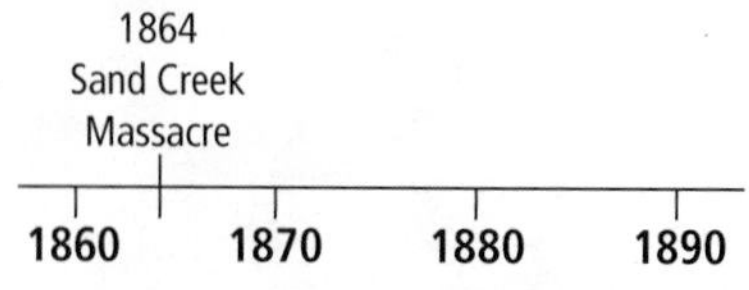

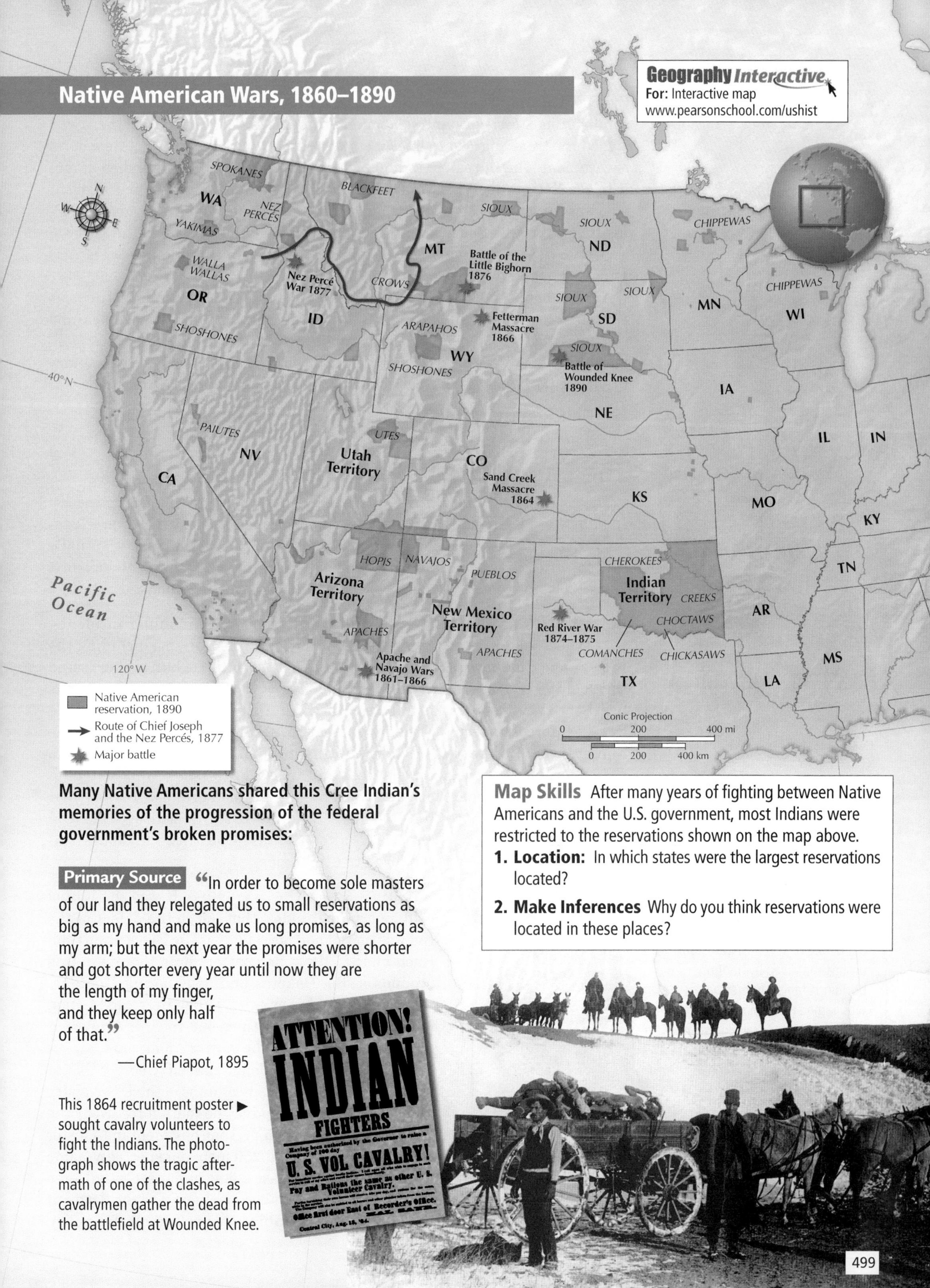

Many Native Americans shared this Cree Indian's memories of the progression of the federal government's broken promises:

Primary Source "In order to become sole masters of our land they relegated us to small reservations as big as my hand and make us long promises, as long as my arm; but the next year the promises were shorter and got shorter every year until now they are the length of my finger, and they keep only half of that."

—Chief Piapot, 1895

This 1864 recruitment poster ▶ sought cavalry volunteers to fight the Indians. The photograph shows the tragic aftermath of one of the clashes, as cavalrymen gather the dead from the battlefield at Wounded Knee.

Map Skills After many years of fighting between Native Americans and the U.S. government, most Indians were restricted to the reservations shown on the map above.

1. **Location:** In which states were the largest reservations located?
2. **Make Inferences** Why do you think reservations were located in these places?

In an effort to pacify the Sioux and to gain more land, the government signed the Fort Laramie Treaty of 1868. The government agreed not to build the road through Sioux territory and to abandon three forts. The Sioux and others who signed the treaty agreed to live on a reservation with support from the federal government. The Bureau of Indian Affairs, established in 1824, handled affairs between Native Americans and the government. The agency appointed an agent who was responsible for distributing land and adequate supplies to anyone willing to farm as well as for maintaining peaceful relations between the reservation and its neighbors. A school and other communal buildings were also promised by the treaty.

Vocabulary Builder
adequate–(AD ih kwuht) *adj.* enough to meet a need

As often happened, some Indians could not live within the imposed restrictions. Unfortunately, many Indian agents were unscrupulous and stole funds and resources that were supposed to be distributed to the Indians. Even the most well-meaning agents often lacked support from the federal government or the military to enforce the terms of the treaties that were beneficial to Native Americans.

✓ **Checkpoint** **Why did tensions exist between settlers and Indians?**

The End of the Indian Wars

The conditions facing Native Americans had all the ingredients for tragedy. Indians were confined to isolated and impoverished areas, which were regularly ravaged by poverty and disease. Promises made to them were eventually broken. Frustration, particularly among young warriors, turned to violence. Guns replaced treaties as the government crushed open rebellions.

Red River War The Red River War, a series of major and minor incidents, led to the final defeat of the powerful southern Plains Indians, including the Kiowas and Comanches. It marked the end of the southern buffalo herds and the opening of the western panhandle of Texas to white settlement. At the heart of the matter was the failure of the United States government to abide by and enforce the terms of the 1867 Treaty of Medicine Lodge. White buffalo hunters were not kept off Indian hunting grounds, food and supplies from the government were not delivered, and white lawlessness was not punished. Hostilities began with an attack by Indians on a group of Texans near the Red River in June 1874. Hostilities ended in June 1875 after the last Comanche holdouts surrendered to U.S. troops.

Battle of the Little Big Horn It was the lure of gold, not animal hides, that led to the defeat of the Indians on the northern Plains. The Black Hills Gold Rush of 1875 drew prospectors onto Sioux hunting grounds in the Dakotas and neighboring Montana. When the Sioux, led by chiefs Crazy Horse and **Sitting Bull,** assembled to drive them out, the U.S. Army sent its own troops against the Native Americans.

In June 1876, a colonel named George Custer rushed ahead of the other columns of the U.S. cavalry and arrived a day ahead of the main force. Near the Little Bighorn River, in present-day Montana, Custer and his force of about 250 men unexpectedly came upon a group of at least 2,000 Indians. Crazy Horse led the charge at what became known as the **Battle of the Little Big Horn,** killing Custer and all of his men.

History Makers

Sitting Bull **(1831?–1890)**
Sitting Bull belonged to the Hunkpapa band, one of seven Lakota Sioux groups that lived by hunting buffalo. A famed fighter, he was named Hunkpapa war chief in his late twenties. Trained as a holy man, he also became a spiritual leader. By the late 1860s, his reputation was so great that the Lakota chose him as the first-ever chief of all seven bands.

Sitting Bull

American Issues Connector

American Indian Policy

TRACK THE ISSUE

How should the federal government deal with Indian nations?

From its earliest days, the federal government has grappled with the issue of relations with Native Americans. Since Indians in the West were forced to move onto reservations, government policy has shifted several times. Use the timeline below to explore this enduring issue.

1787 U.S. Constitution
Federal government given power to regulate trade with Native Americans.

1824 Bureau of Indian Affairs
Agency created to handle relations with Native Americans.

1887 Dawes Act
Government divides reservations into individual land holdings.

1934 Indian Reorganization Act
Tribal governments gain more control over own affairs.

1975 Indian Self-Determination and Educational Assistance Act
Indians win control over schools and other government services.

Comanche girls, 1892

Native Americans in traditional garb press for Indian rights in Washington, D.C.

DEBATE THE ISSUE

Native American Land Claims Today, several Native American nations have made claims to their original lands, arguing that old treaties were illegal. Opponents say that to recognize these claims after so many years would lead to injustice to the people now living on those lands.

"For over 200 years, we have endured hardship and indignities from the unjust taking of our ancestral land. We have been confined to a small reservation. We have suffered the painful loss of our traditional way of life. . . . There will be no actions to evict our neighbors from their homes as we know all too well the pain and suffering displacement causes."

—Tadodaho (Sidney Hill) of the Onondaga Nation, March 10, 2005

"Employing a unique body of laws, today's courts have decided to hear cases based on alleged violations of federal law that occurred over 200 years ago. Even more incredible than the ability and willingness of our judicial system to resurrect these ancient claims, is its [tendency] to apply modern legal interpretations to ancient events and blatantly disregard the historical record."

—Scott Peterman, May 25, 2002

TRANSFER Activities

1. **Compare** How do Tadodaho and Peterman differ on the subject of land claims?
2. **Analyze** How do you think Tadodaho would view the Dawes Act?
3. **Transfer** Use the following Web site to see a video, try a WebQuest, and write in your journal. www.pearsonschool.com/ushist

Cries for revenge motivated army forces to track down the Indians. Sitting Bull and a small group of followers escaped to Canada. Crazy Horse and his followers surrendered, beaten by weather and starvation. By then, the will and the means to wage major resistance had been crushed.

Chief Joseph and the Nez Percés Farther west, in Idaho, another powerful drama played out. In 1877, the federal government decided to move the Nez Percés to a smaller reservation to make room for white settlers. Many of the Nez Percés were Christians and had settled down and become successful horse and cattle breeders. They had pride in themselves and a great deal to lose.

Trying to evade U.S. troops who had come to enforce their relocation, the Nez Percés's leader **Chief Joseph** led a group of refugees on a trek of more than 1,300 miles to Canada. Stopped just short of the border, Chief Joseph surrendered with deeply felt words: "I will fight no more forever." Banished with his group to a barren reservation in Oklahoma, he traveled twice to Washington, D.C., to lobby for mercy for his people.

Wounded Knee With the loss of many leaders and the destruction of their economy, Native Americans' ability to resist diminished. In response, many Indians welcomed a religious revival based on the Ghost Dance. Practitioners preached that the ritual would banish white settlers and restore the buffalo to the Plains. As the popularity of the movement spread, government officials became concerned about where it might lead.

In 1890, in an effort to curtail these activities, the government ordered the arrest of Sitting Bull. In the confrontation, he and several others were killed.

Vocabulary Builder
confrontation–(kahn fruhn TAY shuhn) *n.* hostile encounter

INFOGRAPHIC

ASSIMILATION BY FORCE

By the late 1800s, most Native Americans had been pushed onto reservations where their religions, sacred ceremonies, folklore, and even spoken language were banned. To further rid them of their tribal cultures, some reformers removed young Indians from their homes and sent them to distant boarding schools to learn academics and a trade, but primarily to be "like all other Americans." The forced assimilation, especially of the Indian students, had disastrous results. Ultimately, these children were rejected by both cultures.

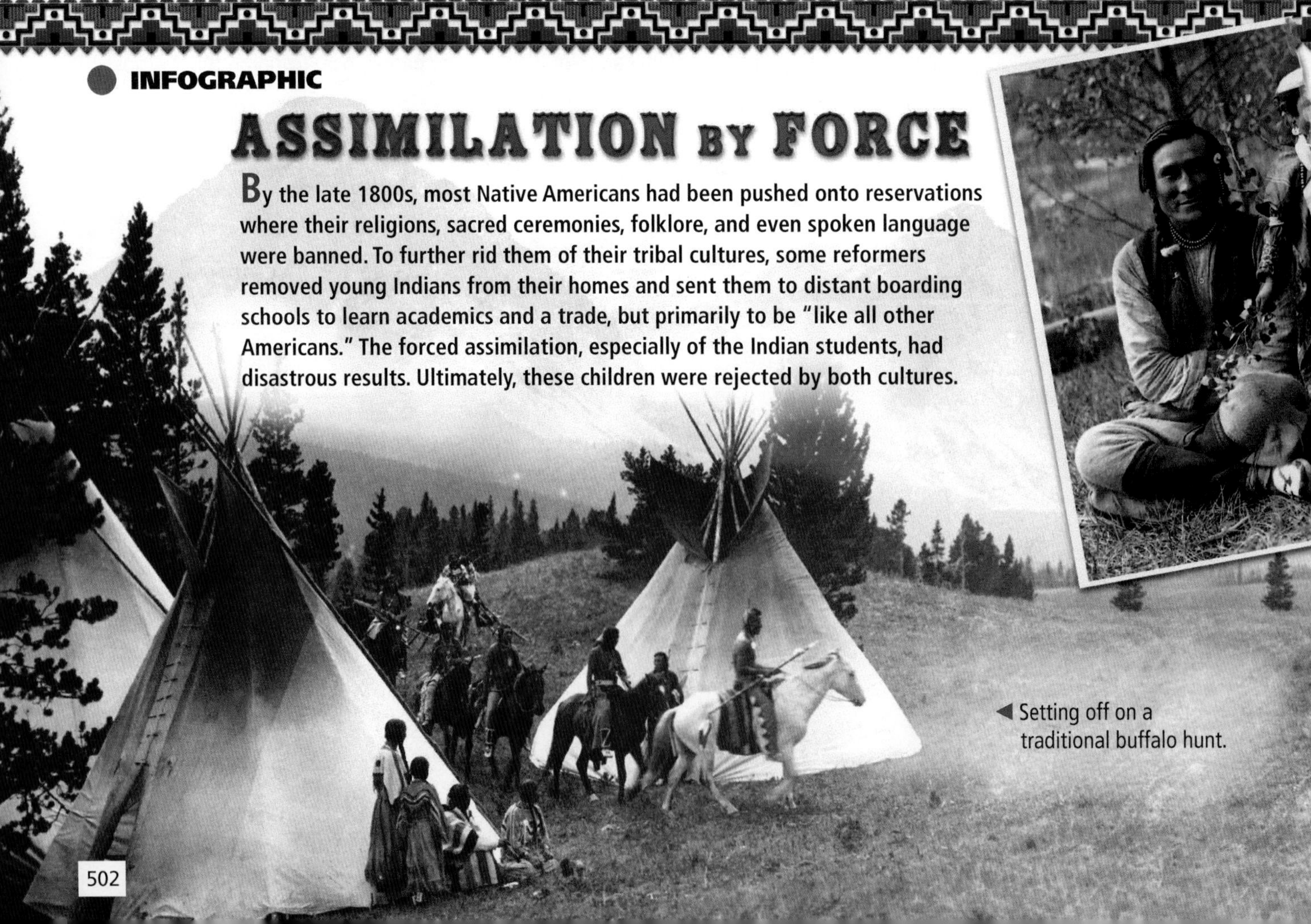

◀ Setting off on a traditional buffalo hunt.

Troops then set out after the group of Indians as they fled. Hostilities broke out at Wounded Knee, South Dakota, when the well-armed cavalry met and outgunned the Indians. The ground was stained with the blood of more than 100 men, women, and children. The tragic end of the Ghost Dance War at **Wounded Knee** sealed the Indians' demise.

✓ Checkpoint What rebellions ended major Indian resistance?

The Government Promotes Assimilation

The reservation policy was a failure. Making Indians live in confined areas as wards of the government was costly in human and economic terms. Policy makers hoped that as the buffalo became extinct, Indians would become farmers and be **assimilated** into national life by adopting the culture and civilization of whites.

Reformers Criticize Government Policy A few outspoken critics defended the Indians' way of life. In *A Century of Dishonor,* Helen Hunt Jackson decried the government's treatment of Native Americans:

> **Primary Source** "There is not among these three hundred bands of Indians one which has not suffered cruelly at the hands either of the Government or of white settlers. The poorer, the more insignificant, the more helpless the band, the more certain the cruelty and outrage to which they have been subjected. . . . It makes little difference where one opens the record of the history of the Indians; every page and every year has its dark stain. . . ."
>
> —Helen Hunt Jackson, 1881

▼ Carlisle Indian Industrial School book cover

◀ Traditional Native American garments (far left) were often replaced with "American" clothes (left), in an effort to assimilate the Native American population.

Established in 1879, the Carlisle Indian Industrial School in Pennsylvania was one of the first boarding schools for Native Americans. Students there were required to change their traditional hairstyles, dress, and language to that of the white American culture.

Thinking Critically

1. **Draw Conclusions** Why do you think it was difficult for assimilated Native Americans to be accepted by their own cultures?
2. **Synthesize Information** Why is forced assimilation destined to fail?

History Makers

Helen Hunt Jackson
(1830–1885)

Helen Hunt Jackson grew up in Massachusetts. In the late 1870s, she heard some Native Americans speak about their peoples' plight. Deeply moved, she was determined to publicize their cause. In *A Century of Dishonor,* she sharply criticized the U.S. government's history of shattered treaties. She elaborated on the situation in a report on Indian policy written for the government and in the highly popular novel *Ramona.* Jackson's work helped build sympathy for the plight of Native Americans.

Susette La Flesche, the granddaughter of a French trader and an Omaha Indian woman, also used her writing and lecturing talents to fight for recognition of the Indians and Indian rights in the courts. Born on the Omaha reservation in Nebraska, she studied in the East and returned to the reservation to teach.

Congress Passes the Dawes Act In 1871, Congress had passed a law stating that "no Indian nation or tribe within the United States would be recognized as an independent nation, tribe or power with whom the United States may contract by treaty." Indians were now to be treated as individuals.

Partly in response to reformers like La Flesche and Jackson and partly to accelerate the process of assimilation, Congress passed the **Dawes General Allotment Act** (sometimes known as the Dawes Severalty Act) in 1887. The Dawes Act replaced the reservation system with an allotment system. Each Indian family was granted a 160-acre farmstead. The size of the farm was based on the eastern experience of how much land was needed to support a family. In the arid West, however, the allotment was not big enough.

To protect the new Indian owners from unscrupulous speculators, the Dawes Act specified that the land could not be sold or transferred from its original family for 25 years. Congress hoped that by the end of that time, younger Indians would embrace farming and individual landownership. To further speed assimilation, missionaries and other reformers established boarding schools, to which Indian parents were encouraged to send their children. Indian children were to learn to live by the rules and culture of white America. The struggle to retain their homeland, freedom, and culture proved tragic. Although Native Americans faced their enemy with courage and determination, tens of thousands died in battle or on squalid reservations. Only a small number were left to carry on their legacy.

✓ **Checkpoint** **How did the Dawes Act change the way Indians were treated?**

Section 2 Assessment

Progress Monitoring *Online*
For: Self-test with vocabulary practice
www.pearsonschool.com/ushist

Comprehension

1. **Terms and People** For each item below, write a sentence explaining its significance to the fate of Native Americans.
   - reservation
   - Sand Creek Massacre
   - Sitting Bull
   - Battle of the Little Big Horn
   - Chief Joseph
   - Wounded Knee
   - assimilate
   - Dawes General Allotment Act
2. **NoteTaking Reading Skill: Identify Supporting Details** Use your concept web and timeline to answer the Section Focus Question: How did the pressures of westward expansion impact Native Americans?

Writing About History

3. **Quick Write: Research an Oral Presentation** Use library or Internet resources to gather information on one of the battles in the Indian Wars. Afterward, list at least two written sources and two images that you might use in an oral presentation.

Critical Thinking

4. **Recognize Cause and Effect** Why did Native Americans and white settlers clash?
5. **Analyze Information** How did Native Americans try but fail to keep their land?
6. **Identify Central Issues** What steps were taken to foster assimilation of Native Americans?

SECTION 3

Locusts were one of the challenges to farming on the Plains. ▶

WITNESS HISTORY

A Test of Courage

Pioneer life in the West in the late 1800s was significantly different from daily life in the East. The challenges were great and survival often difficult. However, according to Lulu Fuhr, a Kansas pioneer, the pioneering spirit met these challenges head-on:

> "There were many tearful occasions for the tearful type. There were days and months without human fellowship, there were frightful blizzards, [drought] destroying seasons . . . and many pitiful deprivations, but there were also compensations for the brave, joyous, determined pioneer."
>
> —Lulu Fuhr

◀ Pioneer woman gathers buffalo chips to use as fuel.

Transforming the West

Objectives

- Analyze the impact of mining and railroads on the settlement of the West.
- Explain how ranching affected western development.
- Discuss the ways various peoples lived in the West and their impact on the environment.

Terms and People

vigilante	open-range system
transcontinental railroad	Homestead Act
land grant	Exoduster

NoteTaking

Reading Skill: Identify Main Ideas Use a chart to record details about changes in the West.

Western Settlement			
Miners	Railroads	Ranchers	Farmers

Why It Matters The West was swept by enormous change after the Civil War. As railroads increased access, settlers, ranchers, and miners permanently transformed millions of acres of western land. **Section Focus Question: What economic and social factors changed the West after the Civil War?**

Miners Hope to Strike It Rich

Mining was the first great boom in the West. Gold and silver were the magnets that attracted a vast number of people. Prospectors from the East were just a part of a flood that included people from all around the world.

Mining Towns Spring Up From the Sierra Nevada to the Black Hills, there was a similar pattern and tempo to the development of mining regions. First came the discovery of gold or silver. Then, as word spread, people began to pour into an area that was ill prepared for their arrival. The discovery of gold at Pikes Peak in Colorado and the Carson River valley in Nevada are classic examples. Mining camps sprang up quickly to house the thousands of people who flooded the region. They were followed by more substantial communities. Miners dreamed of finding riches quickly and easily. Others saw an opportunity to make their fortune by supplying the needs of miners for food, clothing, and supplies.

INFOGRAPHIC

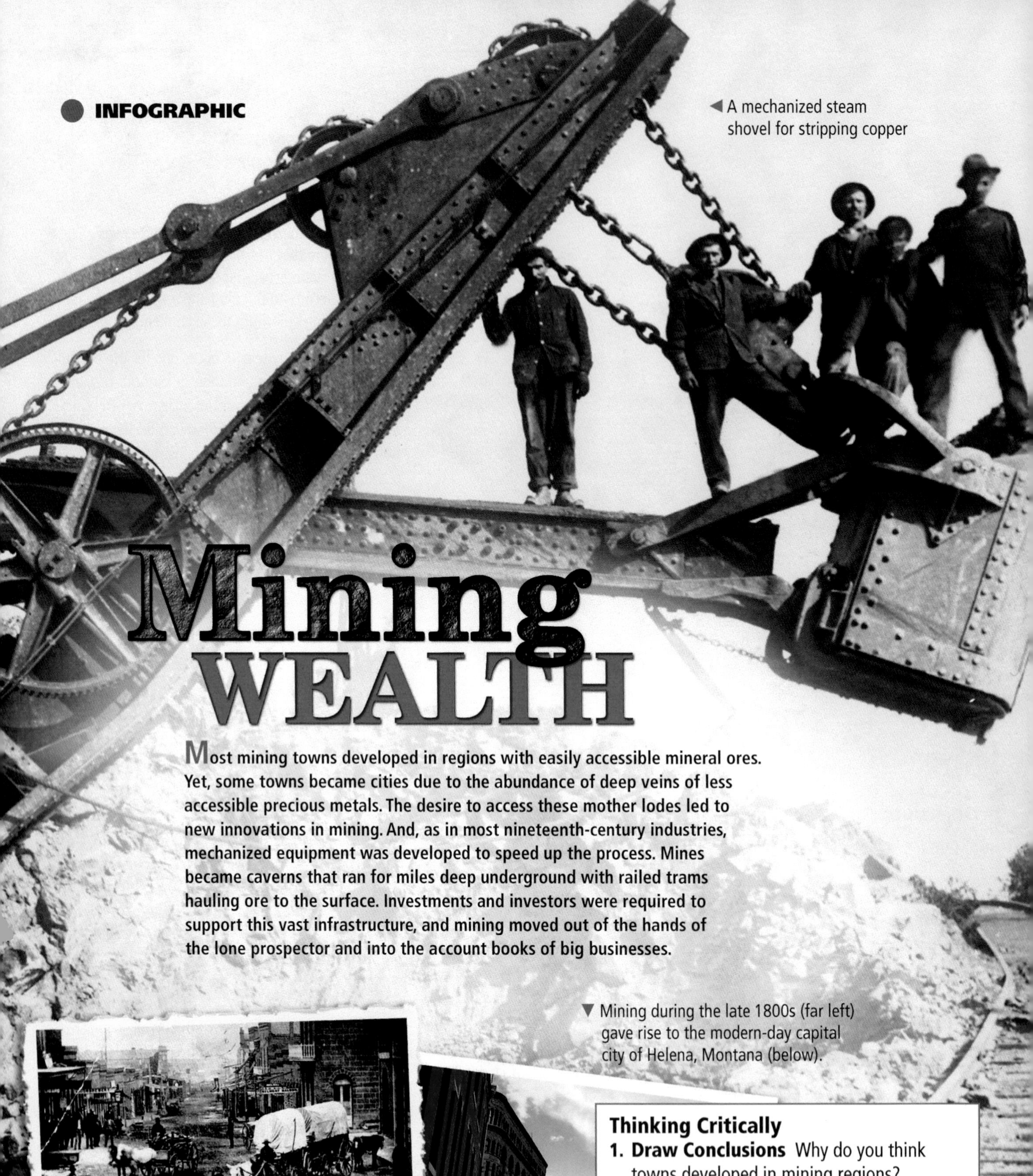

◀ A mechanized steam shovel for stripping copper

Mining WEALTH

Most mining towns developed in regions with easily accessible mineral ores. Yet, some towns became cities due to the abundance of deep veins of less accessible precious metals. The desire to access these mother lodes led to new innovations in mining. And, as in most nineteenth-century industries, mechanized equipment was developed to speed up the process. Mines became caverns that ran for miles deep underground with railed trams hauling ore to the surface. Investments and investors were required to support this vast infrastructure, and mining moved out of the hands of the lone prospector and into the account books of big businesses.

▼ Mining during the late 1800s (far left) gave rise to the modern-day capital city of Helena, Montana (below).

Thinking Critically

1. **Draw Conclusions** Why do you think towns developed in mining regions?
2. **Recognize Cause and Effect** How did the discovery of natural resources contribute to the settlement of the West?

History *Interactive* *

For: To learn more about industry in the West
www.pearsonschool.com/ushist

The rough-and-tumble environment of these communities called out for order. To limit violence and administer justice in areas without judges or jails, miners set up rules of conduct and procedures for settling disputes. In extreme situations, self-appointed law enforcers known as **vigilantes** punished lawbreakers. As towns developed, they hired marshals and sheriffs, like Wyatt Earp and Bat Masterson, to keep the peace. Churches set up committees to address social problems.

Vocabulary Builder
administer–(ad MIHN ihs tuhr) *v.* to manage or direct

Some mining towns—like Leadville, Colorado, and Nevada City, Montana—were "boomtowns." They thrived only as long as the gold and silver held out. Even if a town had developed churches and schools, it might become a ghost town, abandoned when the precious metal disappeared. In contrast, Denver, Colorado; Boise, Idaho; and Helena, Montana, were among the cities that diversified and grew.

Large Companies Make Mining Big Business The first western mining was done by individuals, who extracted the minerals from the surface soil or a streambed. By the 1870s, the remaining mineral wealth was located deep underground. Big companies with the capital to buy mining equipment took over the industry. Machines drilled deep mine shafts. Tracks lined miles of underground tunnels. Crews—often recruited from Mexico and China—worked in dangerous conditions underground.

The arrival of the big mining companies highlighted an issue that would relentlessly plague the West: water and its uses. Large-scale mining required lots of water pumped under high pressure to help separate the precious metals from silt. As the silt washed down the mountains, it fouled water being used by farmers and their livestock. Despite these concerns, the federal government continued to support large mining companies by providing inexpensive land and approving patents for new inventions. Mining wealth helped fuel the nation's industrial development.

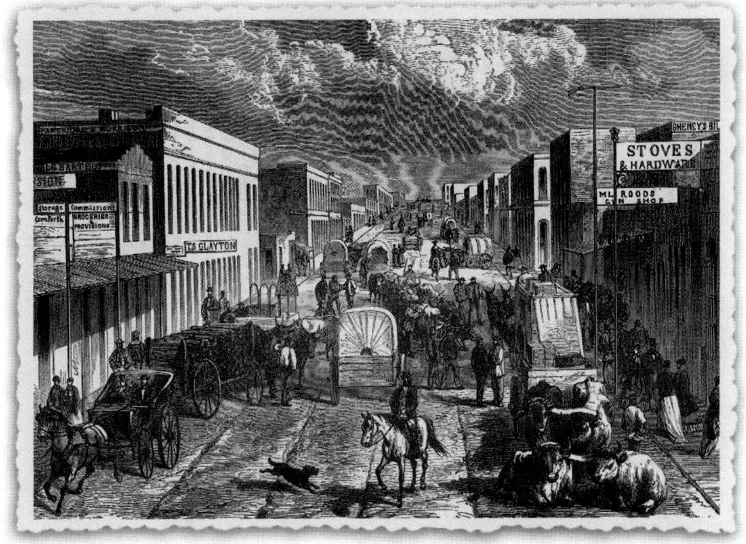

Prosperity in the West
As this 1875 engraving of Denver shows, towns and cities throughout the West grew rapidly. *How does this image illustrate the growth of Denver, Colorado?*

✓ **Checkpoint** **What were the two major phases of mining?**

Railroaders Open the West

As industry in the West grew, the need for a railroad to transport goods increased as well. The idea of a **transcontinental railroad,** a rail link between the East and the West, was not new. Arguments over the route it should take, however, had delayed implementation. While the Civil War kept the South out of the running, Congress finally took action.

Building the Transcontinental Railroad Unlike Europe, where railroads were built and owned by governments, the United States expected its railroads to be built by private enterprise. Congress supported construction of the transcontinental railroad in two ways: It provided money in the form of loans and made **land grants,** giving builders wide stretches of land, alternating on each side of the track route.

Simultaneously in 1863, the Central Pacific started laying track eastward from Sacramento, California, while the Union Pacific headed westward from Omaha, Nebraska. Construction proved to be both difficult and expensive.

The Final Spike
In 1869, the Union Pacific and Central Pacific railroads came together at Promontory, Utah. A symbolic golden spike (above) was the final one driven in to mark the completion of the transcontinental railroad. *How does the photograph above illustrate the mood of this event?*

The human cost of building the railroad was also high. Starved for labor, the Central Pacific Company brought recruits from China and set them to work under harsh contracts and with little regard for their safety. Inch by inch, they chipped and blasted their way through the granite-hard Sierra Nevada and Rockies. Meanwhile, working for the Union Pacific, crews of Irish immigrants crossed the level plains from the East. The two tracks eventually met at Promontory, Utah, in 1869, the same year that the Suez Canal was completed in Egypt. The continent and the world were shrinking in size.

Railroads Intensify Settlement The effects of the railroads were far reaching. They tied the nation together, moved products and people, and spurred industrial development.

The railroads also stimulated the growth of towns and cities. Speculators vied for land in places where a new railroad might be built, and towns already in existence petitioned to become a stop on the western rail route. Railroads intensified the demand for Indians' land and brought white settlers who overwhelmed Mexican American communities in the Southwest. There was no turning back the tide as waves of pioneers moved west.

The addition of states to the Union exemplifies the West's growth. Requirements for statehood included a population of at least 60,000 inhabitants. Between 1864 and 1896, ten territories met those requirements and became states.

 **Checkpoint How did the government encourage the development of a transcontinental railroad?**

Ranchers Build the Cattle Kingdom

Cattle ranching fueled another western boom. This was sparked by the vast acres of grass suitable for feeding herds of cattle. Once the railroad provided the means to move meat to eastern markets, the race was on for land and water.

Vaqueros and Texas Longhorns Long before the arrival of eastern settlers in the West, Mexicans in Texas had developed an efficient system for raising livestock. The Texas longhorn, which originated in Mexico, roamed freely and foraged for its own feed. Each owner marked—or "branded"—the cattle so they could be identified. Under this **open-range system,** property was not fenced in. Though ranchers claimed ownership and knew the boundaries of their property, cattle from any ranch grazed freely across those boundaries. When spring came, the ranchers would hire cowboys to comb thousands of acres of open range, "rounding up" cattle that had roamed all winter. The culture of the cowboy owed its very existence to the Mexican *vaqueros* who had learned to train horses to work with cattle and had developed the roping skills, saddle, lariat, and chaps needed to do the job.

Cowboys and Cattle Drives Once cows were rounded up, cowboys began the long cattle drive to take the animals to a railroad that would transport them to eastern markets. The trek from Texas, Colorado, or Montana to the nearest junction on the transcontinental railroad could take weeks or even months.

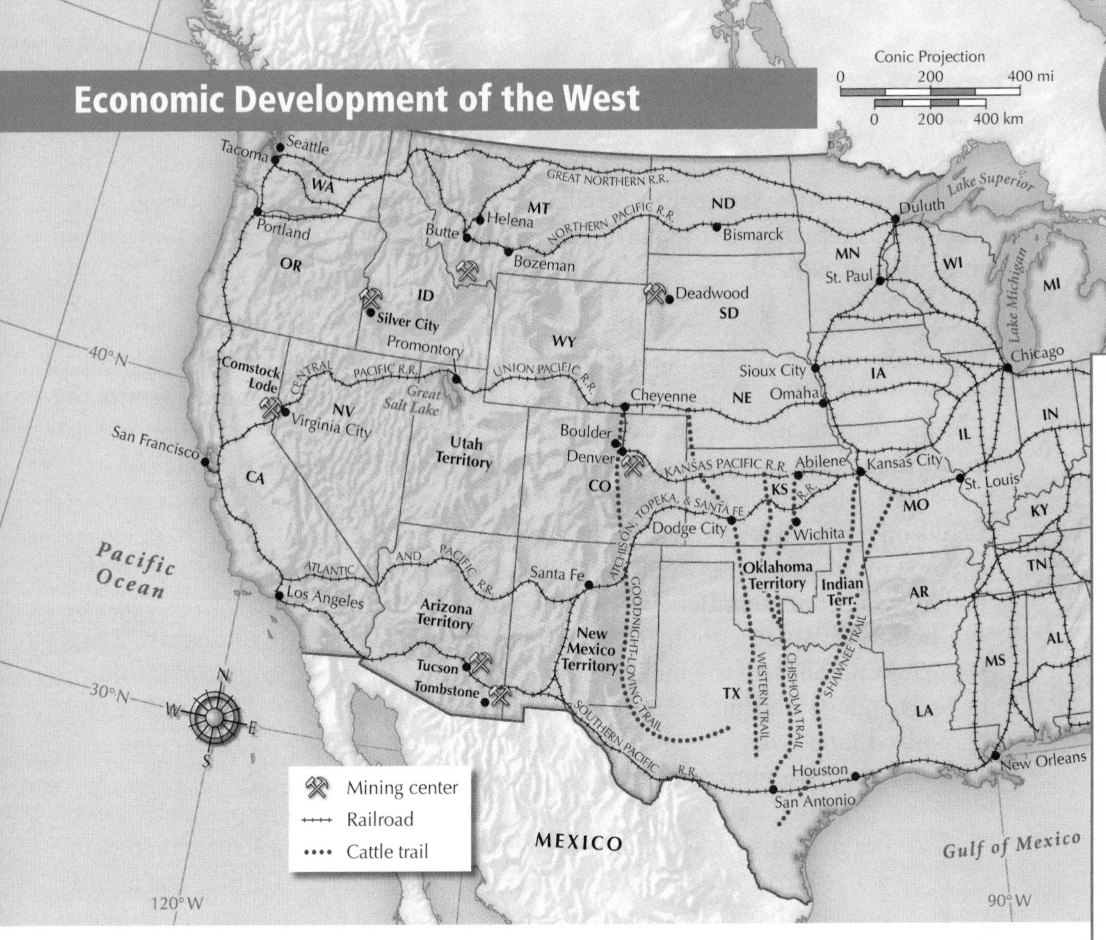

Map Skills Miners, ranchers, and railroads all played a role in the development of the West in the late 1800s.

1. **Locate:** (a) Promontory, (b) Helena, Montana, (c) Chisholm Trail
2. **Location:** Explain how the location of these cities enabled them to become centers of economic activity: Denver, Virginia City, Abilene, Omaha.
3. **Draw Conclusions** How did the railroads contribute to the growth and prosperity of the West?

Geography Interactive
For: Interactive map
www.pearsonschool.com/ushist

The cowboys' work was hard, dangerous, low-paying, and lonely—often involving months of chasing cattle over the countryside. A band of cowboys often included a mix of white, Mexican, and African American men.

The Cow Towns Cattle drives concluded in such railroad towns as Dodge City, Kansas, where the cattle were sold and the cowboys were paid. These cow towns gave rise to stories about colorful characters such as Wild Bill Hickok, Doc Holliday, Wyatt Earp, and Jesse James. They were also the site of rodeos, competitions based on the cowboys' skills of riding, roping, and wrestling cattle. Bill Pickett, an African American cowboy, is credited with inventing bulldogging, in which a cowboy leaps from his horse onto a steer's horns and wrestles the steer to the ground.

▲ Cattle branding irons

The End of Open-Range Ranching Open-range ranching flourished for more than a decade after the Civil War. During that time, several million cattle were driven from Texas north to the railroad stops in Wyoming, Nebraska, and Kansas. However, by the mid-1880s, the heyday of open-ranching came to an end.

Several factors contributed to the demise of the open range. The invention of barbed wire made it possible to fence in huge tracts of land on the treeless plains. The supply of beef exceeded demand, and the price of beef dropped sharply. Added to these factors was a period of extreme weather in the 1880s—brutally freezing winters followed by summer droughts. As springs dried up, herds of cattle starved. The nature of cattle ranching changed as ranchers began to raise hay to feed their stock, and farmers and sheepherders settled on what had been open range.

✓ **Checkpoint** **How did the railroad affect the cattle industry?**

Farmers Settle on Homesteads

The Great Plains were the last part of the country to be heavily settled by white people. It was originally set aside for Indians because it was viewed as too dry for agriculture. Yet, with the coming of the transcontinental railroad, millions of farmers moved into the West in the last huge westward migration in the mid- to late 1800s.

Farmers Move to the Plains The push-and-pull factors that encouraged settlement were varied. Like the miners and cattle ranchers, farmers were looking for a better life. Railroads advertised land for sale, even sending agents to Europe to lure new immigrants, especially from Scandinavia. Other immigrants fled political upheavals in their native lands. Under the **Homestead Act,** passed in 1862, the government offered farm plots of 160 acres to anyone willing to live on the land for five years, dig a well, and build a road.

Some of these new settlers were former slaves who fled the South after the end of Reconstruction. Benjamin Singleton, a black businessman from Tennessee, helped organize a group of African Americans called the "**Exodusters.**" They took their name from the biblical story of Moses leading the exodus of the Jews out of bondage and into a new life in the "Promised Land." The Exodusters' "promised land" was in Kansas and Oklahoma, where they planted crops and founded several enduring all-black towns.

Mining, railroad building, and cattle herding were generally male occupations, so much of the western migration was led by men. But women arrived, too. Everyone had a job to do, either tending the family and farm or working as an entrepreneur running a boardinghouse, laundry, or bakery.

Challenges Demand Solutions The life of homesteaders was hard. Windstorms, blizzards, droughts, plagues of locusts, and heart-rending

Farming the Plains
A family (bottom) poses with their prized possessions in front of their sod house. Some homeowners covered the inside walls with muslin (top) to help keep out the dirt and to prevent bugs, mice, or snakes from crawling in. *How did settlers adapt to the challenges of living on the Plains?*

loneliness tested their endurance. On the treeless plains, few new arrivals could afford to buy lumber to build a home. Instead, they cut 3-foot sections of sod and stacked them like bricks, leaving space for a door and one window. The resulting home was dark, dirty, and dingy.

Necessity is the mother of invention, and farmers on the Plains had many needs beyond housing. The development of barbed wire, a length of wire with twisted barbs, enabled a farmer to fence land cheaply to keep out wandering livestock. The development of a plow that could tackle the sod-covered land, the grain drill that opened furrows and planted seed, the windmill that tapped underground water, and dry-farming techniques were some of the innovations that enabled farmers to succeed. To spur development of better ways to farm, Congress passed the Morrill Act in 1862, which granted land to states for the purpose of establishing agricultural colleges.

Nothing, however, prepared farmers for a series of blizzards and droughts in the 1880s and 1890s that killed animals and ruined harvests. Some of the discouraged and ill-prepared settlers headed back east. The farmers who remained became more commercial and depended more on scientific farming methods.

✓ **Checkpoint** **Why did farmers move to the Plains?**

Competition, Conflict, and Change

There is a sharp contrast between the picture of the West depicted in novels and movies and the reality of life on the Plains. The West was a place of rugged beauty, but it was also a place of diversity and conflict.

Economic Rivalries The various ways that settlers sought to use western land were sometimes at odds with one another. Conflicts between miners, ranchers, sheepherders, and farmers led to violence and acts of sabotage. And no matter who won, Native Americans lost. Grazing cattle ruined farmers' crops, and sheep gnawed grass so close to the ground that cattle could not graze the same land. Although miners did not compete for vast stretches of grassland, runoff from large-scale mining polluted water that ran onto the Plains—and everyone needed water.

Early on, geologist John Wesley Powell recognized water as an important but limited resource. He promoted community control and distribution of water for the common good. Despite his efforts, water usage remained largely unregulated to the benefit of some but not all.

Vocabulary Builder
usage–(YOO sihj) *n.* the act or way something is used

Prejudices and Discrimination From the 1850s onward, the West had the widest diversity of people in the nation. With fewer than 20 percent of the nation's total population, it was home to more than 80 percent of the nation's Asian, Mexican and Mexican American, and Native American residents. Chinese immigrants alone accounted for 100,000 immigrants, almost all of them in the West.

Ethnic tensions often lurked beneath the surface. Many foreign-born white people sought their fortunes on the American frontier, especially in the years following the mid-century revolutions in Europe. Their multiple languages joined the mix of several dozen Native American language groups. Differences in food, religion, and cultural practices reinforced each group's fear and distrust of the others. But mostly it was in the larger cities or towns that discrimination was openly displayed. Chinese immigrants, Mexicans, and Mexican Americans were most often its targets.

Conflict came in many guises. For example, ranchers often belittled homesteaders, labeling them "sodbusters" to mock their work in the soil and their modest houses. Conflict also arose because the view of the ownership of natural

A Diverse Population
Economic opportunities attracted diverse groups to the West. Chinese workers were among the many immigrant groups hired to help build the transcontinental railroad.

resources varied. For many generations, Mexicans had mined salt from the salt beds of the El Paso valley. Mexicans viewed these areas as public property, open to all. However, when Americans arrived in the 1870s, they laid claim to the salt beds and aimed to sell the salt for profit. In 1877, in what became known as the El Paso Salt War, Americans and Mexicans clashed over access to this crucial commodity. When the battles ended, the salt beds were no longer communal property. Now, users would have to buy this natural product.

Closing of the Frontier The last major land rush took place in 1889 when the federal government opened the Oklahoma Territory to homesteaders. On April 22, thousands of "boomers" gathered along the border. When the signal was given, they charged in to stake their claims. However, they found that much of the best land had already been taken by "sooners," who had sneaked into the territory and staked their claims before the official opening.

The following year, the 1890 national census concluded that there was no longer a square mile of the United States that did not have at least a few white residents. The country, the report said, no longer had a "frontier," which at the time was considered an uninhabited wilderness where no white person lived. The era of free western land had come to an end.

However, the challenges and tensions were far from over. Controversies over Indians' land rights were still to come. So, too, were more battles over water and over the mistreatment of minority citizens—especially the Chinese and the Mexican Americans. One historian has described Mexican Americans as "foreigners in their own land." And as the number of African Americans increased in the West, they, too, would battle discrimination.

 **Checkpoint What were some of the causes of prejudice and discrimination in the West?**

SECTION 3 Assessment

Progress Monitoring *Online*
For: Self-test with vocabulary practice
www.pearsonschool.com/ushist

Comprehension

1. **Terms and People** For each of the following terms, write two or three sentences explaining its significance.
   - vigilante
   - transcontinental railroad
   - land grant
   - open-range system
   - Homestead Act
   - Exoduster
2. **NoteTaking Reading Skill: Identify Main Ideas** Use your chart to answer the Section Focus Question: What economic and social factors changed the West after the Civil War?

Writing About History

3. **Quick Write: Outline an Oral Presentation** Make an outline for an oral presentation on the challenges of farming on the Great Plains. Write your main ideas and supporting details on separate note cards. Determine the order in which you will likely deliver your speech, and number each card accordingly. Include any facts and quotations on the cards as well.

Critical Thinking

4. **Make Comparisons** How did mining in the West change over time?
5. **Recognize Cause and Effect** How did railroads contribute to the settlement and growth of the West?
6. **Express Problems Clearly** How did economic and cultural diversity cause conflicts in the West?

Picturing the West

Frederic Remington and Charles Russell were late-nineteenth-century artists who depicted life on the western frontier. Both went west as young men. Remington spent only a few months on a Kansas sheep farm, while Russell worked for nearly a decade as a cowhand. Their experiences on the frontier greatly influenced their art. Remington's and Russell's paintings and sculptures fascinated people on the East Coast and greatly influenced the public's image of the West. However, by the time Remington and Russell were painting, the life they were depicting was either already gone or disappearing swiftly.

▲ Russell, *Smoking Up*

◄ Remington, *The Outlier* (far left)

◄ Remington, *Vaquero* (left)

▼ Remington, *Dash for the Timber*

Thinking Critically

1. **Make Inferences** How do you think this artwork influenced the way people perceived Native Americans and the West?
2. **Connect to Today** How do photographs or paintings of different parts of the world today influence the way we conceive of a place or a culture?

CHAPTER 15

Quick Study Guide

Progress Monitoring *Online*
For: Self-test with vocabulary practice
www.pearsonschool.com/ushist

The New South

Economic Growth	Limits to Growth
• Development of new industries such as textiles, lumber, iron, steel • Expansion of rail lines • Some agricultural diversification to reduce dependence on cotton	• Shortage of skilled workers • Wealth concentrated in hands of a few • Few banks to finance business expansion

Transforming the West

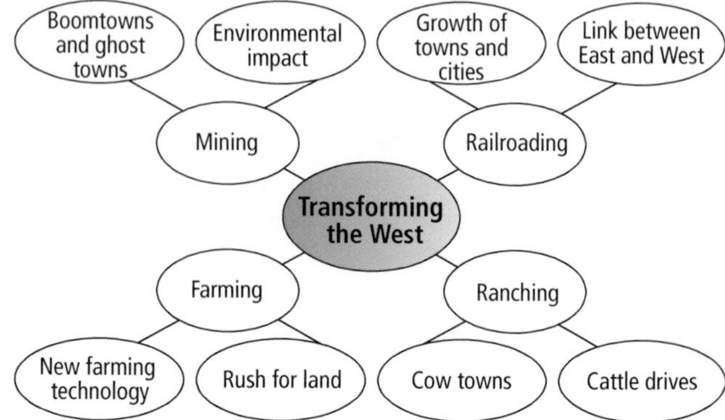

Key Events in the Indian Wars

Event	Description
Sand Creek Massacre, 1864	U.S. troops kill unarmed Cheyenne and Arapaho men, women, and children.
Fetterman Massacre, 1866	Sioux lure Captain William Fetterman and his troops into an ambush.
Red River War, 1874–1875	Series of conflicts ends with defeat of southern Plains Indians. Texas panhandle opened to white settlement.
Battle of the Little Bighorn, 1876	Colonel George Custer meets a huge Sioux force. Custer and all 250 of his men perish.
Nez Percé War, 1877	Rather than relocate to a reservation, Nez Percés flee more than 1,000 miles but are forced to surrender just short of the Canadian border.
Battle of Wounded Knee, 1890	Ghost Dance raises fears of Sioux uprising. More than 100 Sioux are killed at Wounded Knee.

Quick Study Timeline

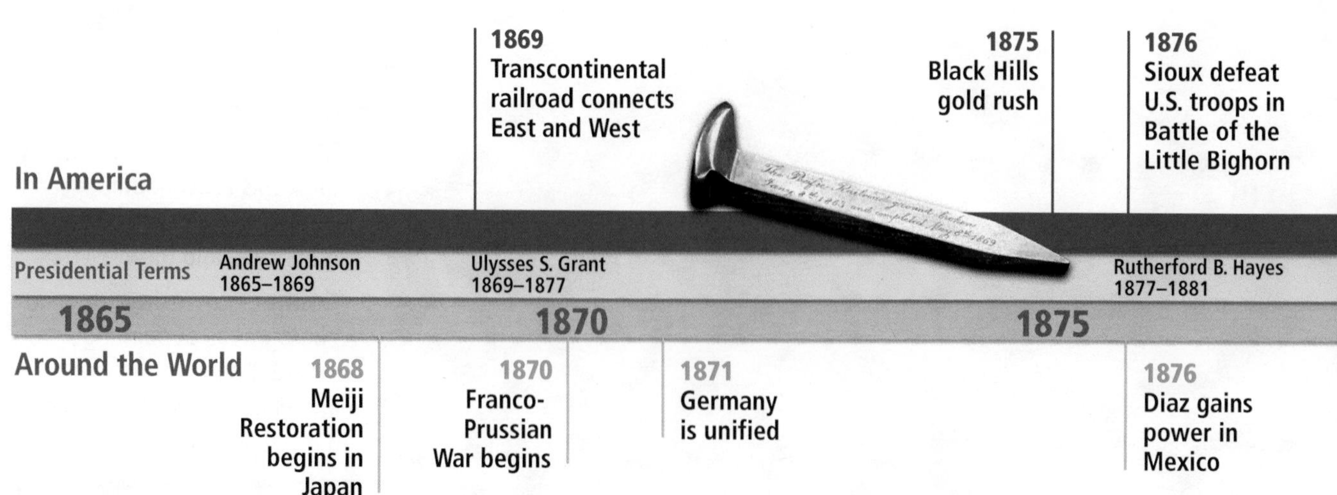

American Issues Connector

By connecting prior knowledge with what you have learned in this chapter, you can gradually build your understanding of enduring questions that still affect America today. Answer the questions below. Then, use your American Issues Connector study guide (or go online: www.pearsonschool.com/ushist).

Issues You Learned About

● **American Indian Policy** As white settlers pushed west, the federal government backed policies to provide them with more land—the land upon which many Native American groups already lived.

1. Write an evaluation of how the U.S. government treated Native Americans in the mid- to late 1800s. Consider:
- the creation of the reservation system
- treaties between Native American groups and the federal government
- clashes between U.S. soldiers and Native Americans
- the Dawes Act

● **Expanding and Protecting Civil Rights** The struggle of a group of people to gain full civil rights may take decades to achieve.

2. What constitutional amendments improved the status of African Americans in the United States? What changes did these amendments bring?

3. How did white southerners in the late 1800s undermine the civil rights that African Americans had gained during Reconstruction?

● **Interaction With the Environment** The American West was a vast land filled with natural resources.

4. What natural resources drew pioneers to the West?

5. How did Native Americans and white settlers differ in their views of the natural environment?

6. What impact did white people have on the buffalo herds of the West?

Connect to Your World — Activity

Technology and Society As you have read, the development of transcontinental railroads changed the ways Americans traveled, transported goods, and did business. Go online or to the local library to learn more about the railroad in the United States today. Find out how many miles of railroad cross the United States. Also, research what the primary use of the railroads is and the problems and opportunities railroads may face in the future. Finally, write a report on the status of the American railroad today.

History *Interactive*
For: Interactive timeline
www.pearsonschool.com/ushist

1879 Exodusters from the South settle in Kansas and Oklahoma

1883 Supreme Court overturns Civil Rights Act of 1875

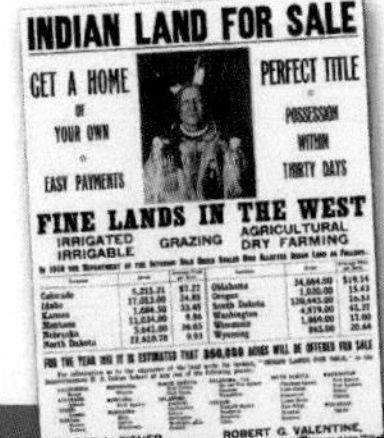

1887 Dawes Act breaks up Indian reservations

1889 Oklahoma is opened to white settlement

1890 Ghost Dance War marks end of Indian resistance

James A. Garfield 1881 | Chester A. Arthur 1881–1885 | Grover Cleveland 1885–1889 | Benjamin Harrison 1889–1893

1880 | **1885** | **1890**

1884 European nations divide Africa at Berlin Conference

1889 Brazil becomes a republic

Chapter Assessment

Terms

1. Define **cash crop.** How did the South's emphasis on cash crops affect its agricultural development?
2. What was the **Sand Creek Massacre**? What effect did it have on the American West?
3. What occurred at **Wounded Knee**? Where and when did it take place, and how was this event significant in the lives of Native Americans?
4. What was the **transcontinental railroad**? What was its purpose, and how did it affect the settlement of the West?
5. What was the **Homestead Act**? What did a family have to do to qualify for the Homestead Act?

Focus Questions

The focus question for this chapter is **How did the economy, society, and culture of the South and West change after the Civil War?** Build an answer to this big question by answering the focus questions for Sections 1 through 3 and the Critical Thinking questions that follow.

Section 1

6. How did the southern economy and society change after the Civil War?

Section 2

7. How did the pressures of westward expansion impact Native Americans?

Section 3

8. What economic and social factors changed the West after the Civil War?

Critical Thinking

9. **Analyze Information** According to Henry Grady, what would characterize the "New South"? In the post–Civil War years, was Grady's vision realized?
10. **Analyze Information** How did Supreme Court rulings in the civil rights cases in 1883 affect the situation of African Americans in the post-Reconstruction South?
11. **Draw Inferences** Why did the federal government encourage Native Americans to assimilate?
12. **Summarize** Summarize the causes and effects of the Indian Wars.
13. **Recognize Cause and Effect** Why did the federal government encourage the construction of the transcontinental railroad? What effect did the new railroad have on the people and the land?
14. **Distinguish False From Accurate Images** The painting below was created in 1914. What emotions do you think the artist is attempting to evoke? Explain your reasoning.

Writing About History

Preparing for an Oral Presentation The post–Civil War years were a complex time in the South and the West, involving a variety of economic, social, and cultural changes. Choose a topic for an oral presentation on some aspect of these changes, and prepare an oral presentation that you might give to classmates to expand on the discussion in your textbook.

Prewriting

- Make a list of possible topics relating to the transformation of the South and the West. Narrow down your list and define a specific topic for your presentation.
- Use library and Internet resources to gather information on your topic. Include both written sources and images.
- Write main ideas and supporting details on note cards.

Drafting

- Develop a working thesis in which you clearly state the purpose of your presentation.
- Write an introduction that clearly defines your topic and what you hope to show.
- Use your note cards to make an outline for your presentation. Clearly indicate the images you would use and when.
- Write a concluding statement that sums up the main point of your presentation.

Revising

- Use the guidelines on page SH31 of the Writing Handbook to revise your presentation.

Document-Based Assessment

U.S. Indian Policy

During the 1800s, most Native Americans were forced to move onto reservations. It was one of the greatest population displacements in modern history. What was the rationale behind this policy? What effects did it have? Use your knowledge of American history and Documents A, B, C, and D to answer questions 1 through 4.

Document A

"... [I]t would be [foolish] to expect that the wild Indians will become industrious and frugal except through a severe course of industrial instruction and exercise, under restraint. The reservation system affords the place for thus dealing with tribes and bands.... [I]t is essential that the right of the Government to keep Indians upon the reservations assigned to them, and to arrest and return them whenever they wander away, should be placed beyond dispute. Without this, whenever these people become restive under compulsion to labor, they will break away in their old roving spirit, and stray off in small bands to neighboring communities, upon which they will prey in a petty fashion, by begging and stealing...."

—*Annual Report of the Commissioner of Indian Affairs,* 1872

Document B

Land Holdings in the U.S., 1871

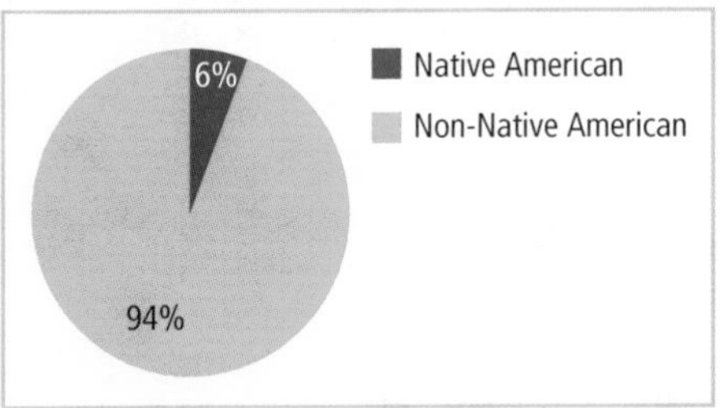

Document C

Navajo student of the Carlisle Indian Industrial School, 1882

Document D

"All men were made by the same Great Spirit Chief. They are all brothers. The earth is the mother of all people, and all people should have equal rights upon it. You might as well expect all rivers to run backward as that any man who was born a free man should be contented penned up and denied liberty to go where he pleases. If you tie a horse to a stake, do you expect he will grow fat? If you pen an Indian up on a small spot of earth and compel him to stay there, he will not be contented nor will he grow and prosper. I have asked some of the Great White Chiefs where they get their authority to say to the Indian that he shall stay in one place, while he sees white men going where they please. They cannot tell me."

—*Chief Joseph, Nez Percé*

---

1. Document B reflects data from the year 1871. How would it be different if it reflected data from a century earlier?
  A The percentage of non–Native American lands would be slightly higher.
  B The percentage of Native American lands would be slightly lower.
  C The percentage of non–Native American lands would be significantly lower.
  D The percentages of Native American and non–Native American lands would be approximately the same.

2. In Document D, Chief Joseph likens a reservation to a
  A mother.
  B stake.
  C horse.
  D river.

3. Which term would a historian most likely use in reference to Document C?
  A assimilation
  B coexistence
  C displacement
  D repatriation

4. **Writing Task** In Document A, the Commissioner of Indian Affairs advocates "a severe course of industrial instruction and exercise." To what was he referring? Use your knowledge of American history and the sources above to develop your answer.

CHAPTER

16 Issues of the Gilded Age 1877–1900

WITNESS HISTORY

Paupers and Millionaires

In 1873, Mark Twain and Charles Dudley Warner published *The Gilded Age.* Disillusioned with the corruption, poverty, and dishonesty around them, Twain and Warner used the novel to express their views. Eventually, the term *Gilded Age* came to define an era in which excessive extravagance and wealth concealed mounting social problems, government corruption, and poverty.

Among the problems were those faced by farmers. In desperation, dissatisfied farmers joined the Populist Party. Ignatius Donnelly, a Populist delegate, addressed his party:

> "We meet in the midst of a nation brought to the verge of moral, political, and material ruin. Corruption dominates the ballot box, the legislatures, the Congress. . . . The people are demoralized. . . . The fruits of the toil of millions are boldly stolen to build up the colossal fortunes. . . . We breed two great classes—paupers and millionaires."
>
> —Ignatius Donnelly, Preamble to the Omaha Platform, 1892

◄ Wealthy people had the pleasure of enjoying leisure time. This group takes a rest from an afternoon of golf.

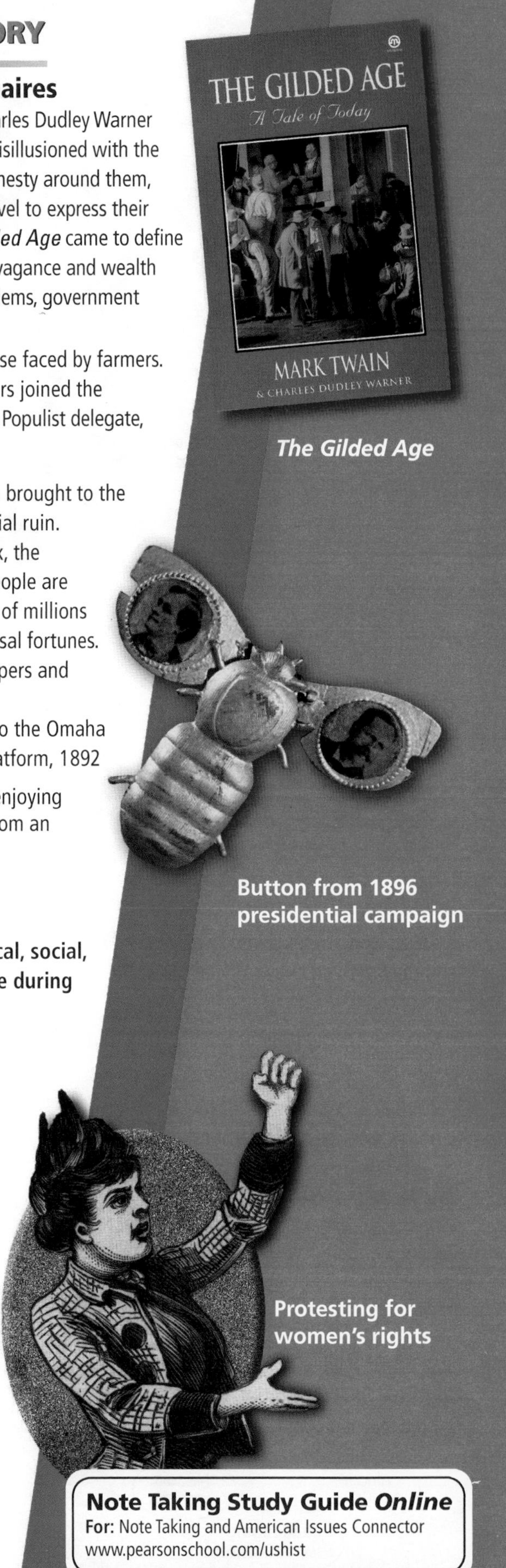

The Gilded Age

Button from 1896 presidential campaign

Protesting for women's rights

Chapter Preview

Chapter Focus Question: What political, social, and economic issues did the nation face during the late 1800s?

Section 1
Segregation and Social Tensions

Section 2
Political and Economic Challenges

Section 3
Farmers and Populism

Use the ☑ Quick Study Timeline at the end of this chapter to preview chapter events.

Note Taking Study Guide *Online*
For: Note Taking and American Issues Connector
www.pearsonschool.com/ushist

SECTION 1

▲ Frederick Douglass

WITNESS HISTORY

Frederick Douglass Laments the Color Line

In 1883, Frederick Douglass, the famous black leader and former runaway slave, addressed a gathering of African Americans in Louisville, Kentucky. Twenty years had passed since Lincoln had issued the Emancipation Proclamation, yet, as Douglass observed, African Americans had not realized their hopes for equality.

"Though we have had war, reconstruction and abolition as a nation, we still linger in the shadow and blight of an extinct institution. Though the colored man is no longer subject to be bought and sold, he is still surrounded by an adverse sentiment, which fetters all his movements. In his downward course he meets with no resistance, but his course upward is resented and resisted at every step of his progress. . . ."

—Frederick Douglass, address in Louisville, Kentucky, 1883

Segregation and Social Tensions

Objectives

- Assess how whites created a segregated society in the South and how African Americans responded.
- Analyze efforts to limit immigration and the effects.
- Compare the situations of Mexican Americans and of women to those of other groups.

Terms and People

Jim Crow laws	Booker T. Washington
poll tax	W.E.B. Du Bois
literacy test	Ida B. Wells
grandfather clause	Las Gorras Blancas

NoteTaking

Reading Skill: Summarize Record the ways in which different groups challenged Reconstruction.

Why It Matters During Reconstruction, the federal government sought to secure equal rights for African Americans. By the time of the Gilded Age (1877–1900), however, African Americans and other minorities experienced a narrowing of their rights. This turn away from equality for all had a lasting impact on society in the United States. **Section Focus Question: How were the civil and political rights of certain groups in America undermined during the years after Reconstruction?**

African Americans Lose Freedoms

Following the disputed presidential election of 1876, President Hayes removed federal troops from the South. This action allowed southern states to reassert their control over African Americans without concern about federal intervention. Southern governments enacted various measures aimed at disenfranchising, or taking away the voting rights of, African Americans and enacted **Jim Crow laws** that kept blacks and whites segregated, or apart.

States' Governments Limit Voting Rights The Fifteenth Amendment, which became part of the United States Constitution in 1870, prohibited state governments from denying someone the right to vote because of "race, color, or previous condition of servitude." After Reconstruction, southern states got around this amendment by passing a number of other restrictive measures. They enacted a **poll tax,** which required voters to pay a tax to vote. The tax, which began in Georgia, cost voters $1 or $2 to vote. Poor African Americans could scarcely afford such a fee. The states also required voters to pass **literacy tests** and "understanding" tests. Because African Americans had been exploited economically and denied an education, these restrictions disqualified many of them as voters.

Vocabulary Builder
exploit–(ehk SPLOYT) *v.* to treat someone unfairly in order to earn money or gain an advantage

Southern states also enacted **grandfather clauses,** which allowed a person to vote as long as his ancestors had voted prior to 1866. Of course, the ancestors of the black freedmen did not vote prior to 1866, but the ancestors of many whites did. In other words, grandfather clauses allowed poor and illiterate whites but not blacks to vote. Some southern states also established all-white primaries, meaning only whites had a voice in selecting who got to run in general elections.

In addition, whites resorted to violence to keep African Americans from participating in the political process. As South Carolina senator Ben Tillman put it: "We have done our level best. We have scratched our heads to find out how we could eliminate the last one of them [black voters]. We stuffed ballot boxes. We shot them."

As a result of these actions, throughout the Deep South, black participation in politics fell dramatically. In Louisiana, for example, the number of blacks registered to vote plummeted from 130,000 in 1894 to just over 1,300 in 1904. On the eve of World War II, in 1940, only 3 percent of all African Americans in the South could vote.

New Laws Force Segregation As the nineteenth century drew to a close, Jim Crow became a way of life in the South. Initially, some white southerners opposed Jim Crow laws on the grounds that if some aspects of life were segregated, in time all aspects of life would become segregated and this would impose an undue burden on society. "If there must be Jim Crow cars [railroad], there should be Jim Crow waiting saloons. And if there were Jim Crow saloons," stated a prominent Charleston newspaper writer, "then there would have to be Jim Crow jury boxes and a Jim Crow Bible for colored witnesses." The whole idea, he concluded, was "absurd."

Nevertheless, widespread segregation became a reality. In addition to Jim Crow railroad cars and waiting stations, southern states established Jim Crow jury boxes and Bibles, as well as cemeteries, restaurants, parks, beaches, and hospitals. Similarly, in northern states, including those that had civil rights laws that outlawed legal segregation, black migrants found many examples of de facto segregation—actual segregation, such as restrictions on where they were allowed to live and work.

During the 1870s, the Supreme Court ruled in cases that undermined the civil rights of African Americans. In *Plessy* v. *Ferguson* (1896), the Supreme Court upheld the constitutionality of Jim Crow laws. (See the feature page at the end of this section.) It did so by arguing that as long as states maintained "separate but equal" facilities, they did not violate the Fourteenth Amendment. Yet, in reality, separate

Rights Denied

As Jim Crow laws spread through the South, African Americans, as shown in the cartoon below, lost freedoms gained during Reconstruction. The change in African American voting patterns evident in South Carolina after 1876 was repeated in other southern states. The graph shows the effects of Jim Crow which kept African Americans from voting.

Voter Turnout in South Carolina, 1876–1896

Percentage of voting-age population: 0, 20, 40, 60, 80, 100
1876 1880 1884 1888 1892 1896
White voters — Black voters

SOURCE: *The Shaping of Southern Politics,* J. Morgan Kousser

facilities were rarely equal. For instance, in 1915, South Carolina spent nearly 14 dollars for every white student but less than 3 dollars for every black student.

✓ **Checkpoint** **In what ways were the rights of African Americans restricted?**

African Americans Oppose Injustices

Vocabulary Builder
status–(STAT uhs) *n.* legal position or condition of a person, group, country, etc.

Even during the darkest days of Jim Crow, African Americans refused to accept the status of second-class citizens. They established black newspapers, women's clubs, fraternal organizations, schools and colleges, and political associations with the goal of securing their freedom. They did not always agree on the best strategies for achieving their goal. However, they were united in their determination to "never turn back" until they had equality.

Booker T. Washington Urges Economic Advancement The most famous black leader during the late nineteenth century was **Booker T. Washington.** Born a slave in 1856, Washington argued that African Americans needed to accommodate themselves to segregation, meaning they should *not* focus their energies on seeking to overturn Jim Crow. Instead, he called for blacks to "pull themselves up from their own bootstraps" by building up their economic resources and establishing their reputations as hardworking and honest citizens.

Primary Source "The wisest among my race understand that the agitation of questions of social equality is the extremest folly, and that progress in the enjoyment of all the privileges that will come to us must be the result of severe and constant struggle rather than artificial forcing. . . . It is important and right that all privileges of the law be ours, but it is vastly more important that we be prepared for the exercises of these privileges."

—Booker T. Washington, Atlanta Exposition address, 1895

History Makers

Booker T. Washington (1856–1915)
As a child, Booker T. Washington worked by day and went to school at night. He was eventually trained as a teacher. After several years of teaching, he was chosen in 1881 to head a normal school, where teachers are trained, in Tuskegee, Alabama. When he arrived, the newly formed school had no buildings or students. Washington went to work finding a space—and persuading 40 students to attend.

Washington led the school for more than 30 years. In that time, the Tuskegee Institute grew to include a hundred buildings, a staff of almost 200 people—all African Americans—and about 1,500 students. It became a model for many similar schools established throughout the country. In the process, Washington became one of the leading figures in the African American community.

In addition to speaking and writing, Washington poured his energies into the Tuskegee Institute, a school in Macon County, Alabama. Under Washington, Tuskegee became known for providing "industrial education," sometimes referred to as vocational education. Such an education, as Washington had suggested in his Atlanta Exposition address, would prepare African Americans to exercise the privileges of citizenship.

W.E.B. Du Bois Attacks Washington's Ideas A native of Great Barrington, Massachusetts, **W.E.B. Du Bois,** who earned his Ph.D. from Harvard University in 1896, criticized Washington's willingness to accommodate southern whites. Echoing the spirit of the abolitionists, he argued that blacks should demand full and immediate equality and not limit themselves to vocational education. Du Bois did not feel that the right to vote was a privilege that blacks needed to earn. He also argued that Washington wrongly shifted the burden of achieving equality from the nation to the "Negro's shoulders" alone. You will learn more about the conflict between Washington and Du Bois in the next chapter.

Ida Wells Crusades Against Lynching One African American woman who fought for justice was **Ida B. Wells.** Born into slavery in 1862, Wells grew up in Holly Springs, Mississippi. Her father, James Wells, became a prominent local businessman and raised her to fight for the rights of African Americans. As a young adult, Wells moved to Memphis, Tennessee, where she worked as a schoolteacher and became active in the African Methodist Episcopal Church. Wells bought a local newspaper, renamed it *Free Speech*, and wrote numerous articles that condemned the mistreatment of blacks.

In 1892, after a mob attack on close friends in Memphis, she wrote an editorial attacking the practice of lynching in the South. "Eight Negroes lynched since last issue of the 'Free Speech,'" Wells declared. "If Southern white men are not careful, they will over-reach themselves and public sentiment will have a reaction."

Local whites responded to Wells's editorial by running her out of town. In exile, Wells embarked on a lifelong crusade against lynching. She wrote three pamphlets aimed at awakening the nation to what she described as the "southern horrors" of legalized murder. She also toured Europe and helped organize women's clubs to fight for African American rights.

 **Checkpoint How did Wells, Washington, and Du Bois protest the mistreatment of African Americans?**

Chinese Immigrants Face Discrimination

During the same time that Jim Crow arose in the South, Chinese immigrants faced racial prejudice on the West Coast. In 1879, California barred cities from employing people of Chinese ancestry. Several years later, San Francisco established a segregated "Oriental" school. Elsewhere, mobs of whites attacked Chinese workers, saying they had taken "white" jobs. Congress responded to these attacks by passing the Chinese Exclusion Act, which prohibited Chinese laborers from entering the country.

Like African Americans, brave Chinese immigrants challenged discrimination. Saum Song Bo questioned why he should support a fund-raising drive to build the Statue of Liberty. "That statue represents Liberty holding a torch which lights the passage of those of all nations who come into this country," Bo wrote in a letter published in *American Missionary* in 1898. "But are the Chinese allowed to come? As for the Chinese who are here, are they allowed to enjoy liberty as men of all other nationalities enjoy it?"

Chinese immigrants also turned to the federal courts to protect their rights but with mixed results. In 1886, in the case of *Yick Wo* v. *Hopkins,* the U.S.

Forging a New Life
Frequently faced with job discrimination, some Chinese immigrants, such as the ones shown here, managed to start their own businesses. These immigrants pose proudly in front of their own grocery store.

Supreme Court sided with a Chinese immigrant who challenged a California law that banned him and other Chinese from operating a laundry. In 1898, the Court ruled that individuals of Chinese descent, born in the United States, could not be stripped of their citizenship. Yet the Court upheld the Chinese Exclusion Act and several other discriminatory measures.

✓ **Checkpoint** **How did Chinese immigrants use the court system to protest discrimination?**

Mexican Americans Struggle in the West

Like African Americans and Asian Americans, Mexican Americans struggled against discrimination in the latter decades of the nineteenth century. At the center of their struggle stood land. The Treaty of Guadalupe Hidalgo, signed at the end of the Mexican-American War, guaranteed the property rights of Mexicans who lived in the Southwest prior to the war. Still, four out of five Mexican Americans who lived in New Mexico lost their land, as did Mexican Americans in other southwestern states.

Abuses and Discrimination Undermine Rights Many factors caused the Mexican Americans to lose most of their land. When Anglo Americans and Mexican Americans laid claim to the same land, U.S. courts put the burden of proof on Mexican Americans to show that they really owned the land. Differences in legal customs, and the fact that much of the land was held communally, not individually, made it difficult for many of them to do so.

In addition, Anglo Americans used political connections to take land away from Mexican Americans. The "Sante Fe Ring," an association of prominent

INFOGRAPHIC

Discrimination in the West

America's move toward integration was neither smooth nor steady. African Americans were not the only group to suffer discrimination. Mexicans and Chinese immigrants also faced harsh and constant discrimination.

After the Treaty of Guadalupe Hidalgo, Mexicans were "thrown among those who were strangers to their language, customs, laws and habits." Although guaranteed the rights of U.S. citizens, Mexicans were subjected to laws limiting their rights as citizens and landowners.

The Burlingame Treaty signed in 1868 guaranteed government protection for Chinese immigrants. Yet, this was hardly the reality. Chinese immigrants were often victims of discrimination and random violence.

Both Mexicans and Chinese immigrants responded to the prejudice with group resistance, lawsuits, and labor strikes.

Surviving harsh conditions, these ▶ Mexican women in San Antonio, Texas, prepare a meal outside their shack.

whites, got the federal government to grant the group control of millions of acres of land in New Mexico. Thousands of Mexican Americans had lived on and farmed this land for many years. Since New Mexico was a territory, not a state, however, Mexican Americans, who comprised the majority of the population, had no representatives in Washington, D.C., to challenge this deal.

Mexican Americans Fight Back Throughout the Southwest—in Texas, New Mexico, Arizona, and California—Mexican Americans fought to maintain their rights. Many Mexicans especially resented the loss of their land. One group, **Las Gorras Blancas,** targeted the property of large ranch owners by cutting holes in barbed-wire fences and burning houses. The group declared: "Our purpose is to protect the rights and interests of the people in general; especially those of the helpless classes." Supported by a national labor organization, the Knights of Labor, the group also had a newspaper to voice their grievances.

As anti-Mexican feelings increased, a group of Hispanic citizens in Tucson, Arizona, formed the Alianza Hispano-Americana in 1894 to protect the culture, interests, and legal rights of Mexican Americans. Within two years, new branches of the organization opened in other cities.

✓ **Checkpoint** **Why did Mexican Americans lose rights to their land?**

Women Make Gains and Suffer Setbacks

Before the Civil War, women played a prominent role in many reform movements, including the drive to abolish slavery. They even began to fight for their own right to vote, to own property, and to receive an education. In the decades that followed the Civil War, women continued to fight for these rights. In some cases, they were successful; in others, they were not.

▼ Violence against Chinese immigrants increased in the West throughout the 1870s and 1880s. In railroad towns and mining camps, angry whites looted and burned Chinese communities.

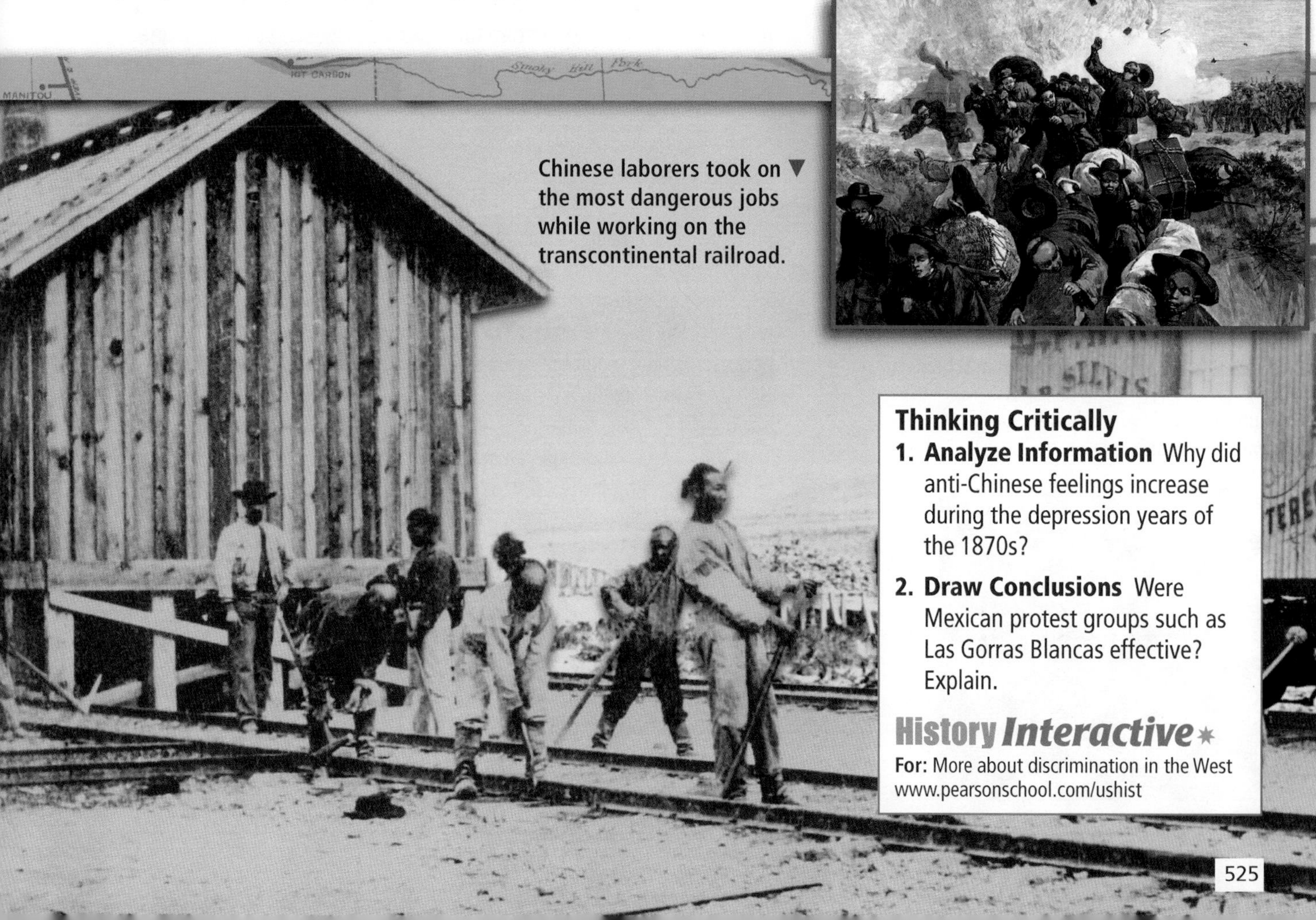

Chinese laborers took on the most dangerous jobs while working on the transcontinental railroad. ▼

Thinking Critically

1. **Analyze Information** Why did anti-Chinese feelings increase during the depression years of the 1870s?
2. **Draw Conclusions** Were Mexican protest groups such as Las Gorras Blancas effective? Explain.

History *Interactive* ✱
For: More about discrimination in the West
www.pearsonschool.com/ushist

American Issues Connector

Women in American Society

TRACK THE ISSUE

Why do Americans disagree over women's rights?

In early America, women had few legal rights. They could not vote, hold office, or work at most jobs. Married women could not own property and were under the legal authority of their husbands. The women's movement helped change all this. Nevertheless, Americans still remain divided over women's rights. Use the timeline below to explore this enduring issue.

1848 Seneca Falls Convention
Women meet in upstate New York to declare support for women's rights

1869 The National Woman Suffrage Association
Anthony and Stanton form organization to fight for women's suffrage

1920 Nineteeth Amendment
Women gain right to vote

1964 Title VII of the Civil Rights Act
Law protects women against job discrimination

1972 Title IX of the Education Codes
Law bans sex discrimination in schools

Supporters of women's suffrage gather in protest.

While many women today have successful careers, some still feel limited in their efforts to land higher positions in their chosen fields.

DEBATE THE ISSUE

Women in the Workplace On average, women earn less than men in the workplace. This wage gap has led to charges of sex discrimination. Feminists also argue that a "glass ceiling" keeps many women from rising to the top of their profession. But other factors may be involved, too.

"The wage gap is the result of a number of factors in addition to discrimination, such as the differences in women's education, their shorter time in the workforce, and their concentration in a narrow range of jobs that are underpaid because women are in them. Nonetheless, a significant portion is attributable to discrimination."

—Sonia Pressman Fuentes, founding member, National Organization for Women

"[Feminists] often portray working women as victims of rampant discrimination [which] [they say] . . . renders women powerless in the face of an impenetrable glass ceiling. While discrimination does exist in the workplace, levels of education . . . and time spent in the workforce play a far greater role in determining women's pay and promotion."

—Naomi Lopez, Director, Center for Enterprise and Opportunity

TRANSFER Activities

1. **Compare** How do the two writers agree? How do they disagree?
2. **Analyze** Affirmative action makes it possible for women and minorities to compete in the workplace. Which of the two women quoted above might support it?
3. **Transfer** Use the following Web site to see a video, try a WebQuest, and write in your journal. www.pearsonschool.com/ushist

Fighting for a Constitutional Amendment

Expanding the rights of African Americans left some women's rights activists, such as Susan B. Anthony, angry. Anthony favored abolishing slavery. Yet she felt betrayed when Radical Republicans did not include women in the Fourteenth and Fifteenth amendments.

In 1869, Anthony and Elizabeth Cady Stanton formed the National Woman Suffrage Association to fight for a constitutional amendment that would grant women the right to vote. In 1872, Anthony voted in an election in Rochester, New York, an illegal act for which she was tried and ultimately convicted in federal court. While awaiting trial, Anthony toured the nation, delivering a speech titled "Is It a Crime for a Citizen of the United States to Vote?" Anthony declared, "Our . . . government is based on . . . the natural right of every individual member . . . to a voice and a vote in making and executing the laws." Anthony's address failed to convince the nation to enact a women's suffrage amendment. By the time of Anthony's death in 1906, only four western states—Wyoming, Utah, Colorado, and Idaho—had granted women the right to vote.

History Makers

Susan B. Anthony (1820–1906)
Originally involved in the temperance movement, reformer Susan B. Anthony joined the fight for women's right to vote in the 1850s. Working closely with her friend Elizabeth Cady Stanton, Anthony spent five decades tirelessly pushing the cause by traveling, writing, speaking, and organizing. To challenge laws that barred women from voting, she cast a ballot in the presidential election of 1872 and then refused to pay the fine when found guilty. Shortly before her death, Anthony urged women to continue the struggle for voting rights with the words "Failure is impossible."

Breaking Down Other Barriers

Women's rights activists, however, did achieve some of their other goals. The number of women attending college jumped. By 1900, one third of all college students, nationwide, were women.

Women also played an increasingly important role in a number of reform movements. Frances Willard led the Women's Christian Temperance Union (WCTU). While temperance, or the ban of the sale of liquor, remained Willard's primary goal, she also supported women's suffrage. She argued that women needed the vote to prohibit the sale of alcohol. Like many of WCTU's members, Willard also promoted other social causes, such as public health and welfare reform.

Checkpoint What successes did women achieve in the years after Reconstruction?

Section 1 Assessment

Progress Monitoring *Online*
For: Self-test with vocabulary practice
www.pearsonschool.com/ushist

Comprehension

1. **Terms and People** Explain how each person or group challenged discrimination.
   - Booker T. Washington
   - W.E.B. Du Bois
   - Ida B. Wells
   - Las Gorras Blancas
2. **NoteTaking Reading Skill: Summarize** Use your concept web to answer the Section Focus Question: How were the civil and political rights of certain groups in America undermined during the years after Reconstruction?

Writing About History

3. **Quick Write: Prepare an Outline** Write down notes to answer the following prompt: Explain how issues such as social reform, civil rights, and the economy dominated local politics in the late 1890s. Then, use your notes to prepare an outline to answer the prompt.

Critical Thinking

4. **Draw Conclusions** How did the *Plessy* v. *Ferguson* decision support the existence of Jim Crow laws?
5. **Recognize Cause and Effect** How did the Treaty of Guadalupe Hidalgo affect relations between Mexican Americans and white Americans in the Southwest?
6. **Analyze Information** Do you think women activists during the late 1800s had any effect on the political or social life of the country? Explain.

Can Separate Treatment Be Equal Treatment?

The Fourteenth Amendment, passed during Reconstruction in 1866, guaranteed equal rights to all citizens. By 1890, civil rights and racial equality were not significant issues for whites in the North and South. Already, the Supreme Court was handing down decisions that overturned Reconstruction legislation and encouraged racial discrimination.

Plessy v. *Ferguson* (1896)

The Facts	The Issue	The Decision
• In 1890, Louisiana passed a law allowing railroads to provide "separate but equal" facilities. • Homer Plessy, an African American, sat in the car reserved for whites. • He was arrested when he refused to move to the "colored" car.	In his appeal to the Supreme Court, Plessy argued that the *Separate Car Act* violated the Fourteenth Amendment.	A 7 to 1 majority declared that state laws requiring separate but equal accommodations for whites and blacks did not violate the Fourteenth Amendment.

Why It Matters

The majority of the Supreme Court reasoned that the Constitution was not intended to protect social equality of race. This interpretation allowed southern states to make laws requiring separate but equal facilities. These racial discrimination laws, known as Jim Crow laws, lasted nearly 60 years before the Court reversed its decision in *Brown* v. *Board of Education* (1954). In this case, the Court ruled that separate but equal facilities violated the Fourteenth Amendment.

JIM CROW LAW.

UPHELD BY THE UNITED STATES SUPREME COURT.

Statute Within the Competency of the Louisiana Legislature and Railroads—Must Furnish Separate Cars for Whites and Blacks.

Washington, May 18.—The Supreme Court today in an opinion read by Justice Brown, sustained the constitutionality of the law in Louisiana requiring the railroads of that State to provide separate cars for white and colored passengers. There was no interstate. commerce feature in the case for the railroad upon which the incident occurred giving rise to case—Plessey vs. Ferguson—East Louisiana railroad. was and is operated wholly within the State, to the laws of Congress of many of the States. The opinion states that by the analogy of the laws of Congress, and of many of states requiring establishment of separate schools for children of two races and other similar laws the

▲ An article from an 1896 newspaper reporting the *Plessy* v. *Ferguson* verdict

Connect to Your World

What does it mean to be treated equally? Are there instances where separate treatment is equal treatment? Consider the following situations. Decide what is equal treatment for the individuals in each case. Discuss your conclusions with the rest of the class.

- Two students enter their high school. One of them is confined to a wheelchair.
- Twelfth graders are required to pass algebra in order to graduate. One student has a documented learning disability in math; the other does not.

For: Supreme Court cases
www.pearsonschool.com/ushist

A young man in a wheelchair faces the difficulty of entering a building. ▶

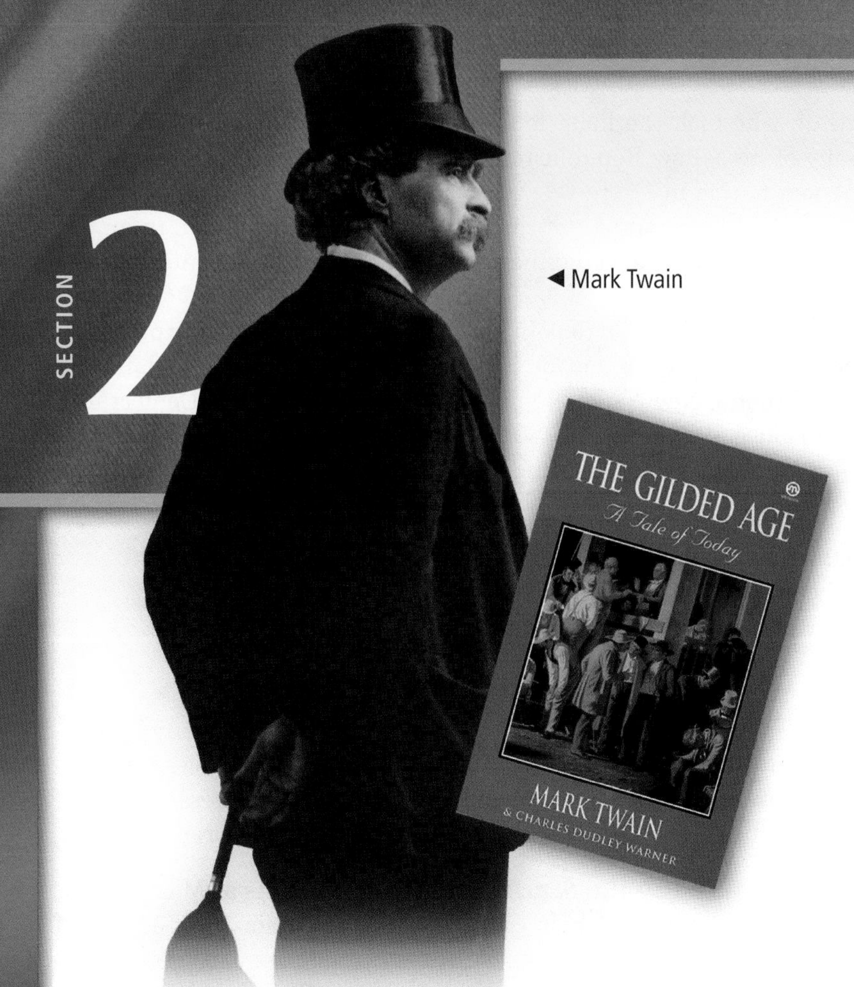

SECTION 2

◀ Mark Twain

WITNESS HISTORY

The Gilded Age

The spoils system, or the practice of giving government positions to political supporters, was the accepted way of staffing federal offices. However, there were demands for reform. Mark Twain and Charles Dudley Warner give their view of the situation in *The Gilded Age*.

“Unless you can get the ear of a Senator . . . and persuade him to use his 'influence' in your behalf, you cannot get an employment of the most trivial nature in Washington. Mere merit, fitness and capability, are useless baggage to you without 'influence.' . . . It would be an odd circumstance to see a girl get employment . . . merely because she was worthy and a competent, and a good citizen of a free country that 'treats all persons alike.'”

—from *The Gilded Age* by Mark Twain and Charles Dudley Warner

Political and Economic Challenges

Objectives

- Analyze the issue of corruption in national politics in the 1870s and 1880s.
- Discuss civil service reform during the 1870s and 1880s.
- Assess the importance of economic issues in the politics of the Gilded Age.

Terms and People

spoils system	Pendleton Civil Service Act
civil service	gold standard

NoteTaking

Reading Skill: Identify Main Ideas As you read, describe the issues that dominated national politics in the 1870s and 1880s.

I. Politics and Economics
  A. Political Stalemate
  B. Corruption in Politics
    1.
    2.

Why It Matters While Congress enacted many major reforms during Reconstruction, it passed very few measures between 1877 and 1900. Instead, inaction and political corruption characterized the political scene during the Gilded Age. This raised questions of whether or not democracy could succeed in a time dominated by large and powerful industrial corporations and men of great wealth. **Section Focus Question: Why did the political structure change during the Gilded Age?**

Balance of Power Creates Stalemate

Party loyalties were so evenly divided that no faction or group gained control for any period of time. Only twice between 1877 and 1897 did either the Republicans or Democrats gain control of the White House and both houses of Congress at the same time. Furthermore, neither held control for more than two years in a row. This made it very difficult to pass new laws. Most of the elections were very close as well, allowing those who lost to block new legislation until they got back in power.

In comparison to Lincoln, the Presidents of the Gilded Age appeared particularly weak. They won by slim margins and seemed to lack integrity. Rutherford B. Hayes owed his election in 1876 to a secret deal. Benjamin Harrison became only the second President in history to lose the popular vote but win the electoral college vote.

Chester Arthur, who took the helm following James Garfield's assassination, upset so many of his fellow Republicans that he failed to win his own party's presidential nomination in 1884.

Vocabulary Builder
integrity–(ihn TEHG ruh tee) *n.* quality of being honest and always having high moral principles

The most noteworthy President of the era was Grover Cleveland. In an era known for its corruption, Cleveland maintained a reputation for integrity. He once observed, "A Democratic thief is as bad as a Republican thief." Cleveland enjoyed an extremely rapid rise to political prominence. In 1881, running as a reformer, he won the race for mayor in Buffalo, New York. A year later, he became the governor of New York, and in 1884, he became the first Democrat to win the White House in 24 years. In 1888, even though he won the popular vote, Cleveland lost to Benjamin Harrison. But Cleveland came back to rewin the presidency in 1892.

 **Checkpoint Why did the federal government fail to make significant political gains between 1877 and 1897?**

Corruption Plagues National Politics

Grover Cleveland's reputation for honesty was the exception. Many government officials routinely accepted bribes. As Henry Adams, the great-grandson of John Adams, observed, "one might search the whole list of Congress, Judiciary, and Executive . . . [from] 1870 to 1895, and find little but damaged reputation."

Political Cartoonists Raise the Alarm Besides such writers as Mark Twain, political cartoonists expressed their concern about the damaging effects of corruption and big money.

"The Bosses of the Senate," one of the most famous political cartoons of the time, drawn by Joseph Keppler, showed a cluster of businessmen representing various trusts, glaring down on the chambers of the Senate.

Thomas Nast did a series of cartoons which exposed the illegal activities of William Marcy "Boss" Tweed, a powerful New York City politician. Eventually, Tweed was arrested. However, he escaped and fled to Spain. While there, Tweed was identified through one of Nast's cartoons.

Analyzing Political Cartoons

The Bosses of the Senate In this political cartoon, Joseph Keppler shows how corporate interests have taken over the business of the Senate.

1. Why do you think the businessmen are drawn so large?
2. How do you think most Americans responded to the political influence of corporations?

The Spoils System Dominates the Government Political parties and the spoils system were central components of politics during the Gilded Age. Under the **spoils system,** which was first used by President Andrew Jackson, politicians awarded government jobs to loyal party workers, with little regard for their qualifications. Parties held elaborate rallies and parades to get out the vote. However, candidates for the presidency did not take part in the campaign. They felt it lowered the reputation of the presidency. Parties developed sophisticated political machines that reached virtually into every ward, in every precinct, in every city in the nation.

The spoils system served as the glue that helped make the parties so powerful. The Postmaster General, who headed the U.S. Postal Service, for example, could reward thousands of supporters with jobs. Likewise, other officials could and did use federal contracts to convince people to vote for their candidates. Ironically, political participation probably got a boost from the spoils system and the fierce partisanship of the era. About 75 to 80 percent of all those who could vote did vote in presidential elections during the Gilded Age.

President Garfield Is Shot
Charles J. Guiteau, unsuccessful at getting a government position, shot President Garfield in a Washington, D.C., train station. *How did Garfield's assassination lead to a change in the civil service system?*

Civil Service Reform Promotes Honest Government The feeling that the spoils system corrupted government, or at least made it terribly inefficient, prompted a number of prominent figures to promote civil service reform. The **civil service** is a system that includes federal jobs in the executive branch. In a reformed system, most government workers would get their jobs due to their expertise and maintain them regardless of which political party won the election. Reforming the spoils system did cause controversy. Without the spoils system, politicians felt they would not attract the people needed to run their parties. Independent attempts by politicians to change the system failed. When Rutherford B. Hayes took office in 1877, he worked for civil service reform. He even placed well-known reformers in high offices. However, the Republican Party did not support his reform efforts. It took the assassination of President James Garfield by Charles J. Guiteau to make civil service reform a reality. Guiteau shot Garfield because he believed that the Republican Party had not fulfilled its promise to give him a government job.

Chester A. Arthur became President after the assassination of Garfield. While Arthur defended the spoils system, he supported the movement for civil service reform, which had been strengthened because of public indignation over Garfield's assassination. Arthur signed the **Pendleton Civil Service Act** in 1883. This act established a Civil Service Commission, which wrote a civil service exam. Individuals who wanted to work for the government had to take the exam, and getting a job depended on doing well on the exam, not on manipulating one's political connections. Initially, the act covered only a small percentage of federal employees, but its reach grew over time, reducing the power of the spoils system.

Vocabulary Builder
manipulate–(muh NIHP yoo layt) *v.* to exert influence or practice deception to obtain some advantage

✓ **Checkpoint How did the spoils system lead to government corruption and, eventually, government reform?**

Economic Issues Challenge the Nation

The tariff and monetary policy were critical economic issues during the Gilded Age. The tariff issue sharply divided the Democrats and Republicans. Monetary policy gave rise to independent political parties or movements that disagreed with the major parties' commitment to the **gold standard.** Using the gold standard meant that the government would use gold as the basis of the nation's currency.

Silver and Gold

By the 1870s, the debate between supporters of the gold or the silver standard began to dominate national politics. At one time, however, the government used both metals to back national currency. Silver and gold certificates, as shown here, were widely circulated.

Americans Debate the Tariff Question The debate over the tariff had deep roots in American history. The tax on imports of manufactured goods and some agricultural products was created to protect newly developed industries. Since then, the debate to lower or increase tariffs continued. Differences over the tariff had divided the Federalists and Jeffersonians and the Democrats and Whigs. During the Gilded Age, it divided the Republicans and Democrats. The tariff question became a major issue during the presidential election of 1888. The Republicans favored a high tariff, arguing that it would allow American industries to grow and promote jobs in manufacturing. Democrats countered that high tariffs increased the costs of goods to consumers and made it harder for American farmers to sell their goods abroad.

Conflicts Develop Over Monetary Policy Two related factors turned monetary policy into a bitter issue during the Gilded Age. During the Civil War, the federal government issued paper money, known as greenbacks. After the war, because they had contributed to wartime inflation (a rise in prices), the government retired, or got rid of, the greenbacks.

Around the same time, Congress passed the Coinage Act of 1873. This law reversed the government policy of making both gold and silver coins. Those who favored the minting of silver—in other words, considering silver as money—protested against what they termed the "Crime of 1873" and prompted Congress to mint silver dollars. Nonetheless, the debate over whether to consider both gold and silver as money or only gold as money continued.

Bankers and others involved in international trade feared that considering silver as money would undermine the economy. In contrast, most farmers favored coining silver to create inflation. They hoped the rise in prices would increase their income. You will read more about this dispute in the next section.

Checkpoint Why did the Republicans and Democrats differ in their view of the tariff issue?

SECTION 2 Assessment

Progress Monitoring *Online*
For: Self-test with vocabulary practice
www.pearsonschool.com/ushist

Comprehension

1. **Terms and People** Explain how each of the following terms describes a political issue during the 1870s and 1880s.
   - spoils system
   - civil service
   - Pendleton Civil Service Act
   - gold standard
2. **NoteTaking Reading Skill: Identify Main Ideas** Use your outline to answer the Section Focus Question: Why did the political structure change during the Gilded Age?

Writing About History

3. **Quick Write: Examine the Question** Look for the key word that will tell you how to focus and organize your response: Summarize the importance of the tariff as a national issue. Write a brief paragraph.

Critical Thinking

4. **Draw Inferences** Why do you think Congress became the strongest branch of the government in the 1880s?
5. **Analyze Information** What were the positive and negative effects of the Pendleton Civil Service Act?
6. **Identify Point of View** President Cleveland called the high tariff "unjust taxation." Why do you think President Cleveland made this statement? Explain his point of view.

SECTION 3

▲ Farmers gather at a Populist rally.

WITNESS HISTORY

Black and White Together

In the late 1800s, a social and political movement made up largely of farmers arose in the South and West. Known as Populists, the biggest obstacle this group faced, especially in the South, was antagonism between blacks and whites. Populist leader Tom Watson tried to persuade the groups to work together.

> “The white tenant lives adjoining the colored tenant. . . . They are equally burdened with heavy taxes. They pay the same high rent. . . . They pay the same enormous prices for farm supplies. . . . Now the People’s Party says to these two men, ‘You are kept apart that you may be separately fleeced of your earnings. . . . You are deceived and blinded that you may not see how this race antagonism perpetuates a monetary system which beggars both.”
>
> —Thomas Watson, “The Negro Question in the South,” 1892

Farmers and Populism

Objectives

- Analyze the problems farmers faced and the groups they formed to address them.
- Assess the goals of the Populists, and explain why the Populist Party did not last.

Terms and People

Oliver H. Kelley
Grange
Populist Party
William Jennings Bryan
William McKinley

NoteTaking

Reading Skill: Identify Causes and Effects As you read, list the reasons that farmers in the South and West felt the need to organize and the effects of their effort.

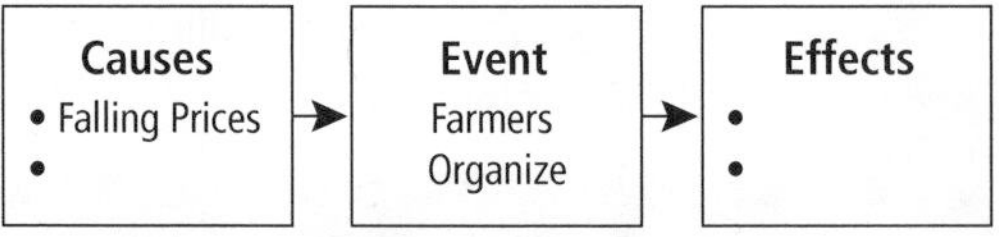

Why It Matters Following the Civil War, millions of men and women migrated west in search of the American dream. However, in the late 1880s and early 1890s, their dream began to turn into a nightmare, which, in turn, sparked a social and political revolt known as populism. This movement displayed the dissatisfaction of millions of ordinary Americans—poor farmers, small landholders, and urban workers—and produced one of the largest third-party movements in American history. **Section Focus Question: What led to the rise of the Populist movement, and what effect did it have?**

Farmers Face Many Problems

The farmers of the West and the South were willing to accept the difficulties of farm life. Yet, farmers discovered that other enormous obstacles stood in the way of realizing their dreams. They received low prices for their crops, yet they had to pay high costs for transportation. Debts mounted while their influence on the political system declined.

Falling Prices and Rising Debt Between 1870 and 1895, farm prices plummeted. Cotton, which sold for about 15 cents a pound in the early 1870s, sold for only about 6 cents a pound in the mid-1890s. Corn and wheat prices declined nearly as rapidly. One study estimated

INFOGRAPHIC

A farmer plows ▶ through hard soil.

Plight of the Farmer

Banks considered mortgage loans a good investment. However, between 1889 and 1893, thousands of farms failed and banks foreclosed on mortgages. ▼

In the 1890s, farmers faced drought, poor harvests, debt, and a drop in the price of wheat, barley, and other crops. Oliver H. Kelley, who would eventually found the Grange organization, hoped to encourage farmers to feel their labor was "honorable" and "farming [was] the highest calling on earth." It was an ambitious goal, since farmers were a discontented group during the late 1800s. Furthermore, as the cartoon at the right shows, the government support that farmers sought was slow in coming. Farm reform was not a primary concern for most lawmakers.

Planting crops on tough prairie soil was hard work for this couple on their farm in Nebraska. ▼

Critical Thinking

1. **Synthesize Information** Why might farmers have readily joined forces with urban workers?
2. **Identify Point of View** Do you think most farmers felt that their work was "the highest calling on earth"? Explain.

that by the early 1890s, it was costing farmers more to produce corn than they could get by selling it, so they burned it and used it as fuel. Planting more crops did not help. On the contrary, the more crops farmers produced, the more prices declined.

During the same time period, the cost of doing business rose. To pay for new machinery, seed, livestock, and other needs, farmers went into debt. An increasing number of farmers mortgaged their farms to raise funds to survive and became tenant farmers—meaning they no longer owned the farm where they worked.

Big Business Practices Also Hurt Farmers blamed big business, especially the railroads and the banks, for their difficulties. They protested that railroads, as monopolies, charged whatever rates they wanted. Likewise, they complained that banks set interest rates at ridiculously high levels. Southern farmers, especially black sharecroppers, faced the added problem of having to deal with dishonest merchants and landlords who paid less for crops and charged more for supplies than promised.

In addition, farmers grew angry because they felt the nation had turned its back on them. The United States had a long tradition of electing leaders from farm states with agricultural backgrounds, like Thomas Jefferson. Yet, it now appeared that most of the nation's leaders came from urban industrial states. Moreover, farmers felt that they performed honest labor and produced necessary goods, while bankers and businessmen were the ones who got rich. One editor for a farmers' newspaper explained:

> **Primary Source** "There are three great crops raised in Nebraska. One is the crop of corn, one a crop of freight rates, and one a crop of interest. One is produced by farmers who sweat and toil to farm the land. The other two are produced by men who sit in their offices and behind their bank counters and farm the farmers."
>
> —*Farmers' Alliance,* 1890

Farmers, however, refused to accept these circumstances. They took action.

 **Checkpoint What were the farmers' major grievances, or complaints?**

Farmers Organize and Seek Change

Farmers created a network of organizations, first in the Midwest and then in the South and West, to address their problems. The Granger movement, also known as the "Patrons of Husbandry," was the first.

Vocabulary Builder
network–(NEHT werk) *n.* group of people, organizations, etc., that work together

The Grange Tries Several Strategies Organized in 1867 by **Oliver H. Kelley**—a Minnesota farmer, businessman, journalist, and government clerk—the organization popularly known as the **Grange** attracted about a million members. The goals of the Grange included providing education on new farming techniques and calling for the regulation of railroad and grain elevator rates.

In the mid-1870s, the states of Illinois, Wisconsin, and Minnesota enacted laws that set maximum rates for shipping freight and for grain storage. The railroad companies challenged these "Grange Laws" in the courts, but the Supreme Court, in general, upheld them. The Grangers also prompted the federal government to establish the Interstate Commerce Commission (ICC) to oversee interstate transportation.

Farmers' Alliances Lead the Protest Although the Grange declined in the late 1870s, farm protest remained strong. Farmers' Alliances, such as the Southern Farmers' Alliance, became important reform organizations. These alliances formed cooperatives to collectively sell their crops, and they called on the federal government to establish "sub-treasuries," or postal banks, to provide farmers with low-interest loans. They hoped the cooperatives would push the costs of doing business down and the prices for crops up. Some of the cooperative efforts succeeded. The Georgia Alliance led a boycott against manufacturers who raised the price of the special cord that farmers used to wrap bundles of cotton.

The Southern Farmers' Alliance organized white farmers. There was also an Alliance network for African American farmers. R. M. Humphrey, a white Baptist minister, headed the Colored Farmers' Alliance, which had been organized by African American and white farmers. Nearly one million African American farmers joined the group by 1891. The Colored Farmers' Alliance recognized that both white and African American farmers shared the same difficulties, but racial tensions prevented any effective cooperation between the groups.

 **Checkpoint** **What reforms did the farmers' organizations introduce?**

The Populist Party Demands Reforms

The spread of the Farmers' Alliances culminated with the formation of the **Populist Party,** or People's Party, in 1892. These Populists sought to build a new political party from the grass roots up. They ran entire slates of candidates for local, state, and national positions. Like a prairie fire, the Populist Party spread rapidly, putting pressure on the two major political parties to consider their demands.

Populists State Their Goals The Populist Party spelled out their views in their platform, which they adopted in Omaha, Nebraska, in July 1892. The platform warned about the dangers of political corruption, an inadequate monetary supply, and an unresponsive government. The Populist Party proposed specific remedies to these problems. To fight low prices, they called for the coinage of silver, or "free silver." To combat high costs, they demanded government ownership of the railroads. Mary Elizabeth Lease, a fiery Populist Party spokesperson, also advanced the cause of women's suffrage.

The Populist Party nominated James B. Weaver of Iowa as their presidential candidate and James Field of Virginia as his running mate. Both had risen to the rank of general in the United States and Confederate armies, respectively, and their nominations represented the party's attempt to overcome the regional divisions that had kept farmers apart since the end of the Civil War. (Southern whites had supported the Democrats; northerners, the Republicans.) The Populist Party also sought to reach out to urban workers, to convince them that they faced the same enemy: the industrial elite.

Populists Achieve Some Successes For a new political party, the Populists did quite well in 1892. Weaver won more than one million votes for the presidency, and the Populists elected three governors, five senators, and ten congressmen. In 1894, the Populist Party continued to expand its base, gaining seats in the state legislatures and prompting the major political parties to consider endorsing its ideas.

In the South, the Populist Party had to unite blacks and whites if it hoped to succeed politically. As noted above, Tom Watson, Georgia's most famous Populist Party leader, made a strong case for casting aside racial prejudice in favor of a political alliance between the races. However, the Democratic Party successfully used racist tactics, such as warning that a Populist victory would lead to "Negro supremacy," to diminish the appeal of the Populist Party.

 **Checkpoint** **What were the goals of the Populist Party?**

The Populist Party, 1890–1900

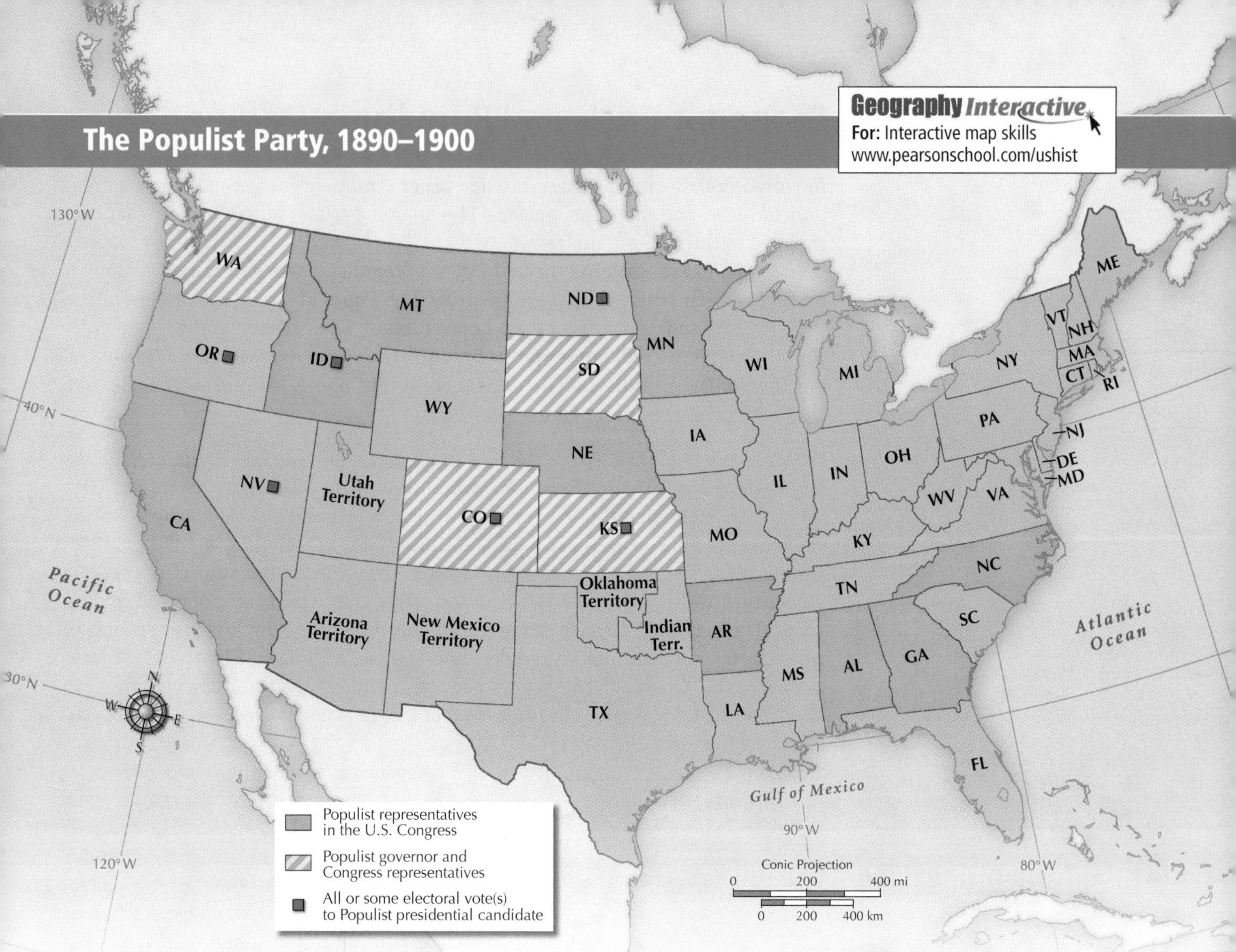

Geography *Interactive*
For: Interactive map skills
www.pearsonschool.com/ushist

130°W 40°N 30°N 120°W 90°W 80°W

WA, OR, ID, MT, ND, SD, WY, MN, WI, MI, NY, ME, VT, NH, MA, CT, RI, PA, NJ, DE, MD, NE, IA, IL, IN, OH, WV, VA, NV, Utah Territory, CO, KS, MO, KY, CA, NC, TN, Oklahoma Territory, Indian Terr., AR, SC, Arizona Territory, New Mexico Territory, MS, AL, GA, LA, TX, FL

Pacific Ocean

Atlantic Ocean

Gulf of Mexico

- Populist representatives in the U.S. Congress
- Populist governor and Congress representatives
- All or some electoral vote(s) to Populist presidential candidate

Conic Projection
0 200 400 mi
0 200 400 km

The Omaha Platform

Distressed farmers did not feel that either the Republican or Democratic parties addressed their problems. As a result, in 1892, farmers attended a convention in Omaha, Nebraska, to set forth their own party platform. Their demands, detailed in The Omaha Platform, are listed below.

- Unlimited coinage of silver
- Graduated income tax
- Government ownership of railroad and telegraph companies
- Bank regulations

Map Skills By the election of 1892, the Populist Party began to draw national attention.

1. **Region** Why did Populists fail to win support in northeastern states?
2. **Draw Conclusions** Based on the map, why might the Democratic and Republican parties have been concerned about the Populist Party in the elections after 1892?

Populist Party supporters wore silver badges to show their stand on free silver.

Economic Crisis and Populism's Decline

In 1893, a four-year-long depression began that not only worsened conditions for already-suffering farmers but for other Americans as well. Labor unrest and violence engulfed the nation. The major parties failed to satisfactorily respond to the nation's distress.

In the midst of national discontent, the Populist Party's dream of forging a broad coalition with urban workers grew. The Populists' relative success at the polls in 1892 and 1894 raised their hopes further. The decision of the Democratic Party to nominate **William Jennings Bryan** as their presidential candidate put the election for the Populists on an entirely different plane, leading some to believe they could win the White House that year.

Bryan and the Election of 1896 Born in Salem, Illinois, William Jennings Bryan moved to Lincoln, Nebraska, where he set up a law practice in 1887. He earned the nickname the "boy orator," in part by displaying his strong debating skills during his successful run for the United States Congress in 1890. In 1896, Bryan addressed the national Democratic convention on the subject of the gold standard, attacking Grover Cleveland and others in the party who opposed coining silver. The audience listened and cheered as Bryan spoke for "the plain people of this country," for "our farms" and declared "we beg no longer." The speech became known as the "Cross of Gold" speech because it ended with the following line: "You shall not press down upon the brow of labor this crown of thorns, you shall not crucify mankind upon a cross of gold."

Geography *Interactive*
For: Interactive map skills
www.pearsonschool.com/ushist

The Presidential Election of 1896

Candidate (Party)	Electoral Vote	Popular Vote	% Electoral Vote	% Popular Vote
William McKinley (Republican)	271	7,104,779	60.6	51.0
William Jennings Bryan (Democratic)	176	6,502,925	39.4	46.7
Other	—	314,226	—	2.3

Map Skills The election of 1896 changed the shape of national politics.

1. **Location** Which two states were split between Bryan and McKinley?
2. **Synthesize Information** Why could the election results be considered a victory of industry over agriculture?

The speech so moved the Democratic delegates that they nominated Bryan as their party's presidential candidate. He was just 36 years old and had not been a contender for the nomination until then. Bryan's advocacy of "free silver," or the coinage of silver as well as gold, and his support of a number of other Populist Party proposals, placed the Populists in a difficult situation. Holding their convention after the Democrats, the Populists had to decide whether to nominate their own presidential candidate and continue to focus on building a broad-based movement from the bottom up or to endorse Bryan with the hope that they could capture the White House in 1896. They chose the latter course.

Bryan's campaign was like none other before. For the first time, a presidential candidate toured the nation, speaking directly to the people. In contrast, **William McKinley,** the Republican candidate, accumulated approximately $15 million, 30 times the amount Bryan had, and allowed party regulars to do the campaigning for him. Marcus Hanna, the political powerhouse who orchestrated McKinley's run, cast Bryan and his Populist Party supporters as a potential dictator and a threat to the Republic. For instance, one cartoon published in the pro-Republican *Los Angeles Times* depicted the Democratic-Populist coalition as a collection of evil witches, who fed the fires of sectionalism, discontent, and prejudice in order to win the election.

✓ **Checkpoint** **How did the nomination of William Jennings Bryan affect the Populist Party?**

Populism's Legacy

McKinley won the election of 1896 and went on to win reelection, again over Bryan, in 1900. Bryan's emphasis on monetary reform, especially free silver, did not appeal to urban workers, and the Populist Party failed to win a state outside of the South and West. Moreover, the decision to endorse Bryan weakened the Populists at the local and state levels, and the party never recovered from its defeat in 1896. The Populist Party lingered for nearly a decade. By the early 1900s, it had disappeared as a feasible alternative to the two major political parties. Most of the voters who supported the Populist Party returned to the Democratic Party in 1896.

Even though the Populist Party fell apart, many of the specific reforms that it advocated became a reality in the early decades of the twentieth century. As we shall see, the Progressives supported a graduated income tax, regulation of the railroads, and a more flexible monetary system. Moreover, populism had a lasting effect on the style of politics in the United States. For a brief time, there was even a coalition of whites and blacks in Texas. They were able to find a common political ground. Increasingly, candidates campaigned directly to the people, and, like Bryan, they emphasized their association with ordinary Americans.

✓ **Checkpoint** **What happened to the Populist Party?**

HISTORY MAKERS

William Jennings Bryan (1860–1925)

William Jennings Bryan practiced law before entering politics. Soon after moving to Nebraska, he was elected to the House of Representatives, where he served two terms. A gifted speaker, Bryan was called "the Great Commoner" because he favored the poor farmers over large corporations. Bryan also backed many Progressive causes, such as the direct election of senators, the adoption of an income tax, Prohibition, and women's suffrage. In 1913, President Woodrow Wilson named him Secretary of State. Committed to keeping peace, Bryan persuaded 31 countries to accept his idea of arbitrating international disputes instead of resorting to war. His hopes for peace were dashed, however, when World War I broke out.

SECTION 3 Assessment

Progress Monitoring *Online*
For: Self-test with vocabulary practice
www.pearsonschool.com/ushist

Comprehension

1. **Terms and People** Explain the significance of these terms and people in establishing support for farmers.
   - Oliver H. Kelley
   - Grange
   - Populist Party
   - William Jennings Bryan
2. **NoteTaking Reading Skill: Identify Causes and Effects** Use your cause-and-effect chart to answer the Section Focus Question: What led to the rise of the Populist movement, and what effect did it have?

Writing About History

3. **Quick Write: Support Your Ideas** Write a paragraph in response to the following: Explain how the election of 1896 ended the political stalemate that began in 1877. Keep in mind that each sentence should support your main idea.

Critical Thinking

4. **Determine Relevance** How did the deflation, or decrease, in the money supply in the late 1800s affect farmers?
5. **Synthesize Information** How did the Farmers' Alliances begin a crusade against big business?
6. **Make Comparisons** In what ways did McKinley represent the old way of politics? In what ways did Bryan represent the new way?

CHAPTER 16

Quick Study Guide

Progress Monitoring *Online*
For: Self-test with vocabulary practice
www.pearsonschool.com/ushist

Segregation and Discrimination

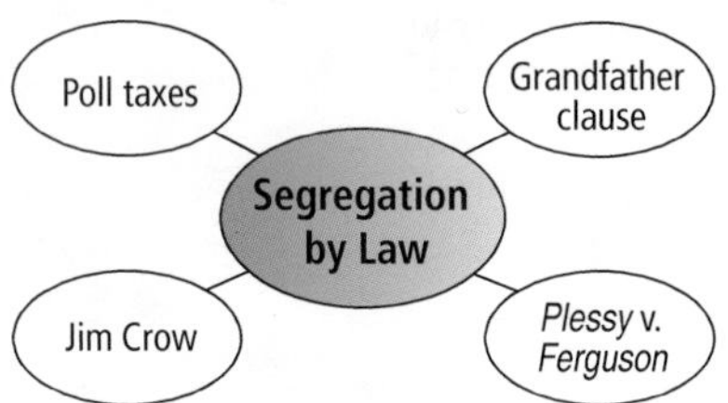

Gold or Silver?

Gold Bugs	Silverites
• Gold standard • Supported by bankers and factory owners • Effects –Prices fall –Less money in circulation	• Bimetallism • Supported by farmers and workers • Effects –Prices rise –More money in circulation

Wheat Prices, 1866–1896

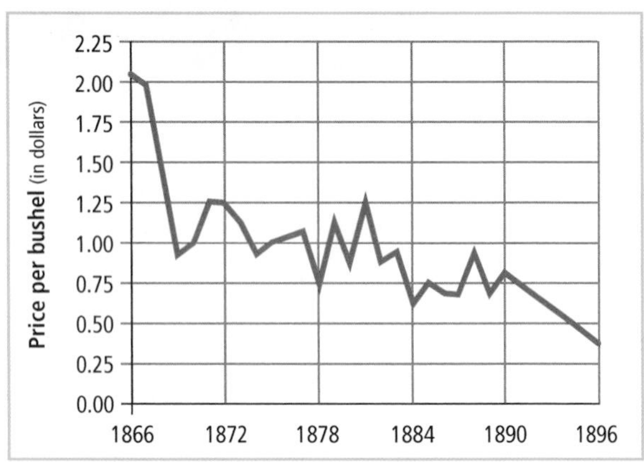

SOURCE: *Historical Statistics of the United States*

Populist Party Platform

- Increase in money supply
- Graduated income tax
- Federal loan program for farmers
- Election of U.S. senators by popular vote
- Eight-hour workday
- Restriction on immigration
- Government ownership of railroads

Quick Study Timeline

In America

1877 First Farmers' Alliance is established

1882 Congress passes Chinese Exclusion Act

Presidential Terms: Ulysses S. Grant 1869–1877; Rutherford B. Hayes 1877–1881; James A. Garfield 1881; Chester A. Arthur 1881–1885

1870 — 1875 — 1880

Around the World

1871 Labor unions legalized in Great Britain

1873 Slave markets abolished in Zanzibar

American Issues Connector

By connecting prior knowledge with what you have learned in this chapter, you can gradually build your understanding of enduring questions that still affect America today. Answer the questions below. Then, use your American Issues Connector study guide (or go online: www.pearsonschool.com/ushist).

Issues You Learned About

● **Women in American Society** Throughout our country's history, women have worked to bring positive change to society.

1. Describe the role that women played in the abolition movement. Why were some women reformers disappointed with the post-Civil War reforms?
2. On the eve of the Declaration of Independence, Abigail Adams wrote to her husband, John Adams: ". . . in the new code of laws . . . , I desire you would remember the ladies and be more generous and favorable to them. . . . Do not put such unlimited power into the hands of the husbands. . . . If . . . attention is not paid to the ladies, we are determined to foment [start] a rebellion, and will not hold ourselves bound by any laws in which we have no voice. . . ." Would Susan B. Anthony and Elizabeth Cady Stanton have agreed with Adams's views? Explain.

● **Expanding and Protecting Civil Rights** Minority groups have worked hard to gain their full civil rights.

3. What was the significance of the Thirteenth, Fourteenth, and Fifteenth amendments?
4. In what ways were African Americans' civil rights violated in the post-Civil War years?
5. How did Chinese immigrants use the legal system to challenge discrimination? How successful were these efforts?

● **Sectionalism and National Politics** Different regions of the country often have varying economic and political needs.

6. By the late 1800s, farmers in the South and Midwest had lost a great deal of their political power. How did this happen?
7. Why and how did the Populist Party seek to expand its message to urban voters?
8. Why was the Populist Party short-lived?

Connect to Your World — Activity

Farmers' Groups

Group	Goal
Grange	Called for states to pass laws setting maximum rates for shipping and storage
Farmers' Alliances	Called on the federal government to establish postal banks to provide farmers with low-interest loans
Populist Party	Called for coinage of silver and demanded government ownership of railroads

During the Gilded Age, the groups listed above worked to bring about laws that were favorable to farmers. What groups are working today to further the interests of farmers? What laws do they support? Go online or to your local library and research current laws and programs that affect agriculture in the United States, as well as laws or programs that farmers would like to see implemented. Compile your findings in a chart.

1883 Civil Service Act establishes a merit system for government jobs

1888 Booker T. Washington opens Tuskegee Institute

1896 In *Plessy* v. *Ferguson*, Supreme Court rules separate but equal facilities legal

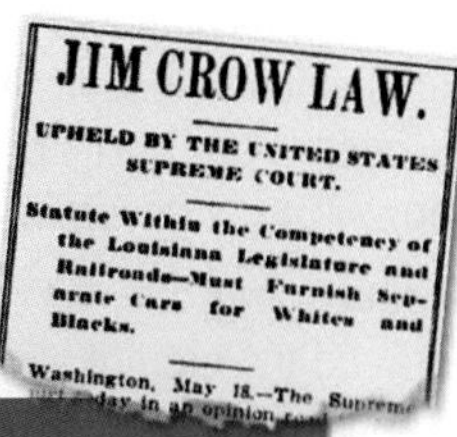

Grover Cleveland 1885–1889 | Benjamin Harrison 1889–1893 | Grover Cleveland 1893–1897

1885 | 1890 | 1895

1885 First Canadian transcontinental railroad completed

1893 Women gain right to vote in New Zealand

History Interactive For: Interactive timeline www.pearsonschool.com/ushist

Chapter Assessment

Terms and People

1. Define **poll tax.** Why did poll taxes have a particularly negative effect on African Americans?
2. What was **Las Gorras Blancas**? What was its goal?
3. What was the **Pendleton Civil Service Act**? What led to its passage?
4. What was the **gold standard**? Which groups of Americans supported it, and which groups opposed it?
5. Who was **William Jennings Bryan**? Why did the Populist Party support him?

Focus Questions

The focus question for this chapter is **What political, social, and economic issues did the nation face during the late 1800s?** Build an answer to this big question by answering the focus questions for Section 1 through 3 and the Critical Thinking questions that follow.

Section 1

6. How were the civil and political rights of certain groups in America undermined during the years after Reconstruction?

Section 2

7. Why did the political structure change during the Gilded Age?

Section 3

8. What led to the rise of the Populist movement, and what effect did it have?

Critical Thinking

9. **Make Comparisons** How were the views of Booker T. Washington and W.E.B. Du Bois similar? How were they different?
10. **Analyze Information** Were the goals of Las Gorras Blancas and the Farmers' Alliance the same? Explain.
11. **Make Generalizations** How would you characterize the American political landscape during the Gilded Age?
12. **Evaluate Credibility of Sources** The *Farmers' Alliance* wrote in 1890 that there were three main ways that people earned money in Nebraska: by raising corn crops, by charging freight rates, and by charging interest on bank loans. Do you think this statement should be taken at face value? Explain.
13. **Analyze Maps** Answer the questions based on the map as well as your reading of this chapter. In the 1896 election, William J. Bryan won the most states but lost the election.
    (a) In which regions did McKinley win?
    (b) Why did the Populist Party fail to win the election?

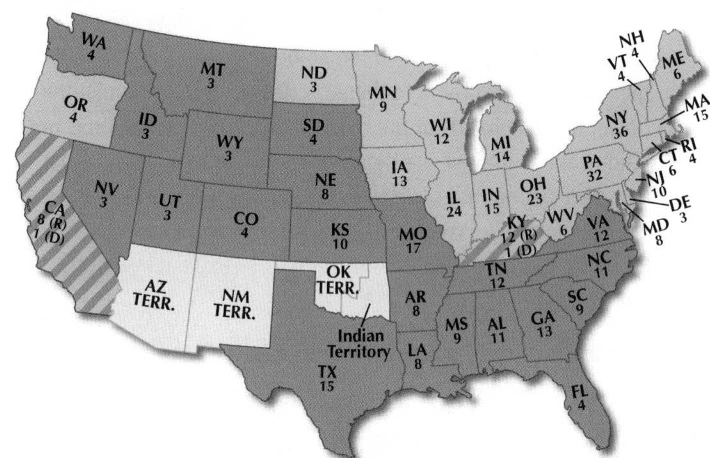

Candidate (Party)	Electoral Vote	Popular Vote	% Electoral Vote	% Popular Vote
McKinley (Republican)	271	7,104,779	60.6	51.0
Bryan (Democratic)	176	6,502,925	39.4	46.7

Writing About History

Writing for Assessment The depression of 1893 had lasting effects on the nation. However, the seeds for these effects began before the collapse of the economy. Write an answer to the following essay topic: Analyze how a demand for a better share of economic and social benefits led Americans to challenge the power of the government and big business before and after 1893.

Prewriting

- Read the prompt and determine what you know about the topic.
- Look for key words, such as "explain," that will tell you what kind of answer to provide.

Drafting

- Focus your time by allowing 10 minutes for prewriting, 20 minutes for drafting, and 10 minutes for revising your response.
- Develop a thesis for your essay, and make sure each piece of information supports it.

Revising

- Use the guidelines on page W22 of the Writing Handbook to revise your essay.

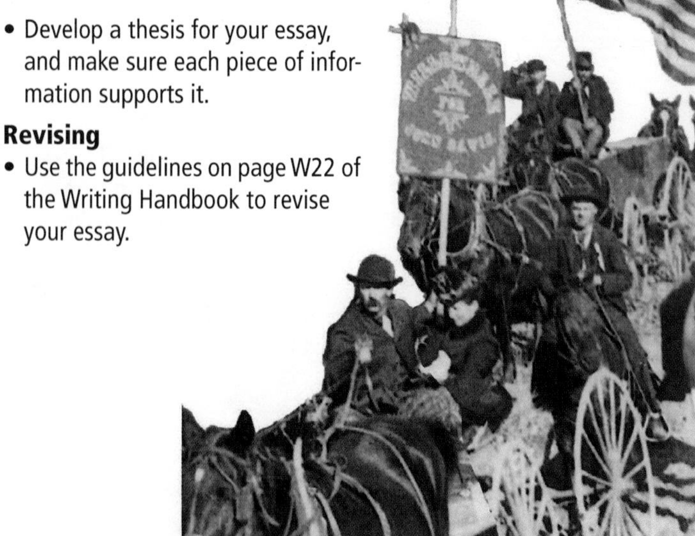

Document-Based Assessment

Populism

What the Populist movement lacked in longevity—it lasted barely a decade—it made up for in passion. Populist fervor swept the country in the 1890s, and People's Party candidates won millions of votes. What made Populist ideas so attractive to so many Americans? Did this short-lived but spirited movement have a lasting effect on the American landscape?

Document A

"The man who is employed for wages is as much a business man as his employer; . . . the merchant at the crossroads store is as much a business man as the merchant of New York; the farmer who goes forth in the morning and toils all day, . . . is as much a business man as the man who goes upon the Board of Trade and bets upon the price of grain; the miners who go down a thousand feet into the earth, or climb two thousand feet upon the cliffs, and bring forth from their hiding places the precious metals . . . are as much business men as the few financial magnates who, in a back room, corner the money of the world. We come to speak of this broader class of business men."

—*William Jennings Bryan, Democratic National Convention, 1896*

Document B

"We realize that, while we [Americans] have political independence, our financial and industrial independence is yet to be attained by restoring to our country the Constitutional control and exercise of the functions necessary to a people's government, which functions have been basely surrendered by our public servants to corporate monopolies. . . .

—*Preamble from the People's Party platform, 1896*

Document C

A Box of Problems

—Los Angeles Times, *September 14, 1896*

Document D

"As the People's party died, many of the disillusioned dropped out of politics. This is part of the reason the percent of eligible voters to cast ballots in presidential races dropped thirty percent between 1896 and 1924. Others continued the egalitarian struggle by joining Eugene V. Debs in the Socialist party. Many, however, returned to the reform wings of their old parties. Several farmer demands [later] became law, . . . namely monopoly regulation, banking/currency reform, and the graduated income tax. Populists had also advocated direct democracy with reforms such as the initiative and referendum. . . . America, however, adopted Populist reforms selectively and piecemeal. The result was hardly the egalitarian vision of Populism in its heyday."

—*Worth Robert Miller,* The Gilded Age: Essays on the Origin of Modern America

---

Reading, Analysis, and Writing Skills

Use your knowledge of populism and Documents A, B, C, and D to answer questions 1 through 4.

1. Which of the documents is a primary source that suggests that Populist ideas would unleash dangerous consequences for the United States?
   A Document A
   B Document B
   C Document C
   D Document D

2. Which primary source documents describe Populist ideas?
   A Documents A and B
   B Documents B and C
   C Documents C and D
   D Documents D and A

3. According to Document D, what became of Populist supporters after the People's Party ceased to exist?
   A They formed a new Populist Party.
   B They re-created the People's Party with new leaders.
   C They joined different political parties.
   D They became farm reformers.

4. **Writing Task** How much did populism impact life in the United States? Use your knowledge of American history and evidence from the sources above to support your position.

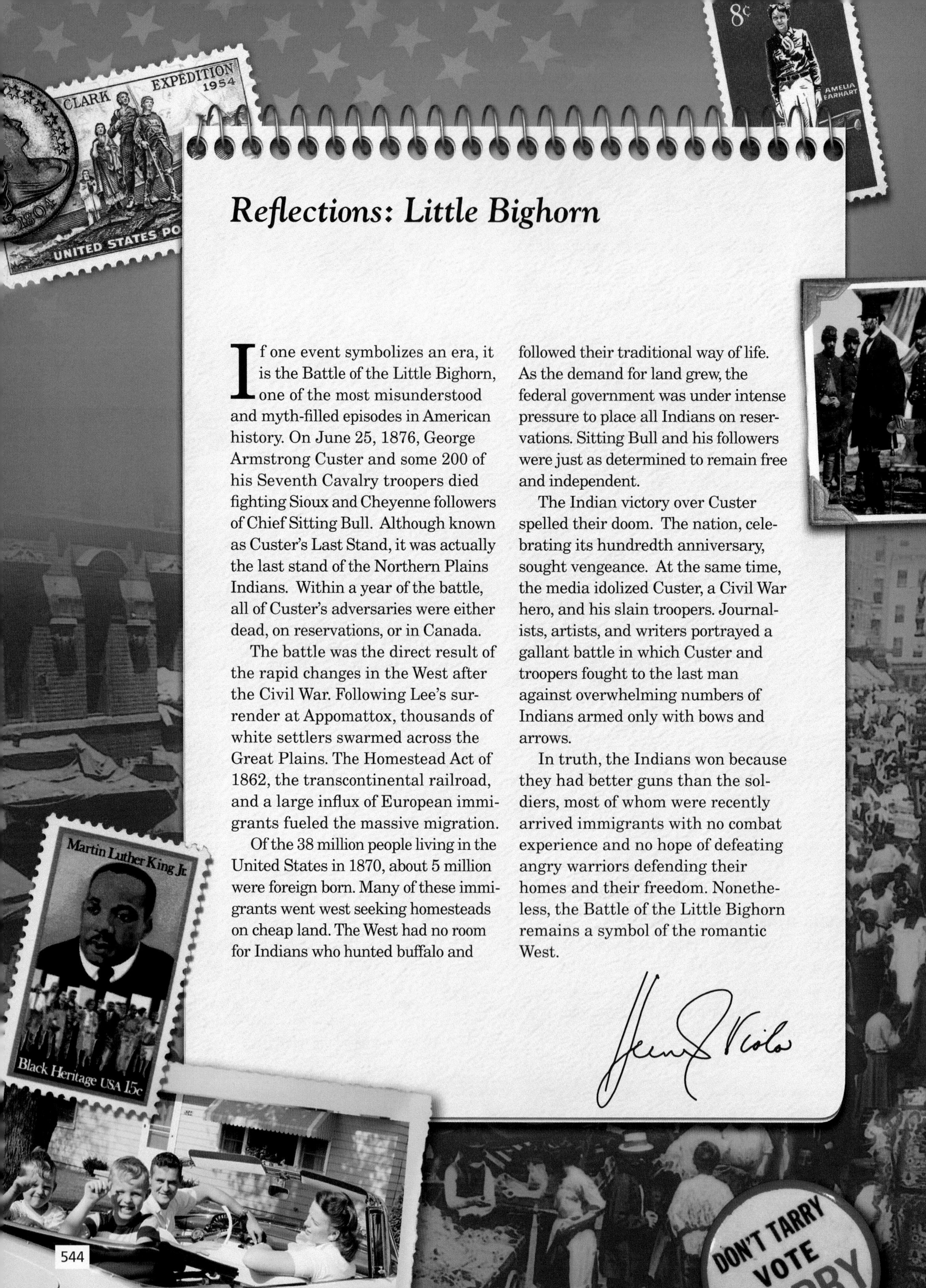

Reflections: Little Bighorn

If one event symbolizes an era, it is the Battle of the Little Bighorn, one of the most misunderstood and myth-filled episodes in American history. On June 25, 1876, George Armstrong Custer and some 200 of his Seventh Cavalry troopers died fighting Sioux and Cheyenne followers of Chief Sitting Bull. Although known as Custer's Last Stand, it was actually the last stand of the Northern Plains Indians. Within a year of the battle, all of Custer's adversaries were either dead, on reservations, or in Canada.

The battle was the direct result of the rapid changes in the West after the Civil War. Following Lee's surrender at Appomattox, thousands of white settlers swarmed across the Great Plains. The Homestead Act of 1862, the transcontinental railroad, and a large influx of European immigrants fueled the massive migration.

Of the 38 million people living in the United States in 1870, about 5 million were foreign born. Many of these immigrants went west seeking homesteads on cheap land. The West had no room for Indians who hunted buffalo and followed their traditional way of life. As the demand for land grew, the federal government was under intense pressure to place all Indians on reservations. Sitting Bull and his followers were just as determined to remain free and independent.

The Indian victory over Custer spelled their doom. The nation, celebrating its hundredth anniversary, sought vengeance. At the same time, the media idolized Custer, a Civil War hero, and his slain troopers. Journalists, artists, and writers portrayed a gallant battle in which Custer and troopers fought to the last man against overwhelming numbers of Indians armed only with bows and arrows.

In truth, the Indians won because they had better guns than the soldiers, most of whom were recently arrived immigrants with no combat experience and no hope of defeating angry warriors defending their homes and their freedom. Nonetheless, the Battle of the Little Bighorn remains a symbol of the romantic West.

Reference Section

Five Themes of Geography

The five themes of geography are tools you can use to analyze geographic information given in photographs, charts, maps, and text. Use these themes to determine the role of geography in U.S. history.

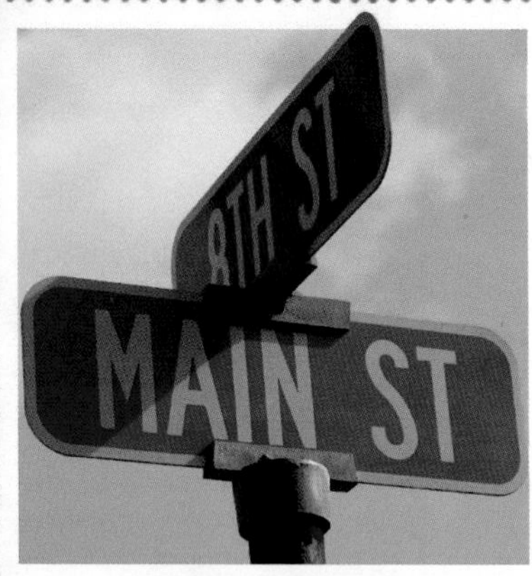

Location answers the question, Where is it? The answer might be an absolute location, such as 167 River Lane, or a relative location, such as six miles west of Mill City.

Place identifies natural and human features that make one place different from another. Landforms and buildings are features that can be used to identify a specific place.

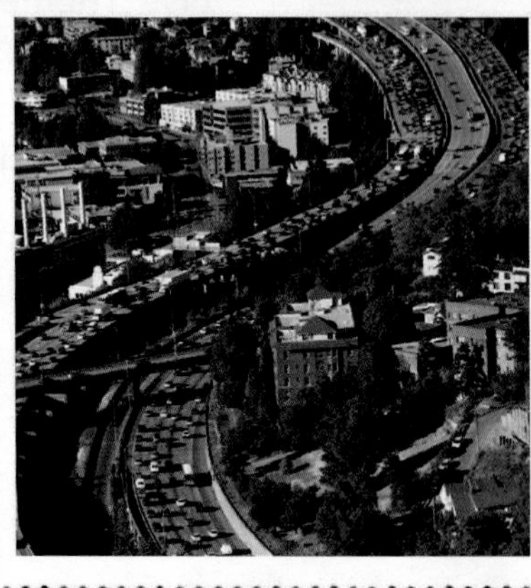

Movement answers the question, How do people, goods, and ideas move from place to place?

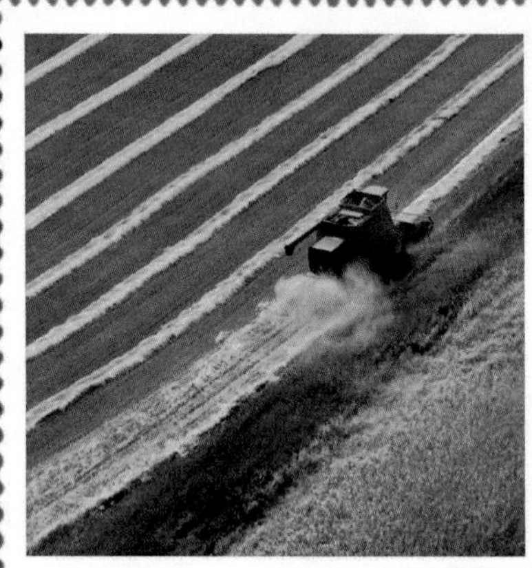

Human-Environment Interaction explores the relationship between people and the natural world. Humans often modify their environment, and the environment affects how they live.

Regions are areas that share at least one common feature. Climate, culture, and government are features that can be used to define regions.

Profile of the Fifty States

State	Capital	Entered Union	Population (2005)	Population Rank	Land Area (Sq. Mi.)	Electoral Votes
Alabama	Montgomery	1819	4,557,808	23	50,744	9
Alaska	Juneau	1959	663,661	47	571,951	3
Arizona	Phoenix	1912	5,939,292	17	113,635	10
Arkansas	Little Rock	1836	2,779,154	32	52,068	6
California	Sacramento	1850	36,132,147	1	155,959	55
Colorado	Denver	1876	4,665,177	22	103,718	9
Connecticut	Hartford	1788	3,510,297	29	4,845	7
Delaware	Dover	1787	843,524	45	1,954	3
District of Columbia	——	——	550,521	——	——	3
Florida	Tallahassee	1845	17,789,864	4	53,927	27
Georgia	Atlanta	1788	9,072,576	9	57,906	15
Hawaii	Honolulu	1959	1,275,194	42	6,423	4
Idaho	Boise	1890	1,429,096	39	82,747	4
Illinois	Springfield	1818	12,763,371	5	55,584	21
Indiana	Indianapolis	1816	6,271,973	15	35,867	11
Iowa	Des Moines	1846	2,966,334	30	55,869	7
Kansas	Topeka	1861	2,744,687	33	81,815	6
Kentucky	Frankfort	1792	4,173,405	26	39,728	8
Louisiana	Baton Rouge	1812	4,523,628	24	43,562	9
Maine	Augusta	1820	1,321,505	40	30,862	4
Maryland	Annapolis	1788	5,600,388	19	9,774	10
Massachusetts	Boston	1788	6,398,743	13	7,840	12
Michigan	Lansing	1837	10,120,860	8	56,804	17
Minnesota	St. Paul	1858	5,132,799	21	79,610	10
Mississippi	Jackson	1817	2,921,088	31	46,907	6
Missouri	Jefferson City	1821	5,800,310	18	68,886	11
Montana	Helena	1889	935,670	44	145,552	3
Nebraska	Lincoln	1867	1,758,787	38	76,872	5
Nevada	Carson City	1864	2,414,807	35	109,826	5
New Hampshire	Concord	1788	1,309,940	41	8,968	4
New Jersey	Trenton	1787	8,717,925	10	7,417	15
New Mexico	Santa Fe	1912	1,928,384	36	121,356	5
New York	Albany	1788	19,254,630	3	47,214	31
North Carolina	Raleigh	1789	8,683,242	11	48,711	15
North Dakota	Bismarck	1889	636,677	48	68,976	3
Ohio	Columbus	1803	11,464,042	7	40,948	20
Oklahoma	Oklahoma City	1907	3,547,884	28	68,667	7
Oregon	Salem	1859	3,641,056	27	95,997	7
Pennsylvania	Harrisburg	1787	12,429,616	6	44,817	21
Rhode Island	Providence	1790	1,076,189	43	1,045	4
South Carolina	Columbia	1788	4,255,083	25	30,110	8
South Dakota	Pierre	1889	775,933	46	75,885	3
Tennessee	Nashville	1796	5,962,959	16	41,217	11
Texas	Austin	1845	22,859,968	2	261,797	34
Utah	Salt Lake City	1896	2,469,585	34	82,144	5
Vermont	Montpelier	1791	623,050	49	9,250	3
Virginia	Richmond	1788	7,567,465	12	39,594	13
Washington	Olympia	1889	6,287,759	14	66,544	11
West Virginia	Charleston	1863	1,816,856	37	24,078	5
Wisconsin	Madison	1848	5,536,201	20	54,310	10
Wyoming	Cheyenne	1890	509,294	50	97,100	3

SOURCES: U.S. Census Bureau, U.S. National Archives, *World Almanac*

The World: Political

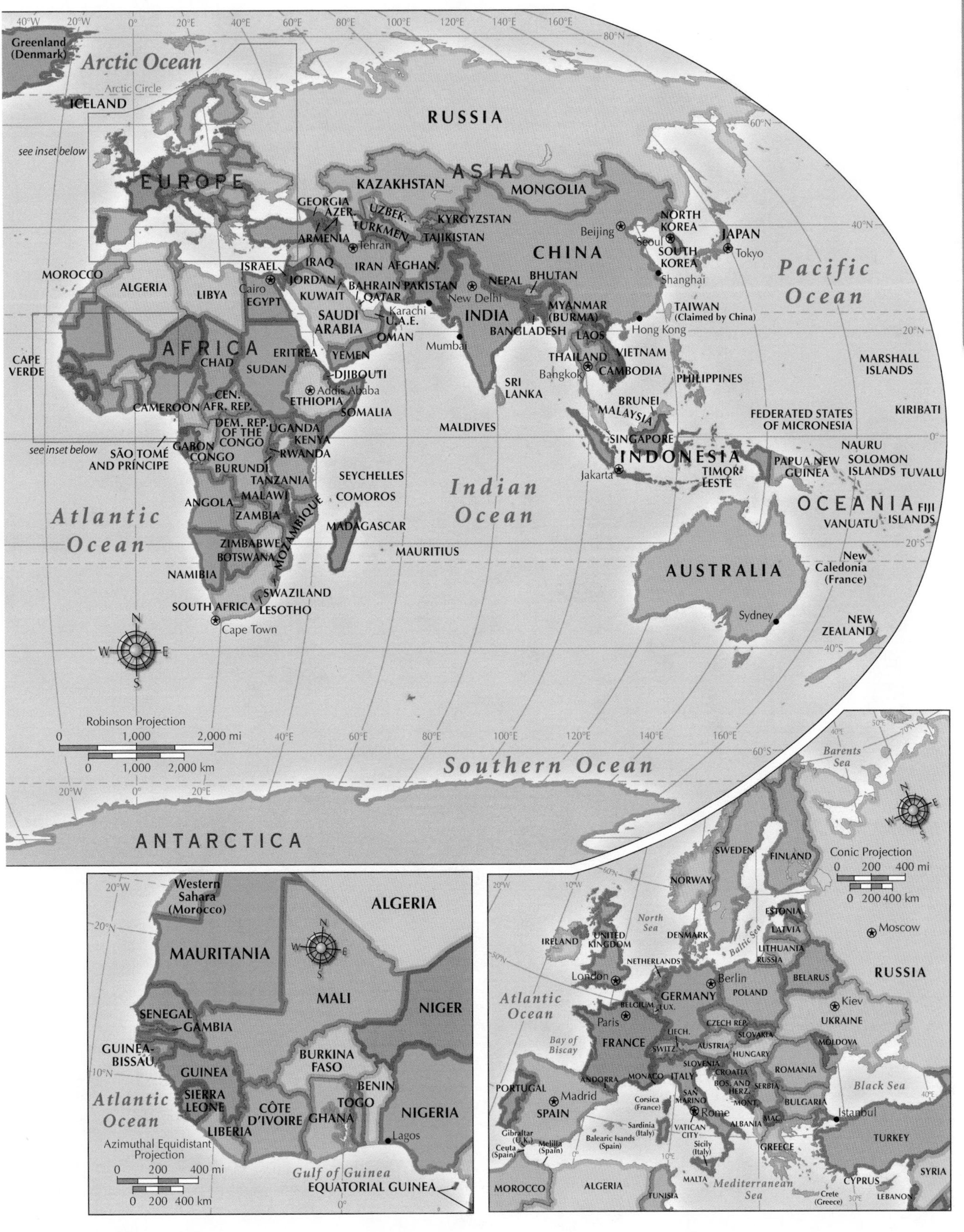
Greenland (Denmark)
Arctic Ocean
Arctic Circle
ICELAND
RUSSIA
see inset below
EUROPE
ASIA
KAZAKHSTAN
MONGOLIA
GEORGIA
AZER.
ARMENIA
UZBEK.
TURKMEN.
KYRGYZSTAN
TAJIKISTAN
Tehran
Beijing
NORTH KOREA
Seoul
SOUTH KOREA
JAPAN
Tokyo
CHINA
Shanghai
Pacific Ocean
MOROCCO
ALGERIA
LIBYA
ISRAEL
Cairo
EGYPT
IRAQ
JORDAN
KUWAIT
IRAN
AFGHAN.
BAHRAIN
QATAR
PAKISTAN
New Delhi
NEPAL
BHUTAN
SAUDI ARABIA
Karachi
U.A.E.
OMAN
INDIA
Mumbai
MYANMAR (BURMA)
BANGLADESH
TAIWAN (Claimed by China)
Hong Kong
LAOS
AFRICA
CHAD
SUDAN
ERITREA
YEMEN
DJIBOUTI
Addis Ababa
ETHIOPIA
SOMALIA
CAPE VERDE
CEN. AFR. REP.
CAMEROON
THAILAND
Bangkok
CAMBODIA
VIETNAM
PHILIPPINES
SRI LANKA
MARSHALL ISLANDS
BRUNEI
MALAYSIA
SINGAPORE
FEDERATED STATES OF MICRONESIA
KIRIBATI
DEM. REP. OF THE CONGO
UGANDA
KENYA
RWANDA
MALDIVES
see inset below
SÃO TOMÉ AND PRÍNCIPE
GABON
CONGO
BURUNDI
TANZANIA
SEYCHELLES
INDONESIA
Jakarta
TIMOR-LESTE
PAPUA NEW GUINEA
NAURU
SOLOMON ISLANDS
TUVALU
ANGOLA
MALAWI
COMOROS
Indian Ocean
OCEANIA
FIJI ISLANDS
VANUATU
Atlantic Ocean
ZAMBIA
MOZAMBIQUE
MADAGASCAR
MAURITIUS
ZIMBABWE
BOTSWANA
NAMIBIA
AUSTRALIA
New Caledonia (France)
SWAZILAND
SOUTH AFRICA
LESOTHO
Cape Town
Sydney
NEW ZEALAND
Robinson Projection
0 1,000 2,000 mi
0 1,000 2,000 km
Southern Ocean
ANTARCTICA
Western Sahara (Morocco)
ALGERIA
MAURITANIA
MALI
NIGER
SENEGAL
GAMBIA
GUINEA-BISSAU
GUINEA
BURKINA FASO
SIERRA LEONE
BENIN
TOGO
CÔTE D'IVOIRE
GHANA
NIGERIA
LIBERIA
Lagos
Atlantic Ocean
Azimuthal Equidistant Projection
0 200 400 mi
0 200 400 km
Gulf of Guinea
EQUATORIAL GUINEA
Barents Sea
SWEDEN
FINLAND
Conic Projection
0 200 400 mi
0 200 400 km
NORWAY
North Sea
ESTONIA
LATVIA
LITHUANIA
RUSSIA
IRELAND
UNITED KINGDOM
DENMARK
Baltic Sea
Moscow
NETHERLANDS
London
Berlin
POLAND
BELARUS
RUSSIA
GERMANY
BELGIUM
LUX.
Atlantic Ocean
Paris
Kiev
UKRAINE
CZECH REP.
SLOVAKIA
Bay of Biscay
FRANCE
LIECH.
SWITZ.
AUSTRIA
HUNGARY
MOLDOVA
SLOVENIA
CROATIA
ROMANIA
ANDORRA
MONACO
ITALY
BOS. AND HERZ.
SERBIA
PORTUGAL
Madrid
SAN MARINO
Corsica (France)
MONT.
Black Sea
SPAIN
Rome
BULGARIA
Istanbul
Sardinia (Italy)
ALBANIA
MAC.
Gibraltar (U.K.)
Ceuta (Spain)
Melilla (Spain)
Balearic Isands (Spain)
VATICAN CITY
Sicily (Italy)
GREECE
TURKEY
MALTA
Mediterranean Sea
CYPRUS
SYRIA
MOROCCO
ALGERIA
TUNISIA
Crete (Greece)
LEBANON

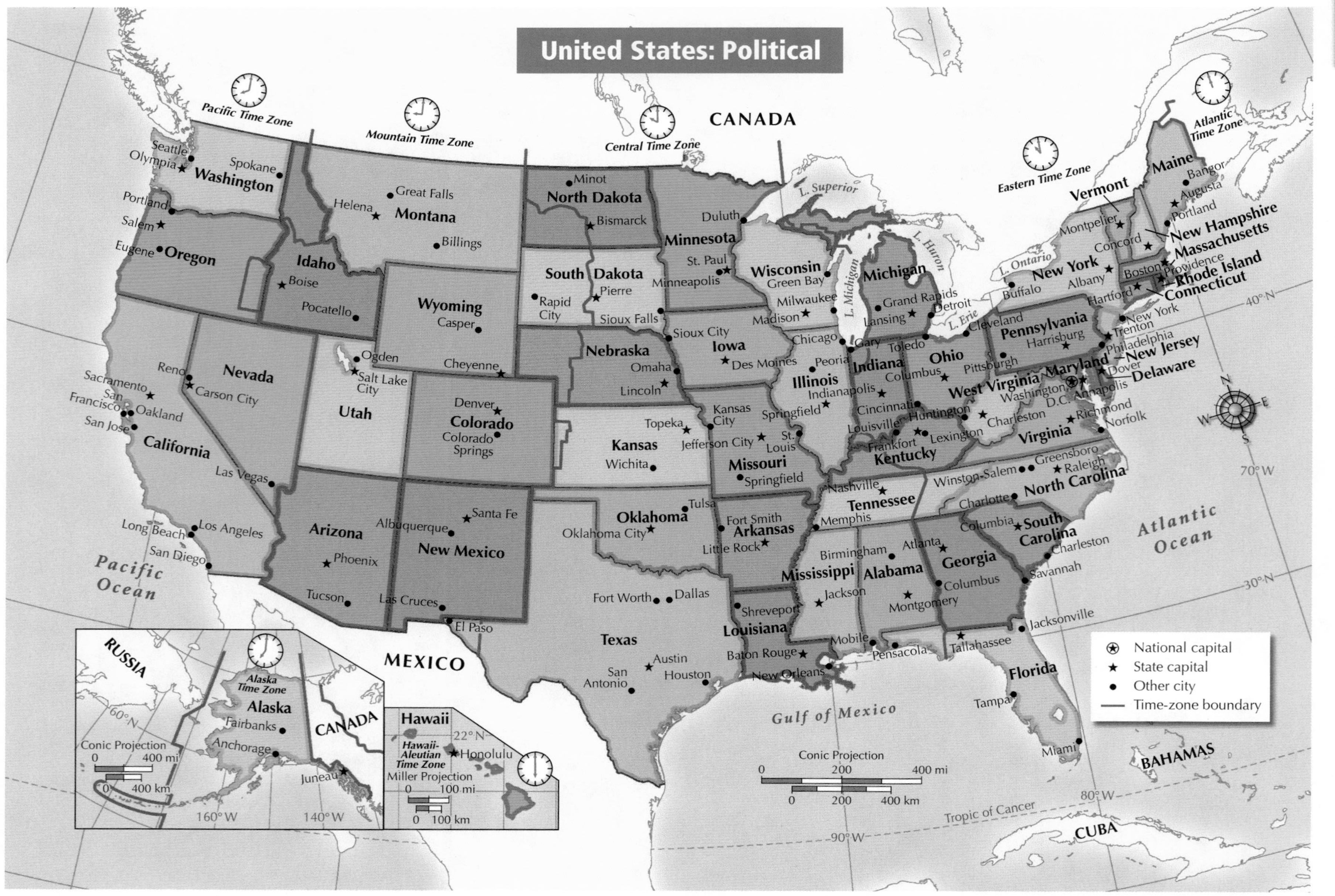
United States: Political
CANADA
MEXICO
RUSSIA
BAHAMAS
CUBA
Pacific Time Zone
Mountain Time Zone
Central Time Zone
Eastern Time Zone
Atlantic Time Zone
Pacific Ocean
Atlantic Ocean
Gulf of Mexico
L. Superior
L. Michigan
L. Huron
L. Erie
L. Ontario
Washington
Seattle
Olympia
Spokane
Oregon
Portland
Salem
Eugene
California
Sacramento
San Francisco
Oakland
San Jose
Los Angeles
Long Beach
San Diego
Nevada
Reno
Carson City
Las Vegas
Idaho
Boise
Pocatello
Montana
Helena
Great Falls
Billings
Wyoming
Casper
Cheyenne
Utah
Ogden
Salt Lake City
Colorado
Denver
Colorado Springs
Arizona
Phoenix
Tucson
New Mexico
Santa Fe
Albuquerque
Las Cruces
El Paso
North Dakota
Minot
Bismarck
South Dakota
Rapid City
Pierre
Sioux Falls
Nebraska
Omaha
Lincoln
Kansas
Topeka
Wichita
Oklahoma
Oklahoma City
Tulsa
Texas
Fort Worth
Dallas
Austin
San Antonio
Houston
Minnesota
Duluth
St. Paul
Minneapolis
Iowa
Sioux City
Des Moines
Missouri
Kansas City
Jefferson City
St. Louis
Springfield
Arkansas
Fort Smith
Little Rock
Louisiana
Shreveport
Baton Rouge
New Orleans
Wisconsin
Green Bay
Milwaukee
Madison
Illinois
Chicago
Peoria
Springfield
Michigan
Grand Rapids
Lansing
Detroit
Indiana
Gary
Indianapolis
Ohio
Toledo
Cleveland
Columbus
Cincinnati
Kentucky
Louisville
Frankfort
Lexington
Tennessee
Nashville
Memphis
Mississippi
Jackson
Alabama
Birmingham
Montgomery
Mobile
Georgia
Atlanta
Columbus
Savannah
Florida
Tallahassee
Pensacola
Jacksonville
Tampa
Miami
South Carolina
Columbia
Charleston
North Carolina
Charlotte
Winston-Salem
Greensboro
Raleigh
Virginia
Richmond
Norfolk
West Virginia
Charleston
Huntington
Pennsylvania
Pittsburgh
Harrisburg
Philadelphia
Maryland
Washington, D.C.
Annapolis
Delaware
Dover
New Jersey
Trenton
New York
Buffalo
Albany
New York
Connecticut
Hartford
Rhode Island
Providence
Massachusetts
Boston
Vermont
Montpelier
New Hampshire
Concord
Maine
Portland
Augusta
Bangor
Alaska
Alaska Time Zone
Fairbanks
Anchorage
Juneau
60° N
160° W
140° W
Conic Projection
0 400 mi
0 400 km
Hawaii
Hawaii-Aleutian Time Zone
Honolulu
22° N
Miller Projection
0 100 mi
0 100 km
Conic Projection
0 200 400 mi
0 200 400 km
40° N
30° N
70° W
80° W
90° W
Tropic of Cancer
National capital
State capital
Other city
Time-zone boundary

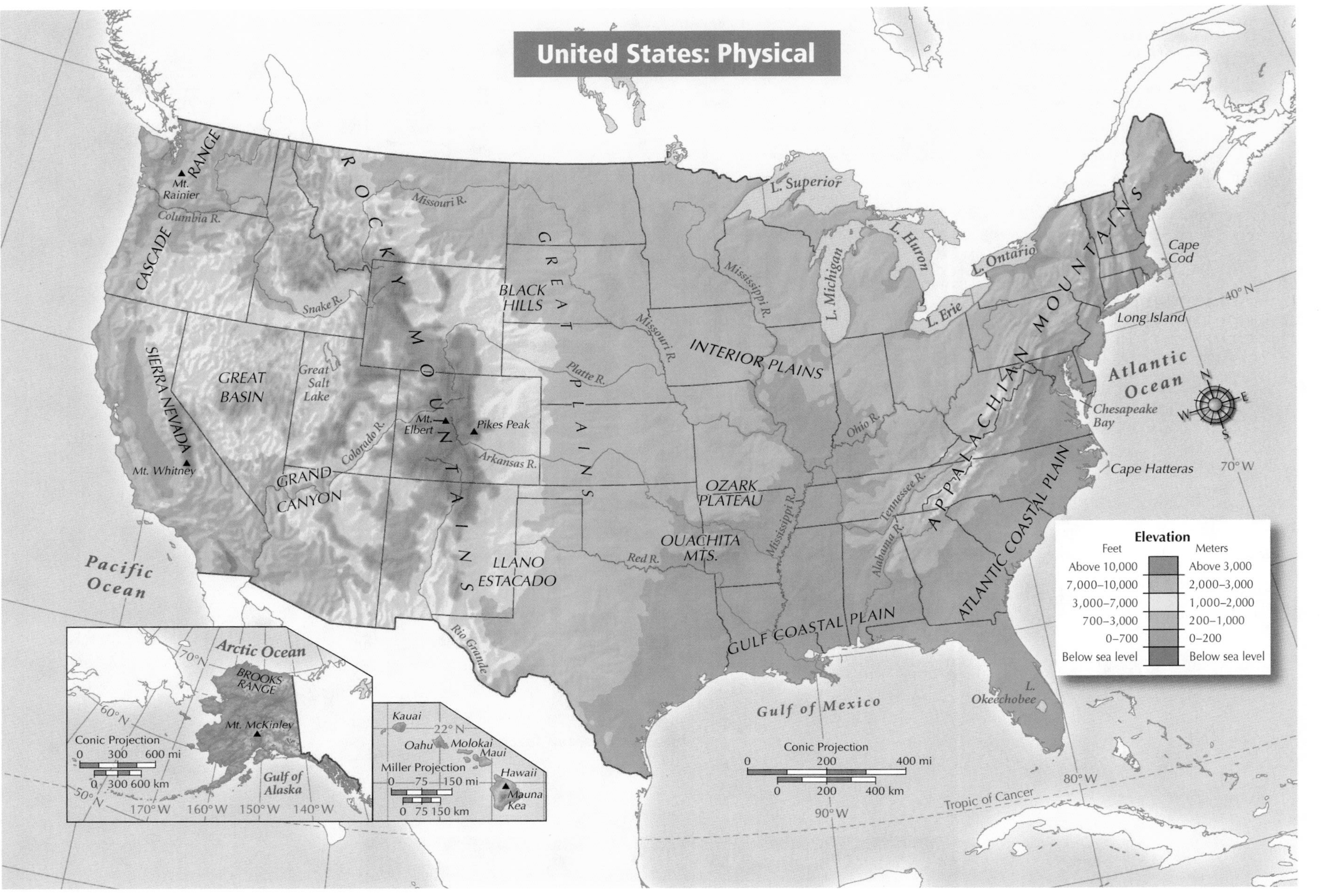
United States: Physical
Elevation
Feet
Meters
Above 10,000
Above 3,000
7,000–10,000
2,000–3,000
3,000–7,000
1,000–2,000
700–3,000
200–1,000
0–700
0–200
Below sea level
Below sea level
Conic Projection
0 200 400 mi
0 200 400 km
Atlantic Ocean
Gulf of Mexico
Pacific Ocean
Cape Cod
Long Island
Chesapeake Bay
Cape Hatteras
L. Okeechobee
Tropic of Cancer
40° N
70° W
80° W
90° W
APPALACHIAN MOUNTAINS
ATLANTIC COASTAL PLAIN
GULF COASTAL PLAIN
INTERIOR PLAINS
OZARK PLATEAU
OUACHITA MTS.
GREAT PLAINS
BLACK HILLS
LLANO ESTACADO
ROCKY MOUNTAINS
GREAT BASIN
GRAND CANYON
SIERRA NEVADA
CASCADE RANGE
L. Superior
L. Michigan
L. Huron
L. Erie
L. Ontario
Ohio R.
Tennessee R.
Alabama R.
Mississippi R.
Missouri R.
Platte R.
Arkansas R.
Red R.
Rio Grande
Colorado R.
Snake R.
Columbia R.
Great Salt Lake
Pikes Peak
Mt. Elbert
Mt. Rainier
Mt. Whitney
Kauai
Oahu
Molokai
Maui
Hawaii
Mauna Kea
22° N
Miller Projection
0 75 150 mi
0 75 150 km
Arctic Ocean
BROOKS RANGE
Mt. McKinley
Gulf of Alaska
70° N
60° N
50° N
170° W
160° W
150° W
140° W
Conic Projection
0 300 600 mi
0 300 600 km

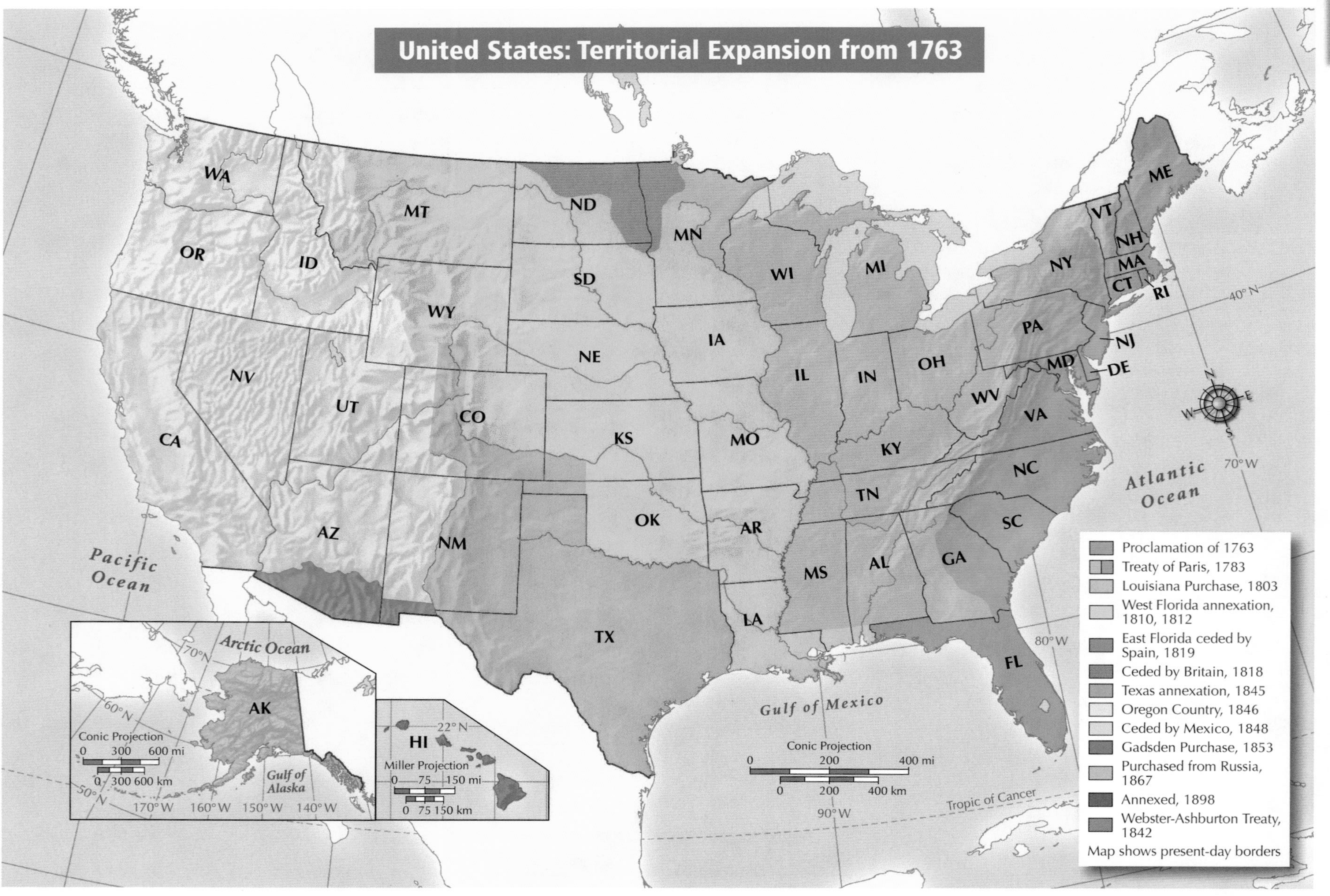
United States: Territorial Expansion from 1763
Proclamation of 1763
Treaty of Paris, 1783
Louisiana Purchase, 1803
West Florida annexation, 1810, 1812
East Florida ceded by Spain, 1819
Ceded by Britain, 1818
Texas annexation, 1845
Oregon Country, 1846
Ceded by Mexico, 1848
Gadsden Purchase, 1853
Purchased from Russia, 1867
Annexed, 1898
Webster-Ashburton Treaty, 1842
Map shows present-day borders
Atlantic Ocean
Pacific Ocean
Gulf of Mexico
Tropic of Cancer
Conic Projection
0 200 400 mi
0 200 400 km
40° N
70° W
80° W
90° W
WA
OR
CA
ID
NV
MT
WY
UT
AZ
CO
NM
ND
SD
NE
KS
OK
TX
MN
IA
MO
AR
LA
WI
IL
MS
MI
IN
KY
TN
AL
OH
WV
VA
NC
SC
GA
FL
PA
NY
MD
DE
NJ
VT
NH
MA
CT
RI
ME
AK
Arctic Ocean
Gulf of Alaska
70° N
60° N
50° N
Conic Projection
0 300 600 mi
0 300 600 km
170° W
160° W
150° W
140° W
HI
22° N
Miller Projection
0 75 150 mi
0 75 150 km

United States: Climates

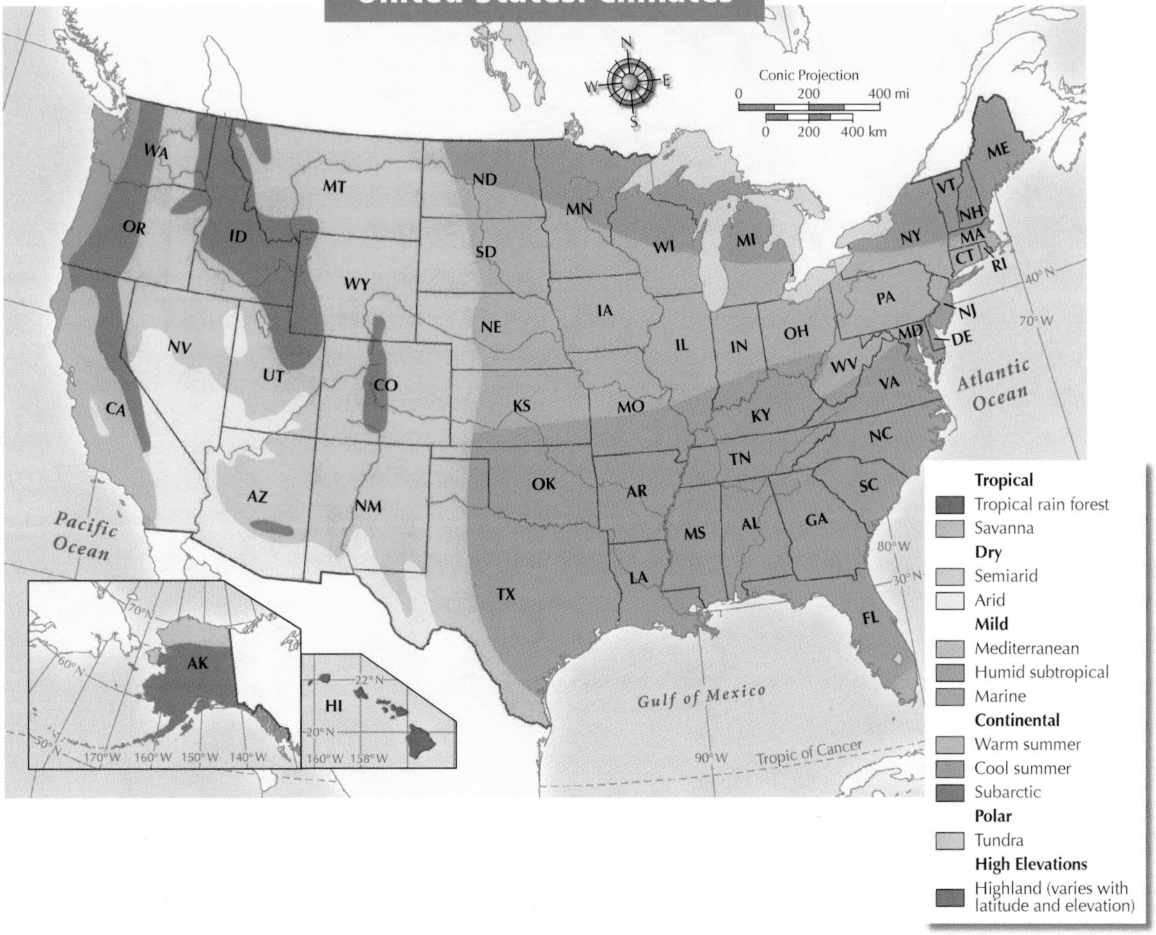

Conic Projection
0 200 400 mi
0 200 400 km

WA, OR, CA, ID, NV, MT, WY, UT, AZ, CO, NM, ND, SD, NE, KS, OK, TX, MN, IA, MO, AR, LA, WI, IL, MI, IN, OH, KY, TN, MS, AL, GA, FL, SC, NC, VA, WV, PA, NY, MD, DE, NJ, CT, RI, MA, VT, NH, ME, AK, HI

Pacific Ocean
Atlantic Ocean
Gulf of Mexico
Tropic of Cancer

Tropical
- Tropical rain forest
- Savanna

Dry
- Semiarid
- Arid

Mild
- Mediterranean
- Humid subtropical
- Marine

Continental
- Warm summer
- Cool summer
- Subarctic

Polar
- Tundra

High Elevations
- Highland (varies with latitude and elevation)

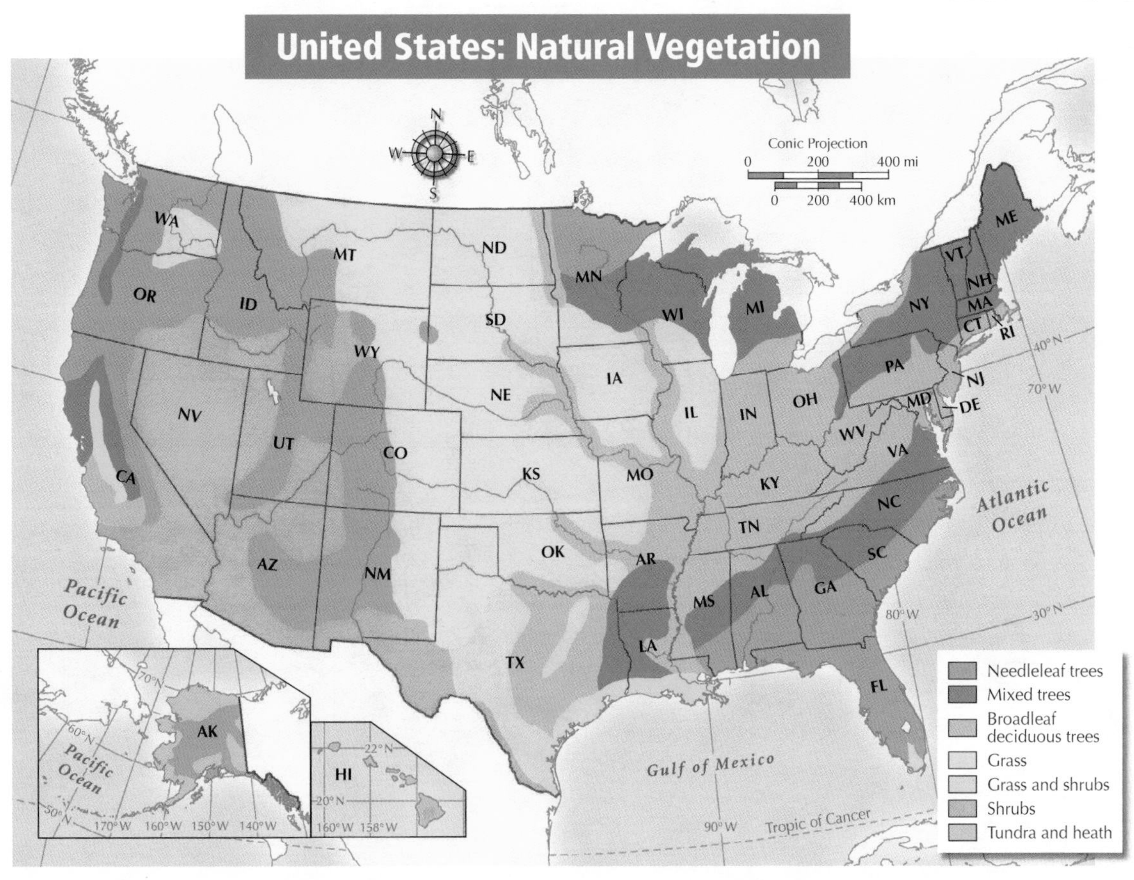

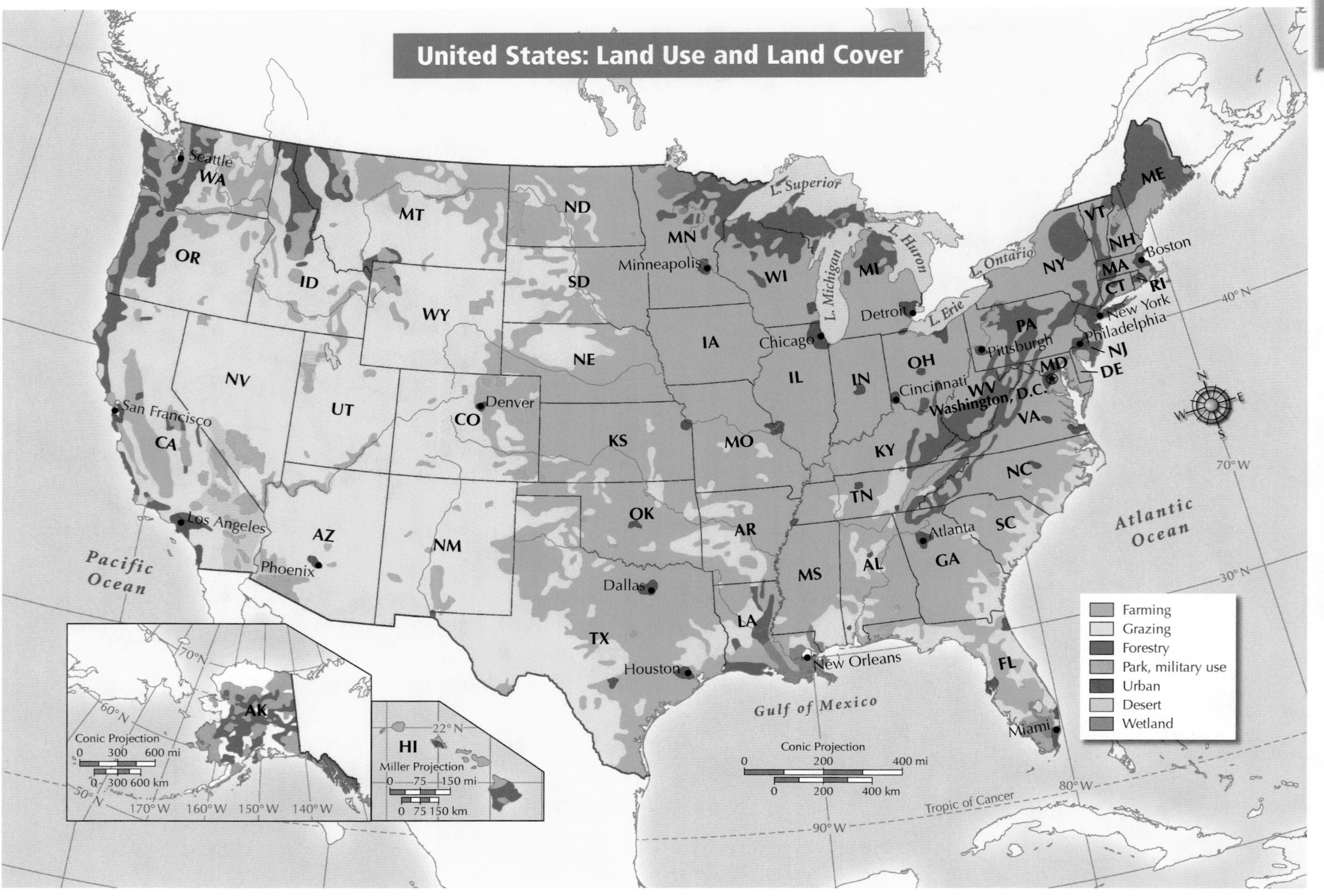
United States: Land Use and Land Cover
Farming
Grazing
Forestry
Park, military use
Urban
Desert
Wetland
Conic Projection
0 200 400 mi
0 200 400 km
Atlantic Ocean
Pacific Ocean
Gulf of Mexico
Tropic of Cancer
L. Superior
L. Michigan
L. Huron
L. Erie
L. Ontario
40° N
30° N
70° W
80° W
90° W
WA
OR
CA
NV
ID
MT
WY
UT
AZ
CO
NM
ND
SD
NE
KS
OK
TX
MN
IA
MO
AR
LA
WI
IL
MI
IN
OH
KY
TN
MS
AL
GA
FL
SC
NC
VA
WV
PA
NY
VT
NH
ME
MA
CT
RI
NJ
DE
MD
Seattle
San Francisco
Los Angeles
Phoenix
Denver
Minneapolis
Dallas
Houston
Chicago
Detroit
New Orleans
Cincinnati
Pittsburgh
Washington, D.C.
Atlanta
Miami
Philadelphia
New York
Boston
AK
Conic Projection
0 300 600 mi
0 300 600 km
60° N
70° N
50° N
170° W
160° W
150° W
140° W
HI
Miller Projection
0 75 150 mi
0 75 150 km
22° N

United States: Natural Resources

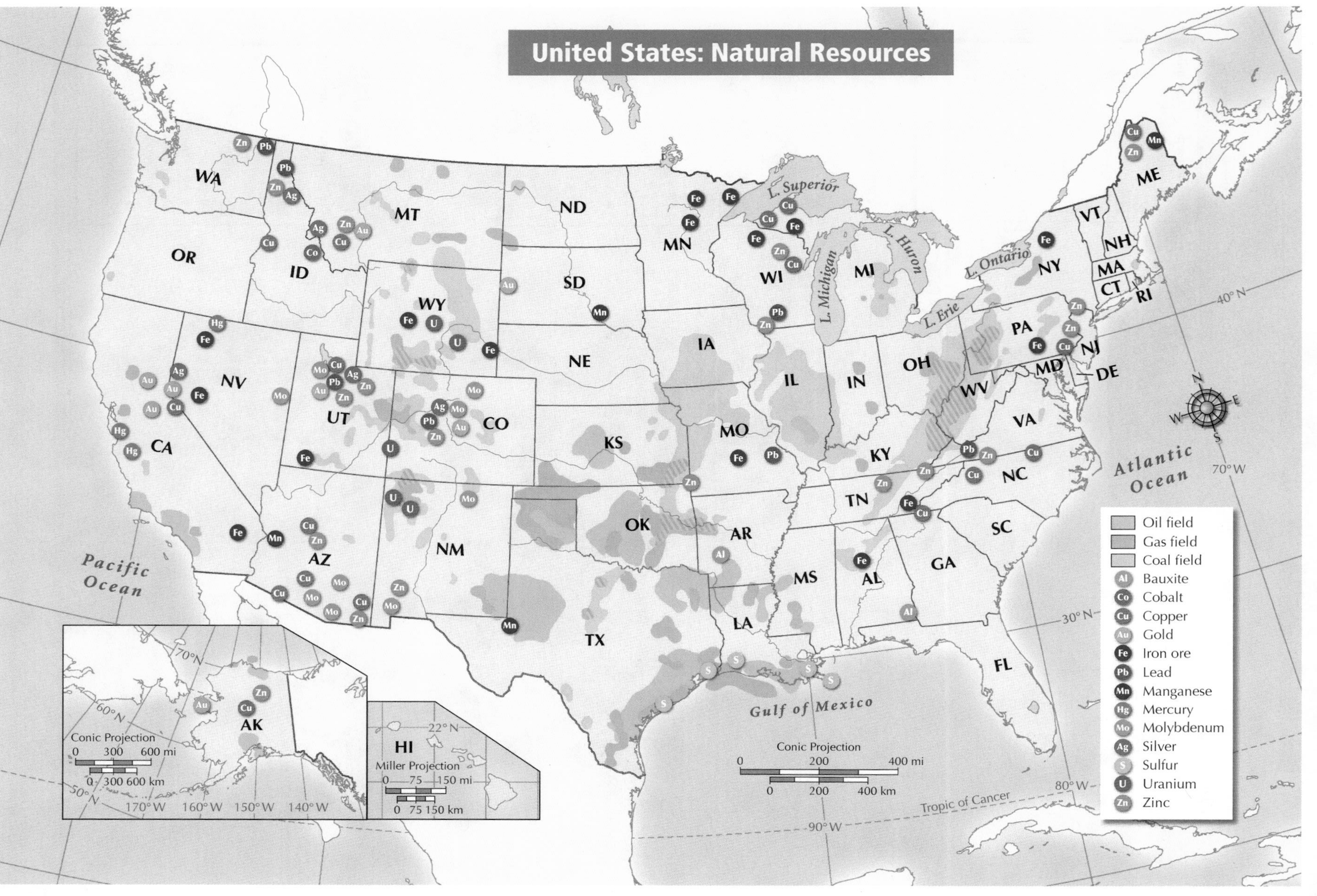

United States: Population Density

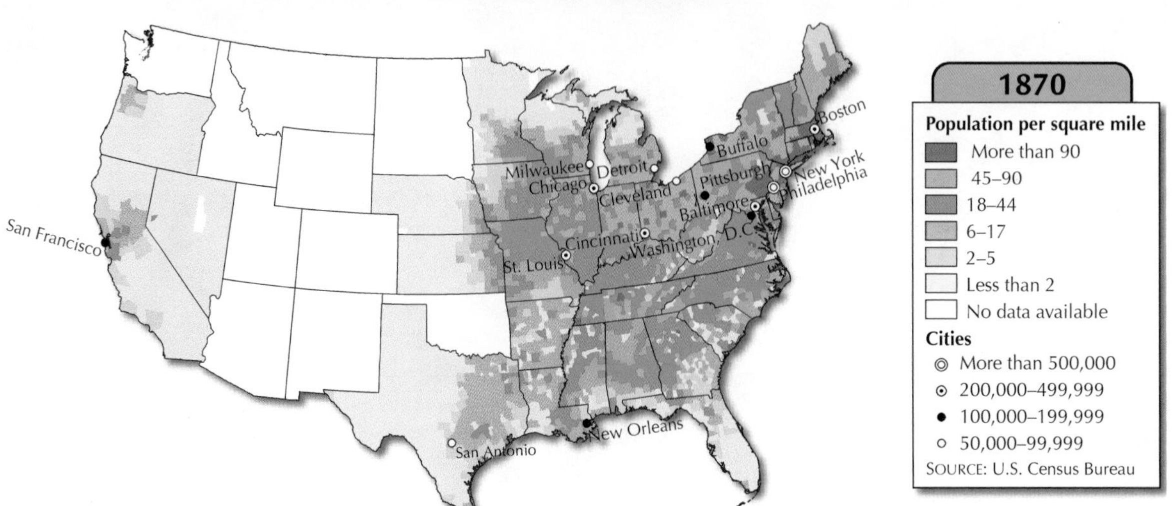

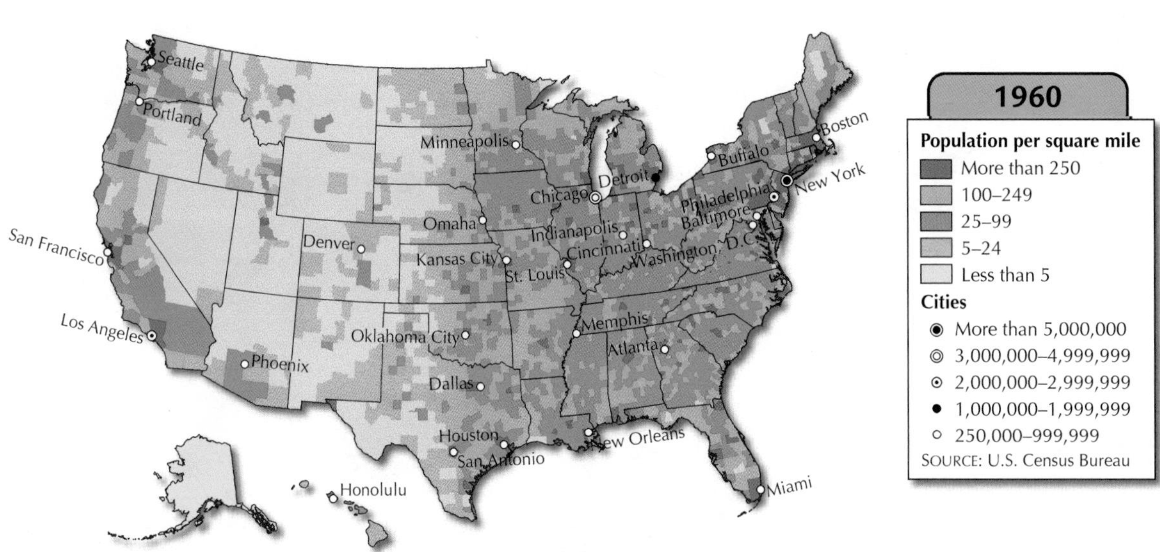

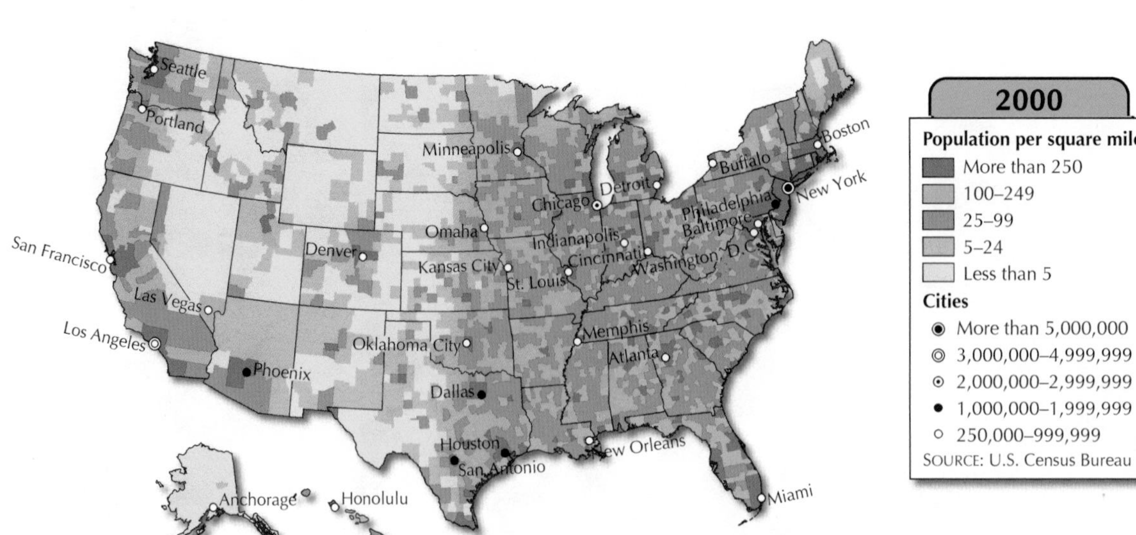

Presidents of the United States

1

George Washington
(1732–1799)

Years in Office: 1789–1797
No political party

Elected from: Virginia
Vice President: John Adams

2

John Adams
(1735–1826)

Years in Office: 1797–1801
Federalist

Elected from: Massachusetts
Vice President: Thomas Jefferson

3

Thomas Jefferson
(1743–1826)

Years in Office: 1801–1809
Democratic Republican

Elected from: Virginia
Vice Presidents: Aaron Burr, George Clinton

4

James Madison
(1751–1836)

Years in Office: 1809–1817
Democratic Republican

Elected from: Virginia
Vice Presidents: George Clinton, Elbridge Gerry

5

James Monroe
(1758–1831)

Years in Office: 1817–1825
National Republican

Elected from: Virginia
Vice President: Daniel Tompkins

6

John Quincy Adams
(1767–1848)

Years in Office: 1825–1829
National Republican

Elected from: Massachusetts
Vice President: John Calhoun

7

Andrew Jackson
(1767–1845)

Years in Office: 1829–1837
Democrat

Elected from: Tennessee
Vice Presidents: John Calhoun, Martin Van Buren

8

Martin Van Buren
(1782–1862)

Years in Office: 1837–1841
Democrat

Elected from: New York
Vice President: Richard Johnson

9

William Henry Harrison*
(1773–1841)

Year in Office: 1841
Whig

Elected from: Ohio
Vice President: John Tyler

10

John Tyler
(1790–1862)

Years in Office: 1841–1845
Whig

Elected from: Virginia
Vice President: none

11

James K. Polk
(1795–1849)

Years in Office: 1845–1849
Democrat

Elected from: Tennessee
Vice President: George Dallas

12

Zachary Taylor*
(1784–1850)

Years in Office: 1849–1850
Whig

Elected from: Louisiana
Vice President: Millard Fillmore

13

Millard Fillmore
(1800–1874)

Years in Office: 1850–1853
Whig

Elected from: New York
Vice President: none

14

Franklin Pierce
(1804–1869)

Years in Office: 1853–1857
Democrat

Elected from: New Hampshire
Vice President: William King

15

James Buchanan
(1791–1868)

Years in Office: 1857–1861
Democrat

Elected from: Pennsylvania
Vice President: John Breckinridge

16

Abraham Lincoln**
(1809–1865)

Years in Office: 1861–1865
Republican

Elected from: Illinois
Vice Presidents: Hannibal Hamlin, Andrew Johnson

Presidents

17

Andrew Johnson
(1808–1875)

Years in Office: 1865–1869
Democrat†

Elected from: Tennessee
Vice President: none

18

Ulysses S. Grant
(1822–1885)

Years in Office: 1869–1877
Republican

Elected from: Illinois
Vice Presidents: Schuyler Colfax, Henry Wilson

19

Rutherford B. Hayes
(1822–1893)

Years in Office: 1877–1881
Republican

Elected from: Ohio
Vice President: William Wheeler

20

James A. Garfield**
(1831–1881)

Year in Office: 1881
Republican

Elected from: Ohio
Vice President: Chester A. Arthur

21

Chester A. Arthur
(1830–1886)

Years in Office: 1881–1885
Republican

Elected from: New York
Vice President: none

22

Grover Cleveland
(1837–1908)

Years in Office: 1885–1889
Democrat

Elected from: New York
Vice President: Thomas Hendricks

23

Benjamin Harrison
(1833–1901)

Years in Office: 1889–1893
Republican

Elected from: Indiana
Vice President: Levi Morton

24

Grover Cleveland
(1837–1908)

Years in Office: 1893–1897
Democrat

Elected from: New York
Vice President: Adlai Stevenson

25

William McKinley**
(1843–1901)

Years in Office: 1897–1901
Republican

Elected from: Ohio
Vice Presidents: Garret Hobart, Theodore Roosevelt

26

Theodore Roosevelt
(1858–1919)

Years in Office: 1901–1909
Republican

Elected from: New York
Vice President: Charles Fairbanks

27

William Howard Taft
(1857–1930)

Years in Office: 1909–1913
Republican

Elected from: Ohio
Vice President: James Sherman

28

Woodrow Wilson
(1856–1924)

Years in Office: 1913–1921
Democrat

Elected from: New Jersey
Vice President: Thomas Marshall

29

Warren G. Harding*
(1865–1923)

Years in Office: 1921–1923
Republican

Elected from: Ohio
Vice President: Calvin Coolidge

30

Calvin Coolidge
(1872–1933)

Years in Office: 1923–1929
Republican

Elected from: Massachusetts
Vice President: Charles Dawes

31

Herbert C. Hoover
(1874–1964)

Years in Office: 1929–1933
Republican

Elected from: New York
Vice President: Charles Curtis

32

Franklin D. Roosevelt*
(1882–1945)

Years in Office: 1933–1945
Democrat

Elected from: New York
Vice Presidents: John Garner, Henry Wallace, Harry S. Truman

33 

Harry S. Truman
(1884–1972)

Years in Office: 1945–1953
Democrat

Elected from: Missouri
Vice President: Alben Barkley

34 

Dwight D. Eisenhower
(1890–1969)

Years in Office: 1953–1961
Republican

Elected from: New York
Vice President: Richard M. Nixon

35 

John F. Kennedy**
(1917–1963)

Years in Office: 1961–1963
Democrat

Elected from: Massachusetts
Vice President: Lyndon B. Johnson

36 

Lyndon B. Johnson
(1908–1973)

Years in Office: 1963–1969
Democrat

Elected from: Texas
Vice President: Hubert Humphrey

37 

Richard M. Nixon***
(1913–1994)

Years in Office: 1969–1974
Republican

Elected from: New York
Vice Presidents: Spiro Agnew, Gerald R. Ford

38 

Gerald R. Ford
(1913–2006)

Years in Office: 1974–1977
Republican

Elected from: Michigan
Vice President: Nelson Rockefeller

39 

James E. Carter
(1924–)

Years in Office: 1977–1981
Democrat

Elected from: Georgia
Vice President: Walter F. Mondale

40 

Ronald W. Reagan
(1911–2004)

Years in Office: 1981–1989
Republican

Elected from: California
Vice President: George H. W. Bush

41 

George H. W. Bush
(1924–)

Years in Office: 1989–1993
Republican

Elected from: Texas
Vice President: J. Danforth Quayle

42 

William J. Clinton
(1946–)

Years in Office: 1993–2001
Democrat

Elected from: Arkansas
Vice President: Albert Gore, Jr.

43 

George W. Bush
(1946–)

Years in Office: 2001–2009
Republican

Elected from: Texas
Vice President: Richard Cheney

44 

Barack H. Obama
(1961–)

Years in Office: 2009–
Democrat

Elected from: Illinois
Vice President: Joseph R. Biden

* Died in office
** Assassinated
*** Resigned
† Elected Vice President on the coalition Union Party ticket

Presidents

Adapted from Prentice Hall's *Economics: Principles in Action* by Arthur O' Sullivan and Steven Sheffrin

Key Economic Questions

In every society, people have access to resources such as water, soil, and human labor. Yet all resources are limited. Economics is the study of how people choose to use their limited resources to meet their wants and needs. Every society must answer three basic economic questions. How a society answers these questions depends on how much it values different economic goals.

Three Key Economic Questions

What goods and services should be produced?	How should goods and services be produced?	Who consumes the goods and services?
How much of our resources should we devote to national defense, education, public health, or consumer goods? Which consumer goods should we produce?	Should we produce food on large corporate farms or on small family farms? Should we produce electricity with oil, nuclear power, coal, or solar power?	How do goods and services get distributed? The question of who gets to consume which goods and services lies at the very heart of the differences between economic systems. Each society answers the question of distribution based on its combination of social values and goals.

Economic Goals

Goal	Description
Economic efficiency	Making the most of resources
Economic freedom	Freedom from government intervention in the production and distribution of goods and services
Economic security and predictability	Assurance that goods and services will be available, payments will be made on time, and a safety net will protect individuals in times of economic disaster
Economic equity	Fair distribution of wealth
Economic growth and innovation	Innovation leads to economic growth, and economic growth leads to a higher standard of living.
Other goals	Societies pursue additional goals, such as environmental protection.

Choices About How to Produce Goods
This wind farm illustrates a society's decision to produce electricity using the power of the wind. What do you think are the benefits and drawbacks of wind power?

Economic Systems

An economic system is the method used by a society to produce and distribute goods and services. A society's economic system reflects how that society answers the three key economic questions and what its economic goals are. Different systems produce different results in terms of productivity, the welfare of workers, and consumer choice.

Modern Economic Systems

	Description	Origin	Location Today
Market (Capitalist, Free-Enterprise)	Economic decisions are made in the marketplace through interactions between buyers and sellers according to the laws of supply and demand. Individual capitalists own the means of production. Government regulates some economic activities and provides such "public goods" as education.	Capitalism has existed since the earliest buying and selling of goods in a market. The market economic system developed in response to Adam Smith's ideas and the shift from agriculture to industry in the 1800s.	Canada, Germany, Japan, United States, and many other nations
Centrally Planned (Command, Socialist, Communist)	Central government planners make most economic decisions for the people. In theory, the workers own the means of production. In practice, the government does. Some private enterprise, but government dominates.	In the 1800s, criticism of capitalism by Karl Marx and others led to calls for distributing wealth according to need. After the 1917 Russian Revolution, the Soviet Union developed the first command economy.	Communist countries, including China, Cuba, and North Korea
Mixed (Social Democratic, Liberal Socialist)	A mix of socialism and free enterprise in which the government plays a significant role in making economic decisions.	The Great Depression of the 1930s ended laissez-faire capitalism in most countries. People insisted that government take a stronger role in fixing economic problems. The fall of communism in Eastern Europe in the 1990s ended central planning in most countries. People insisted on freer markets.	Most nations, including Brazil, France, India, Italy, Poland, Russia, Sweden, and the United Kingdom

Buyers and Sellers in a Free Market

In a market economy, buyers and sellers make decisions on the basis of their own self-interest. They may freely buy and sell goods. In a voluntary exchange, both parties expect to gain from the transaction.

The American Economy

For centuries, people have considered the United States to be a land of opportunity where anyone from any background could achieve success through hard work. Why has the United States been such an economic success? Certainly the open land, natural resources, and uninterrupted flow of immigrant labor have all contributed. But a key factor has also been the tradition of free enterprise—the social and political commitment to giving people the freedom to compete in the marketplace.

Constitutional Protections of Free Enterprise

Property Rights
Property rights are protected by the Fifth Amendment: "No person shall be deprived of life, liberty, or property, without due process; nor shall private property be taken for public use, without just compensation." The Fourteenth Amendment places the same limitation on state governments.

Taxation
Congress can only tax individuals and businesses in the ways the Constitution allows. Article 1 gives Congress the power to levy taxes, but Sections 2 and 9 require that direct taxes be apportioned according to population. The Sixteenth Amendment gave Congress the right to set taxes based on income.

Binding Contracts
Article 1, Section 10, guarantees people and businesses the right to make binding contracts.

▲ Free enterprise in the United States is founded on ideas so basic to our culture that we tend to take them for granted.

Flow of Goods, Services, and Money in a Market Economy

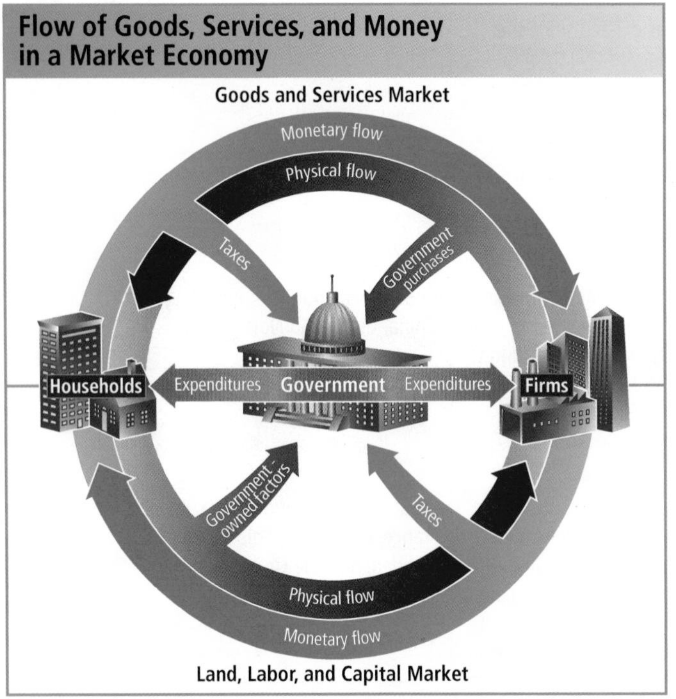

▲ This circular flow model shows how government typically interacts with households and businesses in the marketplace.

United States Workforce, by Occupation, 2005*

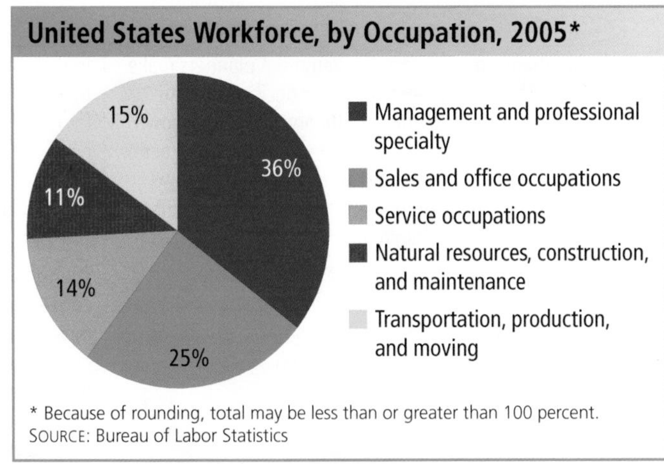

* Because of rounding, total may be less than or greater than 100 percent.
SOURCE: Bureau of Labor Statistics

▲ How do you think this snapshot of the United States labor force would have looked in 1800? In 1900?

Key Events in American Economic History

- **1791** First Bank of the United States chartered
- **1834** Mill girls in Lowell, Massachusetts, protest wage cuts
- **1835** Strike for 10-hour workday in Philadelphia
- **1867** Knights of Labor formed
- **1869** Financial panic sweeps nation
- **1886** American Federation of Labor formed
- **1892** Homestead Strike in Pennsylvania

1780 | 1820 | 1860

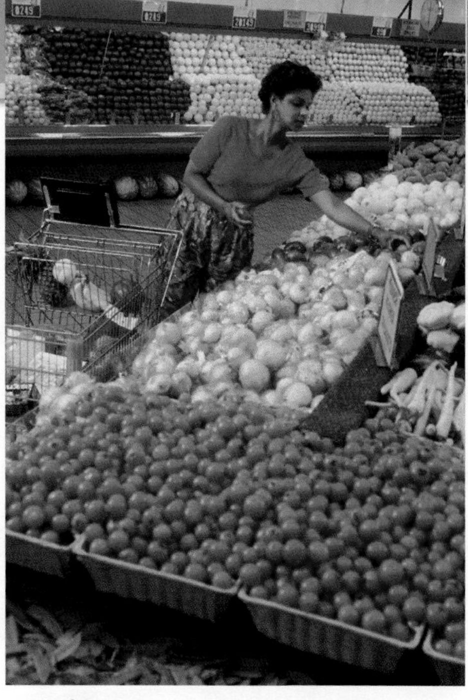

Measuring the Economy's Performance

A modern industrial economy repeatedly experiences cycles of economic growth and decline. Business cycles are of major interest to macroeconomists, who study their causes and effects. Economists use many tools to predict changes in business cycles. The leading indicators are a set of key economic variables including stock prices, interest rates, and manufacturers' new orders for goods.

▲ **Food Prices** An increase in the price of food can signal inflation. What impact do rising food prices have on families?

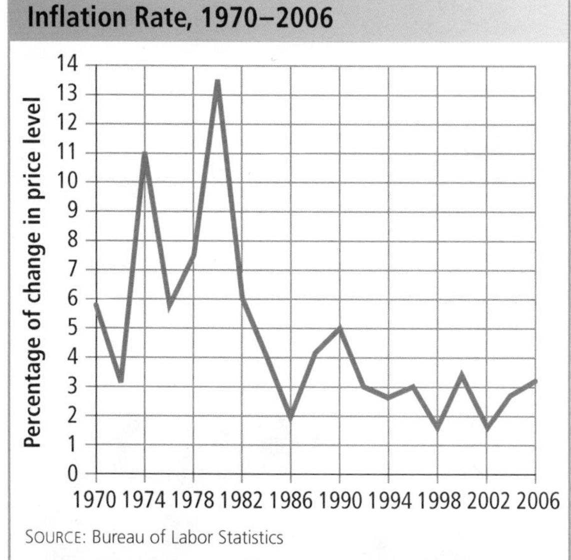

▲ One of the economic indicators economists look at is the economy's level of inflation. Inflation is a general increase in prices. As prices rise, the purchasing power of money declines.

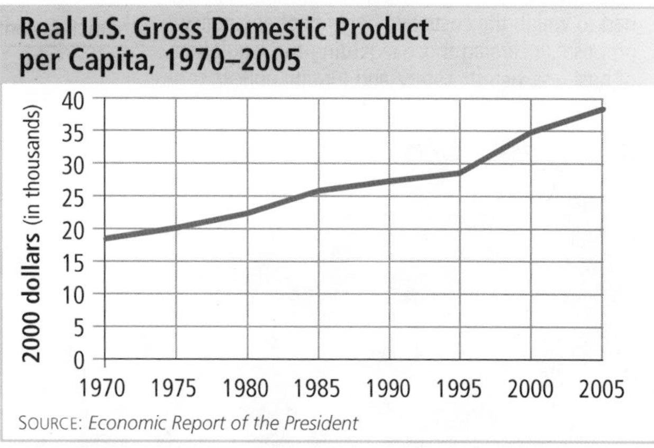

▲ Gross Domestic Product is the dollar value of all final goods and services produced within a country's borders in a given year. GDP per capita equals the GDP divided by the country's total population. Long-term increases in GDP allow an entire society to improve its standard of living.

1913 Federal Reserve System created

1929 Stock market crash

1930 Great Depression begins

1933 Federal Deposit Insurance Corporation (FDIC) created

1947 Taft-Hartley Act

1955 AFL and CIO merge

1963 Equal Pay Act

1980 Savings and Loan crisis begins

1997 More than 160,000 ATMs operate in United States

2001 Office of Faith-Based and Community Initiatives established

2008 Mortgage crisis leads to increase in home foreclosures

1900 1940 1980 2020

Analyzing Costs and Benefits

Economists point out that all individuals, businesses, and large groups of people make decisions that involve trade-offs. Trade-offs are all the alternatives that we give up whenever we choose one course of action over another. One alternative, though, is usually more desirable than all the others. The most desirable alternative given up as the result of a decision is called the opportunity cost. At times, a decision's opportunity cost may be unclear or complicated. Nonetheless, consumers, businesses, and governments must carefully consider trade-offs and opportunity costs before making a decision.

Safety Versus Cost and Convenience Tens of thousands of people are killed every year in auto accidents in the United States. Safety features like antilock brakes, air bags, and seatbelts may save lives, but they also make cars more expensive. Throughout history, government policymakers have had to weigh the costs and benefits of any policy proposal, including those regarding the regulation of business, health, safety, and foreign policy.

Costs of Auto Safety

Safety Feature	Cost
Antilock brakes	$600.00
Side-impact air bags	$350.00
Traction control	$1,200.00

The Federal Budget

The federal budget is a written document indicating the amount of money the government expects to receive during a certain year and authorizing the amount the government can spend that year. Government officials who take part in the budgeting process debate how much should be spent on specific programs such as defense, education, and scientific research.

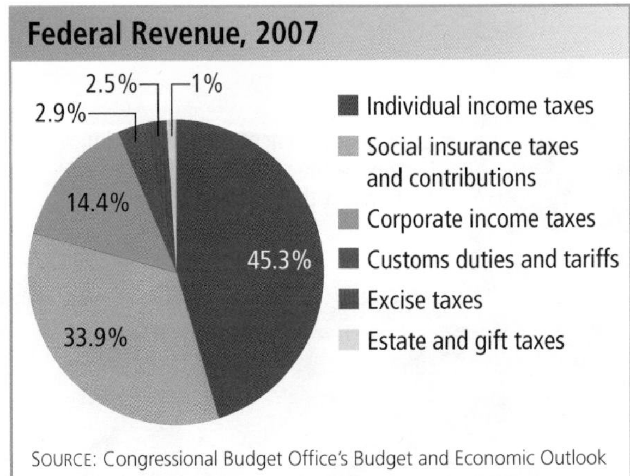

▲ This graph shows the sources of government revenue. What are the largest sources of federal income?

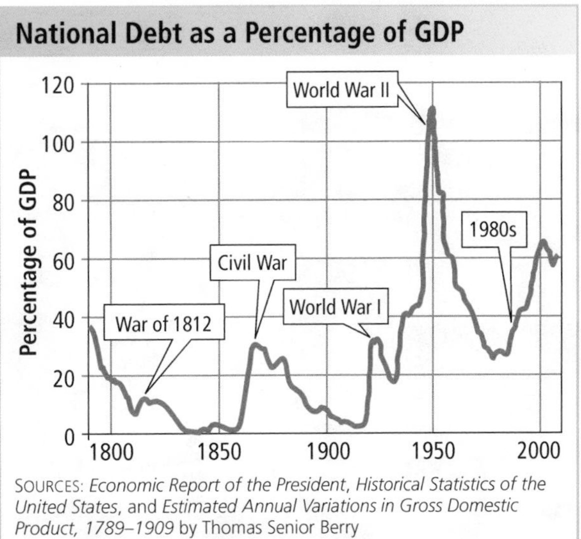

▲ If the federal government's spending is greater than its income in any given year, then the budget is said to be in deficit. The government must then borrow money to pay the shortfall. The total of the government's borrowed money over time is added together to form the national debt.

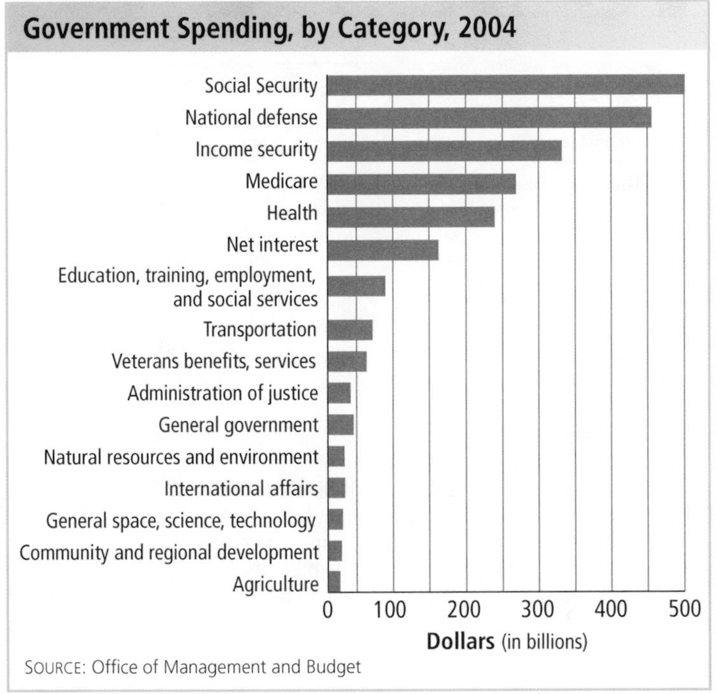

◀ This graph shows how the government spends its money. What are the largest areas of federal spending?

Tools for Moderating the Business Cycle: Fiscal Policy

The federal government takes in money to pay for its spending through taxation and borrowing. The decisions the government makes about taxing and spending can have a powerful impact on the overall economy. Fiscal policy is the use of government spending and revenue collection to influence the economy. Fiscal policies are used to achieve economic growth, full employment, and price stability.

▼ Cutting government spending is difficult because some voters will object to cuts that impact their interests.

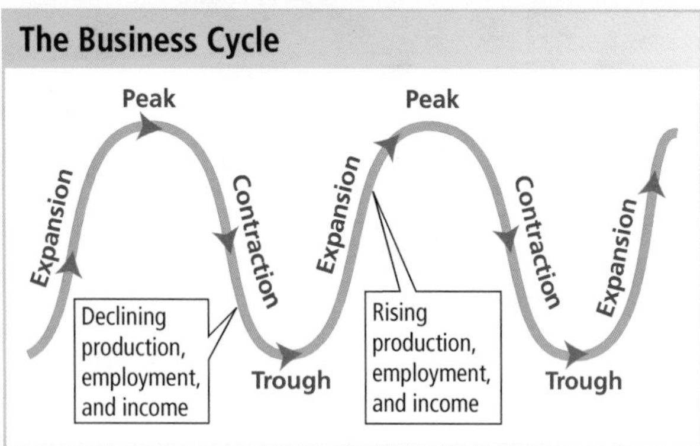

▲ In a business cycle, a period of rising real GDP reaches a peak, then falls into a contraction. When the contraction reaches the low point, or trough, a new expansion begins. From 1854 to 1991, the United States experienced 31 business cycles. Excluding wartimes, the cycles averaged 48 months.

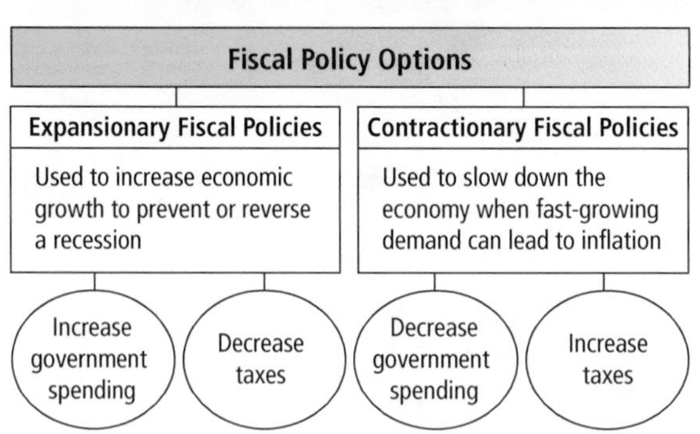

▲ The total level of government spending can be changed to help increase or decrease the output of the economy. Similarly, taxes can be raised or lowered to help increase or decrease the output of the economy. Fiscal policies are difficult to put into practice because many laws dictate spending. Also, it is difficult to predict the business cycle, and there is a significant lag in time before policies take effect.

Tools for Moderating the Business Cycle: Monetary Policy

After the charter of the Second Bank of the United States expired, states chartered some banks while the federal government chartered others. Reserve requirements—the amount of money that banks are required to keep on hand—were difficult to enforce, and bank runs often led to panic. After the Panic of 1907, Congress responded with the Federal Reserve Act of 1913. This act created the Federal Reserve System—a group of twelve independent banks that could lend to other banks in times of need. Monetary policy refers to the actions the Federal Reserve Board takes to influence the level of real GDP and the rate of inflation in the economy.

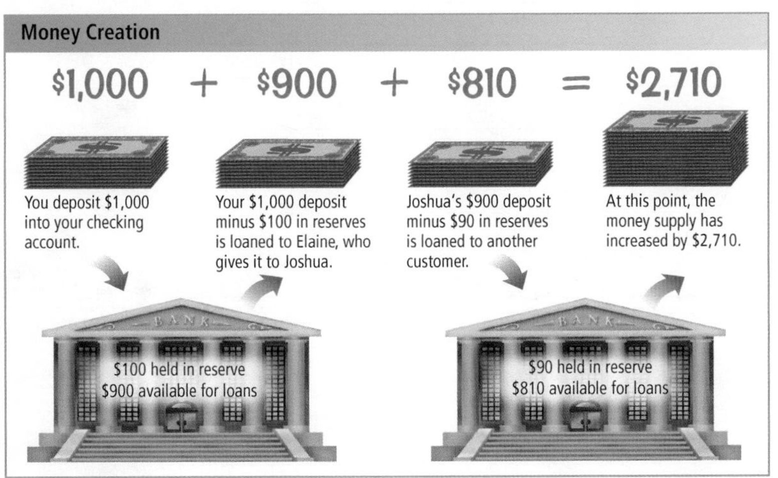

◀ The Federal Reserve is best known for its role in regulating the nation's money supply. Too much money in the economy leads to inflation. This diagram shows how money is created. By altering the amount of money banks are required to keep in reserve, the Fed can increase or shrink the money supply.

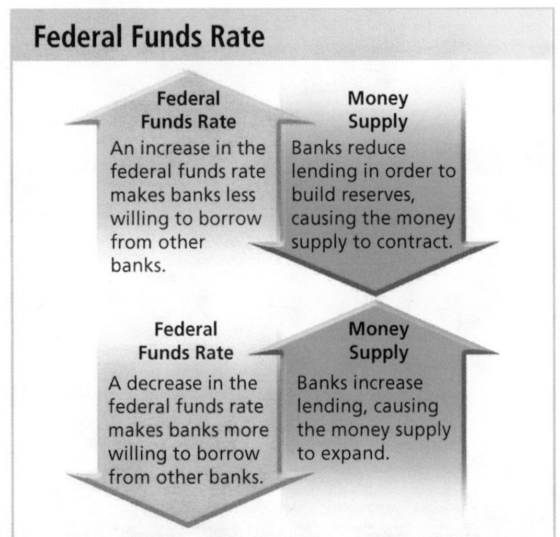

▲ The federal funds rate is the interest rate that banks charge each other when they lend each other reserves. An increase in the federal funds rate makes borrowing more costly, and the monetary supply contracts. Banks are more willing to borrow and lend money when the federal funds rate is low.

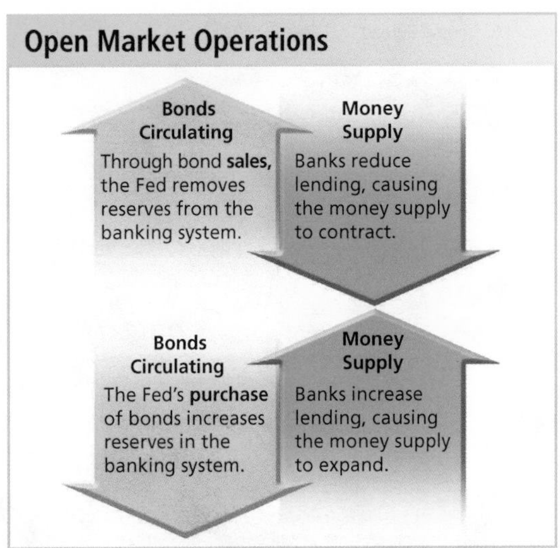

▲ When the Fed purchases government bonds on the open market, the bond seller deposits the money from the bond sale in the bank. In this way, funds enter the banking system, setting in motion money creation. When the Fed sells government bonds that it holds, bond buyers pay for the bonds using money from their bank accounts. When the Fed receives this money, it is taken out of circulation.

U.S. Foreign Trade

Foreign trade has played an important role in the U.S. economy. A free-trade zone is a region where a group of countries agrees to reduce or eliminate trade barriers, such as tariffs or taxes on imports. The North American Free Trade Agreement (NAFTA) set the goal of eliminating all tariffs and trade barriers between Canada, Mexico, and the United States by 2009. Supporters of NAFTA point to increased trade among the countries. About 100 regional trading organizations operate in the world today. Many goods are produced globally by multinational corporations, with parts produced in one country and assembled in another.

Specialization and Trade International trade occurs when one country provides resources that another country needs. By specializing in the production of certain goods and services, nations can use their resources more efficiently. Do research at the library or online to learn more about absolute and comparative advantage to understand why specialization and trade can benefit all nations—even those with few resources.

Balance of Trade
The **balance of trade** is the relationship between a nation's imports and exports.
Historical Context: According to the theory of mercantilism, a nation could increase its wealth by protecting its own industries from foreign competition through tariffs, or taxes on imports, and by striving to export more than it imports. The American colonies provided a market for British-made goods. American colonists were not permitted to trade with countries other than Britain or to manufacture their own goods.
Today: In recent decades, the United States has had an unfavorable balance of trade. It has imported more than it has exported and experienced annual trade deficits. A trade imbalance can be corrected by limiting imports or increasing exports.

Major Exports and Imports, 2007

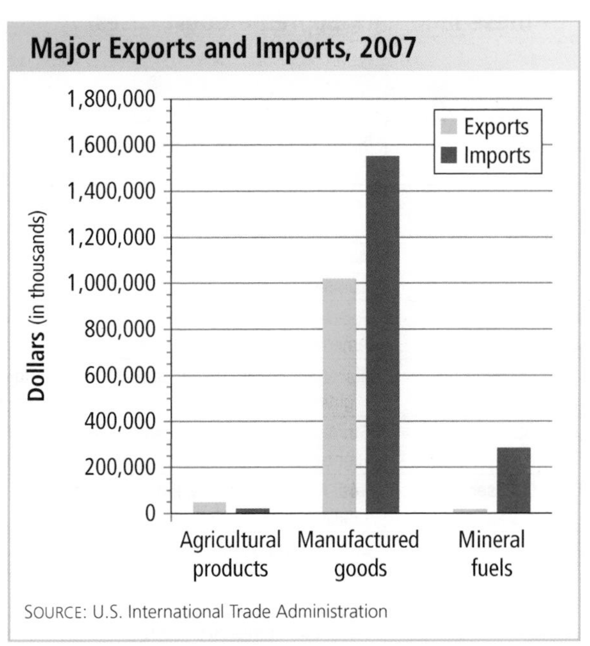

SOURCE: U.S. International Trade Administration

Major Trade Organization Members

Economics Handbook

Landmark Decisions of the Supreme Court

The table below lists key Supreme Court cases, issues, and decisions that have had a lasting impact on the course of the nation's history. Following the table, you will find a more detailed summary of each of these landmark Supreme Court cases.

The Case	The Issues	The Supreme Court's Decision
Marbury v. *Madison* (1803)	Judicial Review, Checks and Balances	First decision to assert judicial review: the power of the Court to interpret the constitutionality of a law
McCulloch v. *Maryland* (1819)	Federalism, States' Rights	Upheld the power of the national government and denied the right of a state to tax a federal agency.
Gibbons v. *Ogden* (1824)	Federalism, States' Rights, Interstate Commerce	Upheld broad congressional power to legislate and regulate commerce between states.
Worcester v. *Georgia* (1832)	Federalism, States' Rights; Native American Sovereignty	Ruled that Georgia had no power to pass laws affecting the Cherokees because federal jurisdiction over the Cherokees was exclusive.
Dred Scott v. *Sandford* (1857)	Slavery, 5th Amendment, Citizens' Rights	Ruled that slaves were property, not citizens and, therefore, Dred Scott was not entitled to use the courts.
Munn v. *Illinois* (1876)	5th Amendment, Public Interest; States' Rights	Upheld an Illinois law regulating railroad rates because the movement of grain was closely related to public interest.
Civil Rights Cases (1883)	14th Amendment Equal Protection Clause, Racial Discrimination	Stated that the 14th Amendment only applied to discriminatory action taken by states, not to discriminatory actions taken by individuals.
Wabash, St. Louis & Pacific R.R. v. *Illinois* (1886)	Federalism, Interstate Commerce	Struck down an Illinois law regulating interstate railroad rates, ruling that it infringed on the federal government's exclusive control over interstate commerce.
United States v. *E.C. Knight Co.* (1895)	Sherman Antitrust Act, Federalism, States' Rights	The Sherman Antitrust Act does not apply to manufacturers located within a single state, because under the 10th Amendment, states have the right to regulate "local activities."
In Re Debs (1895)	Labor Strikes, Interstate Commerce	Ruled that the federal government had the authority to halt a railroad strike because it interfered with interstate commerce and delivery of the mail.
Plessy v. *Ferguson* (1896)	Segregation, 14th Amendment Equal Protection Clause	Permitted segregated public facilities, arguing that separate but equal accommodations did not violate the equal protection clause of the 14th Amendment.
United States v. *Wong Kim Ark* (1898)	Immigration, citizenship,14th Amendment	Affirmed that under the 14th Amendment, all persons born in the United States are citizens of the United States.
Northern Securities Co. v. *United States* (1904)	Sherman Antitrust Act, Interstate Commerce	Sherman Antitrust Act could apply to any company that sought to eliminate competition in interstate commerce, including companies chartered within a single state.
Lochner v. New York(1905)	Labor conditions, property rights, 14th Amendment	Struck down a state law setting a 10-hour day for employees because the law interfered with an employee's right to contract with an employer and violated the protection of liberty guaranteed by the 14th Amendment.
Muller v. *Oregon* (1908)	Women's rights, Labor Conditions, 14th Amendment	In a departure from the *Lochner* case, the Court upheld a state law limiting women's work hours, viewing women as a special class needing special protections.
Standard Oil of New Jersey v. *United States* (1911)	Antitrust	Ruled that Standard Oil was an illegal monopoly and ordered that it be dissolved into smaller, competing companies.
American Tobacco v. *United States* (1911)	Antitrust	Ruled that American Tobacco was an illegal monopoly and ordered that it be dissolved into smaller, competing companies.
Schenck v. *United States* (1919)	1st Amendment freedom of speech, national security	The Court limited free speech in time of war, reasoning that freedom of speech can be limited if the words present a "clear and present danger" to the country.
Abrams v. *United States* (1919)	1st Amendment freedom of speech, national security	Upheld the convictions of persons who distributed antigovernment literature in violation of the Espionage Act. But Justices Holmes and Brandeis dissented, urging more stringent protection of the 1st Amendment.
Gitlow v. *New York* (1925)	1st Amendment freedoms of speech and press, 14th Amendment	Ruled that the freedoms of speech and press were "incorporated" and protected from impairment by the states by the due process clause of the 14th Amendment.
Stromberg v. *California* (1931)	1st Amendment freedom of speech, 14th Amendment	Overturned an anticommunist law that banned the public display of a red flag. This was the first time the Supreme Court struck down a state law under the 1st Amendment as applied to the states by the 14th Amendment.
Near v. *Minnesota* (1931)	1st Amendment freedom of speech, 14th Amendment	The Supreme Court struck down a Minnesota state law, ruling that it infringed upon freedom of the press, guaranteed by the due process clause of the 14th Amendment.

The Case	The Issues	The Supreme Court's Decision
Schechter Poultry Corporation* v. *United States (1935)	New Deal, separation of powers, interstate commerce	The Court held that Congress, not the President, has the power to regulate interstate commerce. The National Industrial Recovery Act was declared unconstitutional for exceeding the commerce power that the Constitution had given to Congress.
West Coast Hotel* v. *Parrish (1937)	Minimum wage laws, 5th Amendment	Ruled that the Constitution allowed the restriction of liberty of contract by state law where such restriction protected the community, health, safety, or vulnerable groups.
West Virginia State Board of Education* v. *Barnette (1943)	Pledge of Allegiance, 1st Amendment	The Court found that a state law requiring students to pledge allegiance to the flag violated freedom of speech and freedom of religion.
Hirabayashi* v. *United States (1943)	5th Amendment, civil liberties, national security	The Supreme Court upheld the legitimacy of travel restrictions imposed on Japanese Americans during World War II.
Korematsu* v. *United States (1944)	5th Amendment, civil liberties, national security	Ruled that the internment of Japanese Americans during World War II did not violate the Constitution.
Everson* v. *Board of Education (1947)	1st Amendment, establishment clause	The New Jersey law allowing reimbursement of money to parents whose children attended Catholic schools did not violate the 1st amendment. Some services "are separate from the religious function."
Dennis* v. *United States (1951)	1st Amendment, civil liberties, national security	The Court ruled that the Smith Act, which prohibited advocation of the overthrow of the U.S. government by force and violence, did not violate the 1st Amendment.
Brown* v. *Board of Education of Topeka (1954)	School segregation, 14th Amendment	The Court found that segregation itself was a violation of the Equal Protection Clause, commenting that "in the field of public education the doctrine of 'separate but equal' has no place."
Watkins* v. *United States (1957)	Rights of the accused, 5th Amendment	The Bill of Rights is applicable to congressional investigations, as it is to all forms of governmental action.
Yates* v. *United States (1957)	1st Amendment freedom of speech, national security	Ruled that the Smith Act did not forbid persons from advocating forcible overthrow of the government; it only forbade actions to achieve that goal.
Cooper* v. *Aaron (1958)	School segregation, 14th Amendment	The Court ruled unanimously against the Little Rock School Board's efforts to not comply with the Brown decision.
Mapp* v. *Ohio (1961)	Search and seizure 4th and 14th amendments	Ruled that evidence obtained by searches and seizures in violation of the Constitution is inadmissible.
Baker* v. *Carr (1962)	Legislative reapportionment, 14th Amendment	Ruled that federal Courts could direct that election-district boundaries be redrawn to ensure citizens' political rights.
Engel* v. *Vitale (1962)	1st Amendment, establishment clause	Ruled that the recitation of a prayer in a public classroom was a violation of the establishment clause of the 1st Amendment.
Gideon* v. *Wainwright (1963)	Rights of the accused, 6th and 14th amendments	The Court said that all states must provide an attorney in all felony and capital cases for people who cannot afford one themselves.
Reynolds* v. *Sims (1964)	Legislative reapportionment, 14th Amendment	Extended the one-person, one-vote principle of *Wesberry* v. *Sanders* (1964) to states, ruling that state legislative districts should be roughly equal in population so that every voter has an equally weighted vote.
Heart of Atlanta Motel* v. *United States (1964)	Racial segregation, interstate commerce	Racial segregation of private facilities engaged in interstate commerce was found unconstitutional.
Miranda* v. *Arizona (1966)	Rights of the accused, 5th, 6th, and 14th amendments	Before questioning suspects held in custody, police must inform suspects that they have the right to remain silent, that anything they say may be used against them, and that they have the right to counsel.
Swann* v. *Charlotte-Mecklenburg Board of Education (1971)	School desegregation, busing	Ruled that busing students to various schools is an acceptable way to integrate segregated school systems. The Court said school districts had broad powers to find solutions to the problem of segregation.
Tinker* v. *Des Moines (1969)	Students' rights, 1st Amendment freedom of speech	Students in school may exercise freedom of speech as long as they do not disrupt classwork, create substantial disorder, or interfere with the rights of others.
New York Times* v. *United States (1971)	1st Amendment freedom of the press	The Court limited censorship through "prior restraint" of the press, noting that it is the obligation of the government to prove that actual harm to the nation's security would be caused by the publication.
Roe* v. *Wade (1973)	Abortion, 9th Amendment, "right to privacy"	Decided that states could regulate abortions only in certain circumstances but otherwise a woman's right to an abortion was protected by her right to privacy.
United States* v. *Nixon (1974)	Executive privilege, separation of powers	Executive privilege was subordinate to "the fundamental demands of due process of law in the fair administration of criminal justice." President Nixon had to surrender audiotapes to a special prosecutor.
Regents of the University of CA* v. *Bakke (1978)	Affirmative action, 14th Amendment,	The Court held that a university could consider an applicant's race in making admissions decisions, but the use of strict racial quotas in affirmative action programs was not permissible.
New Jersey* v. *T.L.O. (1985)	Students' rights, 4th and 14th amendments	School officials, unlike the police, need only "reasonable suspicion" to search students when they believe illegal activity is occurring.
Texas* v. *Johnson (1989)	1st Amendment freedom of speech	Ruled that desecrating the flag as an act of protest is an act of expression protected by the 1st Amendment.
Cruzan* v. *Director, Missouri Department of Health (1990)	"Right to die," 9th Amendment, 14th Amendment	Individuals have the right to refuse medical treatment, but the State can preserve life unless there is "clear and convincing" evidence that the patient desires the withdrawal of medical treatment.

Supreme Court Cases

The Case	The Issues	The Supreme Court's Decision
Board of Education of Westside Community Schools* v. *Mergens (1990)	1st Amendment, Establishment Clause	Allowing students to meet in noncurricular clubs on campus and discuss religion is constitutional because it does not amount to state sponsorship of a religion.
Planned Parenthood of Southeastern Pennsylvania, et al.* v. *Casey (1992)	Abortion, 14th Amendment, "right to privacy"	The Court upheld a woman's "liberty" to have an abortion but also allowed for restrictive state regulations as long as they did not create an "undue burden" or "substantial obstacle" for a woman.
Vernonia School District* v. *Acton (1995)	Students' rights, 4th Amendment search and seizure	The Court decided that drug testing of student athletes was constitutional; students' rights can be lessened at school if it is necessary to maintain student safety.
Reno* v. *American Civil Liberties Union (1997)	Internet, 1st Amendment, freedom of Speech	Ruled that the 1996 Federal Communications Decency Act violated the 1st Amendment's right to freedom of speech by not clearly defining which Internet materials were "indecent."
Bush* v. *Gore (2000)	Election rules, 14th Amendment	Following the controversial 2000 presidential election, the Supreme Court held that the Florida Supreme Court's plan for recounting ballots was unconstitutional.
Mitchell* v. *Helms (2000)	1st Amendment, Establishment Clause	Ruled that a federal law providing funds for educational materials to public and private schools, including Catholic parochial schools, does not violate the 1st Amendment's Establishment Clause.
District of Columbia* v. *Heller (2008)	2nd Amendment	The Court rules that a ban on handguns in the District of Columbia violated the 2nd Amendment right to bear arms.

Abrams v. *United States* (1919)

(1st Amendment freedom of speech, national security) Jacob Abrams and others distributed leaflets attacking the U.S. decision to send troops to Russia, which was experiencing revolution and civil war. They were found guilty of violating the Espionage Act. The Supreme Court upheld the convictions citing Holmes's "clear and present danger" test. But Justices Holmes and Brandeis published a powerful dissenting opinion. Holmes argued that the "silly leaflet" of "poor and puny anonymities" posed no real danger to U.S. efforts, and thus failed to present a "clear and present danger." He urged his colleagues to enforce the 1st Amendment more stringently.

American Tobacco v. *U.S.* (1911)

(antitrust) Federal regulators filed an antitrust suit against American Tobacco, controlled by James Buchanan "Buck" Duke. The company controlled more than 90 percent of the world tobacco market. In 1911, the Supreme Court declared the company was a monopoly in violation of the Sherman Antitrust Act and ordered it to be split into five smaller competing companies.

Baker v. *Carr* (1962)

(legislative reapportionment, 14th Amendment) Rapid population growth had occurred in Tennessee's cities, but the rural-dominated Tennessee legislature did not redraw state legislature districts. Cities with larger populations were underrepresented, while rural communities with smaller populations held the majority of representation. Mayor Baker of Nashville asked for federal court help. The Supreme Court ruled that the apportionment of state legislative districts is within the jurisdiction of federal courts. The Court directed a trial to be held in a Tennessee federal court. The case led to the 1964 *Wesberry* decision, which affirmed voters' right to the equal protection guaranteed by the 14th Amendment and established the principle of "one man, one vote" for the apportionment of congressional districts.

Board of Education of Westside Community Schools v. *Mergens* (1990)

(1st Amendment, establishment clause) A request by Bridget Mergens to form a student Christian religious group at school was denied by an Omaha high school principal. Mergens took legal action, claiming that a 1984 federal law required "equal access" for student religious groups. The Court ordered the school to permit the club, stating that "a high school does not have to permit any extracurricular activities, but when it does, the school is bound by the . . . [Equal Access] Act of 1984. Allowing students to meet on campus and discuss religion is constitutional because it does not amount to 'State sponsorship of a religion.'"

Brown v. *Board of Education of Topeka* (1954)

(school segregation, 14th Amendment) Probably no twentieth-century Supreme Court decision so deeply stirred and changed life in the United States as *Brown*. An eight-year-old girl from Topeka, Kansas, was not permitted to attend her neighborhood school because she was an African American. The Court found that segregation was a violation of the Equal Protection Clause, commenting that "in the field of public education the doctrine of 'separate but equal' has no place. . . . Segregation is a denial of the equal protection of the laws." The decision overturned *Plessy*, 1896.

Bush v. *Gore* (2000)

(election rules, 14th Amendment) Following the controversial 2000 presidential election, the Florida Supreme Court ordered that every county in Florida had to manually recount some ballots. George Bush filed a request for review in the U.S. Supreme Court. The Supreme Court held that the Florida court's plan for recounting ballots was unconstitutional, noting that the Equal Protection Clause guarantees individuals that their ballots cannot be devalued by "later arbitrary and disparate treatment." The Court reasoned that there were too many procedural differences among the various counties for a fair recount to be conducted by the deadline date set by law.

Civil Rights Cases (1883)

(14th Amendment Equal Protection Clause, racial discrimination) The Civil Rights Act of 1875 included punishments for businesses that practiced discrimination. The Court ruled on a number of cases involving the acts in 1883, finding that the Constitution, "while prohibiting discrimination by governments, made no provisions . . . for acts of racial discrimination by private individuals." The decision limited the impact of the Equal Protection Clause, giving tacit approval for segregation in the private sector.

Cooper v. *Aaron* (1958)

(school segregation, 14th Amendment) President Eisenhower sent troops to Little Rock, Arkansas, to protect black students and enforce court-ordered school integration. But the local school board and state government continued to use delaying tactics. Arkansas officials even claimed that a state governor had the same power as the Supreme Court to interpret the Constitution. African American students appealed to the Supreme Court. The Court reaffirmed the *Brown* ruling that segregation was unconstitutional and boldly affirmed the Supreme Court's authority as the ultimate interpreter of the Constitution.

Cruzan v. *Director, Missouri Department of Health* (1990)

("right to die," 9th Amendment, 14th Amendment) After Nancy Beth Cruzan was left in a "persistent vegetative state" by a car accident, Missouri officials refused to comply with her parents' request that the hospital terminate life-support. The Court upheld the State policy under which officials refused to withdraw treatment, rejecting the argument that the Due Process Clause of the 14th Amendment gave the parents the right to refuse treatment on their daughter's behalf. Although individuals have the right to refuse medical treatment, "incompetent" persons are not able to exercise this right; without "clear and convincing" evidence that Cruzan desired the withdrawal of treatment, the State could legally act to preserve her life.

Dennis v. *United States* (1951)

(1st Amendment, civil liberties, national security) Eugene Dennis, a leader of the Communist Party in the United States, was arrested for violation of the Smith Act, which prohibited advocation of the overthrow of the U.S. government by force and violence. Dennis claimed that the law violated his 1st Amendment right to free speech. Reasoning that the Communist Party is a conspiratorial organization with "evil" intent, the Supreme Court upheld the Smith Act and Dennis's conviction. The Court ruled that free speech may be limited if it presents a clear and present danger to overthrow the government of the United States by force or violence.

District of Columbia v. *Heller* (2008)

(2nd Amendment, right to bear arms) The Supreme Court upheld a Court of Appeals decision overturning a District of Columbia law that made it illegal for private citizens to own handguns. The law also required that other firearms be kept either unassembled or with trigger locks in place, thus rendering them unusable. The Court ruled, 5–4, that this law violated a person's Second Amendment right to lawfully own a firearm. Justice Antonin Scalia stated in the Court's opinion "Few laws in the history of our Nation have come close to the severe restriction of the District's handgun ban. . . . Undoubtedly some think that the Second Amendment is outmoded in a society . . . where gun violence is a serious problem. That is perhaps debatable, but what is not debatable is that it is not the role of this Court to pronounce the Second Amendment extinct."

Dred Scott v. *Sandford* (1857)

(slavery, 5th Amendment, citizens' rights) This decision upheld property rights over human rights by saying that Dred Scott, a slave, could not become a free man just because he had traveled in "free soil" states with his master. A badly divided nation was further fragmented by the decision. "Free soil" federal laws and the Missouri Compromise line of 1820 were held unconstitutional because they deprived a slave owner of the right to his "property" without just compensation. This narrow reading of the Constitution, a landmark case of the Court, was most clearly stated by Chief Justice Roger B. Taney, a states' rights advocate.

Engel v. *Vitale* (1962)

(1st Amendment establishment clause) The State Board of Regents of New York required the recitation of a nonsectarian prayer at the beginning of each school day. A group of parents filed suit against the required prayer. The Supreme Court ruled that the recitation of a prayer in a public classroom was a violation of the establishment clause of the 1st Amendment. The Court ruled New York's action unconstitutional, observing, "There can be no doubt that . . . religious beliefs [are] embodied in the Regents' prayer."

Supreme Court Cases

Everson v. *Board of Education* (1947)

(1st Amendment, establishment clause) New Jersey allowed for the reimbursement of transportation costs to parents whose children attended private schools, including parochial Catholic schools. Arch Everson, a taxpaying resident of Ewing Township, sued the local school district, insisting that this reimbursement violated both the New Jersey State Constitution and the First Amendment. In a 5–4 ruling, the Supreme Court upheld the law, stating that the "First Amendment has erected a wall between church and state. . . . New Jersey has not breached it here."

Gibbons v. *Ogden* (1824)

(federalism, states' rights, interstate commerce) Aaron Ogden's exclusive New York ferry license gave him the right to operate steamboats to and from New York. Thomas Gibbons was operating steamboats between New York and New Jersey under a U.S. federal license. Ogden obtained an injunction from a New York court ordering Gibbons to stop operating his boats in New York waters. The Supreme Court invalidated the New York licensing regulations, holding that federal regulations should take precedence under the Constitution's Supremacy Clause (Article VI, Section 2). The decision strengthened the power of the United States to regulate interstate business. Federal regulation of the broadcasting industry, oil pipelines, and banking are all based on *Gibbons*.

Gideon v. *Wainwright* (1963)

(rights of the accused, 6th and 14th amendments) Gideon was charged with breaking into a poolroom. He could not afford a lawyer, and Florida refused to provide counsel for trials not involving the death penalty. Gideon defended himself poorly and was sentenced to five years in prison. The Court called for a new trial, arguing that the Due Process Clause of the 14th Amendment applied to the 6th Amendment's guarantee of counsel for all poor persons facing a felony charge. Gideon later was found not guilty with the help of a court-appointed attorney.

Gitlow v. *New York* (1925)

(1st Amendment freedoms of speech and press, 14th Amendment) Gitlow was convicted for distributing a manifesto that called for the establishment of socialism through strikes and other actions. The Supreme Court considered whether the 1st and 14th amendments had influence on state laws. According to what came to be known as the "incorporation" doctrine, the Court argued that the provisions of the 1st Amendment were "incorporated" by the 14th Amendment. The New York law was not overruled, but the decision clearly indicated that the Court could make such a ruling. Later cases extended the incorporation doctrine. Today, the Supreme Court holds that almost every provision of the Bill of Rights applies to both the federal government and the states.

Heart of Atlanta Motel v. *United States* (1964)

(racial segregation, interstate commerce) The Civil Rights Act of 1964 outlawed racial discrimination in "public accommodations," including motels that refused rooms to blacks. Although local desegregation appeared to fall outside federal authority, the government argued that it was regulating interstate commerce. The Court agreed, declaring, "The power of Congress to promote interstate commerce also includes the power to regulate the local incidents thereof, including local activities . . . which have a substantial and harmful effect upon that commerce." Racial segregation of private facilities engaged in interstate commerce was found unconstitutional.

Hirabayashi v. *United States* (1943)

(5th Amendment, civil liberties, national security) After the Japanese attack on Pearl Harbor, President Roosevelt issued executive orders to protect the West Coast from espionage and sabotage. As a result of these orders, curfews were established, and Japanese Americans were evacuated to relocation centers. Gordon Kiyoshi Hirabayashi, a student at the University of Washington, was convicted of violating a curfew and relocation order. Did the government policies violate the 5th Amendment rights of Americans of Japanese descent? The Supreme Court upheld the curfew, but evaded ruling on the relocation. The Court considered the vulnerability of military installations on the West Coast and the "solidarity" that persons of Japanese descent felt with their motherland, and reasoned that restrictions served an important national interest. Racial discrimination was justified since "in time of war residents having ethnic affiliations with an invading enemy may be a greater source of danger than those of a different ancestry."

In Re Debs (1895)

(labor strikes, interstate commerce) Eugene V. Debs, a leader of the 1894 Pullman Railroad Car workers' strike, refused to halt the strike as ordered by a federal court. Debs appealed his "contempt of court" conviction. Citing Article 1, Section 8 of the Constitution, the Supreme Court ruled that the government had a right to regulate interstate commerce and ensure the operations of the Postal Service. The federal court had a right to stop the strike because the strikers interfered with the railroad's ability to provide interstate commerce and deliver the mail, which benefited the needs and "general welfare" of all Americans.

Korematsu v. *United States* (1944)

(5th Amendment, civil liberties, national security) After the Japanese attack on Pearl Harbor, President Roosevelt issued executive orders to protect the West Coast from acts of espionage and sabotage. As a result of these orders, more than 110,000 Japanese Americans living on the West Coast were forced to abandon their property and live in primitive camps far from the coast. Korematsu refused to report to an assembly center and was arrested. The Court rejected his appeal, noting that "pressing public necessity [World War II] may sometimes justify restrictions which curtail the civil rights of a single racial group" but added that "racial antagonism" never can justify such restrictions. The *Korematsu* decision has been widely criticized, particularly since few Americans of German or Italian descent were interned. In 1988, the U.S. government officially apologized for the internment and paid reparations to survivors.

Lochner v. *New York* (1905)

(labor conditions, property rights, 14th Amendment) A New York law limited bakery employees' working hours to no more than 10 hours a day or 60 hours a week. Lochner claimed that the law infringed on his right to make employer/employee contracts and violated the Due Process Clause of the 14th Amendment. The Supreme Court struck down the New York law, arguing that states have the power to regulate health, safety, and public welfare, but that the New York law was not within the limits of these "police powers." The New York law interfered with citizens' property rights, guaranteed by the 14th Amendment.

Mapp v. *Ohio* (1961)

(search and seizure, 4th and 14th amendments) Admitting evidence gained by illegal searches was permitted by some states before *Mapp*. Cleveland police raided Dollree Mapp's home without a warrant and found obscene materials. She appealed her conviction, saying that the 4th and 14th amendments protected her against improper police behavior. The Court agreed, extending "exclusionary rule" protections to citizens in state courts, saying that the prohibition against unreasonable searches would be "meaningless" unless evidence gained in such searches was "excluded." *Mapp* developed the concept of "incorporation" begun in *Gitlow* v. *New York*, 1925.

Marbury v. *Madison* (1803)

(judicial review, checks and balances) After defeat in the 1800 election, President Adams appointed many Federalists to the federal courts, but James Madison, the new Secretary of State, refused to deliver the commissions. William Marbury, one of the appointees, asked the Supreme Court to enforce the delivery of his commission based on a provision of the Judiciary Act of 1789 that allowed the Court to hear such cases on original jurisdiction. The Court refused Marbury's request, finding that the relevant portion of the Judiciary Act was in conflict with the Constitution. This decision, written by Chief Justice Marshall, established the evaluation of federal laws' constitutionality, or "judicial review," as a power of the Supreme Court.

McCulloch v. *Maryland* (1819)

(federalism, states' rights) This is also known as the "Bank of the United States" case. A Maryland law required federally chartered banks to use only a special paper to print paper money, which amounted to a tax. James McCulloch, the cashier of the Baltimore branch of the bank, refused to use the paper, claiming that states could not tax the federal government. The Court declared the Maryland law unconstitutional, commenting that the "power to tax implies the power to destroy."

Miranda v. *Arizona* (1966)

(rights of the accused; 5th, 6th, and 14th amendments) Arrested for kidnapping and sexual assault, Ernesto Miranda signed a confession including a statement that he had "full knowledge of [his] legal rights." After conviction, he appealed, claiming that without counsel and without warnings, the confession was illegally gained. The Court agreed with Miranda that "he must be warned prior to any questioning that he has the right to remain silent, that anything he says can be used against him in a court of law, that he has the right to . . . an attorney and that if he cannot afford an attorney one will be appointed for him." Although later modified by *Nix* v. *Williams*, 1984, and other cases, *Miranda* firmly upheld citizen rights to fair trials in state courts.

Mitchell v. *Helms* (2000)

(1st Amendment Establishment Clause) Chapter 2 of the Education Consolidation and Improvement Act of 1981 provides for the allocation of funds for educational materials and equipment to public and private schools to implement "secular, neutral, and nonideological" programs. In Jefferson Parish, Louisiana, about 30 percent of Chapter 2 funds are allocated for private schools, most of which are Catholic. Mary Helms and other public school parents filed suit alleging that the policy violated the 1st Amendment's Establishment Clause. The Supreme Court disagreed, ruling that Chapter 2, as applied in Jefferson Parish, is not a law respecting an establishment of religion, noting that "the religious, irreligious, and areligious are all alike eligible for governmental aid."

Muller v. *Oregon* (1908)

(women's rights, labor conditions, 14th Amendment) In 1903, Oregon enacted a law prohibiting women from working in factories or laundries more than 10 hours in any day. After a conviction, Curt Muller claimed that the law violated his freedom of contract, protected by the 14th Amendment. The Court upheld the law, viewing women as a special class that needed special protections. The Court noted that a "woman's physical structure and the functions she performs . . . justify special legislation restricting the conditions under which she should be permitted to toil."

Munn v. *Illinois* (1876)

(5th Amendment, public interest, states' rights) Responding to farmers' complaints about the exorbitant rates they were paying, Illinois passed laws that set maximum rates that railroads and grain storage companies could charge. Munn, a partner in a Chicago warehouse firm, appealed his conviction, contending that the Illinois regulation constituted a taking of property without due process of law. The Supreme Court upheld the Illinois laws, arguing that states may regulate the use of private property "when such regulation becomes necessary for the public good." The case established as constitutional the principle of public regulation of private businesses involved in serving the public interest.

Near v. *Minnesota* (1931)

(1st Amendment freedom of speech, 14th Amendment) Jay Near published a Minneapolis newspaper whose articles charged that local government and police officials were implicated with gangsters. A local official filed a complaint against Near under a Minnesota law that provided permanent injunctions against those who created a "public nuisance," by publishing, selling, or distributing a "malicious, scandalous and defamatory newspaper." The Supreme Court held that the Minnesota law was an infringement of freedom of the press guaranteed by the Due Process Clause of the 14th Amendment.

New Jersey v. *T.L.O.* (1985)

(students' rights, 4th and 14th amendments) After T.L.O., a New Jersey high school student, denied an accusation that she had been smoking in the school lavatory, a vice principal searched her purse and found cigarettes, marijuana, and evidence that T.L.O. had been involved in marijuana dealing at the school. T.L.O. was then sentenced to probation by a juvenile court but appealed on the grounds that the evidence against her had been obtained by an "unreasonable" search. The Court rejected T.L.O.'s arguments, stating that the school had a "legitimate need to maintain an environment in which learning can take place," and that to do this "requires some easing of the restrictions to which searches by public authorities are ordinarily subject." The Court thus created a "reasonable suspicion" rule for school searches, a change from the "probable cause" requirement in the wider society.

New York Times v. *United States* (1971)

(1st Amendment, freedom of the press) In 1971, *The New York Times* obtained copies of classified Defense Department documents, later known as the "Pentagon Papers," which revealed instances in which the Johnson administration had deceived Congress and the American people regarding U.S. policies during the Vietnam War. A U.S. district court issued an injunction against the publication of the documents, claiming that it might endanger national security. On appeal, the Supreme Court cited the 1st Amendment guarantee of a free press and refused to uphold the injunction against publication. The Court noted that it is the obligation of the government to prove that actual harm to the nation's security would be caused by the publication. The decision limited "prior restraint" of the press.

Northern Securities Co. v. *United States* (1904)

(Sherman Antitrust Act, interstate commerce) In 1901, financiers formed the Northern Securities Company as a holding company that controlled the stock of the Great Northern Railway, Northern Pacific Railway, the Chicago, Burlington & Quincy Railroad, and other railroads. Fearing a monopoly, President Theodore Roosevelt's trust-busting government applied the Sherman Antitrust Act. In response to the question of whether the Sherman Act applied to a company chartered by one of the states, the Supreme Court ruled "It cannot be said that any state may give a corporation, created under its laws, authority to restrain interstate or international commerce. . . . Every corporation created by a state is necessarily subject to the supreme law of the land."

Planned Parenthood of Southeastern Pennsylvania, et al. v. *Casey* (1992)

(abortion, 14th Amendment, "right to privacy") The Pennsylvania legislature enacted new regulations limiting abortion. Physicians had to provide patients with antiabortion information and wait at least 24 hours before performing an abortion. In most cases, minors needed the consent of a parent, and married women had to notify their husbands of their intention to abort the fetus. The Supreme Court reaffirmed a woman's "liberty" to have an abortion as it had in the *Roe* decision. However, it upheld most of Pennsylvania's provisions, reasoning that they did not create an "undue burden" or "substantial obstacle" for women seeking an abortion. Under this new "undue burden" test, the only provision to fail was the husband notification requirement.

Plessy v. *Ferguson* (1896)

(segregation, 14th Amendment equal protection) A Louisiana law required separate seating for white and African American citizens on public railroads, a form of segregation. Herman Plessy argued that his right to "equal protection of the laws" was violated. The Court held that segregation was permitted if facilities were equal. The Court interpreted the 14th Amendment as "not intended to give Negroes social equality but only political and civil equality. . . ." The Louisiana law was seen as a "reasonable exercise of (state) police power. . . ." Segregated public facilities were permitted until *Plessy* was overturned by the *Brown* v. *Board of Education* case of 1954.

Regents of the University of California v. *Bakke* (1978)

(affirmative action, 14th Amendment) Under an affirmative action program, the medical school of the University of California at Davis reserved 16 of 100 slots in each class for "disadvantaged citizens." When Bakke, a white applicant, was not accepted by the school, he claimed racial discrimination in violation of the 14th Amendment. The Court ruled narrowly, requiring Bakke's admission but not overturning affirmative action, preferring to review such questions on a case-by-case basis.

Reno v. *American Civil Liberties Union* (1997)

(Internet 1st Amendment, freedom of speech) Seeking to protect minors, the 1996 Federal Communications Decency Act made it a crime to transmit obscene or indecent messages over the Internet. The Supreme Court ruled that the "indecent transmission" provision and the "patently offensive display" provision of the Communications Decency Act violated the 1st Amendment's freedom of speech. The Court reasoned the act did not clearly define "indecent." The Internet does not have the special features (such as historical governmental oversight, limited frequencies, and "invasiveness") that have justified allowing greater regulation of content in radio and television.

Reynolds v. *Sims* (1964)

(legislative reapportionment, 14th Amendment) Voters of Jefferson County, Alabama, filed a suit challenging the apportionment of the Alabama legislature, which was still based on the 1900 federal census. The Supreme Court extended the "one person, one vote" principle that emerged from *Baker* v. *Carr* (1962) and *Wesberry* v. *Sanders* (1964) and applied it to this case, calling for reapportionment based on current census data. Applying the Equal Protection Clause of the 14th Amendment, the Court ruled that state legislative districts should be roughly equal in population so that every voter has an equally weighted vote.

Roe v. *Wade* (1973)

(abortion, 9th Amendment, "right to privacy") A Texas woman challenged a state law forbidding the artificial termination of a pregnancy, saying that she "had a fundamental right to privacy." The Court upheld a woman's right to choose in this case, noting that the state's "important and legitimate interest in protecting the potentiality of human life" became "compelling" at the end of the first trimester, and that before then, ". . . the attending physician, in consultation with his patient, is free to determine, without regulation by the state, that . . . the patient's pregnancy should be terminated." The decision struck down the state regulation of abortion in the first three months of pregnancy and was modified by *Planned Parenthood of Southeastern Pennsylvania* v. *Casey*, 1992.

Schechter Poultry Corporation v. *United States* (1935)

(New Deal, separation of powers, interstate commerce) As part of the New Deal, the National Industrial Recovery Act (NIRA) gave the President authority to regulate aspects of interstate commerce. The government convicted Schechter for not observing minimum wage and hour provisions, selling uninspected chickens, and other violations. The Supreme Court ruled that Congress, not the President, has the power to regulate interstate commerce, and that Congress cannot delegate that power to the President. The Court reversed the conviction of Schechter because his business, which operated almost exclusively in New York State, only indirectly affected interstate commerce. The Court also declared the NIRA to be unconstitutional because it exceeded the commerce power that the Constitution had given to Congress.

Schenck v. *United States* (1919)

(1st Amendment freedom of speech, national security) Schenck, a member of an antiwar group, urged men drafted into military service in World War I to resist and to avoid induction. He was charged with violating the Espionage Act of 1917, which outlawed active opposition to the war. The Court limited free speech in time of war, stating that Schenck's words presented a "clear and present danger. . . ." Although later decisions modified this one, the *Schenck* case created a precedent that 1st Amendment rights are not absolute.

Standard Oil of New Jersey v. *United States* (1911)

(antitrust) The Standard Oil Company of New Jersey, controlled by John D. Rockefeller, owned virtually all the oil-refining companies in the United States and was extending its stranglehold over oil exploration and retail distribution of refined products. The government therefore prosecuted Standard Oil under the Sherman Antitrust Act. The Supreme Court found Standard Oil to be an illegal monopoly that restrained free competition. It fined Rockefeller and others, and ordered that the company be dissolved into smaller, competing companies.

Stromberg v. *California* (1931)

(1st Amendment freedom of speech, 14th Amendment) A California state law, enacted in 1919, prohibited the public display of a red flag. Yetta Stromberg, a member of the Young Communist League and a counselor at a camp for working-class children, was arrested for violating the law. Stromberg had led the youth in raising and pledging allegiance to "the workers' red flag." The Court struck down the law, concluding that a law that permitted the punishment of peaceful opposition exercised in accordance with legal means and constitutional limitations was "repugnant to the guarantee of liberty contained in the 14th Amendment."

Swann v. *Charlotte-Mecklenburg Board of Education* (1971)

(school desegregation, busing) After the *Brown* decision, school desegregation advanced very slowly. The NAACP took the *Swann* case to the Supreme Court on behalf of six-year-old James Swann and other students in the Charlotte-Mecklenburg, North Carolina, school system where the vast majority of black students attended all-black schools. The Court held that all schools in a district need not reflect the district's racial composition, but that the existence of all-white or all-black schools must be shown not to result from segregation policies. It stated that busing students to various schools is an acceptable way to integrate segregated school systems. The Court said school districts had broad powers to find solutions to the problem of segregation.

Texas v. *Johnson* (1989)

(1st Amendment freedom of speech) To protest national policies, Johnson doused a U.S. flag with kerosene and burned it outside the 1984 Republican National Convention in Dallas. He was arrested and convicted under a Texas law prohibiting the desecration of the Texas and U.S. flags. The Court ruled that the Texas law placed an unconstitutional limit on "freedom of expression," noting that ". . . nothing in our precedents suggests that a state may foster its own view of the flag by prohibiting expressive conduct relating to it."

Tinker v. *Des Moines* (1969)

(students' rights, 1st Amendment freedom of speech) Marybeth and John Tinker violated a school rule and wore black armbands to school in protest against the Vietnam War. They were suspended. The Tinkers claimed that their freedom of speech had been violated. The Supreme Court agreed, saying that students do not "shed their constitutional rights to freedom of speech or expression at the schoolhouse gate." Students may express personal opinions as long as they do not disrupt classwork, create substantial disorder, or interfere with the rights of others. Since the wearing of black armbands was a "silent, passive expression of opinion" without these side effects, the Tinkers' action was protected by the 1st Amendment.

United States v. *E. C. Knight Co.* (1895)

(Sherman Antitrust Act, federalism, states' rights) After gaining control of the E. C. Knight Company, the American Sugar Refining Company controlled more than 90 percent of the American sugar-refining industry. The federal government sued the Knight Company under the provisions of the Sherman Antitrust Act. The Court ruled that the Sherman Antitrust Act does not apply to manufacturers located within a single state, because under the 10th Amendment, states have the right to regulate "local activities," such as manufacturing. In later cases, the Court modified its position and permitted Congress greater power to limit monopolies.

United States v. *Nixon* (1974)

(executive privilege, separation of powers) During the investigation of the Watergate scandal, journalists discovered that President Nixon had recorded all of his conversations in the White House, including some with administration officials accused of illegal activities. A special prosecutor subpoenaed the tapes. Nixon refused to release them, citing separation of powers, his need for confidentiality, and executive privilege to immunity from court demands for information. The Supreme Court rejected his arguments and ordered him to surrender the tapes. Executive privilege was subordinate to "the fundamental demands of due process of law in the fair administration of criminal justice."

United States v. *Wong Kim Ark* (1898)

(immigration, citizenship, 14th Amendment) The Chinese Exclusion Act of 1882 denied citizenship to Chinese immigrants. Wong Kim Ark was born in 1873 in California to Chinese parents who were resident aliens. In 1894, Ark visited China. When he returned to the United States, he was denied entrance on grounds that he was not a U.S. citizen. The Supreme Court ruled in favor of Ark. Under the 14th Amendment, all persons born in the United States are citizens of the United States. Since he was born in the United States, Ark was a citizen. The Chinese Exclusion Act could not apply to him because he was a citizen by birth.

Vernonia School District v. *Acton* (1995)

(students' rights, 4th Amendment, search and seizure) The Vernonia school district of Oregon established a student-athlete drug policy that authorized urinalysis drug testing of student athletes. James Acton refused the urinalysis test and was therefore not allowed to participate in the school's junior high football program. Did the school policy violate the 4th Amendment protection against unreasonable search and seizure? The Supreme Court ruled that the school policy was constitutional. The reasonableness of a search is judged by "balancing the intrusion on the individual's 4th Amendment interests against the promotion of legitimate governmental interests." The school's concern over the safety of students under their supervision overrides the minimal intrusion in student-athletes' privacy.

Wabash, St. Louis & Pacific R.R. v. *Illinois* (1886)

(federalism, interstate commerce) An Illinois law regulated railroad rates on the intrastate (within one state) portion of an interstate (two or more states) journey. The Supreme Court declared the state law to be invalid, ruling that continuous transportation across the country is essential and that states should not impose restraints on the freedom of commerce. The Court stated that the regulation of interstate railroad rates is a federal power and that states cannot enact statutes interfering or seriously affecting interstate commerce. Soon afterward, Congress created the Interstate Commerce Commission (ICC).

Watkins v. *United States* (1957)

(rights of the accused, 5th Amendment) In 1954, John Watkins testified in hearings conducted by the House Committee on Un-American Activities. Watkins answered questions about himself but refused to give information on individuals who had left the Communist Party, arguing that such questions were beyond the authority of the committee. After being convicted for refusing to answer the committee's questions, Watkins appealed, arguing that his conviction was a violation of the Due Process Clause of the 5th Amendment. The Supreme Court overturned Watkins's conviction. The Court said that congressional committees had to clearly define the specific purposes of their investigations. Congressional committees must abide by the Bill of Rights. No witness can be made to testify on matters outside the defined scope of a committee's investigation.

West Coast Hotel v. *Parrish* (1937)

(minimum wage laws, 5th Amendment) The case involved Elsie Parrish, an employee of the West Coast Hotel Company, who received wages below the minimum wage fixed by Washington State law. The issue was whether minimum wage laws violated the liberty of contract as construed under the 5th Amendment and applied by the 14th Amendment. The Supreme Court upheld the constitutionality of the minimum wage legislation, ruling that the Constitution allowed the restriction of liberty of contract by state law where such restriction protected the community, health, safety, or vulnerable groups, as in the case of *Muller* v. *Oregon*, 1908.

West Virginia State Board of Education v. *Barnette* (1943)

("Pledge of Allegiance," 1st Amendment) The West Virginia Board of Education required that all teachers and pupils salute the flag. Some children did not comply, saying the requirement went against their religious beliefs. The Court held that compelling public schoolchildren to salute the flag was unconstitutional. "Compulsory unification of opinion," the Court held, was antithetical to 1st Amendment values. The decision noted that Americans could not be forced to demonstrate their allegiance to "what shall be orthodox in politics, nationalism, religion, or other matters of opinion."

Worcester v. *Georgia* (1832)

(federalism, states' rights, Native American sovereignty) Two missionaries were convicted for violating a Georgia law requiring all whites living in Cherokee Indian Territory to obtain a state license. The Supreme Court overturned their convictions, ruling that the state had no power to pass laws affecting the Cherokees because federal jurisdiction over the Cherokees was exclusive. Chief Justice John Marshall argued, "The Cherokee nation, then, is a distinct community occupying its own territory in which the laws of Georgia can have no force. The whole intercourse between the United States and this nation, is, by our constitution and laws, vested in the government of the United States."

Yates v. *United States* (1957)

(1st Amendment, freedom of speech, national security) In 1951, fourteen members of the Communist Party in California were convicted of violating the Smith Act, which said it was illegal to advocate or organize the forceful overthrow or destruction of the U.S. government. Yates claimed that the law violated his 1st Amendment right to freedom of speech. The Supreme Court reversed the convictions, saying that to violate the Smith Act, a person must urge others to do something, not just believe in something. The Court distinguished between speech promoting an idea and speech advocating direct action.

Documents of Our Nation

▲ Signing of the Mayflower Compact

The Mayflower Compact

The Pilgrims arrived at Massachusetts in 1620. Before disembarking, they signed a covenant that established a basis for self-government derived from the consent of the governed. Forty-one men signed the compact, agreeing to abide by the laws of the government. Women, who did not enjoy equal rights, were not asked to sign.

In the name of God, Amen. We, whose names are underwritten, the loyal subjects of our dread Sovereign Lord King James, by the grace of God, of Great Britain, France and Ireland king, defender of the faith, etc. Having undertaken, for the glory of God, and advancement of the Christian faith, and honor of our king and country, a voyage to plant the first colony in the Northern parts of Virginia, do by these presents solemnly and mutually in the presence of God and one of another, covenant and combine ourselves together into a civil body politick, for our better ordering and preservation, and furtherance of the ends aforesaid; and by virtue hereof to enacte, constitute, and frame such just and equal laws, ordinances, acts, constitutions and offices, from time to time, as shall be thought most meet and convenient for the general good of the Colony unto which we promise all due submission and obedience.

In witness whereof we have hereunder subscribed our names at Cape Cod the eleventh of November, in the year of the reign of our Sovereign Lord, King James, of England, France and Ireland, the eighteenth, and of Scotland the fifty-fourth. Anno Dom. 1620.

Patrick Henry
"Liberty or Death"

On March 23, 1775, Patrick Henry urged a Virginia convention to prepare for war against British forces. Decades later, from the recollections of men like Thomas Jefferson, William Wirt wrote a biography of Henry, including the speech below. Henry's passionate speech caused quite a stir, even if we cannot be certain of his exact words.

. . . It is now too late to retire from the contest. There is no retreat but in submission and slavery! Our chains are forged! Their clanking may be heard on the plains of Boston! The war is inevitable—and let it come! I repeat it, sir, let it come!

It is in vain, sir, to extenuate the matter. Gentlemen may cry, Peace, Peace—but there is no peace. The war is actually begun! The next gale that sweeps from the north will bring to our ears the clash of resounding arms! Our brethren are already in the field! Why stand we here idle? What is it that gentlemen wish? What would they have? Is life so dear, or peace so sweet, as to be purchased at the price of chains and slavery? Forbid it, Almighty God! I know not what course others may take; but as for me, give me liberty or give me death!

▲ Patrick Henry addresses fellow Virginians.

Thomas Paine
Common Sense

In 1776, after the battles at Lexington and Concord, Thomas Paine published a fiery fifty-page pamphlet that challenged the authority of the British government and the royal monarchy. Paine appealed to the people of America to seek independence from Great Britain.

. . . As to government matters, it is not in the power of Britain to do this continent justice: The business of it will soon be too weighty, and intricate, to be managed with any tolerable degree of convenience, by a power, so distant from us, and so very ignorant of us. . . .

For as in absolute governments the King is law, so in free countries the law ought to be King; and there ought to be no other. But lest any ill use should afterwards arise, let the crown at the conclusion of the ceremony be demolished, and scattered among the people whose right it is.

A government of our own is our natural right: And when a man seriously reflects on the precariousness of human affairs, he will become convinced, that it is infinitely wiser and safer, to form a constitution of our own in a cool deliberate manner, while we have it in our power, than to trust such an interesting event to time and chance. . . .

▲ Abigail Adams

Abigail Adams
"Remember the Ladies"

John and Abigail Adams spent long periods of time apart during the Revolution and the formation of the United States. During this time, they frequently wrote letters to each other, many discussing the politics of the day. In the following letter, written March 31, 1776, Abigail urges her husband to consider the role of women in the new nation.

. . . I long to hear that you have declared an independency—and by the way in the new Code of Laws which I suppose it will be necessary for you to make I desire you would Remember the Ladies, and be more generous and favorable to them than your ancestors. Do not put such unlimited power into the hands of the Husbands. Remember all Men would be tyrants if they could. If particular care and attention is not paid to the Ladies we are determined to foment a Rebellion, and will not hold ourselves bound by any Laws in which we have no voice, or Representation. . . .

John Adams

"Free and Independent States"

On July 2, 1776, the Second Continental Congress approved a resolution asserting the right of the colonies to be independent of Great Britain. Two days later, Congress would ratify the official Declaration of Independence. In between these two events, John Adams, a member of the Declaration of Independence draft committee, wrote to his wife expressing his excitement.

Yesterday the greatest question was decided, which ever was debated in America, and a greater, perhaps, never was or will be decided among men. A Resolution was passed without one dissenting Colony "that these United Colonies are, and of right ought to be, free and independent States, and as such they have, and of right ought to have, full power to make war, conclude peace, establish commerce, and to do all the other acts and things which other States may rightfully do." You will see, in a few days, a Declaration setting forth the causes which have impelled us to this mighty revolution, and the reasons which will justify it in the sight of God and man. A plan of confederation will be taken up in a few days.

▲ John Adams

Thomas Jefferson

Virginia Statute for Religious Freedom

Thomas Jefferson took great pride in drafting this law in 1777, but it was James Madison who skillfully secured its adoption by the Virginia legislature in 1786. The statute was the basis for the Religion Clauses in the Constitution's Bill of Rights.

. . . Be it enacted by the General Assembly, That no man shall be compelled to frequent or support any religious worship, place, or ministry whatsoever, nor shall be enforced, restrained, molested, or burthened in his body or goods, nor shall otherwise suffer on account of his religious opinions or belief; but that all men shall be free to profess, and by argument to maintain, their opinion in matters of religion, and that the same shall in no wise diminish, enlarge, or affect their civil capacities. . . .

◀ Bruton Parish Church in Virginia

The Northwest Ordinance

Adopted in 1787 by the Second Continental Congress, the Northwest Ordinance created a method for admitting new states to the Union. While the Articles of Confederation lacked a bill of rights, the Ordinance provided one that included many of the basic liberties that would later be included in the Constitution's Bill of Rights.

. . . **ART. 1.** No person, demeaning himself in a peaceable and orderly manner, shall ever be molested on account of his mode of worship or religious sentiments, in the said territory.

ART. 2. The inhabitants of the said territory shall always be entitled to the benefits of the writ of habeas corpus, and of the trial by jury. . . .

ART. 3. Religion, morality, and knowledge, being necessary to good government and the happiness of mankind, schools and the means of education shall forever be encouraged. . . .

ART. 6. There shall be neither slavery nor involuntary servitude in the said territory, otherwise than in the punishment of crimes whereof the party shall have been duly convicted: Provided, always, That any person escaping into the same, from whom labor or service is lawfully claimed in any one of the original States, such fugitive may be lawfully reclaimed and conveyed to the person claiming his or her labor or service as aforesaid.

▲ Settlers moving to the Ohio Territory

The Federalist, No. 51

This Federalist paper was probably written either by James Madison or Alexander Hamilton. It argues that the federal system and the separation of powers proposed in the Constitution provides a system of checks and balances that will protect the rights of the people.

. . . In order to lay a due foundation for that separate and distinct exercise of the different powers of government, which to a certain extent is admitted on all hands to be essential to the preservation of liberty, it is evident that each department should have a will of its own. . . .

But the great security against a gradual concentration of the several powers in the same department, consists in giving to those who administer each department the necessary constitutional means and personal motives to resist encroachments of the others. . . . Ambition must be made to counteract ambition. . . .

The constant aim is to divide and arrange the several offices in such a manner as that each may be a check on the other. . . .

In the compound republic of America, the power surrendered by the people is first divided between two distinct governments, and then the portion allotted to each subdivided among distinct and separate departments. Hence a double security arises to the rights of the people. . . .

Thomas Jefferson
First Inaugural Address

After the hotly contested presidential election of 1800, some expected that Jefferson's inaugural address would attack the defeated Federalists and their policies. Instead, he extended an olive branch of reconciliation. Jefferson praised a society in which people have full freedom to differ. He urged abidance with the will of the majority and respect for the rights of the minority.

Friends and Fellow Citizens:

. . . All . . . will bear in mind this sacred principle, that though the will of the majority is in all cases to prevail, that will, to be rightful, must be reasonable; that the minority possess their equal rights, which equal laws must protect, and to violate which would be oppression. Let us, then, fellow citizens, unite with one heart and one mind. . . . We have called by different names brethren of the same principle. We are all Republicans—we are all Federalists. If there be any among us who would wish to dissolve this Union or to change its republican form, let them stand undisturbed as monuments of the safety with which error of opinion may be tolerated where reason is left free to combat it. . . .

Still one thing more, fellow citizens—a wise and frugal government, which shall restrain men from injuring one another, which shall leave them otherwise free to regulate their own pursuits of industry and improvement, and shall not take from the mouth of labor the bread it has earned. This is the sum of good government. . . .

You should understand what I deem the essential principles of our government, and consequently those which ought to shape its administration. . . . Equal and exact justice to all men, of whatever state or persuasion, religious or political; peace, commerce, and honest friendship, with all nations—entangling alliances with none; the support of the state governments in all their rights . . . absolute acquiescence in the decisions of the majority. . . .

◀ Campaign banner promoting the election of Thomas Jefferson for President

Francis Scott Key
"The Star-Spangled Banner"

▲ Flag that flew over Fort McHenry during the British attack

During the War of 1812, a Maryland attorney named Francis Scott Key witnessed the British attack on Fort McHenry, near Baltimore. In the morning, Key was so delighted to see the American flag still flying over the fort that he composed a poem to commemorate the event. Set to the music of a popular folk tune, "The Star-Spangled Banner" was officially made the national anthem by Congress in 1931.

O say, can you see, by the dawn's early light,
What so proudly we hail'd at the twilight's last gleaming?
Whose broad stripes and bright stars, thro' the perilous fight,
O'er the ramparts we watch'd, were so gallantly streaming?
And the rockets' red glare, the bombs bursting in air,
Gave proof thro' the night that our flag was still there.
O say, does that star-spangled banner yet wave
O'er the land of the free and the home of the brave?

▲ Frederick Douglass

Frederick Douglass
Independence Day Speech

In 1852, Douglass accepted an invitation from the leading citizens of Rochester, New York, to speak at their Fourth of July celebration. Douglass delivered a scathing speech in which he attacked the hypocrisy of celebrating independence and freedom in a nation where millions of people were enslaved.

Fellow citizens, pardon me, allow me to ask, why am I called upon to speak here today? What have I, or those I represent, to do with your national independence? Are the great principles of political freedom and of natural justice, embodied in that Declaration of Independence, extended to us? . . .

What, to the American slave, is your Fourth of July? I answer: a day that reveals to him, more than all other days in the year, the gross injustice and cruelty to which he is the constant victim. To him, your celebration is a sham; your boasted liberty, an unholy license; your national greatness, swelling vanity; your sounds of rejoicing are empty and heartless; your denunciation of tyrants, brass-fronted impudence; your shouts of liberty and equality, hollow mockery; your prayers and hymns, your sermons and thanksgivings, with all your religious parade and solemnity, are, to Him, mere bombast, fraud, deception, impiety, and hypocrisy—a thin veil to cover up crimes which would disgrace a nation of savages. There is not a nation of savages. There is not a nation on the earth guilty of practices more shocking and bloody than are the people of the United States at this very hour. . . .

Sojourner Truth
"Ain't I a Woman?"

▲ Sojourner Truth

Sojourner Truth, an African American woman prominent in both the abolitionist and early feminist movements, delivered her famous speech at a women's rights convention in Akron, Ohio, in 1851. The version below was first published twelve years later in the Anti-Slavery Standard by Frances Gage, a celebrated antislavery fighter and president of the Convention. Although recent scholarship questions the exact wording of the speech, it made a great impact at the time and has endured as a classic statement of women's rights.

. . . I think that 'twixt the Negroes of the South and the women at the North, all talking about rights, the white men will be in a fix pretty soon. But what's all this here talking about?

That man over there says that women need to be helped into carriages, and lifted over ditches, and to have the best place everywhere. Nobody ever helps me into carriages, or over mud-puddles, or gives me any best place! And ain't I a woman? Look at me! Look at my arm! I have ploughed and planted, and gathered into barns, and no man could head me! And ain't I a woman? I could work as much and eat as much as a man—when I could get it—and bear the lash as well! And ain't I a woman? I have borne thirteen children, and seen most all sold off to slavery, and when I cried out with my mother's grief, none but Jesus heard me! And ain't I a woman? . . .

Elizabeth Cady Stanton
Address to the Legislature of New York

In 1854, Elizabeth Cady Stanton presented this speech to the New York State Legislature. She addressed the inequalities faced by all women under the state laws and discussed the specific challenges met by mothers, wives, and widows.

. . . Gentlemen, in republican America, in the nineteenth century, we, the daughters of the revolutionary heroes of '76, demand at your hands the redress of our grievances—a revision of your State Constitution—a new code of laws. Permit us then, as briefly as possible, to call your attention to the legal disabilities under which we labor.

1st. Look at the position of woman as woman. . . . We are persons; native, free-born citizens; property-holders, tax-payers; yet are we denied the exercise of our right to the elective franchise. We support ourselves, and, in part, your schools, colleges, churches, your poor-houses, jails, prisons, the army, the navy, the whole machinery of government, and yet we have no voice in your councils. We have every qualification required by the Constitution, necessary to the legal voter, but the one of sex. . . .

2nd. Look at the position of woman as wife. . . . The wife who inherits no property holds about the same legal position that does the slave on the Southern plantation. She can own nothing, sell nothing. She has no right even to the wages she earns; her person, her time, her services are the property of another. . . .

Abraham Lincoln

The Gettysburg Address

At the Battle of Gettysburg, more than 51,000 Confederate and Union soldiers were listed as wounded, missing, or dead. President Lincoln gave this brief speech at the dedication of The Gettysburg National Cemetery on November 19, 1863. The five known manuscript copies of the speech differ slightly and historians debate which version Lincoln actually delivered. But the address is considered one of the most eloquent and moving speeches in American history. As Lincoln described the significance of the war, he invoked the Declaration of Independence and its principles of liberty and equality, and he spoke of "a new birth of freedom."

Four score and seven years ago our fathers brought forth on this continent, a new nation, conceived in Liberty, and dedicated to the proposition that all men are created equal.

Now we are engaged in a great civil war, testing whether that nation, or any nation so conceived and so dedicated, can long endure. We are met on a great battle-field of that war. We have come to dedicate a portion of that field, as a final resting place for those who here gave their lives that the nation might live. It is altogether fitting and proper that we should do this.

But, in a larger sense, we can not dedicate—we can not consecrate—we can not hallow—this ground. The brave men, living and dead, who struggled here, have consecrated it, far above our poor power to add or detract. The world will little note, nor long remember what we say here, but it can never forget what they did here. It is for us the living, rather, to be dedicated here to the unfinished work which they who fought here have thus far so nobly advanced. It is rather for us to be here dedicated to the great task remaining before us—that from these honored dead we take increased devotion to that cause for which they gave the last full measure of devotion—that we here highly resolve that these dead shall not have died in vain—that this nation, under God, shall have a new birth of freedom—and that government of the people, by the people, for the people, shall not perish from the earth.

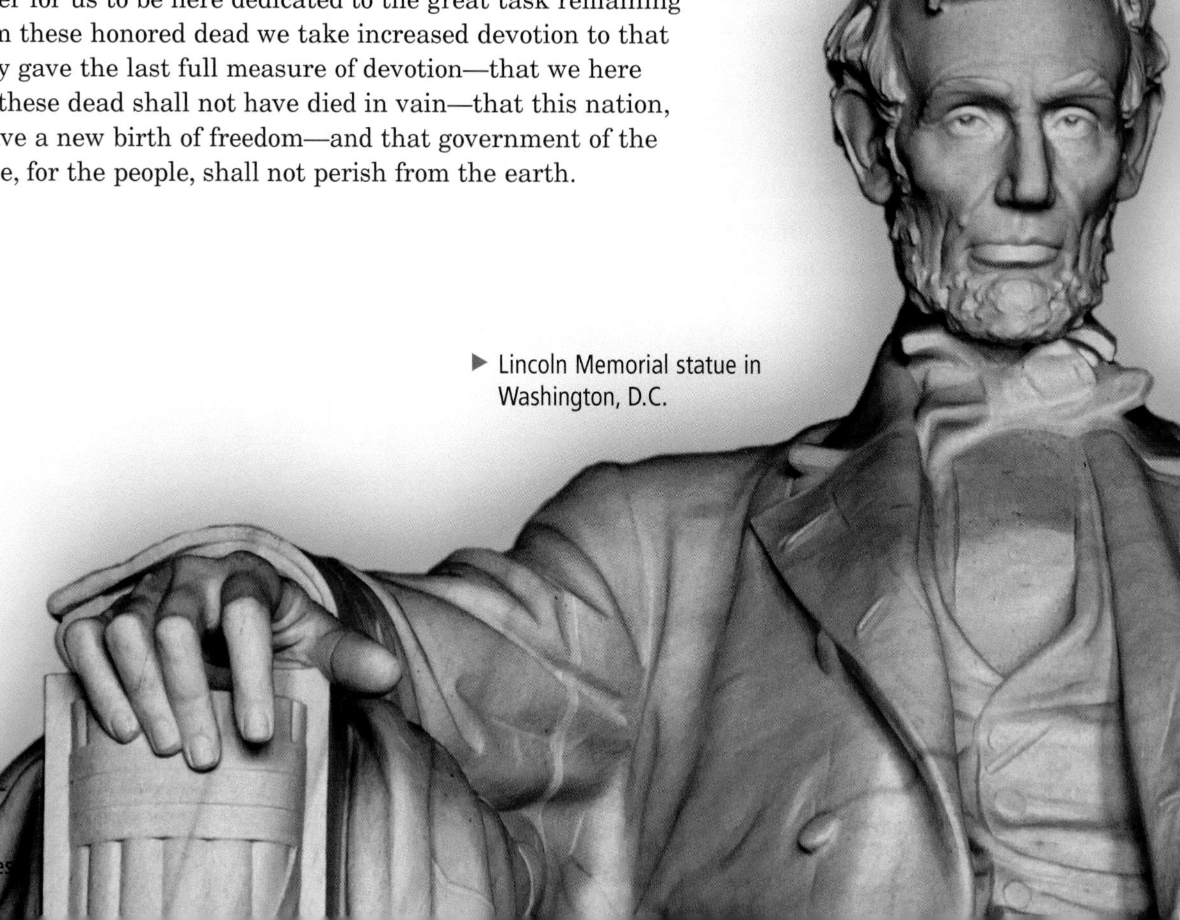

▶ Lincoln Memorial statue in Washington, D.C.

Abraham Lincoln
Second Inaugural Address

Lincoln delivered his second inaugural address just over a month before his death. He spoke about the war, slavery, and the need "to bind up the nation's wounds." The speech's closing words of reconciliation and healing are today carved in the walls of the Lincoln Memorial.

. . . On the occasion corresponding to this four years ago all thoughts were anxiously directed to an impending civil war. All dreaded it, all sought to avert it. While the inaugural address was being delivered from this place, devoted altogether to saving the Union without war, insurgent agents were in the city seeking to destroy it without war—seeking to dissolve the Union and divide effects by negotiation. Both parties deprecated war, but one of them would make war rather than let the nation survive, and the other would accept war rather than let it perish, and the war came.

One-eighth of the whole population were colored slaves, not distributed generally over the Union, but localized in the southern part of it. These slaves constituted a peculiar and powerful interest. All knew that this interest was somehow the cause of the war. To strengthen, perpetuate, and extend this interest was the object for which the insurgents would rend the Union even by war, while the Government claimed no right to do more than to restrict the territorial enlargement of it. Neither party expected for the war the magnitude or the duration which it has already attained. Neither anticipated that the cause of the conflict might cease with or even before the conflict itself should cease. Each looked for an easier triumph, and a result less fundamental and astounding. Both read the same Bible and pray to the same God, and each invokes His aid against the other. . . . Fondly do we hope, fervently do we pray, that this mighty scourge of war may speedily pass away. Yet, if God wills that it continue until all the wealth piled by the bondsman's two hundred and fifty years of unrequited toil shall be sunk, and until every drop of blood drawn with the lash shall be paid by another drawn with the sword, as was said three thousand years ago, so still it must be said "the judgments of the Lord are true and righteous altogether."

With malice toward none, with charity for all, with firmness in the right as God gives us to see the right, let us strive on to finish the work we are in, to bind up the nation's wounds, to care for him who shall have borne the battle and for his widow and his orphan, to do all which may achieve and cherish a just and lasting peace among ourselves and with all nations.

Chief Joseph
"I Will Fight No More Forever"

In 1877, after being ordered to a reservation, Chief Joseph led some 800 of his Nez Percé people in an attempted escape to Canada. They fled more than 1,000 miles across Idaho and Montana, battling the U.S. Army all along the way. Finally, with fewer than 500 of his people remaining and only 40 miles from Canada, Chief Joseph surrendered. General O.O. Howard reported Chief Joseph's poignant words.

I am tired of fighting. Our chiefs are killed. . . . The old men are all dead. . . . It is cold and we have no blankets. The little children are freezing to death. My people, some of them, have run away to the hills, and have no blankets, no food; no one knows where they are—perhaps freezing to death. I want to have time to look for my children and see how many of them I can find. Maybe I shall find them among the dead. Hear me, my chiefs. I am tired; my heart is sick and sad. From where the sun now stands I will fight no more forever.

▲ Chief Joseph

Preamble to the Constitution of the Knights of Labor

The Knights of Labor, which adopted its constitution in 1878, was a national labor union that sought the eight-hour day, abolition of child labor, and equal pay for equal work. The organization grew to more than 700,000 workers, but rapidly declined due to unsuccessful strikes and the formation of the American Federation of Labor in 1886.

The recent alarming development and aggression of aggregated wealth, which, unless checked, will inevitably lead to the pauperization and hopeless degradation of the toiling masses, renders it imperative, if we desire to enjoy the blessings of life, that a check should be placed upon its power and upon unjust accumulation, and a system adopted which will secure to the laborer the fruits of his toil; and as this much-desired object can only be accomplished by the thorough unification of labor, and the united efforts of those who obey the divine injunction that "In the sweat of thy brow shalt thou eat bread," we have formed the Noble Order of the Knights of Labor with a view of securing the organization and direction, by co-operative effort, of the power of the industrial classes; and we submit to the world the objects sought to be accomplished by our organization, calling upon all who believe in securing "the greatest good to the greatest number" to aid and assist us. . . .

Preamble to the Platform of the Populist Party

The People's, or Populist, Party adopted its party platform in 1892 at its national convention in Omaha, Nebraska. The movement, which emerged from the Farmer's Alliance in the 1880s, sought political reforms and a redistribution of political and economic power.

The conditions which surround us best justify our co-operation; we meet in the midst of a nation brought to the verge of moral, political, and material ruin. Corruption dominates the ballot-box, the Legislatures, the Congress, and touches even the ermine of the bench. . . . The fruits of the toil of millions are boldly stolen to build up colossal fortunes for a few, unprecedented in the history of mankind; and the possessors of these, in turn, despise the Republic and endanger liberty. From the same prolific womb of governmental injustice we breed the two great classes—tramps and millionaires. . . .

We have witnessed for more than a quarter of a century the struggles of the two great political parties for power and plunder, while grievous wrongs have been inflicted upon the suffering people. We charge that the controlling influences dominating both these parties have permitted the existing dreadful conditions to develop without serious effort to prevent or restrain them. . . .

We believe that the power of government—in other words, of the people—should be expanded . . . to the end that oppression, injustice, and poverty shall eventually cease in the land. . . .

Emma Lazarus

"The New Colossus"

At the dedication of the Statue of Liberty in 1886, President Grover Cleveland spoke of the Statue of Liberty as a symbol of Franco-American friendship and American ideals. But Jewish American poet Emma Lazarus saw the statue as a shining beacon to the millions who were migrating to the United States. The poem that she wrote to help raise money for the statue's pedestal is today carved on that pedestal for all to read.

Not like the brazen giant of Greek fame,
With conquering limbs astride from land to land;
Here at our sea-washed, sunset gates shall stand
A mighty woman with a torch, whose flame
Is the imprisoned lightning, and her name
Mother of Exiles. From her beacon-hand
Glows world-wide welcome; her mild eyes command
The air-bridged harbor that twin cities frame,
"Keep, ancient lands, your storied pomp!" cries she
With silent lips. "Give me your tired, your poor,
Your huddled masses yearning to breathe free,
The wretched refuse of your teeming shore,
Send these, the homeless, tempest-tossed to me,
I lift my lamp beside the golden door!"

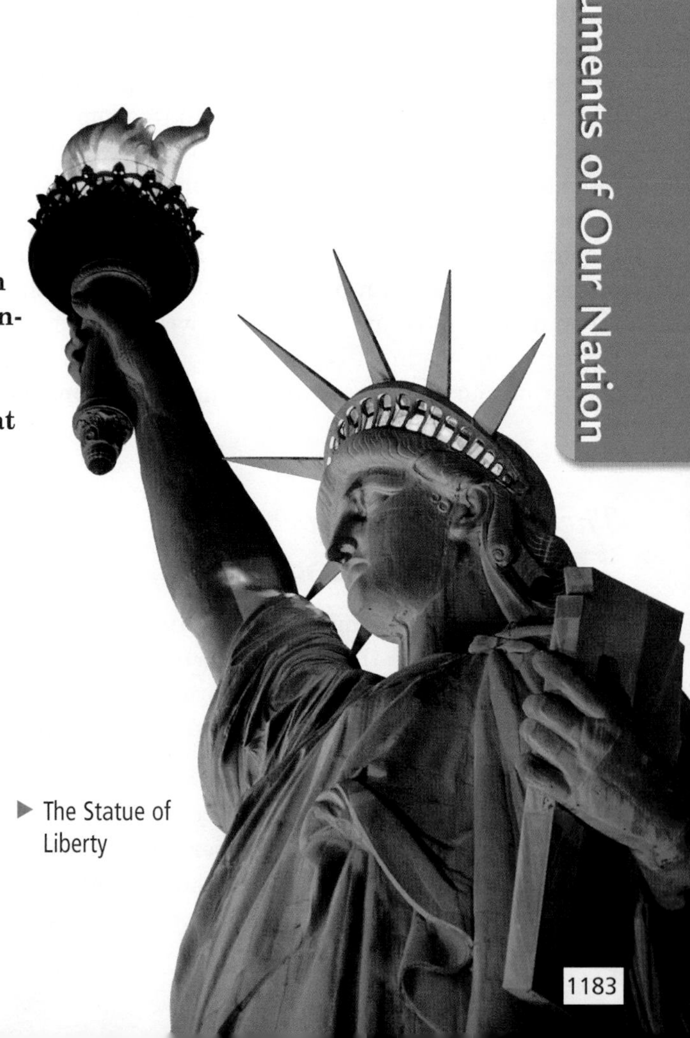

▶ The Statue of Liberty

Booker T. Washington
The Atlantic Exposition Address

In 1895, African American leader Booker T. Washington addressed a predominantly white audience in Atlanta. He urged fellow blacks to build friendly relations with whites and to start "at the bottom" by working at "the common occupations of life." Other black leaders rejected Washington's plan and called it the "Atlanta Compromise."

. . . Ignorant and inexperienced, it is not strange that in the first years of our new life we began at the top instead of at the bottom; that a seat in Congress or the state legislature was more sought than real estate or industrial skill; that the political convention or stump speaking had more attractions than starting a dairy farm or truck garden. . . .

To those of my race who depend on bettering their condition in a foreign land or who underestimate the importance of cultivating friendly relations with the Southern white man, who is their next-door neighbor, I would say: "Cast down your bucket where you are"— cast it down in making friends in every manly way of the people of all races by whom we are surrounded.

Cast it down in agriculture, mechanics, in commerce, in domestic service, and in the professions. And in this connection it is well to bear in mind that whatever other sins the South may be called to bear, when it comes to business, pure and simple, it is in the South that the Negro is given a man's chance in the commercial world. . . . Our greatest danger is that in the great leap from slavery to freedom we may overlook the fact that the masses of us are to live by the productions of our hands, and fail to keep in mind that we shall prosper in proportion as we learn to dignify and glorify common labour, and put brains and skill into the common occupations of life. . . . No race can prosper till it learns that there is as much dignity in tilling a field as in writing a poem. It is at the bottom of life we must begin, and not at the top. Nor should we permit our grievances to overshadow our opportunities. . . .

▲ Booker T. Washington

Theodore Roosevelt
"The New Nationalism"

At Ossowatomie, Kansas, in 1910, Theodore Roosevelt formulated the themes that would guide his 1912 campaign for the presidency. He proposed a New Nationalism that would promote human welfare and counter the power of big business.

. . . Now, this means that our government, National and State, must be freed from the sinister influence or control of special interests. Exactly as the special interests of cotton and slavery threatened our political integrity before the Civil War, so now the great special business interests too often control and corrupt the men and methods of government for their own profit. . . .

It has become entirely clear that we must have government supervision of the capitalization, not only of public-service corporations, including, particularly, railways, but of all corporations doing an interstate business. . . .

Combinations in industry are the result of an imperative economic law which cannot be repealed by political legislation. The effort at prohibiting all combination has substantially failed. The way out lies, not in attempting to prevent such combinations, but in completely controlling them in the interest of the public welfare. . . .

This New Nationalism regards the executive power as the steward of the public welfare. It demands of the judiciary that it shall be interested primarily in human welfare rather than in property, just as it demands that the representative body shall represent all the people rather than any one class or section of the people. . . .

▲ Theodore Roosevelt delivering a campaign speech

Woodrow Wilson
"Peace Without Victory"

On January 22, 1917, before the United States entered World War I, President Wilson spoke to the U.S. Senate about his vision for the future. He called for a "peace without victory." His ideas would later influence international cooperation in the League of Nations.

. . . It must be a peace without victory. . . . Victory would mean peace forced upon the loser, a victor's terms imposed upon the vanquished. It would be accepted in humiliation, under duress, at an intolerable sacrifice, and would leave a sting, a resentment, a bitter memory upon which terms of peace would rest, not permanently but only as upon quicksand. Only a peace between equals can last. . . .

No peace can last, or ought to last, which does not recognize and accept the principle that governments derive all their just powers from the consent of the governed, and that no right anywhere exists to hand peoples about from sovereignty to sovereignty as if they were property. . . .

There can be no sense of safety and equality among the nations if great preponderating armaments are henceforth to continue here and there to be built up and maintained. The statesmen of the world must plan for peace, and nations must adjust and accommodate their policy. . . .

I am proposing that all nations henceforth avoid entangling alliances which would draw them into competitions of power, catch them in a net of intrigue and selfish rivalry, and disturb their own. . . . There is no entangling alliance in a concert of power. When all unite to act in the same sense and with the same purpose, all act in the common interest and are free to live their own lives under a common protection. . . .

Franklin D. Roosevelt
First Inaugural Address

▲ Franklin D. Roosevelt greets supporters.

By 1933, the depression had reached its depth. Roosevelt's first inaugural address outlined in broad terms how he hoped to govern. He advised Americans "that the only thing we have to fear is fear itself." He reminded Americans that the nation's "common difficulties" concerned "only material things."

. . . This great Nation will endure as it has endured, will revive and will prosper. So, first of all, let me assert my firm belief that the only thing we have to fear is fear itself—nameless, unreasoning, unjustified terror which paralyzes needed efforts to convert retreat into advance. In every dark hour of our national life a leadership of frankness and vigor has met with that understanding and support of the people themselves which is essential to victory. I am convinced that you will again give that support to leadership in these critical days. . . .

I am prepared under my constitutional duty to recommend the measures that a stricken nation in the midst of a stricken world may require. These measures, or such other measures as the Congress may build out of its experience and wisdom, I shall seek, within my constitutional authority, to bring to speedy adoption.

But in the event that the Congress shall fail to take one of these two courses, and in the event that the national emergency is still critical, I shall not evade the clear course of duty that will then confront me. I shall ask the Congress for the one remaining instrument to meet the crisis—broad Executive power to wage a war against the emergency, as great as the power that would be given to me if we were in fact invaded by a foreign foe. . . .

George Kennan
"The Sources of Soviet Conduct"

**eorge Kennan published this article anonymously in the July 1947 issue of *Foreign Affairs*. He opposed appeasement and promoted firm opposition to the expansion of communism. His ideas on "containment" became the basis for U.S. policy toward the Soviet Union during the Cold War.**

. . . In these circumstances it is clear that the main element of any United States policy toward the Soviet Union must be that of long-term, patient but firm and vigilant containment of Russian expansive tendencies. . . .

The Soviet pressure against the free institutions of the western world is something that can be contained by the adroit and vigilant application of counter-force at a series of constantly shifting geographical and political points, corresponding to the shifts and maneuvers of Soviet policy, but which cannot be charmed or talked out of existence. The Russians look forward to a duel of infinite duration, and they see that already they have scored great successes. . . .

The issue of Soviet-American relations is in essence a test of the overall worth of the United States as a nation among nations. To avoid destruction the United States need only measure up to its own best traditions and prove itself worthy of preservation as a great nation. . . .

The Pledge of Allegiance

The Pledge of Allegiance was first written in 1892. It was revised twice before 1954, when the words "under God" were added, and it became the version that is still recited today.

I pledge allegiance to the Flag of the United States of America, and to the Republic for which it stands, one Nation under God, indivisible, with liberty and justice for all.

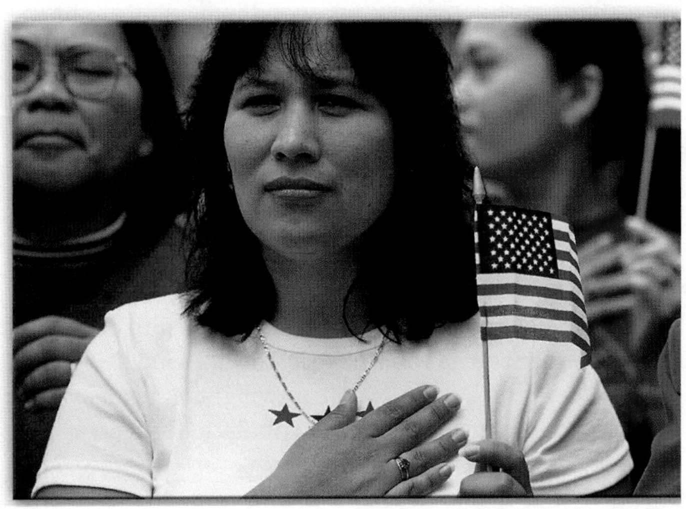

▲ A new citizen salutes the flag.

Dwight D. Eisenhower Farewell Address

On January 17, 1961, President Eisenhower delivered his farewell to the American people on national television. To the surprise of the American people, the general who had led America to victory in World War II issued a strong warning about the dangers of the "military-industrial complex."

. . . Until the latest of our world conflicts, the United States had no armaments industry. American makers of plowshares could, with time and as required, make swords as well. But now we can no longer risk emergency improvisation of national defense; we have been compelled to create a permanent armaments industry of vast proportions. . . .

This conjunction of an immense military establishment and a large arms industry is new in the American experience. The total influence—economic, political, even spiritual—is felt in every city, every state house, every office of the Federal government. We recognize the imperative need for this development. Yet we must not fail to comprehend its grave implications. . . .

We must never let the weight of this combination endanger our liberties or democratic processes. We should take nothing for granted. Only an alert and knowledgeable citizenry can compel the proper meshing of huge industrial and military machinery of defense with our peaceful methods and goals, so that security and liberty may prosper together. . . .

John F. Kennedy
Inaugural Address

On January 20, 1961, President John F. Kennedy delivered his inaugural address in which he announced to the world that "we shall pay any price, bear any burden, meet any hardship, support any friend, oppose any foe, in order to assure the survival and success of liberty."

. . . Let the word go forth from this time and place, to friend and foe alike, that the torch has been passed to a new generation of Americans—born in this century, tempered by war, disciplined by a hard and bitter peace, proud of our ancient heritage—and unwilling to witness or permit the slow undoing of those human rights to which this Nation has always been committed, and to which we are committed today at home and around the world.

Let every nation know, whether it wishes us well or ill, that we shall pay any price, bear any burden, meet any hardship, support any friend, oppose any foe, in order to assure the survival and the success of liberty. . . .

Now the trumpet summons us again—not as a call to bear arms, though arms we need; not as a call to battle, though embattled we are—but a call to bear the burden of a long twilight struggle, year in and year out, "rejoicing in hope, patient in tribulation"—a struggle against the common enemies of man: tyranny, poverty, disease, and war itself. . . .

In the long history of the world, only a few generations have been granted the role of defending freedom in its hour of maximum danger. I do not shrink from this responsibility—I welcome it. . . .

And so, my fellow Americans: ask not what your country can do for you—ask what you can do for your country.

My fellow citizens of the world: ask not what America will do for you, but what together we can do for the freedom of man. . . .

▲ President Kennedy giving his Inaugural Address

Martin Luther King, Jr.
Letter from Birmingham Jail

In 1963, King led a campaign of nonviolent protest against segregation and discrimination in Birmingham, Alabama. Rather than obey a court order to desist, King went to jail. From there, he wrote a response to white Alabama clergymen who were urging King to be more moderate in his struggle. King responded that the wait for civil rights had been too long and that civil disobedience against unjust laws was needed to achieve social justice.

My Dear Fellow Clergymen,

While confined here in the Birmingham City Jail, I came across your recent statement calling our present activities "unwise and untimely." . . .

We have waited for more than 340 years for our constitutional and God-given rights. The nations of Asia and Africa are moving with jetlike speed toward the goal of political independence, and we still creep at horse and buggy pace toward the gaining of a cup of coffee at a lunch counter.

I guess it is easy for those who have never felt the stinging darts of segregation to say wait. But when you have seen vicious mobs lynch your mothers and fathers at will and drown your sisters and brothers at whim; when you have seen hate-filled policemen curse, kick, brutalize, and even kill your black brothers and sisters with impunity; when you see the vast majority of your 20 million Negro brothers smothering in an airtight cage of poverty in the midst of an affluent society; when you suddenly find your tongue twisted and your speech stammering as you seek to explain to your six-year-old daughter why she can't go to the public amusement park that has just been advertised on television, and see the tears welling up in her little eyes when she is told that Funtown is closed to colored children, . . . then you will understand why we find it difficult to wait. . . .

You express a great deal of anxiety over our willingness to break laws. . . . The answer is found in the fact that there are two types of laws: There are just and there are unjust laws. I would agree with Saint Augustine that "An unjust law is no law at all." . . .

All segregation statutes are unjust because segregation distorts the soul and damages the personality. It gives the segregator a false sense of superiority, and the segregated a false sense of inferiority. . . .

Let us all hope that the dark clouds of racial prejudice will soon pass away and the deep fog of misunderstanding will be lifted from our fear-drenched communities and in some not too distant tomorrow the radiant stars of love and brotherhood will shine over our great nation with all their scintillating beauty.

Yours for the cause of Peace and Brotherhood,
Martin Luther King, Jr.

▲ A reflective King in his Birmingham jail cell

Documents of Our Nation

Betty Friedan

The Feminine Mystique

Betty Friedan's book exploded onto the American scene in 1963. Her work sparked a national debate about women's roles and was a pivotal event in the modern women's movement.

◄ Betty Friedan

. . . It . . . is time to stop giving lip service to the idea that there are no battles left to be fought for women in America, that women's rights have already been won. It is ridiculous to tell girls to keep quiet when they enter a new field, or an old one, so the men will not notice they are there. In almost every professional field, in business and in the arts and sciences, women are still treated as second-class citizens. . . . A girl should not expect special privileges because of her sex, but neither should she "adjust" to prejudice and discrimination.

She must learn to compete then, not as a woman, but as a human being. Not until a great many women move out of the fringes into the mainstream will society itself provide the arrangements for their new plan. . . .

Lyndon Johnson
Voting Rights

President Johnson made this speech to Congress on March 15, 1965, a week after deadly racial violence erupted in Selma, Alabama. He used the phrase "we shall overcome," borrowed from African American leaders struggling for equal rights.

. . . There is no Negro problem. There is no Southern problem. There is no Northern problem. There is only an American problem. And we are met here tonight as Americans—not as Democrats or Republicans—we are met here as Americans to solve that problem. . . .

Many of the issues of civil rights are very complex and most difficult. But about this there can and should be no argument. Every American citizen must have an equal right to vote.

Yet the harsh fact is that in many places in this country men and women are kept from voting simply because they are Negroes. . . .

Wednesday I will send to Congress a law designed to eliminate illegal barriers to the right to vote. . . .

But even if we pass this bill, the battle will not be over. What happened in Selma is part of a far larger movement which reaches into every section and State of America. It is the effort of American Negroes to secure for themselves the full blessings of American life.

Their cause must be our cause too. Because it is not just Negroes, but really it is all of us, who must overcome the crippling legacy of bigotry and injustice.

And we shall overcome. . . .

Richard Nixon
Resignation Speech

In the shadow of the Watergate scandal, President Nixon delivered his resignation speech on August 8, 1974. The next morning, he signed the resignation documents, made a final speech to his staff, and stepped onto the Marine One helicopter for the last time, to begin a trip to California as an ex-President.

. . . I have concluded that because of the Watergate matter I might not have the support of the Congress that I would consider necessary to back the very difficult decisions and carry out the duties of this office in the way the interests of the Nation would require. . . .

To continue to fight through the months ahead for my personal vindication would almost totally absorb the time and attention of both the President and the Congress in a period when our entire focus should be on the great issues of peace abroad and prosperity without inflation at home.

Therefore, I shall resign the Presidency effective at noon tomorrow. Vice President Ford will be sworn in as President at that hour in this office. . . .

▲ Richard Nixon leaves the White House after resigning from the presidency.

Jimmy Carter
"Crisis of Confidence"

In the 1970s, Americans struggled with the aftermath of the Vietnam War and the Watergate scandal. Economic problems and an energy crisis added to the malaise. On July 15, 1979, in a nationally televised address, President Carter identified what he believed to be a "crisis of confidence" among the American people.

. . . I want to talk to you right now about a fundamental threat to American democracy. . . . It is a crisis of confidence . . . that strikes at the very heart and soul and spirit of our national will. We can see this crisis in the growing doubt about the meaning of our own lives and in the loss of a unity of purpose for our nation. . . .

In a nation that was proud of hard work, strong families, close-knit communities, and our faith in God, too many of us now tend to worship self-indulgence and consumption. Human identity is no longer defined by what one does, but by what one owns. But we've discovered that owning things and consuming things does not satisfy our longing for meaning. . . .

As you know, there is a growing disrespect for government and for churches and for schools, the news media, and other institutions. This is not a message of happiness or reassurance, but it is the truth and it is a warning. . . .

Documents of Our Nation

Cesar Chavez
Commonwealth Club Address

The Commonwealth Club of California, the nation's oldest public affairs forum, has hosted diverse speakers, including Theodore Roosevelt, Martin Luther King, Jr., Ronald Reagan, and Bill Gates. In 1984, Cesar Chavez spoke about the United Farm Workers and progress for Latinos.

▲ Cesar Chavez

. . . The United Farm Workers is first and foremost a union. . . . But the UFW has always been something more than a union. . . .

The UFW's survival . . . was not in doubt . . . after the union became visible, when Chicanos started entering college in greater numbers, when Hispanics began running for public office in greater numbers, when our people started asserting their rights on a broad range of issues and in many communities across this land. The union survival, its very existence, sent out a signal to all Hispanics that we were fighting for our dignity, that we were challenging and overcoming injustice, that we were empowering the least educated among us, the poorest among us.

The message was clear. If it could happen in the fields, it could happen anywhere: in the cities, in the courts, in the city councils, in the state legislatures. I didn't really appreciate it at the time, but the coming of our union signaled the start of great changes among Hispanics that are only now beginning to be seen. . . .

Like the other immigrant groups, the day will come when we win the economic and political rewards, which are in keeping with our numbers in society. . . .

William Clinton
Second Inaugural Address

President Clinton took the oath of office for a second term on January 20, 1997. This was the last inaugural address of the twentieth century, and Clinton looked optimistically to the challenges that lay ahead in the next century.

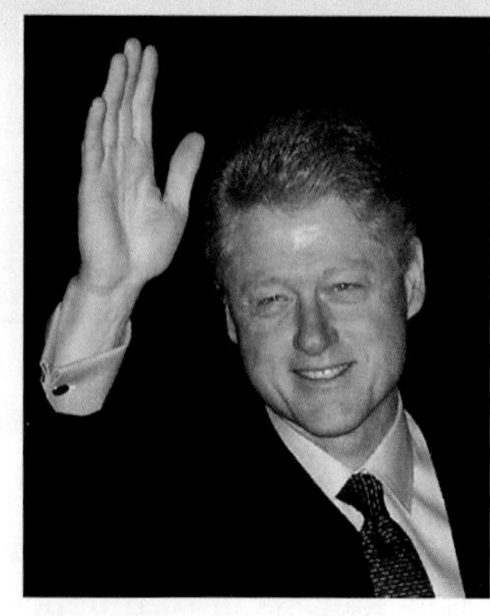

◀ President William Clinton

. . . The world is no longer divided into two hostile camps. Instead, now we are building bonds with nations that once were our adversaries. Growing connections of commerce and culture give us a chance to lift the fortunes and spirits of people the world over. And for the very first time in all of history, more people on this planet live under democracy than dictatorship. . . .

Our land of new promise will be a nation that meets its obligations, a nation that balances its budget, but never loses the balance of its values. A nation where our grandparents have secure retirement and health care, and their grandchildren know we have made the reforms necessary to sustain those benefits for their time. A nation that fortifies the world's most productive economy even as it protects the great natural bounty of our water, air, and majestic land. . . .

George W. Bush
War on Terror Speech

On September 11, 2001, terrorists hijacked and crashed passenger jets into the World Trade Center in New York City and the Pentagon Building in Washington, D.C. On September 20, President Bush addressed a joint session of Congress and announced to the nation a war on terrorism.

. . . Americans have known surprise attacks, but never before on thousands of civilians. All of this was brought upon us in a single day, and night fell on a different world, a world where freedom itself is under attack. . . .

The evidence we have gathered all points to a collection of loosely affiliated terrorist organizations known as al Qaeda.

The terrorists practice a fringe form of Islamic extremism that has been rejected by Muslim scholars and the vast majority of Muslim clerics; a fringe movement that perverts the peaceful teachings of Islam. . . .

Our war on terror begins with al Qaeda, but it does not end there. It will not end until every terrorist group of global reach has been found, stopped and defeated.

Americans are asking "Why do they hate us?" They hate what they see right here in this chamber: a democratically elected government. Their leaders are self-appointed. They hate our freedoms: our freedom of religion, our freedom of speech, our freedom to vote and assemble and disagree. . . .

Our response involves far more than instant retaliation and isolated strikes. Americans should not expect one battle, but a lengthy campaign unlike any other we have ever seen. . . .

We will rally the world to this cause by our efforts, by our courage. We will not tire, we will not falter and we will not fail. . . .

▼ President Bush addresses rescue work at the World Trade Center site.

English/Spanish Glossary

A

abolition movement nineteenth century movement that sought an end to slavery (p. 283)
movimiento de abolición movimiento del siglo XIX que buscaba suprimir la esclavitud

Acquired Immunodeficiency Syndrome (AIDS) a disease with no known cure that attacks the immune system. It began spreading in the early 1980s and remains a serious global health crisis today (p. 1085)
Síndrome de Inmunodeficiencia Adquirida (SIDA) una enfermedad para la que no se conoce cura que ataca el sistema inmunitario de sus víctimas; empezó a extenderse a principios de la década de 1980 y aún hoy sigue representando una seria crisis de salud mundial

Adams-Onís Treaty 1819 treaty in which Spain ceded Florida to the United States (p. 244)
Tratado Adams-Onís tratado de 1819 en el que España cedió Florida a Estados Unidos

administration staff of the executive branch (p. 193)
administración personal del poder ejecutivo

adobe sun-dried brick made from earth, water, and straw (p. 6)
adobe ladrillos hechos de tierra, agua y paja, secados al sol

affirmative action policy that gives special consideration to women and minorities to make up for past discrimination (pp. 1049, 1129)
acción afirmativa política que da trato especial a las mujeres y minorías para resarcirlas de la discriminación del pasado

AFL-CIO in 1955, the American Federation of Labor (AFL) and the Congress of Industrial Organization (CIO) labor unions united (p. 894)
AFL-CIO en 1955 los sindicatos de trabajadores, Federación Estadounidense del Trabajo (AFL) y el Congreso de Organización Industrial (CIO), se unieron

Alamo fortified former mission in San Antonio was the site of the 1836 defeat and slaughter of Texans by Mexican troops (p. 306)
El Álamo antigua misión fortificada en San Antonio, que fue el sitio de la derrota de 1836 y la matanza de tejanos a manos de tropas mexicanas

Albany Plan of Union Benjamin Franklin's 1754 proposal to create one government for the 13 colonies (p. 89)
Plan de la Unión de Albany propuesta de Benjamín Franklin de 1754 para crear un gobierno para las 13 colonias

Alien and Sedition Acts 1798 laws that allowed the government to imprison or deport aliens, and to prosecute its critics (p. 202)
Leyes de Extranjería y Sedición leyes de 1798 que permitieron que el gobierno arrestara o deportara a extranjeros y enjuiciara a sus críticos

Alliance for Progress President Kennedy's program which gave economic aid to Latin America (p. 955)
Alianza para el Progreso programa del presidente Kennedy que daba asistencia económica a América Latina

Allies group of countries led by Britain, France, the United States, and the Soviet Union that fought the Axis Powers in World War II (p. 781)
Aliados grupo de países encabezado por Gran Bretaña, Francia, Estados Unidos, y la Unión Soviética que peleó contra los Poderes del Eje en la Segunda Guerra Mundial

al Qaeda terrorist group established by Osama bin Laden to rid Muslim countries of Western influence (p. 1118)
al Qaida grupo terrorista establecido por Osama bin Laden para eliminar la influencia occidental en los países musulmanes

Alsace-Lorraine territory lost to Germany by France in 1871 (p. 618)
Alsacia y Lorena territorio que Francia perdió ante Alemania en 1871

American Federation of Labor (AFL) labor union that organized skilled workers in a specific trade and made specific demands rather than seeking broad changes (p. 454)
Federación Estadounidense del Trabajo sindicato de trabajadores que organizó a los trabajadores calificados en oficios específicos e hizo pequeñas demandas en lugar de buscar cambios amplios

American Indian Movement (AIM) group that focused on helping Indians, including the securing of legal rights, land, and self-government for Native Americans (p. 583)
Movimiento de Indígenas Estadounidenses grupo que se concentró en ayudar a los indígenas, incluyendo velar por sus derechos legales, tierra y de autodeterminación

American System Henry Clay's federal program designed to stimulate the economy with internal improvements and create a self-sufficient nation (p. 242)
Sistema Estadounidense programa federal de Henry Clay diseñado para estimular la economía con mejoras internas y crear una nación autosuficiente

Americanization belief that assimilating immigrants into American society would make them more loyal citizens (p. 468)
americanización creencia que sostenía que la asimilación de los inmigrantes por la sociedad estadounidense los haría ciudadanos más leales

amnesty general pardon for certain crimes (p. 1057)
amnistía perdón general de ciertos delitos

Anaconda Plan northern Civil War strategy to starve the South by blockading seaports and controlling the Mississippi River (p. 362)
Plan Anaconda estrategia del Norte en la Guerra Civil de llevar al Sur a la rendición por inanición al bloquear los puertos marinos y controlar el río Mississippi

Angel Island immigrant processing station that opened in San Francisco Bay in 1910 (p. 467)
Isla Ángel estación de procesamiento de inmigrantes que abrió sus puertas en la bahía de San Francisco en 1910

Anschluss union of Germany and Austria in 1933 (p. 778)
Anschluss unión de Alemania y Austria en 1933

Anti-Defamation League organization formed in 1913 to defend Jews against physical and verbal attacks and false statements (p. 119)
Liga Antidifamación organización formada en 1913 para defender a los judíos contra los ataques verbales y las falsas declaraciones

English/Spanish Glossary

Antietam 1862 Civil War battle in which 23,000 troops were killed or wounded in one day (p. 368)
Antietam batalla de la Guerra Civil de 1862 en la que murieron o resultaron heridos 23,000 miembros de las tropas en un día de lucha

Antifederalist one who opposed ratification of the Constitution (p. 151)
antifederalista quien se opuso a la ratificación de la Constitución

anti-Semitism prejudice and discrimination against Jewish people (pp. 775, 828)
antisemítismo prejuicios contra las personas judías

apartheid political system of strict segregation by race in South Africa (p. 1094)
apartheid sistema político de segregación intransigente basada en la raza, en Sudáfrica

appeasement policy of granting concessions in order to keep the peace (p. 777)
apaciguamiento política de otorgar concesiones para que mantener la paz

arms race contest in which nations compete to build more powerful weapons (p. 861)
carrera armamentista competencia en la que las naciones se enfrentan para construir armas más poderosas

Articles of Confederation original federal constitution drafted by the Continental Congress in 1777 (p. 136)
Estatutos de la Confederación constitución federal original preparada por el Congreso Continental en 1777

assembly line arrangement of equipment and workers in which work passes from operation to operation in direct line until the product is assembled (p. 661)
línea de ensamblaje organización de equipos y trabajadores en la que el trabajo pasa de una operación a otra en una línea directa hasta que el producto queda ensamblado

assimilate to be absorbed into the main culture of a society (p. 503)
asimilarse ser absorbido por la cultura dominante de una sociedad

Atlantic Charter joint declaration made by Great Britain and the United States during World War II that endorsed national self-determination and an international system of general security (p. 786)
Carta del Atlántico declaración conjunta entre Gran Bretaña y Estados Unidos durante la Segunda Guerra Mundial que aprobaba la autodeterminación nacional y un sistema internacional de seguridad general

autonomy independent control over one's own affairs (p. 306)
autonomía control independiente sobre los asuntos propios

Axis Powers group of countries led by Germany, Italy, and Japan that fought the Allies in World War II (p. 781)
Poderes del Eje grupo de países encabezado por Alemania, Italia y Japón que peleó contra los Aliados en la Segunda Guerra Mundial

B

baby boom increase in births between 1945 and 1964 (p. 435)
baby boom aumento de nacimientos entre 1945 y 1964

Bacon's Rebellion Virginia farmers clashed with both Indians and the colonial government over frontier expansion in 1675 (p. 48)
Rebelión de Bacon Conflicto entre los agricultores de Virginia, los indígenas y el gobierno colonial a causa de la expansión fronteriza en 1675

Barbary War war between the Barbary States and the United States (p. 209)
Guerra Berberisca guerra entre los Estados de Berbería y Estados Unidos

Bataan Death March during World War II, the forced march of American and Filipino prisoners of war under brutal conditions by the Japanese military (p. 793)
Marcha de la Muerte de Batán durante la Segunda Guerra Mundial, la marcha forzada de prisioneros de guerra estadounidenses y filipinos en condiciones brutales impuestas por los militares japoneses

Battle of the Bulge in December 1944, Hitler ordered a counterattack on Allied troops in Belgium, but it crippled Germany by using up reserves and demoralizing its troops (p. 375)
Batalla de las Ardenas en diciembre de 1944, Hitler ordenó un contraataque contra las tropas aliadas en Bélgica, pero esto debilitó a Alemania al usar todas sus reservas y desmoralizar a sus tropas

Battle of Coral Sea World War II battle that took place between Japanese and American aircraft carriers (p. 795)
batalla del Mar del Coral batalla entre aviones japoneses y estadounidenses, durante la Segunda Guerra Mundial, ocurrida en mayo de 1942 en el escenario del Pacífico

Battle of Fallen Timbers 1794 battle in which federal troops defeated the Miami Confederacy of Native Americans (p. 198)
Batalla de Fallen Timbers batalla ocurrida en 1794 en que las tropas federales derrotaron a la Confederación Miami de Indígenas

Battle of Gettysburg battle in 1863 in which Confederate troops were prevented from invading the North and which resulted in more than 50,000 casualties (p. 383)
Batalla de Gettysburg batalla durante 1863 en la que se evitó que las tropas Confederadas invadieran el Norte y que produjo más de 50,000 bajas

Battle of the Little Big Horn 1876 battle in which the Sioux defeated U.S. Army troops (p. 500)
Batalla del Little Big Horn batalla de 1876 durante la cual los sioux derrotaron a las tropas del Ejército de Estados Unidos

Battle of Midway turning point of World War II in the Pacific, in which the Japanese advance was stopped (p. 808)
Batalla de Midway momento decisivo de la Segunda Guerra Mundial en el Pacífico, en que se detuvo el avance de los japoneses

Battle of New Orleans War of 1812 battle when the United States defeated the British in January of 1815 (p. 218)
Batalla de Nueva Orleáns batalla de la Guerra de 1812 en la que Estados Unidos derrotó a los británicos en enero de 1815

Battle of Princeton 1777 Revolutionary War battle in New Jersey, won by the Continental Army (p. 119)

Batalla de Princeton batalla de la Guerra de Independencia ocurrida en Nueva Jersey en 1777 que ganó el Ejército Continental

Battle of Tippecanoe 1811 battle in the Indiana Territory between Native Americans and United States troops in which the Native Americans were defeated (p. 215)

Batalla de Tippecanoe batalla de 1811 en el Territorio de Indiana entre los indígenas y las tropas de Estados Unidos en que los indígenas resultaron derrotados

Battle of Trenton 1776 Revolutionary War battle in New Jersey, won by the Continental Army (p. 119)

Batalla de Trenton batalla de la Guerra de Independencia ocurrida en Nueva Jersey en 1776 que ganó el Ejército Continental

Bay of Pigs invasion 1961 failed invasion of Cuba by a CIA-led force of Cuban exiles (p. 956)

invasión de Bahía de Cochinos invasión de 1961 por exilados cubanos encabezados por la CIA que fracasaron al tratar de invadir Cuba

beatniks small group of writers and artists, in the 1950s and early 1960s, who were critical of American society (p. 456)

beatniks pequeño grupo de escritores y artistas en la década de 1950 y principios de los 1960 que criticaban a la sociedad estadounidense

Berlin airlift program in which U.S. and British pilots flew supplies to West Berlin during a Soviet blockade (p. 852)

puente aéreo de Berlín programa en el que pilotos estadounidenses y británicos volaban llevando suministros a Berlín Occidental durante un bloqueo soviético

Berlin Wall dividing wall built by East Germany in 1961 to isolate West Berlin from Communist-controlled East Berlin (p. 958)

Muro de Berlín pared divisoria construida por Alemania Oriental en 1961 para aislar a Berlín Occidental del Berlín Oriental controlado por los comunistas

Bessemer process method developed in the mid-1800s for making steel more efficiently (p. 439)

proceso Bessemer método desarrollado a mediados del siglo XIX para fabricar más eficientemente el acero

bicameral legislature lawmaking body made up of two houses (p. 135)

legislatura bicameral cuerpo legislativo compuesto de dos cámaras

"big stick" diplomacy Theodore Roosevelt's policy of creating and using, when necessary, a strong military to achieve America's goals (p. 605)

diplomacia de "mano dura" política seguida por Teodoro Roosevelt según la cual se organizaría y usaría, cuando fuera necesario, una fuerza militar poderosa para lograr los objetivos de Estados Unidos

bilingual education system in which students are taught in their native languages as well as in English (p. 1128)

educación bilingüe sistema en el que se enseña a los estudiantes en su idioma nativo así como en inglés

Bill of Rights first ten amendments to the Constitution; written list of freedoms guaranteed to citizens by the government (p. 153)

Declaración de Derechos primeras diez enmiendas a la Constitución; listado escrito de las libertades que el gobierno garantiza a sus ciudadanos

biotechnology application of technology to solving problems affecting living organisms (p. 1105)

biotecnología aplicación de la tecnología para resolver problemas que afectan a los organismos vivos

Black Cabinet group of African American leaders who served as unofficial advisers to Franklin D. Roosevelt (p. 302)

Gabinete Negro grupo de líderes afroestadounidenses que fungieron como consejeros extraoficiales de Franklin D. Roosevelt

black code laws that restricted African Americans' rights and opportunities (p. 405)

códigos negros leyes que restringían los derechos y oportunidades de los afroestadounidenses

blacklist list of persons who were not hired because of suspected communist ties (p. 870)

lista negra lista de personas que no fueron contratadas por sospechas de vínculos comunistas

Black Panthers organization of militant African Americans founded in 1966 (p. 941)

Panteras Negras organización de militantes afroestadounidenses fundada en 1966

black power movement in the 1960s that urged African Americans to use their collective political and economic power to gain equality (p. 941)

poder negro movimiento de la década de 1960 que exhortó a los afroestadounidenses a usar su poder político y económico colectivo para lograr la igualdad

Black Tuesday October 29, 1929, when stock prices fell sharply in the Great Crash (p. 706)

Martes Negro 29 de octubre de 1929, el día en que los precios de las acciones cayeron precipitadamente en la Gran Caída de la Bolsa

"Bleeding Kansas" term used to describe the 1854–1856 violence between proslavery and antislavery supporters in Kansas (p. 336)

"Kansas Sangrante" término usado para describir la violencia de 1854 a 1856 entre los que apoyaban la esclavitud y los que estaban en contra de la esclavitud en Kansas

blitzkrieg "lightning war" that emphasized the use of speed and firepower to penetrate deep into the enemy's territory (p. 781)

blitzkrieg "guerra relámpago" que enfatiza el uso de velocidad y capacidad bélica para penetrar muy adentro en el territorio enemigo

blockade military tactic in which a navy prevents vessels from entering or leaving its enemy's ports (p. 361)

bloqueo táctica militar en la que una fuerza naval evita que los buques entren o salgan de los puertos enemigos

boat people refugees who leave their country by boat (p. 1064)

balseros refugiados que dejan su país en bote

bond certificate bought from the government that promises to pay the holder back the purchase amount plus interest at a future date (p. 374)

bono certificado comprado al gobierno que promete al titular pagar con intereses el monto de la compra en una fecha posterior

Bonus Army group of World War I veterans who marched on Washington, D.C., in 1932 to demand early payment of a bonus promised them by Congress (p. 723)

Ejército del Bono grupo de veteranos de la Primera Guerra Mundial que marcharon sobre Washington, D.C., en 1932, para exigir el pago anticipado de un bono que les prometiera el Congreso

bootlegger one who sells illegal alcohol (p. 678)
contrabandista quien vende alcohol ilegalmente

border state during the Civil War, the states that allowed slavery but remained in the Union: Delaware, Kentucky, Maryland, and Missouri (p. 362)
estados colindantes durante la Guerra Civil, estados donde se toleraba la esclavitud aunque quedaron parte de la Unión: Delaware, Kentucky, Maryland, y Missouri

Boston Massacre incident on March 5, 1770, in which British soldiers killed five colonists in Boston (p. 103)
Masacre de Boston incidente del 5 de marzo de 1770, durante el cual soldados británicos mataron a cinco colonos en Boston

Boston Tea Party December 16, 1773 protest against British taxes in which Bostonians disguised as Native Americans dumped tea into the harbor (p. 103)
Fiesta del Te de Boston protesta del 16 de diciembre de 1773 contra los impuestos británicos en la cual los ciudadanos de Boston disfrazados como nativos estadounidenses botaron te al mar en el puerto

Boxer Rebellion violence started by members of a secret society in China, which prompted the governments of Europe and America to send troops to squash the rebellion (p. 602)
Rebelión de los Bóxer actos de violencia iniciados por miembros de una sociedad secreta en China, que provocó los gobiernos de Europa y América enviaran tropas para sofocar la rebelión

bracero program plan that brought laborers from Mexico to work on American farms (p. 811)
programa de braceros plan que trajo trabajadores de México a trabajar en granjas estadounidenses

Brady Bill law passed in 1993 requiring a waiting period on sales of handguns, along with a criminal background check on the buyer (p. 1111)
Ley Brady ley aprobada en 1993 que exige un período de espera de cinco días para la venta de revólveres, junto con una verificación de los antecedentes delictivos del comprador

bread line line of people waiting for food handouts from charities or public agencies (p. 710)
cola de alimentación fila de personas que esperan alimentos gratuitos de obras caritativas o agencias públicas

brinkmanship belief that only by going to the brink of war could the United States protect itself against communist aggression (p. 862)
política arriesgado creencia según la que sólo estando al borde de la guerra Estados Unidos podía protegerse contra la agresión comunista

budget deficit shortfall between the amount of money spent and the amount taken in by the federal government (p. 1082)
déficit presupuestario faltante entre la cantidad de dinero gastado y la cantidad de dinero captado por el gobierno federal

bull market period of rising stock prices (p. 664)
mercado alcista perfodo durante el cual suben los precios de las acciones

bureaucracy group of departments and officials that make up an organization, such as a government (p. 205)
burocracia grupo de departamentos y personeros que componen una organización, tal como el gobierno

business cycle periodic growth and contraction of the economy (p. 706)
ciclo commercial crecimiento y contracción periódicos de la economía

buying on margin system of buying stocks in which a buyer pays a small percentage of the purchase price while the broker advances the rest (p. 664)
comprando por margen sistema de compra de acciones en el que el comprador paga un pequeño porcentaje del precio de compra mientras que el corredor anticipa el resto

C

Cabinet group of senior officials appointed by the President that heads the executive departments and advises the President (p. 193)
gabinete grupo de personeros de más alto rango nombrados por el presidente que encabezan los departamentos ejecutivos y aconsejan al presidente

California Gold Rush mass migration to California after the discovery of gold in 1848 (p. 313)
Fiebre del Oro de California migración masiva a California después que se descubriera oro en 1848

California Master Plan called for three tiers of higher education: research universities, state colleges, and community colleges, all of which were to be accessible to all of the state's citizens (p. 895)
Plan Maestro de California hizo un llamado para la creación de tres niveles de educación superior: universidades de investigación, universidades estatales, y centros educacionales comunitarios, los cuales deberían ser accesibles para todos los ciudadanos del estado

Camp David Accords 1978 agreement brokered by President Jimmy Carter between Egyptian and Israeli leaders that made a peace treaty between the two nations possible (p. 1066)
Acuerdos de Camp David acuerdo de 1978 agenciado por el presidente Jimmy Carter, entre los lideres de Egipto e Israel que hizo posible un tratado de paz entre ambas naciones

capital money or wealth used to invest in business or enterprise (p. 234)
capital dinero o bienes usados para invertir en un negocio o empresa

carpetbagger negative term for Northerners who moved to the South after the Civil War (p. 411)
carpetbagger término negativo para referirse a norteños que se trasladó al Sur después de la Guerra Civil

cartel association of producers of a good or service that prices and controls stocks in order to monopolize the market (p. 444)
cartel asociación de productores de un bien o servicio que coordina los precios y la producción

cash crop crop grown for sale (p. 494)
cultivo comercial cosecha cultivada para la venta

casualties soldiers killed, wounded, and missing (p. 622)
bajas soldados muertos, heridos y desaparecidos

caucus closed meeting of party members for the purpose of choosing a candidate (p. 249)
comité electoral reunión cerrada de miembros de un partido para efectos de elegir a un candidato

Central Intelligence Agency (CIA) U.S. intelligence-gathering organization (p. 865)
Agencia Central de Inteligencia organización estadounidense para la recolección de inteligencia

charter legal document giving certain rights to a person or company (p. 44)
carta constitucional documento legal que otorga derechos a una persona o compañía

checks and balances system in which each branch of the government has the power to monitor and limit the actions of the other two (p. 155)
controles y equilibrios sistema por el cual cada rama del gobierno tiene el poder de vigilar y limitar las acciones de las otras dos

Chicano movement movement that focused on raising Mexican American consciousness (p. 1030)
movimiento chicano movimiento enfocado en despertar la conciencia de los estadounidenses de origen mexicano

Chinese Exclusion Act 1882 law that prohibited the immigration of Chinese laborers (p. 468)
Ley de Exclusión de Chinos ley de 1882 que prohibía la inmigración de trabajadores chinos

Christian fundamentalist individual who believes in a strict, literal interpretation of the Bible as the foundation of the Christian faith (p. 1056)
fundamentalista cristiano persona que cree en la interpretación estricta y literal de la Biblia como el fundamento de la fe cristiana

Civilian Conservation Corps (CCC) New Deal program that provided young men with relief jobs on environmental conservation projects, including reforestation and flood control (p. 736)
Cuerpos de Conservación Civil programa del Nuevo Trato que proporcionaba ayuda a los jóvenes con trabajo en proyectos de conservación del medio ambiente, incluyendo reforestación y control de inundaciones

Civil Rights Act of 1866 law that established federal guarantees of civil rights for all citizens (p. 406)
Ley de Derechos Civiles de 1866 ley que estableció las garantías federales de los derechos civiles para todos ciudadanos

Civil Rights Act of 1875 law that banned discrimination in public facilities and transportation (p. 495)
Ley de Derechos Civiles de 1875 ley que prohibió la discriminación en instalaciones y transporte públicos

Civil Rights Act of 1957 law that established a federal Civil Rights Commission (p. 921)
Ley de Derechos Civiles de 1957 ley que estableció una Comisión Federal de Derechos Civiles

Civil Rights Act of 1964 outlawed discrimination in public places and employment based on race, religion, or national origin (pp. 932, 966)
Ley de Derechos Civiles de 1964 conjunto de leyes que prohibió la discriminación en lugares y empleos públicos con base en la raza, religión, o nacionalidad

civil service government departments and their nonelected employees (p. 531)
servicio civil departamentos gubernamentales y sus empleados que no son de elección popular

Clayton Antitrust Act 1914 law that strengthened the Sherman Antitrust Act (p. 130)
Ley Clayton Antimonopolio ley de 1914 que fortalecía la Ley Sherman Antimonopolio

Clean Air Act act passed in 1970 that lessened air pollution by limiting the emissions from factories and automobiles (p. 1036)
Ley para el Aire Puro ley aprobada en 1970 que buscaba disminuir la contaminación del aire al limitar las emisiones de fábricas y automóviles

Clean Water Act 1973 law that restricted the pollution of water by industry and agriculture (p. 1036)
Ley para el Agua Limpia ley aprobada en 1973 que buscaba restringir la contaminación industrial y agrícola del agua

Cold War worldwide rivalry between the United States and the Soviet Union (p. 848)
Guerra Fría rivalidad mundial entre Estados Unidos y la Unión Soviética

collective bargaining process in which employers negotiate with labor unions about hours, wages, and other working conditions (p. 453)
negociación colectiva proceso en el que los patronos negocian con los sindicatos sobre los horarios, salarios, y otras condiciones de trabajo

Columbian Exchange the global exchange of goods and ideas between Europe, Africa, and the Americas after Columbus made his first transatlantic voyage in 1492 (p. 25)
intercambio colombino intercambio global de bienes e ideas entre Europa, Africa y las Americas posterior al primer viaje transatlántico de Colón en 1492

Committee on Public Information (CPI) government agency created during World War I to encourage Americans to support the war (p. 630)
Comité de Información Pública organización creada por el gobierno durante la Primera Guerra Mundial para animar al público estadounidense a apoyar la guerra

committees of correspondence network of local groups that informed colonists of British measures and the opposition to them in the years before the Revolutionary War (p. 103)
comités de correspondencia red organizada de grupos locales que informaban a los colonos de las medidas británicas y la oposición a éstas antes de la Guerra Revolucionaria

commune small communities where people share resources (p. 1019)
comunas pequeñas comunidades en las que las personas comparten los recursos

company town community whose residents rely upon one company for jobs, housing, and shopping (p. 451)
pueblo de compañía comunidad cuyos residentes dependen de una compañía para obtener empleo, vivienda, y compras

Compromise of 1850 political agreement that allowed California to be admitted as a free state by allowing popular sovereignty in the territories and enacting a stricter fugitive slave law (p. 328)

Acuerdo de 1850 acuerdo político que permitió la admisión de California como estado libre al permitir la soberanía popular en los territorios y aplicar una ley más estricta a los esclavos fugitivos

Compromise of 1877 agreement by which Rutherford B. Hayes won the 1876 presidential election and in exchange agreed to remove the remaining federal troops from the South (p. 424)

Acuerdo de 1877 acuerdo por el cual Rutheford B. Hayes ganó las elecciones presidenciales de 1876 y a cambio aceptó retirar las tropas federales que permanecían en el Sur

concentration camp camps used by the Nazis to imprison "undesirable" members of society (p. 831)

campo de concentración campos usados por los Nazis para encarcelar a miembros "indeseables" de la sociedad

Confederate States of America government of 11 southern states that seceded from the United States and fought against the Union in the Civil War (p. 350)

Estados Confederados de América gobierno de 11 estados sureños que se separó de Estados Unidos y peleó contra la Unión en la Guerra Civil

Congress of Industrial Organization (CIO) labor organization founded in the 1930s that represented industrial workers (p. 744)

Congreso de Organización Industrial organización de trabajadores fundada en la década de 1930 que representa a los trabajadores industriales

conquistador Spanish conqueror (p. 23)

conquistador conquistador español

conscientious objector person whose moral or religious beliefs forbid him or her to fight in wars (p. 630)

objetor de conciencia persona que rehúsa pelear en una guerra por convicciones morales o religiosas

conscription drafting of citizens into military service (p. 374)

conscripción reclutamiento de ciudadanos en el servicio militar

conservative person who tends to support limited government involvement in the economy, community help for the needy, and traditional values (p. 1076)

conservador persona que tiende a apoyar una participación gubernamental limitada en la economía, favorece la ayuda comunitaria para los necesitados, y mantiene los valores tradicionales

conspicuous consumerism purchasing of goods and services for the purpose of impressing others (p. 480)

consumismo llamativo compra de bienes y servicios para efectos de impresionar a los demás

consumerism large-scale buying, much of it on credit (p. 896)

consumismo compras a gran escala, la mayoría de éstas a crédito

consumer revolution flood of new, affordable goods in the decades after World War I (p. 663)

revolución de consumo flujo de bienes nuevos y asequibles durante las decadas posteriores a la Primera Guerra Mundial

containment policy of keeping communism contained within its existing borders (p. 850)

contención política de mantener el comunismo contenido dentro de sus fronteras existentes

Continental Army army that represented the colonies during the Revolutionary War (p. 109)

Ejército Continental ejército que representó a las colonias durante la Guerra de Independencia

Contract With America Republican plan headed by Newt Gingrich that focused on scaling back the government, balancing the budget, and cutting taxes (p. 1111)

Contrato con Estados Unidos plan republicano encabezado por Newt Gingrich enfocado en la reducción del gobierno, el equilibrio del presupuesto y la reducción de los impuestos

contraband supplies captured from an enemy during wartime (pp. 368, 624)

contrabando suministros confiscados al enemigo en tiempos de guerra

Contras anticommunist counterrevolutionaries who opposed the Sandinista government in Nicaragua in the 1980s (p. 1088)

Contras contrarrevolucionarios anticomunistas opuestos al gobierno Sandinista de Nicaragua en la década de 1980

convoy group of merchant ships sailing together, protected by warships (p. 637)

convoy grupo de buques mercantes que navegan juntos bajo la protección de buques de guerra

Copperhead negative term given to antiwar northern Democrats during the Civil War (p. 375)

Copperheads término peyorativo que se daba a los demócratas del Norte durante la Guerra Civil

corporation company recognized as a legal unit that has rights and liabilities separate from each of its members (p. 443)

corporación compañía reconocida como entidad legal con derechos y responsabilidades separados de los de cada uno de sus miembros

cotton gin machine invented in 1793 to separate the cotton fiber from its hard shell (p. 236)

desmotadora máquina inventada en 1793 para separar la fibra del algodón de la cáscara

counterculture movement that upheld values different from those of mainstream culture (p. 1018)

contracultura movimiento que mantuvo valores diferentes a los de la cultura tradicional

coureurs de bois from the French for "runner of the woods," French colonists who lived in the woods as fur traders (p. 42)

coureurs de bois expresión en francés que significa "corredor de los bosques," que designa a los colonos franceses habitantes de los bosques que comerciaban con pieles

court packing FDR plan to add up to six new justices to the nine-member Supreme Court after the Court had ruled that some New Deal legislation was unconstitutional (p. 746)

plan para llenar las cortes plan de FDR para agregar seis nuevos magistrados a los nueve miembros de la Corte Suprema luego de que la Corte dictaminó que algunas leyes del Nuevo Trato eran inconstitucionales

"credibility gap" American public's growing distrust of statements made by the government during the Vietnam War (p. 994)

"brecha de credibilidad" creciente desconfianza del público estadounidense ante declaraciones del gobierno durante la Guerra de Vietnam

creditor nation country which is owed more money by other countries than it owes other countries (p. 651)
nación acreedora país al que otros países le deben más dinero del que éste les debe

Crittenden Compromise 1861 proposed constitutional amendment that attempted to prevent secession of the southern states by allowing slavery in all territories south of the Missouri Compromise line (p. 352)
Acuerdo Crittenden enmienda constitucional propuesta en 1861 para intentar evitar la secesión de los estados del Sur al proponer que se permitiera la esclavitud en todos los territorios al sur de la línea del Acuerdo de Missouri

Cuban missile crisis 1962 conflict between the U.S. and the Soviet Union resulting from the Soviet installation of nuclear missiles in Cuba (p. 956)
crisis de los misiles de Cuba conflicto entre Estados Unidos y la Unión Soviética en 1962 como resultado de la instalación de misiles nucleares en Cuba por parte de los soviéticos

D

dame school elementary school during colonial times, often operated out of a woman's home (p. 83)
escuela de damas escuela primaria en la época colonial, a menudo con sede en la casa de una mujer

Dawes General Allotment Act 1887 law that divided reservation land into private family plots (p. 504)
Ley de Asignación General Dawes ley de 1887 que dividió las tierras de las reservaciones en parcelas familiares privadas

Dawes Plan agreement in which the United States loaned money to Germany, allowing Germany to make reparation payments to Britain and France (p. 670)
Plan Dawes acuerdo en el que Estados Unidos prestó dinero a Alemania, permitiéndole a ésta hacer pagos de reparación a Gran Bretaña y Francia

D-Day June 6, 1944, the day Allies landed on the beaches of Normandy, France (p. 819)
Día D 6 de junio de 1944, el día en que los Aliados desembarcaron en las playas de Normandía, Francia

death camp Nazi camp designed for the extermination of prisoners (p. 832)
campo de la muerte campo diseñados por los Nazis para el exterminio de prisioneros

Declaration of Independence document drawn up by the Second Continental Congress that announced American independence and the reasons for it (p. 112)
Declaración de Independencia documento redactado por el Segundo Congreso Continental que anunció la independencia de Estados Unidos y las razones para la misma

de facto segregation segregation by unwritten custom or tradition (p. 916)
segregación de facto segregación basada en la costumbre o la tradición no escrita

deficit spending practice of a nation paying out more money than it is receiving in revenues (p. 961)
déficit de gastos práctica de las naciones que gastan más de lo que reciben por ingresos

de jure segregation segregation imposed by law (p. 916)
segregación de iure segregación impuesta por ley

demobilization sending home members of the army (p. 883)
desmovilización enviar a los miembros del ejército de vuelta a casa

Democratic Republican led by Jefferson, one of the first political parties in the United States (p. 197)
Republicano Democrático encabezado por Jefferson, uno de los primeros partidos políticos en Estados Unidos

Department of Homeland Security department created by President Bush to coordinate domestic security efforts (p. 1125)
Departamento de Seguridad Nacional departamento creado por el presidente Bush para coordinar los esfuerzos de seguridad doméstica

deregulation reduction or removal of government controls over an industry (p. 1082)
desregulación reducción o eliminación de los controles gubernamentales en una industria

détente flexible diplomacy adopted by Richard Nixon to ease tensions between the United States, the Soviet Union, and the People's Republic of China (p. 1010)
distensión diplomacia flexible adoptada por Richard Nixon para aliviar las tensiones entre Estados Unidos, la Unión Soviética, y la República Popular China

developing world countries that are less economically advanced than developed countries such as the United States (p. 1065)
mundo en desarrollo países que son menos avanzados económica que los países desarrollados como Estados Unidos

direct primary election in which citizens themselves vote to select nominees for upcoming elections (p. 554)
primarias directas elecciones en las que los ciudadanos votan directamente para elegir los candidatos para las siguientes elecciones.

divest to take away or rid oneself of (p. 1094)
desposeer quitarse o librarse de algo

"dollar diplomacy" President Taft's policy of expanding American investments abroad (p. 609)
"diplomacia del dólar" política exterior del presidente Taft de expandir las inversiones estadounidenses en el exterior

domino theory idea that if a nation falls to communism, its closest neighbors will also fall under communist control (p. 982)
teoría dominó idea que estipulaba que si una nación cae ante el comunismo, sus vecinos más cercanos también caerán bajo el control comunista

dove person who opposed U.S. involvement in the Vietnam War (p. 991)
paloma persona opuesta a la participación estadounidense en la Guerra de Vietnam

draftee young American man drafted into military service (p. 992)
conscripto varón estadounidense joven reclutado para el servicio militar

Dust Bowl term used for the central and southern Great Plains during the 1930s when the region suffered from drought and dust storms (p. 715)

Cuenco de Polvo término usado para describir las Grandes Planicies, durante la década de 1930 cuando la región quedó desolada por la sequía y las tormentas de polvo

E

Earth Day annual event of environmental activism and protest, begun in 1970 (p. 1035)
Día de la Tierra evento anual de activismo y protesta ambiental, empezó en 1970

Economic Opportunity Act law passed in 1964 creating antipoverty programs (p. 966)
Ley de Igualdad de Oportunidades ley aprobada en 1964 que creo programas contra la pobreza

Eighteenth Amendment constitutional amendment banning the manufacture, distribution, and sale of alcohol in the United States (p. 677)
Decimoctava Enmienda enmienda constitucional que prohibió la fabricación, distribución y venta de alcohol en Estados Unidos

Eisenhower Doctrine policy of President Eisenhower that stated that the United States would use force to help any nation threatened by communism (p. 864)
doctrina Eisenhower política del presidente Eisenhower que indicaba que Estados Unidos usaría la fuerza para ayudar a cualquier nación amenazada por el comunismo

electoral college group of persons chosen from each state to indirectly elect the President and Vice President (p. 155)
colegio electoral grupo de personas escogidas de cada estado para elegir el presidente y vicepresidente indirectamente

Ellis Island island in New York Harbor that served as an immigration station for millions of immigrants arriving to the United States (p. 466)
Isla Ellis isla en el puerto de Nueva York que se usó como puesto de migración para millones de inmigrantes que llegaron a Estados Unidos

Emancipation Proclamation decree by President Lincoln that freed enslaved people living in Confederate states still in rebellion (p. 368)
Proclamación de Emancipación decreto del presidente Lincoln que liberó a los esclavos en los territorios confederados aún en rebelión

embargo official ban or restriction on trade (p. 211)
embargo prohibición o restricción oficial del comercio

Endangered Species Act law passed in 1973 to protect endangered plants and animals (p. 1036)
Ley de Especies en Peligro de Extinción ley aprobada en 1973 con el propósito de proteger las plantas y animales en peligro de extinción

Enforcement Acts 1870 and 1871 laws that made it a federal offense to interfere with a citizen's right to vote (p. 417)
Leyes de Aplicación leyes de 1870 y 1871 que hicieron una ofensa federal la interferencia con el derecho de un ciudadano de emitir el voto

English Bill of Rights document signed in 1689 that guaranteed the rights of English citizens (p. 73)
Declaración de Derechos Inglesa documento firmado en 1689 que garantizó los derechos de los ciudadanos ingleses

Enlightenment eighteenth-century movement during which European philosophers believed that society's problems could be solved by reason and science (p. 77)
Ilustración movimiento del siglo XVIII según el cual los filósofos europeos creían que los problemas de la sociedad se podían resolver mediante la razón y la ciencia

entrepreneur person who invests money in a product or business with the goal of making a profit (p. 437)
empresario persona que invierte dinero en un producto o empresa con el fin de obtener una ganancia

Environmental Protection Agency (EPA) government agency committed to cleaning up and protecting the environment (p. 1036)
Agencia de Protección Ambiental agencia gubernamental comprometida con la limpieza y protección del ambiente

Equal Pay Act 1963 law that required both men and women to receive equal pay for equal work (p. 961)
Ley de Pago Equitativo ley de 1963 que exigió que hombres y mujeres reciban la igual paga por un trabajo igual

Equal Rights Amendment (ERA) proposed amendment to the Constitution to guarantee gender equality (p. 1023)
Enmienda de Igualdad de Derechos enmienda propuesta a la Constitución garantizar la igualdad entre los sexos

Erie Canal canal completed in 1825 that connected Lake Erie to the Hudson River (p. 229)
Canal Erie canal terminado en 1825 que conecta el lago Erie con el río Hudson

Espionage Act act passed by Congress in 1917 enacting severe penalties for anyone engaged in disloyal or treasonable activities (p. 632)
Ley de Espionaje ley aprobada por el Congreso en 1917 que estableció penas severas para cualquiera que participara en actividades desleales o de traición

ethnic cleansing systematic effort to purge an area or society of an ethnic group through murder or deportation (p. 1117)
limpieza étnica esfuerzo sistemático para purgar una zona o sociedad de un grupo étnico mediante el asesinato o la deportación

European Union (EU) economic and political union of European nations established in 1993 (p. 1115)
Unión Europea unión económica y política de las naciones europeas establecida en 1993

evangelical style of worship meant to elicit powerful emotions to gain converts (p. 267)
evangélico estilo de culto cuyo fin es suscitar emociones fuertes para atraer conversos

Executive Order 8802 World War II measure that assured fair hiring practices in any job funded by the government (p. 810)
Orden Ejecutiva 8802 medida durante la Segunda Guerra Mundial que garantizaba prácticas justas de empleo en cualquier puesto financiado por el gobierno

executive privilege principle that the President has the right to keep certain communications between himself and other members of the executive branch private (p. 1052)
privilegio ejecutivo principio que indica que el presidente tiene derecho a mantener en privado ciertas comunicaciones con otros miembros del poder ejecutivo

Exodusters African Americans who migrated from the South to the West after the Civil War (p. 510)
Exodusters grupo de afroestadounidenses que emigraron al Oeste después de la Guerra Civil

expansionist person who favors expanding the territory or influence of a country (p. 300)
expansionista persona que favorece la expansión del territorio o influencia de un país

extractive economy economy in a colony where the colonizing country removed raw materials and shipped them back home to benefit its own economy (p. 586)
economía de extracción economía de una colonia donde el país colonizador extraía materias primas y las enviaba a la madre patria para beneficiar su propia economía

F

Fair Deal President Truman's program to expand New Deal reforms (p. 886)
Trato Justo programa del presidente Truman para expandir las reformas del Nuevo Trato

Fair Labor Standards Act 1938 law that set a minimum wage, a maximum workweek of 44 hours, and outlawed child labor (p. 744)
Ley de Normas Laborales Justas ley de 1938 que estableció el salario mínimo, una semana laboral de un máximo de 44 horas, y prohibió el trabajo infantil

Family Medical Leave Act law guaranteeing most full-time employees 12 workweeks of unpaid leave each year for personal or family health reasons (p. 1110)
Ley de Permiso Médico Familiar ley que garantiza a la mayoría de los empleados de tiempo completo 12 semanas laborales de permiso sin goce de sueldo cada año por razones personales o de salud familiar

Farmers' Alliance network of farmers' organizations that worked for political and economic reforms in the late 1800s (p. 494)
Alianza de Granjeros red de organizaciones agrícolas que lucho por alcanzar reformas políticas y económicas a finales del siglo XIX

federal national (p. 136)
federal nacional

Federal Art Project division of the Works Progress Administration that hired unemployed artists to create artworks for public buildings and sponsored art-education programs and exhibitions (p. 761)
Proyecto Federal de Arte división de la Administración de Progreso de Obras que contrató artistas desempleados para crear obras de arte en edificios públicos y patrocinó programas educativos y exhibiciones artísticos

Federal Deposit Insurance Corporation (FDIC) government agency that insures bank deposits, guaranteeing that depositors' money will be safe (p. 735)
Corporación Federal de Aseguramiento de Depósitos agencia gubernamental que asegura los depósitos bancarios, garantizando que el dinero de los depositantes estará seguro

federalism political system in which power is shared between the national government and state governments (p. 147)
federalismo sistema político en el cual el poder se comparte entre el gobierno nacional y los gobiernos estatales

Federalist one who favored ratification of the Constitution (p. 151)
federalista quien favoreció la ratificación de la Constitución

The Federalist series of 85 essays written by Madison, Hamilton, and Jay that explained and defended the Constitution (p. 151)
El Federalista conjunto de 85 ensayos escritos por Madison, Hamilton, y Jay que explicaba y defendía la Constitución

Federal Reserve Act 1913 law that placed national banks under the control of a Federal Reserve Board, which runs regional banks that hold the reserve funds from commercial banks, sets interest rates, and supervises commercial banks (p. 577)
Ley de Reserva Federal ley de 1913 que sometió a todos los bancos del país bajo el control de una Junta de Reserva Federal, que opera los bancos regionales que mantienen un fondo de reserva de los bancos comerciales, fija tasa de intereses, y supervisa a los bancos comerciales

Federal Trade Commission (FTC) government agency established in 1914 to identify monopolistic business practices, false advertising, and dishonest labeling (p. 578)
Comisión Federal de Comercio agencia gubernamental establecida en 1914 para identificar las prácticas comerciales monopolistas, falsa propaganda, y rótulos deshonestos

feminism theory that women and men should have political, social, and economic equality (p. 1022)
feminismo teoría que las mujeres y los hombres deben tener igualdad polítíca, social, y económica

Fifteenth Amendment 1870 constitutional amendment that guaranteed voting rights regardless of race or previous condition of servitude (p. 409)
Decimoquinta Enmienda enmienda constitucional de 1870 que garantizó el derecho al sufragio independientemente de la raza o condición relacionada a la servitud

54th Massachusetts Regiment all-black unit led by Union Colonel Robert Gould Shaw during the Civil War (p. 370)
Regimiento 54o de Massachusetts escuadrón de la Unión dirigido por el coronel Robert Gould Shaw durante la Guerra Civil, compuesto totalmente de soldados negros

filibuster tactic by which senators give long speeches to hold up legislative business (p. 932)
obstruccionismo táctica empleada por los senadores que consistió en hacer prolongados discursos para detener los asuntos legislativos

fireside chat informal radio broadcast in which FDR explained issues and New Deal programs to average Americans (p. 735)
charla junto a la hoguera transmisión informal de radio en que FDR explicaba asuntos y programas del Nuevo Trato a los estadounidenses promedio

First Continental Congress group of delegates that met in 1774 and represented all the American colonies, except Georgia (p. 104)

Primer Congreso Continental grupo de delegados que se reunió en 1774 y representaba a todas las colonias estadounidenses, excepto Georgia

First Seminole War 1817–1818 war between U.S. soldiers and Seminole Indians in Florida (p. 244)
Primera Guerra Seminole guerra de 1817 a 1818 entre soldados estadounidenses e indígenas seminoles en Florida

flapper young woman from the 1920s who defied traditional rules of conduct and dress (p. 684)
chica flapper mujer joven de la década de 1920 que desafiaba las reglas tradicionales de conducta y atuendo

flexible response defense policy allowing for the appropriate action in any type of conflict (p. 955)
respuesta flexible política de defensa que permite acciones apropiadas en conflictos de cualquier tipo

Foraker Act law establishing a civil government in Puerto Rico (p. 604)
Ley Foraker ley que estableció un gobierno civil en Puerto Rico

Fort Sumter federal fort located in Charleston, South Carolina, where the first shots of the Civil War were fired (p. 353)
Fuerte Sumter fuerte federal ubicado en Charleston, Carolina del Sur, donde se dispararon las primeras balas de la Guerra Civil

forty-niners miners who went to California after the discovery of gold in 1848 (p. 313)
forty-niners mineros que se dirigieron a California después del descubrimiento de oro en 1848

442nd Regimental Combat Team World War II unit made up of Japanese American volunteers (p. 813)
Equipo de Combate del Regimiento 442 unidad de la Segunda Guerra Mundial compuesta por voluntarios estadounidenses de origen japonés

Fourteen Points list of terms for resolving World War I and future wars outlined by American President Woodrow Wilson (p. 641)
Catorce Puntos lista de condiciones planteada por el presidente estadounidense Woodrow Wilson para resolver la Primera Guerra Mundial y guerras futuras

Fourteenth Amendment 1868 constitutional amendment which defined citizenship and guaranteed citizens equal protection under the law (p. 407)
Decimocuarta Enmienda enmienda constitucional de 1868 que definió la ciudadanía y garantizó a los ciudadanos protección igual por la ley

franchise business to allow a company to distribute its products or services through retail outlets owned by independent operators (p. 894)
franquicias comerciales permitir que una compañía distribuya sus productos o servicios por medio de establecimientos minoristas y independientes

freedman person who has been freed from slavery (p. 279)
liberto esclavo que ha ganado la libertad

Freedmen's Bureau federal agency designed to aid freed slaves and poor white farmers in the South after the Civil War (p. 405)
Oficina de Hombres Libres agencia federal diseñada para ayudar a los esclavos liberados y los pobres granjeros blancos del Sur luego de la Guerra Civil

freedom ride 1961 protest by activists who rode buses through southern states to test their compliance with the ban on segregation on interstate buses (p. 927)
viaje por la libertad protesta de activistas que en 1961 viajaron en autobuses a través de los estados sureños para probar si acataban la prohibición contra la segregación en autobuses interestatales

Freedom Summer 1964 effort to register African American voters in Mississippi (p. 936)
Verano de Libertad esfuerzo de 1964 por empadronar a votantes afroestadounidenses en Mississippi

Free-Soil Party antislavery political party of the mid-1800s (p. 326)
Partido Tierra Libre partido político antiesclavista de mitad del siglo XIX

French and Indian War war fought from 1754 to 1763 in which Britain and its colonies defeated France and its Indian allies, gaining control of eastern North America (p. 86)
Guerra Franco-Indígena guerra peleada desde 1754 a 1763 en la que Gran Bretaña y sus colonias derrotaron a Francia y sus ailados indígenas, obteniendo el control de la región este de América del Norte

French Revolution republican uprising against the French monarchy that began in 1789 (p. 199)
Revolución Francesa levantamiento republicano contra la monarquía francesa que empezó en 1789

Fugitive Slave Act law that required all citizens to aid in apprehending runaway slaves (p. 329)
Ley de Esclavos Fugitivos ley que obligaba a todos los ciudadanos a aprehender a los esclavos escapados

fundamentalism movement or attitude stressing strict and literal adherence to a set of basic principles (p. 672)
fundamentalismo movimiento o actitud que enfatiza un cumplimiento estricto y literal a un conjunto de principios básicos

G

Gadsden Purchase 1853 purchase of land (present-day Arizona and New Mexico) from Mexico (p. 312)
Compra Gadsden compra que hizo Estados Unidos a México en 1853 de tierras que son actualmente Arizona y Nuevo México

Gag Rule rule lasting from 1836 to 1844 that banned debate about slavery in Congress (p. 285)
Ley de la Mordaza reglamento que prohibía debatir el tema de la esclavitud en el Congreso entre 1836 y 1844

General Agreement on Tariffs and Trade (GATT) international agreement first signed in 1947 aimed at lowering trade barriers (p. 1115)
Acuerdo General sobre Aranceles y Comercio tratado internacional firmado originalmente en 1947 diseñado para disminuir las barreras comerciales

generation gap lack of understanding and communication between older and younger members of society (p. 1019)
brecha generacional falta de entendimiento y comunicación entre los miembros más viejos y los más jóvenes de la sociedad

Geneva Convention international agreement governing the humane treatment of wounded soldiers and prisoners of war (p. 838)

Convención de Ginebra acuerdo internacional que regula el tratamiento humanitario de soldados heridos y prisioneros de guerra

genocide willful annihilation of a racial, political, or cultural group (p. 831)
genocidio aniquilación intencional de un grupo racial, político, o cultural

"Gentlemen's Agreement" pact between the United States and Japan to end segregation of Asian children in San Francisco public schools; in return, Japan agreed to limit the immigration of its citizens to the United States (p. 603)
"Pacto entre Caballeros" acuerdo entre Estados Unidos y Japón para terminar la segregación de niños asiáticos en las escuelas públicas de San Francisco; cambio, Japón aceptó limitar la migración de sus ciudadanos hacia Estados Unidos

Gettysburg Address speech by President Lincoln in which he dedicated a national cemetery at Gettysburg and reaffirmed the ideas for which the Union was fighting (p. 385)
Discurso de Gettysburg discurso del presidente Lincoln durante la inauguración del cementerio nacional en Gettysburg y que reafirmó las ideas por las que la Unión estaba en lucha

Ghana prominent kingdom in West Africa, known for its wealth and trade in gold, lasting from A.D. 800 to A.D. 1200 (p. 16)
Ghana importante reino en África Occidental, conocido por sus riquezas y comercio en oro, existente desde el siglo IX d. C. hasta el siglo XIII d. C

GI Bill of Rights eased the return of World War II veterans by providing education and employment aid (p. 883)
Declaración de Derechos de los Soldados ley que facilitó el retorno de los veteranos de la Segunda Guerra Mundial al brindarles educación y empleo

Gilded Age term coined by Mark Twain to describe the post-Reconstruction era which was characterized by a façade of prosperity (p. 480)
Edad Dorada término usado para describir la era después de la Reconstrucción que se caracterizó por una fachada de prosperidad para el país

glasnost Russian term for "new openness," a policy in the Soviet Union in the 1980s calling for open discussion of national problems (p. 640)
glasnost palabra rusa que significa "apertura", política de la Unión Soviética de finales de la década de 1980 con un llamado a la apertura y discusión de los problemas nacionales

globalization process by which national economies, politics, cultures, and societies mix with those of other nations around the world (p. 1106)
globalización proceso mediante el cual las economías, políticas, culturas, y sociedades de naciónes se mezclan con las de las otras naciones de todo el mundo

gold standard policy of designating monetary units in terms of their value in gold (p. 532)
estándar oro política de designar las unidades monetarias en términos de su valor en oro

grandfather clause law to disqualify African American voters by allowing the vote only to men whose fathers and grandfathers voted before 1867 (p. 521)
cláusula del abuelo ley para descalificar a los votantes afroestadounidenses que permitía votar sólo a los hombres cuyos padres y abuelos habían votado antes de 1867

Grange farmers' organization formed after the Civil War (p. 535)
Grange organización de granjeros formada después de la Guerra Civil

Great Awakening religious movement in the English colonies during the 1730s and 1740s, which was heavily inspired by evangelical preachers (p. 78)
Gran Despertar movimiento religioso en las colonias inglesas durante las décadas de 1730 y 1740, fuertemente inspirado por los predicadores evangélicos

Great Compromise compromise between the Virginia and New Jersey plans for a bicameral legislature; each state would have equal representation in the Senate and varied representation in the House of Representatives based on the state's population (p. 146)
Gran Acuerdo acuerdo mutuo entre los planes de Virginia y Nueva Jersey según el que cada estado tendría una representación equitativa en el Senado y una representación variada en la Casa de Representantes con base en la población del estado

Great Depression period lasting from 1929 to 1941 in which the U.S. economy faltered and unemployment soared (p. 706)
Gran Depresión período entre 1929 y 1941 durante el cual la economía de Estados Unidos falló y el desempleo creció

Great Migration movement of African Americans in the twentieth century from the rural South to the industrial North (p. 634)
Gran Migración desplazamiento de afroestadounidenses durante el siglo XX desde las zonas rurales del Sur hacia las zonas industrializadas del Norte

Great Society President Johnson's goals in the areas of health care, education, the environment, discrimination, and poverty (p. 969)
Gran Sociedad objetivos del presidente Johnson en las áreas de salud, educación, ambiente, discriminación, y pobreza

Great White Fleet battleships sent by Roosevelt in 1907 on a "good will cruise" around the world (p. 603)
Gran Flota Blanca barcos de guerra enviada por Roosevelt en 1907 en una "misión de buena voluntad" alrededor del mundo

guerrilla warfare nontraditional combat methods (p. 599)
guerra de guerrillas método de combate no tradicional constituido por ataques de retirada rápida realizados por grupos pequeños de guerreros

Gulf of Tonkin Resolution 1964 congressional resolution that authorized President Johnson to commit U.S. troops to South Vietnam and fight a war against North Vietnam (p. 984)
Resolución del Golfo de Tonkin resolución del Congreso de 1964 que autorizó al presidente Johnson a enviar tropas estadounidenses a Vietnam del Sur y entrar en guerra contra Vietnam del Norte

English/Spanish Glossary

H

habeas corpus constitutional guarantee that no one can be held in prison without charges being filed (pp. 73, 375)
hábeas corpus garantía constitucional para que nadie permanezca en prisión sin que hayan presentado cargos en su contra

Harlem Renaissance period during the 1920s in which African American novelists, poets, and artists celebrated their culture (p. 693)
Renacimiento de Harlem período durante la década de 1920 en el que los novelistas, poetas, y artistas afroestadounidenses celebraron su cultura

Harpers Ferry town in Virginia (now in West Virginia) where abolitionist John Brown raided a federal arsenal in 1859 (p. 344)
Harpers Ferry pueblo en Virginia (ahora en Virginia Occidental) donde el abolicionista John Brown asaltó un arsenal federal en 1859

Hartford Convention 1814 meeting of Federalists from New England who opposed the War of 1812 and demanded constitutional amendments to empower their region (p. 219)
Convención de Hartford reunión de 1814 de los federalistas de Nueva Inglaterra opuestos a la Guerra de 1812 y que exigió enmiendas constitucionales que daban poder a su región

hawk a person who supported U.S. involvement in the Vietnam War (p. 991)
halcón persona que apoyó la participación estadounidense en la Guerra de Vietnam

Hawley-Smoot Tariff protective import tax authorized by Congress in 1930 (p. 707)
Arancel Hawley-Smoot impuesto de importaciones protector aprobado por el Congreso en 1930

Haymarket Riot 1886 labor-related protest in Chicago which ended in deadly violence (p. 455)
revuelta de Haymarket protesta de 1886 de origen laboral ocurrida en Chicago que terminó con muertes violentas

Helsinki Accords agreement made in 1975 among the United States, Canada, and European nations, including the Soviet Union, in which all nations agreed to support human rights (p. 1063)
Acuerdos de Helsinki acuerdo realizado en 1975 entre Estados Unidos, Canadá, y las naciones de Europa, incluyendo la Unión Soviética, en que todos países acordaron apoyar los derechos humanos

Hepburn Act 1906 law that gave the government the authority to set railroad rates and maximum prices for ferries, bridge tolls, and oil pipelines (p. 571)
Ley Hepburn ley de 1906 que otorgó al gobierno la autoridad de fijar y limitar las tarifas ferroviarias y fijar los precios máximos para trasbordadores, peaje de puentes, y oleoductos

Hollywood Ten group of movie writers, directors, and producers who refused to answer HUAC questions about communist ties (p. 869)
diez de Hollywood grupo de guionistas, directores, y productores que se rehusaron a contestar preguntas del HUAC sobre vínculos comunistas

Holocaust name now used to describe the systematic murder by the Nazis of Jews and others (p. 828)
Holocausto nombre que se usa actualmente para describir el asesinato sistemático de judíos y otros por los Nazis

Homestead Act 1862 law that gave 160 acres of land to citizens willing to live on and cultivate it for five years (pp. 374, 510)
Ley de Repartición de Tierras ley de 1862 que otorgó 160 acres de terreno a los ciudadanos deseosos de habitarlo y cultivarlo por cinco años

Homestead Strike 1892 strike against Carnegie's steelworks in Homestead, Pennsylvania (p. 455)
huelga de Homestead huelga de 1892 contra la acería Carnegie en Homestead, Pennsylvania

Hoover Dam dam on the Colorado River that was built during the Great Depression (p. 722)
Represa Hoover represa en el río Colorado construida durante la Gran Depresión

Hooverville term used to describe makeshift shantytowns set up by homeless people during the Great Depression (p. 712)
Hooverville término usado para describir las barriadas de casuchas establecidas por los desposeídos durante la Gran Depresión.

horizontal integration system of consolidating many firms in the same business (p. 445)
integración horizontal sistema de consolidación de muchas empresas en el mismo ramo de negocios

hot line direct telephone line between the White House and the Kremlin set up after the Cuban missile crisis (p. 956)
línea caliente línea de comunicación telefónica directa entre la Casa Blanca y el Kremlin establecida luego de la crisis de los misiles de Cuba

House of Burgesses representative assembly of colonial Virginia formed in 1619 (p. 46)
Cámara Baja de Virginia asamblea de representantes en la Virginia colonial formada en 1619

House Un-American Activities Committee (HUAC) congressional committee that investigated possible subversive activities within the United States (p. 869)
Comité de la Casa de Representantes de Actividades Anti-Estadounidenses comité del congreso que investigó posibles actividades subversivas dentro de Estados Unidos

human rights basic rights automatically held by every human being, including religious freedom, education, and equality (p. 1063)
derechos humanos derechos básicos que tiene todo ser humano automáticamente y que incluyen la libertad religiosa, la educación, y la igualdad

hydraulic mining use of water to erode gravel hills into long sluices to catch any gold (p. 313)
minería hidráulica uso de agua para erosionar la grava de las laderas y hacer que corra hacia largas esclusas para atrapar el oro

Ice Age period in Earth's history with low global temperatures and glaciers covering large areas (p. 4)
edad del hielo período en la historia de la Tierra caracterizado por bajas temperaturas globales y glaciares que cubrieron grandes áreas

Immigration Act of 1990 law that increased the number of immigrants allowed in the U.S. per year (p. 1127)
Ley de Migración de 1990 ley que aumenta el número de inmigrantes permitidos en Estados Unidos cada año

Immigration and Control Act of 1986 legislation that granted resident status to illegal immigrants residing in the United States since 1982 and penalized employers who hired illegal immigrants (p. 1128)
Ley de Migración y Control de 1986 legislación que otorgó la condición de residente a los inmigrantes ilegales que vivían en Estados Unidos desde 1982 y penaliza a los patronos que contratan inmigrantes ilegales

Immigration and Nationality Act of 1965 law that changed the national quota system to limits of 170,000 immigrants per year from the Eastern Hemisphere and 120,000 per year from the Western Hemisphere (p. 971)
Ley de Migración y Nacionalidad de 1965 ley que cambió el sistema de cuotas nacionales para limitar a 170,000 por año los inmigrantes del hemisferio oriental y 120,000 por año los del hemisferio occidental

impeachment accusation against a public official of wrongdoing in office (pp. 407, 1113)
impugnación acusación contra un empleado público de cometer delitos en la función pública

imperialism political, military, and economic domination of strong nations over weaker territories (p. 586)
imperialismo dominio político, militar y económico de naciones poderosas sobre territorios más débiles

impressment policy of seizing people or property for military or public service (p. 210)
requisa política de capturar personas o propiedades para el servicio militar o público

income tax tax that must be paid by individuals and corporations based on money earned (p. 373)
impuesto sobre la renta impuesto que deben pagar tanto individuos y corporaciones de acuerdo a los ingresos devengados

indentured servant individual who agreed to work without wages for a period of time in exchange for transportation to the colonies (p. 66)
sirviente obligado por contratado persona que aceptaba trabajar sin salario por un tiempo a cambio de transporte a las colonias

Indian New Deal 1930s legislation that gave Indians greater control over their affairs and provided funding for schools and hospitals (p. 751)
Nuevo Trato Indígena legislación de 1930 que otorgó mayor control a los indígenas estadounidenses sobre asuntos y financió escuelas y hospitales

Indian Removal Act act passed by Congress in 1830 that allowed the federal government to negotiate land trades with the Indians in the Southeast (p. 254)
Ley de Remoción de Indígenas ley aprobada por el Congreso en 1830 que permitió al gobierno negociar intercambios de tierras con los indígenas del Sudeste

Industrial Revolution shift from manual labor to mechanized work that began in Great Britain during the 1700s and spread to the United States around 1800 (p. 230)
Revolución Industrial cambio del trabajo manual al trabajo mecanizado que empezó en Gran Bretaña durante el siglo XVIII y llegó a Estados Unidos a principios del siglo XIX

inflation rising prices (pp. 376, 648)
inflación aumento de los precios

influenza flu virus (p. 647)
influenza virus de la gripe

information industry businesses that provide informational services (p. 893)
industrias de la información empresas que brindan servicios de información

initiative process in which citizens put a proposed new law directly on the ballot (p. 555)
iniciativa proceso en el que los ciudadanos proponen directamente una nueva ley en la papeleta de una elección

inner city the older, central part of a city with crowded neighborhoods in which low-income, usually minority groups, live (p. 905)
centro de la ciudad la parte más vieja y central de una ciudad con vecindarios muy poblados en los que viven grupos de bajos recursos, usualmente minorías

installment buying method of purchase in which buyer makes a small down payment and then pays off the rest of the debt in regular monthly payments (p. 664)
plan de pago a plazos método de compra mediante el cual el comprador paga un pequeño enganche y luego paga el resto de la deuda con abonos mensuales regulares

insurrection rebellion (p. 599)
insurrección rebelión

integration process of bringing people of different races, religions, and social classes together (p. 412)
integración proceso de acercar a personas de diferentes razas, religiones, y clases sociales

interchangeable parts identical components that can be used in place of one another (p. 232)
partes intercambiables componentes idénticos que se pueden sustituir unos a otros

Internet a computer network that links people around the world, also called World Wide Web (p. 1106)
Internet red de computadoras que enlaza a personas de todo el mundo, también llamada Red Mundial

internment temporary imprisonment of members of a specific group (p. 813)
reclusión encarcelamiento temporal para miembros de un grupo específico

Interstate Commerce Commission (ICC) first federal agency monitoring business operations, created in 1887 to oversee interstate railroad procedures (p. 448)
Comisión Interestatal de Comercio primera agencia federal en vigilar las operaciones comerciales, creada en 1887 para supervisar los procedimientos del ferrocarril interestatal

Interstate Highway Act 1956 law that authorized the spending of $32 billion to build 41,000 miles of highway (p. 890)
Ley de Carreteras Interestatales ley de 1956 que autorizó el gasto de $32 mil millones para construir 41,000 millas de carreteras

Intolerable Acts American name for the Coercive Acts, which Parliament passed in 1774 to control the colonies (p. 104)
Leyes Intolerables nombre estadounidense para las Leyes Coercitivas que aprobó el Parlamento en 1774 para controlar a las colonias

English/Spanish Glossary

Iran-Contra affair political scandal under President Reagan involving the use of money from secret arms sales to Iran to illegally support the Contras in Nicaragua (p. 1092)
incidente Irán-Contras escándalo político en la administración del presidente Reagan que involucró el uso de dinero procedente de la venta secreta de armas a Irán para apoyar ilegalmente a los Contras en Nicaragua

iron curtain term coined by Winston Churchill to describe the border between the Soviet satellite states and Western Europe (p. 848)
cortina de hierro término acuñado por Winston Churchill para describir la frontera entre los estados satélites soviéticos y Europa Occidental

Iroquois League confederation made up of five Iroquois peoples: the Mohawks, Oneidas, Onondagas, Cayugas, and Senecas (p. 9)
Liga Iroquesa confederación compuesta por los cinco pueblos iroquois: los mohawks, oneidas, onondagas, cayugas y sénecas

"irreconcilables" isolationist senators who opposed any treaty ending World War I that had a League of Nations folded into it (p. 644)
"irreconciliables" senadores aislacionistas opuestos a cualquier tratado para finalizar la Primera Guerra Mundial que involucrara una Sociedad de las Naciones

island hopping World War II strategy that involved seizing selected Japanese-held islands in the Pacific while bypassing others (p. 825)
salto de islas estrategia durante la Segunda Guerra Mundial que involucraba capturar islas selectas que mantenía Japón en el Pacífico a la vez que se evitaban otras

J

Jacksonian Democracy Andrew Jackson and his followers' political philosophy concerned with the interests of the common people and limiting the role of the federal government (p. 251)
Democracia de Jackson filosofía política de Andrew Jackson y sus seguidores que velaba por los intereses de la gente común y la limitación del papel del gobierno federal

jazz American musical form developed by African Americans, based on improvisation and blending blues, ragtime, and European-based popular music (p. 243)
jazz forma musical estadounidense creada por los afroestadounidenses y europeos, basada en la improvisación y la mezcla de el blues, ragtime y música popular de origen europeo

Jazz Singer, The the first movie with sound synchronized to the action (p. 232)
El Cantante de Jazz primera película con sonido y acción sincronizados

Jim Crow Laws segregation laws enacted in the South after Reconstruction (p. 520)
Leyes Jim Crow leyes segregacionistas implantabas en el Sur después de Reconstrucción

jingoism aggressive nationalism; support for warlike foreign policy (p. 145)
patrioterismo nacionalismo agresivo; apoyo a una política exterior belicosa

joint-stock company a company run by a group of investors who share the company's profits and losses (p. 44)
sociedad comanditaria por acciones compañía dirigida por un grupo de inversionistas que se reparten las ganancias y pérdidas de la empresa

judicial review power of the Supreme Court to decide whether the acts of a president or laws passed by Congress are constitutional (p. 206)
revisión judicial poder que le permite a la Corte Suprema decidir si los actos del presidente o las leyes aprobadas por el Congreso son constitucionales

K

kamikazes Japanese pilots who deliberately crashed planes into American ships during World War II (p. 825)
kamikazes pilotos japonéses que deliberadamente chocaban aviones contra buques estadounidenses durante la Segunda Guerra Mundial

Kansas-Nebraska Act 1854 law that divided the Nebraska Territory into Kansas and Nebraska giving each territory the right to decide whether or not to allow slavery (p. 334)
Ley Kansas-Nebraska ley de 1854 que dividió el territorio de Nebraska en Kansas y Nebraska, dándole a cada territorio el derecho de decidir si permitiría la esclavitud o no

Kellogg-Briand Pact 1928 agreement in which many nations agreed to outlaw war (p. 669)
Pacto Kellogg-Briand acuerdo de 1928 en el que los delegados de muchas naciones estuvieron anuentes a prohibir la guerra

Kerner Commission group set up to investigate the causes of race riots in American cities in the 1960s (p. 940)
Comisión Kerner grupo que se formó para investigar las causas de los disturbios raciales en las ciudades estadounidenses en la década de 1960

King Philip's War conflict between English colonists and Native Americans in New England (p. 53)
Guerra del Rey Felipe conflicto que surgió entre los colonos ingleses y los indígenas de Nueva Inglaterra

Kings Mountain a 1780 Revolutionary War battle in South Carolina in which Patriots defeated a Loyalist militia (p. 124)
Kings Mountain batalla de la Guerra de Independencia de 1780 en Carolina del Sur en la cual los patriotas derrotaron a una milicia leal a la corona

Knights of Labor labor union that sought to organize all workers and focused on broad social reforms (p. 453)
Caballeros del Trabajo sindicato de trabajadores que procuró organizar a todos los trabajadores y se enfocó en reformas sociales amplias

Know-Nothings political party of the mid-1800s, officially known as the American Party, that opposed immigration (p. 340)
Know-Nothings partido político efímero a mediados del siglo XIX, oficialmente conocido como el Partido Estadounidense, opuesto a la inmigración

Kristallnacht "Night of the Broken Glass," organized attacks on Jewish communities in Germany on November 9, 1938 (p. 829)
Kristallnacht "noche de los cristales rotos," ataques organizados contra comunidades judías en Alemania, el 9 de noviembre de 1938

Ku Klux Klan organization that promotes hatred and discrimination against specific ethnic and religious groups (pp. 417, 675)
Ku Klux Klan organización que promueve el odio y discriminación contra grupos étnicos y religiosos específicos

L

labor union organization of workers (p. 234)
sindicato de trabajadores organización de trabajadores

laissez-faire lenient, as in the absence of government control over private business (p. 438)
laissez-faire indulgente, por ejemplo, la ausencia de control gubernamental sobre las empresas privadas

land grant land designated by the federal government for building schools, roads, or railroads (p. 507)
tierras en concesión tierras designadas por el gobierno federal para la construcción de escuelas, carreteras, o ferrocarriles

Land Grant College Act 1862 law that made money available to states to establish universities that taught agriculture and mechanical engineering (p. 393)
Ley de Cesión de Terrenos para Universidades ley de 1862 que puso dinero a disposición de los estados para que establecieran universidades que enseñaran agricultura e ingeniería mecánica

Land Ordinance of 1785 law which designed a system for managing and settling lands in the Northwest Territory (p. 137)
Ordenanza de Tierras de 1785 ley mediante la cual designó un sistema para la administración y ocupación de tierras en el Territorio Noroeste

Las Gorras Blancas (the White Caps) group of Mexican Americans living in New Mexico who attempted to protect their land and way of life from encroachment by white landowners (p. 525)
Las Gorras Blancas grupo de estadounidenses de origen mexicano radicados en Nuevo México que intentaron proteger sus tierras y estilo de vida de la expansión de los terratenientes blancos

League of Nations world organization established after World War I to promote peaceful cooperation between countries (p. 642)
Sociedad de las Naciones organización mundial establecida después de a la Primera Guerra Mundial para promover la cooperación pacífica entre los países

Lend-Lease Act act passed in 1941 that allowed President Roosevelt to sell or lend war supplies to any country whose defense he considered vital to the safety of the United States (p. 785)
Ley de Préstamo-Arrendamiento ley aprobada por el Congreso en 1941 que permitió al presidente Franklin Roosevelt vender o prestar suministros bélicos a cualquier país cuya defensa se considerara vital para la seguridad de Estados Unidos

Lewis and Clark Expedition 1804 expedition sent by President Jefferson to explore the newly-acquired Louisiana Purchase (p. 209)
expedición de Lewis y Clark expedición de 1804 mandó por presidente Jefferson a explorar la recién adquirida Compra de Luisiana

liberal a person who tends to support government intervention to help the needy and favor laws protecting the rights of women and minorities (p. 1076)
liberal persona que tiende a apoyar la intervención gubernamental en la ayuda a los necesitados y favorece las leyes que protegen los derechos de las mujeres y las minorías

limited government principle stating that the government has only as much authority as the people give it and, therefore, its power is limited (p. 155)
gobierno limitado principio que declara que el gobierno sólo tiene tanta autoridad como la que le otorga el pueblo y por tanto su poder es limitado

limited war war fought to achieve only specific goals (p. 858)
guerra limitada guerra peleada para alcanzar objetivos específicos

literacy test reading and writing test formerly used in some southern states to prevent African Americans from voting (p. 521)
prueba de alfabetismo prueba de lectura antiguamente usada en algunos estados sureños para evitar que los afroestadounidenses votaran

localism policy relied on by President Hoover in the early years of the Great Depression whereby local and state governments act as primary agents of economic relief (p. 721)
localismo política de la que dependió el presidente Hoover a principios de la Gran Depresión para que los gobiernos locales y estatales actuaran como los principales agentes de asistencia económica

Lone Star Republic nation formed in 1835 by Texans who declared independence from Mexico (p. 306)
República de la Estrella Solitaria nación formada en 1835 por tejanos que le declararon la independencia a México

loose construction belief that the government has any power not forbidden by the Constitution (p. 195)
interpretación libre creencia en que el gobierno tiene cualquier poder que no le prohíba la Constitución

"Lost Generation" term for American writers of the 1920s marked by disillusion with World War I and a search for a new sense of meaning (p. 686)
"Generación Perdida" término usado para referirse a escritores estadounidenses de la década de 1920 marcados por su desilusión con la Primera Guerra Mundial y la búsqueda de un nuevo sentido de la vida

Louisiana Purchase 1803 purchase from France by the United States of the territory between the Mississippi River and the Rocky Mountains (p. 209)
Compra de Luisiana compra que hiciera Estados Unidos en 1803 del territorio entre el río Mississippi y las montañas Rocosas

Lowell girl young woman who worked in the textile mills in Lowell, Massachusetts, in the early 1800s (p. 231)
chica de Lowell mujer joven que trabajaba en las fábricas de textiles de Lowell, Massachusetts, a principios del siglo XIX

Loyalist colonist who remained loyal to Britain during the Revolution (p. 109)
leal a la corona colono que permaneció leal a Gran Bretaña durante la Guerra de Independencia

Lusitania British passenger liner sunk by a German U-boat during World War I (p. 624)
Lusitania trasatlántico británico hundido por un submarino alemán durante la Primera Guerra Mundial.

M

Magna Carta English document from 1215 that limited the power of the king and provided basic rights for citizens (p. 72)
Carta Magna documento inglés de 1215 que limitó el poder del rey y dio derechos básicos a los ciudadanos

Mali West African empire lasting from A.D. 1200 to A.D. 1400 that prospered from the gold trade (p. 16)
Malí imperio del África Occidental existente desde el siglo XIII d. C. hasta el siglo XV que prosperó gracias al comercio del oro

Manhattan Project code name of the project that developed the atomic bomb (p. 826)
Proyecto Manhattan nombre en clave del proyecto que desarrolló la bomba atómica

Manifest Destiny 19th century doctrine that westward expansion of the United States was not only inevitable but a God-given right (p. 301)
Destino Manifiesto doctrina del siglo XIX que establecía que la expansión hacia el Oeste de Estados Unidos no sólo era inevitable sino un derecho Divino

manumission the act of freeing someone from slavery (p. 127)
manumisión acto de liberar a alguien de la esclavitud

Marbury* v. *Madison 1803 Supreme Court case that established the principle of judicial review (p. 206)
Marbury contra Madison caso presentado ante la Corte Suprema en 1803 que estableció el principio de revisión judicial

March on Washington 1963 demonstration in which more than 200,000 people rallied for economic equality and civil rights (p. 930)
Marcha en Washington manifestacíon en 1963 de más de 200,000 personas que marcharon a favor de la igualdad ecońomica y los derechos civiles

Married Women's Property Act 1848 New York State law that guaranteed greater property rights for women; used as a model in other states (p. 290)
Ley del Patrimonio de las Casadas ley aprobada en 1848 en el estado de Nueva York que otorgaba mayores derechos sobre la propiedad a la mujer; sirvió de modelo en otros estados

Marshall Plan foreign policy that offered economic aid to Western European countries after World War II (p. 850)
Plan Marshall política económica y exterior que ofreció ayuda a los países de Europa Occidental después de la Segunda Guerra Mundial

mass culture similar cultural patterns in a society as a result of the spread of transportation, communication, and advertising (p. 482)
cultura de masas patrones similares de cultura en una sociedad como resultado de la propagación del transporte, comunicación, y publicidad

mass production production of goods in large numbers through the use of machinery and assembly lines (pp. 440, 660)
producción en masa producción de bienes en grandes cantidades mediante el uso de maquinaria y líneas de ensamblaje

massive retaliation policy of threatening to use massive force in response to aggression (p. 862)
represalia masiva política de amenazar con el uso de fuerza masiva en respuesta a una agresión

mass transit public transportation systems that carry large numbers of people (p. 475)
transporte de masas sistemas de transporte público que llevan a grandes cantidades de personas

matrilineal when inheritance is passed down through the female side of the family (p. 287)
matrilineal cuando los bienes se heredan por el lado materno de la familia

Mayflower Compact framework for self-government of the Plymouth Colony signed on the ship the *Mayflower* in 1620 (p. 51)
Pacto del Mayflower documento para establecer el sistema de autogobierno de la colonia de Plymouth firmado en el barco *Mayflower* en 1620

McCarthyism negative catchword for extreme, reckless charges of disloyalty (p. 874)
McCarthyismo lema negativo que expresa acusaciones extremas e irresponsables de deslealtad

Meat Inspection Act 1906 law that allowed the federal government to inspect meat sold across state lines and required federal inspection of meat processing plants (p. 572)
Ley de Inspección de Carnes ley de 1906 que permitió al gobierno federal inspeccionar la carne vendida entre los estados y que exigió la inspección federal de las plantas de procesamiento de carne

median family income measure of average family income (p. 896)
mediana del ingreso familiar medida del ingreso familiar promedio

Medicaid federal program created in 1965 to provide low-cost health insurance to poor Americans of any age (p. 970)
Medicaid programa federal creado en 1965 para brindar seguro de salud de bajo costo a los estadounidenses de escasos recursos de cualquier edad

Medicare federal program created in 1965 to provide basic hospital insurance to most Americans over the age of sixty-five (p. 970)
Medicare programa federal creado en 1965 para brindar seguro hospitalario básico a la mayoría de los estadounidenses mayores de sesenta y cinco de edad

melting pot society in which people of different nationalities assimilate to form one culture (p. 468)
crisol de razas una sociedad en la que las personas de diferentes nacionalidades se asimilan para formar una cultura

mercantilism economic policy under which a nation accumulates wealth by exporting more goods than it imports (p. 75)
mercantilismo filosofía económica que sostiene que una nación acumula riquezas al exportar más bienes de los que importa

mercenary professional soldier who is paid to fight in a foreign army (p. 118)
mercenario soldado profesional a quien se le paga por pelear en un ejército extranjero

mestizo person in Spanish colonial America who was of European and Native American descent (p. 35)
mestizo en la Hispanoamérica colonial, persona descendiente de europeo e indígena

metis person in French colonial America who was of French and Native American descent (p. 42)
metis habitante de las colonias francesas en América descendiente de francés e indígena

Middle Ages period in European history from the 5th century through the 14th century (p. 11)
Edad Media período en la historia de Europa que se inicia en el siglo V y termina en el siglo XIV

Middle Passage the forced transport of enslaved Africans from West Africa to the Americas (p. 69)
Travesía Intermedia transporte forzado de esclavos desde África Occidental a las Américas

migrant farmworker person who travels from farm to farm to pick fruits and vegetables (p. 1029)
trabajador agrícola migratorio persona que viaja de una granja a otra para la recolección de frutas y vegetales

militarism glorification of the military (p. 619)
militarismo glorificación de lo militar

Militia Act 1862 law that allowed African American soldiers to serve in the Union military (p. 370)
Ley de Alistamiento ley aprobada en 1862 que permitió a los soldados afroestadounidenses prestar servicio militar en los militares de la Unión

militia trained citizens who serve as soldiers during an emergency (p. 108)
milicia ciudadanos entrenados que fungieron como soldados durante una emergencia

mission religious settlement usually run by Catholic priests and friars in colonial Spanish America (p. 37)
misión asentamiento religioso generalmente manejado por sacerdotes y frailes católicos en la Hispanoamérica colonial

missionary person sent to a foreign country in order to convert others to their religion (p. 35)
misionero persona enviada al país extranjero para convertir a otros a su credo

Missouri Compromise 1820 agreement calling for the admission of Missouri as a slave state and Maine as a free state, and banning slavery in the Louisiana Purchase territory north of the 36°30'N latitude (p. 246)
Acuerdo de Missouri acuerdo de 1820 que hacía un llamado a la admisión de Missouri como estado esclavista y a Maine como estado libre, prohibiendo la esclavitud en el territorio de la Compra de Louisiana al norte de la latitud 36°30'

model T automobile manufactured by Henry Ford to be affordable on the mass market (p. 661)
modelo T automóvil fabricado por Henry Ford para que fuera asequible en el mercado masivo

modernism artistic and literary movement sparked by a break with past conventions (p. 671)
modernismo moda que daba énfasis a la ciencia y los valores seculares por sobre las ideas religiosas tradicionales

Monmouth 1778 Revolutionary War battle site in New Jersey where neither side won a clear victory (p. 120)
Monmouth batalla de la Guerra de Independencia de 1778 en Nueva Jersey en la cual ninguno de los bandos obtuvo una victoria clara

monopoly exclusive control by one company over an entire industry (p. 444)
monopolio control completo de una compañía de una industria

Monroe Doctrine foreign policy doctrine set forth by President Monroe in 1823 that discouraged European intervention in the Western Hemisphere (p. 246)
Doctrina Monroe doctrina de política exterior establecida por el presidente Monroe en 1823 que desalentaba la intervención Europea en el hemisferio Occidental

Montgomery bus boycott 1955–1956 protest by African Americans in Montgomery, Alabama, against racial segregation in the bus system (p. 922)
boicot de los autobuses de Montgomery protesta de 1955 a 1956 de los afroestadounidenses en Montgomery, Alabama, contra la segregación en el sistema de autobuses

"moral diplomacy" Woodrow Wilson's statement that the U.S. would not use force to assert influence in the world, but would instead work to promote human rights (p. 609)
"diplomacia moral" aseveración de Woodrow Wilson en cuanto a que Estados Unidos no usaría la fuerza para ejercer su influencia en el mundo, sino que trabajaría en la promoción de los derechos humanos

Moral Majority political organization established by Reverend Jerry Falwell in 1979 to advance religious goals (p. 1078)
Mayoría Moral organización política establecida por el reverendo Jerry Falwell en 1979 para promover objetivos religiosos

Mormon member of the Church of Jesus Christ of Latter-Day Saints, which was organized in 1830 by Joseph Smith (p. 269)
mormón miembro de la Iglesia de Jesucristo de los Santos de los Últimos Días, fundada en 1830 por José Smith

Mountain Men American trappers who explored the Rocky Mountains area in the early 1800s (p. 301)
montañeses tramperos estadounidenses que exploraron el área de las montañas Rocosas a principios del siglo XIX

muckraker writer who uncovers and exposes misconduct in politics or business (p. 550)
muckraker escritores que descubren y exponen la mala conducta de políticos o empresas

multinational corporation companies that produce and sell their goods and services all over the world (pp. 894, 1106)
corporaciones multinacionales compañías que producen y venden sus bienes y servicios alrededor del mundo

Munich Pact agreement made between Germany, Italy, Great Britain, and France in 1938 that sacrificed the Sudetenland to preserve peace (p. 778)
Pacto de Munich acuerdo de 1938 entre Alemania, Italia, Gran Bretaña, y Francia que sacrificó los Sudetes para preservar la paz

mural a large picture painted directly on a wall or ceiling (p. 761)

mural pintura de grandes dimensiones realizada directamente sobre una pared o cielo raso

mutualistas organized groups of Mexican Americans that make loans and provide legal assistance to other members of their community (p. 567)
mutualistas grupos organizados de estadounidenses de origen mexicano para ofrecer préstamos y asistencia legal a miembros de su comunidad

mutually assured destruction policy in which the United States and the Soviet Union hoped to deter nuclear war by building up enough weapons to destroy one another (p. 861)
destrucción mutua asegurada política con la que Estados Unidos y la Unión Soviética esperaban evitar la guerra nuclear al acumular suficientes armas para destruirse mutuamente

My Lai village in South Vietnam where in 1968 American forces opened fire on unarmed civilians; U.S. soldiers killed between 400 and 500 Vietnamese (p. 1003)
My Lai villa en Vietnam del Sur donde en 1968 fuerzas estadounidenses dispararon contra civiles desarmados; los soldados estadounidenses mataron entre 400 y 500 vietnamitas

N

napalm jellied gasoline dropped in canisters that explode on impact and cover large areas in flames; dropped by U.S. planes during the Vietnam War (p. 986)
napalm gasolina gelatinizada lanzada en latas que explotaban al impactar y dejaban en llamas grandes áreas; lanzadas por aviones estadounidenses durante la Guerra de Vietnam

national debt total amount of money that the federal government owes to the owners of government bonds (p. 1082)
deuda interna cantidad total de dinero que el gobierno federal debe a los dueños de bonos de gobierno

National Aeronautics and Space Administration (NASA) government agency that coordinates U.S. efforts in space (p. 865)
Administración Nacional de Aeronáutica y del Espacio agencia gubernamental formada para coordinar los esfuerzos estadounidenses en el espacio

National American Woman Suffrage Association (NWSA) group founded in 1890 that worked on both the state and national levels to earn women the right to vote (p. 559)
Asociación Nacional para el Sufragio de las Mujeres Estadounidenses grupo fundado en 1890 que funcionó a nivel tanto estatal como nacional para que se otorgara a las mujeres el derecho al voto

National Association for the Advancement of Colored People (NAACP) interracial organization founded in 1909 to abolish segregation and discrimination and to achieve political and civil rights for African Americans (p. 567)
Asociación Nacional para el Avance de los afroestadounidenses organización fundado en 1909 para suprimir la segregación y la discriminización y avanzar los derechos políticos y civiles de los afroestadounidenses

National Consumers League (NCL) group organized in 1899 to investigate the conditions under which goods were made and sold and to promote safe working conditions and a minimum wage (p. 558)
Liga Nacional de Consumidores grupo organizado en 1899 para investigar las condiciones en que se fabricaban y vendían los bienes, así como promover condiciones seguras de trabajo y un salario mínimo

nationalism loyalty and devotion to one's nation (p. 242)
nacionalismo lealtad y devoción hacia la patria

nationalize to place a resource under government control (p. 864)
nacionalización poner un recurso bajo control gubernamental

National Organization for Women (NOW) organization established by Betty Friedan to combat discrimination against women (p. 1023)
Organización Nacional para Mujeres organización establecida por Betty Friedan para derribar las barreras de la discriminación contra mujeres

National Reclamation Act 1902 law that gave the federal government the power to decide where and how water would be distributed through the building and management of dams and irrigation projects (p. 574)
Ley Nacional de Reclamaciones ley de 1902 que otorgó al gobierno federal el poder para decidir adónde y cómo se distribuiría el agua, mediante la construcción y administración de represas y proyectos de irrigación

National Recovery Administration (NRA) New Deal agency that promoted economic recovery by regulating production, prices, and wages (p. 737)
Administración para la Recuperación Nacional agencia del Nuevo Trato que promovió la recuperación económica al instaurar nuevos códigos para controlar la producción, precios y salarios

National Road road built by the federal government in the early 1800s that extended from Maryland to Illinois (p. 228)
Carretera Nacional carretera construida por el gobierno a principios del siglo XIX que se extendía desde Maryland hasta Illinois

Nation of Islam African American religious organization founded in 1930 that advocated separation of the races (p. 940)
Nación Islámica organización afroestadounidense religiosa fundada en 1930 que abogó por la separación de las razas

nativism belief that native-born white Americans are superior to newcomers (p. 468)
nativismo creencia en que los blancos nacidos en Estados Unidos son superiores a los recién llegados

nativist person who favors native-born inhabitants over immigrants (p. 235)
nativista persona que favorece a los habitantes nativos sobre los inmigrantes

natural rights universal rights, such as life and liberty that, according to philosophers, derive from nature rather than a government (p. 112)
derechos naturales derechos universales, como la vida y la libertad, que según los filósofos, se derivan de la naturaleza y no de un gobierno

Navigation Acts British trade laws enacted by Parliament during the mid-1700s that regulated colonial commerce (p. 76)

Leyes de Navegación leyes comerciales británicas establecidas por el Parlamento a mediados del siglo XVIII que regulaban el comercio con las colonias

Neutrality Act of 1939 act that allowed nations at war to buy goods and arms in the United States if they paid cash and carried the merchandise on their own ships (p. 784)

Ley de Neutralidad de 1939 ley que permitió que las naciones en guerra compraran bienes y armas en Estados Unidos si pagaran en efectivo y transportaran la mercadería en sus propios barcos

New Deal programs and legislation enacted by Franklin D. Roosevelt during the Great Depression to promote economic recovery and social reform (p. 733)

Nuevo Trato programas y leyes establecidos por Franklin D. Roosevelt durante la Gran Depresión para promover la recuperación económica y reforma social

New Deal coalition political force formed by diverse groups who united to support Franklin D. Roosevelt and his New Deal (p. 751)

coalición del Nuevo Trato fuerza política formada por grupos diversos unidos para apoyar a Franklin D. Roosevelt y su Nuevo Trato

New Freedom Woodrow Wilson's program to place government controls on corporations in order to benefit small businesses (p. 576)

Nueva Libertad programa de Woodrow Wilson para establecer controles gubernamentales sobre las corporaciones a fin de brindar más oportunidades a las pequeñas empresas

New Frontier President Kennedy's plan aimed at improving the economy, fighting racial discrimination, and exploring space (p. 960)

Nueva Frontera plan del presidente Kennedy dirigido a mejorar la economía, al combatir discriminación racial, y avanzar el programa espacial

"new" immigrant Southern and Eastern European immigrant who arrived in the United States in a great wave between 1880 and 1920 (p. 464)

"nuevos" inmigrante inmigrante del Sur y Este de Europa que llegaró a Estados Unidos en una gran oleada entre 1880 y 1920

New Jersey Plan William Paterson's proposal for a unicameral legislature with each state having one vote (p. 145)

Plan de Nueva Jersey propuesta de William Paterson que requería una legislatura unicameral donde cada estado tendría un voto

New Nationalism President Theodore Roosevelt's plan to restore the government's trust-busting power (p. 575)

Nuevo Nacionalismo plan del presidente Teodoro Roosevelt para restaurar el poder del gobierno de disolver monopolios

New Right political movement supported by reinvigorated conservative groups in the latter half of the twentieth century (p. 1077)

Nueva Derecha movimiento político apoyado por grupos conservadores revigorizados durante la última mitad del siglo XX

Niagara Movement group of African American thinkers founded in 1905 that pushed for immediate racial reforms, particularly in education and voting practices (p. 566)

Movimiento Niágara grupo de pensadores afroestadounidenses fundado en 1905 que presionó para obtener reformas raciales inmediatas, particularmente en cuanto a la educación y el voto

Nineteenth Amendment constitutional amendment that gave women the right to vote (p. 561)

Décimonovena Enmienda enmienda constitucional que otorgó a las mujeres el derecho al voto

No Child Left Behind Act 2002 law aimed at improving the performance of primary and secondary schools particularly through mandated sanctions against schools not reaching federal performance standards (p. 1121)

Ley Que Ningún Niño Se Quede Atrás ley del año 2000 destinada a mejorar el desempeño de escuelas primarias y secundarias particularmente mediante sanciones por mandato contra las escuelas que no cumplan las normas federales de desempeño

nonimportation agreements colonial consumer boycotts of British exports as a response to taxes passed by Parliament (p. 101)

acuerdos de no importación boicots de los consumidores coloniales contra las exportaciones británicas como respuesta a los impuestos aprobados por el Parlamento

North American Free Trade Agreement (NAFTA) agreement signed in 1993 calling for the removal of trade restrictions among Canada, Mexico, and the United States (p. 1115)

Tratado de Libre Comercio de América del Norte (TLCAN) acuerdo firmado en 1993 para la remoción de las restricciones comerciales entre Canadá, México y Estados Unidos

North Atlantic Treaty Organization (NATO) military alliance formed to counter Soviet expansion (p. 852)

Organización del Tratado del Atlántico Norte (OTAN) alianza militar formada parar la expansión soviética

Northwest Ordinance of 1787 law which provided a basis for governing the Northwest Territory (p. 137)

Ordenanza del Noroeste de 1787 ley que estableció la base para el gobierno del Territorio del Noroeste

Northwest Territory vast territory north of the Ohio River and west of Pennsylvania as far as the Mississippi River (p. 136)

Territorio Noroeste vasto territorio al norte del río Ohio y al oeste de Pennsylvania hasta llegar al río Mississippi

nuclear family ideal or typical household with a father, mother, and children (p. 897)

núcleo familiar hogar ideal o típico con un padre, una madre, y niños

Nuclear Test Ban Treaty 1963 nuclear-weapons agreement, which banned aboveground nuclear tests (p. 958)

Tratado de Prohibición de Pruebas Nucleares acuerdo de 1963 sobre armas nucleares que prohibió las pruebas nucleares en la superficie de la Tierra

nullification concept in which states could nullify, or void, any federal law they deemed unconstitutional (p. 256)

anulación concepto por el que los estados podrían anular o vetar cualquier ley federal que consideraran inconstitucional

Nuremberg Laws laws enacted by Hitler that denied German citizenship to Jews (p. 829)

Leyes de Nuremberg leyes impuestas por Hitler que negaban la ciudadanía alemana a los judíos

Nuremberg Trials trials in which Nazi leaders were charged with war crimes (p. 838)

Juicios de Nuremberg juicios en los que se acusó a los líderes Nazis de crímenes de guerra

Office of War Information (OWI) government agency that encouraged support of the war effort during World War II (p. 814)

Oficina de Información de Guerra agencia gubernamental que animaba el apoyo al esfuerzo bélico durante la Segunda Guerra Mundial

Okies general term used to describe Dust Bowl refugees (p. 715)

Okies término general usado para describir a los refugiados del Cuenco de Polvo

Open Door Policy American statement that the government did not want colonies in China, but favored free trade there (p. 602)

política de puertas abiertas declaración estadounidense que proclamaba que el gobierno no deseaba colonias en China, pero favorecía el libre comercio ahí

open range vast area of grassland on which livestock roamed and grazed (p. 508)

praderas vastas áreas de pastizales en las que el ganado paseaba y pastaba

Operation Desert Storm 1991 American-led attack on Iraqi forces after Iraq refused to withdraw its troops from Kuwait (p. 1097)

Operación Tormenta del Desierto ataque que comandaron los estadounidenses en 1991 contra las fuerzas iraquíes luego que Irak rehusó a retirar sus tropas de Kuwait

Oregon Trail trail from Independence, Missouri, to Oregon that was used by pioneers in the mid-1800s (p. 302)

Sendero de Oregón ruta desde Independence, Missouri, hasta Oregón usada por los pioneros a mediados del siglo XIX

Organization of Petroleum Exporting Countries (OPEC) group of countries which sell oil to other nations and cooperate to regulate the price and supply of oil (p. 1048)

Organización de Países Exportadores de Petróleo grupo de países que venden petróleo a otras naciones y que coopera en la regulación del precio y suministro del crudo

P

Palmer Raids the series of raids in the early 1920s initiated by Attorney General A. Mitchell Palmer, against suspected radicals and communists (p. 201)

Redadas Palmer redadas de principios de la década de 1920 iniciadas por el fiscal general del estado A. Mitchell Palmer contra personas sospechosas de ser radicales o comunistas

Panama Canal human-made waterway linking the Atlantic to the Pacific across the Isthmus of Panama (p. 607)

Canal de Panamá vía acuática hecha por los humanos que une el Atlántico y el Pacífico a través del istmo de Panamá

pardon official forgiveness of a crime and its punishment (p. 1056)

indulto perdón oficial de un delito y su castigo

Paris Peace Accords 1973 peace agreement between the United States, South Vietnam, North Vietnam, and the Vietcong that effectively ended the Vietnam War (p. 1004)

Acuerdos de Paz de París acuerdo de paz de 1973 entre Estados Unidos, Vietnam del Sur, Vietnam del Norte, y el Vietcong que de hecho finalizó la Guerra de Vietnam

parliament legislative body of a country (p. 73)

parlamento entidad legislativa de un país

patent official rights given by the government to an inventor for the exclusive right to develop, use, and sell an invention for a set period of time (p. 438)

patente derechos oficiales otorgados por el gobierno a un inventor para que tenga los derechos exclusivos para desarrollar, usar, y vender un invento durante un plazo determinado

Patriot Act law passed following September 11, 2001, giving law enforcement broader powers in monitoring possible terrorist activities (p. 1125)

Ley Patriótica ley aprobada después del 11 de septiembre del 2001 que otorgó mayores poderes a los agentes de la ley para vigilar posibles actividades terroristas

Peace Corps American government organization that sends volunteers to provide technical, educational, and medical services in developing countries (p. 955)

Cuerpo de Paz organización del gobierno de Estados Unidos que envía voluntarios para que brinden servicios técnicos, educativos, y médicos en países en vías de desarrollo

Pearl Harbor American military base attacked by the Japanese on December 7, 1941 (p. 789)

Pearl Harbor base militar estadounidense atacada por los japoneses el 7 de diciembre de 1941

Pendleton Civil Service Act 1883 law that created a civil service system for the federal government in an attempt to hire employees on a merit system rather than on a spoils system (p. 531)

Ley Pendleton del Servicio Civil ley de 1883 que creó un sistema de servicio civil para el gobierno federal en un intento por contratar empleados con un sistema de méritos en lugar del clientelismo

penitentiary movement movement aimed at structuring prisons so that prisoners will feel penitent for their crimes (p. 276)

movimiento penitenciario movimiento encaminado a estructurar las prisiones de tal modo que los presos se sientan arrepentidos por los delitos cometidos

Pentagon Papers classified U.S. government study that revealed American leaders intentionally involved the United States in Vietnam without fully informing the American people; leaked to *The New York Times* in 1971 (p. 1003)

Documentos del Pentágono estudio clasificado del gobierno estadounidense que reveló que los líderes estadounidenses intencionalmente involucraron a Estados

Unidos en Vietnam sin haber informado completamente a la ciudadanía estadounidense; lo filtró al *The New York Times* en 1971

Pequot War war between Puritans and Pequot tribe in 1636 over trade rights and territorial expansion (p. 53)
Guerra de los Pequot guerra que ocurrió en 1636 entre los puritanos y la tribu Pequot, debido a los derechos comerciales y la expansión de territorio

perestroika a policy in the Soviet Union in the late 1980s calling for restructuring of the stagnant Soviet economy (p. 1088)
perestroika política de la Unión Soviética de finales de la década de 1980 que abogó por la reestructuración de la estancada economía soviética

personal computer small computer intended for individual use (p. 1105)
computadora personal computadora pequeña destinada al uso personal

personal liberty laws laws enacted by northern states to counteract the Fugitive Slave Act by granting rights to escaped slaves and free blacks (p. 331)
leyes de libertad individual leyes instauradas por los estados del Norte para contrarrestar la Ley de Esclavos Fugitivos, al otorgar derechos tanto a los esclavos escapados como a los negros libertos

Pilgrims English Puritans who sought religious freedom and founded Plymouth Colony in 1620 (p. 51)
peregrinos puritanos ingleses que buscaban la libertad de credo y que fundaron la colonia de Plymouth en 1620

placer mining use of metal pans, picks, and shovels to harvest gold from the banks and bottoms of rivers and streams (p. 313)
minería de placer uso de bandejas de metal, picos y palas para extraer el oro de las márgenes y fondos de ríos y arroyos

Platt Amendment set of conditions under which Cuba was granted independence in 1902, including restrictions on rights of Cubans and granting to the U.S. the "right to intervene" to preserve order in Cuba (p. 605)
Enmienda Platt grupo de condiciones con las que se le otorgó la independencia a Cuba en 1902, que incluían restricciones de los derechos de los cubanos y que otorgaban a EE.UU. el "derecho de intervenir" a fin de conservar el orden en Cuba

political party organization of people that seeks to win elections and hold public office in order to shape government policy (p. 197)
partido político organización de personas que busca ganar elecciones y ocupar puestos públicos a fin de dirigir las políticas gubernamentales

poll tax sum of money to be paid before a person could vote (p. 521)
impuesto electoral suma de dinero a pagar antes que una persona pudiera votar

Pontiac's Rebellion uprising in 1763 by Indians in the Great Lakes region (p. 88)
Rebelión de Pontiac levantamiento en 1763 de los indígenas en la región de los Grandes Lagos

popular sovereignty principle in which the people are the only source of government power (p. 155)
soberanía popular principio por el cual las personas son la única fuente de poder gubernamental

popular sovereignty political policy that permitted the residents of federal territories to decide on whether to enter the union as free or slave states (p. 326)
soberanía popular doctrina política que permitió a los residentes de los territorios federales decidir si ingresaban a la unión como estados libres o esclavistas

Populist Party People's Party; political party formed in 1891 to advocate a larger money supply and other economic reforms (p. 536)
Partido Populista Partido del Pueblo; partido político formado en 1891 para abogar por un mayor suministro de dinero y otras reformas económicas

precedent act or statement that becomes an example, rule, or tradition to be followed (p. 193)
precedente acción o declaración que se convierte en el ejemplo, regla o tradición a seguir

presidio fort built by the Spanish in colonial America, usually in what is today the U.S. Southwest and California (p. 35)
presidio fortín construido por los españoles en la América colonial, usualmente situado en lo que hoy día son el Sudoeste de Estados Unidos y California

privatize to transfer from governmental ownership or control to private interests (p. 1131)
privatizar transferir la propiedad o control gubernamental a intereses privados

Proclamation of 1763 declaration by the British king ordering all colonists to remain east of the Appalachian Mountains (p. 88)
Proclamación de 1763 declaración del rey de Gran Bretaña para que los colonos permanecieran al este de los montes Apalaches

productivity the rate at which goods are produced or services performed (p. 884)
productividad velocidad a la que se producen bienes o se brindan servicios

Progressive Party political party that emerged from the Taft-Roosevelt battle that split the Republican Party in 1912 (p. 575)
Partido Progresivo partido político surgido de la batalla entre Taft y Roosevelt que dividió al Partido Republicano en 1912

Progressivism movement that responded to the pressures of industrialization and urbanization by promoting reforms (p. 548)
Progresivismo movimiento surgido como respuesta a las presiones de la industrialización y urbanización, que promovía nuevas ideas y reformas políticas

Prohibition the forbidding by law of the manufacture, transport, and sale of alcohol (p. 677)
Prohibición ley para prohibir la fabricación, transporte, y venta de alcohol

proprietary colony English colony granted to an individual or group by the Crown (p. 47)
colonia concedida colonia inglesa cedida por la Corona a un individuo o grupo

protective tariff tax on imported goods making the price high enough to protect domestic goods from foreign competition (p. 438)
arancel proteccionista impuesto sobre bienes importados que sube lo suficiente su precio a fin de proteger a los bienes domésticos de la competencia extranjera

public school movement movement aimed at providing greater educational opportunities through the establishment of tax-supported public schools (p. 275)
movimiento de educación pública movimiento orientado a ofrecer mayores oportunidades educativas mediante la fundación de escuelas públicas financiadas con los impuestos

Public Works Administration (PWA) New Deal agency that provided millions of jobs constructing public buildings (p. 737)
Administración de Obras Públicas agencia del Nuevo Trato que brindó millones de empleos en la construcción de obras públicas

pull factor factors that attract people to a new location (p. 56)
factor de atracción causa que atrae a la población hacia una nueva ubicación

Pullman Strike violent 1894 railway workers' strike which began outside of Chicago and spread nationwide (p. 457)
huelga de Pullman violenta huelga de los trabajadores ferrocarrileros de 1894 que empezó en las afueras de Chicago y se extendió por todo el país

pump priming economic theory that favored public works projects because they put money into the hands of consumers who would buy more goods, stimulating the economy (p. 741)
cebado de bomba teoría económica que favorece los proyectos de obras públicas porque ponen dinero en manos de los consumidores que comprarán más bienes, estimulando así la economía

Pure Food and Drug Act 1906 law that allowed federal inspection of food and medicine and banned the interstate shipment and sale of impure food and the mislabeling of food and drugs (p. 572)
Ley de Alimentos y Fármacos Puros Ley de 1906 que permitió la inspección federal de los alimentos y medicinas y prohibió el transporte y venta interestatal de alimentos impuros así como el rotulado erróneo de alimentos y fármacos

Puritans English Protestants who believed in strict religious discipline and the simplification of worship; settlers of the Massachusetts Bay Colony (p. 50)
puritanos protestantes ingleses que observaban una disciplina religiosa estricta y profesaban la simplificación del culto; pobladores de la Colonia de la Bahía de Massachusetts

push factor factors that motivate people to leave their home countries (p. 56)
factor de empuje causa que hace que la población deje su país de origen

Q

quota system arrangement that limited the number of immigrants who could enter the United States from specific countries (p. 673)
sistema de cuotas acuerdo que limitó el número de inmigrantes provenientes de países específicos que podían ingresar a Estados Unidos

R

Radical Republicans congressmen who advocated full citizenship rights for African Americans along with a harsh Reconstruction policy toward the South (p. 404)
Republicanos Radicales congresistas que abogaban por derechos ciudadanos íntegros para los afroestadounidenses junto con una política dura de Reconstrucción en el Sur

ratification official approval (p. 150)
ratificación aprobación oficial

rationing government-controlled limits on the amount of certain goods that civilians could buy during wartime (p. 814)
racionamiento límites controlados por el gobierno sobre la cantidad de ciertos bienes que podían comprar los civiles en tiempos de guerra

realpolitik a foreign policy promoted by Henry Kissinger during the Nixon administration based on concrete national interests instead of abstract ideologies (p. 1009)
realpolitik política exterior promovida por Henry Kissinger durante la administración Nixon con base en intereses nacionales concretos en lugar de ideologías abstractas

recall process by which voters can remove elected officials from office before their terms end (p. 555)
destitución proceso por el cual los electores pueden remover a funcionarios electos antes de terminar su período

Reconquista battle, ending in 1492, that reestablished Spanish Christian rule on the Iberian Peninsula after 700 years of Muslim dominance (p. 14)
la Reconquista batalla, finalizada en 1492, que volvió a establecer el poder cristiano español en la península Ibérica después de 700 años de dominio musulmán

Reconstruction program implemented by the federal government between 1865 and 1877 to repair damage to the South caused by the Civil War and restore the southern states to the Union (p. 402)
Reconstrucción programa implementado por el gobierno federal entre 1865 y 1877 para reparar los daños al Sur que causó la Guerra Civil y reincorporar los estados sureños a la Unión

Reconstruction Finance Corporation (RFC) federal agency set up by Congress in 1932 to provide emergency government credit to banks, railroads, and other large businesses (p. 722)
Corporación de Financiamiento para la Reconstrucción agencia federal establecida por el Congreso en 1932 para brindar créditos gubernamentales de emergencia a los bancos, ferrocarriles, y otras grandes empresas

Redeemer term for white southern Democrats who returned to power after 1870 (p. 422)
redentores término usado para los demócratas blancos sureños que regresaron al poder después de 1870

Red Scare fear that communists were working to destroy the American way of life (pp. 649, 868)
miedo rojo miedo a que los comunistas están empeñados en destruir la forma de vida estadounidense

referendum process that allows citizens to approve or reject a law passed by a legislature (p. 555)

referendo proceso que permite que los ciudadanos aprueben o rechacen una ley que ha aprobado por una legislatura

Renaissance period in European history lasting from the fourteenth to the sixteenth century, which ushered in a more secular age and encouraged freedom of thought, the importance of the individual, and renewed interest in classical learning (p. 13)

Renacimiento período en la historia de Europa que cubre desde el siglo XIV hasta el siglo XVI y que introdujo una edad más secular, alentó la libertad de pensamiento y la importancia del individuo, y renovó el interés en la educación clásica

reparations payment for war damages (p. 642)

reparaciones pago por los daños causados por la guerra

repatriation process by which Mexican Americans were encouraged, or forced, by local, state, and federal officials to return to Mexico during the 1930s (p. 717)

repatriación proceso por el cual los estadounidenses de origen mexicano fueron animados, o forzados, por los oficiales locales, estatales, y federales para que regresaran a México durante la década de 1930

republic form of government in which officials are elected by the people (p. 134)

república forma de gobierno en la que el pueblo elige a los funcionarios

Republican Party political party established around an antislavery platform in 1854 (p. 340)

Partido Republicano partido político establecido en 1854 en torno a una plataforma antiesclavista

reservationists a group of Senators, led by Henry Cabot Lodge, who opposed the Treaty of Versailles, to end World War I, unless specific changes were included (p. 196)

reservasionistas grupo de senadores encabezados por Henry Cabot que se oponía a terminar la Primera Guerra Mundial con el Tratado de Versalles a menos que éste inlcuyera ciertos cambios

reservation public lands where Native Americans were forced to live by the federal government (p. 497)

reservación tierras públicas donde el gobierno federal obligó a vivir a los indígenas

revivalist preacher who works to renew the importance of religion in American life (p. 266)

renovador de la fe predicador dedicado a renovar la importancia de la religión en el modo de vida estadounidense

rock-and-roll music originated in the gospel and blues traditions of African Americans (p. 901)

rock-and-roll música originada en las tradiciones del gospel y blues de los afroestadounidenses

Roosevelt Corollary President Theodore Roosevelt's reassertion of the Monroe Doctrine to keep the Western Hemisphere free from intervention by European powers (p. 607)

Corolario Roosevelt replanteamiento del presidente Teodoro Roosevelt de la Doctrina Monroe, según la cual la política de Estados Unidos era mantener al hemisferio occidental libre de la intervención de las potencias europeas

Rough Riders group of men, consisting of rugged westerners and upper-class easterners who fought during the Spanish-American War (p. 596)

jinetes rudos grupo de hombres fuertes provenientes del Oeste y de la clase alta del Este que pelearon durante la Guerra entre España y Estados Unidos

royal colony English colony that was under direct control of the Crown (p. 47)

colonia real colonia inglesa controlada directamente por la Corona

rural-to-urban migrant a person who moves from an agricultural area to a city (p. 474)

inmigrante del campo a la ciudad persona que se traslada de las áreas rurales a la ciudad

Russo-Japanese War a war between Japan and Russia in 1904 over the presence of Russian troops in Manchuria (p. 603)

Guerra Ruso-Japonesa guerra entre Japón y Rusia durante 1904 por la presencia de tropas Rusas en Manchuria

S

salutary neglect British policy in early 1700s which allowed the colonies virtual self-rule as long as Great Britain was gaining economically (p. 75)

negligencia benigna política británica de principios del siglo XVIII que permitió que las colonias virtualmente se autogobernaran en tanto que Gran Bretaña tuviera ganancias económicas

sanctions penalties (p. 1064)

sanciones castigos

Sand Creek Massacre 1864 incident in which Colorado militia killed a camp of Cheyenne and Arapaho Indians (p. 498)

Masacre de Sand Creek incidente de 1864 durante el cual una milicia de Colorado asesinó a un campamento de indígenas cheyene y arapaho

Santa Fe Trail trail developed by traders in the mid-1800s, connecting Independence, Missouri, to Santa Fe, New Mexico (p. 301)

Sendero de Santa Fe ruta creada por comerciantes a mediados del siglo XIX que unía a Independence, Missouri, con Santa Fe, Nuevo México

Saratoga 1777 Revolutionary War battle considered to be the turning point in the war because the Patriot win convinced the French to aid the United States (p. 120)

Saratoga una batalla en 1777 de la Guerra de Independencia considerada el punto crucial de la guerra porque el triunfo de los patriotas convenció a Francia de reconocer a Estados Unidos como nación

satellite a mechanical device that orbits Earth receiving and sending communication signals or transmitting scientific data (p. 1106)

satélite dispositivo mecánico que orbita la Tierra y que recibe y envía señales de comunicación o transmite datos científicos

satellite state independent nation under the control of a more powerful nation (p. 847)

estado satélite nación independiente bajo el control de una nación más poderosa

saturation bombing tactic of dropping massive amounts of bombs in order to inflict maximum damage (p. 807)

saturación de bombardeos táctica de dejar caer cantidades masivas de bombas a fin de infligir el máximo daño

Savings and Loan crisis the failure of about 1,000 savings and loan banks as a result of risky business practices (p. 1082)
crisis financiera fracaso de cerca de 1,000 bancos de ahorro y préstamo como resultado de prácticas comerciales riesgosas

scalawag negative term for a southern white who supported the Republican Party after the Civil War (p. 411)
scalawag término negativo para referirse a un blanco sureño que apoyó al Partido Republicano después de la Guerra Civil

scientific management approach to improving efficiency, in which experts looked at every step of a manufacturing process, trying to find ways to reduce time, effort, and expense (p. 661)
administración científica enfoque para mejorar la eficiencia, en el que los expertos observaban cada paso de un proceso de manufactura y buscaban formas de reducir el tiempo, esfuerzo, y costo

Scopes Trial 1925 trial of a Tennessee schoolteacher for teaching Darwin's theory of evolution (p. 672)
Juicio Scopes juicio al que fue sometido, en 1925, un maestro de Tennessee por enseñar la teoría de Darwin sobre la evolución

secede to withdraw formally from a membership in a group or an organization (p. 327)
separarse retirir formalmente de la membresía en un grupo u organización

Second Continental Congress assembly of delegates representing every colony that met in 1775 in Philadelphia (p. 109)
Segundo Congreso Continental asamblea de delegados con representación de cada colonia que se reunió en 1775 en Filadelfia

Second Great Awakening religious revival movement in the first half of the 1800s (p. 266)
Segundo Gran Despertar movimiento de renovación religiosa que se dio en la primera mitad del siglo XIX

Second New Deal legislative activity begun by Franklin D. Roosevelt in 1935 to solve problems created by the Great Depression (p. 740)
Segundo Nuevo Trato actividad legislativa iniciada por Franklin D. Roosevelt en 1935 para lidiar con los problemas creados por la Gran Depresión

segregation forced separation, oftentimes by race (p. 412)
segregación separación forzada, a menudo con base en la raza

Selective Service Act act passed by Congress in 1917 authorizing a draft of men for military service (p. 628)
Ley de Servicio ley aprobada por el Congreso en 1917 que autorizó el reclutamiento de hombres para el servicio militar

self-determination the right of people to choose their own form of government (p. 642)
autodeterminación derecho de las personas de elegir su propia forma de gobierno

Seneca Falls Convention held in New York in 1848, the first women's rights convention in the United States (p. 290)
Convención de Seneca Falls la primera convención sobre los derechos de la mujer realizada en Estados Unidos, celebrada en Nueva York en 1848

separation of powers principle that divides power among the executive, legislative, and judicial branches of government (p. 155)
separación de poderes principio que divide el poder entre las ramas ejecutiva, legislativa, y judicial

Separatists groups who wished to separate from the Anglican Church to begin their own churches (p. 50)
separatistas grupos que querían separarse de la iglesia Anglicana para fundar sus propias iglesias

service economy an economic system focused on the buying and selling of services (p. 1108)
economía de servicio sistema económico enfocado en la compra y venta de servicios

service sector businesses that provide services rather than manufactured goods (p. 893)
sector de servicios empresas que brindan servicios en lugar de fabricar bienes

settlement house community center organized at the turn of the twentieth century to provide social services to the urban poor (p. 552)
casa de asentamiento centro comunal organizado a inicios del siglo XX para ofrecer servicios sociales a los pobres de la ciudad

sharecropping system in which a farmer tended a portion of a planter's land in return for a share of the crop (p. 415)
aparcería sistema en el cual un granjero atiende una porción de la tierra del propietario a cambio de una parte de la cosecha

share-tenancy much like sharecropping, except that the farmer chose what crop he would plant and bought his own supplies (p. 416)
arrendamiento por aparcería similar a la aparcería, excepto que el granjero elige qué cultivar y compra sus propios ínsumos

Shays' Rebellion farmers' rebellion led by Daniel Shays against higher taxes in Massachusetts (p. 141)
Rebelión de Shays rebelión de granjeros conducida por Daniel Shays en contra del aumento de impuestos en Massachusetts

Sherman Antitrust Act 1890 law banning any trust that restrained interstate trade or commerce (p. 448)
Ley Antimonopolios Sherman ley de 1890 que prohibió los consorcios que restringían el comercio o negocios interestatales

Shiloh 1862 Civil War battle where nearly 25,000 Union and Confederate troops were killed or wounded (p. 364)
Shiloh batalla de 1862 de la Guerra Civil en la que cerca de 25,000 miembros de las tropas de la Unión y la Confederación murieron o fueron heridos

siege military tactic in which an enemy is surrounded and all supplies are cut off in an attempt to force a surrender (p. 381)
sitio táctica militar según la cual se rodea al enemigo cerrando por completo el acceso de abastecimientos a fin de obligarlo a rendirse

silent majority phrase introduced by President Richard Nixon to refer to a significant number of Americans who supported his policies but chose not to express their views (p. 1047)
mayoría silenciosa frase introducida por el presidente Richard Nixon para referirse a un número significativo de

estadounidenses que apoyaban sus políticas pero eligieron no expresar su opinión

sit-down strike labor protest in which workers stop working and occupy the workplace until their demands are met (p. 745)
huelga de brazos caídos protesta laboral en que los trabajadores dejan de trabajar y ocupan el lugar de trabajo hasta que se satisfacen sus demandas

sit-in form of protest where participants sit and refuse to move (p. 925)
sentada forma de protesta en que los participantes se sientan y rehúsan moverse

Sixteenth Amendment 1913 constitutional amendment that gave Congress the authority to levy an income tax (p. 577)
Décimosexta Enmienda enmienda constitucional de 1913 que otorgó al Congreso la autoridad para establecer un impuesto a las rentas

skyscraper very tall building (p. 475)
rascacielos edificio muy alto

Smith Act law that made it unlawful to teach or advocate the violent overthrow of the United States government (p. 869)
Ley Smith ley que prohibió la enseñanza o defensa de un derrocamiento violento del gobierno estadounidense

Social Darwinism the belief held by some in the late nineteenth century that certain nations and races were superior to others and therefore destined to rule over them (p. 447)
darwinismo social creencia de algunos a finales del siglo XIX según la que algunas naciones o razas eran superiores a otras y por lo tanto estaban destinadas a gobernar

Social Gospel reform movement that emerged in the late nineteenth century that sought to improve society by applying Christian principles (p. 552)
Evangelio Social movimiento reformista surgido a finales del siglo XIX cuyo fin era mejorar la sociedad al aplicarse principios cristianos

socialism system or theory under which the means of production are publicly controlled and regulated rather than owned by individuals (p. 453)
socialismo sistema o teoría según la cual los medios de producción son controlados y regulados públicamente en lugar de ser propiedad de individuos

Social Security Act 1935 law that set up a pension system for retirees, established unemployment insurance, and created insurance for victims of work-related accidents. It also provided aid for poverty-stricken mothers and children, the blind, and the disabled (p. 741)
Ley del Seguro Social ley de 1935 que crea un sistema de pensión para jubilados, establece un seguro de desempleo y crea seguros para las víctimas de accidentes laborales. También suministra ayuda a las madres y niños pobres, ciegos, y discapacitados

Songhai large West African empire lasting from 1400 to 1600 (p. 16)
Songhai gran imperio del África Occidental existente entre el siglo XV d. C. y el siglo XVII d. C.

Sons of Liberty organization of colonists formed in opposition to the Stamp Act and other British laws and taxes (p. 101)
Hijos de la Libertad organización de colonos formada para oponerse a la Ley del Timbre y otras leyes e impuestos británicos

Southeast Asia Treaty Organization (SEATO) defensive alliance aimed at preventing communist aggression in Asia (pp. 859, 983)
Organización del Tratado del Sudeste Asiático alianza defensiva orientada a prevenir la agresión comunista en Asia

southern strategy tactic of the Republican Party for winning presidential elections by securing the electoral votes of southern states (p. 1048)
estrategia sureña táctica del Partido Republicano para ganar las elecciones presidenciales al asegurarse los votos electorales de los estados del Sur

"space race" the competition between the United States and the Soviet Union to develop the technology to successfully land on the moon (p. 961)
"carrera espacial" competencia entre Estados Unidos y la Unión Soviética en el desarrollo de la tecnología para aterrizar exitosamente en la Luna

Spanish Civil War Nationalist forces led by General Francisco Franco rebelled against the democratic Republican government of Spain (p. 777)
Guerra Civil Española conflicto en España, en el que las fuerzas Nacionalistas dirigidas por el General Francisco Franco se rebelaron contra el gobierno democrático Republicano

speculation practice of making high-risk investments in hopes of obtaining large profits (p. 706)
especulación la práctica de hacer inversiones de alto riesgo con la esperanza de obtener grandes ganancias

sphere of influence a region dominated and controlled by an outside power (p. 601)
esfera de influencia región dominada y controlada por un poder externo

spoils system practice of the political party in power giving jobs and appointments to its supporters, rather than to people based on their qualifications (pp. 252, 531)
clientelismo práctica del partido político en el poder de asignar los puestos y nombramientos a sus seguidores en lugar de basarlos en las calificaciones

Square Deal President Theodore Roosevelt's program of reforms to keep the wealthy and powerful from taking advantage of small business owners and the poor (p. 570)
Trato Justo programa de reformas del presidente Teodoro Roosevelt para evitar que los ricos y poderosos se aprovecharan de los propietarios de pequeñas empresas y de los pobres

stagflation term for the economic condition created in the late 1960s and 1970s by high inflation combined with stagnant economic growth and high unemployment (p. 1047)
estanflación término para la condición económica creada a finales de las décadas de 1960 y 1970 por una alta inflación combinada con el estancamiento del crecimiento económico y el alto desempleo

Stamp Act 1765 law passed by Parliament that required colonists to pay taxes on printed materials (p. 100)
Ley del Timbre ley de 1765 aprobada por el Parlamento para exigir a los colonos el pago de impuestos sobre los materiales impresos

"Star-Spangled Banner" poem written by Francis Scott Key in 1814 that became the national anthem in 1931 (p. 217)

"Bandera de Estrellas Centelleantes" poema escrito por Francis Scott Key en 1814 que se convirtió en el himno nacional en 1931

steerage third-class accommodations on a steamship (p. 466)
compartimento de tercera clase alojamiento de tercera clase en un barco de vapor

Strategic Arms Limitation Treaty (SALT I) 1972 treaty between the United States and the Soviet Union that froze the deployment of intercontinental ballistic missiles and placed limits on antiballistic missiles (p. 1010)
Tratado de Limitación de Armas Estratégicas tratado de 1972 entre los Estados Unidos y la Unión Soviética que congeló el despliegue de misiles balísticos intercontinentales y puso límites a los misiles antibalísticos

Strategic Arms Limitation Treaty II (SALT II) proposed agreement between the United States and the Soviet Union to limit certain types of nuclear arms production; it was never ratified by the United States Senate (p. 1064)
Tratado de Limitación de Armas Estratégicas II acuerdo propuesto entre los Estados Unidos y la Unión Soviética para limitar la producción de ciertos tipos de armas nucleares; nunca fué ratíficado por el Senado de los Estados Unidos

strategic bombing tactic of dropping bombs on key political and industrial targets (p. 807)
bombardeo estratégico táctica de dejar caer bombas en blancos políticos e industriales clave

Strategic Defense Initiative (SDI) plan to develop innovative defenses to guard the United States against nuclear missile attacks (p. 1088)
Iniciativa de Defensa Estratégica Plan para desarrollar las defensas innovadoras para salvaguardar a Estados los Unidos contra los ataques de misiles nucleares

strict construction belief that the government is limited to powers clearly stated in the Constitution (p. 195)
interpretación estricta creencia en que el gobierno está limitado a los poderes establecidos en la Constitución

Student Nonviolent Coordinating Committee (SNCC) grass-roots movement founded in 1960 by young civil rights activists (p. 926)
Comité Estudiantil Coordinador de la No Violencia movimiento de base compuesto fundado en 1960 por jóvenes activistas a favor de los derechos humanos

Students for a Democratic Society (SDS) organization founded in 1960 at the University of Michigan to fight racism and poverty (p. 994)
Estudiantes a Favor de una Sociedad Democrática organización fundada en 1960 en la Universidad de Michigan para combatir el racismo y la pobreza

suburb residential areas surrounding a city (p. 476)
suburbios áreas residenciales que rodean una ciudad

Suez crisis attempt by France and Great Britain to seize control of the Suez Canal in 1956 (p. 864)
crisis de Suez intento de Francia y Gran Bretaña para tomar control del Canal de Suez en 1956

suffrage the right to vote (p. 290)
sufragio derecho al voto

Sunbelt name given to the region of states in the South and the Southwest (p. 891)
Cinturón del Sol nombre dado a la región de los estados del sur y suroeste

superpower powerful country that plays a dominant economic, political, and military role in the world (p. 836)
superpotencia un país poderoso que juega un papel dominante en el mundo en terminos economicos, politicos, y militares

supply-side economics economic theory which says that reducing tax rates stimulates economic growth (p. 1081)
economía de la oferta teoría económica que mantiene que reduciendo impuestos estimula el crecimiento conomico

suspension bridge bridge that has a roadway suspended by cables (p. 439)
puente colgante un puente cuya carretera está suspendida por cables

sweatshop small factory where employees have to work long hours under poor conditions for little pay (p. 451)
taller del sudor fábrica pequeña donde los empleados tienen que trabajar muchas horas bajo condiciones deficientes y por poco sueldo

T

Taft Hartley Act a law that restricted the power of labor unions (p. 885)
Ley Taft Hartley ley que restringió el poder de los sindicatos de trabajadores

Taliban Islamic fundamentalist faction that controlled most of Afghanistan from 1996–2001 (p. 1124)
Talibán fracción fundamentalista islámica que controló la mayor parte de Afganistán entre 1996 a 2001

tariff tax on imported goods (p. 194)
arancel impuesto sobre bienes importados

Tariff of Abominations 1828 protective tariff, so-named by its southern opponents (p. 255)
Arancel de Abominaciones arancel protector de 1828, llamado así por sus oponentes sureños

Tariff of 1816 protective tariff established by Congress to encourage Americans to buy goods made in the U.S. (p. 233)
Arancel de 1816 arancel protector establecido por el Congreso para estimular a los estadounidenses a comprar bienes hechos en los Estados Unidos

Tea Party Movement informal movement made up of local groups who want to reduce the size and scope of the federal government
movimiento Tea Party movimiento informal compuesto por grupos locales que quieren reducir el tamaño y el alcance del gobierno federal

Teapot Dome scandal Harding Administration scandal in which the Interior Secretary leased government oil reserves to private oilmen for bribes (p. 668)
escándalo Teapot Dome el escándalo durante la administración Harding en que el secretario del interior arrendó las reservas de petróleo del gobierno a cambio de un soborno

televangelist minister who uses the television to preach (p. 1061)

teleevangelista pastor que usa el formato para predicar

temperance movement movement aimed at stopping alcohol abuse and the problems created by it (p. 277)
movimiento de temperancia movimiento encausado a eliminar el abuso del alcohol y los problemas que éste genera

tenant farming system in which a farmer paid rent to a landowner for the use of the land (p. 416)
agricultura de arrendamiento sistema en el que un agricultor paga un alquiler por el uso de la tierra a un propietario

tenement multistory building divided into apartments to house as many families as possible (p. 476)
vecindad edificio de varios pisos dividido en departamentos para albergar a varias familias

Tennessee Valley Authority (TVA) government agency that built dams in the Tennessee River valley to control flooding and generate electric power (p. 736)
Autoridad del Valle del Tennessee agencia gubernamental que construye represas en el valle del río Tennessee para controlar las inundaciones y generar energía eléctrica

termination policy ended all programs monitored by the Bureau of Indian Affairs. It also ended federal responsibility for the health and welfare of Native Americans (p. 907)
política de terminación política que cerró todos los programas a cargo de la Oficina de Asuntos Indígenas. También dio por terminada la responsabilidad federal en cuanto a la salud y bienestar de los indígenas estadounidenses

Tet Offensive communist assault on a large number of South Vietnamese cities in early 1968 (p. 995)
Ofensiva Tet asalto comunista contra un gran número de ciudades de Vietnam del Sur a principios de 1968

Thirteenth Amendment 1865 constitutional amendment that abolished slavery (p. 391)
Decimotercera Enmienda enmienda constitucional de 1865 que abolió la esclavitud

38th parallel dividing line between North and South Korea (p. 855)
paralelo 38 línea divisoria entre Corea del Norte y Corea del Sur

Three-Fifths Compromise compromise in which each enslaved person would be counted as three fifths of a person for the purposes of legislative representation (p. 148)
Acuerdo de Tres Quintos acuerdo según el que cada esclavo se contaría como tres quintos de una persona para efectos de la representación legislativa

Tiananmen Square site in Beijing where Chinese students' prodemocracy protests were put down by the Chinese government in 1989 (p. 1094)
Plaza Tiananmen lugar en Pekín donde las protestas de los estudiantes chinos a favor de la democracia fueron aplacadas por el gobierno chino en 1989

time zone any of the 24 longitudinal areas of the world within which the same time is used (p. 440)
huso horario cualquiera de las veinticuatro zonas del mundo en la que se usa la misma hora

totalitarianism a theory of government in which a single party or leader controls the economic, social, and cultural lives of its people (p. 772)
totalitarismo teoría de gobierno según la que un solo partido o líder controla la vida económica, social, y cultural de la poblacíon

total war military strategy in which an army attacks not only enemy troops but the economic and civilian resources that support them (p. 386)
guerra total estrategia militar en la cual, además de atacar a las tropas enemigas, un ejército arremete también contra los recursos económicos y civiles que las sostienen

toxic waste poisonous byproducts of human activity (p. 1035)
desechos tóxicos productos de desecho venenosos resultantes de la actividad humana

Trail of Tears forced march of the Cherokee Indians to move west of the Mississippi in the 1830s (p. 254)
Sendero del Llanto marcha forzada de los indígenas cherokee para mudarlos al oeste del Mississippi en la década de 1830

Transcendentalist person who follows the literary and philosophical movement based on finding spiritual reality through nature and consciousness of self (p. 272)
trascendentalista seguidor del movimiento literario y filosófico que buscaba hallar la realización espiritual a través de la naturaleza y la consciencia del propio ser

transcontinental railroad rail link between the eastern and the western United States (p. 507)
ferrocarril transcontinental enlace ferroviario entre el este y el oeste de los Estados Unidos

Treaty of Fort Laramie 1851 treaty that restricted Indians to specific areas away from the major trails (p. 304)
Tratado del Fuerte Laramie tratado de 1851 que restringía a los indígenas a áreas específicas alejadas de los senderos mayores

Treaty of Ghent 1814 agreement that ended the War of 1812 (p. 218)
Tratado de Gante acuerdo de 1814 que finalizó la Guerra de 1812

Treaty of Guadalupe-Hidalgo 1848 treaty ending the Mexican-American War (p. 311)
Tratado Guadalupe-Hidalgo tratado de 1848 que finalizó la Guerra México-Estadounidense

Treaty of Paris 1783 peace treaty that ended the Revolutionary War and affirmed American independence (p. 125)
Tratado de París tratado de paz de 1783 que dió por finalizada la Guerra de Independencia y estableció la independencia de Estados Unidos

Treaty of Paris an agreement signed by the United States and Spain in 1898, which officially ended the Spanish-American War (p. 597)
Tratado de París acuerdo firmado por Estados Unidos y España en 1898 que marcó el final oficial de la Guerra entre España y Estados Unidos

triangular trade three-way pattern of trade that involved England, English colonies in the Americas, and West Africa (p. 69)
comercio triangular patrón trilateral de comercio que involucró a Inglaterra, las colonias inglesas en las Américas, y África Occidental

trickle-down economics economic theory that holds that money lent to banks and businesses will trickle down to consumers (p. 722)
economía por goteo teoría económica que mantiene que el dinero prestado a los bancos y empresas llegará a los consumidores

Tripartite Pact agreement that created an alliance between Germany, Italy, and Japan during World War II (p. 784)
Pacto Tripartito acuerdo que creó una alianza entre Alemania, Italia, y Japón durante la Segunda Guerra Mundial

Truman Doctrine President Truman's promise to help nations struggling against communist movements (p. 848)
doctrina Truman promesa del Presidente Truman de ayudar a las naciones en lucha contra los movimientos comunistas

trust group of separate companies that are placed under the control of a single managing board in order to form a monopoly (p. 445)
trust grupo de distintas compañías bajo el control de una sola junta administrativa

turnpike road that requires users to pay a toll (p. 228)
autopista de peaje carretera que exige el pago de una cuota a sus usuarios

Tuskegee Airmen African American squadron that escorted bombers in the air war over Europe during World War II (p. 807)
Aviadores de Tuskegee escuadrón de afroestadounidenses que escoltaba a los bombarderos en la guerra aérea en cielos de Europa durante la Segunda Guerra Mundial

Twenty-fifth Amendment constitutional amendment ratified in 1967 that deals with presidential succession, vice presidential vacancy, and presidential inability (p. 1051)
Vigésima Quinta Enmienda enmienda constitucional ratificada en 1967 que trata de la sucesión presidencial, vacantes de vicepresidentes, e incapacidad presidencial

Twenty-fourth Amendment constitutional amendment that banned the poll tax as a voting requirement (p. 938)
Vigésima Cuarta Enmienda enmienda constitucional que prohibió el impuesto electoral como requisito para votar

U

U-boat German submarine (p. 624)
buque submarino U submarino alemán

unconditional surrender giving up completely without any concessions (p. 805)
rendición incondicional darse por vencido completamente sin concesiones

Underground Railroad system that existed before the Civil War, in which black and white abolitionists helped escaped slaves travel to safe areas, especially Canada (p. 333)
Ferrocarril Subterráneo sistema que existió antes de la Guerra Civil en el que negros y blancos abolicionistas socorrían a los esclavos escapados a llegar a zonas seguras, especialmente Canadá

unfunded mandate program or action required but not paid for by the federal government (p. 1078)
mandatos sin fondos programas o acciones requeridos pero que no paga el gobierno federal

unicameral legislature lawmaking body made up of a single house (p. 134)
legislatura unicameral cuerpo legislativo compuesto de una sola cámara

Unitarian members of the Unitarian religion, which is based on the belief that God is a single divine being rather than a trinity (p. 269)
unitarios miembros del unitarismo, una religión basada en la creencia en que Dios es un ser único divino y no una trinidad

United Farm Workers (UFW) labor union of farm workers that used nonviolent tactics, including a workers' strike and a consumer boycott of table grapes (p. 1029)
Trabajadores Agrícolas Unidos sindicato de trabajadores agrícolas que usó tácticas pacíficas, incluyendo una huelga de trabajadores y un boicot por los consumidores de uvas

United Nations (UN) organization founded in 1945 to promote peace (p. 837)
Naciones Unidas (ONU) organización fundada en 1945 para promover la paz

Universal Declaration of Human Rights document issued by the UN to promote basic human rights and freedoms (p. 837)
Declaración Universal de los Derechos Humanos documento emitido por la ONU para promover los derechos y libertades humanos básicos

urbanization expansion of cities and/or an increase in the number of people living in them (p. 472)
urbanización expansión de ciudades y/o aumento del número de sus habitantes

Urban League network of churches and clubs that set up employment agencies and relief efforts to help African Americans get settled and find work in the cities (p. 567)
Liga Urbana red de iglesias y clubes que estableció agencias de empleo y esfuerzos de asistencia para ayudar a que los afroestadounidenses se asentaran y encontraran empleo en las ciudades

urban renewal government programs for redevelopment of urban areas (p. 905)
renovación urbana programas gubernamentales para el desarrollo de las áreas urbanas

utopian community separate settlement established with the goal of moral perfection (p. 271)
comunidad utópica asentamiento independiente fundado para alcanzar la perfección moral

V

Valley Forge location in Pennsylvania where Washington's army spent a difficult winter in 1777–1778 (p. 120)
Valle Forge lugar en Pennsylvania donde el ejército de Washington pasó un invierno difícil de 1777 a 1778

vaudeville type of show, including dancing, singing, and comedy sketches, that became popular in the late nineteenth century (p. 485)
vodevil tipo de espectáculo que incluye baile, canto, y comedia que se popularizó a finales del siglo XIX

vertical integration system of consolidating firms involved in all steps of a product's manufacture (p. 445)
integración vertical sistema de consolidación de empresas involucradas en todos los pasos de la manufactura de un producto

viceroy in colonial Spanish America, king-appointed official who governs a province, colony, or country (p. 35)
virrey en la Hispanoamérica colonial, funcionario nombrado por el rey para gobernar una provincia, colonia, o país

Vicksburg Confederate stronghold on the Mississippi River that surrendered to Union forces in 1863 after a siege (p. 381)
Vicksburg baluarte confederado en el río Mississippi que se rindió a las fuerzas de la Unión en 1863 luego de un sitio

Vietcong South Vietnamese communist rebels that waged a guerrilla war against the government of South Vietnam throughout the Vietnam War (p. 983)
Vietcong rebeldes comunistas sudvietnamitas que hicieron guerra de guerrillas contra el gobierno de Vietnam del Sur durante la Guerra de Vietnam

Vietnamization President Nixon's plan for gradual withdrawal of U.S. forces as South Vietnamese troops assumed more combat duties (p. 1001)
vietnamización plan del presidente Nixon para terminar gradualmente la participación estadounidense en Vietnam, a medida que las tropas sudvietnamitas asumían más deberes de combate

vigilante self-appointed law enforcer (p. 507)
vigilante persona autonombrada para hacer cumplir la ley

Violence Against Women Act law passed in 1994 that increased federal resources to apprehend and prosecute men guilty of violent acts against women (p. 1131)
Ley contra la Violencia hacia las Mujeres ley aprobada en 1994 que aumentó los recursos federales para arrestar y enjuiciar a los hombres culpables de actos violentos contra las mujeres

Virginia and Kentucky resolutions state resolutions passed in 1798 declaring the Alien and Sedition Acts unconstitutional (p. 202)
resoluciones de Virginia y Kentucky resoluciones estatales aprobadas en 1798 que declararon inconstitucionales las Leyes de Extranjería y Sedición

Virginia Plan James Madison's proposal for a bicameral legislature with representation based upon population (p. 144)
Plan de Virginia propuesta de James Madison para legislatura bicameral con representación basada en la cantidad de habitantes

Volstead Act law enacted by Congress to enforce the Eighteenth Amendment (p. 677)
Ley Volstead ley impuesta por el Congreso para hacer cumplir la Decimoctava Enmienda

Voting Rights Act law that banned literacy tests and empowered the federal government to oversee voter registration (p. 938)
Ley de Derechos Electorales ley que prohibió las pruebas de alfabetismo y dio poder al gobierno federal de vigilar el empadronamiento de los votantes

voucher certificates or other documents that can be used as money (p. 1085)
vales certificados u otros documentos que pueden ser usados como dinero

W

Wade-Davis Bill required that a majority of prewar voters in the Confederate states swear loyalty to the Union before restoration could begin (p. 404)
Proyecto de Ley Wade-Davis proyecto de ley que requería a los votantes de los estados Confederados de antes de la guerra jurar lealtad a la Unión para que comenzara la restauración

Wagner Act New Deal law that abolished unfair labor practices, recognized the right of employees to organize labor unions, and gave workers the right to collective bargaining (p. 744)
Ley Wagner ley que abolió las prácticas laborales injustas, reconoció el derecho de los trabajadores de organizar sindicatos, y dió a los trabajadores el derecho a las negociaciones colectivas

War Hawks members of Congress who pushed for war against Great Britain beginning in 1810 (p. 215)
halcones de guerra miembros del Congreso que presionaron por una guerra contra Gran Bretaña a partir de 1810

War of 1812 war between the United States and Great Britain (p. 216)
Guerra de 1812 guerra entre Estados Unidos y Gran Bretaña

War on Poverty President Johnson's programs aimed at aiding the country's poor through education, job training, proper health care, and nutrition (p. 966)
Guerra Contra la Pobreza programas del presidente Johnson enfocados en ayudar a los pobres de la nación mediante la educación, entrenamiento laboral, servicios de salud, y nutrición adecuados

War Powers Act 1973 law passed by Congress restricting the President's war-making powers; the law requires the President to consult with Congress before committing American forces to a foreign conflict (p. 1007)
Ley de Poderes Bélicos ley aprobada por el Congreso en 1973 que restringió los poderes bélicos del presidente; la ley exige que el presidente consulte con el Congreso dentro de un período de 48 horas antes de comprometer fuerzas estadounidenses en un conflicto extranjero

War Refugee Board U.S. government agency founded in 1944 to save Eastern European Jews (p. 833)
Junta de Refugiados de Guerra agencia del gobierno de Estados Unidos fundada en 1944 para salvar a los judíos de Europa Oriental

Warren Commission committee that investigated the assassination of President Kennedy (p. 963)
Comisión Warren comité que investigó el asesinato del presidente Kennedy

"Warren Court" Supreme Court of the 1960s under Chief Justice Earl Warren, whose decisions supported civil rights (p. 971)
"Corte Warren" Corte Suprema de la década de 1960 bajo el mandato del presidente de los magistrados Earl Warren, cuyas decisiones apoyaron los derechos civiles, libertades civiles, derecho al sufragio y privacidad personal

Warsaw Pact military alliance of the Soviet Union and its satellite states (p. 852)
Pacto de Varsovia alianza militar de la Unión Soviética y sus estados satélites

Washington Naval Disarmament Conference meeting held in 1921 and 1922 where world leaders agreed to limit construction of warships (p. 669)
Conferencia de Desarme Naval de Washington reunión realizada en 1921 y 1922 durante la cual los líderes mundiales acordaron limitar la construcción de buques de guerra

Watergate political scandal involving illegal activities that ultimately led to the resignation of President Nixon in 1974 (p. 1049)
Watergate escándalo político que involucró actividades ilegales que al final condujeron a la renuncia del presidente Nixon en 1974

Weapons of Mass Destruction (WMD) nuclear, biological, and chemical weapons intended to kill or harm on a large scale (p. 1125)
armas de destrucción masiva armas nucleares, biológicas, y químicas destinadas a matar o lesionar a gran escala

welfare state government that assumes responsibility for providing for the welfare of the poor, elderly, sick, and unemployed (p. 755)
estado de bienestar gobierno que asume la responsabilidad de velar por el bienestar de los pobres, ancianos, enfermos, y desempleados

Western Front battle front between the Allies and Central Powers in western Europe during World War I (p. 621)
Frente Occidental frente de batalla entre los Aliados y los Poderes Centrales en Europa occidental durante la Primera Guerra Mundial

Whig member of the nationalist political party formed in 1832 in opposition to the Democrats (p. 257)
Whig miembro del partido político nacionalista formado en 1832 en oposición a los demócratas

Whiskey Rebellion 1794 uprising in western Pennsylvania that opposed the federal excise tax on whiskey (p. 195)
Rebelión del Whiskey levantamiento de 1794 al oeste de Pennsylvania en oposición al impuesto federal indirecto sobre el whiskey

Wilmot Proviso proposed, but rejected, 1846 bill that would have banned slavery in the territory won from Mexico in the Mexican War (pp. 312, 325)
Condición Wilmot ley propuesta pero rechazada de 1846 que habría prohibido la esclavitud en los territorios ganados a México en la Guerra México-Estadounidense

Women's Army Corps (WAC) U.S. Army group established during World War II so that women could serve in noncombat roles (p. 792)
Cuerpo Femenino del Ejército grupo del Ejército de Estados Unidos establecido durante la Segunda Guerra Mundial para que las mujeres pudieran dar servicio en papeles no combativos

women's movement movement beginning in the mid-1800s in the United States that sought greater rights and opportunities for women (p. 288)
movimiento femenino movimiento iniciado a mediados del siglo XIX en Estados Unidos que buscaba conquistar mayores derechos y oportunidades para las mujeres

Works Progress Administration (WPA) key New Deal agency that provided work relief through various public-works projects (p. 292)
Administración del Progreso de Obras agencia clave del Nuevo Trato que brindó ayuda laboral a través de varios proyectos de obras públicas

World Trade Organization (WTO) international organization formed in 1995 to encourage the expansion of world trade (p. 667)
Organización Mundial del Comercio (OMC) organización internacional formada en 1995 para estimular la expansión del comercio mundial

Wounded Knee 1890 confrontation between U.S. cavalry and Sioux that marked the end of Indian resistance (p. 503)
Wounded Knee enfrentamiento de 1890 entre la caballería de Estados Unidos y los sioux que marcó el fin de la resistencia indígena

XYZ Affair diplomatic controversy in 1798 in which French officials demanded bribes of American negotiators (p. 202)
Asunto XYZ controversia diplomática en 1798 en la cual oficiales franceses exigieron sobornos de los negociadores estadounidenses

Yalta Conference 1945 strategy meeting between Roosevelt, Churchill, and Stalin (p. 834)
Conferencia de Yalta reunión sobre estrategia realizada en 1945 entre Roosevelt, Churchill, y Stalin

Yellow Press newspapers that used sensational headlines and exaggerated stories in order to promote readership (p. 594)
prensa amarillista periódicos que utilizaban titulares sensacionales e historias exageradas para promover su circulación

Yorktown site in Virginia where Cornwallis's army surrendered to Washington (p. 124)
Yorktown lugar en Virginia donde el ejército de Cornwallis se rindió ante Washington

Z

Zimmermann note telegram written by German Foreign Minister Zimmermann proposing an alliance between Germany and Mexico against the United States during World War I (p. 627)
telegrama de Zimmermann telegrama escrito por el ministro del exterior alemán Zimmermann en el que proponía una alianza entre Alemania y México contra Estados Unidos en la Primera Guerra Mundial

Note: Page numbers followed by *b* refer to box; *c,* chart; *g,* graph; *m,* map; *i,* illustration; *p,* photo; *q,* quotation; *t,* table.

Index

C

Index

D

E

F

Index

I

M

Index

N

O

P

S

Index

U

Z

Acknowledgments

Staff Credits

The people who make up the **United States History** team—representing design services, editorial, editorial services, education technology, manufacturing and inventory planning, market research, marketing services, planning and budgeting, product planning, production services, project office, publishing processes, and rights and permissions—are listed below. Bold type denotes core team members.

Ernie Albanese, Mary Aldridge, Diane Alimena, Leann Davis Alspaugh, Michele Angelucci, Jasjit Arneja, **Margaret Antonini,** Rosalyn Arcilla, Alan Asarch, Helene Avraham, Penny Baker, Renée Beach, Peter Brooks, Lois Brown, Kerry Buckley, Pradeep Byram, Rui Camarinha, Lisa Carrillo, Sarah Carroll, Kerry Cashman, Justin Contursi, Jason Cuoco, Harold DelMonte, **James Doris,** Laura Edgerton-Riser, Leanne Esterly, Anne Falzone, Libby Forsyth, Phillip Gagler, Doreen Galbraith, Joe Galka, Kathy Gavilanes, Julie Gecha, Allen Gold, Holly Gordon, Mary Ann Gundersen, Mary Hanisco, Rick Hickox, Karen Holtzman, **Kristan Hoskins,** Beth Hyslip, Katharine Ingram, Linda Johnson, **John Kingston,** Stephanie Krol, Courtney Lane, Mary Sue Langan, Julian Libysen, **Salena LiBritz,** Marian Manners, Grace Massey, Patrick McCarthy, John McClure, Mike McLaughlin, Rich McMahon, Kathleen Mercandetti, Art Mkrtchyan, Karyl Murray, Ken Myett, Deborah Nicholls, Xavier W. Niz, Kim Ortell, Jennifer Paley, Ray Parenteau, **Judi Pinkham,** Linda Punskovsky, Matthew J. Raycroft, Maureen Raymond , **Ryan Richards,** Bruce Rolff, **Laura Ross,** Robyn Salbo, Donna Schindler, Gerry Schrenk, Mildred Schulte, **Melissa Shustyk,** Siri Schwartzman, Ann Shea, Robert Siek, **Laurel Smith,** Lisa Smith-Ruvalcaba, Kara Stokes, Frank Tangredi, Elizabeth Torjussen, Humberto Ugarte, Ellen Welch Granter, Rachel Winter

Additional Credits

Steve Apple, Karen Beck, Meg Ceccolini, Donna DiCuffa, Lynette Haggard, Stuart Kirschenbaum, Beth Kun, Carol Maglitta, Karen Mancinelli-Paige, Caroline McDonnell, Lesley Pierson, Rachel Ross, Ted Smykal, Alfred Voto, Marc Wezdecki

Art Credits

Kerry Cashman **SH12, 7, 19, 26, 28–29, 37, 38, 44, 46, 51, 60–61, 68–69, 75, 83, 92–93, 102–103, 112–113, 115, 122–123, 132–133, 142, 146–147, 152–153, 158–159, 162, 164–165, 171, 176–177, 178, 183, 186, 192–193, 204–205, 214, 226, 228–229, 235, 240–241, 248–249, 256–257, 263, 266, 270–271, 275, 278–279, 285, 294–295, 305, 316–317, 326–327, 342–343, 348–349, 356, 358–359, 368–369, 372–373, 382, 392–393, 403, 414, 418–419, 422–423, 424, 428–429, 436–437, 442–443, 451, 460–461, 474, 479, 482–483, 486–487, 491, 494, 498–499, 514, 519, 520–521, 526–527, 540–541, 549, 556–557, 558, 564–565, 572, 582–583, 590, 592–593, 602–603, 612, 618–619, 620–621, 634, 636, 642–643, 650–651, 668, 674–675, 682, 684–685, 706–707;** Ellen Welch Granter **398, 402, 406, 411, 412, 413, 420, 428, 430;** Hefflin Agency/Ilene Winn-Lederer **10;** Kevin Jones Associates **358–359;** Steve McEntee **659;** Rich McMahon **C3, C6, C9, C12, C14, C17, 92, 443, 598, 601, 607, 615, 620, 640, 707, 708, 709, 710, 711, 712, 713;** Jen Paley, **SH11, SH12, SH13, SH14, SH15, SH16, SH17, SH18, SH19, SH20, SH21, SH26, SH27, SH28, SH31, 4, 9, 13, 15, 18, 20, 21, 28, 29, 31, 34, 35, 42, 48, 50, 54, 55, 59, 60, 62, 66, 73, 80, 87, 92, 100, 105, 106, 109, 116, 121, 126, 128, 130, 132, 135, 138, 140, 144, 147, 149, 151, 156, 159, 161, 164, 165, 166, 170, 174, 180, 181, 183, 189, 193, 194, 198, 199, 204, 212, 213, 216, 217, 218, 221, 223, 224, 231, 234, 235, 237, 238, 240, 241, 242, 248, 254, 256, 257, 259, 260, 261, 262, 263, 266, 272, 274, 278, 280, 284, 286, 292, 293, 295, 296, 297, 299, 300, 303, 305, 308, 309, 310, 316, 318, 324, 325, 329, 331, 337, 340, 344, 345, 348, 350, 351, 354, 358, 361, 365, 370, 377, 380, 384, 386, 390, 392, 395, 400, 423, 428, 434, 435, 437, 440, 441, 448, 455, 458, 460, 463, 468, 476, 477, 488, 490, 496, 498, 504, 505, 508, 511, 512, 517, 518, 526, 528, 529, 532, 537, 539, 544, 545, 549, 552, 553, 559, 560, 564, 566, 570, 572, 574, 578, 580, 581, 583, 584, 586, 589, 592, 594, 599, 603, 605, 609, 610, 611, 613, 628, 629, 633, 639, 644, 645, 648, 650, 652, 653, 656, 658, 660, 661, 663, 664, 666, 668, 671, 678, 679, 680, 681, 682, 684, 691, 704, 705, 706, 710, 714–715, 751, 906, 1026, 1101, 1129, 1154–1155, 1157, 1160, 1161;** XNR Productions, Inc. **SH22, 5, 11, 13, 24, 26, 28, 40, 46, 53, 85, 114, 125, 129, 141, 149, 158, 160, 162, 164, 172, 176, 186, 191, 195, 200, 214, 266, 281, 287, 306–307, 328, 333, 343, 346, 356, 364, 372, 374, 376, 383, 388, 401, 403, 408, 409, 416, 428, 438, 444, 460, 470, 479, 500, 509, 533, 539, 547, 550, 564, 565, 588, 601, 611, 632, 646, 648, 650, 669, 672, 676, 684, 692, 693, 694, 695, 696, 697, 698, 699, 700, 713, 892, 1036, 1132**

Photographs

Every effort has been made to secure permission and provide appropriate credit for photographic material. The publisher deeply regrets any omission and pledges to correct errors called to its attention in subsequent editions.

Unless otherwise acknowledged, all photographs are the property of Pearson Education, Inc. Photo locators denoted as follows: Top (T), Center (C), Bottom (B), Left (L), Right (R), Background (Bkgd)

Cover (Bkgrd) Corbis, (CCL) Getty Images, (BL) Barry Rosenthal/Getty Images, (BL) Bettmann/Corbis, (TR) Corbis, (TC) Michael J. Deas, (BR) Corbis, (B) Getty Images, (BC) NASA; **vi** ©The Granger Collection, NY; **viii** ©Walters Art Museum, Baltimore, USA/Bridgeman Art Library; ix (L) Getty Images, Library of Congress; **x** ©SuperStock/SuperStock; xi (T) ©Bettmann/Corbis, (B) Judith Miller/Larry & Dianna Elman/©DK Images; **xii** (L) Getty Images, (C) ©Blank Archives/Getty Images, (R) Bettmann/Corbis, (B) Tim Ridley/collection of the Louisiana State Museum, Gift of the New Orleans Jazz Club/©DK Images; **xiii** Getty Images; **xiv** (R) ©Time Life Pictures/Getty Images, (L) Charles Gatewood/The Image Works, Inc.; **xv** (L) Peter Turnley/Corbis, (R) Reuters/Corbis; **xvi** Getty Images; **xviii** The New York Public Library/Art Resource, NY; **xix** Photofest; **xxxii** (R) Dirk Anschutz/Getty Images, George Doyle/Getty Images, (L) Library of Congress; **SH01** Darius Ramazani/zefa; **SH02** Jose Luis Pelaez, Inc./Corbis; **SH06** Tom Stewart/Corbis; **SH12** Fox Photos/Getty Images; **SH19** zhu difeng/Shutterstock; **SH23** Bettmann/Corbis; **SH24** ©The Granger Collection, NY; **SH26** Library of Congress; **SH29** ©The Granger Collection, NY; **SH30** Dynamic Graphics Group/IT Stock Free/Alamy; **SH32** (TR, TC, CL) ©The Granger Collection, NY, (BL) Bettmann/Corbis, (CR) Bettmann/Corbis, (TL) Corbis, (Bkgrd) The Art Archive/National Archives Washington DC/The Kobal Collection; 0 (T) ©Christopher Hurst/The Image Works, Inc.; **1** SuperStock; **2** The Granger Collection, NY; **3** (C) ©Peabody Essex Museum, Salem, Massachusetts, USA/Bridgeman Art Library, (B) ©Richard A. Cooke/Corbis, (T) Image copyright ©The Metropolitan Museum of Art/Art Resource, NY; **4** Smithsonian American Art Museum, Washington, DC/Art Resource, NY; **7** (BR) ©George H.H. Huey/Alamy Images, (BR) David Muench/Corbis, (L) George H. H. Huey/Corbis, (TR) IRA BLOCK/National Geographic Image Collection; **9** The Art Archive; **11** (R, L) ©The Granger Collection, NY; **12** AKG London Ltd.; **14** ©The Granger Collection, NY; **15** The Granger Collection, NY; **17** (TL) ©P.Hussenot/photocuisine/Corbis, (border) Ariadne Van Zandbergen/Lonely Planet/Getty Images, (C) Musée des Arts Africains et Océaniens/Gianni Dagli Orti/The Art Archive, (B) Nik Wheeler/Corbis, (TR) Stockbyte/Getty Images; **19** (B) North Wind Picture Archives, (T) Werner Forman/Art Resource, NY; **20** Corbis; **22** The Granger Collection, NY; **23** The Art Archive; **25** (BL) ©Courtesy of the Bancroft Library, University of California, Berkeley, (T, CL) ©The Granger Collection, NY, (BR) Chas Howson ©The British Museum/©DK Images, (CR) The Image Works, Inc.; **27** (T) Sherwin Crasto/Rueters/Corbis, (B) The Granger Collection, NY; **28** (L) ©George H.H. Huey/Alamy Images, (L) David Muench/Corbis, (R) The Granger Collection, NY; **29** (L) ©Underwood & Underwood/Corbis, (R) The Granger Collection, NY; **30** (T) Antiquarian Images, (T) British Library, (B) Chas Howson ©The British Museum/©DK Images; **32** ©The Granger Collection, NY; **33** (B) Ashmolean Museum/The Art Archive, (T) J.Bedmar/Iberfoto/Photoaisa, (C) Pilgrim Society; **34** (L) ©The Granger Collection, NY, (R) Bettmann/Corbis; **35** Gilles Mermet/AKG London Ltd.; **37** North Wind Picture Archives; **38** (TR) Courtesy Florida Museum of Natural History, (TL, C, B) Mission San Luis de Apalachee; **39** ©Associated Press; **40** (R) Corbis, (R) Tom McHugh/Photo Researchers, Inc.; **41** Erich Lessing/Art Resource, NY; **42** North Wind Picture Archives/Alamy Images; **43** Mary Evans Picture Library; **44** ©Bettmann/Corbis; **45** Bettmann/Corbis; **46** (BL) ©Jeremy Horner/Corbis, (BR) ©North Wind Picture Archives/Alamy Images, (TL, CL) APVA Preservation Virginia, (TR) Getty Images; **47** (L) MPI/Hulton Archive/Getty Images, (R) Private Collection/Bridgeman Art Library; **48** ©The Granger Collection, NY; **50** ©The Granger Collection, NY; **51** Kevin Fleming/Corbis; **52** (R, L) North Wind Picture Archives; **53** North Wind Picture Archives; **55** ©The Granger Collection, NY; **57** Library of Congress; **58** (C) Private Collection, John Noott Galleries, Broadway, Worcestershire, UK/Bridgeman Art Library, (B) Bridgeman-Giraudon/Art Resource, NY, (TR) Getty Images, (TL) The New York Public Library/Art Resource, NY; **60** Private Collection/Bridgeman Art Library; **61** (R) ©Associated Press, (L) North Wind Picture Archives; **62** Bettmann/Corbis; **64** Bettmann/Corbis, Collection of The New-York Historical Society; **65** (C, B) ©The Granger Collection, NY, (T) The Granger Collection, NY; **66** ©The Granger Collection, NY; **68** North Wind Picture Archives, Science Faction/SuperStock; **69** (B) ©Wilberforce House Museum, Hull City Council, UK/©DK Images, (BL) Private Collection/©Michael Graham-Stewart/Bridgeman Art Library, (T) Royal Albert Memorial Museum, Exeter, Devon, UK/Bridgeman Art Library; **70** ©The Granger Collection, NY; **72** (R) ©The Granger Collection, NY, (L) Colonial Williamsburg Foundation; **73** ©Michael Nicholson/Corbis; **75** (T) Courtesy of the Charlestown Shipwreck and Heritage Centre, Cornwall, Alex Wilson/©DK Images, (BL) Martin Cameron/©DK Images, (BR) Philip Dowel/©DK Images; **76** ©The Granger Collection, NY, (T) S.J. Shrubsole, Corp.; **78** (T) ©The Granger Collection, NY, (B) The New York Public Library/Art Resource, NY; **79** The Granger Collection, NY; **80** ©The Granger Collection, NY, (R) S.J. Shrubsole, Corp.; **81** ©The Granger Collection, NY; **82** (C, B) ©The Granger Collection, NY, (BC) New Jersey Historical Society, (T) North Wind Picture Archives; **84** (T) ©The Granger Collection, NY, (B) The Granger Collection, NY; **85** (R) Corbis, (B) Private Collection/©Look and Learn/Bridgeman Art Library; **86** ©The Granger Collection, NY; **87** North Wind Picture Archives, Paramount Press, Inc.; **89** (B) ©The Granger Collection, NY, (T) The Philadelphia Museum of Art/Art Resource, NY; **90** North Wind Picture Archives; **91** The Granger Collection, NY; **92** (T, B) ©The Granger Collection, NY; **94** (TR,) ©The Granger Collection, NY, (BL) Bettmann/Corbis, (CR, BR) Bettmann/Corbis, Corbis, (BC) The Art Archive/National Archives Washington DC/The Kobal Collection; **95** SuperStock; **96** ©SuperStock/SuperStock; **97** (B) Collection of Guilford Courthouse National Military Park, NC, (T) Colonial Williamsburg Foundation, (C) The National Park Service, Museum Management Program; **98** (L) Library of Congress, (R) Scottish National Portrait Gallery, Edinburgh, Scotland/Bridgeman Art Library; **100** (CL&B) Corbis, (TR) Courtesy of The Boston Society/Old State House, (T) Library of Congress, (CR) North Wind Picture Archives, (TL&B) North Wind/North Wind Picture Archives; **101** Art Resource, NY; **102** ©The Granger Collection, NY; **103** (B) Collection of The New-York Historical Society, (T) Library of Congress; **104** ©Bettmann/Corbis, (T) Dumbarton House/The National Society of The Colonial Dames of America; **105** ©The Granger Collection, NY; **106** (BL) ©The Granger

Collection, NY, (T, BR, BC) Getty Images, (TC) North Wind Picture Archives; **107** (B) Bettmann/Corbis, (TL) Library of Congress, (TR) North Wind Picture Archives; **108** ©The Granger Collection, NY; **109** (B) Private Collection/Bridgeman Art Library, (T) Chip Fanelli/Concord Museum, Concord, MA; **110** North Wind Picture Archives; **111** (TR) ©The Granger Collection, NY, (L) Getty Images, (BR, Bkgrd) The New York Public Library/Art Resource, NY; **112** Library of Congress; **116** The Art Archive/The Kobal Collection; **117** (L) ©SuperStock/SuperStock, (R) The National Park Service, Museum Management Program; **118** ©SuperStock/SuperStock; **119** ©Atwater Kent Museum of Philadelphia/Courtesy of Historical Society of Pennsylvania Collection/Bridgeman Art Library; **120** ©The Granger Collection, NY; **122** (T, B) The National Park Service, Museum Management Program; **123** ©The Granger Collection, NY, (CR) Dave King/©Confederate Memorial Hall, New Orleans/©DK Images; **124** HIP/Art Resource, NY; **125** (T) ©North Wind Picture Archives/Alamy Images, (BL) ©The Granger Collection, NY, (BC) Bibliotheque Nationale, Paris, France/Giraudon/Bridgeman Art Library, (BR) Getty Images; **127** ©The Granger Collection, NY; **128** (R) Dumbarton House/The National Society of The Colonial Dames of America, Scottish National Portrait Gallery, Edinburgh, Scotland/Bridgeman Art Library; **130** The National Park Service, Museum Management Program; **132** State Museum of Pennsylvania ; **133** (B) Collection of The New-York Historical Society, (C) Smithsonian National Museum of American History, Division of Politics and Reform, (T) The National Park Service; **134 135** Private Collection/Peter Newark American Pictures/Bridgeman Art Library; **136** Private Collection/©Dreweatt Neate Fine Art Auctioneers, Newbury, Berks, UK/Bridgeman Art Library, Stephen & Carol Huber; **137** (B) Smithsonian National Museum of American History, Division of Politics and Reform; (T, C) Clements Library, University of Michigan; **138** Jim Wark/PhotoLibrary Group, Inc.; **139** Clements Library/University of Michigan; **141** National Portrait Gallery, Smithsonian Institution/Art Resource, NY; **142** (T) ©The Granger Collection, NY, (B) The National Park Service; **143** Corel; **144** Library of Congress; **147** (R) ©Archivo Iconografico, S. A./Corbis, (L) Corbis, (R) SuperStock; **149** (T, B) ©The Granger Collection, NY; **150** (T) National Archives, (B) The Corcoran Gallery of Art/Corbis; **152** (L) ©Chateau de Blerancourt/Dagli Orti/The Art Archive, (R) ©Collection of the New-York Historical Society, USA/Bridgeman Art Library, (C) Bettmann/Corbis; **153** ©The Granger Collection, NY; **154** (T) Getty Images, (B) Getty Images; **157** The Pierpont Morgan Library/Art Resource, NY; **158** National Portrait Gallery, Smithsonian Institution/Art Resource, NY; **159** ©Brooklyn Museum/Corbis; **160** (T) ©Bettmann/Corbis, (B) State Museum of Pennsylvania ; **162** Art Resource, NY; **163** The Art Archive/The Kobal Collection; **164** (T) ©Danilo Calilung/Corbis, (B) Swim Ink 2, LLC/Corbis; **169** (T, C) ©The Granger Collection, NY, (B) Bettmann/Corbis; **180** (B) Corbis, (T) Getty Images; **184** Corbis; **190** Gift of Edgar Williams and Bernice Chrysler Garbisch./National Gallery of Art, Washington, DC; **191** (B) ©The Granger Collection, NY, (T) Scott W. Dolson, (C) The Granger Collection, New York; **192** (L) Library of Congress, (R) Scott W. Dolson; **193** ©The Granger Collection, NY; **194** (B) Federal Reserve Bank of Richmond, (T) Lee Snider/Photo Images/Corbis; **195** ©The Granger Collection, NY; **196** (TL, B) ©The Granger Collection, NY, (TR) Private Collection/ Giraudon/Bridgeman Art Library; **198** (R) Buffalo and Erie County Historical Society, Hal Sherman; **199** (B)/©The Granger Collection, NY, (T) Kevin Fleming/Corbis; **200** (B) Archiving Early America, Snark/Art Resource, NY; **201** (T) American Antiquarian Society, (B) Chateau de Versailles, France/Bridgeman Art Library, (C) The Library Company of Philadelphia; **202**/©The Granger Collection, NY; **204** (Inset) ©Brooklyn Museum/ Corbis, Library of Congress; **205** (R, L) ©The Granger Collection, NY; **207** (B) Getty Images, (T) Stapleton Collection/Corbis; **209** (B) ©The Granger Collection, NY, (T) Thomas Jefferson Foundation, Inc.; **210** ©The Granger Collection, NY; **211** ©Leonard de Selva/Corbis; **212** (#2) ©Royal Geographical Society, London, UK/Bridgeman Art Library, (TR) ©Ocean/Corbis, (#1) ©Royal Geographical Society, London, UK/Bridgeman Art Library, (#4) ©Stone Nature Photography/Alamy Images, (#3) Division of Political History/National Museum of American History/Smithsonian Institution, (#4) Ernst Mayr Library of the Museum of Comparative Zoology - Special Collections, Harvard University, (#6) North Wind Picture Archives, (#5) North Wind Picture Archives/Alamy Images, (CR) Steve Hurst @ USDA-NRCS PLANTS Database/USDA; **213** (#7) North Wind Picture Archives, (#8) Smithsonian American Art Museum, Washington, DC/Art Resource, NY; **214** North Wind Picture Archives/Alamy Images; **215** (L) Corbis, (Bkgrd) Courtesy National Park Service, Statue of Liberty National Monument, (L) Library of Congress, (R) Stapleton Collection/Corbis; **216**/©The Granger Collection, NY; **217** Composite photograph of the almost 200-year-old Star-Spangled Banner, the flag that inspired the national anthem. Smithsonianís National Museum of American History, 2004/National Museum of American History/Smithsonian Institution; **218** ©The Granger Collection, NY; **218** ©The Granger Collection, NY; **220** (L) Scott W. Dolson, (R) The Granger Collection, New York; **221** Composite photograph of the almost 200-year-old Star-Spangled Banner, the flag that inspired the national anthem. Smithsonianís National Museum of American History, 2004/National Museum of American History/Smithsonian Institution; **222** ©Brooklyn Museum/Corbis; **224** (TR, CL) ©The Granger Collection, NY, (BL) Bettmann/Corbis, (CR, BR) Bettmann/Corbis, (TL) Corbis, (Bkgrd) The Art Archive/National Archives Washington DC/The Kobal Collection; **226** ©Bettmann/ Corbis; **227** ©Bettmann/Corbis, (C) ©The Granger Collection, NY, (T) Smithsonian National Museum of American History, Division of Politics and Reform; **228** (R) American Textile History Museum, (L) North Wind Picture Archives; **229** (B) ©Bettmann/Corbis, (T) ©SSPL/The Image Works, Inc.; **230** Robertstock; **231** Bettmann/Corbis; **232** ©Bettmann/Corbis; **233** Hulton Archive Inc./Getty Images, (Inset) Library of Congress; **234** Smithsonian National Museum of American History, Division of Politics and Reform; **235** (T) ©Bernie Epstein/Alamy Images, (B) ©The Granger Collection, NY, (T) Tzaud photo/Photographers Direct; **237** (R, Bkgrd) ©Bettmann/Corbis, (L) ©The Granger Collection, NY; **239** ©The Granger Collection, NY; **240** (Bkgrd) ©Archive Images/Alamy Images, (T) ©Visions of America, LLC/Alamy, Old Slave Mart; **241** (T) ©Owaki/Kulla/Corbis, (B) ©Richard Cummins/Corbis; **242** (R) Bettmann/Corbis, (L) Smithsonian National Museum of American History, Division of Politics and Reform; **245** (T) ©The Granger Collection, NY, (C) ©Walters Art Museum, Baltimore, USA/Bridgeman Art Library, (B) The Granger Collection, New York; **248** (B) ©Bob Daemmrich/The Image Works, Inc., (T) ©The Granger Collection, NY; **249** (R) ©Collection of the New-York Historical Society, USA/Bridgeman Art Library, (L) Library of Congress; **250** Private Collection/Photo ©Christie's Images/Bridgeman Art Library; **251** ©The Granger Collection, NY; **252** ©The Granger Collection, NY, Courtesy, National Museum of the American Indian, Smithsonian Institution (17/9690). Photo by David Heald./National Museum of the American Indian, Smithsonian Institution; **255** ©Niday Picture Library/Alamy Images, Seny Norasingh/Clemson University; **257** ©The Granger Collection, NY; **258** (R, L) ©The Granger Collection, NY; **259** ©The Granger Collection, NY; **260** ©The Granger Collection, NY; **261** ©Collection of the New-York Historical Society, USA/Bridgeman Art Library; **262** North Wind Picture Archives; **263** (C) ©David J. & Janice L. Frent Collection/Corbis, Picture History; **264** ©The Granger Collection, NY; **265** (B) ©DK Images, (T) Ames Historical Society, (C) Adelaide Johnson, Portrait monument to Lucretia Mott, Elizabeth Cady Stanton and Susan B. Anthony. Marble, c. 1920./Architect of the Capitol; **266** Corbis; **267** ©The Granger Collection, NY; **268** (B) ©The Granger Collection, NY, (T) Steve Liss//Time Life Pictures/Getty Images; **269** ©The Granger Collection, NY; **270** Getty Images; **271** ©Peabody Essex Museum, Salem, Massachusetts, USA/Bridgeman Art Library, (Bkgrd) G.Mushinsky/Shutterstock, (Bkgrd) Massachusetts Historical Society; **272** Getty Images; **273** (B) ©The Granger Collection, NY, (T) Lebrecht Collection; **274** Bloomer Waltz, (costume for summer). Composed by William Dessier. Op 29./Lith. of Sarony & Major, N.Y./Collection #LC-USZC4-3591/Library of Congress; **275** (B) ©The Granger Collection, NY, (T) Ames Historical Society; **276** Library of Congress; **277** Corbis; **278** ©The Granger Collection, NY; **279** ©The Granger Collection, NY; **280** Corbis; **281** (T) ©The Granger Collection, NY, (B) Research Center, Acc. No. 1960.46/The Historic New Orleans Collection, (B) Time & Life Pictures/Getty Images, (T) Virginia Historical Society, Richmond, Virginia; **282** (L) ©Bettmann/Corbis, (R) The National Park Service; **283** ©The Granger Collection, NY; **284** (L) ©The Granger Collection, NY, (R) Bettmann/Corbis, (BC) Cover illustration, Farmer's Alliance Songs, by E.O Excell and Dr. Reid Parker . Chicago, IL: E.O. Excell, Publisher, 1890), Elias Carr Papers (#160.29.c.); **286** Library of Congress; **287** ©Bettmann/Corbis; **288** (R, L) ©The Granger Collection, NY; **289** (L) Corbis, (B) Courtesy of the Elizabeth Cady Stanton Trust, (R) Mary Evans Picture Library; **290** Library of Congress; **291** (T) Dept. of Rare Books & Special Collections, Rush Rhees Library/University of Rochester, (B) Adelaide Johnson, Portrait monument to Lucretia Mott, Elizabeth Cady Stanton and Susan B. Anthony. Marble, c. 1920./Architect of the Capitol; **292** ©The Granger Collection, NY; **293** Library of Congress; **294** ©The Granger Collection, NY; **296** Scotts Bluff National Monument/Scotts Bluff National Monument; **297** (B) ©Gunter Marx/Alamy Images, (T) ©The Granger Collection, NY, (C) Chicago Historical Society: 1920.38/Chicago History Museum; **298** Getty Images; **299** ©Richard Cummins/Corbis; **300** ©The Granger Collection, NY; **301** ©North Wind Picture Archives/Alamy Images; **302** Travelsite/ Global/The Art Archive; **303** (BR) James L. Amos/National Geographic Image Collection, (T) Mary Evans Picture Library, (BL) North Wind Picture Archives; **304** Bettmann/Corbis; **305** (R) ©The Granger Collection, NY, (L) Bettmann/Corbis; **306** Corbis; **307** (L) ©The Granger Collection, NY, (R) Bettmann/Corbis; **310** (B) Chicago Historical Society: 1920.38/Chicago History Museum, (T) Getty Images; **311** (R) ©Gunter Marx/Alamy Images, (L) Courtesy of the California History Room, California State Library, Sacramento, California. Image has been colorized.; **313** (TL) Bettmann/Corbis, (TR) Courtesy of the California History Room, California State Library, Sacramento, California, (B) Seaver Center for Western History Research, Natural History Museum of Los Angeles County. Museum Collection Number 277; **314** (BR) ©SuperStock/SuperStock, (BL) EB Crocker Art Gallery Sacramento/Laurie Platt Winfrey/The Art Archive, (TL) Pascal Goetgheluck/Photo Researchers, Inc., (C) Private Collection/Peter Newark American Pictures/Bridgeman Art Library, (TR) Private Collection/Peter Newark Western Americana/Bridgeman Art Library; **315** ©The Granger Collection, NY; **316** (L) ©North Wind Picture Archives/Alamy Images, (R) ©The Granger Collection, NY; **317** Getty Images; **318** Bettmann/Corbis; **320** (TR, TC, CL) ©The Granger Collection, NY, (BL) Bettmann/Corbis, (CR, BR) Bettmann/Corbis, (TL) Corbis, (Bkgrd) The Art Archive/National Archives Washington DC/The Kobal Collection; **321** Library of Congress; **322** Art Resource, NY; **323** (C) ©The Granger Collection, NY, (T) ©Tom Uhlman/Alamy Images, (B) The Granger Collection; **324** ©The Granger Collection, NY; **325** (B) Brown Brothers, (T) The Granger Collection, NY; **326** ©The Granger Collection, NY; **327** The Granger Collection, NY; **328** ©The Granger Collection, NY; **329** Courtesy of the California History Room, California State Library, Sacramento, California; **330** (B)

Acknowledgments

©The Granger Collection, NY, (T) T. Wrangler; **331** ©The Granger Collection, NY; **332** (BL, BC) ©The Granger Collection, NY, (TR) Collection of the Louisiana State Museum/Louisiana State Museum, (C) Culver Pictures/The Art Archive/The Kobal Collection, (T) Library of Congress, (BR) North Wind Picture Archives, (TC) ©SuperStock; **336** (Inset) ©The Granger Collection, NY; **337** ©The Granger Collection, NY; **338** (T, B) ©The Granger Collection, NY; **339** ©The Granger Collection, NY; **341** (Inset) ©The Granger Collection, NY; **342** ©The Granger Collection, NY, Corbis; **343** (L) ©The Granger Collection, NY, (R) Library of Congress; **344** (R, L, C) ©The Granger Collection, NY; **346** ©The Granger Collection, NY; **347** (R, L, CR, CL) ©The Granger Collection, NY, (Bkgrd) iStockphoto; **348** (B) Library of Congress, (T) The Granger Collection; **349** Library of Congress; **351** Collection of The New-York Historical Society,; **352** (L) Bettmann/Corbis, (R) Corbis; **353** (R) ©The Granger Collection, NY, (L) United States Dept. of the Interior/United States Department of the Interior; **354** Courtesy of the California History Room, California State Library, Sacramento, California; **355** ©The Granger Collection, NY; **356** ©The Granger Collection, NY; **357** ©The Granger Collection, NY; **359** (B) Corbis, (T) Courtesy National Park Service, Museum Management Program and Gettysburg National Military Park, Blood-stained diary of Alfred S. Rowe, Company C, 6th Maryland, GETT 7304/The National Park Service, (C) Dave King/US Army Military History Institute; **358** Don Troiani; **360** Library of Congress; **361** (R) Bettmann/Corbis, (L) Library of Congress; **363** (TR) ARPL/HIP/The Image Works, Inc., (TL) Civil War Minie Ball, Scottsville Museum, Scottsville, VA, (B) From the collection of the Behringer-Crawford Museum, Covington, KY, (CR) Medford Historical Society Collection/Corbis, (BC) Military History/National Museum of American History/Smithsonian Institution; **364** Library of Congress; **366** Dave King/US Army Military History Institute; **367** (R) Bettmann/Corbis, (L) Library of Congress; **369** Bettmann/Corbis; **370** (R) Chicago History Museum, (L) Corbis, (L) Library of Congress; **371** (C) Angus Oborn/Rough Guides/©DK Images, (R) Columbia TriStar/Photofest; **372** (T, B) Library of Congress; **373** (L) ©The Granger Collection, NY, (R) National Museum of American History/Smithsonian Institution; **374** (BR) ©The Granger Collection, NY, (BL) Bettmann/Corbis, (T) Ohio Historical Society/Ohio Historical Society; **375** (L) Library of Congress, (R) The British Museum/ Topham-HIP/The Image Works, Inc.; **376** Library of Congress; **377** (BL) Courtesy National Park Service, Museum Management Program and Gettysburg National Military Park, "Union Playing Cards" used by Assistant Surgeon Platte Brush,/Gettysburg National Military Park, (BR) Courtesy National Park Service, Museum Management Program and Gettysburg National Military Park, Blood-stained diary of Alfred S. Rowe, Company C, 6th Maryland, GETT 7304/The National Park Service, (TR) Courtesy National Park Service, Museum Management Program and Gettysburg National Military Park, Tin Cup, GETT 3471, The National Park Service, (TL) Library of Congress; **378** Library of Congress; **379** (T) Bettmann/Corbis, (B) Corbis, (CR) Dave King/©Confederate Memorial Hall, New Orleans/©DK Images, (CL) Gettysburg National Military Park/Gettysburg National Military Park; **380** (L) Corbis, (R) Courtesy National Park Service, Courtesy National Park Service, Museum Management Program and Gettysburg National Military Park, Drum carried by John Unger, Company B, 40th Regiment New York, Veteran Volunteer Infantry Mozart Regiment, December 20, 1863,GETT 32847; **382** MPI/Getty Images; **383** ©The Granger Collection, NY; **384** (BR) Corbis, (T) Library of Congress, (BL) The Museum of the Confederacy Richmond Virginia/Katherine Wetzel/Museum of the Confederacy, Richmond, VA; **385** (R) Getty Images, (L) Library of Congress; **386** (L) Corbis, (R) Library of Congress; **388** (Bkgrd) Getty Images, (B) ©The Granger Collection, NY, (C) Collection of State Historical Museum/Mississippi Department of Archives and History/Mississippi Department of Archives and History, (T) L. M. Strayer Collection; **389** (B) Greenwich Workshop, Inc., (T) L. M. Strayer Collection, (C) Old Court House Museum, Vicksburg MS/Old Court House Museum; **390** Snark/Art Resource, NY; **391** (BL) ©Hulton-Deutsch Collection/Corbis, (BR) Corbis, (T) Smithsonian American Art Museum, Washington, DC/Art Resource, NY; **392** (L,) Corbis, (C) Library of Congress; **393** Bettmann/Corbis; **395** Paul A. Souders/Corbis; **396** (R, L) Library of Congress; **397** (L) Corbis, (R) Smithsonian American Art Museum, Washington, DC/Art Resource, NY; **398** (B) Corbis, (T) Library of Congress; **399** The New York Public Library/Art Resource, NY; **400** Bettmann/Corbis; **401** (T) ©The Granger Collection, NY, (C) Antique Textile Resource, (B) Library of Congress; **402** ©The Granger Collection, NY; **403** Library of Congress; **404** Library of Congress; **405** Getty Images; **406** Library of Congress; **407** Corbis; **408** (B) ©The Granger Collection, NY, (T, BC) Corel Professional Photos CD-ROM™/Corel, (TC) iStockphoto, (Bkgrd) National Archives and Records Administration/ Courtesy National Archives of the United States; **410** (B) Library of Congress, (T) The Granger Collection, New York; **411** ©The Granger Collection, NY; **412** Associated Press; **413** The Granger Collection, NY; **414** (BL) ©The Granger Collection, NY, (T) Hulton Archive/Getty Images, (TR) Hulton Archives/Getty Images, (CR) LSU Shreveport Archives-Noel Memorial Library, (CR) National Archives and Records Administration/Courtesy National Archives of the United States, (BR) William Holmes McGuffey Museum, Miami University, Oxford, Ohio; **416** ©The Granger Collection, NY; **417** Corbis; **418** (B) Mississippi Department of Archives and History, (T) Picture History/Picture History; **419** Library of Congress; **420** (L) Library of Congress, (R) National Archives and Records Administration/ Courtesy National Archives of the United States; **421** (R)/©The Granger Collection, NY, (L) Library of Congress; **422** Wadsworth Atheneum Museum of Art/Art Resource, NY; **423** (T) Corbis, (B) David Pollack/Corbis; **425** Library of Congress; **426** ©The Granger Collection, NY; **428** Corbis; **429** The Granger Collection, New York; **430** (T) Bettmann/Corbis, (B) Library of Congress; **431** (B) Corbis, (T) Picture History/Picture History; **432** (TR, TC, CL) ©The Granger Collection, NY, (BL) Bettmann/Corbis, (CR, BR) Bettmann/Corbis, (TL) Corbis, (Bkgrd) The Art Archive/National Archives Washington DC/The Kobal Collection; **433** Getty Images; **434** Museum of the City of New York/Getty Images; **435** (T) Collection of Ralph Brunke, (C) Corbis, (B) Museum of the City of New York/29.100.1752/The Art Archive; **436** (L) ©The Granger Collection, NY, (R) Bettmann/Corbis; **437** Library of Congress; **438** (L) ©Bettmann/Corbis, (R) Bettmann/Corbis; **439** (BL) Bettmann/Corbis, (BC) Corbis, (T) Library of Congress, (L) no credit necessary; **440** Rand McNally and Company. "Burlington Route." 1892. Map Collections:1544-1999/Library of Congress; **441** (C, BR) Corbis, (T, BL) Library of Congress; **442** Bettmann/Corbis; **443** (L) ©The Granger Collection, NY, (R) American Textile History Museum, Lowell, Massachusetts/American Textile History Museum; **444** (L) Mary Evans Picture Library/The Image Works, Inc., (Bkgrd) Bettmann/Corbis, (R) Bettmann/Corbis; **445** Bettmann/Corbis; **446** (B) Corbis, (TR) Underwood & Underwood/Corbis, (TL) ©Associated Press; **447** (T, B) Getty Images; **449** (BL) Bettman/Corbis, (R) Bettmann/Corbis, (TL) Carnegie Autograph Collection, Manuscripts and Archives Division, The New York Public Library, Astor, Lenox and Tilden Foundations/New York Public Library Picture Collection; 450 Brown Brothers; **451** Hulton Archive/Getty Images; **452** (B) ©The Granger Collection, NY, (T) Corbis; **453** Collection of Ralph Brunke; **455** Special Collections & Archives; **456** (BR) Corbis, (BL) Getty Images, (C) Library of Congress, (T) Mary Evans Picture Library/The Image Works, Inc.; **459** Bettmann/Corbis; **460** Library of Congress; **461** Provided courtesy HarpWeek, LLC/Courtesy of HarpWeek, LLC; **462** (L) Library of Congress; **463** (T) Cheap emigrant ticket to San Francisco, 1876(print),American School, (19th century)/Private Collection, Peter Newark American Pictures/Bridgeman Art Library, (C, B) Corbis; **464** Bettmann/Corbis; **465** The Jewish Museum, NY/Art Resource, NY; **466** (R) Bettmann/Corbis, (L) Cheap emigrant ticket to San Francisco, 1876(print),American School, (19th century)/Private Collection, Peter Newark American Pictures/Bridgeman Art Library; **467** ©The Granger Collection, NY; **468** The New York Public Library/Art Resource, NY; **469** (T) Library of Congress, (B) The New York Public Library/Art Resource, NY; **470** (B) Topham/ HIP/The Image Works, Inc., (T) Photo by Lewis W. Hine/Museum of the City of New York/Getty Images, (C) Topham/The Image Works, Inc.; **471** (TL) Bettmann/Corbis, (C) Corbis, (TR) Paul A. Souders/Corbis; **472** Brown Brothers; **474** (B) Bettmann/Corbis, (TR) Bettmann/Corbis, (TL) Library of Congress; **475** Bettmann/Corbis; **477** (T) Lester Lefkowitz/Corbis, (B) Library of Congress; **478** Corbis; **479** (C) ©The Granger Collection, NY, (B) Brown Brothers, (T) Corbis; **480** (B) Bettmann/Corbis, (T) Corbis; **481** (B) ©Schenectady Museum; Hall of Electrical History Foundation/Corbis, (T) Image courtesy of The Advertising Archives/The Advertising Archive; **482** (CR) Swim Ink 2, LLC , (Bkgrd) Getty Images, (T) Sears; **483** Corbis; **484** (T) Corbis, (B) Photo by Wallace G. Levison//Time Life Pictures)/Getty Images; **485** Library of Congress; **487** ©The Granger Collection, NY; **488** (T) Getty Images, (B) Bettmann/Corbis; **489** Michigan State University Archives/Michigan State University; **490** (L) From the collections of Henry Ford Museum & Greenfield Village/From the Collections of The Henry Ford; **491** (T) Courtesy of The National Museum of the American Indian/Smithsonian Institution, (neg #)/National Museum of the American Indian, Smithsonian Institution, (C) Geoff Brightling/©DK Images, (B) Union Pacific Museum/Union Pacific Railroad Historical Collection; **492** Library of Congress; **493** Getty Images; **494** Corbis; **495** ©The Granger Collection, NY; **496** (R) Courtesy of The National Museum of the American Indian/Smithsonian Institution, (neg #)/National Museum of the American Indian, Smithsonian Institution, (L) Library of Congress; **497** Hulton Archive Inc./Getty Images; **498** Library of Congress; **499** (L) Getty Images, (R) Copyright 1995-2005 Denver Public Library, Colorado Historical Society, and Denver Art Museum/Denver Public Library, Western History Collection; **500** (R, L) ©The Granger Collection, NY; **501** (B) ©The Granger Collection, NY, (T) ©Associated Press; **502** (R) ©The Granger Collection, NY, (L) Bettmann/Corbis; **503** (B) ©The Granger Collection, NY, (TL) Bill Manns/The Art Archive, (TR) Cumberland County Historical Society/Cumberland County Historical Society, Carlisle, PA; **504** Helen Hunt Jackson, ca. 1875. William S. Jackson Photograph Collection, PP 85-30s, Part 3, Folder 1, Photo 2, photographed by Marshall, Boston. Special Collections, Colorado College, Colorado Springs, Colorado; **505** (R) Frank Greenaway/©DK Images, (L) U.S. Department of Agriculture/U.S. Department of Agriculture; **506** (BL) Bettmann/Corbis, (T) Corbis, (BR) courtesy westernmininghistory; **507** ©Image Asset Management Ltd./ SuperStock; **508** (B) ©The Granger Collection, NY, (T) Corbis; **509** ©Geoff Brightling/©DK Images; **510** (B) Bettmann/Corbis, (T) Philip Gould/Corbis; **512** ©Huntington Library/ SuperStock; **513** (B) ©SuperStock/SuperStock, (CL) Brooklyn Museum of Art, New York, USA/Bequest of Miss Charlotte R. Stillman/Bridgeman Art Library, (CR) Frederic Remington Christie's Images/Corbis, (T) Judith Miller/The Coeur d'Alene Art/©DK Images; **514** ©The Granger Collection, NY; **515** (R) Frank Greenaway/©DK Images, (L) Library of Congress; **516** (T) The Navajo (oil on canvas), Dixon, Maynard (1875-1946)/Private Collection, Christie's Images/Bridgeman Art Library, (B) U.S. Department of Agriculture/U.S. Department of Agriculture; **517** (L) Cumberland County Historical Society, Carlisle, PA, (R) John N. Choate/Cumberland County Historical Society, Carlisle, PA; **518** (L) ©The Granger Collection, NY; **519** (C) ©David J. & Janice L. Frent Collection/Corbis, (B) Bettmann/Corbis, (T) Meridian Book 1994. Cover design by Robin Locke Monda.; **520** J. R. Eyerman/Time Life Pictures/Getty Images, (Inset) The Granger Collection, NY; **521** The Granger Collection, New York; **522** ©Archive Pics/Alamy Images; **523** North Wind Picture Archives; **524** Corbis, (Bkgrd) The New York Public Library/Art Resource, NY; **525** (R) North Wind Picture Archives, (L) Topham/The Image Works, Inc.; **526** (B) Bettmann/Corbis, (T) Corbis; **527** The Granger Collection, NY; **528** (T) ©The Granger Collection, NY, (B) SuperStock; **529** (R) Meridian

Book 1994. Cover design by Robin Locke Monda., (L) The Image Works, Inc.; **530** ©The Granger Collection, NY; **531** ©The Granger Collection, NY; **532** Federal Reserve Bank, USA, Federal Reserve Bank, USA/Federal Reserve Bank of San Francisco; **533** Kansas State Historical Society/Kansas State Historical Society; **534** (T) Alland/The Image Works, Inc., (BC) ©The Granger Collection, NY, (B) Bettmann/Corbis, (TC) Minnesota Historical Society/Corbis; **537** ©David J. & Janice L. Frent Collection/Corbis; **539** Corbis; **541** (L) ©Archive Pics/Alamy Images, (R) ©The Granger Collection, NY; **542** Kansas State Historical Society/Kansas State Historical Society; **543** Los Angeles Times, September 14, 1896; **544** (TR, TC, CL) ©The Granger Collection, NY, (BL) Bettmann/Corbis, (CR, BR) Bettmann/Corbis, (TL) Corbis, (Bkgrd) The Art Archive/National Archives Washington DC/The Kobal Collection; **545** Library of Congress/Corbis; **546** Library of Congress; **547** (C) Getty Images, (B) ©The Granger Collection, NY, (T) Dartmouth College Library; **548** Bettmann/Corbis; **549** Corbis; **550** (C, B) ©The Granger Collection, NY, (T) Library of Congress; **551** (T) ©The Granger Collection, NY, (B) Hulton-Deutsch Collection/Corbis; **552** (R) Library of Congress, (C) The Granger Collection, NY, (L) Underwood & Underwood/Corbis; **554** Courtesy of The Rosenberg Library, Galveston, TX/Courtesy of the Rosenberg Library, Galveston,Texas; **556** (T) Dartmouth College Library, (B) Library of Congress; **557** (T) Lewis W. Hine/George Eastman House/Getty Images, (B) Melissa Shustyk; **558** Corbis; **559** ©The Granger Collection, NY; **560** (BC) ©Bettmann/Corbis, (B) David J. & Janice L. Frent/Corbis, (Bkgrd) Library of Congress, (T) Underwood & Underwood/Corbis; **561** (TR) Bettmann/Corbis, (TL) Courtesy of the Historic National Woman's Party, Sewall-Belmont House and Museum, Washington, D.C./Library of Congress; **562** Library of Congress; **563** (T) Ariel Skelley/Corbis, (B) National Archives and Records Administration/Courtesy National Archives of the United States; **564** San Diego Historical Society, EH Davis Collection/ ©San Diego Historical Society Photo Collection; **565** (L) Corbis, (R) Cornelius M/. Battey/Library of Congress; **566** (T) ©The Granger Collection, NY, (B) Courtesy of the Abraham Lincoln Presidential Library/Courtesy of The Abraham Lincoln Presidential Library; **567** Library of Congress; **568** Brown Brothers; **569** (L) ©Ann Ronan Picture Library/HIP/The Image Works, Inc., (R) Paul & Rosemary Volpp; **570** (BR) ©The Granger Collection, NY, (T, BL) Bettmann/Corbis; **571** (TL) ©The Granger Collection, NY, (TR) Corbis, (BL) Courtesy Kansas State Historical Society/Kansas State Historical Society, (BR) Science Museum/SSPL/The Image Works, Inc.; **573** Library of Congress; **574** Brown Brothers; **575** ©The Granger Collection, NY; **576** (B) Judith Miller/Larry & Dianna Elman/©DK Images, (T) Library of Congress; **577** Getty Images; **578** ©The Granger Collection, NY; **580** Library of Congress; **581** (R) ©The Granger Collection, NY, (L) Cornelius M/. Battey/Library of Congress; **582** David J. & Janice L. Frent/Corbis; **584** (L) Bettmann/Corbis; **585** (T) Getty Images, (C) ©The Granger Collection, NY, (B) SCHOMBURG CENTER/Art Resource, NY; **586** Michael Maslan Historic Photographs/Corbis; **587** (T) Bettmann/Corbis, (B) Corbis; **588** Library of Congress; **589** Getty Images; **590** (B) Corbis, (T) Victor Jose Cobo/©Associated Press; **592** (L) Bettmann/Corbis, (R) National Museum of American History/Smithsonian Institution; **594** (T) ©The Granger Collection, NY, (B) Chicago History Museum; **595** (R) Bettmann/Corbis, (L, C) The New York Historical Society; **596** (R) Corbis, (L) SCHOMBURG CENTER/Art Resource, NY; **599** Library of Congress; **600** (L) Getty Images, (R) Bettmann/Corbis; **601** (TL) Library of Congress, (TR) Rare Books, Manuscript & Special Collections Library, Duke University, (B) University of Wisconsin - Madison/Library of Congress; **602** Bettmann/Corbis; **603** ©The Granger Collection, NY; **604** Bettmann/Corbis; **605** Bettmann/Corbis; **607** (T) ©The Granger Collection, NY, (BR) Bettmann/Corbis, (BL) Corbis; **608** Corbis; **610** (T) Getty Images, (B) Culver Pictures/The Art Archive/The Kobal Collection; **612** (T) Bettmann/Corbis, (B) Corbis; **613** (R) Getty Images, (L) ©The Granger Collection, NY; **614** Bettmann/Corbis; **615** (R, L) ©The Granger Collection, NY, (Bkgrd) Courtesy of Conelrad; **616** National Archives and Records Administration/Courtesy National Archives of the United States; **617** (B) Brown Brothers, (C) Library of Congress; **618** Mary Evans Picture Library; **619** ©The Granger Collection, NY; **621** Bettmann/Corbis; **622** Hulton-Deutsch Collection/Corbis; **623** ©The Granger Collection, NY; **624** (B) Courtesy Motorbuch Verlag and Eberhard Moeller. Photo from The Encyclopedia of U-Boats; From 1904 to the Present., Imperial War Museum/Eileen Tweedy/The Art Archive/The Kobal Collection; **625** (C) Gary Ombler/Imperial War Museum/©DK Images, (B) Library of Congress, (T) Three Lions/Getty Images; **626** (B) Bettmann/Corbis, (T) Ceerwan Aziz/Reuters/Corbis; **627** Hulton Archive Inc./Getty Images; **628** (R) Historical Pictures/Stock Montage/Stock Montage Inc., (L) Library of Congress; **629** Brown Brothers; **630** Rykoff Collection/Corbis; **631** (BR) ©The Granger Collection, NY, (TR) Bettmann/Corbis, (BL) Corbis, (TL) Library of Congress; **632** ©Bettmann/Corbis; **633** (T) ©The Granger Collection, NY, (B) Library of Congress; **634** Chicago History Museum/Hulton Archive/Getty Images; **636** (B) Bettmann/Corbis, (Bkgrd) Corbis, (T) Library of Congress; **637** (R) ©The Granger Collection, NY, (L) Library of Congress; **638** ©The Granger Collection, NY; **640** (B) Bettmann/Corbis, (Bkgrd) The Art Archive; **641** (R) Ann Ronan Picture Library/HIP/The Image Works, Inc., (C) The National World War I Museum, Kansas City, Missouri; **642** Corbis; **644** Library of Congress; **646** Bettmann/Corbis; **647** (L) Library of Congress, (R) National Archives and Records Administration/Courtesy National Archives of the United States; **648** (L) Getty Images, (R) Underwood & Underwood/Corbis; **649** Bettmann/Corbis; **650** Library of Congress; **651** (B) Bettmann/Corbis, (T) David I. & Janice L. Frent Collection/Corbis; **652** The National World War I Museum, Kansas City, Missouri; **653** (L) Bettmann/Corbis, (R) Library of Congress; **654** (B) ©The Granger Collection, NY, (T) Library of Congress; **655** ©The Granger Collection, NY; **656** (TR, TC, CL) ©The Granger Collection, NY, (BL) Bettmann/Corbis, (CR, BR) Bettmann/Corbis, (TL) Corbis, (Bkgrd) The Art Archive/National Archives Washington DC/The Kobal Collection; **657** The Art Archive/Laurie Platt Winfrey/The Kobal Collection; **658** Getty Images; **659** (C) Getty Images, (T) Bettmann/Corbis, (B) The Granger Collection; **660** (L) akg-images/The Image Works, Inc., (R) Image courtesy of The Advertising Archives/The Advertising Archive; **661** Bettmann/Corbis; **662** (C) Bettmann/Corbis, (Inset) Blue Lantern Studio/Corbis, (T) Corbis, (BR) Image courtesy of The Advertising Archives/The Advertising Archive, (BL) Lake County Museum/Corbis, (CL) Visions of America, LLC/Alamy Images; **664** Museum of the City of New York/Corbis; **665** USDA/U.S. Department of Agriculture; **666** (R) Getty Images, (L) Corbis; **667** ©The Granger Collection, NY; **668** Getty Images; 671 (R) Getty Images, (L) Prints & Photographs Division/Library of Congress; **672** Getty Images; **673** ©The Granger Collection, NY; **674** (B) Bettmann/Corbis, (T) Ramin Talaie/Corbis; **675** Library of Congress; **676** (BL) Bettmann/Corbis, (T) Drug Enforcement Administration, (BR) Library of Congress; **677** (B) ©Bettmann/Corbis, (TR) Library of Congress, (TL) The Art Archive/National Archives Washington/The Kobal Collection; **678** K.J. Historical/Corbis; **679** (R) ©The Granger Collection, NY, (L) Schenectady Museum;Hall of Electrical History Foundation/Corbis; **680** (BR) Bettmann/Corbis, (TR) Bettmann/Corbis, (TL, BL) Image courtesy of The Advertising Archives/The Advertising Archive; **681** (L) Behring Center/ National Museum of American History/Smithsonian Institution, (R) Underwood & Underwood/Corbis; **682** (B) Bettmann/Corbis, (T) The Art Archive/Culver Pictures/The Kobal Collection; **683** (C) ©The Granger Collection, NY, (TL) Bettmann/Corbis, (B) Culver Pictures/The Art Archive/The Kobal Collection, (TR) The Jewish Museum, NY/Art Resource, NY; **685** (L) ©Francis G. Mayer/Corbis, (R) The Newark Museum/Art Resource, NY; **686** (T) Getty Images, (B) ©Steve Skjold/Alamy Images; **687** Getty Images; **688** (B) ©John Springer Collection/Corbis, (TC) Bettmann/Corbis, (T) Bettmann/Corbis; **689** (C) ©The Granger Collection, NY, (R) Bettmann/Corbis, (L) Sarah Fabian-Baddiel/HIP/The Image Works, Inc.; **690** Schomburg Center, The New York Public Library/Art Resource, NY; **691** Bettmann/Corbis; **692** (L) ©Blank Archives/Getty Images, (R) Frank Driggs Collection/Getty Images, (C) Tim Ridley/collection of the Louisiana State Museum, Gift of the New Orleans Jazz Club/©DK Images; **693** Getty Images; **694** The Granger Collection; **695** (B) Brown Brothers, (T) Winold Reiss, Portrait of Langston Hughes (1902-1967) 1925. National Portrait Gallery, Washington DC, USA./Art Resource, NY; **696** (R) Getty Images, (L) Bettmann/Corbis; **697** (R) ©The Granger Collection, NY, (L) Bettmann/Corbis; **698** The Jewish Museum, NY/Art Resource, NY; **699** Hulton Archive Inc./Getty Images; **700** Corbis; **701** (T) Getty Images, (C) Corbis; **702** (L) Blank Archives/Getty Images, (R) Getty Images; **703** ©The Granger Collection, NY; **704** Bettmann/Corbis; **705** (R) Condé Nast Archive/Corbis, (L) Minnesota Historical Society/Corbis; **706** (B) ©The Granger Collection, NY, (T) FPG/Staff/Hulton Archive/Getty Images; **707** Bettmann/Corbis; 709 Library of Congress; **711** (C) ©The Granger Collection, NY, (T, B) Bettmann/Corbis, (Inset) Horace Bristol/Corbis; **712** (B) Corbis, (T) Library of Congress, (Bkgrd) Museum of History and Industry/Corbis; **713** ©The Granger Collection, NY; **714** ©Associated Press; **715** ©The Granger Collection, NY; **716** ©The Granger Collection, NY; **717** Library of Congress; **718** (B) Mary Evans Picture Library/The Image Works, Inc., (T) ©Associated Press; **719** (TL) ©The Granger Collection, NY, (TR) ©Associated Press, (BL) Corbis; **720** (T) Hulton Archive Inc./Getty Images; **721** Corbis; **722** CORBIS/Corbis; **723** (B) Bettmann/Corbis, (Bkgrd) Bettmann/Corbis, (T) Getty Images; **725** (B) Getty Images, (T) Peter Anderson/©DK Images; **726** Corbis; **727** ©The Granger Collection, NY; **728** Minnesota Historical Society/Corbis; **730** Bettmann/Corbis; **731** (T) ©The Granger Collection, NY, (C) Blank Archives/Getty Images, (B) David J. & Janice L. Frent Collection; **732** (L) ©The Granger Collection, NY, (R) Getty Images; **733** Getty/Getty Images; **734** (BR, BL) Corbis, (BC) The Granger Collection, NY, (T) Topham/The Image Works, Inc.; **735** ©Bettmann/Corbis; 736 (R, L) Corbis; **737** ©The Granger Collection, NY; **738** (R) Bettmann/Corbis, (L) Bettmann/Corbis; **739** (T) ©Associated Press, (B) no credit necessary; **740** Minnesota Historical Society/Corbis; **741** Corbis; **742** (TL) ©Bettmann/Corbis, (BL) ©Associated Press, (BR) Bettmann/Corbis, (TR) Library of Congress; **743** (CR) Dennis MacDonald/PhotoEdit, Inc., (CL) Mark Antman/The Image Works, Inc., (B) Michael Newman/PhotoEdit, Inc., (T) Monika Graff/The Image Works, Inc.; **744** (Inset, B) ©Bettmann/Corbis; **745** ©The Granger Collection, NY; 746 Library of Congress; **747** ©Associated Press; **748** ©Bettmann/Corbis; **749** (L) Corbis, (R) Library of Congress; **750** ©Associated Press; **751** ©Associated Press; **753** Tim Boyle/Getty Images; 757 White House Photo Office/The White House; **758** MGM/The Art Archive/The Kobal Collection; **759** (BR) Bettmann/Corbis, (BL) Getty Images, (T) Image courtesy of The Advertising Archives/The Advertising Archive; **760** Art Resource, NY, Corbis; **761** Kelly-Mooney Photography/ Corbis; **762** ©The Granger Collection, NY; **763** (T) ©The Granger Collection, NY, (CR) Everett Collection, Inc., (CL) SELZNICK/MGM/The Art Archive/The Kobal Collection, (B) United Artists/Photofest; **764** (R) ©Bettmann/Corbis, (L) Getty Images; **765** (L) ©Bettmann/Corbis, (R) SELZNICK/MGM/The Art Archive/The Kobal Collection; **766** Corbis; **767** Library of Congress; **768** (TR, TC, CL) ©The Granger Collection, NY, (BL) Bettmann/Corbis, (CR, BR) Bettmann/Corbis, (TL) Corbis, (Bkgrd) The Art Archive/National Archives Washington DC/The Kobal Collection; **769** Alfred Eisenstaedt/Pix

Acknowledgments

Inc./Time & Life Pictures/Getty Images; **770** Hulton-Deutsch Collection/Corbis; **771** (C) Getty Images, (T) The Art Archive/Imperial War Museum/The Kobal Collection, (B) The New York Public Library/Art Resource, NY; **772** Bettmann/Corbis; **773** Getty Images; **774** (T, BL) AKG London Ltd., (BR) Bettmann/Corbis; **775** (R) Bettmann/Corbis, (TL) Bettmann/Corbis, (BL) Mary Evans Picture Library; **777** Bettmann/Corbis; **778** Corbis; **779** ©Bettmann/Corbis; **780** (L) Bettmann/Corbis, (R) Corbis; **781** Corbis; **782** Corbis; **783** (L) Bettman/Corbis, (C) Bettmann/Corbis, (R) Hulton-Deutsch Collection/Corbis; **784** ©The Granger Collection, NY; **785** (B) Bettmann/Corbis, (T) Time Life Pictures/Getty Images; **786** ©Associated Press; **787** Printed by permission for the Norman Rockwell Family Agency Copyright 1943 the Norman Rockwell Family Entities/Corbis; **788** ©Bettmann/Corbis; **789** (B) Bettman/Corbis, (T) The Art Archive/Imperial War Museum/The Kobal Collection; **790** (T) Check Six/Getty Images, (BR) Naval Historical Center-Image #NH97379/Navy Art Collection, Naval Historical Center, (BL) ©Associated Press; **791** (BL) Getty Images, (T) Photo by Three Lions/Getty Images, (BR) SuperStock; **792** Courtesy National Archives and Records Administration, College Park, Maryland, photo no. (NWDNS-208-AA-352QQ(5))/Courtesy National Archives of the United States; **793** Corbis; **794** Getty Images; **796** Bettmann/Corbis; **797** (L) Corbis, (R) Getty Images; **798** ©Bettmann/Corbis; **799** Corbis; **800** Corbis; **801** (B) Dorling Kindersley, Courtesy of the Museum of the Regiments, Calgary/Peter Wilson/©DK Images, (C) Getty Images, (T) Ron Edmonds/AP/Wide World Photos; **802** (L) Getty Images, (R) Getty Images; **803** Corbis; **804** (T) DRAGESCO-JOFFE, ALAIN/Animals Animals/Earth Scenes, (B) National Archives and Records Administration/Courtesy National Archives of the United States, (B) ©Associated Press; **805** Bettmann/Corbis; **806** (L) ©Associated Press; **807** Getty Images, (Bkgrd) National Archives and Records Administration/Courtesy National Archives of the United States ; **808** Picture Desk/The Kobal Collection; **809** (R) Library of Congress, (L) Time Life Pictures/National Archives/Getty Images; **810** Hulton Archive Inc./Getty Images; **811** Corbis; **812** (L) Bettmann/Corbis, (R) ©Associated Press; **813** Dorling Kindersley, Courtesy of the Museum of the Regiments, Calgary/Peter Wilson/©DK Images; **814** (T, B) Everett Collection, Inc.; **815** (B) ©Associated Press, (T) Brown Brothers; **816** (BR, BL) ©Associated Press, (TR) Library of Congress, (TL) National Archives and Records Administration/Courtesy National Archives of the United States , (BC) SuperStock, (C) The Granger Collection, NY; **817** (Inset) SuperStock, (Bkgrd) ©Associated Press; **818** (L) ©Topham/The Image Works, Inc., (R) Time Life Pictures/Getty Images; 819 Bettmann/Corbis; **820** (BR) Corbis; **821** (B) by ROBERT CAPA 2001 By Cornell Capa/Magnum Photos/©Magnum Photos, (T) MYCHELE DANIAU/AFP/Getty Images; **823** (T) Corbis, (B) Ron Edmonds/AP/Wide World Photos; **825** Getty Images; **826** U.S. Air Force/U. S. Air Force Photo; 827 (B) ©DK Images, (T) Bettmann/Corbis; **828** Corbis; **829** (R) Andy Crawford/Imperial War Museum, London, (L) Bettmann/Corbis; **830** (TC) AKG London Ltd., (CL) Corbis, (T) Keystone/GettyImages/Getty Images, (TR) Topham/The Image Works, Inc., (CR) US Holocaust Memorial Museum. The views or opinions expressed in this book and the context in which the image is used, do not necessarily reflect the views or policy of, not imply approval or endorsement by, The United States Holocaust Memorial Museum./United States Holocaust Museum; (CC) US National Archives/Roger-Viollet/The Image Works, Inc., (B) USHMM, courtesy of Robert A. Schmuhl/United States Holocaust Museum; **833** Vincent Kessler/Corbis; **834** ©The Granger Collection, NY, (C) Corbis; **835** Corbis; **837** Bettmann/Corbis; **839** Getty Images; **840** (R) Dorling Kindersley, Courtesy of the Museum of the Regiments, Calgary/Peter Wilson/©DK Images, (L) SuperStock; **841** (L) Bettmann/Corbis, (R) Corbis; **842** (B) Corbis, (T) Used with permission from the Stars and Stripes a DoD publication. @ 2005 Stars and Stripes; **844** Bettmann/Corbis; **845** (T) Corbis, (B) Courtesy of Conelrad, (C) Getty Images; **846** (R, L) Getty Images; **847** Bettmann/Corbis; **849** Time & Life Pictures/Getty Images; **850** Corbis; **851** (B) Bettmann/Corbis, (T) Keystone/Getty Images; **853** (B) Bettmann/Corbis, (T) National Archives and Records Administration/Courtesy National Archives of the United States; **854** (R, L) Corbis; **855** ©Associated Press; **856** Corbis; **858** Bettmann/Corbis; **859** John Nordell/The Image Works, Inc.; **860** (R) Getty Images, (L) Courtesy of Conelrad; **862** (Bkgrd, B) ©Jerry Cooke/Corbis, (TR, TL) Bettmann/Corbis; **863** Erich Lessing/©Magnum Photos; **865** (B) Getty Images, (T) Sovfoto/Eastfoto; **866** (CL) Bettmann/Corbis, (B) Bettmann/Corbis, (CR) Corbis, (TR) ©Associated Press, (T) Courtesy of Conelrad; **867** (T) U.S. Govt. Printing Office 1960/civildefensemusem collection, (B) Courtesy of Conelrad; **868** Courtesy of Conelrad; **869** ©The Granger Collection, NY; **870** (L) Image courtesy of The Advertising Archives/2006 Marvel Characters, Inc. Used with permission/The Advertising Archive, (R) Courtesy of Conelrad; **871** (Bkgrd) Courtesy of Conelrad, (R) Allied Artists/The Art Archive/The Kobal Collection, (L) Everett Collection, Inc.; **872** (T) AFP/Getty Images, (B) Time Life Pictures/Getty Images; **873** ©The Granger Collection, NY; **874** ©Marvin Koner/Corbis; **875** Getty Images; **876** (B) Bettmann/Corbis, (T) Corbis; **877** (T) Getty Images, (B) John Nordell/The Image Works, Inc.; **878** Corbis; **879** ©The Granger Collection, NY; **880** Getty Images; **881** (T) ©The Granger Collection, NY, (B) Bettmann/Corbis, (C) Dwight D. Eisenhower Library; Bob Paull, Staff Photographer/Courtesy National Archives of the United States; **882** Gamma-Keystone/Getty Images; **883** Getty Images; **884** Underwood & Underwood/Corbis; **885** (R) Ewing Galloway/Photolibrary Group/PhotoLibrary Group, Inc., (L) WILLARD CULVER/National Geographic Image Collection; **886** (R) Ron Wade Political Memorabilia, (L) W. Eugene Smith/Time & Life Pictures/Getty Images; **887** Bettmann/Corbis; **888** (R) Photo by J. R. Eyerman/Time LifePictures/Getty Images, (L) Time & Life Pictures/Getty Images; **889** Bettmann/Corbis; **890** (R) H. Armstrong Roberts/Corbis, (L) H. Armstrong Roberts/Classicstock/Robertstock; **891** (L) H. Armstrong Roberts/Classicstock/Robertstock, (R) Philip Gendreau/Corbis; **892** H. Armstrong Roberts/Classicstock/Robertstock; **893** Corbis; **894** Bettmann/Corbis; **895** Getty Images; **896** (L) Behring Center/National Museum of American History/Smithsonian Institution, (R) Getty Images; **897** (T) ©The Granger Collection, NY, (B) Tom Kelley/Hulton Archive/Getty Images; **898** Bettmann/Corbis; **899** (CR)/Getty Images, (CL) CBS Photo Archive/Getty Images, (T) H. Armstrong Roberts/Classicstock/Robertstock, (CC) Penguin USA/Courtesy, Penguin Books, (B) Time & Life Pictures/Getty Images; **900** (TC) Getty Images, (TR) CBS Photo Archive/Getty Images, (B) Image courtesy of The Advertising Archives/The Advertising Archive, (TL) Wrather Corp/Apex Film Corp/The Art Archive/The Kobal Collection; **901** Dunigan/Classicstock/Robertstock; **902** (B) Don Wright/Time & Life Pictures/Getty Images, (CL) Everett Collection, Inc., (T) MICHAEL OCHS ARCHIVES/Getty/Getty Images, (CR) Redferns/Getty Images; **903** (R) Bettmann/Corbis, (L) Bob Adelman/Magnum Photos & Simon & Schuster/©Magnum Photos; **904** Photofest; **905** (L) Bruce Davidson/Magnum Photos/©Magnum Photos, (R) ©Associated Press; **906** Bettmann/Corbis; **907** Library of Congress; **908** (L) Library of Congress, (R) Time & Life Pictures/Getty Images; **910** (B) MICHAEL OCHS ARCHIVES/Getty/Getty Images, (T) Ron Wade Political Memorabilia; **911** (R) State Museum of PA, PA Historical and Museum Commission/State Museum of Pennsylvania, Pennsylvania Historical and Museum Commission, (L) ©Associated Press; **912** (TR, TC, CL) ©The Granger Collection, NY, (BL) Bettmann/Corbis, (CR, BR) Bettmann/Corbis, (TL) Corbis, (Bkgrd) The Art Archive/National Archives Washington DC/The Kobal Collection; **913** ©1976 George Ballis/Take Stock/The Image Works, Inc.; **914** Bettmann/Corbis; **915** (C) Bettmann/Corbis, (T) Bettmann/Corbis, (B) David J. & Janice L. Frent Collections/Corbis; **916** (B) Corbis, (T) ©Associated Press; **917** (R) Bettmann/Corbis, (L) Elliott Erwitt/©Magnum Photos; **918** Carl Iwasaki/Time Life Pictures/Getty Images; **919** Time Life Pictures/Getty Images; **920** ©The Granger Collection, NY; **921** ©Bettmann/Corbis; **922** (C) ©The Granger Collection, NY, (B) Time Life Pictures/Getty Images; **924** (B) Bob Daemmrich/The Image Works, Inc., (T) Time Life Pictures/Getty Images; **925** ©Associated Press; **926** (R) Bettmann/Corbis, (L) Bettmann/Corbis; **927** (BR, BL) Bettmann/Corbis, (T) Bruce Davidson/Magnum Photos/©Magnum Photos; **928** ©Associated Press; **929** ©Associated Press; **930** (R) Flip Schulke Archi/Black Star, (L) Photo by Francis Miller/Time & Life Pictures/Getty Images; **931** (BR) ©Flip Schulke/Corbis, (BL) John F. Kennedy Library, National Archives, document MS 2003-036, (T) National Museum of American History/Smithsonian Institution; **933** (B) ©Time Life Pictures/Getty Images, (T) Flip Schulke/Corbis; **934** (T) Bettmann/Corbis, (L, B) ©Associated Press; **935** Bettmann/Corbis; **936** (L) David J. & Janice L. Frent Collection/Corbis, (R) Time Life Pictures/Getty Images; **937** ©Associated Press; **938** Flip Schulke/Corbis; **939** (T) ©Associated Press, (B) Flip Schulke/Corbis; **940** (T) Bettmann/Corbis, (B) David J. & Janice L. Frent Collections/Corbis; **940** ©Associated Press; **942** (T) ©Associated Press, (Inset) Bob Adelman/Magnum Photos/©Magnum Photos, (B) POPPERFOTO/Alamy Images; 945 Photofest; **946** (R) ©The Granger Collection, NY, (L) Time Life Pictures/Getty Images; **947** (R) ©Time Life Pictures/Getty Images, (L) Bettmann/Corbis; **948** ©Associated Press; **949** ©Associated Press; **950** ©Associated Press; **951** (T) David J. & Janice L. Frent Collection/Corbis, (C) The Peace Corps/Peace Corps, (B) Time & Life Pictures/Getty Images; **952** David J. and Janice L. Frent Collection/Corbis; **953** Getty Images, (Inset) Bettmann/Corbis; **954** Corbis; **955** (L) JP Laffont/Sygma/Corbis, (R) PhotoEdit, Inc.; **957** Corbis; **959** Bettmann/Corbis; **960** (B) Corbis, (T) Zuma Press, Inc.; **961** A 1963 Herblock Cartoon, copyright by The Herb Block Foundation/The Herb Block Foundation; **962** (TR, CL) GRIN Great Images in NASA/NASA, (B) NASA, (CR) NASA/NASA, (TL) NIX/NASA Image Exchange/NASA Image Exchange; **963** Bettmann/Corbis; **964** (T) Flip Schulke/Black Star, (B) Larry Kolvoord/The Image Works, Inc.; **965** Bettmann/Corbis; **966** Bettmann/Corbis; **967** (B) Bettmann/Corbis, (T) James Leynse/Corbis; **968** (T) ©AP Images, (BR) Banana Stock/AGE Fotostock, (BL) Marty Heitner/The Image Works, Inc.; **969** (T) ArenaPal/Topham/The Image Works, Inc., (B) Hulton Archive/Getty Images, (C) Sesame Street and associated characters, trademarks and design elements are owned and licensed by Sesame Workshop. ©2007 Sesame Workshop. All rights reserved.; **970** (R) Leah-Anne Thompson/Shutterstock, (L) Stockbyte/Thinkstock; **971** Corbis; **973** (T) Paul S. Conklin/PhotoEdit, Inc., (B) Robert Houston/©AP Images; **974** (R) National Portrait Gallery, Smithsonian Institution/Art Resource, NY, (L) The Peace Corps/Peace Corps; **975** Robert Houston/©AP Images; **976** Corbis; **978** ©The Granger Collection, NY; **979** (C) Library of Congress, (T) National Museum of American History/Smithsonian Institution, (B) West Point Museum Collection, United States Military Academy, West Point, New York/West Point Museum Collection, United States Military Academy, West Point, New York.; **980** Topham/The Image Works, Inc.; **981** WolfgangKaehler/Corbis; **982** (R) AFP/Getty Images, (L) The Image Works, Inc.; **983** ©Associated Press; **985** (R) National Archives and Records Administration, Records of the U.S. Marine Corps/Courtesy National Archives of the United States , (L) West Point Museum Collection, United States Military Academy, West Point, New York/West Point Museum Collection, United States Military Academy, West Point, New York.; **987** ©Associated Press; **988** (B) ©Associated Press, (T) National Archives and Records Administration/Courtesy National Archives of the United States , (Bkgrd) Time Life Pictures/Getty Images; **989** (L) ©Associated Press, (R) ©The Granger Collection, NY; **990** Reuters/Corbis; **991** A 1967 Herblock Cartoon, copyright by The Herb Block Foundation/The Herb Block Foundation; **992** (L) Getty Images, (Inset) CBS Photo Archive/Getty Images, (R) Leif Skoogfors/Corbis; **993** Topham/The Image Works, Inc.; **994** Bernard Gotfryd/Getty Images; **996** Basset/National Archives and Records Administration/Courtesy National Archives of the United States; **997** (BL) ©The Granger Collection, NY, (CR, B) Bettmann/Corbis, (TL) Getty Images, (TR) ©Associated Press; **998** Bob Peterson/Time Life Pictures/Getty Images; **999** (B) ©David J. & Janice L. Frent Collection/Corbis, (T) Time & Life Pictures/Getty Images; **1000** (R) David J. & Janice L. Frent Collection/Corbis, (L) Leif Skoogfors/Corbis; **1001** USAF; **1002** Getty Images; **1003** Ronald S. Haeberle/Time Life Pictures/Getty Images; **1004** (BL) Getty Images, (TL)

AbsoluteStockPhoto/Alamy, (R) Charles Pefley/Mira; **1005** (C) Brand X Pictures/Alamy, (L) ©Associated Press; **1006** (T) AHMAD MASOOD/Reuters/Corbis, (B) James Pickerell/Black Star; **1008** (L) Bettmann/Corbis, (R, C) Corel Professional Photos CD-ROM™; **1009** Corbis; **1010** National Museum of American History/Smithsonian Institution; **1011** Dirck Halstead/Liaison/Getty Images; **1012** ©Associated Press; **1013** (R, C) Corel Professional Photos CD-ROM™, (L) Getty Images; **1014** James Pickerell/Black Star; **1015** ©Associated Press; **1016** Time Life Pictures/Getty Images; **1017** (T) Charles Gatewood/The Image Works, Inc., (C) Redferns/Getty Images, (B) Wally McNamee/Corbis; **1018** (L) Getty Images, (R) John Dominis/The Image Works, Inc., (Bkgrd) Time Life Pictures/Getty Images; **1020** (BL) Corbis, (LC) Douglas J. Gilford's Mad Cover site, (TR) H. Armstrong Roberts/Classicstock/Robertstock, (TCR) Hulton Archive/Getty Images, (BR) Jason Reed/Reuters/Corbis, (TCL) Redferns/Getty Images, (BC) The Granger Collection, NY; **1022** (R) Bettmann/Corbis, (L) Charles Gatewood/ The Image Works, Inc.; **1023** Bettmann/Corbis; **1024** (L) Reprinted by permission of Ms. magazine, 1972, (R) ©Associated Press; **1025** (L) Bettmann/Corbis, (R) ©Associated Press; **1027** (T) Getty Images, (B) Mary Kate Denny/PhotoEdit, Inc.; **1028** Tribute to Diego Rivera/1998 and **2006** City of Philadelphia Mural Arts Program/Jane Golden/Delia King/Photo by Jack Ramsdale/Reprinted by permission; **1029** (B) Arthur Schatz/Time Life Pictures/Getty Images, (T) Barry Sweet/©AP Photo; **1030** (L) ©Associated Press; **1031** (B) ©Associated Press, (TR) Ed Kashi/Corbis; **1032** (R) ©Associated Press, (L) ©Bettmann/ Corbis; **1033** The Post and Courier,Mic Smith/©Associated Press; **1034** (B) Bettmann/Corbis, (R) Library of Congress, (L) Photofest; **1035** Nature Consortium, Ron Wurzer/©Associated Press; **1036** Getty Images; **1037** Ohio EPA; **1038** (T) ©WorldFoto/Alamy Images, (B) Thomas Moran, The Grand Canyon of the Yellowstone, 1872, The U.S. Department of the Interior Museum, Washington D.C./United States Department of the Interior; **1040** Arthur Schatz/Time Life Pictures/Getty Images; **1041** Henry Diltz/Corbis; **1042** Photofest; **1043** 1998 by Lalo Alcaraz, All Rights Reserved; **1044** Bettmann/Corbis; **1045** (T) Connie Ricca/Corbis, (B) Dennis Brack Ltd./Black Star, (C) ©Associated Press; **1046** Corbis; **1047** ©Bettmann/Corbis; **1048** (R, L) Bettmann/Corbis; **1050** (C) Bettmann/Corbis, (BR) Mark Godfrey/The Image Works, Inc., (BL) ©Associated Press; **1051** (TR) Bettmann/Corbis, (TL) ©Associated Press, (BL) Charles Gatewood/The Image Works, Inc., (BR) Mark Godfrey/The Image Works, Inc.; **1052** Time & Life Pictures/Getty Images; **1054** ©Associated Press; **1055** Mark Godfrey/The Image Works, Inc.; **1056** (B) Bettmann/Corbis, (T) Corbis; **1057** (T) Dennis Brack Ltd./Black Star, (B) Larry Lee Photography/Corbis; **1058** Nathan Benn/Corbis; **1059** (C) Cleo Photography/PhotoEdit, Inc., (T) Jeffrey D. Smith, (B) Mark Richards/PhotoEdit, Inc.; **1060** (#5) ABC-TV/The Art Archive/The Kobal Collection, (BR) PARAMOUNT TELEVISION/ The Art Archive/The Kobal Collection, (B) Bettmann/Corbis, (#4 L) CBS, (#4 R, #1) CBS/Landov LLC, (TR, #3, #2) Everett Collection, Inc.; 1062 (B) ©Michael Pole/Corbis, (T) Bettmann/ Corbis; **1063** ©Associated Press; **1064** Bettmann/Corbis; **1065** ©Mark Peterson/Corbis; **1066** (T) Bettmann/Corbis, (BR) Kaveh Kazemi , The Image Works, Inc.; **1067** (R) ©Associated Press; (L) Wally McNamee/Corbis; **1068** (L) Dennis Brack Ltd./Black Star, (R) Wally McNamee/Corbis; **1070** Dennis Brack Ltd./Black Star; **1071 A** 1974 Herblock Cartoon, copyright by The Herb Block Foundation/The Herb Block Foundation; **1072** (TR, TC, CL) ©The Granger Collection, NY, (BL) Bettmann/Corbis, (CR, BR) Bettmann/Corbis, (TL) Corbis, (Bkgrd) The Art Archive/National Archives Washington DC/The Kobal Collection; **1073** ©mood-board/Alamy; **1074** Corbis; **1075** (C) Plambeck/NewsCom, (B) SPELLING/ABC/The Art Archive/The Kobal Collection; 1076 (R) Bettmann/Corbis, (L) David J. & Janice L. Frent Collection/Corbis; **1078** Wally McNamee/Corbis; **1079** Bettmann/Corbis; **1081** (L) The Ronald Reagan Presidential Library and Museum; **1083** Ron Edmonds; **1084** (CT) Barry Thumma, (BC) Bill Hudson, (BL) Judi Sheppard Missett, (BR) NASA, (TL) SPELLING/ABC/The Art Archive/The Kobal Collection, (TR) STOCKFOLIO/Alamy Images; **1085** Charles Tasnadi; **1086** (B) Time Life Pictures/Getty Images, (T) ©Associated Press; **1087** Leif Skoogfors/ Corbis; **1088** Bill Gentile/Corbis; **1089** Library of Congress; **1090** (BL) AFP/Getty Images, (BR) AFP/Getty Images; **1091** (RB) ©Lionel Cironneau/AP Images, (LB) Charles Steiner/The Image Works, Inc., (RT) Doug Mills, (LT) Peter Turnley/Corbis; **1093** J.L. Atlan/Sygma/Corbis; **1094** Time Life Pictures/Getty Images; **1095** (L) Bettmann/Corbis, (C) Betty Press, (R) Jacques Langevin SYGMA/Corbis; **1096** Ben Gibson-Katz; **1097** Corbis; **1098** The Ronald Reagan Presidential Library and Museum; **1099** (T) AFP/Getty Images, (B) Plambeck/ NewsCom; **1100** ©Lionel Cironneau/AP Images; **1102** Ann Johansson/©Associated Press; **1103** (C) Mark Avery/Orange Country Register/Corbis, (B) NASA/Photo Researchers, Inc., (T) Patrick Robert/Corbis; **1104** Courtesy of Dell Inc.; **1105** (T) Steven Senne/©Associated Press, (B) The Fort Wayne Journal Gazette, Samuel Hoffman/©Associated Press; **1109** (L) Arnie Sachs/Corbis; **1110** Susan Ragan; **1111** ©Associated Press; **1112** Reuters/Corbis; **1114** Robert Mecea/©Associated Press; **1115** Whittemore/Rothco Cartoons; **1116** (Border) Ariadne Van Zandbergen/Lonely Planet/Getty Images, (#1) ARKO DATTA/AFP/Getty Images, (B, #3, #2) Scott Wallace; **1117** VALDRIN XHEMAJ/AFP/NewsCom; **1118** Reuters/Corbis; **1119** (L) KEVIN LAMARQUE/Reuters/Corbis, (R) Mark Avery/Orange Country Register/Corbis; **1121** ©Associated Press, (Inset) REUTERS/Sean Adair/Files SV/Reuters Media; **1122** Corbis; **1124** Kathleen Flynn/St. Petersburg Times/PSG/NewsCom; **1125** ©Associated Press; **1126** US Coast Guard/©AP Images; **1127** (R, L) Courtesy Linda and Eddie Tran/Kathy Burnett; **1128** Matt York; **1130** The Image Works, Inc.; **1131** ©James Berglie/Zuma Press, Inc.; **1133** (C) Christophe Calais/In Visu/Corbis, (L) Mario Tama/Getty Images, (R) REUTERS/Larry Downing/Landov LLC; **1134** (T) Charles Bennett/AP/Wide World Photos, (B) Matt York; **1135** Tribune Media Services, Inc. All Rights Reserved. Reprinted with permission./Tribune Media Services; **1136** (TR, TC, CL) ©The Granger Collection, NY, (CR, BL) Bettmann/Corbis, (TL) Corbis, (Bkgrd) The Art Archive/National Archives Washington DC/The Kobal Collection; **1137** Richard Rowan/Photo Researchers, Inc./Photo Researchers, Inc.; **1138** (C) Comstock Images/Thinkstock, (TC) Henrik Winther Andersen/Shutterstock, (B) Jeff Greenberg/Omni-Photo Communications, Inc./Omni Photo Communications, (Bkgrd) John A. Anderson/ Shutterstock, (TL) Richard Paul Kane/Shutterstock, (TC) Thinkstock; **1149** (#2) Art Resource, NY, (#3, #7, #8, #11, #13) The White House Historical Association (White House Collection); (Bkgrd) Corel, (#5) National Portrait Gallery, Smithsonian Institution/Art Resource, NY/Art Resource, NY, (#6, #10, #1) National Portrait Gallery, Smithsonian Institution/Art Resource, NY, (#9, #4, #16, #15, #14, #12) National Portrait Gallery, Smithsonian Institution/Art Resource, NY; **1150** (#17, #19, #22, #23, #28, #29, #30, #31, #32) The White House Historical Association (White House Collection); (#27) Art Resource, NY, (T) Corel, (#25) National Portrait Gallery, Smithsonian Institution/Art Resource, NY, (#26, #21, #20, #18) National Portrait Gallery, Smithsonian Institution/Art Resource, NY; 1151 (#33, #34, #36, #37, #38, #39, #40, #41) The White House Historical Association (White House Collection); (#44) ©Associated Press, (B) ©The Granger Collection, NY, (T) Corel, (#35) National Portrait Gallery, Smithsonian Institution/Art Resource, NY, (#43) The White House; **1152** Lester Lefkowitz/Corbis; **1153** George Doyle/Stockbyte/Getty Images; 1154 North Wind Picture Archives; **1155** (T) Blair Seitz/Stock Connection/Stock Connection, (B) Blank Archives/Getty Images; 1156 Michael Newman/PhotoEdit, Inc.; **1158** Nature Consortium, Ron Wurzer/ ©Associated Press; **1160** ©Associated Press; **1173** (T) ©The Granger Collection, NY, (B) Bettmann/Corbis; **1174** Corbis; **1175** (B) Colonial Williamsburg Foundation, Williamsburg, VA, (T) Réunion des Musées Nationaux/Art Resource, NY; **1176** North Wind Picture Archives; **1177** ©The Granger Collection, NY; **1178** (B) ©The Granger Collection, NY, (T) Composite photograph of the almost 200-year-old Star-Spangled Banner, the flag that inspired the national anthem. Smithsonianís National Museum of American History, 2004/National Museum of American History/Smithsonian Institution; **1179** Bettmann/Corbis; **1180** patrimo-nio designs limited/Shutterstock; **1182** ©Christie's Images/Corbis; **1183** Alan Schein/ZEFA; **1184** Corbis; **1185** ©Ann Ronan Picture Library/HIP/The Image Works, Inc.; **1186** Bettmann/Corbis; **1187** Corbis; **1188** Bettmann/Corbis; **1189** (T) Bettmann/Corbis, (B) JP Laffont/Sygma/Corbis; **1190** Reuters/Corbis; **1191** Arthur Schatz/Time Life Pictures/ Getty Images; **1192** (T) Reuters/Corbis, (B) Reuters/Corbis.

Grateful acknowledgement is made to the following for copyrighted material:

Alfred A. Knopf, a division of Random House and Harold Ober Associates
"Beaumont to Detroit: 1943," "My People," "The Negro Speaks of Rivers" from *The Collected Poems Of Langston Hughes* by Langston Hughes, edited by Arnold Rampersad with David Roessel, Associate Editor, copyright © 1994 by the Estate of Langston Hughes. Used by permission of Alfred A. Knopf, a division of Random House, Inc. and Harold Ober Incorporated.

Paul Brians
Reading About the World, Volume 2, edited and translated by Paul Brians, et al. (Harcourt Brace Custom Publishing, 1999). Used by permission of Paul Brians.

Alfred Music Publishing Co, Inc.
Over the Rainbow (from "The Wizard of Oz"). Music by HAROLD ARLEN lyrics by E.Y. HARBURG. Copyright © 1938 (Renewed) METRO-GOLDWYN-MAYER INC. Copyright © 1939 (Renewed) EMI FEIST CATALOG INC. All rights controlled and administered by EMI FEIST CATALOG INC. (Publishing) and ALFRED MUSIC PUBLISHING CO., INC. (Print). All rights reserved. Used by permission.

David Higham Associates Ltd.
The Benefits Conferred on Portugal translated and edited by George H. T. Kimble for The Hakluyt Society. Copyright © The Hakluyt Society. Used by permission of David Higham Associates Ltd.

Amy Goodman
"Independent Media in a Time of War" by Amy Goodman from *Voices of a People's History of The United States.* Copyright © 2003 by Amy Goodman. Used by permission of the author.

Estate of Lorraine Hansberry, Methuen & Co., Ltd. and Random House, Inc.
A Raisin in the Sun by Lorraine Hansberry. Copyright © 1958 by Robert Nemiroff, as an unpublished work. Copyright © 1959, 1966, 1984 by Robert Nemiroff. Copyright © renewed 1986, 1987 by Robert Nemiroff. Used by permission of the Estate of Lorraine Hansberry, Methuen Drama, an imprint of A&C Black Publishers Ltd and Random House, Inc.

Estate of Michael Harrington and Simon & Schuster, Inc.
The Other American: Poverty In The United States by Michael Harrington. Copyright © 1962, 1969, 1981 by Michael Harrington. Copyright © renewed 1990 by Stephanie Harrington. All rights reserved. Used by permission of the Estate of Michael Harrington and Scribner, a Division of Simon & Schuster, Inc.

Acknowledgments

James Lockhart
We People Here: Nahuatl Accounts of the Conquest Mexico by James Lockhart, ed. & tr. Copyright © James Lockhart. Used by permission.

Ludlow Music, Inc.
ROLL ON COLUMBIA by Woody Guthrie. Music based on GOODNIGHT, IRENE by Huddie Ledbetter and John A. Lomax. TRO-©-Copyright 1936 (Renewed) 1957 (Renewed) and 1963 (Renewed). Ludlow Music, Inc., New York, New York. Used by permission.

Next Decade Music, Glocca Morra Music & Gorney Music
"Brother Can You Spare a Dime?" by E.Y. "Yip" Harburg and Jay Gorney. Published by Glocca Morra Music (ASCAP) and Gorney Music (ASCAP). Administered by Next Decade Entertainment, Inc. All rights reserved. Used by permission.

Richard Overy
"World War II: Why the Allies Won" by Professor Richard Overy. Copyright © Professor Richard Overy. Used by permission.

Oxford University Press
Packaging the Presidency 3rd Edition by Jamieson (1996) 66w from p. 451 as an epigraph © 1984, 1992, 1996 by Kathleen Hall Jamieson. Used by permission of Oxford University Press, Inc.

Penguin Books, Ltd., London And Viking Penguin, a division of Penguin Group (USA), Inc.
The Grapes of Wrath by John Steinbeck, copyright © 1939, renewed © 1967 by John Steinbeck. Used by permission of Penguins Books, Ltd. and Viking Penguin, a division of Penguin Group (USA) Inc.

Perseus Books Group
Almost A Woman by Esmeralda Santiago. Copyright © 1994 Esmeralda Santiago. Used by permission of Da Capo Press, a member of Perseus Books Group.

Progressive Labor Party
"The Great Flint Sit Down Strike Against GM 1936–1937" by Walter Linder. Copyright © The Progressive Labor Party. Used by permission of Walter Linder.

Simon & Schuster
Manchild in the Promised Land by Claude Brown. Copyright © 1965 by Claude Brown. All rights reserved. Used by permission of Scribner, a Division of Simon & Schuster, Inc., from

South Caroliniana Library
"E.B. Heyward Letter, January 22, 1866." Copyright © The South Caroliniana Library. Used by permission of the South Caroliniana Library.

University of Exeter Press
"Description of an Early Nazi Rally by Louise Solmitz, Schoolteacher" edited by J. Noakes and G. Pridham from *Nazism Series Volume 1 1919–1945: The Rise To Power: A Documentary Reader.* Copyright © University of Exeter Press. Used by permission.

University of Washington Press
"A Poem written by a Taoist from the Town of Iron" from *Island: Poetry and History of Chinese Immigrants on Angel Island, 1910–1940* by Him Mark Lai, et at. Copyright © The University of Washington Press. Used by permission.

Writer's House
"I Have a Dream," "Letter from Birmingham Jail," "Pilgrimage to Non-Violence," "A Time to Break Silence" and "When Peace Becomes Obnoxious" by Dr. Martin Luther King Jr. Copyright © 1956, 1958, 1967, 1963 Dr. Martin Luther King Jr., copyright © renewed 1986, 1991, 1995 Coretta Scott King. Used by permission of The Heirs to the Estate of Martin Luther King Jr., c/o Writers House as agent for the proprietor New York, N.Y.

Note: Every effort has been made to locate the copyright owner of material reproduced in this component. Omissions brought to our attention will be corrected in subsequent editions.